Trade Associations and Professional Bodies of the United Kingdom & Eire

Trade Associations and Professional Bodies of the United Kingdom & Eire

An alphabetical and subject classified guide to 5,000 organisations that promote and foster business, commerce, trade, science, and related activities in the United Kingdom and Eire.

Consulting Editor
Verne Thompson

Graham & Whiteside
Cengage Learning

Australia • Brazil • Japan • Korea • Mexico • Singapore • Spain • United Kingdom • United States

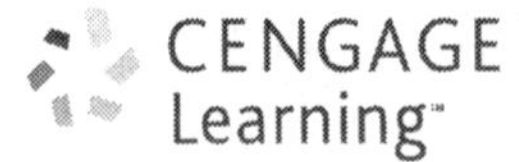

Trade Associations and Professional Bodies of the UK and Eire
Consulting Editor: Verne Thompson

Publisher: Victoria Bentley

Content Project Editor: Verne Thompson

Head of Production and Manufacturing: Alissa Chappell

Production Controller: Tom Relf

Typesetter: M. Wündisch, Leipzig, Germany

Cover design: Jackie Wrout

British Library Cataloguing-in-Publication Data
A catalogue record for this book is available from the British Library.

ISBN: 978-1-86099-6870

Cengage Learning EMEA
Cheriton House, North Way
Andover SP10 5BE

Cengage Learning products are represented in Canada by Nelson Education Ltd.

For your lifelong learning solutions, visit
www.cengage.co.uk

Printed by TJ International, Padstow, Cornwall
1 2 3 4 5 6 7 8 9 10 – 13 12 11

Contents

Introduction

This updated and expanded directory, a co-publication between the Gale Group and Graham & Whiteside, provides essential information on nearly 5,000 trade associations and professional bodies in Eire (Republic of Ireland), England, Northern Ireland, Scotland and Wales in the following sectors: trade, business, and commercial; environmental and agricultural; legal, government, public administration and military; engineering, technological, natural and social sciences; educational; health and medical; public affairs; labour unions associations, and federations.

Typical entries include as available: name, address, phone, fax, e-mail, website, year founded, number of members; number of staff, contact name, fee, description of activities, library type, details of meetings and conventions.

Indexes cover: associations by regions, by subject classification; and by acronym.

In order to keep our information as up-to-date and reliable as possible, we would appreciate hearing about any changes in the entries included in this edition. We would also be grateful to know about any new or existing associations which are not currently included.

Please contact the Publisher:

Trade Associations and Professional Bodies
of the United Kingdom & Eire
Graham & Whiteside
Cheriton House, North Way
Andover SP10 5BE

We also welcome any comments or suggestions.

Ireland

Ireland

Acadamh Rioga na hEireann
see Royal Irish Academy

00001
access Cinema
The Studio Bldg., Meeting House Sq., Temple Bar, Dublin 2, Ireland
Tel: 01 6794420
Fax: 01 6794166
Email: info@accesscinema.ie
Website: http://www.accesscinema.ie
Members: 4000
Staff: 3
Contact: Maeve Cooke, Dir.
Description: Aims to create an awareness and understanding of films as an art form in Ireland; encourage the production, distribution, and exhibition of films in Ireland including the work of Irish film-makers; promote the understanding of other cultures through film. Arranges film seasons, seminars, lectures and special screenings. Imports and distributes films to member societies and others. Organizes and assists in the development of new film societies.
Formerly: Formerly, Federation of Irish Film Societies

00002
Accounting Technicians Ireland
47-49 Pearse St., Dublin 2, Ireland
Tel: 01 6498100
Fax: 01 6336846
Email: info@accountingtechniciansireland.ie
Website: http://www.accountingtechniciansireland.ie
Members: 10000
Staff: 13
Contact: Gay Sheehan, CEO
Fee: £175
Membership Type: regular
Description: Aims to provide a qualification in accounting and information skills for persons working in firms in public practice, in industry and commerce and in public sector. Provides members services to support professional work.
Library Subject: business accounting
Library Type: reference
Formerly: Formerly, Institute of Accounting Technicians in Ireland

00003
Action from Ireland
AFRI
134 Phibsborough Rd., Phibsboro, Dublin 7, Ireland
Tel: 01 8827563
Fax: 01 8827576
Email: afri@iol.ie
Website: http://www.afri.ie
Members: 3000
Staff: 3
Contact: Andy Storey, Chm.
Description: Non-partisan political organization. Works to increase awareness of the causes of poverty. Believes these causes include: unfair distribution of wealth; misuse of the earth's resources; exploitation of the economically disadvantaged; waste of resources caused by international arms races and debt crises.
Publication: Book
Publication title: Just a Second

00004
Action on Smoking and Health - Ireland
ASH-NI
43/45 Northumberland Rd., Ballsbridge, Dublin 4, Ireland
Tel: 01 2310521
Email: ashire@iol.ie
Website: http://www.ash.ie
Staff: 40
Contact: Luke Clancy, Chm.
Description: Supports cancer research/prevention and care. Individuals united to disseminate information on the dangers of smoking. Seeks to establish smoke-free public areas and help those addicted to smoking. Works with medical and health groups in support of its aims. Support groups for cancer patients and families, nurses in cancer centres and units, patient advocacy.

00005
Active Retirement Ireland
ARI
Shamrock Chambers, 1-2 Eustace St., Dublin 2, Ireland
Tel: 01 6792142
Fax: 01 6799636
Email: fara@eircom.ie
Website: http://www.activeirl.ie
Members: 25000
Staff: 2
Description: Retired individuals over 55 years of age. Encourages member to "lead a full, happy and healthy retirement." Organizes outings, social activities, sports activities, educational programs, and community service activities.
Formerly: Formerly, Federation of Active Retirement Association

00006
Adelaide Hospital Society
The Adelaide and Meath Hospital, Tallaght, Dublin 24, Ireland
Tel: 01 4142072
Fax: 01 4142070
Email: roisin.whiting@amnch.ie
Website: http://www.adelaide.ie
Members: 1000
Staff: 2
Contact: Fergus O'Ferrall, Dir.
Fee: £40
Membership Type: individual
Fee: £50
Membership Type: family
Description: Promotes the participation of the Protestant community in the Irish health system. Makes available financial support to Adelaide and Meath Hospital. Conducts fundraising activities; sponsors charitable programs.
Publication: Newsletter
Publication title: Adelaide Diary

00007
Age Action Ireland
AAI
30/31 Lower Camden St., Dublin 2, Ireland
Tel: 01 4756989
Fax: 01 4756011
Email: info@ageaction.ie
Website: http://www.ageaction.ie
Members: 1500
Staff: 73
Contact: Robin Webster, Chief Exec.
Fee: £10
Membership Type: individual (retired, unwaged)
Fee: £30
Membership Type: individual (employed)
Description: Works to improve the quality of life of all older people, especially those who are most disadvantaged and vulnerable, by enabling them to live full, independent and satisfying lives for as long as they wish in their own homes. Membership is open to all organizations and individuals concerned with aging and older people. Main activities include advocacy, information and publishing, library, education and training, U3A, Carer Support Programme, innovative projects, research, policy development and campaigning.

00008
Aircraft Owners and Pilots Association - Ireland
AOPA
Curramore, Kiltoom, Athlone, Roscommon, Ireland
Tel: 01 2875867
Fax: 01 2875893
Email: secretary@aopaireland.com
Website: http://www.iaopa.org/map-continents.cfm
Members: 275
Contact: Jim Breslin, Pres.
Description: Provides government representation and safety seminars. Protects general aviation airports. Campaigns to control the cost of flying for general aviation pilots.
Publication: Booklet
Publication title: Airport Guide

00009
Alliance For Animal Rights
AFAR
PO Box 4734, Dublin 1, Ireland
Tel: 085 7371810
Email: berniew@esatclear.ie
Website: http://www.afarireland.org
Description: Promotes public awareness of animal exploitation and abuse. Encourages the public to take up the vegan lifestyle. Campaigns for cruelty free products.

00010
Alzheimer Society of Ireland
ASI
Temple Rd., Blackrock, Dublin, Ireland
Tel: 01 2073800
Fax: 01 2103772
Email: info@alzheimer.ie
Website: http://www.alzheimer.ie
Members: 5000
Staff: 140
Contact: Maurice A. O'Connell, CEO
Fee: £15
Membership Type: regular
Description: Individuals and organizations. Seeks to improve the quality of life of people with Alzheimer's disease and their families; promotes advancement in the diagnosis and treatment of Alzheimer's disease. Makes available home support and day care service to people with Alzheimer's disease and their families; maintains respite home; serves as a clearinghouse on Alzheimer's disease and services available to people with the disease.
Publication: Newsletter
Publication title: Alzheimer Society of Ireland Newsletter

00011

American Chamber of Commerce Ireland
AMCHAM IRELAND

6 Wilton Pl., Dublin 2, Ireland
Tel: 01 6616201
Fax: 01 6616217
Email: info@amcham.ie
Website: http://www.amcham.ie
Members: 410
Staff: 5
Contact: Lionel Alexander, Pres.
Fee: £2500
Membership Type: corporate
Description: Represents companies and individuals engaged in trading and investing between the United States and Ireland. Aims to promote a business environment that is attractive to all companies engaged in trade and commerce between the U.S. and Ireland. Provides a forum through which ideas and information can be shared.
Library Subject: Ireland-U.S. trade
Library Type: reference
Publication: Directory
Publication title: American Business Directory: Directory and Year Book of American Business in Ireland. Advertisements.
Meetings/Conventions: monthly meeting

00012

American Women's Club of Dublin

PO Box 2545, Dublin 4, Ireland
Email: info@awcd.net
Website: http://www.awcd.net
Members: 180
Fee: £60
Membership Type: regular
Fee: £45
Membership Type: pensioner, student
Description: Promotes American-Irish relations and cross-cultural understanding among North American women and their families living in Ireland. Helps North American women, as well as Irish who have lived in North America, to make the personal and lifestyle adjustments necessary for positive experiences living in Ireland.

00013

Amnesty International - Ireland

Sean MacBride House, 48 Fleet St., Dublin 2, Ireland
Tel: 01 8638300
Fax: 01 6751731
Email: info@amnesty.ie
Website: http://www.amnesty.ie/live/irish/default.asp
Description: Irish section of Amnesty International. Promotes human rights.

An Oige

see Irish Youth Hostel Association

An Taisce

see National Trust for Ireland

00014

Animal and Plant Health Association
APHA

8 Woodbine Pk., Blackrock, Dublin, Ireland
Tel: 01 2603050
Fax: 01 2603021
Email: info@apha.ie
Website: http://www.apha.ie
Members: 31
Staff: 3
Contact: Brendan Barnes, Dir.
Description: Promotes awareness of animal and plant health issues.
Publication: Book
Publication title: Veterinary Data Sheet Compendium

00015

Ankylosing Spondylitis Association of Ireland
ASAI

Carmichael Ctre., N Brunswick St., Dublin 7, Ireland
Tel: 01 8376614
Email: info@ankylosing-spondylitis.ie
Website: http://www.asif.rheumanet.org/ireland.htm
Members: 120
Contact: Hugh Cassidy, Chm.
Fee: £14
Membership Type: regular
Description: Educates and heightens awareness of the general public, patients and medical professions with regard to Ankylosing Spondylitis. Provides support, advice and answers to anybody and ultimately to support or aid research into this illness.

Aontas Innealtoireacht Bithleighis na hEireann

see Biomedical Engineering Association of Ireland

Aontas Muinteoiri Eireann

see Teachers' Union of Ireland

Aos-Oideachas Naisiunta Tri Aontu Soarlach

see National Association of Adult Education

00016

Aosdana

70 Merrion Sq., Dublin 2, Ireland
Tel: 01 6180200
Fax: 01 6761302
Email: aosdana@artscouncil.ie
Website: http://aosdana.artscouncil.ie
Members: 246
Staff: 2
Contact: Toby Dennett, Registrar
Description: Artists, composers, and writers of Irish birth or residence.

00017

Architectural Association of Ireland
AAI

Office No. 1, 43-44 Temple Bar, Dublin 2, Ireland
Tel: 01 6351428
Fax: 01 6351429
Email: aaiadmin@eircom.net
Website: http://architecturalassociation.ie/index.php/aai/index-past
Contact: Hugo Lamont, Pres.
Fee: £80
Membership Type: full
Fee: £20
Membership Type: retired, unemployed, associated organization, student (over 2nd year)
Description: Architects and those interested in the progress of architecture in Ireland. Promotes and affords facilities for the study of architecture and the allied sciences and arts. Provides a medium of communication between members; sponsors a public lecture series.

00018

Arthritis Ireland
AI

1 Clanwilliam Sq., Grand Canal Quay, Dublin 2, Ireland
Tel: 01 6618188
Fax: 01 6618261
Email: info@arthritisireland.ie
Website: http://www.arthritisireland.ie
Contact: Louise Moran, Contact
Fee: £15
Membership Type: senior
Fee: £30
Membership Type: individual
Description: Individuals and organizations with an interest in arthritis. Seeks to improve the quality of life of people with arthritis; promotes advancement in the diagnosis and treatment of arthritis. Serves as a clearinghouse on arthritis, its treatment, and services available to people with arthritis; makes available aids and appliance to make life easier for people with arthritis; conducts educational programs; sponsors children's services; provides financial support to arthritis research programs.
Formerly: Formerly, Arthritis Foundation of Ireland
Publication: Newsletter
Publication title: Arthritis News

00019

Arts Council of Ireland
AC

70 Merrion Sq., Dublin 2, Ireland
Tel: 01 6180200
Fax: 01 6761302
Email: info@artscouncil.ie
Website: http://www.artscouncil.ie/en/homepage.aspx
Members: 17
Staff: 13
Contact: Mary Cloake, Dir.
Description: Independent statutory body assisting and promoting the arts. Assists promoters of musical events and publishers of translations of contemporary Irish literature.
Publication: Brochure
Publication title: Bursaries Brochure

00020

Asperger Syndrome Association of Ireland
ASPIRE

Coleraine House, Carmichael Centre, Coleraine St., Dublin 7, Ireland
Tel: 01 8780027
Fax: 01 8780029
Email: admin@aspireireland.ie
Website: http://www.aspireireland.ie
Members: 300
Staff: 3
Contact: Des McKernan, Honorary Sec.
Fee: £70
Membership Type: regular
Description: People with Asperger Syndrome and their families; health care providers and other individuals providing support and services to people with Asperger Syndrome. Seeks to improve the quality of life of people with Asperger Syndrome. Functions as a support network for people with Asperger Syndrome and their families; facilitates research projects.
Library Subject: Asperger Syndrome, autistic spectrum disorder
Library Type: open to the public
Meetings/Conventions: Parent's Day – semiannual meeting

00021

Association for Common European Nursing Diagnoses, Interventions and Outcomes
ACENDIO

School of Nursing and Midwifery, Trinity College Dublin, 24 D'Olier St., Dublin 2, Ireland
Email: secretariat@acendio.net
Website: http://www.acendio.net
Contact: Fintan Sheerin, Sec.
Fee: £58
Membership Type: individual
Fee: £580
Membership Type: institution
Description: Nurses and nursing organizations. Provides network and development of resources towards standards supporting sharing and comparison of data about nursing.

00022

Association for Dental Education in Europe
ADEE

Dublin Dental School and Hospital, Trinity College, Lincoln Pl., Dublin 2, Ireland
Tel: 01 6127287
Fax: 01 6127294
Email: administrator@adee.org
Website: http://www.adee.org/cms
Contact: Majella Giles, Admin.
Fee: £30
Membership Type: individual
Description: Promotes the advancement of dental education.
Meetings/Conventions: annual meeting September 7 to 10, 2011. Antalya Turkey

00023

Association for French Language Studies
AFLS

School of Languages and Literatures, John Henry Newman Bldg., Rm. D303, Belfield 4, Dublin, Ireland
Tel: 01 7168448
Fax: 01 7161175
Email: vera.regan@ucd.ie
Website: http://www.afls.net
Members: 150
Contact: Vera Regan, Pres.
Fee: £42
Membership Type: standard
Fee: £25
Membership Type: reduced
Description: Promotes language teaching and research in French language and linguistics in Higher Education.
Publication: Journal
Publication title: Cahiers de l'AFLS

00024

Association for Higher Education Access and Disability
AHEAD

East Hall, UCD, Carysfort Ave., Blackrock, Dublin, Ireland
Tel: 01 7164396
Email: ahead@ahead.ie
Website: http://www.ahead.ie
Members: 70
Staff: 8
Contact: Ann Heelan, Exec. Dir.
Description: Individuals and organizations. Promotes increased access to higher education for people with disabilities. Lobbies for more stringent statutes mandating accessibility of educational institutions; represents the interests of people with disabilities before institutions of higher education.

00025

Association for Purchasing and Supply
APS

141 Clonliffe Rd., Dublin 3, Ireland
Tel: 01 8369685
Email: info@irishpurchasing.com
Website: http://www.irishpurchasing.com
Fee: £130
Membership Type: individual
Fee: £580
Membership Type: corporate
Description: Provides individuals and organizations an opportunity to express views on the profession, ask questions and seek support across a global network of like minded professionals within materials management, supply chain and logistics.
Publication: Journal
Publication title: Purchasing and Supply Solutions. Advertisements.

Association internationale des critiques d'art - Irlande

see International Association of Art Critics - Ireland

00026

Association of Advertisers in Ireland
AAI

Fitzwilliam Business Centre, 26 Upper Pembroke St., Dublin 2, Ireland
Tel: 01 6373950
Fax: 01 6373954
Email: info@aai.ie
Website: http://www.aai.ie
Members: 100
Staff: 3
Contact: Fiona Curtin, Pres.
Fee: £850-5850
Membership Type: business (based on total commercial communications spend)
Description: Commercial organizations supplying advertising goods or services. Encourages greater understanding and confidence in the role advertising plays in society. Fosters self-regulatory practices as a means to higher industry standards. Defends members' interests. Provides advisory services; disseminates information on agencies, media, rates, and services.
Library Type: reference
Publication: Directory
Publication title: MAPS Directory - Media, Advertising, Promotions, Sponsorship. Advertisements.

00027

Association of Approved Tourist Guides of Ireland
AATGI

PO Box 6156, Dublin 13, Ireland
Tel: 01 2781626
Fax: 01 2781626
Email: bookings@tourguides.ie
Website: http://www.tourguides.ie
Members: 200
Contact: Georgina Boylan, Pres.
Fee: £190
Membership Type: regular
Description: Plays a representative role in the guiding sector of Ireland.

00028

Association of Chartered Certified Accountants - Ireland
ACCA

9 Leeson Park, Dublin 6, Ireland
Tel: 01 4988900
Fax: 01 4963615
Email: info@ie.accaglobal.com
Website: http://ireland.accaglobal.com
Members: 131500
Contact: Liz Hughes, Hd.
Description: Aims to provide professional opportunities to people of ability and application and be a leader in the development of the global accountancy profession. Promotes the highest ethical and governance standards and works in the public interest.

00029
Association of Community and Comprehensive Schools
ACCS
10H Centerpoint Business Park, Oak Dr., Dublin 12, Ireland
Tel: 01 4601150
Fax: 01 4601203
Email: office@accs.ie
Website: http://www.accs.ie
Members: 91
Staff: 4
Contact: Malachy Molloy, Pres.
Description: School boards of management. Seeks to advance education and the concept of broad comprehensive curricula. Promotes the wider "community" concept of schools.
Publication: Newsletter
Publication title: ACCS Newsletter

00030
Association of Consulting Engineers of Ireland
ACEI
46 Merrion Sq., Dublin 2, Ireland
Tel: 01 6425588
Fax: 01 6425590
Email: info@acei.ie
Website: http://www.acei.ie
Contact: John Lombard, Pres.
Description: Independent consulting firms and principal engineers within such firms in Republic of Ireland and Northern Ireland; degreed engineers or individuals with equivalent experience. Promotes the practice, profession, and procedures of engineering (particularly consultative); encourages professional advancement of individuals in the field. Works to develop public awareness of the usefulness of engineering.
Meetings/Conventions: annual convention

00031
Association of Electrical Contractors - Ireland
AECI
Woodview Centre, Main St., Celbridge, Kildare, Ireland
Tel: 01 2886499
Fax: 01 2885870
Email: aeci@indigo.ie
Website: http://www.aeci.ie
Members: 351
Staff: 3
Contact: Brian Flangan, Pres.
Description: Association of electrical contractors in Ireland. Promotes economic development of members through training in commercial and physical areas. Represents members' interests in industrial relations. Makes legal services and insurance available to members at group rates.
Library Subject: wiring rules, emergency lighting, fire alarm regulations
Library Type: reference
Meetings/Conventions: annual conference – Exhibits.

00032
Association of Hunt Saboteurs - Ireland
PO Box 4734, Dublin 1, Ireland
Tel: 087 2651720
Email: associationofhuntsaboteurs@gmail.com
Website: http://www.huntsabsireland.org
Contact: John Tierney, Contact
Description: Promotes public awareness of hunt sabotage and the fight against animal abuse in Ireland. Studies how hunters operate in the field. Develops tactics and strategies.
Publication: Booklet
Publication title: HSA Tactics Manual

00033
Association of Irish Composers
AIC
Association of Irish Composers, Pembroke Row, Dublin 2, Ireland
Tel: 074 9383734
Fax: 074 9383734
Email: info@composers.ie
Website: http://www.composers.ie
Contact: John McLachlan, Exec. Dir.
Fee: £50
Membership Type: composer
Fee: £30
Membership Type: student/unwaged
Description: Represents the interests of composers in all areas of copyright. Seeks to enhance the professional status of Irish composers. Promotes better awareness of new Irish music. Supports and lobbies in all areas that affect composers' material good.
Publication: Handbook
Publication title: Young Composers Handbook

00034
Association of Irish Musical Societies
AIMS
Slieve Bloom, Kavanagh Pl., Co. Tipperary, Thurles, Tipperary, Ireland
Tel: 0504 22364
Email: mary.butler@aims.ie
Website: http://www.aims.ie
Members: 130
Contact: Mary Butler, Natl. Sec.
Description: Aims to improve the standard of presentation and production of amateur musicals. Provides advice, education and information about production and technical personnel, performers, and other aspects of show production to members. Commissions new works. Conducts summer schools and workshops. Runs annual youth summer school.
Publication: Journal
Publication title: Show Times. Advertisements.

00035
Association of Occupational Therapists of Ireland
AOTI
PO Box 11555, Ground Fl., Bow Bridge House, Bow Ln., Kilmainham 8, Dublin, Ireland
Tel: 0163 37222
Email: aoti@eircom.net
Website: http://www.aoti.ie
Contact: Valerie Flattery, Chair
Fee: £160
Membership Type: full practicing
Fee: £110
Membership Type: part time practicing (up to 20 hours)
Description: Promotes occupational therapy as an art and science. Facilitates the exchange of information. Aims to advance the practice and standards of occupational therapy. Promotes the education and training of therapists.

00036
Association of Secondary Teachers Ireland
ASTI
Thomas MacDonagh House, Winetavern St., Dublin 8, Ireland
Tel: 01 6040160
Fax: 01 8972760
Email: info@asti.ie
Website: http://www.asti.ie
Members: 17000
Staff: 22
Contact: Patrick King, Gen. Sec.
Description: Second level school teachers. Promotes second level education. Works to enhance the professional status of teachers. Represents members' interests before government agencies, school administrative bodies, and the public.
Formerly: Formerly, Association of Secondary Teachers
Publication: Magazine
Publication title: ASTI Review. Advertisements.

00037
Asthma Society of Ireland
ASI
26 Mountjoy Sq., Dublin 1, Ireland
Tel: 01 8788511
Fax: 01 8788128
Email: office@asthmasociety.ie
Website: http://www.asthmasociety.ie
Staff: 3
Contact: Jean Holohan, CEO
Fee: £25
Membership Type: regular
Fee: £15
Membership Type: unwaged
Description: Individuals with asthma; health care personnel and other individuals providing support and services to people with asthma. Seeks to improve the quality of life of people with asthma. Serves as a clearinghouse on asthma and its treatment; supports health professionals treating people with asthma.
Library Subject: asthma, allergy, COPD, eczema
Library Type: open to the public
Publication: Magazine
Publication title: Asthma Society News. Advertisements.
Meetings/Conventions: Asthma Information Day – annual seminar

00038
Astronomy Ireland
PO Box 2888, Dublin 5, Ireland
Tel: 01 8470777
Fax: 01 8470771
Email: sec@astronomy.ie
Website: http://www.astronomy.ie
Members: 11000
Staff: 30
Contact: David Moore, Chm.
Fee: £48
Membership Type: full, household
Fee: £40
Membership Type: student, person under 18 years old, unwaged, person over 65 years old

Description: Individuals interested in astronomy and outer space. Conducts educational programs; makes available children's services; maintains speakers' bureau. Makes and sells telescopes.
Publication: Magazine
Publication title: Astronomy and Space Magazine. Advertisements.

00039

Bakers, Food and Allied Workers' Union - Ireland
BFAWU

143 Lower Drumcondra Rd., Dublin 9, Ireland
Tel: 01 8844811
Fax: 01 884417
Email: info@bfawu.org
Website: http://www.bfawu.org
Members: 1200
Contact: M. Hanlon, Regional Off.
Description: Assists and protects workers. Conducts training for members.

00040

Biomedical Engineering Association of Ireland
BEAI

Cork University Hospital, Biomedical Engineering Department, Wilton, Cork, Ireland
Tel: 021 4922849
Email: noel.murphy@hse.ie
Website: http://www.beai.org
Contact: Bernard Murphy, Chm.
Fee: £30
Membership Type: full
Fee: £20
Membership Type: associate, retired
Description: Promotes biomedical and clinical engineering in Ireland.
Publication: Newsletter
Publication title: Spectrum

00041

BirdWatch Ireland
BWI

Unit 20, Block D, Bullford Business Campus, Kilcoole, Wicklow, Ireland
Tel: 01 2819878
Fax: 01 2810997
Email: info@birdwatchireland.ie
Website: http://www.birdwatchireland.ie
Members: 14000
Staff: 25
Contact: John Cromie, Chm.
Fee: £40
Membership Type: individual
Fee: £50
Membership Type: family
Description: Promotes conservation and protection of wild birds in their natural habitat in Ireland.
Publication: Journal
Publication title: Irish Birds

00042

BODYWHYS: The Eating Disorders Association of Ireland

PO Box 105, Dublin, Ireland
Tel: 01 2834963
Fax: 01 2056959
Email: info@bodywhys.ie
Website: http://www.bodywhys.ie
Staff: 5
Contact: Jacinta Hastings, CEO
Description: Offers support to people with/affected by eating disorders. Disseminates information to promote a better understanding of eating disorders. Runs self-help and support groups. Operates telephone helpline.
Library Subject: eating disorders, related issues
Library Type: not open to the public
Formerly: Formerly, BODYWHYS: Help, Support, Understanding for Anorexia and Bulimia Nervousa

00043

Brainwave The Irish Epilepsy Association
BIEA

249 Crumlin Rd., Dublin 12, Ireland
Tel: 01 4557500
Fax: 01 4557013
Email: info@epilepsy.ie
Website: http://www.epilepsy.ie
Members: 8000
Staff: 24
Contact: Mike Glynn, CEO
Fee: £12.7
Membership Type: regular
Description: Seeks to improve the health of people with epilepsy; committed to working for and meeting the needs of everyone with epilepsy in Ireland. Strives for the creation of a society in which people with epilepsy have the right and opportunity to participate in at all levels. Works to empower people to make a difference in their lives.
Publication: Magazine
Publication title: Epilepsy News. Advertisements.

00044

Bram Stoker Club
BSC

Regent House, Trinity Coll., Dublin 2, Ireland
Fax: 01 6719003
Email: dlass@tcd.ie
Website: http://benecke.com/stoker.html
Members: 20
Contact: David M. Lass, Hon. Sec.
Description: Affiliated with the Bram Stoker Society, Encourages the study, appreciation, and presentation of the works of Abraham (Bram) Stoker (1847-1912), Irish author noted for his use of Gothic tradition with supernatural themes, as in his book *Dracula*. Studies works of Irish writers influenced by Stoker; conducts research on the Stoker family; campaigns for plaques to be placed on Irish sites associated with the Stoker family; promotes tourist visits to such locales as well as to sites associated with other Gothic novelists.

00045

Bram Stoker Society - Ireland
BSS

Regent House, Trinity College, Dublin 2, Ireland
Fax: 01 6719003
Email: dlass@tcd.ie
Website: http://benecke.com/stoker.html
Members: 120
Contact: David Lass, Honorary Sec.
Fee: £10
Membership Type: in EU zone
Fee: £10
Membership Type: in UK
Description: Enthusiasts of the works of Abraham (Bram) Stoker (1847-1912), Irish author noted for his use of Gothic tradition with supernatural themes, as in his book *Dracula*. Encourages the study and appreciation of the life and works of Bram Stoker and other Irish authors of the Gothic and Supernatural tradition including, Charles Robert Maturin (1780-1824), Joseph Sheridan Le Fanu (1814-1873), and Lord Dunsany (1878-1957). Sponsors film shows and lectures.

00046

Building Materials Federation
BMF

Confederation House, 84-86 Lower Baggot St., Dublin 2, Ireland
Tel: 01 6051652
Fax: 01 6381652
Email: mark.macauley@ibec.ie
Website: http://www.ibec.ie/bmf
Members: 35
Contact: Mark McAuley, Dir.
Description: Represents the interests of producers of building materials in Ireland, both nationally and internationally. Promotes the interests of all sectors of the building materials industry in Ireland and encourages the growth and development of each to its full potential.
Publication: Newsletter
Publication title: BMF Update

Bureau Europeen pour les Langues Moins Repandues

see European Bureau for Lesser-Used Languages

00047

Burma Action Ireland
BAI

PO Box 6786, Dublin 1, Ireland
Tel: 087 1261857
Fax: 01 8559753
Email: info@burmaactionireland.org
Website: http://www.burmaactionireland.org
Contact: John Boorman, Hon. Pres.
Fee: £50
Membership Type: organization
Fee: £25
Membership Type: full-time waged
Description: Raises public awareness of the current situation in Burma and the nature of the ruling regime. Campaigns for democracy and human rights in Burma. Provides material and moral assistance to those forces involved in the struggle for democracy and human rights in Burma. Lobbies the Irish government on its stand on Burma.
Publication: Newsletter
Publication title: The Burma Action Ireland Newsletter

00048

Call Centre Management Association, Ireland
CCMA

PO Box 1016, Naas 18, Kildare, Ireland
Tel: 087 2256055
Fax: 01 2938957
Email: info@ccma.ie
Website: http://www.ccma.ie
Contact: Annette Hickey, Chair
Fee: £100
Membership Type: individual
Fee: £800
Membership Type: corporate
Description: Promotes the profession and recognition of contact center management. Develops a system of benchmarking and standards for courses and training available to the industry. Creates awareness for all relevant legislation being passed on the industry at the European and local levels. Provides education to members.

00049

Car Rental Council of Ireland

5 Upper Pembroke St., Dublin 2, Ireland
Tel: 01 6761690
Fax: 01 6619213
Email: predmond@simi.ie
Website: http://www.carrentalcouncil.ie
Description: Represents car hire companies operating in the Republic of Ireland.
Library Subject: gay, lesbian, straight travel publications, travel in North America and international
Library Type: not open to the public
Meetings/Conventions: biennial meeting

00050

Carers Association

National Office, Market Sq., Tullamore, Offaly, Ireland
Tel: 057 9322920
Fax: 057 9323623
Email: info@carersireland.com
Website: http://www.carersireland.com
Members: 8000
Staff: 106
Contact: Enda Egan, CEO
Description: Represents caregivers who provide high levels of care in their own homes for family members and neighbors. Provides home-based respite services. Disseminates information; conducts educational programs.
Library Subject: welfare, home-care
Library Type: reference

Ceardchumann Teicniuil, Innealtoireachta and Leictreachais

see Technical, Engineering and Electrical Union

00051

Chambers of Commerce of Ireland
CCI

17 Merrion Sq., Dublin 2, Ireland
Tel: 01 4004300
Fax: 01 6612811
Email: info@chambers.ie
Website: http://www.chambers.ie/index.php?id=1
Members: 60
Contact: Ian Talbot, Chief Exec.
Description: Local chambers of commerce representing 11,000 companies in the Republic of Ireland. Promotes, develops, and represents Irish industry and commerce. Provides lobbying services for members. Conducts training seminars and programs. Seeks to stimulate and facilitate the growth and development of the Irish chamber network. Runs several business development projects.
Formerly: Also Known As, Chambers Ireland
Publication: Newsletter
Publication title: The Bulletin

00052

Chartered Institute of Logistics and Transport in Ireland
CILTI

1 Fitzwilliam Pl., Dublin 2, Ireland
Tel: 01 6763188
Fax: 01 6764099
Email: info@cilt.ie
Website: http://www.cilt.ie
Members: 1250
Staff: 6
Contact: Colm Holmes, CEO
Fee: £103
Membership Type: regular
Fee: £134
Membership Type: chartered
Description: Aims to advance and promote the science and art of logistics and transport.
Publication: Magazine
Publication title: LINKLINE. Advertisements.

00053

Chartered Institute of Management Accountants - Ireland
CIMA

45-47 Pembroke Rd., Ballsbridge 4, Dublin, Ireland
Tel: 01 6430400
Fax: 01 6430401
Email: dublin@cimaglobal.com
Website: http://www.cimaglobal.com/our-locations/ireland
Contact: Fiona Arnold, Student Recruitment Mgr.
Description: Represents financial managers and accountants who work in industry, commerce, not-for-profit and public sector organizations.

00054

Cheshire Ireland
CI

Block 4 Bracken Business Park, Bracken Rd., Sandyford Industrial Estate, Dublin 18, Ireland
Tel: 01 2974100
Fax: 01 2052060
Email: info@cheshire.ie
Website: http://www.cheshire.ie
Contact: Mark Blake Knox, Chief Exec.
Description: Strives to provide accommodation and respite and other support services to adults with physical disabilities in the Republic of Ireland.
Formerly: Formerly, Cheshire Foundation in Ireland

00055

ChildFund Ireland

63 Lower Mount St., Dublin 2, Ireland
Tel: 01 6762128
Fax: 01 6761072
Email: info@childfund.ie
Website: http://www.childfund.ie
Contact: Michael Kiely, CEO
Description: Dedicated to supporting children in developing countries.
Formerly: Formerly, Christian Children's Fund of Ireland

00056

Childminding Ireland

9 Bulford Business Campus, Kilcoole, Wicklow, Ireland
Tel: 01 2878466
Fax: 01 2878465
Email: info@childminding.ie
Website: http://www.childminding.ie
Contact: Patricia Murray, Chief Exec.
Fee: £55
Membership Type: full
Fee: £20
Membership Type: general, associate
Description: Promotes high standards in family-based day care for children. Promotes public awareness of childminders as an important component in the workforce. Provides training, support and advice for childminders and parents. Maintains a register of childminders.

00057

Children at Risk in Ireland
CARI

110 Lower Drumcondra Rd., Dublin 9, Ireland
Tel: 01 8308529
Fax: 01 8306309
Email: info@cari.ie
Website: http://www.cari.ie
Staff: 50
Contact: Mary Flaherty, Natl. Dir.
Description: Provides post-assessment therapy services for children (up to 18 years old) who have experienced child sexual abuse. Provides an information service, outreach presentations and workshops. Operates confidential telephone advice and support line.

00058

Children's Books Ireland
CBI

17 N Great Georges St., 1st Fl., Dublin 1, Ireland
Tel: 01 8727475
Fax: 01 8727476
Email: info@childrensbooksireland.com
Website: http://www.childrensbooksireland.com
Members: 1000
Staff: 3
Contact: Mags Walsh, Dir.
Fee: £30
Membership Type: individual
Fee: £60
Membership Type: overseas institutional/overseas individual
Description: Parents, teachers, librarians, booksellers, authors, and illustrators. Promotes children's books and reading.
Publication: Magazine
Publication title: Inis. Advertisements.
Meetings/Conventions: Irish Children's Book Festival – festival

00059
Children's Rights Alliance
4 Upper Mount St., Dublin 2, Ireland
Tel: 01 6629400
Fax: 01 6629355
Email: info@childrensrights.ie
Website: http://www.childrensrights.ie
Members: 80
Contact: Paul Gilligan, Chm.
Description: Seeks to secure the implementation in Ireland of the principles and provisions of the UN Convention on the Rights of the Child. Advances the effort to eliminate child poverty in Ireland. Promotes awareness and understanding of the convention and training in children's rights for relevant statutory personnel. Seeks to incorporate into Irish law the principles and provisions of the UN Convention on the Rights of the Child.

00060
Clanwilliam Institute
CI
18 Clanwilliam Terr., Grand Canal Quay, Dublin 2, Ireland
Tel: 01 6761363
Email: office@clanwilliam.ie
Website: http://www.clanwilliam.ie
Members: 24
Staff: 21
Contact: Aileen Tierney, CEO
Description: Psychologists, family therapists, and other mental health and family service providers. Promotes healthy and happy family relations. Provides consulting services, therapy, and mediation to families in crisis; offers substance abuse, stress management, parenting and adult education programs. Conducts family enrichment activities; sponsors professional training courses for mental health and family service providers. Sponsors public education campaigns to raise awareness of family issues; lobbies government agencies on issues relating to families and family life. Offers counseling and training programmes for organizations' staff.

00061
Clare Animal Welfare
CAW
Ahish, Ballinruan, Crusheen, Clare, Ireland
Tel: 087 1315904
Email: sheena@clareanimalwelfare.net
Website: http://www.clareanimalwelfare.net
Contact: Sarah Mortimer, Contact
Fee: £10
Membership Type: employed
Fee: £7
Membership Type: student, unwaged
Description: Creates positive public awareness of the rights of animals. Offers support to individuals and groups who are concerned about animals in the community. Seeks to highlight the inadequacies for animals in the community.

00062
Classical Association of Ireland
CAI
c/o Simon Spence, Membership Sec.
University College of Dublin, Department of Classics, Dublin 4, Ireland
Email: website@classicalassociation.com
Website: http://www.classicalassociation.com/index.html
Contact: Vincent Twomey, Honorary Pres.
Fee: £30
Membership Type: individual
Fee: £40
Membership Type: family
Description: Individuals with a general interest in ancient Greek and Roman civilizations and those who teach Classics at the second and third levels. Seeks to cultivate and further an interest in classical studies in Ireland. Provides lectures and field trips; organizes social events; promotes the study of Classics in the curriculum; assists in the development of study aids; raises community awareness.

00063
Cleft Lip and Palate Association of Ireland
CLAPAI
36 Woodlands Ave., Dun Laoghaire, Dublin, Ireland
Tel: 087 1319803
Email: info@cleft.ie
Website: http://www.cleft.ie
Contact: Enda Barrett, Chair
Description: Provides support and information for parents and children affected by cleft lip and palate; provides support to new parents and advice on feeding and ongoing medical care throughout treatment.
Publication: Booklet
Publication title: Information on CLEFT LIP & PALATE

00064
Clonmel Chamber of Commerce
8 Sarsfield St., Clonmel, Tipperary, Ireland
Tel: 052 6126500
Email: info@clonmelchmanber.com
Website: http://www.clonmelchamber.com
Contact: Brian Cleary, CEO
Description: Promotes commerce and industry in Ireland.

00065
Cluid Housing Association - North East
Shanowen Business Centre, Shanowen Rd., Ste. 6, Santry, Dublin 9, Ireland
Tel: 01 8578030
Fax: 01 8579653
Email: northeast@cluid.ie
Website: http://www.cluid.ie
Contact: Simon Brooke, Chm.
Description: Seeks to design, build and manage affordable housing. Facilitates the creation of homes and sustainable communities for those in housing need. Aims to create mixed, sustainable communities.

00066
Coeliac Society of Ireland
4 N Brunswick St., Carmichael House, Dublin 7, Ireland
Tel: 01 8721471
Fax: 01 8735737
Email: info@coeliac.ie
Website: http://www.coeliac.ie
Members: 4500
Staff: 1
Contact: Gerry Flaherty, Chm.
Fee: £25
Membership Type: individual
Fee: £30
Membership Type: family, professional
Description: Promotes, safeguards, and protects members' interests in relation to Coeliac disease. Produces a list of gluten free foods, information leaflets, and cookbooks.
Library Subject: Coeliac disease, food list, cookery
Library Type: reference

00067
COFORD: National Council for Forest Research and Development
Arena House, Arena Rd., Sandyford, Dublin 18, Ireland
Tel: 01 2130725
Fax: 01 2130611
Email: info@coford.ie
Website: http://www.coford.ie/iopen24
Staff: 5
Contact: Eugene Hendrick, Dir.
Description: Harvesters and manufacturers of forest products; forestry research and educational programs and institutions. Promotes improved communication and cooperation among forest industries and forestry researchers; seeks to ensure sustainable use of forestry resources. Monitors and evaluates forest research projects; facilitates innovation in the practice of forestry and the harvesting and manufacturing of forest products; sponsors research and educational programs. Represents the Republic of Ireland in international forestry and research organizations; maintains liaison with European Union forestry agencies.
Publication: Newsletter
Publication title: Forestry and Wood Update

Comhairle Chaomhnaithe Phortaigh na hEireann
see Irish Peatland Conservation Council

Comhairle Naisiunta na mBan in Eirinn
see National Women's Council of Ireland

Comhairle Naisiunta na Nog
see National Youth Council of Ireland

Comhairle Treidlianna na Heireann
see Veterinary Council of Ireland

Comhaltas Ceoltoiri Eireann
see Traditional Irish Music, Singing and Dancing Society

Comhaontas na Siochana is Neodrachta
see Peace and Neutrality Alliance

00068

Comhlamh

Ballast House, 2nd Fl., Aston Quay, Dublin 2, Ireland
Tel: 01 4783490
Fax: 01 4783738
Email: info@comhlamh.org
Website: http://www.comhlamh.org
Members: 800
Staff: 15
Contact: Deirdre Murray, Dir.
Description: Citizens of the Republic of Ireland who have participated in development work overseas; interested others. Promotes international cooperation in development. Works to increase awareness and understanding of development issues. Offers a support and information service to returning development workers. Offers support to volunteers involved in development education.
Publication: Magazine
Publication title: Focus on Ireland and the Wider World. Advertisements.

00069

Compassion In World Farming - Ireland
CIWF

PO Box 750, Togher, Cork, Ireland
Tel: 021 4639038
Email: info@ciwf.ie
Website: http://www.ciwf.ie
Contact: Mary-Anne Bartlett, Dir.
Description: Campaigns for improvements in farm animal welfare. Seeks to end industrialized farming of animals. Strives to end the live export trade. Opposes generic engineering and cloning of farm animals. Highlights particular issues in the media.
Publication: Video
Publication title: Good For Farm Animals, Good For Us!

Conaidhm Eireannach na Muinteoiri Ollscoile
see Irish Federation of University Teachers

00070

Connemara Pony Breeders Society
CPBS

4 Lenaboy Pk., Salthill, Galway, Ireland
Tel: 09521863
Email: enquiries@cpbs.ie
Website: http://www.cpbs.ie
Members: 850
Staff: 2
Contact: Dermot Power, Pres.
Description: Breeders of Connemara ponies.
Publication: Newsletter
Publication title: An Capaillin. Advertisements.

00071

Construction Industry Federation
CIF

Construction House, Canal Rd., Dublin 6, Ireland
Tel: 01 4066000
Fax: 01 4966953
Email: cif@cif.ie
Website: http://www.cif.ie/asp/section.asp?s=1
Members: 3000
Contact: Gerald Purcell, Pres.
Description: General contractors, mechanical and electrical contractors, specialist contractors, and home-builders. Provides problem-solving expertise for the industry, monitors issues and trends, and initiates proposals.
Publication: Newsletter
Publication title: CIF News Update

00072

Consumers Association of Ireland
CAI

43-44 Chelmsford Rd., Dublin 6, Ireland
Tel: 01 4978600
Fax: 01 4978601
Email: cai@consumerassociation.ie
Website: http://www.consumerassociation.ie
Members: 9500
Staff: 9
Contact: Dermott Jewell, Chief Exec.
Fee: £96
Membership Type: regular
Description: Works on behalf of the interest of Irish consumers. Runs a telephone advice and information service to help consumers with complaints.
Publication: Magazine
Publication title: Consumer Choice

00073

CREATE

10-11 Earl St. S, Dublin 8, Ireland
Tel: 01 4736600
Fax: 01 4736599
Email: info@create-ireland.ie
Website: http://www.create-ireland.ie
Members: 200
Staff: 6
Contact: Arthur Duignan, Asst. Dir.
Fee: £60
Membership Type: community, organization
Fee: £30
Membership Type: individual associate
Description: Supports arts development in Ireland. Offers free public arts information service, work referrals for artists and skilled practitioners, specialist training for artists and organizations, project advice and career development, consulting, administrative and research services.
Formerly: Formerly, Creative Activity for Everyone
Publication: Newsletter
Publication title: CAFEnews

00074

Cuba Support Group - Ireland

15 Merrion Sq., Dublin 2, Ireland
Tel: 087 6785842
Email: cubasupport@eircom.net
Website: http://www.cubasupport.com
Staff: 2
Contact: Simon McGuinness, Coor.
Fee: £20
Membership Type: employed
Fee: £10
Membership Type: unwaged
Description: Brings together people across the political spectrum who believe in Cuba's right to trade, develop and self-determination.
Publication: Newsletter
Publication title: Cuba Today

Cumann Bainistiocht Eolaiocht na h-Eireann
see Management Science Society of Ireland

Cumann Cheol Tire Eireann
see Folk Music Society of Ireland

Cumann Comhshaoil Dhoctuiri na heireann
see Irish Doctors Environmental Association

Cumann Corpoideachais na hEireann
see Physical Education Association of Ireland

Cumann Innealtoiri Comhairle na h Eirann
see Association of Consulting Engineers of Ireland

Cumann Leabharlann na hEireann
see Library Association of Ireland

Cumann Lucht Capaillini Chonamara
see Connemara Pony Breeders Society

Cumann Muinteoiri Eireann
see Irish National Teachers' Organisation

Cumann na Meanmhuinteori Eire
see Association of Secondary Teachers Ireland

Cumann na Scoileanna Pobail agus Cuimsitheacha
see Association of Community and Comprehensive Schools

Cumann Tireolaiochta na hEireann
see Geographical Society of Ireland

00075

Cystic Fibrosis Association of Ireland CFAI

CF House, 24 Lower Rathmines Rd., Dublin 6, Ireland
Tel: 01 4962433
Fax: 01 4962201
Email: info@cfireland.ie
Website: http://www.cfireland.ie
Members: 2000
Staff: 7
Contact: Philip Watt, CEO
Description: People with cystic fibrosis and their families; individuals and organizations providing support and services to people with cystic fibrosis. Seeks to improve the quality of life of people with cystic fibrosis. Provides backup services for people with cystic fibrosis.
Library Type: reference
Publication: Magazine
Publication title: Future Force. Advertisements.

00076

DeafHear.ie

35 N Frederick St., Dublin 1, Ireland
Tel: 01 8175700
Fax: 01 8783629
Email: info@deafhear.ie
Website: http://www.deafhear.ie
Staff: 70
Fee: £20
Description: Individuals and organizations. Seeks to improve the quality of life of people with hearing impairments; promotes full recognition of the rights of people with hearing loss. Makes available support and services; conducts educational and advocacy campaigns. Offers a job coaching service; operates Family Resource Centre; conducts sign language classes.
Library Subject: deaf issues
Library Type: open to the public
Formerly: Formerly, National Association for Deaf People
Publication: Magazine
Publication title: DeafHear Matters. Advertisements.

00077

DEBRA Ireland

La Touche House, 1 Grove Rd., Rathmines, Dublin 6, Ireland
Tel: 01 4126924
Fax: 01 6335104
Email: info@debraireland.org
Website: http://www.debraireland.org
Staff: 15
Contact: Michael Griffith, Contact
Description: Individuals and organizations. Seeks to improve the quality of life of people with EB and their families. Makes available specialist care; conducts educational programs for health care personnel and the public.
Publication: Newsletters

00078

Dental Health Foundation

1st Fl. Corrigan House, Fenian St., Dublin 2, Ireland
Tel: 01 6629123
Fax: 01 6618721
Email: info@dentalhealth.ie
Website: http://www.dentalhealth.ie
Contact: Brendan Pigott, Chm.
Description: Promotes oral health in Ireland.
Publication: Report
Publication title: Mouthpiece

00079

Diabetes Federation of Ireland

76 Lower Gardiner St., Dublin 1, Ireland
Tel: 01 8363022
Fax: 01 8365182
Email: info@diabetes.ie
Website: http://www.diabetes.ie/Website/content/default.aspx
Members: 5000
Staff: 6
Contact: Kieran O'Leary, CEO
Description: Represents people with diabetes. Provides information, creates awareness encourages research and ongoing support of people with diabetes.
Publication: Magazine
Publication title: Diabetes Ireland

00080

Disability Federation of Ireland DFI

Fumbally Ct., Fumbally Ln., Dublin 8, Ireland
Tel: 01 4547978
Fax: 01 4547981
Email: info@disability-federation.ie
Website: http://www.disability-federation.ie
Staff: 7
Contact: John Dolan, CEO
Description: Voluntary and nonstatutory agencies providing support services to people with disabilities. Seeks to increase the availability and quality of services for people with disabilities; promotes development of the full potential of all people. Provides support and assistance to members; facilitates communication and networking among members; develops training programs for people providing services to people with disabilities; serves as a liaison linking members with public agencies responsible for statutes affecting people with disabilities. Makes available resource services; sponsors research and educational programs; conducts lobbying activities.
Publication: Newsletter
Publication title: DFI Newsletter

00081

Disabled Drivers' Association of Ireland DDAI

Ballendine, Claremorris, Mayo, Ireland
Tel: 094 9364054
Fax: 094 9364336
Email: info@ddai.ie
Website: http://www.ddai.ie
Members: 5500
Staff: 5
Contact: Kenneth Fox, CEO
Description: Individuals and organizations. Promotes improve mobility for people with disabilities. Lobbies to safeguard the right of people with disabilities to obtain drivers' licenses; conducts educational and training programs.
Publication: Magazine
Publication title: Steering Wheel. Advertisements.

00082

DOCHAS, The Irish Association of Non-Governmental Development Organisations

12 Harcourt St., Dublin 2, Ireland
Tel: 01 4053801
Fax: 01 4053802
Email: anna@dochas.ie
Website: http://www.dochas.ie
Members: 38
Staff: 3
Contact: Helen Keogh, Chair
Description: Brings together 38 Irish NGDO involved in development and relief overseas and/or in the provision of development education. Aims to provide a forum for consultation and cooperation between its members and acts as the Irish Assembly of Development and Relief Organisations in relation to the CONCORD - a European Confederation for relief and development.

00083

Down Syndrome Ireland

Citylink Business Park, Old Naas Rd., Dublin 12, Ireland
Tel: 01 4266500
Fax: 01 4266501
Email: info@downsyndrome.ie
Website: http://www.downsyndrome.ie
Members: 3000
Staff: 9
Contact: Christina Riordan, Gen. Mgr.
Description: Unites to improve the quality of life of people with Down Syndrome. Provides support and services to people with Down Syndrome and their families. Conducts educational programs.
Library Subject: down syndrome
Library Type: reference
Formerly: Formerly, FootSteps: Down Syndrome Ireland

00084

Driving Instructor Register of Ireland DIR

105 Shanliss Rd., Santry, Dublin 9, Ireland
Tel: 01 8622278
Fax: 01 8622279
Email: info@dir.ie
Website: http://www.dir.ie
Members: 1400
Staff: 4
Contact: Des Cummins, Chm.
Description: Represents driving instructors in Ireland.
Publication: Newsletter
Publication title: RDI Update. Advertisements.

00085

Dublin Chamber of Commerce

7 Clare St., Dublin 2, Ireland
Tel: 01 6447200
Fax: 01 6766043
Email: info@dubchamber.ie
Website: http://www.dublinchamber.ie
Members: 1600
Staff: 17
Contact: Gina Quin, Chief Exec.
Fee: £550
Membership Type: small and medium enterprise
Fee: £1500
Membership Type: business
Description: Promotes commerce and industry in Dublin, Ireland.
Publication: Magazine
Publication title: Business Ireland

00086

Dublin City Business Association DCBA

21 Dawson St., Dublin 2, Ireland
Tel: 01 6622995
Email: info@dcba.ie
Website: http://www.dcba.ie
Members: 800
Staff: 3
Contact: Tom Coffey, CEO
Description: Retail Federation in the city of Dublin. Promotes a sustainable city centre that is attractive to live, work, visit, and shop in centre.
Library Subject: cities, Dublin
Library Type: by appointment only
Publication: Booklet
Publication title: Dublin Map & Visitor Guide. Advertisements.

00087

Dyspraxia Association of Ireland

Carmichael House, North Brunswick St., Dublin 7, Ireland
Tel: 01 8747085
Email: dyspraxiaireland@eircom.net
Website: http://www.dyspraxiaireland.com
Contact: Tom McCarthy, Chair
Fee: £30
Membership Type: parent, adult
Fee: £35
Membership Type: professional
Description: Parents of children with dyspraxia. Seeks to raise awareness of dyspraxia in Ireland and to create a better understanding of the difficulties children and parents face. Ensures adequate professional and medical resources are available to parents; provides information and a support network; works to improve diagnostic services.

Eagras Um Chearta Cheolta

see Irish Music Rights Organisation

00088

Economic and Social History Society of Ireland ESHSI

c/o Dr. Margaret O'Hogartaigh, Membership Sec.
Department of Modern History, Trinity College, Dublin 2, Ireland
Email: eshsireland@gmail.com
Website: http://eh.net/eshsi
Members: 650
Staff: 12
Contact: David Dickson, Pres.
Fee: £26
Membership Type: individual
Fee: £32
Membership Type: institution
Description: Encourages the study of Irish economic and social history at all levels. Brings together individuals engaged in teaching and research.
Publication: Journal
Publication title: Irish Economic and Social History

00089

Economic and Social Research Institute ESRI

Whitaker Sq., Sir John Rogerson's Quay, Dublin 2, Ireland
Tel: 01 8632000
Fax: 01 8632100
Email: admin@esri.ie
Website: http://www.esri.ie
Members: 500
Staff: 85
Contact: Frances Ruane, Dir.
Fee: £400-2600
Membership Type: corporate (based on number of staff)
Fee: £400
Membership Type: library
Description: Applies current thinking in economics and the social sciences to the actual and potential problems of Irish society ESRI. Research is a vital constituent in the national debate on economic and social issues.

Eigse Eireann

see Poetry Ireland

00090

EIL Intercultural Learning EIL

1 Empress Pl., Summerhill N, Cork, Ireland
Tel: 021 4551535
Fax: 021 4551587
Email: info@eilireland.org
Website: http://www.eilireland.org
Members: 2000
Staff: 6
Contact: Kevin Hickey, Dir.
Description: Works to establish peace and understanding among different cultures through cooperation with government agencies and schools. Sponsors cultural immersion and volunteer programs.
Formerly: Formerly, Experiment in International Living - Ireland

00091

Electro-Technical Council of Ireland ETCI

Unit H12, Centrepoint Business Park, Oak Rd., Dublin 12, Ireland
Tel: 01 4290088
Fax: 01 4290090
Email: info@etci.ie
Website: http://www.etci.ie
Contact: Michael Hanly, Chm.
Description: Represents all aspects of electrotechnology in Ireland and the Irish member of the International Electrotechnical Commission (IEC) and the European Committee for Electrotechnical Standardisation (CENELEC). Involves everyone associated with the electrical industry, seeking comment, input and suggestions of the industry. Prepares rules, guides, and codes of practice and through consultation achieves agreement on a consensus basis.

00092

Enable - Ireland

32nd Fl., Rosemount Park Dr., Rosemount Business Park, Ballycoolin Rd., Dublin 11, Ireland
Tel: 01 8727155
Fax: 01 8665222
Email: communications@enableireland.ie
Website: http://www.enableireland.ie
Contact: Donal Cashman, Chm.
Description: Provides support services for people with disabilities and their families. Aims for a holistic approach in service delivery. Helps individuals make choices and reduce dependence.

00093

Energy Action EA

IDA Unit 14, Newmarket, Dublin 8, Ireland
Tel: 01 4545464
Fax: 01 4549797
Email: info@energyaction.ie
Website: http://www.energyaction.ie/home.html
Members: 14
Staff: 61
Contact: David McCarthy, Chm.
Description: Individuals interested in meeting the energy needs of the elderly. Seeks to improve energy efficiency in the homes of elderly people. Provides home insulation services at no cost to elderly individuals. Trains unemployed people to install insulation in accordance with building codes and safety standards.

00094

Energy Research Group ERG

University College Dublin, Richview, Clonskeagh, Dublin 14, Ireland
Tel: 01 2692750
Fax: 01 7162690
Email: erg@erg.ucd.ie
Website: http://erg.ucd.ie
Staff: 20
Contact: J. Owen Lewis, Dir.
Description: Promotes architectural innovation and technical change in the construction industries leading to more energy-efficient buildings. Conducts research and development activities; makes available consulting services; provides technical support to architects and designers; current projects focus on application of solar energy technologies to architectural designs. Gathers and disseminates information to raise public awareness of energy efficiency in architecture; sponsors educational programs.
Publication: Video
Publication title: Solar Architecture in Europe

00095

Engineers Ireland IEI

22 Clyde Rd., Ballsbridge, Dublin 4, Ireland
Tel: 01 6651300
Fax: 01 6685508
Email: info@engineersireland.ie
Website: http://www.engineersireland.ie
Members: 24000
Contact: John Power, Dir. Gen.
Fee: £60
Membership Type: retired
Fee: £35

Membership Type: volunteer, postgraduate, unemployed
Description: Engineers and engineering students. Seeks to advance the engineering professions; promotes continuing professional development of members. Facilitates communication and collaboration among members; sponsors educational programs; conducts golf tournaments and other social activities. Conducts qualifying examinations; promulgates standards of competence, ethics, and practice for the engineering professions.
Library Subject: engineering
Library Type: reference
Formerly: Formerly, Institution of Engineers of - Ireland
Publication: Journal
Publication title: The Engineers Journal

00096

Erb's Palsy Association of Ireland

Seafield Rd., Blackrock, Louth, Ireland
Tel: 042 9322198
Email: info@erbspalsy.ie
Website: http://www.erbspalsy.ie
Members: 200
Contact: Phillip Murtagh, Sec.
Description: Parents of children born with Erb's Palsy. Seeks to raise awareness of and provide information on Erb's Palsy, a childbirth injury causing temporary and sometimes permanent paralysis in the arm.

00097

Estuarine and Coastal Sciences Association
ECSA

Zoology Dept., Trinity Coll., Dublin 2, Ireland
Tel: 01 6081640
Email: jwilson@tcd.ie
Website: http://www.ecsa-news.org
Members: 700
Contact: Jim Wilson, Sec.
Fee: £31
Membership Type: full
Fee: £11
Membership Type: student
Description: Professional scientists, estuarine and coastal managers, students, and interested individuals and organizations in 24 countries. Promotes: the production and dissemination of scientific knowledge and understanding of estuaries and other brackish and coastal waters; the prevention of environmental deterioration; management of natural resources for the public benefit. Fosters cooperation, coordination, and communication between producers and users of scientific information and among specialists from different disciplines. Sponsors professional training courses in estuarine methodology; holds symposia and workshops on such topics as numerical analyses, physical methods, and taxonomy of invertebrate groups.
Formerly: Formerly, Estuarine and Brackish-Water Biological Association
Publication: Bulletin
Publication title: ECSA Bulletin. Advertisements.

00098

European Academy of Paediatric Dentistry
EAPD

Department of Public and Child Dental Health, Dublin Dental School and Hospital, Lincoln Pl., Dublin 2, Ireland
Email: pfleming@dental.tcd.ie
Website: http://www.eapd.gr
Members: 550
Contact: Paddy Fleming, Sec.
Fee: £100
Membership Type: active, associate
Fee: £40
Membership Type: retired, student
Description: Individuals whose primary concern is in the areas of practice, education, and research related to pediatric dentistry. Works to improve the oral health of children.
Publication: Journal
Publication title: European Archives of Paediatric Dentistry. Advertisements.
Meetings/Conventions: biennial congress May 24 to 27, 2012. Strasbourg France

00099

European Association for Computer Assisted Language Learning
EUROCALL

University of Ulster, School of Languages, Literatures and Cultures, Coleraine, Ireland
Email: eurocall@ulster.ac.uk
Website: http://www.eurocall-languages.org
Members: 410
Staff: 2
Contact: Margaret Gammell, Sec.
Fee: £90
Membership Type: individual
Fee: £225
Membership Type: corporate
Description: Language teaching professionals. Promotes the use of foreign languages in Europe. Disseminates information and offers advice on all aspects of the use of technology for language learning, for those involved in education and training.
Publication: Newsletter
Publication title: EUROCALL Review
Meetings/Conventions: Networked Language Learning – annual conference

00100

European Bureau for Lesser-Used Languages
EBLUL

Sr. Chill Dara - Kildare St. 46, Baile Atha Cliath, Dublin 2, Ireland
Tel: 01 6794764
Website: http://www.eblul.org
Members: 26
Staff: 7
Contact: John McIntyre, VP
Description: Member states of the Commission of the European Communities. Preserves and promotes the minority cultures and languages of Europe. Believes that minority languages are integral to Europe's general cultural heritage; rejects linguistic and cultural conformity and envisions a "unity in diversity" in Europe. Works for the creation of legal and political structures that would protect minority language communities; seeks to cultivate solidarity among such communities through the exchange of information; provides and encourages practical assistance to these communities. Sponsors study visits for minority language activists. Has researched the status of minority languages in pre-school education.
Publication: Booklet
Publication title: Language Rights: Individual & Collective

00101

European College of Veterinary Internal Medicine - Companion Animals
ECVIM-CA

c/o Dr. Carmel T. Mooney, Exec. Sec.
University Colorado Dublin, Faculty of Veterinary Medicine, Department of Small Animal Studies, Belfield, Dublin 4, Ireland
Tel: 01 6687988
Email: carmel.mooney@ucd.ie
Website: http://www.ecvim-ca.org
Contact: Michele Borgarelli, Pres.
Description: Works to advance companion animal internal medicine in Europe.
Publication: Brochure
Publication title: Information Brochure for Residents and Supervisors

00102

European Computer Driving License Foundation
ECDL-F

Portview House, Thorncastle St., Dublin 4, Ireland
Tel: 01 6306000
Fax: 01 6306001
Website: http://www.ecdl.org/publisher/index.jsp
Description: Promotes knowledge about information technology; works to increase the level of competence in using computers and common computer applications worldwide; aims to provide certification for global information technology standards.

00103

European Foot and Ankle Society
EFAS

76a Upper Georges St., Dun Laoghaire, Dublin, Ireland
Tel: 01 2302591
Fax: 01 2302594
Email: efas@eventplus.ie
Website: http://www.efas.co.uk
Members: 2850
Contact: Hakon Kofoed, Pres.
Fee: £160
Membership Type: individual
Fee: £60
Membership Type: corresponding/associate
Description: Promotes the development of foot and ankle surgery; aims to advance education, study and research in the foot and ankle surgery specialty.

00104

European Foundation for the Improvement of Living and Working Conditions

Wyattville Rd., Loughlinstown 18, Dublin, Ireland
Tel: 01 2043100
Fax: 01 2826456
Email: information@eurofound.europa.eu
Website: http://www.eurofound.europa.eu
Staff: 100
Contact: Jorma Karppinen, Dir.
Description: Promotes research management and information and communication to improve the living and working conditions of people living in Europe; maintains support in the areas of administration, human

resources, operational services, information and communication technologies with governments, employers, trade unions, and the European Commission.
Library Subject: quality of life, quality of work, industrial relations, restructuring, equal opportunities
Library Type: by appointment only
Publication: Newsletters
Publication title: Communique

00105
European Movement - Ireland
EMI
6 Merrion Sq., Dublin 2, Ireland
Tel: 01 6625815
Fax: 01 6625817
Email: info@europeanmovement.ie
Website: http://www.europeanmovement.ie
Members: 800
Staff: 4
Contact: Andrea Pappin, Exec. Dir.
Fee: £60
Membership Type: individual
Fee: £10
Membership Type: student
Description: Promotes the economic, political and social development of Europe. Plays an active role in shaping Irish attitudes to Europe. Works to influence policy process; promotes public discussion on key issues relating to Europe's development, and their implications for Ireland. Disseminates information on European Union issues.
Publication: Journal
Publication title: Bulletin

00106
European Society for Cataract and Refractive Surgeons
ESCRS
Temple House, Temple Rd., Blackrock, Dublin 2, Ireland
Tel: 01 2091100
Fax: 01 2091112
Email: escrs@escrs.org
Website: http://www.escrs.org
Members: 4000
Contact: Josep Guell, Pres.
Fee: £150
Membership Type: full, international, non-medical visual scientist
Fee: £50
Membership Type: trainee
Description: Strives to advance scientific knowledge in the field of intraocular lens implantation and in the art and practice of such surgery.
Publication: Magazine
Publication title: Eurotimes. Advertisements.
Meetings/Conventions: annual congress – Exhibits.

00107
European Society of Domestic Animal Reproduction
ESDAR
University College Dublin, School of Agriculture, Food Science and Veterinary Medicine, College of Life Sciences, Rm. 249, Belfield 4, Dublin, Ireland
Tel: 01 7166255
Fax: 01 7166253
Email: mark.crowe@ucd.ie
Website: http://www.esdar.org
Contact: Mark A. Crowe, Sec.
Fee: £60
Membership Type: regular
Description: Promotes education and research in domestic animal reproduction, especially for clinical aspects, biotechnology and physiology of reproduction.
Publication: Journal
Publication title: Reproduction in Domestic Animals

00108
Farm Tractor and Machinery Trade Association
FTMTA
Unit 3, Rd. D, Tougher's Business Park, Newhall, Naas 12, Kildare, Ireland
Tel: 045 409309
Fax: 045 409308
Email: info@ftmta.ie
Website: http://www.ftmta.ie
Members: 275
Staff: 2
Contact: Gary Ryan, Chief Exec.
Description: Provides information, advice and lobbying services for those involved in the farm machinery industry in Ireland.

Federacion Internacional de Patologia Cervical y Colposcopia
see International Federation for Cervical Pathology and Colposcopy

00109
Federation of Aerospace Enterprises in Ireland
FAEI
Confederation House, 84-86 Lower Baggot St., Dublin 2, Ireland
Tel: 01 6051652
Fax: 01 6381652
Email: mark.mcauley@ibec.ie
Website: http://www.faei.ie
Members: 50
Contact: Mark McAuley, Contact
Description: Promotes the Irish Aerospace Industry at home and abroad as a world class provider of products and services. Develops education and training needs to meet the future demands of the industry. Coordinates with the Irish Aviation Authority on issues which impact the development of European and other airworthiness regulatory requirements.
Publication: Newsletter
Publication title: Aerospace Enterprise

00110
Federation of Irish Beekeepers Associations
FIBA
Ballinakill, Enfield, Meath, Ireland
Tel: 046 9541433
Email: mgglee@eircom.net
Website: http://www.irishbeekeeping.ie
Members: 1500
Contact: Michael G. Gleeson, Sec.
Description: Local authorities representing 1500 beekeepers. Promotes growth and development of domestic apiculture; seeks to advance beekeeping techniques and related sciences. Represents members' collective interests; conducts research and educational programs; operates labelling scheme for Irish bee products; maintains speakers' bureau; makes available discounts on insurance and apicultural supplies to members; formulates beekeeping standards and conducts certification examinations; undertakes lobbying campaigns.
Publication: Journal
Publication title: An Beachaire
Meetings/Conventions: Summer Course – annual seminar

00111
Fertilizer Association of Ireland
FAI
c/o Grassland Fertilizers Ltd.
Carrigrohane Rd., Cork, Ireland
Tel: 087 2755625
Website: http://www.fertilizer-assoc.ie/default.htm
Members: 120
Description: Provides a forum for the exchange of scientific and technical information in relation to the production and use of fertilizers. Promotes the efficient use of fertilizers in Ireland.

00112
FIABCI - Ireland
14 Millbrook Village, Dublin 6, Ireland
Tel: 087 6686124
Fax: 01 2604196
Email: pauljackson10@eircom.net
Website: http://www.fiabci.com
Contact: Eddie Barrett, Pres.
Description: Represents professionals involved in the property industry. Gives members access to information on real estate markets all over the world. Disseminates general and technical information and recommends solutions to problems facing the real estate profession. Provides assistance to members whenever the rules of the profession are called into question. Encourages private property ownership.

00113
Fianna Fail
65-66 Lower Mount St., Dublin 2, Ireland
Tel: 01 6761551
Email: info@briancrowleymep.ie
Website: http://www.fiannafail.ie
Contact: Mary White, Contact
Description: Fosters equal rights for women in Ireland.

Foilsiu Eireann
see Publishing Ireland

00114
Folk Music Society of Ireland
FMSI
c/o The Irish Traditional Music Archive
63 Merrion Sq., Dublin 2, Ireland
Tel: 01 6619699
Email: sales@itma.ie
Website: http://homepage.tinet.ie/~shields/fmsi
Members: 250
Staff: 1
Contact: Seoirse Bodley, Chm.
Description: Individuals in 10 countries interested in the practice and study of traditional Celtic folk music. Gathers previously unpublished collections of traditional Irish music. Conducts lectures and recitals.

00115

Food and Drink Industry Ireland FDII

Confederation House, 84-86 Lower Baggot St., Dublin 2, Ireland
Tel: 01 6051621
Fax: 01 6381621
Email: info@ibec.ie
Website: http://www.fdii.ie
Members: 26
Contact: Paul Kelly, Dir.
Description: Agribusiness, meat, dairy, baby food, sugar, cereals and cold-storage, drinks, brewing and distilling industries, food processors and suppliers, non-food grocery products, including health and beauty and tobacco. Advocates for members in regulatory matters, business representation, and human resources.
Publication: Newsletter
Publication title: Focus

Foras Oiliuna agus Forbartha Eireann

see Irish Institute of Training and Development

00116

Foroige, National Youth Development Organisation

Block 12D, Joyce Way, Park West, Dublin 12, Ireland
Tel: 01 6301560
Fax: 01 6301568
Email: info@foroige.ie
Website: http://www.foroige.ie
Members: 40000
Staff: 100
Contact: Sean Campbell, CEO
Description: Youth and their volunteer leaders united for self-improvement and the development of the community. Works with youth and volunteer leaders in educational programs in areas including agriculture, horticulture, youth cooperative education, citizenship, culture, family and life skills, health, leadership, and science. Provides support and services to at-risk youth, exchange program and study trips.

00117

Friedreichs Ataxia Society of Ireland FASI

San Martino, Mart Ln., Foxrock, Dublin 18, Ireland
Tel: 01 2894788
Fax: 01 2898845
Email: info@ataxia.ie
Website: http://ataxia.ie
Members: 250
Staff: 3
Contact: Barbara Flynn, Contact
Description: Individuals and organizations. Seeks to improve the quality of life of people with Friedreich's Ataxia and their families. Makes available support and services; conducts educational and advocacy campaigns.
Library Type: reference

00118

Friends of St. Luke's Hospital

Highfield Rd., Rathgar, Dublin 6, Ireland
Tel: 01 4065102
Fax: 01 4065237
Email: info@friendsofstlukes.ie
Website: http://www.friendsofstlukes.ie/index.php/events/21
Members: 15
Staff: 5
Contact: Fiona Campbell, Office Mgr.
Description: Seeks to enhance the care, comfort and management of cancer patients at Dublin's St. Luke's Hospital. Works to ensure that patients benefit to the fullest extent from the advances in techniques and equipment.

00119

Friends of the Earth - Ireland

9 Upper Mount St., Dublin 2, Ireland
Tel: 01 6394652
Email: info@foe.ie
Website: http://www.foe.ie
Members: 400
Staff: 12
Contact: Cathy Maguire, Chair
Fee: £48
Membership Type: individual
Fee: £60
Membership Type: household
Description: Works to increase public awareness of environmental problems. Conducts media and educational campaigns on topics such as air pollution, toxic waste issues, alternative energy, and climate change. Maintains an information service.
Formerly: Formerly, Earthwatch
Publication: Magazine
Publication title: Earthwatch. Advertisements.

00120

Front Line

81 Main St., Blackrock, Dublin, Ireland
Tel: 01 2123750
Fax: 01 2121001
Email: info@frontlinedefenders.org
Website: http://www.frontlinedefenders.org
Staff: 24
Contact: Mary Lawlor, Dir.
Description: Provides for the security needs on behalf of human rights defenders. Mobilizes campaigning and lobbying on behalf of defenders at immediate risk. Facilitates temporary relocation.
Publication: Manual
Publication title: Economic, Social and Cultural Rights Online Manual

Gaillimhe in Aghaidh an Chogaidh

see Galway Alliance Against War

00121

Galway Alliance Against War GAAW

PO Box 9260, Dublin, Ireland
Tel: 018727912
Email: gaaw1@eircom.net
Website: http://irishantiwar.org/node/727
Contact: Niall Farrell, Contact
Description: Promotes the use of judicial procedures in any campaign against terrorism. Opposes the waging of war in any campaign against terrorism. Seeks to address the underlying causes of conflict in the Middle East.

00122

Galway Chamber of Commerce and Industry

Commerce House, Merchants Rd., Galway, Ireland
Tel: 091 563536
Fax: 091 561963
Email: info@galwaychamber.com
Website: http://www.galwaychamber.com
Contact: Michael Coyle, CEO
Description: Promotes commerce and industry in County Galway, Ireland.

00123

Gay HIV Strategies

Fumbally Ct., Tower One, Fumbally Ln., Dublin 8, Ireland
Tel: 01 4730599
Fax: 01 4730597
Email: ghs@nexus.ie
Website: http://www.iol.ie/nexus/ghs.htm
Members: 10
Staff: 1
Contact: Kieran Rose, Proj. Dir.
Description: Facilitates new programs, resources and linkages between the Statutory, Nongovernmental Organizations, and other agencies and the gay community for HIV prevention strategies for gay men.

00124

Geographical Society of Ireland

School of Geography, Planning and Environmental Policy, University College Dublin, E001 Newman Bldg., Belfield 4, Dublin, Ireland
Tel: 01 7168179
Email: david.meredith@teagasc.ie
Website: http://www.geographical-society-ireland.org
Contact: David Meredith, Hon. Sec.
Fee: £30
Membership Type: full
Fee: £15
Membership Type: student, retired, unwaged
Description: Geographers, geography students and educators, and other individuals with an interest in geography. Promotes geographical studies in Ireland. Serves as forum for the exchange of information among members; functions as a clearinghouse on geography. Conducts field trips and other educational programs.
Publication: Newsletter
Publication title: Geonews

00125

Geophysical Association of Ireland GAI

c/o Hartmut Krahn, Sec.
Unit F4, Maynooth Business Campus, Maynooth, Kildare, Ireland
Email: secretary@gai.ie
Website: http://www.gai.ie
Members: 141
Staff: 11
Contact: Yvonne O'Connell, Pres.
Description: Acts as a forum for technical discussion and exchange on geophysical topics.

00126
Geotechnical Society of Ireland
GSI
H5 Ctre. point Business Park, Oak Rd., Dublin 12, Ireland
Tel: 01 4564370
Fax: 01 4564306
Email: mlacy@blp.ie
Website: http://www.engineersireland.ie/community/societies/geotechnical
Contact: Michael Lacy, Sec.
Description: Aims to promote international cooperation among engineers and scientists for the advancement and dissemination of knowledge in the field of geotechnics, as well as its engineering and environmental applications.

00127
GOAL
12 Cumberland St., Dun Laoghaire, Dublin, Ireland
Tel: 01 2809779
Fax: 01 2809215
Email: info@goal.ie
Website: http://www.goal.ie
Staff: 2500
Contact: John O'Shea, Chief Exec.
Description: Supports people affected by humanitarian crisis around the world. Provides emergency supplies, life-saving services and rehabilitation programmes.
Publication: Newsletter
Publication title: Goal Post

00128
Green Book of Ireland
55 Park Ave., Ballsbridge 4, Dublin, Ireland
Tel: 01 6762555
Fax: 01 2837877
Email: ireland@greenbook.ie
Website: http://www.greenbook.ie/index.html
Description: Promotes the hospitality industry in Ireland, including private hotels, castles and country houses.

Grupa Tacaiochta Cuba - Eire
see Cuba Support Group - Ireland

00129
GS1 Ireland
The Nutley Bldg., Merrion Rd., Dublin 4, Ireland
Tel: 01 2080660
Fax: 01 2080670
Email: info@gs1ie.org
Website: http://www.gs1ie.org
Members: 2800
Staff: 5
Contact: Jim Bracken, CEO
Fee: £502.15
Membership Type: once off registration fee
Description: Develops and promotes open, global multi sectoral standards for supply and demand chain management. Covers the section of item identifications, bar code symbols, e-commerce messages and RFID applications. Engages in retail grocery, general merchandise, healthcare and D.I.Y.
Formerly: Formerly, Article Numbering Association of Ireland
Publication: Newsletter

00130
Guild of Agricultural Journalists of Ireland
Irish Food Publishers Media, 31 Deansgrange Rd., Blackrock, Dublin, Ireland
Tel: 01 2893305
Email: margaret@ifpmedia.com
Website: http://www.agriguild.ie
Contact: Margaret Donnelly, Chair
Description: Promotes agricultural journalism in Ireland.

00131
Habitat for Humanity - Ireland
Quadrant House, Chapelizod, Dublin 20, Ireland
Tel: 01 6299611
Fax: 01 6299648
Email: info@habitatireland.ie
Website: http://www.habitatireland.ie
Contact: Karen Kennedy, Exec. Dir.
Description: Works in partnership with volunteers from all faiths who are committed to its goal of eliminating poverty housing. Brings families and communities in need together with volunteers and resources to build decent shelter sold with no profit.

00132
Headway Ireland - National Association for Acquired Brain Injury
HINHIA
1-3 Manor St., Business Park, Dublin 7, Ireland
Tel: 01 8102066
Fax: 01 8102070
Email: loughrank@headway.ie
Website: http://www.headway.ie
Staff: 50
Contact: Kieran Loughran, CEO
Description: Individuals and organizations. Seeks to improve the quality of life of people with head injuries and their families. Makes available support and services; conducts educational and advocacy campaigns; sponsors training programs for providers of care and services to people with head injuries.
Library Type: reference

00133
Health Research Board
HRB
73 Lower Baggot St., Dublin 2, Ireland
Tel: 01 2345000
Fax: 01 6612335
Email: hrb@hrb.ie
Website: http://www.hrb.ie
Contact: Reg Shaw, Chm.
Description: Promotes, assists, commissions or conducts medical, epidemiological, health and health services research.
Publication: Newsletter
Publication title: Research Funding News

00134
Healthcare Informatics Society of Ireland
HISI
Crescent Hall, Mt. St. Crescent, Dublin 2, Ireland
Tel: 01 6447820
Email: hisi@hisi.ie
Website: http://www.hisi.ie
Members: 700
Contact: Gerry Lyons, Pres.
Fee: £25
Membership Type: general
Description: Fosters international exchange of knowledge concerning health care and biomedical research through medical informatics. Sponsors conferences.

00135
Higher Education and Training Awards Council
HETAC
26-27 Denzille Ln., Dublin 2, Ireland
Tel: 01 6314567
Fax: 01 6314577
Email: info@hetac.ie
Website: http://www.hetac.ie
Contact: Gearoid O Conluain, Chief Exec.
Description: Works as the qualifications awarding body for third-level educational and training institutions outside the university sector in Ireland. Sets standards for higher education and training awards; validates higher education and training programmes; monitors institutional quality assurance procedures; delegates awarding powers to recognized institutions and ensures that student assessment procedures are fair and consistent.
Formerly: Formerly, National Council for Educational Awards

00136
Home Birth Association of Ireland
HBA
30 Cushla Downs, Monkslands, Athlone, Roscommon, Ireland
Tel: 090 6405267
Email: enquiries@homebirth.ie
Website: http://www.homebirth.ie
Members: 210
Contact: Marguerite Hannon, Sec.
Fee: £20
Membership Type: regular
Description: Individuals interested in home birthing. Seeks to increase the awareness of birth as a normal physiological process, while incorporating home birthing into mainstream maternity services. Produces information booklets, midwives' directory, and holds conferences and support group meetings.
Library Subject: birth, pregnancy, breastfeeding, diet, vaccination
Library Type: not open to the public

00137
Horse Racing Ireland
HRI
Ballymany, The Curragh, Newbridge, Kildare, Ireland
Tel: 045 455455
Fax: 045 455456
Email: info@hri.ie
Website: http://www.goracing.ie
Contact: Brian Kavanagh, Chief Exec.
Description: Promotes horse racing in Ireland.

00138
Human Life International - Ireland
6 Belvedere Pl., Dublin 1, Ireland
Tel: 01 8552504
Website: http://www.hli.org
Contact: Patrick McCrystal, Exec. Dir.
Description: Promotes the sanctity of life and dignity of the family through prayer, education and support services.

00139
Huntington's Disease Association of Ireland
HDAI
Carmichael House, N Brunswick St., Dublin 7, Ireland
Tel: 01 8721303
Fax: 01 8729931
Email: hdai@indigo.ie
Website: http://www.huntingtons.ie
Contact: Catherine Paradise, Chair
Description: Individuals and organizations. Seeks to improve the quality of life of people with Huntington's disease and their families. Makes available support and services; conducts educational and advocacy campaigns; serves as a clearinghouse on Huntington's disease.
Publication: Handbook
Publication title: Facing Huntington's Disease

00140
IFA Aquaculture
c/o Irish Farmers Association
Irish Farm Centre, Bluebell 12, Dublin, Ireland
Tel: 01 4508755
Fax: 01 4551043
Email: richieflynn@ifa.ie
Website: http://www.ifa.ie/Sectors/Aquaculture.aspx
Members: 100
Contact: Richie Flynn, Exec. Sec.
Description: Campaigns for the removal of local authority rates from fish farms and lobby for the re-launch of a national shellfish biotoxin scheme. Encourages and promotes the orderly and transparent introduction of Special Areas of Conservation.
Formerly: Formerly, Ifa Fish Farming Section

00141
Inclusion Ireland
Unit C2, The Steelworks, Foley St., Dublin 1, Ireland
Tel: 01 8559891
Fax: 01 8559904
Email: info@inclusionireland.ie
Website: http://www.inclusionireland.ie
Members: 160
Staff: 4
Contact: Deirdre Carroll, CEO
Fee: £40
Membership Type: individual
Description: Voluntary organizations. Promotes the welfare of people with intellectual disability; works as an umbrella group for organizations working in the field of intellectual disability.
Formerly: Formerly, National Association for the Mentally Handicapped of Ireland
Publication: Directory
Publication title: Directory of Services for People with Intellectual Disability

00142
Independent Workers Union
IWU
55 N Main St., Cork, Ireland
Tel: 021 4277151
Email: info@union.ie
Website: http://union.ie
Members: 120
Staff: 1
Fee: £20
Membership Type: full
Fee: £10
Membership Type: support, solidarity
Description: Represents butchers in the Cork area.
Formerly: Formerly, Cork Operative Butchers Society

00143
Industrial Heritage Association of Ireland
IHAI
c/o Dr. Ron Cox, Membership Sec.
Trinity College, Museum Bldg., Dublin, Ireland
Email: info@ihai.ie
Website: http://www.ihai.ie
Members: 120
Contact: Colin Rynne, Pres.
Fee: £20
Membership Type: individual
Fee: £50
Membership Type: heritage centre
Description: Individuals, associations, and corporations interested in preserving Ireland's industrial heritage. Seeks to foster a greater understanding and appreciation of the sites, monuments, and machinery that constitute Ireland's industrial heritage. Promotes a nationwide inventory, survey, and record of all industrial sites.
Publication: Newsletter

00144
Information and Communications Technology Ireland
84-86 Lower Baggot St., Dublin 2, Ireland
Tel: 01 6051582
Fax: 01 6381582
Email: info@ictireland.ie
Website: http://www.ictireland.ie
Contact: Paul Sweetman, Dir.
Description: Raises awareness of the importance of information and communications technology sector. Ensures that Ireland is an attractive location for ICT investment by both foreign and indigenous companies. Promotes education, research and development, sales and marketing and networking opportunities.
Publication: Bulletin
Publication title: e-Link

00145
Inland Waterways Association of Ireland
IWAI
c/o Brenda Ainsworth, Membership Sec.
25 Ellesmere Ave., N Circular Rd., Dublin 7, Ireland
Tel: 01 8682609
Email: membership@iwai.ie
Website: http://www.iwai.ie
Members: 4400
Contact: Paul Garland, Pres.
Fee: £44
Membership Type: single
Fee: £55
Membership Type: family
Description: Promotes the development, use, and maintenance of Ireland's navigable rivers and canals. Lobbies and advises national and local governments and other organizations on issues concerning waterways, including pollution and future developments.
Publication: Magazine
Publication title: Inland Waterways News. Advertisements.

Institiuid Ceimice Na hEireann
see Institute of Chemistry of Ireland

00146
Institute for Numerical Computation and Analysis
INCA
7-9 Dame Ct., Dublin 2, Ireland
Email: info@incaireland.org
Website: http://www.incaireland.org
Members: 25
Staff: 5
Contact: Diarmuid Herlihy, Sec.
Description: Encourages the development of numerical analysis, computation, and related areas. Maintains association with Royal College of Surgeons in Ireland and is accredited by University of Buckingham, U.K.

00147
Institute of Advertising Practitioners in Ireland
IAPI
8 Upper Fitzwilliam St., Dublin 2, Ireland
Tel: 01 6765991
Fax: 01 6614589
Email: info@iapi.com
Website: http://www.iapi.ie
Members: 48
Staff: 7
Contact: Brian Swords, Pres.
Description: Advertising agencies and professionals. Promotes growth and development of the domestic advertising industries. Represents members before industrial organizations and government agencies; sponsors continuing professional development programs for advertisers; conducts promotional activities.
Library Subject: advertising
Library Type: open to the public

00148
Institute of Bankers in Ireland
1 N Wall Quay, Dublin 1, Ireland
Tel: 01 6116500
Fax: 01 6116565
Email: info@bankers.ie
Website: http://www.bankers.ie
Members: 35050
Contact: Andrew Healy, Pres.
Description: Works to develop fully the professional potential of the men and women working in banking and financial services by enhancing their knowledge and skills through education and training programs and recognizing with appropriate qualifications those who achieve the required standards.

00149
Institute of Chemistry of Ireland
ICI
PO Box 9322, Cardiff Ln., Dublin 2, Ireland
Email: info@instituteofchemistry.org
Website: http://www.chemistryireland.org
Members: 800
Staff: 1
Contact: James P. Ryan, Hon. Sec.
Fee: £300-800
Membership Type: company (based on the number of employees)
Fee: £30
Membership Type: association
Description: Chemists, Chemical technicians, students of chemistry, and chemical companies. Promotes interest in all branches and applications of chemistry, including industry. Disseminates information.
Library Subject: archive material
Library Type: reference
Publication: Journal
Publication title: Irish Chemical News

00150
Institute of Designers in Ireland
IDI
The Digital Hub, Roe Ln., Thomas St., Dublin 8, Ireland
Tel: 01 4893650
Fax: 01 4885801
Email: info@idi-design.ie
Website: http://www.idi-design.ie
Members: 300
Staff: 1
Contact: Rachael Murtagh, Exec. Off.
Fee: £225
Membership Type: individual
Fee: £85
Membership Type: associate
Description: Represents designers of consumer products, interiors, exhibitions, textiles and fashion; photographers; theater, film and television set designers; graphic designers; design educators and administrators. Promotes the design industry in the Republic of Ireland. Seeks to maintain standards of professional practice, conduct and integrity; further the education in the field; provide a forum for the discussion of design matters.
Formerly: Formerly, Society of Designers in Ireland
Publication: Directory
Publication title: Design Directory Ireland
Meetings/Conventions: Design Awards – annual competition

00151
Institute of Directors in Ireland
IOD
Europa House, Harcourt St., Dublin 2, Ireland
Tel: 01 4110010
Fax: 01 4110090
Email: info@iodireland.ie
Website: http://www.iodireland.ie
Contact: Maura Quinn, Chief Exec.
Fee: £295
Membership Type: full, associate
Description: Provides a forum for the exchange of ideas and information, encourages members to improve the standards and performance as directors and represents the views of business leaders to government and other associations. Supports the provision of a wealth-creating environment in Ireland.
Publication: Magazine
Publication title: Irish Director

00152
Institute of Geologists of Ireland
IGI
University College Dublin, UCD School of Geological Sciences, Dublin 4, Ireland
Tel: 01 7162085
Fax: 01 2837733
Email: info@igi.ie
Website: http://www.igi.ie
Members: 155
Staff: 2
Contact: John Kelly, Pres.
Fee: £145
Membership Type: professional
Fee: £35
Membership Type: associate, member-in-training
Description: Aims to promote the science and profession of geology in Ireland, to raise the awareness and importance of geosciences to society and to represent the professional interests of members.
Publication: Newsletter

00153
Institute of Incorporated Public Accountants
IIPA
2 Abbey Moat House, Abbey St., Naas, Kildare, Ireland
Tel: 045 895936
Fax: 045 895830
Email: info@iipa.ie
Website: http://www.iipa.ie
Contact: Richard O'Callaghan, CEO
Fee: £300
Membership Type: associate
Description: Aims to develop and enhance businesses in Ireland and internationally through the provision of accountancy and auditing services.

00154
Institute of Industrial Engineers Ireland
IIE
PO Box 790, Sandyford, Dublin 18, Ireland
Tel: 01 2943156
Fax: 01 2943131
Email: enquiries@iie.ie
Website: http://www.iie.ie
Members: 500
Contact: Seamus O'Sullivan, Pres.
Fee: £198
Membership Type: senior
Description: Provides leadership in developing industrial engineering; enhances the capabilities of those who are involved in or manage the application, education, training, research or development of industrial engineering, and in representing the industrial engineering profession.

00155
Institute of International Trade of Ireland
IITI
26 Merrion Sq., Dublin 2, Ireland
Tel: 01 6612474
Email: info@iiti.ie
Website: http://www.iiti.ie
Members: 360
Staff: 3
Contact: John Whelan, Chm.
Fee: £500
Membership Type: academic, corporate
Fee: £150
Membership Type: associate, student
Description: Professionals engaged in international trade and marketing. Promotes professional development of members; seeks to increase international trade involving the Republic of Ireland. Formulates and maintains professional standards for international trade and marketing practitioners; conducts research and educational programs.
Publication: Newsletter
Publication title: Export Link. Advertisements.

00156
Institute of Management Consultants and Advisers
IMCA
19 Elgin Rd., Dublin 2, Ireland
Tel: 01 6349636
Fax: 01 2815330
Email: info@imca.ie
Website: http://www.imca.ie
Members: 600
Staff: 2
Contact: Tom Moriarty, Development Exec.
Fee: £195
Membership Type: associate (less than 3 years)
Fee: £250
Membership Type: individual, consultant, associate (3 years or more)
Description: Aims to advance the management consultancy profession in Ireland. Provides Code of Professional Conduct to ensure that the members render the highest standards of performance and service.

00157
Institute of Public Administration
IPA
57-61 Lansdowne Rd., Dublin 4, Ireland
Tel: 01 2403600
Fax: 01 6689135
Email: information@ipa.ie
Website: http://www.ipa.ie
Contact: Nicolas Marcoux, Mgr.
Description: Provides training, education, research, and publications.
Publication: Yearbook
Publication title: Administration Yearbook & Diary

00158
Insurance Institute of Ireland
39 Molesworth St., Dublin 2, Ireland
Tel: 01 6456600
Email: info@insurance-institute.ie
Website: http://www.insurance-institute.ie
Members: 5600
Staff: 14
Contact: Denis Kelleher, Pres.
Fee: £140
Membership Type: ordinary
Fee: £245
Membership Type: chartered
Description: Represents brokers, insurance agents, and companies engaged in all aspects of the insurance and financial services professions. Promotes efficiency and improvement in business practice among members.

Provides education, training, and professional development programs, including exams. Encourages a high standard of ethical behavior.

00159

International Adoption Association - Ireland
IAA

Terenure Enterprise Centre, 17 Rathfarnham Rd., Dublin, 6W2, Ireland
Tel: 01 4992206
Email: info@iaaireland.org
Website: http://www.iaaireland.org
Members: 750
Description: Provides help and guidance to Irish families who have adopted abroad or are intending to do so.

00160

International Association of Art Critics - Ireland

224 Larkhill Rd., Dublin 9, Ireland
Tel: 01 68370116
Email: president@aica.ie
Website: http://www.aica.ie
Contact: Ciaran Bennett, Pres.
Description: Acts as a voice for the visual arts in Ireland. Seeks to promote excellence in writing on the visual arts. Supports members' careers as art critics.

00161

International Association of Broadcast Meteorology
IABM

30 Parkview, Wexford, Ireland
Email: chairman@iabm.org
Website: http://www.iabm.org
Contact: Claire Martin, Chair
Fee: £75
Membership Type: full, associate
Fee: £500
Membership Type: corporate
Description: Works to improve the status of broadcast meteorology. Represents the views of weather broadcasters. Aims to establish and maintain a register of members as a resource.

00162

International Association of Hydrogeologists - Ireland
IAH

c/o Orla McAlister, Treas.
Tobin Consulting Engineers, Block 10-4, Blanchardstown Corporate Park, Dublin 15, Ireland
Tel: 01 8030401
Website: http://www.iah-ireland.org
Members: 130
Contact: Teri Hayes, Pres.
Fee: £72
Membership Type: general
Fee: £36
Membership Type: student
Description: Promotes the science and engineering of groundwater issues. Enhances the science, technology, and profession of hydrogeology. Increases public awareness of the role and value of hydrogeologist and hydrogeology in society.

00163

International Association of Technological University Libraries
IATUL

Dublin City University Library, Dublin 9, Ireland
Email: paul.sheehan@dcu.ie
Website: http://www.iatul.org
Contact: Paul Sheehan, Sec.
Fee: £500
Membership Type: sustaining
Fee: £150
Membership Type: ordinary, associate (band 1 library)
Description: Libraries of academic institutions in 41 countries that offer courses in engineering or technology at the doctoral level; nonvoting associate members are libraries of academic institutions that offer such courses to the Master's or equivalent level; observer members are libraries housed in national patent offices and science museums with technological collections that meet research standards. Works to facilitate international cooperation among member libraries to stimulate and develop library projects of international and regional importance.
Publication: Journal
Publication title: IATUL Conference Proceedings

00164

International Bureau for Epilepsy
IBE

11 Priory Hall, Stillorgan, Dublin 18, Ireland
Tel: 01 2108850
Fax: 01 2108450
Email: ibedublin@eircom.net
Website: http://www.ibe-epilepsy.org
Members: 112
Staff: 2
Contact: Mike Glynn, Pres.
Fee: £150
Membership Type: full
Fee: £100
Membership Type: associate
Description: National organizations and individuals interested in the medical, social, and scientific aspects of Epilepsy. Focuses on aspects of daily life with epilepsy. Facilitates exchange of information and experience regarding the care of persons with epilepsy. Provides material on how to organize and finance non-medical societies. Organizes training sessions.
Library Type: not open to the public
Publication: Magazine
Publication title: International Epilepsy News
Meetings/Conventions: International Epilepsy Congress – biennial congress

00165

International Federation for Cervical Pathology and Colposcopy
IFCPC

Royal Colorado of Surgeons in Ireland, Coombe Women and Infants University Hospital, Dublin 8, Ireland
Tel: 04085355
Fax: 014538777
Email: prendiville.walter@gmail.com
Website: http://www.ifcpc.org
Members: 34
Contact: Walter Prendiville, Sec. Gen.
Description: Federation of national societies. Encourages basic and applied research. Disseminates information concerning uterine cervical pathology and colposcopy.

00166

International Federation of Surgical Colleges
IFSC

123 St. Stephen's Green, Dublin 2, Ireland
Tel: 01 4022707
Fax: 01 4022230
Email: ifsc@rcsi.ie
Website: http://www.ifsc-net.org
Members: 795
Staff: 1
Contact: S.W.A. Gunn, Sec. Gen.
Description: National colleges, academies, and associations of surgery in 77 countries. Works to improve standards of surgery throughout the world. Promotes cooperation and exchange of medical and surgical information among surgical institutions. Encourages high standards of education, training, and research in surgery and its allied sciences. Supports clinical and scientific congresses in the surgical community. Fosters cooperation in developing the best possible standards of surgical facilities and treatment, and in providing appropriate scholarships and surgical training in countries requesting aid. Collaborates with the World Health Organization to strengthen rural surgical health services in developing countries; maintains distribution facility for journals to Third World nations.
Library Type: reference
Publication: Newsletter
Publication title: IFSC News
Meetings/Conventions: Surgical Outreach to Developing Countries – annual symposium

00167

International Fiscal Association - Ireland

Matheson Ormsby and Prentice, 30 Herbert St., Dublin 2, Ireland
Tel: 01 6199000
Fax: 01 6199010
Email: shane.hogan@mop.ie
Website: http://www.ifa.nl
Contact: Shane Hogan, Chm.
Description: Promotes the study and advancement of international and comparative law with regard to public finance, specifically international, comparative fiscal law and the financial and economic aspects of taxation. Plays an active role in international taxation.

00168

International Organization for Migration (Dublin, Ireland)
IOM

7 Hill St., Dublin 1, Ireland
Tel: 01 8787900
Fax: 01 8787901
Email: info@iomdublin.org
Website: http://www.iomdublin.org
Description: Carries out operational assistance programs for migrants. Encourages social and economic development through migration. Prevents trafficking and smuggling of persons. Fosters orderly and planned migration of refugees, displaced persons and other individuals to countries offering resettlement opportunities. Upholds the human dignity and well-being of migrants.
Publication: Newsletter
Publication title: IOM Dublin Newsletter

00169

International Society for Quality in Healthcare
ISQua

2 Parnell Sq. E, Dublin 1, Ireland
Tel: 01 8717049
Fax: 01 8783845
Email: isqua@isqua.org
Website: http://www.isqua.org
Members: 700
Staff: 5
Contact: Roisin Boland, CEO
Fee: £200
Membership Type: individual
Fee: £1000
Membership Type: institutional
Description: Works to provide services to guide health professionals, health providers, researchers, agencies, policymakers and consumers to achieve excellence in healthcare delivery to all people and to continuously improve the quality and safety of care.
Publication: Journal
Publication title: International Journal Quality in Healthcare

00170

International Songwriters Association
ISA

PO Box 46, Limerick, Ireland
Tel: 061 228837
Fax: 061 2288379
Email: jliddane@songwriter.iol.ie
Website: http://www.songwriter.co.uk
Description: Songwriters, professional, semi-professional and amateur. Works as a protective and advisory organization for songwriters, with members in more than 50 countries.
Publication: Magazine
Publication title: Songwriter Magazine

00171

International Union for Quaternary Research
INQUA

Trinity College, Dept. of Geography, Museum Bldg., Dublin 2, Ireland
Tel: 01 8961213
Email: pcoxon@tcd.ie
Website: http://www.inqua.tcd.ie
Members: 35
Contact: Peter Coxon, Sec. Gen.
Description: National academies. Encourages interdisciplinary study of problems dealing with the Quaternary Period as defined in geologic stratigraphy. Maintains 16 commissions. Conducts research programs.
Library Subject: quaternary research
Library Type: not open to the public
Publication: Journal
Publication title: Quaternary International

00172

Ireland China Association
ICA

28 Merrion Sq., Dublin 2, Ireland
Tel: 01 6612182
Fax: 01 6612315
Email: info@irelandchina.org
Website: http://www.irelandchina.org
Contact: Brendan Waldron, Chair
Fee: £75
Membership Type: individual
Fee: £400
Membership Type: corporate
Description: Aims to bring together Irish and Chinese businesspeople for the purpose of exploring business opportunities and making contracts. Promotes greater economic ties and increases trade and commerce between Ireland and China. Furthers the cultural links and greater knowledge of both countries.
Meetings/Conventions: Evening Briefing – periodic meeting

00173

Ireland Japan Association
IJA

c/o Irish Exporters Association
28 Merrion Sq., Dublin 2, Ireland
Tel: 01 6612182
Fax: 01 6612315
Email: info@ija.ie
Website: http://www.ija.ie
Contact: Darina Slattery, Chair
Fee: £400
Membership Type: corporate
Fee: £75
Membership Type: family, individual
Description: Aims to enhance and develop relations between Ireland and Japan. Promotes economic and business ties and increases trade and commerce between Ireland and Japan. Fosters mutual understanding between the peoples of both countries. Creates a forum for Irish and Japanese people to interact in both business and social environments.

00174

Irish Angus Cattle Society

24 Hawthorn Crescent, Boyle Rd., Carrick-On-Shannon, Leitrim, Ireland
Tel: 071 9620253
Fax: 071 9620406
Email: angus@iol.ie
Website: http://www.irishangus.ie
Contact: Michael O'Connell, Pres.
Fee: £50
Membership Type: regular
Fee: £500
Membership Type: life
Description: Works for the development and improvement of the breed in Ireland.

00175

Irish Anti-Vivisection Society
IAVS

PO Box 13, Greystones, Wicklow, Ireland
Tel: 01 2820154
Email: info@irishantivivisection.org
Website: http://www.irishantivivisection.org
Fee: £10
Membership Type: adult
Fee: £5
Membership Type: individual under 18, senior citizen
Description: Strives for the total abolition of all experiments causing distress or suffering to animals. Promotes measures of partial reform. Encourages scientists to use existing alternative methods that do not require the use of living animals. Lobbies public representatives and officials to change the law.

00176

Irish Antique Dealers Association
IADA

c/o Ian Haslem, Sec.
The Silver Shop, 23B Powerscourt Townhouse, Dublin 2, Ireland
Tel: 061 6794147
Email: info@iada.ie
Website: http://www.iada.ie
Contact: George Stacpoole, Pres.
Description: Works to encourage artistic development and economic expansion. Represents the interests of associations, syndicates, chambers of commerce and federations of art and antique dealers. Fosters communication among members.

00177

Irish Association for American Studies
IAAS

4 Preston Close, Naas, Kilmeague, Kildare, Ireland
Email: jon.mitchell@nuim.ie
Website: http://www.americanstudiesinireland.materdei.ie
Members: 43
Contact: Jonathan Mitchell, Treas.
Fee: £30
Membership Type: full
Fee: £10
Membership Type: concession
Description: Represents scholars and teachers involved in research or teaching concerning U.S. culture and society.
Publication: Journal
Publication title: Irish Journal of American Studies. Advertisements.

00178

Irish Association for Counselling and Psychotherapy
IACP

21 Dublin Rd., Bray, Dublin, Ireland
Tel: 01 2723427
Fax: 01 2869933
Email: iacp@iacp.ie
Website: http://www.irish-counselling.ie
Members: 3000
Contact: Claire Missen, Contact
Fee: £275
Membership Type: accredited
Fee: £230
Membership Type: associate organization
Description: Professional counselors and therapists in Ireland. Seeks to set, maintain, and regulate standards for the profession of counseling and therapy in order to protect the public. Operates accreditation schemes; operates a complaints procedure.
Publication: Magazine
Publication title: Eisteach. Advertisements.

00179
Irish Association for Economic Geology
IAEG
c/o Paul Gordon, Treas.
Lundin Mining Exploration, Castletown, Galmoy, Crosspatrick, Kilkenny 4, Ireland
Tel: 056 8831533
Fax: 056 8831525
Email: paul.gordon@lundinmining.com
Website: http://www.iaeg.org
Members: 320
Contact: Robin Taggart, Treas.
Fee: £15
Membership Type: student
Fee: £40
Membership Type: associate, overseas
Description: Economic geologists and other interested individuals. Compiles statistics. Conducts educational programs.
Library Subject: economics, exploration, mine geology
Library Type: reference
Meetings/Conventions: periodic workshop

00180
Irish Association for Nurses in Oncology
IANO
PO Box 1499, Dublin 4, Ireland
Tel: 01 8735702
Email: info@iano.ie
Website: http://www.iano.ie
Members: 200
Contact: Frieda Clinton, Pres.
Fee: £35
Membership Type: registered nurse
Description: Provides education and information exchange for members of the nursing profession, particularly those caring for people with cancer.
Publication: Booklet
Publication title: Cancer Nursing News

00181
Irish Association for Spina Bifida and Hydrocephalus
IASBAH
Old Nangor Rd., Clondalkin, Dublin 22, Ireland
Tel: 01 4572329
Fax: 01 4572328
Email: gkennedy@iasbah.ie
Website: http://www.sbhi.ie
Members: 1500
Staff: 6
Contact: George Kennedy, CEO
Description: Individuals and organizations. Seeks to improve the quality of life of people with spina bifida or hydrocephalus and their families. Makes available support and services; conducts educational and advocacy campaigns.

00182
Irish Association of Creative Arts Therapists
IACAT
PO Box 4176, Dublin 1, Ireland
Tel: 087 9921746
Email: info@iacat.ie
Website: http://www.iacat.ie
Contact: Vanessa Smith, Chair
Fee: £96
Membership Type: professional
Fee: £60
Membership Type: associate
Description: Represents the interests of art therapists in Ireland. Aims to promote, regulate and support the work of creative art therapists. Establishes professional standard for education and ethical practice of art therapy.

00183
Irish Association of Dermatologists
IAD
c/o Dr. Gillian Murphy, Pres.
Beaumont Hospital, Department of Dermatology, Dublin 9, Ireland
Tel: 091 542379
Email: trevor.markham@hse.ie
Website: http://www.irishdermatologists.ie
Contact: Trevor Markham, Sec.
Description: Works to stimulate cooperation between dermatological societies. Promotes advancement of the profession in the field of dermatology. Encourages personal and professional relations among dermatologists. Provides educational programs.

00184
Irish Association of Investment Managers
IAIM
35 Fitzwilliam Pl., Dublin 2, Ireland
Tel: 01 6761919
Fax: 01 6761954
Email: info@iaim.ie
Website: http://www.iaim.ie
Members: 14
Contact: Gerry Keenan, Chm.
Description: Promotes the investment management industry to ensure the best working practices. Represents members' interests to government, regulatory bodies, and other organizations.

00185
Irish Association of Pension Funds
IAPF
Slane House, Ste. 2, 25 Lower Mount St., Dublin 2, Ireland
Tel: 01 6612427
Fax: 01 6621196
Email: info@iapf.ie
Website: http://www.iapf.ie
Members: 350
Staff: 3
Contact: Marie Burke, Chm.
Fee: £415-1420
Membership Type: non-practitioner (based on the number of members)
Fee: £775-3450
Membership Type: service provider
Description: Acts as a forum for discussion relating to legislative and practical aspects of occupational pension schemes. Liaises with governmental bodies and other professional bodies.
Publication: Magazine
Publication title: Irish Pensions

00186
Irish Association of Physicists in Medicine
IAPM
St. Vincents University Hospital, Elm Park, Dublin 4, Ireland
Website: http://www.theiapm.ie
Contact: Linda Gray, Co-Sec.
Fee: £40
Membership Type: professional, allied-professional
Fee: £20
Membership Type: retired
Description: Aims to promote the application of physical scientists in medicine. Provides education, training and professional development.

00187
Irish Association of Social Workers
IASW
114-116 Pearse St., Dublin 2, Ireland
Tel: 01 6774838
Email: office@iasw.ie
Website: http://www.iasw.ie
Fee: £170
Membership Type: full (direct debit)
Fee: £100
Membership Type: associate
Description: Seeks to improve the standards and equality of social work. Provides support to social workers in the practice of their profession. Represents the views of social workers on matters of social policy at the national and international levels.

00188
Irish Association of Suicidology
IAS
PO Box 11634, Ballsbridge 4, Dublin, Ireland
Tel: 01 6674900
Email: info@ias.ie
Website: http://www.ias.ie
Contact: Declan Behan, CEO
Fee: £40
Membership Type: general
Description: Works to facilitate communication between clinicians, volunteers, survivors, and researchers in all matters relating to suicide and suicide behavior; promotes public awareness of problems of suicide and suicidal behavior.
Publication: Booklet
Publication title: Conference Proceedings. Advertisements.

00189
Irish Association of Teachers in Special Education
IATSE
c/o Drumcondra Education Centre
Drumconda, Dublin 9, Ireland
Email: info@iatse.ie
Website: http://www.iatse.ie
Members: 700
Contact: Jerry Pierce, Ed.
Fee: £40
Membership Type: full
Fee: £30
Membership Type: associate/student
Description: Disseminates knowledge and information to teachers and others involved in special education. Provides opportunities for communication, cooperation and exchange of ideas. Encourages research

and projects for special education. Provides in-service courses and/or seminars for teachers, parents and others involved in special education. Organises annual international conference.
Publication: Journal
Publication title: Reach

00190
Irish Astronomical Association
IAA
3 Vaddegan Ave., Antrim, Glengormley, BT36 7SP, Ireland
Email: iaa@irishastro.com
Website: http://irishastro.org.uk
Members: 200
Staff: 6
Contact: Daniel Collins, Sec.
Description: Encourages public awareness of astronomy.
Formerly: Formerly, Irish Astronomical Society
Publication: Newsletter
Publication title: Newssheets. Advertisements.

00191
Irish Auctioneers' and Valuers' Institute
IAVI
38 Merrion Sq., Dublin 2, Ireland
Tel: 01 6611794
Email: info@iavi.ie
Website: http://www.iavi.ie
Members: 1800
Contact: Alan Cooke, Chief Exec.
Description: Represents the majority of real estate agents and auctioneers in Ireland. Serves the interests of members and the profession and safeguards those of the public, interacting between the groups to the benefit of both.
Publication: Magazine
Publication title: The Property Valuer. Advertisements.

00192
Irish Banking Federation
IBF
Nassau House, Nassau St., Dublin 2, Ireland
Tel: 01 6715311
Fax: 01 6796680
Email: ibf@ibf.ie
Website: http://www.ibf.ie
Members: 60
Contact: Pat Farrell, Chief Exec.
Description: Financial institutions, including licensed domestic and foreign banks and institutions operating in the international Financial Services Centre. Represents and promotes the interests of the Irish banking industry in Ireland and abroad. Liaises with national authorities; disseminates information; represents Irish banking abroad, particularly in the EU.
Publication: Magazine
Publication title: About Banking

00193
Irish Bioenergy Association
IrBEA
c/o Vicky Heslop
Methan O Gen, Ltd., Tooracurragh, Ballymacarbry, Waterford, Ireland
Tel: 05236304
Email: contact@irbea.org
Website: http://www.irbea.org
Contact: Tom Bruton, Pres.
Fee: £300-1000
Membership Type: corporate
Fee: £100
Membership Type: individual
Description: Promotes the bioenergy industry in the Republic of Ireland and Northern Ireland. Improves public awareness of biomass as a realistic option for energy supply. Influences policy makers to promote the development of bioenergy. Facilitates networking and information sharing among those interested in bioenergy development.

00194
Irish Blue Cross
15A Goldenbridge Industrial Estate, Tyrconnell Rd., Inchicore, Dublin 8, Ireland
Tel: 01 4163030
Fax: 01 4163035
Email: info@bluecross.ie
Website: http://www.bluecross.ie
Members: 40
Contact: Gerry O'Sullivan, Chm.
Description: Dedicated to the care of sick and needy animals; operates a horse ambulance service.

00195
Irish Brokers Association
IBA
87 Merrion Sq., Dublin 2, Ireland
Tel: 01 6613067
Fax: 01 6619955
Email: info@iba.ie
Website: http://www.iba.ie
Members: 600
Staff: 5
Contact: Ciaran Phelan, CEO
Description: Comprises of representative and regulatory body for insurance brokers in Ireland.

00196
Irish Business and Employers Confederation
IBEC
Confederation House, 84/86 Lower Baggot St., Dublin 2, Ireland
Tel: 01 6051500
Fax: 01 6381500
Email: info@ibec.ie
Website: http://www.ibec.ie/IBEC/IBEC.nsf/vPages/Home?OpenDocument
Members: 7500
Contact: Leo Crawford, Pres.
Description: Firms: industrial, commercial, and public sector firms that manufacture products or provide services. Promotes the growth and development of Irish industry and commercial activity. Advises the government and represents interests of industry on relevant legislative issues. Maintains the Irish Business Bureau in conjunction with Irish Business and Employers Confederation and the Chambers of Commerce of Ireland. Develops public awareness of the role of industry in national development through press, radio, television, and public meetings. Monitors technological developments; compiles statistics; provides advice and assistance to members; maintains speakers' bureau.
Library Subject: industrial relations, government, training, statistics
Library Type: not open to the public
Formerly: Formerly, Conference of Irish Industry
Publication: Magazine
Publication title: Economic Trends
Meetings/Conventions: Managing Absence – periodic workshop

00197
Irish Campaign for Nuclear Disarmament
ICND
PO Box 6327, Dublin 6, Ireland
Email: irishcnd@ireland.com
Website: http://indigo.ie/~goodwill/icnd.html
Members: 150
Contact: Emily Doherty, Sec.
Fee: £15
Membership Type: individual
Fee: £20
Membership Type: household
Description: Coordinates activities in the Republic of Ireland to encourage nuclear disarmament. Conducts demonstrations, campaigns, and lobbying activities. Maintains speakers' bureau.
Publication: Newsletter
Publication title: PeaceWork

00198
Irish Cancer Society
ICS
43/45 Northumberland Rd., Dublin 4, Ireland
Tel: 01 2310500
Fax: 01 2310555
Email: reception@irishcancer.ie
Website: http://www.cancer.ie
Contact: Bill McCabe, Chm.
Description: Seeks to prevent cancer, save lives from cancer and improve the quality of life of those living with cancer through patient care research and education.
Library Subject: cancer
Library Type: by appointment only

00199
Irish Cardiac Society
ICS
c/o Ms. Stella Lawlor, Exec. Sec.
Irish Heart Foundation, 4 Clyde Rd., Ballsbridge, Dublin 4, Ireland
Tel: 01 6685001
Fax: 01 6685896
Email: slawlor@irishheart.ie
Website: http://www.irishcardiacsociety.com
Members: 135
Contact: Declan Sugrue, Pres.
Fee: £100
Membership Type: individual
Description: Promotes the study of cardiology in Ireland.

00200

Irish Cattle and Sheep Farmers Association
ICSA

9 Lyster House, Lyster Sq., Portlaoise, Laois, Ireland
Tel: 0502 62120
Fax: 0502 62121
Email: info@icsaireland.com
Website: http://www.icsaireland.com
Members: 9000
Staff: 6
Contact: Gabriel Gilmartin, Pres.
Description: Livestock producers. Represents the beef and lamb sectors in the political arena.
Formerly: Formerly, Irish Cattle Traders' and Stockowners Association
Publication: Magazine
Publication title: The Drystock Farmer

00201

Irish Centre for European Law
ICEL

Law School, House 39, Trinity College, Dublin 2, Ireland
Tel: 01 8961845
Email: icel@tcd.ie
Website: http://www.icel.ie
Members: 300
Staff: 2
Contact: Andrew Beck, Dir.
Fee: £395
Membership Type: corporate
Fee: £180
Membership Type: individual
Description: Promotes the knowledge, study, and discussion of European Union and European Human Rights law in Ireland. Organizes conferences and continuing education programs. Disseminates information.
Publication: Book
Publication title: European Initiatives in Intellectual Property

00202

Irish Chamber of Shipping

c/o Quality Freight Ltd.
Port Centre Alexandra Rd., Dublin 1, Ireland
Tel: 01 8366233
Fax: 01 8366061
Email: rmccann@qualityfreight.ie
Website: http://www.ecsa.be/members.asp
Description: National branch of the European Community Shipowners' Associations. Promotes the interests of water freight and passenger shipping concerns in the Republic of Ireland.

00203

Irish Christmas Tree Growers
ICTG

PO Box 8581, Glenageary, Dublin, Ireland
Tel: 01 2304973
Fax: 01 2304973
Email: info@christmastreesireland.com
Website: http://www.christmastreesireland.com
Members: 92
Description: Christmas tree growers are full members; individuals and corporations in related fields are associate members. Promotes growth and development in the Christmas tree industry. Represents members' interests before national and international government agencies. Establishes quality standards for Christmas trees; makes available technical support and assistance to members; maintains contact with related associations and agencies worldwide. Facilitates communication among members.
Publication: Catalog
Publication title: Buy and Sell Catalogue. Advertisements.

00204

Irish Computer Society
ICS

Crescent Hall, Mt. St. Crescent, Dublin 2, Ireland
Tel: 01 6447820
Fax: 01 6620224
Website: http://www.ics.ie
Members: 1065
Staff: 1
Contact: Fintan Swanton, Pres.
Fee: £25
Membership Type: student
Fee: £105
Membership Type: associate, affiliate
Description: Information technology professionals, educators, and students. Promotes development and use of computers and computer-related techniques; establishes and maintains standards of practice for computer professionals. Facilitates exchange of information among members; represents members' interests before government agencies and international technical and scientific organizations.
Publication: Newsletter
Publication title: Irish Computer Society Newsletter

00205

Irish Congress of Trade Unions
ICTU

31/32 Parnell Sq., Dublin 1, Ireland
Tel: 01 8897777
Fax: 01 8872012
Email: congress@ictu.ie
Website: http://www.ictu.ie
Members: 56
Contact: David Begg, Gen. Sec.
Description: Represents trade unions in Ireland. Provides information, advice and training to the unions and members. Assists with the resolution of disputes between unions and employers.

00206

Irish Copyright Licensing Agency
ICLA

25 Denzille Ln., Dublin 2, Ireland
Tel: 01 6624211
Fax: 01 6624213
Email: info@icla.ie
Website: http://www.icla.ie
Contact: Samantha Holman, Exec. Dir.
Description: Fosters the creation of Reproduction Rights Organizations (RROs). Facilitates the collective management of reproduction and other rights relevant to copyrighted works. Works to develop and increase public awareness of the need for effective RROs. Supports joint attempts by publishers, authors and other rightholders to create and develop rights management systems worldwide.

00207

Irish Cosmetics, Detergent and Allied Products Association
ICDA

84-86 Lower Baggot St., Dublin 2, Ireland
Tel: 01 6051671
Fax: 01 6381671
Email: sandra.browne@energizer.com
Website: http://www.icda.ie
Contact: Sandra Browne, Chair
Description: Represents the interests of companies in Ireland engaged in the manufacture, distribution or sales of cosmetics, toiletries, detergents and allied household products.

00208

Irish Council for Civil Liberties
ICCL

9-13 Blackhall Pl., Dublin 7, Ireland
Tel: 01 7994504
Fax: 01 7994512
Email: info@iccl.ie
Website: http://www.iccl.ie
Members: 450
Staff: 7
Contact: Mark Kelly, Dir.
Description: Conducts campaigns in support of civil liberties. Stresses the importance of preserving and extending civil liberties and examines relevant laws and official practices. Sponsors seminars.
Publication: Journal
Publication title: Journal of Rights

00209

Irish Creamery Milk Suppliers' Association
ICMSA

John Feely House, Dublin Rd., Castletroy, Limerick, Ireland
Tel: 061 314677
Fax: 061 315737
Email: info@icmsa.ie
Website: http://www.icmsa.ie
Members: 40000
Contact: Jackie Cahill, Pres.
Description: Represents dairy farmers in Ireland.

00210

Irish Dairy Board
IDB

Grattan House, Mount St. Lower, Dublin 2, Ireland
Tel: 01 6619599
Fax: 01 6612778
Email: idb@idb.ie
Website: http://www.idb.ie
Members: 24
Contact: Vincent Buckley, Chm.
Description: Serves the needs and quality demands of dairy consumers worldwide. Works to increase sales within Europe through improved distribution and marketing structures.

00211
Irish Deaf Society
IDS
30 Blessington St., Dublin 7, Ireland
Tel: 01 8601878
Fax: 01 8601960
Email: info@irishdeafsociety.ie
Website: http://www.irishdeafsociety.ie
Members: 300
Staff: 15
Contact: John Mangan, CEO
Fee: £15
Membership Type: individual (in Ireland)
Fee: £25
Membership Type: individual (rest of the world), organization
Description: Representative organization of Deaf people, seeks recognition of Irish sign language and conducts various educational and advocacy campaigns.
Library Subject: deafness, sign language, culture, interpreting
Library Type: open to the public
Publication: Magazine
Publication title: Irish Deaf Journal. Advertisements.

00212
Irish Dental Association
IDA
Leopardstown Office Park, Unit 2, Sandyford, Dublin 18, Ireland
Tel: 01 2950072
Fax: 01 2950092
Email: info@irishdentalassoc.ie
Website: http://www.dentist.ie
Members: 1200
Contact: Mena Sherlock, Sec./Admin.
Fee: £720
Membership Type: general practice, limited practice, specialist practice, hospital dental surgeon (consultant)
Fee: £550
Membership Type: public dental surgeon, hospital dental surgeon (non consultant)
Description: Represents dental practitioners, specialists and health board dental surgeons. Promotes the advancement of the dental profession. Helps the population to attain optimum oral health.

00213
Irish Direct Marketing Association
IDMA
8 Upper Fitzwilliam St., Dublin 2, Ireland
Tel: 01 6610470
Fax: 01 8308914
Email: services@idma.ie
Website: http://www.directbrand.ie/idma
Members: 500
Contact: Brian O'Kennedy, Chm.
Fee: £650
Membership Type: corporate, overseas
Fee: £350
Membership Type: associate, charity
Description: Promotes, develops and defends the interests of members by providing an interactive communication and information forum. Ensures the highest standards of integrity and fair trading.

00214
Irish Doctors Environmental Association
IDEA
Millbrook Clinic, County Cork, Bandon, Cork, Ireland
Tel: 023 8841132
Email: info@ideaireland.org
Website: http://www.ideaireland.org
Contact: Philip Michael, Honorary Sec.
Fee: £40
Membership Type: regular, associate
Fee: £20
Membership Type: student, unwaged, pensioner
Description: Educates and updates physicians and the general public on ecological problems impinging health and safety of individuals. Promotes human health through the protection and restoration of the environment.

00215
Irish Economic Association
IEA
Rm. D202, Economics Dept., Arts Bldg., Belfield 4, Dublin, Ireland
Email: info@iea.ie
Website: http://www.iea.ie
Contact: John Sheehan, Sec.
Description: Aims for the development of economics in Ireland. Organises conferences, publishes a newsletter and supports economic researches.
Publication: Journal
Publication title: Economic and Social Review

00216
Irish Engineering Enterprises Federation
IEEF
Confederation House, 84-86 Lower Baggot St., Dublin 2, Ireland
Tel: 01 6051500
Fax: 01 6381638
Email: info@ibec.ie
Website: http://www.ibec.ie/ieef
Contact: Marian Byron, Dir.
Description: Promotes and supports the competitiveness and prosperity of the engineering sector in Ireland. Represents the sector's interests to national government and EU institutions as well as the provision of business and market information to companies, and development of specific programmes on key business issues.
Formerly: Formerly, Engineering Industry Association
Publication: Newsletter
Publication title: IEEF Update

00217
Irish Epilepsy League
IEL
Beaumont Hospital, Neurology Dept., Dublin 9, Ireland
Email: normandelanty@eircom.net
Website: http://www.ilae-epilepsy.org/visitors/chapters/index.cfm
Contact: Norman Delanty, Pres.
Description: Seeks to advance and disseminate knowledge about epilepsy. Aims to improve services and care for patients. Strives to increase public awareness of epilepsy as a treatable brain disorder. Fosters the development of and cooperation among associations with common interests.

00218
Irish Ergonomics Society
IES
University of Limerick, Manufacturing and Operations Manufacturing, Limerick, Ireland
Tel: 061 202900
Fax: 061 202913
Email: wkright@indigo.ie
Website: http://www.ergonomics.ie/IES.html
Members: 65
Contact: Eilish Duggan, Sec.
Fee: £55
Membership Type: fellow
Fee: £50
Membership Type: regular
Description: Professionals involved in the ergonomics field promoting the discovery and exchange of knowledge concerning the characteristics of human beings that are applicable to the design of systems and devices of all kinds.
Publication: Newsletter
Publication title: The Irish Ergonomist

00219
Irish Exporters Association
IEA
28 Merrion Sq., Dublin 2, Ireland
Tel: 01 6612182
Fax: 01 6612315
Email: iea@irishexporters.ie
Website: http://www.irishexporters.ie
Members: 400
Staff: 15
Contact: John Whelan, Chief Exec.
Fee: £350-990
Membership Type: company (depends on annual turnover)
Description: Facilitates national and international trade by providing companies and industries with information on Irish exports. Conducts education and training programs. Lobbies government, the European Union and the World Trade Organization. Hosts European Information Centers.
Publication: Magazine
Publication title: Export Link. Advertisements.
Meetings/Conventions: National Export Forum – annual general assembly – Exhibits.

00220
Irish Family History Society
IFHS
PO Box 36, Naas, Kildare, Ireland
Email: ifhs@eircom.net
Website: http://homepage.eircom.net/~ifhs
Members: 400
Contact: Gerry Cahill, Honorable Chm.
Fee: £25
Membership Type: regular (with Irish addresses)
Fee: £25
Membership Type: regular (overseas)
Description: Aims to promote the study of Irish Family History and genealogy. Promotes the recording of gravestone inscriptions. Aims to promote the preservation, security and accessibility of archival material. Advises all those interested in seeking their Irish roots. Encourages the repatriation of information from overseas on Irish emigrants. Maintains a reference library for the use of members. Collaborates with and supports other societies with similar aims.
Publication: Journal
Publication title: Irish Family History

00221

Irish Family Planning Association

IFPA

60 Amiens St., Dublin 1, Ireland
Tel: 01 8069444
Fax: 01 8069445
Email: post@ifpa.ie
Website: http://www.ifpa.ie
Contact: Fiona Tyrrell, Communications and Development Off.
Fee: £10
Membership Type: unwaged
Fee: £25
Membership Type: waged
Description: Works to improve the quality of life for individuals living in Ireland by promoting family planning and responsible parenthood. Advocates family planning as a basic human right. Offers programs in sex education, family planning, and health. Provides contraceptive and health care services. Conducts research.

00222

Irish Farmers' Association

IFA

Irish Farm Centre, Bluebell 12, Dublin, Ireland
Tel: 01 4500266
Fax: 01 4551043
Email: postmaster@ifa.ie
Website: http://www.ifa.ie
Members: 3000
Staff: 2
Contact: Padraig Walshe, Pres.
Fee: £55
Membership Type: general
Description: Members include the Irish Mushroom Growers Association, Irish Handy Nursery Stock Association, Irish Field Vegetable Producers Association, Irish Bedding Plant Producers Association, Irish Protected Vegetable Producers Association, Irish Apple Growers Association, Irish Soft Fruit Growers Association and Irish Bulb Producers Association. Provides representative services for members on a local, national and international level. Activities include lobbying Government at all levels, compiling weekly market reports and analyses, liaising with other representative bodies across Europe and assisting with the promotion of Irish Horticultural produce around the world.
Formerly: Absorbed, Irish Commercial Horticultural Association

00223

Irish Federation of University Teachers

IFUT

11 Merrion Sq., Dublin 2, Ireland
Tel: 01 6610910
Fax: 01 6610909
Email: ifut@eircom.net
Website: http://www.ifut.ie
Members: 1600
Staff: 2
Contact: Mike Jennings, Gen. Sec.
Fee: £29
Membership Type: postgraduate
Fee: £33
Membership Type: retired
Description: Professors and other educators employed at the postsecondary level. Promotes effective postsecondary education. Works to enhance the professional status of members' interest before government agencies, college and university administrative bodies, and the public.
Publication title: Equality Issues

00224

Irish Federation of University Women

IrFUW

5 Rowan Park Ave., Blackrock, Dublin, Ireland
Tel: 012805176
Email: irishfuw@gmail.com
Website: http://www.ifuw.org/nfas/ireland/index.htm
Description: Women university graduates. Advocates women's pursuit of higher education in Ireland.

00225

Irish Fish Producers Organization

IFPO

77 Sir John Rogerson's Quay, Dublin 2, Ireland
Tel: 01 6401850
Fax: 01 6401851
Email: ifpo@eircom.net
Website: http://www.ifpo.ie
Members: 83
Staff: 3
Contact: Lorcan O'Cinneide, CEO
Description: Owners of commercial sea-fishing vessels. Works to make the best use of the available fish stocks to optimize returns.

00226

Irish Foster Care Association

IFCA

Village Green, Unit 23, Tallaght Village, Dublin 24, Ireland
Tel: 01 4599474
Fax: 01 4628014
Email: info@ifca.ie
Website: http://www.ifca.ie
Staff: 7
Contact: Deirdre McTeigue, Dir.
Description: Helps to coordinate the work of all those interested in foster care. Provides a forum to effectively promote the welfare of children already in foster care. Provides information on fostering related issues. Seeks to draw more families into fostering.
Publication: Pamphlet
Publication title: Fostering Facts

00227

Irish Fragile X Society

IFXS

c/o Inclusion Ireland
The Steel Works, Unit C2, Foley St., Dublin 1, Ireland
Email: info@fragilex-ireland.org
Website: http://www.fragilex-ireland.org
Contact: Mary Smith, Co-Founder
Fee: £13
Membership Type: family
Fee: £20
Membership Type: associate
Description: Works to improve the quality of life of all people affected by Fragile X syndrome; provides mutual support and information to families, promotes public awareness of Fragile X syndrome.

00228

Irish Franchise Association

Kandoy House, 2 Fairview Strand, Dublin 3, Ireland
Tel: 01 8134555
Fax: 01 8134575
Email: info@irishfranchiseassociation.com
Website: http://www.irishfranchiseassociation.com
Contact: Tom Shanahan, Exec. Dir.
Description: Promotes the development of franchising in Ireland. Protects the interests of franchising companies. Works to establish a clear definition of ethical franchising standards.
Publication: Newsletter
Publication title: Franchise Ireland

00229

Irish Funds Industry Association

IFIA

1 Gandon House, Mayor St., Dublin 1, Ireland
Tel: 01 6701077
Fax: 01 6701092
Email: info@irishfunds.ie
Website: http://www.irishfunds.ie
Contact: Carin Bryans, Chair
Description: Represents individuals and firms involved in international fund services industry. Supports and complements the development of fund services. Promotes awareness and encourages training and professional development of personnel within the industry.

00230

Irish Georgian Society

IGS

74 Merrion Sq., Dublin 2, Ireland
Tel: 01 6767053
Fax: 01 6620290
Email: info@igs.ie
Website: http://www.igs.ie
Members: 3500
Staff: 5
Contact: Desmond Fitzgerald, Pres.
Fee: £2000
Membership Type: benefactor
Fee: £350
Membership Type: patron
Description: International society of individuals, firms, and libraries from 23 countries united to preserve Irish art and architecture, especially that of the Georgian period. Conducts rescue, repair and restoration work on buildings in need. Promotes tourism as a means of preserving the Irish heritage. Arranges expeditions to buildings of interest.
Formerly: Formerly, Irelands Architectural Heritage Society
Publication: Journal
Publication title: Irish Architectural and Decorative Studies

00231

Irish Gerontological Society

IGS

St. Vincent's University Hospital, Dept. of Medicine for the Elderly, Our Lady's Ward, Elm Park, Dublin 4, Ireland
Tel: 087 7463310
Email: marianhughes@ireland.com
Website: http://www.gerontology.ie
Members: 300
Staff: 3
Contact: Marian Hughes, Admin. Off.
Fee: £25
Membership Type: full

Description: Health care professionals treating the elderly; scientists and clinicians with an interest in the aging process and diseases of the aged. Promotes gerontological research and increased availability of gerontological care; facilitates training of gerontology specialists. Represents the interests of gerontologists and gerontological organizations.

00232

Irish Girl Guides
IGG

27 Pembroke Pk., Dublin 4, Ireland
Tel: 01 6683898
Fax: 01 6602779
Email: info@irishgirlguides.ie
Website: http://www.irishgirlguides.ie
Members: 12000
Staff: 14
Contact: Linda Peters, CEO
Description: Provides a meeting place for girls from a variety of backgrounds. Works to help girls grow in self-confidence and develop leadership skills. Teaches girls practical indoor and outdoor skills. Encourages community service activities.

00233

Irish Grain and Feed Association
IGFA

19 Carrick Hill, Portlaoise 2, Laois, Ireland
Tel: 0502 67022
Fax: 0502 68690
Email: info@eorna.ie
Website: http://www.eorna.ie
Contact: Jerry Clifford, Pres.
Description: Ensures the commercial function in the different sectors of the cereals, rice, animal feed, oil seeds, olive oil, oils and fats, and agrosupply trade.

00234

Irish Guide Dogs for the Blind
IGDB

Model Farm Rd., Cork, Ireland
Tel: 021 4878200
Fax: 021 4874152
Email: info@guidedogs.ie
Website: http://www.guidedogs.ie
Contact: Jim Dennehy, Pres.
Description: Dog trainers and individuals providing support and services to people with impaired vision. Seeks to improve the quality of life of people with impaired vision. Makes available trained guide dogs to people with impaired vision; conducts training programs for people wishing to use guide dogs.

00235

Irish Haemophilia Society
IHS

1st Fl., Cathedral Ct., New St., Dublin 8, Ireland
Tel: 01 6579900
Fax: 01 6579901
Email: info@haemophilia.ie
Website: http://www.haemophilia.ie
Members: 300
Staff: 5
Contact: Brian O'Mahony, Chief Exec.
Fee: £30
Membership Type: ordinary/family
Fee: £650
Membership Type: life
Description: Individuals and organizations. Seeks to improve the quality of life of people with hemophilia and their families. Makes available support and services; conducts educational and advocacy campaigns; supports hematological research.
Library Subject: all aspects of Haemophilia
Library Type: reference

00236

Irish Hard of Hearing Association
IHHA

35 N Frederick St., Dublin 1, Ireland
Tel: 01 8175700
Fax: 01 8723816
Email: ihha@deafhear.ie
Website: http://ihha.ie
Contact: Maggie Fitzgerald, Pres.
Fee: £10
Membership Type: individual
Description: Serves as a national organization for hearing impaired people from all walks of life.
Publication: Magazine
Publication title: Hearsay

00237

Irish Hardware and Building Materials Association
IHBMA

Elmville, Upper Kilmacud Rd., Dendrum, Dublin 14, Ireland
Tel: 01 2980969
Fax: 01 2986103
Email: info@ihbma.ie
Website: http://www.ihbma.ie
Members: 600
Contact: John Murphy, Pres.
Description: Provides training, education and advisory services to members to improve their businesses and services to consumers.
Meetings/Conventions: President's Ball – semiannual banquet

00238

Irish Holstein Friesian Association
IHFA

Ballymacowen, Clonakilty, Cork, Ireland
Tel: 023 33443
Email: enquiries@ihfa.ie
Website: http://www.ihfa.ie
Members: 3500
Contact: Richard Whelan, Chm.
Description: Validates and upkeeps the herdbook of Holstein Friesian Cattle. Gives direction to the development and promotion of the breed in Ireland.

00239

Irish Home Builders Association
IHBA

c/o Construction Industry Federation
Construction House, Canal Rd., Dublin 6, Ireland
Tel: 01 4066000
Fax: 01 4966953
Email: ihba@cif.ie
Website: http://www.cif.ie/asp/section.asp?s=1
Members: 1500
Staff: 5
Contact: Hubert Fitzpatrick, Dir.
Description: Represents and promotes the economic interests of residential building contractors in the Republic of Ireland. Conducts lobbying and advocacy campaigns. Gathers and disseminates industry information.
Publication: Newsletter
Publication title: Homebuilder Magazine

00240

Irish Hospital Consultants Association
IHCA

Heritage House, Dundrum Office Park, Dublin 14, Ireland
Tel: 01 2989123
Fax: 01 2989395
Email: info@ihca.ie
Website: http://www.ihca.ie
Members: 1800
Contact: Finbarr Fitzpatrick, Sec. Gen.
Fee: £58
Membership Type: regular
Fee: £700
Membership Type: regular
Description: Represents hospital consultants working in public and private practice in Ireland.

00241

Irish Hospitality Institute
IHI

8 Herbert Ln., Dublin 2, Ireland
Tel: 01 6624790
Fax: 01 6624789
Email: info@ihi.ie
Website: http://www.ihi.ie
Contact: Natasha Kinsella, Chief Exec.
Fee: £220
Membership Type: fellow
Fee: £170
Membership Type: full, associate
Description: Works to encourage hospitality professionals to take responsibility for professional development and to promote professionalism.
Formerly: Formerly, Irish Hotel and Catering Institute
Publication: Newsletter
Publication title: IHI News

00242

Irish Hotels Federation
IHF

13 Northbrook Rd., Dublin 6, Ireland
Tel: 01 4976459
Fax: 01 4974613
Email: info@ihf.ie
Website: http://www.ihf.ie
Members: 1000
Staff: 11
Contact: Tim Fenn, Chief Exec.
Fee: £260
Membership Type: guesthouse
Fee: £360
Membership Type: hotel
Description: Hotel and guesthouse proprietors in the Republic of Ireland. Promotes and protects members' interests and represents the industry. Offers advisory services to members on legal, technical, and economic matters including fire precautions, marketing, labor relations, and business promotions. Works with the Irish Tourist Board. Makes recommendations to government agencies on industry issues. Monitors trends in the

European Economic Community and their application to Irish affairs.
Publication: Booklet
Publication title: Be Our Guest - Hotel and Guesthouse Guide

00243
Irish Institute of Credit Management
IICM
17 Kildare St., Dublin 2, Ireland
Tel: 01 6099444
Fax: 01 6099445
Email: info@iicm.ie
Website: http://www.iicm.ie
Contact: Sean Mac Mahon, Pres.
Description: Represents the credit management profession in Ireland by holding conferences and seminars on credit management issues. Provides education and training for all credit personnel; makes representations to government on items relevant to credit professionals.

00244
Irish Institute of Training and Development
IITD
Millennium Business Park, 4 Sycamore House, Naas, Kildare, Ireland
Tel: 045 881166
Fax: 045 881192
Email: info@iitd.com
Website: http://www.iitd.com
Members: 2000
Staff: 2
Contact: John Gorman, Pres.
Fee: £195
Membership Type: fellow
Fee: £180
Membership Type: full
Description: Individuals working in human resource development in Ireland. Fosters communication among members. Conducts educational programs.
Publication: Magazine
Publication title: T&D. Advertisements.

00245
Irish Insurance Federation
IIF
Insurance House, 39 Molesworth St., Dublin 2, Ireland
Tel: 01 6761820
Fax: 01 6761943
Email: fed@iif.ie
Website: http://www.iif.ie
Members: 64
Staff: 14
Contact: Michael Kemp, Chief Exec.
Description: Promotes life and non-life insurance companies in Ireland; works to influence the domestic and international regulatory, legal, political and social environments in order to advance the interests of the insurance industry and consumers.

00246
Irish International Freight Association
IIFA
Strand House, Strand St., Malahide, Dublin, Ireland
Tel: 01 8455411
Fax: 01 8455534
Email: iifa@eircom.net
Website: http://www.iifa.ie
Members: 100
Contact: Colm Walsh, CEO
Description: Represents Freight Forwarders in Ireland. Promotes among the membership, the need to improve professional status and to ensure high standards of professional conduct and practice.

00247
Irish Internet Association
IIA
The Digital Hub, 101 James St., Dublin 8, Ireland
Tel: 01 5424154
Email: info@iia.ie
Website: http://www.iia.ie
Members: 3400
Staff: 3
Contact: Joan Mulvilhill, CEO
Fee: £695
Membership Type: corporate
Fee: £350
Membership Type: SME
Description: Companies and organizations involved with electronic commerce and Internet-related services. Promotes and represents the Internet industry in Ireland.
Publication: Magazine
Publication title: IIA Digital Digest. Advertisements.

00248
Irish Kidney Association
IKA
Donor House, Block 43A, Parkwest, Dublin 12, Ireland
Tel: 01 6205306
Fax: 01 6205366
Website: http://www.ika.ie
Members: 2500
Staff: 16
Contact: Patricia May, Chair
Description: Provides support for those with end-stage renal disease and kidney transplants. Prints and distributes Organ Donor Cards. Irish representative of the World Transplant Games; maintains five-apartment Holiday Centre in Tramore for all kidney patients; offers counseling and financial assistance. Provides accommodation and support to family members of inpatients while in the hospital.
Publication: Magazine
Publication title: Support

00249
Irish Labour Party
17 Ely Pl., Dublin 2, Ireland
Tel: 01 6784700
Fax: 01 6612640
Email: membership@labour.ie
Website: http://www.labour.ie
Members: 7000
Staff: 45
Contact: Michael Allen, Gen. Sec.
Fee: £15
Membership Type: individual - standard
Fee: £10
Membership Type: individual (over 65 years old)
Description: Political party advocating democratic socialism in the Republic of Ireland.
Publication: Newsletter
Publication title: Labour News

00250
Irish Landscape Institute
ILI
PO Box 11068, Dublin 2, Ireland
Tel: 01 6627409
Email: ili@irishlandscapeinstitute.com
Website: http://www.irishlandscapeinstitute.com
Members: 160
Contact: Dave Kirkwood, Pres.
Fee: £85
Membership Type: graduate
Fee: £170
Membership Type: full
Description: Promotes the growth of the landscape architecture profession. Fosters high standards of quality in design, planning, development, and conservation in the field. Encourages the role of landscape architects as an instrument of aesthetic achievement and social change for the public welfare. Promotes the exchange of technical information and supports scientific research in all aspects of landscape architecture.

00251
Irish LP Gas Association
ILPGA
c/o Flogas Ireland Ltd.
Dublin Rd., Drogheda, Louth, Ireland
Tel: 041 9831041
Fax: 041 9831043
Email: info@flogas.ie
Website: http://www.ilpga.ie
Members: 2
Contact: Paul O'Connell, Chm.
Description: Promotes safe storage, distribution, and use of LP gas.

00252
Irish Management Institute
IMI
Sandyford Rd., Dublin 16, Ireland
Tel: 01 2078400
Fax: 01 2955147
Email: sharon.byrne@imi.ie
Website: http://www.imi.ie
Contact: Tom MCCarthy, Chief Exec.
Fee: £500
Membership Type: personal
Fee: £350
Membership Type: associate (retired/student)
Description: Works with individuals and organisations to improve the practice of management in Ireland.

00253
Irish Marine Federation
IMF
Confederation House, 84/86 Lower Baggot St., Dublin 2, Ireland
Tel: 01 6051652
Fax: 01 6381652

Email: mark.mcauley@ibec.ie
Website: http://www.irishmarinefederation.com
Contact: Mark McAuley, Sec.
Fee: £540
Membership Type: general
Description: Seeks to promote the interests of all sectors of the marine industry in Ireland and to encourage its growth and development. Provides advice, information and services to members. Promotes the image of the industry through quality awareness, public statements and the organization of Boat Shows.

00254

Irish Mathematical Society
IMS

St. Patrick's College, Rm. Mov30A, Drumcondra, Dublin 9, Ireland
Email: sinead.breen@spd.dcu.ie
Website: http://www.maths.tcd.ie/pub/ims
Contact: Sinead Breen, Treas.
Fee: £25
Membership Type: ordinary
Fee: £12.5
Membership Type: student
Description: Aims to further mathematics and mathematical research in Ireland.
Publication: Bulletin

00255

Irish Medical Devices Association
IMDA

Confederation House, 84-86 Lower Baggot St., Dublin 2, Ireland
Tel: 01 6051529
Fax: 01 6381529
Email: imda@ibec.ie
Website: http://www.ibec.ie/imda
Members: 80
Contact: Sharon Higgins, Dir.
Description: Represents the medical device and diagnostic companies in Ireland. Promotes the development and growth of the industry. Encourages research and development, manufacture and marketing of products in the medical device and diagnostic sectors.
Publication: Newsletter
Publication title: IMDA Update

00256

Irish Medical Organisation
IMO

10 Fitzwilliam Pl., Dublin 2, Ireland
Tel: 01 6767273
Fax: 01 6612758
Email: imo@imo.ie
Website: http://www.imo.ie
Members: 5000
Contact: George McNeice, CEO
Fee: £1308
Membership Type: consultant, general practitioner (individual)
Fee: £1026
Membership Type: consultant (no clinical academics)
Description: Physicians and medical students and their families. Seeks to develop a "caring, efficient and effective health service". Serves as a professional body representing physicians in Ireland; facilitates exchange of information among members; encourages medical research.
Publication: Journal
Publication title: Irish Medical Journal

00257

Irish Meteorological Society
IMS

c/o Met Eireann
Glasnevin Hill, Dublin 9, Ireland
Tel: 01 806426
Email: climate.enquiries@met.ie
Website: http://www.irishmetsociety.org/cms
Contact: Emily Gleeson, Sec.
Fee: £15
Membership Type: adult in Dublin
Fee: £10
Membership Type: adult outside Dublin
Description: Promotes interest in all areas of meteorology and dissemination of meteorological knowledge. Consists of members working in the related areas such as meteorology, aviation, marine and agriculture, and the environment.
Meetings/Conventions: annual meeting

00258

Irish Mining and Quarrying Society
IMQS

UCD School of Geological Sciences, Rm. G16A, Belfield 4, Dublin, Ireland
Tel: 01 7162085
Fax: 01 2837733
Email: info@imqs.ie
Website: http://www.imqs.ie
Members: 300
Contact: Sean Finlay, Pres.
Fee: £40
Membership Type: ordinary
Fee: £80
Membership Type: fellow
Description: Represents and promotes the extractive industry in Ireland. Fosters discovery, development, processing and marketing of the mineral and other geological natural resources in an environmentally compatible manner.
Publication: Magazine
Publication title: Extractive Industry Review

00259

Irish Motor Neurone Disease Association
IMNDA

Coleraine House, Coleraine St., Dublin 7, Ireland
Email: info@imnda.ie
Website: http://www.imnda.ie
Staff: 5
Contact: Ciara Hudson, Office Mgr.
Description: Promotes interest in Motor Neurone Disease (MND) research among medical and scientific communities and the public in Ireland. Offers support services to MND sufferers and their families. Disseminates information about the disease.
Publication: Newsletter
Publication title: IMNDA Newsletter

00260

Irish Music Rights Organisation
IMRO

Copyright House, Pembroke Row, Lower Baggot St., Dublin 2, Ireland
Tel: 01 6614844
Fax: 01 6763125
Email: info@imro.ie
Website: http://www.imro.ie
Contact: Keith Donald, Chm.
Description: Musicians, music publishers, and other individuals, agencies, and organizations with an interest in the intellectual property rights of musicians and composers. Promotes broadening and strengthening of existing intellectual property laws governing music rights. Serves as a clearinghouse on the intellectual property rights of musicians and composers; conducts educational and advocacy programs; provides licensing assistance to musicians and composers.

00261

Irish National Teachers' Organisation
INTO

35 Parnell Sq., Dublin 1, Ireland
Tel: 01 8047700
Fax: 01 8722462
Email: info@into.ie
Website: http://www.into.ie
Members: 37871
Staff: 38
Contact: Sheila Nunan, Gen. Sec.
Fee: £100
Membership Type: substitute teacher
Fee: £50
Membership Type: career break
Description: Union of primary school teachers in the Republic of Ireland and primary and postprimary school teachers in Northern Ireland. Seeks to express a collective opinion on education and teaching; safeguard and improve employment conditions; advise and assist on professional matters; promote interests and the raising of educational standards. Administers funds for assistance of members.
Publication: Magazine
Publication title: Intouch. Advertisements.

00262

Irish Nutrition and Dietetic Institute
INDI

Ashgrove House, Kill Ave., Dun Laoghaire, Ireland
Tel: 01 2804839
Fax: 01 2892353
Email: info@indi.ie
Website: http://www.indi.ie
Members: 400
Contact: Janis Morrissey, Pres.
Fee: £231.5
Membership Type: practicing
Fee: £88
Membership Type: retired/non practicing
Description: Professional dietitians. Promotes growth in the number of dietary and nutrition-related positions in the Republic of Ireland. Represents the interests of members.
Publication: Newsletter
Publication title: In Focus

00263
Irish Offshore Operators' Association
IOOA

c/o Brendan Sheehan, Sec.
Tramway House, Dartry Rd., Dublin 6, Ireland
Tel: 01 4975716
Email: info@iooa.ie
Website: http://www.iooa.ie
Contact: Fergus Cahill, Chm.
Description: Represents the oil and gas companies with operating interests in Ireland's offshore hydrocarbon industry. Provides a forum for representatives of member companies to work together in identifying and tackling issues facing Ireland's offshore industry. Cooperates and provides a united approach to issues such as safety, the environment, legislation and employment. Assists in the growth of oil and gas exploration and production in Ireland's waters.

00264
Irish Organic Farmers and Growers Association
IOFGA

Main St., Newtownforbes, Longford, Ireland
Tel: 04342495
Fax: 04342496
Email: info@iofga.org
Website: http://www.iofga.org
Members: 1050
Staff: 13
Contact: Angela Clarke, Contact
Description: Organic farmers. Promotes production and consumption of organic food. Maintains a set of rigorous production standards and operates an inspection program.
Publication: Magazine
Publication title: Organic Matters. Advertisements.

00265
Irish Organisation for Geographic Information
IRLOGI

1 Roseville, Naas, Kildare, Ireland
Tel: 045 871950
Fax: 086 8110101
Email: info@irlogi.ie
Website: http://www.irlogi.ie
Contact: Bruce McCormack, Pres.
Description: Stimulates the development and effective use of geographic information in Ireland. Aims to be the focus for the collection, exchange and dissemination of geographic information. Encourages the development and adoption of quality and reliability standards for Geographic Information (GI). Encourages and supports education and training in GI.

00266
Irish Pain Society
IPS

22, Merrion Sq., Dublin 2, Ireland
Fax: 01 6614374
Email: ips@rcsi.ie
Website: http://www.iasp-pain.org/AM/Template.cfm?Section=Chapters
Members: 120
Contact: Liam Conroy, Pres.
Fee: £50
Membership Type: consultant
Fee: £25
Membership Type: non-consultant
Description: Promotes research on pain. Seeks to improve the health care given to patients with pain. Provides information on pain and its related topics.
Publication: Articles
Publication title: PainWise

00267
Irish Payment Services Organisation
IPSO

14 Cumberland St., 2nd Fl., Dun Laoghaire, Dublin, Ireland
Tel: 01 6636740
Fax: 01 2843409
Email: info@ipso.ie
Website: http://www.ipso.ie
Contact: Pat McLoughlin, CEO
Description: Represents payment industry. Promotes the development of payment services for financial institutions in the Irish industry. Provides strategic and technical support to the payments industry.
Publication: Newsletter
Publication title: IPSO Facto

00268
Irish Peatland Conservation Council
IPCC

Bog of Allen Nature Centre, Lullymore, Rathangan, Kildare, Ireland
Tel: 045 860133
Fax: 045 860481
Email: bogs@ipcc.ie
Website: http://www.ipcc.ie
Members: 1500
Staff: 4
Contact: Catherine O'Connell, Chief Exec.
Fee: £40
Membership Type: individual
Fee: £45
Membership Type: family, joint, friend
Description: Works to conserve living intact Irish bogs and peatlands. Purchases bogland nature reserves and repairs damaged bogs. Encourages a lifestyle in harmony with the environment.
Publication: Newsletter
Publication title: Peatland News. Advertisements.

00269
Irish Pharmaceutical Healthcare Association
IPHA

Franklin House, 140 Pembroke Rd., Dublin 4, Ireland
Tel: 01 6603350
Fax: 01 6686672
Email: info@ipha.ie
Website: http://www.ipha.ie
Contact: Anne Nolan, Chief Exec.
Description: Promotes the economic and political environment of the pharmaceutical industry in Ireland in order to provide quality medicines and healthcare to patients.
Publication: Newsletter
Publication title: Medicines Matter

00270
Irish Playwrights and Screenwriters Guild
IPSG

Art House, Curved St., Temple Bar, Dublin 2, Ireland
Tel: 01 6709970
Email: info@script.ie
Website: http://www.script.ie
Members: 150
Staff: 1
Contact: Audrey O'Reilly, Chair
Description: Irish dramatists writing for theatre, radio, and television. Promotes and protects the rights of Irish dramatists and encourages and promotes aspiring writers. Negotiates terms and conditions of employment in TV and radio. Hosts guest speakers who talk about various scriptwriting topics.

00271
Irish Productivity Centre
IPC

Alexandra House, The Sweepstakes, Ballsbridge, Dublin 4, Ireland
Tel: 01 6319320
Fax: 01 6319001
Email: partners@ipcconsulting.ie
Website: http://www.ipc.ie
Description: Unites to help Irish businesses to improve productivity and competitiveness strategies through the provision of high quality and relevant consultancy, facilitation, training and research services.

00272
Irish Quaternary Association
IQUA

Department of Geography, National University of Ireland, Maynooth, Kildare, Ireland
Tel: 01 7086147
Email: stephen.mccarron@nuim.ie
Website: http://www.tcd.ie/geography/IQUA/Index.htm
Members: 150
Contact: Stephen McCarron, Sec.
Fee: £15
Membership Type: general
Fee: £10
Membership Type: student, unwaged
Description: Aims to promote quaternary studies in Ireland through publications and the activities of the organization.
Formerly: Formerly, Irish Association for Quaternery Studies

00273
Irish Raynaud's and Scleroderma Society
IRSS

PO Box 2958, Foxrock, Dublin 18, Ireland
Tel: 01 2020184
Email: info@irishraynauds.com
Website: http://www.irishraynauds.com
Members: 400
Staff: 2
Contact: Irene Bergin, CEO
Fee: £25
Membership Type: regular
Description: Individuals and organizations. Seeks to improve the quality of life of people with Raynaud's disease or scleroderma and their families. Promotes better

physician-patient communication. Makes available support and services; conducts educational and advocacy campaigns.

00274

Irish Recorded Music Association IRMA

1 Corrig Ave., Dun Laoghaire, Ireland
Tel: 01 2806571
Fax: 01 2806579
Email: irma_info@irma.ie
Website: http://www.irma.ie
Fee: £150
Membership Type: small company
Fee: £750
Membership Type: medium company
Description: Promotes the interests of members through the use of statutes, case law, contracts, and agreements. Represents members on national and international copyright issues; coordinates anti-piracy actions; compiles statistical information on the international recording industry; and provides industry contacts and advisory services.

00275

Irish Refugee Council IRC

Ballast House, 2nd Fl., Aston Quay, Dublin 2, Ireland
Tel: 01 7645854
Fax: 01 6725927
Email: info@irishrefugeecouncil.ie
Website: http://www.irishrefugeecouncil.ie
Contact: Robin Hanan, CEO
Fee: £20
Membership Type: individual
Fee: £35
Membership Type: household
Description: Seeks to ensure that all aspects of Ireland's asylum and refugee policy and practice fully respect international law and the human rights of asylum-seekers and refugees. Promotes public awareness and understanding of asylum and refugee issues.

00276

Irish Road Haulage Association IRHA

Gowna Plaza, Ste. 6, Bracetown Business Park, Clonee, Meath, Ireland
Tel: 01 8013380
Fax: 01 8253080
Email: info@irha.ie
Website: http://www.irha.ie
Contact: Vincent Caulfield, Pres.
Fee: £220
Membership Type: company (based on number of vehicles)
Description: Works to represent and promote the interests of the licensed transport industry in Ireland and abroad.
Publication: Newsletter
Publication title: Knights of the Road

00277

Irish Salmon Growers' Association ISGA

c/o Irish Farmers Association
Irish Farm Centre, Bluebell, Dublin 12, Ireland
Tel: 01 4500266
Fax: 01 4551043
Email: postmaster@ifa.ie
Website: http://www.ifa.ie
Members: 30
Contact: Teresa Curran, Regional Office Admin.
Description: Represents the salmon growers in Ireland. Aims to diversify and meet the needs of the market.

00278

Irish Security Industry Association ISIA

42-44, Northumberland Rd., Dublin 4, Ireland
Tel: 01 6905736
Fax: 01 6905739
Email: info@isia.ie
Website: http://www.isia.ie
Members: 63
Staff: 1
Contact: Barry Brady, Exec. Dir.
Fee: £450-5900
Membership Type: guarding, electronic, transport, monitoring (based on the turnover)
Fee: £450
Membership Type: investigator, surveillance, private detective
Description: Supports a wide spectrum of security services; acts as self-regulatory body with quality assurance scheme and national training for employees. Represents members to government and police and generally provides lobby services on many issues.

00279

Irish Small and Medium Enterprises Association ISME

17 Kildare St., Dublin 2, Ireland
Tel: 01 6622755
Fax: 01 6612157
Email: info@isme.ie
Website: http://www.isme.ie
Members: 4600
Staff: 9
Contact: Mark Fielding, Chief Exec.
Description: Independent Representative and Lobbying body for small and medium size businesses. Promotes the development of small enterprises. Acts as a liaison with government agencies. Conducts Educational, Training and Network programs. Provides Professional Advice and Support, Saving, Discount and Affiliate Schemes to all member companies.
Library Type: by appointment only
Publication: Book
Publication title: Irish Employers Obligations Procedures and Practices Guide

00280

Irish Society for Archives ISA

c/o Antoinette Doran, Membership Sec.
IVRLA Project Office, Rm. 327, James Joyce Library, UCD, Belfield, Dublin 4, Ireland
Email: antoinette.doran@ucd.ie
Website: http://www.ucd.ie/archives/isa/isa-index.html
Members: 150
Contact: Raymond Refausse, Chm.
Fee: £10
Membership Type: student
Fee: £25
Membership Type: ordinary
Description: Individuals and institutions with an interest in archives. Promotes the place of archives in Irish society and acts as a forum for the discussion of archival matters in Ireland. Represents archives before government agencies and lobbies for free access to archival materials. Supports research and educational programs on archival collections in Ireland.
Publication: Journal
Publication title: Irish Archives

00281

Irish Society for Autism ISA

Unity Bldg., 16/17 Lower O'Connell St., Dublin 1, Ireland
Tel: 01 8744684
Website: http://www.autism.ie
Staff: 100
Contact: Pat Matthews, Exec. Dir.
Description: Individuals and organizations. Seeks to improve the quality of life of people with autism and their families. Makes available support and services; conducts educational and advocacy campaigns.

00282

Irish Society for Disability and Oral Health ISDH

c/o Sarah Roux, Honorary Sec.
HSE Ballymun Healthcare Facility, Ballymun Civic Centre, Main St., Ballymun 9, Dublin, Ireland
Tel: 01 8467231
Fax: 01 8467531
Email: sarah.roux@hse.ie
Website: http://www.isdh.ie
Contact: Tina Gorman, Pres.
Fee: £50
Membership Type: dentist
Fee: £30
Membership Type: profession complimentary to dentistry
Description: Seeks to promote, preserve and protect the oral health of people with disabilities. Consults with disability groups to identify their needs and the demands of people with disabilities. Encourages undergraduate and postgraduate teaching and training of oral health care for people with disabilities. Fosters research in the field of oral health care for people with disabilities.

00283

Irish Society for Quality and Safety in Healthcare ISQSH

Blanchardstown Corporate Park, No. 12, Block 8, Dublin 15, Ireland
Tel: 01 8855897
Fax: 01 8208487
Email: info@isqsh.ie
Website: http://www.isqsh.ie
Staff: 4
Contact: Brian Scollard, Hon. Treas.
Description: Promotes improvement of quality and safety in healthcare.

00284

Irish Society for Rheumatology
ISR

c/o ISR Secretariat, Arthritis Foundation of Ireland
Mesphil House, 37 Adelaide Rd., Dublin 2, Ireland
Tel: 01 2315251
Fax: 01 2315502
Email: info@isr.ie
Website: http://www.isr.ie/home/default.asp
Members: 150
Staff: 1
Contact: Gaye Cunanne, Pres.
Description: Promotes the specialty medical field of rheumatology in Ireland.

00285

Irish Society for the Prevention of Cruelty to Animals
ISPCA

Natl. Animal Centre, Derryglogher Lodge, Keenagh, Longford, Ireland
Tel: 01 4325035
Fax: 01 4325024
Email: info@ispca.ie
Website: http://www.ispca.ie
Members: 300
Staff: 4
Contact: Mark Beazley, Chief Exec.
Fee: £50
Membership Type: associate
Description: Individuals with an interest in the well-being of animals. Promotes humane treatment of animals and works to uphold and expand the rights of animals.

00286

Irish Society of Chartered Physiotherapists
ISCP

Royal College of Surgeons, 123, St. Stephen's Green, Dublin 2, Ireland
Tel: 01 4022148
Fax: 01 4022160
Email: info@iscp.ie
Website: http://www.iscp.ie
Members: 3000
Staff: 6
Contact: Ruaidhri O'Connor, CEO
Fee: £290
Membership Type: practicing
Fee: £80
Membership Type: non-practicing, overseas
Description: Represents the interests of physiotherapists.
Publication: Newsletter
Publication title: Firsthand. Advertisements.

00287

Irish Society of Homeopaths
ISH

Regus House, Harcourt Rd., Dublin 2, Ireland
Tel: 01 4773193
Email: info@irishhomeopathy.ie
Website: http://www.irishhomeopathy.ie/homeopaths/index.php
Members: 400
Contact: Michael Smith, Chm.
Description: Represents lay homeopaths in Ireland. Works to make homeopathy accessible to all, increase awareness and understanding about Homeopathy, regulate standards and ethics of professional practice, provide continuing professional development, and work towards integration of Homeopathy within the Irish health care system.

00288

Irish Society of Human Genetics
ISHG

c/o Anne Parle-McDermott, Sec.
Dublin City University, School of Biotechnology, Dublin 9, Ireland
Tel: 01 7008499
Fax: 01 7005284
Email: anne.parle-mcdermott@dcu.ie
Website: http://irishsocietyofhumangenetics.blogspot.com
Contact: Collette Hand, Pres.
Fee: £35
Membership Type: ordinary, overseas
Fee: £25
Membership Type: reduced ordinary
Description: Geneticists, molecular biologists, medical doctors, laboratory scientists, epidemiologists, ethicists, and lawyers. Promotes study and research in human genetics as it relates to health and disease. Conducts research; disseminates information.

00289

Irish Society of Occupational Medicine
ISOM

c/o Dr. David Madden, Hon. Treas.
PO Box 7453, Ballsbridge, Dublin 4, Ireland
Email: isom@eircom.net
Website: http://www.iol.ie/~isom
Members: 270
Contact: Fiona Donnelly, Hon. Sec.
Description: Occupational physicians and doctors promoting occupational medicine in Ireland.

00290

Irish Society of Periodontology

c/o Dr. John Molloy, Sec.
7b Dock Road Galway, Galway, Ireland
Tel: 091 569110
Fax: 091 569112
Website: http://www.efp.net
Contact: Patricia Shalloe, Pres.
Description: Works as professional organization that brings together Irish dentists to promote excellence in dentistry and the importance of periodontology in dental health.

00291

Irish Society of Surveying, Photogrammetry and Remote Sensing
ISSPRS

Bolton St., Department of Surveying, Dublin 1, Ireland
Tel: 01 4023730
Fax: 01 4023999
Email: issprs@indigo.ie
Website: http://www.isprs.org
Members: 50
Contact: Richard Kirwan, Pres.
Description: Promotes the advancement of photogrammetry and remote sensing and their applications. Initiates and coordinates research in photogrammetry and remote sensing. Fosters cooperation and coordination with related international scientific organizations. Promotes scientific interests focusing on photogrammetry, remote sensing and related disciplines, as well as applications in cartography, geodesy, surveying, natural, Earth and engineering sciences.

00292

Irish South and West Fish Producers Organisation
IS&WFPO

The Pier, Castletownbere, Cork, Ireland
Tel: 027 70670
Fax: 027 70771
Email: southwest@eircom.net
Website: http://www.irishsouthandwest.ie
Description: Represents fishermen in the South and West Coast of Ireland.

00293

Irish Stammering Association
ISA

Carmichael House, N Brunswick St., Dublin 7, Ireland
Tel: 01 8724405
Fax: 01 8735737
Email: mail@stammeringireland.ie
Website: http://www.stammeringireland.ie
Contact: Patrick Kelly, Contact
Fee: £20
Membership Type: regular
Description: Works to promote awareness of stuttering in Ireland.

00294

Irish Sudden Infant Death Association
ISIDA

Carmichael House, 4 N Brunswick St., Dublin 7, Ireland
Tel: 01 8732711
Fax: 01 8726056
Email: isida@eircom.net
Website: http://www.isida.ie
Contact: Kevin O'Meara, Chm.
Description: Provides information and support to families bereaved by sudden infant death and others affected by it; supports research into the causes and prevention of sudden infant death syndrome. Offers bereavement group therapy, befriending service, annual memorial service, SIDS Model of Care, speakers' bureau.
Publication: Book
Publication title: A Book of Remembrance

00295

Irish Taxation Institute
ITI

South Block, Longboat Quay, Grand Canal Harbour, Dublin 2, Ireland
Tel: 01 6631700
Fax: 01 6688387
Email: info@taxireland.ie
Website: http://www.taxireland.ie
Contact: Mark Redmond, CEO
Description: Educates, informs, represents and sets standards for tax consultants in Ireland. Serves as the examining and professional standards body for the tax consultancy profession. Offers a range of professional training programs.

00296

Irish Timber Growers' Association
ITGA

17 Castle St., Dalkey, Dublin, Ireland
Tel: 01 2350520
Fax: 01 2350416
Email: info@itga.ie
Website: http://www.itga.ie
Contact: Brendan Lacey, Chm.
Fee: £99-299
Membership Type: associate, individual (based on hectares of forestry)
Fee: £170
Membership Type: corporate (two foresters employed)
Description: Represents private woodland owners in Ireland. Aims to support the development and expansion of private sector forestry in Ireland.

00297

Irish Tour Operators Association
ITOA

PO Box 65, Bray, Wicklow, Ireland
Tel: 01 2861113
Fax: 01 2861107
Email: info@itoa-ireland.com
Website: http://www.irishtouroperators.com
Members: 35
Description: Promotes Ireland as a destination among its overseas partners including tour operators and major retail travel groups. Packages and promotes the various elements of the Irish tourism products for marketing overseas. Acts as the Irish representative of overseas tour operators, wholesalers and traffic generators. Provides packaging, booking and reservations services for the overseas travel trade.

00298

Irish Tourist Industry Confederation
ITIC

Sandyford Office Park, Unit 5, Dublin, Ireland
Tel: 01 2934950
Fax: 01 2934991
Email: itic@eircom.net
Website: http://www.itic.ie
Members: 30
Contact: Eamonn McKeon, CEO
Description: Represents the Irish tourist industry and works with the government on issues influencing tourism policy and performance, investment strategies and funding priorities, particularly for international marketing and product development.

00299

Irish Travel Agents Association
ITAA

32 S William St., Dublin 2, Ireland
Tel: 01 6794179
Fax: 01 6719897
Email: info@itaa.ie
Website: http://www.itaa.ie
Members: 366
Contact: Simon Nugent, Chief Exec.
Fee: £250
Membership Type: general
Description: Retail travel agents and tour operators in Ireland. Promotes the travel and tourism industry in Ireland and high standards of excellence and ethics among members.

00300

Irish Visual Artists' Rights Organisation
IVARO

37 N Great, George's St., Dublin 1, Ireland
Tel: 01 8722296
Fax: 01 8722364
Email: info@ivaro.ie
Website: http://www.ivaro.ie
Contact: Robert Ballagh, Chm.
Description: Protects the rights of painters, sculptors, photographers and other visual artists. Provides members with copyright information that will help them vouch for the originality of their work. Coordinates with other international organizations and the media regarding the current issues involved in copyright laws. Informs the public about copyright infringement.

00301

Irish Vocational Education Association
IVEA

McCann House, 99 Marlborough Rd., Donnybrook, Dublin 4, Ireland
Tel: 01 4966033
Fax: 01 4966460
Email: info@ivea.ie
Website: http://www.ivea.ie
Contact: Mary Bohan, Pres.
Description: Promotes the development and implementation of appropriate education and training policies for the vocational education sector. Contributes to the drafting and publication of legislation, which promotes the interests of the vocational education sector. Offers education and training programs.
Publication: Booklet
Publication title: Managing Allegations of Child Sexual Abuse

00302

Irish Wheelchair Association
IWA

Aras Chuchulainn, Blackheath Dr., Clontarf, Dublin 3, Ireland
Tel: 01 8186400
Fax: 01 8333873
Email: info@iwa.ie
Website: http://www.iwa.ie
Members: 20000
Staff: 1300
Contact: Kathleen McLoughlin, CEO
Description: Individuals and organizations. Seeks to improve the social, economic, and legal status of people with disabilities. Makes available support and services; conducts educational and advocacy campaigns.
Publication: Magazine
Publication title: Spokeout. Advertisements.

00303

Irish Wind Energy Association
IWEA

Kilowen House, Southernlink Business Pk., Jigginstown, Naas, Kildare, Ireland
Tel: 045 899341
Fax: 045 854958
Email: office@iwea.com
Website: http://www.iwea.com
Members: 300
Contact: Stephen Wheeler, Chm.
Fee: £115
Membership Type: ordinary
Fee: £2300
Membership Type: associate
Description: Promotes the use of wind energy in Ireland. Advances the development and application of wind energy. Influences the government policy in renewable energy.
Publication: Newsletter
Publication title: In The Wind

00304

Irish Woodturners' Guild
IWG

40 Broadford Crescent, Ballinteer, Dublin 16, Ireland
Email: secretary@irishwoodturnersguild.com
Website: http://www.irishwoodturnersguild.com
Members: 800
Contact: Eugene Grimley, Honorary Sec.
Fee: £54
Membership Type: individual
Fee: £57
Membership Type: family
Description: Works for the advancement and promotion of woodturning. Provides education, information and organization to those interested in woodturning. Encourages communication and exchange of views among woodturners of all nations. Encourages and participates in the development of training standards and educational facilities for turning.

00305

Irish Youth Foundation
IYF

56 Fitzwilliam Sq., 2nd Fl., Dublin 2, Ireland
Tel: 01 6766535
Fax: 01 6769893
Email: info@iyf.ie
Website: http://www.iyf.ie/intro.html
Staff: 3
Contact: Liam O'Dwyer, Chief Exec.
Description: Supports projects and programs that make a positive difference in the lives of vulnerable children and young people in Ireland. Raises funds through private donations, gifts, campaigns and events. Develops facilities and amenities for young people; provides necessary equipment to youth projects.

00306

Irish Youth Hostel Association
IYHA

61 Mountjoy St., Dublin 7, Ireland
Tel: 01 8304555
Fax: 01 8305808
Email: mailbox@anoige.ie
Website: http://www.anoige.ie
Members: 6000
Staff: 60
Fee: £30
Membership Type: senior
Fee: £20
Membership Type: family
Description: Represents 24 youth hostels throughout Ireland. Provides inexpensive accommodation for young visitors to Ireland. Helps in organizing group and individual tours around the country. Conducts educational programs, leader courses, environmental walks, tree plantings and photography club.

Library Subject: tourism literature, Ireland
Library Type: reference
Publication: Newsletter
Publication title: The Hosteller

00307

JCI Dublin

7 Clare St., Dublin 2, Ireland
Tel: 087 9529050
Email: info@jcdublin.com
Website: http://jcidublin.com
Contact: Laura Borlea, Pres.
Description: Provides opportunities for young people to develop leadership skills, responsibility, fellowship and entrepreneurship. Conducts individual development courses. Conducts charitable programs and sponsors competitions.

00308

Junior Achievement Ireland

8 Longford Pl., Monkstown, Dublin, Ireland
Tel: 01 2366644
Fax: 01 2803758
Email: info@juniorachievement.ie
Website: http://www.juniorachievement.ie
Staff: 25
Contact: Della Clancy, Exec. Dir.
Description: Aims to build a bridge between classroom and workplace. Provides young people the opportunity to participate in educational programs. Recruits persons who are qualified to teach students about business.

00309

Junior Chamber International Ireland
JCI Ireland

28-32 Upper Pembroke St., Dublin 2, Ireland
Tel: 01 2342514
Fax: 01 2342400
Email: president@jci-ireland.org
Website: http://www.jci-ireland.org/website/index.php
Members: 200
Contact: Mark Kelly, Pres.
Description: Provides opportunities for young people to develop leadership skills, responsibility, fellowship and entrepreneurship. Conducts individual development courses. Conducts charitable programs and sponsors competitions.

00310

Junior Chamber International Limerick
JCI Limerick

PO Box 111, Limerick, Ireland
Tel: 087 3162251
Email: juniorchamberlimerick@eircom.net
Website: http://www.jci.cc/local/limerick
Contact: Emmeline Searson, Pres.
Description: Provides opportunities for young people to develop leadership skills, responsibility, fellowship and entrepreneurship. Conducts individual development courses. Conducts charitable programs and sponsors competitions.

00311

Junior Chamber International Waterford

PO Box 33, Waterford, Ireland
Tel: 086 3955727
Email: waterford@jci-ireland.org
Website: http://jci-ireland.org/waterford
Contact: Ronan Gingles, Acting Chm.
Description: Provides opportunities for young people to develop leadership skills, responsibility, fellowship and entrepreneurship. Conducts individual development courses. Conducts charitable programs and sponsors competitions.

00312

Law Society of Ireland

Blackhall Pl., Dublin 7, Ireland
Tel: 01 6724800
Fax: 01 6724801
Email: general@lawsociety.ie
Website: http://www.lawsociety.ie
Members: 5000
Contact: Ken Murphy, Dir. Gen.
Description: Solicitors, law students and scholars, and other individuals with an interest in the law. Seeks to "improve access to the law". Represents the professional interests of, and provides support and services to, solicitors. Handles public complaints regarding the conduct of members; administers statutory compensation fund. Develops guidelines for legal practice and education. Sponsors continuing professional development courses for solicitors.
Publication: Magazine
Publication title: Law Society Gazette

00313

Leinster Society of Chartered Accountants
LSCA

CA House, Pearse St., Dublin 2, Ireland
Tel: 01 6377219
Fax: 01 6685685
Email: leinstersociety@icai.ie
Website: http://leinster.charteredaccountants.ie
Members: 9000
Contact: David Connolly, Chm.
Description: Develops and supports the Chartered Accountant as the premier provider of business services and excellence for whatever sector they serve. Provides both educational and social services for its members.

00314

Library Association of Ireland
LAI

53 Upper Mount St., Dublin 2, Ireland
Tel: 01 4597834
Fax: 01 6762346
Email: president@libraryassociation.ie
Website: http://www2.libraryassociation.ie
Members: 600
Contact: Siobhan Fitzpatrick, Pres.
Fee: £25-110
Membership Type: personal
Fee: £15
Membership Type: unemployed, retired, student
Description: Libraries and individuals employed in libraries and information service industries in the Republic of Ireland. Promotes librarianship and high standards of practice. Represents members' interests. Monitors relevant legislation and conducts research.
Formerly: Absorbed, Online Users' Group/Ireland
Publication: Journal
Publication title: An Leabharlann. Advertisements.
Meetings/Conventions: Celtic Connection – annual conference

00315

Licensed Vintners' Association
LVA

Anglesea House, Anglesea Rd., Ballsbridge, Dublin 4, Ireland
Tel: 01 6680215
Fax: 01 6680448
Website: http://www.lva.ie
Members: 700
Contact: Charlie Chawke, Chm.
Description: Protects and develops the strategic business interests of the members.

00316

Limerick Chamber of Commerce

96 O'Connell St., Limerick, Ireland
Tel: 061 415180
Fax: 061 415785
Email: info@limerickchamber.ie
Website: http://www.limerickchamber.ie
Contact: Reginald Freake, Dir.
Fee: £200-1200
Membership Type: general (based on number of employees)
Description: Promotes commerce and trade in County Limerick, Ireland.

00317

Macra Na Feirme

Irish Farm Ctre., Bluebell, Dublin 12, Ireland
Tel: 01 4268900
Email: macra@macra.ie
Website: http://www.macra.ie
Members: 11000
Staff: 25
Contact: Terry Cooke, Office Mgr.
Description: Youths interested in agriculture and rural development. Promotes the education of members in agriculture and related fields. Offers courses in agriculture, leadership training, public speaking, drama, machinery maintenance, and animal husbandry. Sends delegations and representatives to seminars, courses, and conferences in several countries. Maintains charitable programs; operates placement service.
Publication: Directory
Publication title: Discount Directory

00318

Magazines Ireland

25 Denzille Ln., Dublin 2, Ireland
Tel: 01 6675579
Email: grace@magazinesireland.ie
Website: http://www.ppa.ie
Contact: Grace Aungier, Chief Exec.
Fee: £1150-2850
Membership Type: full (based on annual turnover)
Fee: £2500
Membership Type: associate
Description: Publishers of consumer, business, and professional magazines in Ireland. Promotes members' interests.

Formerly: Formerly, Periodical Publishers Association of Ireland
Publication: Newsletter
Publication title: The Newspread

00319
Management Science Society of Ireland
MSSI

University College Dublin, UCD School of Business, Colorado of Business and Law, Dublin 4, Ireland
Tel: 01 7164706
Fax: 01 7164783
Email: cathal.brugha@ucd.ie
Website: http://mis.ucd.ie/mssi
Members: 112
Contact: Cathal Brugha, Contact
Description: Promotes operational research, management science, decision science and systems science as an academic discipline and a profession. Encourages teachings and acts as a forum for the exchange of information related to these. Is a node for connecting people involved academically and in practice in Ireland with the international community, particularly the European Association of Operational Research Societies and the International Federation for Systems Research.

00320
Mandate Trade Union

O'Lehane House, 9 Cavendish Row, Dublin 1, Ireland
Tel: 01 8746321
Fax: 01 8729581
Email: mandate@mandate.ie
Website: http://www.mandate.ie
Members: 38000
Staff: 40
Contact: John Douglas, Gen. Sec.
Description: Represents the interests of individuals working in retail, bar and administrative positions in the Republic of Ireland. Conducts educational programs.
Formerly: Formerly, Irish Distributive and Administrative Trade Union
Publication: Magazine
Publication title: Mandate News
Meetings/Conventions: Delegate Conference – biennial conference

00321
Marketing Society of Ireland
MS

PO Box 58, Bray, Wicklow, Ireland
Tel: 01 2761995
Fax: 01 2761995
Email: info@marketingsociety.ie
Website: http://www.marketingsociety.ie
Members: 400
Contact: Valda Boardman, Chair
Fee: £150
Membership Type: individual
Fee: £375
Membership Type: corporate
Description: Senior managers and other interested professionals. Advances marketing as the key to successful business growth. Organizes debates and seminars; maintains speakers' bureau. Fosters exchange among members.
Publication: Newsletter

00322
Mediators Institute Ireland
MII

Montana House, Whitechurch, Dublin 16, Ireland
Tel: 01 6099190
Fax: 01 4930595
Email: info@themii.ie
Website: http://www.themii.ie
Members: 120
Staff: 1
Contact: Karen Erwin, Pres.
Fee: £180
Membership Type: practitioner
Fee: £100
Membership Type: general, associate practitioner
Description: Professional association for business, community and family mediators. Maintains register of accredited practitioner mediators and sets accreditation for professional mediators.
Publication: Newsletter
Publication title: Agreement

00323
Mental Health Ireland
MHI

6 Adelaide St., Dun Laoghaire, Dublin, Ireland
Tel: 01 2841166
Fax: 01 2841736
Email: info@mentalhealthireland.ie
Website: http://www.mentalhealthireland.ie
Contact: Brian Howard, CEO
Description: Seeks to help those who are mentally ill and to promote positive mental health in Ireland. Works to provide various types of accommodation outside the hospital, to set-up workshops, to visit and befriend those affected, and to arrange social events.
Publication: Newsletter
Publication title: Mensana News

00324
Microscopical Society of Ireland
MSI

c/o Dr. Fiona Lyng, Treas.
MSI, Focas Institute, Dublin Institute of Technology, Kevin St., Dublin 8, Ireland
Website: http://www.ifsm.uconn.edu
Contact: Thomas Flannagan, Sec.
Fee: £16
Membership Type: full
Fee: £12
Membership Type: student
Description: Works to promote advances in microscopy, including the science and practice of all microscopical imaging, analysis and diffraction techniques. Facilitates communication and cooperation among microscopists.

00325
Migraine Association of Ireland
MAI

Unit 14, Block 5, Port Tunnel Business Park, Clonshaugh, Dublin 17, Ireland
Tel: 01 8941280
Fax: 01 8064122
Email: info@migraine.ie
Website: http://www.migraine.ie
Members: 1700
Staff: 5
Contact: Patrick Little, CEO
Fee: £30
Membership Type: regular (in UK and Ireland)
Fee: £10
Membership Type: student
Description: Seeks to share information and provide support for those affected by chronic migraine headaches in Ireland. Encourages medical research; lobbies for a national headache/migraine specialist clinic in Ireland; maintains relationships with other related societies and associations.
Library Subject: migraine
Library Type: not open to the public
Publication: Newsletter
Meetings/Conventions: semiannual meeting

00326
Military History Society of Ireland
MHSI

Newman House, 86 St. Stephens Green, Dublin 2, Ireland
Email: alanaoif@indigo.ie
Website: http://www.mhsi.ie
Members: 900
Contact: Harman Murtagh, Pres.
Fee: £32
Membership Type: individual
Fee: £16
Membership Type: student
Description: Individuals with an interest in Irish military history. Promotes study and interest in the topics of Irish military history and the history of the Irish at war. Facilitates exchange of information among members. Serves as a clearinghouse on Irish military history. Sponsors research and educational programs. Conducts field trips to battle sites.
Publication: Journal
Publication title: Irish Sword

00327
Miscarriage Association of Ireland
MAI

Carmichael Ctre., N Brunswick St., Dublin 7, Ireland
Tel: 01 8735702
Fax: 01 8735737
Email: info@miscarriage.ie
Website: http://www.miscarriage.ie
Fee: £15
Membership Type: general
Description: Seeks to provide support to women (and men) who are dealing with miscarriage.

00328
Monaghan Photographic Society
MPS

Belbroid Centre, North Rd., Monaghan, Ireland
Email: info@monaghanphotographicsociety.com
Website: http://www.monaghanphotographicsociety.com/index2.html
Description: Promotes photography in Ireland.
Library Subject: photography
Library Type: reference
Meetings/Conventions: weekly workshop

00329

Multiple Sclerosis Society of Ireland MSI

MS Resource Centre, 80 Northumberland Rd., Dublin 4, Ireland
Tel: 01 6781600
Fax: 01 6781601
Email: info@ms-society.ie
Website: http://www.ms-society.ie
Members: 5000
Staff: 65
Contact: Allen O'Connor, Chm.
Description: Seeks to improve the quality of life of people with multiple sclerosis and their families. Works to facilitate people with Multiple Sclerosis to control their lives and environment, to live with dignity and participate in the community. Provides a range of services to meet the needs of the MS Community.
Library Subject: multiple sclerosis
Library Type: reference
Publication: Magazine
Publication title: MS News. Advertisements.

00330

Muscular Dystrophy Ireland MDI

71/72 N Brunswick St., Dublin 7, Ireland
Tel: 01 8721501
Fax: 01 8724482
Email: info@mdi.ie
Website: http://www.mdi.ie
Members: 560
Staff: 21
Contact: Joe Mooney, CEO
Description: Provides support and information to individuals with muscular dystrophy and their families. Support services include family support, information, respite, youth activities and transportation. Funds research into the condition.
Publication: Newsletter
Publication title: MDI News Update. Advertisements.

00331

Music Network

The Coach House, Dublin Castle, Dublin 2, Ireland
Tel: 01 6719429
Fax: 01 6719430
Email: admin@musicnetwork.ie
Website: http://www.musicnetwork.ie/myc/cms/pages
Members: 8
Staff: 7
Contact: Deirdre McCrea, CEO
Description: Aims to make music accessible to all people, regardless of geographic location. Organizes tours for classical, traditional and jazz musicians. Develops and publicizes musical education. Operates information service publishing online directories of music sector and music education in Ireland.
Publication: Book
Publication title: Irish Music Handbook 2nd Edition

00332

Narcotics Anonymous Ireland NA

29 Bride St., Dublin 8, Ireland
Tel: 01 6728000
Email: info@na-ireland.org
Website: http://www.na-ireland.org
Description: Provides a recovery process and support network for drug addicts. Facilitates and stabilizes the recovery of the members. Uses 12-step program adapted from Alcoholics Anonymous to aid in the recovery process.

00333

National Association for Youth Drama NAYD

7 N Great George's St., Dublin 1, Ireland
Tel: 01 8781301
Fax: 01 8749816
Email: info@nayd.ie
Website: http://nayd.ie
Contact: Orlaith McBride, Dir.
Fee: £30
Membership Type: individual
Fee: £10
Membership Type: student
Description: Fosters the establishment and sustained development of youth theatres. Promotes youth drama projects and festivals. Offers training in youth drama practices for leaders, directors and teachers. Develops guidelines for protecting members from abuse and exploitation.
Publication: Newsletter
Publication title: Intermission

00334

National Association of Adult Education

2nd Fl., 83-87 Main St., Ranelagh, Dublin 6, Ireland
Tel: 01 4068220
Fax: 01 4068227
Email: mail@aontas.com
Website: http://www.aontas.com
Members: 500
Staff: 11
Contact: Berni Brady, Dir.
Description: Organizations and individuals interested in adult education. Seeks to develop a system of lifelong learning which is accessible to all adults, particularly those who are considered socially or educationally disadvantaged. Conducts research on education for women, older learners, and adult education and the unemployed. Formulates adult education policies; promotes positive public attitudes toward adult education. Provides referral service.
Publication: Journal
Publication title: Adult Learner

00335

National Association of Building Cooperatives Society NABCo

33 Lower Baggot St., Dublin 2, Ireland
Tel: 01 6612877
Fax: 01 6614462
Email: admin@nabco.ie
Website: http://www.nabco.ie
Members: 25
Staff: 7
Description: Promotes the cooperative housing movement in Ireland.
Library Subject: housing, cooperative housing
Library Type: not open to the public
Publication: Newsletter
Publication title: Co-operative Housing News

00336

National Association of Tenants' Organisations NATO

35 Meath Pl., Dublin 8, Ireland
Tel: 01 4543842
Fax: 01 4543842
Email: mail@tuq.org.au
Members: 100180
Contact: Christy Hynes, Pres.

00337

National Association of the Ovulation Method of Ireland NAOMI

11 Marlborough Ct., Marlborough St., Dublin 1, Ireland
Tel: 01 8786156
Fax: 01 8788158
Email: inforequest@naomi.ie
Website: http://www.naomi.ie
Members: 50
Staff: 2
Description: Promotes natural family planning (ovulation method/Billings) among engaged and married couples. Conducts pre-marriage courses. Offers educational programs on menopause, infertility, subfertility, and natural family planning.

00338

National Children's Nurseries Association NCNA

Unit 12c, Bluebell Business Park, Old Naas Rd., Bluebell, Dublin 12, Ireland
Tel: 01 4601138
Fax: 01 4601185
Email: info@ncna.ie
Website: http://www.ncna.ie
Members: 400
Contact: Sally O'Donnell, Chm.
Description: Raises public awareness of issues affecting the childcare sector. Works to increase the quality of day-care in Ireland. Highlights the value of nurseries in providing support for families. Educates nursery owners, staff, parents and legislators. Keeps abreast of new developments, new methods, and new approaches in the field of childcare.
Publication: Book
Publication title: After School - The Way Forward

00339

National Council for the Blind of Ireland NCBI

Whitworth Rd., Drumcondra 9, Dublin, Ireland
Tel: 01 8307033
Fax: 01 8307787
Email: info@ncbi.ie
Website: http://www.ncbi.ie
Members: 15000
Staff: 150
Contact: Des Kenny, CEO
Description: Works to promote the full independence of people with impaired vision and to minimize the disabling effects of vision impairment.
Publication: Magazine
Publication title: NCBI News

00340

National Council for the Professional Development of Nursing and Midwifery
NCNM

Unit 6-7 Manor Business Park, Manor St., Dublin 7, Ireland
Tel: 01 8825300
Fax: 01 8680366
Email: admin@ncnm.ie
Website: http://www.ncnm.ie
Contact: Yvonne O'Shea, CEO
Description: Promotes and develops the professional role of nurses and midwives. Works to ensure the delivery of quality nursing and midwifery care to patients and clients. Seeks to expand communication and support among nurses and midwives.

00341

National Dairy Council
NDC

3 Arkle Rd.., Dublin 18, Ireland
Tel: 01 2902451
Fax: 01 2902452
Email: info@ndc.ie
Website: http://www.ndc.ie
Members: 18
Contact: Dominic Cronin, Chm.
Description: Acts as the essential interface between producers and consumers in the generic promotion of dairy products in Ireland. Ensures that consumers continue to receive the latest scientific information about dairy products and the role in a healthy, balanced diet.

00342

National Federation of Arch Clubs
NFAC

74 Meadow Grove, Dublin 16, Ireland
Tel: 01 2951081
Fax: 01 2963049
Email: archclubs@eircom.net
Website: http://www.archclubs.com/Default.aspx?AspxAutoDetectCookieSupport=1
Members: 2000
Description: Individuals and organizations. Seeks to improve the quality of life of people with learning disabilities and their families. Makes available recreational facilities for people with learning disabilities.
Publication: Newsletter
Publication title: Archbeat

00343

National Federation of Services for Unmarried Parents and Their Children

14 Gandon House, Custom House Sq., Dublin 1, Ireland
Tel: 01 6700120
Fax: 01 6700199
Email: info@treoir.ie
Website: http://www.treoir.ie
Members: 50
Staff: 6
Contact: Margaret Dromey, CEO
Description: Aims to improve the standards of care for unmarried parents and their children in Ireland.

00344

National Guild of Master Craftsmen
NGMC

3 Greenmount Ln., Harold's Cross, Dublin 12, Ireland
Tel: 01 4732543
Fax: 01 4732018
Email: info@nationalguild.ie
Website: http://www.nationalguild.ie
Members: 6500
Staff: 6
Contact: Pat Doyle, Managing Dir.
Description: Represents skilled tradesmen. Aims to protect the skills and integrity of its members and clearly define the skilled from the non-skilled thus enabling the general public to choose a National Guild of Master Craftsmen member to facilitate the service they require.

00345

National Irish Safety Organisation
NISO

A11 Calmount Park, Calmount Ave., Ballymount, Dublin 12, Ireland
Tel: 01 4659760
Fax: 01 4659765
Email: info@niso.ie
Website: http://www.niso.ie
Members: 1800
Staff: 5
Contact: Pauric Corrigan, Pres.
Fee: £450
Membership Type: corporate (with 50 or more employees)
Fee: £190-280
Membership Type: corporate (with less than 50 employees)
Description: Promotes occupational health and safety.
Publication: Magazine
Publication title: Health and Safety Times

00346

National Newspapers of Ireland
NNI

Clyde Lodge, 15 Clyde Rd., Ballsbridge, Dublin 4, Ireland
Tel: 01 6689099
Fax: 01 6689872
Email: fcullen@cullencommunications.ie
Website: http://www.nni.ie
Members: 18
Contact: Frank Cullen, Coordinating Dir.
Description: Promotes the benefits of newspaper advertising.

00347

National Parents and Siblings Alliance
NPSA

31, Magenta Hall, Santry, Dublin 9, Ireland
Tel: 01 8624100
Email: npsa@eircom.net
Website: http://www.npsa.ie
Contact: Seamus Greene, Dir.
Description: Seeks to inform and unite parents and siblings of people with intellectual disabilities and autism living in Ireland. Aims to campaign and lobby for the rights of people with intellectual disabilities and autism. Works with other groups representing people with learning and other disabilities toward the development of a united voice for people with disabilities.
Publication: Newsletter
Publication title: NPSA Newsletter

00348

National Standards Authority of Ireland
NSAI

1 Swift Sq., Northwood, Santry, Dublin 9, Ireland
Tel: 01 8073800
Fax: 01 8073838
Email: info@nsai.ie
Website: http://www.nsai.ie
Contact: Maurice Buckley, CEO
Description: Provides a national standards authority in Ireland; supports enterprise, trade and consumers in the areas of standards, legal metrology, and agreements.

00349

National Trust for Ireland

The Tailors Hall, Back Ln., Dublin 8, Ireland
Tel: 01 4541786
Fax: 01 4533255
Email: admin@antaisce.org
Website: http://www.antaisce.org
Members: 5000
Staff: 12
Contact: Carol O'Connor, Admin.
Fee: £45
Membership Type: individual
Fee: £55
Membership Type: family
Description: Individuals and others interested in conserving and protecting Ireland's natural environment and built heritage. Lobbies politicians and government departments to improve legislation, funding, and other policies to protect the environment. Conducts educational programs.

00350

National Women's Council of Ireland
NWCI

9 Marlborough Ct., Marlborough St., Dublin 1, Ireland
Tel: 01 8787248
Fax: 01 8787301
Email: info@nwci.ie
Website: http://www.nwci.ie
Members: 167
Staff: 13
Contact: Clare Treacy, Chair
Fee: £30-1000
Membership Type: affiliate
Fee: £30
Membership Type: supporting
Description: Represents women and women's groups in Ireland; works to create a society where women can participate equally in all aspects of social and economic life; addresses important and controversial issues affecting women.

00351

National Youth Council of Ireland
NYCI

3 Montague St., Dublin 2, Ireland
Tel: 01 4784122
Fax: 01 4783974
Email: info@nyci.ie
Website: http://www.youth.ie
Staff: 15
Contact: Mary Cunningham, Dir.
Description: Youth organizations. Promotes healthy physical, social, and spiritual growth among youth. Represents members before government agencies and the public; coordinates members' activities; lobbies for more effective public policies affecting youth. Conducts research and educational programs; makes available children's services; maintains speakers' bureau; compiles statistics.
Publication: Newsletter
Publication title: Clar Na Og

00352

Neurofibromatosis Association of Ireland
NAI

Carmichael Centre, N Brunswick St., Dublin 7, Ireland
Tel: 01 8726338
Fax: 01 8735737
Email: nfaireland@eircom.net
Website: http://www.nfaireland.ie
Members: 480
Staff: 1
Contact: Fergal Griffin, Admin.
Fee: £15
Membership Type: individual, family
Fee: £30
Membership Type: overseas
Description: Individuals and organizations. Seeks to improve the quality of life of people with neurofibromatosis and their families; promotes increased awareness of neurofibromatosis among health care providers and the public. Makes available support and services; conducts educational and advocacy campaigns; sponsors research.
Publication: Newsletter
Publication title: Neuro News. Advertisements.

00353

New Zealand Ireland Association
NZIA

9 Belair Village, Ashford, Wicklow, Ireland
Email: info@newzealand.ie
Website: http://www.newzealand.ie
Contact: Maija Tweeddale, Contact
Fee: £25
Membership Type: individual
Fee: £35
Membership Type: family
Description: Purpose Promotes the culture of New Zealand for New Zealanders living in Ireland and for Irish people interested in New Zealand.

00354

One Family

c/o Cherish House
2 Lower Pembroke St., Dublin 2, Ireland
Tel: 01 6629212
Fax: 01 6629096
Email: info@onefamily.ie
Website: http://onefamily.ie
Members: 400
Staff: 10
Contact: Karen Kiernan, Dir.
Description: Single parents. Provides a support, advice, information, and counseling to single parent families. Campaigns for legal reform in the areas of single parents and children's rights. Offers the following services: information service, practical support, parenting support, outreach, unmarried fathers support, single parent counseling, support groups, computer training, personal development, professional training, campaigning and lobbying, and pregnancy counseling.
Formerly: Formerly, Cherish
Publication: Newsletter
Publication title: Cherish News. Advertisements.

00355

Operation Smile - Ireland

31 Pembroke Rd., Dublin 4, Ireland
Tel: 01 6676659
Fax: 01 6670119
Email: teri@operationsmile.ie
Website: http://ireland.operationsmile.org
Contact: Teresa Cosgrove, CEO
Description: Works to increase the availability of cosmetic and reconstructive surgery among impoverished children. Performs free reconstructive surgery on needy children. Conducts training programs for surgeons. Distributes medical equipment and supplies to indigenous health care centers.

00356

Orthodontic Society of Ireland
OSI

c/o Aideen McCallum
Aiken's Village, 58 Grianan Fidh, Sandyford, Dublin 18, Ireland
Tel: 01 2963638
Email: info@orthodontics.ie
Website: http://www.orthodontics.ie
Contact: Paul Dowling, Pres.
Description: Works to advance all aspects of orthodontics and its relations with the collateral arts and sciences for the public benefit. Seeks for the furtherance of orthodontics among all branches of the dental profession working in private practice, hospitals, and universities.

00357

Oxfam - Ireland

9 Burgh Quay, Dublin 2, Ireland
Tel: 01 6727662
Fax: 01 6727680
Email: info@oxfamireland.org
Website: http://www.oxfamireland.org
Staff: 85
Contact: Jim Clarken, CEO
Description: Autonomous national branch of international organization. Sponsors development and relief projects. Strives to reduce hunger and poverty. Promotes community development projects that foster self-sufficiency.

00358

Parkinson's Association of Ireland
PAI

Carmichael House, North Brunswick St., Dublin 7, Ireland
Email: info@parkinsons.ie
Website: http://www.parkinsons.ie
Contact: Joe Lynch, CEO
Fee: £25
Membership Type: regular
Description: Seeks to provide comfort and assistance to those living with Parkinson's Disease in Ireland.

00359

Pax Christi - Ireland

Pax Christi Ctre., 52 Lower Rathmines Rd., Dublin 6, Ireland
Tel: 01 4965293
Website: http://www.paxchristi.net/international/eng/show_mo.php?id=48
Contact: Tony D'Costa, Contact
Description: Works for peace while bearing witness to the peace of Christ. Contributes to the construction of a more genuinely humane world, with respect for the life of each human being. Collaborates with other Christian groups and peace movements. Struggles against sources of injustice such as violence, war, hatred, and economic inequality. Condemns the arms race. Urges arms control and disarmament. Stresses the importance of detente between the East and West, human rights, the Catholic Church's duty to emphasize peace, and the problems of the Third World.

00360

Peace and Neutrality Alliance
PANA

17 Castle St., Dalkey, Dublin, Ireland
Tel: 01 2351512
Email: info@pana.ie
Website: http://www.pana.ie
Members: 26
Contact: Roger Cole, Chm.
Fee: £40
Membership Type: waged individual
Fee: £15
Membership Type: unwaged individual
Description: Advocates for an independent Irish policy. Opposes policies that associate Ireland with any military alliance such as the WEU or NATO. Promotes European and international security through a policy of disarmament and demilitarization. Opposes the militarization of the European Union.

00361

People with Disabilities - Ireland
PwDI

Jervis House, Jervis St., 4th Fl., Dublin 1, Ireland
Tel: 01 8721744
Fax: 01 8721771
Email: info@pwdi.ie
Website: http://www.pwdi.ie
Contact: James McClean, Chm.
Description: Seeks to improve the status of people with disabilities in Ireland. Provides support to people with disabilities, their families and caregivers. Works to lobby for changes that will promote equality for people with disabilities.
Publication: Newsletter
Publication title: Cumhacht

00362

Pharmaceutical Society of Ireland
PSI

18 Shrewsbury Rd., Ballsbridge, Dublin 4, Ireland
Tel: 01 2184000
Fax: 01 2837678
Email: info@pharmaceuticalsociety.ie
Website: http://www.pharmaceuticalsociety.ie
Members: 3500
Contact: Ambrose McLoughlin, Registrar/CEO
Description: Individuals working in community retail pharmacies, hospital pharmacies, and pharmaceutical industries. Promotes the development of higher standards of practice in the pharmaceutical industries; seeks to safeguard public health. Enforces laws governing the retail sale of medicines; conducts site inspections of premises where medicines are sold or supplied to insure compliance with legal and professional standards. Promulgates and enforces standards of ethics and practice for the pharmaceutical industries. Conducts continuing professional education programs for pharmacists.

00363

Pharmachemical Ireland

Confederation House, 84-86 Lower Baggot St., Dublin 2, Ireland
Tel: 01 6051584
Fax: 01 6381584
Email: matt.moran@ibec.ie
Website: http://www.pharmachemicalireland.ie
Contact: Matt Moran, Dir.
Description: Represents the needs of the pharmaceutical and chemical manufacturing industries in Ireland. Works to take the lead in environmental performance, to expand and develop the sectors' business activities to maintain international competitiveness, and to improve the industry's communications with all sectors of society, especially local communities.
Formerly: Formerly, Irish Pharmaceutical and Chemical Manufacturers' Federation
Publication: Newsletter
Publication title: Horizons

00364

Physical Education Association of Ireland
PEAI

University of Limerick, The National Technology Park, Limerick, Ireland
Tel: 087 6480475
Fax: 087 1346115
Email: peai@peai.org
Website: http://www.peai.org
Members: 350
Contact: Ann MacPhail, Pres.
Fee: £50
Membership Type: ordinary
Fee: £40
Membership Type: associate
Description: Physical education teachers in the Republic of Ireland. Promotes physical education and works in conjunction with education officials to construct effective curriculums and practical teaching techniques; grants honorary lifetime memberships to individuals in the field. Maintains hall of fame.
Publication: Newsletter
Publication title: PEAI Newsletter. Advertisements.
Meetings/Conventions: National Physical Education Conference – annual conference – Exhibits.

00365

Pioneer Total Abstinence Association
PTAA

27 Upper Sherrard St., Dublin 1, Ireland
Tel: 01 8749464
Fax: 01 8748485
Email: enquiries@pioneertotal.ie
Website: http://www.pioneerassociation.ie
Members: 500000
Staff: 7
Contact: Padraig Brady, CEO
Description: Promotes sobriety, principally by prayer and consecrated abstinence from alcohol. Encourages members to engage in good works.
Publication: Magazine
Publication title: Pioneer. Advertisements.

00366

Poetry Ireland

No. 2, Prouds Ln., St. Stephen's Green, Dublin 2, Ireland
Tel: 01 4789974
Fax: 01 4780205
Email: info@poetryireland.ie
Website: http://www.poetryireland.ie
Staff: 5
Contact: Jane O'Hanlon, Contact
Description: Develops, supports and promotes poetry throughout Ireland. Acts as a resource and information point for those interested in poetry. Promotes opportunity for poets working or living in Ireland.

00367

Polio Fellowship of Ireland
PFI

Park House, Stillorgan Grove, Dublin, Ireland
Tel: 01 2888366
Fax: 01 2836128
Email: parkhouse@rehab.ie
Website: http://www.irishhealth.com/psg/polio.html
Staff: 16
Contact: Thomas J. Stephens, Chm.
Description: Seeks to improve the quality of life of people who have physical disabilities, including polio, and mental health learning difficulties. Provides day activities, training, and residential accommodation.

00368

Political Studies Association of Ireland
PSAI

University College Cork, Dept. of Government, O'Rahilly Bldg., Dublin, Ireland
Tel: 021 4903028
Fax: 021 4903135
Email: t.reidy@ucc.ie
Website: http://www.psai.ie
Members: 270
Contact: Theresa Reidy, Sec.
Fee: £50
Membership Type: full
Fee: £30
Membership Type: student
Description: Membership Professional staff of third-level institutions, research organizations, and similar bodies who are engaged in research in the area of politics, and to post-graduate students. Purpose Promotes the study and research of political studies in Ireland.

00369

Psychiatric Nurses Association of Ireland
PNA

Station House, The Waterways, Sallins 1, Kildare, Ireland
Tel: 045 852300
Fax: 045 855750
Email: info@pna.ie
Website: http://www.pna.ie
Members: 5500
Staff: 6
Contact: Des Kavanagh, Gen. Sec.
Description: Psychiatric nurses in Ireland. Seeks to advance the study and practice of psychiatric nursing. Encourages professional advancement for psychiatric nurses. Liaises with the Department of Health, Department of Environment, Health Boards and Hospitals.
Library Subject: industrial relations
Library Type: not open to the public
Publication: Journal
Publication title: Psychiatric Nursing. Advertisements.
Meetings/Conventions: annual conference

00370

Psychological Society of Ireland
PSI

CX House, 2A Corn Exchange Pl., Poolbeg St., Dublin 2, Ireland
Tel: 01 4749160
Fax: 01 4749161
Email: info@psihq.ie
Website: http://www.psihq.org
Members: 2000
Staff: 3
Contact: Ronan Yore, Pres.
Fee: £40
Membership Type: student
Fee: £65
Membership Type: full time post graduate student, graduate in the first 3 years of post-graduation, retired graduate
Description: Strives to advance psychology as a pure and applied science. Maintains a code of ethics and standards of conduct. Provides professional diploma schemes.
Library Type: reference

00371

Publishing Ireland

Guinness Enterprise Center, Taylor's Ln., Dublin 8, Ireland
Tel: 01 4151210
Email: info@publishingireland.com
Website: http://www.publishingireland.com
Members: 90
Staff: 2
Contact: Jean Harrington, Pres.
Fee: £100-1800
Membership Type: business (based on the number of employees)
Description: Book publishers. Promotes the sale, distribution, and export of books published in the Republic of Ireland. Facilitates communication and cooperation among members; advises members on copyright laws and related issues.

00372

Register of Electrical Contractors of Ireland
RECI

Unit 9, KCR Industrial Estate, Ravensdale Park, Dublin 12, Ireland
Tel: 01 4929966
Fax: 01 4929983
Email: info@reci.ie
Website: http://www.reci.ie
Contact: Denise McAuley, Contact
Description: Protects the interests of the users of electrical service. Monitors the work and competence of its registered contractors to achieve the standards set in the electrical industry.
Publication: Newsletter
Publication title: RECI News

00373

Restaurants Association of Ireland
RAI

11 Bridge Ct., City Gate, St. Augustine St., Dublin 8, Ireland
Tel: 01 6779901
Fax: 01 6718414
Email: info@rai.ie
Website: http://www.rai.ie
Members: 500
Staff: 5
Contact: Paul Cadden, Pres.
Description: Restaurant owners. Develops policies and goals to ensure future legislation that would assist members in the development of the restaurant sector.
Publication: Newsletter
Publication title: Food For Thought

00374

Retail Grocery, Dairy and Allied Trades Association
RGDATA

Rock House, Blackrock, Dublin, Ireland
Tel: 01 2887584
Fax: 01 2832206
Email: rgdata@rgdata.ie
Website: http://www.rgdata.ie
Members: 4500
Contact: Tara Buckley, Dir. Gen.
Description: Supports interests of retail, independent grocers in Ireland, including trade to government, media, consumers, and suppliers.

00375

Royal Academy of Medicine in Ireland
RAMI

Frederick House, 4th Fl., 19 S Frederick St., Dublin 2, Ireland
Tel: 01 6334820
Fax: 01 6334918
Email: secretary@rami.ie
Website: http://www.rami.ie
Members: 2000
Staff: 3
Contact: John J. O'Connor, Gen. Sec./Treas./Asst. Ed.
Description: Physicians, medical researchers, and other scientists with an interest in medicine. Seeks to advance medical study, teaching, and practice. Serves as a forum for the exchange of information among members; sponsors research and educational programs.
Publication: Journal
Publication title: Irish Journal of Medical Science. Advertisements.

00376

Royal College of Physicians of Ireland
RCPI

Frederick House, 19 S Frederick St., Dublin 2, Ireland
Tel: 01 8639700
Fax: 01 6724707
Email: college@rcpi.ie
Website: http://www.rcpi.ie/pages/home.aspx
Members: 4500
Staff: 50
Contact: John Donohoe, Pres.
Description: Makes available postgraduate medical education and training.
Library Subject: medical history
Library Type: by appointment only

00377

Royal College of Surgeons in Ireland
RCSI

123 St. Stephens Green, Dublin 2, Ireland
Tel: 01 4022100
Email: info@rcsi.ie
Website: http://www.rcsi.ie
Contact: Cathal Kelly, CEO/Registrar
Description: Seeks to maintain the highest standards in education and training.
Library Subject: medicine
Library Type: lending

00378

Royal Dublin Society
RDS

Anglesea Rd., Ballsbridge, Dublin 4, Ireland
Tel: 01 6680866
Fax: 01 6604014
Email: info@rds.ie
Website: http://www.rds.ie
Members: 5500
Staff: 60
Contact: Michael Duffy, Chief Exec.
Description: Seeks to advance Ireland in the areas of agriculture, arts, science and industry through a programme of foundation events, including National Crafts Competition, the Gold Medal for Industry, Boyle Medal, Science Live Lectures, Forestry Award and the Dublin Horse Show. Promotes an interest in Irish culture, history and development.
Publication: Magazine
Publication title: Minerva

00379

Royal Institute of the Architects of Ireland
RIAI

8 Merrion Sq., Dublin 2, Ireland
Tel: 01 6761703
Fax: 01 6628593
Email: info@riai.ie
Website: http://www.riai.ie
Members: 2100
Contact: Paul Keogh, Pres.
Description: Represents professionally qualified architects in Ireland. Works for the advancement of Architecture and the associated Arts and Sciences, the promotion of high standards of professional conduct and practice and the protection of the interests of architectural training and education.

00380

Royal Irish Academy
RIA

19 Dawson St., Dublin 2, Ireland
Tel: 01 6762570
Fax: 01 6762346
Email: p.buckley@ria.ie
Website: http://www.ria.ie
Contact: Patrick Buckley, Exec. Sec.
Description: Promotes the advancement of science, humanities and learning. Facilitates cultural exchanges and conducts joint programs with academies in other countries. Acts as the national affiliating body to international scientific unions and organizations. Advises government agencies on allocation of funds for archaeological research and other projects. Maintains over 30 national committees in the areas of science and humanities.
Publication: Journal
Publication title: Eriu

00381

Royal Irish Academy of Music
RIAM

36-38 Westland Row, Dublin 2, Ireland
Tel: 01 6764412
Fax: 01 6622798
Email: info@riam.ie
Website: http://www.riam.ie
Contact: John O'Conor, Dir.
Description: Transmits and maintains highest standards of performance and appreciation in all musical disciplines. Embodies and reflects the tradition and heritage of Irish music.

00382

Royal Irish Automobile Club
RIAC

34 Dawson St., Dublin 2, Ireland
Tel: 01 6775628
Fax: 01 6710793
Email: info@motorsportireland.com
Website: http://www.motorsportireland.com
Contact: J. Naylor, Dir.
Description: Promotes motorsport in Ireland.

00383

Royal National Lifeboat Institution - Ireland
RNLI Ireland

Dun Laoghaire Lifeboat Station, Queens Rd., Dun Laoghaire, Dublin, Ireland
Tel: 01 2802667
Email: dun-laoghaire@rnli.org.uk
Website: http://www.rnli.org.uk
Members: 4800
Staff: 45

Contact: Stephen Wynne, Contact
Description: Works to save lives at sea by ensuring the volunteer staffing and operation of 41 lifeboat stations around the coast and inland of Ireland.
Publication: Yearbook
Publication title: Lifeboats Ireland. Advertisements.

00384

Royal Society of Antiquaries of Ireland

63 Merrion Sq., Dublin 2, Ireland
Tel: 01 6761749
Email: rsai@rsai.ie
Website: http://www.rsai.ie
Members: 1100
Staff: 2
Contact: Charles Doherty, Pres.
Fee: £60
Membership Type: individual
Fee: £30
Membership Type: family, retired
Description: Aims to preserve, examine, and illustrate all ancient monuments and memorials of the arts, manners, and customs of the past.
Library Subject: Irish and UK archaeology and history, Society archive material, Du noyer collection of drawings and sketches of archaeology and antiquities
Library Type: reference

00385

Schizophrenia Ireland
SI

38 Blessington St., Dublin 7, Ireland
Tel: 01 8601620
Fax: 01 8601602
Email: info@sirl.ie
Website: http://www.shineonline.ie
Contact: John Saunders, Dir.
Fee: £10
Membership Type: individual
Fee: £20
Membership Type: family
Description: Individuals and organizations. Seeks to improve the quality of life of people with schizophrenia and their families. Provides support and services; conducts educational and advocacy campaigns.

00386

Scouting Ireland CSI

Larch Hill, Dublin 16, Ireland
Tel: 01 4956300
Fax: 01 4956301
Email: questions@scouts.ie
Website: http://www.scouts.ie
Members: 30072
Staff: 16
Contact: Michael Devins, Natl. Sec.
Description: Aims to help young people develop physically, intellectually, socially, spiritually and culturally so that they may take a constructive place in society as mature adults. Trains members to be responsible and active members of their local, national and international communities. Emphasizes international understanding, cooperation, and brotherhood.

00387

Screen Producers Ireland
SPI

77 Merrion Sq., Dublin 2, Ireland
Tel: 01 6621114
Fax: 01 6619949
Email: info@screenproducersireland.com
Website: http://www.screenproducersireland.com
Members: 150
Contact: Gaby Smyth, Chm.
Fee: £300
Membership Type: company
Description: Acts as the representative body for independent film, television, animation and digital content producers in Ireland.

00388

Services, Industrial Professional and Technical Union
SIPTU

Liberty Hall, Dublin 1, Ireland
Tel: 01 8586300
Fax: 01 8749466
Email: info@siptu.ie
Website: http://www.siptu.ie
Members: 200000
Staff: 280
Contact: Jack O'Connor, Gen. Pres.
Description: Workers in Northern Ireland and the Republic of Ireland. Monitors developments in wages, industry, commerce, and society. Reports on economic and social events. Sponsors the Irish Trade Union Trust, which assists unemployed people and funds job creation initiatives. Sponsors training courses in industrial relations for union officials and activists.
Formerly: Formerly, Federated Workers Union
Publication title: Equality Review

00389

Sligo Chamber of Commerce and Industry

16 Quay St., Sligo, Ireland
Tel: 071 9161274
Fax: 071 9160912
Email: info@sligochamber.ie
Website: http://www.sligochamber.com
Contact: Rebecca Stevens, CEO
Description: Promotes commerce and industry in County Sligo, Ireland.

00390

Small Firms Association
SFA

Confederation House, 84-86 Lower Baggot St., Dublin 2, Ireland
Tel: 01 6051500
Fax: 01 6381667
Email: info@sfa.ie
Website: http://www.sfa.ie
Members: 8000
Contact: Patricia Callan, Dir.
Fee: £535-775
Membership Type: regular (based on number of employees)
Description: Represents the small enterprises in Ireland. Provides economic, commercial, employee relations and social affairs advice and assistance.

00391

Social Workers in the Field of Learning Disability

c/o Irish Association of Social Workers
IASW Offices, 114/116 Pearse St., Dublin 2, Ireland
Tel: 01 6774838
Email: iasw@eircom.net
Website: http://www.iasw.ie
Description: Social workers working with people with learning disabilities. Seeks to improve the quality of life of people with learning disabilities; works to insure respect for the human rights of people with learning disabilities. Serves as a forum for the exchange of information among members; assists public agencies in devising public policies impacting people with learning disabilities.
Library Subject: social work, learning disabilities
Library Type: not open to the public

00392

Society of Archivists - Ireland
SOAI

Cathal Brugha Barracks, Dublin 6, Ireland
Tel: 01 8046081
Email: itscecile@gmail.com
Website: http://www.archives.org.uk/thesociety/regions/ireland.html
Members: 1800
Contact: Cecile Chemin, Chair
Description: Archivists, records managers, and conservators. Encourages preservation of archives and works to advance their administration. Fosters development of professional expertise and contributions to the body of professional knowledge. Provides a forum for communication among members.
Publication: Book
Publication title: Standards for the Development of Archives Services in Ireland

00393

Society of Chartered Surveyors in the Republic of Ireland
SCS

5 Wilton Pl., Dublin 2, Ireland
Tel: 01 6765500
Fax: 01 6761412
Email: info@scs.ie
Website: http://www.scs.ie/home
Contact: Peter Stapleton, Pres.
Description: Acts as the professional body for chartered surveyors practicing in the Republic of Ireland. Strives to maintain the highest professional standards. Encourages members to carry professional indemnity insurance.

00394

Society of Saint Vincent de Paul - Ireland
SVP

91/92 Sean McDermott St., Dublin 1, Ireland
Tel: 01 8386990
Fax: 01 8387355
Email: info@svp.ie
Website: http://www.svp.ie/Home.aspx
Members: 9500
Contact: Mairead Bushnell, Pres.

Description: Christian lay persons engaged in a spirit of justice and charity and united by a personal commitment to serve those who suffer. Seeks, through personal contact, to relieve suffering and promote the dignity and integrity of the individual. Conducts research.
Publication: Journal
Publication title: The Bulletin

00395

Society of the Irish Motor Industry SIMI

5 Upper Pembroke St., Dublin 2, Ireland
Tel: 01 6761690
Fax: 01 6619213
Email: info@simi.ie
Website: http://www.simi.ie
Contact: Alan Nolan, Dir. Gen.
Fee: £1256-12268
Membership Type: vehicle distributor
Fee: £1979-3393
Membership Type: accessory component manufacturer
Description: Represents the interests of automobile manufacturers in the Republic of Ireland.
Publication: Magazine
Publication title: Irish Motor Management. Advertisements.

00396

Society of Trust and Estate Practitioners Ireland

10 Clare St., Dublin 2, Ireland
Tel: 01 6761185
Email: info@step.ie
Website: http://www.step.ie
Contact: Mary Condell, Chair
Fee: £185
Membership Type: full
Fee: £75
Membership Type: student
Description: Aims to bring together all practitioners in the field of trusts and estates. Raises the public profile of trust and estate work as a profession in its own right. Advances knowledge and learning in trusts, estates and allied subjects. Encourages and promotes the study of trusts and estate practice. Provides education, training, representation and networking for its members.

00397

Sociological Association of Ireland SAI

Dept. of Sociology, University College Cork, Safari, Donovans Rd., Cork, Ireland
Tel: 021 4903756
Email: sai@ucd.ie
Website: http://www.sociology.ie
Members: 150
Staff: 1
Contact: Ciaran McCullagh, Pres.
Fee: £85
Membership Type: full
Fee: £35
Membership Type: student
Description: Graduates in sociology; social/cultural anthropology; political science; demography; human/social geography/social psychology; economics/political economy; history; social administration; linguistics and education. Provides a forum.
Publication: Journal
Publication title: Irish Journal of Sociology. Advertisements.

00398

South Dublin Chamber of Commerce

Tallaght Business Ctre., Whitestown Industrial Estate, Tallaght, Dublin 24, Ireland
Tel: 01 4622107
Fax: 01 4599512
Email: business@sdchamber.ie
Website: http://www.sdchamber.ie
Members: 400
Staff: 20
Contact: Peter Byrne, Chief Exec.
Fee: £138
Membership Type: associate
Fee: £3411
Membership Type: corporate
Description: Promotes and encourages investment in the local economy at all levels.
Library Subject: business
Library Type: reference
Publication: Newsletter
Publication title: ChamberLink. Advertisements.

00399

Spinal Injuries Action Association SIAA

National Rehabilitation Hospital, Rochestown Ave., Dun Laoghaire Co., Dublin, Ireland
Tel: 01 2355317
Email: info@spinalinjuries.ie
Website: http://www.siairl.org/spinal/Main/Home.htm
Members: 1200
Staff: 9
Contact: Colm Whooley, CEO
Description: Individuals and organizations. Seeks to improve the quality of life of people with spinal injuries and their families. Makes available support and services; conducts educational and advocacy campaigns.
Publication: Newsletter
Publication title: Spinal News

00400

Statistical and Social Inquiry Society of Ireland SSISI

c/o Sean Lyons, Honorary Sec.
ESRI, Whitaker Sq., Sir John Rogerson's Quay, Dublin 2, Ireland
Tel: 01 8632019
Email: sean.lyons@esri.ie
Website: http://www.ssisi.ie
Contact: D. De Buitleir, Pres.
Fee: £30
Membership Type: ordinary
Fee: £250
Membership Type: life
Description: Promotes the study of statistics, economics and social science in Ireland. Organizes public meetings where papers are presented and discussed. Publishes proceedings of the meetings.

00401

Support Organisation for Trisomy 13/18 Ireland SOFT Ireland

17 Bramble Close, Athlone, Westmeath, Ireland
Tel: 086 3656461
Email: info@softireland.com
Website: http://www.softireland.com
Contact: Carmel Reilly, Chair
Description: Provides support for families of children born with Patau's Syndrome (Trisomy 13), Edwards' Syndrome (Trisomy 18) and related chromosomal disorders. Raises public awareness and understanding of these syndromes. Offers assistance and encouragement to families of affected individuals.
Publication: Booklet
Publication title: Why My Baby

00402

Teachers' Union of Ireland TUI

73 Orwell Rd., Rathgar, Dublin 6, Ireland
Tel: 01 4922588
Fax: 01 4922953
Email: tui@tui.ie
Website: http://www.tui.ie
Members: 12000
Contact: Peter MacMenamin, Gen. Sec.
Description: Teachers and other educational personnel. Promotes effective second and third level education. Works to enhance the professional status of members. Represents members' interests before government agencies, management bodies, and the public.

00403

Technical, Engineering and Electrical Union TEEU

6 Gardiner Row, Dublin 1, Ireland
Tel: 01 8747047
Fax: 01 8747048
Email: info@teeu.ie
Website: http://www.teeu.ie
Members: 40000
Contact: Eamon Devoy, Gen. Sec.
Fee: £4.5
Membership Type: general, craft, trade
Description: Maintains and improves the skills, safety, working conditions, pay and general welfare of the members. Provides representation, advice and guidance in all aspects of industrial relations, labor law, health and welfare at work, new forms of work organization, partnership at workplace level, pensions, financial services, education and training for workplace representatives.

00404

Traditional Irish Music, Singing and Dancing Society

32 Belgrave Sq., Monkstown, Dublin, Ireland
Tel: 01 2800295
Fax: 01 2803759
Email: eolas@comhaltas.ie
Website: http://comhaltas.ie
Description: Irish musicians, singers, dancers, and those who wish to promote the Irish tradition in these areas. Fosters friendship among all lovers of Irish music, particularly the music of the Irish harp and the uilleann (elbow) pipes. Conducts research and educational programs. Holds concerts, festivals, and music competitions.
Formerly: Formerly, Traditional Irish Singing and Dancing Society
Publication: Magazine
Publication title: Treoir. Advertisements.

00405
Transparency International - Ireland
Trinity College Dublin, School of Business, Aras an Phiarsaigh, Dublin 2, Ireland
Tel: 01 6127067
Email: info@transparency.ie
Website: http://www.transparency.ie
Contact: John Devitt, Chief Exec.
Fee: £120
Membership Type: foundation
Fee: £40
Membership Type: standard
Description: Aims to promote good governance and fight against corruption. Seeks to raise public awareness of anti-corruption measures and influence legislation regulating international business transactions. Provides anti-corruption tools, strategies and programs.
Publication: Newsletter
Publication title: TIQ Ireland

00406
Transport Salaried Staffs' Association - Ireland TSSA
Nerney's Ct., Temple St., Dublin 1, Ireland
Tel: 01 8743467
Fax: 01 8745662
Email: enquiries@tssa.ie
Website: http://www.tssa.ie
Members: 1880
Contact: Carla McCambridge, Contact
Fee: £4.55
Membership Type: full (Ireland)
Fee: £2.28
Membership Type: fewer than 26 hours per week (Ireland)
Description: Represents transport and travel trade workers in Ireland. Strives to improve the working conditions of its members.

00407
Tyrone Guthrie Centre TGC
Annaghmakerrig, Newbliss, Monaghan, Ireland
Tel: 047 54003
Fax: 047 54380
Email: info@tyroneguthrie.ie
Website: http://www.tyroneguthrie.ie
Contact: Pat Donlon, Dir.
Description: Artists. Promotes development of the artistic talents of members, particularly those of Irish descent. Makes available residences for artists of all disciplines Irish and International. Provides studio space and other assistance to aspiring artists.
Publication: Magazine
Publication title: The Regent

00408
UNICEF - Ireland
33 Lower Ormond Quay, Dublin 1, Ireland
Tel: 01 8783000
Email: info@unicef.ie
Website: http://www.unicef.ie
Contact: Melanie Verwoerd, Exec. Dir.
Description: Works with local communities to provide emergency relief and run long-term development programs in areas such as health, education and child protection; works specifically for children.
Publication: Book
Publication title: For the Children - A Celebration of Families

Union Internationale pour l'Etude du Quarternaire
see International Union for Quaternary Research

00409
Union of Students in Ireland USI
3-4 St. Agnes Rd., Crumlin, Dublin 12, Ireland
Tel: 01 7099300
Fax: 01 7099302
Email: press@usi.ie
Website: http://www.usi.ie
Members: 250000
Staff: 3
Contact: Peter Manion, Pres.
Fee: £5
Membership Type: full time student
Description: Students attending postsecondary institutions in the Republic of Ireland and Northern Ireland. Promotes improvements in education and the quality of life of students. Represents members before educational institutions and government agencies regulating education.

00410
University Philosophical Society UPS
Trinity College Dublin, Dublin 2, Ireland
Email: president@tcdphil.com
Website: http://www.tcdphil.com
Members: 2500
Contact: Brendan Curran, Pres.
Description: Provides members the opportunity to discuss and debate on a particular subject. Awards the members with the best papers for every session.
Publication: Magazine
Publication title: Philander

00411
Vegetarian Society of Ireland VSI
c/o Dublin Food Coop.
12 Newmarket, Dublin 8, Ireland
Tel: 01 328834
Email: vegsoc@ireland.com
Website: http://www.vegetarian.ie
Members: 300
Fee: £20
Membership Type: regular
Fee: £300
Membership Type: life
Description: Seeks to inform the people of Ireland about vegetarianism and to cooperate with other organizations promoting vegetarianism, animal welfare and animal rights.
Publication: Newsletter
Publication title: The Irish Vegetarian. Advertisements.

00412
Veterinary Council of Ireland
53 Lansdowne Rd., Ballsbridge, Dublin 4, Ireland
Tel: 01 6684402
Fax: 01 6604373
Email: info@vci.ie
Website: http://www.vci.ie
Members: 19
Contact: Valerie Beatty, Registrar
Description: Represents the veterinary surgeons in Ireland. Aims to control the practise of veterinary surgery and registry of persons engaged in the practice.

00413
Vintners' Federation of Ireland VFI
VFI House, Castleside Dr., Rathfarnham, Dublin 14, Ireland
Tel: 01 4923400
Fax: 01 4923577
Email: enquiries@vintners.ie
Website: http://www.vfi.ie
Members: 5000
Staff: 20
Contact: Padraig Cribben, CEO
Description: Works as a trade association representing bars and taverns.

00414
Visual Artists Ireland
37 N Great George's St., Dublin 1, Ireland
Tel: 01 8722296
Fax: 01 8722364
Email: info@visualartists.ie
Website: http://www.visualartists.ie
Members: 1100
Staff: 7
Contact: Niamh Looney, Information and Communications Off.
Fee: £60
Membership Type: friend
Fee: £25
Membership Type: concession
Description: Professional visual artists. Provides services, facilitates and resources for artists. Acts as an advocate for the interests of artists and initiates projects and publications.
Formerly: Formerly, Sculptors Society of Ireland

00415
Voluntary Service International VSI
30 Mountjoy Sq., Dublin 1, Ireland
Tel: 01 8551011
Fax: 01 8551012
Email: info@vsi.ie
Website: http://www.vsi.ie
Members: 450
Staff: 4
Contact: Tom Ryder, Coor.
Fee: £27
Membership Type: wage earner
Fee: £14
Membership Type: non-wage earner
Description: Volunteers working for peace and international understanding through voluntary service. Coordinates the activities of Service Civil International in the Republic of Ireland.

00416
Volunteering Ireland
18 Eustace St., Temple Bar, Dublin 7, Ireland
Tel: 01 6369446
Fax: 01 6729198
Email: info@volunteeringireland.ie
Website: http://www.volunteeringireland.ie
Contact: Elaine Bradley, CEO
Description: Represents individuals and organizations interested in action through voluntary commitment to human service. Provides networking for volunteer program development. Promotes understanding through volunteer effort.

00417
Waterford Chamber
2 George's St., Waterford, Ireland
Tel: 051 872639
Fax: 051 876002
Email: info@waterfordchamber.ie
Website: http://www.waterfordchamber.com
Members: 650
Staff: 10
Contact: Michael Garland, Chief Exec.
Fee: £229-4493
Membership Type: individual (based on number of employees)
Fee: £107
Membership Type: charity
Description: Promotes commerce and trade in County Waterford, Ireland.

00418
Wexford Chamber of Industry and Commerce
The Ballast Office, Crescent Quayay, Wexford, Ireland
Tel: 053 9122226
Fax: 053 9121478
Email: info@wexfordchamber.ie
Website: http://www.wexfordchamber.ie
Contact: Madeleine Quirke, Chief Exec.
Description: Promotes trade and commerce in County Wexford, Ireland.

00419
Wine Development Board of Ireland
14 Whitefriars, Peter's Row, Aungiers St., Dublin 2, Ireland
Tel: 01 4757580
Fax: 01 4759274
Email: info@wineboard.ie
Website: http://www.wineboard.com
Members: 37
Description: Promotes knowledge and understanding of wine through extensive training and education programs for consumers and trade personnel. Provides statistics of the Irish wine market to trade members.

00420
WITH/Curam, Parent and Carer NGO in Ireland
11 Wyattville Pk., Loughlinstown, Dun Laoghaire, Ireland
Tel: 01 2826460
Fax: 046 9430314
Email: withcare@eircom.net
Website: http://homepage.eircom.net/~WITH
Members: 400
Contact: Caitriona Lynch, Pres.
Description: Parents/carers. Supports and encourages all who choose to stay at home to care for their families. Works to achieve equality for those working in the home. Establishes friendship groups for homemakers within their communities and functions as a forum for at-home parents and careers, most of who are women, to express opinions and influence society. Disseminates information. Conducts seminars and meetings. Provides speakers at conferences, meetings and for the media.
Formerly: Formerly, Women in the Home

00421
Women in Technology and Science WITS
PO Box 3783, Dublin 4, Ireland
Tel: 087 7690319
Email: info@witsireland.com
Website: http://www.witsireland.com
Contact: Charlotte O'Kelly, Chair
Fee: £50
Membership Type: individual
Fee: £20
Membership Type: retired/unemployed/student
Description: Promotes women's participation in science and technology. Encourages cooperation between women scientists and technologists in all aspects of scientific and technological endeavor. Promotes the investigation of the role and influence of women in Irish science and technology. Provides a support and information network for women working in science and technology.
Publication: Directory
Publication title: Talent Bank

00422
Women's Aid - Ireland
Everton House, 47 Old Cabra Rd., Dublin 7, Ireland
Tel: 01 8684721
Fax: 01 8684722
Email: info@womensaid.ie
Website: http://www.womensaid.ie
Members: 60
Staff: 40
Contact: Margaret Martin, Dir.
Description: Provides information, support and access to accommodations for women experiencing violence; works to eradicate violence against women through political, cultural and social advocacy.
Publication: Book
Publication title: Making the Links

00423
Women's International League for Peace and Freedom - Ireland
Ballinacloona Cottage, Ballyneal, Carrick-on-Suir, Tipperary, Ireland
Tel: 051 647061
Email: gloriafrankel@eircom.net
Website: http://www.wilpf.int.ch/world/ireland.htm
Contact: Gloria Frankel, Chair
Description: Works on issues of peace, human rights and disarmament at the local, national and international levels. Promotes political and social equality and economic equity. Supports the continuous development and implementation of international and humanitarian law.

00424
World Vision Ireland
The Mews, Garland House, Rathmines Park, Dublin 6, Ireland
Tel: 01 4980800
Fax: 01 4980801
Email: ireland@wvi.org
Website: http://www.worldvision.ie
Staff: 10
Contact: Stella Mew, CEO
Description: Helps transform the lives of children and families in need, irrespective of religious beliefs, gender, race, or ethnic background. Provides opportunity to every Irish household to be involved in child-focused work.

00425
Yeats Society Sligo YSS
Douglas Hyde Bridge, Sligo, Dublin, Ireland
Tel: 07191 42693
Fax: 07191 42780
Email: info@yeats-sligo.com
Website: http://www.yeats-sligo.com
Contact: Joe Cox, Pres.
Fee: £25
Membership Type: single
Fee: £40
Membership Type: family (two people)
Description: Furthers study of the life and poetical work of W.B. Yeats and Anglo-Irish literature.
Formerly: Formerly, Yeats Society

00426
Young Women's Christian Association - Ireland
64 Lower Baggot St., Dublin 2, Ireland
Tel: 01 6449536
Fax: 01 6449537
Email: ywcaofireland@eircom.net
Website: http://www.ywcaofireland.ie
Members: 150
Staff: 1
Description: Works to promote Christian fellowship and service among young women in Ireland. Advocates justice, peace, and unity.

00427
Zoological Society of Ireland ZSI
Phoenix Park, Dublin 8, Ireland
Tel: 01 4748900
Fax: 01 6771660
Email: info@dublinzoo.ie
Website: http://www.dublinzoo.ie/inside.asp?sectionId=1
Members: 1500
Staff: 80
Contact: Leo Oosterweghel, Dir.
Fee: £160
Membership Type: family
Fee: £100
Membership Type: individual
Description: Works to conserve, study and breed the endangered species of animals.
Publication: Magazine
Publication title: Zoo Matters. Advertisements.

United Kingdom

United Kingdom

00428

4Children

City Reach, 5 Greenwich View Pl., London, E14 9NN, UK
Tel: 020 75122112
Fax: 020 75376012
Email: info@4children.org.uk
Website: http://www.4children.org.uk
Members: 4000
Staff: 50
Fee: £21.5
Membership Type: individual
Fee: £32
Membership Type: small/medium setting
Description: Supports individuals and groups setting up out of school care by providing information, publications, training and advice.
Formerly: Formerly, Kid's Clubs Network

00429

A Rocha International

3 Hooper St., Cambridge, CB1 2NZ, UK
Tel: 01387 710286
Email: international@arocha.org
Website: http://www.arocha.org/int-en/2-DSY.html
Members: 2500
Staff: 40
Contact: Ghillean Prance, Chm.
Description: International conservation organization working to share God's love for all creation, Bulgaria, Ghana, India, the Netherlands, Portugal, Lebanon, Finland, France, Kenya, the UK, Canada, the USA, the Czech Republic, Switzerland, South Africa, Brazil, Peru and New Zealand.
Publication: Newsletter
Publication title: A Rocha International News

00430

Aberdeen and Grampian Chamber of Commerce AGCC

Greenhole Pl., Bridge of Don, Aberdeen, AB23 8EU, UK
Tel: 01224 343900
Fax: 01224 343943
Email: info@agcc.co.uk
Website: http://www.agcc.co.uk
Members: 1700
Staff: 30
Contact: Robert Collier, Chief Exec.
Fee: £316.08
Membership Type: local trading (minimum; based on number of full time employees)
Fee: £2792.98
Membership Type: local trading (maximum; based on number of full time employees)
Description: Supports and promotes the interests of business and commerce in Northeastern Scotland.
Publication: Bulletin
Publication title: Chamber's Business Bulletin

00431

Aberdeen Formation Evaluation Society AFES

c/o Anika Ephraim
Altens Industrial Estate, Souterhead Rd., Aberdeen, AB21 3LF, UK
Tel: 01224 380669
Email: anika.ephraim@eu.weatherford.com
Website: http://www.afes.org.uk
Contact: Casper van den Nouland, Pres.
Description: Dedicated to the promotion for the public benefit, education and knowledge in the scientific and technical aspects of formation evaluation, including reservoir characteristics of exposures from a geological and petrophysical perspective. Conducts career talks and a field trip to the Fife coast.

00432

Aberdeen Geological Society AGS

30 Hillview Terr., Cults, Aberdeen, AB15 9HJ, UK
Email: stella.bain@idnet.com
Website: http://www.aberdeengeolsoc.org.uk
Contact: Stella Bain, Treas.
Fee: £10
Membership Type: ordinary
Fee: £5
Membership Type: student, unwaged, OAP
Description: Amateur geologists, academics, students and professional geologists promoting the study of geology; conducts field trips to exotic geological locations around Scotland.
Meetings/Conventions: Members' Night – annual meeting

00433

Aberdeen-Angus Cattle Society AACS

Pedigree House, 6 King's Pl., Perth, PH2 8AD, UK
Tel: 01738 622477
Fax: 01738 636436
Email: info@aberdeen-angus.co.uk
Website: http://www.aberdeen-angus.co.uk
Members: 1800
Staff: 6
Contact: Ron McHattie, Chief Exec.
Fee: £828.75
Membership Type: life
Fee: £33.15
Membership Type: general
Description: Breeders of Aberdeen-Angus cattle in Great Britain and Ireland. Promotes the breed; maintains pedigree records.
Publication title: Aberdeen-Angus Review. Advertisements.

00434

Abortion Rights

18 Ashwin St., London, E8 3DL, UK
Tel: 020 79239792
Fax: 020 79239792
Email: choice@abortionrights.org.uk
Website: http://www.abortionrights.org.uk
Members: 1000
Staff: 2
Contact: Anne Quesney, Dir.
Fee: £20
Membership Type: standard
Fee: £10
Membership Type: concession
Description: Individuals and organizations in England united to liberalize the Abortion Act passed in Parliament in 1967, which permits a woman to terminate her pregnancy only if she can prove continuing it would involve a medical risk. Seeks to extend and protect women's right to choose to terminate her pregnancy. Distributes information to schools and the public. Monitors legislation on abortion and related issues and expresses concerns to the British Parliament, Department of Health, and National Health Service. Lobbies for extension of British laws to Northern Ireland.
Publication: Newsletter
Publication title: ALRA Newsletter

00435

Academi - Yr Academi Gymreig

3rd Fl., Mt. Stuart House, Mt. Stuart Sq., Cardiff, CF10 SFQ, UK
Tel: 029 20472266
Fax: 029 20492930
Email: post@academi.org
Website: http://www.academi.org
Members: 1500
Staff: 15
Contact: Peter Finch, Chief Exec.
Fee: £15
Membership Type: waged
Fee: £7.5
Membership Type: unwaged
Description: Fellow - an honorary position; member - open by invitation to those who are deemed to have made a contribution to literature of Wales; associates - open to all interested in the Academy's work. Exists in order to promote literature in Wales.
Publication: Journal
Publication title: A470. Advertisements.

00436

Academia Europaea

4th Fl., 21 Albemarle St., London, W1S 4HS, UK
Tel: 020 74953717
Fax: 020 76295442
Website: http://www.acadeuro.org
Members: 2300
Staff: 4
Contact: David Coates, Exec. Sec.
Description: Academics and other individuals with an interest in European issues. Promotes increased understanding and appreciation of European science, culture and scholarship. Facilitates communication and cooperation among members; sponsors research and educational programs.
Publication: Journal
Publication title: European Review. Advertisements.

00437

Academy of Experts

3 Gray's Inn Sq., London, WC1R 5AH, UK
Tel: 020 74300333
Fax: 020 74300666
Email: admin@academy-experts.org
Website: http://www.academy-experts.org
Members: 2000
Staff: 3
Contact: Phillippa Rowe, Chair
Fee: £105
Membership Type: forensic practitioner
Fee: £450
Membership Type: corporate

Description: Professionals from multi disciplines all specializing in their own fields but all practiced in the giving, preparing of experts' reports. A professional society and qualifying body for independent experts experienced in a wide range of professional, commercial and industrial disciplines. The Academy provides an expert matching service as well as maintaining a register of qualified mediators.
Library Type: not open to the public
Formerly: Formerly, The British Academy of Experts
Publication: Journal
Publication title: The Expert and Dispute Resolver. Advertisements.

00438

Academy of Learned Societies for the Social Sciences AcSS

Academy of Social Sciences, 30 Tabernacle St., London, EC2A 4UE, UK
Tel: 0207 3300898
Email: administrator@acss.org.uk
Website: http://www.acss.org.uk
Members: 400
Contact: Stephen Anderson, Exec. Dir.
Description: Social science organizations representing more than 35,000 social scientists in the United Kingdom. Seeks to advance the social sciences; promotes the professional interests of members. Facilitates exchange of information among members; sponsors research and educational programs.
Formerly: Formerly, Association of Learned Societies in the Social Sciences
Publication: Journal
Publication title: 21st Century Society

00439

Access Flooring Association AFA

PO Box 386, Hull, HU9 5WX, UK
Tel: 0845 1200068
Email: information@theafa.com
Website: http://www.theafa.com
Members: 8
Description: Manufacturers or installers of and contractors for access flooring. Promotes the manufacture and installation of access flooring to the highest possible standard and represents the industry with any bodies involved in the production of standards.
Publication: Handbook
Publication title: Platform Floor Performance Specifications MOB PF2 PS/SPU

00440

ACFO

35 Lavant St., Petersfield, GU32 3LL, UK
Tel: 01730 260162
Email: info@acfo.org
Website: http://www.acfo.org
Contact: Julie Jenner, Contact
Description: Represents the professional interests of vehicle fleet operators. Provides support and advice in all areas of fleet operations. Develops expertise in fleet management through meetings, informed debate and training.
Publication: Journal
Publication title: Fleet Operator

00441

Achievers International

Enterprise Education Trust, Enterprise House, 1-2 Hatfields, London, SE1 9PG, UK
Tel: 0207 6200735
Fax: 0207 2614539
Website: http://www.achieversinternational.org
Description: Works to assist students to form small companies and export and import locally manufactured products to and from a foreign partner group.

00442

Acronym Institute for Disarmament Diplomacy

24 Colvestone Crescent, London, E8 2LH, UK
Tel: 020 75038857
Fax: 020 75038857
Email: katb@acronym.org.uk
Website: http://www.acronym.org.uk
Contact: Rebecca Johnson, Founding Dir./Ed.
Description: Works with policymakers and non-governmental organizations to promote non-proliferation and nuclear disarmament; disseminates information. Promotes talks among nuclear weapon states to identify measures for further progress in transparency, arms control and confidence building, focusing on unilateral initiatives.
Publication: Reports
Publication title: ACRONYM Reports

00443

Act Together

PO Box 34728, London, N7 6XE, UK
Email: info@acttogether.org
Website: http://www.acttogether.org
Contact: Nadje Al-Ali, Contact
Description: Represents UK-based Iraqi and non-Iraqi women. Campaigns against the economic sanctions imposed on Iraq after the 1991 Gulf war. Promotes women's initiatives in Iraq. Raises the consciousness about the current situation of women in Iraq.

00444

Action Against Allergy AAA

PO Box 278, Twickenham, TW1 4QQ, UK
Tel: 020 88922711
Fax: 020 88924950
Email: aaa@actionagainstallergy.freeserve.co.uk
Website: http://www.actionagainstallergy.co.uk
Members: 1200
Contact: Patricia Schooling, Exec. Dir.
Fee: £15
Membership Type: individual (in UK)
Fee: £250
Membership Type: life
Description: Campaigns for diagnosis and treatment of allergies through the British national health service institutions and physicians. Provides information to chronic allergy sufferers. Coordinates medical reference center.
Library Subject: allergies
Library Type: reference
Publication: Newsletter
Publication title: Allergy Newsletter. Advertisements.
Meetings/Conventions: annual convention – Exhibits.

00445

Action Against Medical Accidents AvMA

44 High St., Surrey, Croydon, CR0 1YB, UK
Tel: 020 86889555
Fax: 020 86679065
Email: advice@avma.org.uk
Website: http://www.avma.org.uk
Members: 12
Contact: Peter Walsh, Chief Exec.
Description: Provides independent advice and support to anyone who has suffered a medical accident.
Formerly: Formerly, Action for Victims of Medical Accidents

00446

Action Aid, Bretton Woods Project BWP

33-39 Bowling Green Lane, London, EC1R 0BJ, UK
Tel: 020 32207729
Email: info@brettonwoodsproject.org
Website: http://www.brettonwoodsproject.org
Staff: 3
Contact: Jesse Griffiths, Coor.
Description: Serves as a clearinghouse and advocacy organisation on World Bank and International Monetary Fund issues. Works with a range of non-government organisations and researchers. Produces bimonthly Bretton Woods Update newsletter.
Publication: Report
Publication title: Blinding with Science: How World Bank analysis determines PRSP policies

00447

Action Cancer

1 Marlborough Park, Belfast, BT9 6XS, UK
Tel: 028 90803344
Fax: 028 90803356
Email: info@actioncancer.org
Website: http://www.actioncancer.org
Staff: 42
Contact: Robin McRoberts, Chief Exec.
Description: Works to heighten awareness of the importance of early cancer detection. Offers breast and cervical cancer screening services for women, and testicular and prostatic screening services for men. Provides counselling for cancer patients, families, and friends. Maintains research lab. Disseminates information.
Publication: Magazine
Publication title: Action Cancer News Update
Meetings/Conventions: seminar

00448

Action for Blind People

14-16 Verney Rd., London, SE16 3DZ, UK
Tel: 020 76354800
Fax: 020 76354900
Email: info@actionforblindpeople.org.uk
Website: http://www.actionforblindpeople.org.uk
Staff: 400
Contact: Stephen Remington, CEO
Description: Provides services for visually impaired people in the UK, including employment services, hotels and holidays accommodation, and information and welfare rights advice.
Library Subject: visual impairment
Library Type: reference

00449

Action for Children in Conflict AFCiC

Victoria House, 10 Broad St., Abingdon, OX14 3LH, UK
Tel: 01235 539319
Email: info@actionchildren.org
Website: http://www.actionchildren.org
Contact: Christopher Le Fevre, Chm.
Description: Provides psychological, emotional and educational support to the survivors of conflict.

00450

Action for Market Towns AMT

5 Baxter Ct., High Baxter St., Bury St. Edmunds, IP33 1ES, UK
Tel: 01284 756567
Fax: 01284 761816
Email: info@towns.org.uk
Website: http://towns.org.uk
Contact: Chris Wade, Chief Exec.
Fee: £113-210
Membership Type: town (based on population)
Fee: £318
Membership Type: individual organization
Description: Represents and promotes the interests of market towns to government and media. Promotes the vitality and viability of small towns. Serves as a voice for all market towns. Provides information, advice and support to market towns.
Publication: Newsletter
Publication title: Strategy

00451

Action for Sick Children

High Ln., 32b Buxton Rd., Stockport, SK6 8BH, UK
Tel: 01663 763004
Email: pamela.barnes@actionforsickchildren.org
Website: http://www.actionforsickchildren.org
Members: 800
Staff: 4
Contact: Pamela Barnes, Chair
Description: Individual members (voting rights) and subscribers to library service. Membership categories are individual, family, affiliate, statutory, CHC, voluntary organization, overseas. A partnership of parents and professionals working to promote the best health care for children at home or in hospital.

00452

Action for Southern Africa ACTSA

231 Vauxhall Bridge Rd., London, SW1V 1EH, UK
Tel: 020 32632001
Fax: 020 79319398
Email: actsa@actsa.org
Website: http://www.actsa.org
Members: 3500
Staff: 8
Contact: Tony Dykes, Dir.
Fee: £17
Membership Type: individual
Fee: £22
Membership Type: joint
Description: Campaigns with people of Southern Africa to build a better future; influences decision makers in Britain and Europe on policies affecting Southern Africa; aims to keep the region in the public and political spotlight.

00453

Action on Disability and Development ADD

Vallis House, 57 Vallis Rd., Somerset, Frome, BA11 3EG, UK
Tel: 01373 473064
Fax: 01373 452075
Email: add@add.org.uk
Website: http://www.add.org.uk
Staff: 90
Contact: Jabulani Ncube, Chief Exec.
Description: Development organizations. Seeks to increase participation by people with disabilities in the development process. Conducts educational and training courses to enhance the income-generation potential of people with disabilities; supports inclusion of people with disabilities in community rehabilitation initiatives.

00454

Action on Elder Abuse AEA

PO Box 60001, London, SW16 9BY, UK
Tel: 020 88359280
Fax: 020 86969328
Email: enquiries@elderabuse.org.uk
Website: http://www.elderabuse.org.uk
Contact: Gary FitzGerald, Chief Exec.
Fee: £21
Membership Type: individual (in UK and Ireland)
Fee: £14
Membership Type: full-time student/retired individual (in UK and Ireland)
Description: Prevents abuse in old age by raising awareness, education, promoting research and the collection and dissemination of information. Provides a national information and advice service and provides guidance for the prevention of, and action on, the abuse of older people.
Publication: Bulletin
Publication title: Action Points

00455

Action on Smoking and Health - England ASH

144-145 Shoreditch High St., London, E1 6JE, UK
Tel: 020 77395902
Fax: 020 77294732
Email: enquiries@ash.org.uk
Website: http://www.ash.org.uk
Members: 1000
Staff: 7
Contact: Deborah Arnott, Chief Exec.
Description: Publicizes the dangers of smoking. Campaigns for smoke-free public areas and for tobacco control legislation. Liaises with medical charities, health promotion organizations, and private groups. Disseminates information; monitors media, scientific, and trade publications.
Library Subject: smoking, health
Library Type: reference
Publication: Newsletter
Publication title: Political Bulletin

00456

Action on Smoking and Health - Scotland ASH Scotland

8 Frederick St., Edinburgh, EH2 2HB, UK
Tel: 0131 2254725
Fax: 0131 2254759
Email: ashscotland@ashscotland.org.uk
Website: http://www.ashscotland.org.uk
Staff: 27
Contact: Sheila Duffy, Chief Exec.
Description: National organization dedicated to campaigning for a tobacco-free Scotland. Aims to keep the tobacco issue on the public agenda. Promotes non-smoking as the norm. Contributes to the reduction in the uptake of smoking. Supports stop smoking initiatives.
Library Subject: smoking and health, tobacco and society
Library Type: reference
Formerly: Formerly, Scottish Committee Action on Smoking and Health
Publication: Annual Report
Publication title: ASH Scotland Annual Report

00457

ActionAid

Hamlyn House, Macdonald Rd., Archway, London, N19 5PG, UK
Tel: 020 31220561
Fax: 020 72785667
Email: mail@actionaid.org
Website: http://www.actionaid.org.uk
Contact: Richard Miller, Dir.
Description: Promotes human rights worldwide.

00458

Active Learning Network for Accountability and Performance in Humanitarian Action ALNAP

Overseas Development Institute, 111 Westminster Bridge Rd., London, SE1 7JD, UK
Tel: 020 79220300
Fax: 020 79220399
Email: alnap@alnap.org
Website: http://www.alnap.org
Contact: John Mitchell, Dir.
Description: Aims to improve humanitarian performance through increased learning and accountability. Incorporates humanitarian organizations and experts from across the humanitarian sector. Serves as a collective response by the humanitarian sector.
Publication: Handbook
Publication title: Participation by Crisis-affected Populations in Humanitarian Action Practitioners' Handbook

00459

Ada Cole Rescue Stables

Broadlands, Broadley Common, Nr Nazeing, Essex, Waltham Abbey, EN9 2DH, UK
Tel: 01992 892133
Fax: 01992 893841
Website: http://www.nwnet.co.uk/terryreader/Ada_Cole/Ada_Cole.htm
Description: Advocates for equine justice; seeks to prevent cruelty to horses; rehabilitates horses with the aim of placing rescued animals into caring foster homes.

00460
Adam Smith Institute
ASI
23 Great Smith St., London, SW1P 3BL, UK
Tel: 020 72224995
Email: info@adamsmith.org
Website: http://www.adamsmith.org
Contact: Madsen Pirie, Pres.
Fee: £500
Membership Type: executive
Fee: £1000
Membership Type: premium
Description: Researches and develops practical initiatives to inject choice and competition into public services, extend personal freedom, reduce taxes, prune back regulation and cut government waste.
Publication: Paper
Publication title: A Cloudy Energy Future

00461
Addison's Disease Self Help Group
ADSHG
PO Box 1083, Guildford, GU1 4NP, UK
Email: deana@addison.org.uk
Website: http://www.addisons.org.uk
Members: 850
Contact: Deana Kenward, Pres.
Fee: £12
Membership Type: local
Fee: £20
Membership Type: international
Description: Serves as a support group for men, women, and children with adrenal insufficiency caused by autoimmune destruction of the glands.

00462
Adopt-A-Minefield
c/o No More Landmines Trust
Charles House, 4th Fl., 375 Kensington High St., London, W14 8QH, UK
Tel: 020 74715580
Email: info@landmines.org.uk
Website: http://www.minesawareness.org
Description: Promotes awareness for mine clearance and rehabilitation of landmine survivors.

00463
Adult Residential Colleges Association
ARCA
6 Bath Rd., Felixstowe, IP11 7JW, UK
Tel: 01394 278161
Fax: 01394 271083
Email: arcasec@aol.com
Website: http://www.arca.uk.net
Members: 30
Staff: 2
Description: Short-term residential colleges, mainly for adult education, offering weekend, mid-week and one week courses. Promotes and disseminates knowledge of the work of member adult education organisations, their primary aim being to provide short-term residential liberal adult education.

00464
Advertising Association of the United Kingdom
AA
Artillery House, 7th Fl. N, 11-19 Artillery Row, London, SW1P 1RT, UK
Tel: 020 73401100
Fax: 020 72221504
Email: aa@adassoc.org.uk
Website: http://www.adassoc.org.uk
Members: 31
Staff: 14
Contact: Penny Hughes, Pres.
Description: Represents the advertising and promotional marketing industry, including advertisers, agencies, the media, and support services. Campaigns to maintain the freedom to advertise and to improve public attitudes toward advertising. Maintains information center on advertising and related topics. Compiles advertising statistics; conducts seminars and courses; coordinates research on advertising issues.
Library Type: by appointment only
Publication: Yearbook
Publication title: Advertising Statistics Yearbook

00465
Advertising Producers Association
APA
47 Beak St., London, W1F 9SE, UK
Tel: 020 74342651
Fax: 020 74349002
Email: info@a-p-a.net
Website: http://www.a-p-a.net
Members: 127
Staff: 3
Contact: Stephen Davies, Chief Exec.
Description: Production companies who make television commercials. Represents the producers of television commercials.
Formerly: Formerly, Advertising Film and Videotape Producers Association

00466
Advertising Standards Authority
ASA
Mid City Pl., 71 High Holborn, London, WC1V 6QT, UK
Tel: 020 74922222
Fax: 020 72423696
Email: enquiries@asa.org.uk
Website: http://www.asa.org.uk/asa
Staff: 101
Contact: Chris Smith, Chm.
Description: Upholds standards in all media advertising in the UK. Acting independently of both the government and the industry, it ensures compliance with the advertising codes by investigating complaints, issuing pre-publication advice to non-broadcast advertisers and publishers, and conducting extensive research and monitoring programmes.
Publication title: The CAP Code (the British Code of Advertising, Sales Promotion and Direct Marketing)

00467
Advice UK
63 St. Mary Ave., 6th Fl., London, EC3A 8AA, UK
Tel: 020 74695700
Fax: 020 74695701
Email: mail@adviceuk.org.uk
Website: http://www.adviceuk.org.uk/home
Members: 1000
Staff: 21
Contact: Steve Johnson, Chief Exec.
Description: Provides support services to independent advice centres providing direct access and free services to the public in all areas of welfare law. Promotes the availability of quality advice and represents the interests of independent advice centres nationally.
Formerly: Formerly, Federation of Independent Advice Centres
Publication: Bulletin
Publication title: Advice UK Mailing

00468
Advisory Centre for Education
ACE
1C Aberdeen Studios, 22 Highbury Grove, London, N5 2DQ, UK
Tel: 020 77043370
Fax: 020 73549069
Email: enquiries@ace-ed.org.uk
Website: http://www.ace-ed.org.uk
Staff: 25
Contact: Sam Murray, Contact
Fee: £50
Membership Type: individual
Fee: £75
Membership Type: professional
Description: Independent national advice centre for parents of children aged 5-16 in state education in England and Wales.
Publication: Journal
Publication title: ACE Education Now

00469
Advisory Committee on Protection of the Sea
ACOPS
13-14 Trumpington St., Cambridge, CB2 1QA, UK
Tel: 01223 748811
Email: acopsadmin@googlemail.com
Website: http://www.acops.org.uk
Members: 70
Staff: 5
Contact: Trevor Dixon, Contact
Description: Local authority associations, port and fishery associations, industry and tourist organizations, trade unions, and wildlife groups in 18 countries. Promotes preservation and protection of the world's seas from pollution by human activities. Compiles statistics. Sponsors seminars for local authority representatives. Organizes international conferences on sustainable tourism and national and global plans of action to reduce marine pollution from land based activities.
Formerly: Formerly, Advisory Committee on Oil Pollution of the Sea
Publication: Report
Publication title: ACOPS Annual UK Oil Pollution Survey

00470
Advocates for Animals
10 Queensferry St., Edinburgh, EH2 4PG, UK
Tel: 0131 2256039
Fax: 0131 2206377
Email: info@advocatesforanimals.org
Website: http://www.advocatesforanimals.org.uk
Staff: 6
Contact: Fiona Ogg, CEO

Description: Seeks to protect animals from cruelty and prevent of the infliction of suffering, the abolition of vivisection.

00471

Aerosol Society

c/o Sheila Coates, Sec.
PO Box 34, Portishead, Bristol, BS20 7FE, UK
Tel: 01275 849019
Fax: 01275 844877
Email: admin@aerosol-soc.org.uk
Website: http://www.aerosol-soc.org.uk
Members: 500
Staff: 1
Contact: Virginia Foot, Pres.
Fee: £15
Membership Type: ordinary
Fee: £200
Membership Type: corporate
Description: Promotes aerosol science.

00472

AFASIC - England

1st Fl., 20 Bowling Green Ln., London, EC1R 0BD, UK
Tel: 020 74909410
Fax: 020 72512834
Website: http://www.afasicengland.org.uk
Members: 20000
Staff: 15
Contact: Linda Lascelles, Chief Exec.
Fee: £15
Membership Type: family
Fee: £35
Membership Type: institutional
Description: Promotes the interests of young people with speech and/or language difficulties. Seeks to enhance understanding of speech and language disorders and improve educational and employment opportunities for young adults with such disorders. Offers advice and support for parents of individuals with speech and language disorders. Conducts research on children's language development. Organizes international symposia, national seminars, and workshops. Maintains speakers' bureau; compiles statistics.
Formerly: Formerly, AFASIC - Overcoming Speech Impairments
Publication: Newsletter
Publication title: Afasic Abstract

00473

Afghan Paiwand Association

Moran House, 2nd Fl., Ste. 7-9, 449-451 High Rd., Willesden, NW10 2JJ, UK
Tel: 020 8459 6691
Fax: 020 8905 8770
Email: info@paiwand.com
Website: http://www.paiwand.com
Contact: Ahmad Washeed, Sec.
Fee: £5
Membership Type: general
Description: Seeks to improve the quality of life and promote the physical, social and mental well being of members of the Afghan community living in the United Kingdom. Works to integrate Afghan community into the greater community in the United Kingdom and to maintain links with other Afghan communities around the world. Provides all-around assistance and service to the Afghan community members in the United Kingdom.
Publication: Newsletter
Publication title: Paiwand Newsletter

00474

Afghanaid

Development House, 56-64 Leonard St., London, EC2A 4LT, UK
Tel: 020 70650825
Email: info@afghanaid.org.uk
Website: http://www.afghanaid.org.uk
Contact: Amanda Curley, UK Fundraising Mgr.
Description: Assists rural communities in Afghanistan by involving members of the community; promotes income generation through beekeeping; improved wheat seed, vegetable gardens, and tree planting; veterinary work; vocational training of women; food security; health education; sanitation; and road and bridge building.
Publication: Annual Report
Publication title: Annual Review

00475

Africa Centre

38 King St., Covent Garden, London, WC2E 8IT, UK
Tel: 020 78361973
Fax: 020 78361975
Email: info@businessofculture.com
Website: http://www.africacentre.org.uk
Staff: 9
Contact: Graeme Jennings, Interim Mgr.
Description: Represents individuals and organizations with an interest in Africa. Promotes increased understanding of, and appreciation for, African current events, culture, and history among the people of the United Kingdom. Presents programs and activities highlighting African cultures; supports and promotes cultural activities of African communities in Britain and Europe. Maintains library, and conducts educational and charitable programs.
Publication: Newsletter
Publication title: Events Sheet. Advertisements.

00476

Africa-Europe Group for Interdisciplinary Studies AEGIS

Centre of African Studies, School of Oriental and African Studies, Thornhaugh St., Russell Sq., London, WC1H 0XG, UK
Tel: 020 78984370
Fax: 020 78984369
Email: cas@soas.ac.uk
Website: http://www.aegis-eu.org
Contact: Paul Nugent, Pres.
Description: Aims to create synergies between experts and institutions, particularly on social sciences and humanities, in order to improve understanding about contemporary African societies.

00477

African Bird Club ABC

c/o BirdLife International
Wellbrook Ct., Girton Rd., Cambridge, CB3 0NA, UK
Email: chairman@africanbirdclub.org
Website: http://www.africanbirdclub.org
Members: 1200
Contact: Keith Betton, Chm.
Fee: £21
Membership Type: individual (Europe and Africa)
Fee: £24
Membership Type: family (Europe and Africa)
Description: Promotes conservation of African birds; provides a worldwide focus for African ornithology; encourages conservation of birds of the region.

00478

African Books Collective ABC

PO Box 721, Oxford, OX1 9EN, UK
Tel: 01869 349110
Fax: 01869 349110
Email: orders@africanbookscollective.com
Website: http://www.africanbookscollective.com
Members: 100
Staff: 11
Contact: Mary Jay, CEO
Description: Owned by African publishers. Marketing and distribution of African published books outside Africa. Facilitates exchange of information among African book publishers.
Library Type: reference

00479

African Child Association ACA

5 Westminster Bridge Rd., London, SE1 7XW, UK
Tel: 020 72526655
Fax: 020 76201431
Email: enquiries@acaint.org
Website: http://www.cridoc.net/african_child_association.php
Description: Seeks to promote and protect the rights of African children. Improves the intellectual and social skills of African children. Provides educational and training programs on issues and matters concerning children's rights. Raises public awareness of general welfare of African children.
Publication: Journal
Publication title: The African Child

00480

African Community Involvement Association ACIA

Justin Plz. 3, Viceroy, Ste. 1, 341 London Rd., Mitcham, Surrey, CR4 4BE, UK
Tel: 0208 6872400
Fax: 0208 6464363
Email: info@acia-uk.org
Website: http://www.acia-uk.org
Description: Aims to deliver culturally appropriate quality of health care and support services for Africans living HIV/AIDS. Ensures the relief of sickness among people living with HIV/AIDS infection. Provide facilities for recreation and other leisure time activities for young people to improve their life condition. Provides education and training for refugees and asylum seekers living in the UK.

00481

African Foundation for Development AFFORD

Castle Works, 21 St. Georges Rd., London, SE1 6ES, UK
Tel: 0207 5823578
Fax: 0207 5873919
Email: afford@afford-uk.org

Website: http://www.afford-uk.org
Contact: Chukwu-Emeka Chikezie, Exec. Dir.
Description: Fosters development programs in Africa.

00482

African Health For Empowerment and Development
AHEAD

1st Fl., 130 Powis St., Woolwich, London, SE18 6NN, UK
Tel: 020 83170865
Fax: 020 83164042
Email: info@africanhealth.org.uk
Website: http://www.africanhealth.org.uk
Description: Addresses the health and social care needs of African communities in South London. Aims to make a major contribution towards achieving equality of access to health for Africans, refugees and asylum seekers in the greater London Area. Provides health promotion, advocacy and support services to mainly African communities in the areas of HIV and sexual health.
Publication: Newsletter

00483

African Studies Association of the United Kingdom
ASAUK

36 Gordon Sq., London, WC1H 0PD, UK
Tel: 020 30738335
Fax: 020 30738340
Email: secretary@asauk.net
Website: http://www.asauk.net
Members: 500
Staff: 1
Contact: Gemma Haxby, Sec.
Fee: £49
Membership Type: joint
Fee: £20
Membership Type: student
Description: Academics, educators, students, and other individuals with and interest in international studies. Seeks to advance study and teaching in the field. Conducts research and educational programs.
Publication: Journal
Publication title: African Affairs (The Journal of the Royal African Society). Advertisements.

00484

Afro-Asian Society of Nematologists
AASN

24 Brantwood Rd., Luton, LU1 1JJ, UK
Tel: 01582 726724
Fax: 01582 760981
Email: rsiddiqi@dialstart.net
Website: http://www.ifns.org/membership/aasn.html
Members: 200
Contact: M.R. Siddiqi, Ed.-in-Chief
Description: Promotes and enhances the science of plant and insect nematology, particularly in the areas of Africa and Asia.
Publication: Journal
Publication title: International Journal of Nematology. Advertisements.

00485

Age Concern England
ACE

Astral House, 1268 London Rd., London, SW16 4ER, UK
Tel: 020 87657200
Email: customer.relations@acent.co.uk
Website: http://www.ageconcern.org.uk
Members: 98
Contact: Gordon Lishman, Dir. Gen.
Description: Involved in campaigning, parliamentary work, policy analysis, research, specialist information and advice provision and publishing. Raises funds. Member of the federation of over 400 Age Concern organizations operating in England. Provides both financial and development support to assist the other members in their provision of vital local services.

00486

Age Concern Scotland
ACS

Causewayside House, 160 Causewayside, Edinburgh, EH9 1PR, UK
Tel: 0845 8330200
Fax: 0845 8330759
Email: info@agescotland.org.uk
Website: http://www.ageconcernandhelptheagedscotland.org.uk
Members: 1000
Staff: 74
Contact: David Manion, Chief Exec.
Description: Works to make the lives of older people in Scotland more secure, comfortable, dignified and enjoyable.

Agence Internationale ISBN
see International ISBN Agency

Agencia de Informacao de Mocambique
see Mozambique News Agency

00487

Agents Association of Great Britain

54 Keyes House, Dolphin Sq., London, SW1V 3NA, UK
Tel: 020 78340515
Fax: 020 78210261
Email: association@agents-uk.com
Website: http://www.agents-uk.com
Members: 460
Staff: 3
Contact: Michael Vine, Pres.
Description: Theatrical agents. Professional association for theatrical employment agents, including membership agents dealing with all sections of the industry from legitimate to contemporary artists. A collective voice for negotiations with unions and government and EC legislation.
Library Type: not open to the public
Formerly: Formerly, Entertainment Agents Association

00488

Agricultural Economics Society
AES

Holtwood, Red Lion St., Cropredy, Banbury, OX17 1PD, UK
Tel: 01295 750182
Fax: 01295 750182
Email: aes@cingnet.org.uk
Website: http://www.aes.ac.uk
Members: 450
Contact: David Blandford, Pres.
Fee: £48
Membership Type: ordinary
Fee: £24
Membership Type: student, retired
Description: Agricultural economists in the UK, students of agricultural economics, and interested individuals. Promotes the study and teaching of all disciplines relevant to agricultural economics. Areas of interest include agricultural industry; food and related industries; rural communities. Conducts studies in fields of economics, statistics, marketing, business management, politics, history, and sociology.
Publication: Journal
Publication title: Journal of Agricultural Economics. Advertisements.
Meetings/Conventions: annual competition

00489

Agricultural Engineers' Association
AEA

Samuelson House, 62 Forder Way, Hampton, Peterborough, PE7 8JB, UK
Tel: 08456 448748
Fax: 01733 314767
Email: ab@aea.uk.com
Website: http://www.aea.uk.com
Members: 250
Staff: 11
Contact: Roger Lane-Nott, Dir. Gen.
Fee: £200
Membership Type: regular (based on turnover)
Description: Manufacturers, wholesale distributors and importers of tractors, machinery, implements, equipment and used in agriculture, horticulture, forestry, aquaculture, the cultivation of parks and gardens and in the outdoor leisure industry; providers of parts and services to the above. Aims to safeguard and promote the interests of manufacturers and wholesale distributors. The areas covered are technical standards and legislation; legal - patents monitor, EC directives, distribution; economics - market information and statistics; export missions overseas and UK Government funding for export activities; shows and demonstrations.
Publication: Directory
Publication title: Outdoor Power Equipment Directory and Price Guide
Meetings/Conventions: Outlook Conference – semiannual meeting

00490

Agricultural Law Association
ALA

Kimblewick Cottage, Prince Albert Rd., West Mersea, Colchester, CO5 8AZ, UK
Tel: 01206 383521
Email: enquiries@ala.org.uk
Website: http://www.ala.org.uk
Members: 1000
Contact: Geoff Whittaker, Consultant/Advisor

Fee: £70
Membership Type: regular
Description: Membership is open to all qualified members of the professions associated with giving advice on the subjects of agriculture, environment, farming, forestry and the rural community to students and trainees in those professions and to any others interested in the fields of operation as Council may approve. Promotes the study, knowledge and understanding of the law relating to Agriculture, the Environment, Farming, Forestry and the Rural Community.
Publication: Magazine
Publication title: The Bulletin

00491

Agricultural Lime Association ALA

Gillingham House, 38-44 Gillingham St., London, SW1V 1HU, UK
Tel: 020 79638000
Fax: 020 79638001
Email: ala@mineralproducts.org
Website: http://www.aglime.org.uk
Members: 9
Contact: Eileen Pullinger, Dir.
Description: Represents the interests of members on all aspects of the industry such as technical and environmental issues related to the promotion of the final product.
Publication: Booklet
Publication title: Agricultural Lime, the Natural Solution

00492

Air League AL

Broadway House, Tothill St., London, SW1H 9NS, UK
Tel: 020 72228463
Email: exec@airleague.co.uk
Website: http://www.airleague.co.uk
Members: 1800
Staff: 8
Contact: Andrew Brookes, Dir.
Fee: £29
Membership Type: student
Fee: £55
Membership Type: full
Description: Individuals involved in the aerospace industry, civil and military aviation, and government agencies. Supports British aviation and the British aerospace industry. Represents members' interests before government authorities and the press.
Publication: Newsletter
Publication title: Air League Newsletter. Advertisements.

00493

Air-Britain Historians AB

Blacklands Ln., Sudbourne, Suffolk, Woodbridge, IP12 2AX, UK
Tel: 01394 450767
Email: membership@air-britain.co.uk
Website: http://www.air-britain.com
Members: 4000
Contact: Howard J. Nash, Membership Sec.
Fee: £20
Membership Type: in UK
Fee: £23
Membership Type: in Europe
Description: Aviation enthusiasts seeking to encourage the preservation of records of aeronautical development and history.
Publication: Magazine
Publication title: Aeromilitaria

00494

Aircraft Owners and Pilots Association - United Kingdom AOPA UK

50a Cambridge St., London, SW1V 4QQ, UK
Tel: 020 78345631
Fax: 020 78348623
Email: info@aopa.co.uk
Website: http://www.aopa.co.uk
Members: 400000
Staff: 3
Contact: Martin Robinson, CEO
Fee: £72
Membership Type: pilot (overseas)
Fee: £62
Membership Type: instructor
Description: Aircraft owners - corporate and private - and all pilots in the general aviation sector. Protects and develops the requirements of UK General Aviation, including pilot training and licensing, aircraft certification, airspace and aerodromes. Provides the coordinating office for the UK General Aviation Awareness Council.
Publication: Magazine
Publication title: General Aviation

00495

Aircraft Research Association ARA

Manton Ln., Bedfordshire, Bedford, MK41 7PF, UK
Tel: 01234 350681
Fax: 01234 328584
Email: ara@ara.co.uk
Website: http://www.ara.co.uk
Members: 4
Staff: 130
Contact: Dougie Hunter, Chief Exec.
Description: Conducts research and engineering work to produce both theoretical and practical model designs. Manufactures models and conducts wind tunnel testing for member companies and others.
Library Subject: aerodynamics
Library Type: reference
Publication: Newsletter
Publication title: ARA Update

00496

Airfields Environment Trust AET

Broken Wharf House, 2 Broken Wharf, London, EC4V 3DT, UK
Tel: 020 72482223
Fax: 020 73298160
Email: info@aet.org.uk
Website: http://www.aet.org.uk
Description: Undertakes research on aviation's environmental impacts.

00497

Airport Operators Association AOA

3 Birdcage Walk, London, SW1H 9JJ, UK
Tel: 020 77993171
Fax: 020 73400999
Email: info@aoa.org.uk
Website: http://www.aoa.org.uk/home/index.asp
Members: 200
Staff: 6
Contact: Ed Anderson, Chm.
Description: Airports and associated companies. Represents the interests of UK airport and aerodrome operators.
Publication: Journal
Publication title: Airport Operator. Advertisements.

00498

Airship Association

P.O. Box 715, Folkestone, CT20 9ER, UK
Email: secretary@airship-association.org
Members: 500
Fee: £25
Membership Type: individual in UK
Fee: £15
Membership Type: student, senior citizen
Description: Aeronautical engineers, aircraft and flight professionals, and individuals interested in the development of airships. Provides a forum for the exchange of information among those who believe that there is a future for the use of modern airships as surveillance and coastal patrol craft, freight and passenger transports, ferries, and film and television platforms. Maintains contacts with organizations and individuals who study, build, or promote airships.
Publication: Booklet
Publication title: Airships Today
Meetings/Conventions: International Airship Convention – biennial convention – Exhibits.

Airts Cooncil o Norlin Airlann

see Arts Council of Northern Ireland

00499

Al-Anon Family Groups - United Kingdom and Eire

61 Great Dover St., London, SE1 4YF, UK
Tel: 020 74030888
Fax: 020 73789910
Email: enquiries@al-anonuk.org.uk
Website: http://www.al-anonuk.org.uk
Description: Offers understanding and support for families and friends of problem drinkers, whether alcoholic is still drinking or not.
Publication: Brochure
Publication title: Al-Anon - A Community Resource

00500

Alcohol Concern AC

64 Leman St., London, E1 8EU, UK
Tel: 020 72640510
Fax: 020 74889213
Email: contact@alcoholconcern.org.uk
Website: http://www.alcoholconcern.org.uk
Members: 250
Staff: 24

Contact: Don Shenker, Chief Exec.
Fee: £25
Membership Type: student, unwaged
Fee: £65
Membership Type: individual
Description: Acts as the national umbrella body for 500 local agencies tackling alcohol-related harm. Offers help to the families and friends of those with alcohol problems. Promotes the development of a national alcohol policy. Increases of alcohol issues.
Publication: Paper
Publication title: Factsheets

00501
Alcohol Focus Scotland
AFS
166 Buchanan St., 2nd Fl., Glasgow, G1 2LW, UK
Tel: 0141 5726700
Fax: 0141 3331606
Email: enquiries@alcohol-focus-scotland.org.uk
Website: http://www.alcohol-focus-scotland.org.uk
Staff: 20
Contact: Peter Brunt, Chm.
Fee: £25
Membership Type: individual
Fee: £60
Membership Type: organization
Description: Improves the quality of people's lives by changing Scotland's drinking culture. Promotes responsible drinking behaviour and discourages drinking to excess.
Formerly: Formerly, Scottish Council on Alcohol
Publication: Newsletter
Publication title: Alcohol Update

00502
Alcoholics Anonymous - England
AA
PO Box 1, Stonebow House, Stonebow, York, YO1 7NJ, UK
Tel: 01904 644026
Email: help@alcoholics-anonymous.org.uk
Website: http://www.alcoholics-anonymous.org.uk
Members: 2000000
Contact: Ann N., Contact
Description: Individuals recovering from alcoholism in the United Kingdom and the Republic of Ireland. Members believe that they can free themselves from alcohol abuse by following a 12-step program that includes sharing of experiences, strength, and hope with fellow members. Refuses alliance with any sect, denomination, political organization, or institution and does not endorse or oppose any cause.
Formerly: Formerly, Alcoholics Anonymous World Services - United Kingdom and Eire General Services Office

00503
Alexander Thomson Society
7 Walmer Crescent, Glasgow, G51 1AT, UK
Email: info@greekthomson.org.uk
Website: http://www.greekthomson.org.uk
Members: 400
Contact: Sally White, Sec.
Fee: £20
Membership Type: individual
Fee: £30
Membership Type: joint
Description: Promotes and protects the work of the architect Alexander Thomson.
Publication: Video
Publication title: Nineveh on the Cycle

00504
Alkan Society
AS
c/o Nicholas King, Sec.
42 St. Alban's Hill, Hemel Hempstead, HP3 9NG, UK
Email: info@alkansociety.org
Website: http://www.alkansociety.org
Members: 180
Staff: 6
Contact: Eliot Levin, Chm.
Fee: £10
Membership Type: regular
Description: Individuals dedicated to the advancement of public knowledge, understanding, and appreciation of the life and works of Charles Valentin Alkan (1813-88), French composer and pianist. Organizes concerts and lectures.
Publication: Bibliography

00505
Alliance Against IP Theft
c/o BPI
Riverside Bldg., County Hall, Westminster Bridge Rd., London, SE1 7JA, UK
Tel: 020 78031324
Fax: 020 78031310
Email: info@allianceagainstiptheft.co.uk
Website: http://www.allianceagainstiptheft.co.uk
Members: 500
Contact: Lavina Carey, Chair
Description: Provides a single voice for people who share an interest in preventing intellectual property theft in the UK. Protects the rights of businessmen and consumers against counterfeiting and piracy.
Formerly: Formerly, Alliance Against Counterfeiting and Piracy

00506
Alliance for Beverage Cartons and the Environment - United Kingdom
ACE
c/o Tetra Pak UK Ltd.
Bedwell Rd., Cross Lanes, Wrexham, LL13 0UT, UK
Tel: 0870 4426000
Email: enquiries@ace-uk.co.uk
Website: http://www.ace-uk.co.uk
Members: 3
Contact: Richard Hands, Chm.
Description: Major manufacturers of liquid food cartons in the UK. Lobbies both UK and European governments on issues relevant to the beverage carton industry to avoid legislative discrimination. Promotes the environmental and other benefits of the beverage carton and acts as an information service.
Formerly: Also Known As, Liquid Food Carton Manufacturers Association

00507
Alliance of International Market Research Institutes
AIMRI
26 Granard Ave., London, SW15 6HJ, UK
Tel: 020 87803343
Fax: 020 82466893
Email: rtchilton@aol.com
Website: http://www.aimri.net
Members: 103
Staff: 2
Contact: Richard T. Chilton, Sec.
Fee: £550-815
Membership Type: full (based on annual turnover)
Fee: £315
Membership Type: consultant
Description: Professional international market research agencies. Represents corporate interests of members. Offers conferences and training courses.
Formerly: Formerly, Association of European Market Research Institutes
Publication: Newsletter
Publication title: Synergie Plus

00508
Alliance of Literary Societies
ALS
22 Beeches Rd., Kidderminster, DY11 5HF, UK
Tel: 01562 748996
Email: johnshorland@aol.com
Website: http://www.allianceofliterarysocieties.org.uk
Members: 125
Contact: Julie Shorland, Membership Sec.
Membership Type: society/group
Description: Open to Literary Societies only. Strives to initiate or support action aimed at preserving literary heritage. Acts as a liaison body between member societies. Maintains an up-to-date directory of Literary Societies. Supports action aimed at preserving buildings, places, etc. with literary connections.

00509
Alliance of Registered Homeopaths
ARH
Millbrook, Millbrook Hill, Nutley, TN22 3PJ, UK
Tel: 01825 714506
Fax: 01825 714506
Email: info@a-r-h.org
Website: http://www.a-r-h.org
Contact: Karin Mont, Chair
Fee: £295
Membership Type: registered homeopath
Fee: £75
Membership Type: new graduate
Description: Advocates for safe and effective homeopathic practice. Increases public awareness regarding homeopathic treatment.
Publication: Journal
Publication title: Homeopathy in Practice. Advertisements.

00510
Alliance of Religions and Conservation
ARC
The House, Kelston Park, Bath, BA1 9AE, UK
Tel: 01225 758004
Fax: 01225 442962
Email: info@arcworld.org
Website: http://www.arcworld.org
Contact: Martin Palmer, Dir.
Description: Individuals and organizations. Promotes the development and implementation of practical educational projects designed to further the involvement of religions in environmental protection. Produces materials exploring the links between religion and environmental protection.
Publication: Newsletter
Publication title: Faith in Conservation

00511

Alliance Party of Northern Ireland APNI

88 University St., Belfast, BT7 1HE, UK
Tel: 028 90324274
Fax: 028 90333147
Email: alliance@allianceparty.org
Website: http://www.allianceparty.org
Members: 3000
Staff: 6
Contact: Gerry Lynch, Exec. Dir.
Fee: £43.5
Membership Type: regular
Fee: £75
Membership Type: joint
Description: Cross-community party in Northern Ireland dedicated to a non-sectarian society.
Publication: Newsletter
Publication title: Alliance News

00512

Almshouse Association

Billingbear Lodge, Maidenhead Rd., Berkshire, Wokingham, RG40 5RU, UK
Tel: 01344 452922
Fax: 01344 862062
Email: naa@almshouses.org
Website: http://www.almshouses.info
Members: 1900
Staff: 9
Fee: £20
Membership Type: bronze level friend
Fee: £50
Membership Type: silver level friend
Description: Members are almshouse foundations, which provide accommodation for the elderly. Advises members on any matters, concerning almshouses and the welfare of the elderly; promotes improvements in almshouses; promotes study and research into all matters affecting almshouses; makes grants or loans to members.

00513

Alstrom Syndrome International - United Kingdom AS UK

49 Southfield Ave., Devon, Paignton, TQ3 1LH, UK
Tel: 01803 524238
Email: info@alstrom.org.uk
Website: http://www.alstrom.org.uk
Members: 50
Contact: Kay Parkinson, Chief Exec.
Description: Provides support to those affected by Alstrom Syndrome and their families, friends, and professionals worldwide.
Meetings/Conventions: International Family Conference – triennial conference

00514

Alternative Investment Management Association AIMA

167 Fleet St., 2nd Fl., London, EC4A 2EA, UK
Tel: 020 78228380
Fax: 020 78228381
Email: info@aima.org
Website: http://www.aima.org
Members: 1200
Contact: Andrew Baker, CEO
Description: Represents alternative investment fund managers, service providers, institutional investors, and regulators. Aims to increase investor education, work with regulators and other interested parties in order to promote and control the use of alternative investments.
Formerly: Formerly, European Managed Futures Association
Publication: Journal
Publication title: AIMA Journal. Advertisements.

00515

Aluminium Extruders Association AEA

c/o Aluminium Federation
47 Birmingham Rd., West Bromwich, B70 6PY, UK
Tel: 0121 6016363
Fax: 0870 1389714
Email: alfed@alfed.org.uk
Website: http://www.alfed.org.uk/page.asp?node=1&dec=Home
Members: 8
Contact: Will Savage, CEO
Description: Represents members' interests.

00516

Aluminium Federation ALFED

National Metalforming Centre, 47 Birmingham Rd., West Midlands, West Bromwich, B70 6PY, UK
Tel: 0121 6016363
Fax: 0870 1389714
Email: alfed@alfed.org.uk
Website: http://www.alfed.org.uk/page.asp?node=1&dec=Home
Members: 220
Staff: 6
Contact: Will Savage, Chief Exec.
Description: Member companies represent most sectors of the UK aluminium industry, which has a total workforce of over 30,000. Provides a wide range of services, helping members to improve productivity, operate safe working practices in an environmentally acceptable way. Assists in the search for new markets and increased usage of aluminium. Represents the interests of the industry with the UK government, EC and the European Parliament.
Library Subject: information club
Library Type: not open to the public
Publication: Annual Report

00517

Aluminium Packaging Recycling Organization ALUPRO

1 Brockhill Ct., Brockhill Ln., Redditch, B97 6RB, UK
Tel: 01527 597757
Fax: 01527 594140
Email: info@alupro.org.uk
Website: http://www.alupro.org.uk
Members: 350
Staff: 7
Description: Recycling centres across the UK which buy aluminium cans from the general public. Promotes the aluminium can package and, mainly, its recyclability. Supports collectors and has a register of over 350 Recycling centres who buy aluminium cans from the public. Aiming for a 50% recycling rate for aluminium cans by the year 2000.
Publication: Brochure
Publication title: Schools Information Pack

00518

Alzheimer Scotland-Action on Dementia ASAD

22 Drumsheugh Gardens, Edinburgh, EH3 7RN, UK
Tel: 0131 2431453
Fax: 0131 2431450
Email: alzheimer@alzscot.org
Website: http://www.alzscot.org
Members: 2100
Staff: 600
Contact: Henry Simmons, Chief Exec.
Fee: £20
Membership Type: individual (ordinary)
Fee: £25
Membership Type: group
Description: Works to help individuals with dementia and their carers in Scotland.
Publication: Newsletter
Publication title: Dementia in Scotland

00519

Alzheimer's Disease International ADI

64 Great Suffolk St., London, SE1 0BL, UK
Tel: 020 79810880
Fax: 020 79282357
Email: info@alz.co.uk
Website: http://www.alz.co.uk
Staff: 4
Contact: Marc Wortmann, Exec. Dir.
Description: Aims to help establish and strengthen Alzheimer associations worldwide. Raises global awareness of Alzheimer's disease and other causes of dementia.
Publication: Newsletter
Publication title: Global Perspective

00520

Alzheimer's Society AS

Devon House, 58 St. Katherine's way, London, E1W 1LB, UK
Tel: 020 74233500
Fax: 020 74233501
Email: enquiries@alzheimers.org.uk
Website: http://www.alzheimers.org.uk
Members: 25000
Staff: 1500
Contact: Ruth Sutherland, Interim Chief Exec.
Description: Provides care and research charity for people with Alzheimer's disease and other forms of dementia, their families and carers.
Library Subject: health and social care relating to Alzheimer's disease and other dementias
Library Type: not open to the public
Formerly: Formerly, Alzheimer's Disease Society

00521

Amateur Entomologists' Society
AES

PO Box 8774, London, SW7 5ZG, UK
Website: http://www.amentsoc.org
Members: 1500
Contact: Dafydd Lewis, Sec.
Fee: £20
Membership Type: ordinary
Fee: £12
Membership Type: junior
Description: Works to promote and disseminate entomological knowledge; promotes interest in entomology to youth.
Publication: Magazine
Publication title: AES Bug Club Magazine. Advertisements.
Meetings/Conventions: Northern Exhibition – annual trade show – Exhibits.

00522

American Academy of Optometry - British Chapter
ACABC

2 Doric Pl., Woodbridge, IP12 1BT, UK
Tel: 01394 380139
Fax: 0796 7446413
Email: academy@debenlogic.net
Website: http://www.academy.org.uk
Members: 125
Contact: Andrew Field, Sec.
Fee: £260
Membership Type: regular
Description: Optometrists. Seeks to advance the study, teaching, and practice of optometry. Maintains standards of training, ethics, and practice for members; conducts continuing professional development courses for optometrists.
Meetings/Conventions: Clinical Conference – biennial conference

00523

American Civil War Round Table - United Kingdom
ACWRT-UK

34 Linden Rd., London, N10 3DH, UK
Email: tonybrown@americancivilwar.org.uk
Website: http://www.americancivilwar.org.uk
Members: 200
Contact: Tony Brown, Treas.
Fee: £25
Membership Type: in United Kingdom
Fee: £50
Membership Type: international
Description: Promotes study of the American Civil War (1861-65). Conducts research on purchasing and naval activities in Great Britain and Europe as well as on the post-war careers of Americans remaining in Great Britain.
Publication: Newsletter
Publication title: Crossfire. Advertisements.

00524

American Peanut Council - European Office

Grosvenor Gardens House, 35-37 Grosvenor Gardens, London, SW1W 0BS, UK
Tel: 020 78280838
Fax: 020 78280839
Email: lmckerchar@peanutsusa.org.uk
Website: http://www.peanuts.org.uk
Contact: Louise McKerchar, VP/European Marketing Dir.
Description: Aims for market development and dissemination of information about the peanut industry. Supports research for improvement of the quality of U.S. peanuts.

00525

American Women of Berkshire and Surrey
AWBS

PO Box 10, Virginia Water, GU25 4YP, UK
Email: president@awbs.org.uk
Website: http://www.awbs.org.uk
Members: 700
Contact: Norma Ascroft, Pres.
Fee: £50
Membership Type: regular
Fee: £35
Membership Type: senior (60 years old and over)
Description: Serves as a support network and umbrella organization for members of American women's groups residing in the Berkshire/Surrey area. Promotes friendship and interaction among members and the furtherance of knowledge and understanding of England.
Publication: Magazine
Publication title: Common Ground. Advertisements.

00526

American Women of Surrey
AWS

PO Box 170, Surrey, Cobham, KT11 2YJ, UK
Website: http://www.awsurrey.org
Members: 500
Contact: Kelly Thomas, Webmaster
Fee: £55
Membership Type: single
Fee: £35
Membership Type: senior
Description: Promotes friendship and cooperation among members. Works to further members' knowledge and understanding of England. Provides financial and material support to philanthropic projects.
Publication: Newsletter
Publication title: Roundabout Surrey

00527

American Women's Club of Central Scotland
AWCCS

PO Box 231, 44-46 Morningside Rd., Edinburgh, EH10 4BF, UK
Email: getinfo@awccs.org
Website: http://www.awccs.org
Members: 114
Fee: £30
Membership Type: active, associate
Fee: £24
Membership Type: full-time student, spouse, senior
Description: Promotes intellectual, social and charitable contacts by and for Americans and their families living in Central Scotland.

00528

American Women's Club of London
AWC

68 Old Brompton Rd., London, SW7 3LQ, UK
Tel: 020 75898292
Fax: 020 78239006
Email: awc@awclondon.org
Website: http://www.awclondon.org
Fee: £60
Membership Type: individual (plus processing fee)
Description: Provides social, cultural, educational, and philanthropic activities for expatriates living in London.

00529

Amnesty International - International Secretariat

1 Easton St., Peter Benson House, London, WC1X 0DW, UK
Tel: 020 74135500
Fax: 020 79561157
Email: amnestyis@amnesty.org
Website: http://www.amnesty.org
Members: 2200000
Staff: 430
Contact: Irene Khan, Sec. Gen.
Description: Promotes human rights. Works for the release of nonviolent "prisoners of conscience".

00530

Amnesty International - United Kingdom
AIUK

The Human Rights Action Ctre., 17-25 New Inn Yard, London, EC2A 3EA, UK
Tel: 020 70331500
Fax: 020 70331503
Email: sct@amnesty.org.uk
Website: http://www.amnesty.org.uk
Staff: 320
Contact: Irene Khan, Sec. Gen.
Fee: £7.5
Membership Type: student
Fee: £5
Membership Type: youth (14-18 of age)
Description: Serves as a human rights movement working to secure the immediate and unconditional release of all prisoners of conscience (individuals who have not used or advocated violence and have been imprisoned due to their beliefs, color, sex, religion, ethnic origin, or language); urges immediate, fair trials of political prisoners. Seeks an end to torture, executions and "disappearances", abuses by opposition groups, hostage taking, arbitrary killing, and other inhuman, cruel, or degrading treatment or punishment. Conducts research and organizes worldwide action by local members on behalf of prisoners held in countries other than their own; initiates national and international campaigns to publicize patterns of human rights abuses; sends delegates to observe trials and visit countries to interview prisoners and meet with government officials.
Formerly: Formerly, Amnesty International - England
Publication: Report
Publication title: Amnesty International Report

00531
Amnesty International - United Kingdom Scottish Office
Rosebery House, 9 Haymarket Terr., Edinburgh, EH12 5EZ, UK
Tel: 0844 8009088
Fax: 0131 3137000
Email: scotland@amnesty.org.uk
Website: http://www.amnesty.org.uk/scotland
Members: 15000
Staff: 3
Description: National branch of Amnesty International. Works to promote and defend human rights.

Amnistia Internacional
see Amnesty International - United Kingdom

00532
Anaesthetic Research Society
ARS
University Division of Anesthesia and Intensive Care, Queen's Medical Centre, Nottingham, NG7 2UH, UK
Tel: 0115 8231002
Fax: 0115 9700739
Email: j.hardman@nottingham.ac.uk
Website: http://www.ars.ac.uk
Members: 700
Staff: 11
Contact: Jonathan G. Hardman, Honorary Sec.
Fee: £30
Membership Type: regular
Description: Facilitates the presentation of members' research in anesthesiology (clinical or experimental, completed or in progress).
Publication: Journal
Publication title: Proceedings. Advertisements.
Meetings/Conventions: meeting

00533
Anatomical Society of Great Britain and Ireland
ASGBI
c/o Ms. Mary-Anne Piggott, BSc, Exec. Admin.
Dept. of Anatomy, King's College, London, SE1 1UL, UK
Tel: 020 78488234
Fax: 020 78488234
Email: maryanne.piggott@kcl.ac.uk
Website: http://www.anatsoc.org.uk
Members: 650
Contact: Susan Standring, Pres.
Fee: £35
Membership Type: ordinary
Fee: £65
Membership Type: with journal
Description: Individuals involved in anatomical science. Promotes development and advancement in anatomy and related science through research and education. Offers program for graduate students.
Publication: Journal
Publication title: Journal of Anatomy

00534
Ancient Egypt and Middle East Society
AEMES
2 Seathorne Crescent, Skegness, PE25 1RP, UK
Tel: 01754 765341
Fax: 01754 765341
Email: khepera@tamador.freeserve.co.uk
Website: http://www.aemes.co.uk
Members: 95
Contact: Sue Kirk, Sec.
Fee: £15.5
Membership Type: individual
Fee: £21.5
Membership Type: family
Description: Promotes and encourages interest in the history, archaeology, and cultures of the ancient civilizations of the Middle East.
Publication: Journal
Publication title: AEMES Journal

00535
Ancient Monuments Society
AMS
St. Ann's Vestry Hall, 2 Church Entry, London, EC4V 5HB, UK
Tel: 020 72363934
Email: office@ancientmonumentssociety.org.uk
Website: http://www.ancientmonumentssociety.org.uk
Members: 2000
Staff: 3
Contact: Matthew Saunders, Sec.
Fee: £24
Membership Type: individual or institutional
Fee: £16
Membership Type: senior citizen/junior/student
Description: Individuals and institutions united for the study and conservation of ancient monuments and historic buildings of all types and ages. Forms a working partnership with the Friends of Friendless Churches, which owns 38 architecturally important but redundant places of worship.
Publication title: Transactions of the Ancient Monuments Society

00536
Anderson Association
Three Pears Rd., Guildford, Surrey, Merrow, UK
Tel: 01483 570475
Email: iaa@anderson-assoc.org
Website: http://www.anderson-assoc.org
Contact: Ian A. Anderson, Sec.-Treas.
Description: Promotes humanitarian activities in Rwanda. Improves the health, education and moral leadership development of Rwandese people. Provides health and medical services and ensures that the community has access to doctors and medical facilities.

00537
Anglican Pacifist Fellowship
APF
11 Weavers End, Hanslope, Milton Keynes, MK19 7PA, UK
Email: ajkempster@aol.com
Website: http://www.anglicanpeacemaker.org.uk
Members: 1400
Contact: Tony Kempster, Honorary Sec.
Description: Communicant members, from 27 countries, of the Church of England, or of a church in full communion with it, who believe their membership in the Christian Church involves the complete repudiation of modern war and preparation for it. Promotes Christianity, especially through the study and application of Christian gospel in its relation to war and allied social issues. Works towards the establishment of peace in the world. Propagates the belief that pacifism is inherent in Christianity. Provides members, in times of war and peace, with opportunities to apply the Christian faith by relieving human suffering. Organizes lecture schools.
Publication: Newsletter
Publication title: The Anglican Peacemaker. Advertisements.

00538
Anglo Chilean Society
ACS
12 Devonshire St., London, W1N 2DS, UK
Tel: 020 75801271
Fax: 020 75805901
Email: info@anglochileansociety.org
Website: http://www.anglochileansociety.org
Members: 350
Staff: 1
Contact: Richard Wilkinson, Chm.
Fee: £15
Membership Type: single
Fee: £20
Membership Type: couple
Description: Individuals (350) and corporations (12). Seeks to foster friendly relations between England and Chile and disseminate information in England about Chile and its culture. Organizes art exhibitions, and film shows. Sends prizes to Chilean schools; conducts essay competitions. Provides information on Chile to individuals and institutions.
Publication: Newsletter
Publication title: Chilean News

00539
Anglo Danish Society
43 Maresfield Ave., London, NW3 5TF, UK
Tel: 020 77948781
Email: info@anglo-danishsociety.org.uk
Website: http://www.anglo-danishsociety.org.uk
Members: 320
Staff: 1
Fee: £20
Membership Type: family
Fee: £15
Membership Type: individual
Description: Promotes closer understanding between the United Kingdom and Denmark.

00540
Anglo-Austrian Music Society
c/o Richard Tauber Prize Committee
158 Rosendale Rd., London, SE21 8LG, UK
Tel: 020 87610444
Fax: 020 87666151
Email: info@aams.org.uk
Website: http://www.aams.org.uk/index.htm
Contact: Walter J. Foster, Sec. Gen.
Description: Promotes the value of Austrian music in Britain. Composes a small group of Austrian refugee musicians and few English people. Involves British musicians and British music.

00541
Anglo-European College of Chiropractic
AECC
13-15 Parkwood Rd., Bournemouth, BH5 2DF, UK
Tel: 01202 436200
Fax: 01202 436312
Email: aecc@aecc.ac.uk
Website: http://www.aecc.ac.uk
Members: 25
Staff: 100
Contact: Kenneth Vall, Principal
Description: Chiropractic practitioners, educators, and students. Seeks to advance the study, teaching, and practice of chiropractic. Facilitates communication among members; sponsors research and educational programs.

00542
Anglo-German Foundation for the Study of Industrial Society
AGF
34 Belgrave Sq., London, SW1X 8DZ, UK
Tel: 020 78231123
Fax: 020 78232324
Email: info@agf.org.uk
Website: http://www.agf.org.uk
Staff: 4
Contact: Ray Cunningham, Dir.
Description: Government agencies of Great Britain and Germany. Promotes comparative research in the fields of industrial, economic, and social policy in the United Kingdom and Germany. Provides financial and other support to bilateral research programs; cultivates better understanding and closer relations between the two countries; works to establish practical and durable links between industry, academics, government, and the media in Great Britain and Germany.

00543
Animal Care College
Index House, Berkshire, Ascot, SL5 7ET, UK
Tel: 01344 636436
Fax: 01344 622771
Email: info@animalcarecollege.co.uk
Website: http://www.animalcarecollege.co.uk
Contact: David Cavill, Principal
Fee: £25
Membership Type: associate
Description: Open to all those who have gained certification in recognized courses. Aims to improve the quality of standards of animal care.

00544
Animal Health Distributors Association
AHDA
Belmesthorpe Grange, Newstead Ln., Stamford, PE9 4JJ, UK
Tel: 01780 767757
Fax: 01780 767221
Email: ian@ahda.co.uk
Website: http://www.ahda.co.uk
Members: 150
Staff: 2
Contact: Ian Scott, Sec. Gen.
Description: Agricultural Merchants who are registered and qualified to distribute animal medicines to farmers and horse owners together with several wholesalers of such products. Aims to prevent the EC legislating members from going out of business and to ensure an appropriate number of animal medicines which are classified for distribution by registered distributors.

00545
Animal Health Information Specialists
AHIS
Royal Veterinary College Library, Hawkshead Ln., North Mymms, Herts, Hatfield, AL9 7TA, UK
Tel: 01707 6666535
Email: ekeith@rvc.ac.uk
Website: http://www.ahis.org
Contact: Elspeth Keith, Hon. Sec.
Fee: £25
Membership Type: regular
Description: Fosters cooperation and exchange among individuals interested in animal health information.

00546
Animal Health Trust
AHT
Lanwades Park, Kentford, Suffolk, Newmarket, CB8 7UU, UK
Tel: 01638 751000
Fax: 01638 750410
Email: info@aht.org.uk
Website: http://www.aht.org.uk
Staff: 220
Contact: Farrah Stevens, Contact
Description: Aims to push back the frontiers of veterinary science. Develops new technology and knowledge for the better diagnosis, prevention and cure of diseases. Provides a referral service for veterinary surgeons in practice.
Library Subject: veterinarian
Library Type: by appointment only
Publication: Newsletter
Publication title: AHT News

00547
Animal Mission
Highlands, Brighton Rd., Lr Kingswood, Tadworth, Surrey, KT20 6XL, UK
Tel: 01737 243472
Website: http://www.animalmission.org.uk
Description: Committed to assisting families whose changing circumstances cause them to part with a loved pet, these pets are cared for in a rural, family environment until suitable permanent homes can be found. No accepted animal is destroyed.

00548
Animal Samaritans
AS
PO Box 154, Bexleyheath, DA16 2WS, UK
Tel: 020 83031859
Email: info@animalsamaritans.org.uk
Website: http://www.animalsamaritans.org.uk
Members: 1000
Contact: Chris Bishop, Chm.
Fee: £8
Membership Type: adult
Fee: £5
Membership Type: child, senior citizen, concession
Description: Provides re-homing of unwanted and ill-treated animals in the south-east London and north-west Kent areas; offers a pet bereavement scheme.
Publication: Newsletter
Publication title: AS News

00549
Animals in Distress Sanctuary
55 Silver St., Manchester, M44 6HT, UK
Tel: 0161 7752221
Email: irlam@animals-in-distress.net
Website: http://www.animals-in-distress.net
Contact: Sylvia Durham, Founder/Chair
Membership Type: adult
Fee: £60-120
Membership Type: life
Description: Provides the strays, abandoned, neglected, injured, sick or old animals and unwanted pets in the northwest of England, a better quality of life through a new home or long-term shelter at the Field of Dreams retirement home.

00550
Animals in Mind
AIM
31 Magdalen Way, North Somerset, Worle, BS22 7PG, UK
Tel: 01934 516714
Email: info@animalsinmind.org.uk
Website: http://aim.aimcosoftware.co.uk
Contact: Alan Bach, Contact
Fee: £10
Membership Type: individual
Description: Committed to helping pet owners understand their pets better to avoid them having to be re-homed or destroyed due to behavior problems; promotes gentle methods of teaching for pets.
Publication: Booklet
Publication title: There Must be an Easier Way

00551
Anthropological Association of Ireland
AAI
c/o Sheila Fitzgerald, Treas.
National University of Ireland, 17 Rosses Quay, Rostrevor, BT34 3GL, UK
Email: jrollins02@qub.ac.uk
Website: http://www.anthropologyireland.org
Contact: Andrew Finlay, Chm.
Fee: £30
Membership Type: standard
Fee: £15
Membership Type: student
Description: Promotes the study of anthropology in Ireland.
Publication: Journal
Publication title: Irish Journal of Anthropology

00552
Anti Copying In Design
ACID
PO Box 5078, Gloucester, GL19 3YB, UK
Tel: 0845 6443617
Fax: 0845 6443618
Email: help@acid.uk.com
Website: http://acid.eu.com
Contact: Dids Macdonald, CEO
Fee: £125

Membership Type: student/recent graduate, associate
Fee: £225-1500
Membership Type: organization
Description: Combats the growing threats of plagiarism in the design and creative industries. Works to end intellectual property rights abuse. Provides education and shares knowledge of intellectual property rights. Helps understand and protect the rights of members.

00553
Anti-Counterfeiting Group
ACG
PO Box 578, High Wycombe, HP11 1YD, UK
Tel: 01494 449165
Fax: 01494 465052
Email: info@a-cg.com
Website: http://www.a-cg.org
Members: 200
Staff: 5
Contact: Ruth Orchard, Dir. Gen.
Fee: £2000
Membership Type: associate, Brand Protection Group
Fee: £2100
Membership Type: full
Description: Represents nearly 200 manufacturers and distributors of branded products, firms of intellectual property lawyers and agents, and providers of product security technology and services. Campaigns for improved resources for investigations of counterfeiting and the enforcement of anti-counterfeiting legislation; communicates the message about the damage counterfeiting does to the national economy, business generally and to the consumer. Serves as the hub of a national and international network of information, advice and contacts on anti-counterfeiting activity.

00554
Anti-Slavery International
Thomas Clarkson House, The Stableyard, Broomgrove Rd., London, SW9 9TL, UK
Tel: 020 75018920
Fax: 020 77384110
Email: info@antislavery.org
Website: http://www.antislavery.org/english/default.aspx
Members: 2000
Staff: 19
Contact: Aidan McQuade, Dir.
Fee: £35
Membership Type: waged
Fee: £11
Membership Type: unwaged
Description: Aims to eliminate all forms of slavery in the world today. Works to end slavery by exposing current cases of slavery and campaigning for their eradication. Supports the initiatives of local organizations to release people enslaved. Promotes more effective implementation of international laws against slavery and presses governments of countries where there is slavery to develop and implement measures to end it.
Formerly: Absorbed, Aborigines' Protection Society
Publication: Newsletter
Publication title: The Reporter

00555
Antiquarian Booksellers Association of the United Kingdom
ABA
Sackville House, 40 Piccadilly, London, W1J 0DR, UK
Tel: 020 74393118
Fax: 020 74393119
Email: admin@aba.org.uk
Website: http://www.abainternational.com
Members: 265
Contact: Julian Rota, Pres.
Fee: £436.96
Membership Type: domestic
Fee: £218.48
Membership Type: overseas
Description: Bookselling firms and dealers in rare books and manuscripts with a minimum of 5 years trading experience. Seeks to uphold the standards of antiquarian book trade. Serves as a liaison between potential book collectors and members; disseminates information and advice.
Library Type: by appointment only
Meetings/Conventions: Bath Book Fair – annual trade show

00556
Antiquarian Horological Society
AHS
New House, High St., Ticehurst, Sussex, TN5 7AL, UK
Tel: 01580 200155
Fax: 01580 201323
Email: secretary@ahsoc.demon.co.uk
Website: http://www.ahsoc.demon.co.uk
Staff: 2
Contact: Arnold Wolfendale, Pres.
Fee: £37
Membership Type: junior (under 25 years of age)
Fee: £65
Membership Type: ordinary
Description: Brings together those who share a common interest in antiquarian horology ranging from the earliest time pieces to 20th century mechanisms.
Publication: Journal
Publication title: Antiquarian Horology. Advertisements.

00557
Anxiety UK
AUK
Zion Community Resource Ctre., 339 Stretford Rd., Hulme, Manchester, M15 4ZY, UK
Tel: 08444 775774
Email: info@anxietyuk.org.uk
Website: http://www.anxietyuk.org.uk
Members: 6000
Staff: 3
Contact: Nicky Lidbetter, Chief Exec.
Fee: £20
Membership Type: individual
Description: Provides information, support, and advice to anyone affected by anxiety disorders, including panic attacks, OCD, BDD, agoraphobia, social phobia, and PTSD.
Formerly: Formerly, National Phobics Society
Publication: Newsletter
Publication title: Anxious times. Advertisements.

00558
Applied Vision Association
AVA
University of Bristol, Dept. of Experimental Psychology, 12 A Priory Rd., Bristol, BS8 1TU, UK
Tel: 0117 9288565
Fax: 0117 9288588
Email: tom.troscianko@bristol.ac.uk
Website: http://www.theava.net
Contact: Tom Troscianko, Sec.
Fee: £25
Membership Type: life (ordinary)
Fee: £15
Membership Type: life (retired)
Description: Works to advance, promote, develop and improve the study and knowledge of human vision including medical problems relating to vision.
Publication: Newsletter
Publication title: Bulletin of the Applied Vision Association. Advertisements.

00559
Appropriate Technology ASIA
ATA
80 Westbourne Rd., Cambridgeshire, Chatteris, PE16 6HQ, UK
Email: info@atasia.org.uk
Website: http://www.atasia.org.uk/web/index.aspx
Staff: 25
Description: Seeks to find marginal and threatened populations in environmentally challenging situations in Asia and help them to meet their basic needs for housing, household energy, safe water, food and good health. Seeking out the poorest and using participatory practice, ATA will apply technology and knowledge that is appropriate and environmentally sustainable while embedding skills in the communities with which it works.

00560
Approved Driving Instructors National Joint Council
ADINJC
16 Grosvenor Close, Staffordshire, Lichfield, WS14 9SR, UK
Tel: 01543 256578
Fax: 01747 855091
Email: lynne@lbsom.co.uk
Website: http://www.adinjc.org.uk
Members: 26
Staff: 2
Contact: Lynne Barrie, Gen. Sec.
Fee: £75
Membership Type: regular
Description: Represents the interests of National or local associations of driving instructors. Acts as united voice for members, dealing with government departments and acting as representatives on their behalf.

00561
APT Enterprise Development
29 Northwick Business Centre, Gloucestershire, Moreton-in-Marsh, GL56 9RF, UK
Tel: 01386 700130
Fax: 01386 701010
Email: info@aptenterprise.org.uk
Website: http://www.aptenterprise.org.uk
Staff: 5
Contact: Andy Jeans, Chief Exec.
Description: Dedicated to the elimination of poverty in developing countries and specializes in educating people to help themselves by providing skills training, technology transfer and support for the development of their own small enterprises. Maximizes benefit to those in need by formulating and implementing sustainable projects that address the real roots of the problems in the most appropriate way.

00562

Arab Horse Society
AHS

Windsor House, The Square, Ramsbury, Marlborough, SN8 2PE, UK
Tel: 01672 521411
Email: areeves@reevesfinancial.co.uk
Website: http://www.arabhorsesociety.com
Members: 3000
Staff: 7
Contact: Maggie Court, Office Mgr.
Fee: £49
Membership Type: single
Fee: £66
Membership Type: double
Description: Promotes the welfare of horses and ponies by organizing educational courses with topics on veterinary, judging and racing. Adopts a "Premium Scheme" to promote the use of Arab blood.
Publication: Journal
Publication title: Arab Horse Society Journal. Advertisements.

00563

Arab International Women's Forum
AIWF

4th Fl., 45 Albemarle St., London, W1S 4JL, UK
Tel: 0207 4097788
Fax: 0207 4097575
Email: info@aiwfonline.com
Website: http://www.aiwfonline.co.uk
Contact: Haifa Fahoum Al Kaylani, Founder/Chair
Fee: £50
Membership Type: individual
Fee: £100
Membership Type: association
Description: Promotes the role of women in the economy and society. Serves as a link between the Arab business and professional women and their counterparts in the international community.

00564

Arboricultural Association
AA

Ullenwood Ct., Cheltenham, GL53 9QS, UK
Tel: 01242 522152
Fax: 01242 577766
Email: admin@trees.org.uk
Website: http://www.trees.org.uk
Members: 2000
Staff: 23
Contact: Nick Eden, Dir.
Fee: £26
Membership Type: student
Fee: £108
Membership Type: associate
Description: Arboriculturists and conservationists; forestry experts; representatives of government departments; interested individuals. Promotes the study of arboriculture (the conservation, planting, and care of trees and woodlands). Works to conserve the forests and woodlands of the United Kingdom Great Britain particularly trees and woods grown for amenity. Strives to raise the standards of arboriculture, to advance knowledge of trees, and to foster community interest in conservation. Makes recommendations to government authorities on matters of arboricultural concern. Coordinates training programs; conducts examinations; stimulates research and development. Organizes lectures; conduct competitions.
Publication: Directory
Publication title: Arboricultural Consultants
Meetings/Conventions: National Arboriculture Conference – annual conference – Exhibits.

00565

Archaeology Abroad
AA

31-34 Gordon Sq., London, WC1H 0PY, UK
Tel: 020 85370849
Fax: 020 85370849
Email: arch.abroad@ucl.ac.uk
Website: http://www.britarch.ac.uk/archabroad
Members: 500
Staff: 4
Fee: £22
Membership Type: individual
Description: Provides lists of opportunities for archaeological fieldwork outside the UK.

00566

Archaeology Scotland

Stuart House, Ste. 1a, Eskmills, Station Rd., Musselburgh, EH21 7PB, UK
Tel: 0845 8723333
Fax: 0845 8723334
Email: info@archaeologyscotland.org.uk
Website: http://www.archaeologyscotland.org.uk
Members: 1000
Staff: 9
Contact: Eila MacQueen, Dir.
Fee: £28
Membership Type: individual
Fee: £45-110
Membership Type: society (based on number of members)
Description: Individuals and organizations including museums and public archeological and historic preservation associations. Promotes increased public awareness of Scottish archeological heritage and encourages identification and preservation of archeological sites. Lobbies for improved public policies governing the preservation of archeological and historic sites. Conducts research and educational programs and serves as liaison linking members and organizations pursuing similar goals. Maintains office at the Royal Museum in Edinburgh.
Formerly: Formerly, Council for Scottish Archaeology
Publication: Journal
Publication title: Discovery and Excavation in Scotland. Advertisements.
Meetings/Conventions: Archaeological Research in Progress – annual conference

00567

Architects Registration Board
ARB

8 Weymouth St., London, W1W 5BU, UK
Tel: 020 75805861
Fax: 020 74365269
Email: info@arb.org.uk
Website: http://www.arb.org.uk
Members: 33000
Staff: 15
Contact: Alison Carr, Chief Exec./Registrar
Description: Architects must have obtained recognized qualifications and have passed a professional practice exam. Maintains a register of architects. Concerned with the recognition of examinations qualifying for registration; discipline of the profession; the prosecution of persons unlawfully using the name, style or title 'architect'. Provides scholarships and maintenance grants for students and supports the furtherance of education and research in architecture.
Formerly: Formerly, Architects Registration Council of the UK
Publication: Directory
Publication title: Register of Architects

00568

Architectural and Specialist Door Manufacturers Association
ASDMA

Burnside House, 3 Coates Ln., High Wycombe, HP13 5EY, UK
Tel: 01494 447370
Fax: 01494 462094
Email: specialdoors@gmail.com
Website: http://www.asdma.com
Members: 29
Staff: 1
Contact: Lin Parry, Contact
Fee: £1000
Membership Type: full
Fee: £500
Membership Type: associate
Description: Specialist timber door manufacturers and businesses engaged in allied industries. Promotes the benefits of using independently tested and quality assured doors which meet necessary fire, safety and other performance criteria. Offers advice and information to end users.

00569

Architectural Association
AA

36 Bedford Sq., London, WC1B 3ES, UK
Tel: 020 78874000
Fax: 020 74140782
Email: membership@aaschool.ac.uk
Website: http://www.aaschool.ac.uk
Members: 3200
Contact: Brett Steele, Dir.
Fee: £120
Membership Type: professional
Description: Works to improve standards of architectural engineering and to assemble an architectural space to create a school of significant architectural diversity, and intelligence.

00570

Architectural Cladding Association
ACA

60 Charles St., 4th Fl., Leicestershire, Leicester, LE1 1FB, UK
Tel: 0116 2536161
Fax: 0116 2514568
Email: aca@britishprecast.org
Website: http://www.architectural-cladding-association.org.uk
Members: 4
Staff: 2
Contact: Stephen Maddalena, Chm.
Description: Represents manufacturers of precast concrete architectural cladding.
Publication: Book
Publication title: Cast in Concrete

00571

Architectural Heritage Society of Scotland
AHSS

The Glasite Meeting House, 33 Barony St., Edinburgh, EH3 6NX, UK
Tel: 0131 5570019
Fax: 0131 5550049
Email: nationaloffice@ahss.org.uk
Website: http://www.ahss.org.uk
Members: 1100
Staff: 2
Contact: Laura Gutierrez, Dir.
Fee: £14.5
Membership Type: student, unemployed
Fee: £30
Membership Type: single
Description: People interested in historical buildings, architects. Works with the study and protection of Scottish architecture.
Formerly: Formerly, Scottish Georgian Society
Publication: Journal
Publication title: Architectural Heritage

00572

Aristotelian Society
AS

Rm. 281, Stewart House, Russel Sq., London, WC1B 5DN, UK
Tel: 020 78628685
Fax: 020 78628685
Email: mail@aristoteliansociety.org.uk
Website: http://www.aristoteliansociety.org.uk
Members: 700
Staff: 2
Contact: Mark Cortes Favis, Exec. Admin.
Fee: £17.5
Membership Type: ordinary
Fee: £9
Membership Type: student
Description: Academics, students and amateur philosophers in English-speaking countries. Promotes the study of philosophy. Holds biweekly discussions.
Meetings/Conventions: Joint Session of the Aristotelian Society and the Mind Association – annual conference

00573

Arkleton Trust
AT

The Old Golf House, Rectory Rd., Berkshire, Streatley, RG8 9QA, UK
Tel: 01491 872147
Fax: 0870 2884783
Email: mail@arkletontrust.co.uk
Website: http://www.arkletontrust.co.uk
Staff: 5
Contact: Caroline Higgs, Chair
Description: Promotes creation and implementation of sustainable rural development projects. Serves as a clearinghouse on rural development; sponsors development and agricultural research. Serves as a liaison between development organizations and government agencies overseeing development. Conducts seminars for development personnel and administrators.

00574

ARLIS/UK and Ireland: Art Libraries Society of the United Kingdom and Ireland

The National Art Library, Victoria and Albert Museum, Cromwell Rd., South Kensington, London, SW7 2RL, UK
Tel: 020 79422317
Email: arlis@vam.ac.uk
Website: http://www.arlis.org.uk
Members: 700
Staff: 1
Contact: Pat Christie, Chair
Fee: £45
Membership Type: enhanced
Fee: £30
Membership Type: enhanced retired/student/unwaged
Description: Seeks for the development and promotion of the librarianship of the visual arts, including architecture and design. Works for the professional development of members to enable them to provide the best possible art library resources and services for educational and cultural development within the UK and Ireland.
Publication: Newsletter
Publication title: ARLIS/UK & Ireland News-sheet. Advertisements.
Meetings/Conventions: annual lecture

00575

Army Families Federation
AFF

Trenchard Lines, Upavon, Pewsey, SN9 6BE, UK
Tel: 01980 615525
Fax: 01980 615526
Email: us@aff.org.uk
Website: http://www.aff.org.uk
Staff: 70
Contact: Julie McCarthy, Chief Exec.
Description: Promotes communication, information, and liaison between the Army, its families and the policy makers, representing the views of the families and arguing for change where necessary.
Formerly: Formerly, Federation of Army Wives
Publication: Report
Publication title: Accompanied Service Survey 1997. Advertisements.

00576

Army Records Society
ARS

PO Box 21, Baldock, SG7 5SH, UK
Tel: 01462 896688
Fax: 01462 896677
Email: ars@hall-mccartney.co.uk
Website: http://www.armyrecordssociety.org.uk
Members: 525
Contact: Jim Beach, Honorary Sec.
Fee: £25
Membership Type: individual
Fee: £35
Membership Type: individual, institution (overseas/in British Isles)
Description: Individuals and organizations in the United Kingdom interested in British military history. Publishes official papers and correspondences of military figures and eyewitness accounts of battles and campaigns.
Publication: Book
Publication title: The Army and the Curragh Incident, 1914

00577

Aromatherapy Trade Council
ATC

PO Box 387, Ipswich, IP2 9AN, UK
Tel: 01473 603630
Fax: 01473 603630
Email: info@a-t-c.org.uk
Website: http://www.a-t-c.org.uk
Members: 54
Contact: Geoff Lyth, Chm.
Description: Serves as the UK trade association for the specialist aromatherapy essential oil trade. Establishes guidelines for safety, labeling and packaging for the aromatherapy trade and publishes Guidelines on Legislation for people setting up businesses. Promotes responsible use of aromatherapy products.

00578

Art Through Touch
ATT

c/o Pocklington Resource Centre
1c Yukon Rd., London, SW12 9PZ, UK
Tel: 020 86752666
Email: goto@art-through-touch.co.uk
Website: http://www.art-through-touch.org.uk
Fee: £10
Membership Type: ordinary
Description: Promotes access to art activity for people who are visually impaired. Organizes visits to museums and galleries. Conducts research in the area of educational practice in art and visual impairment.

00579

Artfoundation

c/o Transfrontiers
27 Old Gloucester St., London, WC1N 3XX, UK
Tel: 0709 2272402
Fax: 0709 2087367
Email: information@xtmt.com
Website: http://www.artfoundation.org.uk
Description: Promotes cross-cultural understanding through art; assists and promotes promising artists; provides art courses.

00580

Arthritis Care
AC

18 Stephenson Way, London, NW1 2HD, UK
Tel: 020 73806500
Email: info@arthritiscare.org.uk
Website: http://www.arthritiscare.org.uk/Home
Members: 70000
Staff: 350
Contact: Jane Asher, Pres.
Fee: £26
Membership Type: individual
Fee: £14
Membership Type: concessionary
Description: Individuals with arthritis and concerned others. Seeks to: increase awareness of the problems associated with rheumatic diseases; disseminate information; establish a nationwide network of branches; improve welfare facilities; provide information, advice and practical aid. Maintains hotels.
Library Subject: arthritis, daily living, equipment, disability issues
Library Type: not open to the public
Formerly: Formerly, British Rheumatism and Arthritis Association

Publication: Magazine
Publication title: Arthritis News. Advertisements.

00581
Arthritis Care - Central England
Carlton Business and Technology Ctre., Unit 7, Station Rd., Carlton, Nottingham, NG4 3AT, UK
Tel: 0115 9525522
Fax: 0115 9520336
Email: centralengland@arthritiscare.org.uk
Website: http://www.arthritiscare.org.uk/Home
Description: Aims to empower all people with arthritis by providing high quality information and support. Provides self-management training programs and campaigns for greater awareness of the needs of all people with arthritis.

00582
Arthritis Care - North England
Belle Vue Business Ctre., Ste. 1, Elm Tree St., Wakefield, WF1 5EP, UK
Tel: 01924 882150
Email: northengland@arthritiscare.org.uk
Website: http://www.arthritiscare.org.uk/Home
Contact: Gill Laidler, Volunteer Development Mgr.
Description: Promotes independence and empowers people with arthritis to live positive lives. Raises awareness of arthritis.

00583
Arthritis Care - Scotland
Unit 25A, Anniesland Business Park, Glasgow, G13 1EU, UK
Tel: 0141 9547776
Fax: 0141 9546171
Email: scotland@arthritiscare.org.uk
Website: http://www.arthritiscare.org.uk/InyourArea/Scotland/Contactus
Description: Promotes independence and empowers people with arthritis to live positive lives. Raises awareness of arthritis.

00584
Arthritis Care - South England
18 Stephenson Way, 1st Fl., London, NW1 2HD, UK
Tel: 020 73806509
Fax: 020 73806511
Email: southengland@arthritiscare.org.uk
Website: http://www.arthritiscare.org.uk/inyourarea/southengland
Contact: Pippa Nelson, Operations Mgr.
Fee: £20
Membership Type: full
Fee: £10
Membership Type: concession (below 25 years old)
Description: Promotes independence and empowers people with arthritis to live positive lives. Raises awareness of arthritis.
Publication: Magazine
Publication title: Arthritis News

00585
Arthritis Care - Southeast England
18 Stephenson Way, London, NW1 2HD, UK
Tel: 0207 3806500
Email: seregoffice@arthritiscare.org.uk
Website: http://www.arthritiscare.org.uk/Home
Description: Promotes independence and empowers people with arthritis to live positive lives. Raises awareness of arthritis.

00586
Arthritis Care - Wales
1 Caspian Point, Pierhead St., Cardiff Bay, Cardiff, CF10 4DQ, UK
Tel: 02920 444155
Email: wales@arthritiscare.org.uk
Website: http://www.arthritiscare.org.uk/inyourarea/wales
Contact: Lorraine Fletcher, Admin.
Description: Promotes independence and empowers people with arthritis to live positive lives. Raises awareness of arthritis.

00587
Arthritis Research Campaign
ARC
Copeman House, St. Mary's Ct., St. Mary's Gate, Chesterfield, S41 7TD, UK
Tel: 01246 558033
Fax: 01246 558007
Email: enquiries@arthritisresearchuk.org
Website: http://www.arc.org.uk
Members: 40000
Staff: 71
Contact: Charles Maisey, Chm.
Description: Raises funds to: promote medical research into the cause, treatment and cure of arthritis and related musculoskeletal conditions; educate medical students, doctors and allied health professional about arthritis; provide information to people affected by arthritis and to the general public. Has a wide-ranging research program involving people, projects and centers usually at university medical schools. Produces educational literature aimed at medical professionals and the general public.
Formerly: Formerly, Arthritis and Rheumatism Council for Research

00588
Article 19 - Global Campaign for Free Expression
A19
Free Word Ctre., 60 Farrington Rd., London, EC1R 3GA, UK
Tel: 020 73242500
Email: info@article19.org
Website: http://www.article19.org
Contact: Agnes Callamard, Exec. Dir.
Description: Named for Article 19 of the Universal Declaration of Human Rights, organization unites individuals in 32 countries to advocate the right to freedom to hold opinions without interference and to receive and disseminate information through any media. Works to eradicate censorship worldwide. Pressures governments for greater freedom of information and expression; encourages improved national and international standards to protect such freedoms. Maintains a network of contacts and correspondents for information exchange regarding censorship. Campaigns on behalf of censorship victims. Conducts research programs.
Publication: Annual Report
Publication title: ARTICLE 19

00589
Arts and Business
A&B
Nutmeg House, 60 Gainsford St., Butler's Wharf, London, SE1 2NY, UK
Tel: 020 73788143
Fax: 020 74077527
Email: contactus@artsandbusiness.org.uk
Website: http://artsandbusiness.org.uk
Members: 361
Staff: 70
Contact: Colin Tweedy, Chief Exec.
Fee: £700
Membership Type: business
Fee: £2000
Membership Type: business patron
Description: Promotes and encourages partnerships between the private sector and the arts, to their mutual benefit and to that of the community at large. Provides a wide range of services to its member organizations and businesses as well as to 700 arts professionals through the Arts and Business Development Forum. Aims to enable individual business people to share their skills with the arts, manages the Skills Bank and the Board Bank through its Arts at Work program. Manages, on behalf of the Arts Council England, which can make financial awards to new or established sponsors of the arts. Runs programs from London and through a network of offices nationwide.
Formerly: Formerly, Association for Business Sponsorship of the Arts

00590
Arts Centre Group
ACG
Menier Chocolate Factory, 1st Fl., 51 Southwark St., London, SE1 1RU, UK
Tel: 0845 4581881
Email: info@artscentregroup.org.uk
Website: http://www.artscentregroup.org.uk
Members: 600
Staff: 1
Contact: Susanne Scott, Chair
Fee: £50
Membership Type: professional, group
Fee: £25
Membership Type: student/concession
Description: Christians in 12 countries working professionally in the arts, the media, and entertainment. Promotes an understanding of the link between members' Christian identities and their artistic expression. Encourages Christian artists to develop their professional abilities and assists them in merging their faith and careers. Evangelizes other artists by encouraging them to express Christian ideals through their works. Organizes events ranging from debates, discussions and performance to an annual lecture, an annual poetry competition, prayer and bible studies and social events.
Publication: Newsletters
Publication title: E-info

00591
Arts Council of England
ACE
14 Great Peter St., London, SW1P 3NQ, UK
Tel: 0845 3006200
Fax: 020 79736564
Email: enquiries@artscouncil.org.uk
Website: http://www.artscouncil.org.uk
Contact: Alan Davey, Chief Exec.
Description: National strategic policy body for the arts in England. Works in partnership with the Regional Arts Board, which is responsible for funding and development of the arts in England.
Formerly: Formerly, Arts Council of Great Britain

00592

Arts Council of Northern Ireland

MacNeice House, 77 Malone Rd., Belfast, BT9 6AQ, UK
Tel: 028 90385200
Fax: 028 90661715
Email: info@artscouncil-ni.org
Website: http://www.artscouncil-ni.org
Contact: Roisin McDonough, Chief Exec.
Description: Supports the artists and art organizations in Northern Ireland, UK. Provides funding programs and grants for members.

00593

Arts Council of Wales
ACW

Bute Pl., Cardiff, CF10 5AL, UK
Tel: 0845 8734900
Fax: 029 20441400
Email: info@artswales.org.uk
Website: http://www.artswales.org
Members: 18
Staff: 80
Contact: Dai Smith, Chm.
Description: Promotes development and appreciation of the arts in Wales; works to make the arts more accessible to the public; makes recommendations to government and other bodies on issues affecting the arts. Provides financial and other assistance to arts programs.
Publication: Newsletter
Publication title: Crefft/Craft

00594

Arts Marketing Association
AMA

7A Clifton Ct., Clifton Rd., Cambridge, CB1 7BN, UK
Tel: 01223 578078
Fax: 01223 245862
Email: info@a-m-a.co.uk
Website: http://www.a-m-a.org.uk
Members: 1900
Staff: 10
Contact: Julie Aldridge, Exec. Dir.
Fee: £30.08
Membership Type: student, unwaged (including VAT)
Fee: £59-157
Membership Type: individual (based on amount of earnings)
Description: Represents professionals involved in the arts. Aims to support the professional development of its members through training, events and networking opportunities.
Publication: Journal
Publication title: JAM

Arts Sans Frontieres

see Artfoundation

00595

Asbestos Removal Contractors Association
ARCA

237 Branston Rd., Staffordshire, Burton-on-Trent, DE14 3BT, UK
Tel: 01283 531126
Fax: 01283 568228
Email: info@arca.org.uk
Website: http://www.arca.org.uk
Members: 160
Staff: 2
Contact: Steve Sadley, Chief Exec.
Description: Asbestos contracting managers and individuals in 9 countries. Monitors and recommends guidelines for asbestos handling and disposal. Disseminates information on protective clothing, respiratory equipment, and methods of decontamination. Offers residential and in-house training courses for line managers and supervisory staff.
Library Subject: asbestos removal
Library Type: not open to the public
Publication: Journal
Publication title: ARCA & ATAC Journal

Asociacion Internacional de Estudios en Comunicacion Social

see International Association for Media and Communication Research

Asociacion Mundial de las Guias Scouts (AMGS)

see World Association of Girl Guides and Girl Scouts

00596

Asparagus Growers Association
AGA

133 Eastgate, Lincolnshire, Louth, LN11 9QG, UK
Tel: 01507 602427
Email: jayne.dyas@pvga.co.uk
Website: http://www.british-asparagus.co.uk
Contact: Jayne Dyas, Sec.
Description: Membership Growers of asparagus. Purpose Provides help to UK asparagus growers both in growing and marketing.

00597

Asset Based Finance Association
ABFA

Boston House, The Little Green, Surrey, Richmond, TW9 1QE, UK
Tel: 0208 3329955
Fax: 0208 3322585
Email: kate.sharp@abfa.org.uk
Website: http://www.abfa.org.uk
Members: 43
Staff: 5
Contact: Kate Sharp, CEO
Description: Brokers, business agents, and factors in the United Kingdom. Promotes and protects members' interests in the fields of factoring and invoice discounting. Conducts educational and research programs. Maintains a code of conduct; fosters the advancement of knowledge and experience; awards diplomas to students. Disseminates information; compiles statistics.
Formerly: Formerly, Association of British Factors and Discounters
Publication: Newsletter
Publication title: Insight

00598

Associated Society of Locomotive Engineers and Firemen
ASLEF

9 Arkwright Rd., Hampstead, London, NW3 6AB, UK
Tel: 020 73178600
Fax: 020 77946406
Email: info@aslef.org.uk
Website: http://www.aslef.org.uk
Members: 18500
Contact: Keith Norman, Gen. Sec.
Fee: £9.32-24.39
Membership Type: individual (based on salaries)
Description: Train drivers or others on the footplate employed on UK railways, London Underground and Tyne; Wear Metro. Negotiates terms and conditions of employment; provides legal services and representation; political representation; pensions representation.
Publication: Journal
Publication title: Freight Journal

Association Cartographique Internationale

see International Cartographic Association

Association d'Experts Europeens du Batiment et de la Construction

see Association of European Building Surveyors and Construction Experts

Association de Droit International

see International Law Association

Association de Litterature et de Linguistique Computationnelles

see Association for Literary and Linguistic Computing

00599

Association des Chercheurs Iraniens
ACI

PO Box 7630, London, NW6 3ZB, UK
Tel: 020 73288415
Fax: 020 73281484
Email: london@aciiran.com
Website: http://www.aciiran.com
Contact: Hossein Ladjevardi, Pres.
Description: Works to identify the problems concerning the future of Iran and Iranians. Offers a framework for social, political, cultural, and economic planning for the future of Iran. Recognizes the rights of all Iranians to equality and self determination.

Association des Experts-Comptables Internationaux

see Association of International Accountants

Association des Juristes Franco-Britanniques
see Franco-British Lawyers Society

Association des Secretaires Generaux des Parlements
see Association of Secretaries General of Parliaments

Association europeene de societies de neurochirugie
see European Association of Neurosurgical Societies

Association Europeene des Galvanisateurs
see European General Galvanizers Association

Association Europeenne des Anthropologues Sociaux
see European Association of Social Anthropologists

Association Europeenne des Enseignants
see European Association of Teachers - UK Section

Association Europeenne des Etudes Juives
see European Association for Jewish Studies

Association Europeenne pour la Protection Passive contre l'Incendie
see European Association for Passive Fire Protection

00600

Association for Achievement and Improvement through Assessment
AAIA

2 Laneside Dr., Hinckley, LE10 1TG, UK
Email: current.membership@aaia.org.uk
Website: http://www.aaia.org.uk
Contact: Elizabeth Lewin, Membership Sec.
Fee: £75
Membership Type: full
Fee: £37.5
Membership Type: associate
Description: Promotes pupil achievement through the development of effective assessment practice. Works to further the educational practice and professional development of members. Develops a professional response to issues that may influence assessment, recording and reporting.

00601

Association for Astronomy Education
AAE

c/o Royal Astronomical Society
Burlington House, Piccadilly, London, W1J 0BQ, UK
Email: secretary@aae.org.uk
Website: http://www.aae.org.uk
Members: 240
Contact: Robert Massey, Pres.
Fee: £12
Membership Type: individual
Fee: £10
Membership Type: retired, senior citizen
Description: Teachers, lecturers, astronomy professionals and amateurs who have links with education via either formal tuition or local or commercial links e.g. planetaria. Aims to promote and support astronomy education at all levels and to provide a forum for discussion and curriculum development in astronomy education.

00602

Association for Careers Education and Guidance
ACEG

9 Lawrence Leys, Bloxham, Banbury, OX15 4NU, UK
Tel: 01295 720809
Fax: 01295 720809
Email: info@aceg.org.uk
Website: http://www.aceg.org.uk
Members: 2000
Contact: Alan Vincent, Gen. Sec.
Fee: £60
Membership Type: general
Description: Teachers or other individuals involved in careers and guidance work in education. Represents the views of members in regular meetings with various branches of Government and Government agencies and has continuing links with other professional careers associations in Europe.
Formerly: Formerly, National Association of Careers and Guidance Teachers
Publication: Journal
Publication title: Careers Education and Guidance

00603

Association for Catering Excellence
ACE

Bourne House, Horsell Park, Surrey, Woking, GU21 4LY, UK
Tel: 01483 765111
Fax: 01483 751991
Email: admin@acegb.org
Website: http://www.acegb.org
Contact: Sean Valentine, Chm.
Fee: £50
Membership Type: individual professional
Fee: £75
Membership Type: individual allied
Description: Represents managers, chefs, accountants, consultants, students, suppliers etc., from the wide domain of the Food Service Sector. Encourages caterers and associates from all sectors of the industry to network, exchange ideas, socialize and keep in touch.

00604

Association for Child and Adolescent Mental Health
ACAMH

c/o Ingrid King, Exec. Dir.
St. Saviour's House, 39-41 Union St., London, SE1 1SD, UK
Tel: 020 74037458
Fax: 020 74037081
Email: ingrid.king@acamh.org.uk
Website: http://www.acamh.org.uk
Contact: Eric Taylor, Chm.
Fee: £60
Membership Type: ordinary, in UK
Fee: £66
Membership Type: ordinary, in Eire and rest of Europe
Description: Professionals working in the field of child mental health. Encourages dissemination of scientific research and information. Aims to further scientific study of the mental health of children, young people and their families. Promotes best practice and provides training and opportunities for continuing professional development for everyone working with children.
Formerly: Formerly, Association for Child Psychology and Psychiatry
Publication: Newsletter
Publication title: The Bridge

00605

Association for Clinical Biochemistry
ACB

130-132 Tooley St., London, SE1 2TU, UK
Tel: 020 74038001
Fax: 020 74038006
Email: admin@acb.org.uk
Website: http://www.acb.org.uk
Members: 2300
Staff: 5
Contact: Julian Barth, Pres.
Fee: £120
Membership Type: ordinary-band 1
Fee: £158
Membership Type: ordinary-band 2
Description: University graduates in science or medicine occupied in the practice of clinical biochemistry, mainly in district, general and teaching hospitals. Associate members from related disciplines, such as cytogenetics, microbiology and immunology. Promotes the advancement of clinical biochemistry.
Publication: Handbook
Publication title: ACB Members Handbook. Advertisements.

00606

Association for Clinical Data Management
ACDM

105 St. Peter's St., Hertfordshire, St. Albans, AL1 3EJ, UK
Tel: 01727 896080
Fax: 01727 896026
Email: admin@acdm.org.uk

Website: http://www.acdm.org.uk
Members: 1095
Fee: £45
Membership Type: general
Description: Promotes the professional identity of Clinical Data Management. Advances and provides technical knowledge and education in Clinical Data Management.

00607

Association for Conferences and Events
ACE

Riverside House, High St., Cambridgeshire, Huntingdon, PE29 3SG, UK
Tel: 07827 472309
Website: http://www.aceinternational.org
Members: 500
Staff: 3
Contact: Michael Sharp, Chm.
Fee: £200
Membership Type: venue, supplier, corporate
Fee: £160
Membership Type: individual
Description: Corporate companies, charities and associations, hotels and venues, conference and event organisers, service suppliers, tourist bodies. Provides a forum for member organisations involved in all aspects of the meetings business. Services include: monthly newsletter, events calendar, job spot, discounts, magazine, information sheets, publications, help line. Activities include seminars, socials, study weekends, inspection visits, networking opportunities. Training programme includes courses on Meetings Planning and on First Aid at Events.
Library Subject: conferences, events, exhibitions, venues, surveys
Library Type: not open to the public
Formerly: Formerly, Association of Conference Executives
Publication: Newsletter
Publication title: ACE Newsletter. Advertisements.

00608

Association for Consultancy and Engineering
ACE

Alliance House, 12 Caxton St., London, SW1H 0QL, UK
Tel: 020 72226557
Fax: 020 79909202
Email: consult@acenet.co.uk
Website: http://www.acenet.co.uk
Members: 800
Contact: Nelson Ogunshakin, Chief Exec.
Description: National associations of independent consulting engineers. Promotes the interests of independent consulting engineers; represents electrical, civil, environmental, geotechnical, metallurgical, cultural, and other engineering fields. Standardizes forms of agreement, contracts, and guidelines for consulting engineers; acts as clearinghouse.
Publication: Directory

00609

Association for Continence Advice
ACA

c/o Fitwise Management Limited
Drumcross Hall, West Lothian, Bathgate, EH48 4JT, UK
Tel: 01506 811077
Fax: 01506 811477
Email: aca@fitwise.co.uk
Website: http://www.aca.uk.com
Members: 850
Staff: 2
Contact: Doreen McClurg, Chair
Fee: £45
Membership Type: full
Fee: £60
Membership Type: full (overseas)
Description: Professionals with an interest in the health and social care of people with continence problems. Aims to provide a means of communication and support between members and other interested groups; to promote educational activities; to produce and distribute a newsletter; to promote research activities and disseminate research findings; to liaise and maintain dialogue with relevant manufacturers; to promote public awareness and positive attitudes within society.
Publication: Journal
Publication title: Continence

00610

Association for Cultural Exchange, ACE Cultural Tours

Babraham, Cambridge, CB22 3AP, UK
Tel: 01223 835055
Fax: 01223 837394
Email: ace@aceculturaltours.co.uk
Website: http://www.acestudytours.co.uk
Staff: 20
Description: Promotes the study of different cultures and lifestyles through study tours and courses in art, architecture, and archaeology history. Offers about 150 educational programs every year, usually lasting from 1 to 3 weeks.
Formerly: Formerly, Association for Cultural Exchange, ACE Study Tours
Publication: Newsletter
Publication title: ACE Newsletter

00611

Association for Dance Movement Psychotherapy - United Kingdom
ADMPUK

32 Meadfoot Ln., Torquay, TQ1 2BW, UK
Email: admin@admt.org.uk
Website: http://www.admt.org.uk
Contact: Shirley Mawer, Chair
Fee: £35
Membership Type: associate
Fee: £40
Membership Type: student
Description: Individuals united to promote dance movement therapy. Monitors and promotes training. Offers professional services.
Publication: Newsletter
Publication title: E-Motion. Advertisements.

00612

Association for Environment Conscious Building
AECB

PO Box 32, Llandysul, SA44 5ZA, UK
Tel: 0845 4569773
Email: sally@aecb.net
Website: http://www.aecb.net
Members: 1300
Staff: 1
Contact: Chris Herring, Chm.
Fee: £50
Membership Type: individual
Fee: £100-250
Membership Type: company
Description: Building companies, developers, architects, local authorities, consultants, etc. Generates more environmental awareness with the building and construction industry and to encourage greener building.
Library Type: by appointment only
Publication: Magazine
Publication title: Building for a Future

00613

Association for Environmental Archaeology
AEA

Rm. 211, 8 Kirkby Pl. Drake Circus, Devon, Plymouth, PL4 8AA, UK
Tel: 01752 233129
Fax: 01752 233054
Email: membership@envarch.net
Website: http://www.envarch.net
Members: 400
Contact: Ralph Fyfe, Membership Sec.
Fee: £37
Membership Type: student, unwaged
Fee: £50
Membership Type: waged
Description: Seeks to understand past ecology, with emphasis on man's role, and past human economy and living conditions. Analyzes the remains of plants and animals, and the sediments in which they are buried. Interests include anthropology, palaeopathology, parasitology, zooarchaeology, palaeobotany, and the study of prehistoric economy.
Publication: Newsletter

00614

Association for European Transport
AET

1 Vernon Mews, Vernon St., West Kensington, London, W14 0RL, UK
Tel: 020 73481978
Fax: 020 73481989
Email: info@aetransport.org
Website: http://www.aetransport.org/lc_cms/page_view.asp?id=22
Members: 300
Staff: 1
Contact: Tom van Vuren, Chm.
Fee: £84
Membership Type: individual
Fee: £670-2120
Membership Type: organization
Description: Professionals working in the transportation industries; transportations firms; libraries and information centers. Seeks to advance the business and regulatory interests of the European transportation industries. Serves as a clearinghouse on transportation and transportation research. Facilitates communication and cooperation among members; organizes the annual European Transport Conference.

00615
Association for Financial Markets in Europe
AFME
St. Michael's House, 1 George Yard, London, EC3V 9DH, UK
Tel: 020 77439300
Fax: 020 77439301
Website: http://www.afme.eu
Members: 52
Staff: 20
Contact: Gael De Boissard, Chm.
Description: Principal trade association in the UK for firms active in the investment banking and securities industry. Represents the interests of its members on all aspects of their business and promotes their views to the authorities in the UK, the European Union, and elsewhere.
Formerly: Formerly, British Merchants Banking and Securities Houses Association

00616
Association for Geographic Information
AGI
5 St. Helen's Pl., Bishopsgate, London, EC3A 6AU, UK
Tel: 020 70360430
Fax: 020 70360301
Email: info@agi.org.uk
Website: http://www.agi.org.uk
Members: 1200
Staff: 4
Contact: Chris Holcroft, Dir./CEO
Fee: £75
Membership Type: individual
Fee: £1055
Membership Type: corporate
Description: Vendors and users of geographic information and geographic information systems (GIS). Spreads the benefits of geographic information throughout the community. Helps all users and vendors of geographic information and GIS. Holds events and seminars for information exchange and networking within the sector.
Library Subject: geographic
Library Type: not open to the public
Publication: Book
Publication title: AGI Source Book for GIS. Advertisements.

00617
Association for German Studies in Great Britain and Ireland
AGS
University of Leeds, Dept. of German, Leeds, LS2 9JT, UK
Email: f.j.finlay@leeds.ac.uk
Website: http://www.cutg.ac.uk
Contact: Frank Finlay, Pres.
Fee: £25
Membership Type: ordinary in UK
Fee: £10
Membership Type: associate in UK
Description: Promotes and fosters high standard of competence among university teachers of German.
Formerly: Formerly, Conference of University Teachers of German in Great Britain and Ireland

00618
Association for Group and Individual Psychotherapy
AGIP
1 Fairbridge Rd., London, N19 3EW, UK
Tel: 020 72727013
Fax: 020 72726945
Email: office@agip.org.uk
Website: http://www.agip.org.uk
Description: Provides psychoanalytic psychotherapy services and training programs.

00619
Association for Heritage Interpretation
AHI
54 Balmoral Rd., Kent, ME7 4PG, UK
Tel: 05602 747737
Email: admin@ahi.org.uk
Website: http://www.ahi.org.uk
Members: 500
Staff: 1
Contact: Aaron Lwaton, Chm.
Fee: £60
Membership Type: full
Fee: £50
Membership Type: associate
Description: Encourages excellence in the presentation and management of natural and cultural environments through promoting high standards of professional practice in interpretation and raising the profile of interpretation as a profession.
Publication: Journal
Publication title: Interpretation Journal. Advertisements.

00620
Association for History and Computing UK Branch
AHC
Liverpool Hope University, Deanery of Business and Computer Sciences, Hope Park, Liverpool, L16 9JD, UK
Email: farrimb@hope.ac.uk
Website: http://www.ahc.ac.uk
Contact: Brian Farrimond, Contact
Fee: £18
Membership Type: full
Fee: £8
Membership Type: student, retired, and unwaged
Description: Promotes the use of applied information science in historical research.
Publication: Journal
Publication title: History and Computing

00621
Association for Improvements in the Maternity Services
AIMS
5 Ann's Ct., Grove Rd., Surrey, Surbiton, KT6 4BE, UK
Tel: 0208 3909534
Fax: 0208 3904381
Email: chair@aims.org.uk
Website: http://www.aims.org.uk
Contact: Beverley Lawrence Beech, Chair
Fee: £25
Membership Type: individual (in UK and Europe)
Fee: £30
Membership Type: group, institution, overseas (outside Europe)
Description: Offers information, support and advice to parents on maternity care, including parents' rights, the choices available, technological interventions, natural childbirth and complaints procedures.
Publication: Journal

00622
Association for Industrial Archaeology
AIA
Ironbridge Institute, Ironbridge Gorge Museum, Coalbrookdale, Telford, TF8 7DX, UK
Tel: 0132 5359846
Email: aia-enquiries@contacts.bham.ac.uk
Website: http://www.industrial-archaeology.org
Contact: Anne Lowes, Liaison Off.
Fee: £21
Membership Type: student (overseas)
Fee: £18
Membership Type: student (in UK)
Description: Individuals and institutions in 7 countries interested in the archaeology of industry. Stresses the importance of the study and preservation of historic industrial sites. Represents the interests of local industrial archaeological societies. Sponsors specialized discussions, annual training weekends, and workshops.
Publication title: Conference Guide

00623
Association for Infant Mental Health, United Kingdom
AIMH UK
Knowle Clinic, Broadfield Rd., Bristol, BS4 2UH, UK
Tel: 0208 1442386
Email: info@aimh.org.uk
Website: http://www.aimh.org.uk
Contact: Shirley Gracias, Chair
Fee: £15
Membership Type: general
Description: Creates a network for professionals working to promote the mental health of infants. Increases awareness of infants' mental health. Provides support and information to prevent mental impairment during infancy.

00624
Association for Information Management
ASLIB
Howard House, Wagon Ln., Bingley, Bradford, BD16 1WA, UK
Tel: 01274 777700
Fax: 01274 785201
Email: gcoult@aslib.com
Website: http://www.aslib.co.uk
Members: 2250
Staff: 30
Contact: Graham Coult, Contact
Fee: £52.5
Membership Type: affiliate
Fee: £30
Membership Type: student
Description: Information users and providers in industry, commerce, research, government, education, and the professions in 70 countries. Operates information

service. Conducts seminars; offers training courses; provides recruiting and job placement assistance.
Library Type: reference
Publication title: Forthcoming International Scientific and Technical Conferences

00625
Association for International Cancer Research
AICR
Madras House, Fife, St. Andrews, KY16 9EH, UK
Tel: 01334 477910
Fax: 01334 478667
Email: enquiries@aicr.org.uk
Website: http://www.aicr.org.uk
Staff: 11
Contact: J. Murray, Chm.
Description: Supports fundamental research into the causes, mechanisms, diagnosis, treatment and prevention of cancer. Disseminates research results.
Publication: Annual Report
Publication title: AICR Annual Review

00626
Association for Language Learning
ALL
University of Leicester, University Rd., Leicester, LE1 7RH, UK
Tel: 0116 2297600
Fax: 0116 2231488
Email: info@all-languages.org.uk
Website: http://www.all-languages.org.uk
Members: 5000
Staff: 5
Contact: Sheila James, Proj. Admin.
Fee: £50
Membership Type: full
Fee: £34
Membership Type: retired, unwaged, part-time
Description: Language teachers and lecturers, advisers, teacher trainers, inspectors in all sectors of education from primary to higher, adult education and training. Aims to support language teachers, lecturers and trainers and to promote languages in the education systems of the UK. Offers advice, publications and in-service training courses.
Publication: Journal
Publication title: Deutsch Lehren und Lernen. Advertisements.

00627
Association for Learning Languages en Famille
ALLEF
7 Lucas Ct., Biddenham, Bedford, MK40 4RN, UK
Tel: 01325 359954
Email: jturley@allef.org.uk
Website: http://www.allef.org.uk
Contact: Janet Turley, Contact
Description: Exchange program for British and French children, ages 9 to 11. Promotes total culture immersion to achieve English/French bilingualism.

00628
Association for Learning Technology
ALT
ALT Administration, Gipsy Ln., Headington, Oxford, OX3 0BP, UK
Tel: 01865 484125
Fax: 01865 484165
Email: admin@alt.ac.uk
Website: http://www.alt.ac.uk
Members: 700
Staff: 4
Contact: Cathy Ellis, Dir.
Fee: £56
Membership Type: educational (inside UK), non-educational (inside UK)
Fee: £69
Membership Type: educational (overseas), non-educational (overseas)
Description: Learning technology practitioners in tertiary education, including researchers, publishers, manufacturers, service providers, librarians and policy makers. Promotes good practice in the use and development of learning technologies in tertiary education; facilitates interchange between practitioners, researchers and policymakers in education and industry; represents the membership in areas of policy (such as infrastructure provision and resource allocation).

00629
Association for Literary and Linguistic Computing
ALLC
King's College London, Centre for Computing in the Humanities, Strand, London, WC2R 2LS, UK
Tel: 020 78365454
Email: paul.spence@kcl.ac.uk
Website: http://www.allc.org
Members: 360
Contact: Paul Spence, Honorary Treas.
Fee: £64
Membership Type: individual
Description: Individuals who are graduates in languages and/or computing (450); universities that process languages by computer and companies that provide language processing services or market-related products and equipment (350). Seeks to further literary and linguistic research by computer and to provide a means of communication for all those concerned with such research.
Library Type: reference
Publication: Journal
Publication title: Literary and Linguistic Computing
Meetings/Conventions: periodic symposium

00630
Association for Low Countries Studies in Great Britain and Ireland
ALCS
University of Sheffield, Department of Germanic Studies, 1 Upper Hanover St., Sheffield, S3 7RA, UK
Tel: 0114 2224396
Fax: 0114 2222160
Email: alcs@shef.ac.uk
Website: http://alcs.group.shef.ac.uk/index.php
Contact: Nicola McLelland, Proc.
Description: Promotes the study of the language, culture and history of the Low Countries. Represents the interests of Low Countries Studies in higher education at the national and international levels. Encourages research in Low Countries Studies. Increases public awareness of the Low Countries, especially the Dutch language, Dutch and Flemish culture, history and society.
Publication: Journal
Publication title: Dutch Crossing: A Journal for Low Countries Studies

00631
Association for Low Flow Anaesthesia
ALFA
Department of Anaesthesia, General Infirmary at Leeds, Leeds, LS1 3EX, UK
Tel: 0113 3926672
Email: gfnunn@alfanospamnaes.org
Website: http://www.alfanaes.org/alfa-1.htm
Members: 300
Contact: Geoffrey Nunn, Pres./Membership Sec.
Description: Promotes the use and understanding of methods of inhalational anesthesia involving recirculation of exhaled gases and reduced fresh gas input. Fosters continuing education for anesthesiologists. Conducts research.

00632
Association for Measurement and Evaluation of Communication
AMEC
26 York St., London, W1U 6PZ, UK
Tel: 0126 8412414
Fax: 0207 6813820
Email: barryleggetter@amecorg.com
Website: http://www.amecorg.com/amec/index.asp
Contact: Barry Leggetter, Exec. Dir.
Fee: £20-40
Membership Type: student, associate - individual
Fee: £80
Membership Type: full - individual
Description: Represents a global trade body and professional institute for agencies and practitioners. Provides media evaluation and communication research. Defines and develops the industry with better professional standards for both companies and individuals.
Publication: Annual Report
Publication title: Annual Review

00633
Association for Medical Education in Europe
AMEE
Tay Park House, 484 Perth Rd., Dundee, DD2 1LR, UK
Tel: 01382 381953
Fax: 01382 381987
Email: amee@dundee.ac.uk
Website: http://www.amee.org/index.asp?cookies=True
Contact: Ronald M. Harden, Gen. Sec.-Treas.
Fee: £39
Membership Type: student
Fee: £85
Membership Type: individual
Description: Medical schools, educators, and students. Seeks to advance medical scholarship and practice. Serves as a clearinghouse on medical education; encourages communication and cooperation among

members; sponsors research programs and continuing professional development courses.
Publication: Journal
Publication title: Medical Teacher. Advertisements.

00634
Association for Medical Humanities
AMH
c/o Dr. Joseph O'Dwyer, Treas.
Dept. of Anaesthesia, Worthing Hospital, Lyndhurst Rd., West Sussex, Worthing, BN11 2DH, UK
Email: jodwyer@doctors.org.uk
Website: http://www.gla.ac.uk/departments/amh
Contact: Paul Lazarus, Pres.
Fee: £47
Membership Type: individual
Fee: £100
Membership Type: corporate
Description: Represents professionals who work in the field of medical humanities. Promotes medical humanities in education, healthcare and research. Provides information, degree programs and research results relevant to medical humanities.

00635
Association for Multiple Endocrine Neoplasia Disorders
AMEND
No. 1 Draper St., Southborough, Kent, Tunbridge Wells, TN4 0PG, UK
Tel: 01892 516076
Fax: 01892 516076
Email: info@amend.org.uk
Website: http://www.amend.org.uk
Contact: Jo Grey, Chair
Description: Improves the well-being of persons suffering from Multiple Endocrine Neoplasia (MEN) by providing information on genetic disease, emotional and practical support, and funding for future research programs. Promotes the earlier diagnosis of MEN by raising awareness of the condition among relevant health professionals.

00636
Association for Neuro-Linguistic Programming
ANLP
41 Marlowes, Hertfordshire, Hemel Hempstead, HP1 1LD, UK
Tel: 0845 0531162
Fax: 0845 0531176
Email: admin@anlp.org
Website: http://www.anlp.org
Members: 960
Staff: 1
Contact: Karen Moxom, Managing Dir.
Fee: £75
Membership Type: affiliate
Fee: £85
Membership Type: diploma
Description: Provides methods and models on how people think.

00637
Association for Palliative Medicine of Great Britain and Ireland
APM
76 Botley Rd., Park Gate, Southampton, SO31 1BA, UK
Tel: 01489 565665
Email: sabine.tuck@apmonline.org
Website: http://www.palliative-medicine.org
Members: 1000
Staff: 1
Description: Aims to promote the advancement and development of palliative medicine and is recognized as representing physicians at all grades who work in palliative medicine and those with an interest in the specialty.

00638
Association for Payment Clearing Services
APACS
Mercury House, Triton Ct., 14 Finsbury Sq., London, EC2A 1LQ, UK
Tel: 020 77116200
Fax: 020 72565527
Email: corpcomms@apacs.org.uk
Website: http://www.apacs.org.uk
Members: 31
Staff: 140
Contact: Paul Smee, Chief Exec.
Description: Forecasts payment trends, conducts market research, carries out lobbying activities, collates industry statistics and gets involved in developing industry standards and best practices.
Publication: Annual Report
Publication title: UK Payment Statistics

00639
Association for Perioperative Practice
AFPP
Daisy Ayris House, 6 Grove Park Ct., Harrogate, HG1 4DP, UK
Tel: 01423 508079
Fax: 01423 531613
Email: hq@afpp.org.uk
Website: http://www.afpp.org.uk/home
Members: 8000
Staff: 19
Contact: Diane Gilmour, Pres.
Fee: £45
Membership Type: regular (non registered), student, retired
Fee: £84
Membership Type: regular (registered)
Description: Operating theatre nurses. Workshops and study days are organized locally and nationally throughout the year.
Formerly: Formerly, National Association of Theatre Nurses
Publication: Journal
Publication title: Journal of Perioperative Practice. Advertisements.
Meetings/Conventions: annual congress – Exhibits.

00640
Association for Petroleum and Explosives Administration
APEA
PO Box 106, Saffron Walden, CB11 3XT, UK
Tel: 00845 6035507
Fax: 00845 6035507
Email: admin@apea.org.uk
Website: http://www.apea.org.uk
Members: 1200
Contact: Jane A. Mardell, Business Mgr.
Fee: £30
Membership Type: individual
Fee: £130
Membership Type: corporate
Description: Petroleum officers, trading standards officers, government officers, equipment suppliers, installation/service contractors, equipment operators, environment agency consultants, and users and oil company engineers. Aims to advance scientific, technical and legal knowledge; to facilitate information exchange; to promote uniformity; to focus attention of legislative requirements, within the petroleum and explosives industry.
Publication: Book
Publication title: Guidance for Design, Construction, Modification, Maintenance and Decommissioning of Filling Stations

00641
Association for Post Natal Illness
APNI
145 Dawes Rd., Fulham, London, SW6 7EB, UK
Tel: 020 73860868
Fax: 020 73868885
Website: http://apni.org
Contact: Merton Sandler, Pres.
Description: Provides support to mothers suffering from post-natal illness; strives to promote public awareness of post-natal illness; encourages research in post-natal illness.
Publication: Brochures

00642
Association for Professionals in Services for Adolescents
APSA
Holtwood, Red Lion St., Cropredy, Banbury, OX171PD, UK
Tel: 01295 750182
Fax: 01295 750182
Email: contact@apsa-web.info
Website: http://www.apsa-web.info
Members: 500
Fee: £200
Membership Type: team
Fee: £42
Membership Type: individual
Description: Aims to promote the study, understanding and care of adolescents, generate new thinking about adolescent care, both residential and community-based and provide a forum for discussion and exchange of ideas and views.

00643
Association for Project Management
APM
Ibis House, Regent Park, Summerleys Rd., Buckinghamshire, Princes Risborough, HP27 9L3, UK
Tel: 0845 4581944
Fax: 01844 274509
Email: info@apm.org.uk
Website: http://www.apm.org.uk
Members: 15950
Staff: 25
Contact: Martin Barnes, Pres.
Fee: £109
Membership Type: associate
Fee: £135
Membership Type: full
Description: Strives to develop and promote the professional disciplines of project and programme management for the public benefit.
Library Subject: project management
Library Type: not open to the public
Publication: Journal
Publication title: International Journal of Project Management

00644
Association for Project Safety
APS
Stanhope House, 12 Stanhope Pl., Edinburgh, EH12 5HH, UK
Tel: 08456 121290
Fax: 08456 121291
Email: info@aps.org.uk
Website: http://www.associationforprojectsafety.co.uk/home.php
Members: 5000
Staff: 8
Contact: Philip Baker, Pres./Dir.
Fee: £130-135
Membership Type: full
Fee: £115-120
Membership Type: full (with corporate)
Description: Across all disciplines within the construction industry subject to the CDM Regulations 1994. Aims to provide a centre of expertise and forum for information and research exchange for all those undertaking duties as Planning Supervisors under the CDM (Construction, Design & Management) Regulations 1994.
Formerly: Formerly, Association of Planning Supervisors
Publication title: Form of Appointment
Meetings/Conventions: bimonthly meeting

00645
Association for Public Service Excellence
APSE
Washbrook House, 2nd Fl., Lancastrian Office Ctre., Talbot Rd., Old Trafford, Manchester, M32 0FP, UK
Tel: 0161 7721810
Fax: 0161 7721811
Email: enquiries@apse.org.uk
Website: http://www.apse.org.uk
Members: 270
Staff: 25
Contact: Paul O'Brien, Chief Exec.
Fee: £1820-2875
Membership Type: two-tier authority (population related formula)
Fee: £2202-3033
Membership Type: unitary authority (population related formula)
Description: Local authorities and other organisations subscribing to aims and objectives. Advises local authorities on best practice in delivery of public services. Provides a wide range of services for its members which includes comprehensive briefings and publications on latest developments. Offers advice and research facilities.
Library Type: not open to the public
Publication: Newsletter
Publication title: Direct News. Advertisements.
Meetings/Conventions: annual conference – Exhibits.

00646
Association for Radiation Research
ARR
University of Manchester, School Of Pharmacy and Pharmaceutical Sciences, Oxford Rd., Manchester, M13 9PL, UK
Tel: 0116 2752128
Fax: 0116 2752396
Email: kaye.williams@manchester.ac.uk
Website: http://www.le.ac.uk/cm/arr/home.html
Members: 150
Contact: Kaye J. Williams, Chm.
Fee: £20
Membership Type: general
Fee: £10
Membership Type: student, retired
Description: Scientific, medical, and technical professionals interested in ionizing radiation in 16 countries. Works to increase and disseminate knowledge pertaining to ionizing radiation in the fields of biology, chemistry, and physics. Stimulates research; grants bursaries to students wishing to attend the association's conference.
Library Type: reference
Meetings/Conventions: annual meeting

00647
Association for Real Change
ARC
ARC House, Marsden St., Derbyshire, Chesterfield, S40 1JY, UK
Tel: 01246 555043
Fax: 01246 555045
Email: contact.us@arcuk.org.uk
Website: http://www.arcuk.org.uk
Members: 300
Staff: 23
Contact: Gill Braime, Contact
Description: Organizations providing care facilities for people with learning disabilities. Seeks to ensure quality care for people with learning disabilities. Encourages diversity and high standards in day care and residential programs. Offers training programs for working with people with learning disabilities.
Formerly: Formerly, Association for Residential Care
Publication: Bulletin
Publication title: In the Spotlight

00648
Association for Rehabilitation of Communication and Oral Skills
ARCOS
Whitbourne Lodge, 137 Church St., Worcestershire, Malvern, WR14 2AN, UK
Tel: 01684 576795
Email: arcos@arcos.org.uk
Website: http://www.arcos.org.uk
Contact: Kay Alexander, Patron
Description: Provides support and comprehensive therapy for people with communication or swallowing problems, including those with multiple disabilities resulting from developmental or acquired brain injury.

00649
Association for Research in the Voluntary and Community Sector
ARVAC
c/o School of Business and Society Science
Roehampton University, Southlands College, 80 Roehampton Ln., London, SW15 5SL, UK
Website: http://www.arvac.org.uk
Contact: Steven Howlett, Chm.
Description: Provides training and facilitation in basic research methods for small community groups in the UK. Disseminates information on community sector research. Holds conferences and workshops.

00650
Association for Road Traffic Safety and Management
ARTSM
c/o Radix Traffic Limited
Unit D3, Premier Centre, Romsey, Hampshire, SO51 9DG, UK
Tel: 020 89776952
Fax: 020 89778339
Email: philip.crickmay@artsm.org.uk
Website: http://www.artsm.org.uk
Members: 45
Staff: 3
Fee: £550
Membership Type: company (based on annual turnover of less than 500,000)
Fee: £840
Membership Type: affiliate
Description: Road sign manufacturers in the United Kingdom. Conducts educational programs.
Formerly: Formerly, Association for Road Traffic Sign Makers

00651
Association for Roman Archaeology
ARA
75 York Rd., Wiltshire, Swindon, SN1 2JU, UK
Tel: 01793 534008
Fax: 01793 534008
Email: ara.enquiry@hotmail.com
Website: http://www.associationromanarchaeology.org
Members: 3000
Staff: 6
Contact: Bryn Walters, Dir./Sec.
Fee: £17.5
Membership Type: single
Fee: £22.5
Membership Type: couple
Description: Promotes Roman studies and archaeology.
Publication: Magazine
Publication title: Bulletin on Roman Discoveries. Advertisements.

00652

Association for Sandwich Education and Training
ASET

W11, 1 Moorfoot, Sheffield, S1 4PQ, UK
Tel: 0114 2212902
Fax: 0114 2212903
Email: aset@asetonline.org
Website: http://www.asetonline.org
Members: 85
Staff: 1
Contact: Keith Fildes, Admin.
Fee: £40
Membership Type: individual
Fee: £95
Membership Type: SME (less than 250 employees)
Description: Promotes the concept of integrating work and learning in higher and further education, as well as the implementation of best practice for work placements. The professional body for placement and employability professionals, ASET provides support, advice and training for all practitioners working in the field.

00653

Association for Science Education
ASE

College Ln., Hatfield, AL10 9AA, UK
Tel: 01707 283000
Fax: 01707 266532
Email: info@ase.org.uk
Website: http://www.ase.org.uk
Members: 10828
Staff: 47
Contact: Annette Smith, Chief Exec.
Fee: £80
Membership Type: secondary teacher
Description: Membership Teachers of science in the primary, secondary and tertiary sectors of education. There are some industrial members and members from abroad. Purpose Covers the teaching of science in schools and colleges at all levels - the aim being to help teachers in their work and provide a forum for communication between teachers.
Publication: Journal
Publication title: ASE Primary Science

00654

Association for Scottish Literary Studies
ASLS

University of Glasgow, Department of Scottish Literature, 7 University Gardens, Glasgow, G12 8QH, UK
Tel: 0141 3305309
Fax: 0141 3305309
Email: d.jones@scothist.arts.gla.ac.uk
Website: http://www.asls.org.uk
Members: 800
Staff: 2
Contact: Duncan Jones, Gen. Mgr.
Fee: £40
Membership Type: individual
Fee: £67
Membership Type: institution
Description: Academics, teachers, writers, and other individuals in 22 countries interested in Scottish language and literature. Aims to promote the study, teaching, and writing of Scottish language and literature. Furthers the study of the languages of Scotland.
Publication: Magazine
Publication title: The Bottle Imp
Meetings/Conventions: annual conference

00655

Association for Shared Parenting
ASP

PO Box 2000, Dudley, DY1 1YZ, UK
Tel: 0178 9751157
Fax: 0178 9751081
Email: spring.cott@btopenworld.com
Website: http://www.sharedparenting.f9.co.uk
Members: 60
Staff: 6
Fee: £20
Membership Type: waged
Fee: £10
Membership Type: unwaged
Description: Promotes children's right to the nurture of both parents after separation or divorce. Operates a Contact Centre, with facilities available on Saturdays for children to enjoy contact with their non-residential parent.

00656

Association for Skeptical Enquiry
ASKE

PO Box 4650, Sheffield, S11 0EE, UK
Email: aske1@talktalk.net
Website: http://www.aske-skeptics.org.uk
Contact: Michael Heap, Chm.
Fee: £10
Membership Type: in United Kingdom
Fee: £14
Membership Type: overseas
Description: Promotes the use of scientific methods in the analysis of ideas, claims and practices which are paranormal in nature. Raises public awareness of the rational and scientific understanding of extraordinary and paranormal claims. Opposes the misinterpretation and misrepresentation of science for purposes which deceive the public.
Publication: Newsletter
Publication title: Skeptical Adversaria

00657

Association for Specialist Fire Protection
ASFP

Kingsley House, Ganders Business Park, Kingsley, Hampshire, Bordon, GU35 9LU, UK
Tel: 01420 471612
Fax: 01420 471611
Email: info@asfp.org.uk
Website: http://www.asfp.org.uk
Members: 57
Staff: 4
Contact: Wilf Butcher, CEO
Description: Manufacturers, contractors, distributors, regulatory, certification, consultant bodies in specialist fire protection for construction industry. Represents the majority of UK structural fire protection companies with associate members representing regulatory certification, testing and consulting bodies.
Publication: Manual
Publication title: Fire Protection for Structural Steel in Building

00658

Association for Spina Bifida and Hydrocephalus
ASBAH

42 Park Rd., Peterborough, PE1 2UQ, UK
Tel: 08454 507755
Fax: 01733 555985
Email: helpline@asbah.org
Website: http://www.asbah.org
Staff: 100
Contact: Jeffrey Tate, Pres.
Description: Provides help and information to individuals/families with spina bifida and/or hydrocephalus in England, Wales and Northern Ireland only; trained advisers visit families; team of specialist advisers in continence, education, medical matters. Organizes study days for professionals and families. Produces fact sheets and magazines.
Library Type: not open to the public
Publication: Magazine
Publication title: LINK

00659

Association for Studies in the Conservation of Historic Buildings
ASCHB

70 Cowcross St., London, EC1M 6EL, UK
Email: info@aschb.org.uk
Website: http://www.aschb.org.uk
Members: 350
Contact: John Thorneycroft, Pres.
Fee: £35
Membership Type: individual
Description: Professionals engaged in the conservation of historic buildings. Membership by invitation only. Provides a forum for the dissemination of knowledge generated by the members in the course of their work on historic buildings.

00660

Association for Teaching Psychology
ATP

c/o Wendy Wood, Membership Chair
40, Rothbury Terr., Heaton, Newcastle upon Tyne, NE6 5XH, UK
Tel: 0191 2650304
Email: wendywood@blueyonder.co.uk
Website: http://www.theatp.org
Contact: Deb Gajic, Chair
Fee: £25
Membership Type: regular
Description: Teachers of psychology in Secondary Schools, Further Education Colleges and Colleges of Higher Education. Supports teachers of psychology at pre-degree level. Provides help and advice. Organizes an annual updating conference for members and distributes resources produced by teachers for teachers.

00661

Association for the Conservation of Energy
ACE

Westgate House, 2a Prebend St., London, N1 8PT, UK
Tel: 020 73598000
Fax: 020 73590863
Email: info@ukace.org
Website: http://www.ukace.org
Members: 24
Staff: 9
Contact: Andrew Warren, Dir.
Description: UK-based companies that have substantial interests in energy conservation equipment and services. Current members include controls manufacturers, energy service companies, manufacturers and distributors of insulation materials. Acts as a lobby group which carries out policy research on energy conservation. Works to promote wider awareness of the need for and the benefits of using energy more efficiently in buildings, and to help establish a sensible and consistent national energy efficiency policy and programme.
Publication: Newsletter
Publication title: FACE Newsletter

00662

Association for the Protection of Rural Scotland

Gladstone's Land, 3rd Fl., 483 Lawnmarket, Edinburgh, EH1 2NT, UK
Tel: 0131 2257012
Email: info@ruralscotland.org
Website: http://www.ruralscotland.btik.com
Members: 750
Staff: 3
Contact: John Mayhew, Dir.
Fee: £32
Membership Type: individual
Fee: £20
Membership Type: individual (over 65)
Description: Seeks to protect Scotland's countryside and to promote ideas for its care and improvement by means of constructive proposals, careful research and active involvement in the maintenance of landscape features.
Formerly: Formerly, Association for the Protection of Rural Scotland
Publication title: Costs and Benefits: The Role of Community Councils as Statutory Consultant for Planning Applications (June 1996)

00663

Association for the Scientific Study of Anomalous Phenomena
ASSAP

27 Old Gloucester St., London, WC1N 3XX, UK
Tel: 0845 6521648
Email: assapmembership@assap.org
Website: http://www.assap.org
Members: 350
Contact: Dave Wood, Chm.
Fee: £15
Membership Type: standard
Fee: £25
Membership Type: overseas
Description: Open to anyone interested in the aims of the organization. Research into all paranormal, anomalous and related phenomena.
Library Subject: paranormal, anomalous
Library Type: not open to the public
Publication: Journal
Publication title: Anomaly

00664

Association for the Study and Preservation of Roman Mosaics
ASPROM

61 Norwich St., Cambridge, CB2 1ND, UK
Email: honsec@asprom.org
Website: http://www.asprom.org
Members: 200
Contact: Janet Huskinson, Sec.
Fee: £20
Membership Type: corporate
Fee: £17.5
Membership Type: joint
Description: Academics, mosaic specialists, conservators, students, institutional members, lay people interested in Romano-British mosaic art. Aims to advance education amongst the general public by fostering the study and preservation of Roman mosaics and related material.
Publication: Newsletter
Publication title: ASPROM Newsletter

00665

Association for the Study of Animal Behaviour
ASAB

University of St. Andrews, Saint Mary's Colorado, South St., St. Andrews, KY16 9JP, UK
Email: susan.healy@st-andrews.ac.uk
Website: http://asab.nottingham.ac.uk
Members: 2000
Contact: Sue Healy, Membership Sec.
Fee: £15-25
Membership Type: student/unwaged
Fee: £35-45
Membership Type: ordinary
Description: Professionals and students in 20 countries engaged in the scientific study of animal behavior. Promotes the study of animal behavior.
Publication: Journal
Publication title: Animal Behaviour

00666

Association for the Study of Medical Education
ASME

12 Queen St., Edinburgh, EH2 1JE, UK
Tel: 0131 2259111
Fax: 0131 2259444
Email: info@asme.org.uk
Website: http://www.asme.org.uk
Members: 970
Staff: 3
Contact: David Blaney, Chief Exec.
Fee: £10.25
Membership Type: student
Fee: £92
Membership Type: non-clinical/training grade
Description: Individuals engaged in medical education at the undergraduate, postgraduate, and continuing professional development levels. Promotes "knowledge and expertise in medical education." Facilitates information exchange and the establishment of formal networks linking members; serves as a forum for the debate of issues impacting the field of medical education.

00667

Association for the Study of Modern and Contemporary France
ASMCF

University of Bradford, Department of Modern Languages, Bradford, BD7 1DP, UK
Email: membership@asmcf.org
Website: http://www.asmcf.org
Contact: Maggie Allison, Membership Sec.
Fee: £46
Membership Type: individual
Fee: £10
Membership Type: postgraduate, unwaged
Description: Develops research and education concerning modern and contemporary France in the United Kingdom. Provides a forum for those involved in teaching and researching modern France and the Francophone world.

00668

Association for the Study of Obesity
ASO

Eversheds House, 70 Great Bridgewater St., Manchester, M1 5ES, UK
Tel: 01304 367788
Email: catherine.stone@aso.org.uk
Website: http://www.aso.org.uk
Members: 520
Staff: 2
Contact: Susan Jebb, Chair
Fee: £55
Membership Type: individual
Fee: £22
Membership Type: student
Description: Scientists, researchers, dieticians, health education workers, and students in England. Promotes information exchange between members; promotes research into the causes, prevention and treatment of obesity; seeks to encourage action to reduce the prevalence of obesity and to enhance treatment.

00669

Association for the Study of Travel in Egypt and the Near East
ASTENE

26 Millington Rd., Cambridge, CB3 9HP, UK
Fax: 020 74354911
Email: astene@dsl.pipex.com
Website: http://www.astene.org.uk
Contact: Jaromir Malek, Pres.
Description: Promotes education and learning with particular reference to the history of travel and travellers in Egypt and the Near East. Acts as a focus for the collection of materials, information, and contacts by holding conferences, seminars, exhibitions, lectures and visits.

00670

Association for the Teaching of the Social Sciences
ATSS

Old Hall Ln., Manchester, M13 0XT, UK
Tel: 0161 2489375
Email: atss@btconnect.com
Website: http://www.le.ac.uk/education/centres/ATSS/atss.html
Members: 700
Staff: 2
Contact: Frances Rippin, Chair
Fee: £20
Membership Type: unwaged
Fee: £50
Membership Type: overseas
Description: Individual teachers of social science in schools and in further and higher education; educational institutions concerned with the delivery of the social science curriculum; those involved in teacher training, publishing and academic research relating to the social sciences. Supports the class teacher and promotes the social sciences in schools and colleges. Organizes annual national and regional conferences for teachers and students and works closely with other social science organizations. Assists in the development of good classroom practice and in syllabus and resource development.

00671

Association for Veterinary Teaching and Research Work
AVT&RW

PO Box 320, Bridgwater, TA7 9XJ, UK
Tel: 01458 210818
Fax: 01458 210040
Email: enquiries@avtrw.co.uk
Website: http://www.avtrw.co.uk
Members: 500
Contact: Adrian Philbey, Sec.
Fee: £25
Membership Type: individual
Description: Represents individuals engaged primarily in veterinary teaching and research in UK and Eire. Works to further contact between research workers and teachers in animal research. Promotes and influences veterinary education. Provides and maintains the technical excellence of veterinary teaching and research.
Publication: Proceedings
Publication title: AVT and RW Annual Conference. Advertisements.

00672

Association in Scotland to Research into Astronautics
ASTRA

Flat 65, Dalriada House, Anderston, Glasgow, G2 7PE, UK
Tel: 0141 2217658
Email: duncanlunan@talktalk.net
Members: 100
Contact: Duncan A. Lunan, Sec.
Fee: £15
Membership Type: adult
Fee: £10
Membership Type: unwaged
Description: Amateur and professional scientists from nine countries active in the field of space research. Promotes, stimulates, and conducts space research. Engages in amateur astronomy and practical research such as waverider aerodynamics, lightsails and asteroid deflection. Sponsors discussion projects as a basis for books on different aspects of space exploration; conducts scientific exhibitions and model rocketry for young members.
Library Subject: astronomy, spaceflight, aviation
Library Type: reference
Formerly: Formerly, Scottish Branch of the British Interplanetary Society
Publication: Journal
Publication title: Asgard. Advertisements.
Meetings/Conventions: periodic competition

Association Internationale Contre les Experiences Douloureuses sur les Animaux

see International Association Against Painful Experiments on Animals

Association Internationale de Recherche Apicole

see International Bee Research Association

Association Internationale des Approvisionneurs de Navires

see International Ship Suppliers and Services Association

Association Internationale des Avocats du Monde et des Industries du Spectacle

see International Association of Entertainment Lawyers - France

Association Internationale des Etudes et Recherches sur L'Information et la Communication

see International Association for Media and Communications Research

Association Internationale des Instituts de Navigation

see Royal Institute of Navigation

Association Internationale des Laboratoires Textiles Lainiers

see International Association of Wool Textile Laboratories

Association Internationale des Services d'Installations Electriques sur lesBateaux

see International Ship Electrical and Engineering Service Association

Association Internationale du Barreau

see International Bar Association

00673

Association of Accounting Technicians
AAT

140 Aldersgate St., London, EC1A 4HY, UK
Tel: 020 73973000
Fax: 020 73973009
Email: aat@aat.org.uk
Website: http://www.aat.org.uk
Members: 100000
Staff: 90
Contact: Jane Scott Paul, Chief Exec.
Fee: £69
Membership Type: student/affiliate (UK only)
Description: Provides a recognized professional qualification for accounting technicians. Seeks to improve standards of competence and professional development in accounting and related areas.
Library Subject: accountancy and related areas
Library Type: not open to the public
Formerly: Formerly, Accounting Technicians in Finance and Accounting
Publication: Magazine
Publication title: Accounting Technician. Advertisements.
Meetings/Conventions: Presidential Conference – quarterly conference – Exhibits.

00674

Association of Anaesthetists of Great Britain and Ireland
AAGBI

21 Portland Pl., London, W1B 1PY, UK
Tel: 020 76311650
Fax: 020 76314352
Email: info@aagbi.org
Website: http://www.aagbi.org
Members: 10000
Staff: 18
Contact: Richard Birks, Pres.
Fee: £76-235
Membership Type: ordinary (based on salary)
Fee: £173
Membership Type: joint ordinary
Description: Aims to promote education and research in anaesthesia and to bring together as many members as possible at the three annual meetings to disseminate relevant information both at home and abroad. Fosters research in anaesthesia and allied subjects; encourages collaborative ventures involving members; represents members' interests.
Publication: Journal
Publication title: Anaesthesia

00675

Association of Applied Biologists AAB

Warwick Enterprise Park, Warwick, CV35 9EF, UK
Tel: 01789 472020
Fax: 01789 470234
Email: rebecca@aab.org.uk
Website: http://www.aab.org.uk
Members: 800
Contact: Mike Jeger, Pres.
Fee: £53
Membership Type: full
Fee: £26.5
Membership Type: student
Description: Research scientists in private and state applied biology institutes and universities in 60 countries interested in the furthering development of applied biology.
Publication: Newsletter
Publication title: AAB News

00676

Association of Art and Antique Dealers LAPADA

535 King's Rd., Chelsea, London, SW10 0SZ, UK
Tel: 020 78233511
Fax: 020 78233522
Email: drhodes@lapada.org
Website: http://www.lapada.org
Members: 650
Staff: 5
Contact: Sarah Percy-Davis, Chief Exec.
Fee: £470
Description: Represents dealers in art, antiques and works of art from antiquities to contemporary fine art. Provides professional services to members including specialist insurance cover, legal advice and promotion. Offers free advice service to the public about specialist dealers.
Formerly: Formerly, London & Provincial Antique Dealers Association
Publication: Magazine
Publication title: LAPADA Views. Advertisements.

00677

Association of Art Historians AAH

Cowcross Ct., 70 Cowcross St., London, EC1M 6EJ, UK
Tel: 020 74903211
Fax: 020 74903277
Email: admin@aah.org.uk
Website: http://www.aah.org.uk
Members: 1100
Staff: 3
Contact: Evelyn Welch, Acting Chair
Fee: £45
Membership Type: individual
Fee: £20
Membership Type: concessionary
Description: Formed to promote the study of art history and ensure wider public recognition of the field. Serves an organization for professional art historians and researchers including all those who are working in education, museums and galleries. For independent art historians and for all who are studying the subject.
Publication: Magazine
Publication title: The Art Book. Advertisements.

00678

Association of Authorised Public Accountants AAPA

10 Lincoln's Inn Fields, London, WC2A 3BP, UK
Tel: 020 70595895
Fax: 020 70595916
Website: http://www.accaglobal.com/aapa/aapa
Members: 608
Staff: 8
Contact: Stuart Tye, Pres.
Fee: £181
Membership Type: individual
Description: Auditors in 20 countries. Seeks to "improve and advance the professional and ethical status and the technical standards of statutory authorized auditors". Represents members' interests. Maintains close liaison with government ministry responsible for trade and industry. Conducts research and educational programs. Compiles statistics.
Library Type: reference

00679

Association of Authors' Agents AAA

David Higham Associates Ltd., Golden Sq., 5-8 Lower John St., London, W1F 9HA, UK
Tel: 020 74345900
Email: anthonygoff@davidhigham.co.uk
Website: http://www.agentsassoc.co.uk/index.php
Members: 75
Contact: Anthony Goff, Pres.
Description: British literary agencies and individual agents. Promotes discussion and cooperation between members; encourages high standards of professional conduct; represents members' interests before other professional organizations.
Publication: Yearbook
Publication title: The Writers and Artists' Yearbook

00680

Association of Average Adjusters AAA

c/o The Baltic Exchange
St. Mary Axe, London, EC3A 8BH, UK
Tel: 020 76235501
Fax: 020 76231623
Email: aaa@balticexchange.com
Website: http://www.average-adjusters.com
Members: 560
Staff: 2
Contact: David Taylor, Sec.
Description: Prepares marine insurance claims and general average statements on an independent and impartial basis.

00681

Association of Bakery Ingredients Manufacturers ABIM

c/o Food and Drink Federation
6 Catherine St., London, WC2B 5JJ, UK
Tel: 020 78362460
Fax: 020 78360580
Website: http://www.abim.org.uk
Members: 21
Staff: 3
Contact: Geraldine Smith, Exec. Sec.
Description: Promotes and represents members' interest in relation to European technical and legislative matters affecting the bakery ingredients manufacturing industry.

00682

Association of Blind and Partially Sighted Teachers and Students ABAPSTAS

BM Box 6727, London, WC1N 3XX, UK
Tel: 0117 9664839
Email: chair@abapstas.org.uk
Website: http://www.abapstas.org.uk
Members: 350
Contact: Elisabeth Standen, Chair
Description: Visually impaired teachers, trainers, students, and people looking for work or who have an interest in education. Provides mutual support through the exchange of ideas and experience of education and employment, promotes the needs and strengths of visually impaired teachers and students and campaigns on relevant issues.
Publication: Newsletter
Publication title: The Bulletin
Meetings/Conventions: annual conference

00683

Association of Blind Piano Tuners ABPT

31 Wyre Crescent, Lynwood, Lancashire, Darwen, BB3 0JG, UK
Tel: 0844 7361976
Fax: 01254 773158
Email: abpt@uk-piano.org
Website: http://www.uk-piano.org
Members: 110
Contact: Richard Foster, Chm.
Fee: £55
Membership Type: full
Fee: £25
Membership Type: overseas, associate
Description: Serves the professional and particular needs of blind and partially sighted piano tuners.

00684

Association of Breastfeeding Mothers ABM

PO Box 207, Somerset, Bridgwater, TA6 7YT, UK
Tel: 08444 122948
Email: info@abm.me.uk
Website: http://www.abm.me.uk
Members: 430
Contact: Pam Lacey, Chair
Fee: £18
Membership Type: standard
Fee: £25
Membership Type: overseas
Description: Mothers who have breastfed their babies and are trained as counselors. Believes that breast milk is "the perfect food for infants" because it promotes the health of infant and mother and is inexpensive, convenient, and allows a mother time to relax with her baby. Offers support and encouragement to mothers who wish to breastfeed. Operates support groups; fosters exchange of information and friendly contact among nursing mothers; provides solutions to non-medical problems of breast-feeding. Offers services such as

24-hour counseling; arranges for speakers to tour schools and clinics.
Publication: Annual Report
Publication title: ABM Annual Report
Meetings/Conventions: periodic meeting

00685
Association of British Certification Bodies
ABCB
129 A Whitehorse Hill, Kent, Chislehurst, BR7 6DQ, UK
Tel: 020 82951128
Fax: 020 84678095
Email: trevor.nash@abcb.org.uk
Website: http://www.abcb.org.uk
Members: 30
Staff: 2
Contact: Trevor Nash, Chief Exec.
Description: Independent accredited certification bodies who undertake impartial certification of quality and environmental management systems, products, and personnel. Aims to provide a forum for the discussion and formulation of policy on matters of common concern; to represent the collective interests of members and, where consistent with such interests, those of individual members, in appropriate quarters; and to adopt, if thought fit, a code of professional practice in certification matters.
Publication: Newsletter
Publication title: ABCB News

00686
Association of British Choral Directors
ABCD
15 Granville Way, Sherborne, DT9 4AS, UK
Tel: 01935 389482
Email: rachel.greaves@abcd.org.uk
Website: http://www.abcd.org.uk
Members: 755
Staff: 3
Contact: Rachel Greaves, Gen. Sec.
Fee: £20
Membership Type: student
Fee: £50
Membership Type: individual
Description: Amateur and professional choral conductors and choral trainers, individual, music publishers and music services organizations. Aims to promote, improve and maintain the education, training and development of choral directors with a view to improving standards in all sectors of choral activity within the United Kingdom by organising regional and national training courses.
Publication: Journal
Publication title: Mastersinger. Advertisements.

00687
Association of British Climatologists
ABC
c/o Royal Meteorological Society
104 Oxford Rd., Reading, RG1 7LL, UK
Tel: 0118 9568500
Fax: 0118 9568571
Email: chiefexec@tarmets.org
Website: http://www.rmets.org/activities/groups/SIG/detail.php?ID=6
Members: 125
Fee: £6
Membership Type: inside United Kingdom
Fee: £7
Membership Type: outside United Kingdom
Description: Specialist group of the Royal Meteorological Society. Individuals working in climatology and related fields. Encourages research and information exchange in all aspects of climatology. Areas of concern include climatology of the British Isles, atmospheric pollution, and climatic change and variability. Sponsors annual competition for the best undergraduate dissertation on a climatological subject.
Publication: Newsletter
Publication title: Climate News

00688
Association of British Climbing Walls
ABC
Mile End Climbing Wall, Haverfield Rd., Bow, London, E3 5BE, UK
Tel: 020 89800289
Email: andrew.reid@mileendwall.org.uk
Website: http://www.abcclimbingwalls.co.uk
Contact: Andrew Reid, Chm.
Fee: £200
Membership Type: aspirant, full, trade
Description: Represents the interests of owners and managers of climbing centres in the United Kingdom. Develops safe practice and management processes for operating climbing centres. Provides a forum for members to share their experiences on accidents and near misses.

00689
Association of British Credit Unions Limited
ABCUL
Holyoake House, Hanover St., Manchester, M60 OAS, UK
Tel: 0161 8323694
Fax: 0161 8323706
Email: info@abcul.org
Website: http://www.abcul.coop/page/index.cfm
Description: Serves as the voice of the credit union movement in UK. Promotes credit unions as the first choice for low-cost, high quality, and ethical financial services. Improves the day to day operations, legislation, and regulation for all credit unions.

00690
Association of British Dispensing Opticians
ABDO
199 Gloucester Terr., London, W2 6LD, UK
Tel: 020 72985100
Fax: 020 72985111
Email: general@abdo.org.uk
Website: http://www.abdo.org.uk
Members: 7400
Staff: 30
Contact: Barry Duncan, Pres.
Fee: £250
Membership Type: full
Fee: £170
Membership Type: reduced full
Description: Aims to support, protect and advance the character, status and interests of dispensing opticians. Promotes better education and training of dispensing opticians.
Publication: Journal
Publication title: Dispensing Optics. Advertisements.

00691
Association of British Drivers
ABD
PO Box 2228, Kenley, CR8 5ZT, UK
Tel: 0870 4442535
Fax: 0870 1362370
Email: brian.gregory@abd.org.uk
Website: http://www.abd.org.uk
Members: 2500
Contact: Brian Gregory, Chm.
Fee: £30
Membership Type: individual
Fee: £50
Membership Type: affiliate (under 500 members)
Description: Automobile drivers in the United Kingdom. Seeks to "provide an active, responsible voice to lobby for the beleaguered British car driver." Promotes "recognition of the fact that roads are an essential part of the UK transport system." Conducts lobbying activities to secure: improved standards of drivers' training; more realistic speed limits; improvements in road and vehicle safety; and the abolition of toll roads and Gatso cameras.
Publication: Newsletter
Publication title: On the Road

00692
Association of British Healthcare Industries
ABHI
111 Westminster Bridge Rd., London, SE1 7HR, UK
Tel: 020 79604360
Fax: 020 79604361
Email: enquiries@abhi.org.uk
Website: http://www.abhi.org.uk
Members: 200
Contact: Peter Ellingworth, Chief Exec.
Description: Sterilizing equipment manufacturers in England. Provides a forum for the exchange of information on market conditions. Prepares industry standards in conjunction with other organizations.
Formerly: Formerly, Association of Sterilizer and Disinfector Equipment Manufacturers Association
Meetings/Conventions: quarterly meeting

00693
Association of British Insurers
ABI
51 Gresham St., London, EC2V 7HQ, UK
Tel: 020 76003333
Fax: 020 76968999
Email: info@abi.org.uk
Website: http://www.abi.org.uk
Members: 400
Staff: 100
Contact: Tim Breedon, Chm.
Description: Trade association representing 420 insurance companies in the United Kingdom. Promotes and protects the interests of members. Monitors government actions which may affect members. Cooperates with other associations having similar objectives. Conducts educational programs.
Library Subject: statistics, financial services
Library Type: not open to the public

00694

Association of British Investigators
ABI

295/297 Church St., Lancashire, Blackpool, FY1 3PJ, UK
Tel: 01253 297502
Fax: 01253 752185
Email: info@theabi.org.uk
Website: http://www.theabi.org.uk
Members: 400
Staff: 1
Contact: Eric Shelmerdine, Gen. Sec.
Fee: £165
Membership Type: full, associate, affiliate, provisional, overseas
Description: Private investigators in Britain with more than 2 years of experience. Promotes adherence to association's code of ethics. Conducts seminars.
Formerly: Formerly, British Detectives Association
Publication: Directory
Publication title: Directory of Registered Members

00695

Association of British Mining Equipment Companies
ABMEC

Unit 1, Thornes Office Park, Monckton Rd., W Yorkshire, Wakefield, WF2 7AN, UK
Tel: 01924 360200
Fax: 01924 380553
Email: ruth.bailey@abmec.org.uk
Website: http://www.abmec.org.uk
Members: 40
Staff: 6
Contact: Ruth Bailey, Dir. Gen.
Description: Companies in the United Kingdom involved in the manufacture of mining equipment. Promotes the sale of British-made mining equipment in Great Britain and abroad. Disseminates information on mining equipment to customers.

00696

Association of British Neurologists
ABN

Ormond House, 4th Fl., 27 Boswell St., London, WC1N 3JZ, UK
Tel: 020 74054060
Fax: 020 74054070
Email: info@theabn.org
Website: http://www.theabn.org
Members: 1139
Staff: 2
Contact: Karen Reeves, Admin.
Fee: £185
Membership Type: ordinary
Fee: £70
Membership Type: associate, affiliate
Description: Trainee and consultant in the neurological sciences. Promotes the advancement of the neurological sciences, including the practice of neurology in the British Isles.

00697

Association of British Offshore Industries
ABOI

28-29 Threadneedle St., London, EC2R 8AY, UK
Tel: 020 76282555
Fax: 020 76384376
Email: info@maritimeindustries.org
Website: http://www.maritimeindustries.org
Members: 65
Staff: 1
Contact: Ken Gibbons, Dir.
Description: Aims to provide a global market cultivation and new business pursuit service to member companies engaged in support of investment and operations in oil and gas and offshore sectors.
Formerly: Formerly, Association of British Offshore Industries
Publication: Membership Directory
Publication title: Handbook and Members Directory. Advertisements.

00698

Association of British Orchestras
ABO

20 Rupert St., London, W1D 6DF, UK
Tel: 020 72870333
Fax: 020 72870444
Email: info@abo.org.uk
Website: http://www.abo.org.uk
Members: 150
Staff: 4
Contact: Mark Pemberton, Dir.
Fee: £320-5100
Membership Type: full
Fee: £415
Membership Type: associate
Description: Supports, develops and advances the interests and activities of the orchestral profession in the U.K. Seeks to influence and improve the environment in which orchestras operate. Ensures that orchestras flourish and achieve maximum potential. Key activities include advocacy, services, information and learning that are delivered through conferences, seminars, negotiations, training opportunities, education initiatives and representation.
Publication: Bulletin
Publication title: Update

00699

Association of British Professional Conference Organisers
ABPCO

9 Wellington Park, Belfast, BT9 6DJ, UK
Tel: 028 90387475
Email: info@abpco.org
Website: http://www.abpco.org
Members: 95
Staff: 1
Contact: Lesley Maltman, Exec. Dir.
Fee: £300
Membership Type: individual (full)
Fee: £200
Membership Type: individual (associate)
Description: Provides meetings for members who are proprietors/directors of their own conference organizing companies or the conference directors/managers of professional or trade associations, corporations, educational or public sector bodies. Trains personnel directly or indirectly involved with the conference industry. Offers a variety of marketing and business development services.
Meetings/Conventions: Think Tank Weekend – annual meeting

00700

Association of British Science Writers
ABSW

The Dana Centre, 165 Queen's Gate, London, SW7 5HD, UK
Email: absw@absw.org.uk
Website: http://www.absw.org.uk
Members: 500
Staff: 1
Contact: Angela Nicolaides, Contact
Fee: £40
Membership Type: ordinary
Fee: £36
Membership Type: associate
Description: Represents medical and scientific journalists. Aims to increase the standard of science journalism in the UK, written and broadcast media.
Publication: Report
Publication title: The Science Reporter. Advertisements.

00701

Association of British Theatre Technicians
ABTT

55 Farringdon Rd., London, EC1M 3JB, UK
Tel: 020 72429200
Fax: 020 72429303
Email: info@abtt.org.uk
Website: http://www.abtt.org.uk
Members: 1700
Staff: 3
Contact: Mark White, Chm.
Fee: £15
Membership Type: student, retired
Fee: £45
Membership Type: associate, regular
Description: Individuals concerned with the technical side of theatre. Covers theatre planning and all technical aspects of theatrical presentation.
Publication title: Codes of Practice for the Theatre Industry

00702

Association of British Theological and Philosophical Libraries
ABTAPL

London School of Theology, Green Ln., London, HA6 2UW, UK
Tel: 01923 456192
Email: a.linfield@lst.ac.uk
Website: http://www.abtapl.org.uk
Members: 200
Contact: Alan Linfield, Chm.
Fee: £25
Membership Type: institutional
Fee: £15
Membership Type: personal
Description: Librarians, philosophers, and theologians; philosophy and theology libraries; divinity schools. Promotes discussion and exchange of information among librarians working with theological, philosophical, and related materials. Organizes visits to a variety of libraries to encourage familiarity with modern library practice. Provides members with an informal network for consultation, advice, and support.
Publication title: A Guide to the Theological Libraries of Great Britain and Ireland

00703
Association of British Travel Agents
ABTA
68-71 Newman St., London, W1T 3AH, UK
Tel: 020 73071900
Fax: 020 73071920
Email: abta@abta.co.uk
Website: http://www.abta.com/home
Members: 8956
Staff: 60
Contact: Daniele Broccoli, Contact
Fee: £540
Membership Type: full
Fee: £1000
Membership Type: travel industry partner
Description: Travel agents and tour operators working to create a favorable business environment and ensure high standards of service and accountability to the traveling public. Mandates the use of precise financial parameters for travel and tour services. Offers complaint conciliation and arbitration services. Liaises and negotiates with trade and governmental regulatory bodies.
Library Subject: travel
Library Type: not open to the public
Publication: Handbook
Publication title: Members Handbook
Meetings/Conventions: Travel Convention – annual convention – Exhibits.

00704
Association of British Wild Animal Keepers
ABWAK
Edinburgh Zoo, Education Department, 134 Corstorphine Rd., Edinburgh, EH12 6TS, UK
Email: abwak-enquiries@live.co.uk
Website: http://www.abwak.co.uk
Members: 400
Contact: Alaina Macri, Membership Sec.
Fee: £25-45
Membership Type: professional, associate
Fee: £45
Membership Type: joint
Description: Wild animal keepers in Great Britain. Promotes communication and exchange among members.
Publication: Journal
Publication title: RATEL

00705
Association of Broadcasting Doctors
ABD
1 Lark Bank, Prickwillow, Cambridge, Ely, CB7 4SW, UK
Tel: 01353 687966
Email: jackiepetts@oneservice.co.uk
Website: http://www.broadcasting-doctor.org
Members: 680
Staff: 3
Contact: Jackie Petts, Admin.
Description: Practicing clinicians - consultants and GPs - who also broadcast in local, regional and national radio and television. Provides training and support for members with the aim of improving the standards of medical broadcasting; acts as a clearing house for broadcasting organizations seeking medical contributors; updates members on medical advances which might attract public attention; acts on behalf of members in their relationships with broadcasting organizations.
Publication: Newsletter
Publication title: Broadcasting Doctor
Meetings/Conventions: Radio Training Session – quarterly workshop

00706
Association of Brokers and Yacht Agents
ABYA
Glass Works, Penns Rd., Petersfield, GU32 2EW, UK
Tel: 01730 710425
Fax: 01730 710423
Email: info@abya.co.uk
Website: http://www.ybdsa.co.uk
Members: 155
Staff: 5
Contact: Jane Gentry, Chief Exec./Company Sec.
Description: Professional association for small craft brokers and agents. Promotes membership of the association, use of standard documentation and maintenance of knowledge through training. Organizes training events, seminars, and others for its members. Operates Customs Warehousing scheme for ex-VAT boats being offered for sale in the UK.
Library Subject: surveying, brokerage
Library Type: reference
Publication title: Codes of Practice
Meetings/Conventions: annual conference

00707
Association of Building Engineers
ABE
Lutyens House, Billing Brook Rd., Weston Favell, Northamptonshire, Northampton, NN3 8NW, UK
Tel: 0845 1261058
Fax: 01604 784220
Email: building.engineers@abe.org.uk
Website: http://www.abe.org.uk
Members: 7000
Staff: 25
Contact: Simon Lawes, Pres.
Fee: £45
Membership Type: student, retired
Fee: £185
Membership Type: regular
Description: Promotes and advances the knowledge, study and practice of each and all of the arts and sciences concerned with building technology, planning, design, construction, maintenance and repair of the built environment and the creation and maintenance of a high standard of professional qualification, conduct and practice.
Library Subject: building engineering
Library Type: not open to the public
Formerly: Formerly, Incorporated Association of Architects and Surveyors
Publication: Journal
Publication title: Building Engineer. Advertisements.

00708
Association of Business Executives
ABE
5th Fl., CI Tower, St. George Sq., New Maiden, Surrey, London, KT3 4TE, UK
Tel: 020 83292930
Fax: 020 83292945
Email: complaints@abeuk.com
Website: http://www.abeuk.com
Members: 50000
Staff: 35
Contact: Lyndon Jones, Founder/Chm.
Fee: £25
Membership Type: student
Fee: £30
Membership Type: associate
Description: Student membership sitting examinations.
Publication title: Business Executive

00709
Association of Business Psychologists
ABP
180 Piccadilly, London, W1J 9ER, UK
Tel: 0207 9171733
Website: http://www.theabp.org.uk
Contact: Steve Whiddett, Chm.
Fee: £30
Membership Type: full
Description: Represents a community of professionals who are business-led, and psychology-focused. Disseminates information about psychological practices in business. Provides a forum for exploring the potential impact of psychology-based research on business.

00710
Association of Business Recovery Professionals
R3
8th Fl., 120 Aldersgate St., London, EC1A 4JQ, UK
Tel: 020 75664200
Fax: 020 75664224
Email: association@r3.org.uk
Website: http://www.r3.org.uk
Members: 3400
Staff: 12
Contact: Graham Rumney, CEO
Fee: £67
Membership Type: student
Fee: £395
Membership Type: full
Description: Professional association for insolvency, business recovery, and turnaround specialists in the UK. Works to promote the best practice for professionals working with financially troubled individuals and businesses. Represents the interest of its members. Provides a forum for debate on key issues facing the profession.
Formerly: Formerly, Society of Practitioners of Insolvency
Publication: Journal
Publication title: Recovery. Advertisements.

00711
Association of Business Schools
ABS
137 Euston Rd., London, NW1 2AA, UK
Tel: 0207 3880007
Fax: 0207 3880009
Email: abs@the-abs.org.uk
Website: http://www.the-abs.org.uk
Members: 100
Staff: 4
Contact: Jonathan Slack, Chief Exec.
Fee: £2800
Membership Type: full
Fee: £700

Membership Type: associate
Description: Educational institutions offering business and management education programs in the United Kingdom. Seeks to advance the study, teaching, and practice of business, management, and related disciplines. Facilitates exchange of information among members; sponsors research and educational programs.

00712
Association of C and C Users
ACCU
23 Wordsworth Rd., Abingdon, OX14 5NY, UK
Email: accumembership@accu.org
Website: http://accu.org
Members: 1000
Contact: Mick Brooks, Contact
Fee: £17.5
Membership Type: student
Fee: £35
Membership Type: full
Description: Developers, trainers and implementers of C, C, and Java products (compilers, libraries) and programmers using these products. Aims to support good programming practice in C, C, and Java. It also represents the views of C, C, and Java users at national and international level on committees concerned with standards for these languages.
Publication: Journal
Publication title: C Vu. Advertisements.

00713
Association of Camphill Communities
AOCC
Murtle House, Bieldside, Aberdeen, AB15 8TT, UK
Tel: 01384 441680
Fax: 01224 868420
Email: sam@camphillscotland.org.uk
Website: http://www.camphill.org.uk
Members: 75000
Description: Individuals interested in the development of children and adults with learning disabilities. Promotes full cultural, social, and economic integration of all people, particularly those with learning disabilities or other vulnerabilities. Maintains egalitarian communities in which individuals can improve their self-esteem and social and economic skills in a supportive environment. Conducts educational programs; provides support and services to people with learning disabilities and other vulnerable individuals.
Publication: Brochure
Publication title: An Introduction to Camphill Communities

00714
Association of Car Rental Industry Systems Standards
ACRISS
Aslan Rise, 8 St. Mary's Garth, Buxted, East Sussex, Uckfield, TN22 4LY, UK
Tel: 0791 2344305
Email: acrisseeig@aol.com
Website: http://www.acriss.org
Fee: £16000
Membership Type: principal
Fee: £3000
Membership Type: associate
Description: Aims to facilitate the use of computerized reservation systems for car rental services in Europe; formulates and recommends standards for use in the design, installation, and use of computerized systems used by travel agents, car rental reservations, including systems using ticketing and invoicing facilities.

00715
Association of Cardiothoracic Anaesthetists
ACTA
Royal College of Anaesthetists, Churchill House, 35 Red Lion Sq., London, WC1R 4SG, UK
Email: acta@rcoa.ac.uk
Website: http://www.acta.org.uk
Members: 400
Contact: Clare Bunnell, Admin
Fee: £40
Membership Type: consultant, overseas (with hard copy of newsletter)
Fee: £25
Membership Type: associate, overseas (with electronic copy of newsletter)
Description: Consultants who are currently engaged in the practice of cardiothoracic anaesthesia. Aims to further the development of the art and science of caring for patients undergoing heart and chest surgery.
Publication: Newsletter
Publication title: ACTA News

00716
Association of Certified Fraud Examiners, United Kingdom Chapter
26 York St., London, W1U 6PZ, UK
Tel: 0207 8732209
Fax: 0207 1837843
Email: info@acfeuk.co.uk
Website: http://www.acfeuk.co.uk
Contact: David Alexander, Pres.
Description: Aims to reduce the incidence of fraud and white-collar crimes. Works to set high standards and strict code of professional conduct among fraud examiners. Provides members the opportunity to enhance their capabilities through educational tools, networking opportunities and career development.

00717
Association of Charitable Foundations
ACF
Central House, 14 Upper Woburn Pl., London, WC1H 0AE, UK
Tel: 020 72554499
Email: acf@acf.org.uk
Website: http://www.acf.org.uk
Members: 300
Staff: 8
Contact: John Kingston, Chm.
Fee: £95-4950
Membership Type: full (based on grant expenditure)
Fee: £95-3610
Membership Type: associate, affiliate (based on grant expenditure)
Description: Grant-making trusts and foundations. Supports the work of grant-making charitable trusts and foundations in the U.K.
Library Subject: charitable grant-making
Library Type: not open to the public
Publication: Magazine
Publication title: Trust & Foundation News
Meetings/Conventions: Better Giving – biennial conference

00718
Association of Charity Officers
ACO
Five Ways, 57/59 Hatfield Rd., Hertfordshire, Potters Bar, EN6 1HS, UK
Tel: 01707 651777
Fax: 01707 660477
Email: info@aco.uk.net
Website: http://www.aco.uk.net
Members: 200
Staff: 5
Description: Executive officers or secretaries of benevolent funds and registered exempt charities giving non-contributory relief to individuals in need. Seeks to: encourage and improve liaison and cooperation between charities; represent charities on legislative issues; discover those in need and solicit help from members' funds. Informs and advises individuals, governmental and statutory bodies, and voluntary organizations; sponsors discussion groups; disseminates information and provides training classes.
Publication title: Individuals in Need: Guidelines for Grantmakers

00719
Association of Chartered Certified Accountants - United Kingdom
ACCA UK
29 Lincoln's Inn Fields, London, WC2A 3EE, UK
Tel: 020 70595000
Fax: 020 70595050
Email: info@accaglobal.com
Website: http://www.uk.accaglobal.com
Members: 131500
Contact: Branden Murtagh, Chief Exec.
Description: Represents accountants and accounting students. Promotes quality accounting and financial qualifications. Strives to provide professional opportunities and access to people of ability around.
Library Subject: accounting, business
Library Type: reference
Publication: Journal
Publication title: Accounting and Business. Advertisements.

00720
Association of Chief Estate Surveyors and Property Managers in Local Government
ACES
23 Athol Rd., Bramhall, Cheshire, SK7 1BR, UK
Tel: 0161 4399589
Fax: 0161 4407383
Email: secretary@aces.org.uk
Website: http://www.aces.org.uk
Members: 352
Contact: Tim Foster, Sec.
Fee: £100
Membership Type: regular
Description: Serving and former local government valuers and estate surveyors. Seeks to co-ordinate the application of the principles and practice of valuation and estate management in the interest of Local Authorities. Provides a forum for discussion and dissemination of information. Encourages an exchange of views with other Associations and bodies dealing with matters of valuation and estate management.
Publication: Magazine
Publication title: The Terrier. Advertisements.

00721
Association of Chief Executives of Voluntary Organisations
ACEVO
1 New Oxford St., London, WC1A 1NU, UK
Tel: 020 72804960
Fax: 020 72804989
Email: info@acevo.org.uk
Website: http://www.acevo.org.uk
Members: 1700
Staff: 14
Contact: Lesley-Anne Alexander, Chair
Fee: £190-610
Membership Type: full (based on annual income of organization)
Fee: £190
Membership Type: associate
Description: Chief executives of voluntary organizations. Aims to improve standards within the voluntary sector by improving the professionalism and effectiveness of chief executives of voluntary organizations.
Publication: Book
Publication title: And Why Not? Tapping The Talent of Not-for-profit Chief Executives
Meetings/Conventions: North West Regional Forum – annual meeting

00722
Association of Chief Police Officers in Scotland
ACPOS
26 Holland St., Glasgow, G2 4NH, UK
Tel: 0141 4351230
Email: secretariat@acpos.pnn.police.uk
Website: http://www.acpos.police.uk
Contact: Pat Shearer, Pres.
Description: Represents Scottish police officers.

00723
Association of Chief Police Officers of England, Wales and Northern Ireland
ACPO
10 Victoria St., 1st Fl., London, SW1H 0NN, UK
Tel: 020 70848950
Fax: 020 70848951
Email: info@acpo.pnn.police.uk
Website: http://www.acpo.police.uk
Members: 336
Staff: 20
Contact: Hugh Orde, Pres.
Description: Chief police officers in England, Wales and Northern Ireland.
Publication: Journal
Publication title: Policing Today. Advertisements.

00724
Association of Child Abuse Lawyers
ACAL
Ste. 13, Claremont House, 22 - 24 Claremont Rd., Surbiton, KT6 4QU, UK
Tel: 020 83904701
Fax: 020 83991152
Email: info@childabuselawyers.com
Website: http://www.childabuselawyers.com
Contact: Peter Garsden, Pres.
Fee: £40
Membership Type: student
Fee: £85
Membership Type: non-practicing
Description: Represents and improves the standards of lawyers, experts and other professionals involved in obtaining compensation for the physical, sexual or emotional abuse of children and adults. Provides practical support for professionals and survivors in the field of abuse.

00725
Association of Child Psychotherapists
ACP
120 W Heath Rd., London, NW3 7TU, UK
Tel: 020 84581609
Fax: 020 84581482
Email: contactus@childpsychotherapy.org.uk
Website: http://www.childpsychotherapy.org.uk
Members: 760
Contact: Angie Lee Lazone, Admin.
Description: Safeguards the interests of psychotherapists and fosters the exchange of information on the treatments of psychological disturbances of behavior, thinking, and feeling. Provides a forum for discussion.
Publication: Journal
Publication title: Journal of Child Psychotherapy. Advertisements.
Meetings/Conventions: annual conference – Exhibits.

00726
Association of Christian Teachers
ACT
94A London Rd., St. Albans, AL1 1NX, UK
Tel: 01727 840298
Fax: 01727 848966
Email: act@christians-in-education.org.uk
Website: http://www.christians-in-education.org.uk
Members: 2450
Staff: 3
Contact: Arthur Jones, Chm.
Fee: £40
Membership Type: standard
Fee: £20
Membership Type: unwaged, retired, low income, working overseas as a missionary
Description: Works to serve, inspire and equip Christian teachers in England and around the world.
Publication: Magazine
Publication title: ACT Now. Advertisements.

00727
Association of Cities and Regions for Recycling and Sustainable Resource Management
ACR
Ave. d'Auderghem 63, Skipton, BD23 1EP, UK
Tel: 032 22346500
Fax: 032 22346501
Email: info@acrplus.org
Website: http://www.acrplus.org
Members: 98
Staff: 5
Contact: Jean-Pierre Hannequart, Pres.
Description: Cities and regions operating recycling programs. Promotes increased recycling of municipal waste to reduce the buildup of solid wastes in landfill sites. Serves as a clearinghouse on municipal recycling programs; provides consulting services to cities wishing to establish prevention and recycling schemes; advocates for the increased use of recyclable packaging.
Formerly: Formerly, Association of Cities for Recycling
Publication: Newsletter

00728
Association of Clinical Embryologists
ACE
Kelmer Court House, 102 Sale Ln., Manchester, M29 8PZ, UK
Tel: 0161 17902020
Fax: 0161 17902020
Email: support@embryologists.org.uk
Website: http://www.embryologists.org.uk
Members: 400
Contact: Mike Hooper, Sec.
Fee: £40
Membership Type: full
Fee: £20
Membership Type: associate - UK
Description: Supports the professional interests of embryologists working in the UK. Promotes high standards of practice in clinical embryology. Advances the education and training of persons engaged in the profession. Conducts and makes public the results of research about embryology. Supports persons suffering from subfertility.
Publication: Newsletter
Publication title: The Embryologist. Advertisements.

00729
Association of Clinical Pathologists
ACP
189 Dyke Rd., Hove, BN3 1TL, UK
Tel: 01273 775700
Fax: 01273 773303
Email: info@pathologists.org.uk
Website: http://www.pathologists.org.uk
Contact: Robin Reid, Pres.
Fee: £127
Membership Type: ordinary
Fee: £77
Membership Type: trainee
Description: Promotes the study and practice of clinical pathology. Seeks to improve the status of clinical pathologists and make them equal to other consultants. Assists medical schools. Aims to provide a forum where members could exchange views on work and research.
Publication: Newsletter
Publication title: ACP News. Advertisements.

00730
Association of Colleges
AoC
2-5 Stedham Pl., London, WC1A 1HU, UK
Tel: 020 70349900
Fax: 020 70349950
Email: enquiries@aoc.co.uk
Website: http://www.aoc.co.uk
Members: 400
Staff: 4
Contact: Martin Doel, Chief Exec.
Description: FE colleges throughout the UK.

00731

Association of Coloproctology of Great Britain and Ireland ACPGBI

c/o The Royal College of Surgeons of England
35-43 Lincoln's Inn Fields, London, WC2A 3PE, UK
Tel: 020 79730307
Fax: 020 74309235
Email: acpgbi@asgbi.org.uk
Website: http://www.acpgbi.org.uk
Members: 1272
Staff: 1
Contact: Najib Y. Haboubi, Pres.
Fee: £250
Membership Type: ordinary surgical
Fee: £80
Membership Type: associate, staff grade
Description: Acts as a multidisciplinary association that promotes standards and training in coloproctology.
Publication: Journal
Publication title: Colorectal Disease. Advertisements.

00732

Association of Commonwealth Archivists and Records Managers ACARM

7 Ln. Close, Dollis Hill, London, NW2 6QZ, UK
Tel: 020 30845736
Fax: 020 78316303
Email: newsletter@acarm.org
Website: http://www.acarm.org
Members: 120
Contact: Luis De Carvalho, Membership Sec./Admin.
Fee: £15
Membership Type: individual
Fee: £100
Membership Type: national archive
Description: Individual archivists and others representing 57 archives institutions or other specialized repositories in 32 Commonwealth countries. Facilitates exchange of information and experience among archivists and records managers with a common archival heritage, and promotes better understanding of the Commonwealth through the use of records. Works to reaffirm the importance of archives in the national heritage of member countries. Encourages the dissemination of archival material among member institutions. Seeks to establish professional training programs and set high standards in an effort to further the development of archival knowledge and skill.
Formerly: Formerly, Commonwealth Archivists Association
Publication: Newsletter
Publication title: ACARM Newsletter. Advertisements.

00733

Association of Commonwealth Universities ACU

Woburn House, 20-24 Tavistock Sq., London, WC1H 9HF, UK
Tel: 020 73806700
Fax: 020 73872655
Email: info@acu.ac.uk
Website: http://www.acu.ac.uk
Members: 500
Contact: John Wood, Sec. Gen.
Description: Voluntary association of 500 universities in 35 Commonwealth countries or regions. Promotes contact and cooperation among universities of the Commonwealth. Provides information about universities. Administers scholarship and fellowship programs (including the Commonwealth Scholarship and Fellowship Plan (CSFP)). Also publicizes vacancies in member universities and certain other institutions through its advertising and publicity services section. Policy and research unit coordinates and disseminates research on higher education.
Formerly: Formerly, Universities Bureau of the British Empire
Publication: Magazine
Publication title: ACU Bulletin
Meetings/Conventions: Conference of Executive Heads – periodic conference

00734

Association of Community Rail Partnerships ACORP

Rail and River Centre, Canal Side, Civic Hall, 15a New St., Slaithwaite, Huddersfield, HD7 5AB, UK
Tel: 01484 847790
Fax: 01484 847877
Email: office@acorp.uk.com
Website: http://www.acorp.uk.com
Contact: Neil Buxton, Gen. Mgr.
Fee: £150
Membership Type: funded organization
Fee: £75
Membership Type: not funded voluntary organization
Description: Improves station facilities, train services and effectiveness of local railways. Helps identify innovative solutions for local railways. Disseminates examples of good practice and organizes training sessions for local railway management.
Publication: Magazine
Publication title: Train Times

00735

Association of Computer Professionals ACP

Chilverbridge House, East Sussex, Arlington, BN26 6SB, UK
Tel: 01323 871874
Fax: 01323 871875
Email: admin@acpexamboard.com
Website: http://www.acpexamboard.com
Members: 6000
Staff: 18
Contact: N. Keats, Sec. Gen.
Fee: £42
Membership Type: student group, practitioner
Fee: £50
Membership Type: licentiate, graduate
Description: Mainly student membership. Prepares candidates through examination for a successful career in computing up to Higher National Diploma Standard.

00736

Association of Consultant Architects ACA

60 Godwin Rd., Kent, Bromley, BR2 9LQ, UK
Tel: 020 83251402
Fax: 020 84669079
Email: office@acarchitects.co.uk
Website: http://www.acarchitects.co.uk
Contact: Alison Low, Sec. Gen.
Description: Architectural consultants in the U.K. Seeks to encourage excellence in the quality of service that is offered to clients. Represents exclusively the aims and interests of architects in private practice on issues of practice.
Publication: Handbook
Publication title: ACA Form of Building Agreement

00737

Association of Consulting Actuaries ACA

St. Clement's House, 27-28 Clement's Ln., London, EC4N 7AE, UK
Tel: 020 32079380
Fax: 020 32079134
Email: acahelp@aca.org.uk
Website: http://www.aca.org.uk
Members: 1700
Contact: Stuart Southall, Chm.
Description: Independent actuaries engaged in private practice. Facilitates the exchange of views and information between consulting trustees, actuaries and the organizations they represent. Advises pension scheme trustee companies, life and general insurance companies in the United Kingdom and overseas.
Publication: Newsletter
Publication title: Placard

00738

Association of Consulting Scientists ACS

5 Willow Heights, Cradley Health, West Midlands, B64 7PL, UK
Tel: 0121 6023515
Fax: 0121 6021062
Email: sgc@sgconsult.co.uk
Website: http://www.consultsci.uku.co.uk
Members: 25
Description: Firms engaged in scientific consultancy, the provision of analytical and testing services, the undertaking of contract research.

00739

Association of Contact Lens Manufacturers ACLM

PO Box 735, Devizes, SN10 3TQ, UK
Tel: 01380 860418
Fax: 01380 860863
Email: secgen@aclm.org.uk
Website: http://www.aclm.org.uk
Members: 30
Contact: Simon Rodwell, Sec. Gen.
Description: Manufacturers of contact lenses. Promotes the growth and development of the domestic contact lens industry. Facilitates communication and cooperation among members; represents members before government agencies, labor, professional, medical, and industrial organizations, and the public.

00740
Association of Convenience Stores
ACS

17 Farnborough St., Federation House, Hampshire, Farnborough, GU14 8AG, UK
Tel: 01252 515001
Fax: 01252 515002
Email: acs@acs.org.uk
Website: http://www.acs.org.uk
Members: 32000
Staff: 12
Contact: James Lowman, Chief Exec.
Fee: £148
Membership Type: full, associate
Description: Represents the interest of over 25,000 convenience and small store operators. Represents members' interests in matters relating to national and EU legislation and also provides a number of retail services.
Publication: Newsletter
Publication title: thelocalshop.com. Advertisements.

00741
Association of Corporate Treasurers
ACT

51 Moorgate, London, EC2R 6BH, UK
Tel: 020 78472540
Fax: 020 73748744
Email: enquiries@treasurers.org
Website: http://www.treasurers.org
Members: 4000
Contact: Matthew Hurn, Pres.
Fee: £253
Membership Type: fellow
Fee: £232
Membership Type: associate
Description: Professional body supporting those working in treasury, risk and corporate finance in the international marketplace. Promotes the study and best practice of finance and treasury management; offers education and examination, conferences, publications and training for financial professionals.
Library Subject: finance and treasury
Library Type: not open to the public
Publication: Magazine
Publication title: The Treasurer. Advertisements.
Meetings/Conventions: conference

00742
Association of Cost Engineers
ACOSTE

Lea House, 5 Middlewich Rd., Cheshire, Sandbach, CW11 1XL, UK
Tel: 01270 764798
Fax: 01270 766180
Email: enquiries@acoste.org.uk
Website: http://www.acoste.org.uk
Members: 2140
Staff: 4
Contact: Rajkumar Roy, Pres.
Fee: £105
Membership Type: fellow
Fee: £95
Membership Type: regular
Description: Membership is from the client, contracting and professional areas of industry. Covers planning, project management and cost control. Different grades: fellows, members, associates, graduates, students. Cost engineering embraces activities such as estimating, cost control, construction management, investment appraisal and risk analysis.
Library Subject: cost engineering
Library Type: not open to the public
Publication: Journal
Publication title: Project Control Professional

00743
Association of Council Secretaries and Solicitors
ACSeS

Afon Bldg., Worthing Rd., Horsham, RH12 1TL, UK
Tel: 01403 788249
Fax: 01403 788241
Email: tonykilner@acses.org.uk
Website: http://www.acses.org.uk
Members: 515
Staff: 1
Contact: Mirza Ahmad, Pres.
Fee: £250-300
Membership Type: full (based on the geographical branch)
Fee: £185-200
Membership Type: past service employed (based on the geographical branch)
Description: Chief officers or officers of comparable status and deputies wholly or substantially responsible for the management of the administrative, secretarial and legal functions of local, police and fire authorities in England and Wales. Confers on all matters affecting local government, promotes and develops professional knowledge and talent, and gives advice to any association of local authorities or any other body.
Formerly: Formed by Merger of, Society of County Secretaries
Meetings/Conventions: annual conference

00744
Association of Cycle Traders
ACT

PO Box 5110, Hove, BN52 9EB, UK
Tel: 08456 187256
Email: info@actsmart.biz
Website: http://www.thecyclingexperts.co.uk
Members: 850
Contact: David Wilsher, Pres.
Description: Cycle retailers and individuals in related fields united to improve the safety standards of cycles. Negotiates with government departments, media, and manufacturers to provide a safe environment for cyclists. Seeks to develop new initiative, which endeavors to increase awareness and understandings of the benefits local bike shops have to offer. Supports the future of cycling in the UK. Campaigns actively on behalf of independent cycle shops to ensure that their voice is heard and understood.
Formerly: Formerly, National Association of Cycle and Motorcycle Traders
Publication: Newsletter
Publication title: The Independent

00745
Association of Directors of Children's Services
ADCS

The Triangle, 3rd Fl., Exchange Sq., Manchester, M4 3TR, UK
Tel: 0161 8385757
Fax: 0161 8385756
Email: info@adcs.org.uk
Website: http://www.adcs.org.uk
Contact: Edwina Grant, Honorary Sec.
Description: Represents statutory directors of children's services (DCS) and other children's services professionals in leadership roles. Provides a national leadership for DCSs appointed under the provisions of the Children Act 2004. Serves as a voice for children with local and central government and with the public. Promotes research, development, innovation and learning across children's services.

00746
Association of Directors of Social Work
ADSW

Rosebery House, 9 Haymarket Terr., Edinburgh, EH12 5EZ, UK
Tel: 0131 4749220
Email: sophie.mills@adsw.org.uk
Website: http://www.adsw.org.uk
Contact: Sophie Mills, Admin.
Description: Promotes social welfare and social inclusion and the interests of users, carers and vulnerable people. Establishes internal networks to discuss policy and to address social work issues. Seeks to encourage innovation, share developments and issues, and disseminate good practice across Scotland. Organizes and disseminates research into methods and standards.

00747
Association of Disabled Professionals
ADP

BCM ADP, London, WC1N 3XX, UK
Tel: 01204 431638
Fax: 01204 431638
Email: info@adp.org.uk
Website: http://www.adp.org.uk
Members: 250
Staff: 1
Contact: Kath Sutherland, Development Off.
Fee: £20
Membership Type: full
Fee: £25
Membership Type: sustaining/international
Description: Professionals and students with disabilities. Offers advice and information especially on employment and educational issues. Provides means to disabled professionals and those in managerial positions to network and offer advice and support. Maintains liaisons with government authorities.
Publication title: ADP Quarterly

00748
Association of Drainage Authorities
ADA

Wellington House, Manby Park, Lincolnshire, Manby, LN11 8UU, UK
Fax: 0150 7328097
Email: admin@ada.org.uk
Website: http://www.ada.org.uk
Members: 300
Contact: Jean Venables, Chief Exec.
Description: Flood defense and drainage authorities in England and Wales with associate membership extended to local authorities, manufacturers, suppliers

and other bodies interested in flood defense and land drainage. Represents the interests of flood defense and land drainage in consultation with government departments and other national bodies and to provide an advisory service to the membership. Interests are served through Finance and Administration, Technical and Environmental and Publicity Committees.

00749

Association of Ductwork Contractors and Allied Services ADCAS

Federation of Environmental Trade Association, Milley Ln., Hare Hatch, 2 Waltham Ct., Reading, RG10 9TH, UK
Tel: 0118 9403416
Fax: 0118 9406258
Email: info@feta.co.uk
Website: http://www.feta.co.uk/adcas/index.htm
Contact: Malcolm Moss, Pres.
Fee: £200-2400
Membership Type: full
Fee: £400-800
Membership Type: associate
Description: Represents ductwork contractors' allied suppliers and manufacturers of equipment for ventilation and air conditioning systems. Provides training and continuing education. Introduces effective responses to changes in legislation, government standards and regulations and industry best practice.

00750

Association of Educational Psychologists AEP

4 The Riverside Ctre., Frankland Ln., Durham, DH1 4ED, UK
Tel: 0191 3849512
Fax: 0191 3865287
Email: enquiries@aep.org.uk
Website: http://www.aep.org.uk
Members: 2600
Staff: 6
Contact: Sean O'Donoghue, Pres.
Fee: £165
Membership Type: full
Fee: £108
Membership Type: affiliate
Description: Professional association and trade union for educational psychologists in the United Kingdom.
Publication: Journal
Publication title: Educational Psychology in Practice

00751

Association of Electoral Administrators AEA

c/o Gina Armstrong, Administration and Finance Mgr.
PO Box 201, South Eastern, Liverpool, L16 5HH, UK
Tel: 0151 2818246
Fax: 0151 2818246
Email: gina.armstong@aea-elections.co.uk
Website: http://www.aea-elections.co.uk/default.jsp
Members: 1600
Contact: John Turner, Chief Exec.
Description: Represents electoral administrators in Scotland. Aims to encourage training and education of the development of experience in members. Fosters the advancement of consistent and efficient administration of electoral registration and the conduct of elections.

00752

Association of Electrical and Mechanical Trades AEMT

St. Saviours House, St. Saviours Pl., York, YO1 7PJ, UK
Tel: 01904 674899
Fax: 01904 674896
Email: admin@aemt.co.uk
Website: http://www.aemt.co.uk
Description: Represents companies who supply, repair or service electrical and mechanical equipment. Provides meetings, training courses and programmes for members to maintain the highest standard of business practice and integrity.

00753

Association of Electricity Producers AEP

Charles House, 5-11 Regent St., London, SW1Y 4LR, UK
Tel: 020 79309390
Fax: 020 79309391
Email: enquiries@aepuk.com
Website: http://www.aepuk.com
Members: 106
Staff: 12
Contact: David Porter, Chief Exec.
Description: Companies using nearly all types of generating technology and all scales of production. Represents companies that generate and sell electricity.
Library Type: not open to the public
Formerly: Formerly, Association of Independent Electricity Producers

00754

Association of European Building Surveyors and Construction Experts

c/o The Royal Institution of Chartered Surveyors
12 Great George St., Parliament Sq., London, SW1P 3AD, UK
Tel: 020 73343734
Fax: 020 76951526
Email: aeebc@rics.org
Website: http://www.aeebc.org
Contact: Kevin Sheridan, Pres.
Fee: £100
Membership Type: affiliate individual
Fee: £300
Membership Type: affiliate organization
Description: Represents professional building surveyors and construction experts. Establishes standard practices for professionals working across European Union. Promotes training, education, and professional development of surveyors and experts who provide construction and property services in accordance with EU policy.

00755

Association of European Trade Mark Owners MARQUES

840 Melton Rd., Thurmaston, Leicester, LE4 8BN, UK
Tel: 0116 2640080
Fax: 0116 2640141
Email: info@marques.org
Website: http://www.marques.org
Contact: Guido Baumgartner, Chm.
Fee: £370
Membership Type: corporate
Fee: £650
Membership Type: expert
Description: Works to educate and promote the professional development of brand owners in the selection, management and protection of trademarks within a global economy.

00756

Association of Event Organisers AEO

119 High St., Hertfordshire, Berkhamsted, HP4 2DJ, UK
Tel: 01442 285810
Fax: 01442 875551
Email: info@aeo.org.uk
Website: http://www.aeo.org.uk
Members: 206
Staff: 10
Contact: Austen Hawkins, CEO
Fee: £720
Membership Type: organizer, associate
Description: Cross section of exhibition organizing companies and companies, which provide a service to exhibition organizers. Serves as the focal point for firms and people, who organize exhibitions in the UK, Europe and worldwide. Aims to safeguard and promote the interests of its members and to ensure that exhibitors and visitors to shows are guaranteed the highest quality service.
Formerly: Formerly, Association of Exhibition Organisers
Publication: Newsletter
Publication title: Exhibition Issues. Advertisements.

00757

Association of Festival Organisers AFO

c/o FolkArts England
PO Box 296, Derbyshire, Matlock, DE4 3XU, UK
Tel: 01629 827014
Fax: 01629 821874
Email: info@folkarts-england.org
Website: http://www.folkarts-england.org
Contact: Steve Heap, Dir.
Fee: £60
Membership Type: organization
Fee: £90
Membership Type: associate
Description: Works for and with the festival and event organisers. Supports live music, dance, song, arts, crafts and theatre.

00758

Association of Football Statisticians AFS

53a St. Philip St., London, SW8 3SR, UK
Tel: 020 77205079
Email: enquiries@11v11.com
Website: http://www.11v11.co.uk
Members: 1200
Staff: 12
Fee: £19.99
Membership Type: regular
Description: Soccer statisticians in 38 countries. Promotes increased interest in the sport of soccer and its history. Compiles statistics; develops and distributes educational materials.
Publication: Report
Publication title: AFS Report

00759
Association of Foreign Banks
AFB
1 Bengal Ct., London, EC3V 9DD, UK
Tel: 020 72838300
Fax: 020 72838302
Email: secretariat@foreignbanks.org.uk
Website: http://www.foreignbanks.org.uk
Members: 166
Staff: 3
Contact: Roger Gifford, Chm.
Description: Represents foreign banks and securities houses.
Formerly: Formerly, Foreign Banks and Securities Houses Association

00760
Association of Gardens Trusts
AGT
70 Cowcross St., London, EC1M 6EJ, UK
Tel: 020 72512610
Fax: 020 72512610
Email: gardenstrusts@agt.org.uk
Website: http://www.gardenstrusts.org.uk
Contact: Gilly M. Drummond, Pres.
Description: Assists in the protection, conservation, restoration or creation of garden land in United Kingdom for the education and enjoyment of the public. Promotes the formation of a new county gardens trust. Organizes workshops, seminars and annual conference.

00761
Association of Geotechnical and Geoenvironmental Specialists
AGS
c/o Forum Court
83 Copers Cope Rd., Beckenham, BR3 1NR, UK
Tel: 020 86588212
Fax: 020 86630949
Email: ags@ags.org.uk
Website: http://www.ags.org.uk/site/home/index.cfm
Members: 120
Staff: 2
Contact: Matthew Warner, Chm.
Fee: £250
Membership Type: associate, affiliate
Fee: £60
Membership Type: personal
Description: Consultants and contractors offering specialist services in site investigation, geotechnics, engineering geology, foundation design and construction, geoenvironmental engineering, geochemistry and hydrogeology. Promotes and enhances the quality of professional practice in geotechnical engineering. Facilitates liaison between all organizations operating in the field of geotechnics. Publishes guidelines on good practice and on ethical or professional matters.

00762
Association of Golf Writers
AGW
1 Pilgrims Bungalow, Mulberry Hill, Chilham, CT4 8AH, UK
Tel: 01227 732496
Fax: 01227 732496
Email: enquiries@agwgolf.org
Website: http://www.agwgolf.org
Members: 150
Contact: Andy Farrell, Admin.
Description: Journalists covering golf. Seeks to ensure good working conditions at events; gives advice on proper press facilities.

00763
Association of Governing Bodies of Independent Schools
AGBIS
3 Codicote Road, Hertfordshire, Welwyn, AL6 9LY, UK
Tel: 01438 840730
Fax: 00560 3432632
Email: admin@agbis.org.uk
Website: http://www.agbis.org.uk
Members: 730
Staff: 4
Contact: Stuart Westley, Gen. Sec.
Fee: £235
Description: Membership is restricted to the Governing Bodies of Independent Schools in the United Kingdom, which are constituted as educational charities. There are minimum requirements as to the number of pupils and academic achievement. Purpose Aims to advance education in Independent Schools; to discuss matters concerning the policy and administration of Independent schools, and to encourage co-operation between their governing bodies; to consider the relationship of such schools to the general educational interests of the community; to express the views of governing bodies on the foregoing matters, and to take such action as may be expedient.
Formerly: Formerly, Governing Bodies Association
Publication: Handbook
Publication title: Guidelines for Governors

00764
Association of Graduate Careers Advisory Services
AGCAS
Millennium House, 30 Junction Rd., Sheffield, S11 8XB, UK
Tel: 0114 2515750
Fax: 0114 2515751
Email: anne-marie.martin@careers.lon.ac.uk
Website: http://www.agcas.org.uk
Members: 1200
Staff: 12
Contact: Anne-Marie Martin, Pres.
Description: Represents higher education career services and professional staff in all United Kingdom and Irish universities and most of the major degree-awarding institutions of higher education. Provides a framework through which those involved in careers advisory work can exchange information and organize collaborative activities to lead and support the delivery of the highest quality career education, information and guidance for students and graduates.

00765
Association of Graduate Recruiters
AGR
The Innovation Ctre., Warwick Technology Park, Gallows Hill, Warwick, CV34 6UW, UK
Tel: 01926 623236
Fax: 01926 623237
Email: info@agr.org.uk
Website: http://www.agr.org.uk
Members: 700
Staff: 4
Contact: Carl Gilleard, Chief Exec.
Fee: £705
Membership Type: full
Fee: £105.75
Membership Type: company affiliate
Description: Aims to support employers in all aspects of graduate recruitment.
Publication title: A Newcomer's Guide to Graduate Recruitment

00766
Association of Guilds of Weavers, Spinners and Dyers
AGWSD
17 St. Marys Close, Henley-on-Thames, RG9 1RD, UK
Email: info@wsd.org.uk
Website: http://www.wsd.org.uk
Members: 5000
Contact: Matty Smith, Hon. Sec.
Description: Members belong to one of the country wide 103 affiliated guilds. Concerned with the preservation and improvement of craftsmanship in handweaving, spinning and dying for the benefit of the members and the promotion of public awareness in such craftsmanship. Provides opportunities for the exchange of information and widening of knowledge through specific schools, courses, conferences and exhibitions, lectures and library facilities.
Library Subject: spinning, weaving, tapestry weaving, dyeing with plants, synthetic dyeing, design, preparing fibre for spinning, wool and other fibres, weaving equipment
Library Type: reference
Publication: Magazine
Publication title: The Journal. Advertisements.

00767
Association of Heads of Outdoor Education Centres
AHOEC
Bendrigg Trust, Bendrigg Lodge, Old Hutton, Kendal, Cumbria, LA8 0NR, UK
Tel: 01539 723766
Email: trevor@bendrigg.org.uk
Website: http://www.ahoec.org/index.htm
Members: 150
Contact: Trevor Clark, Contact
Description: LEA and Private Centres, Outdoor Pursuits/Outward Bound/Environmental Study. Full time Heads or Deputy Heads in the UK. Promotes all-around personal development through outdoor education and residential provision; aims to develop, establish and maintain good and safe practice in outdoor education. Provides a regional and national forum for members. Encourages awareness of, and active respect for environment. Speaks publicly as a national authoritative body.
Publication title: Adventure Education

00768

Association of Healthcare Professionals
AHCP

Prospect House, 148 Lawrence St., York, YO10 3EB, UK
Tel: 07946 772620
Email: helpdesk@ahcp.co.uk
Website: http://www.ahcp.co.uk
Members: 800
Staff: 1
Contact: Penny Harrison, Natl. Sec.
Fee: £55
Membership Type: individual
Fee: £450
Membership Type: group
Description: Managers in cleaning and support services. Supplies, maintains and encourages an efficient domestic service to support the principal business operated in any building. Provides a national code of practice to complement professional and occupational training.
Library Type: reference
Formerly: Formerly, Association of Domestic Management

00769

Association of Hispanists of Great Britain and Ireland
AHGBI

Newcastle University, School of Modern Languages, Old Library Bldg., Newcastle upon Tyne, NE1 7RU, UK
Email: ann.davies@newcastle.ac.uk
Website: http://www.hispanists.org.uk
Members: 600
Contact: Ann Davies, Membership Sec.
Fee: £25
Membership Type: full
Fee: £10
Membership Type: retired
Description: Promotes the interests of lecturers in Hispanic Studies (including Catalan, Galician, Basque, Portuguese and Latin American) in universities in the UK and Ireland.

00770

Association of Holistic Biodynamic Massage Therapists
AHBMT

c/o Hayley Merron, Membership Sec.
Flat 4, St. Peters House, Windmill St., Macclesfield, SK11 7HS, UK
Email: enquiries@ahbmt.org
Website: http://www.ahbmt.org
Members: 60
Contact: Pam Bilinge, Chm.
Fee: £55
Membership Type: full
Fee: £27.5
Membership Type: student/associate/affiliate
Description: Represents the interests of people trained or training in biodynamic massage. Educates the public and other professionals about the nature and benefits of biodynamic massage. Provides a support network for members.
Publication: Journal
Publication title: Biodynamic Massage. Advertisements.

00771

Association of Home Information Pack Providers
AHIPP

Britannia House, Fernie Rd., Market Harborough, LE16 7PH, UK
Tel: 0870 9507739
Fax: 01604 743249
Email: info@hipassociation.co.uk
Website: http://www.hipassociation.co.uk
Members: 100
Contact: Mike Ockenden, Dir. Gen.
Fee: £12000
Membership Type: executive
Fee: £6000
Membership Type: associate
Description: Encourages and promotes standards for the production and provision of home information packs. Provides assistance to the government and others in the effective introduction of home information packs. Produces and disseminates policies, proposals and information about the industry. Facilitates a forum for the exchange of non-competitive information.

00772

Association of Humanistic Psychology Practitioners
AHPP

Box BCM AHPP, London, WC1N 3XX, UK
Tel: 08457 660326
Email: admin.ahpp@btinternet.com
Website: http://www.ahpp.org
Contact: John Gloster Smith, Gen. Sec.
Fee: £60-90
Membership Type: associate
Fee: £200
Membership Type: full
Description: Provides accreditation of humanistic psychotherapists as member organization of the U.K. Council for Psychotherapy and for other therapists and counselors; makes available referral services; conducts training and professional development programs. Disseminates information to members.

00773

Association of Illustrators
AOI

2nd Fl., Back Bldg., 150 Curtain Rd., London, EC2A 3AT, UK
Tel: 020 76134328
Email: info@theaoi.com
Website: http://www.theaoi.com
Members: 1300
Staff: 2
Contact: Derek Brazell, Interim Mgr.
Fee: £156
Membership Type: full
Description: Represents illustrators and those with an interest in illustration. Aims to support illustrators and promote British illustration.

00774

Association of Independent Computer Specialists
AICS

Honeyhill Bismore, Eastcombe, Stroud, GL6 7DG, UK
Tel: 0845 1235399
Email: honsec@aics.org.uk
Website: http://www.aics.org.uk
Contact: R.K. Brooks, Honorary Sec.
Fee: £70.5
Membership Type: associate, full
Description: Consultants, computer programmers, software designers, and training, communications, web designers and documentation specialists. Promotes high professional standards of conduct in independent computer services. Provides technical updates to members.

00775

Association of Independent Crop Consultants
AICC

Agriculture Pl., Drayton Farm, E Meon, Hampshire, Petersfield, GU32 1PN, UK
Tel: 01730 823881
Fax: 01730 823882
Email: aicc@farmline.com
Website: http://www.aicc.org.uk
Members: 230
Contact: Peter Taylor, Exec. Pres.
Description: Independent crop consultants and specialists connected with arable farming. Acts as a professional organization for the truly independent crop consultant. Aims to maintain professional standards and reinforce the independence of its members who provide all aspects of advice in agronomy, covering production, protection, planning and marketing. Full consideration is always given to the technical and practical implications, together with the importance of conservation and the environment, in the decision-making process.

00776

Association of Independent European Lawyers
AIEL

Burwood House, 2nd Fl., 14-16 Caxton St., London, SW1H 0QY, UK
Tel: 020 78731000
Fax: 020 78731000
Email: john.gray@williamsturges.co.uk
Website: http://www.aiel.com
Members: 14
Contact: John Gray, Sec.
Description: Independent attorneys. Promotes adherence to high standards of ethics and practice by members. Represents members' professional interests; sponsors continuing professional development courses.

00777

Association of Independent Financial Advisers
AIFA

2-6 Austin Friars House, Austin Friars, London, EC2N 2HD, UK
Tel: 020 76281287
Email: info@aifa.net
Website: http://www.aifa.net
Members: 17000
Staff: 8
Contact: Chris Cummings, Dir. Gen.
Fee: £295
Membership Type: individual (minimum)
Fee: £280
Membership Type: company (minimum)

Description: Trade association. Represents full time IFAs to government, EEC and regulators.
Formerly: Formerly, IFA Association
Publication: Magazine
Publication title: Selling Financial Services. Advertisements.

00778
Association of Independent Libraries
AIL
The Leeds Library, 18 Commercial St., Leeds, LS1 6AL, UK
Tel: 0113 2453071
Email: enquiries@theleedslibrary.co.uk
Website: http://www.independentlibraries.co.uk
Members: 30
Contact: Catherine Levy, Contact
Description: Historic and independent libraries, currently active and providing a general collection for a general readership. Helps maintain contact within the body of independent libraries, and seeks to enhance public awareness of the location and role of independent libraries as a vital part of national heritage and an important educational resource.
Publication: Newsletter
Publication title: AIL Newsletter

00779
Association of Independent Museums
AIM
4 Clayhall Rd., Gosport, PO12 2BY, UK
Tel: 02392 587751
Email: aimadmin@aim-museums.co.uk
Website: http://www.aim-museums.co.uk
Members: 900
Contact: Roger Hornshaw, Admin.
Fee: £30
Membership Type: individual
Fee: £30-70
Membership Type: museum (based on the number of visitors)
Description: Connects, supports and represents Independent museums. Unites museums not directly administered by government. Encourages exchange of experience and advice; represents members' interests. Organizes seminars and study visits.
Publication: Bulletin
Publication title: AIM Bulletin. Advertisements.

00780
Association of Independent Research and Technology Organisations
AIRTO
c/o CCFRA
Gloucestershire, Chipping Campden, GL55 6LD, UK
Tel: 01386 842247
Fax: 01386 842010
Email: airto@campden.co.uk
Website: http://www.airto.co.uk
Members: 35
Contact: Richard Brook, Pres.
Description: Represents the interests of techno-business consultants and contract research organisations in Europe.
Meetings/Conventions: periodic meeting

00781
Association of Independent Tour Operators
AITO
133A St. Margaret's Rd., Middlesex, Twickenham, TW1 1RG, UK
Tel: 020 87449280
Fax: 020 87443187
Email: info@aito.co.uk
Website: http://www.aito.co.uk
Members: 157
Staff: 9
Contact: Peter Burgess, Membership Mgr.
Fee: £411.25
Membership Type: individual
Description: Smaller specialist tour operators, all fully bonded for client protection, who offer the widest choice possible of quality products to their clients. Lobbies on behalf of small specialist tour operators. Helps them to market their products, arranges press functions, helps keep them up-to-date on industry issues that affect them and uses their joint purchasing power to buy a variety of products and services at good rates, particularly training courses and insurance. Upholds guidelines of the Quality Charter and Code of Business Practice. Promotes environmentally responsible tourism.
Publication: Newsletter
Publication title: Consumer

00782
Association of Industrial Laser Users
AILU
Oxford House, 100 Ock St., Oxfordshire, Abingdon, OX14 5DH, UK
Tel: 01235 539595
Fax: 01235 550499
Website: http://www.ailu.org.uk
Members: 270
Staff: 2
Contact: Mike Green, Exec. Sec.
Fee: £295
Membership Type: corporate
Fee: £70
Membership Type: individual
Description: Aims to foster cooperation and collaboration on non-competitive technical matters and provide a forum and mechanisms for sharing experience and expertise. Represents and promotes the interests of industrial laser users. Disseminates professional and other information to members. Promotes the best practice in the industrial applications of lasers in materials processing and allied technologies. Supports the maintenance and improvement of standards of safety and performance in the industrial user of lasers.
Publication: Magazine
Publication title: The Laser User

00783
Association of Industrial Road Safety Officers
AIRSO
68 The Blvd., Worthing, BN13 1LA, UK
Tel: 01903 506095
Email: airso@talk21.com
Website: http://www.airso.co.uk
Members: 400
Contact: Graham Feest, Sec.
Fee: £40
Membership Type: basic
Description: Open to individuals whose work is or has been connected with the promotion of road safety particularly in the areas of education, training and publicity. Acts as a professional organization for road safety in industry and represents the views of the Association's membership when in consultation with government bodies and agencies. Keeps members informed of current road safety policies and practices.

00784
Association of Insurance and Risk Managers
AIRMIC
6 Lloyd's Ave., London, EC3N 3AX, UK
Tel: 020 74807610
Fax: 020 77023752
Email: enquiries@airmic.co.uk
Website: http://www.airmic.com
Members: 1000
Contact: John Hurrell, CEO
Fee: £395
Membership Type: individual
Fee: £1130
Membership Type: corporate (based on the number members)
Description: Managers or senior members of risk management or insurance departments in industry, commerce, or government are members; junior members of risk management or insurance departments are associate members; instructors in risk management and other interested individuals are affiliate members. Serves as a forum for the exchange of ideas and information among members; disseminates information on technical matters and new practices in risk management and insurance. Represents members' interests before trade and market associations and government bodies; promotes public understanding of programs the nature and purposes of risk management; provides educational.
Publication: Magazine
Publication title: AIRMIC News
Meetings/Conventions: annual conference

00785
Association of Interior Specialists
AIS
Olton Bridge, 245 Warwick Rd., Solihull, B92 7AH, UK
Tel: 0121 7070077
Fax: 0121 7061949
Email: info@ais-interiors.org.uk
Website: http://ais-interiors.org.uk
Members: 400
Staff: 6
Contact: Martin Romaine, Pres.
Fee: £300
Membership Type: associate
Fee: £650
Membership Type: contractor
Description: Represents companies involved in the manufacture, supply and installation of all aspects of interior fit-outs and refurbishment, from main interior contractors to specialist fit-out contractors, and interior systems manufacturers to distributors. Maintains and works to improve the standards, quality of workmanship, training and technical expertise to benefit members and clients.
Formerly: Formerly, Partitioning and Interiors Association
Publication: Handbook
Publication title: AIS Site Guide for Partitioning

00786

Association of International Accountants
AIA

Staithes 3, The Watermark, Metro Riverside, Newcastle upon Tyne, NE11 9SN, UK
Tel: 0191 4930277
Fax: 0191 4930278
Website: http://www.aiaworldwide.com
Staff: 20
Contact: Andrew Lamb, Pres.
Description: Offers an internationally recognized qualification for professional accountants. Works to promote and support the progress of the accountancy profession in UK and other countries. Seeks to ensure that its examinations and membership requirements support the development of the accountancy profession in the countries in which it examines.
Publication: Journal
Publication title: International Accountant. Advertisements.
Meetings/Conventions: annual meeting

00787

Association of International Couriers and Express Services
AICES

1st Fl., Unit 6, Poyle 14 Newlands Dr., Colnbrook, SL3 0DX, UK
Tel: 01753 680550
Fax: 01753 687033
Email: info@aices.org
Website: http://www.aices.org
Contact: Anne De Courcy, Sec. Gen.
Description: International courier and express services companies. Seeks to: represent and promote the industry; improve and maintain professional standards; serve as a negotiating body; promote development of similar overseas associations.
Formerly: Formerly, Association of International Air Courier Services

00788

Association of Investment Companies
AIC

9th Fl., 24 Chiswell St., London, EC1Y 4YY, UK
Tel: 020 72825555
Fax: 020 72825556
Email: enquiries@theaic.co.uk
Website: http://www.theaic.co.uk
Members: 300
Staff: 25
Contact: Lori Fox, Membership Dir.
Description: Investment trust companies which are approved by the Inland Revenue under s842 ICTA 1988, or under S842AA ICTA and also certain closed-end funds which are not so approved but nonetheless satisfy all the tests in S842. Eligible companies must be closed-end, listed on the London Stock Exchange and whose business is primarily the management of a portfolio consisting mainly of shares and securities. Concerned with the promotion, protection and advancement of the interests of closed-ended investment trust companies and their shareholders by influencing developments in legislation and practice affecting investors, companies and the stock market, by political lobbying and by promotion of their merits, in particular to private investors and independent financial advisers.
Formerly: Formerly, Association of Investment Trust Companies - England
Publication: Booklet
Publication title: AIC Stats

00789

Association of Labour Providers

102 Frimley House, 5 The Parade, High St., Frimley, GU16 7JQ, UK
Tel: 01276 509306
Fax: 01276 761076
Email: info@labourproviders.org.uk
Website: http://www.labourproviders.org.uk
Contact: David Camp, Dir.
Fee: £300-1500
Membership Type: organization
Fee: £500
Membership Type: associate
Description: Seeks to promote labour providers. Represents the views of labour providers to growers, packhouses, supermarkets and government departments and agencies. Provides commentary, guidance and advice on legal and regulatory developments relevant to the provision of labor. Establishes, endorses and enforces codes of practice for the provision of labor.

00790

Association of Landscape Contractors of Ireland
ALCI

22 Summerhill Park, Bangor, BT20 5QQ, UK
Tel: 028 91272823
Fax: 028 91272823
Email: secretary@alci.org.uk
Website: http://www.alci.org.uk
Members: 120
Contact: Lyn Sherriff, Coor.
Description: Represents and supports landscape contractors in Ireland.

00791

Association of Language Testers in Europe
ALTE

1 Hills Rd., Cambridge, CB1 2EU, UK
Tel: 01223 552780
Fax: 01223 553036
Email: info@alte.org
Website: http://www.alte.org
Members: 31
Contact: Michael Milanovic, Mgr.
Fee: £2000
Membership Type: full
Fee: £1000
Membership Type: associate
Description: Works to establish common standards and fairness for all stages of the language testing process, including test development, test administration, marking and grading, reporting of test results, test analysis, and reports of findings.

00792

Association of Laparoscopic Surgeons of Great Britain and Ireland
ALS

c/o The Royal College of Surgeons of England
35-43 Lincoln's Inn Fields, London, WC2A 3PE, UK
Tel: 020 79730305
Fax: 020 74309235
Email: jtreglohan@asgbi.org.uk
Website: http://www.alsgbi.org
Contact: Jenny Treglohan, Exec. Off.
Fee: £195
Membership Type: full (with EAES and journal)
Fee: £130
Membership Type: full (without EAES and journal)
Description: Represents surgeons in all aspects of laparoscopic surgery. Aims to foster developments in laparoscopic surgery. Supports training, maintenance of clinical standards and research and development of new laparoscopic techniques.
Meetings/Conventions: annual meeting November 16 to 17, 2011. Norwich United Kingdom

00793

Association of Law Costs Draftsmen
ALCD

Church Cottage, Church Ln., Stuston, Diss, IP21 4AG, UK
Tel: 01379 741404
Fax: 01379 742702
Email: enquiries@alcd.org.uk
Website: http://www.alcd.org.uk
Members: 800
Contact: Iain Stark, Chm.
Fee: £50
Membership Type: student
Description: Voluntary membership to a professional body of Law Costs Draftsmen, which enables members to take examinations to associate/fellowship level.
Publication: Journal
Publication title: ALCD Journal. Advertisements.

00794

Association of Law Teachers
ALT

BPP Law School, 68-70 Red Lion St., Plymouth, WC1R 4NY, UK
Email: chrismaguire@bppls.com
Website: http://www.lawteacher.ac.uk
Members: 850
Contact: Chris Maguire, Chm.
Fee: £30
Membership Type: individual (UK and other EU states)
Fee: £35
Membership Type: individual (non-EU)
Description: Law teachers from higher and further education. Furthers the study, understanding and reform of educational aspects of law and its teaching, and represents members' views on the teaching of law and the general support and encouragement of activities of benefit to law teachers.
Publication: Journal
Publication title: The Law Teacher. Advertisements.

00795

Association of Lawyers for Children
ALC

PO Box 283, East Molesey, KT8 0WH, UK
Tel: 0208 2247071
Email: admin@alc.org.uk
Website: http://www.alc.org.uk
Members: 1200
Contact: Julia Higgins, Admin.
Fee: £85
Membership Type: full
Fee: £40
Membership Type: associate
Description: Lawyers, social workers, children's guardians, doctors, and others who work with or for children. Offers training, consultation and research, to improve knowledge, furthering best practice, and encouraging inter-agency understanding in work with and for children. Upholds the welfare of children, and raises awareness of children's rights and needs.
Publication: Newsletter
Publication title: ALC Newsletter. Advertisements.
Meetings/Conventions: Making Contact Work – meeting

00796

Association of Learned and Professional Society Publishers
ALPSP

51 Middletons Rd., Yaxley, Peterborough, PE7 3NU, UK
Tel: 01733 247178
Fax: 08707 626178
Email: admin@alpsp.org
Website: http://www.alpsp.org/ngen_public
Members: 360
Contact: Ian Russel, Chief Exec.
Fee: £210-5505
Membership Type: full, associate (based on band limits)
Description: Represents not-for-profit publishers and those who work with them.
Publication: Journal
Publication title: Learned Publishing. Advertisements.
Meetings/Conventions: annual international conference

00797

Association of Licensed Aircraft Engineers
ALAE

Bourn House, 8 Park St., Surrey, Bagshot, GU19 5AQ, UK
Tel: 01276 474888
Fax: 01276 452767
Email: alae@alae.org
Website: http://www.alae.org
Members: 2100
Staff: 2
Contact: Robert Alway, Chm.
Fee: £85
Membership Type: general
Fee: £10
Membership Type: student
Description: Licensed Aircraft Engineers. Aims to maintain the professional status of the licensed aircraft engineer; represent the licensed aircraft engineer within the aviation industry; promote the advancement of technical knowledge, safety and skills of those engaged in civil aviation.
Publication: Newsletter
Publication title: LPRA News. Advertisements.
Meetings/Conventions: Radio Solutions – annual conference – Exhibits.

00798

Association of Licensed Multiple Retailers
ALMR

9B Walpole Ct., Ealing Studios, London, W5 5ED, UK
Tel: 020 85792080
Fax: 020 85797579
Email: info@almr.org.uk
Website: http://www.almr.org.uk
Contact: Alexander Salussolia, Pres.
Description: Works to promote the interests of the independent companies within licensed retailing.

00799

Association of Lighting Designers
ALD

PO Box 680, Oxford, OX1 9DG, UK
Tel: 07817 60189
Email: office@ald.org.uk
Website: http://www.ald.org.uk
Members: 700
Contact: Ian Saunders, Admin. Sec.
Fee: £25
Membership Type: student
Fee: £40
Membership Type: associate
Description: Professional lighting designers in theatre, performance arts and architecture. Associate membership for any interested persons. Provides a resource and forum for discussion and development of artistic and creative aims.
Publication: Magazine
Publication title: Focus. Advertisements.

00800

Association of Lloyd's Members
ALM

100 Fenchurch St., London, EC3M 5LG, UK
Tel: 020 74887500
Fax: 020 74887555
Email: mail@alm.ltd.uk
Website: http://www.alm.ltd.uk
Contact: Anthony Young, Chief Exec./Sec.
Fee: £455
Membership Type: individual underwriting
Fee: £130
Membership Type: individual non-underwriting
Description: Aims to work for the creation of a more dynamic and profitable Lloyd's. Maximizes the income of its members from their underwriting and to increase the value of their capacity.
Publication: Newspaper
Publication title: ALM News

00801

Association of Loading and Elevating Equipment Manufacturers
ALEM

Airport House, Purley Way, Surrey, Croydon, CR0 0XZ, UK
Tel: 020 82534501
Fax: 020 82534510
Email: alem@admin.co.uk
Website: http://www.alem.org.uk
Members: 26
Contact: Tim Faithfull, Sec.
Description: Serves as a trade association for manufacturers of loading and elevating equipment in the United Kingdom. Represents members' interests.
Publication: Membership Directory
Publication title: Product Guide

00802

Association of Management and Professional Staffs
AMPS

AEEU House, Borough Rd., West Yorkshire, Wakefield, WF1 3AZ, UK
Tel: 01924 371765
Fax: 01924 290327
Email: sec@amps.demon.co.uk
Website: http://www.amps.demon.co.uk
Members: 150000
Contact: Gordon H. Hopwood, Exec. Sec.
Description: Represents the interests of management personnel and professionals.
Formerly: Formerly, Council of Managerial and Professional Staffs

00803

Association of Manufacturers of Domestic Appliances
AMDEA

Rapier House, 40-46 Lambs Conduit St., London, WC1N 3NW, UK
Tel: 020 74050666
Fax: 020 74056609
Email: info@amdea.org.uk
Website: http://www.amdea.org.uk
Members: 60
Staff: 5
Contact: Douglas Herbison, Chief Exec.
Description: National trade association representing domestic appliance manufacturers.

00804

Association of Manufacturers of Power Generating Systems
AMPS

Samuelson House, Forder Way, Hampton, Peterborough, PE7 8JB, UK
Tel: 08456 448748
Fax: 01733 314767
Email: ab@amps.org.uk
Website: http://www.amps.org.uk
Members: 65
Staff: 4
Contact: R. Lane-Nott, Dir. Gen.
Fee: £1056
Membership Type: full
Fee: £528
Membership Type: affiliate
Description: Companies specializing in the design, manufacture, supply, installation, commission and maintenance of reciprocating diesel and gas engine and gas turbine driven electrical generating systems for prime power and emergency standby applications.
Publication: Manual
Publication title: The Amps Guide to ISO 8528

00805
Association of Master Upholsterers and Soft Furnishers
AMU
Q1 Capital Point, Capital Business Park, Parkway, Cardiff, CF3 2PU, UK
Tel: 02920 778918
Fax: 02920 793508
Email: susans@upholsterers.co.uk
Website: http://www.upholsterers.co.uk
Members: 500
Contact: Bob Bishton, Pres.
Fee: £50
Membership Type: full
Description: Craft upholsterers, upholstered furniture manufacturers, chair frame manufacturers, soft furnishing retailers, contractors, and others associated with the craft of upholstery.

00806
Association of MBA's
25 Hosier Ln., London, EC1A 9LQ, UK
Tel: 020 72462686
Fax: 020 72462687
Email: info@mbaworld.com
Website: http://www.mbaworld.com
Members: 14000
Staff: 16
Contact: Hilary Sears, Chair
Fee: £120
Membership Type: alumni, (UK resident)
Fee: £95
Membership Type: student, alumni (non-UK resident)
Description: Individual membership is open to students and graduates of Association of MBAs-approved MBA programmes. Corporate membership is encouraged for business schools appearing on the Association's approved list and for companies and other organisations who share the objectives of the Association and who wish to contribute towards them. Committed to enhancing quality in management and to providing a unique network of contacts for members. Services and activities include: a membership book; circa 70 networking/educational events pa; career opportunities; accreditation of MBA programmes; salary research; administration of a preferential rate MBA loan scheme for students of accredited programmes; an MBA information service.
Publication: Book
Publication title: Guide to Business Schools. Advertisements.
Meetings/Conventions: Accredited MBA Fair – semiannual convention – Exhibits.

00807
Association of Medical Research Charities
AMRC
61 Gray's Inn Rd., London, WC1X 8TL, UK
Tel: 020 72698820
Fax: 020 72698821
Website: http://www.amrc.org.uk/homepage
Members: 113
Contact: Simon Denegri, Chief Exec.
Fee: £330
Membership Type: regular
Description: Works together with member charities and partners in order to support the sector's effectiveness and advance medical research by developing best practice, providing information and guidance, improving public dialogue about research and science, and influencing government. Conducts research on heart disease, cancer, diabetes, as well as cystic fibrosis and motor neurone disease.

00808
Association of Medical Secretaries, Practice Managers, Administrators and Receptionists
AMSPAR
Tavistock House N, Tavistock Sq., London, WC1H 9LN, UK
Tel: 020 73876005
Fax: 020 73882648
Email: info@amspar.com
Website: http://www.amspar.com
Members: 5000
Staff: 6
Contact: Elaine Guy, Pres.
Fee: £48
Membership Type: full
Description: Those who have successfully completed examinations or qualify by the experience gained through working in the medical field. encourages high standards among persons engaged in medical administrative employment.
Formerly: Formerly, Association of Medical Secretaries, Practice Administration and Receptionists
Publication: Magazine
Publication title: AMSPAR Professional

00809
Association of Mining Analysts
AMA
Bankside plc., 1 Frederick's Pl., London, EC2R 8AE, UK
Tel: 020 88782308
Fax: 020 83921220
Email: info@ama.org.uk
Website: http://www.ama.org.uk
Members: 300
Contact: Tony Mahalski, Chm.
Fee: £50
Membership Type: regular
Description: Aims to improve the quality of mining investment research. Organizes presentations and seminars on mining companies and operational issues. Promotes better understanding of the mining industry and its activities.

00810
Association of Motion Picture Sound
AMPS
28 Knox St., London, W1H 1FS, UK
Tel: 020 77236727
Email: info@amps.net
Website: http://www.amps.net
Members: 350
Staff: 1
Contact: Chris Roberts, Chm.
Description: Persons employed in the production of sound tracks associated with moving images, recording the original dialogue music and sound effects, editing these sounds and rerecording them to accompany the moving picture images. Promotes and encourages the science technology and creative application of all aspects of motion picture sound recording and reproduction and seeks to promote and enhance the status and recognition of the contribution of those engaged therein.
Publication: Newsletter
Publication title: AMPS Newsletter

00811
Association of Municipal Engineers
AME
c/o The Institution of Civil Engineers
1 Great George St., Westminster, London, SW1P 3AA, UK
Tel: 020 72227722
Email: engineering@ice.org.uk
Website: http://www.ice.org.uk/homepage/index.asp
Members: 11500
Staff: 4
Contact: Jean Venables, Pres.
Description: Members of the Institution of Civil Engineers employed in public services. Provides a focus for the development of technical and management excellence of municipal and public sector civil engineers and the promotion of professional competence for the benefit of the community. Seeks to promote and enhance the identity, contribution and influence of members within and outside the profession.
Library Subject: engineering
Library Type: by appointment only
Publication: Journal
Publication title: Municipal Engineer

00812
Association of Muslim Lawyers
AML
PO Box 148, High Wycombe, HP13 5WJ, UK
Tel: 0778 7136495
Email: info@aml.org.uk
Website: http://www.aml.org.uk
Contact: Ifath Nawaz, Pres.
Fee: £90
Membership Type: solicitor, barrister, judge
Fee: £50
Membership Type: non-practicing lawyer
Description: Represents lawyers, students, practitioners, Muslims and non-Muslims who work on issues of importance and significance to Muslims. Highlights issues that affect Muslims. Promotes the provision of legal advice and assistance. Protects the legal rights of Muslims and the availability of advice in accordance with Shari'an of Islam.

00813
Association of National Park Authorities
ANPA
126 Bute St., Cardiff Bay, Cardiff, CF10 5LE, UK
Tel: 029 20499966
Email: info@anpa.gov.uk
Website: http://www.nationalparks.gov.uk
Members: 15
Staff: 6
Contact: Cathryn Marcus, Coor.
Description: Chairmen of the 11 National Parks in England and Wales. Represents national parks in dealings with government and campaigns on their behalf nationally and internationally.
Formerly: Formerly, Association of National Parks

00814
Association of National Tourist Office Representatives UK
ANTOR
39 Pennington Close, Golden Common, Winchester, SO21 1UR, UK
Tel: 0870 2419084
Fax: 0196 2711239
Email: esther@antor.com
Website: http://www.antor.com
Members: 70
Contact: Esther Smith, Exec. Sec.
Description: Serves as lobbying and social group for overseas national and regional tourist offices based in the UK.

00815
Association of Natural Burial Grounds
ANBG
The Natural Death Centre charity, In The Hill House, Watley Ln., Twyford, Winchester, SO21 1QX, UK
Tel: 0962 712690
Email: rosie@naturaldeath.org.uk
Website: http://www.naturaldeath.org.uk
Staff: 1
Contact: Rosie Inman-Cook, Mgr.
Fee: £50
Membership Type: full, provisional
Description: Assists natural burial grounds in the UK by putting forward a code of practice for its members, providing referral, advice, and information services, and publicity.
Formerly: Absorbed, natural death centre, nicholas albery foundation
Publication: Book
Publication title: The New Natural Death Handbook

00816
Association of Newspaper and Magazine Wholesalers
ANMW
Wakefield House, Pipers Way, Swindon, SN3 1RF, UK
Tel: 01793 563692
Email: howard.birch@smithsnews.co.uk
Website: http://www.anmw.co.uk
Members: 26
Staff: 5
Contact: Mark Charlton, Sec.
Description: Wholesalers of newspapers, periodicals and magazines situated within the United Kingdom. Represents the wholesale newspaper trade and provides a forum for its membership.

00817
Association of Noise Consultants
The Old Pump House, 1A Stonecross, St. Albans, AL1 4AA, UK
Tel: 020 82534518
Email: anc@kingstonsmith.co.uk
Website: http://www.association-of-noise-consultants.co.uk
Members: 105
Contact: Adrian James, Contact
Description: Consultancy practices. Aims to provide a corporate organization for independent firms of consultants offering professional services in the field of noise and also vibration.
Publication: Book
Publication title: ANC Guidelines - Measurement and Assessment of Groundborne Noise and Vibration

00818
Association of Optometrists
AOP
61 Southwark St., London, SE1 0HL, UK
Tel: 020 72619661
Fax: 020 72610228
Email: bobhughes@aop.org.uk
Website: http://www.assoc-optometrists.org
Members: 7000
Staff: 27
Contact: Bob Hughes, Chief Exec.
Fee: £581
Membership Type: full, overseas insured, retired block
Fee: £349
Membership Type: full (reduced), honorary insured, dispensing associate
Description: Optometrists and dispensing opticians and students. Aims to support, promote and protect interests of members individually and corporately; to encourage high standards of practice; to make suitable arrangements for the defence of members in disciplinary and professional matters. Advises on commercial, legal and administrative aspects of practice.
Publication: Journal
Publication title: Optometry Today. Advertisements.

00819
Association of Paediatric Anaesthetists of Great Britain and Ireland
APAGBI
21 Portland Pl., London, W1B 1PY, UK
Tel: 020 76318887
Fax: 020 76314352
Email: apagbiadministration@aagbi.org
Website: http://www.apagbi.org.uk
Members: 650
Contact: R. Bingham, Treas.
Fee: £64
Membership Type: consultant
Fee: £43
Membership Type: affiliate, trainee
Description: Pediatric anesthetists practicing in Great Britain and Ireland and outside the British Isles. Promotes the study of pediatric anesthesiology. Collects and disseminates information; conducts research; advises other professional bodies on matters pertaining to pediatric anesthesiology.

00820
Association of Painting Craft Teachers
APCT
Shrewsbury College of Arts and Technology, London Rd., Shrewsbury, SY2 6PR, UK
Tel: 01743 342501
Email: barrym@shrewsbury.ac.uk
Website: http://www.apct.co.uk
Members: 250
Contact: Barry Mason, Natl. Sec.
Fee: £50
Membership Type: full, affiliate
Fee: £150
Membership Type: centre
Description: Individuals engaged in education and training throughout the painting and decorating industry, including technology and related skills associated with interior and exterior decoration, vehicle painting, industrial finishing and signwork. Advances education and training in the craft skills throughout the painting and decorating industry; furthers the interests of all who teach these skills; acts as a representative body in consultation with awarding bodies on all matters connected with the teaching of painting and decorating and allied subjects.
Publication: Magazine
Publication title: The Artisan. Advertisements.

00821
Association of Pakistani Physicians and Surgeons of the United Kingdom
APPS
17A Cobra Ct., Blackmore Rd., Stretford, Manchester, M32 0QY, UK
Tel: 0161 8645609
Email: admin@appsuk.org
Website: http://www.appsuk.org
Contact: Anwaar Ahmad Chahal, Contact
Fee: £10
Membership Type: standard
Fee: £5
Membership Type: spouse, retired
Description: Seeks to protect and promote Pakistani physicians and surgeons of UK. Encourages continued medical education and research among doctors. Raises awareness of health issues among ethnic communities. Improves relations and fosters understanding among doctors. Delivers better healthcare and promotes patient safety.

00822
Association of Pension Lawyers
APL
c/o Jill Clucas, Sec.
PMI House, Rm. 10, 4-10 Artillery Ln., London, E1 7LS, UK
Email: pensionlawyers@runbox.com
Website: http://www.apl.org.uk
Members: 900
Contact: Alastair Meeks, Chm.
Description: Lawyers satisfying certain criteria, specializing in pensions law. Promotes awareness of the importance of the rule of law in the provision of pensions and in regulating and defining the relationships between pension scheme trustees, employers and beneficiaries.

00823
Association of Personal Injury Lawyers
APIL
11 Castle Quay, Nottingham, NG7 1FW, UK
Tel: 0115 9580585
Fax: 0115 9580885
Email: sharon.smith@apil.org.uk
Website: http://www.apil.org.uk
Contact: Denise Kitchener, Chief Exec.
Fee: £224.25
Membership Type: practitioner
Fee: £115
Membership Type: non-practicing legal practitioner, paralegal/legal support staff

Description: Represents lawyers working on behalf of personal injury victims. Provides accreditation to lawyers specializing in the area of personal injury law. Campaigns for better laws to help people who are injured or ill through no fault of their own.

00824

Association of Pet Behavior Counsellors APBC

PO Box 46, Worcester, WR8 9YS, UK
Tel: 01386 751151
Fax: 01386 750743
Email: info@apbc.org.uk
Website: http://www.apbc.org.uk
Contact: David Ryan, Chm.
Fee: £40
Membership Type: academic/student
Fee: £80
Membership Type: provisional
Description: Improves the welfare of pets. Promotes the practice of pet behavior therapy as a recognized profession. Offers advice and information on understanding pet behavior. Acts as a forum for exchange of information and ideas about pet behavior.

00825

Association of Pet Dog Trainers - United Kingdom APDT

PO Box 17, Kempsford, Fairford, GL7 4WZ, UK
Tel: 01285 810811
Email: info@apdt.co.uk
Website: http://www.apdt.co.uk
Fee: £45
Membership Type: regular
Description: Seeks to establish and maintain standards for the practice of dog training. Advises and informs veterinary surgeons and members of the public seeking dog training. Furthers the understanding and advancement of good practice in dog training of members.

00826

Association of Pharmacy Technicians of United Kingdom APTUK

4th Fl., 1 Mabledon Pl., London, WC1H 9AJ, UK
Tel: 020 75511551
Email: president@aptuk.org
Website: http://www.aptuk.org
Contact: Steve Acres, Pres.
Fee: £35
Membership Type: full
Fee: £15
Membership Type: student
Description: Represents and promotes pharmacy technicians. Maintains, safeguards and enhances the professional standards of pharmacy technicians and other healthcare staff. Seeks registration and improves the education of technicians. Promotes safe and cost effective dispensing, distribution and use of medicines.
Publication: Journal
Publication title: Pharmacy Technician Journal

00827

Association of Photographers AOP

81 Leonard St., London, EC2A 4QS, UK
Tel: 020 77396669
Fax: 020 77398707
Email: general@aophoto.co.uk
Website: http://home.the-aop.org
Members: 1800
Contact: Kingsley Marten, Managing Dir.
Fee: £315
Membership Type: regular
Fee: £240
Membership Type: provisional
Description: Professional photographers working in advertising, editorial, or fashion photography. Conducts monthly workshops and organizes exhibitions. Maintains gallery. Provides education programs and membership legal assistance and awards competitions. Strives to protect the rights of professional photographers. Provides information services. Seeks to build an effective network of communications with photographers from around the world.
Library Subject: photography
Library Type: reference
Formerly: Formerly, Association of Fashion, Advertising, and Editorial Photographers
Publication: Book
Publication title: ABCD of Copyright
Meetings/Conventions: Careers Talk – monthly lecture

00828

Association of Plumbing and Heating Contractors APHC

12 The Pavillions, Cranmore Dr., Solihull, B90 4SB, UK
Tel: 021 7115030
Fax: 021 7057871
Email: info@aphc.co.uk
Website: http://www.competentpersonsscheme.co.uk
Members: 2200
Staff: 22
Contact: Clive Dickin, CEO
Fee: £112
Membership Type: probationary
Fee: £305
Membership Type: licensed
Description: Aims to assist plumbing and heating contractors in providing information that is essential to plumbing and heating contractors and giving them competitive advantage elements such as technical and safety advice to marketing and customer service tips. Provides a range of value added affinity schemes by assisting in competition commercially. Represents the needs and interests of members at a local, regional, national, and European level.
Library Type: reference
Formerly: Formerly, National Association of Plumbing, Heating and Mechanical Services Contractors
Publication: Newsletter
Publication title: Hot & Cold

00829

Association of Police Authorities APA

15 Greycoat Pl., London, SW1P 1BN, UK
Tel: 020 76643096
Fax: 020 76643191
Email: apa.info@lga.gov.uk
Website: http://www.apa.police.uk/apa
Contact: Rob Garnham, Chm.
Description: Acts as the national voice of all police authorities. Influences the national policing agenda on behalf of police authorities and local communities. Promotes awareness of policing needs and the roles and achievements of police authorities.

00830

Association of Policy Market Makers APMM

PO Box 6717, Sturminster Newton, DT10 9AR, UK
Tel: 0845 8330088
Fax: 0845 8330089
Email: enquiries@apmm.org
Website: http://www.apmm.co.uk
Members: 6
Description: Represents firms that buy and sell with profits endowments and whole-of-life policies. Provides Practice Guidelines for its members to adhere to.

00831

Association of Port Health Authorities APHA

Walbrook Wharf, 3rd Fl., 78-83 Upper Thames St., London, EC4R 3TD, UK
Tel: 08707 444505
Fax: 02072 482114
Email: apha@porthealth.co.uk
Website: http://www.apha.org.uk
Members: 61
Staff: 2
Fee: £895
Membership Type: corporate
Fee: £746
Membership Type: associate
Description: Local authorities, port health authorities in the United Kingdom, Ireland and the Channel Islands. Promotes the health and safety of seafarers. Discusses issues on imported food, environmental health, etc. with central government, EU organisations, etc.
Publication: Handbook
Publication title: Port Health Handbook

00832

Association of Principal Fire Officers APFO

9-11 Pebble Close, Amington, Tamworth, B77 4RD, UK
Tel: 01827 302300
Fax: 01827 302399
Email: enquiries@apfo.org.uk
Website: http://www.apfo.org.uk
Description: Exists to promote and protect the interests of individuals who lead the British fire and rescue service. Negotiates the settlement of disputes where members are involved. Assists members in matters concerning employment or work related injury.

00833

Association of Private Client Investment Managers and Stockbrokers
APCIMS

22 City Rd., Finsbury Sq., London, EC1Y 2AJ, UK
Tel: 020 74487100
Fax: 020 76384636
Email: info@apcims.co.uk
Website: http://www.apcims.co.uk
Members: 217
Staff: 9
Contact: David Bennett, Chief Exec.
Description: Represents the interests of investment managers and stockbrokers serving the UK's 12 million private investors.
Publication: Magazine
Publication title: Q Review

00834

Association of Professional Landscapers
APL

Horticulture House, 19 High St., Theale, Berkshire, Reading, RG7 5AH, UK
Tel: 0118 9303132
Fax: 0118 9323453
Email: apl@the-hta.org.uk
Website: http://www.landscaper.org.uk
Members: 197
Contact: Alison Smith, Admin.
Description: Serves the customer demands for landscaping services and responds to the range of influences on the UK gardening market.

00835

Association of Professional Music Therapists
APMT

24-27 White Lion St., London, N1 9PD, UK
Tel: 020 78376100
Fax: 020 78376100
Email: apmtoffice@aol.com
Website: http://www.apmt.org
Members: 535
Staff: 1
Contact: Stephen Sandford, Chm.
Fee: £155
Membership Type: full
Fee: £93
Membership Type: full cash break
Description: Professional music therapists and music therapy students. Aims to fulfill the needs of qualified music therapists in Great Britain. Focuses on employment and sharing of information. Works to protect music therapists already in work and to assist in the creation of new posts. Sets standards of practice and training.
Publication: Journal
Publication title: British Journal of Music Therapy. Advertisements.

00836

Association of Professional Recording Services
APRS

PO Box 22, Totnes, TQ9 7YZ, UK
Tel: 01803 868600
Fax: 01803 868444
Website: http://www2.aprs.co.uk
Members: 380
Staff: 1
Contact: George Martin, Pres.
Fee: £64.63
Membership Type: associate
Fee: £352.5
Membership Type: company, affiliate
Description: Companies and people working in the professional audio industry who meet APRS entrance criteria. Acts as the trade association for firms and persons professionally/commercially involved in sound recording and post production in the UK.
Publication: Newsletter
Publication title: APRS Bulletin

00837

Association of Public Analysts
APA

Burlington House, Piccadilly, London, W1V 0BA, UK
Email: apaweb@nmichie.co.uk
Website: http://www.publicanalyst.com
Members: 250
Contact: D. Campbell, Pres.
Fee: £190
Membership Type: regular
Fee: £175
Membership Type: Scottish
Description: Public analysts and staff. Assists in upholding and maintaining the character and position of public analysts and promotes co-operation between them.

00838

Association of Publishing Agencies
APA

Queens House, 3rd Fl., 55/56 Lincoln's Inn Fields, London, WC2A 3LJ, UK
Tel: 020 74044166
Fax: 020 74044167
Email: patrick.fuller@apa.co.uk
Website: http://www.apa.co.uk
Members: 31
Staff: 2
Contact: Patrick Fuller, CEO
Description: Members must be financially sound and must have the resources to provide three or more of the following services: editorial, design, advertising, sales, production and distribution management. Members must abide by the Code of Practice and must deal fairly and honestly with clients, employees, suppliers, intermediaries and readers. Aims to promote awareness of the effectiveness of a customer magazine as a marketing medium; to maintain high standards of work and business practice; and to act as a central source of information.
Publication title: A to Z of Customer Publishing, Showcase, Research Guide
Meetings/Conventions: Relationship Marketing – annual conference

00839

Association of Qualitative Research
AQR

Davey House, 31 St. Neots Rd., Eaton Ford, Cambs, St. Neots, PE19 7BA, UK
Tel: 01480 407227
Fax: 01480 211267
Email: info@aqr.org.uk
Website: http://www.aqr.org.uk
Members: 1150
Contact: Peter Lovett, Chair
Fee: £115
Membership Type: regular (with VAT)
Fee: £100
Membership Type: overseas (no VAT)
Description: Practitioners of qualitative market research including those in research agencies, freelancers, field managers and purchasers of market research. Serves as the UK's specialist professional study for Provides a forum for debate, promotes good practice and helps to train/educate at all levels.
Library Subject: research
Library Type: reference
Publication: Directory
Publication title: Directory & Handbook. Advertisements.

00840

Association of Radical Midwives
ARM

c/o Ishbel Kargar, Membership Sec.
62 Greetby Hill, Ormskirk, L39 2DT, UK
Tel: 01695 571748
Email: ikargar@tiscali.co.uk
Website: http://www.midwifery.org.uk
Members: 1300
Staff: 1
Contact: Sarah Montagu, Admin. Sec.
Fee: £35
Membership Type: outside UK
Fee: £30
Membership Type: in UK
Description: Midwives, mothers, health professionals, and interested individuals. Supports the interests of midwives. Provides supportive services and information to women experiencing difficulty in securing adequate and sympathetic maternity care.
Publication: Booklet
Publication title: Choices in Childbirth

00841

Association of Railway Training Providers
ARTP

22 Headfort Pl., London, SW1X 7RY, UK
Tel: 020 72010778
Fax: 020 72355777
Email: info@artp.co.uk
Website: http://www.artp.co.uk
Contact: Andy McKenna, Chm.
Fee: £495
Membership Type: corporate
Description: Represents the interests of railway training providers and competence assessors. Provides a forum to increase understanding of the need for and the means of developing standards of quality and technical specifications in the railway industry sector. Encourages and supports members to develop their businesses through training and assessment.

00842

Association of Real Estate Funds AREF

65 Kingsway, London, WC2B 6TD, UK
Tel: 020 72694677
Email: jcartwright@aref.org.uk
Website: http://www.aref.org.uk
Members: 56
Contact: John Cartwright, Chief Exec.
Fee: £2500
Description: Aims to raise awareness of Real Estate Funds and demonstrate the advantages of these funds as effective real estate investment vehicles. Represents its members' interests on legislative, regulatory and fiscal matters affecting the real estate industry.
Formerly: Formerly, Association of Property Unit Trusts

00843

Association of Reflexologists AoR

5 Fore St., Somerset, Taunton, TA1 1HX, UK
Tel: 01823 351010
Fax: 01823 336646
Email: info@aor.org.uk
Website: http://www.aor.org.uk
Members: 6000
Staff: 10
Contact: Carolyn Story, Chief Exec.
Fee: £36
Membership Type: student/friend inside UK
Fee: £45.56
Membership Type: full overseas
Description: Promotes reflexology to the public.
Publication: Journal
Publication title: Reflexions. Advertisements.
Meetings/Conventions: seminar

00844

Association of Relocation Professionals ARP

PO Box 189, Diss, IP22 1PE, UK
Tel: 08700 737475
Fax: 08700 718719
Email: enquiries@arp-relocation.com
Website: http://www.arp-relocation.com
Members: 200
Staff: 2
Contact: Tad Zurlinden, Chief Exec.
Fee: £311-934
Membership Type: full, associate (based on the number of employee)
Fee: £411
Membership Type: affiliate
Description: Companies, partnerships, individuals offering relocation services to companies, their employees and individuals moving within the UK and overseas; affiliate members, those offering products or services that may be of use to those relocating. Works to encourage and promote companies offering relocation services, ensure the professional integrity of its members and high standards of service, to both the private and corporate sectors.
Formerly: Formerly, Association of Relocation Agents
Publication: Book
Publication title: ARP Guide to the UK. Advertisements.

00845

Association of Researchers in Medicine and Science ARMS

c/o Dunhill Research Laboratories
Thomas Guy House, 5th Fl., Guys Hospital, London, SE1 9RT, UK
Email: david.jessop@bristol.ac.uk
Website: http://www.hope-academic.org.uk/arms
Contact: David Jessop, Chm.
Fee: £10
Membership Type: individual
Description: Promotes higher degree of professional competence in research within academic and allied institutions in the U.K. Supports the professional and scientific interests of researchers; works to establish a satisfactory career structure for researchers in medicine and science; conducts educational programs to raise public awareness of research and the role of the researcher in society. Conducts surveys, maintains lobbying body at the national level.
Publication: Newsletter
Publication title: ARMS Newsletter

00846

Association of Residential Letting Agents ARLA

Arbon House, 6 Tournament Ct., Edge Hill Dr., Warwick, CV34 6LG, UK
Tel: 0844 3870555
Fax: 01926 417789
Email: info@arla.co.uk
Website: http://www.arla.co.uk
Members: 1800
Fee: £175
Membership Type: regular, fellow (working in an ARLA firm)
Fee: £115
Membership Type: student
Description: Firms that meet defined criteria and complying with a code of practice. Provides training courses, holds seminars, conducts surveys and promotes the profession through the media. Consulted prior to legislation and always available for comment on rented housing throughout the UK.
Publication: Magazine
Publication title: Agreement. Advertisements.

00847

Association of Residential Managing Agents ARMA

178 Battersea Park Rd., London, SW11 4ND, UK
Tel: 020 79782607
Fax: 020 74986153
Email: info@arma.org.uk
Website: http://www.arma.org.uk
Members: 185
Contact: Brett Williams, Chm.
Description: Corporate members must hold professional indemnity insurance and provide an annual audit certificate; members must be involved in the management of blocks of flats.

00848

Association of Retirement Housing Managers ARHM

Southbank House, Black Prince Rd., London, SE1 7SJ, UK
Tel: 020 74630660
Email: enquiries@arhm.org
Website: http://www.arhm.org/home.php
Fee: £625
Membership Type: full
Fee: £900
Membership Type: affiliate
Description: Aims to achieve high standards and ethics in the management of private retirement and sheltered housing. Provides Code of Practice for members that includes information and advice when managing leasehold properties.

00849

Association of School and College Leaders ASCL

130 Regent Rd., Leicester, LE1 7PG, UK
Tel: 0116 2991122
Fax: 0116 2991123
Email: info@ascl.org.uk
Website: http://www.ascl.org.uk
Members: 13000
Staff: 25
Contact: Sara Gadzik, Communications Dir.
Description: Represents principals, heads, deputies, assistant heads and senior teachers in secondary schools and colleges.
Formerly: Formerly, Secondary Heads Association
Publication: Magazine
Publication title: Leader. Advertisements.

00850

Association of Scottish Visitor Attractions ASVA

Epic House, 28-32 Cadogan St., Glasgow, G2 7LP, UK
Tel: 01412 290923
Fax: 01412 487693
Email: info@asva.co.uk
Website: http://www.asva.co.uk
Staff: 3
Description: Visitor attractions companies and individuals interested in visitor attractions and suppliers of goods and services to visitor attractions. Represents the visitor attraction industry in Scotland. Aims to improve the quality and performance of existing attractions and inform the development of new ones, to promote attractions in a more effective way; develops staff and management skills through conferences, regular communication and the provision of a development helpline as well as on-site visits.
Publication: Newsletter
Publication title: ASVA Reporter

00851

Association of Sealant Applicators ASA

Grovedell House, 15 Knightswick Rd., Canvey Island, SS8 9PA, UK
Tel: 01268 696878
Fax: 01268 511247

Email: arichardson@rowlandhall.co.uk
Website: http://www.associationofsealantapplicators.org
Members: 50
Staff: 2
Contact: Tony Richardson, Sec.
Fee: £530
Membership Type: applicator, manufacturer, affiliate
Description: Promotes the highest standards of building design, specifications of material, and applicators workmanship. Provides an organized forum for advanced training and the circulation of ideals and techniques.

00852

Association of Secretaries General of Parliaments
ASGP

c/o Steven Mark, Sec.
House of Commons, 7 Millbank, London, SW1P P3JA, UK
Tel: 020 72193498
Fax: 020 72192681
Email: asgp@parliament.uk
Website: http://www.asgp.info/en/home
Members: 225
Contact: Amrani Hafnaoui, Pres.
Description: Secretaries general from parliamentary assemblies in 95 countries, and/or their deputies. Facilitates contacts between secretaries general for the purposes of studying the law, procedure, practice and working methods of different parliaments; proposes measures for improving those methods and for securing cooperation between the services of different parliaments.
Publication: Journal
Publication title: Constitutional and Parliamentary Information

00853

Association of Security Consultants
ASC

42 Amis Ave., New Haw, Addlestone, KT15 3ET, UK
Tel: 07071 224865
Email: info@securityconsultants.org.uk
Website: http://www.securityconsultants.org.uk
Members: 71
Staff: 1
Contact: Laurie Doust, Sec.
Fee: £125
Membership Type: affiliate
Fee: £150
Membership Type: full
Description: Serves as professional organization for independent security consultants. Represents and promotes the interests of independent security consultants. Aims to set and maintain the highest standards of quality in all its undertakings through adherence to its code of conduct.
Library Subject: British and European security standards
Library Type: reference
Publication: Directory
Publication title: Consultants Resources Directory

00854

Association of Show and Agricultural Organisations
ASAO

Oakley Farm, Merstham, Surrey, Redhill, RH1 3QN, UK
Tel: 01737 645857
Fax: 01737 645121
Website: http://www.asao.co.uk
Members: 200
Contact: Richard Cuzens, Chm.
Fee: £80
Membership Type: organization (not holding events/shows)
Fee: £55
Membership Type: organization (holding events with 5000 or below attendees)
Description: Organizes agricultural, equine and horticultural shows ranging from small local one-day events to major four-day national shows. Helps show organizers stage successful events.
Publication: Booklet
Publication title: List of Shows and Events

00855

Association of Sign Language Interpreters
ASLI

Fortuna House, S Fifth St., Milton Keynes, MK9 2EU, UK
Tel: 0871 4740522
Fax: 01908 325259
Email: chair@asli.org.uk
Website: http://www.asli.org.uk/default.aspx
Contact: Sarah Haynes, Chm.
Fee: £204
Membership Type: full
Fee: £180
Membership Type: associate
Description: Encourages good practice in sign language interpreting. Represents the interests and views of sign language interpreters. Provides discussion of issues on language interpreting. Assists and supports sign language interpreters.
Publication: Magazine
Publication title: NEWSLI

00856

Association of Social Anthropologists of the UK and the Commonwealth
ASA

PO Box 5233, Brighton, BN50 9YW, UK
Email: admin@theasa.org
Website: http://www.theasa.org
Contact: Rohan Jackson, Admin.
Fee: £50
Membership Type: individual (inside Great Britain)
Fee: £35
Membership Type: individual (inside Europe)
Description: Represents professional social anthropologists in 42 countries. Promotes study and teaching of social anthropology. Sponsors seminars on professional training and current advances in the field. Seeks to present the interest of social anthropology and maintains its professional status.
Publication: Report
Publication title: Annals of the ASA
Meetings/Conventions: annual conference September 12 to 16, 2011. Lampeter United Kingdom

00857

Association of Solicitors and Investment Managers
ASIM

North House, 198 High St., Tonbridge, TN9 1BE, UK
Tel: 01892 864391
Fax: 01732 362626
Email: elisabeth@asim.org.uk
Website: http://www.asim.org.uk
Members: 88
Contact: Elisabeth Andreasson, Admin.
Description: Solicitors' firms conducting investment management, usually for private clients. Encourages provision of portfolio investment services by solicitors' firms subject to appropriate expertise and high standards; increases awareness of such firms among the general public; lobbies the government and self-regulatory or professional bodies on behalf of members; provides a forum for the exchange of information and experience.
Publication: Newsletter
Publication title: ASIM Newsletter

00858

Association of South East Asian Studies in the UK
ASEASUK

School of Oriental and African Studies, University of London, Thornhaugh St., Russell Sq., London, WC1H 0XG, UK
Email: sc66@soas.ac.uk
Website: http://aseasuk.org.uk
Members: 150
Staff: 2
Contact: Susan Conway, Honorary Sec.
Fee: £20
Membership Type: full, associate (outside UK)
Fee: £12
Membership Type: associate (inside UK)
Description: Represents academics specializing in the South East Asian region. Advises Higher Education Funding Council for England on issues connected with South-East Asian Studies.
Publication: Newsletter
Publication title: ASEASUK News

00859

Association of Speakers Clubs
ASC

27 Hamilton Dr., Whitley Bay, NE26 1JQ, UK
Tel: 0191 2513740
Fax: 0191 2513740
Email: jjames9241@aol.com
Website: http://www.the-asc.org.uk
Members: 1800
Contact: Joe James, Pres.
Fee: £8
Membership Type: regular
Description: Covers training in public speaking.

00860

Association of Subscription Agents and Intermediaries
ASA

Field Cottage, School Ln., Suffolk, IP17 1HE, UK
Tel: 01728 633196
Email: info@subscription-agents.org
Website: http://www.subscription-agents.org
Members: 49
Staff: 1
Contact: Sarah Durrant, Sec. Gen.
Description: Open to any company whose main occupation, or a substantial part of it, is that of a subscription agent or an electronic intermediary; Membership may be initiated by invitation or direct application to the Secretary. Exists to ensure that members achieve the

highest standards of service for the customers and improve relationships, service and terms with the publishers.
Publication: Newsletter
Publication title: ASA News

00861
Association of Suppliers to the British Clothing Industry
ASBCI
Unit 5, 25 Square Rd., West Yorkshire, Halifax, HX1 1QG, UK
Tel: 01422 354666
Fax: 01422 381184
Email: info@asbci.co.uk
Website: http://www.asbci.co.uk
Members: 125
Staff: 2
Contact: Stephanie Ingham, Sec.
Fee: £575
Membership Type: within United Kingdom
Fee: £35
Membership Type: student in United Kingdom
Description: Companies that are suppliers to the BCI retail, manufacturing, chemical, finishers, fabric manufacturers, interlinings, drycleaners, universities. Aims to raise profitability of member companies by effective use of modern technology; to enhance continuously the quality of goods delivered by ASBCI members; to provide exchange of information between the sectors; to continue to improve consumer satisfaction with goods before and after cleaning and laundering.
Library Subject: clothing manufacture
Library Type: by appointment only
Formerly: Formerly, British Interlining Manufacturers Association
Publication: Booklet
Publication title: Introduction to Colour in Clothing and Textiles

00862
Association of Surgeons of Great Britain and Ireland
ASGBI
35-43 Lincoln's Inn Fields, London, WC2A 3PE, UK
Tel: 020 79730300
Fax: 020 74309235
Email: admin@asgbi.org.uk
Website: http://www.asgbi.org.uk
Members: 2000
Staff: 8
Contact: Michael Horrocks, Pres.
Fee: £325
Membership Type: full fellow
Fee: £90-190
Membership Type: corresponding fellow
Description: General surgeons. Concerned with the advancement of the science and art of surgery and the promoting of friendship amongst surgeons. Specializes in general surgery and is recognized as such by Government and by the profession.
Publication: Journal
Publication title: British Journal of Surgery

00863
Association of Systematic Kinesiology
ASK
104a Sedlescombe Rd. N, East Sussex, TN37 7EN, UK
Tel: 0845 0200383
Email: admin@systematic-kinesiology.co.uk
Website: http://www.systematic-kinesiology.co.uk
Members: 400
Contact: Marie Cheshire, Admin.
Fee: £30
Membership Type: friend
Fee: £50
Membership Type: associate/student
Description: Strives to educate the public about the value of kinesiology. Keeps a register of qualified and insured practitioners. Refers people who are trying to find a kinesiologist in their area.

00864
Association of Tank and Cistern Manufacturers
ATCM
22 Grange Park, St. Arvans, Chepstow, NP16 6EA, UK
Tel: 01291 623634
Email: imcc@atcmtanks.org.uk
Website: http://www.atcmtanks.org.uk
Members: 13
Staff: 2
Contact: Ian McCrone, Chm.
Fee: £1200
Membership Type: full
Description: Manufacturers of tanks and cisterns in a variety of materials including thermoplastics, GRP and metal products. Promotes good practice concerning the manufacture and installation of tanks and cisterns, primarily for water storage.
Library Subject: international and European water regulations and standards
Library Type: reference
Publication: Newsletter
Publication title: ATCM News Update

00865
Association of Teachers and Lecturers
ATL
7 Northumberland St., London, WC2N 5RD, UK
Tel: 020 79306441
Fax: 020 79301359
Email: info@atl.org.uk
Website: http://www.atl.org.uk
Members: 160000
Staff: 70
Contact: Mary Bousted, Gen. Sec.
Description: Represents and supports education practitioners, including teachers, lecturers and education support professionals working in all school levels throughout England, Wales, Northern Ireland and the Channel Islands. Promotes the cause of education; protects and improves the status of the profession; offers legal and professional advice and assistance to members.
Formerly: Formerly, Association of Assistant Mistresses
Publication: Magazine
Publication title: Report. Advertisements.

00866
Association of Teachers of Lipreading to Adults
ATLA
c/o Hearing Concern LINK
19 Hartfield Rd., Eastbourne, East Sussex, BN21 2AR, UK
Email: atla@lipreading.org.uk
Website: http://www.lipreading.org.uk
Members: 250
Contact: Heidi Walsh, Chair
Fee: £30
Membership Type: full
Fee: £15
Membership Type: retired
Description: Professional association for teachers of lipreading for adults who become deaf or hard of hearing; aims to promote understanding of the special needs of people with an acquired hearing loss; seeks to advance the awareness of the benefits of lipreading and other communication skills in the rehabilitation of people with an acquired hearing loss.
Publication: Magazine
Publication title: Catchword

00867
Association of Teachers of Mathematics
ATM
Unit 7, Prime Industrial Park, Shaftesbury St., Derby, DE23 8YB, UK
Tel: 01332 346599
Fax: 01332 204357
Email: admin@atm.org.uk
Website: http://www.atm.org.uk
Members: 4000
Staff: 7
Contact: Su Strange, Sr. Admin. Off.
Fee: £58
Membership Type: personal
Fee: £86
Membership Type: secondary school
Description: Teachers, students, colleges, schools, libraries, advisers, inspectors, and educational publishers interested in mathematics in 30 countries. Encourages changes in mathematical education relevant to the needs of students. Organizes working groups to address mathematical issues.
Formerly: Formerly, Association for Teaching Aids in Mathematics
Publication: Journal
Publication title: Mathematics Teaching. Advertisements.

00868
Association of Teachers of Singing
AOTOS
18 Syon Park Gardens, Isleworth, Middlesex, TW7 5NB, UK
Tel: 020 87589422
Website: http://aotos.org.uk
Members: 453
Contact: Heidi Pegler, Membership Sec.
Fee: £40
Membership Type: individual
Fee: £80
Membership Type: corporate
Description: Teachers of singing, private and college/institution orientated. Aims to promote, for the benefit of its members and for wider dissemination, understanding of the matters connected with the teaching of singing and to bring together people who are occupied in this work.
Publication: Magazine
Publication title: Singing-Voice of AOTOS

00869

Association of Technical Lightning and Access Specialists ATLAS

Royal London House, 22-25 Finsbury Sq., London, EC2A 1DX, UK
Tel: 0844 2490026
Fax: 0844 2490027
Email: info@atlas.org.uk
Website: http://www.atlas.org.uk
Members: 59
Contact: Graeme Fisher, Pres.
Description: Members, affiliates, (with less than 2 years trading) and special members (suppliers to the industry). Promotes safety methods for working at height which result in quality of service to clients.
Formerly: Formerly, National Federation of Master Steeplejacks and Lightning Conductor Engineers

00870

Association of the British Pharmaceutical Industry ABPI

12 Whitehall, London, SW1A 2DY, UK
Tel: 0870 8904333
Fax: 020 77471414
Email: manderson@abpi.org.uk
Website: http://www.abpi.org.uk
Members: 72
Staff: 65
Contact: Martin Anderson, Dir. of Commercial Affairs
Description: Pharmaceutical companies conducting business in the United Kingdom involved in research and development, or those companies interested in pharmaceutical matters. Represents manufacturers of medicines not advertised to the public.
Library Subject: pharmaceutical industry, medicine, health economics
Library Type: not open to the public

00871

Association of Therapeutic Communities ATC

Barns Centre, Church Ln., Toddington, Glos, Cheltenham, GL54 5DQ, UK
Tel: 01242 620077
Fax: 01242 620077
Email: post@therapeuticcommunities.org
Website: http://www.therapeuticcommunities.org
Members: 200
Contact: Chris Holman, Chm.
Fee: £50
Membership Type: individual in UK
Fee: £60
Membership Type: individual elsewhere
Description: Represents nurses, social workers, researchers, psychologists, creative therapists, managers, residential care staff, teachers, psychotherapists, psychiatrists, and academics. Conducts training and education programs.
Publication: Newsletter
Publication title: The Joint

00872

Association of Town Centre Management ATCM

1 Queen Anne's Gate, Westminster, London, SW1H 9BT, UK
Tel: 020 72220120
Fax: 020 72273460
Email: info@atcm.org
Website: http://www.atcm.org
Members: 520
Staff: 13
Contact: Simon Quin, Chief Exec.
Fee: £343.75
Membership Type: affiliate, academic, overseas
Fee: £2937.5
Membership Type: corporate
Description: Aims to promote town and city centers as environmentally sustainable, socially inclusive and economically vital and viable.
Library Subject: town centre management
Library Type: reference

00873

Association of Translation Companies ATC

Unit 24, Level 6 N, New England House, New England St., Brighton, BN1 4GH, UK
Tel: 01273 676777
Fax: 08450 582590
Email: admin@atc.org.uk
Website: http://www.atc.org.uk
Contact: Geoffrey Bowden, Gen. Sec.
Description: Promotes the use of professionally produced translations by those seeking to communicate effectively with markets worldwide. Seeks to raise standards and encourage the adoption of quality systems.
Publication: Newsletter
Publication title: Communicate. Advertisements.

00874

Association of United Kingdom Media Librarians AUKML

PO Box 14254, London, SE1 9WL, UK
Tel: 020 78733920
Email: chair@aukml.org.uk
Website: http://www.aukml.org.uk
Members: 120
Contact: Richard Nelsson, Chm.
Fee: £15
Membership Type: student/unwaged
Fee: £20
Membership Type: associate
Description: Librarians working in UK newspaper and broadcasting companies. Exists to keep members informed of developments in text and picture librarianship that directly affect their industry.
Publication: Newsletter
Publication title: Deadline

00875

Association of University Administrators AUA

University of Manchester, Oxford Rd., Manchester, M13 9PL, UK
Tel: 0161 2752063
Fax: 0161 2752036
Email: aua@manchester.ac.uk
Website: http://www.aua.ac.uk
Members: 4100
Staff: 7
Contact: Christopher Hallas, Chair
Fee: £52-98
Membership Type: full (based on annual salary)
Fee: £63
Membership Type: associate
Description: Administrators and managers in virtually all Higher Education institutions in the UK and Republic of Ireland drawn from all areas of administration including secretariat, registration, estates, and student services. Concerned with the development of sound methods of administration in higher education and encouragement of the professional development of individual administrators and managers in all areas of administration by providing courses, seminars, conferences and opportunities for the exchange of ideas and discussion of current problems in higher education including study visits abroad.
Publication: Newsletter
Publication title: Newslink. Advertisements.

00876

Association of University Professors of French and Heads of Departments of French in Universities in the UK and Ireland AUPHF

University of Durham, French Department, Elvet Riverside, New Elvet, Durham, DH1 3JT, UK
Tel: 0191 3343420
Fax: 0191 3343421
Email: lucille.cairns@durham.ac.uk
Website: http://www.auphf.ac.uk
Members: 185
Contact: Lucille Cairns, VP
Fee: £30
Membership Type: regular
Description: Professors of French and Heads of French Departments in UK Universities. Aims to keep members informed of the latest developments in educational policy affecting the discipline and organization of French studies and to make representations on members' behalf on these matters to Government and Funding Councils.
Formerly: Formerly, Association of University Professors of French and Heads of French Departments
Publication: Proceedings
Publication title: French in the '90s

00877

Association of University Research and Industry Links AURIL

Queen's University Belfast, Lanyon North, University Rd., Belfast, BT7 1NN, UK
Tel: 028 90972589
Fax: 028 90972570

Email: auril@qub.ac.uk
Website: http://www.auril.org.uk/pages/home.php
Contact: Philip Graham, Exec. Dir.
Fee: £700
Membership Type: university, public sector (based on number of members), international
Fee: £900
Membership Type: associate
Description: Represents all practitioners involved in knowledge creation, development, and exchange in the UK. Works to ensure that new ideas, technologies and innovations flow into the market place.

00878

Association of University Teachers - Scotland
UCU - Scotland

6 Castle St., Edinburgh, EH2 3AT, UK
Tel: 0131 2266694
Fax: 0131 2262066
Email: edinburgh@ucu.org.uk
Website: http://www.ucu.org.uk
Members: 6500
Contact: Eleanor McGowan, Sec.
Description: University academic and related staff. Acts as a trade union and professional association.

00879

Association of Upper Gastrointestinal Surgeons
AUGIS

The Royal College Of Surgeons, 35-43 Lincoln's Inn Fields, London, WC2A 3PE, UK
Tel: 020 73044773
Fax: 020 74309235
Email: manager@augis.org
Website: http://www.augis.org
Contact: Graeme Poston, Pres.
Fee: £130
Membership Type: full
Fee: £70
Membership Type: overseas, trainee
Description: Aims to improve the delivery, results and outcomes of conditions of the oesophagus, stomach, duodenum, pancreas, liver and biliary tract requiring surgical treatment. Provides a structure for training objectives and fosters developments in upper gastrointestinal surgery. Advances the quality of care to patients with upper gastrointestinal diseases.
Meetings/Conventions: annual conference September 15 to 16, 2011. Belfast United Kingdom

00880

Association of Valuers of Licensed Property
AVLP

c/o Fleurets
Wellesley House, 96 E St., Suffolk, Sudbury, CO10 2TP, UK
Tel: 01787 378050
Email: bob.whittle@fleurets.com
Website: http://www.avlp.com
Members: 125
Contact: Roger Thomson, Pres.
Description: Experts in valuation of licensed premises, public houses, restaurants and hotels. Promotes professional and proper understanding of value of licensed premises.

00881

Association of Veterinary Anaesthetists
AVA

The Royal Veterinary Coll., Hawkshead Ln., North Mymms, Herts, Hatfield, AL9 7TA, UK
Tel: 01707 666333
Fax: 01707 649384
Email: dbrodbelt@rvc.ac.uk
Website: http://www.ava.eu.com
Members: 400
Staff: 1
Contact: Karen Walsh, Sec.
Fee: £80
Membership Type: full (UK and Europe)
Fee: £68
Membership Type: affiliate, retired (UK and Europe)
Description: Veterinary surgeons; medics, anaesthetists, those with medical university qualifications and scientists, animal technicians and veterinary nurses. Furthers teaching and research in veterinary anaesthetics.
Formerly: Formerly, Association of Veterinary Anaesthetists of Great Britain and Ireland
Publication: Journal
Publication title: Journal of Veterinary Anaesthesia and Analgesia. Advertisements.
Meetings/Conventions: World Congress – semiannual congress – Exhibits.

00882

Association of Welding Distributors
AWD

Secure Hold Business Centre, Studley Rd., Redditch, B98 7LG, UK
Tel: 01952 290036
Fax: 01952 290037
Email: info@awd.org.uk
Website: http://www.awd.org.uk
Members: 150
Staff: 2
Contact: Mike Hill, Dir.
Description: Distributors, manufacturers and importers of welding equipment and consumables. Aims to enhance the status of members and encourage end users to deal only with the association's approved suppliers; improve tangible benefits available to members; develop communications by offering a regular newsletter service to the membership. Continues to liaise more closely with METCOM and take full advantage of facilities available to association.
Library Subject: welding science, application, finance, administration, trade publications
Library Type: not open to the public
Publication: Newsletter
Publication title: AWD Business Bulletin

00883

Association of Wheelchair Children
AWC

6 Woodman Parade, N Woolwich, London, E16 2LL, UK
Tel: 0207 4733684
Email: colin@go-kids.go.org.uk
Website: http://www.go-kids-go.org.uk
Contact: Owen McGhee, Trainer
Description: Helps children with wheelchairs to become independently mobile. Provides training, advice and advocacy support to children with wheelchairs and to the parents of these children.

00884

Association of Wholesale Electrical Bulk Buyers
AWEBB

2 Kensington Works, Hallam Fields Rd., Derbyshire, Ilkeston, DE7 4BR, UK
Tel: 0115 9441088
Fax: 0115 9301036
Email: info@awebb.org.uk
Website: http://www.awebb.org.uk
Members: 59
Staff: 8
Description: Wholesale electrical bulk buyers.

00885

Association of Wireless Technology
AOWT

1 Grove Rd., Maidenhead, SL6 1LW, UK
Tel: 01628 666399
Email: enquiries@aowt.org
Website: http://www.aowt.org
Contact: Christopher D. Love, Chm.
Fee: £550
Membership Type: general
Description: Promotes wireless technology software development and deployment. Negotiates with government and legislative bodies to support or oppose undertakings that affects the industry and executes scientific research and technical development.

00886

Association of Women Solicitors
AWS

The Law Society, 113 Chancery Ln., London, WC2A 1PL, UK
Tel: 0207 3205793
Email: enquiries@womensolicitors.org.uk
Website: http://www.womensolicitors.org.uk
Members: 11000
Contact: Judith McDermott, Contact
Description: Promotes the professional and business interests of women attorneys.

00887

Association of Woodturners of Great Britain
AWGB

c/o Sandra Needham, Membership Sec.
114 Slough Rd., Berkshire, Datchet, SL3 9AF, UK
Tel: 01753 593771
Email: ray.key@btopenworld.com
Website: http://www.woodturners.co.uk
Members: 3000
Contact: Ray Key, Pres.
Fee: £16
Membership Type: individual
Fee: £26
Membership Type: family, overseas
Description: Anyone interested in woodturning, most professionals are members but 90% of membership are hobbyists. Fosters greater awareness of art and craft of woodturning, provides a forum for exchange of information on turning and turners; encourages training and development and acts as the national body and voice of woodturning in the UK.
Library Subject: various aspects of woodturning

Library Type: not open to the public
Publication: Newsletter
Publication title: Revolutions. Advertisements.

00888

Association of Zimbabwe Journalists in the United Kingdom AZJ-UK

83 Glendale Dr., Surrey, Burpham, GU4 7JA, UK
Email: feedback@zimbabwejournalists.com
Website: http://www.zimbabwejournalists.com
Description: Expands the shrinking democratic space in Zimbabwe; offers an independent outlet for news for and by the people of Zimbabwe; and provides a source for balanced, authoritative, accurate and in-depth information about Zimbabwe.

Association Parlementaire du Commonwealth

see Commonwealth Parliamentary Association

Association Psychanalytique Internationale

see International Psychoanalytical Association

Association Sans But Lucrative

see Anderson Association

00889

Ataxia - UK

Lincoln House, Kennington Park, 1-3 Brixton Rd., London, SW9 6DE, UK
Tel: 020 75821444
Fax: 020 75829444
Email: office@ataxia.org.uk
Website: http://www.ataxia.org.uk
Members: 1900
Staff: 12
Contact: Hillary Box, PR Mgr.
Description: Works as a charity that supports people affected by ataxia by funding world class research into causes and treatments; and by providing a range of services that includes helpline, publications, local groups, individual contact, welfare grants. Supports people with ataxia and their families, friends and carers.
Publication: Magazine
Publication title: Ataxian. Advertisements.

00890

Ataxia-Telangiectasia Society

IACR - Rothamsted, Harpenden, AL5 2JQ, UK
Tel: 0582 760733
Fax: 0582 760162
Email: atsociety@btconnect.com
Website: http://www.atsociety.org.uk
Members: 150
Staff: 3
Contact: Kay Atkins, Family Support Worker
Description: Seeks to alleviate the suffering caused by Ataxia-Telangiectasia by supporting families, raising awareness of the disease and funding research. Conducts fundraising activities.
Publication: Newsletter
Publication title: A-T Society News. Advertisements.

00891

Attend

11-13 Cavendish Sq., London, W1G 0AN, UK
Tel: 0845 4500285
Email: info@attend.org.uk
Website: http://www.attend.org.uk/home.aspx
Members: 767
Staff: 17
Contact: David Wood, Chief Exec.
Fee: £300-459
Membership Type: group (based on the gross income)
Fee: £25
Membership Type: individual
Description: Partners with nearly 700 United Kingdom charities working to enhance the quality of life for people suffering ill health, disability or social disadvantage; aims to promote and support the work of members through professional Regional Coordinators, grants, information and guidance on best practice, high rate deposit scheme, comprehensive low cost insurance, conferences, publications, negotiated discounts with suppliers, merchandise and support materials for fundraising; also takes an active interest in lobbying government and other health and social care agencies to make effective policy.
Formerly: Formerly, National Association of Leagues of Hospital Friends
Publication: Magazine
Publication title: Friends Connect

00892

Audio Engineering Society - British Section AES

PO Box 645, Slough, SL1 8BJ, UK
Tel: 01628 663725
Email: uk@aes.org
Website: http://www.aes.org/sections/uk
Members: 700
Staff: 2
Contact: Nathan Bentall, Chm.
Description: Members are involved in various areas of audio engineering. Acts as a subsidiary of parent body which has its headquarters in New York, USA.
Publication: Newsletter
Publication title: British Section Newsletter

00893

Audit Bureau of Circulations - United Kingdom ABC

Saxon House, 211 High St., Berkhamsted, HP4 1AD, UK
Tel: 01442 870800
Email: marketing@abc.org.uk
Website: http://www.abc.org.uk
Members: 3000
Contact: Jerry Wright, Chief Exec.
Fee: £450
Membership Type: in UK
Fee: £583
Membership Type: worldwide
Description: Provides an independent currency for the buying and selling of media.
Publication: Report
Publication title: National Newspaper

00894

Australasian Plant Society

1 Iffin Cottages, Iffin Ln., Canterbury, CT4 7BE, UK
Tel: 01227 780038
Email: secretary@anzplantsoc.org.uk
Website: http://anzplantsoc.org.uk
Contact: Jeremy R. Spon, Sec.
Fee: £10
Membership Type: regular in UK, overseas
Description: Aims to encourage an awareness of the garden qualities of Australasian plants and try to grow as many plants as possible.
Publication title: Seed List

00895

Authors' Licensing and Collecting Society ALCS

The Writers House, 13 Haydon St., London, EC3N 1DB, UK
Tel: 020 72645700
Fax: 020 72645755
Email: alcs@alcs.co.uk
Website: http://www.alcs.co.uk
Members: 60000
Staff: 37
Contact: Owen Atkinson, Chief Exec./Exec. Dir.
Fee: £25
Membership Type: ordinary (full)
Description: Open to all writers and their successors. Concerned with the collection and distribution of royalties to writers.
Publication: Newsletter
Publication title: ALCS News

00896

Autism Independent UK

199-203 Blandford Ave., Kettering, NN16 9AT, UK
Tel: 01536 523274
Fax: 01536 523274
Email: autism@autismuk.com
Website: http://www.autismuk.com
Members: 4000
Staff: 7
Description: Individuals with autism and their families. Seeks to increase awareness of autism; promotes development of improved diagnosis and treatment of people with autism. Works to improve the quality of life of people with autism. Serves as a nonmedical information center on autism and its treatment; sponsors research and educational programs; provides support and services to people with autism and their families. Maintains Diagnosis and Assessment Resource Centre, where interested individuals can access information on autism and its treatment. Collaborates with county agencies in the development of public health policies impacting people with autism.
Library Subject: autism
Library Type: reference
Formerly: Formerly, Society of the Autistically Handicapped

00897

Autism Initiatives UK

7 Chesterfield Rd., Crosby, Liverpool, L23 9XL, UK
Tel: 0151 3309500
Fax: 0151 3309501
Email: headoffice@autisminitiatives.org
Website: http://www.autisminitiatives.org
Contact: Keith Roberts, Contact
Fee: £10

Membership Type: individual
Description: Provides information on autism from behavior management to diagnosis.

00898

Automated Material Handling Systems Association
AMHSA

PO Box 7113, Leicester, LE7 9XX, UK
Tel: 0116 2598518
Fax: 0870 7877439
Email: secretary@amhsa.co.uk
Website: http://www.amhsa.co.uk
Members: 21
Staff: 1
Description: UK companies which have designed, installed and commissioned at least one automated material handling system and UK suppliers of unit load conveying equipment and systems. Provides a forum for members to discuss matters of mutual interest and to work together to promote ever-improving standards of quality, safety and commercial practice.
Publication title: Seven Codes of Practice

00899

Automatic Door Suppliers Association
ADSA

411 Limpsfield Rd., The Green, Surrey, Warlingham, CR6 9HA, UK
Tel: 01883 624961
Fax: 01883 626841
Website: http://adsa.org.uk
Members: 20
Staff: 1
Description: Suppliers of automatic doors: swing, sliding and revolving. Promotes standards of safety in the installation and use of automatic doors.

00900

Automatic Identification Manufacturers - United Kingdom
AIM UK

The Old Vicarage, All Souls Rd., Halifax, HX3 6DR, UK
Tel: 01422 368368
Fax: 01422 355604
Email: ian@aimuk.org
Website: http://www.aimuk.org
Contact: Ian Smith, Pres.
Fee: £500-2500
Membership Type: organization (based on turnover)
Description: Manufacturers, suppliers, systems integrators and consultants in the field of automatic identification/data capture (bar coding, RF tags, RF data communication, portable terminals, magnetic stripe, OCR, smart cards, vision systems, voice recognition, etc.) Educates the marketplace in automatic identification/data capture technologies and thereby to increase the market for the products and services of its members. Participates in the standardization process to ensure the best use can be made of these technologies.
Publication title: Update and Focus Europe

00901

Automatic Vending Association
AVA

1 Villiers Ct., 40 Upper Mulgrave Rd., Cheam, Sutton, SM2 7AJ, UK
Tel: 020 86611112
Fax: 020 86612224
Email: bridget@ava-vending.co.uk
Website: http://www.ava-vending.co.uk
Members: 200
Staff: 9
Contact: Andy Porter, Chm.
Description: Producers, suppliers, importers, exporters, and distributors involved in the vending machine industry in the United Kingdom. Represents members' interests; promotes the vending industry.
Formerly: Formerly, Automatic Vending Association of Britain
Meetings/Conventions: AVEX – biennial trade show – Exhibits.

00902

Automotive Distribution Federation
ADF

Aftermarket House, 5 Marlin Office Village, 1250 Chester Rd., Castle Bromwich, Birmingham, B35 7AZ, UK
Tel: 0845 3131506
Fax: 0845 3131508
Email: admin@adf.org.uk
Website: http://www.adf.org.uk/index.php
Members: 350
Staff: 3
Contact: Quintin Cornforth, Pres./Chm.
Fee: £400
Membership Type: agent
Fee: £760
Membership Type: service
Description: Members are wholesale distributors and manufacturers of motor components and accessories for the independent automotive aftermarket. Aims to serve, promote and strengthen the independent automotive aftermarket and improve the quality of products and services available to the ultimate benefit of the consumer. Also represents the interests of members, by forging links with Government, European Community, all authoritative bodies and other organizations both nationally and internationally.
Library Type: reference
Formerly: Formerly, Motor Factors Association
Publication: Magazine
Publication title: Eyes and Ears. Advertisements.
Meetings/Conventions: Aftermarket Workout – annual conference

00903

Automotive Manufactures' Racing Association
AMRA

The Nook, 27 Topside, Grenoside, Sheffield, S35 8RD, UK
Tel: 0114 2464878
Fax: 0114 2464858
Email: info@amrauk.com
Website: http://www.amrauk.com
Members: 130
Staff: 1
Contact: Stuart A. Barnes, Coor.
Description: Provides collective representation for the automotive manufacturing industry by liaison with motor sports governing bodies, event organizers, and circuit owners in the UK.

00904

AVERT

4 Brighton Rd., Horsham, W Sussex, London, RH13 5BA, UK
Tel: 01403 210202
Email: info@avert.org
Website: http://www.avert.org
Staff: 7
Contact: Annabel Kanabus, Dir.
Description: Seeks to improve the quality of life for persons with AIDS. Conducts research and educational programs. Provides free information and conducts programs regarding AIDS, both within the U.K. and overseas.
Library Subject: AIDS and related subjects
Library Type: reference
Formerly: Formerly, AIDS Education and Research Trust
Publication: Newsletter

00905

Aviation Environment Federation
AEF

Broken Wharf House, 2 Broken Wharf, London, EC4V 3DT, UK
Tel: 020 72482223
Fax: 020 73298160
Email: info@aef.org.uk
Website: http://www.aef.org.uk
Members: 150
Staff: 3
Contact: Tim Johnson, Dir.
Fee: £20
Membership Type: individual
Fee: £30-36
Membership Type: association (based on the number of members)
Description: Represents local authorities, parish councils, amenity societies; airfield management pilots; and individuals concerned with the protection of the environment. Seeks to see aviation develop in a way which allows reasonable protection of people and the environment from its adverse effects. Explores consequences of aviation policies by taking part in public enquiries, evaluating noise and environmental impact, and studying community response. Encourages good consultative practices and represents environmental interests before civil aviation authorities. Makes recommendations on such issues as environmental protection factors, technical and operational methods of noise reduction, good relations between airfields and neighbors, and careful planning of the use and siting of airfields.
Library Subject: aviation, environmental matters
Library Type: reference
Formerly: Formerly, Airfields Environment Federation
Publication: Newsletter
Publication title: Flying Green

00906

Avicultural Society

c/o Peter Stocks, Sec.-Treas.
Sheraton Lodge, Station Rd., Southminster, CM0 7EW, UK
Email: admin@avisoc.co.uk
Website: http://www.avisoc.co.uk
Members: 1000
Contact: Raymond Sawyer, Pres.
Fee: £21
Membership Type: overseas
Fee: £18
Membership Type: regular
Description: Studies British and foreign birds in freedom and captivity.
Publication: Magazine
Publication title: Avicultural Magazine

00907

Avon and Border Counties Welsh Pony and Cob Association

Hursley House, Hursley Hill, Bristol, BS14 0QZ, UK
Tel: 07711 545964
Email: sue.hole@simplyhealth.co.uk
Website: http://www.avonbc.com
Contact: Susan Hole, Sec.
Fee: £8
Membership Type: single
Fee: £10
Membership Type: joint, family
Description: Records the breeding details of Welsh ponies and cobs. Seeks to improve and promote the breed.

00908

Babraham Institute

Babraham Research Campus, Cambridge, CB22 3AT, UK
Tel: 01223 496000
Fax: 01223 496002
Email: babraham.contact@bbsrc.ac.uk
Website: http://www.babraham.ac.uk
Staff: 450
Contact: Caroline Edmonds, Deputy Dir./Sec.
Description: Focuses on life science research with biotechnological, pharmaceutical and biomedical applications.
Library Subject: biological science
Library Type: not open to the public
Formerly: Formerly, Institute of Animal Physiology
Publication title: The Babraham Institute Corporate Plan
Meetings/Conventions: Babraham Bioenterprise Award Lecture – annual lecture

00909

Baby Milk Action

34 Trumpington St., Cambridge, CB2 1QY, UK
Tel: 01223 464420
Email: info@babymilkaction.org
Website: http://www.babymilkaction.org
Members: 2000
Staff: 4
Contact: Sarah Hansen, Office Mgr.
Fee: £7
Membership Type: unwaged individual
Fee: £18
Membership Type: waged individual
Description: Works to protect mothers and their babies worldwide. Promotes breastfeeding and promotes awareness of the potential for health damage inherent in artificial infant feeding. Seeks to strengthen national and international controls on the marketing of baby foods and formulae; monitors promotional campaigns for baby formulae and challenges companies that violate the World Health Organization's International Code of Marketing of Breastmilk Substitutes. Works with other international organizations to protect and support local breastfeeding initiatives worldwide. Lobbies British government agencies and the European Union on behalf of increased protection of breastfeeding and maternity benefits.
Publication: Newsletter
Publication title: Update

00910

Baby Products Association BPA

2 Carrera House, Merlin Ct., Gatehouse Close, Aylesbury, HP19 8DP, UK
Tel: 0845 4569570
Fax: 0845 4569573
Email: info@b-p-a.org
Website: http://www.b-p-a.org
Members: 120
Staff: 5
Contact: Julie James, Contact
Description: Promotes the industry to the general public and the trade as being professional and responsible; provides support to member organizations; represents the industry to government departments (in the UK, the EC and elsewhere), to local authorities and other organizations that have an interest in this field.
Library Subject: British, European standards relating to baby products
Library Type: not open to the public
Publication: Yearbook
Publication title: BPA Yearbook. Advertisements.

00911

BackCare, The Charity for Healthier Backs

16 Elmtree Rd., Middlesex, Teddington, TW11 8ST, UK
Tel: 020 89775474
Fax: 020 89435318
Email: info@backcare.org.uk
Website: http://www.backcare.org.uk
Staff: 16
Contact: Sash Newman, Chief Exec.
Fee: £12.5
Membership Type: individual supporter
Fee: £15
Membership Type: professional
Description: Back pain sufferers, osteopaths, chiropractors, medical doctors, and safety and training officers in 12 countries. Sponsors research on the causes and treatment of back pain. Teaches an individual to use one's body sensibly in order to prevent spinal damage. Promotes the formation of local branches. Keeps back pain sufferers informed on current developments in research, education, treatment and equipment.
Formerly: Formerly, National Back Pain Association
Publication: Booklet
Publication title: A Carer's Guide to the Safer Moving and Handling of Patients

00912

Badger Face Welsh Mountain Sheep Society

Stall House, Vowchurch, Hereford, HR2 0QE, UK
Tel: 01981 550685
Email: lucylevinge@btinternet.com
Website: http://www.badgerfacesheep.co.uk
Members: 230
Contact: Lucy Levinge, Gen. Sec.
Fee: £15
Membership Type: full
Fee: £5
Membership Type: junior
Description: Promotes the breeding and improvement of the Badger Face Welsh Mountain Sheep.

00913

Bagpipe Society

11 Queens Pl., West Yorkshire, Otley, LS21 3HY, UK
Email: bagpipes@snozz.com
Website: http://www.bagpipesociety.org.uk
Members: 250
Contact: Michael Ross, Treas./Membership Sec.
Fee: £17
Membership Type: waged, family
Fee: £9
Membership Type: unwaged
Description: Promotes bagpipes and the music of bagpipes.
Publication: Newsletter
Publication title: Chanter. Advertisements.

00914

Bakers, Food and Allied Workers' Union - United Kingdom BFAWU

Stanborough House, Great North Rd., Stanborough, Welwyn Garden City, AL8 7TA, UK
Tel: 01707 260150
Fax: 01707 261570
Email: info@bfawu.org
Website: http://www.bfawu.org
Members: 36000
Staff: 16
Contact: Joe Marino, Gen. Sec.
Description: Individuals employed in the field of baking and related industries. Works to eliminate night work, to set the minimum wage rate, and to nationalize the baking industry. Provides legal assistance to members; offers financial support to members in the case of death, sickness, or unemployment. Organizes biennial apprentice competition; sponsors educational programs.
Publication: Manual
Publication title: Book of Rules, Health, and Safety

00915

Balint Society

c/o Dr. D. Watt
Tollgate Health Centre, 220 Tollgate Rd., London, E6 4JS, UK
Email: david.watt@gp-f84093.nhs.uk
Website: http://balint.co.uk
Contact: Andrew Elder, Pres.
Description: Helps practitioners understand patients better. Conducts focus group discussion, training and research.

00916

Ball and Roller Bearing Manufacturers Association BRBMA

Heathcote House, 136 Hagley Rd., Edgbaston, Birmingham, B16 9PN, UK
Tel: 0121 4544141
Fax: 0121 4544949
Email: info@brbma.org
Website: http://www.brbma.org
Description: Ball and roller bearing manufacturers. Facilitates technical cooperation for the benefit of the industry and its customers.

00917

Baltic Air Charter Association BACA

c/o Mr. Willem van der Pol, Council Member
Baltic Exchange, 38 St. Mary Axe, London, EC3A 8BH, UK
Tel: 020 76235501
Fax: 020 73691622
Email: baca@balticexchange.com
Website: http://www.baca.org.uk
Members: 210

Contact: Dick Gilbert, Chm.
Fee: £285
Membership Type: regular
Description: Represents the commercial aviation industry in UK. Promotes ethical business practices and involves itself in political issues that may affect the industry.

00918

Baltic Exchange

38 St. Mary Axe, London, EC3A 8BH, UK
Tel: 020 76235501
Fax: 020 73691622
Email: enquiries@balticexchange.com
Website: http://www.balticexchange.com
Members: 670
Staff: 25
Contact: Mark Jackson, Chm.
Description: International shipping exchange. Provides independent daily shipping market information.
Publication: Magazine
Publication title: The Baltic. Advertisements.

00919

Banana Link

Sackville Pl., Ste. 201, 44-48 Magdalen St., Norwich, NR3 1JU, UK
Tel: 01603 765670
Fax: 01603 761645
Email: info@bananalink.org.uk
Website: http://www.bananalink.org.uk
Description: Aims to alleviate poverty and prevent environment degradation in banana exporting communities. Works toward a sustainable banana economy. Facilitates fair trade.
Publication: Bulletin
Publication title: Banana Trade News

00920

Bankruptcy Association of England and Wales BAGBI

4 Johnson Close, Abraham Heights, Lancashire, Lancaster, LA1 5BR, UK
Tel: 01539 469474
Email: johnmcqueen@theba.org.uk
Website: http://www.theba.org.uk/index.php
Members: 1500
Staff: 3
Contact: John McQueen, Founder/CEO
Fee: £15
Membership Type: general
Description: Campaigns for reform of the United Kingdom's insolvency laws. Advises and assists debtors and bankrupts.
Formerly: Formerly, Association of Bankrupts
Publication: Book
Publication title: Bankruptcy Explained

00921

Bar Association for Local Government and the Public Service BALGPS

Ingleby House, 11-14 Cannon St., Birmingham, B2 5EN, UK
Tel: 0121 3039991
Fax: 0121 3031312
Email: chairman@balgps.org.uk
Website: http://www.balgps.org.uk
Members: 100
Contact: Mirza F.N. Ahmad, Chm.
Description: Represents barristers in local government and the public sector. Focuses on the protection and promotion of the professional rights, and interests of barristers employed in local government and public sector by giving advice to barristers seeking a career in the public sector, making representations to the Bar Council and elsewhere relating to training, rights of audience and direct access to counsel and by promoting professional knowledge.

00922

Barbers Company

Barber-Surgeons' Hall, 1 Monkwell Sq., Wood St., London, EC2Y 5BL, UK
Tel: 020 76060741
Fax: 020 76063857
Email: clerk@barberscompany.org
Website: http://www.barberscompany.org
Contact: Peter J. Durrant, Clerk
Description: Organizes charitable work with priority to those with medical, barbers or city background. Awards scholarships and recognitions to professionals of medicine.

00923

BAREMA

The Stables, Sugworth Ln., Oxfordshire, Radley, OX14 2HX, UK
Tel: 01865 736393
Fax: 01865 736393
Email: barema@btinternet.com
Website: http://www.barema.org.uk
Members: 36
Staff: 2
Contact: Harrie Cooke, Sec.
Description: Maintains close links with government departments, Standards Organisation and professional bodies within its specialty while actively supporting ABHI in all matters of general interest.
Formerly: Formerly, British Anaesthetic and Respiratory Equipment Manufacturers Association

00924

Barnsley and Rotherham Chamber of Commerce

Innovation Ctre., Innovation Way, Wilthorpe, Barnsley, S75 lJL, UK
Tel: 0844 4145100
Fax: 0844 8465102
Email: sball@brchamber.co.uk
Website: http://www.brchamber.co.uk
Members: 800
Staff: 13
Contact: Sue Ball, Membership Admin.
Fee: £249
Membership Type: silver
Fee: £499
Membership Type: gold
Description: Promotes business and commerce.
Formerly: Formerly, Barnsley Chamber of Commerce and Industry

00925

Basingstoke Conservation Volunteers BCV

68 Grainger Close, Basingstoke, RG22 4EA, UK
Tel: 01635 268482
Email: mike@basingstokecv.org.uk
Website: http://www.basingstokecv.org.uk
Members: 40
Contact: Mike Norman, Membership Sec.
Fee: £3
Membership Type: adult
Fee: £2
Membership Type: student, retired, unwaged
Description: Works to carry out practical habitat conservation projects in North Hampshire. Conducts light clearance tasks such as coppicing in woodland and scrub-bashing on downland sites, hedge-laying, boardwalk construction and pond clearance. Much of work done in cooperation with Hampshire Wildlife Trust.
Publication: Newsletter

00926

BASO - Association for Cancer Surgery BASO-ACS

c/o Royal College of Surgeons
35-43 Lincoln's Inn Fields, London, WC2A 3PE, UK
Tel: 020 74055612
Fax: 020 74046574
Email: lucydavies@baso.org.uk
Website: http://www.baso.org
Members: 700
Contact: Lucy Davies, Admin.
Description: Specialises in the treatment of breast cancer. Provides services to cancer surgeons and to the public in general.
Formerly: Formerly, British Association of Surgical Oncology

00927

Bat Conservation Trust - UK BCT

15 Cloisters House, 8 Battersea Park Rd., London, SW8 4BG, UK
Tel: 020 76272629
Fax: 020 76272628
Email: enquiries@bats.org.uk
Website: http://www.bats.org.uk
Members: 5000
Staff: 7
Contact: Chris Packham, Pres.
Fee: £24.5
Membership Type: individual
Fee: £33
Membership Type: family (with/without children)
Description: Coordinates bat conservation and research in the United Kingdom. Sponsors public education programs to encourage protection of the animals and their roosting sites.
Formerly: Formerly, Bat Conservation Trust - England

00928
Bates Association for Vision Education
BAVE
95 Brodrick Rd., Eastbourne, BN22 9NY, UK
Tel: 0800 0556130
Fax: 0845 2255098
Email: bave@seeing.org
Website: http://www.seeing.org
Members: 20
Contact: Julia Galvin, Sec.
Description: Teachers of Bates Method vision education. Seeks to advance the knowledge and practice of vision education for the improvement of eyesight without lenses or surgery.
Library Type: not open to the public
Formerly: Formerly, London Association of Eyesight Training
Publication: Magazine
Publication title: Vision Education News

00929
Bath Institute for Rheumatic Diseases
BIRD
1 Trim Bridge, Allan Dixon Bldg., Bath, BA1 1HD, UK
Tel: 01225 448444
Fax: 01225 336809
Email: fundraising@birdbath.org.uk
Website: http://www.birdbath.org.uk
Contact: Libby Gawith, Sec.
Description: Promotes the study of rheumatic diseases.

00930
Bathroom Manufacturers Association
BMA
Federation House, Station Rd., Stoke-on-Trent, ST4 2RT, UK
Tel: 01782 747123
Fax: 01782 747161
Email: info@bathroom-association.org.uk
Website: http://www.bathroom-association.org
Members: 20
Staff: 4
Contact: Yvonne Orgill, Chief Exec.
Description: Promotes the bathroom industry through representation; provides continuous dialogue between members and the industry.

00931
Battery Vehicle Society
BVS
17, Novello Close, Brighton Hill, Basingstoke, RG22 4LF, UK
Tel: 07711 252971
Email: membership@batteryvehiclesociety.org.uk
Website: http://www.BatteryVehicleSociety.org.uk/wordpress/?page_id=2
Contact: Robert Sharpe, Membership Sec.
Fee: £15
Membership Type: ordinary
Fee: £10
Membership Type: unemployed, registered disabled, individual (under 18 or over 65)
Description: Represents the interests of both the amateur and professional electric vehicle owners. Provides a forum for the exchange of information and ideas between members.
Library Subject: electric vehicles, battery vehicles, batteries, charging points, historic vehicles
Library Type: reference

00932
BCPC
7 Omni Business Ctre., Omega Park, Alton, GU34 2QD, UK
Tel: 01420 593200
Fax: 01420 593209
Email: md@bcpc.org
Website: http://www.bcpc.org
Staff: 5
Contact: Colin Ruscoe, Chm.
Description: Promotes the knowledge and understanding of crop protection/production through conferences, publications, teaching resources for schools, training manuals, identifying R&D needs for policy makers.
Formerly: Formerly, British Crop Protection Council
Publication: Book
Publication title: Pesticide Manual

00933
BEAMA Capacitor Manufacturer's Association
BCMA
Westminster Tower, 3 Albert Embankment, London, SE1 7SL, UK
Tel: 020 77933000
Fax: 020 77933003
Email: info@beama.org.uk
Website: http://www.beama.org.uk/en/other-associations/bcma.cfm
Contact: Howard Porter, CEO
Description: Wound capacitors of film, paper, or mixed dielectric construction.

00934
BEAMA Electroheat Manufacturers Association of BEAMA
EMAB
Westminster Tower, 3 Albert Embankment, London, SE1 7SL, UK
Tel: 020 77933000
Fax: 020 77933003
Email: info@beama.org.uk
Website: http://www.beama.org.uk
Contact: Howard Porter, Dir.
Description: Manufacturers and suppliers of electroheat equipment including, industrial heading elements and induction and infrared and electric surface heating.

00935
BEAMA Installation
Westminster Tower, 3 Albert Embankment, London, SE1 7SL, UK
Tel: 020 77933013
Fax: 020 77933003
Email: cac@beama.org.uk
Website: http://www.beamainstallation.org.uk
Members: 66
Staff: 6
Contact: David P. Dossett, Chm.
Description: Trade association for manufacturers of electrical installation equipment and cable management products.
Formerly: Formerly, Electrical Installation Equipment Manufacturers' Association

00936
BEAMA Metering and Communications Association
BEMCA
Westminster Tower, 3 Albert Embankment, London, SE1 7SL, UK
Tel: 020 77933000
Fax: 020 77933003
Email: hp@beama.org.uk
Website: http://www.bemca.org.uk
Contact: Howard Porter, Dir.
Description: Focuses on integrating electricity meters and all matters affecting the design, manufacture, supply, and operation of electricity metering equipment for the supply utilities.

00937
BEAMA Transmission and Distribution Association
BTDA
Westminster Tower, 3 Albert Embankment, London, SE1 7SL, UK
Tel: 020 77933000
Fax: 020 77933003
Email: info@beama.org.uk
Website: http://www.beama.org.uk
Members: 30
Staff: 2
Contact: Howard Porter, Dir.
Description: Manufacturers of high voltage, transmission and distribution equipment.

00938
Beating Disorders Association
BEAT
Wensum House, 1st Fl., 103 Prince of Wales Rd., Norwich, NR1 1DW, UK
Tel: 01603 619090
Fax: 01603 664915
Email: info@b-eat.co.uk
Website: http://www.b-eat.co.uk/Home
Members: 3000
Staff: 32
Contact: Susan Ringwood, Chief Exec.
Fee: £21
Membership Type: regular
Description: Individuals affected by anorexia, bulimia nervosa, and related eating disorders, their families, and friends. Offers information, help, and support. Seeks to enhance awareness and understanding of these illnesses. Communicates with related organizations and individuals in the medical and counseling professions. Disseminates information. Organizes regional support days. Offers training for professionals.
Formerly: Formerly, Anorexic Aid
Publication: Journal
Publication title: European Eating Disorders Review. Advertisements.
Meetings/Conventions: annual conference

00939
Beaumont Society
BS
27 Old Gloucester St., London, WC1N 3XX, UK
Tel: 01582 412220
Email: enquiries@beaumontsociety.org.uk
Website: http://www.beaumontsociety.org.uk
Members: 800
Staff: 14
Contact: Shirley Keel, Pres.
Fee: £29
Membership Type: UK resident
Fee: £35
Membership Type: Europe resident
Description: Transvestites and transsexuals. Promotes improved public understanding of transvestism and gender dysphoria. Seeks to assist members in becoming functional members of society. Serves as a support group for members; conducts educational programs for health care and social workers and other individuals working with people with gender dysphoria. Maintains national information line.

00940
Beaver Water World
Waylands Farm, Approach Rd., Tatsfield, North Westerham, Kent, TN16 2JT, UK
Tel: 01959 577747
Website: http://www.beaverwaterworld.com
Description: Seeks to be a refuge for rare and rescued reptiles. Provides rescue facilities for unwanted reptiles and other animals; works to discourage the public from purchasing wild caught animals; promotes conservation projects; works towards providing an animal hospital for reptiles; aims to create near natural conditions for rescued reptiles.

00941
Bedfordshire and Luton Chamber of Commerce, Training and Enterprise
Kimpton Rd., Bedfordshire, Luton, LU2 0SX, UK
Tel: 01582 522448
Fax: 01582 522450
Email: info@chamber-business.com
Website: http://www.chamber-business.com
Members: 1600
Staff: 34
Contact: Brian Hibbert, Chm.
Fee: £233.22
Membership Type: sole trader
Fee: £1612.53
Membership Type: business (maximum)
Description: Promotes business and commerce.
Publication: Magazine
Publication title: Business Focus

00942
Bee Improvement and Bee Breeders' Association
BIBBA
75 Newhall Rd., Doncaster, DN3 1QQ, UK
Tel: 01302 88581350
Email: membershipsecretary@bibba.com
Website: http://www.bibba.com
Members: 357
Contact: David Allen, Membership Sec.
Fee: £20
Membership Type: ordinary
Description: Concerned with the conservation, restoration, study, selection and improvement of the native and near native honeybees of Britain and Ireland.
Formerly: Formerly, Village Bee Breeders Association
Publication: Magazine
Publication title: Bee Improvement. Advertisements.

00943
Befrienders Worldwide
BI
Upper Mill, Kingston Rd., Ewell, KT17 2AF, UK
Tel: 0208 3948300
Fax: 0208 3948301
Email: international@samaritans.org
Website: http://www.befrienders.org
Members: 30000
Staff: 5
Description: Aims to build effective suicide prevention services resourced by volunteers throughout the world.
Formerly: Formerly, Befrienders International Samaritans Worldwide

00944
Belgian Luxembourg Chamber of Commerce in Great Britain
BLCC
Westwood House, Annie Med Ln., South Cave, HU15 2HG, UK
Tel: 0207 1274292
Fax: 0870 4292148
Email: info@blcc.co.uk
Website: http://www.blcc.co.uk
Members: 190
Contact: Michel Vanhoonacker, Chm.
Fee: £350
Membership Type: corporate (with less than 100 employees)
Fee: £650
Membership Type: corporate (with more than 99 employees)
Description: Works to improve and strengthen two-way commercial and trade relations between London and UK. Offers networking activities, corporate events, virtual office facilities, administration services, salary administration, company registration and recruitment services.
Publication: Magazine
Publication title: Belux. Advertisements.

00945
Benevolent Fund of the College of Optometrists and the Association of Optometrists
PO Box 10, Swanley, BR8 8ZF, UK
Tel: 01322 660388
Email: info@opticalbenfund.com
Website: http://www.opticalbenfund.com
Staff: 1
Contact: David Lacey, Contact
Description: Members/former members of the optical profession and their dependents.
Formerly: Formerly, Benevolent Fund of the College of Optometrists

00946
Berkshire Conservation Volunteers
BeC
PO Box 165, Berkshire, Reading, RG1 4LD, UK
Tel: 01189 751528
Email: membership@berkshire-conservation-volunteers.org.uk
Website: http://www.berkshire-conservation-volunteers.org.uk
Contact: Neil Frankum, Membership Sec.
Fee: £5
Membership Type: individual
Description: Works to carry out voluntary environmental work on local nature reserves in Reading, Berkshire and North Hampshire. Conducts woodland type work during winter like coppicing, shrub clearance, tree planting, hedge laying etc. with more varied work during the summer like path construction, hay making, pond clearance, fencing and dry stone walling.

00947
Beverage Service Association
BSA
Hartfield Pl., 40-44 High St., Middlesex, Northwood, HA6 1BN, UK
Tel: 01923 848392
Fax: 01923 848391
Email: info@beverageserviceassociation.com
Website: http://www.beverageserviceassociation.com
Contact: Jim Devlin, Exec. Dir.
Fee: £99-735
Membership Type: distributor (based on annual turnover)
Fee: £55-1320
Membership Type: retailer (based on the number of outlets)
Description: Fosters the growth of the UK out-of-home, non-vending refreshment industry. Raises the quality of beverages produced and the standard of service provided by the industry. Provides education, training, information and communication to all sectors engaged in beverage services.
Publication: Magazine
Publication title: In the Cup. Advertisements.

00948
BHR Group
The Fluid Engineering Centre, Cranfield, Bedford, MK43 0AJ, UK
Tel: 01234 750422
Fax: 01234 750074
Email: contactus@bhrgroup.co.uk
Website: http://www.bhrgroup.com
Members: 25
Staff: 80
Contact: J. Alistair R. Muir, Gen. Mgr.
Description: Individuals and companies interested in developments in fluid engineering technology. Disseminates technical information to the industry. Represents members' interests. Conducts research programs.
Library Subject: fluid engineering
Library Type: reference
Formerly: Formerly, British Hydromechanics Research Association
Publication: Newsletter
Publication title: BHR Group News

00949

Bhutan Society of the United Kingdom

c/o Mrs. Elizabeth Lee
13, Albury House, Sells Close, Surrey, Guilford, GU1 3JY, UK
Tel: 01483 455764
Email: info@bhutansociety.org
Website: http://www.bhutansociety.org
Contact: Michael Rutland, Chm.
Fee: £15
Membership Type: individual
Fee: £20
Membership Type: household
Description: Promotes knowledge and understanding of the Kingdom of Bhutan, its history and culture. Seeks to encourage cultural and educational links and foster good relations between the peoples of Bhutan and the United Kingdom.
Publication: Newsletter

00950

Bibliographical Society - United Kingdom

c/o Margaret Ford, Honorary Sec.
Institute of English Studies, University of London, Senate House, Malet St., London, WC1E 7HU, UK
Email: secretary@bibsoc.org.uk
Website: http://www.bibsoc.org.uk
Members: 1050
Contact: John Barnard, Pres.
Fee: £37
Membership Type: overseas
Fee: £33
Membership Type: regular
Description: Bibliographers, booksellers, book collectors, academics of all kinds; everyone interested in historical and critical bibliography. Promotes and encourages study and research in the fields of historical, analytical, descriptive and textual bibliography and the history of printing, publishing, bookselling, bookbinding and collecting. Holds meetings at which papers are read and discussed and publishes works concerned with bibliography.
Publication: Journal
Publication title: The Library. Advertisements.

00951

Biochemical Society - England BS

3rd Fl., Eagle House, 16 Procter St., London, WC1V 6NX, UK
Tel: 020 72804100
Fax: 020 72804170
Email: genadmin@biochemistry.org
Website: http://www.biochemistry.org
Members: 7000
Contact: Chris Kirk, Chief Exec.
Fee: £62
Membership Type: full
Fee: £16
Membership Type: student/emeritus
Description: Seeks to promote biochemistry and to provide a forum for information exchange and discussion of teaching and research in biochemistry. Maintains 7 specialized theme panels.
Publication: Journal
Publication title: Biochemical Journal. Advertisements.
Meetings/Conventions: Life Sciences – annual meeting – Exhibits.

00952

Biodynamic Agricultural Association BDAA

c/o The Painswick Inn Project
Gloucester St., Stroud, GL5 1QG, UK
Tel: 01453 759501
Fax: 01453 759501
Email: office@biodynamic.org.uk
Website: http://www.biodynamic.org.uk
Members: 800
Staff: 4
Contact: Bernard Jarman, Exec. Dir.
Description: Farmers, growers, foresters, gardeners, and anyone interested in food, nutrition, the environment and a meaning-filled life. Promotes and develops biodynamic agriculture, a unique organic approach inspired by Rudolf Steiner's spiritual scientific research.
Publication title: Bio-Dynamic Farming Practice

00953

BioIndustry Association BIA

14/15 Belgrave Sq., London, SW1X 8PS, UK
Tel: 020 75657190
Fax: 020 75657191
Email: admin@bioindustry.org
Website: http://www.bioindustry.org
Members: 350
Staff: 8
Contact: Clive Dix, Chm.
Fee: £1680-23400
Membership Type: corporate
Fee: £1838-7875
Membership Type: associate
Description: Individuals interested in contributing to the development of biotechnology in the United Kingdom. Represents members' interests concerning regulatory affairs, policy, and funding. Maintains liaison with trade associations and biotechnology organizations. Provide a forum for idea and information exchange. Sponsors exhibitions.
Library Subject: business, bioscience
Library Type: reference
Formerly: Formerly, Association for the Advancement of British Biotechnology

00954

Bird Life International - United Kingdom

Wellbrook Ct., Girton Rd., Cambridge, CB3 0NA, UK
Tel: 01223 277318
Fax: 01223 277200
Email: birdlife@birdlife.org
Website: http://www.birdlife.org
Members: 2500000
Staff: 4000
Contact: Michael Rands, Dir./Chief Exec.
Description: A partnership of natural conservation organisations. Conserves all bird species on earth and their habitats, and through this, to work for the world's biological diversity and the sustainability of human use of natural resources. Advises governments and private bodies on significant national and international bird conservation issues.
Publication: Journal
Publication title: Bird Conservation International. Advertisements.

00955

BirdLife International

Wellbrook Ct., Girton Rd., Cambridge, CB3 0NA, UK
Tel: 01223 277318
Fax: 01223 277200
Email: birdlife@birdlife.org
Website: http://www.birdlife.org
Contact: Marco Lambertini, Contact
Description: Aims to prevent the extinction of any bird species. Maintains and improves the conservation status of all bird species. Integrates bird conservation into sustaining people's livelihoods and helps conserve biodiversity.
Publication: Journal
Publication title: Bird Conservation International. Advertisements.

00956

Birmingham Chamber of Commerce and Industry BCI

75 Harborne Rd., Birmingham, B15 3DH, UK
Tel: 0121 4546171
Fax: 0121 4558670
Email: info@birmingham-chamber.com
Website: http://www.birmingham-chamber.com
Members: 4000
Contact: Paul Bassi, Pres.
Fee: £311.38
Membership Type: company (with 1-5 employees)
Fee: £346.63
Membership Type: company (with 6-10 employees)
Description: Promotes and supports business and commerce.
Publication: Journal
Publication title: Chamberlink

00957

Birmingham Natural History Society BNHS

23 Crosbie Rd., Birmingham, B17 9BG, UK
Tel: 0121 4271010
Email: peterjarvis668@googlemail.com
Website: http://freespace.virgin.net/clare.h/bnhs.htm
Members: 120
Contact: Peter Coxhead, Pres.
Fee: £6
Membership Type: individual
Description: Promotes the understanding of general natural history and conservation topics.
Library Subject: general natural history, country floras
Library Type: not open to the public
Publication: Journal
Publication title: Proceedings of BNHS

00958

Bitumen Waterproofing Association BWA

19 Regina Crescent, Ravenshead, Nottingham, NG15 9AE, UK
Tel: 01623 430574
Fax: 01623 798098
Email: info@bwa-europe.com
Website: http://www.bwa-europe.com
Members: 35
Staff: 5
Contact: Paul K. Newman, Chief Exec.
Fee: £5000-45000
Membership Type: company
Fee: £5000
Membership Type: non-active company
Description: National waterproofing contractors' associations and waterproofing materials manufacturers in 21 countries. Coordinates and undertakes research on rain waterproofing and sealing against underground water of construction or civil engineering works; establishes centers for documentation, information, and research; disseminates information on waterproofing to aid in the advancement of its application. Maintains contact with governments and bodies representing the construction industry and the civil engineering profession in order to inform them of decisions reached at international congresses. Organizes special projects, courses, and exhibitions.
Formerly: Formerly, International Waterproofing Association

00959

BKSTS - The Moving Image Society

Pinewood Studios, Pinewood Rd., Iver Heath, SL0 0NH, UK
Tel: 01753 656656
Email: info@bksts.com
Website: http://nt12.orbital.net/bksts/about.asp
Members: 2000
Staff: 3
Contact: Roland Brown, Pres.
Fee: £96
Membership Type: full, associate
Fee: £24
Membership Type: student
Description: Technicians and management in the film, television and related industries. Assists in establishing technical standards, recommended practices and processes of production. Encourages study and research in all aspects of film and television production and distribution of allied arts and sciences. Holds meetings and conferences and organizes training courses and seminars.
Library Subject: film, television, technical
Library Type: not open to the public
Formerly: Formerly, British Kinematograph Sound and TV Society
Publication: Journal
Publication title: Cinema Technology. Advertisements.

00960

Black and Asian Studies Association BASA

18 Ridge Rd., Mitcham, CR4 2ET, UK
Email: jonah.albert@bl.uk
Website: http://www.blackandasianstudies.org.uk
Members: 200
Contact: Jonah Albert, Sec.
Fee: £30
Membership Type: institution
Fee: £10
Membership Type: individual
Description: Encourages and disseminates information on the history of Black and Asian people in Britain.
Publication: Newsletter

00961

Black Country Chamber of Commerce

Ward St., Walsall, WS1 2AG, UK
Tel: 0845 0021234
Fax: 01922 645721
Email: info@blackcountrychamber.co.uk
Website: http://forums.blackcountrychamberonline.co.uk
Members: 3200
Staff: 18
Contact: Mike Dell, Pres.
Description: Offers a wide range of business support services and networking opportunities. Helps owners and managers to maximize their business potential.

00962

Blackwater Wildlife Rescue

Woobinda, 8 Randell Close, Blackwater, Surrey, GU17 9HF, UK
Tel: 01276 31477
Website: http://www.e.volve.org.uk/directoryitem.aspx?dataitem=2966
Contact: Carole Waite, Co-Founder/Mgr.
Fee: £8
Membership Type: individual
Fee: £10
Membership Type: sponsorship
Description: Works to rescue and rehabilitate the British wildlife.

00963

BLC Leather Technology Centre

Kings Park Rd., Moulton Park, Northampton, NN3 6JD, UK
Tel: 01604 679999
Fax: 01604 679998
Email: info@blcleathertech.com
Website: http://www.blcleathertech.com
Members: 400
Staff: 60
Fee: £1495
Membership Type: research associate (group minimum)
Description: Provides essential support services to leather manufacturers, users and retailers. Ensures fast accurate solutions to technical, management or environmental problems of its members.
Library Subject: leather technology, management, health and safety, environment
Library Type: not open to the public
Publication: Journal
Publication title: BLC Journal
Meetings/Conventions: seminar

00964

Bliss Classification Association BCA

c/o Vanda Broughton, Hon. Sec.
University Colorado London, School of Library, Archives & Information Studies, Gower Tower St., London, WC1E 6BT, UK
Tel: 020 76792291
Email: v.broughton@ucl.ac.uk
Website: http://www.blissclassification.org.uk
Members: 95
Contact: Vanda Broughton, Hon. Sec.
Fee: £10
Membership Type: individual
Fee: £30
Membership Type: institution
Description: Individuals and institutions around the world seeking to promote the use and development of the Bliss Bibliographic Classification System. Provides a detailed classification for use in libraries and information centers of all kind. Maintains a fully faceted notation allowing very specific classification and is highly flexible. Offers training courses on the scheme's application, provides updates to the scheme, and organizes lectures.
Publication: Bulletin
Publication title: Bliss Bibliographic Classification. Advertisements.

00965

Blue Cross

Shilton Rd., Oxon, Burford, OX18 4PF, UK
Tel: 01993 822651
Fax: 01993 823083
Email: info@bluecross.org.uk
Website: http://www.bluecross.org.uk
Contact: Diane Sinclair, Chair
Description: Seeks to ensure the welfare of companion animals, provides practical care, promotes responsible animal ownership, provides treatment for those who cannot afford private veterinary services, finds permanent homes for unwanted or abandoned pets.
Publication: Report
Publication title: Annual Review

00966

Blue Ventures Conservation - Madagascar

2D Aberdeen Studios, Aberdeen Centre, 22-24 Highbury Grove, London, N5 2EA, UK
Tel: 020 31760548
Fax: 0800 0664032
Website: http://www.blueventures.org
Contact: Richard Nimmo, Managing Dir.
Description: Works to enhance global coral reef conservation in Madagascar, Tanzania, New Zealand, South Africa and the Comoros Islands.

00967

Bluefaced Leicester Sheep Breeders Association BFL

Riverside View, Warwick Rd., Carlisle, CA1 2BS, UK
Tel: 01228 598022
Fax: 01228 598021
Email: info@blueleicester.co.uk
Website: http://www.blueleicester.co.uk
Members: 1700
Staff: 2
Contact: Helen Carr-Smith, Sec.
Description: Encourages the breeding and maintaining the purity of the Bluefaced Leicester sheep. Maintains registry of purebred progeny of the Bluefaced Leicester sheep.
Publication: Magazine
Publication title: Looking Ahead

00968

Board of Airline Representatives in the United Kingdom
BAR UK

5 Hobart Pl., London, SW1W 0HU, UK
Tel: 020 77520200
Fax: 020 72450055
Email: office@bar-uk.org
Website: http://www.bar-uk.org
Members: 90
Contact: Elisabeth Haddow, Exec. Asst.
Fee: £98-1130
Membership Type: full (based on month started as a member)
Fee: £49-565
Membership Type: associate (based on month started as a member)
Description: Represents the airline industry in UK. Lobbies on issues that affect the industry and keeps members up to date with industrial and governmental developments.

00969

Boarding Schools Association
BSA

Grosvenor Gardens House, 35-37, Grosvenor Gardens, London, SW1W 0BS, UK
Tel: 020 77981580
Fax: 020 77981581
Email: bsa@boarding.org.uk
Website: http://www.boarding.org.uk
Members: 509
Staff: 4
Contact: Hilary Moriaty, Natl. Dir.
Description: Independent and maintained boarding schools, associations which have an active interest in boarding education. Covers schools, both maintained and independent, with boarding facilities. Ten conferences annually are arranged, to include INSET Training for boarding pastoral work. Research projects commissioned.
Publication: Magazine
Publication title: Boarding School. Advertisements.

00970

Body Positive Tayside
BPT

13 Main St., Dundee, DD3 7EY, UK
Tel: 01382 226860
Fax: 01382 322606
Email: admin@bodypositivetayside.org
Website: http://www.bodypositivetayside.org
Staff: 3
Description: Empowers HIV positive and HCV positive people and those affected by HIV or HCV, to eliminate the stigma associated with HIV/HCV. Provides opportunities for people to come together for peer support. Provides awareness raising and anti-discrimination training for staff, volunteers and members.
Publication: Newsletter

00971

Body Stress Release Association - UK

9 Shrublands Dr., Lightwater, GU18 5QS, UK
Tel: 01276 475651
Email: paul@bodystressrelease.org.uk
Website: http://www.bodystressrelease.org.uk
Contact: Paul Masureik, Contact
Description: Increases awareness of the general public, health professionals and the media of body release technique. Provides information about developments in body stress release. Encourages practitioners to be engaged in continuing professional development.

00972

Bone Research Society
BRS

c/o Portland Customer Services
Commerce Way, Colchester, CO2 8HP, UK
Tel: 01206 796351
Fax: 01206 799331
Email: jon.tobias@bristol.ac.uk
Website: http://www.brsoc.org.uk
Contact: Jon Tobias, Pres.
Fee: £50
Membership Type: full
Fee: £25
Membership Type: student
Description: Works to advance the understanding of osteoporosis. Promotes prevention, diagnosis and treatment of the disease.

00973

Book Aid International
BAI

39-41 Coldharbour Ln., Camberwell, London, SE5 9NR, UK
Tel: 020 77333577
Fax: 020 79788006
Email: info@bookaid.org
Website: http://www.bookaid.org/cms.cgi/site/index.htm
Staff: 34
Contact: Clive Nettleton, Dir.
Description: Works in conjunction with organizations in developing countries to support their work in literacy, education, training, and publishing by providing books and journals at their request. Over 750,000 selected books and journals each year are targeted to enable learning and skills development in around 50 developing countries throughout the world.
Formerly: Formerly, Ranfurly Library Service
Publication: Newsletter
Publication title: Interchange

00974

Books for Keeps
BfK

1 Effingham Rd., London, SE12 8NZ, UK
Tel: 0208 8524953
Fax: 0208 3187580
Email: enquiries@booksforkeeps.co.uk
Website: http://www.booksforkeeps.co.uk
Staff: 3
Contact: Richard Hill, Managing Dir.
Description: Schools, libraries, bookshops, publishers, authors and parents concerned with the importance of book use and availability.
Formerly: Also Known As, School Bookshop Association

00975

Booksellers Association of the United Kingdom and Ireland
BA

Minster House, 272 Vauxhall Bridge Rd., London, SW1V 1BA, UK
Tel: 020 78020802
Fax: 020 78020803
Email: mail@booksellers.org.uk
Website: http://www.booksellers.org.uk
Members: 3200
Staff: 40
Contact: Jane Streeter, Pres.
Description: Companies engaged in bookselling. Promotes and protects members' interests. Researches methods to increase efficiency and profitability while reducing costs. Disseminates information and advice. Organizes marketing programs. Provides products and services designed to assist members in the smooth and efficient running of their bookshops.
Publication: Newsletter
Publication title: Bookselling Essentials

00976

Border Collie Rescue
BCR

57 Market Pl., Richmond, DL10 4JQ, UK
Tel: 0870 4445838
Email: hq@bordercollierescue.org
Website: http://www.bordercollierescue.org
Members: 387
Contact: Nicki Oliver, Contact
Description: Exists to work internationally to rescue, provide care, shelter and sanctuary for stray, lost, neglected, abandoned, ill-treated and unwanted Border Collies and other working Sheepdogs and to re-home these dogs in environments suitable for their well-being; seeks justice for these dogs, works to alleviate their suffering, encourages responsible dog ownership through education and example, discourages irresponsible breeding, cruelty and neglect of such dogs. Seeks to improve the breed, its behavior and requirements, promotes the breed in character and bloodline.

00977

Born Free Foundation

3 Grove House, Foundry Ln., West Sussex, Horsham, RH13 5PL, UK
Tel: 01403 240170
Email: info@bornfree.org.uk
Website: http://www.bornfree.org.uk
Contact: Will Travers, CEO
Fee: £78
Membership Type: platinum
Fee: £39
Membership Type: gold
Description: Promotes animal welfare and conservation; campaigns for the protection and conservation of animals in their natural habitat and against keeping animals in zoos and circuses or as exotic pets.

00978
Botanical Gardens Conservation International
BGCI
Descanso House, 199 Kew Rd., Surrey, Richmond, TW9 3BW, UK
Tel: 020 83325953
Fax: 020 83325956
Email: info@bgci.org
Website: http://www.bgci.org
Members: 700
Staff: 13
Contact: Sara Oldfield, Sec. Gen.
Fee: £15-750
Membership Type: patron institution (based on institution's budget)
Fee: £40
Membership Type: associate
Description: Works to raise the awareness on botanical conservation. Communicates with the government on topics affecting the importance of plant conservation.
Publication: Journal
Publication title: BG Journal

00979
Botanical Society of Scotland
BSS
c/o Royal Botanic Garden
20a Inverleith Row, Edinburgh, EH3 5LR, UK
Tel: 0131 5527171
Email: barbra.harvie@ed.ac.uk
Website: http://www.botsocscot.org.uk
Members: 300
Contact: Barbra Harvie, Gen. Sec.
Fee: £32
Membership Type: standard
Fee: £28
Membership Type: standard (student)
Description: Promotes botany in Scotland.
Formerly: Formerly, Botanical Society of Edinburgh
Publication: Newsletter
Publication title: BSS News

00980
Botanical Society of the British Isles
BSBI
Botany Dept., Natural History Museum, Cromwell Rd., London, SW7 5BD, UK
Email: coordinator@bsbi.org.uk
Website: http://www.bsbi.org.uk
Members: 2700
Contact: M.E. Braithwaite, Pres.
Fee: £25
Membership Type: ordinary, institutional
Fee: £3
Membership Type: family (for each additional member)
Description: Represents amateur and professional botanists in Great Britain and Ireland. Promotes the study of British and Irish flowering plants and ferns. Organizes field visits and symposia; conducts surveys.
Formerly: Formerly, Botanical Society of London
Publication title: BSBI Abstracts

00981
Box Culvert Association
BoxCA
60 Charles St., Leicestershire, Leicester, LE1 1FB, UK
Tel: 0116 2536161
Fax: 0116 2514568
Email: boxca@britishprecast.org
Website: http://www.boxculvert.org.uk
Members: 6
Staff: 2
Description: Represents manufacturers of precast concrete box culverts.
Publication title: Applications Guide

00982
Boys' and Girls' Clubs of Northern Ireland
Musgrave Park Industrial Estate, 22 Stockmans Way, Ground Fl., Belfast, BT9 7JU, UK
Tel: 028 90663321
Fax: 028 90663306
Email: office@boysandgirlsclubs-ni.org.uk
Website: http://www.boysandgirlsclubs-ni.org.uk
Members: 18000
Staff: 6
Contact: Paul Curran, Chief Exec.
Description: Provides young people with positive opportunities that will enhance personal and social growth to adulthood.

00983
Boys' Brigade
BB
Felden Lodge, Herts, Hemel Hempstead, HP3 0BL, UK
Tel: 01442 231681
Fax: 01442 235391
Email: enquiries@boys-brigade.org.uk
Website: http://www.boys-brigade.org.uk
Members: 400000
Contact: Steve Dickinson, Sec.
Description: Promotes Christian ideals among boys in 66 countries. Organizes community projects; offers training for officers and full-time staff. Sponsors competitions; bestows awards. Compiles statistics.

00984
BPIF Cartons
c/o British Printing Industries Federation
Farringdon Point, 29-35 Farringdon Rd., London, EC1M 3JF, UK
Tel: 0192 4203331
Email: chris.selby@bpif.org.uk
Website: http://www.britishprint.com/page.asp?node=160&sec=BPIF_Cartons
Members: 50
Staff: 1
Contact: John Monks, Pres.
Description: Carton manufacturers and suppliers. Covers the folding carton and paperboard packaging industry. Provides information and guidance and represents members to outside organizations and government.
Formerly: Formerly, British Carton Association

00985
Bradford Chamber of Commerce
Devere House, Vicar Ln., Little Germany, West Yorkshire, Bradford, BD1 5AH, UK
Tel: 01274 772777
Fax: 01274 771081
Email: information@bradfordchamber.co.uk
Website: http://www.bradfordchamber.co.uk
Members: 1100
Staff: 46
Contact: Harold C. Robinson, Pres.
Fee: £232-1557
Membership Type: business (based on the number of employees of 1 - above 1000)
Fee: £200
Membership Type: new business (with less than 10 staff)
Description: Promotes business and commerce.
Publication: Magazine
Publication title: Businessplus

00986
Brazilian Chamber of Commerce in Great Britain
32 Green St., London, W1K 7AT, UK
Tel: 020 73999281
Fax: 020 74990186
Email: brazilianchamber@brazilianchamber.org.uk
Website: http://www.brazilianchamber.org.uk
Members: 208
Staff: 3
Contact: Jaime Gornsztejn, Chm.
Fee: £510
Membership Type: corporate
Fee: £306
Membership Type: company
Description: Promotes business and commerce.
Publication: Magazine
Publication title: Brazilian Business Brief
Meetings/Conventions: annual dinner

00987
Breast Cancer Care
BCC
5-13 Great Suffolk St., London, SE1 0NS, UK
Tel: 0845 0920800
Email: info@breastcancercare.org.uk
Website: http://www.breastcancercare.org.uk
Contact: Samia Al Qadhi, Chief Exec.
Description: Provides information and support to those affected by breast cancer. Operates advice line, one-to-one volunteer support, and aftercare services, including prosthesis fitting.
Formerly: Formerly, Breast Care and Masectomy Association

00988
Breast Cancer Support Service - Northern Ireland
c/o Ulster Cancer Foundation
40-44 Eglantine Ave., Belfast, BT9 6DX, UK
Tel: 02890 663281
Fax: 02890 668715
Email: info@ulstercancer.org
Website: http://www.ulstercancer.org
Staff: 50
Contact: Eileen Creery, Contact
Description: Promotes awareness of breast care and early detection of breast cancer. Supports the rehabilitation of women who have breast cancer and breast surgery.

Formerly: Formerly, Breast Care and Mastectomy Support Service
Publication: Booklet
Publication title: Coping with Breast Cancer

00989

Brecknock Federation of Young Farmers Clubs

Rm. 15, Neuadd Brycheiniog, Cambrian Way, Powys, Brecon, LD3 7HR, UK
Tel: 01874 612207
Fax: 01874 612389
Email: brecknock@yfc-wales.org.uk
Website: http://www.yfc-wales.org.uk/brecknock.php
Members: 500
Contact: Joanne Evans, Chair
Description: Promotes the personal development of young people living in rural areas, understanding of cultural diversity of Wales and equality of opportunities. Works to raise the profile of Welsh language.

00990

Brecon and Borders Welsh Pony and Cob Breeders Association

Upper Wenallt, Talybont on Usk, Powys, Brecon, LD3 7YU, UK
Tel: 01874 676298
Email: secretary@bbwpcba.com
Website: http://www.bbwpcba.com
Contact: Lynne Williams, Sec.
Description: Records the breeding details of Welsh ponies and cobs. Seeks to improve and promote the breed.

00991

Brewing, Food and Beverage Industry Suppliers Association BFBi

3 Brewery Rd., W Midlands, Wolverhampton, WV1 4JT, UK
Tel: 01902 422303
Fax: 01902 795744
Email: info@bfbi.org.uk
Website: http://www.bfbi.org.uk
Members: 450
Staff: 4
Contact: Ruth E. Evans, Chief Exec.
Fee: £460
Membership Type: regular
Description: Full membership available to companies engaged in supplying the brewing, and food and beverage and distilling industries. Associate Membership is available to individuals or sole traders. Applicants must have been trading within the industry for minimum of 12 months and have to be proposed by an existing full member. Aims to enable its members to act together in all matters appertaining to their trade or professional interests; to monitor legislative proposals, to form a centre for obtaining and diffusing information; to offer members the opportunity to explore overseas markets; to create a social forum to maintain customer contact.
Formerly: Formerly, Allied Brewery Traders Association
Publication: Directory
Publication title: ABTA Directory

00992

Brick Development Association BDA

The Building Ctre., 26 Store St., London, WC1E 7BT, UK
Tel: 020 73237030
Fax: 020 75803795
Email: brick@brick.org.uk
Website: http://www.brick.org.uk
Members: 21
Staff: 10
Description: UK clay and calcium silicate brick manufacturers. Promotes the use of brick. Works to establish and maintain British and European Standards.
Publication: Bulletin
Publication title: Brick Bulletin

00993

Bridge Joint Association

Riverside House, 4 Meadows Business Park, Station Approach, Blackwater, Surrey, Camberley, GU17 9AB, UK
Tel: 01276 33777
Fax: 01276 38899
Email: secretary@bridgejoints.org.uk
Website: http://www.bridgejoints.org.uk
Members: 10
Staff: 1
Contact: Colin Cleverly, Sec.
Description: Companies supplying and installing bridge expansion joints. Aims to maintain and improve standards of design, manufacture and installation of bridge expansion joints, to cooperate with purchasers and specifiers and to represent the interests of members.
Library Subject: standards for bridge joint
Library Type: open to the public
Publication title: Joint Data Sheets

00994

Bridport Arts Centre

South St., Dorset, Bridport, DT6 3NR, UK
Tel: 01308 427183
Email: info@bridport-arts.com
Website: http://www.bridport-arts.com
Contact: Polly Gifford, Dir.
Description: Provides a forum for the discussion and presentation of the arts.

00995

Bristol Chamber of Commerce and Initiative

c/o GWE Business West - Leigh Court
Leigh Ct., Abbots Leigh, Bristol, BS8 3RA, UK
Tel: 01275 373373
Fax: 01275 370706
Email: info@gwebusinesswest.co.uk
Website: http://www.gwebusinesswest.co.uk/chambers_of_commerce/bristol.aspx
Members: 2500
Staff: 150
Contact: Michael Bothamley, Pres.
Description: Promotes business and commerce.
Publication: Magazine
Publication title: Business West Update. Advertisements.

00996

Bristol Industrial Archaeological Society BIAS

The Museum of Bath at Work, Julian Rd., Bath, BA1 2RH, UK
Email: gsandg.sheppard@btopenworld.com
Website: http://b-i-a-s.org.uk
Members: 250
Contact: Stuart Burroughs, Vice Chm.
Fee: £15
Membership Type: ordinary
Fee: £13
Membership Type: retired
Description: Concerned with the recording and interpreting of materials related to the industrial development of Bristol, Bath, North Somerset, and South Gloucestershire. Prints an annual Journal and quarterly bulletins. Organizes visits, lecture program, research programs, and advises local organizations.
Publication: Journal
Publication title: BIAS Journal

00997

Britain - Nepal Medical Trust BNMT

Export House, 130 Vale Rd., Kent, Tonbridge, TN9 1SP, UK
Tel: 01732 360284
Fax: 01732 363876
Email: info@britainnepalmedicaltrust.org.uk
Website: http://www.britainnepalmedicaltrust.org.uk
Staff: 135
Contact: Jeffrey Mecaskey, Chm.
Description: Represents health care professionals and health organizations. Seeks to improve the health of the people of Nepal. Works with Nepalese government agencies to increase delivery of health services in underserved areas. Evaluates health programs and makes recommendations for their improvement. Distributes medical equipment, medications, and other supplies.

00998

Britain-Nepal Chamber of Commerce BNCC

35 St. Philip's Ave., Worcester Park, London, KT4 8JS, UK
Tel: 020 83306446
Fax: 020 83307447
Email: barry@tamgroup.co.uk
Website: http://www.nepal-trade.org.uk
Members: 107
Staff: 1
Contact: Peter Fowler, Chm.
Fee: £12
Membership Type: student
Fee: £95
Membership Type: associate (sole trader, non-UK company)
Description: Promotes trade and commerce between Nepal and Great Britain.

00999

British - German Jurists Association BGJA

14 New St., London, EC2M 4HE, UK
Tel: 020 79729727

Fax: 020 79729721
Email: rvaldinger@bgja.org.uk
Website: http://www.bgja.org.uk
Contact: Lord Mance, Honorary Pres.
Fee: £35
Membership Type: individual
Fee: £10
Membership Type: student, pupil, trainee solicitor
Description: Promotes recognition of the German and British legal systems in the spirit of European unification. Represents the interests of lawyers in both Germany and throughout Great Britain.

01000
British Abrasives Federation
BAF
Toad Hall, Hilton Rd., Berkshire, Hurst, RG10 0BS, UK
Tel: 08456 121380
Fax: 08456 121380
Email: info@thebaf.org.uk
Website: http://www.thebaf.org.uk
Members: 35
Staff: 1
Contact: Stuart Lane, Sec.
Description: Coated abrasive, bonded abrasive, superabrasive, and suppliers. Develops standards related to the abrasives industry. Offers guidance on issues related to training of end-users.
Library Subject: international standards for abrasives
Library Type: reference

01001
British Academy
10 Carlton House Terr., London, SW1Y 5AH, UK
Tel: 020 79695200
Fax: 020 79695300
Email: chiefexec@britac.ac.uk
Website: http://www.britac.ac.uk
Contact: Robin Jackson, Chief Exec./Sec.
Description: Scholars in the social sciences and the humanities. Promotes research and scholarship in the social sciences and humanities. Represents members at the national and international levels, supports research programs and facilitates international co-operation and exchange among social sciences and humanities scholars. Provides advice to government and other public bodies on questions affecting social science and humanities research. Conducts academic competitions.

01002
British Academy of Film and Television Arts
BAFTA
195 Piccadilly, London, W1J 9LN, UK
Tel: 020 77340022
Fax: 020 77341792
Email: info@bafta.org
Website: http://www.bafta.org
Members: 6500
Staff: 42
Contact: Tim Corrie, Chm.
Description: Represents those who work actively within the film, television and video games industries and have worked for not less than four years in those industries; companies who wish to demonstrate an exceptional level of support for the Academy and its work.
Library Type: not open to the public
Publication: Magazine
Publication title: ACADEMY. Advertisements.

01003
British Academy of Film and Television Arts - Scotland
BAFTA
249 W George St., Glasgow, G2 4QE, UK
Tel: 0141 3021770
Fax: 0141 3021771
Email: infoscotland@bafta.org
Website: http://www.baftascotland.co.uk
Contact: Ewan Angus, Chm.
Fee: £240
Membership Type: regular
Fee: £105
Membership Type: associate
Description: Promotes and rewards excellence in Scotland's screen industry. Arranges preview screenings of major new films, specialist film showcases and other industry events. Provides opportunities for the exchange of information and networking within Scotland's screen industry.

01004
British Academy of Forensic Sciences
BAFS
Queen's Mary School of Medicine and Dentistry, Haematology ICMS, 4 Newark St., London, E1 2AT, UK
Tel: 020 78822276
Email: y.d.syndercombe-court@qmul.ac.uk
Website: http://www.bafs.org.uk
Contact: Denise Syndercombe Court, Sec. Gen.
Fee: £60
Membership Type: full, associate
Fee: £35
Membership Type: student
Description: Aims to advance the knowledge of forensic science and medicine. Promotes better cooperation between lawyers and expert witnesses concerned with court proceedings. Utilizes the skills and knowledge within the membership to promote the solution of national and international problems in forensic science.
Publication: Journal
Publication title: Medicine Science and the Law

01005
British Academy of Songwriters, Composers and Authors
BASCA
British Music House, 26 Berners St., London, W1T 3LR, UK
Tel: 020 76362929
Fax: 020 76362212
Email: info@basca.org.uk
Website: http://www.basca.org.uk
Members: 2000
Staff: 10
Contact: Patrick Rackow, Chief Exec.
Fee: £141.38
Membership Type: professional
Fee: £45
Membership Type: friend
Description: Represents songwriters, lyricists and composers of all types of music. Lobbies for developments in legislation both in UK and Europe. Presents the annual Ivor Novello Awards and British Composer Awards; provides a range of member services; is represented on all the major music industry boards.
Formerly: Formerly, British Academy of Songwriters, Composers and Authors
Publication: Magazine
Publication title: The Works

01006
British ACM Chapter
City University, Dept. of Computing, Northampton Sq., London, EC1V 0HB, UK
Tel: 020 70408445
Email: mjh1@cam.ac.uk
Website: http://www.acm.org
Contact: Martin Hughes, Chm.
Fee: £15
Membership Type: regular
Fee: £5
Membership Type: student/unemployed
Description: Represents a diverse group of researchers, artists, developers, filmmakers, scientists, and other professionals who share an interest in computer graphics and interactive techniques. Values integrity, passion, excellence, volunteerism and cross-disciplinary interaction.

01007
British Activity Holiday Association
BAHA
The Hollies, Oak Bank Ln., Hoole Village, Chester, CH2 4ER, UK
Tel: 01244 301342
Email: info@baha.org.uk
Website: http://www.baha.org.uk
Members: 31
Description: Members are organizations which provide activity holidays within the United Kingdom. Inspects members' establishments annually to ensure set standards are maintained, offers a consumers' advice service and represents and advises members on specific areas of interest.
Publication title: Consumer Guide

01008
British Actors' Equity Association
Guild House, Upper St., Martin's Ln., London, WC2H 9EG, UK
Tel: 0207 3796000
Fax: 0207 3797001
Email: info@equity.org.uk
Website: http://www.equity.org.uk
Contact: Duncan Smith, Finance Mgr.
Description: Represents artists in the fields of arts and entertainment.

01009
British Acupuncture Council
BAcC
63 Jeddo Rd., London, W12 9HQ, UK
Tel: 020 87350400
Fax: 020 87350404
Email: info@acupuncture.org.uk
Website: http://www.acupuncture.org.uk
Members: 3000
Contact: Rita Lewis, Chair
Fee: £255
Membership Type: in UK
Fee: £80
Membership Type: outside UK
Description: British acupuncturists. Represents professional acupuncturists who have an extensive training in

acupuncture and the biomedical sciences appropriate to the practice of this therapy. Promotes research.
Publication: Newsletter
Publication title: The Acupuncturist

01010
British Adhesives and Sealants Association
BASA
5 Alderson Rd., Worksop, S80 1UZ, UK
Tel: 01909 480888
Fax: 01909 473834
Email: secretary@basaonline.org
Website: http://www.basaonline.org/Home.aspx
Members: 95
Staff: 1
Contact: John Murdoch, Sec.
Fee: £780-7005
Membership Type: full (adhesives and sealants manufacturer)
Fee: £1895
Membership Type: full (supplier)
Description: Represents manufacturers, their suppliers and associated companies in the adhesive and sealant industry in the UK and Ireland.
Library Type: reference
Publication: Yearbook
Publication title: Yearbook and Directory. Advertisements.

01011
British Aerobiology Federation
BAF
University of Worcester, National Pollen and Aerobiology Research Unit, Henwick Grove, Worcester, WR2 6AJ, UK
Tel: 01905 855200
Fax: 01905 855234
Email: pollen@worc.ac.uk
Website: http://www.nri.org/baf/contact.html
Contact: Janette Bartle, Membership Sec.
Description: Promotes awareness and scientific research in Aerobiology; provides a channel of communication between aerobiologists.

01012
British Aerosol Manufacturers' Association
BAMA
King's Bldgs., Smith Sq., London, SW1P 3JJ, UK
Tel: 020 78285111
Fax: 020 78348436
Email: enquiries@bama.co.uk
Website: http://www.bama.co.uk
Members: 70
Staff: 4
Contact: Sue Rogers, Dir.
Fee: £35218.76
Membership Type: company (based on aerosol-related turnover)
Description: Aerosol manufacturers in the United Kingdom. Promotes and protects members' interests.
Publication title: Industry Codes of Practice

01013
British Agricultural and Garden Machinery Association
BAGMA
Middleton House, 2 Main Rd., Middleton Cheney, Oxfordshire, Banbury, OX17 2TN, UK
Tel: 01295 713344
Fax: 01295 711665
Email: info@bagma.com
Website: http://www.bagma.com
Members: 850
Staff: 3
Contact: Howard Pullen, Pres.
Fee: £182-756
Membership Type: retail (based on number of employees)
Fee: £404.2
Membership Type: associate
Description: Full members are specialist dealers and service engineers for agricultural machinery; associate members are repairers and service engineers; affiliate members are manufacturers and wholesalers. Exists to promote the interests of specialists in agricultural and garden machinery; to maintain high standards in the trade so that customers receive professional attention at all times.
Publication: Manual
Publication title: Garden Machinery Price Guide

01014
British Agricultural History Society
BAHS
University of Exeter, Dept. of History, Amory Bldg., Rennes Dr., Exeter, EX4 4RJ, UK
Tel: 01392 263284
Fax: 01392 263305
Email: bahs@exeter.ac.uk
Website: http://www.bahs.org.uk
Members: 850
Staff: 1
Contact: J.A. Chartes, Pres.
Fee: £20
Membership Type: individual
Fee: £5
Membership Type: student, unemployed
Description: Scholars, persons concerned with agriculture and the rural sector, and local historians. Covers all aspects of rural and agricultural history - technical, social, economic, ethnographical, environmental - in Britain and overseas.
Publication: Journal
Publication title: Agricultural History Review. Advertisements.

01015
British Air Line Pilots Association
BALPA
BALPA House, 5 Heathrow Blvd., 278 Bath Rd., West Drayton, UB7 0DQ, UK
Tel: 020 84764000
Fax: 020 84764077
Email: balpa@balpa.org
Website: http://www.balpa.org
Members: 9000
Staff: 30
Contact: Mark Searle, Chm.
Fee: £24
Membership Type: associate
Description: British civil airline pilots and flight engineers. Protects and improves the professional status of members.
Publication: Journal
Publication title: The Log. Advertisements.

01016
British Airports Group
BAG
Salamanca Sq., 9 Albert Embankment, London, SE1 7SP, UK
Tel: 020 70914540
Fax: 020 70914545
Email: bag@sbac.co.uk
Website: http://www.sbac.co.uk/pages/87011355.asp
Members: 200
Staff: 2
Contact: Alan Lamond, Chm.
Fee: £255
Membership Type: affiliate
Fee: £525-2510
Membership Type: band A-F
Description: Helps UK companies win business in overseas airport developments. Organizes trade missions and overseas exhibitions for member companies. Disseminates market intelligence and assists high level foreign visitors looking to source UK products, services and partnerships.

01017
British American Security Information Council - United Kingdom
BASIC UK
Grayston Centre, 2nd Fl., 28 Charles Sq., London, N1 6HT, UK
Tel: 020 73244680
Fax: 020 73244681
Email: basicuk@basicint.org
Website: http://www.basicint.org
Staff: 11
Contact: Paul Ingram, Exec. Dir.
Description: Promotes public awareness of defense disarmament, military strategy, and nuclear policies in order to foster informed debate on these issues.
Library Subject: international security
Library Type: reference
Publication: Reports
Publication title: BASIC Reports

01018
British Amusement Catering Trade Association
BACTA
Alders House, 133 Aldersgate St., London, EC1A 4JA, UK
Tel: 020 77269826
Fax: 020 77269822
Email: info@bacta.org.uk
Website: http://www.bacta.org.uk
Members: 1855
Staff: 7
Contact: Neil Chinn, Pres.
Description: Manufacturers, distributors and operators of coin-operated amusement equipment together with owners of inland and seaside amusement centers and arcades. Promotes and protects the interests of members.
Publication: Brochure
Publication title: Annual Review. Advertisements.

01019

British and International Federation of Festivals

Festivals House, 198 Park Ln., Cheshire, Macclesfield, SK11 6UD, UK
Tel: 0870 7744290
Fax: 0870 7744292
Website: http://web.mac.com/bpme/BIFF/Welcome.html
Members: 1075
Staff: 4
Contact: Liz Whitehead, Chief Exec.
Description: Amateur festivals of music, dance and speech, professional adjudicator and accompanist members. Concerned with the advancement of the amateur performing arts by providing a platform for performance combined with the teaching of an expert adjudicator.

01020

British and International Golf Greenkeepers Association BIGGA

BIGGA House, Aldwark, Alne, York, YO61 1UF, UK
Tel: 01347 833800
Fax: 01347 833801
Email: info@bigga.co.uk
Website: http://www.bigga.org.uk
Members: 7300
Staff: 21
Contact: John Pemberton, Chief Exec.
Fee: £90
Membership Type: international
Fee: £75-125
Membership Type: full
Description: Golf Greenkeepers, together with those working or interested in the fine turf industries. Promotes and advances all aspects of greenkeeping. Assists and encourages the proficiency of members.
Library Subject: greenkeeping
Library Type: not open to the public
Publication: Magazine
Publication title: Greenkeeper International. Advertisements.
Meetings/Conventions: annual trade show – Exhibits.

01021

British and Irish Association of Law Librarians BIALL

12 S Bridge, Box 123, Edinburgh, EH1 1DD, UK
Email: admin@biall.org.uk
Website: http://www.biall.org.uk
Members: 900
Staff: 1
Contact: Elaine Bird, Sec.
Fee: £52.5
Membership Type: personal
Fee: £157.5
Membership Type: institutional
Description: Unites and coordinates the interests, opinions and activities of law library professionals into a single, influential voice, ensuring that members' views are fully taken into account by decision-makers at all levels. Seeks to achieve aims through a variety of activities: represents members' interests in informal discussions with the government and other organizations on relevant policy issues; interacts with other organizations worldwide to exchange views and information; regularly contacts legal professionals, publishers, data providers, and academics; offers training on a range of professional topics and skills and educational support, including bibliographical study and research in law and librarianship; provides informal advice and support through a network of professional contacts and colleagues.
Publication: Directory
Publication title: Directory of Law Libraries

01022

British and Irish Law, Education and Technology Association BILETA

University of Warwick, UK Centre for Legal Education, Coventry, CV4 7AL, UK
Tel: 024 76523117
Fax: 024 76523290
Email: ukcle@warwick.ac.uk
Website: http://www.bileta.ac.uk/default.aspx
Members: 100
Contact: Stephen Cooper, Membership Sec.-Treas.
Fee: £25
Membership Type: individual
Fee: £125
Membership Type: institution, associate
Description: Law teaching institutions in the United Kingdom and overseas. Promotes the use of technology in legal education. Promotes research; supports the development and distribution of legal software; provides information on technology in legal developments; liaises with other related organizations.

01023

British and Irish Ombudsman Association BIOA

PO Box 308, Twickenham, TW1 9BE, UK
Tel: 0208 88949272
Email: secretary@bioa.org.uk
Website: http://www.bioa.org.uk
Members: 151
Staff: 1
Description: Ombudsman and complaint handling organizations.
Publication: Newsletter
Publication title: The Ombudsman

01024

British and Irish Orthoptic Society BIOS

c/o Chartered Society of Physiotherapists
14 Bedford Row, London, WC1R 4ED, UK
Tel: 0207 3061135
Fax: 0207 2428452
Email: bios@orthoptics.org.uk
Website: http://www.orthoptics.org.uk/home/home
Members: 1400
Staff: 3
Contact: Dariel Cross, Membership Sec./Office Mgr.
Fee: £294
Membership Type: full
Fee: £144
Membership Type: overseas
Description: Represents orthoptists, including students and retired orthoptists; members work in both NHS and private practice.
Formerly: Formerly, British Orthoptic Society
Publication: Journal
Publication title: British and Irish Orthoptic Journal. Advertisements.
Meetings/Conventions: BOS Scientific Conference – annual conference – Exhibits.

01025

British Andrology Society BAS

Sheffield University, Academic Unit of Reproductive and Developmental Medicine, Level 4, Jessop Wing, Tree Root Walk, Sheffield, S10 2SF, UK
Tel: 0114 2268195
Fax: 0114 2268538
Email: a.fazeli@sheffield.ac.uk
Website: http://www.britishandrology.org.uk
Contact: Alireza Fazeli, Chair
Fee: £25
Membership Type: full
Fee: £15
Membership Type: student, retired
Description: Scientists and clinicians working in the fields of human and mammalian reproduction with an interest in the male. Promotes the interests of members. Research is an important activity in the organization.

01026

British Angora Goat Society

5 The Langlands, Hampton Lucy, Warwick, CV35 8BN, UK
Tel: 01789 841930
Fax: 01789 841219
Email: secretary.bags@btinternet.com
Website: http://www.britishangoragoats.org.uk
Members: 350
Contact: E. Graham, Sec.
Description: Owners and breeders of Angora goats.

01027

British Antique Dealers' Association BADA

20 Rutland Gate, London, SW7 1BD, UK
Tel: 020 75894128
Fax: 020 75819083
Website: http://www.bada.org
Members: 400
Staff: 5
Contact: Ian H. Walker, Chm.
Fee: £495
Membership Type: general
Description: Members comprise 400 antiques dealers in the United Kingdom. Represents the interests of antiques dealers in Britain. Aims to establish and maintain confidence between its members and the public in both buying and selling.
Publication: Handbook
Publication title: The British Antique Dealers' Association Handbook. Advertisements.

01028

British Antique Furniture Restorers Association BAFRA

The Old Rectory, Warmwell, Dorchester, DT2 8HQ, UK
Tel: 01305 854822
Fax: 01305 854822
Email: headoffice@bafra.org.uk
Website: http://www.bafra.org.uk
Members: 390
Staff: 1
Contact: Michael Barrington, Chm.
Fee: £50
Membership Type: individual
Fee: £85
Membership Type: joint
Description: Promotes the highest standards in furniture conservation and restoration; provides support to members; and educates members and the public in matters of furniture conservation, restoration, and historical aspects.
Library Subject: furniture conservation, restoration, history, design
Library Type: not open to the public

01029

British Appaloosa Society

7 Newbridge St., Wolverhampton, WV6 0EE, UK
Tel: 01902 761654
Email: c4r14@hotmail.co.uk
Website: http://www.appaloosa.org.uk
Members: 500
Contact: Carla Ankiah, Membership Sec.
Fee: £10
Membership Type: single (junior/student)
Fee: £25
Membership Type: joint (junior/senior)
Description: Seeks to improve the quality of the Appaloosa breed.

01030

British Approvals Board for Telecommunications BABT

Forsyth House, Churchfield Rd., Surrey, Walton-on-Thames, KT12 2TD, UK
Tel: 01932 251200
Fax: 01932 251201
Email: info@babt.com
Website: http://www.babt.com
Staff: 30
Contact: Jean-Louis Evans, Managing Dir.
Description: Assessment evaluation and approval for telecommunications apparatus intended for connection to the UK public networks. UK notified body for approval of terminal equipment in EEC; UK notified body for electromagnetic compatibility for radio communications terminal equipment in EEC; UK notified body under the Low Voltage Directive. Provides approval of metering/billing systems for UK public networks.
Publication: Newsletter
Publication title: BABT Newsletter

01031

British Approvals for Fire Equipment BAFE

Bridges 2, The Fire Service College, London St., Gloucestershire, Moreton-in-Marsh, GL56 0RH, UK
Tel: 0844 3350897
Fax: 01608 653359
Email: info@bafe.org.uk
Website: http://www.bafe.org.uk
Staff: 5
Contact: Stephen Adams, Gen. and Marketing Mgr.
Description: Promotes the quality assurance of fire protection equipment and services.

01032

British Arachnological Society BAS

31 Duxford Close, Worcestershire, Redditch, B97 5BY, UK
Tel: 01527 544952
Email: secretary@britishspiders.org.uk
Website: http://wiki.britishspiders.org.uk/index.php5?title=Main_Page
Contact: John Partridge, Sec.
Fee: £15
Membership Type: in UK
Fee: £18
Membership Type: overseas
Description: Promotes the study of arachnida, especially spiders, pseudoscorpions and harvestmen.
Library Subject: arachnology
Library Type: reference
Publication: Bulletin
Publication title: Bulletin of the British Arachnological Society

01033

British Art Medal Society

PO Box 43888, London, NW6 6WL, UK
Email: membership@bams.org.uk
Website: http://www.bams.org.uk
Contact: Charles Franklyn, Membership Sec.
Fee: £20
Membership Type: ordinary
Fee: £35
Membership Type: associate
Description: Encourages, develops and supports the practice and study of medallic art.
Publication: Journal
Publication title: The Medal. Advertisements.

01034

British Artist Blacksmiths Association BABA

60 Buchanan St., Balfron, Glasgow, G63 0TW, UK
Tel: 01360 440830
Fax: 07740 951608
Email: elspeth@ironhorse-studios.co.uk
Website: http://www.baba.org.uk
Members: 700
Contact: Elspeth Bennie, Treas.
Fee: £70
Membership Type: professional, amateur, supporter, non-profit corporate
Fee: £45
Membership Type: student, retired
Description: Mainly working blacksmiths/metalworkers specializing in pieces which are both utility and artistic. Members come from all parts of the UK, mainland Europe, USA, Australia and New Zealand. Encourages the hand skills associated with the hot working of metals, and fosters an appreciation of art blacksmith work among potential customers. Organizes exhibitions of members' work and working, social gatherings in many parts of the UK.
Publication: Magazine
Publication title: British Blacksmith. Advertisements.

01035

British Arts Festivals Association BAFA

28 Charing Cross Rd., 2nd Fl., London, WC2H 0DB, UK
Tel: 020 72404532
Email: info@artsfestivals.co.uk
Website: http://www.artsfestivals.co.uk
Members: 110
Staff: 1
Contact: Stewart Collins, Chm.
Fee: £125
Membership Type: regular
Fee: £135-1080
Membership Type: festival, corporate (based on annual turnover)
Description: Wide range of arts festivals in the United Kingdom. Provides a forum for exchange of experience between festivals, a representative voice and a source of central information for press and public.
Publication: Brochure

01036

British Association and College of Occupational Therapists BAOT/COT

106-114 Borough High St., Southwark, London, SE1 1LB, UK
Tel: 020 73576480
Email: membership@cot.co.uk
Website: http://www.cot.org.uk/Homepage
Members: 29000
Staff: 60
Contact: Julia Scott, Chief Exec.
Fee: £20.33
Membership Type: professional
Fee: £15.25
Membership Type: discounted professional
Description: State registered Occupational Therapists, Occupational Therapy Helpers and Technical Instructors. Acts as a professional association in the field of rehabilitative medicine. Promotes occupational therapy education, honorable practice, and repression of malpractice. Provides the facilities for the advancement of the science of occupational therapy.
Library Subject: occupational therapy and related topics
Library Type: not open to the public
Publication: Journal
Publication title: British Journal of Occupational Therapy. Advertisements.
Meetings/Conventions: Broadeninct Horizons – annual conference – Exhibits.

01037
British Association for Adoption and Fostering
BAAF
Saffron House, 6-10 Kirby St., London, EC1N 8TS, UK
Tel: 020 74212600
Fax: 020 74212601
Email: mail@baaf.org.uk
Website: http://www.baaf.org.uk
Members: 1900
Staff: 71
Contact: David Holmes, Chief Exec.
Fee: £75.5
Membership Type: full (inside UK and Ireland)
Fee: £44.5
Membership Type: retired (inside UK and Ireland)
Description: Members include local authority and voluntary adoption agencies and professionals working in adoption, fostering and social work with children. Aims to extend the opportunities for family life for all children being looked after away from their families; to become the major inter-disciplinary and educational force for professionals working with these children; to promote high standards of practice in adoption, fostering and child care social work and increase public understanding of the issues involved.
Formerly: Formerly, BAAF
Publication: Journal
Publication title: Adoption and Fostering Journal. Advertisements.

01038
British Association for American Studies
BAAS
University of Leicester, Department of English, University Rd., Leicester, LE1 7RH, UK
Tel: 0116 2231068
Fax: 0116 2577199
Email: catherine.morley@baas.ac.uk
Website: http://www.baas.ac.uk
Members: 500
Contact: Catherine Morley, Sec.
Fee: £48
Membership Type: individual
Fee: £34
Membership Type: student, retired, unwaged (with journal)
Description: Professional organization concerned with university level conferences.
Publication: Newsletter
Publication title: American Studies in Britain. Advertisements.

01039
British Association for Applied Linguistics
BAAL
c/o Dovetail Management Consultancy
PO Box 6688, London, SE15 3WB, UK
Tel: 0207 6390090
Fax: 0207 6356014
Email: admin@baal.org.uk
Website: http://www.baal.org.uk
Members: 690
Contact: Jeanie Taylor, Admin.
Fee: £40
Membership Type: individual
Fee: £15
Membership Type: student, retired, unemployed
Description: Language teachers, lexicologists, teachers, speech therapists, and forensic linguists. Promotes research into language use. Seeks to foster the understanding of languages among non-linguists.
Meetings/Conventions: annual meeting – Exhibits.

01040
British Association for Behavioural and Cognitive Psychotherapies
BABCP
Victoria Buildings, 9-13 Silver St., Bury, BL9 0EU, UK
Tel: 0161 7974484
Fax: 0161 7972670
Email: babcp@babcp.com
Website: http://www.babcp.com
Members: 7500
Contact: John Taylor, Pres.
Fee: £54-62
Membership Type: full (in UK and Ireland)
Fee: £62-70
Membership Type: full (overseas)
Description: Health, Social Service, education staff and therapists in private practice; individuals interested in psychotherapies and accredited/registered psychotherapists. Promotion of behavioural and cognitive therapy approaches in health, educational and social problem areas.
Publication: Journal
Publication title: Behavioural & Cognitive Psychotherapy Journal. Advertisements.

01041
British Association for Biological Anthropology and Osteoarchaeology
BABAO
c/o Dr. Tina Jakob, Membership Sec.
Durham University, Department of Archaeology, South Rd., Durham, DH1 3LE, UK
Website: http://www.babao.org.uk
Contact: Holger Schutkowski, Chm.
Fee: £16
Membership Type: full
Fee: £11
Membership Type: unwaged, student
Description: Promotes the study of human bioarchaelogy. Aims to provide a forum for the exchange of ideas and information concerning biological anthropology and osteoarchaeology. Improves standards in all aspects of the study of biological remains of past and present people.
Publication: Annual Report
Publication title: Annual Review

01042
British Association for Canadian Studies
BACS
University of London, Senate House, Rm. 212, S Block, Male St., London, WC1E 7HU, UK
Tel: 020 78628687
Email: canstuds@gmail.com
Website: http://www.canadian-studies.info/main
Members: 500
Staff: 1
Contact: Jodie Robson, Admin.
Fee: £30
Membership Type: regular
Fee: £15
Membership Type: student/unwaged, concessionary
Description: Provides a forum for Canadian studies in the UK.

01043
British Association for Cancer Research
BACR
c/o Leeds Institute of Molecular Medicine
St. James's University Hospital, Clinical Sciences Bldg., Beckett St., Leeds, LS9 7TF, UK
Tel: 0113 2065611
Fax: 0113 2429886
Email: bacr@leeds.ac.uk
Website: http://www.bacr.org.uk
Members: 1200
Staff: 1
Contact: Robert Souhami, Pres.
Fee: £50
Membership Type: full
Fee: £25
Membership Type: student
Description: Laboratory and clinical cancer research workers. Conducts and promotes research into the prevention, causes, treatment, and cure of cancer.

01044
British Association for Cemeteries in South Asia
BACSA
c/o Dr. Rosie Llewellyn-Jones, Hon. Sec.
135 Burntwood Ln., London, SW17 0AJ, UK
Tel: 020 89479131
Email: rosieljai@clara.co.uk
Website: http://www.bacsa.org.uk
Members: 1800
Contact: Alan Tritton, Pres.
Fee: £7.5
Membership Type: student, single
Fee: £100
Membership Type: life
Description: Historians, genealogists, and individuals interested in the preservation of cemeteries in South Asia that hold bodies of Europeans.
Publication: Book
Publication title: The Gordon Creeds in Afghanistan

01045
British Association for Chemical Specialities
BACS
Simpson House, Windsor Ct., Clarence Dr., Harrogate, HG1 2PE, UK
Tel: 01423 700249
Fax: 01423 520297
Email: enquiries@bacsnet.org
Website: http://www.bacsnet.org
Members: 135
Staff: 3
Contact: Jackie Hall, Contact
Description: Trade association representing manufacturers of specialty and performance chemicals, including: maintenance products for institutional, industrial, and consumer use; biocides; disinfectants; specialty surfactant and water treatment. Promotes high standards for health, safety, and environmental impact in the chemical industry. Addresses legislative and regulatory

issues at the national and international levels. Provides technical and legal guidance to members. Creates opportunities for members to share ideas and experience. Promotes the prosperity of its members.
Formerly: Formerly, British Disinfectant Manufacturers Association
Publication title: BACS Annual Review
Meetings/Conventions: monthly meeting

01046
British Association for Chinese Studies
BACS

School of Modern Languages and Cultures, University of Leeds, Woodhouse Lane, Leeds, LS2 9JT, UK
Tel: 0113 3433468
Fax: 0113 3436741
Email: d.pattinson@leeds.ac.uk
Website: http://www.bacsuk.org.uk
Members: 200
Contact: David Pattinson, Treas.
Fee: £30
Membership Type: individual
Fee: £40
Membership Type: family
Description: Students, faculty, museum and library staff, journalists, and others with an interest in Chinese studies. Encourages and promotes the study of China in schools and colleges in Britain; represents the interest of teachers of Chinese at the university level; administers scholarship for study in Taiwan. Encompasses the China Postgraduate Network; provides an organizational framework for all postgraduates whose research concerns China; aims to disseminate information; offers advice; maintains a database of postgraduates in Britain. Strives to pursue links with similar organizations in other countries.

01047
British Association for Counselling and Psychotherapy
BACP

BACP House, 15 St. John's Business Park, Leicestershire, Lutterworth, LE17 4HB, UK
Tel: 01455 883300
Fax: 01455 550243
Email: bacp@bacp.co.uk
Website: http://www.bacp.co.uk
Members: 32000
Staff: 45
Contact: Cary Cooper, Pres.
Fee: £94
Membership Type: affiliate
Fee: £142
Membership Type: regular
Description: Individual or organizational membership for counsellors or people using counselling skills. Aims to promote awareness of counselling internationally and raise standards of training and practice through its Ethical Framework for Good Practice in Counselling and Psychotherapy. Provides support including an information service for members and the public.
Formerly: Formerly, British Association for Counselling

01048
British Association for Early Childhood Education

136 Cavell St., London, E1 2JA, UK
Tel: 020 75395400
Fax: 020 75395409
Email: office@early-education.org.uk
Website: http://www.early-education.org.uk
Members: 6500
Staff: 6
Contact: Jenny Rabin, Operations Mgr.
Fee: £18
Membership Type: student individual
Fee: £45
Membership Type: overseas individual
Description: Teachers, parents, nursery nurses, day nursery and family center staff, playgroup workers, social workers, Local Authority administrators, University and College lecturers, health visitors, doctors and psychologists. Concerned with all aspects of children's learning between 0-9 years. Organizes national conferences, publishes a journal and literature, carries out research and through 55 branches arranges meetings, seminars and conferences.
Publication: Newsletter
Publication title: Early Education. Advertisements.

01049
British Association for Fair Trade Shops
BAFTS

66, Longstomps Ave., Chelmsford, CM2 9LA, UK
Tel: 0786 6759201
Email: info@bafts.org.uk
Website: http://www.bafts.org.uk
Members: 190
Staff: 2
Description: Promotes fair trade retailing in Britain. Raises the profile of fair trade shops which adheres to the national framework of agreed criteria, both on the high street and as an economic and political reality. Contributes to sustainable development by offering better trading conditions to, and securing the rights of, marginalized producers and workers. Improves the livelihoods and well being of producers by improving market access, strengthening producer organizations and paying a better price.
Publication: Newsletter
Publication title: Fair Trading News

01050
British Association for Immediate Care
BASICS

Turret House, Turret Ln., Suffolk, Ipswich, IP4 1DL, UK
Tel: 01473 218407
Fax: 01473 280585
Email: admin@basics.org.uk
Website: http://www.basics.org.uk
Members: 2500
Staff: 3
Contact: Richard Steyn, Chm.
Fee: £98-177
Membership Type: full
Fee: £57-136
Membership Type: associate
Description: Medical practitioners and non-medical practitioners (e.g., ambulance, nurse, emergency planning personnel) involved in pre-hospital immediate medical care. Aims to foster cooperation between existing Immediate Care Schemes and to encourage and aid the formation and extension of schemes in the UK; to develop and strengthen co-operation between all services in dealing with emergencies and to encourage and assist research into all aspects of pre-hospital immediate medical care and accident prevention.

01051
British Association for Japanese Studies
BAJS

University of Essex, Wivenhoe Park, Essex, Colchester, C04 3SQ, UK
Tel: 01206 872543
Fax: 01206 873965
Email: bajs@bajs.org.uk
Website: http://www.bajs.org.uk
Members: 230
Contact: Lynn Baird, Sec.
Description: Seeks to further interest in Japanese studies.
Publication: Journal
Publication title: Japan Forum. Advertisements.

01052
British Association for Local History
BALH

PO Box 6549, Somersal Herbert, Ashbourne, DE6 5WH, UK
Tel: 01283 585947
Email: info@balh.co.uk
Website: http://www.balh.co.uk/index.php
Members: 2500
Staff: 5
Contact: David Hey, Pres.
Fee: £25
Membership Type: individual
Fee: £18
Membership Type: student
Description: People working, individually or in a group, on the history of their house, family, village or town; searching in the archives at a local record office; attending evening classes on local history or the local environment; or visiting buildings and sites of historical interest. Promotes local history for the complementary purpose of academic study and leisure activity.
Publication: Journal
Publication title: The Local Historian. Advertisements.

01053
British Association for Lung Research
BALR

c/o Dr. Deborah Clarke, Membership Sec.
9 Red Lion Ct., London, EC4A 3EF, UK
Email: deborah.clarke@imperial.ac.uk
Website: http://www.balr.org.uk
Contact: Ann Millar, Chair
Fee: £35
Membership Type: ordinary, associate (overseas)
Fee: £20
Membership Type: student (registered for higher degree, requires research supervisor's counter signature)
Description: Promotes interest and encourages studies in the field of experimental research.

01054
British Association for Modern Mosaic
BAMM
2B Bodiam Business Park, Robertsbridge, East Sussex, TN32 5UP, UK
Email: buddmosaics@googlemail.com
Website: http://www.bamm.org.uk
Contact: Oliver Budd, Pres.
Fee: £25
Membership Type: standard
Fee: £60
Membership Type: corporate, education
Description: Promotes, encourages and supports excellence in contemporary mosaic art. Raises public awareness of modern mosaic art through exhibitions, publications, events and related educational activities.
Publication: Newsletter
Publication title: Grout

01055
British Association for Nutritional Therapy
BANT
27 Old Gloucester St., London, WC1N 3XX, UK
Tel: 0870 6061284
Fax: 0870 6061284
Email: theadministrator@bant.org.uk
Website: http://www.bant.org.uk
Contact: Catherine Honeywell, Chair
Fee: £75
Membership Type: full (practicing, non-practicing), fellow
Fee: £25
Membership Type: student
Description: Assists members in attaining the highest standards of integrity, knowledge, competence and professional practice. Holds a register of practitioners who are fully qualified in both the science of nutrition as well as clinical practice. Promotes high standards of education in Nutritional Therapy and high standards of practice and ethics within the profession.

01056
British Association for Paediatric Nephrology
BAPN
Bristol Royal Hospital for Children, Upper Maudlin St., Bristol, BS2 8BJ, UK
Tel: 0117 3428881
Email: jane.tizard@ubht.nhs.uk
Website: http://www.bapn.org
Members: 70
Contact: Jane Tizard, Sec.
Fee: £50
Membership Type: regular
Description: Paediatricians participating in the care of children with kidney diseases. Aims to promote policies concerning the care of children with renal disease, to conduct scientific meetings, to consider manpower and training issues and to conduct multicentre trials and other collaborative research.

01057
British Association for Performing Arts Medicine
BAPAM
Totara Park House, 4th Fl., 34-36 Grays Inn Rd., London, WC1X 8HR, UK
Tel: 020 74045888
Fax: 020 74043222
Email: enquiries@bapam.org.uk
Website: http://www.bapam.org.uk/index.php
Members: 700
Staff: 5
Contact: Richard Price, Chm.
Fee: £35
Membership Type: individual
Description: Provides helpline and free assessment and diagnosis for performers with performance-related injuries and illnesses.
Formerly: Formerly, British Association for Performing Arts Medicine

01058
British Association for Psychopharmacology
BAP
36 Cambridge Pl., Hills Rd., Cambridge, CB2 1NS, UK
Tel: 01223 358396
Fax: 01223 321268
Email: susan@bap.org.uk
Website: http://www.bap.org.uk
Members: 1200
Staff: 2
Contact: Susan Chandler, Exec. Off.
Fee: £80
Membership Type: full
Fee: £20
Membership Type: training
Description: Represents psychopharmacologists, psychiatrists, neuropharmacologists, psychologists, and neurochemists. Brings together scientists working in academic, clinical, and industrial applications of psychopharmacology. Arranges scientific meetings, study groups, and seminars; encourages basic research and pharmaceutical development. Offers professional guidance to the public on matters related to psychopharmacology.
Publication: Journal
Publication title: Journal of Psychopharmacology. Advertisements.

01059
British Association for Sexual and Relationship Therapy
BASRT
PO Box 13686, London, SW20 9ZH, UK
Tel: 020 85432707
Fax: 020 85432707
Email: info@basrt.org.uk
Website: http://www.basrt.org.uk
Members: 750
Staff: 2
Contact: Peter Bell, Chm.
Fee: £128
Membership Type: general
Fee: £70
Membership Type: student, affiliate
Description: Professional psychosexual therapists, clinicians, and medics working in the field of sexual and marital therapy. Aims to advance the education and training of persons engaged in sexual, marital and relationship therapy; to promote research in this field; to advance public education about sexual, marital and relationship therapy.
Formerly: Formerly, British Association for Sexual and Marital Therapy
Publication: Journal
Publication title: Sexual and Relationship Therapy

01060
British Association for Sexual Health and HIV
BASHH
1 Wimpole St., London, W1G 0AE, UK
Tel: 020 72902968
Fax: 020 72902989
Email: bashh@rsm.ac.uk
Website: http://www.bashh.org
Members: 1000
Contact: Keith Radcliffe, Pres.
Fee: £68-270
Membership Type: fellow (with subscription to both journals)
Fee: £29-115
Membership Type: clinical assistant (with subscription to both journals)
Description: Promotes the study and practice of diagnosing and treating sexually transmitted diseases. Educates the public in all matters concerning the management of HIV infections and sexual health.
Formerly: Formerly, Association for Genito-Urinary Medicine

01061
British Association for Slavonic and East European Studies
BASEES
University of Wales, Department of International Politics, Aberystwyth, SY23 3DA, UK
Website: http://www.basees.org.uk
Members: 500
Contact: Elena Korosteleva-Polglase, Membership Sec.
Fee: £25
Membership Type: full
Fee: £15
Membership Type: associate, retired
Description: Advances education for the public benefit in the humanities and social sciences; relates to the former Soviet Union and the countries of Eastern Europe.

01062
British Association for South Asian Studies
BASAS
14 Stephenson Way, London, NW1 2HD, UK
Tel: 020 73885490
Email: basas@basas.org.uk
Website: http://www.basas.org.uk
Members: 250
Staff: 12
Contact: Kunal Sen, Chm.
Fee: £15
Membership Type: full
Fee: £25
Membership Type: concessionaire
Description: Individuals interested in the "art, culture, economies, history, religion, sociology and/or politics of India, Pakistan, Bangladesh, Sri Lanka, Nepal, Bhutan, and the Maldives." Seeks to advance scholarship and teaching in the field of south Asian studies. Facilitates exchange of information among members; sponsors research and educational programs.
Publication: Newsletter
Publication title: BASAS Bulletin

01063
British Association for the Study of Headache
BASH

c/o The Migraine Trust
55-56 Russell Sq., 2nd Fl., London, WC1B 4HP, UK
Email: r.peatfield@imperial.ac.uk
Website: http://www.bash.org.uk
Contact: Richard Peatfield, Chm.
Fee: £150
Membership Type: full
Fee: £50
Membership Type: student
Description: Represents the interests of all health care professionals with an interest in headache. Aims to relieve persons suffering from headache by advancing the scientific study of this condition. Collaborates with international research institutions engaged in advancing the study of headache.
Publication: Article
Publication title: Management Guidelines

01064
British Association for the Study of Religions
BASR

Bangor University, School of Theology and Religious Studies, College Rd., Bangor, LL57 2DG, UK
Email: b.schmidt@bangor.ac.uk
Website: http://www.basr.ac.uk
Members: 254
Contact: Bettina Schmidt, Honorary Sec.
Fee: £20
Membership Type: regular
Fee: £10
Membership Type: student, unwaged
Description: Promotes the academic study of religions through international collaboration of all scholars whose research has a bearing on the subject.
Publication: Journal
Publication title: Diskus: the Journal of the British Association for the Study of Religions

01065
British Association in Forensic Medicine
BAFM

University of Glasgow, Department of Forensic Medicine and Science, Glasgow, G12 8QQ, UK
Tel: 0141 3304145
Email: j.clark@formed.gla.ac.uk
Website: http://www.bafm.org
Members: 170
Contact: J.C. Clark, Sec.
Fee: £50
Membership Type: medical/dental practitioner
Description: Promotes the specialty of forensic pathology. Represents members' interests.

01066
British Association of Academic Phoneticians
BAAP

University of Cambridge, Department of Linguistics, Sidgewik Ave., Cambridge, CB3 9DA, UK
Tel: 01223 335060
Fax: 01223 335053
Email: fjn1@cam.ac.uk
Website: http://www.baap.ac.uk
Members: 150
Contact: Francis Nolan, Pres.
Description: Seeks to further the academic study of phonetics.

01067
British Association of Aesthetic Plastic Surgeons
BAAPS

The Royal College of Surgeons of England, 35-43 Lincoln's Inn Fields, London, WC2A 3PE, UK
Tel: 020 74301840
Fax: 020 72424922
Email: info@baaps.org.uk
Website: http://www.baaps.org.uk
Contact: Nigel Mercer, Pres.
Description: Fosters exchange of information among surgeons for the advancement of aesthetic plastic surgery. Encourages specialized training among plastic surgeons. Develops and advocates high standards of professional conduct; advises, promotes, and disseminates information on aesthetic plastic surgery. Provides educational programs for general practitioners and the press; conducts semiannual educational program for trainees and consultants.

01068
British Association of Art Therapists
BAAT

24-27 White Lion St., London, N1 9PD, UK
Tel: 020 76864216
Fax: 020 78377945
Email: info@baat.org
Website: http://www.baat.org
Contact: Diane Waller, Pres.
Fee: £150
Membership Type: full, corporate
Fee: £40
Membership Type: trainee, unemployed, retired
Description: Art therapists. Maintains a comprehensive directory of qualified art therapists and works to promote art therapy in the UK.
Publication: Brochure
Publication title: Art Therapy in Education Guidelines

01069
British Association of Aviation Consultants
BAAC

16 Connaught Pl., London, W2 2ES, UK
Email: committee@baac.org.uk
Website: http://www.baac.org.uk
Members: 70
Staff: 1
Contact: John Wheeler, Chm.
Fee: £125
Membership Type: regular
Fee: £65
Membership Type: associate
Description: Represents the views and furthers the interest of members. Advances the status of the profession of registered aviation consultants.
Publication: Membership Directory
Publication title: Register of Members

01070
British Association of Barbershop Singers
BABS

Druids Lea, Upper Stanton Drew, Bristol, BS39 4EG, UK
Email: chairman@singbarbershop.com
Website: http://www.singbarbershop.com
Contact: Alan Goldsmith, Chm.
Fee: £23
Membership Type: individual associate
Fee: £120
Membership Type: associate club
Description: Fosters barbershop harmony singing in the United Kingdom; coordinates the activities of barbershop clubs. Offers Young Men in Harmony educational program and judge training program. Sponsors competitions.
Meetings/Conventions: annual convention – Exhibits.

01071
British Association of Beauty Therapy and Cosmetology
BABTAC

Ambrose House, Unit 1, Meteor Ct., Barnett Way, Barnwood, Gloucester, GL4 3GG, UK
Tel: 01452 623110
Fax: 01452 611599
Email: enquiries@babtac.com
Website: http://www.babtac.com
Members: 8500
Staff: 6
Contact: Julie Speed, Gen. Mgr.
Fee: £45
Membership Type: overseas, associate
Fee: £95.5
Membership Type: full
Description: Qualified and student beauty therapists. Aims to inject a new enthusiasm and dedication to the work; to present a strong united front to increase respect from the general public and press; to maintain and raise the standard of training; to publicizes and streamline the confederation education system; to encourage pride in the presentation and rendering of service to clients.
Publication: Magazine
Publication title: Vitality
Meetings/Conventions: Beauty Therapy Exhibition and Congress – annual congress – Exhibits.

01072
British Association of Behavioral Optometrists
BABO

21 Hartlebury Way, Charlton Kings, Cheltenham, Gloucestershire, GL52 6YB, UK
Tel: 001242 575107
Email: admin@babo.co.uk
Website: http://www.babo.co.uk
Members: 93
Contact: Mary Hayward, Sec.
Description: Seeks to improve understanding of Behavioral Optometry, through continuing education and training and by providing an accredited list of trained optometrists.
Library Subject: behavioral optometry
Library Type: reference

01073

British Association of Brain Injury Case Managers
BABICM

PO Box 199, Bury, BL8 9EJ, UK
Tel: 07002 222426
Email: secretary@babicm.org
Website: http://www.babicm.org
Contact: Anne Cossar, Treas.
Fee: £100
Membership Type: advanced, advanced process, regular
Fee: £300
Membership Type: corporate
Description: Represents the professional interests of case managers. Promotes the development of case management in the field of acquired brain injury. Advances the knowledge, skills and techniques of case management through education and training. Offers advice and support to people with brain injury and other complex conditions.

01074

British Association of Clinical Anatomists
BACA

University of E Anglia, School of Medicine, Health Policy and Practice, Norwich, NR4 7TJ, UK
Tel: 0603 591104
Fax: 0603 593752
Email: d.heylings@uea.ac.uk
Website: http://www.liv.ac.uk/HumanAnatomy/phd/baca
Contact: David Heylings, Honorary Sec.
Description: Represents the interests of members.

01075

British Association of Colliery Management - Technical, Energy and Administrative Management
BACM-TEAM

6a S Parade, Doncaster, DN1 2DY, UK
Tel: 01302 815551
Fax: 01302 815552
Email: gs@bacmteam.org.uk
Website: http://bacmteam.org.uk/public/about.php
Members: 6078
Staff: 15
Contact: Patrick Carragher, Gen. Sec.
Fee: £300
Membership Type: full (maximum)
Description: Union of individuals in the mining and associated industries in Great Britain. Promotes and protects the interests of members. Regulates relations between members, their employers, and other employees in the mining industry. Disseminates information concerning legislation affecting members. Provides legal advice and assistance.
Formerly: Formerly, British Association of Colliery Management

01076

British Association of Conference Destinations
BACD

Charles House, 6th Fl., 148-149 Great Charles St., Birmingham, B3 3HT, UK
Tel: 0121 2121400
Fax: 0121 2123131
Email: info@bacd.org.uk
Website: http://www.bacd.biz
Members: 80
Staff: 5
Contact: Tony Rogers, Chief Exec.
Description: Aims to promote British conference, meetings, exhibition and incentive travel facilities. Offers free and impartial venue finding service. Organizes an annual exhibition. Runs education courses.
Library Subject: conference and exhibition industry
Library Type: reference
Publication: Directory
Publication title: British Conference Destinations Directory. Advertisements.

01077

British Association of Cosmetic Doctors
BACD

Shorne Village Surgery, Crown Ln., Shorne, DA12 3DY, UK
Tel: 01474 823900
Email: info@cosmeticdoctors.co.uk
Website: http://www.cosmeticdoctors.co.uk
Contact: Sharon Turner-Fry, Sec.
Fee: £325
Membership Type: associate
Description: Represents cosmetic medical practitioners. Aims to advance safe and ethical images of cosmetic medicine. Maintains standards in cosmetic medicine. Offers medical cosmetic advice to the public.

01078

British Association of Crystal Growth
BACG

University of Manchester, School of Chemical Engineering and Materials Science, Molecular Materials Ctre., Manchester, M60 1QD, UK
Email: info@bacg.org.uk
Website: http://www.bacg.org.uk/BACG.NET/Home.aspx?
Contact: Roger Davey, Pres.
Fee: £8
Membership Type: regular
Description: Promotes semiconductor science and technology.

01079

British Association of Day Surgery
BADS

35-43 Lincoln's Inn Fields, London, WC2A 3PE, UK
Tel: 020 79730308
Fax: 020 79730314
Email: bads@bads.co.uk
Website: http://www.daysurgeryuk.org/bads/joomla
Members: 720
Staff: 1
Contact: Ian Smith, Pres.
Fee: £52.5
Membership Type: nurse, manager, doctor
Fee: £102.5
Membership Type: permanent medical staff
Description: Nurses, managers, surgeons and anesthetists. Encourages expansion of day surgery. Seeks to promote education, research and high-quality treatment in the field of surgery. Offers advice to Royal Colleges, NHS Executive, regional commissions and trusts including private health organizations.
Publication: Journal
Publication title: Journal of One-Day Surgery. Advertisements.

01080

British Association of Dental Nurses
BADN

PO Box 4, Hillhouse Intl. Business Ctre., Rm. 200, Lancashire, Thornton-Cleveleys, FY5 4QD, UK
Tel: 01253 38360
Email: admin@badn.org.uk
Website: http://www.badn.org.uk
Staff: 5
Contact: Sue Bruckel, Pres.
Fee: £70
Membership Type: full
Fee: £30
Membership Type: associate
Description: Professional association representing dental nurses in the UK and overseas as well as other members of the dental industry. Represents members working in specialist areas such as training, orthodontics, special care, and the armed forces. Aims to support, encourage, and provide advice to dental nurses; to develop and maintain nationally recognized standards; to protect the professional status of the dental nurse; and to maintain contact with the necessary bodies to achieve the above.
Library Subject: dental nursing, dentistry
Library Type: reference
Formerly: Formerly, ABDSA
Publication: Journal
Publication title: The British Dental Nurses Journal. Advertisements.
Meetings/Conventions: Dental Nursing Conference – annual conference – Exhibits.

01081

British Association of Dermatologists
BAD

4 Fitzroy Sq., London, W1T 5HQ, UK
Tel: 020 73830266
Fax: 020 73885263
Email: admin@bad.org.uk
Website: http://www.bad.org.uk
Members: 1000
Staff: 20
Contact: Marilyn Benham, CEO
Fee: £128
Membership Type: associate, trainee, associate trainee
Fee: £246
Membership Type: ordinary
Description: Medical professionals united to further the knowledge and teaching of dermatology. Promotes the interests of members and their patients. Conducts medical and scientific research; disseminates information.
Library Type: reference
Publication: Handbook
Publication title: BAD Members Handbook

01082

British Association of Dramatherapists BADth

Waverley, Battledown Approach, Gloucestershire, Cheltenham, GL52 6RE, UK
Tel: 01242 235515
Email: enquiries@badth.org.uk
Website: http://www.badth.org.uk
Members: 670
Staff: 2
Contact: Madeline Andersen-Warren, Chair
Fee: £100
Membership Type: full
Fee: £90
Membership Type: associate/overseas
Description: Aims to educate the public about dramatherapy, to support dramatherapists and to increase the availability of properly-trained and supervised dramatherapists. Also aims to ensure that high standards are maintained and to implement Equal Opportunities policies. Responds to the increasing demands for information and represents dramatherapy at national and international level.
Publication: Journal
Publication title: The Journal of Dramatherapy. Advertisements.

01083

British Association of Former United Nations Civil Servants BAFUNCS

6 The Lawn, Ealing Green, London, W5 5ER, UK
Tel: 020 88406657
Email: bengoabc@talktalk.net
Website: http://bafuncs.imo.org
Members: 920
Contact: Michael Davies, Exec. Pres.
Description: Encourages members to keep in touch with former colleagues through social, cultural and sporting activities. Extends welfare to former employees of the United Nations Civil Service and spouses in need. Represents members' interests in relations with the United Nations and its Specialized Agencies and British Government authorities. Protects the value of UN pensions through representation on Federation of Associations of Former International Civil Servants.

01084

British Association of Friends of Museums BAFM

7 Northbrook House, Free St., Bishop's Waltham, S032 1NP, UK
Tel: 0870 2248905
Email: admin@bafm.org.uk
Website: http://www.bafm.org.uk
Members: 554
Contact: Sue Hall, Hon. Sec.
Fee: £50-150
Membership Type: group (based on number of members)
Fee: £30
Membership Type: institutional
Description: Groups of Friends of museums, libraries, art galleries, archives, and other institutions preserving the United Kingdom's cultural heritage. Acts as an umbrella and supports all Friends Groupings around the United Kingdom sharing news, advice, help and good practices. Offers rewarding volunteer activities. Provides a start up guide.
Publication: Handbook
Publication title: BAFM Friends

01085

British Association of Golf Course Constructors BAGCC

32 New Rd., Ringwood, Hampshire, BH24 3AU, UK
Tel: 01425 475584
Fax: 01425 475643
Email: secretary@bagcc.org.uk
Website: http://www.bagcc.org.uk
Contact: Brian D. Pierson, Chm.
Description: Promotes and develops golf course constructions in the UK and overseas. Adopts policy that will ensure high quality workmanship.

01086

British Association of Green Crop Driers BAGCD

The Old Stalbes, Hillhurst Farm, Westenhanger, Hythe, CT21 4HT, UK
Tel: 01522 523322
Email: info@bagcd.org
Website: http://www.bagcd.org
Members: 25
Staff: 1
Contact: Liz Harding, Sec.
Description: Producers of dried green crops. Promotes the dehydration and processing of forage crops.

01087

British Association of Head and Neck Oncologists BAHNO

PO Box 85, Midhurst, GU29 9WS, UK
Tel: 01730 813700
Fax: 01730 812042
Email: secretariat@bahno.org.uk
Website: http://www.bahno.org.uk
Members: 340
Contact: Jill McFarland, Sec.
Fee: £50
Membership Type: full
Fee: £25
Membership Type: associate, overseas
Description: Represents specialists with a major interest in head and neck oncology. Encourages discussion and the sharing of knowledge in the various clinical and research specialties involved in the management of head and neck cancer.

01088

British Association of Homoeopathic Veterinary Surgeons BAHVS

103 Golf Dr., Nuneaton, CV11 6ND, UK
Tel: 07768 322075
Email: sec@bahvs.com
Website: http://www.bahvs.com
Members: 110
Contact: Stuart Marston, Honorary Sec.
Fee: £15
Membership Type: student
Fee: £70
Membership Type: full
Description: Composed of veterinary surgeons and veterinary students. Works to stimulate the awareness of veterinary surgeons. Inform its members of the practices and other issues relating to veterinary homeopathy.

01089

British Association of Hospitality Accountants BAHA

Merley House Business Ctre., Ste. 6, Merley House Ln., Dorset, Wimborne, BH21 3AA, UK
Tel: 01202 889430
Fax: 01202 887967
Email: admin@baha-uk.org
Website: http://www.baha-uk.org
Members: 700
Staff: 2
Contact: David Cook, Pres.
Fee: £99.87
Membership Type: ordinary
Fee: £105.75
Membership Type: associate
Description: Financial directors, financial controllers, accountants and consultants in the hospitality sector. Promotes the highest professional standards in financial management in the hospitality industry and to underwrite and develop those standards by the provision of education programmes.
Formerly: Formerly, British Association of Hotel Accountants
Publication: Book
Publication title: Uniform System of Accounts for the Lodging Industry

01090

British Association of Indian Anaesthetists BAOIA

PO Box 520, Sandal, Wakefield, WF1 9BX, UK
Email: maheshnagar@hotmail.com
Website: http://www.baoia.org
Contact: Anil Kumar Gupta, Pres.
Fee: £10
Membership Type: regular
Description: Represents the interests of Indian anaesthetists. Improves communication and networking among Indian anaesthetists in UK. Promotes research and education in the field of anaesthesia. Supports the development and improvement of anaesthetic practice.

01091

British Association of Journalists BAJ

89 Fleet St., London, EC4Y 1DH, UK
Tel: 020 73533003
Fax: 020 73532310
Email: office@bajunion.org.uk
Website: http://www.bajunion.org.uk
Contact: Steve Turner, Gen. Sec.
Fee: £17.5
Membership Type: national newspaper/broadcasting/news agency staff
Fee: £10
Membership Type: other senior
Description: Provides excellence in trade union representation and legal advocacy for freelance and staff

journalists, including fees, employment and copyright matters.
Publication: Newsletter
Publication title: BAJ News

01092
British Association of Landscape Industries
BALI

Landscape House, Stoneleigh Park, Warwickshire, Coventry, CV8 2LG, UK
Tel: 024 76690333
Fax: 024 76690077
Email: contact@bali.org.uk
Website: http://www.bali.org.uk
Members: 700
Staff: 8
Contact: Richard Gardiner, Chm.
Fee: £200
Membership Type: probationary contractor, branch, overseas
Fee: £130
Membership Type: corresponding
Description: Landscapers in the United Kingdom. Promotes practice of professional landscaping. Defends industry interests.
Publication: Newsletter
Publication title: Landscape News

01093
British Association of Leisure Parks, Piers and Attractions
BALPPA

37 Tanner St., Ste. 12, London, SE1 3LF, UK
Tel: 0207 4034455
Fax: 0207 4034022
Email: balppa5@btconnect.com
Website: http://www.balppa.org
Members: 300
Staff: 2
Contact: Martin Barratt, Chief Exec.
Description: Park membership, UK private sector leisure parks, piers and attractions; Trade associate membership, suppliers of goods and services to the parks sector. Aims to promote and defend the interests of the industry; to represent the needs and concerns of the industry to HM Government departments and elsewhere at national level; to provide advice, information and other services to its members, to provide forums for discussion of their interests and concerns and to promote best practice in the industry.
Publication: Directory
Publication title: BALPPA Group Travel Guide

01094
British Association of Medical Managers
BAMM

Petersgate House, 64 St. Petersgate, Cheshire, Stockport, SK1 1HE, UK
Tel: 0161 4741141
Fax: 0161 4747167
Email: bamm@bamm.co.uk
Website: http://www.bamm.co.uk
Members: 1200
Staff: 10
Contact: Jenny Simpson, Chief Exec.
Fee: £195
Membership Type: full
Fee: £171.5
Membership Type: associate
Description: Doctors from all specialties and at all levels of interest in management are invited to apply for membership. Junior doctors are warmly welcomed and non-medical managers are welcome to apply for associate membership. Concerned with the promotion of quality healthcare by improving and supporting the contribution of doctors in management. Unites doctors with an interest in healthcare management. Members are keen to learn from, and work with each other to ensure a meaningful and effective contribution to the management of organisations.
Publication: Journal
Publication title: Clinician in Management

01095
British Association of Neuroscience Nurses
BANN

c/o Neal Cook
University of Ulster, Magee Campus Northland Rd., Londonderry, BT48 7JL, UK
Tel: 028 71375463
Email: nf.cook@ulster.ac.uk
Website: http://www.bann.org.uk
Members: 310
Contact: Anne Preece, Pres.
Fee: £30
Membership Type: full
Description: Promotes high standards of patient care in the Neurosciences field. Provides opportunities for knowledge transfer between neuroscience nurses. Encourages clinical research and promotes interest in the neuroscience area.

01096
British Association of Occupational Therapists
BAOT

106-114 Borough High St., Southwark, London, SE1 1LB, UK
Tel: 020 73576480
Fax: 020 74502299
Email: membership@cot.co.uk
Website: http://www.cot.co.uk/Homepage
Members: 29000
Staff: 50
Contact: Julia Scott, Chief Exec.
Fee: £20.94
Membership Type: professional
Fee: £5.19
Membership Type: retired
Description: Promotes high standards among occupational therapists. Supports the provision of efficient, reliable, and effective services that benefit all users of occupational therapy. Encourages personal and intellectual development of occupational therapists and support staff.
Publication: Journal
Publication title: British Journal of Occupation Therapy. Advertisements.

01097
British Association of Oral and Maxillofacial Surgeons
BAOMS

c/o Royal College of Surgeons of England
35-43 Lincoln's Inn Fields, London, WC2A 3PE, UK
Tel: 020 74058074
Fax: 020 74309997
Email: office@baoms.org.uk
Website: http://www.baoms.org.uk
Members: 1200
Contact: Marie E. Morton, Pres.
Fee: £85
Membership Type: individual, overseas
Fee: £105
Membership Type: associate fellow
Description: Aims to promote the advancement of education and research into the development of oral and maxillofacial surgery in the British Isles; to encourage, and assist postgraduate education, study and research in oral and maxillofacial surgery. Arranges regular meetings at which lectures and demonstrations will be given.
Publication: Journal
Publication title: British Journal of Oral and Maxillofacial Surgery

01098
British Association of Otorhinolaryngologists - Head and Neck Surgeons
ENT UK

c/o Royal College of Surgeons
35-43 Lincoln's Inn Fields, London, WC2A 3PE, UK
Tel: 020 74048373
Fax: 020 74044200
Email: admin@entuk.org
Website: http://www.entuk.org
Members: 1300
Staff: 4
Contact: Nechama Lewis, Admin. Mgr.
Fee: £37
Membership Type: affiliate, corresponding
Fee: £170
Membership Type: trainee/associate
Description: Consultant ENT and head and neck surgeons, consultant audiological physicians as well as medical practitioners engaged in the practice of otorhinolaryngology and head and neck surgery in grades other than that of consultant and healthcare professionals in other allied disciplines. Aims to support and encourage education, research, development and audit in otorhinolaryngology, head and neck surgery. Promotes the highest standards of medical and surgical practice within otorhinolarynglogy, head and neck surgery, for the benefit of patients.
Publication: Newsletter
Publication title: The BAO-HNS Newsletter
Meetings/Conventions: British Academy Conference in Otolaryngology – triennial meeting – Exhibits.

01099

British Association of Paediatric Surgeons of England
BAPS

35-43 Lincoln's Inn Fields, London, WC2A 3PN, UK
Tel: 020 78696915
Fax: 020 78696919
Email: honsec@baps.org.uk
Website: http://www.baps.org.uk
Members: 700
Staff: 1
Contact: David Drake, Pres.
Fee: £275
Membership Type: full (UK and Ireland)
Fee: £100
Membership Type: full (international), associate (UK and Ireland)
Description: Pediatric surgeons, consultants, and trainees. Works to improve the techniques of study, practice, and research in paediatric surgery; fosters professional relations among paediatric surgeons. Sponsors training program.
Publication: Journal
Publication title: Journal of Pediatric Surgery
Meetings/Conventions: annual congress – Exhibits.

01100

British Association of Paintings Conservator-Restorers
BAPCR

PO Box 258, Norwich, NR13 4WY, UK
Tel: 01603 516237
Fax: 01603 510985
Email: secretary@bapcr.org.uk
Website: http://www.bapcr.org.uk
Members: 400
Staff: 1
Contact: Lucy Tetlow, Sec.
Fee: £70
Membership Type: fellowship
Fee: £45
Membership Type: associate
Description: Aims to sustain and improve high standards of excellence in the practice of picture conservation and restoration. Encourages the investigation of new methods and materials. Protects the interests of the public and the profession in relevant matters. Promotes a high standard of conduct by members of the profession.
Formerly: Formerly, Association of British Picture Restorers

01101

British Association of Paper Historians
BAPH

Smithy Cottage, Hilton, Blandford Forum, Dorset, DT11 0DB, UK
Email: terry@baph.org.uk
Website: http://www.baph.org.uk
Contact: Shulla Jacques, Sec.
Fee: £36
Membership Type: individual (in UK)
Fee: £50
Membership Type: joint (in UK)
Description: Aims to act as a focal point for sharing information on historical paper research, both voluntary and professional, by promoting contact between those involved and by providing information on current developments.
Publication: Journal
Publication title: The Quarterly

01102

British Association of Perinatal Medicine
BAPM

c/o Lisa Nandi, Exec. Off.
5 - 11 Theobalds Rd., London, WC1X 8SH, UK
Tel: 020 70926085
Fax: 020 70926001
Email: bapm@rcpch.ac.uk
Website: http://www.bapm.org
Members: 800
Contact: David Field, Pres.
Fee: £25-100
Membership Type: medical
Fee: £25-50
Membership Type: non-medical
Description: Works to improve the standard of perinatal care in the British Isles.
Publication: Newsletter
Publication title: BAPM News
Meetings/Conventions: annual meeting

01103

British Association of Pharmaceutical Physicians
BRAPP

Royal Station Ct., Station Rd., Twyford, Reading, RG10 9NF, UK
Tel: 0118 9341943
Fax: 0118 9320981
Email: info@brapp.org
Website: http://www.brapp.org.uk
Members: 700
Staff: 3
Contact: Jane Barrett, Chm.
Description: Fully registered medical practitioners practising pharmaceutical medicine in, or on behalf of, the pharmaceutical industry or in the statutory regulatory authority. Assists and advises members in all matters pertaining to the execution of their professional duties relating to the pharmaceutical industry.
Publication: Journal
Publication title: Pharmaceutical Physician

01104

British Association of Pharmaceutical Wholesalers
BAPW

90 Long Acre, London, WC2E 9RA, UK
Tel: 020 70310590
Fax: 020 70310591
Email: mail@bapw.net
Website: http://www.bapw.net
Members: 65
Staff: 3
Contact: Martin Sawer, Exec. Dir.
Fee: £1500
Membership Type: associate
Description: Works as a representative body for all full-time pharmaceutical wholesalers in discussion with Department of Health, manufacturers and other pharmaceutical industry bodies.
Publication: Newsletter
Publication title: The BAPW Bulletin

01105

British Association of Picture Libraries and Agencies
BAPLA

59 Tranquil Vale, Blackheath, London, SE3 0BS, UK
Tel: 020 77131780
Fax: 020 77131211
Email: enquiries@bapla.org.uk
Website: http://www.bapla.org.uk
Members: 350
Staff: 4
Contact: Paul Brown, Chm.
Description: Works in diverse areas of marketing, industry surveys, industry statistics, lobbying, and setting standards in business practice and technology. Operates referral service to assist picture researchers to locate the best source of photographic images.

01106

British Association of Plastic, Reconstructive and Aesthetic Surgeons
BAPRAS

The Royal College of Surgeons, 35-43 Lincoln's Inn Fields, London, WC2A 3PE, UK
Tel: 020 78315161
Fax: 020 78314041
Email: secretariat@bapras.org.uk
Website: http://www.bapras.org.uk
Members: 650
Staff: 5
Contact: D.J. Coleman, Hon. Sec.
Fee: £70
Membership Type: overseas associate
Fee: £100
Membership Type: allied associate
Description: Plastic Surgeons. Promotes and directs the development of plastic surgery and aims to foster and co-ordinate education, study and research in plastic surgery.
Publication: Journal
Publication title: Journal of Plastic, Reconstructive and Aesthetic Surgery

01107

British Association of Play Therapists
BAPT

1, Beacon Mews, South Rd., Weybridge, Surrey, KT13 9DZ, UK
Tel: 01932 828638
Fax: 01932 820100
Email: info@bapt.uk.com
Website: http://www.bapt.info
Members: 400
Contact: Inge Roberts, Vice Chair
Fee: £50
Membership Type: associate
Fee: £100
Membership Type: full
Description: Develops and advances the profession and practice of play therapy in the UK. Raises public and professional awareness of the value of play therapy for enhancing the mental health and emotional well-being of children and young people. Promotes safe, ethical and effective practice of play therapy through training, professional development and evidence-based research.
Publication: Booklet
Publication title: BAPT Guide to Play Therapy

01108
British Association of Prosthetists and Orthotists
BAPO

Sir James Clark Bldg., Abbey Mills Business Ctre., Paisley, PA1 1TJ, UK
Tel: 0845 1668490
Email: lorna@bapo.com
Website: http://www.bapo.com/site
Members: 900
Staff: 4
Contact: Lorna Graham, Secretariat Mgr.
Fee: £220
Membership Type: technician associate
Fee: £35
Membership Type: student associate
Description: Orthotists and prosthetists. Seeks to protect the prosthetic and orthotic profession with regard to its status and interests. Encourages high standards of ethics and practice among members; conducts continuing professional education and training programs; serves as a clearinghouse on orthotics and prosthetics; provides advice and assistance to members.
Publication: Magazine
Publication title: BAPOMAG

01109
British Association of Psychotherapists
BAP

37 Mapesbury Rd., London, NW2 4HJ, UK
Tel: 020 84529823
Fax: 020 84520310
Email: mail@bap-psychotherapy.org
Website: http://www.bap-psychotherapy.org/content.jsp
Members: 500
Staff: 6
Contact: Elise Ormerod, CEO
Description: Full, associate and student members, trained and qualified by the organization in either adult or child psychotherapy. Aims to promote the knowledge and application of psychotherapy and the training of both Adult and Child Psychotherapists. Administers external courses since 1989 for the benefit of interested members of the helping professions. Operates a clinical service to help people find a qualified psychotherapist. Conducts trainings.
Library Subject: psychoanalytical psychotherapy, analytical psychology, child psychotherapy
Library Type: not open to the public
Publication: Journal
Publication title: British Journal Of Psychotherapists

01110
British Association of Record Dealers
BARD

Colonnade House, 1st Fl., 2 Westover Rd., Bournemouth, BH1 2BY, UK
Tel: 01202 292063
Fax: 01202 292067
Email: admin@bardltd.org
Website: http://www.bardltd.org
Contact: Kim Bayley, Dir. Gen.
Fee: £90-649
Membership Type: retailer associate
Fee: £23298
Membership Type: retailer full (maximum)
Description: Represents retailers that sell entertainment products in UK. Acts as a forum for its members and helps in promoting the entertainment industry.
Meetings/Conventions: BVA Liaison Committee Meeting – quarterly meeting

01111
British Association of Removers
BAR

Tangent House, 62 Exchange Rd., Hertfordshire, Watford, WD18 0TG, UK
Tel: 01923 699480
Fax: 01923 699481
Email: info@bar.co.uk
Website: http://www.bar.co.uk
Members: 900
Staff: 12
Description: Trade association representing approved, professional companies in the furniture removal and associated industries. Provides a customer conciliation service. Acts as a forum for the exchange of information concerning the industry. Conducts research and educational programs.
Formerly: Formerly, British Association of Removers
Publication: Magazine
Publication title: Removals and Storage. Advertisements.

01112
British Association of Research Quality Assurance
BARQA

3 Wherry Ln., Ipswich, IP4 1LG, UK
Tel: 01473 221411
Fax: 01473 221412
Email: info@barqa.com
Website: http://www.barqa.com/cms.php?pageid=390&index=1
Members: 1650
Staff: 5
Contact: David Weller, Contact
Fee: £62
Membership Type: general, inside UK
Fee: £74
Membership Type: general, outside UK
Description: Promotes members' interests.
Publication: Magazine
Publication title: QUASAR. Advertisements.

01113
British Association of Retinal Screeners
BARS

Ward 25, Ninewells Hospital, Dundee, DD1 9SY, UK
Tel: 01 382632713
Email: info@eyescreening.org.uk
Website: http://www.eyescreening.org.uk
Contact: Alison Simpson, Admin. Sec.
Fee: £20
Membership Type: regular
Fee: £40
Membership Type: associate
Description: Represents the interests of retinal screeners. Provides retinal screening services for people with diabetes. Offers support and continuing education for individuals involved in retinal screening.

01114
British Association of Settlements and Social Action Centres
BASSAC

33 Corsham St., London, N1 6DR, UK
Tel: 0845 2410375
Fax: 0845 2410376
Email: info@bassac.org.uk
Website: http://www.bassac.org.uk
Members: 75
Staff: 10
Contact: Ben Hughes, Chief Exec.
Fee: £200
Membership Type: basic
Description: National network of multi-purpose organisations seeking to tackle the causes and effects of poverty and social exclusion, primarily in inner city and urban areas. Provides a range of services to members of the local communities in which these organisations are located.
Publication: Directory
Publication title: BASSAC Directory

01115
British Association of Skin Camouflage
BASC

PO Box 3671, Chester, CH1 9QH, UK
Tel: 01254 703107
Website: http://www.skin-camouflage.net
Members: 100
Staff: 1
Description: Trains professionals. Encourages and supports members. Informs and provides remedial camouflage service for patients.
Meetings/Conventions: Training Initiatives – triennial meeting

01116
British Association of Social Workers
BASW

16 Kent St., Birmingham, B5 6RD, UK
Tel: 0121 6223911
Fax: 0121 6224860
Email: info@basw.co.uk
Website: http://www.basw.co.uk
Members: 10000
Staff: 20
Contact: Hilton Dawson, Chief Exec.
Description: Social workers in the UK. Concerned to promote the social work profession in UK on issues of social work policy and practice. Services to members include advice and representation, publications and the association's journal Professional Social Work.
Publication: Magazine
Publication title: Professional Social Work

01117
British Association of Sport Rehabilitators and Trainers
BASRAT

University of Salford, School of Healthcare Professions, Frederick Rd., Salford, M6 6PU, UK
Email: chair@basrat.org
Website: http://www.basrat.org

Contact: Steve Aspinall, Chm.
Fee: £20
Membership Type: student
Fee: £50
Membership Type: associate, affiliate
Description: Represents healthcare practitioners and people participating in sport and exercise at all levels. Provides a platform from which sports rehabilitators can promote their work, both nationally and internationally.

01118

British Association of Stroke Physicians
BASP

c/o Trish O'Neill, Admin.
PO Box 259, Wallasey, CH27 9DY, UK
Email: basp@basp.ac.uk
Website: http://www.basp.ac.uk
Contact: Martin James, Pres.
Fee: £40
Membership Type: full
Fee: £20
Membership Type: associate/affiliate
Description: Promotes the advancement of stroke medicine. Develops guidelines for the training of junior doctors in the field of stroke medicine. Encourages members to provide and organize education and training about stroke care. Facilitates basic and clinical research relevant to stroke. Provides advice regarding stroke health policy and service delivery.

01119

British Association of Symphonic Bands and Wind Ensembles
BASBWE

c/o Richard Edwards
Fron, Llansadwrn, Anglesey, LL59 5SL, UK
Tel: 01248 811285
Email: membership@basbwe.org
Website: http://www.basbwe.org
Members: 850
Contact: Philip Robinson, Chm.
Fee: £20
Membership Type: individual in UK
Fee: £35
Membership Type: individual outside UK
Description: Organizations, companies, and individuals in the U.K. dedicated to advance symphonic bands and wind ensembles. Fosters contact between members and encourages information exchange. Organizes clinics on topics including the administrative aspects of running a band or ensemble, conducting, programming, fundraising, and specialist and non-specialist skills; sponsors workshops on instrument maintenance, jazz orchestras, wind ensembles, chamber groups, and arranging for ensembles.
Publication: Magazine
Publication title: Winds. Advertisements.

01120

British Association of Teachers of Dancing
BATD

Pavilion 8, Upper Level, Watermark Business Park, 315 Govan Rd., Glasgow, G51 2SE, UK
Tel: 0141 4273699
Fax: 0141 4199783
Email: enquiries@batd.co.uk
Website: http://www.batd.co.uk
Contact: Shelagh Connolly, Pres.
Description: Represents and assists professionals in the field of dancing. Organizes refresher courses, festivals, seminars, championship, instructional sessions and annual conferences for its members.

01121

British Association of Teachers of the Deaf
BATOD

21, Keating Close, Medway, Kent, Rochester, ME1 1EQ, UK
Tel: 0845 6435181
Fax: 0845 6435181
Email: secretary@batod.org.uk
Website: http://www.batod.org.uk
Members: 1786
Staff: 1
Contact: Paul Simpson, Natl. Sec.
Fee: £70
Membership Type: full, associate
Fee: £35
Membership Type: full (taking a career break), associate (unwaged), retired
Description: Promotes excellence in the education of deaf children and young people. Represents the interests of teachers of the deaf in Britain.
Publication: Magazine
Meetings/Conventions: annual conference – Exhibits.

01122

British Association of Urological Surgeons
BAUS

35/43 Lincoln's Inn Fields, London, WC2A 3PE, UK
Tel: 020 78696950
Fax: 020 74045048
Email: admin@baus.org.uk
Website: http://www.baus.org.uk
Members: 1500
Staff: 7
Contact: Adrian Joyce, Pres.
Fee: £320
Membership Type: full (in UK)
Fee: £250
Membership Type: associate (in UK and overseas), full, corresponding (overseas)
Description: Urological surgeons from the UK and overseas. Medical practitioners in other specialties with an interest in urology. Aims to promote a high standard in the practice of urology.
Publication: Newsletter
Publication title: The Bulletin
Meetings/Conventions: Section of Andrology – annual meeting

01123

British Association of Veterinary Ophthalmologists
BrAVO

Animal Health Trust, Lanwades Park, Kentford, Newmarket, Suffolk, CB8 7UU, UK
Tel: 08700 502540
Fax: 08700 502541
Email: secretary@bravo.org.uk
Website: http://www.bravo.org.uk
Contact: Claudia Hartley, Sec.
Fee: £35
Membership Type: regular
Description: Seeks to improve veterinary ophthalmology. Educates and trains veterinary surgeons in veterinary ophthalmology. Promotes the practice, teaching and research of animal ophthalmology.
Publication: Journal
Publication title: Veterinary Ophthalmology

01124

British Association of Women Entrepreneurs
BAWE

112 John Player Bldg., Stirling, FK7 7RP, UK
Tel: 01827 312812
Fax: 01827 261022
Email: president@bawe-uk.org
Website: http://www.bawe-uk.org
Contact: Tatjana Hine, Pres.
Fee: £150
Membership Type: general
Description: Encourages the personal development of member entrepreneurs. Provides opportunities for members to expand their business through informal and formal networking. Represents and promotes British entrepreneurship worldwide.

01125

British Astronomical Association
BAA

Burlington House, Piccadilly, London, W1J 0DU, UK
Tel: 020 77344145
Fax: 020 74394629
Email: office@britastro.org
Website: http://www.britastro.org/baa
Members: 3000
Contact: David Boyd, Pres.
Fee: £44
Membership Type: ordinary (aged 22-65)
Fee: £31
Membership Type: senior (aged 65 or over)
Description: Astronomical societies and amateur astronomers. Supports modern techniques for observation, data handling, and scientific presentation of results. Facilitates information exchange. Organizes residential weekend courses. Provides information service. Loans instruments to members.
Library Type: reference
Publication: Journal
Publication title: Journal of the British Astronomical Association. Advertisements.

01126

British Atherosclerosis Society
BAS

British Heart Institute, University of Bristol, Level 7, Bristol Royal Infirmary, Bristol, BS2 8HW, UK
Tel: 0117 9283154
Email: s.j.george@bristol.ac.uk
Website: http://www.britathsoc.org
Contact: Sarah Jane George, Sec.
Description: Aims to promote atherosclerosis research. Encourages exchange of knowledge and education of the public in all matters relating to the cause and treatment of atherosclerosis diseases in humans. Provides a forum for the presentation of novel scientific and clinical results in atherosclerosis research.

01127

British Audio-Visual Dealers Association BADA

33 High St., Hampton Wick, London, KT1 4DA, UK
Tel: 020 81506741
Website: http://www.bada.co.uk
Members: 102
Staff: 1
Contact: Phil Hansen, Operations and Marketing Mgr.
Description: Specialist hi-fi retailers. Associate members are manufacturers and distributors of real hi-fi and specialist press. Maintains a Professional Standards of Conduct Charter which members are obliged to display in their shops. Members help customers identify, clarify and satisfy their needs through demonstration of selected (often British) Hi-Fi products. Information and advice to Media available.
Formerly: Formerly, British Audio Dealers Association

01128

British Automatic Fire Sprinkler Association BAFSA

Richmond House, Broad St., Ely, CB7 4AH, UK
Tel: 01353 659187
Fax: 01353 666619
Email: info@bafsa.org.uk
Website: http://www.bafsa.org.uk
Members: 80
Contact: Peter Armstrong, Chm.
Fee: £1100-3300
Membership Type: installer
Fee: £10000
Membership Type: sprinkler head manufacturer
Description: Concerned with the promotion of the greater and more efficient use of automatic sprinkler and other systems using water as a means for the control and extinguishing of fires.
Formerly: Formerly, British Automatic Sprinkler Association
Publication: Pamphlet
Publication title: BAFSA Information File

01129

British Automation and Robot Association BARA

c/o PPMA Ltd.
New Progress House, 34 Stafford Rd., Wallington, SM6 9AA, UK
Tel: 020 87738111
Fax: 020 87730022
Email: bara@bara.org.uk
Website: http://www.bara.org.uk
Contact: Mike Wilson, Pres.
Fee: £750
Membership Type: large supplier (with a turnover greater than $2M)
Fee: £400
Membership Type: small supplier (with turnover less than $2M)
Description: Promotes robotics and automation. Facilitates the exchange of information and experience. Conducts research events. Compiles statistics.
Formerly: Formerly, British Association for Robotics and Automation

01130

British Ballet Organization BBO

Woolborough House, 39 Lonsdale Rd., Barnes, London, SW13 9JP, UK
Tel: 020 87481241
Fax: 020 87481301
Email: info@bbo.org.uk
Website: http://www.bbo.org.uk
Members: 806
Staff: 5
Contact: John Travis, Chief Exec.
Fee: £120
Membership Type: teacher
Fee: £12
Membership Type: student
Description: Teachers, executants, and students. Offers exams in ballet, tap, jazz, and modern dance. Validated by the Council for Dance Education and Training. Provides teaching examinations in ballet, tap, and jazz.
Publication: Magazine
Publication title: Dancer. Advertisements.

01131

British Bankers' Association BBA

Pinners Hall, 105-108 Old Broad St., London, EC2N 1EX, UK
Tel: 020 72168800
Fax: 020 72168811
Email: info@bba.org.uk
Website: http://www.bba.org.uk
Members: 223
Staff: 60
Contact: Angela Knight, Chief Exec.
Description: Trade association representing banks conducting business in the United Kingdom.
Publication: Book
Publication title: Annual Abstract of Banking Statistics

01132

British Bedding and Pot Plant Association BBPA

PO Box 475, Huntingdon, PE28 3YP, UK
Tel: 08702 416526
Fax: 08702 416526
Email: bpoa@btconnect.com
Website: http://www.bpoaonline.co.uk
Contact: Dawn Smith, Exec. Off.
Description: Those involved with production (growing) bedding, pot and ornamental plants. Also those in associated trades. Promotes bedding and pot plants through generic promotion of industry and participation in gardening events; Technical advice and discussion and representation through National Farmers' Union.

01133

British Bee-Keepers' Association BBKA

c/o National Beekeeper Centre
National Agricultural Centre, Stoneleigh Park, Warwickshire, Kenilworth, CV8 2LG, UK
Tel: 02476 696679
Fax: 02476 690682
Email: admin@britishbeekeepers.com
Website: http://www.britishbee.org.uk
Members: 9000
Staff: 2
Contact: Mike Harris, Gen. Sec.
Fee: £33
Membership Type: individual
Fee: £18
Membership Type: outside UK
Description: Nearly all county and district associations in England (as well as a few outside England) are Area Member Associations of the organization and members of those organizations automatically become indirect members of the organization. Aims to promote and further the craft of beekeeping. Its activities thus serve the interests of all beekeepers, but members of the organization also benefit from a number of specific services which are provided, including insurance.
Publication: Newsletter
Publication title: BBKA News. Advertisements.

01134

British Beer and Pub Association BBPA

Market Towers, 1 Nine Elms Ln., London, SW8 5NQ, UK
Tel: 020 76279191
Fax: 020 76279123
Email: web@beerandpub.com
Website: http://www.beerandpub.com
Members: 72
Staff: 18
Contact: Ralph Findlay, Chm.
Description: Members are brewery companies and multiple licensed retailers in the United Kingdom.
Formerly: Formerly, Brewers and Licensed Retailers Association
Publication title: Beer and Pubs Facts

01135

British Belgian Blue Cattle Society BBB

Fell View, Blencarn, Cumbria, Penrith, CA10 1TX, UK
Tel: 01768 88775
Fax: 01768 88779
Email: info@britishbluecattle.org
Website: http://www.britishbluecattle.org
Contact: John Fleming, Sec.
Description: Promotes the Belgian Blue breed of cattle in the United Kingdom. Establishes standards of Belgian Blue cattle. Ensures the excellence of meat products obtained from the breed.

01136

British Biophysical Society BBS

University of Sheffield, Molecular Biology and Biotechnology, Sheffield, S10 2TN, UK
Email: bbs@britishbiophysics.org.uk
Website: http://www.britishbiophysics.org.uk
Contact: C. Jeremy Craven, Treas.
Fee: £15
Membership Type: full
Fee: £10
Membership Type: student/retired
Description: Represents scientists engaged in the study, research and teaching of biophysics and its related studies. Works for the advancement of the science of biophysics.

01137
British Blind and Shutter Association
BBSA
PO Box 232, Suffolk, Stowmarket, IP14 9AR, UK
Tel: 01449 780444
Fax: 08712 647220
Email: info@bbsa.org.uk
Website: http://www.bbsa.org.uk
Members: 380
Staff: 3
Contact: Tony Edmondson, Contact
Fee: £305-1082
Membership Type: full (based on number of employees)
Fee: £503.17
Membership Type: service
Description: Manufacturers and suppliers of internal and external blinds, awnings and shutters. Represents around 360 member companies involved in the manufacture of blinds and/or shutters in the UK. Representation on BSI and CEN committees regarding standards work. Organizes a trade exhibition.
Library Subject: technical research
Library Type: not open to the public
Publication: Magazine
Publication title: Blinds and Shutters

01138
British Blood Transfusion Society
BBTS
Enterprise House, Manchester Science Park, Lloyd St., N, Manchester, M15 6SE, UK
Tel: 0161 2327999
Fax: 0161 2327979
Email: bbts@bbts.org.uk
Website: http://www.bbts.org.uk
Members: 1712
Staff: 4
Contact: Dafydd Thomas, Pres.
Fee: £72
Membership Type: full
Fee: £82
Membership Type: overseas
Description: Promotes knowledge and advances understanding of all aspects of transfusion medicine for the public benefit.
Publication: Journal
Publication title: Transfusion Medicine

01139
British Bluegrass Music Association
BBMA
c/o David Rozzell
26 Martin Rd., Copnor, Portsmouth, PO3 6JZ, UK
Tel: 023 92651265
Email: contact@britishbluegrass.co.uk
Website: http://www.britishbluegrass.co.uk/index.html
Members: 600
Staff: 8
Contact: John Wirtz, Chm.
Fee: £24
Membership Type: individual
Fee: £30
Membership Type: family
Description: Promotes Bluegrass music in Britain. Encourages new markets for Bluegrass music. Coordinates efforts to improve the public image and awareness of Bluegrass music. Establishes and maintains a Bluegrass Directory. Encourages existing festivals, show promoters, radio and media outlets to increase their exposure of Bluegrass music. Acts as a communications resource, assisting members in their activities.
Publication: Magazine
Publication title: British Bluegrass News. Advertisements.

01140
British Board of Film Classification
BBFC
3 Soho Sq., London, W1D 3HD, UK
Tel: 020 74401570
Fax: 020 72870141
Email: feedback@bbfc.co.uk
Website: http://www.bbfc.co.uk
Staff: 70
Contact: David Cooke, Dir.
Description: Recommends and formulates regulations for films, videos, and some computer games produced or marketed in the United Kingdom. Conducts research programs.

01141
British Brands Group
BBG
100 Victoria Embankment, London, EC4Y 0DH, UK
Tel: 07020 934250
Fax: 07020 934252
Email: info@britishbrandsgroup.org.uk
Website: http://www.britishbrandsgroup.org.uk
Members: 25
Staff: 1
Contact: John Noble, Dir.
Fee: £515-22660
Membership Type: full
Fee: £1290
Membership Type: associate
Description: Branded product manufacturers. Represents members' interests.
Publication: Newsletter
Publication title: British Brands

01142
British Bryological Society
BBS
6 Darnford Close, Stafford, ST16 1LR, UK
Email: membership@britishbryologicalsociety.org.uk
Website: http://www.britishbryologicalsociety.org.uk
Members: 615
Contact: M.F. Godfrey, Membership Sec.
Fee: £20
Membership Type: ordinary
Fee: £10
Membership Type: concessionary
Description: Individuals interested in bryology, the study of mosses and liverworts. Promotes a wider interest in all aspects of bryology. Serves as a clearinghouse on bryology; facilitates exchange of information among members; conducts research and educational programs; keeps records of bryophyte distribution and endangered bryophyte species. Maintains panel of referees to assist in the identification of bryophytes; operates herbarium of voucher specimens for consultation by members.
Library Subject: bryology
Library Type: reference
Publication: Bulletin
Publication title: Field Bryology
Meetings/Conventions: Field Work Week – annual meeting

01143
British Business and General Aviation Association
BBGA
19 Church St., Brill, Aylesbury, HP18 9RT, UK
Tel: 01844 238020
Fax: 01844 238087
Email: info@bbga.aero
Website: http://www.bbga.aero
Members: 160
Description: Aircraft operators; individuals and companies concerned with air taxi, charter, and commuter flight transportation. Promotes and represents members' interests before regulatory bodies. Maintains liaisons with other organizations in the air transport industry.
Formerly: Also Known As, General Aviation Manufacturers and Traders Association

01144
British Cactus and Succulent Society
BCSS
49 Chestnut Glen, Hornchurch, RM12 4HL, UK
Tel: 01708 447778
Email: secretary@bcss.org.uk
Website: http://www.bcss.org.uk
Members: 3000
Contact: Eddy A. Harris, Sec.
Fee: £15
Membership Type: full
Fee: £12
Membership Type: senior, junior
Description: Advances the education of the public by the study, culture and preparation of succulent plants and to promote the conservation of such plants.

01145
British Camelids Association
Puckpitts Farm, Tredington, Shipston-on-Stour, Warwickshire, CV36 4NH, UK
Tel: 01608 661893
Fax: 01608 661893
Email: camelids@btinternet.com
Website: http://www.llama.co.uk
Members: 244
Contact: Jane Brown, Sec.
Description: Represents owners, breeders and enthusiasts of llamas, alpacas, vicunas, guanacos and camels in the United Kingdom.
Formerly: Formerly, British Camelids Owners and Breeders Association
Publication: Journal
Publication title: Camelids Chronicle

01146
British Cardiovascular Society
BCS
9 Fitzroy Sq., London, W1T 5HW, UK
Tel: 020 73833887
Fax: 020 73880903
Email: enquiries@bcs.com
Website: http://www.bcs.com/pages
Contact: Keith Fox, Pres.
Fee: £220
Membership Type: ordinary
Fee: £140
Membership Type: non-physician, affiliate

Description: Strives to promote cardiovascular health. Sets clinical standards and conducts research in heart and circulatory diseases.
Formerly: Formerly, British Cardiac Society
Publication: Journal
Publication title: Heart

01147
British Cartographic Society
BCS

c/o Royal Geographical Society
1 Kensington Gore, London, SW9 2AR, UK
Tel: 0115 9328684
Fax: 0115 9328684
Email: admin@cartography.org.uk
Website: http://www.cartography.org.uk
Members: 700
Contact: Bob Lilley, Pres.
Fee: £35
Membership Type: ordinary
Fee: £15
Membership Type: associate
Description: Promotes the development of cartography. Facilitates pool information and exchange ideas on cartography. Stimulates the discussion on technical developments and advances of cartography.
Library Subject: cartography, GIS
Library Type: by appointment only
Publication: Journal
Publication title: The Cartographic Journal. Advertisements.
Meetings/Conventions: annual symposium – Exhibits.

01148
British Casino Association
BCA

38, Grosvenor Gardens, London, SW1W 0EB, UK
Tel: 020 77301055
Fax: 020 77301050
Email: director@nci-forum.co.uk
Website: http://www.britishcasinoassociation.org.uk
Members: 117
Contact: Penelope Cobham, Chm.
Fee: £17504
Membership Type: London casino
Fee: £1680
Membership Type: provincial casino, affiliate
Description: All licensed casinos in the UK. Provides a national trade association for holders of UK casino licenses.

01149
British Cattle Veterinary Association
BCVA

The Green, Gloucestershire, Frampton-on-Severn, GL2 7EP, UK
Tel: 01452 740816
Fax: 01452 741117
Email: office@cattlevet.co.uk
Website: http://www.bcva.eu
Members: 1400
Staff: 3
Contact: Keith Cutler, Pres.
Fee: £135
Membership Type: full (in UK)
Fee: £145
Membership Type: full (overseas including Ireland)
Description: Veterinary surgeons, research workers; mostly professional veterinary surgeons in practice. Concerned with education; promotion; research into cattle topics; promotion of cattle veterinarian; political opinion on cattle matters; source of information And reference on cattle topics.
Publication: Journal
Publication title: Cattle Practice
Meetings/Conventions: annual congress – Exhibits.

01150
British Cave Research Association
BCRA

The Old Methodist Chapel, Great Hucklow, Derbyshire, Buxton, SK17 8RG, UK
Tel: 01298 873810
Fax: 01298 873801
Email: bcra-enquiries@bcra.org.uk
Website: http://www.bcra.org.uk
Members: 1000
Contact: David Checkley, Chm.
Description: Scientists and sporting cavers interested in the scientific aspects of caves and karst. Aims to promote the study of caves and associated phenomena, and to publish the results of the researches carried out in the furtherance of these objects, for the benefit of the public.
Library Subject: caves, caving, karst
Library Type: reference
Publication: Journal
Publication title: Cave and Karst Science
Meetings/Conventions: British National Caving Conference – annual conference – Exhibits.

01151
British Caving Association
BCA

The Old Methodist Chapel, Great Hucklow, Derbyshire, Buxton, SK17 8RG, UK
Email: chairman@british-caving.org.uk
Website: http://www.british-caving.org.uk
Members: 9
Contact: Andy Eavis, Chm.
Description: Consists of 5 regional Caving Councils in the UK, plus 4 other, national caving bodies, which covers, education, research, cave rescue and mine exploration; 340 caving clubs. Covers, safety, conservation, equipment, training, access and liaison with many bodies such as the Sports Council, Central Council for Physical Recreation, English Nature, etc.
Library Subject: caving, training, conservation
Library Type: not open to the public
Publication: Handbook
Publication title: Cave Conservation Handbook

01152
British Cement Association
BCA

Riverside House, 4 Meadows Business Park, Station Approach, Blackwater, Surrey, Camberley, GU17 9AB, UK
Tel: 01276 608700
Fax: 01276 608701
Email: mpacement@mineralproducts.org
Website: http://www.cementindustry.co.uk
Members: 4
Staff: 32
Contact: Mike Gilbert, CEO
Description: Represents the interests of the UK's cement industry in its relations with government, the European Union and other relevant organizations.
Library Subject: concrete materials, technology
Library Type: reference
Formerly: Formerly, Cement and Concrete Association
Publication: Journal
Publication title: Concrete Quarterly

01153
British Centre of the International Theatre Institute

Goldsmith College, Univ. of London, Lewisham Way, New Cross, London, SE14 6NW, UK
Tel: 020 79197171
Email: iti@gold.ac.uk
Website: http://www.gold.ac.uk
Members: 400
Staff: 1
Contact: Neville Shulman, Dir.
Fee: £10
Membership Type: student
Fee: £85
Membership Type: organization, large company, university department
Description: Arts professionals, academics and anyone with an interest in international performing arts. Aims to promote cultural exchange between nations and thereby deepen mutual understanding and participate in the strengthening of peace. Provides information and contacts worldwide.

01154
British Ceramic Confederation
BCC

Federation House, Station Rd., Stoke-on-Trent, ST4 2SA, UK
Tel: 01782 744631
Fax: 01782 744102
Email: bcc@ceramfed.co.uk
Website: http://www.ceramfed.co.uk
Members: 150
Staff: 9
Contact: Laura Cohen, Chief Exec.
Description: Manufacturers of ceramic products in the United Kingdom. Representative body for manufacturers of ceramic products in the United Kingdom, providing representation and services in the areas of industrial relations, health and safety, environment, energy, trade etc.

01155
British Chambers of Commerce
BCC

65 Petty France, London, SW1H 9EU, UK
Tel: 020 76545800
Fax: 020 76545819
Email: info@britishchambers.org.uk
Website: http://www.britishchambers.org.uk
Members: 61
Staff: 20
Contact: Neville Reyner, Pres.
Description: Represents businesses of all sizes and sectors in UK. Works for a positive business environment.
Publication: Survey
Publication title: Economic Survey
Meetings/Conventions: World of Business – annual conference – Exhibits.

01156

British Chelonia Group

BCG

PO Box 1176, Chippenham, SN15 1XB, UK
Email: enquiries@britishcheloniagroup.org.uk
Website: http://www.britishcheloniagroup.org.uk
Contact: Don Freeman, Chm.
Fee: £13
Membership Type: regular
Fee: £18
Membership Type: family, regular contributing
Description: Promotes research on tortoises, terrapins and turtles.
Publication: Journal
Publication title: Testudo

01157

British Chemical Engineering Contractors Association

BCECA

1 Regent St., London, SW1Y 4NR, UK
Tel: 020 78396514
Fax: 020 79303466
Email: rod.dean@bceca.org.uk
Website: http://www.bceca.org.uk
Members: 18
Staff: 2
Contact: Rod Dean, Dir.
Description: Principal companies in the UK which provide engineering, procurement, construction and project management services to all the process industries, i.e. oil, gas, chemical, pharmaceutical, power, water etc. Aims to improve public understanding of members' activities and to provide a focal point for representation of members' interests to clients, the UK Government, European Community and international institutions and other interested parties.
Publication: Magazine
Publication title: Target

01158

British Cheque Cashers Association

BCCA

PO Box 3414, Chester, CH1 9BF, UK
Tel: 01244 505904
Fax: 01244 505909
Email: info@bcca.co.uk
Website: http://www.bcca.co.uk
Members: 400
Staff: 2
Contact: Geoff Holland, Chief Exec.
Description: Provides representation of its members' interests to government whether in London or Brussels - and its regulatory bodies. Also seeks to enhance understanding of the industry and to promote the interests of check cashers generally by helping to shape a climate of opinion which enables members to conduct their business profitably.
Publication: Newsletter
Publication title: BCCA News. Advertisements.

01159

British Chiropractic Association

BCA

59 Castle St., Berkshire, Reading, RG1 7SN, UK
Tel: 0118 9505950
Fax: 0118 9588946
Email: enquiries@chiropractic-uk.co.uk
Website: http://www.chiropractic-uk.co.uk/default.aspx?m=1&mi=1
Members: 860
Staff: 4
Description: Complementary medicine practitioners/chiropractors. Concerned with treatment of spinal disorders by specialised manipulative techniques.
Publication title: Contact

01160

British Christmas Tree Growers Association

13 Wolrige Rd., Edinburgh, EH16 6HX, UK
Tel: 0131 6641100
Fax: 0131 6642669
Email: rogermhay@btinternet.com
Website: http://www.christmastree.org.uk
Members: 350
Staff: 1
Fee: £150
Membership Type: associate
Fee: £125
Membership Type: grower (with sales of less than 5,000 trees)
Description: Christmas tree growers, (landowners, farmers, small holders) associate members, nurserymen, wholesalers etc. Aims to ensure that British growers produce top quality trees. Carries out market research, assists and co-ordinates marketing and reviews prospects. Represents the interests of British growers, advises on the growing and care of Christmas trees and organizes Open Days, Symposiums and overseas visits.

01161

British Cleaning Council

BCC

478-480 Salisbury House, London Wall, London, EC2M 5QQ, UK
Tel: 020 79209640
Fax: 020 76386990
Email: info@britishcleaningcouncil.org
Website: http://www.britishcleaningcouncil.org
Members: 19
Contact: Trevor Iles, Pres.
Description: Any recognized trade association or research or educational body or institution concerned with industrial, commercial or institutional cleaning. Provides a forum for all constituent bodies to meet together to further the aims of their industry as a whole and takes responsibility for external relations at home and abroad on matters of common interest to members.
Publication: Newsletter
Publication title: The Voice

01162

British Coatings Federation

BCF

The Stables, Thorncroft Manor, Thorncroft Dr., Surrey, Leatherhead, KT22 8JB, UK
Tel: 01372 700848
Fax: 01372 700851
Email: enquiry@bcf.co.uk
Website: http://www.coatings.org.uk
Members: 130
Staff: 12
Contact: Tony Mash, CEO
Fee: £772.5
Membership Type: associate (minimum)
Fee: £4892.5
Membership Type: associate (maximum)
Description: Full - paint and printing ink manufacturers within UK. Promotes the interests of the UK coatings manufacturing industry. Provides a forum for discussing environmental health safety and technical and commercial issues. Provides legislative advice and information.
Formerly: Formerly, Paintmakers Association

01163

British Colour Makers Association

BCMA

19, Wyatville Ave., Derbyshire, Buxton, SK17 6WJ, UK
Tel: 01298 27028
Email: info@bcma.org.uk
Website: http://www.bcma.org.uk
Members: 20
Staff: 1
Contact: Adrian Baker, Chm.
Description: Major UK pigment manufacturers. Aims to maintain contact with legislative bodies; to ensure that the pigment industry is fully up to date with current government and EC policy. Also responsible for ensuring that the industry acts in a responsible manner.

01164

British Comparative Literature Association

BCLA

University of Manchester, Dept. of French Studies, Oxford Rd., Manchester, M13 9PL, UK
Email: penny.brown@manchester.ac.uk
Website: http://www.bcla.org
Contact: Penny Brown, Sec.
Fee: £35
Membership Type: employed
Fee: £21
Membership Type: postgraduate, unwaged
Description: Promotes the scholarly study of literature without confinement to national and linguistic boundaries, and in relation to other disciplines.
Publication: Journal
Publication title: Comparative Criticism

01165

British Compressed Air Society

BCAS

33/34 Devonshire St., London, W1G 6PY, UK
Tel: 020 79352464
Fax: 020 79353077
Email: enquiries@bcas.org.uk
Website: http://www.bcas.org.uk
Members: 93
Staff: 3
Contact: Chris Dee, Exec. Dir.
Fee: £1495
Membership Type: full company
Fee: £975
Membership Type: associate company
Description: Manufacturers and distributors and end-users of compressed air, gas, vacuum, and related equipment in the UK. Seeks to help members develop their professional competence.
Library Subject: compressors, vacuum pumps
Library Type: open to the public
Publication: Book
Publication title: Installation Guide, 5th Ed.

01166

British Compressed Gases Association BCGA

1 Gleneagles House, Vernongate, Derby, DE1 1UP, UK
Tel: 01332 225120
Fax: 01332 225101
Email: bcga.admin@bcga.co.uk
Website: http://www.bcga.co.uk
Members: 60
Staff: 3
Description: Trade Association representing companies engaged in the manufacture, containment, distribution and application of industrial, food and medical gases. Promotes the advancement of technology and safe practice in the manufacture, containment, distribution and application of industrial, food and medical gases; to participate and provide advice in UK and European Standards-making and legislative processes; to offer practical guidance to users of industrial gases and equipment.
Library Subject: codes of practice, guidance notes
Library Type: open to the public
Publication: Manuals
Publication title: Codes of Practice
Meetings/Conventions: annual conference – Exhibits.

01167

British Computer Association of the Blind BCAB

c/o RNIB
58-72 John Bright St., Birmingham, B1 1BN, UK
Tel: 0845 4308627
Email: info@bcab.org.uk
Website: http://www.bcab.org.uk
Members: 230
Contact: Mike Townsend, Pres.
Fee: £21
Membership Type: full
Fee: £10.5
Membership Type: associate
Description: Provides general assistance and advice on information technology issues for blind and visually impaired persons. Organizes training courses. Engages in lobbying.

01168

British Computer Society BCS

North Star House, 1st Fl., Block D, N Star Ave., Swindon, SN2 1FA, UK
Tel: 01793 417417
Fax: 01793 417444
Email: bcshq@hq.bcs.org.uk
Website: http://www.bcs.org
Members: 70000
Staff: 120
Contact: David Clarke, Chief Exec.
Fee: £52
Membership Type: associate
Fee: £25
Membership Type: student
Description: Information technology professionals accredited by the society or by society-approved courses. Aims to compile and keep members abreast of technical developments so as to influence computing in computing professions. Strives to further information exchange and to inspire high technical and ethical standards. Acts as a professional qualifying body by accrediting degree and diploma courses; offers accreditation exams. Disseminates expert advice to European Economic Community and British government and industry representatives on issues such as computer misuse, safety-critical systems, computers for the disabled, and quality control of software engineering.
Library Subject: engineering, electronics, manufacturing
Library Type: open to the public
Publication: Journal
Publication title: Computer Journal

01169

British Confectioners' Association BCA

Home Farm Business Centre, Unit 4, Brighton, BN1 9HU, UK
Website: http://www.the-bca.com
Members: 60
Contact: Tim Cutress, Sec.
Description: Promotes the study of the art of flour confectionery and baking. Conducts lectures, demonstrations and discussions and provides opportunities of social intercourse among the members. Protects and promotes the interests of the flour confectionery trade.

01170

British Constructional Steelwork Association BCSA

4 Whitehall Ct., Westminster, London, SW1A 2ES, UK
Tel: 020 78398566
Fax: 020 79761634
Email: gillian.mitchell@steelconstruction.org
Website: http://www.steelconstruction.org
Members: 200
Staff: 10
Contact: Gillian Mitchell, Deputy Dir. Gen.
Description: Represents the steel construction industry.
Publication: Directory
Publication title: Directory for Specifiers and Buyers

01171

British Contact Lens Association BCLA

7/8 Market Pl., London, W1W 8AG, UK
Tel: 020 75806661
Fax: 020 75806669
Email: vfreeman@bcla.org.uk
Website: http://www.bcla.org.uk
Members: 1800
Contact: Vivien Freeman, Sec. Gen.
Fee: £101-110
Membership Type: individual
Fee: £20
Membership Type: student
Description: Promotes the contact lens industry. Educates the public and the industry about contact lens technology, its features and benefits. Supports research and development of quality contact lens materials. Participates in seminars and conferences dealing with eye health care.

01172

British Contract Furnishing Association BCFA

Project House, 25 W Wycombe Rd., Buckinghamshire, High Wycombe, HP11 2LQ, UK
Tel: 01494 896790
Fax: 01494 896799
Email: enquiries@bcfa.org.uk
Website: http://www.thebcfa.com
Members: 223
Staff: 5
Contact: Colin Watson, Managing Dir.
Fee: £500-5560
Membership Type: company (based on contract sales turnover)
Description: Trade association of manufacturers and suppliers of contract furnishings, including carpets, lighting, furniture, bedding, blinds, wallcoverings, and floor coverings. Promotes and protects members' interests.
Library Type: reference
Publication: Membership Directory
Publication title: Contract Furnishing Directory. Advertisements.

01173

British Contract Manufacturers and Packers Association BCMPA

St. Mary's Ct., The Broadway, Buckinghamshire, Amersham, HP7 0UT, UK
Tel: 01494 582013
Fax: 01494 726256
Email: info@bcmpa.org.uk
Website: http://www.bcmpa.org.uk
Members: 43
Staff: 1
Contact: Rodney Steel, Chief Exec.
Fee: £600-1938
Membership Type: company (based on annual turnover)
Description: Promotes the technical, trade, and commercial interests of British contract manufacturers and packers.

01174

British Copyright Council

29-33 Berners St., London, W1T 3AB, UK
Tel: 01986 788122
Fax: 01986 788847
Email: secretary@britishcopyright.org
Website: http://www.britishcopyright.org
Members: 34
Staff: 1
Contact: Janet Ibbotson, CEO/Sec.
Description: Serves as a forum for the bodies speaking for those who create or hold interests or copyright in literary, dramatic, musical or artistic works and those who perform them.
Publication: Booklet
Publication title: Guide to the Law of Copyright and Rights in Performances

01175

British Council BC

10 Spring Gardens, London, SW1A 2BN, UK
Tel: 0161 9577755
Fax: 0161 9577762

Email: general.enquiries@britishcouncil.org
Website: http://www.britishcouncil.org/new
Staff: 7500
Contact: Martin Davidson, Chief Exec.
Description: Promotes increased understanding of the United Kingdom and the English language worldwide. Facilitates educational, technological, cultural, and scientific cooperation between the United Kingdom and other countries.

01176

British Council for Offices
BCO

78-79 Leadenhall St., London, EC3A 3DH, UK
Tel: 020 72830125
Fax: 020 76261553
Email: mail@bco.org.uk
Website: http://www.bco.org.uk
Contact: Gerald Kaye, Pres.
Fee: £845
Membership Type: corporate
Fee: £195
Membership Type: individual
Description: Seeks to research, develop and communicate best practice in all aspects of the office sector. Provides a forum for the discussion and debate of issues affecting office sector. Advances understanding of effective office space.
Publication: Annual Report
Publication title: Annual Review

01177

British Council of Shopping Centres
BCSC

1 Queen Anne's Gate, Westminster, London, SW1H 9BT, UK
Tel: 020 72221122
Fax: 020 72273452
Email: info@bcsc.org.uk
Website: http://www.bcsc.org.uk/index.asp
Members: 1450
Contact: Michael Green, Chief Exec.
Fee: £770
Membership Type: corporate
Fee: £135
Membership Type: affiliate (35 or over), local authority, retailer, shopping centre manager
Description: Represents the shopping center industry, i.e., funding institutions, managing agents, designers, retailers, architects, lawyers and construction/engineering. Promotes the development and improvement of shopping facilities.

01178

British Cryogenics Council
BCC

PO Box 41, Leatherhead, KT22 9YY, UK
Tel: 01372 376544
Fax: 01372 376544
Email: admin@bcryo.org.uk
Website: http://www.bcryo.org.uk/index.php
Members: 100
Staff: 1
Contact: John Vandore, Treas.
Fee: £10
Membership Type: regular
Fee: £5
Membership Type: student, unemployed, retired individual
Description: Promotes knowledge in low temperature science and technology. Supports the application of cryogenic processes.
Formerly: Formerly, British Cryoengineering Society
Publication: Book
Publication title: Cryogenics Fluids Databook

01179

British Crystallographic Association
BCA

c/o Northern Networking Events
Braeview House, 9/11 Braeview Pl., Glenfinnan Ste., East Kilbride, G74 3XH, UK
Tel: 01355 244966
Fax: 01355 249959
Email: bca@glasconf.demon.co.uk
Website: http://crystallography.org.uk
Members: 800
Contact: Elspeth F. Garman, Pres.
Fee: £20
Membership Type: full
Fee: £10
Membership Type: concession
Description: Crystallographers in universities, research establishments and industry, with interests in the field of molecular biology, chemistry, physics, mineralogy, materials science, etc. Aims to advance the science of crystallography.
Publication: Newsletter
Publication title: Crystallography News. Advertisements.

01180

British Culinary Federation
BCF

PO Box 10532, Alcester, B50 4ZY, UK
Tel: 01789 491218
Email: secretary@britishculinaryfederation.co.uk
Website: http://www.britishculinaryfederation.co.uk
Contact: Jayne Mottram, Admin.
Fee: £20
Membership Type: junior
Fee: £40
Membership Type: associate
Description: Membership is available at several levels, starting with students up through retired members of the catering community. Promotes culinary skills throughout the industry, and gain recognition for members as high skilled professionals in the catering industry. Hosts luncheons, competitions and conferences.

01181

British Dam Society
BDS

c/o Institution of Civil Engineers
1 Great George St., Westminster, London, SW1P 3AA, UK
Tel: 020 76652234
Fax: 020 77991325
Email: bds@ice.org.uk
Website: http://www.britishdams.org
Members: 500
Contact: Peter Mason, Chm.
Fee: £35
Membership Type: standard
Fee: £16
Membership Type: retired
Description: Aims to give access to worldwide experience and knowledge in the field of dam and reservoir engineering.
Formerly: Formerly, British National Committee on Large Dams
Meetings/Conventions: annual meeting

01182

British Dance Council
BDC

Terpsichore House, 240 Merton Rd., S Wimbledon, London, SW19 1EQ, UK
Tel: 020 85450085
Fax: 020 85450225
Email: secretary@british-dance-council.org
Website: http://www.british-dance-council.org
Members: 18
Staff: 2
Contact: Len Armstrong, Hon. Pres.
Description: Amateur and professional dancers' associations; dance teaching associations; companies with a professional interest in the ballroom dancing world; honorary members elected by virtue of a lifetime commitment to dancing. Enables teachers to work together on uniform lines. Formulates and administers the rules for competition dancing and co-ordinates the promotion of schemes to publicise the social styles of ballroom dancing.
Formerly: Formerly, British Council of Ballroom Dancing

01183

British Deaf Association
BDA

10 Fl. Coventry Point, Market Way, Coventry, CV1 1EA, UK
Tel: 024 76550936
Fax: 024 76221541
Email: bda@bda.org.uk
Website: http://bda.org.uk
Members: 6500
Staff: 50
Contact: Terry Riley, Chm.
Fee: £2.5
Membership Type: youth (up to 17 years old)
Fee: £5
Membership Type: standard
Description: Mainly profoundly deaf people who use sign language as their means of communication. Aims to serve and protect the deaf community.
Publication: Newsletter
Publication title: British Deaf News. Advertisements.

01184

British Deer Society
BDS

The Walled Garden, Burgate Manor, Fordingbridge, SP6 1EF, UK
Tel: 01425 655434
Email: h.q@bds.org.uk
Website: http://www.bds.org.uk
Members: 6000
Staff: 5
Contact: Mark Nicolson, Chm.
Fee: £53
Membership Type: individual - full
Fee: £20
Membership Type: student
Description: Concerned with the study and the dissemination of the knowledge of deer, the promotion of proper and humane methods of management of deer and the provision of advice on all matters related to deer.
Publication: Journal
Publication title: Deer Journal

01185

British Dental Association BDA

64 Wimpole St., London, W1G 8YS, UK
Tel: 0207 9350875
Fax: 0207 4875232
Email: enquiries@bda.org
Website: http://www.bda.org
Members: 20000
Staff: 70
Contact: Amarjit Gill, Pres.
Fee: £483
Membership Type: ordinary
Fee: £45
Membership Type: student (studying for 4-5 years)
Description: Professional association and trade union for dental surgeons in the United Kingdom. Promotes dentistry and the provision of dental services to the public. Represents members' interests individually and collectively before the government.
Library Subject: dentistry
Library Type: reference
Publication: Newsletter
Publication title: BDA News. Advertisements.

01186

British Dental Practice Managers' Association BDPMA

3 Kestrel Ct., Waterwells Dr., Waterwells Business Park, Gloucester, GL2 2AT, UK
Tel: 01452 886364
Fax: 01452 886468
Email: info@bdpma.org.uk
Website: http://www.bdpma.org.uk
Members: 700
Staff: 1
Contact: Amelia Bray, Chair
Description: Promotes cooperation and provides a way to communicate and support those actively involved in Dental Practice Management.
Publication: Magazine
Publication title: Networking. Advertisements.

01187

British Dental Trade Association BDTA

Mineral Ln., Chesham, HP5 1NL, UK
Tel: 01494 782873
Fax: 01494 786659
Email: admin@bdta.org.uk
Website: http://www.bdta.org.uk
Members: 106
Staff: 4
Contact: Tony Reed, Exec. Dir.
Description: Companies manufacturing dental equipment and supplies. Establishes international standards and technical harmonization for dental equipment. Represents members' interests before government bodies, international agencies, and the public. Maintains liaison with organizations representing dentists, dental technicians, and dental supply dealers and distributors. Compiles statistics.
Library Type: not open to the public
Publication: Magazine
Publication title: Dental Trader. Advertisements.
Meetings/Conventions: Dental Showcase – biennial meeting – Exhibits.

01188

British Design and Art Direction D&AD

9 Graphite Sq., Vauxhall Walk, London, SE11 5EE, UK
Tel: 020 78401111
Fax: 020 78400840
Email: contact@dandad.co.uk
Website: http://www.dandad.org
Members: 2300
Staff: 22
Fee: £160
Membership Type: full, associate
Fee: £40
Membership Type: student
Description: Leading creatives from design and advertising communities are full members; non creatives who are recognized as encouraging and supporting D&AD's aims are associate members. Works on behalf of the advertising and design communities. Sets standards of creative excellence, promotes this concept in the business arena and educates and inspires the next creative generation.
Formerly: Formerly, Designers and Art Directors Association of the U.K.
Publication title: British Design & Art Direction Showreel of Award Winning Ads

01189

British Dietetic Association BDA

Charles House, 5th Fl., 148/9 Great Charles St. Queensway, Birmingham, B3 3HT, UK
Tel: 0121 2008080
Fax: 0121 2008081
Email: info@bda.uk.com
Website: http://www.bda.uk.com
Members: 5500
Staff: 25
Contact: Dame Barbara Clayton, Pres.
Fee: £240
Membership Type: full
Fee: £121
Membership Type: affiliate
Description: Professional registered dietitians. Promotes advancement of the science and practice of dietetics and related subjects. Sponsors training and educational programs. Arranges meetings, refresher courses, and study conferences. Provides liaison between dietitians in the United Kingdom and other countries.
Publication: Magazine
Publication title: Career Choices. Advertisements.

01190

British Display Society BDS

14-18 Heralds Way, Town Ctre., South Woodham Ferrers, Essex, CM3 5TQ, UK
Tel: 020 88562030
Email: enquiries@britishdisplay.co.uk
Website: http://www.britishdisplaysociety.co.uk
Staff: 2
Contact: Bernard Brandham, Chm.
Description: Practitioners in display - retail, point of sale, exhibition design -tutors and students of display design. Concerned with the education and promotion of display standards.
Publication: Newsletter
Publication title: BDS Newsletter

01191

British Doll Artists Association BDA

26 Foxholes, Rudgwick, RH12 3DX, UK
Tel: 01403 823596
Email: mahar.likha@virgin.net
Website: http://www.britishdollartists.org.uk/index.htm
Members: 34
Contact: Marian Paiso-Ironmonger, Sec.
Fee: £30
Membership Type: full
Fee: £35
Membership Type: foreign associate
Description: Artists who make totally original dolls. Promotes the work of members via annual exhibitions, slide presentations and the illustrated BDA Directory.

01192

British Dragonfly Society BDS

c/o Henry Curry, Sec.
23, Bowker Way, Whittlesey, Peterborough, PE7 1PY, UK
Tel: 017 33204286
Email: bdssecretary@dragonflysoc.org.uk
Website: http://www.dragonflysoc.org.uk/index.html
Members: 1507
Staff: 1
Contact: Pam Taylor, Pres.
Fee: £15
Membership Type: local
Fee: £20
Membership Type: overseas
Description: Amateur and professional naturalists and conservation enthusiasts. Aims to promote and encourage the study and conservation of dragonflies and their natural habitats, especially in the United Kingdom.
Publication: Journal
Publication title: British Dragonfly Society Journal

01193

British Driving Society BDS

83 New Rd., Helmingham, Suffolk, Stowmarket, IP14 6EA, UK
Tel: 01473 892001
Fax: 01473 892005
Email: email@britishdrivingsociety.co.uk
Website: http://www.britishdrivingsociety.co.uk
Members: 5750
Staff: 2
Contact: Tess Styles, Exec. Sec.
Fee: £28
Membership Type: adult
Fee: £45
Membership Type: dual
Description: Encourages and assists those interested in the driving of all equines.
Publication: Yearbook
Publication title: Annual Shows Almanac. Advertisements.

01194
British Dyslexia Association
BDA

Unit 8, Bracknell Beeches, Old Bracknell Ln., Bracknell, RG12 7BW, UK
Tel: 0845 2519003
Fax: 0845 2519005
Email: admin@bdadyslexia.org.uk
Website: http://www.bdadyslexia.org.uk
Members: 10000
Staff: 39
Contact: Paul Marsden, Chief Exec.
Fee: £40
Membership Type: individual (in UK)
Fee: £50
Membership Type: individual (overseas)
Description: Empowers all dyslexic people to reach their full potential. Disseminates all the latest thinking on dyslexia through its wide and diverse networks and uses its knowledge and experience to influence policy and bring about lasting change. Works to advise and support dyslexic people and those they come into contact with at a local level. Works both on the strategic and operational levels to ensure that dyslexic people are heard, valued and recognised as being major assets to society.
Publication: Magazine
Publication title: Contact

01195
British Ecological Society
BES

12 Roger St., London, WC1N 2JU, UK
Tel: 0207 6852500
Fax: 0207 6852501
Email: info@britishecologicalsociety.org
Website: http://www.britishecologicalsociety.org
Members: 4000
Staff: 13
Contact: Hazel J. Norman, Exec. Dir.
Fee: £20
Membership Type: student/reduced/retired
Fee: £40
Membership Type: regular
Description: Teachers, local authority ecologists, research scientists, conservationists, environmental consultants, and others with an interest in ecology, natural history, or the environment. Promotes the science of ecology through research, publications and conferences and uses findings of such research to educate the public and influence policy decisions that involve ecological matters.
Publication: Journal
Publication title: Journal of Animal Ecology

01196
British Educational Communications and Technology Agency
BECTA

Science Park, Millburn Hill Rd., Coventry, CV4 7JJ, UK
Tel: 024 76416994
Fax: 024 76411418
Email: customerservices@becta.org.uk
Website: http://www.becta.org.uk
Contact: Stephen Crowne, Chief Exec.
Description: Supports the UK government and national organizations in the use and development of ICT in education in order to raise standards, widen access, improve skills, and encourage effective management. Works in partnership to develop the National Grid for Learning strategy.
Formerly: Formerly, National Council for Educational Technology

01197
British Educational Leadership, Management and Administration Society
BELMAS

Victoria Hall, Rm. 50, Norfolk St., Sheffield, S1 2JB, UK
Tel: 0114 2799926
Fax: 0114 2796868
Email: info@belmas.org.uk
Website: http://www.belmas.org.uk
Members: 550
Contact: Richard Davis, Business Mgr.
Fee: £49
Membership Type: individual, fellowship
Fee: £30
Membership Type: student, retired
Description: Promotes leadership in organizations with an educational purpose and provides training, advice and consultancy in leadership. Conducts research.
Publication: Journal
Publication title: Educational Management Administration & Leadership

01198
British Educational Research Association
BERA

S Pk. Rd., Cheshire, Macclesfield, SK11 6SH, UK
Tel: 01625 664543
Fax: 01625 664510
Email: admin@bera.ac.uk
Website: http://www.bera.ac.uk
Members: 2200
Contact: John Gardner, Pres.
Fee: £65
Membership Type: ordinary
Fee: £24
Membership Type: student, retired
Description: Educational researchers in UK and abroad. Encourages the pursuit of educational research and its applications for the improvement of educational practice and the general benefit of the community.
Publication: Journal
Publication title: British Educational Research Journal

01199
British Educational Suppliers Association
BESA

20 Beaufort Ct., Admirals Way, London, E14 9XL, UK
Tel: 020 75374997
Fax: 020 75374846
Email: besa@besa.org.uk
Website: http://www.besa.org.uk/besa/home/index.jsp
Members: 300
Staff: 10
Contact: Dominic Savage, Dir. Gen.
Description: Represents United Kingdom-based manufacturers and distributors of equipment, materials, consumables, furniture, technology, ICT hardware and software related services for the education market.
Publication: Book
Publication title: BESABook

01200
British Egg Industry Council
BEIC

c/o British Egg Information Service
52A Cromwell Rd., London, SW7 5BE, UK
Tel: 020 70528899
Website: http://www.britegg.co.uk
Members: 12
Staff: 4
Description: Represents the interests of the egg industry. Lobbies government and the European Commission. Fosters research.

01201
British Electrostatic Control Association
BECA

136 Hagley Rd., Edgbaston, Birmingham, B16 9PN, UK
Tel: 0121 4544141
Fax: 0121 4544949
Email: sparker@cvdfk.com
Website: http://www.beca.co.uk
Fee: £250
Membership Type: full
Fee: £50
Membership Type: associate
Description: Works to advance the theory and practice of electrical overstress avoidance, with emphasis on electrostatic discharge phenomena. Focuses on the effects of both material and manmade electromagnetic threats on electronic components, subsystems, and systems. Promotes exchange of technical information and cooperation among members. Develops standards; conducts educational programs.

01202
British Electrotechnical and Allied Manufacturers' Association
BEAMA

Westminster Tower, 3 Albert Embankment, London, SE1 7SL, UK
Tel: 020 77933000
Fax: 020 77933003
Email: info@beama.org.uk
Website: http://www.beama.org.uk
Members: 500
Contact: Howard Porter, CEO
Description: Provides a wide range of services to both members and to the industry including legal, statistics, standards, commercials, oversea marketing, technology, environmental and much more.

01203
British Endodontic Society
BES

PO Box 707, Gerrards Cross, SL9 0XS, UK
Tel: 01494 581542
Fax: 01494 581542
Website: http://www.britishendodonticsociety.org.uk
Contact: Howard Lloyd, Pres.
Fee: £90
Membership Type: regular
Fee: £120
Membership Type: joint
Description: Works to promote and advanced endodontology. Assists the dental profession, institutes guidelines on the standard of care and current good practice, and

offers advice on the training requirements in endodontics.
Publication: Journal
Publication title: International Endodontic Journal

01204
British Engraved Stationery Association
BESA
Farringdon Point, 29-35 Farringdon Rd., London, EC1M 3JF, UK
Tel: 0207 9158400
Email: chris.patefield@bpif.org.uk
Website: http://www.engravedstationery.org
Members: 45
Contact: Chris Patefield, Contact
Description: Promotes the British Engraved Stationery industry more widely throughout the print and design industries. Encourages best practice and creates an environment which enables the exchange of views and information.

01205
British Entomological and Natural History Society
BENHS
c/o The Pelham-Clinton Bldg.
Dinton Pastures Country Park, Davis St., Hurst, Reading, RG10 0TH, UK
Email: enquiries@benhs.org.uk
Website: http://www.benhs.org.uk
Members: 900
Contact: John Muggleton, Hon. Sec.
Fee: £19
Membership Type: ordinary, corporate
Fee: £6
Membership Type: junior, under 18 years old
Description: Amateur and professional entomologists, seeks to promote and advance research in the field of entomology, invertebrate conservation and taxonomy, primarily in the British Isles and mainland Europe.
Publication: Journal
Publication title: British Journal of Entomology and Natural History
Meetings/Conventions: monthly meeting

01206
British Epilepsy Association
New Anstey House, Gate Way Dr., Yeadon, Leeds, LS19 7XY, UK
Tel: 0113 2108800
Fax: 0113 3910300
Email: helpline@epilepsy.org.uk
Website: http://www.epilepsy.org.uk
Members: 14000
Staff: 66
Contact: Margaret Anstey, VP
Fee: £17
Membership Type: individual
Fee: £45
Membership Type: professional
Description: Association is owned by its members. Provides care in the community for the country's estimated 456,000 people with epilepsy. Provides epilepsy counselling, advice, information, and the National Epilepsy Helpline. Maintains around 100 regional groups and branches - regional office in Northern Ireland and Wales. National information centre provides extensive service to public and professionals.
Formerly: Also Known As, Epilepsy Action
Publication: Magazine
Publication title: Epilepsy Professional

01207
British Equestrian Trade Association
BETA
Stockeld Pk., W Yorkshire, Wetherby, LS22 4AW, UK
Tel: 01937 587062
Fax: 01937 582728
Email: claire@beta-uk.org
Website: http://www.beta-uk.org
Members: 700
Staff: 11
Contact: Claire Williams, Exec. Dir./Sec.
Description: Members are equestrian retailers and manufacturers. Represents and promotes the British equestrian trade, nationally and internationally; promotes safer riding through better equipment and protection; promotes riding generally and offers the riding public improving standards of service.
Publication: Catalog
Publication title: The Beta International Trade Fair

01208
British Equine Veterinary Association
BEVA
Mulberry House, 31 Market St., Cambridgeshire, Fordham, CB7 5LQ, UK
Tel: 01638 723555
Fax: 01638 724043
Email: info@beva.org.uk
Website: http://www.beva.org.uk
Members: 1400
Contact: Sandy Love, Chm.
Fee: £199-220
Membership Type: ordinary
Fee: £275-325
Membership Type: associate
Description: Practising equine vets, members of academia, veterinary universities and members of pharmaceutical companies, home and overseas. Promotes the cultural, scientific and professional activities of veterinary surgeons and others interested in equine practice, welfare, teaching and research.
Publication: Newsletter
Publication title: BEVA Newsletter

01209
British Expertise
10 Grosvenor Gardens, London, SW1W 0DH, UK
Tel: 020 78241920
Fax: 020 78241929
Email: mail@britishexpertise.org
Website: http://www.britishexpertise.org/bx/pages/bx.php
Members: 280
Staff: 11
Contact: David Howell, Chm.
Fee: £543
Membership Type: individual
Fee: £750-9995
Membership Type: corporate (based on the number of staff)
Description: Promotes British consultancy and construction companies worldwide. Facilitates contact with members seeking consultancy or contractor contacts and advice. Maintains contact with governments and international institutions.
Formerly: Formerly, British Consultants and Construction Bureau
Publication: Annual Report
Publication title: Annual Review

01210
British Exporters Association
BEXA
Broadway House, Tothill St., London, SW1H 9NQ, UK
Tel: 020 72225419
Fax: 020 77992468
Email: hughbailey@bexa.co.uk
Website: http://www.bexa.co.uk
Contact: Richard Needham, Pres.
Description: Capital goods manufacturers; international trading/export houses; banks interested in international trade finance; export credit insurers. Lobbying on behalf of export houses, and larger manufacturing exporters and banks involved in international trade finance; puts manufacturers in touch with export houses.
Publication: Directory
Publication title: Directory of Export Buyers in the UK

01211
British False Memory Society
BFMS
Wiltshire, Bradford-on-Avon, BA15 1NF, UK
Tel: 01225 868682
Fax: 01225 862251
Email: bfms@bfms.org.uk
Website: http://www.bfms.org.uk
Members: 1200
Staff: 4
Contact: Madeline Greenhalgh, Dir.
Description: Seeks to raise awareness of the dangers of recovered memory therapy. Collaborates with associated organizations. Offers telephone support to family members falsely accused of childhood sexual abuse. Fosters research.
Library Subject: childhood sexual abuse, recovered memory therapy
Library Type: reference

01212
British Federation of Audio
BFA
PO Box 365, Farnham, GU10 2BD, UK
Tel: 01428 714616
Fax: 01428 717599
Website: http://www.british-audio.org.uk
Members: 44
Staff: 3
Contact: Lord Gowrie, Honorary Pres.
Description: Represents manufacturers and distributors of branded hi-fi/audio goods. Works to promote the audio industry through collective action. Collects statistics and other data relating to the trade and serves as a forum for communications between manufacturers, distributors and dealers.

01213
British Federation of Brass Bands
BFBB
Maple Estate, Unit 12, Stocks Ln., Barnsley, S75 2BL, UK
Tel: 01226 771015
Email: natoffice@bfbb.co.uk
Website: http://www.bfbb.co.uk
Members: 326
Staff: 4
Contact: Peter Parkes, Pres.
Fee: £100
Membership Type: band
Fee: £20
Membership Type: associate
Description: Represents the interests of brass bands in the United Kingdom.
Publication: Directory
Publication title: Directory of Brass Bands. Advertisements.

01214
British Federation of Women Graduates
BFWG
4 Mandeville Courtyard, 142 Battersea Park Rd., London, SW11 4NB, UK
Tel: 020 74988037
Email: office@bfwg.org.uk
Website: http://www.bfwg.org.uk
Members: 600
Contact: Marianne Haslegrave, Pres.
Fee: £29
Membership Type: ordinary, junior
Fee: £48
Membership Type: ordinary
Description: Promotes women's opportunities in education and public life. Works as part of an international organization to improve the lives of women and girls. Fosters local, national and international friendship.
Formerly: Formerly, British Federation of University Women

01215
British Fertility Society
BFS
22 Apex Ct., Bradley Stoke, Bristol, BS32 4JT, UK
Tel: 01454 642217
Fax: 01454 642222
Email: bfs@bioscientifica.com
Website: http://www.fertility.org.uk
Members: 800
Contact: Peter Brinsden, Pres.
Fee: £135
Membership Type: associate, clinician
Fee: £65
Membership Type: counsellor, nurse, scientist, retired
Description: Promotes the practice, training, education and research in the field of infertility and reproductive medicine.
Library Subject: reproductive medicine, infertility
Library Type: reference
Publication: Newsletter

01216
British Film Institute
BFI
21 Stephen St., London, W1T 1LN, UK
Tel: 020 72551444
Website: http://www.bfi.org.uk
Staff: 500
Contact: Greg Dyke, Chm.
Fee: £40
Membership Type: regular
Fee: £1200
Membership Type: patron
Description: Promotes access to, and appreciation of film culture.

01217
British Flue and Chimney Manufacturers' Association
BFCMA
2 Waltham Ct., Milley Ln., Hare Hatch, Reading, RG10 9TH, UK
Tel: 0118 9403416
Fax: 0118 9406258
Email: info@feta.co.uk
Website: http://www.feta.co.uk/bfcma/index.htm
Members: 16
Staff: 5
Contact: Robert Burke, Pres.
Description: Promotes the advantages and proper use of factory-made, conventional and natural draught flue and chimney systems. Aims to influence building regulations, standards and codes of practice relevant to flue and chimney systems.
Publication: Handbook
Publication title: Guide to Flues & Chimneys

01218
British Fluid Power Association
BFPA
Cheriton House, Cromwell Park, Oxfordshire, Chipping Norton, OX7 5SR, UK
Tel: 01608 647900
Fax: 01608 647919
Email: enquiries@bfpa.co.uk
Website: http://www.bfpa.co.uk
Contact: J.C. Serkumian, Pres.
Description: Hydraulic and pneumatic equipment suppliers and manufacturers; individuals involved or interested in the fluid power industries. Promotes cooperation in the field; sets technical standards and guidelines. Represents members' interests. Operates educational programs; conducts research; maintains advisory and information service; disseminates marketing data, statistics, and exporting information.
Formerly: Formerly, Association of Hydraulic Equipment Manufacturers
Meetings/Conventions: Motion and Control Exhibition – quadrennial meeting

01219
British Fluid Power Distributors Association
BFPDA
Cheriton House, Cromwell Park, Oxfordshire, Chipping Norton, OX7 5SR, UK
Tel: 01608 647900
Fax: 01608 647919
Email: enquiries@bfpa.co.uk
Website: http://www.bfpa.co.uk
Members: 100
Staff: 4
Contact: N. Ord, Chm.
Description: Quality assurance; support of manufacturers, forum for discussion; code of professional conduct; promotion of training and education, marketing information; technical guidelines; liaison with government and other organisations.

01220
British Fluoridation Society
BFS
Ashton Leigh and Wigan PCT, Bryan House, Standishgate, Wigan, WN1 1AH, UK
Tel: 01942 483099
Email: bfs@bfsweb.org
Website: http://www.bfsweb.org
Contact: Raman Bedi, Chief Dental Off.
Description: Promotes fluoridation of the water supplies to improve dental health and reduce health inequalities.

01221
British Flute Society
BFS
c/o Anna Munks, Sec.
27 Eskdale Gardens, Purley, Surrey, CR8 1ET, UK
Tel: 020 86683360
Email: secretary@bfs.org.uk
Website: http://www.bfs.org.uk
Members: 2000
Contact: James Galway, Pres.
Fee: £25
Membership Type: individual in UK/school in UK/flute club
Fee: £15
Membership Type: student in UK/senior citizen/disabled in UK
Description: Professional players, teachers, amateur players. Promotes flute playing at all levels. Holds events for flute players throughout the country.
Publication: Journal
Publication title: Flute

01222
British Footwear Association
BFA
3 Burystead Pl., Wellingborough, NN8 1AH, UK
Tel: 01933 229005
Fax: 01933 225009
Email: info@britfoot.com
Website: http://www.britfoot.com
Members: 80
Staff: 5
Description: Fosters a favorable trading climate for footwear from British brands, both in the UK and overseas.
Publication: Booklet
Publication title: Footwear for Special Needs. Advertisements.

01223

British Fragrance Association
BFA

PO Box 173, Surrey, Cranleigh, GU6 8WU, UK
Tel: 01483 275411
Fax: 01483 275411
Email: secretariat@bfaorg.org
Website: http://www.bfaorg.org
Members: 29
Staff: 1
Contact: Julie Young, Exec. Sec.
Fee: £1000
Membership Type: associate
Fee: £400
Membership Type: consultant
Description: Manufacturers of fragrance ingredients, producers and companies marketing fragrance compounds and aroma chemicals. Promotes and protects the interests of the industry, encourages members to maintain high standards and to appropriately promote, support or oppose legislation affecting the industry or its members. Co-operates with government departments and other bodies interested in or having association with the industry. Collects and disseminates technical, statistical and other information.

01224

British Franchise Association
BFA

Centurion Ct., 85F Milton Park, Abingdon, OX14 4RY, UK
Tel: 01235 820470
Fax: 01235 832158
Email: mailroom@thebfa.org
Website: http://www.thebfa.org
Members: 231
Staff: 9
Contact: Johanna Roughley, Communications Mgr.
Fee: £2560
Membership Type: full, affiliate
Fee: £2455
Membership Type: associate
Description: Members are engaged in the distribution of goods and services through independent outlets under franchise agreements.
Publication: Handbook
Publication title: Franchisee Pack
Meetings/Conventions: annual conference

01225

British Frozen Food Federation
BFFF

Warwick House, Unit 7, Long Bennington Business Park, Main Rd., Long Bennington, Newark, NG23 5JR, UK
Tel: 01400 283090
Fax: 01400 283097
Email: brianyoung@bfff.co.uk
Website: http://www.bfff.co.uk
Contact: Brian Young, Dir. Gen.
Fee: £2781.37
Membership Type: band A-D (based on annual U.K. frozen food turnover)
Fee: £1338.66
Membership Type: associate
Description: Encourages development of the British frozen food industry with high standards.

01226

British Fur Trade Association
BFTA

Brookstone House, 6 Elthorne Rd., London, N19 4AG, UK
Email: info@britishfur.co.uk
Website: http://www.britishfur.co.uk
Members: 40
Description: Aims to build greater awareness of the für trade and related issues. Helps to dispel the myths about für production.

01227

British Furniture Manufacturers
BFM

Wycombe House, 9 Amersham Hill, High Wycombe, HP13 6NR, UK
Tel: 01494 523021
Fax: 01494 474270
Email: adam.mason@fm.org.uk
Website: http://www.bfm.org.uk
Members: 383
Staff: 8
Contact: Roger Mason, Managing Dir.
Description: British furniture manufacturers including exhibition, and export division. Acts as the trade association for British furniture manufacturers. Organizes exhibitions, home and overseas, plus supporting export promotions. Acts as the public voice for the industry on all matters from safety to the environment and as industry training body.
Publication: Directory
Publication title: Furniture From Britain
Meetings/Conventions: Summer Furniture Show – annual trade show – Exhibits.

01228

British Gear Association
BGA

IMEX Business Park, Ste. 59, Shobnall Rd., Staffordshire, Burton-on-Trent, DE14 2AU, UK
Tel: 01283 515521
Fax: 01283 515841
Email: admin@bga.org.uk
Website: http://www.bga.org.uk
Members: 105
Staff: 4
Contact: Peter Wright, Chm.
Description: Represents manufacturers of gears and power transmission products; suppliers to the power transmission industry; users of gears and related power transmission products; academic, educational and research establishments actively involved in research, design, and development of the industry; and those providing specialized services that advance the use of gearing. Promotes the competitive position of the UK gear and power transmission industry; promotes such technical research, educational and training activities as deemed necessary in the overall interest of the industry; cooperates with government and other industries on matters of urgency and interest to the industry.
Formerly: Formerly, British Gear Association
Publication: Handbook
Publication title: Buyers Guide & Members Handbook. Advertisements.

01229

British Geological Survey
BGS

Kingsley Dunham Centre, Keyworth, Nottingham, NG12 5GG, UK
Tel: 0115 9363100
Fax: 0115 9363200
Email: enquiries@bgs.ac.uk
Website: http://www.bgs.ac.uk
Staff: 800
Contact: John Ludden, Exec. Dir.
Description: Approximately 507 of the staff are scientists, the rest is made up of administration and technical support. Contributes to the economic competitiveness of the UK, the effectiveness of public services and policy (including international policy) and the quality of life by providing the geoscience information and advice for the UK both onshore, offshore and internationally.
Library Subject: earth sciences
Library Type: reference
Publication: Survey
Publication title: British Geological Survey Annual Report

01230

British Geophysical Association
BGA

University of Bristol, Department of Earth Sciences, Wills Memorial Bldg., Queen's Rd., Bristol, BS8 1RJ, UK
Tel: 0117 33 15126
Email: gljmk@bristol.ac.uk
Website: http://www.geophysics.org.uk
Contact: Michael Kendall, Pres.
Description: Promotes the subject of geophysics in order to strengthen the relationship between geology and geophysics in the U.K. Holds meetings and courses, encourages the publication of the results of research, responds to consultations, promotes geophysics education.

01231

British Geotechnical Association
BGA

c/o Institution of Civil Engineers
1 Great George St., London, SW1P 3AA, UK
Tel: 020 76652233
Fax: 020 77991325
Email: bga@britishgeotech.org.uk
Website: http://www.britishgeotech.org.uk
Members: 1392
Staff: 1
Contact: Sarah Stallebrass, Chair
Fee: £32
Membership Type: student, retired
Fee: £50
Membership Type: individual
Description: Individuals, corporate and student members who are geotechnical engineers or otherwise engaged or interested in geotechnics. Concerned with the advancement of public education in the subject of soil and rock mechanics and engineering geology and in their application to engineering.
Formerly: Formerly, British Geotechnical Society

01232
British Geriatrics Society
BGS
Marjory Warren House, 31 St. John's Sq., London, EC1M 4DN, UK
Tel: 020 76081369
Fax: 020 76081041
Email: general.information@bgs.org.uk
Website: http://www.bgs.org.uk
Members: 2500
Staff: 5
Contact: Graham Mulley, Pres.
Fee: £178
Membership Type: consultant in UK
Fee: £106
Membership Type: trainee, research fellow, clinical assistant
Description: Consultant geriatricians and other doctors, scientists and professionals with an interest in geriatric medicine and care of older individuals. Aims to promote scientific developments of geriatric medicine, improve medical and social services for older individuals and promote measures, which will improve health throughout adult life to ensure better fitness on achieving old age.
Publication: Journal
Publication title: Age and Ageing. Advertisements.
Meetings/Conventions: semiannual conference – Exhibits.

01233
British Glass
BG
9 Churchill Way, Sheffield, S35 2PY, UK
Tel: 0114 2901850
Fax: 0114 2901851
Email: d.dalton@britglass.co.uk
Website: http://www.britglass.org.uk/index.html
Contact: Dave Dalton, CEO
Description: Trade federation with research arm. Conducts research programs. Compiles statistics on sales of glass containers. Offers consultancy services and technical support.
Library Subject: glass technology
Library Type: reference
Formerly: Formerly, British Glass Manufacturers' Confederation

01234
British Glove Association
BGA
32 Park Hill Rd., Harborne, Birmingham, B17 9SL, UK
Tel: 0121 2422602
Fax: 0121 4275358
Email: info@gloveassociation.org
Website: http://www.gloveassociation.org
Members: 50
Staff: 1
Contact: Ray Fiveash, Sec.
Fee: £55
Membership Type: individual
Fee: £144
Membership Type: small business (with less than 5 employees)
Description: Glove manufacturers, traders, and suppliers of leather and fabrics to the industry. Promotes glove manufacturing and trading in the United Kingdom.
Formerly: Formerly, National Association of Glove Manufacturers

01235
British Goat Society
BGS
34-36 Fore St., Bovey Tracey, Devon, Newton Abbot, TQ13 9AD, UK
Tel: 01626 833168
Fax: 01626 834536
Email: secretary@allgoats.com
Website: http://www.allgoats.com
Members: 2000
Staff: 2
Contact: Sue Knowles, Sec.
Fee: £30
Membership Type: single
Fee: £10
Membership Type: family
Description: Aims to circulate knowledge and general information upon goats, to extend and encourage the keeping of goats, so as to increase the production and use of their products. Also to improve the various breeds of goats, and especially to develop those qualities which are generally recognized and valued and to safeguard against cruelty from whatever source.

01236
British Grassland Society
BGS
c/o Ms. Jessica Buss
Unit 32 C, StoneLeigh Deer Park, Stareton, Warwickshire, Kenilworth, CV8 2LY, UK
Tel: 02476 696600
Email: office@britishgrassland.com
Website: http://www.britishgrassland.com
Members: 1000
Staff: 2
Contact: Tony Evans, Pres.
Fee: £40
Membership Type: full (non-farmer)
Fee: £30
Membership Type: farmer
Description: Represents farmers, research scientists, and other individuals in 35 countries involved in agricultural education and advisory services. Seeks to advance methods of production and use of grass and forage crops in agriculture through research and education. Conducts educational and summer tours.
Publication: Magazine
Publication title: Grass and Forage Farmer
Meetings/Conventions: periodic conference

01237
British Guild of Travel Writers
BGTW
26 Needwood House, Woodberry Down, London, N4 2TN, UK
Tel: 020 81448713
Email: secretariat@bgtw.org
Website: http://www.bgtw.org
Members: 270
Contact: Robert Ellison, Sec.
Fee: £125
Membership Type: general
Description: Professional travel journalists (including writers, photographers and broadcasters). Holds regular meetings (about once a month) on subjects of interest to members.
Publication: Magazine
Publication title: Globetrotter

01238
British Hallmarking Council
No. 1 Colmore Sq., Birmingham, B4 6AA, UK
Tel: 0870 7631414
Fax: 0870 7631814
Email: david.gwyther@martjohn.com
Website: http://www.britishhallmarkingcouncil.gov.uk
Members: 19
Contact: David Gwyther, Sec.
Description: Oversees the activities of the assay offices in Great Britain. Advises HM Government on legislation. Seeks to fix maximum price for assaying and hallmarking articles of precious metal.

01239
British Hardware and Housewares Manufacturers' Association
BHHMA
Brooke House, 4 The Lakes, Bedford Rd., Northampton, NN4 7YD, UK
Tel: 01604 622023
Fax: 01604 631252
Email: info@bhhma.com
Website: http://www.bhhma.co.uk
Members: 360
Staff: 9
Contact: Andrew Weiss, Pres.
Description: Manufacturers or suppliers of hardware and housewares to the UK consumer market. Supports the needs of manufacturers of hardware and housewares in the United Kingdom. Offers a wide range of membership and consultancy services including export assistance, parliamentary and legal and market information.
Formerly: Formerly, BHHMA
Publication: Newsletter
Publication title: BHHMA Newsletter

01240
British Hardware Federation
BHF
225 Bristol Rd., Edgbaston, Birmingham, B5 7UB, UK
Tel: 0121 4466688
Fax: 0121 4465215
Email: information@bhfgroup.co.uk
Website: http://www.bhfgroup.co.uk
Members: 5000
Staff: 64
Contact: John Morris, Natl. Pres.
Description: Hardware retailers including d-i-y, gardening, tools, ironmongers, housewares, electrical, plumbing. Aims to identify and promote the interests of hardware retailers in the UK.
Library Subject: hardware, housewares, garden products
Library Type: not open to the public
Publication: Catalog
Publication title: Architects and Builders Ironmongery Catalogue

01241

British Hat Guild
BHG

PO Box 48664, London, NW8 6WS, UK
Tel: 07932 678003
Fax: 01582 481821
Email: info@britishhatguild.co.uk
Website: http://www.britishhatguild.co.uk
Members: 70
Staff: 1
Fee: £25
Membership Type: model milliner, student
Fee: £65
Membership Type: small company
Description: Members are manufacturers, milliners, wholesalers and retailers. Dedicated to the design, manufacture and promotion of hats.
Library Type: open to the public
Publication: Manual
Publication title: The Guide to a Career in Hat Manufacturing

01242

British Health Care Association
BHCA

PO Box 6752, Elgin, IV30 9BN, UK
Tel: 01343 544841
Email: info@bhca.org.uk
Website: http://www.bhca.org.uk
Members: 30
Staff: 2
Contact: Steve Fritz, Contact
Description: Represents hospital cash plan insurance programs, health benefits providers and health maintenance organizations in the United Kingdom. Promotes effective hospitalization coverage for the public and other health care benefits.
Formerly: Formerly, British Hospitals Contributory Schemes Association

01243

British Healthcare Business Intelligence Association
BHBIA

105 St. Peter's St., Hertfordshire, St. Albans, AL1 3EJ, UK
Tel: 01727 896085
Fax: 01727 896026
Email: admin@bhbia.org.uk
Website: http://www.bhbia.org.uk
Contact: Julie Curphey, Chair
Fee: £395
Membership Type: corporate
Fee: £126
Membership Type: personal
Description: Works to promote and enhance the professionalism and value of Business Intelligence within the Healthcare Industry.
Publication: Handbook

01244

British Heart Foundation
BHF

Greater London House, 180 Hampstead Rd., London, NW1 7AW, UK
Tel: 020 75540000
Fax: 020 74865820
Email: internet@bhf.org.uk
Website: http://www.bhf.org.uk
Contact: Peter Hollins, Chief Exec.
Description: Funds research into the causes and prevention diagnosis and treatment of cardiovascular disease. Sponsors postgraduate medical education; distributes fellowships and research funds. Organizes symposia, and workshops for health care and research professionals. Provides cardiac equipment for hospitals and ambulance services. Supports heart patients through rehabilitation programmes, heart support groups and nurses. Conducts fundraising events. Compiles statistics.
Meetings/Conventions: BUPA Great North Run – annual competition

01245

British Hedgehog Preservation Society
BHPS

Hedgehog House, Dhustone, Ludlow, SY8 3PL, UK
Tel: 01584 890801
Email: info@britishhedgehogs.org.uk
Website: http://www.britishhedgehogs.org.uk
Staff: 4
Contact: Fay Vass, Chief Exec.
Fee: £7.5
Membership Type: ordinary
Fee: £12.5
Membership Type: family
Description: Advises on the care of hedgehogs and has a network of carers nationwide; supplies education packs to schools, libraries, and wildlife groups. Arranges talks to interested groups; funds research on the behavioral habits of hedgehogs.
Publication: Catalog
Publication title: Hogalogue. Advertisements.

01246

British Helicopter Advisory Board
BHAB

Graham Ste., West Entrance, Fairoaks Airport, Chobham, Surrey, Woking, GU24 8HX, UK
Tel: 01276 856100
Fax: 01276 856126
Email: info@britishhelicopterassociation.org
Website: http://www.britishhelicopterassociation.org
Staff: 3
Fee: £14456
Membership Type: full (major commercial helicopter operating company)
Fee: £529-1108
Membership Type: full (corporate body, company operating helicopters by professional pilot/emergency services)
Description: Membership covers the majority of helicopter operating companies, manufacturers, equipment manufacturers, sales and service companies, corporate and private owners, the Helicopter Club of Great Britain, together with a wide variety of companies with. an interest in helicopter operations including heliport and helipad operators. Represents the British civil helicopter industry and advises on all aspects of civil helicopter operation.
Publication: Handbook
Publication title: BHAB Information Handbook. Advertisements.

01247

British Herb Trade Association
BHTA

133 Eastgate, Lincolnshire, Louth, LN11 9QG, UK
Tel: 01507 602427
Fax: 01507 600101
Email: info@bhta.org.uk
Website: http://www.bhta.org.uk
Members: 80
Staff: 1
Contact: Tim Mudge, Contact
Description: Individuals, firms and organizations who are commercially or professionally involved in the business of herbs in the UK. Aims to encourage improvement and maintenance of standards of product, presentation and business methods within the industry; to assist members in the development of their skills and with the profitable growth of their enterprises; to promote knowledge of and the increased use and cultivation of herbs in Great Britain; to foster co-operation between all actively involved in, or with an interest in, the herb industry.
Library Subject: herb production and uses
Library Type: reference

01248

British Herbal Medicine Association
BHMA

PO Box 583, Exeter, EX1 9GX, UK
Tel: 08456 801134
Fax: 08456 801136
Email: secretary@bhma.info
Website: http://www.bhma.info
Contact: Ray Hill, Chm.
Fee: £19.5
Membership Type: student
Fee: £64.34
Membership Type: individual
Description: Members are importers, manufacturers, herbal practitioners, herbal retailers, wholesalers and health food shops. Ensures herbal medicine is available to all who seek it and fosters herbal research.
Publication: Book
Publication title: A Guide to Traditional Herbal Medicines

01249

British Herpetological Society
BHS

11, Strathmore Pl., Montrose, DD10 8LQ, UK
Email: info@thebhs.org
Website: http://www.thebhs.org
Members: 1100
Contact: Trevor J.C. Beebee, Pres.
Fee: £35
Membership Type: full
Fee: £25
Membership Type: ordinary
Description: Private individuals, university libraries. Conservation, captive breeding, scientific group and junior sections all very active. Meetings held regularly and a library is available.
Publication: Bulletin
Publication title: BHS Bulletin. Advertisements.

01250
British HIV Association
BHIVA
c/o Mediscript
1 Mountview Ct., 310 Friern Barnet Ln., London, N20 0LD, UK
Tel: 020 83695380
Fax: 020 84469194
Website: http://www.bhiva.org
Contact: Ian G. Williams, Chm.
Fee: £175
Membership Type: consultant
Fee: £85
Membership Type: non-consultant
Description: Relieves sickness and aims to protect and preserve health through the development and promotion of good practice in the treatment of HIV and HIV-related illnesses. Advances public education in the subject of HIV and the symptoms, causes, treatment and prevention of HIV-related illnesses. Promotes research and dissemination of information about HIV/AIDS.
Publication: Journal
Publication title: HIV Medicine

01251
British Holiday and Home Parks Association
BH&HPA
Chichester House, 6 Pullman Ct., Great Western Rd., Gloucester, GL1 3ND, UK
Tel: 01452 526911
Fax: 01452 508508
Email: membership@bhhpa.org.uk
Website: http://www.bhhpa.org.uk
Members: 2100
Staff: 11
Fee: £230
Membership Type: individual
Description: Owners and managers of residential, caravan, chalet, tent and self-catering parks. Representation to national, European and local authorities; information and advice to members through journal, handbook, convention, telephone advice line; marketing and promotions - generic promotions campaign; commercial services - special offer/discount schemes.

01252
British Holistic Medical Association
BHMA
PO Box 371, Bridgwater, TA6 9BG, UK
Tel: 01278 722000
Email: admin@bhma.org
Website: http://www.bhma.org
Members: 600
Staff: 4
Contact: Craig Brown, Admin.
Fee: £48
Membership Type: standard
Fee: £20
Membership Type: overseas supplement
Description: Professional corporate/associate membership (for the lay public), nurse/student membership and overseas membership. Works to educate doctors and other healthcare professionals in the principles and practice of holistic medicine, to encourage research studies and publication of work carried out in the field of holistic medicine and to bring together holistic healthcare practitioners for mutual support and further personal and professional development.
Publication: Journal
Publication title: Journal of Holistic Healthcare. Advertisements.

01253
British Homeopathic Association
BHA
Hahnemann House, 29 Park St. W, London, LU1 3BE, UK
Tel: 01582 408675
Fax: 01582 723032
Email: info@britishhomeopathic.org
Website: http://www.trusthomeopathy.org
Members: 3000
Staff: 3
Contact: John Cook, Chm.
Fee: £20
Membership Type: retired/unwaged
Fee: £25
Membership Type: in UK and Ireland
Description: The Association is a registered charity supported by a membership of people who, being convinced of the efficacy of the homoeopathic system of medicine, give regular subscriptions or donations for its maintenance. Aims to support, extend and develop homoeopathy. Puts the general public in touch with homoeopathic doctors, veterinary surgeons and pharmacies. Also book publishers, maintaining in print a number of books on various aspects of homoeopathy as well as the magazine.
Library Subject: homoeopathy
Library Type: not open to the public
Publication: Magazine
Publication title: Health and Homoeopathy. Advertisements.

01254
British Horn Society
c/o CAF Administration Service
Kings Hill, Kent, West Malling, ME19 4TA, UK
Email: mike@british-horn.org
Website: http://www.british-horn.org
Members: 700
Contact: Barry Tuckwell, Pres.
Description: Professional musicians, amateur musicians and students.
Publication: Magazine
Publication title: Horn Player

01255
British Horological Federation
11 Daytron Close, Bidforn On Avon, Warwickshire, NG23 5TE, UK
Tel: 01789 490725
Fax: 01636 706965
Email: scchild.bhf@virgin.net
Website: http://www.b-h-f.org
Members: 50
Contact: Sid Child, Sec. Gen.
Description: Horological companies. Promotes high standards for member companies. Helps member companies achieve fair trading around the world, particularly in the UK and the European Union. Represents the British Industry on the Horological Industries Committee of Europe. Also on British and International Standards Committees.

01256
British Horological Institute
BHI
Upton Hall, Upton, Newark, NG23 5TE, UK
Tel: 01636 813795
Fax: 01636 812258
Email: info@bhi.co.uk
Website: http://www.bhi.co.uk
Members: 3000
Contact: Martin Taylor, Gen. Mgr.
Fee: £100
Membership Type: associate (in UK)
Fee: £120
Membership Type: associate (overseas)
Description: Serves as professional body for individuals.
Publication: Journal
Publication title: Horological Journal. Advertisements.

01257
British Horse Society
BHS
Stoneleigh Deer Park, Warwickshire, Kenilworth, CV8 2XZ, UK
Tel: 0844 8481666
Fax: 01926 707800
Email: enquiry@bhs.org.uk
Website: http://www.bhs.org.uk
Members: 56000
Staff: 75
Contact: Graham Cory, Chief Exec.
Description: Any person with an interest in the equine world - from the horse's welfare, through to road safety and training. Promotes the welfare, care and use of the horse and pony. Encourages horsemanship and the improvement of horse management and breeding. Represents all equine interests.
Publication: Yearbook
Publication title: BHS Yearbook. Advertisements.

01258
British Hospitality Association
BHA
Queens House, 55-56 Lincoln's Inn Fields, London, WC2A 3BH, UK
Tel: 020 74047744
Fax: 020 74047799
Email: bha@bha.org.uk
Website: http://www.bha.org.uk
Members: 39000
Staff: 11
Contact: Ufi Ibrahim, Chief Exec.
Description: Proprietors of group and individually owned hotels, restaurants and catering businesses. Also trade membership open to suppliers to the hospitality industry. Represents the British hospitality industry -hotels, restaurants, contract caterers and Motorway Service Areas. Provides a wide range of advisory and other services for members and puts forward their views to UK and European policymakers.
Publication: Survey
Publication title: British Hospitality: Trends and Statistics

01259
British Housewives' League
17 Osbourne Rd., London, N13 5PT, UK
Email: housewives@freeuk.com
Website: http://www.housewives.freeuk.com
Contact: Stella Masters, Contact
Fee: £20

Membership Type: associate
Description: Works to provide women with a voice in social issues. Encourages "development of personality in accordance with Christian tradition". Acts politically to defend traditional values of family, nation and democracy.

01260
British Humanist Association
BHA
1 Gower St., London, WC1E 6HD, UK
Tel: 020 70793580
Fax: 020 70793588
Email: info@humanism.org.uk
Website: http://www.humanism.org.uk/home
Members: 4100
Staff: 7
Contact: Andrew Copson, Chief Exec.
Fee: £35
Membership Type: full
Fee: £20
Membership Type: concessionary
Description: Promotes Humanism as a valid ethical life stance and an alternative to religion. Provides non-religious ceremonies across Great Britain. Seeks to promote Humanism particularly in education and the media.
Publication: Magazine
Publication title: BHA News Members Newsletter

01261
British Hydrological Society
BHS
1 Great George St., Westminster, London, SW1P 3AA, UK
Tel: 020 72227722
Fax: 020 72227500
Email: bhs@ice.org.uk
Website: http://www.hydrology.org.uk
Members: 1080
Contact: Tim Fuller, Sec.
Fee: £25
Membership Type: individual
Fee: £12.5
Membership Type: student, retired
Description: Works to promote interest and scholarship in scientific and applied aspect of hydrology.
Publication: Newsletter
Publication title: Circulation
Meetings/Conventions: National Hydrology Symposium – biennial symposium

01262
British Hydropower Association
BHA
12 Riverside Park, Station Rd., Dorset, Wimborne, BH21 1QU, UK
Tel: 01202 880333
Fax: 01202 886609
Email: info@british-hydro.org
Website: http://www.british-hydro.org
Members: 220
Contact: David Williams, CEO
Fee: £5000
Membership Type: sponsoring
Fee: £2060
Membership Type: principal company
Description: Water power users, (i.e. millers, weavers, electricity generators), consultants and manufacturers of hydro power equipment. Protects water power users (from the depredation of Government etc.) and promotes the use of water power.

01263
British Hypertension Society
BHS
PO Box 65, Leicester, LE2 7LX, UK
Tel: 07717 467973
Fax: 020 89796700
Email: bhs@le.ac.uk
Website: http://www.bhsoc.org
Members: 250
Staff: 1
Contact: Jackie Howarth, Admin. Off.
Fee: £50
Membership Type: individual
Description: Provides a medical and scientific research forum to enable sharing of cutting edge research in order to understand the origin of high blood pressure and improve its treatment. Produces guidelines for the management of hypertension which are widely adopted in primary care in the UK and elsewhere. Undertakes active validation of new blood pressure devices for the measurement of blood pressure. Establishes educational programs to support scientists, doctors and other healthcare workers involved in understanding the basis of high blood pressure and improving its treatment.

01264
British In-Vitro Diagnostics Association
BIVDA
1 Queen Anne's Gate, London, SW1H 9BT, UK
Tel: 020 79574633
Fax: 020 79574644
Email: enquiries@bivda.co.uk
Website: http://www.bivda.co.uk
Members: 107
Staff: 3
Contact: Doris-Ann Williams, Dir. Gen.
Description: Represents the interests of companies with major involvement and interest in the In-Vitro Diagnostics industry.
Publication: Newsletter
Publication title: Diagnostics in Healthcare

01265
British Indian Psychiatric Association
BIPA
c/o Dr. Seshagiri Rao Nimmagadda, Gen. Sec.
Thornford Park, Crookham Hill, Berkshire, RG19 8ET, UK
Email: srnimmagadda@doctors.org.uk
Website: http://www.bipa.org.uk
Members: 500
Contact: Subodh Dave, Chm.
Fee: £175
Membership Type: life
Fee: £40
Membership Type: regular, associate
Description: Promotes education and research in psychiatry in the UK. Improves mental health services for people of Indian origin. Serves as a forum for Indian psychiatrists in UK for mutual support. Liaises with IPS and IAPA to encourage international collaboration in research and training.

01266
British Industrial Truck Association
BITA
5-7 High St., Sunninghill, Berkshire, Ascot, SL5 9NQ, UK
Tel: 01344 623800
Fax: 01344 291197
Email: info@bita.org.uk
Website: http://www.bita.org.uk
Staff: 5
Contact: James Clark, Sec. Gen.
Fee: £1360
Membership Type: truck supplier group, component/services group
Fee: £535
Membership Type: associate, affiliate
Description: Industrial truck manufacturers, suppliers, and importers in the United Kingdom. Promotes the interests of the industrial truck industry in the United Kingdom.
Publication: Newsletter
Publication title: BITA Members' Newsletter
Meetings/Conventions: International Materials Handling Exhibition – annual meeting

01267
British Infection Society
BIS
Hartley Taylor Ltd., Henderson House, New Rd., Bucks, Princes Risborough, HP27 0JN, UK
Tel: 01844 275650
Fax: 01494 274407
Email: secretariat@britishinfection.org
Website: http://www.britishinfection.org/drupal
Members: 900
Contact: Jane Stockley, Pres.
Fee: £60
Membership Type: full
Fee: £65
Membership Type: overseas
Description: Members of the medical profession and others working in related spheres which are relevant to the Society's objectives. Established to relieve sickness by the study of all aspects of infection and to promote the wide dissemination of relevant knowledge.
Formerly: Formerly, British Society for the Study of Infection
Publication: Journal
Publication title: The Journal of Infection. Advertisements.
Meetings/Conventions: annual meeting

01268
British Infertility Counselling Association
BICA
c/o Dr. Jim Monach, Membership Sec.
100 Bole Hill Ln., Sheffield, S10 1SD, UK
Tel: 01372 451626
Email: info@bica.net
Website: http://www.bica.net
Contact: Sandra Hewett, Information Off.
Fee: £45
Membership Type: full
Fee: £50
Membership Type: organization, overseas
Description: Acts as the professional association for infertility counsellors in the UK. Seeks to promote the highest standards of counselling for those considering or undergoing infertility treatment. Offers training and education services. Helps people with fertility problems.

Conducts an accreditation programme for infertility counsellors in the UK.
Publication: Book
Publication title: Implications for People Considering Donor-Assisted Conception

01269
British Institute of Agricultural Consultants
BIAC
c/o The Estate Office
Torry Hill, Milstead, Kent, Sittingbourne, ME9 0SP, UK
Tel: 01795 830100
Fax: 01795 830243
Email: info@biac.co.uk
Website: http://www.biac.co.uk
Members: 305
Staff: 3
Contact: David Leaver, Pres.
Description: Professionals giving advice and consultancy services in agriculture, horticulture, forestry, amenity, rural planning, etc. Also expert witnesses. Aims to advance the profession of agricultural consultancy and promote and publicize the services of members.
Publication: Newsletter
Publication title: Expert Witness Directory

01270
British Institute of Cleaning Science
BICSc
9 Premier Ct., Boarden Close, Moulton Park, Northampton, NN3 6LF, UK
Tel: 01604 678710
Fax: 01604 645988
Email: info@bics.org.uk
Website: http://www.bics.org.uk
Members: 4500
Staff: 9
Contact: Lynn Webster, Chair
Fee: £33.5
Membership Type: practitioner
Fee: £45
Membership Type: associate
Description: Open to those qualified within the cleaning industry. Professional body promoting training and education in the cleaning industry.

01271
British Institute of Dental and Surgical Technologists
BIDST
4 Thompson Green, W Yorkshire, Shipley, BD17 7PR, UK
Tel: 0845 6443726
Website: http://www.bidst.org
Members: 300
Contact: Steve Taylor, Chm.
Fee: £65
Membership Type: licentiate, fellow, associate
Fee: £25
Membership Type: student
Description: Maintains standards as a professional institute for dental and surgical technicians.
Formerly: Formerly, British Institute of Surgical Technologists
Publication: Journal
Publication title: Journal of the British Institute of Surgical Technologists

01272
British Institute of Energy Economics
BIEE
c/o Debbie Heywood
Stars Cottage, Stars Ln., Bucks, Aylesbury, HP17 8UL, UK
Tel: 01296 747916
Fax: 01296 747916
Email: admin@biee.org
Website: http://www.biee.org
Contact: Tony Scanlan, Membership Sec.
Fee: £85
Membership Type: full
Fee: £50
Membership Type: regular
Description: Aims to encourage the study of energy economics and energy policy by bringing together individuals with a wide range of energy expertise and encouraging the exchange of ideas and information.

01273
British Institute of Facilities Management
BIFM
No. 1 Bldg., The Causeway, Bishop's Stortford, CM23 2ER, UK
Tel: 0845 0581356
Fax: 01279 712669
Email: info@bifm.org.uk
Website: http://www.bifm.org.uk/bifm/home
Members: 12546
Staff: 15
Contact: Ian R. Fielder, Chief Exec.
Fee: £67
Membership Type: student
Fee: £122
Membership Type: associate
Description: Professional practicing facilities managers and those in related professions with an interest in facilities management. Represents the interests of professional facilities managers, whom it supports, through education, training and research in facilities management. Conducts regional based CPD programme and monthly meetings.
Publication title: Guides on FM issues

01274
British Institute of Graphologists
BIG
PO Box 3060, Gerrards Cross, SL9 9XP, UK
Tel: 01753 891241
Email: contact@britishgraphology.org
Website: http://www.britishgraphology.org
Contact: John Beck, Chm.
Fee: £60
Membership Type: elected, graduate
Fee: £50
Membership Type: affiliate
Description: Works to promote and enrich the science of graphology. Provides facilities for the study of graphology through tutorial courses, lectures, and seminars in UK.
Publication: Journal
Publication title: The Graphologist

01275
British Institute of Human Rights
BIHR
King's Coll. London, Melbourne House, 7th Fl., 46 Aldwych, London, WC2B 4LL, UK
Tel: 020 78481818
Fax: 020 78481814
Email: info@bihr.org.uk
Website: http://www.bihr.org.uk
Members: 170
Staff: 3
Contact: Katie Ghose, Dir.
Fee: £25
Membership Type: friend
Fee: £50
Membership Type: legal friend
Description: Strives to develop and improve human rights protection at home and abroad. Promotes public awareness of human rights through developing community outreach programs to help those socially or economically isolated. Provides specialized human rights education and training and undertakes effective research with a view to contributing to the development of policy from a human rights perspective.
Publication: Newsletter
Publication title: BIHR Brief

01276
British Institute of Innkeeping
BII
Wessex House, 80 Park St., Surrey, Camberley, GU15 3PT, UK
Tel: 01276 684449
Fax: 01276 23045
Email: reception@bii.org
Website: http://www.bii.org/home
Members: 13500
Staff: 58
Contact: Neil Robertson, Chief Exec.
Fee: £88.13
Membership Type: associate
Fee: £99.88
Membership Type: member
Description: Represents those who directly involved in supervising the day-to-day running of public houses. Promotes nationally recognized levels of professional competence amongst the membership and develops business skills. Has an awarding body, BIIAB, which produces nationally recognized qualifications for the licensed retail sector.
Publication: Magazine
Publication title: bII BUSINESS. Advertisements.

01277
British Institute of International and Comparative Law
BIICL
Charles Clore House, 17 Russell Sq., London, WC1B 5JP, UK
Tel: 020 78625151
Fax: 020 78625152
Website: http://www.biicl.org
Members: 560
Staff: 15
Contact: Robert McCorquodale, Dir.
Description: Academic, student, practicing lawyers throughout the world. Through its meetings, publications and research and training programmes, it serves to familiarize lawyers with legal systems other than their

own (particularly within the EU) and to provide opportunities to contribute by widened experience, comparison and analysis of these systems to the development of national, international and regional law.
Publication: Bulletin
Publication title: Bulletin of International Legal Developments. Advertisements.

01278
British Institute of Learning Disabilities
BILD
Campion House, Green St., Kidderminster, DY10 1JL, UK
Tel: 01562 723010
Fax: 01562 723029
Email: enquiries@bild.org.uk
Website: http://www.bild.org.uk
Members: 1200
Staff: 31
Contact: Keith Smith, Chief Exec.
Fee: £21
Membership Type: student, personal, voluntary group
Fee: £52-77
Membership Type: professional, teacher (in UK, Europe, worldwide)
Description: Works towards improving the quality of life of people with learning disabilities, by the promotion and provision of education and training; information; research; books and journals. Provides consultancy.
Publication: Journal
Publication title: British Journal of Learning Disabilities. Advertisements.

01279
British Institute of Musculoskeletal Medicine
BIMM
PO Box 116, Bushey, WD23 9BY, UK
Tel: 020 84219910
Fax: 020 83864183
Email: deena@bimm.org.uk
Website: http://www.bimm.org.uk
Members: 360
Contact: Deena Harris, Admin./Education Coor.
Fee: £75
Membership Type: ordinary
Fee: £175
Membership Type: higher rate (earning more than 10,000 from musculoskeletal practice)
Description: Doctors involved in musculoskeletal medicine. Concerned with the furtherance of knowledge and expertise in musculoskeletal medicine which includes treatment of sports injuries, back pain and other conditions of the locomotor system by osteopathy, injections and other physical modalities.
Publication: Journal
Publication title: Journal of Orthopaedic Medicine

01280
British Institute of Non-Destructive Testing
BINDT
Newton Bldg., St. George's Ave., Northampton, NN2 6JB, UK
Tel: 01604 893811
Fax: 01604 893861
Email: info@bindt.org
Website: http://www.bindt.org
Members: 2200
Contact: Matt Gallagher, Chief Exec.
Fee: £79.5
Membership Type: regular
Fee: £64.5
Membership Type: graduate, affiliate, practitioner
Description: Engineers, industrial organizations, students, and other interested organizations and individuals. Advances the science and practice of non-destructive testing and condition monitoring in the UK and worldwide. Sets national industry standards and issues certificates of competence to qualified engineers practicing non-destructive testing.
Formerly: Formerly, NDT Society of Great Britain
Publication: Journal
Publication title: Insight-Non-Destructive Testing and Condition Monitoring. Advertisements.
Meetings/Conventions: biennial conference – Exhibits.

01281
British Institute of Organ Studies
BIOS
15 Baxendale, London, N20 0EG, UK
Tel: 02084 450801
Email: john@jnorman.me.uk
Website: http://www.duresme.org.uk/BIOS/bios1.htm
Members: 675
Contact: John Norman, Chm.
Fee: £30
Membership Type: ordinary
Fee: £24
Membership Type: concession
Description: Amenity society for the British pipe organ. Purpose Works for the faithful restoration of historic organs, particularly in Britain. Promotes scholarly research into the history of the organ and its music. Conserves sources and materials related to the history of the organ and makes them accessible to scholars. Encourages exchange of information with similar bodies and individuals outside Britain.
Publication: Journal
Publication title: Journal of the BIOS

01282
British Institute of Persian Studies - United Kingdom
c/o The British Academy
10 Carlton House Terr., London, SW1Y 5AH, UK
Tel: 020 79695203
Fax: 020 79695401
Email: bips@britac.ac.uk
Website: http://www.bips.ac.uk
Contact: Vesta Sarkhosh Curtis, Pres.
Fee: £40
Membership Type: full (UK and overseas)
Fee: £50
Membership Type: joint
Description: Promotes scholarship and research in all aspects of Iranian studies.
Publication: Journal
Publication title: Iran

01283
British Institute of Professional Photography
BIPP
1 Prebendal Ct., Oxford Rd., Aylesbury, HP19 8EY, UK
Tel: 01296 718530
Fax: 01296 336367
Email: info@bipp.com
Website: http://www.bipp.com
Members: 3500
Staff: 5
Contact: Chris Harper, Chief Exec.
Fee: £50
Membership Type: student
Fee: £75
Membership Type: retired
Description: Professional photographers, photographic technicians and others involved in professional photography. Represents the professional photography industry to the government and aims to improve the technical knowledge and professional status of people in the photography industry. Aims to achieve and maintain standards in professional practice and conduct.
Publication: Directory
Publication title: Directory of Professional Photography. Advertisements.

01284
British Institute of Radiology
BIR
36 Portland Pl., London, W1B 1AT, UK
Tel: 020 73071400
Fax: 020 73071414
Email: admin@bir.org.uk
Website: http://www.bir.org.uk
Members: 2000
Staff: 16
Contact: S. Green, Pres.
Fee: £164
Membership Type: full
Fee: £45
Membership Type: associate
Description: Medical radiologists, scientists, and allied professionals in 55 countries. Conducts seminars.
Library Subject: diagnostic radiology, radiotherapy/oncology, magnetic resonance imaging
Library Type: reference
Publication: Journal
Publication title: British Journal of Radiology. Advertisements.
Meetings/Conventions: Scientific Congress – annual congress – Exhibits.

01285
British Insurance Broker's Association
BIBA
BIBA House, 8th Fl., 18 Bevis Marks, London, EC3A 7JB, UK
Tel: 020 73970201
Fax: 020 76269676
Email: enquiries@biba.org.uk
Website: http://www.biba.org.uk
Members: 2000
Staff: 20
Contact: Eric Galbraith, Chief Exec.
Description: Insurance brokers in the United Kingdom. Promotes the interests of members.
Formerly: Formerly, British Insurance and Investment Brokers' Association
Publication: Magazine
Publication title: The Broker. Advertisements.

01286
British Insurance Law Association
BILA
47 Bury St., Suffolk, Stowmarket, IP14 1HD, UK
Tel: 07776 115795
Fax: 01449 770941
Email: secretariat@bila.org.uk
Website: http://www.bila.org.uk
Contact: Stephen Lewis, Chm.
Fee: £60
Membership Type: individual
Fee: £225-800
Membership Type: corporate (based on number of nominated members)
Description: Represents insurers, insurance brokers and other intermediaries, academic lawyers, solicitors and barristers promoting changes in the field of insurance. Holds talks and conferences on insurance law.
Publication: Journal

01287
British Interactive Media Association
BIMA
The Lightwell, 12-16 Laystall St., London, EC1R 4PF, UK
Tel: 020 78436797
Email: info@bima.co.uk
Website: http://www.bima.co.uk
Members: 200
Staff: 2
Contact: Justin Cooke, CEO
Fee: £40
Membership Type: individual
Fee: £320
Membership Type: associate corporate
Description: Open to any person or organization with an interest in multimedia. Members come from fields of application development, hardware manufacturing, publishing, distribution, disc pressing, programming and consultancy. Promotes wider understanding of the benefits of multimedia to industry, government and education. Provides a forum for the exchange of views amongst members.
Publication: Newsletter
Publication title: BIMA News

01288
British Interior Design Association
BIDA
Units 109-111 The Chambers, Chelsea Harbour, London, SW10 0XF, UK
Tel: 020 73490800
Fax: 020 73490500
Email: enquiries@bida.org
Website: http://www.bida.org
Staff: 3
Contact: Joy Whittaker, Exec. Mgr.
Fee: £395
Membership Type: designer
Fee: £145
Membership Type: associate
Description: Represents interior decorators and designers worldwide. Promotes the interior decorating and design industry.
Library Type: open to the public
Formerly: Formerly, Interior Decorators and Designers Association
Publication: Magazine
Publication title: De-Zine Student Magazine

01289
British Interior Textiles Association
BITA
5 Portland Pl., London, W1B 1PW, UK
Tel: 020 76367788
Fax: 020 76367515
Email: enquiries@interiortextiles.com
Website: http://www.interiortextiles.co.uk
Members: 105
Description: Manufacturers, converters and major distributors of furnishing fabrics and household textiles. Promotes, safeguards and protects the interests of members. Provides meeting points for members.
Publication: Newsletter
Publication title: BITA Newsletter

01290
British International Freight Association
BIFA
Redfern House, Browells Ln., Middlesex, Feltham, TW13 7EP, UK
Tel: 020 88442266
Fax: 020 88905546
Email: bifa@bifa.org
Website: http://www.bifa.org
Members: 1400
Staff: 18
Contact: Peter Quantrill, Dir. Gen.
Fee: £725
Membership Type: trading (minimum fee)
Fee: £720
Membership Type: associate
Description: Companies involved in the freight industry in the United Kingdom. Represents members' interest.
Library Subject: multi-modal international freight transport
Library Type: reference
Publication: Directory
Publication title: BIFA Freight Services Directory. Advertisements.

01291
British International Spa Association
BISA
SPA House, Winchett Hill, Kent, Goudhurst, TN17 1JY, UK
Tel: 01580 212954
Email: spahouse@spaassociation.org.uk
Website: http://www.spaassociation.org.uk
Contact: Lord Thurso, Pres.
Fee: £25
Membership Type: student
Fee: £85
Membership Type: individual
Description: Promotes minimum standards of quality and service within the spa industry. Improves and promotes education for spa therapists. Acts as an educational platform for the public and for the trade outlets involved in spa services.

01292
British International Studies Association
BISA
International Politics Bldg., Aberystwyth University, Penglais, Aberystwyth, SY23 3DA, UK
Tel: 01970 628672
Fax: 01970 622709
Email: bisa@aber.ac.uk
Website: http://www.bisa.ac.uk
Members: 900
Contact: Gail Birkett, Admin.
Fee: £50
Membership Type: full
Fee: £25
Membership Type: associate
Description: Promotes the study of international relations and related subjects through teaching, research and the facilitation of contact between scholars.
Publication: Journal
Publication title: Review of International Studies

01293
British Interplanetary Society
BIS
27/29 S Lambeth Rd., London, SW8 1SZ, UK
Tel: 020 77353160
Fax: 020 75875118
Email: mail@bis-spaceflight.com
Website: http://www.bis-spaceflight.com
Members: 3000
Staff: 6
Contact: Robert Charles Parkinson, Pres.
Fee: £18
Membership Type: student (under 22 years old)
Fee: £37
Membership Type: individual (over 65 years old)
Description: Academic, scientific, and technical professionals involved in space research, exploration, and technology. Disseminates information to members on current research.
Library Type: lending
Publication: Journal
Publication title: Journal of the British Interplanetary Society

01294
British Jewellers' Association
BJA
Federation House, 10 Vyse St., Birmingham, B18 6LT, UK
Tel: 0121 2371110
Fax: 0121 2371113
Email: info@bja.org.uk
Website: http://www.bja.org.uk
Members: 700
Staff: 4
Contact: Simon Rainer, Chief Exec.
Fee: £270-1500
Membership Type: full (based on number of employees)
Fee: £118
Membership Type: design/craft
Description: Manufacturing jewellers, silversmiths, designer craftsmen, bullion dealers and companies offering service to the trade. Aims to be the voice of the industry representing members' interests in the media and government. Provides certain benefits and services for members. Close liaison with trade fairs for and with members. Acts for members, individually and collectively on issues of importance.
Publication: Newsletter
Publication title: Jewellery in Britain. Advertisements.

01295

British Jewellery, Giftware and Finishing Federation BJGF

Federation House, 10 Vyse St., Birmingham, B18 6LT, UK
Tel: 0121 2362657
Fax: 0121 2363921
Email: enquiries@bjgf.org.uk
Website: http://www.bjgf.org.uk
Members: 2500
Staff: 31
Contact: David Metcalfe, Pres.
Fee: £150
Description: Manufacturers and distributors of jewellery, silverware, giftware, art metalware, luggage, leather goods; also metal finishers. Works as an employers' federation comprising six trade associations, namely British Jewellers' Association, Jewellery Distributors' Association, The Giftware Association, Art Metalware Manufacturers' Association, British Luggage and Leathergoods Association and Metal Finishing Association. Activities include trade promotion by exhibiting at trade fairs in UK and overseas; trade protection; trade training and publishing.
Formerly: Formerly, British Jewellery and Giftware Federation

01296

British Laminate Fabricators Association BLFA

PO Box 8841, Nottingham, NG11 1AJ, UK
Tel: 0115 9213889
Email: info@blfa.co.uk
Website: http://www.blfa.co.uk
Members: 54
Contact: Christopher D. Thomas, Vice Chm./Treas.
Fee: £550
Membership Type: general
Description: Members are actively engaged in the production of laminate, the working of laminate or the provision of necessary chemicals therefore. Promotes the quality of laminate fabrication. Undertakes work of all types, from flat panel to sophisticated postforming techniques.
Formerly: Formerly, British Laminated Plastic Fabricators Association

01297

British Leafy Salads Association BLSA

133 Eastgate, Louth, LN11 9QG, UK
Website: http://www.britishleafysalads.co.uk
Members: 24
Staff: 1
Contact: David Piccaver, Chm.
Description: Marketing information and bulk purchasing.
Formerly: Formerly, British Iceberg Growers' Association

01298

British Leprosy Relief Association LEPRA

28 Middleborough, Essex, Colchester, CO1 1TG, UK
Tel: 01206 216700
Fax: 01206 762151
Email: lepra@leprahealthinaction.org
Website: http://www.lepra.org.uk/home.asp
Contact: Terry Vasey, Chief Exec.
Description: Seeks to restore health, hope, and dignity to people affected by leprosy. Offers social and economic rehabilitation programs. Sponsors research into the causes, prevention, and treatment of leprosy and allied diseases.

01299

British Lichen Society BLS

Natural History Museum, Department of Botany, Cromwell Rd., London, SW7 5BD, UK
Fax: 0207 9425529
Email: bls@nhm.ac.uk
Website: http://www.thebls.org.uk
Members: 620
Contact: S. Ward, Pres.
Fee: £30
Membership Type: ordinary
Fee: £85
Membership Type: ordinary (3 years, 2008-2010)
Description: International society for all persons interested in taxonomy, ecology, physiology, or environmental issues relating to lichens. Organizes field and lecture meetings.
Library Subject: lichenology
Library Type: reference
Publication: Journal
Publication title: The Lichenologist

01300

British Lime Association BLA

Gillingham House, 38-44 Gillingham St., London, SW1V 1HU, UK
Tel: 020 79638000
Fax: 020 79638001
Email: bla@mineralproducts.org
Website: http://www.britishlime.org
Members: 6
Contact: Gwil Neal, Contact
Description: Represents the interest of the UK lime industry in technical, promotional and general matters. Aims to broaden the public's knowledge of the benefits of lime.

01301

British Llama and Alpaca Association

Puckpitts Farm, Shipston-on-Stour, Warwickshire, Tredington, CV36 4NH, UK
Tel: 01608 661893
Fax: 01608 661893
Email: camelids@btinternet.com
Website: http://www.llama.co.uk
Members: 350
Staff: 10
Contact: Jane Brown, Assoc. Sec.
Fee: £30
Membership Type: single
Fee: £45
Membership Type: family
Description: Breeders, owners and general enthusiasts from farmers to surgeons -ages 20 to 70 who own or are interested in South American camelids (i.e. llamas, alpacas, vicunas, guanacos). Works to promote good husbandry practices, and the establishment of sound breeding programs for the continued improvement and increase of British stock. Membership offers owners and enthusiasts the opportunity to swap information at numerous organized social events, seminars, lectures and conferences.
Publication: Magazine
Publication title: The Camelids Chronicle. Advertisements.

01302

British Lung Foundation BLF

73-75 Goswell Rd., London, EC1V 7ER, UK
Tel: 020 76885555
Email: membership@blf-uk.org
Website: http://www.lunguk.org
Members: 22000
Staff: 35
Contact: Dame Helena Shovelton, CEO
Description: Individuals and organizations. Seeks to advance the prevention, diagnosis, and treatment of lung diseases. Maintains support groups for people with lung disease; provides financial and other assistance to lung disease research; conducts educational programs; participates in charitable activities; compiles statistics.

01303

British Machine Vision Association and Society for Pattern Recognition BMVA

c/o Royston Parkin, Membership Sec.
95 Queen St., Sheffield, S1 1WG, UK
Tel: 0114 2720306
Fax: 0114 2726158
Email: chair@bmva.org
Website: http://www.iapr.org
Members: 510
Contact: Andrew Fitzgibbon, Chm.
Fee: £20
Membership Type: personal
Fee: £200
Membership Type: corporate
Description: Promotes pattern recognition and the allied branches of engineering together with its related arts and sciences. Stimulates research, development and the application of pattern recognition in science and human activity.
Publication: Newsletter
Publication title: BMVA News

01304

British Marine Federation BMF

Marine House, Thorpe Lea Rd., Egham, TW20 8BF, UK
Tel: 01784 473377
Fax: 01784 439678
Email: info@britishmarine.co.uk
Website: http://www.britishmarine.co.uk
Members: 1550
Staff: 49
Contact: Alan Morgan, Pres.
Description: Companies engaged in all sectors of the United Kingdom's marine industry. Promotes and protects members' interests.
Publication: Newsletter
Publication title: British Marine News

01305

British Marine Federation - Scotland
BMF

Fl. 3, Apt. 7, 354 Meadowside Quay Walk, Glasgow, G11 6ED, UK
Tel: 0141 334 5153
Email: mike@clydemarinepress.co.uk
Website: http://www.britishmarine.co.uk
Members: 60
Staff: 1
Contact: Mike Balmforth, Sec.
Description: Members of the marine industry in Scotland who are members of the British Marine Industries Association.
Formerly: Formerly, Scottish Marine Industries Association

01306

British Marine Life Study Society
BMLSS

Glaucus House, 14 Corbyn Crescent, Sussex, Shoreham-by-Sea, BN43 6PQ, UK
Tel: 01273 465433
Fax: 01273 465433
Email: enquiries@glaucus.org.uk
Website: http://www.glaucus.org.uk
Members: 97
Staff: 1
Contact: Andy Horton, Webmaster/Ed.
Fee: £25
Membership Type: individual, family, corporate, school
Fee: £30
Membership Type: individual (inside Europe)
Description: Represents public aquaria, zoos, ecologists, marine biologists, museums, marine laboratories, education, libraries, general public, local authorities, rockpoolers, fishermen, divers, biological recorders. Studies the marine fauna and flora of the shore and seas surrounding the British Isles. Provides publication and distribution of knowledge of marine fauna and flora. Promotes ideas and projects concerning the conservation of the British marine environment.
Library Subject: marine wildlife, oceanography, marine biology, geology, aquariology
Library Type: reference
Publication: Journal
Publication title: Glaucus. Advertisements.
Meetings/Conventions: periodic workshop – Exhibits.

01307

British Maritime Law Association
BMLA

c/o ReedSmith Richards Butler
Beaufort House, 15 Botolph St., London, EC3A 7EE, UK
Tel: 020 77725881
Fax: 020 72475091
Email: p.griggs@incelaw.com
Website: http://www.bmla.org.uk
Members: 280
Staff: 2
Contact: Anthony Diamond, Chm.
Fee: £30
Membership Type: individual
Fee: £1500
Membership Type: institution
Description: Association of Average Adjusters; British Insurance Brokers Association; The Chamber of Shipping; Institute of London Underwriters; Lloyd's Underwriters Association; Protection and Indemnity Clubs; university law departments, solicitors, barristers and loss adjusters. Promotes uniformity of maritime law (private rather than public). Co-ordinates contributions to international and national maritime legislation and informs members of latest developments in maritime law.

01308

British Materials Handling Federation
BMHF

National Metalforming Centre, 47 Birmingham Rd., West Bromwich, B70 6PY, UK
Tel: 0121 6016350
Fax: 0121 6016387
Email: enquiry@bmhf.org.uk
Website: http://www.bmhf.org.uk/page.asp?node=1&dec=Home
Description: British associations of materials handling equipment manufacturers.
Publication: Journal
Publication title: BMHF Yearbook and Directory. Advertisements.

01309

British Measurement and Testing Association
BMTA

East Malling Enterprise Centre, New Rd., East Malling, Kent, ME19 6BJ, UK
Tel: 01732 897452
Fax: 01732 897453
Email: enquiries@bmta.co.uk
Website: http://www.bmta.co.uk
Members: 90
Contact: Peter Russell, Technical Sec.
Fee: £275
Membership Type: organization (with 7-24 full time employees or partners)
Fee: £470
Membership Type: organization (with 25-250 employees)
Description: Organisations and individuals who have an interest in measurement or testing. Focuses on measurement and testing in the UK. Keeps its members informed on activities affecting measurement going on at home, in Europe and internationally, and represents the UK interests in the European scene.
Publication: Newsletter
Publication title: BMTA News
Meetings/Conventions: periodic workshop – Exhibits.

01310

British Medical Acupuncture Society
BMAS

BMAS House, 3 Winnington Ct., Cheshire, Northwich, CW8 1AQ, UK
Tel: 01606 786782
Fax: 01606 786783
Email: admin@medical-acupuncture.org.uk
Website: http://www.medical-acupuncture.co.uk
Members: 2000
Staff: 9
Contact: Dianne Hough, Sr. Admin.
Fee: £115
Membership Type: regular, accredited
Fee: £79
Membership Type: overseas, dental, veterinary
Description: Medically qualified practitioners. Concerned with the training of medical practitioners in acupuncture. Geographic listings of medically qualified practitioners of acupuncture.
Library Subject: acupuncture in medicine
Library Type: not open to the public
Publication: Journal
Publication title: Acupuncture in Medicine. Advertisements.
Meetings/Conventions: semiannual conference – Exhibits.

01311

British Medical Association
BMA

c/o BMA House
Tavistock Sq., London, WC1H 9JP, UK
Tel: 020 73874499
Email: bmanews@bma.org.uk
Website: http://www.bma.org.uk
Contact: Hamish Meldrum, Chm.
Fee: £417
Membership Type: standard
Fee: £107-311
Membership Type: concessionary (based on years of qualification)
Description: Doctors' trade union and professional association. Scientific and educational body and a publishing house.
Library Subject: clinical medicine, health services management and policy
Library Type: reference
Publication: Journal
Publication title: BMJ Specialist Journals

01312

British Medical Laser Association
BMLA

c/o Mr. Vasant H. Oswal, VP
Far Shirby, Upleatham Redcar, Cleveland, TS11 8AG, UK
Tel: 01382 632240
Fax: 01382 646047
Email: h.moseley@dundee.ac.uk
Website: http://www.bmla.co.uk
Contact: Harry Moseley, Pres.
Description: Strives to promote the use of lasers for treatment of human disease. Promotes the development of laser technology in medicine. Works for understanding between clinical and scientific disciplines in laser application.
Publication: Journal
Publication title: Lasers in Medical Science

01313

British Medical Ultrasound Society
BMUS

36 Portland Pl., London, W1B 1LS, UK
Tel: 020 76363714
Fax: 020 73232175
Email: drj@bmus.org
Website: http://www.bmus.org/intro/home.asp
Members: 2230
Staff: 3
Contact: David Roberts, CEO
Fee: £80
Membership Type: overseas, consultant sonographer, consultant clinical scientist
Fee: £20
Membership Type: student

Description: Medical practitioners, physicists/scientists, sonographers, radiographers, veterinarians, and manufacturers of sonographic equipment. Seeks to advance the science and technology of ultrasound and to improve education in the field.
Formerly: Formerly, British Medical Ultrasound Group
Publication: Newsletter
Publication title: BMUS Bulletin. Advertisements.
Meetings/Conventions: annual convention – Exhibits.

01314

British Menopause Society
BMS

4-6 Eton Pl., Buckinghamshire, Marlow, SL7 2QA, UK
Tel: 01628 890199
Fax: 01628 474042
Email: admin@thebms.org.uk
Website: http://www.thebms.org.uk
Contact: Mary Ann Lumsden, Chair
Fee: £80
Membership Type: nurse in UK
Fee: £100
Membership Type: nurse outside UK
Description: Works to increase the awareness of post-menopausal healthcare issues. Promotes optimal management through conferences, roadshows, and publications.
Publication: Journal

01315

British Menswear Guild
BMG

5 Portland Pl., London, W1B 1PW, UK
Email: director@british-menswear-guild.co.uk
Website: http://www.british-menswear-guild.co.uk
Members: 32
Staff: 2
Contact: David Challinor, Dir.
Description: Top quality manufacturers of men's clothing and accessories. Aims to promote the export of top quality British men's wear to leading shops and stores throughout the world.

01316

British Metals Recycling Association
BMRA

16 High St., Brampton, Huntingdon, PE28 4TU, UK
Tel: 01480 455249
Fax: 01480 453680
Email: admin@recyclemetals.org
Website: http://www.recyclemetals.org
Members: 300
Staff: 4
Contact: Ian Hetherington, Dir. Gen.
Fee: £1280
Membership Type: service, international (plus VAT)
Description: Promotes and maintains a high standard of conduct between members; promotes the welfare and prosperity of the ferrous and non-ferrous scrap industry; promotes improvements in processing the products of the industry through research and exchange of information; represents the common interests of the industry with suppliers, consumers and government.

01317

British Mexican Society
BMS

PO Box 251, Morpeth, NE61 9DH, UK
Tel: 0870 9220679
Email: enquiries@britishmexicansociety.org.uk
Website: http://www.britishmexicansociety.org.uk
Contact: Richard Maudslay, Chm.
Fee: £15
Membership Type: student
Fee: £30
Membership Type: individual
Description: Aims to foster and promote knowledge and appreciation of the rich cultural heritage of Mexico by offering a forum for all United Kingdom residents interested in Mexico and its traditions. Aims to raise funds from various sources and activities in order to support charitable projects in Mexico specially for children and focusing in health and education.

01318

British Microcirculation Society
BMS

c/o Dr. Jim Middleton, Membership Sec.
Keele University, Research Institute for Science & Technology in Medicine, Keele, ST5 5BG, UK
Tel: 01691 404149
Email: lopa.leach@nottingham.ac.uk
Website: http://www.microcirculation.org.uk
Members: 260
Contact: Lopa Leach, Exec. Sec.
Fee: £15
Membership Type: student
Fee: £40
Membership Type: ordinary
Description: Individuals interested in the study of microcirculation and endothelium. Conducts clinical and scientific research.
Library Subject: microcirculation
Library Type: not open to the public
Meetings/Conventions: annual meeting – Exhibits.

01319

British Mule Society
BMS

2 Boscombe Rd., Swindon, SN25 3EY, UK
Tel: 0179 3615478
Email: ann@britishmulesociety.org.uk
Website: http://www.britishmulesociety.org.uk
Members: 150
Contact: Ann Hunter, Sec.
Fee: £15-20
Membership Type: individual (UK and overseas)
Fee: £20-25
Membership Type: family (UK and overseas)
Description: Individuals interested in mules, hinnies, or mule-breeding donkeys. Encourages the breeding of good quality mules through selection of parents; promotes appreciation and well-being of mules. Provides advice and assistance to mule owners and admirers; maintains mule registry. Produces mule-related memorabilia; facilitates communication among members.
Meetings/Conventions: Mule Day – annual show

01320

British Music Hall Society
BMHS

c/o Howard Lee, Honorary Membership Sec.
Thurston Lodge, Thurston Park, Kent, Whitstable, CT5 1RE, UK
Email: actorlee@btinternet.com
Website: http://www.music-hall-society.com
Members: 1000
Contact: Doreen Hermitage, Chm.
Fee: £20
Membership Type: UK, worldwide
Fee: £25
Membership Type: couple (overseas)
Description: Anyone interested in light entertainment, past and present who are united in encouraging interest in music hall and variety. Aims to preserve the history of music hall and variety, to recall the artists who were part of the scene and support entertainers of the present day. Holds regular Music Hall Shows with professional and/or membership participation, and a monthly study group meeting. Occasional Field trips are also arranged.
Publication: Magazine
Publication title: Call Boy. Advertisements.

01321

British Music Rights
BMR

British Music House, 26 Berners St., London, W1T 3LR, UK
Tel: 020 73064446
Fax: 020 73064449
Email: contact@ukmusic.org
Website: http://www.bmr.org
Staff: 7
Contact: Andy Heath, Chm.
Description: Represents the interests of Britain's composers, songwriters, and music publishers. Promotes awareness of the rights and rewards for creativity in the music business. Promotes the value of these rights to the UK economy.

01322

British Music Society
BMS

c/o Stephen Trowell, Treas.
7 Tudor Gardens, Upminster, RM14 3DE, UK
Tel: 01708 224795
Email: sct.bms1943@amserve.com
Website: http://www.britishmusicsociety.com
Members: 600
Contact: John McCabe, Pres.
Fee: £18
Membership Type: ordinary
Fee: £25
Membership Type: patron
Description: Libraries, institutions, students, and other interested individuals in 21 countries. Promotes the work of lesser-known British composers, primarily from the years 1850-1975 by means of quarterly newsletter and annual journal. Publishes other books and issues, audiotape and compact discs. Sponsors competitions.
Publication: Book
Publication title: British Choral Music
Meetings/Conventions: annual meeting

01323
British Mycological Society
BMS
City View House, Union St., Manchester, M12 4JD, UK
Tel: 0161 2777638
Fax: 0161 2777634
Email: admin@britmycolsoc.info
Website: http://www.britmycolsoc.org.uk
Members: 1400
Contact: Lynne Boddy, Pres.
Fee: £30
Membership Type: regular
Fee: £20
Membership Type: postgraduate student
Description: Microbiologists, mycologists, and other scientists organized to promote mycology, the study of fungi.
Library Subject: mycology and plant pathology
Library Type: reference
Publication: Journal
Publication title: Field Mycology

01324
British Natural Hygiene Society
BNHS
Shalimar, 3 Ahlrold Grove, Essex, Frinton-on-Sea, CO13 9BD, UK
Tel: 01636 682941
Website: http://www.bnhs.ms11.net/bnhs
Contact: Keki R. Sidhwa, Pres./Co-Founder
Fee: £10.5
Membership Type: associate
Fee: £12.5
Membership Type: associate (Eire & European countries)
Description: Promotes holistic and complementary health care as an alternative to conventional medical approaches to health disease.
Publication: Magazine
Publication title: The Hygienist

01325
British Naturalists' Association
BNA
PO Box 5682, Corby, NN17 2ZW, UK
Tel: 01536 262977
Email: info@bna-naturalists.org
Website: http://www.bna-naturalists.org
Staff: 1
Contact: David Bellamy, Honorary Pres.
Fee: £20
Membership Type: ordinary
Fee: £24
Membership Type: family
Description: Professional and amateur naturalists. Serves as the national body for both novice and experienced naturalists. Offers its members field activities, lectures, branch programmes throughout the country, field trips in the UK and abroad, and natural history publications at reduced prices. Established Blake Shield BNA Trust Fund which organizes Blake Shield Competition for groups of young people.
Publication title: British Naturalist

01326
British Neuropathological Society
BNS
Derriford Hospital, Histopathology Department, Derriford Rd., Plymouth, PL6 8DH, UK
Email: david.hilton@phnt.swest.nhs.uk
Website: http://www.bns.org.uk
Members: 190
Contact: David Hilton, Sec.
Fee: £70
Membership Type: ordinary
Description: Promotes science and clinical practice related to neuropathology and diseases of the nervous system and skeletal muscle.

01327
British Neuropsychiatry Association
BNPA
c/o Jackie Ashmenall, Admin. Asst.
Lion House, 51 Sheen Ln., London, SW14 8AB, UK
Tel: 020 88780573
Fax: 020 88780573
Email: admin@bnpa.org.uk
Website: http://www.bnpa.org.uk
Contact: Eileen Joyce, Chm.
Fee: £35
Membership Type: general
Fee: £10
Membership Type: individual (under 30 years old)
Description: Provides a forum for the exchange of ideas on neuropsychiatry. Encourages cross-disciplinary discussion of clinical and academic issues. Improves the understanding and treatment of people with neuropsychiatric disorders.

01328
British Neuroscience Association
BNA
University of Cambridge, Department of Experimental Psychology, Cambridge, CB2 3EB, UK
Tel: 01223 766450
Fax: 01223 333564
Email: bnaoffice@neuroscience.cam.ac.uk
Website: http://www.bna.org.uk
Members: 2000
Contact: David Nutt, Pres.-Elect
Fee: £69
Membership Type: full (direct debit)
Fee: £75
Membership Type: full (check and credit card)
Description: Promotes study of the structure and functions of the nervous system. Assist in the training of neuroscientists and other professionals engaged in neuroscience teaching and research.
Publication: Booklet
Publication title: Science of the Brain

01329
British Nuclear Medicine Society
BNMS
Regent House, 291 Kirkdale, London, SE26 4QD, UK
Tel: 020 86767864
Fax: 020 86768417
Email: office@bnms.org.uk
Website: http://www.bnms.org.uk
Contact: Alan C. Perkins, Pres.
Fee: £132
Membership Type: full, in UK
Fee: £172
Membership Type: full, outside UK
Description: Promotes nuclear medicine within the medical community. Provides forum for the advancement of nuclear medicine.
Publication: Newsletter
Publication title: News and Views

01330
British Nutrition Foundation
BNF
High Holborn House, 52-54 High Holborn, London, WC1V 6RQ, UK
Tel: 020 74046504
Fax: 020 74046747
Email: postbox@nutrition.org.uk
Website: http://www.nutrition.org.uk
Members: 49
Staff: 16
Contact: Alan Shenkin, Honorary Pres.
Description: Provides reliable information and scientifically based advice on nutrition and related health matters. Aims to help individuals understand how they may best match their diet with their lifestyle. Produces a wide range of publications on many aspects of diet and health.
Library Subject: nutrition as food science
Library Type: reference
Publication: Bulletin
Publication title: BNF Nutrition Bulletin

01331
British Obesity Surgery Patient Association
BOSPA
PO Box 805, Taunton, TA1 9DU, UK
Tel: 0845 6020446
Email: enquiries@bospa.org
Website: http://www.bospa.org
Contact: Chrissie Palmer, Chair
Fee: £50
Membership Type: professional, affiliate
Fee: £20
Membership Type: life (personal)
Description: Provides support and information to patients in UK for whom obesity surgery can provide an enormous benefit. Seeks to encourage action to reduce the prevalence of obesity. Aims to promote research about obesity. Enhances the understanding and treatment of obesity. Empowers individuals with access to surgery services.

01332
British Occupational Hygiene Society
BOHS
5/6 Melbourne Business Ct., Millennium Way, Pride Park, Derby, DE24 8LZ, UK
Tel: 01332 298101
Fax: 01332 298099
Email: admin@bohs.org
Website: http://www.bohs.org/standardTemplate.aspx
Members: 1300
Staff: 11
Contact: Rob Turner, Pres.
Fee: £40
Membership Type: individual
Fee: £20
Membership Type: retired
Description: Promotes public and professional awareness of occupational and environmental hygiene practices and standards. Provides access to specialist information and outside consultants. Conducts seminars. Offers a wide range of qualifications in occupational hygiene and allied subjects. Maintains Faculty of Occupational Hygiene.
Publication: Journal
Publication title: Annals of Occupational Hygiene

01333
British Office Supplies and Services Federation
BOSS

29-35 Farringdon Rd., London, EC1M 3JF, UK
Tel: 0845 4501565
Fax: 0207 9158414
Email: info@bossfederation.co.uk
Website: http://www.bossfederation.com/page.asp?node=1
Members: 1200
Staff: 2
Contact: Alan Barclay, Chm.
Description: Retailers, manufacturers, associates and wholesalers of office and stationery equipment. Concerned with all aspects of stationery, office products, office furniture, and office machinery including computer hardware and software.
Formerly: Formerly, British Office Systems and Stationery Federation
Publication: Newsletter
Publication title: Environmental Newsletter

01334
British Oil Spill Control Association
BOSCA

Society of Maritime Industries, 28 - 29 Threadneedle St., London, EC2R 8AY, UK
Tel: 020 76282555
Fax: 020 76384376
Email: info@maritimeindustries.org
Website: http://www.maritimeindustries.org/about/oil_spill.jsp
Members: 45
Staff: 2
Contact: John Murray, Chief Exec.
Description: Represents the United Kingdom spill response industry. Membership includes equipment manufacturers, service contractors and consultants and covers every aspect of oil pollution prevention, control and clean-up at sea, along coastlines and inland. Maintains service contracts with both the Maritime and Coastguard Agency (MCA) and the environment regulators, under the terms of which it maintains the national equipment database for use in spill incidents. Plays an active role in clean-up operations undertaken by these organizations. Provides round-the-clock spill response services for commercial organizations and the general public.
Publication: Directory
Publication title: British Oil Spill Control Association Guide to Suppliers

01335
British Orchid Growers Association
BOGA

David Stead Orchids, Greenscapes Horticultural Centre, Brandon Crescent, Shadwell, Leeds, LS17 9JH, UK
Tel: 0113 2893933
Fax: 0113 2893944
Email: info@davidsteadorchids.co.uk
Website: http://www.boga.org.uk
Members: 12
Contact: David Stead, Sec.
Description: Represents orchid nurseries and sundries traders. Promotes and maintains the highest standards of orchid fair trading.

01336
British Origami Society
BOS

c/o Mrs. Penny Groom
2A The Chestnuts, Countesthorpe, Leicester, LE8 5TL, UK
Email: tsurumailbox-origami@yahoo.co.uk
Website: http://www.britishorigami.info
Members: 700
Contact: Mick Guy, Chm.
Fee: £26
Membership Type: ordinary
Fee: £20
Membership Type: junior, student
Description: Seeks to encourage, inform, and educate on origami.
Publication: Magazine
Publication title: British Origami

01337
British Ornithologists' Union
BOU

PO Box 417, Peterborough, PE7 3FX, UK
Tel: 0733 844820
Email: bou@bou.org.uk
Website: http://www.bou.org.uk
Members: 1800
Staff: 2
Contact: Alistair Dawson, Pres.
Fee: £35
Membership Type: ordinary
Fee: £22
Membership Type: junior
Description: Professional and interested amateur ornithologists. Aims to further the science of ornithology throughout the world.
Library Subject: ornithology
Library Type: not open to the public
Publication: Journal
Publication title: IBIS Journal. Advertisements.
Meetings/Conventions: Birds and Disturbance – annual conference – Exhibits.

01338
British Orthodontic Society
BOS

12, Bridewell Pl., London, EC4V 6AP, UK
Tel: 020 73538680
Fax: 020 73538682
Website: http://www.bos.org.uk
Members: 1600
Staff: 1
Contact: Nigel Harradine, Chm.
Fee: £295
Membership Type: associate, trade, laboratory
Fee: £200
Membership Type: international
Description: Persons interested in orthodontics eligible for membership. Members (normally resident in the UK), honorary members, life members, international members, associate members, retired members, laboratory and trades members. Concerned with the promotion of the study and practice of orthodontics. Orthodontics is a specialty of dentistry and involves the treatment of abnormalities of jaw size and dental arch relationship and irregularities of tooth position.
Publication: Newsletter
Publication title: BOS Newsletter

01339
British Orthopaedic Foot and Ankle Society
BOFAS

c/o British Orthopaedic Association
Royal Orthopaedic Association, 35-43 Lincoln's Inn Fields, London, WC2A 3PN, UK
Website: http://www.bofas.org.uk
Contact: Fred Robinson, Pres.
Description: Represents foot and ankle surgeons in the British Orthopaedic Association, as well as in other health related and professional bodies. Encourages interest in foot and ankle surgery.
Formerly: Formerly, British Orthopaedic Foot Surgery Society
Publication: Journal
Publication title: Foot and Ankle Surgery

01340
British Osteopathic Association
BOA

3 Park Terr., Manor Rd., Luton, LU1 3HN, UK
Tel: 0158 2488455
Fax: 0158 2481533
Email: boa@osteopathy.org
Website: http://www.osteopathy.org
Members: 2000
Staff: 4
Contact: Michael Watson, Chief Exec.
Fee: £50
Membership Type: student
Fee: £60
Membership Type: first year graduate
Description: Provides independent representation, care and support.
Publication: Newspaper
Publication title: Osteopathy Today. Advertisements.

01341
British Overseas NGOs for Development
BOND

Regent's Wharf, 8 All Saints St., London, N1 9RL, UK
Tel: 020 78378344
Fax: 020 78374220
Email: bond@bond.org.uk
Website: http://www.bond.org.uk
Members: 340
Staff: 24
Contact: Nick Roseveare, CEO
Fee: £110-4500
Membership Type: full (based on annual expenditure)
Fee: £45
Membership Type: provisional
Description: Aims to improve the United Kingdom's contributions to international development. Collaborates with nongovernmental organizations (NGOs) internationally.

01342
British Packaging Association
BPA

24 Grange St., Kilmarnock, KA1 2AR, UK
Tel: 01563 570518
Fax: 01563 572728
Email: npc@natpack.org.uk
Website: http://www.boxpackaging.org.uk
Members: 100

Staff: 2
Fee: £300-700
Membership Type: regular (based on turnovers)
Description: Represents members' interests.
Formerly: Absorbed, Packaging Distributors Association

01343

British Pain Society
BPS

Churchill House, 3rd Fl., 35 Red Lion Sq., London, WC1R 4SG, UK
Tel: 020 72697840
Fax: 020 78310859
Email: info@britishpainsociety.org
Website: http://www.britishpainsociety.org
Members: 1652
Staff: 2
Contact: Michael Bond, Pres.
Fee: £144
Membership Type: general (based on income)
Description: Professional body representing healthcare professionals working in chronic and acute pain. Aims to relieve the suffering of pain by the promotion of education, training and research. Supplies general information and a list of pain clinics by county.
Formerly: Formerly, Pain Society
Publication: Newsletter
Publication title: Pain Society Newsletter. Advertisements.
Meetings/Conventions: annual international conference – Exhibits.

01344

British Palomino Society
BPS

Penrhiwllan, Llandysul, SA44 5NZ, UK
Tel: 01239 851387
Fax: 01239 851040
Email: britpal@lineone.net
Website: http://www.britishpalominosociety.co.uk
Members: 551
Staff: 1
Contact: A. Langley, Contact
Fee: £35
Membership Type: regular, family
Fee: £17.5
Membership Type: junior
Description: Promotes the advancement of Palominos and their breeding.
Publication: Magazine
Publication title: Palomino. Advertisements.
Meetings/Conventions: Royal Norfolk – annual show

01345

British Parking Association
BPA

Stuart House, 41-43 Perrymount Rd., Haywards Heath, RH16 3BN, UK
Tel: 01444 447300
Fax: 01444 454105
Email: info@britishparking.co.uk
Website: http://www.britishparking.co.uk
Members: 600
Staff: 20
Contact: Keith Banbury, Chief Exec.
Description: Members represent central and local government, consultants, contractors, engineers, planners, architects, car park operators and equipment manufacturers. Holds exhibitions and meetings, publishes information on all aspects of parking and provides services to members. Consulted by official bodies on matters affecting parking and is available for consultation by decision makers and thus serves as a channel through which those with parking interests can make their views known in the appropriate quarters. Operates technical information service; maintains speakers' bureau.
Publication: Journal
Publication title: Parking News. Advertisements.

01346

British Peanut Council
BPC

20 St. Dunstan's Hill, 1st Fl., London, EC3R 8NQ, UK
Tel: 020 72832707
Fax: 020 76231310
Email: info@peanuts.org.uk
Website: http://www.peanuts.org.uk
Members: 45
Staff: 2
Contact: Geoff Street, Chm.
Fee: £250
Membership Type: trade
Fee: £200
Membership Type: overseas
Description: Promotes and protects the interests of the British peanut industry.

01347

British Pest Control Association
BPCA

1 Gleneagles House, Ground Fl., Vernongate S St., Derby, DE1 1UP, UK
Tel: 01332 294288
Fax: 01332 225101
Email: enquiry@bpca.org.uk
Website: http://www.bpca.org.uk/home.asp?parent_id=1
Members: 250
Staff: 12
Contact: Martina Flynn, Pres.
Fee: £7705.65
Membership Type: full (based on relevant turnover)
Fee: £205.63
Membership Type: provisional scheme
Description: Companies in Great Britain providing products and services to the pest control industry, including fumigation equipment, silo cleaning, and bird control.
Publication: Membership Directory

01348

British Pharmacological Society
BPS

16 Angel Gate, City Rd., London, EC1V 2PT, UK
Tel: 020 74170110
Fax: 020 74170114
Email: info@bps.ac.uk
Website: http://www.bps.ac.uk
Members: 2650
Staff: 11
Contact: Kate Baillie, Chief Exec.
Fee: £90
Membership Type: ordinary
Fee: £150
Membership Type: fellow
Description: Pharmacologists and clinical pharmacologists in academia and industry in 20 countries. Conducts educational symposia and lectures; makes available travel bursaries.
Publication: Journal
Publication title: British Journal of Clinical Pharmacology. Advertisements.
Meetings/Conventions: James Black Conference – annual conference

01349

British Philosophical Association
BPA

University of Birmingham, Dept. of Philosophy, London, B15 2TT, UK
Tel: 0121 4146054
Fax: 0121 4148453
Email: philosophy@bham.ac.uk
Website: http://www.bpa.ac.uk
Contact: Helen Beebee, Dir.
Fee: £15
Membership Type: full (waged)
Fee: £8
Membership Type: full (unwaged)
Description: Promotes the study of philosophy, particularly within higher education. Assists professional philosophers in their teaching, scholarship and research in philosophy. Fosters interest in and appreciation of philosophy in the wider community. Expresses the views of the community of professional philosophers in Britain to relevant bodies.

01350

British Phonographic Industry
BPI

Riverside Bldg., County Hall, Westminster Bridge Rd., London, SE1 7JA, UK
Tel: 020 78031300
Fax: 020 78031310
Email: general@bpi.co.uk
Website: http://www.bpi.co.uk
Members: 231
Staff: 23
Contact: Tony Wadsworth, Chm.
Fee: £67.5
Membership Type: full
Fee: £500
Membership Type: associate
Description: Trade Association for British record companies. Acts as a focal point both for its members and for individuals and organizations dealing with the record industry. Promotes the interests of the industry both in Westminster and Brussels.
Library Subject: music
Library Type: by appointment only
Publication: Handbook
Publication title: Statistical Handbook

01351

British Photodermatology Group
BPG

Gloucestershire Royal Hospital, Medical Physics Dept., Great Western Rd., Gloucester, GL1 3NN, UK
Tel: 08454 225976
Fax: 08454 226489
Email: david.taylor@glos.nhs.uk
Website: http://www.bpg.org.uk
Contact: David Taylor, Sec.-Treas.
Description: Works for the advancement of photodermatological education by dissemination of the results of research into or relevant to effects, in health and disease, of ultraviolet and visible radiation on the skin.

01352
British Phycological Society
BPS
Department of Botany, The Natural History Museum, Cromwell Rd., London, SW7 5BD, UK
Tel: 020 79425910
Fax: 020 79425529
Email: j.brodie@nhm.ac.uk
Website: http://www.brphycsoc.org
Members: 470
Contact: Juliet Brodie, Pres.
Fee: £10.5
Membership Type: ordinary (without journal)
Fee: £36.5
Membership Type: ordinary (with journal)
Description: Scientists, students, and other interested persons organized to further phycology, the study of algae. Conducts conservation activities and field excursions. Assists in mapping the geographical distributions of seaweeds of the British Isles. Maintains a scientific meeting fund to enable students to attend society meetings.
Publication: Journal
Publication title: European Journal of Phycology
Meetings/Conventions: annual conference – Exhibits.

01353
British Pig Association
BPA
Trumpington Mews, 40B High St., Trumpington, Cambridge, CB2 2LS, UK
Tel: 01223 845100
Fax: 01223 846235
Email: bpa@britishpigs.org
Website: http://www.britishpigs.org.uk
Members: 650
Staff: 4
Contact: Robert Overend, Chm.
Fee: £20
Membership Type: individual
Description: Participants in the pig industry - principally pedigree pig farmers, representative body for the pedigree pig industry. Operates the UK's longest established, proven Herd Book recording service.

01354
British Plastics Federation
BPF
5-6 Bath Pl., Rivington St., London, EC2A 3JE, UK
Tel: 020 74575000
Fax: 020 74575020
Email: reception@bpf.co.uk
Website: http://www.bpf.co.uk
Members: 400
Staff: 24
Contact: Peter Davis, Dir. Gen.
Description: Open to all UK companies with an involvement in the plastics sector, whether polymer, machinery or additive producers or plastics processors. Exists to promote the growth and profitability of the UK Plastics Industry. Encourages cooperation between manufacturers to ensure a coordinated industry response to common opportunities and challenges. Represents its members' interests to UK government and EC institutions. Information service 9061 908070.
Publication title: Codes of Practice on Health & Safety

01355
British Porphyria Association
BPA
136 Devonshire Rd., Durham, DH1 2BL, UK
Tel: 01474 369231
Email: helpline@porphyria.org.uk
Website: http://www.porphyria.org.uk
Contact: Mike Badminton, Contact
Description: Represents the interests of Porphyria patients and their relatives. Seeks to raise awareness and improve understanding of Porphyria. Provides support services to patients and their families. Maintains contact with other Porphyria support groups in other countries. Sponsors research and education. Provides patients and practitioners with details of doctors specializing in Porphyria.

01356
British Ports Association
BPA
4th Fl. Carthusian Ct., 12 Carthusian St., London, EC1M 6EZ, UK
Tel: 020 72601780
Fax: 020 72601784
Email: info@britishports.org.uk
Website: http://www.britishports.org.uk
Members: 89
Staff: 3
Contact: David Whitehead, Dir.
Fee: £909
Membership Type: associate
Description: Includes ports, terminal operators and port facilities. Represents a broad cross-section of port types in terms of ownership, size and operations in the UK ports industry. Works to address the diverse issues face by the industry.

01357
British Poultry Council
BPC
5 - 11 Lavington St., London, SE1 0NZ, UK
Tel: 0845 3022833
Email: bpc@poultry.uk.com
Website: http://www.poultry.uk.com
Contact: Ted Wright, Chm.
Description: Conducts parliamentary and legislative lobbying on issues of research and development, farm animal welfare, trading standards, and import regulation. Analyzes poultry industry statistics covering the United Kingdom, European, and world markets. Monitors poultry diseases that could disrupt the industry; commissions clinical research.
Formerly: Formerly, British Poultry Meat Federation

01358
British Precast Concrete Federation
BPCF
60 Charles St., Leicester, LE1 1FB, UK
Tel: 0116 2536161
Fax: 0116 2514568
Email: info@britishprecast.org
Website: http://www.britishprecast.org
Contact: Martin Clarke, Chief Exec.
Description: Manufacturers of precast concrete products in factories in the United Kingdom. Represents members' interests before government bodies and regulatory agencies. Acts as forum for the exchange of technical information. Sponsors tours.
Formerly: Formerly, British Cast Concrete Federation
Publication: Directory
Publication title: Products Directory

01359
British Press Photographers Association
BPPA
2 Lansdowne Crescent, Ste. 219, Bournemouth, BH1 1SA, UK
Email: info@thebppa.com
Website: http://www.thebppa.com
Members: 400
Contact: Jeff Moore, Chm.
Fee: £75
Membership Type: individual
Description: Represents the press photographers in UK. Promotes press photography by exhibiting and publishing the members' work.

01360
British Printing Industries Federation
BPIF
Farringdon Point, 29-35 Farringdon Rd., London, EC1M 3JF, UK
Tel: 020 79158300
Fax: 020 74057784
Email: info@britishprint.com
Website: http://www.britishprint.com
Members: 3000
Staff: 120
Contact: Michael Johnson, Chief Exec.
Fee: £160-3590
Membership Type: silver (based on number of employees)
Fee: £310-6140
Membership Type: gold (based on number of employees)
Description: Promotes and represents the interests of the printing, packaging, and graphic communications industry in the United Kingdom. Offers technical and legal consulting services. Sponsors competitions. Compiles statistics. Conducts seminars.

01361
British Professional Toastmasters' Authority
BPTA
12 Little Bornes, Dulwich, London, SE21 8SE, UK
Tel: 020 86705585
Fax: 020 86700055
Website: http://www.ivorspencer.com
Contact: Ivor Spencer, Pres.
Description: Represents the interests of professional public speakers in the United Kingdom. Promotes the art of public speaking.

01362
British Promotional Merchandise Association
BPMA

52-53 Russell Sq., London, WC1B 4HP, UK
Tel: 020 76316960
Fax: 020 76316944
Email: enquiries@bpma.co.uk
Website: http://www.bpma.co.uk
Members: 700
Contact: Gordon Glenister, Dir. Gen.
Fee: £1028.13
Membership Type: company (turnover is 1 million)
Fee: £543.44
Membership Type: company (turnover is less than 1 million)
Description: Represents suppliers of promotional merchandise and services. Provides Code of Conduct for its members to follow.
Publication: Yearbook
Publication title: BPMA Directory. Advertisements.
Meetings/Conventions: The ASI Show – periodic show

01363
British Property Federation
BPF

5th Fl., St. Albans House, 57-59 Haymarket, London, SW1Y 4QX, UK
Tel: 020 78280111
Fax: 020 78343442
Email: info@bpf.org.uk
Website: http://www.bpf.org.uk
Members: 500
Staff: 13
Contact: Liz Peace, Chief Exec.
Fee: £750-6400
Membership Type: property company (gross assets of 5 million to over 100 million)
Fee: £9900-39500
Membership Type: property company (gross assets of over 150 million to over 3 billion)
Description: Acts as the trade association of the property industry, membership includes property development companies, property investment companies, banks, insurance companies, pension funds, residential landlords, multiple retailers and professional firms.

01364
British Psychoanalytical Society
BPAS

112A Shirland Rd., London, W9 2EQ, UK
Tel: 020 75635000
Fax: 020 75635001
Email: ginette@goulston-lincoln.com
Website: http://www.psychoanalysis.org.uk
Contact: Ginette Goulston Lincoln, Contact
Fee: £380
Membership Type: full
Fee: £190
Membership Type: associate, retired, guest
Description: Psychoanalysts in the United Kingdom. Offers instructional programs. Promotes members' interests.
Library Subject: psychoanalysis
Library Type: open to the public
Publication: Brochure
Publication title: Beyond the Couch
Meetings/Conventions: English-Speaking Weekend Conference – biennial conference

01365
British Psychodrama Association
BPA

8 Douglas Dr. E, Helensburgh, G84 9BG, UK
Tel: 07794 125602
Email: james@bpad.co.uk
Website: http://www.psychodrama.org.uk
Members: 250
Contact: James Scanlan, Admin.
Fee: £50
Membership Type: individual (in UK)
Fee: £100
Membership Type: trainee
Description: Promotes the use of psychodrama and sociodrama as a creative and effective approach to working with a wide range of people in a variety of different settings. Psychodrama, sociometry, and group psychotherapy developed from the work of Jacob Levy Moreno (1889-1974).
Library Subject: psychodrama, sociodrama
Library Type: reference
Publication: Journal
Publication title: British Journal of Psychodrama and Sociodrama

01366
British Psychological Society
BPS

St. Andrews House, 48 Princess Rd. E, Leicester, LE1 7DR, UK
Tel: 0116 2549568
Fax: 0116 2771314
Email: enquiries@bps.org.uk
Website: http://www.bps.org.uk
Members: 45000
Contact: Sue Gardner, Pres.
Fee: £100
Membership Type: fellow, ordinary, associate, graduate
Fee: £48
Membership Type: graduate (during the first three years after the eligibility on application)
Description: Academic, research, and all branches of applied psychology. Promotes the advancement of psychological study and works to ensure high standards of professional education and conduct.
Publication: Journal
Publication title: British Journal of Clinical Psychology

01367
British Psychosocial Oncology Society
BPOS

Lynda Jackson Macmillan Centre, Mt. Vernon Cancer Centre, Middlesex, Northwood, HA6 2RN, UK
Tel: 01923 844878
Fax: 01923 844172
Email: teresa.young2@nhs.net
Website: http://www.bpos.org
Contact: Teresa Young, Sec.
Fee: £85
Membership Type: full
Fee: £25
Membership Type: associate
Description: Advances education and research in psychosocial oncology. Improves the quality of care of people with cancer by promoting better information-giving, communication and psychosocial support. Promotes knowledge and implementation of the principles of psychosocial oncology among healthcare providers working with people with cancer and their families.
Publication: Journal
Publication title: Psycho-Oncology

01368
British Pteridological Society
BPS

c/o Mike G. Taylor, Membership Sec.
Westlea, Kyleakin, Isle of Skye, IV41 8PH, UK
Tel: 01599 534391
Email: membership@ebps.org.uk
Website: http://www.nhm.ac.uk/hosted_sites/bps
Members: 800
Contact: Yvonne C. Golding, Gen. Sec.
Fee: £20
Membership Type: full
Fee: £10
Membership Type: student
Description: Amateur and professional pteridologists interested in all aspects of the botany, natural history and cultivation of ferns and fern allies. Promotes the growing, study and conservation of fern and fern allies, and encourages interest in their taxonomy, distribution and ecology.
Publication: Journal
Publication title: American Fern Journal

01369
British Pump Manufacturers' Association
BPMA

National Metalforming Ctre., 47 Birmingham Rd., West Bromwich, B70 6PY, UK
Tel: 0121 6016350
Fax: 0121 6016387
Email: enquiry@bpma.org.uk
Website: http://www.bpma.org.uk/page.asp?node=18&sec=Home
Members: 60
Staff: 3
Contact: Brian Huxley, Dir.
Fee: £927-9884
Membership Type: regular (based on annual turnover)
Fee: £500
Membership Type: associate
Description: Trade association for manufacturers and suppliers of pumps in Great Britain. Promotes pump manufacturing industry. Encourages exchange of information between members.
Publication: Newsletter
Publication title: BPMA News
Meetings/Conventions: International Pump Technical Conference – biennial conference

01370
British Puppet and Model Theatre Guild

65 Kingsley Ave., London, W13 0EH, UK
Tel: 020 89978236
Email: peter@peterpuppet.co.uk
Website: http://www.puppetguild.org.uk
Members: 250
Contact: Peter Charlton, Chm.
Fee: £18
Membership Type: full, adult
Fee: £12
Membership Type: junior (below 16 years old)
Description: Promotes puppetry and toy theatre.
Publication: Magazine
Publication title: The Puppet Master

01371
British Pyrotechnists Association
BPA
8 Aragon Pl., Kimbolton, Huntingdon, Cambridge, PE28 0JD, UK
Tel: 01480 878621
Fax: 01480 878650
Email: info@bpa-fmg.org.uk
Website: http://www.bpa-fmg.org.uk
Members: 28
Staff: 1
Contact: Tom A. Smith, Sec.
Description: Works as an umbrella organization incorporating the Firework Makers' Guild. Collects and passes on to all firework manufacturers information concerning Government and other regulations etc. Acts as a source of information to the industry and promotes the safe handling of fireworks in the UK.
Publication: Video
Publication title: Celebrate Safely

01372
British Rabbit Council
BRC
Purefoy House, 7, Kirkgate, Notts, Newark, NG24 1AD, UK
Tel: 01636 676042
Fax: 01636 611683
Email: info@thebrc.org
Website: http://www.thebrc.org
Members: 5042
Staff: 2
Contact: G. Webb-Bailey, Pres.
Fee: £2
Membership Type: junior
Fee: £8.75
Membership Type: adult
Description: Protects, furthers and co-ordinates the interests of all British rabbit breeders; assists and extends the exhibition of rabbits. Influences, advises and co-operates with central and local authorities, departments of education and other committees and schools in promoting the extension of the breeding of rabbits and to promote and encourage education and research of a scientific and/or practical nature.
Publication title: Breeds Standard. Advertisements.

01373
British Record Society
BRS
London School of Economics, Houghton St., London, WC2A 2AE, UK
Email: p.h.wallis@lse.ac.uk
Website: http://www.britishrecordsociety.org
Contact: Patrick Wallis, Honorary Sec.
Fee: £28
Membership Type: individual
Fee: £46
Membership Type: institutional
Description: Concerned with the publishing of indexes to historical records.

01374
British Records Association
BRA
c/o Finsbury Library
245 St. John St., London, EC1V 4NB, UK
Tel: 020 78330428
Fax: 020 78330416
Email: brrecass@btconnect.com
Website: http://www.britishrecordsassociation.org.uk
Members: 875
Staff: 2
Contact: M.V. Roberts, Chm.
Fee: £25
Membership Type: individual
Fee: £55
Membership Type: institutional
Description: Individuals and institutions involved in the use and preservation of historical documents. Aims to further the study of history through maintenance of public and private archives. Acts to rescue and preserve documents that might otherwise be destroyed. Generates public interest in matters pertaining to archive preservation. Facilitates access to historical archives for interested students, authors, and other researchers.
Publication: Journal
Publication title: Archives. Advertisements.

01375
British Red Cross
44 Moorfields, London, EC2Y 9AL, UK
Tel: 0844 8711111
Fax: 020 75622000
Email: information@redcross.org.uk
Website: http://www.redcross.org.uk
Members: 40000
Staff: 2500
Contact: Nicholas Young, CEO
Description: Provides services in local communities across UK such as responding to emergencies, training first aiders, helping vulnerable people regain their independence and assisting refugees and asylum seekers. Responds rapidly to disasters and conflicts around the world.
Publication: Newsletter

01376
British Reflexology Association
BRA
Monks Orchard, Whitbourne, Worcester, WR6 5RB, UK
Tel: 01886 821207
Fax: 01886 822017
Email: bra@britreflex.co.uk
Website: http://www.britreflex.co.uk
Members: 750
Contact: Diane Morgan, Contact
Fee: £45
Membership Type: ordinary
Description: Represents individuals involved in practicing the method of reflexology as a profession.
Publication: Newsletter
Publication title: Footprints. Advertisements.
Meetings/Conventions: lecture

01377
British Refrigeration Association
BRA
Federation of Environmental Trade Associations, Milley Ln., 2 Waltham Ct., Berkshire, Reading, RG10 9TH, UK
Tel: 0118 9403416
Fax: 0118 9406258
Email: info@feta.co.uk
Website: http://www.feta.co.uk
Members: 120
Staff: 5
Contact: Cedric Sloan, Dir. Gen.
Description: Manufacturers, distributors, contractors and training organizations working in the refrigeration industry. Works closely with government, public bodies and other organisations, both in the UK and overseas, to further the interests of the refrigeration industry.

01378
British Retail Consortium
BRC
21 Dartmouth St., London, SW1H 9BP, UK
Tel: 020 78548900
Fax: 020 78548901
Email: onlinehelp@brc.org.uk
Website: http://www.brc.org.uk
Staff: 40
Contact: Stephen Robertson, Dir. Gen.
Fee: £1265
Membership Type: retail (minimum)
Fee: £3462
Membership Type: trade association (minimum)
Description: Represents 90 percent of the retail industry in the UK.
Library Type: reference
Formerly: Formerly, Retail Consortium
Publication: Newsletter
Publication title: Broadcast

01379
British Retinitis Pigmentosa Society
BRPS
PO Box 350, Buckingham, MK18 1GZ, UK
Tel: 0128 0821334
Fax: 0128 0815900
Email: info@brps.org.uk
Website: http://www.brps.org.uk/home.php?home=yes
Members: 3000
Staff: 3
Contact: David Head, Chief Exec.
Fee: £20
Membership Type: individual
Description: RP sufferers and their families and interested multidisciplinary members. Aims to help RP sufferers and their families cope with RP. Raises money for medical research.
Publication: Annual Report
Publication title: Annual Trustees Report and Research Report

01380
British Rig Owners' Association
BROA
Carthusian Ct., 12 Carthusian St., London, EC1M 6EZ, UK
Tel: 020 74172827
Fax: 020 76001534
Email: postmaster@broa.org
Website: http://www.broa.org
Members: 8
Contact: Paul King, Chm.
Description: Owners/managers of mobile offshore units. Aims to promote and protect the interests of British rig owners/managers in respect of all aspects of design, construction, equipment and operation of mobile offshore units.

01381
British Safety Council
70 Chancellors Rd., London, W6 9RS, UK
Tel: 020 87411231
Fax: 020 87414555
Email: mail@britsafe.org
Website: http://www.britsafe.org
Members: 10000
Staff: 90
Contact: Julie Nerney, Chief Exec.
Fee: £350-650
Membership Type: standard (based on number of employees)
Description: Aims to promote health, safety and environmental best practice for the benefit of society and the increase of productivity.

01382
British Sandwich Association
BSA
Association House, 18c Moor St., Chepstow, NP16 5DB, UK
Tel: 01291 636331
Fax: 01291 630402
Email: jim@jandmgroup.co.uk
Website: http://www.sandwich.org.uk
Members: 1280
Staff: 6
Contact: Jim Winship, Dir.
Description: Represents suppliers to the sandwich industry (meat, cheese, salad, mayonnaise, and bread packaging, refrigeration, distribution etc.), sandwich manufacturers, and sandwich bars/retail buyers. Promotes sandwich consumption as well as quality standards. Has developed its own Code of Practice for the industry which has the approval of the Institution of Environmental Health Officers and many retailers.
Publication: Magazine
Publication title: Sandwich and Snack News. Advertisements.
Meetings/Conventions: Food on the Move – periodic conference – Exhibits.

01383
British Science Association
Wellcome Wolfson Bldg., 165 Queen's Gate, London, SW7 5HD, UK
Tel: 0870 7707101
Fax: 0870 7707102
Email: supporters@britishscienceassociation.org
Website: http://www.britishscienceassociation.org
Contact: Roland Jackson, Chief Exec.
Fee: £250
Membership Type: corporate (based on company size)
Fee: £250
Membership Type: institutional
Description: Scientists; corporations; individuals interested in science. Seeks to enhance public understanding and awareness of science and technology and their impact on society. Maintains 16 subject sections.
Formerly: Formerly, British Association for the Advancement of Science
Publication: Magazine
Publication title: Science and the Public Affairs
Meetings/Conventions: Festival of Science – annual meeting – Exhibits.

01384
British Science Fiction Association
BSFA
39 Glyn Ave., Herts, New Barnet, EN4 9PJ, UK
Email: bsfamembership@yahoo.co.uk
Website: http://www.bsfa.co.uk
Members: 600
Contact: Peter Wilkinson, Membership Sec.
Fee: £26
Membership Type: in UK
Fee: £32
Membership Type: outside UK
Description: Promotes and encourages the reading, writing and publishing of science fiction, and provides a forum where SF fans, authors, publishers and critics can maintain contact and exchange ideas. Other services include writers' postal workshops and information service.
Publication: Magazine
Publication title: Focus. Advertisements.

01385
British Security Industry Association
BSIA
Kirkham House, John Comyn Dr., Worcester, WR3 7NS, UK
Tel: 0845 3893889
Fax: 0845 3890761
Email: c.brooks@bsia.co.uk
Website: http://www.bsia.co.uk
Members: 570
Staff: 22
Contact: James Kelly, Chief Exec.
Fee: £795.63
Membership Type: principal section
Fee: £1495
Membership Type: overseas associate
Description: Trade association for manufacturers and suppliers of security products and services in Great Britain, including safes, alarms, guard and patrol services access control, closed circuit television, information destruction, and physical security.
Library Type: by appointment only
Publication: Membership Directory
Publication title: Security Direct. Advertisements.

01386
British Sheep Dairying Association
BSDA
Treemans Rd., Horsted Keynes, RH17 7EA, UK
Tel: 01825 791636
Email: office@sheepdairying.co.uk
Website: http://www.sheepdairying.co.uk
Members: 200
Staff: 1
Contact: John Ryrie, Chm.
Fee: £50
Description: Individuals and companies with an interest in sheep dairying. Promotes sheep dairying in the UK and worldwide.
Publication: Journal
Publication title: Sheep Dairy News. Advertisements.

01387
British Shops and Stores Association
BSSA
Middleton House, 2 Main Rd., Middleton Cheney, Oxon, Banbury, OX17 2TN, UK
Tel: 01295 712277
Fax: 01295 711665
Email: membership@bssa.co.uk
Website: http://www.british-shops.co.uk
Members: 4750
Staff: 45000
Contact: Alan Hawkins, CEO
Fee: £195-1093
Membership Type: full (based on annual turnover)
Fee: £404.2
Membership Type: associate (based on annual turnover)
Description: Non-food retailers. Represents non-food retailers nationwide with specific sectors covering fashions and fabrics, men's and boys' wear, and furnishings. Services include clearing house, insurance, training, general advisory services and regular bulletins.
Publication: Newsletter
Publication title: Retail Review

01388
British Show Pony Society
BSPS
124 Green End Rd., Sawtry, Huntingdon, PE28 5XS, UK
Tel: 01487 831376
Fax: 01487 832779
Email: info@bsps.com
Website: http://www.britishshowponysociety.co.uk
Description: Aims to improve children's shows by promoting classes and competitions.

01389
British Sign and Graphics Association
BSGA
5 Orton Enterprise Centre, Bakewell Rd., Orton Southgate, Cambridgeshire, Peterborough, PE2 6XU, UK
Tel: 01733 230033
Email: info@bsga.co.uk
Website: http://www.bsga.co.uk
Members: 230
Staff: 3
Contact: Ian Drinkwater, Natl. Pres.
Fee: £352-2525
Membership Type: full (based on turnover)
Fee: £382-1039
Membership Type: associate (based on turnover)
Description: Any company or firm engaged in manufacturing illuminated or non-illuminated advertising signs, any company or firm who supplies raw materials, components, equipment or services to the sign-making industry, or, any college or educational establishment which provides training or qualification courses for the sign industry. Aims to promote, develop, consolidate and protect the interests of sign manufacturers or suppliers to the industry. Promotes a high standard of quality, design, workmanship and good commercial practice within the sign industry.
Formerly: Formerly, British Sign Association
Publication: Newsletter
Publication title: BSGA News

01390

British Sleep Society
BSS

PO Box 247, Huntingdon, PE28 3UZ, UK
Email: enquiries@sleeping.org.uk
Website: http://www.sleeping.org.uk
Contact: John Shneerson, Pres.
Fee: £25
Membership Type: regular
Description: Represents medical, healthcare and scientific workers who have an interest in sleep and medical disorders. Aims to improve public health by promoting education into sleep and its disorders. Promotes knowledge and research in sleep, its disorders and treatment.

01391

British Small Animal Veterinary Association
BSAVA

Woodrow House, 1 Telford Way, Waterwells Business Park, Quedgeley, Gloucester, GL2 2AB, UK
Tel: 01452 726700
Fax: 01452 726701
Email: administration@bsava.com
Website: http://www.bsava.com
Members: 5500
Staff: 20
Contact: Grant Petrie, Pres.
Fee: £194
Membership Type: full
Fee: £129
Membership Type: postgraduate
Description: Veterinarians in 20 countries. Operates speakers' bureau; sponsors educational programs. Compiles statistics. Sponsors competitions; conducts charitable activities.
Library Type: reference
Publication: Newsletter
Publication title: BSAVA News

01392

British Society for Allergy and Clinical Immunology
BSACI

Elliot House, 10-12 Allington St., London, SW1E 5EH, UK
Tel: 020 78087135
Fax: 020 78087139
Email: info@bsaci.org
Website: http://www.bsaci.org
Contact: Fiona Rayner, Chief Exec.
Fee: £117
Membership Type: overseas
Fee: £112
Membership Type: full (UK)
Description: Works to improve the management of allergic and related diseases in the United Kingdom. Provides a curriculum for the training of allergy specialists and supports research into the causes and treatment of allergic disease.
Publication: Newsletter
Publication title: Allergy Update
Meetings/Conventions: annual meeting

01393

British Society for Allergy, Environmental and Nutritional Medicine
BSAENM

PO Box 7, Powys, Knighton, LD7 1WF, UK
Tel: 01547 550380
Website: http://www.jnem.demon.co.uk
Fee: £65
Membership Type: full, scientific
Fee: £25
Membership Type: associate
Description: Provides support and contact for medical and other health professionals. Organizes scientific meetings at both national and international level. Points doctors to sources of information in the form of books, clinical papers, etc.
Publication: Journal
Publication title: Journal of Nutritional and Environmental Medicine

01394

British Society for Antimicrobial Chemotherapy
BSAC

Griffin House, 53 Regent Pl., Birmingham, B1 3NJ, UK
Tel: 0121 2361988
Fax: 0121 2129822
Email: enquiries@bsac.org.uk
Website: http://www.bsac.org.uk
Members: 800
Staff: 5
Contact: Tracey Guise, Exec. Off.
Fee: £83
Membership Type: regular (with printed and online versions of the jac)
Fee: £44
Membership Type: regular (with online access only)
Description: Individuals in 33 countries working in the field of antimicrobial chemotherapy. Furthers research and understanding of antimicrobial chemotherapy.
Publication: Journal
Publication title: Journal of Antimicrobial Chemotherapy. Advertisements.

01395

British Society for Cell Biology
BSCB

Institute of Cancer Research, 237 Fulham Rd., London, SW3 6JB, UK
Tel: 020 71535510
Fax: 020 71535340
Email: clare.isacke@icr.ac.uk
Website: http://www.bscb.org
Contact: Clare Isacke, Pres.
Fee: £35
Membership Type: regular (direct/overseas)
Fee: £35
Membership Type: regular (non-direct debit payer)
Description: Promotes cell biology through scientific meetings and encourages understanding through public discussion of cell biology aims and achievements.

01396

British Society for Clinical Cytology
BSCC

12 Coldbath Sq., London, EC1R 5HL, UK
Tel: 020 72786907
Email: mail@bscc.uk.net
Website: http://www.clinicalcytology.co.uk
Contact: J.H.F Smith, Pres.
Fee: £75
Membership Type: regular
Fee: £125
Membership Type: ordinary
Description: Aims to advance the science and art of clinical cytology by encouraging higher standards in clinical cytology for the benefit of the public.

01397

British Society for Clinical Neurophysiology
BSCN

Frenchay Hospital, Clinical Neurophysiology Department, Bristol, BS16 1LE, UK
Email: nick.kane@nbt.nhs.uk
Website: http://www.clinicalneurophysiology.org.uk
Members: 350
Contact: Peter Heath, Pres.
Fee: £100
Membership Type: individual
Fee: £15
Membership Type: subscriber
Description: Medical practitioners, scientists and technologists. Medical and scientific study of electrical activity that can be recorded from the nervous system. Promotes research, education and training in clinical neurophysiology.
Formerly: Formerly, EEG Society

01398

British Society for Clinical Psychophysiology
BSCP

26 Wervin Rd., Prenton, Birkenhead, CH43 0UZ, UK
Tel: 0151 2018428
Fax: 0151 2018428
Email: admin@the-bscp.com
Website: http://www.the-bscp.com
Members: 4
Contact: Steve Richards, Founder
Description: Represents psychotherapists working in the field of integrative medicine and mind-body therapy. Accredits training courses in holistic-medical psychotherapy. Maintains a registry of individual practitioners.

01399

British Society for Dental and Maxillofacial Radiology
BSDMFR

Dundee Dental Hospital, 2 Park Pl., Scotland, Dundee, DD1 4HR, UK
Email: alison.menhinick@tuht.scot.nhs.uk
Website: http://www.liv.ac.uk/~ppnixon
Members: 150
Contact: Alison Menhinick, Honorary Sec.
Fee: £30

Membership Type: ordinary
Fee: £20
Membership Type: associate
Description: Dental radiologists. Offers educational and public service programs. Conducts research.

01400
British Society for Disability and Oral Health
BSDH

19 Hazelmere Ave., Melton Park, Gosforth, NE3 5QL, UK
Email: katherine.wilson@newcastle.ac.uk
Website: http://www.bsdh.org.uk
Contact: Kathy Wilson, Honorary Sec.
Fee: £50
Membership Type: full
Fee: £25
Membership Type: category A
Description: Promotes the oral health of disabled people of all ages. Fosters research and education in the field of oral health for disabled people. Encourages networking and communication of individuals interested in the oral care of people with disabilities.
Publication: Journal
Publication title: Journal of Disability and Oral Health

01401
British Society for Eighteenth Century Studies
BSECS

University of Hertfordshire, English Division, School of Humanities, College Ln., Hatfield, AL10 9AB, UK
Email: ssmith2@wiley.com
Website: http://www.bsecs.org.uk
Contact: Gavin Budge, Exec. Sec.
Fee: £40
Membership Type: ordinary
Fee: £20
Membership Type: retired, student
Description: Represents people interested in the literature, history, art, politics and society of the Long Eighteenth Century.
Publication: Journal
Publication title: British Journal for Eighteenth Century Studies

01402
British Society for Geomorphology
BSG

Royal Geographical Society, 1 Kensington Gore, London, SW7 2AR, UK
Email: d.a.robinson@sussex.ac.uk
Website: http://www.geomorphology.org.uk
Contact: David Robinson, Honorary Treas.
Fee: £45
Membership Type: postgraduate
Fee: £12
Membership Type: student, retired, unwaged
Description: Develops geomorphology through international cooperation; promotes the study and development of geomorphology in all aspects; fosters the dissemination of knowledge of geomorphology. Fosters better communication among those working in the geomorphic sciences, especially in geography.
Formerly: Formerly, British Geomorphological Research Group
Publication: Newsletter
Publication title: Geophemera
Meetings/Conventions: Geomorphology and Earth System – annual conference

01403
British Society for Haematology
BSH

100 White Lion St., London, N1 9PF, UK
Tel: 020 77130990
Email: info@b-s-h.org.uk
Website: http://www.b-s-h.org.uk
Members: 1300
Staff: 3
Contact: D. Linch, Pres.
Fee: £70
Membership Type: associate
Fee: £140
Membership Type: full
Description: Committed to advancing the practice and study of haematology; promotes good haematological practice and communication.
Publication: Journal
Publication title: British Journal of Haematology. Advertisements.

01404
British Society for Histocompatibility and Immunogenetics
BSHI

12 Coldbath Sq., London, EC1R 5HL, UK
Email: secretary@bshi.org.uk
Website: http://www.bshi.org.uk
Members: 450
Contact: Jackie Cornish, Pres.
Description: Promotes service and research activities in Histocompatibility and Immunogenetics (H&I), especially in the fields of transplantation and disease susceptibility. Promotes and maintains the highest possible professional standards in H&I. Establishes and promotes training in all theoretical and practical aspects of H&I.
Publication: Newsletter

01405
British Society for Human Genetics
BSHG

Birmingham Women's Hospital, Clinical Genetics Unit, Birmingham, B15 2TG, UK
Tel: 0121 6272634
Fax: 0121 6236971
Email: bshg@bshg.org.uk
Website: http://www.bshg.org.uk
Members: 2000
Staff: 2
Contact: Dina Kotecha, Exec. Off.
Fee: £55
Membership Type: regular
Description: Aims to advance the science of human genetics; promotes research and public awareness of human genetics related to health and disease; guides professionals contributing to genetics in healthcare; offers informed opinion on issues of public interest.
Publication: Newsletter
Publication title: BSHG Newsletter

01406
British Society for Immunology
BSI

Vintage House, 37 Albert Embankment, London, SE1 7TL, UK
Tel: 020 30319800
Fax: 020 75822882
Email: bsi@immunology.org
Website: http://bsi.immunology.org/Page.aspx?pid=1417
Members: 4000
Staff: 16
Contact: Judith Willets, CEO
Fee: £60
Membership Type: ordinary
Fee: £20
Membership Type: concessionary
Description: Immunologists. Aims to advance the science of immunology for the benefit of the public.
Publication: Journal
Publication title: Clinical and Experimental Immunology. Advertisements.
Meetings/Conventions: Congress of Immunology – annual congress – Exhibits.

01407
British Society for Medical Mycology
BSMM

St. John's Institute of Dermatology, Department of Mycology, GSTS Pathology, St. Thomas Hospital, London, SE1 7EH, UK
Tel: 0207 1886400
Email: susan.howell@kcl.ac.uk
Website: http://www.bsmm.org
Members: 327
Contact: Susan A. Howell, Honorary Sec.
Fee: £20
Membership Type: individual
Description: Advances research on medical and veterinary mycology for the public benefit. Sponsors scientific activities including symposia, meetings and training courses.

01408
British Society for Middle Eastern Studies
BRISMES

University of Durham, Institute for Middle Eastern and Islamic Studies, Elvet Hill Rd., Durham, DH1 3TU, UK
Tel: 0191 3345179
Fax: 0191 3345661
Email: a.l.haysey@dur.ac.uk
Website: http://www.brismes.ac.uk
Contact: Zahia Salhi, Exec. Dir.
Fee: £90
Membership Type: fellow
Fee: £75
Membership Type: associate
Description: Teachers, researchers, students, diplomats, journalists, and other individuals with an interest in the Middle East. Promotes increased interest in Middle Eastern studies.
Publication: Newsletter
Publication title: BRISMES Newsletter

01409

British Society for Music Therapy
BSMT

24-27 White Lion St., 2nd Fl., London, N1 9PD, UK
Tel: 020 78386100
Fax: 020 78376142
Email: info@bsmt.org
Website: http://www.bsmt.org
Members: 850
Staff: 4
Contact: Juliette Alvin, Founder
Fee: £50
Membership Type: individual
Fee: £35
Membership Type: student
Description: Open to all interested in music therapy. Promotes the use and development of music therapy in treatment and rehabilitation of children and adults suffering from emotional, physical or mental handicap. Holds meetings and conferences. Displays and sells books and videos on music therapy.
Library Subject: music therapy
Library Type: not open to the public
Publication: Journal
Publication title: British Journal of Music Therapy. Advertisements.

01410

British Society for Neuroendocrinology
BSN

School of Biomedical Sciences, University of Nottingham Medical School, Queen's Medical Centre, Nottingham, NG7 2UH, UK
Tel: 0115 8230164
Fax: 0115 8230142
Email: fran.ebling@nottingham.ac.uk
Website: http://www.neuroendo.org.uk
Contact: Fran Ebling, Chm.
Fee: £75
Membership Type: full, overseas (with journal)
Fee: £100
Membership Type: overseas (not entitled to standard subscription)
Description: Promotes the advancement of research on the endocrine and nervous systems. Aims to provide therapies for many neuroendocrine diseases and disorders and bring forward methods that are beneficial to regulate normal neuroendocrine function in man and animals.
Publication: Journal
Publication title: Journal of Neuroendocrinology. Advertisements.

01411

British Society for Oral Medicine
BSOM

c/o Dr. Alan J. Mighell, Honorary Sec.
Leeds Dental Institute, Dept. of Oral Medicine, Leeds, LS2 9LU, UK
Fax: 0113 3436165
Email: sec@bsom.org.uk
Website: http://www.bsom.org.uk
Contact: Farida Fortune, Pres.
Fee: £30
Membership Type: fellow-in-training, regular
Fee: £50
Membership Type: fellow
Description: Promotes the communication, practice and development of Oral Medicine within Great Britain and Ireland.

01412

British Society for Parasitology
BSP

87 Gladstone St., Bedford, MK41 7RS, UK
Tel: 01234 211015
Fax: 01234 211015
Email: info@bsp.uk.net
Website: http://www.bsp.uk.net
Members: 1300
Contact: Jan Bradley, Pres.
Fee: £40
Membership Type: full
Fee: £12
Membership Type: student, retired, unwaged
Description: Parasitologists employed in government agencies, pharmaceutical companies, research laboratories, and universities; students of parasitology. Promotes the study of parasitology and provides a forum for the exchange of ideas and experiences. Disseminates information on advances in the field.
Publication: Book
Publication title: Autumn Symposium
Meetings/Conventions: Malaria Meeting – annual conference – Exhibits.

01413

British Society for Plant Pathology
BSPP

Marlborough House, Basingstoke Rd., Spencers Wood, Reading, RG7 1AG, UK
Tel: 01603 880313
Fax: 01603 208493
Email: secretary@bspp.org.uk
Website: http://www.bspp.org.uk
Members: 800
Contact: Sarah Gurr, Pres.
Fee: £150
Membership Type: individual (with one journal subscription)
Fee: £300
Membership Type: individual (both journals)
Description: Individuals with an interest in any aspect of plant pathology. Promotes the study and advancement of plant pathology. Serves as a clearinghouse on plant pathology; encourages interaction and cooperation among members.
Publication: Newsletter
Publication title: BSPP News
Meetings/Conventions: Presidential Conference – annual conference

01414

British Society for Protist Biology
BSPB

c/o Dr. Stephen Coupe, Membership Sec.
Coventry University, James Starley Bldg., Priory St., Coventry, CV1 5FB, UK
Tel: 0117 9288249
Fax: 0117 9257374
Email: w.gibson@bristol.ac.uk
Website: http://www.protist.org.uk
Contact: Wendy Gibson, Pres.
Fee: £25
Membership Type: full
Fee: £15
Membership Type: student
Description: Works to promote the study, teaching and dissemination of all aspects of protozoology.
Formerly: Formerly, British Section of Society of Protozoologists

01415

British Society for Research on Ageing
BSRA

University of Hull, Dept. Biological Sciences, Cottingham Rd., Kingston Upon Hull, HU6 7RX, UK
Email: secretary@bsra.org.uk
Website: http://www.bsra.org.uk
Members: 150
Contact: Sandra Jones, Sec.
Fee: £25
Membership Type: individual
Fee: £10
Membership Type: student
Description: Biological scientists and clinicians involved in the study of aging. Promotes knowledge of the biology of aging and effective treatment of age-related diseases. Works to increase public awareness of the aging process. Sponsors annual postgraduate award competition.
Publication: Journal
Publication title: Lifespan

01416

British Society for Restorative Dentistry
BSRD

c/o Ms. Becky Rowe, Membership Admin. Sec.
Bristol Dental Hospital, 3rd Fl., Chapter House, Lower Maudlin St., Bristol, BS1 2LY, UK
Tel: 0117 3424400
Fax: 0117 3424443
Email: matthew.garrett@nhs.net
Website: http://www.bsrd.org.uk
Members: 987
Contact: Matthew Garrett, Hon. Sec.
Description: Aims to promote high standards in restorative dentistry among all practitioners, through meetings and publications. Provides an opportunity to meet with colleagues who share a common interest in keeping abreast of all the changes taking place in this aspect of dentistry, particularly in the field of fixed prosthodontics. Encourages continuing education in Restorative Dentistry.

01417

British Society for Rheumatology
BSR

Bride House, 18-20 Bride Ln., London, EC4Y 8EE, UK
Tel: 020 78420900
Fax: 020 78420901
Email: bsr@rheumatology.org.uk
Website: http://www.rheumatology.org.uk
Members: 1500
Staff: 14
Contact: Samantha Peters, Chief Exec.
Fee: £190
Membership Type: ordinary
Fee: £95
Membership Type: retired (with journal)
Description: Committed to advancing knowledge and practice in the field of rheumatology; aims to improve awareness and understanding of arthritis and other musculoskeletal conditions; works at national and local level to promote high quality standards of care with these conditions.
Library Subject: rheumatology
Library Type: not open to the public
Publication: Journal
Publication title: Rheumatology. Advertisements.

Meetings/Conventions: annual general assembly – Exhibits.

01418
British Society for Strain Measurement
BSSM
22 St. Georges Rd., Bedford, MK40 2LS, UK
Tel: 01234 347778
Fax: 01234 347778
Email: bianagale@bssm.org
Website: http://www.bssm.org
Members: 300
Staff: 2
Contact: Jerry Lord, Chm.
Fee: £80.5
Membership Type: individual
Fee: £629
Membership Type: corporate 1 (industrial)
Description: Seeks to advance the knowledge of strain measurement, stress analysis and associated technologies. Provides a forum for the exchange of information between practising engineers and technicians. Promotes quality engineering design and safety and reliability through properly conducted measurement, testing and analysis. Arranges conferences, national and regional meetings and courses on all relevant topics. Validates engineers and technicians working in the stress and strain measurement fields.
Publication: Journal
Publication title: Strain. Advertisements.
Meetings/Conventions: bimonthly conference

01419
British Society for Surgery of the Hand
BSSH
Royal College of Surgeons of England, 35-43 Lincoln's Inn Fields, London, WC2A 3PE, UK
Tel: 020 78315162
Fax: 020 78314041
Email: secretariat@bssh.ac.uk
Website: http://www.bssh.ac.uk
Members: 653
Staff: 5
Description: The membership is drawn from the two major parent specialties of orthopedic and plastic surgery; all members share an interest in the hand. Promote and direct the development of hand surgery and foster and coordinate education, study and research in hand surgery including the dissemination and diffusion of knowledge of hand surgery among members of the Society and the medical profession.
Publication: Journal
Publication title: Journal of Hand Surgery
Meetings/Conventions: annual conference – Exhibits.

01420
British Society for the History of Mathematics
BSHM
c/o Andrew Thurburn and Co.
38 Tamworth Rd., Surrey, Croydon, CR0 1XU, UK
Email: a.mann@gre.ac.uk
Website: http://www.bshm.org
Members: 430
Staff: 12
Contact: Tony Mann, Pres.
Fee: £30
Membership Type: ordinary
Fee: £20
Membership Type: retired/unwaged
Description: Researchers, educators, students, and other individuals with an interest in the history of mathematics. Promotes historical study of mathematics and seeks to further the use of history in the teaching of mathematics. Gathers and disseminates information on mathematics history, education, and research. Facilitates communication and cooperation among members. Conducts study tours of museum and library collections.
Meetings/Conventions: Research in Progress Day – annual lecture

01421
British Society for the History of Medicine
BSHM
c/o Dr. Fiona Davidson, MD, Sec.
24 Foxes Dale, Blackheath, London, SE3 9BQ, UK
Tel: 020 88526245
Email: drfdavidson@yahoo.co.uk
Website: http://www.bshm.org.uk
Contact: Sue Weir, Pres.
Description: Promotes meetings on the subject of the History of Medicine on a national scale and represents Britain in the affairs of the International Society for the History of Medicine.
Publication: Newsletter
Publication title: BHSM News. Advertisements.

01422
British Society for the History of Pharmacy
BSHP
840 Melton Rd., Thurmaston, Leicester, LE4 8BN, UK
Tel: 0116 2640083
Fax: 0116 2640141
Email: bshp@associationhq.org.uk
Website: http://www.bshp.org
Fee: £20
Membership Type: regular
Description: Strives to propagate understanding of the history of pharmacy. Collaborates with related professions and local historians on medico-pharmaceutical topics.
Publication: Journal
Publication title: Pharmaceutical Historian

01423
British Society for the History of Science
BSHS
PO Box 3401, Norwich, NR7 7JF, UK
Tel: 01603 516236
Fax: 01603 208563
Email: office@bshs.org.uk
Website: http://www.bshs.org.uk
Members: 700
Contact: Sally Horrocks, Pres.
Fee: £33
Membership Type: ordinary in Europe
Fee: £41
Membership Type: outside UK and Europe
Description: Aims to promote and further the study of the history and philosophy of science.
Publication: Journal
Publication title: British Journal for the History of Science. Advertisements.

01424
British Society for the Study of Prosthetic Dentistry
BSSPD
c/o Mrs. Linda Erickson, Admin.
School of Dental Sciences, Framlington Pl., Newcastle upon Tyne, NE2 4BW, UK
Tel: 0191 2228140
Fax: 0191 2228140
Email: l.e.erickson@newcastle.ac.uk
Website: http://www.bsspd.org
Members: 490
Contact: D. Walmsley, Pres.
Fee: £60
Membership Type: full
Description: Ordinary and honorary members. Ordinary membership is available to those dentists, doctors or scientists who profess an interest in prosthetic dentistry and shall be by election. Established to advance education in prosthetic dentistry for the benefit of the public.
Publication: Proceedings
Publication title: BSSPD Proceedings

01425
British Society of Animal Science
BSAS
PO Box 3, Penicuik, EH26 0RZ, UK
Tel: 0131 4454508
Fax: 0131 5353103
Email: bsas@sac.ac.uk
Website: http://www.bsas.org.uk
Members: 1000
Contact: Mike A. Steele, Chief Exec.
Fee: £65
Membership Type: individual
Fee: £32.5
Membership Type: post-graduate, retired
Description: Individuals concerned with animal science. Provides opportunities for information exchange among members relating to animals and animal products.
Publication: Journal
Publication title: Animal

01426
British Society of Audiology
BSA
80 Brighton Rd., Reading, RG8 1PS, UK
Tel: 0118 9660622
Fax: 0118 9351915
Email: bsa@thebsa.org.uk
Website: http://www.thebsa.org.uk
Members: 1400
Staff: 3
Contact: David Baguley, Chm.
Fee: £61
Membership Type: full, associate
Fee: £10
Membership Type: student
Description: Individuals interested in audiology. Promotes the science of audiology (i.e. the study of hearing and balance) and the diagnosis, alleviation and prevention of hearing and balance impairment. Promotes the advancement of education in audiology and the furtherance of research in audiology and the publication of the results of such research.
Publication: Magazine
Publication title: BSA News. Advertisements.
Meetings/Conventions: annual conference

01427
British Society of Baking
BSB
Vine Cottage, Tompkins Ln., Bicester, OX27 0EX, UK
Tel: 01869 277094
Fax: 01869 242979
Email: bsb@freeuk.com
Website: http://www.bsb.org.uk
Members: 350
Contact: Keith Houliston, Contact
Fee: £55
Membership Type: regular
Description: Retail bakers, small craft bakers, independent group plant bakers, supermarket groups, research organizations, flour millers, ingredient and equipment suppliers. Provides a forum for learning more about the baking industry through conferences and associated events.
Library Type: not open to the public
Meetings/Conventions: Golf Day – annual competition

01428
British Society of Cinematographers
BSC
PO Box 2587, Gerrards Cross, SL9 7WZ, UK
Tel: 01753 888052
Fax: 01753 891486
Email: office@bscine.com
Website: http://www.bscine.com
Members: 290
Staff: 3
Contact: Frances Russell, Sec.-Treas.
Fee: £300
Membership Type: full
Fee: £150
Membership Type: associate
Description: Directors of photography working in motion pictures. Promotes and encourages the pursuit of the highest standards in the craft of motion picture photography. Aims to further the application by others of high standards and to encourage original and outstanding work. It also provides facilities for social intercourse between the members and arranges lectures, debates and meetings.
Publication: Magazine
Publication title: British Cinematographer. Advertisements.

01429
British Society of Clinical and Academic Hypnosis
BSCAH
Inspiration House, Redbrook Grove, Sheffield, S20 6RR, UK
Tel: 0844 8843116
Fax: 0844 8843116
Email: bscah@btinternet.com
Website: http://www.bscah.com
Members: 369
Staff: 1
Contact: Angela Morris, Sec.
Description: Qualified doctors, dentists and other registered health professionals Promotes the study and training in the principles and practice of hypnosis. It encourages research and publication of work relating to hypnosis.
Library Type: not open to the public
Formerly: Formerly, British Society of Medical and Dental Hypnosis
Publication: Newsletter

01430
British Society of Criminology
BSC
2-6 Cannon St., London, EC4M 6YH, UK
Tel: 07896 347183
Email: kate.williams@wlv.ac.uk
Website: http://www.britsoccrim.org
Members: 1000
Contact: Kate Williams, Exec. Sec.
Fee: £88.5
Membership Type: full
Fee: £76.5
Membership Type: full (student, retired)
Description: Works to advance the interests and knowledge of persons engaged in teaching, research, and public education about crime, criminal behavior, and the criminal justice system in United Kingdom.
Publication: Journal
Publication title: Criminology and Criminal Justice

01431
British Society of Dental Hygiene and Therapy
BSDHT
3 Kestrel Ct., Waterwells Business Park, Waterwells Dr., Quedgley, Gloucester, GL2 2AT, UK
Tel: 01452 886365
Fax: 01452 886468
Email: enquiries@bsdht.org.uk
Website: http://www.bsdht.org.uk/index.html
Members: 2500
Contact: Sally Simpson, Pres.
Fee: £90
Membership Type: full
Fee: £45
Membership Type: just qualified
Description: Strives to promote the study of Oral Health and to provide a consultative body to which reference may be made by public or private bodies for guidance in connection with the Dental Hygienist Profession.

01432
British Society of Dowsers
BSD
4/5 Cygnet Ctr., Worcester Rd., Worcs, Hanley Swan, WR8 0EA, UK
Tel: 01684 576969
Fax: 01684 311388
Email: info@britishdowsers.org
Website: http://www.britishdowsers.org
Members: 1440
Staff: 2
Contact: Grahame Gardner, Pres.
Fee: £30
Membership Type: individual
Fee: £38
Membership Type: joint
Description: Anyone who is interested in dowsing. Promotes the scientific principles of dowsing including the knowledge of its application to the search for subterranean watercourses, cavities, tunnels, ores and other entities.
Library Subject: dowsing
Library Type: open to the public
Publication: Journal
Publication title: Dowsing Today. Advertisements.

01433
British Society of Echocardiography
BSE
Docklands Business Centre, 10-16 Tiller Rd., London, E14 8PX, UK
Tel: 020 73455185
Fax: 020 73455186
Email: admin@bsecho.org
Website: http://www.bsecho.org
Members: 2300
Contact: Navroz Masani, Pres.
Fee: £60
Membership Type: basic
Description: Represents the interests of professionals working in the field of clinical echocardiography. Aims to promote the study and advancement of ultrasound imaging and Doppler techniques in cardiology. Facilitates training and education of physicians.

01434
British Society of Enamellers
BSOE
17 Aubert Rd., London, N5 1TX, UK
Email: secretary@enamellers.org
Website: http://www.enamellers.org
Members: 80
Contact: Melissa Rigby, Chair
Fee: £25
Membership Type: associate
Fee: £54
Membership Type: full
Description: Promotes the interests of professional enamellers.
Library Subject: enamel historical, members work
Library Type: reference

01435
British Society of Flavourists
BSF
1 Wansford Close, Brentwood, CM14 4PU, UK
Tel: 01277 224587
Email: christogoddard@aol.com
Website: http://www.bsf.org.uk
Members: 600
Contact: Christopher A. Goddard, Hon. Sec.
Fee: £39
Membership Type: fellow
Fee: £34
Membership Type: associate, affiliate
Description: Promotes and protects the interests of individuals working within the flavour industry. Advances the science and art of flavour technology and application. Encourages the education and development of flavourists, with the co-operation of training boards or universities as appropriate. Provides a responsible and informed body of professional opinion to comment on all aspects of legislation which affects the science and art of flavour technology.
Publication: Newsletter
Publication title: News and Views. Advertisements.

01436
British Society of Gastroenterology
BSG
3 St. Andrews Pl., Regent's Park, London, NW1 4LB, UK
Tel: 020 79353150
Fax: 020 74873734
Email: t.smith@bsg.org.uk
Website: http://www.bsg.org.uk
Members: 2600
Staff: 3
Contact: Tom Smith, Chief Exec.
Fee: £195
Membership Type: full, international
Fee: £97.5
Membership Type: trainee
Description: Physicians and surgeons with a special interest in gastroenterology. Associate nurse/clinical members. Concerned with the advancement of gastroenterology and the promotion of friendship amongst those who have a special interest in the subject.
Library Type: reference
Publication: Newsletter
Publication title: BSG News

01437
British Society of Gerontology
BSG
PO Box 607, 8 Queenswood Grove, York, YO24 4PP, UK
Tel: 07535 248835
Email: britishgerontology@yahoo.co.uk
Website: http://www.britishgerontology.org
Contact: Miriam Bernard, Pres.
Fee: £50
Membership Type: UK waged
Fee: £20
Membership Type: full time student, retired/unwaged
Description: Promotes understanding of human aging and later life through research and communication in order to improve quality of life in old age.
Publication: Journal
Publication title: Ageing and Society

01438
British Society of Hearing Aid Audiologists
BSHAA
Remo House, 6th Fl., 310-312 Regent St., London, W1B 3BS, UK
Email: secretary@bshaa.com
Website: http://www.bshaa.com
Members: 1200
Contact: Roger Lewin, Pres.
Fee: £165
Membership Type: regular
Description: Educational and trade association for private hearing aid dispensers. Promotion of ethical standards through training, examination and codes of practice.
Formerly: Formerly, BSHAA
Publication: Newsletter
Publication title: BSHAA News. Advertisements.
Meetings/Conventions: annual congress – Exhibits.

01439
British Society of Hypnotherapists
BSH
37 Orbain Rd., London, SW6 7JZ, UK
Tel: 020 73851166
Fax: 020 73851166
Email: enquiries@britishhypnotherapists.org.uk
Website: http://www.britishhypnotherapists.org.uk
Members: 20
Contact: John Butler, Contact
Description: Specializes in the treatment of nervous disorders and addictions. Provides information service for public; conducts research on behalf of members and distributes information to them.

01440
British Society of Magazine Editors
BSME
137 Hale Ln., Edgware, Middlesex, HA8 9QP, UK
Tel: 020 89064664
Email: admin@bsme.com
Website: http://www.bsme.com
Members: 300
Contact: Gill Branston, Admin.
Fee: £94
Membership Type: full
Fee: £64.63
Membership Type: associate
Description: Represents the needs and views of all magazine editors, and enhances their status, acting as a voice for the industry.

01441
British Society of Master Glass Painters
BSMGP
c/o Chris Wyard, Hon. Sec./Newsletter Ed.
PO Box 15, Minehead, TA24 8ZX, UK
Tel: 01643 862807
Email: secretary@bsmgp.org.uk
Website: http://www.bsmgp.org.uk
Members: 600
Contact: Caroline Benyon, Chair
Fee: £45
Membership Type: in UK
Fee: £50
Membership Type: overseas (posted newsletter)
Description: Represents the interests of stained glass designers, painters and makers, historians, researchers and other academics, conservators, restorers, students, and amateur stained glass makers. Promotes and encourages high standards in the art and craft of stained glass painting and staining. Seeks to preserve the stained glass heritage of Britain.
Publication: Journal
Publication title: The Journal of Stained Glass. Advertisements.

01442
British Society of Periodontology
BSP
PO Box 334, Leeds, LS19 9FJ, UK
Tel: 0844 3351915
Website: http://www.bsperio.org.uk
Members: 790
Contact: Helen Clough, Admin. Mgr.
Fee: £80
Membership Type: full (postgraduate student/hygienist/therapist), associate (other dental care professional)
Fee: £120
Membership Type: full (dentist with access to electronic journal only)
Description: Members are dental surgeons. Promotes the art and science of dentistry and, in particular, the art and science of periodontology for the benefit of the public.
Publication: Journal
Publication title: Journal of Clinical Periodontology

01443
British Society of Plant Breeders
BSPB
Woolpack Chambers, 16 Market St., Ely, CB7 4ND, UK
Tel: 01353 653200
Fax: 01353 661156
Email: enquiries@bspb.co.uk
Website: http://www.bspb.co.uk/index.asp
Members: 50
Staff: 15
Contact: Penny Maplestone, Chief Exec.
Description: Represents members' interests; licenses and collects royalties on production of protected crop varieties.

01444
British Society of Psychosomatic Obstetrics, Gynaecology and Andrology
BSPOGA
U.S. Department of of Obstetrics and Gynaecology, Russells Hall Hospital, Dudley, DY1 2QH, UK
Email: chairman@bspoga.org
Website: http://www.bspoga.org
Contact: Mira Lal, Chair
Fee: £50
Membership Type: medical
Fee: £25
Membership Type: non-medical
Description: Promotes the study of psychobiological and psychosocial, ethical and cross-cultural problems in the fields of obstetrics and gynecology, women's health and reproductive health; facilitates the dissemination of new information in these fields.

01445
British Society of Rehabilitation Medicine
BSRM
c/o Royal College of Physicians
11 St. Andrews Pl., London, NW1 4LE, UK
Tel: 01992 638865
Fax: 01992 638674
Email: admin@bsrm.co.uk
Website: http://www.bsrm.co.uk
Contact: Christopher Roy, Pres.
Fee: £215
Membership Type: ordinary (EC)
Fee: £221
Membership Type: non-EC
Description: Encourages doctors' involvement in management of disability through research and education.

01446
British Society of Rheology
BSR
c/o David M. Binding
Institute of Mathematical and Physical Sciences, University of Wales, Ceredigion, Aberystwyth, SY23 3BZ, UK
Tel: 01970 622775
Fax: 01970 622826
Email: dmb@aber.ac.uk
Website: http://www.bsr.org.uk
Members: 600
Contact: Oliver Guy Harlen, Pres.
Fee: £25
Membership Type: regular
Description: Represents people interested in rheology whether theoretical, experimental and scientists in academia and industry. Promotes the science and dissemination of knowledge in areas of pure and applied rheology.
Library Type: open to the public
Publication: Journal
Publication title: Annual Rheology Reviews. Advertisements.

01447
British Society of Scientific Glassblowers
BSSG
c/o Mr. Ian Pearson
Glendale, Sinclair St., Caithness, Thurso, KW14 7AQ, UK
Tel: 01847 802629
Fax: 01847 802971
Email: ian.pearson@dounreay.com
Website: http://www.bssg.co.uk
Members: 250
Contact: William Fludgate, Chm.
Fee: £12.5
Membership Type: student, retired
Fee: £25
Membership Type: full craft, associate
Description: Individuals engaged in scientific glassblowing and associated professions. Aims to uphold and further the status of scientific glassblowers; holds meetings, presents papers and encourages and promotes higher standards of skill and technical knowledge.
Library Type: not open to the public
Publication: Journal
Publication title: Journal of the British Society of Scientific Glassblowers. Advertisements.

01448
British Society of Soil Science
BSSS
Cranfield University, Bldg. 53, Cranfield, MK43 0AL, UK
Tel: 01234 752983
Fax: 01234 752970
Email: admin@soils.org.uk
Website: http://www.soils.org.uk
Members: 1000
Staff: 8
Contact: Keith Goulding, Pres.
Fee: £50
Membership Type: ordinary
Fee: £30
Membership Type: student
Description: Individuals in 48 countries interested in advancing the study of soil science. Encourages exchange of information.
Publication: Journal
Publication title: European Journal of Soil Science. Advertisements.

01449
British Society of Toxicological Pathologists
BSTP
PO Box 6356, Isle of Skye, IV41 8WZ, UK
Tel: 07894 123533
Fax: 01599 530331
Email: bstpoffice@aol.com
Website: http://www.bstp.org.uk
Members: 240
Fee: £50
Membership Type: full (without journal)
Fee: £25
Membership Type: associate (without journal)
Description: Educates pathologists who work in the field of human safety assessment.

01450
British Sociological Association
BSA
Bailey Ste., Palantine House, Belmont Business Park, Durham, DH1 1TW, UK
Tel: 0191 3830839
Fax: 0191 3830782
Email: enquiries@britsoc.org.uk
Website: http://www.britsoc.co.uk
Members: 2993
Staff: 9
Contact: Judith Mudd, Chief Exec.
Fee: £40
Membership Type: concessionary (full-time student, unwaged), retired
Fee: £74
Membership Type: UK standard A
Description: Individuals interested or employed in the fields of psychology, sociology, and other social sciences. Promotes the study of sociology and works to create a favorable climate for sociological research. Acts as a communication and information network.
Publication: Journal
Publication title: Cultural Sociology Journal
Meetings/Conventions: annual conference – Exhibits.

01451
British Soft Drinks Association
BSDA
20-22 Stukeley St., London, WC2B 5LR, UK
Tel: 020 74300356
Fax: 020 78316014
Email: bsda@britishsoftdrinks.com
Website: http://www.britishsoftdrinks.com
Members: 108
Staff: 11
Contact: Roger White, Pres.
Fee: £767
Membership Type: manufacturer (minimum)
Fee: £890.7
Membership Type: associate
Description: Members are manufacturers, factors and franchisers of still and carbonated soft drinks, concentrates, freeze drinks, fruit juices and packaged waters. Provides an efficient, cost effective service to members which promotes, protects and represents their common industry interests.

01452
British Sound Recording Association
BSRA
28 Millway Ave., Norfolk, Roydon, IP22 4QL, UK
Email: bsra@soundhunters.com
Website: http://www.soundhunters.com/bsra/index.html
Contact: Tony Faulkner, Pres.
Fee: £23
Membership Type: individual
Fee: £28.5
Membership Type: family, overseas
Description: Includes individuals and clubs interested in creative sound recording. Organizes drama realizations, documentaries and recordings.
Publication: Newsletter
Publication title: Recording News

01453
British Stainless Steel Association
BSSA
Broomgrove, 59 Clarkehouse Rd., Sheffield, S10 2LE, UK
Tel: 0114 2671260
Fax: 0114 2661252
Email: enquiry@bssa.org.uk
Website: http://www.bssa.org.uk
Members: 100
Staff: 3
Contact: Nigel Ward, Dir.
Fee: £360-1040
Membership Type: regular (depends on the total company turnover)
Description: Membership is open to companies or individuals involved with stainless steel. Promotes and develops the use of stainless steel to the benefit of all members.

01454
British Stammering Association
BSA
15 Old Ford Rd., London, E2 9PJ, UK
Tel: 020 89831003
Fax: 020 89833591
Email: mail@stammering.org
Website: http://www.stammering.org
Contact: Leys Geddes, Chm.
Fee: £15
Membership Type: general
Fee: £5
Membership Type: unemployed, student, individual receiving income support
Description: Supplies free information packs for adults, teenagers, parents, teachers and employers. Helpline staffed by people who stammer. Operates facilities and activities for members. Projects on early referral to speech therapy for stammering children, and stammering pupils project.
Library Subject: stammering
Library Type: reference
Publication: Magazine
Publication title: Speaking Out

01455

British Stammering Association - Scotland
BSA

8 Barclay Terr., Edinburgh, EH10 4HP, UK
Tel: 0845 3303800
Email: bsascotland@stammering.org
Website: http://www.stammering.org/scotland
Contact: Jan Anderson, Development Mgr.
Fee: £15
Membership Type: regular
Description: Raises awareness and understanding of stammering. Provides accessible support services for people in Scotland who stammer, their families and the speech and language therapists who seek to help them.
Library Type: lending
Publication: Magazine
Publication title: Speaking Out

01456

British Standards Institution
BSI

389 Chiswick High Rd., London, W4 4AL, UK
Tel: 020 89969001
Fax: 020 89967001
Email: cservices@bsi-group.com
Website: http://www.bsigroup.com
Members: 28000
Staff: 2301
Contact: Howard Kerr, Chief Exec.
Description: Corporations, associations, individuals, and local governments. Produces private, national, and international standards for British industry; conducts testing, certification, and quality assessment programs; provides information to exporters. Cooperates with the Joint European Standards Institution to develop uniform standards for the European union. Conducts research and educational programs.
Publication title: Bibliotech

01457

British Stickmakers Guild
BSG

9 Princess Pl., Clay Cross, Derbyshire, Chesterfield, S49 9EJ, UK
Email: alanbsg@aol.com
Website: http://www.your-adviser.com/bsg/home.html
Members: 2105
Contact: Alan Bradshaw, Chm.
Fee: £10
Membership Type: full
Fee: £15
Membership Type: overseas
Description: Open to all persons having an interest in making sticks, canes, and crooks for interest and pleasure and the promotion of this art. Promotes the art of stick-making and joins together all persons with an interest in the subject. Demonstrates this craft throughout the country and encourages all persons with an interest to join and promote the craft.
Publication: Magazine
Publication title: The Stickmaker. Advertisements.

01458

British Sugarcraft Guild
BSG

Wellington House, Messeter Pl., Eltham, London, SE9 5DP, UK
Tel: 020 88596943
Email: nationaloffice@bsguk.org
Website: http://www.bsguk.org
Members: 5000
Staff: 2
Contact: Marilyn Hill, Chair
Fee: £28.5
Membership Type: international
Fee: £22.5
Membership Type: branch, individual
Description: Branch, individual and overseas membership open to anyone interested in the art of sugarcraft. Aims to promote and stimulate interest in sugarcraft as an art form, share knowledge, develop talent and improve standards.
Publication: Newsletter
Publication title: British Sugarcraft News. Advertisements.

01459

British Sundial Society
BSS

4 New Wokingham Rd., Crowthorne, RG45 7NR, UK
Tel: 01663 762415
Email: graham@sheardhall.co.uk
Website: http://www.sundialsoc.org.uk
Members: 500
Contact: G. Aldred, Gen. Sec.
Fee: £33
Membership Type: individual (outside Europe), family (within Europe)
Fee: £37
Membership Type: family (outside Europe)
Description: Promotes the science and knowledge of all types of sundials.

01460

British Suzuki Institute
BSI

The Lightbox, Unit 1.01, 111 Power Rd., Chiswick, London, W4 5PY, UK
Tel: 020 31764170
Fax: 020 31764175
Email: info@britishsuzuki.com
Website: http://www.britishsuzuki.com
Members: 1850
Staff: 3
Contact: Minette Joyce, Admin.
Fee: £30
Membership Type: overseas associate
Fee: £25
Membership Type: associate
Description: Music teachers, specialized educators, parents, and interested individuals in England. Promotes musical education among children using the educational philosophy and ideas of Shinichi Suzuki, a Japanese musician. (The Suzuki method teaches music as a language.) Sponsors and runs training programs using the Suzuki method for teachers of cello, flute, piano, and violin. Makes available children's services; participates in charitable programs.
Publication: Journal
Publication title: Ability

01461

British Tarantula Society
BTS

c/o Angela Hale, Sec.
3 Shepham Ln., Polegate, BN26 6LZ, UK
Email: angehale@thebts.co.uk
Website: http://www.thebts.co.uk
Contact: Andrew Smith, Chm.
Fee: £15
Membership Type: in UK and Europe
Fee: £20
Membership Type: international
Description: Advances public and professional knowledge on correct keeping and breeding of tarantulas and other associated fauna.
Publication: Journal

01462

British Textile Machinery Association
BTMA

Mt. Pleasant, Glazebrook Ln., Glazebrook, Warrington, WA3 5BN, UK
Tel: 0161 7755740
Fax: 0161 7755485
Email: btma@btma.org.uk
Website: http://www.btma.org.uk
Members: 110
Staff: 5
Description: Aims to promote the interests, both at home and abroad, of the British textile machinery industry.
Meetings/Conventions: annual meeting

01463

British Tinnitus Association
BTA

Acorn Business Park, Ground Fl., Unit 5, Woodseats Close, Sheffield, S8 0TB, UK
Tel: 0114 2509922
Fax: 0114 2582279
Email: info@tinnitus.org.uk
Website: http://www.tinnitus.org.uk
Members: 9000
Staff: 6
Contact: Roy Bratby, Chm.
Fee: £15
Membership Type: in UK
Fee: £20
Membership Type: outside UK
Description: Individual Members or via a network of 80 local self-help groups and contacts. Offers information about tinnitus and helps to found and implement self-help groups to provide mutual support and varying degrees of counseling. Campaigns for better services for people with tinnitus and for more tinnitus clinics. A national conference is held annually.
Publication: Magazine
Publication title: Quiet

01464

British Toilet Association
BTA

PO Box 847, West Sussex, RH12 5AL, UK
Tel: 01403 258779
Fax: 01403 258779
Email: enquiries@britloos.co.uk
Website: http://www.britloos.co.uk
Contact: Mike Bone, Dir.
Fee: £620
Membership Type: commercial company
Fee: £410
Membership Type: local authority
Description: Represents the interests and aspirations of 'away from home' toilet providers, suppliers and users of all types. Acts as the catalyst for change in

the pursuit of standards of excellence in all areas of public toilet provision and management. Campaigns for legislation relating to the provision of public toilets and adequate number of facilities for men and women. Provides a forum for public toilet providers, contractors, suppliers, and users to share concern and ideas and communicate best practices.

01465

British Toxicology Society
BTS

PO Box 10371, Colchester, CO1 9GL, UK
Tel: 01206 226059
Fax: 01206 226057
Email: secretariat@thebts.org
Website: http://www.thebts.org
Members: 950
Contact: Nora Green, Contact
Fee: £60
Membership Type: full
Fee: £10
Membership Type: student
Description: Promotes the science of toxicology through epidemiological evaluation of the prevalence of the chemical toxicity, bioanalysis of exposure to potentially harmful chemicals, and prediction of the toxicity of chemicals.

01466

British Toy and Hobby Association
BTHA

80 Camberwell Rd., London, SE5 OEG, UK
Tel: 0207 7017271
Fax: 0207 7082437
Email: queries@btha.co.uk
Website: http://www.btha.co.uk
Members: 138
Staff: 9
Contact: Roland Earl, Sec.
Description: Manufacturers of toys and hobby-related items in the U.K. Promotes the toy and hobby industry; represents members' interests.
Publication: Brochure
Publication title: Membership and Information
Meetings/Conventions: Toy Fair – annual trade show

01467

British Toymakers Guild
BTG

PO Box 240, Uckfield, TN22 9AS, UK
Tel: 01225 442440
Fax: 01825 769321
Email: info@toymakersguild.co.uk
Website: http://www.toymakersguild.co.uk
Members: 220
Staff: 1
Contact: Robert Nathan, Mgr.
Fee: £110
Membership Type: regular
Fee: £60
Membership Type: associate
Description: Members are craftsmen toy makers, shops, galleries, and collectors. Promotes and encourages excellence in toy making and the making of miniatures.
Publication title: The Toymaker

01468

British Transplantation Society
BTS

Chester House, 68 Chestergate, Cheshire, Macclesfield, SK11 6DY, UK
Tel: 01625 664547
Fax: 01625 664510
Email: secretariat@bts.org.uk
Website: http://www.bts.org.uk
Members: 800
Contact: Keith Rigg, Pres.
Fee: £20
Membership Type: reduced (with income of less than 30,000)
Fee: £60
Membership Type: ordinary
Description: Aims to advance the study of biological and clinical problems of tissue and organ transplantation; facilitates contact between persons interested in transplantation; makes new knowledge available to any person for the good of community.
Meetings/Conventions: annual congress

01469

British Travelgoods and Accessories Association
BTAA

Federation House, 10 Vyse St., Hockley, Birmingham, B18 6LT, UK
Tel: 0121 2371107
Fax: 0121 2363921
Email: info@btaa.org.uk
Website: http://www.btaa.org.uk
Members: 59
Staff: 1
Contact: Diana Fiveash, Chief Exec.
Fee: £265-1400
Membership Type: full (based on turnover)
Fee: £270
Membership Type: overseas
Description: Represents manufacturers, designers, importers, exporters, agents and distributors of luggage, belts, small leather goods, handbags. Aims to provide services which will benefit the commercial interests of members; promotes the interests of members; works to facilitate export activities and negotiate minimum terms and conditions of employment.
Formerly: Formerly, British Luggage and Leathergoods Association
Publication: Magazine
Publication title: Fashion Extras

01470

British Trombone Society
BTS

1-3 Church St., Hutton, Yorkshire, Driffield, YO25 9PR, UK
Tel: 01377 202209
Email: secretary@britishtrombonesociety.org
Website: http://www.britishtrombonesociety.org
Members: 1000
Contact: Geoff Wolmark, Sec.
Fee: £18
Membership Type: retired/student
Fee: £24
Membership Type: regular
Description: Maintains and develops contact amongst trombonists.
Publication: Magazine
Publication title: The Trombonist. Advertisements.

01471

British Trout Association
BTA

The Rural Centre, West Mains, Ingliston, Midlothian, EH28 8NZ, UK
Tel: 0131 4724080
Fax: 0131 4724083
Email: mail@britishtrout.co.uk
Website: http://www.britishtrout.co.uk
Members: 100
Contact: David Bassett, Contact
Description: Trout producers in Britain. Conducts research and educational programs; represents members' interests.

01472

British Trust for Conservation Volunteers
BCTV

Sedum House, Mallard Way, Doncaster, DN4 8DB, UK
Tel: 01 302388883
Fax: 01 302311531
Email: information@btcv.org.uk
Website: http://www2.btcv.org.uk
Staff: 514
Contact: Rupert Evenett, Chm.
Fee: £35
Membership Type: individual
Description: Offers practical conservation opportunities. Works to support and advice local people and community groups. Provides training and learning management opportunities and practical land management for conservation.

01473

British Trust for Ornithology
BTO

The Nunnery, Norfolk, Thetford, IP24 2PU, UK
Tel: 01842 750050
Fax: 01842 750030
Email: info@bto.org
Website: http://www.bto.org
Members: 12000
Staff: 80
Contact: Andy Clements, Dir.
Fee: £29
Membership Type: individual - ordinary
Fee: £23
Membership Type: individual - concession
Description: Birdwatchers and bird ringers. Promotes and encourages the wider understanding, appreciation and conservation of birds through scientific studies using the combined skills and enthusiasm of members, other bird watchers and staff.
Library Subject: ornithology, ecology, statistics
Library Type: not open to the public
Publication: Annual Report
Publication title: Annual Report and Accounts
Meetings/Conventions: annual dinner

01474

British Tunnelling Society
BTS

1 Great George St., London, SW1P 3AA, UK
Email: bts@britishtunnelling.org.uk
Website: http://www.britishtunnelling.org.uk
Members: 750
Staff: 1
Contact: Owen Meredith, Sec.
Fee: £390-1005
Membership Type: corporate in UK (based on number of employees)
Fee: £30
Membership Type: retired in UK
Description: Individuals, corporate, students and companies in tunnelling/tunnelling equipment. Advances the education of the public in and promotes the art and science of tunnelling, including the creation and use of underground space by fostering, understanding experience, interest and research therein.
Publication: Magazine
Publication title: Tunnels and Tunnelling. Advertisements.

01475

British Turf and Landscape Irrigation Association
BTLIA

41 Pennine Way, Great Eccleston, Lancashire, Preston, PR3 0YS, UK
Tel: 01995 670675
Website: http://www.btlia.org.uk
Members: 40
Contact: Roger Davey, Chm.
Description: For those concerned with manufacture, installation or maintenance of turf and landscape irrigation equipment or design of irrigation systems.

01476

British Turned-Parts Manufacturers Association
BTMA

Pear Tree Cottage, Snitterfield Ln., Norton Lindsey, Warwick, CV35 8JQ, UK
Tel: 01789 730877
Fax: 01789 730899
Email: info@btma.org
Website: http://www.btma.org
Members: 100
Staff: 1
Contact: Brian Owen, Pres.
Description: Represents precision turned parts and components manufacturers.
Publication title: Buyers Guide

01477

British UFO Research Association
BUFORA

41 Castlebar Rd., Ealing, London, W5 2DJ, UK
Tel: 020 89973496
Email: enquiries@bufora.org.uk
Website: http://www.bufora.org.uk
Contact: Tony Eccles, Chm.
Description: Promotes and conducts investigations into the UFO phenomenon across the United Kingdom. Compiles and disseminates UFO reports and related data. Fosters ongoing cooperation and exchange in the field of ufology. Offers a field investigation training course.
Library Subject: UFOs
Library Type: not open to the public

01478

British Union for the Abolition of Vivisection
BUAV

16a Crane Grove, London, N7 8NN, UK
Tel: 020 77004888
Fax: 020 77000252
Email: info@buav.org
Website: http://www.buav.org
Staff: 25
Contact: Michelle Thew, CEO
Description: Campaigns to end animal experiments.
Publication: Magazine
Publication title: Campaign Report. Advertisements.

01479

British Universities Film and Video Council
BUFVC

77 Wells St., London, W1T 3QJ, UK
Tel: 020 73931500
Fax: 020 73931555
Email: ask@bufvc.ac.uk
Website: http://bufvc.ac.uk
Members: 220
Staff: 17
Contact: Murray Weston, Chief Exec.
Description: Schools, colleges, polytechnics, universities, local education authorities, hospitals, industries, television companies, and individuals in 9 countries. Promotes the use of television and video for educational purposes; encourages careers in educational television; organizes training programs.
Formerly: Formerly, British Universities Film and Video Council and Society for Screen-Based Learning
Publication: Journal
Publication title: Viewfinder. Advertisements.

01480

British Urban Regeneration Association
BURA

63-66 Hatton Garden, 4th Fl., London, EC1N 8LE, UK
Tel: 020 75394030
Fax: 020 74049614
Email: info@bura.org.uk
Website: http://www.bura.org.uk
Contact: Jeremy Beecham, Pres.
Fee: £1000
Membership Type: private sector, whitehall department, executive agency, non departmental Public Body
Fee: £500
Membership Type: local public sector organization
Description: Serves as a forum for the exchange of ideas, experiences, and information for the emerging regeneration sector.
Publication: Newsletter
Publication title: Regeneration

01481

British Vacuum Council
BVC

76 Portland Pl., London, W1N 3DH, UK
Email: bvc@british-vacuum-council.org.uk
Website: http://www.british-vacuum-council.org.uk
Members: 18
Staff: 1
Contact: Mark Bowden, Sec.
Description: Two representatives from each of the 2 bodies affiliated to the Council which are: The Institute of Physics and the Faraday Division of The Royal Society of Chemistry. Aims to promote and advance the understanding and teaching of vacuum science, technology and applications by coordinating and promoting conferences, seminars and courses and publications in these fields; encouraging excellence amongst postgraduate students and other young research workers in these fields.

01482

British Valve and Actuator Association
BVAA

9 Manor Park, Banbury, OX16 3TB, UK
Tel: 01295 221270
Fax: 01295 268965
Email: enquiry@bvaa.org.uk
Website: http://www.bvaa.org.uk
Members: 67
Staff: 3
Contact: Bill Whiteley, Chm.
Description: Covers industrial valves and actuators for the control of fluids and gases.
Formerly: Formerly, British Valve and Actuator Association
Publication: Directory
Publication title: Buyers Guide

01483

British Vehicle Rental and Leasing Association
BVRLA

River Lodge, Badminton Ct., Amersham, HP7 0DD, UK
Tel: 01494 434747
Fax: 01494 434499
Email: info@bvrla.co.uk
Website: http://www.bvrla.co.uk
Members: 800
Staff: 14
Contact: John Lewis, CEO
Fee: £950
Membership Type: intermediary
Fee: £415-3305
Membership Type: group (with 10000 fleet size or below)
Description: Trade association for the vehicle (cars/vans/commercial vehicles) rental and leasing/contract hire and vehicle management industries and other associated businesses. Promotes/supports the corporate objectives of members by interfacing with Government/Civil Service on strategic, economic and legislative issues relating to the industry. Offers support and advisory services, seminars and training; enforces Codes of Conduct and Quality Assurance Schemes.
Library Type: not open to the public
Publication: Magazine
Publication title: BVRLA News

01484

British Venture Capital Association BVCA

1st Fl. N, Brettenham House, Lancaster Pl., London, WC2E 7EN, UK
Tel: 020 74201800
Fax: 020 74201801
Email: bvca@bvca.co.uk
Website: http://www.bvca.co.uk/home
Members: 410
Staff: 11
Contact: Simon Walker, CEO
Fee: £1100-85000
Membership Type: full
Fee: £2200-11000
Membership Type: associate financial/investor
Description: Venture capital, private equity, and professional firms connected with the venture capital industry. Represents virtually every major source of venture capital in the UK. Provides information about members to entrepreneurs and investors; represents members' views in discussions with Government and other bodies; provides a forum for the exchange of views among members; develops and maintains the highest standards of professional practice and provides training for members' employees.
Library Type: not open to the public
Publication: Directory
Publication title: BVCA Directory of Members

01485

British Veterinary Association BVA

7 Mansfield St., London, W1G 9NQ, UK
Tel: 020 76366541
Fax: 020 79086349
Email: bvahq@bva.co.uk
Website: http://www.bva.co.uk
Members: 11500
Staff: 38
Contact: Harvey Locke, Pres.-Elect
Fee: £30-60
Membership Type: student
Fee: £348
Membership Type: joint (UK)
Description: Veterinarians and veterinary students. Promotes interests of members and the animals in their care. Monitors activities of, provides advice to, and develops and maintains contact with organizations interested in animal health including government agencies, local authorities, professional societies, animal rights groups, and universities. Disseminates information to the public and the media. Conducts charitable programs. Sponsors seminars and symposia. Maintains 20 specialist divisions.
Library Type: reference
Formerly: Formerly, National Veterinary Medical Association
Publication: Journal
Publication title: In Practice

01486

British Veterinary Dental Association BVDA

53-55 Maidstone Rd., Footscray, Kent, Sidcup, DA14 5HBY, UK
Tel: 020 83008111
Email: secretary@bvda.co.uk
Website: http://www.bvda.co.uk
Contact: Andrew Perry, Sec.
Fee: £60
Membership Type: full
Fee: £75
Membership Type: practice
Description: Promotes the practice and teaching of animal dentistry. Educates and trains veterinary and dental surgeons. Advocates for animal dental health in United Kingdom.

01487

British Veterinary Nursing Association BVNA

82 Greenway Business Ctre., Harlow Business Park, Harlow, CM19 5QE, UK
Tel: 01279 408644
Fax: 01279 408645
Email: bvna@bvna.co.uk
Website: http://www.bvna.org.uk
Members: 4500
Staff: 7
Contact: Donna Lewis, Pres.
Fee: £28
Membership Type: student
Fee: £35
Membership Type: associate
Description: Full membership qualified veterinary nurses; students; associate; supporter. Aims to foster and promote the status of the veterinary nurse; representation on associated professional committees, and government committees. Gives advice on a career as a veterinary nurse. Membership benefits include an employment register, annual congress, reduced entry into regional and national meetings, and educational courses.
Publication: Journal
Publication title: VNJ
Meetings/Conventions: annual congress – Exhibits.

01488

British Video Association BVA

167 Great Portland St., London, W1W 5PE, UK
Tel: 020 74360041
Fax: 020 74360043
Email: lavinia@bva.org.uk
Website: http://www.bva.org.uk
Members: 30
Staff: 3
Contact: Lavinia Carey, Dir. Gen.
Description: Full members are copyright owners of product for the pre-recorded video market. Associate members have affiliated operations, such as box manufacturers, wholesalers, printers, duplicators, etc. Represents, promotes and protects the collective interests of copyright owning companies who produce and/or distribute videos in the UK.
Publication: Brochure
Publication title: A Parent's Guide to Video

01489

British Violin Making Association BVMA

c/o John Topham, Treas.
114 Mid St., South Nutfield, Redhill, RH1 4JH, UK
Tel: 01737 822341
Website: http://www.bvma.org.uk
Members: 500
Contact: Marc Soubeyran, Chm.
Fee: £45
Membership Type: individual (in UK)
Fee: £20
Membership Type: student (in UK)
Description: Raises the standard of skill and expertise of makers and restorers of violins. Promotes violin making to the general public. Conducts fellowship among individuals interested in violins and bows. Shares information among makers and restorers of violins.
Publication: Newsletter
Publication title: The British Violin

01490

British Water

1 Queen Anne's Gate, London, SW1H 9BT, UK
Tel: 020 79574554
Fax: 020 79574565
Email: info@britishwater.co.uk
Website: http://www.britishwater.co.uk
Members: 200
Staff: 9
Contact: David Neil-Gallacher, Chief Exec.
Description: UK water and waste water industries, designers, contractors, manufacturers, and suppliers of water purification plant equipment and chemicals, financial institutions, law firms, and training and research organizations, media, and travel service providers. Promotes involvement of members in water-related projects of British companies and organizations worldwide. Works with government bodies to establish water quality standards and methods of treatment; provides technical support to water quality programs of other organizations.
Formerly: Formerly, British Effluent Water Association and British Water Industries Group

01491

British Women Pilots' Association BWPA

Brooklands Museum, Brooklands Rd., Weybridge, KT13 0QN, UK
Email: info@bwpa.co.uk
Website: http://www.bwpa.co.uk
Members: 400
Contact: Caroline Gough-Cooper, Chair
Membership Type: regular (18 or over, based on date of joining)
Fee: £3.35-40
Membership Type: family (based on date of joining)
Description: Assists women to gain pilots' licenses of all types. Advise women on training required and openings available to them. Promotes training and employment of women in aviation.
Library Subject: aviation
Library Type: by appointment only

01492

British Woodworking Federation BWF

Royal London House, 22-25 Finsbury Sq., London, SW1P 3QL, UK
Tel: 0844 2092610
Fax: 0870 2092611
Email: bwf@bwf.org.uk
Website: http://www.bwf.org.uk
Members: 500
Staff: 10
Contact: David Campbell, Chief Exec.

Description: Represents manufacturers, distributors and installers of timber doors, windows, conservatories, staircases, all forms of architectural joinery including shopfitting, timber frame buildings and engineered timber components, as well as suppliers to the industry. Provides advice to members regarding technical issues, employment and contractual law, health and safety, tax issues, and environmental matters.

01493

British Wool Marketing Board
BWMB

Wool House, Roydsdale Way, Euroway Trading Estate, West Yorkshire, Bradford, BD4 6SE, UK
Tel: 01274 688666
Fax: 01274 652233
Email: mail@britishwool.org.uk
Website: http://www.britishwool.org.uk
Members: 59078
Contact: Frank Langrish, Chm.
Description: Operates a central marketing system for UK fleece wool. Aims to achieve the best possible net return for wool producers.
Library Type: open to the public

01494

British-Yemeni Society
BYS

c/o Rebecca Johnson, Honorary Sec.
2 Lisgar Terr., London, W14 8SJ, UK
Tel: 020 76038895
Website: http://www.al-bab.com/bys
Contact: Abdulla Mohamed Ali Al-Radhi, Co-Pres.
Fee: £20
Membership Type: ordinary
Fee: £10
Membership Type: student
Description: Promotes friendship and understanding between Yemen and the United Kingdom. Aims to advance the knowledge in Britain about the Republic of Yemen, its history, geography, economy and culture. Provides a contact between individuals of both countries for the development of cultural, commercial and humanitarian activities.

01495

BritishAmerican Business Inc.
BABi

75 Brook St., London, W1K 4AD, UK
Tel: 020 72909888
Email: ukinfo@babinc.org
Website: http://www.babinc.org
Members: 700
Staff: 16
Contact: Richard Fursland, CEO
Fee: £3970
Membership Type: London Transatlantic Council
Fee: £1690
Membership Type: London - sponsor
Description: Helps member companies build and expand international business.
Library Type: reference
Formerly: Formerly, American Chamber of Commerce - United Kingdom
Publication: Magazine
Publication title: Network. Advertisements.

01496

Brittle Bone Society
BBS

30 Guthrie St., Dundee, DD1 5BS, UK
Tel: 01382 204446
Fax: 01382 206771
Email: contact@brittlebone.org
Website: http://www.brittlebone.org
Members: 2000
Staff: 5
Contact: Patricia Osborne, Chief Exec.
Description: Supports research into osteogenesis imperfecta and related conditions. Supplies or identifies alternative sources of accurate information on genetics and other medical issues associated with OI.

01497

Broadcasting Entertainment Cinematograph and Theatre Union
BECTU

373-377 Clapham Rd., London, SW9 9BT, UK
Tel: 020 73460900
Fax: 020 73460901
Email: info@bectu.org.uk
Website: http://www.bectu.org.uk/home
Members: 26500
Staff: 50
Contact: Gerry Morrissey, Gen. Sec.
Fee: £135-400
Membership Type: general (based on annual income)
Description: Represents the interests of workers in the film, broadcasting, theatre and related industries.
Formerly: Formerly, Association of Cinematograph, Television and Allied Technicians
Publication: Magazine
Publication title: Stage Screen & Radio. Advertisements.

01498

Bronte Society
BS

Bronte Parsonage Museum, Church St., Haworth, West Yorkshire, Keighley, BD22 8DR, UK
Tel: 01535 642323
Fax: 01535 647131
Email: info@bronte.org.uk
Website: http://www.bronte.info
Members: 2000
Staff: 26
Contact: Margaret McCarthy, Contact
Fee: £24
Membership Type: single adult in U.K. and Europe
Fee: £40
Membership Type: joint adult overseas
Description: Preserves the literary works, manuscripts, and other objects of the Bronte sisters (Charlotte, 1816-55, Emily, 1818-48, and Anne, 1820-49). Maintains the Bronte Parsonage Museum. Provides research facilities by appointment.
Publication: Newsletter
Publication title: Gazette. Advertisements.

01499

BTCV

Sedum House, Mallard Way, Doncaster, DN4 8DB, UK
Tel: 01302 388883
Fax: 01302 311531
Email: information@btcv.org.uk
Website: http://www2.btcv.org.uk
Members: 8300
Staff: 339
Contact: Tom Flood, Chief Exec.
Fee: £23
Membership Type: individual
Fee: £35
Membership Type: local group
Description: Charity protecting the environment through practical action. A network of over 150 field offices allows volunteers of all ages and from all sections of the community to train and take part in a wide range of environmental projects, including planting trees and hedges, repairing footpaths and drystone walls, improving access to the countryside. Organizes conservation working holidays both in the UK and worldwide.
Formerly: Formerly, British Trust for Conservation Volunteers

01500

BTCV Scotland

Balallan House, 24 Allan Park, Stirling, FK8 2QG, UK
Tel: 01786 479697
Email: scotland@btcv.org.uk
Website: http://www2.btcv.org.uk/display/btcv_scotland
Description: Delivers a range of volunteering opportunities and community support services across Scotland as well as waste minimization schemes in the Highlands and Islands in Central Scotland through Action Recycle. Provides opportunities for individuals and communities to improve their local environment through practical action.

01501

Builders Merchants Federation
BMF

15 Soho Sq., London, W1D 3HL, UK
Tel: 020 74391753
Fax: 020 77342766
Email: info@bmf.org.uk
Website: http://www.bmf.org.uk
Contact: Terry Parker, Chm.
Description: Merchants specializing in the distribution of building materials in the United Kingdom. Promotes members' interests.
Publication: Yearbook
Publication title: Year Book and Buyers Guide

01502

Building Cost Information Service of the Royal Institution of Chartered Surveyors
BCIS

12 Great George St., London, SW1P 3AD, UK
Tel: 020 76951500
Fax: 020 76951501
Email: contact@bcis.co.uk
Website: http://www.bcis.co.uk/site/index.aspx
Contact: Joe Martin, Exec. Dir.
Description: Aims to provide a center of expertise and information exchange on building costs.
Publication title: BCIS Quarterly Review of Building Prices

01503
Building Research Establishment
BRE

Bucknalls Ln., Watford, WD25 9XX, UK
Tel: 01923 664000
Email: enquiries@bre.co.uk
Website: http://www.bre.co.uk
Staff: 650
Contact: Peter Bonfield, Chief Exec.
Description: Centre of expertise for construction, fire, the built environment and risk sciences that provides research, consultancy, training, and information services to clients worldwide.
Publication: Newsletter
Publication title: Constructing the Future
Meetings/Conventions: Cabin Air Quality in Passenger Aircraft – conference

01504
Building Services Research and Information Association
BSRIA

Old Bracknell Ln. W, Bracknell, RG12 7AH, UK
Tel: 01344 465600
Fax: 01344 465626
Email: bsria@bsria.co.uk
Website: http://www.bsria.co.uk
Members: 720
Staff: 120
Contact: Andrew Eastwell, Chief Exec.
Fee: £625-5515
Membership Type: company (based on size and type of organization)
Description: Works with construction and building services companies. Provides services to improve confidence in design, profitable construction, added value in manufacture, competitive advantage in marketing, effective commissioning and accurate measurement, efficient building occupation, operation and maintenance.
Library Subject: building services
Library Type: by appointment only
Publication: Manual
Publication title: Application Guide

01505
Building Societies Association - England
BSA

6th Fl., York House, 23 Kingsway, London, WC2B 6UJ, UK
Tel: 020 75205900
Fax: 020 72405290
Email: information@bsa.org.uk
Website: http://www.bsa.org.uk
Members: 65
Staff: 20
Contact: Rachel Blackmore, External Affairs Mgr.
Description: Association of building societies in the United Kingdom. Promotes and protects members' interests.
Library Subject: savings, mortgages, housing
Library Type: by appointment only
Publication: Yearbook
Publication title: Building Societies Yearbook

01506
Bureau of Freelance Photographers
BFP

Focus House, 497 Green Lanes, London, N13 4BP, UK
Tel: 020 88823315
Email: info@thebfp.com
Website: http://www.thebfp.com
Members: 6500
Staff: 3
Contact: John Tracy, Chief Exec.
Fee: £70
Membership Type: outside UK
Fee: £54
Membership Type: in UK
Description: Freelance photographers supplying editorial/publishing markets. Assists and advises members.
Publication: Handbook
Publication title: Freelance Photographer's Market Handbook

01507
Bus Users UK

PO Box 2950, Stoke-on-Trent, ST4 9EW, UK
Tel: 01782 442855
Fax: 01782 442856
Email: enquiries@bususers.org
Website: http://www.nfbu.org
Members: 750
Staff: 6
Contact: Caroline Cahm, Pres.
Fee: £13
Membership Type: individual
Fee: £17
Membership Type: family
Description: Individual bus passengers, passenger groups, and groups/organisations interested in public transport. Helps to set up local user groups and provides them with help and advice in dealing with local bus issues. Develops links between passengers and those responsible for provision of local bus services as well as bus manufacturers. Campaigns for government policies to encourage improvements in both the level and quality of bus transport.
Formerly: Formerly, National Federation of Bus Users
Publication: Newsletter
Publication title: Bus User

01508
Business and Professional Women - UK
BPW UK

74, Fairfield Rise, Essex, Billericay, CM12 9NU, UK
Tel: 01277 623867
Email: hq@bpwuk.co.uk
Website: http://www.bpwuk.co.uk
Staff: 2
Contact: Sue Ashmore, Natl. Pres.
Fee: £70
Membership Type: individual
Description: Serves as networking and lobbying organization. Aims to enable business and professional women to achieve in their careers. Encourages women to take an active part in public life and decision making at all levels. Evaluates changing work patterns and press for development in education and training to meet them. Strives to ensure that the same opportunities and facilities are available to both men and women. Undertakes studies of problems common to business and professional women in Europe and worldwide.
Formerly: Formerly, Business and Professional Women of the United Kingdom
Publication: Magazine
Publication title: BPW News

01509
Business and Professional Women International
BPW

PO Box 568, Horsham, RH13 9ZP, UK
Email: members.services@bpw-international.org
Website: http://www.bpw-international.org
Members: 100000
Staff: 3
Contact: Elizabeth Benham, Pres.
Description: Promotes the status of women worldwide. Seeks higher business and professional standards.
Library Subject: organization history, statistics on business and professional women, health, housing, crime, development projects
Library Type: not open to the public
Formerly: Formerly, International Federation of Business and Professional Women
Publication: Book
Publication title: A Measure Filled

01510
Business Application Software Developers Association
BASDA

92 High St., Buckinghamshire, Great Missenden, HP16 0AN, UK
Tel: 01494 868030
Fax: 01494 868031
Email: info@basda.org
Website: http://websites.uk-plc.net/BASDA
Members: 200
Staff: 2
Contact: Jairo Rojas, Dir. Gen.
Fee: £300-8600
Membership Type: full, associate (based on annual revenues)
Fee: £1000
Membership Type: corporate, affiliate
Description: Open to developers of recognized accountancy or business application software products - as full members. Also available to other organizations that have an interest in the development of the industry as associate members. Aims to bring together organizations with an interest in the development, accreditation and marketing of business and accounting software products and to provide a forum for members to influence the direction of the industry.
Formerly: Formerly, Business and Accounting Software Developers Association
Publication: Handbook
Publication title: Changeover to the Euro

01511
Business Archives Council
BAC

Lloyds TSB Group Archives, 48 Chiswell St., 2nd Fl., London, EC1Y 4XX, UK
Tel: 020 78605762
Website: http://www.businessarchivescouncil.org.uk
Members: 300
Contact: Karen Sampson, Hon. Sec.
Fee: £145
Membership Type: corporate

Fee: £55
Membership Type: institutional
Description: Records managers, archivists and anyone connected with the records of business. Aims to encourage the preservation of archives of the business community and to promote the study of business history.
Publication: Newsletter
Publication title: BAC Newsletter

01512
Business Council for Africa BCA

2 Vincent St., London, SW1P 4LD, UK
Tel: 020 78285544
Fax: 020 78285251
Email: info@bcafrica.co.uk
Website: http://www.bcafrica.co.uk
Members: 180
Staff: 5
Fee: £550
Membership Type: small business
Fee: £800
Membership Type: medium sized company
Description: Firms and companies located outside West Africa with substantial commercial interests in the area's countries. Seeks to aid and stimulate the economic development of West African countries. Represents overseas private sector operators considering operations in West Africa that are mutually beneficial to the operators and the countries involved. Represents members' interests before governmental bodies. Provides information to members on economic and political developments in West African countries.
Formerly: Formerly, West Africa Business Association
Publication: Reports
Publication title: Country Reports

01513
Butchers' Company

Butchers' Hall, 87 Bartholomew Close, London, EC1A 7EB, UK
Tel: 020 76004106
Fax: 020 76064108
Email: clerk@butchershall.com
Website: http://www.butchershall.com
Members: 1600
Staff: 8
Contact: Jeffrey Davies, Master
Fee: £55
Membership Type: fellow, graduate
Fee: £49
Membership Type: associate, affiliate
Description: Seeks to maintain and apply professional code of conduct in meat trading; promote education and training throughout the meat/food industry; promote excellence via technical presentations.
Library Subject: meat industry
Library Type: not open to the public

01514
Butterfly Conservation BC

Manor Yard, E Lulworth, Wareham, BH20 5QP, UK
Tel: 01929 400209
Fax: 01929 400210
Email: info@butterfly-conservation.org
Website: http://www.butterfly-conservation.org
Members: 11500
Staff: 35
Contact: Martin Warren, Chief Exec.
Fee: £28
Membership Type: single
Fee: £20
Membership Type: student
Description: Dedicated to saving butterflies, moths and their habitats. Aims to preserve these insects for future generations to enjoy by making people aware of their declining numbers, funding research and by setting up reserves for the rarer species.
Publication: Magazine
Publication title: Butterfly Conservation News. Advertisements.

01515
CABI

Nosworthy Way, Oxfordshire, Wallingford, OX10 8DE, UK
Tel: 01491 832111
Fax: 01491 833508
Email: cabi@cabi.org
Website: http://www.cabi.org
Contact: John Regazzi, Chm.
Description: Entomologists, agricultural scientists, and other organizations and individuals with an interest in pest control. Promotes development and implementation of biological pest control strategies and techniques. Conducts research; gathers and disseminates information; provides technical support and assistance to local pest control organizations and projects worldwide.
Formerly: Absorbed, International Institute of Biological Control

01516
CABI Bioscience Switzerland Centre

Nosworhy Way, Oxfordshire, Wallingford, OX10 8DE, UK
Tel: 0149 1832111
Fax: 0149 1829292
Email: europe-ch@cabi.org
Website: http://www.cabi.org
Contact: Matthew J.W. Cock, Regional Dir.
Description: Promotes the development and implementation of biological pest control strategies and techniques. Conducts research and disseminates information to members. Provides technical support and assistance to local pest control organizations and projects worldwide.

01517
Calibre Audio Library

New Rd., Weston Turville, Aylesbury, HP22 5XQ, UK
Tel: 01296 432339
Fax: 01296 392599
Website: http://www.calibre.org.uk
Members: 15000
Staff: 37
Contact: Martin Findlay, Chm.
Description: Provides a free postal library service of unabridged books on cassette and audio for the blind and print disabled.
Formerly: Formerly, CALIBRE - Cassette Library for the Blind and Print Handicapped

01518
Call Centre Management Association CCMA

PO Box 125, Sandbach, CW11 2FF, UK
Tel: 01477 500826
Website: http://www.ccma.org.uk
Members: 300
Contact: Ann Marie Stagg, Chair
Fee: £95
Membership Type: regular
Description: Individuals responsible for the management or supervision of a call centre. Promotes the profession and recognition of call centre management; acts as the professional body for call centre managers and supervisors, offers education and training, leading to professional qualifications.
Library Type: open to the public
Publication: Newsletter
Publication title: Call Centered
Meetings/Conventions: meeting

01519
Calligraphy and Lettering Arts Society CLAS

54 Boileau Rd., London, SW13 9BL, UK
Email: sue@clas.co.uk
Website: http://www.clas.co.uk
Members: 1500
Contact: Janet Mehigan, Contact
Fee: £30
Membership Type: individual in UK
Fee: £37
Membership Type: individual outside UK
Description: Promotes the practice and teaching of calligraphy and lettering.
Publication: Magazine
Publication title: The Edge. Advertisements.

Camara Oficial de Comercio de Espana en Gran Bretana

see Spanish Chamber of Commerce in Great Britain

01520
Cambridge Philosophical Society CPS

Central Science Library, Arts School, Bene't St., Cambridge, CB2 3PY, UK
Tel: 01223 334743
Email: philosoc@hermes.cam.ac.uk
Website: http://www.cambridgephilosophicalsociety.org
Contact: B. Larner, Exec. Sec.
Fee: £10
Membership Type: fellow
Description: Aims to promote scientific inquiry.

01521
Cambridge Refrigeration Technology
CRT
140 Newmarket Rd., Cambridge, CB5 8HE, UK
Tel: 01223 365101
Fax: 01223 461522
Email: crt@crtech.co.uk
Website: http://www.crtech.co.uk
Members: 60
Staff: 12
Description: Shipowners carrying refrigerated cargoes (full). Any interested party (associate) including consultants, leasing companies, insurance companies and P & I Clubs. Covers research, development, testing, consultancy and information services related to all forms of refrigerated transport; also cargo care & insurance & claims issues. Includes full size vehicle thermal test chambers.
Library Subject: environmental testing, refrigerated transport, shipping, storage, commodities, perishables, equipment, legislation, standards, patents
Library Type: not open to the public
Formerly: Formerly, Shipowners Refrigerated Cargo Research Association
Publication: Newsletter
Publication title: RTIS CD-ROM
Meetings/Conventions: periodic meeting

01522
Cambridgeshire Chamber of Commerce and Industry
CCCI
Enterprise House, The Vision Park, Histon, Cambridge, CB4 9ZR, UK
Tel: 01223 237414
Fax: 01223 237405
Email: enquiries@cambscci.co.uk
Website: http://www.cambridgeshirechamber.co.uk
Members: 1600
Staff: 15
Contact: John Bridge, CEO
Fee: £217.38
Membership Type: sole trader
Fee: £246.75
Membership Type: company (minimum; based on number of employees)
Description: Promotes business and commerce.

01523
Campaign Against Arms Trade
CAAT
11 Goodwin St., Finsbury Park, London, N4 3HQ, UK
Tel: 020 72810297
Fax: 020 72814369
Email: enquiries@caat.org.uk
Website: http://www.caat.org.uk
Members: 4000
Staff: 7
Contact: Symon Hill, Contact
Description: Coalition of organizations and individuals united to end the international arms trade and Britain's role in it. Works in coordination with other peace organizations to promote awareness of the dangers of arms exports. Exchanges information with European anti-arms organizations. Seeks to convert the military industry to "socially-useful" production.
Publication: Magazine
Publication title: CAAT News

01524
Campaign for National Parks
CNP
6-7 Barnard Mews, London, SW11 1QU, UK
Tel: 020 79244077
Fax: 020 79245761
Email: info@cnp.org.uk
Website: http://www.cnp.org.uk
Members: 2500
Staff: 9
Contact: Kathy Moore, Chief Exec.
Description: Campaigns to protect and promote National Parks for the benefit and quiet enjoyment of all. Friends of the Campaign for National Parks support the work of the Campaign for National Parks.
Formerly: Formerly, Council for National Parks

01525
Campaign for Nuclear Disarmament
CND
162 Holloway Rd., London, N7 8DQ, UK
Tel: 020 77002393
Fax: 020 77002357
Email: enquiries@cnduk.org
Website: http://www.cnduk.org
Members: 45000
Staff: 12
Fee: £8
Membership Type: youth (under 25 years), student (donor only)
Fee: £24
Membership Type: waged individual
Description: Coordinates nuclear disarmament efforts in the United Kingdom through local groups. Includes activities such as: street campaigning, lobbying and elections work, public information and press campaigns, public relations, and information dissemination. Maintains speakers' bureau.
Publication: Newsletter
Publication title: Campaign

01526
Campaign for Press and Broadcasting Freedom
CPBF
Vi and Garner Smith House, 23 Orford Rd., 2nd Fl., Walthamstow, London, E17 9NL, UK
Tel: 020 85215932
Email: freepress@cpbf.org.uk
Website: http://www.cpbf.org.uk
Members: 700
Staff: 2
Contact: Barry White, Natl. Organizer
Fee: £15
Membership Type: individual
Fee: £25-450
Membership Type: organization
Description: Promotes media democracy.
Publication: Newsletter
Publication title: Free Press. Advertisements.

01527
Campaign for the Accountability of American Bases
CAAB
59 Swarcliffe Rd., Harrogate, HG1 4QZ, UK
Tel: 01423 884076
Email: mail@caab.corner.org.uk
Website: http://www.caab.org.uk
Contact: Lindis Percy, Coor.
Description: Committed to raising public awareness, scrutiny and accountability of the presence of the United States Visiting Forces and their Agencies in the UK and worldwide. Aims to send the US military back to within their borders.

01528
Campaign for the Protection of Rural Wales
CPRW
Ty Gwyn, 31 High St., Welshpool, SY21 7YD, UK
Tel: 01938 552525
Fax: 01938 871552
Email: info@cprwmail.org.uk
Website: http://www.cprw.org.uk
Members: 4000
Staff: 7
Contact: Jean Rosenfeld, Chm.
Fee: £24
Membership Type: individual
Fee: £36
Membership Type: joint
Description: Rural conservationists in Wales. Opposes industrial and real estate developments that would diminish the natural landscape of the countryside of Wales. Monitors European Economic Community policies cooperatively with the European Environmental Bureau. Examines government proposals and legislative efforts to encourage environmental protection.
Formerly: Formerly, Council for the Protection of Rural Wales
Publication: Magazine
Publication title: Caring for Today and Tomorrow

01529
Campaign to Protect Rural England
CPRE
128 Southwark St., London, SE1 0SW, UK
Tel: 020 79812800
Fax: 020 79812899
Email: info@cpre.org.uk
Website: http://www.cpre.org.uk/home
Members: 60000
Staff: 40
Contact: Bill Bryson, Pres.
Fee: £29
Membership Type: individual, Parish Council
Fee: £38
Membership Type: joint
Description: Promotes the beauty, tranquility and diversity of rural England; encourages the sustainable use of land and other natural resources in town and country.
Formerly: Formerly, Council for Preservation of Rural England
Publication: Magazine
Publication title: Countryside Voice. Advertisements.

Campana de Solidaridad con Nicaragua
see Nicaragua Solidarity Campaign

01530
Campden BRI
Station Rd., Chipping Campden, GL55 6LD, UK
Tel: 01386 842000
Fax: 01386 842100
Email: info@campden.co.uk
Website: http://www.campden.co.uk
Members: 1700
Staff: 380
Contact: Steven Walker, Dir. Gen.
Description: Members are companies involved in agri-food, drink and allied industries including packaging and process innovation. Covers research, consultancy, and training into all areas of food and drink production, processing and preservation, including microbial and chemical contamination, quality management systems, sensory analysis and food hygiene requirements.
Library Type: not open to the public
Publication: Newsletter

01531
Can Makers
Lynton House, 7-12 Tavistock Sq., London, WC1H 9LT, UK
Tel: 020 73312369
Email: canmakers@cohnwolfe.com
Website: http://www.canmakers.co.uk
Members: 17
Staff: 3
Contact: Vince Major, Chm.
Description: Drinks can manufacturers, raw material suppliers (steel, aluminum and coatings), destining interests and secondary (multi-pack) suppliers. Represents the interests of the manufacturers of drinks cans and raw material suppliers to promote the benefits of drinks cans and the environmental advantages.
Library Type: open to the public
Publication: Report
Publication title: Market Review

01532
Canada-UK Chamber of Commerce
38 Grosvenor St., London, W1K 4DP, UK
Tel: 020 72586578
Fax: 020 72586594
Email: info@canada-uk.org
Website: http://www.canada-uk.org
Members: 330
Staff: 2
Contact: Nigel Bacon, Exec. Dir.
Fee: £5500
Membership Type: charter
Fee: £600
Membership Type: group
Description: Provides business networking forum for companies and individuals engaged in trade and commerce involving Canada, the UK and Europe. Offers business networking opportunity to subscribers and guests through a variety of events such as breakfast meetings, lunches, and seminars.

Canolfan Gymreig Materion Rhyngwladol
see Welsh Centre for International Affairs

01533
Captain Cook Society
CCS
13 Cowdry Close, Dewsbury, W Yorkshire, Thornhill, WF12 0LW, UK
Email: secretary@captaincooksociety.com
Website: http://www.captaincooksociety.com
Members: 500
Contact: Alwyn Peel, Sec.
Fee: £14
Membership Type: in UK
Fee: £28
Membership Type: in U.S.
Description: Individuals from 20 countries interested in the collection and study of material portraying the life and times of Captain James Cook (1728-79), English mariner and explorer. Conducts research on maritime history; disseminates information; announces related exhibitions; collects historical information on Cook and his sea voyages; reviews related maritime books.
Publication: Journal
Publication title: Cook's Log. Advertisements.

01534
Care for the Wild International
CWI
The Granary, Tickfold Farm, Kingsfold, W Sussex, Horsham, RH12 3SE, UK
Tel: 01306 627900
Fax: 01306 627901
Email: info@careforthewild.com
Website: http://www.careforthewild.com
Members: 30000
Staff: 10
Contact: Barbara Maas, Chief Exec.
Description: Promotes the conservation and welfare of wildlife in Britain and abroad, particularly Africa and Asia. Provides fast, direct practical aid to animals in need by assisting to make areas safe from poachers, rehabilitation of sick or injured animals, and providing sanctuary for those unable to return to the wild. Work in the U.K. includes badgers, foxes, hedgehogs, seals and wild birds; abroad work focuses on the protection of tigers, elephants, rhinos, chimps, gibbons, orangutans, langurs, bears and wildcats.

01535
Care Forum Wales
PO Box 2195, Wrexham, LL13 7WL, UK
Tel: 01978 755400
Email: enquiries@careforumwales.co.uk
Website: http://www.careforumwales.co.uk
Contact: Sue Thomas, Contact
Fee: £300
Membership Type: regular
Description: Open to all interested in the care sector in Wales. To organize and maintain a coherent and proactive strategy, in order to influence health and social policy in Wales; and to promote common standards and high quality training and education for staff in the care sector. Hosts an annual conference.

01536
CARE International UK
10-13 Rushworth St., London, SE1 0RB, UK
Tel: 0207 9349334
Fax: 0207 9349335
Website: http://www.careinternational.org.uk
Staff: 61
Contact: Geoffrey Dennis, Chief Exec.
Description: National branch of the international organization. Individuals and organizations working to assist and provide relief to the underprivileged, victims of natural disasters, and others in need. Assists communities in achieving long-term economic and social development while conserving natural resources through cooperation with community members and local organizations. Operates programs in health education, water sanitation, small business development, and education.
Formerly: Formerly, CARE Britain
Publication: Bulletin

01537
Careers Research and Advisory Centre
CRAC
Sheraton House, 2nd Fl., Castle Park, Cambridge, CB3 0AX, UK
Tel: 01223 460277
Fax: 01223 311708
Email: web.enquiries@crac.org.uk
Website: http://www.crac.org.uk
Members: 300
Staff: 45
Contact: Jeffrey Defries, Chief Exec.
Fee: £3000
Membership Type: corporate
Fee: £1500
Membership Type: not for profit, charity
Description: Aims to support lifelong learning and career development through building strong links between education, training, and employment.
Publication: Newsletter
Publication title: Connections. Advertisements.

01538
Carers Northern Ireland
58 Howard St., Belfast, BT1 6PJ, UK
Tel: 028 90439843
Email: info@carersni.org
Website: http://www.carersni.org/Home
Staff: 5
Contact: Helen Ferguson, Dir.
Description: Individuals and organizations involved in caring. Seeks to raise the awareness of the needs of carers. Works with all levels of government and society to inform, support and advise.
Publication: Magazine
Publication title: Caring

01539
Carers UK
20 Great Dover St., London, SE1 4LX, UK
Tel: 020 73784999
Fax: 020 73789781
Email: info@carersuk.org
Website: http://www.carersuk.org/Home
Members: 10000
Staff: 54
Contact: Imelda Redmond, Chief Exec.
Description: Provides information and support to carers, persons who provide assistance and support to ill, disabled, or elderly individuals. Encourages carers to recognize and work towards meeting their needs as caregivers through actively participating in social issues and legislative development that affects care givers and recipients. Offers training programs for professionals.
Formerly: Formerly, Carers National Association
Publication: Newsletter
Publication title: Caring. Advertisements.

01540

Caretakers of the Environment International - Scotland
CEI

c/o Dyce Academy
Riverview Dr., Dyce, Aberdeen, AB21 7NF, UK
Tel: 01224 725118
Fax: 01224 772571
Email: 100260.3676@compuserve.com
Website: http://www.caretakers4all.org/scotland
Contact: Raymond Jowett, Coor.
Description: Represents secondary school teachers and students active in environmental education. Promotes environmental awareness among youth and adults. Seeks to create global environmental education networks. Gathers and disseminates information on successful environmental education techniques and curricula. Develops projects enabling teachers and students to take direct action to improve environmental quality.

01541

Caribbean Banana Exporters Association
CBEA

Flagship Consulting, 67 Pall Mall, London, SW1Y 5ES, UK
Tel: 0208 4286773
Fax: 0208 4280014
Email: gem.cbea@btinternet.com
Website: http://www.cbea.org
Members: 4
Staff: 45
Contact: Gordon Myers, Exec. Sec.
Description: Banana associations of the Windward Islands, Belize, and Jamaica. Strives to improve and develop the banana industry. Studies agronomic, economic, and statistical aspects of the banana industry; conducts research on plant pathology and fruit quality.
Formerly: Formerly, Commonwealth Banana Exporters Association

01542

Carmarthenshire Welsh Pony and Cob Association

Brynteg, Bryncethin Rd., Garnant, Carmarthenshire, Ammanford, UK
Tel: 01269 826353
Email: chairman@cwpca.org
Website: http://www.cwpca.org
Contact: Robert Buchanan, Chm.
Fee: £8
Membership Type: single
Fee: £10
Membership Type: joint
Description: Records the breeding details of Welsh ponies and cobs. Seeks to improve and promote the breed.

01543

Carpenters' Company

c/o Carpenters' Hall
Throgmorton Ave., London, EC2N 2JJ, UK
Tel: 020 75887001
Fax: 020 73821683
Email: info@carpentersco.com
Website: http://www.thecarpenterscompany.co.uk
Members: 250
Description: Promotes the craft of carpentry and runs a building crafts college where courses are run in fine woodwork, shoplifting and stonemasonry. Runs a convalescent home and alms houses.
Library Subject: historic carpentry
Library Type: reference

01544

Casino Operators Association of the UK
COA

c/o Philip Lowther, Gen. Sec.
15 Livesey St., Sheffield, S6 2BL, UK
Tel: 0114 2816209
Fax: 0114 2816199
Email: coa.generalsecretary@tiscali.co.uk
Website: http://www.casinooperatorsassociation.org.uk
Members: 9
Contact: Andrew M. Love, Chm.
Description: Promotes the business of gaming in the United Kingdom. Protects the rights and interests of small casino operators. Expresses members' views on casino gaming issues.

01545

Cast Metals Federation
CMF

The National Metalforming Centre, 47 Birmingham Rd., West Bromwich, B70 6PY, UK
Tel: 0121 6016397
Fax: 0121 6016391
Email: admin@cmfed.co.uk
Website: http://www.castmetalsfederation.com/home.asp
Members: 200
Staff: 5
Contact: John Parker, Contact
Description: UK Foundries. Assists and encourages industry profitability; promotes image of the British Foundry Industry; extends membership with the Metal Casting Industry.
Formerly: Absorbed, British Investment Casting Trade Association
Publication: Directory
Publication title: Castings Buyers' Guide

01546

Castings Technology International
CTI

Advanced Manufacturing Park Brunel Way, South Yorkshire, Rotherham, S60 5WG, UK
Tel: 0114 2541144
Fax: 0114 2541155
Email: info@castingstechnology.com
Website: http://www.castingstechnology.com
Members: 300
Staff: 110
Contact: Mike C. Ashton, Chief Exec.
Fee: £2500
Membership Type: casting producer, casting user
Fee: £1250
Membership Type: small casting producer
Description: Carries out research and provides impartial expertise on all aspects of the design, materials, manufacture, use, quality, and performance of castings. Maintains facilities for design, prototype manufacture and testing.
Library Subject: casting
Library Type: reference
Formerly: Formerly, Steel Castings Association
Publication: Book
Publication title: Specifications for Steel Castings

01547

Catering Equipment Distributors Association of Great Britain
CEDA

PO Box 683, Worcestershire, Inkberrow, BD16 2XW, UK
Tel: 01386 793911
Email: peterkay@ceda.co.uk
Website: http://www.ceda.co.uk
Staff: 1
Contact: Peter Kay, Dir.
Fee: £865
Membership Type: full/service (under 1 million sales turnover)
Fee: £1130
Membership Type: full/service (with 1 million to 3 million sales turnover)
Description: Companies primarily engaged in the distribution of commercial catering equipment. Works to promote and advance the interests and status of members; to foster the highest standards of efficiency; to encourage, support and promote technical education for the benefit of members. Provides communication between members and foster discussion on matters of common interest.
Publication: Newsletter
Publication title: CEDA News. Advertisements.

01548

Catering Equipment Suppliers Association
CESA

3 Albert Embankment, Westminster Tower, London, SE1 7SL, UK
Tel: 020 77933030
Fax: 020 77933031
Email: enquiries@cesa.org.uk
Website: http://www.cesa.org.uk
Members: 100
Staff: 3
Contact: Malcolm Harling, Chm.
Description: Manufacturers of commercial catering equipment and/or suppliers of goods and services to the industry. Promotes cooperation and coordination between those engaged in the catering equipment manufacturing industry; makes representations to government departments and authorities, whether international, national or local on matters affecting members.

01549

Catholic Agency for Overseas Development
CAFOD

Romero Close, Stockwell Rd., London, SW9 9TY, UK
Tel: 020 77337900
Fax: 020 72749630
Email: cafod@cafod.org.uk
Website: http://www.cafod.org.uk
Contact: John Rawsthorne, Chm.
Description: Promotes human development and social justice. Raises funds from Catholic communities to fund long-term development projects in poor areas. Responds to emergencies brought by conflict and natural disasters. Supports schools and parishes throughout England and Wales.

01550
Cats Protection
CP
National Cat Centre, Chelwood Gate, Haywards Heath, Sussex, RH17 7TT, UK
Tel: 08702 099099
Fax: 01825 741004
Email: helpline@cats.org.uk
Website: http://www.cats.org.uk
Members: 46000
Staff: 275
Fee: £15
Membership Type: individual (in UK)
Fee: £24
Membership Type: individual (outside UK)
Description: Cat lovers, for the most part subscribers to the Charity's publications and passive supporters of the Charity's aims. A small percentage (around 5%) actively involved in cat rescue work on an unpaid voluntary basis. Aims to rescue stray and unwanted cats and kittens, rehabilitating and rehoming them where possible; to encourage the neutering of cats not required for breeding; to inform the public on the care of cats and kittens.
Publication: Magazine
Publication title: The Cat

01551
Celtic Film and Television Festival
CFTF
249 W George St., Glasgow, G12 4QE, UK
Tel: 0141 3021737
Email: info@celticmediafestival.co.uk
Website: http://www.celticfilm.co.uk
Members: 262
Staff: 1
Contact: Cathal Goan, Chm.
Description: Film and programme makers working in the Celtic countries; particular emphasis is given to productions in the indigenous languages. Promotes film and programme making in the Celtic countries and about Celtic countries. Promotes the education and training of skills relevant to production and encourages cooperation between members.
Formerly: Formerly, Celtic Film and Television Association

01552
Cement Admixtures Association
CAA
38A Tilehouse Green Ln., Knowle, Solihull, B93 9EY, UK
Tel: 01564 776362
Fax: 01564 776362
Email: info@admixtures.org.uk
Website: http://www.admixtures.org.uk
Members: 11
Staff: 1
Contact: John Dransfield, Sec.
Description: Cement admixtures production and marketing companies in the United Kingdom are full members; suppliers of materials and testing services to the cement admixtures industries are associate members. Encourages the safe and effective use of admixtures in concrete, cement, and sand mixes. Cooperates with government departments in the creation and monitoring of industry standards.
Publication: Handbook
Publication title: Admixture Data Sheet

01553
Cementitious Slag Makers Association
CSMA
Coach House, West Hill, Surrey, Oxted, RH8 9JB, UK
Tel: 01708 682439
Email: standard@ukcsma.co.uk
Website: http://www.ukcsma.co.uk
Members: 7
Description: Promotes the use of Ground Granulated Blast-furnace Slag (GGBS) in the UK. Provides technical input into British and European Standards, and gives advice on existing and potential applications. Coordinates and disseminates research and development of GGBS. Represents views of member companies to government.

01554
Central Association of Agricultural Valuers
CAAV
Market Chambers, 35 Market Pl., Coleford, GL16 8AA, UK
Tel: 01594 832979
Fax: 01594 810701
Email: enquire@caav.org.uk
Website: http://www.caav.org.uk
Members: 2000
Contact: Jeremy Moody, Sec./Advisor
Fee: £285
Membership Type: fellow
Fee: £110
Membership Type: probationer
Description: Members are land agents, agricultural valuers and auctioneers which awards the qualification FAAV on examination. Publishes technical guidance and briefings. Engages with government and others in professional matters.

01555
Central Association of Bee-Keepers
CABK
8 Frank's Cottages, St. Mary's Ln., Essex, Upminster, RM14 3NU, UK
Tel: 01708 220897
Email: secretary@cabk.org.uk
Website: http://www.cabk.org.uk
Members: 200
Contact: Pat Allen, Sec.
Fee: £10
Membership Type: single
Fee: £12
Membership Type: dual
Description: Enables beekeepers and others interested in bees and other social insects to keep in touch with the latest research and ideas about bees and related topics. Acts as a bridge between the beekeeper and the scientist. Invites as its speakers those who are acknowledged experts, both nationally and internationally, in their fields. Publishes and distributes free to its members a selection of the lectures given to the association; these lecture booklets are offered for sale to other beekeepers and additional copies may be purchased by members at a reduced rate. Organizes more than ten lectures per year.
Publication: Book
Publication title: Honeybee Biology 1982

01556
Centre for Agricultural Strategy
CAS
c/o The University of Reading
PO Box 237, Reading, RG6 6AR, UK
Tel: 0118 3788150
Fax: 0118 9353423
Email: casagri@reading.ac.uk
Website: http://www.apd.reading.ac.uk/AgriStrat/index.html
Staff: 9
Contact: Richard Tranter, Dir.
Description: Provides independent and continuing assessments of agricultural and food industries across the countryside. Facilitates strategic planning for the agricultural, food, and ancillary industries, together with relevant government departments and agencies.

01557
Centre for Alternative Technology
CAT
Powys, Machynlleth, SY20 9AZ, UK
Tel: 01654 705950
Fax: 01654 702782
Email: info@cat.org.uk
Website: http://www.cat.org.uk/index.tmpl?refer=index&init=1
Members: 5500
Staff: 90
Contact: Charlotte Cosserat, Information Off.
Fee: £22
Membership Type: individual
Fee: £27
Membership Type: joint
Description: Promotes sustainability, including renewable energy, environmental building, energy efficiency, alternative sewage and wastewater treatment, and organic growing. Provides visitor center, courses, consultancy, and educational facilities.
Publication: Journal
Publication title: Practical Journal of Sustainable Living

01558
Centre for Deaf Studies
CDS
8 Woodland Rd., Bristol, BS8 1TN, UK
Tel: 0117 9546900
Fax: 0117 9546921
Email: enquiries-cds@bristol.ac.uk
Website: http://www.bris.ac.uk/deaf
Contact: Claire Holder, Programme Admin.
Description: Works with deaf people to understand deafness, language and behavior. Facilitates deaf-hearing inter-working; creates a learning environment that is effective for deaf and hearing students; allows the development of Deaf Studies as an academic discipline by allowing deaf people to take leading roles in teaching and research.

01559
Centre for Ecology and Hydrology
CEH
Maclean Bldg., Benson Ln., Crowmarsh Gifford, Wallingford, OX10 8BB, UK
Tel: 01491 838800
Fax: 01491 692424
Email: enquiries@ceh.ac.uk
Website: http://www.ceh.ac.uk

Contact: Patricia Nuttall, Dir.
Description: Represents ecologists and other natural and social scientists. Promotes high-quality, interdisciplinary research in areas including environmental impact assessment, habitat restoration, and conservation. Conducts research; gathers and disseminates information.
Formerly: Formerly, Institute of Terrestrial Ecology

01560
Centre for Economic Policy Research
CEPR
53-56 Great Sutton St., London, EC1V 0DG, UK
Tel: 020 71838801
Fax: 020 71838820
Email: cepr@cepr.org
Website: http://www.cepr.org/default_static.htm
Members: 500
Staff: 23
Contact: Stephen Yeo, CEO
Fee: £6000
Membership Type: corporate (silver)
Fee: £10000
Membership Type: corporate (gold)
Description: Research fellows throughout Europe. Enables members to collaborate in economic research; disseminates results to the public. Areas of interest include open economy macroeconomics, trade policy, and European economic integration.
Publication: Bulletin
Publication title: CEPR Bulletin

01561
Centre for Interfirm Comparison
32 St. Thomas St., Winchester, SO23 9HJ, UK
Tel: 01962 844144
Fax: 01962 843180
Email: enquiries@cifc.co.uk
Website: http://www.cifc.co.uk
Staff: 12
Description: Provides expertise in performance measurement and financial control of companies and other organizations. Services include interfirm comparison; benchmarking; development of performance indicators; surveys, statistics and business information; and training in these topics.

01562
Centre for Photographic Conservation
233 Stanstead Rd., Forest Hill, London, SE23 1HU, UK
Tel: 020 86903678
Fax: 020 83141940
Email: cphotoconservation@cpc-moor.com
Website: http://www.cpc.moor.dial.pipex.com
Contact: Ian Moor, Contact
Description: Works to develop preservation and conservation techniques for photographic materials. Conducts research in historic process and material photographic technologies.

01563
Centre for Policy on Ageing
CPA
25-31 Ironmonger Row, London, EC1V 3QP, UK
Tel: 020 75536500
Fax: 020 75536501
Email: cpa@cpa.org.uk
Website: http://www.cpa.org.uk
Members: 102
Staff: 7
Contact: Gillian Crosby, Dir.
Description: Works with practitioners, academics, central and local governments and all working with and on behalf of older individuals; promotes policies in the United Kingdom which will result in higher standards of care and quality of life for older people. Encourages informed debate on issues affecting older persons and stimulates public awareness of their needs. Conducts studies and makes recommendations to policymakers.
Publication: Report
Publication title: CPA Report

01564
Centre for Women's Health
c/o Sandyford Initiative
2-6 Sandyford Pl., Sauchiehall St., Glasgow, G3 7NB, UK
Tel: 0141 2118130
Website: http://www.sandyford.org
Description: Seeks to promote women's health. Offers counseling services and groups for women. Provides a training center and meeting place. Conducts studies on the quality of existing women's health services. Disseminates information, and provides library services and links to health services.
Library Subject: health and well-being of men and women
Library Type: open to the public

Centre Seismologique International
see International Seismological Centre

01565
CERAM
Queens Rd., Penkhull, Stoke-on-Trent, ST4 7LQ, UK
Tel: 0845 0260902
Fax: 01782 412331
Email: enquiries@ceram.com
Website: http://www.ceram.com
Contact: Graham Small, Contact
Description: Works to test, research and develop ceramic products and materials. Disseminates information to members. Conducts training.
Library Type: reference
Formerly: Formerly, British Ceramics Research
Publication: Newsletter
Publication title: Progress

01566
Ceredigion Welsh Pony and Cob Association
Swn-y-Nant, Tregaron, Ceredigion, SY25 6NG, UK
Tel: 01974 298443
Email: kath@telecomplus.org.uk
Website: http://www.ceredigionwpca.com
Contact: Kath Davies, Sec.
Fee: £5
Membership Type: single
Fee: £8
Membership Type: dual
Description: Records the breeding details of Welsh ponies and cobs. Seeks to improve the breed and promote its excellence.

01567
CFA Society of the UK
CFA UK
2nd Fl., 135 Cannon St., London, EC4N 5BP, UK
Tel: 0207 2809620
Fax: 0207 2809636
Email: info@cfauk.org
Website: http://www.uksip.org
Members: 6000
Staff: 10
Contact: Will Goodhart, Chief Exec.
Fee: £140
Membership Type: regular, affiliate (employed)
Fee: £70
Membership Type: regular, affiliate (retired or unemployed)
Description: Investment analysts and fund managers. Acts as the professional body for members of the investment community applying formal analytical skills to research, portfolio management and related activities.
Library Subject: investment fund management
Library Type: not open to the public
Formerly: Formerly, Institute of Investment Management and Research
Publication: Journal
Publication title: Professional Investor. Advertisements.

01568
CFFI Ceredigion YFC
1 Ffordd y Gogledd, Ceredigion, Aberaeron, SA46 0JD, UK
Tel: 01545 571333
Fax: 01545 571444
Email: ceredigion@yfc-wales.org.uk
Website: http://www.yfc-ceredigion.org.uk
Contact: Haydn Richards, Pres.
Description: Promotes the personal development of young people living in rural areas. Promotes the understanding of the cultural diversity of Wales. Works to raise the profile of the Welsh language.

01569
Challenger Society for Marine Science
CSMS
National Oceanography Centre, Waterfront Campus, Rm. 346/10, Southampton, SO14 3ZH, UK
Email: jxj@noc.soton.ac.uk
Website: http://www.challenger-society.org.uk/the_society
Members: 550
Contact: Jennifer Jones, Exec. Sec.
Fee: £20
Membership Type: student, retired
Fee: £40
Membership Type: full, overseas
Description: Scientists. Works to advance the study and application of marine science through research and education. Maintains specialist groups in different disciplines to provide a forum for technical discussion. Provides marine science information to the public in order to encourage study of the seas. Offers financial assistance to marine science students. Sponsors competitions.
Formerly: Formerly, Challenger Society
Publication: Newsletter
Publication title: Challenger Wave. Advertisements.

01570

Challenges Worldwide
CWW

54 Manor Pl., Edinburgh, EH3 7EH, UK
Tel: 0845 2000342
Email: info@challengesworldwide.com
Website: http://www.challengesworldwide.com
Staff: 5
Contact: Eoghan Mackie, Chief Exec./Founder
Description: Matches dynamic, motivated and skilled individuals to volunteer assignments in developing countries. Matches volunteers to sustainable short-term placements, offering technical assistance to host organisations in developing countries in a mutually beneficial way. Matches volunteers to a placement opportunity in local initiatives specifically addressing local priorities. Work is currently concentrated to several specific locations within Central America, Central and South Asia and West Africa in order to derive as much benefit in each location.

01571

Chamber of Commerce East Lancashire

Red Rose Ct., Clayton Business Park, Lancashire, Accrington, BB5 5JR, UK
Tel: 01254 356400
Fax: 01254 388900
Email: info@chamberelancs.co.uk
Website: http://www.chamberelancs.co.uk
Members: 1000
Staff: 23
Contact: Michael Damms, Chief Exec.
Fee: £873.03
Membership Type: business (maximum; based on number of employees)
Fee: £157.45
Membership Type: sole trader
Description: Promotes business and commerce.

01572

Chamber of Commerce, Herefordshire and Worcestershire

Severn House, Prescott Dr., Warndon Business Park, Worcester, WR4 9NE, UK
Tel: 0845 6411641
Fax: 0845 6414641
Email: enquiries@hwchamber.co.uk
Website: http://www.hwchamber.co.uk
Members: 2000
Staff: 185
Contact: Mike Ashton, Chief Exec.
Fee: £111.63
Membership Type: voluntary
Fee: £129.25
Membership Type: start-up business
Description: Promotes business and commerce. Represents its members' interests.
Library Subject: business, employment law
Library Type: reference
Publication: Newspaper
Publication title: New Direction. Advertisements.

01573

Chamber of Shipping
CoS

Carthusian Ct., 12 Carthusian St., London, EC1M 6EZ, UK
Tel: 020 74172800
Fax: 020 76001534
Email: postmaster@british-shipping.org
Website: http://www.british-shipping.org/home
Members: 133
Staff: 35
Contact: Jan Kopernicki, Pres.
Description: United Kingdom-based ship owners and managers, and associates from across the maritime sector. Promotes and protects members' interests. Represents the shipping industry before government agencies, international regulatory bodies.
Formerly: Formerly, General Council of British Shipping
Publication: Journal
Publication title: Annual Review

Chambre de Commerce Francaise de Grande Bretagne (CCFGB)
see French Chamber of Commerce in Great Britain

Chambre Internationale de la Marine Marchande
see International Chamber of Shipping

01574

Channel Chamber of Commerce

Shepway Business Ctre., Shearway Rd., Kent, Folkestone, CT19 4RH, UK
Tel: 01303 270022
Fax: 01303 270476
Email: info@shepwaybc.co.uk
Website: http://www.shepwaybc.co.uk
Members: 360
Contact: Peter Hobbs, Chief Exec.
Fee: £170-290
Membership Type: company (1-49 employees)
Fee: £400-580
Membership Type: company (50-199 employees)
Description: Represents members at local, regional and national level on matters concerning trade, commerce and industry and lobbying. Facilitates networking, forums and events to enable members to exchange ideas, information, views and business practice.
Formerly: Formerly, Shepway Chamber of Commerce and Industry
Publication: Magazine
Publication title: Rapport in Business. Advertisements.

01575

Charity Law Association

Hempsons, The Exchange, Sta. Parade, Harrogate, HG1 1DY, UK
Tel: 01634 373253
Email: admin@charitylawassociation.org.uk
Website: http://www.charitylawassociation.org.uk/en/default.aspx
Members: 615
Staff: 1
Contact: Catherine Rustomji, Honorary Sec.
Fee: £50
Membership Type: individual
Fee: £130
Membership Type: group
Description: Solicitors and barristers practicing in the field of charity law, other professionals such as accountants having an interest in the development of charity law, charities and charity trustees. Aims to advance the education of the public in charity law and matters relating thereto and to improve the administration of charities.

01576

Charles Rennie Mackintosh Society
CRMS

Queen's Cross Church, 870 Garscube Rd., Glasgow, G20 7EL, UK
Tel: 0141 9466600
Fax: 0141 9467276
Email: trish@crmsociety.com
Website: http://www.crmsociety.com
Members: 1600
Staff: 3
Contact: Stuart Robertson, Exec. Dir./Sec.
Fee: £35
Membership Type: individual
Fee: £15
Membership Type: student
Description: Individuals in 29 countries united to foster interest in the art and architecture of Charles Rennie Mackintosh (1868-1928), Scottish architect, artist, and designer. Aims to conserve and improve the condition of buildings and artifacts designed by Mackintosh; develop an interest in his works. Conducts lectures and tours.
Publication: Newsletter
Publication title: CRM Society Newsletter

01577

Charles Williams Society
CWS

35 Broomfield, Stacey Bushes, Milton Keynes, MK12 6HA, UK
Email: charles_wms_soc@yahoo.co.uk
Website: http://www.charleswilliamssociety.org.uk
Members: 114
Contact: Richard Sturch, Sec.
Fee: £15
Membership Type: single
Fee: £20
Membership Type: joint, single outside UK
Description: Individuals interested in literary activities and in promoting interest in the life and works of Charles Walter Stansby Williams (1886-1945), writer and lay theologian.

01578

Chart and Nautical Instrument Trade Association
CNITA

Priory Ct., Pilgrim St., London, EC4V 6DR, UK
Tel: 020 76189178
Fax: 020 73297302
Email: info@cnita.com
Website: http://www.cnita.com
Description: Represents members' interests.
Formerly: Formerly, British Nautical Instrument Trade Association

01579

Chartered Institute of Arbitrators CIArb

12 Bloomsbury Sq., London, WC1A 2LP, UK
Tel: 020 74217444
Fax: 020 74044023
Email: info@ciarb.org
Website: http://www.ciarb.org
Members: 12000
Staff: 30
Contact: Michael Forbes Smith, Dir. Gen.
Fee: £330
Membership Type: fellow
Fee: £210
Membership Type: associate
Description: Serves as the professional home for all dispute resolvers and a resource centre for those who benefit from cost effective and private dispute resolution. Offers individuals from a variety of sectors, internationally recognised standards of excellence.
Publication: Journal
Publication title: Arbitration

01580

Chartered Institute of Architectural Technologists CIAT

397 City Rd., London, EC1V 1NH, UK
Tel: 020 72782206
Fax: 020 78373194
Email: info@ciat.org.uk
Website: http://www2.ciat.org.uk
Members: 8000
Staff: 12
Contact: Francesca Berriman, Chief Exec.
Description: Represents 6,800 professionals working and studying in the field of architectural technology in the UK and overseas. Serves as the qualifying body for Chartered Architectural Technologists (MCIAT) and Architectural Technicians (TCIAT). Sets standards of competence for the profession, representing the interests of its members to ensure that their skills receive suitable recognition.
Formerly: Formerly, Society of Architectural and Associated Technicians
Publication: Magazine
Publication title: Architectural Technology. Advertisements.

01581

Chartered Institute of Bankers in Scotland CIOBS

Drumsheugh House, 38b Drumsheugh Gardens, Edinburgh, EH3 7SW, UK
Tel: 0131 4737777
Fax: 0131 4737788
Email: info@charteredbanker.com
Website: http://www.charteredbanker.com
Members: 13000
Staff: 24
Contact: Philip Grant, Pres.
Fee: £100
Membership Type: personal
Fee: £82
Membership Type: associate
Description: Students and qualified members from the financial services sector. Serves as a professional educational body for those employed in the financial services sector. Publishes a wide range of study materials.
Library Subject: banking, finance, economics
Library Type: not open to the public
Publication: Journal
Publication title: The Scottish Banker. Advertisements.

01582

Chartered Institute of Building CIOB

Englemere, Kings Ride, Berkshire, Ascot, SL5 7TB, UK
Tel: 01344 630700
Fax: 01344 630777
Email: reception@ciob.org.uk
Website: http://www.ciob.org.uk/home
Members: 42000
Staff: 100
Contact: Chris Blythe, Chief Exec.
Description: Skilled managers and professionals with a common commitment to achieve and maintain the highest possible standards. Focuses on the promotion, for the public benefit, of the science and practice of building; the advancement of education in the science and practice of building including all necessary research and the publication of the results of all such research; the establishment and maintenance of appropriate standards of competence and conduct of those engaged, or about to engage, in the science and practice of building.
Library Subject: construction management
Library Type: not open to the public
Formerly: Absorbed, Architecture and Surveying Institute
Publication: Magazine
Publication title: Construction Information Quarterly

01583

Chartered Institute of Environmental Health CIEH

Chadwick Ct., 15 Hatfields, London, SE1 8DJ, UK
Tel: 020 79286006
Fax: 020 79285862
Email: info@cieh.org
Website: http://www.cieh.org
Members: 10500
Staff: 110
Contact: Graham Jukes, Chief Exec.
Fee: £161
Membership Type: fellow, voting, graduate, accredited associate
Fee: £88
Membership Type: associate
Description: Enforces a wide range of legislation on issues such as food safety, pollution, housing standards and safety at work. Educates the public on matters of hygiene and safety. Enhances training and professional development of environmental health officers. Promotes environmental health and the dissemination of knowledge about environmental health issues.
Library Subject: environmental health
Library Type: by appointment only
Formerly: Formerly, Institution of Environmental Health Offices
Publication: Journal
Publication title: Environmental Health. Advertisements.

01584

Chartered Institute of Housing CIH

Octavia House, Westwood Way, Coventry, CV4 8JP, UK
Tel: 024 76851700
Fax: 024 76695110
Email: customer.services@cih.org
Website: http://www.cih.org
Members: 22000
Staff: 120
Contact: Sarah Webb, CEO
Fee: £48
Membership Type: student, career break
Fee: £144
Membership Type: affiliate
Description: Aims to promote the highest standards of service in housing through education and training as the professional body for people working in all sectors of housing.
Publication: Journal
Publication title: Housing. Advertisements.

01585

Chartered Institute of Journalists CIOJ

2 Dock Offices, Surrey Quays Rd., London, SE16 2XU, UK
Tel: 020 72521187
Fax: 020 72322302
Email: memberservices@cioj.co.uk
Website: http://cioj.co.uk
Members: 1250
Staff: 3
Contact: Dominic Cooper, Gen. Sec.
Fee: £195
Membership Type: regular
Fee: £133
Membership Type: affiliate
Description: Print journalists, broadcasters, Internet communications, photographers, and public relations practitioners. Upholds and seeks to improve standards in journalism and also acts as an independent trade union.
Publication: Journal
Publication title: The Journal. Advertisements.

01586

Chartered Institute of Library and Information Professionals CILIP

7 Ridgmount St., London, WC1E 7AE, UK
Tel: 020 72550500
Fax: 020 72550501
Email: info@cilip.org.uk
Website: http://www.cilip.org.uk/pages/default.aspx
Staff: 70
Contact: Biddy Fisher, Pres.
Fee: £38-184
Membership Type: associate, charter, affiliate
Fee: £575
Membership Type: life
Description: Information specialists, librarians and consultants working in the field of librarianship and information services. The main UK body for library and information professionals, concerned with education, training and standards of practice.
Formerly: Formerly, Chartered Association of Library and Information Professionals
Publication: Yearbook
Publication title: CILIP Yearbook
Meetings/Conventions: biennial conference – Exhibits.

01587

Chartered Institute of Library and Information Professionals in Scotland
CILIPS

1st Fl., Bldg. C, Brandon Gate, Leechlee Rd., Hamilton, ML3 6AU, UK
Tel: 01698 458888
Email: e.fulton@slainte.org.uk
Website: http://www.slainte.org.uk
Members: 2500
Staff: 3
Contact: Elaine Fulton, Dir.
Description: Individuals active in library and information industries. Promotes libraries and librarianship in Scotland. Seeks to: improve library services and the qualifications and status of librarians; strengthen the role of library services in the community. Represents members' interests; offers advice on salary levels, trade unions, and working conditions. Disseminates information on recent developments in library science; organizes weekend schools.
Formerly: Formerly, Scottish Library Association
Publication: Journal
Publication title: Information Scotland. Advertisements.

01588

Chartered Institute of Linguists
IoL

Saxon House, 48 Southwark St., London, SE1 1UN, UK
Tel: 020 79403100
Fax: 020 79403101
Email: info@iol.org.uk
Website: http://www.iol.org.uk
Members: 6500
Staff: 50
Contact: Lady Brewer, Pres.
Fee: £49
Membership Type: student
Fee: £85
Membership Type: associate
Description: Promotes proficiency in modern languages worldwide amongst professional linguists, including translators, interpreters and educationalists, as well as those in the public and private sectors for whom languages are an important skill.
Publication: Journal
Publication title: The Linguist. Advertisements.

01589

Chartered Institute of Logistics and Transport
CILT

Earlstrees Ct., Earlstrees Rd., Northants, Corby, NN17 4AX, UK
Tel: 01536 740100
Fax: 01536 740101
Email: enquiry@ciltuk.org.uk
Website: http://www.cilt-international.com/web/pages/home
Members: 33000
Contact: Leonard John Harper, Pres.
Description: Managers and others in 60 countries engaged in transport or logistics. Contributes to professional education in the field through the development of qualifications for those involved in the movement of people and goods. Promotes and coordinates the study and advancement of the science of transportation. Stimulates debate on transport issues and logistics with governments and the public. Sponsors studies undertaken by individuals. Administers exams and grants diplomas. Conducts student essay competitions.
Library Subject: transport, logistics
Library Type: reference
Publication: Journal
Publication title: CILT World. Advertisements.

01590

Chartered Institute of Loss Adjusters
CILA

Warwick House, 65/66 Queen St., London, EC4R 1EB, UK
Tel: 020 73379960
Fax: 020 79293082
Email: info@cila.co.uk
Website: http://www.cila.co.uk
Members: 3214
Staff: 6
Contact: Malcolm Hyde, Exec. Dir.
Fee: £30
Membership Type: ordinary, student
Fee: £290
Membership Type: associate, fellow
Description: Member institute for chartered loss adjusters.

01591

Chartered Institute of Management Accountants
CIMA

26 Chapter St., London, SW1P 4NP, UK
Tel: 020 88492251
Fax: 020 88492450
Email: cima.contact@cimaglobal.com
Website: http://www.cimaglobal.com
Members: 172000
Staff: 220
Contact: George Glass, Chm./Pres.
Description: Serves as a professional body devoted to the science and skill of management accountancy. Represents Chartered Management Accountants work in industry, commerce and the public sector. Comprises commercially focused financial managers responsible for managing the resources of business enterprises. Offers professional qualification evaluation services.
Formerly: Formerly, Institute of Cost and Management Accountants
Publication: Magazine
Publication title: Insight

01592

Chartered Institute of Marketing
CIM

Moor Hall, Cookham, Berkshire, Maidenhead, SL6 9QH, UK
Tel: 01628 427120
Fax: 01628 427499
Email: qualifications@cim.co.uk
Website: http://www.cim.co.uk/home.aspx
Members: 60000
Staff: 150
Contact: Paul Judge, Pres.
Fee: £135-145
Membership Type: affiliate professional
Description: Seeks to increase knowledge of the principles and practices of marketing through the "delivery of world class professional support to marketing professionals". Organizes residential training courses on all aspects of marketing; offers certificates and postgraduate diploma in Marketing.
Library Subject: marketing, business
Library Type: reference
Publication: Magazine
Publication title: Marketing Business. Advertisements.

01593

Chartered Institute of Patent Agents
CIPA

95 Chancery Ln., London, WC2A 1DT, UK
Tel: 020 74059450
Fax: 020 74300471
Email: mail@cipa.org.uk
Website: http://www.cipa.org.uk/pages/home
Members: 3000
Staff: 11
Contact: Michael Ralph, Sec./Registrar
Description: Fellows are registered UK patent agents; Associates are part-qualified trainees, or members of associated professions; British Overseas or Foreign Members are patent attorneys qualified abroad. The professional body for patent agents and others in the intellectual property field.

01594

Chartered Institute of Personnel and Development
CIPD

151 The Broadway, London, SW19 1JQ, UK
Tel: 0208 6126200
Fax: 0208 6126201
Email: cipd@cipd.co.uk
Website: http://www.cipd.co.uk/default.cipd
Members: 134680
Staff: 280
Contact: Kristina Ingate, Sec.
Fee: £125
Membership Type: non-studying, studying, affiliate
Fee: £62
Membership Type: career bridge register
Description: Those involved in the management and development of people in the UK and the Republic of Ireland. Aims to position the institute as the leading organization in the United Kingdom and the Republic of Ireland responsible for the management and development of people and the dissemination of information on this.
Formerly: Formerly, Institute of Personnel Management
Publication: Magazine
Publication title: People Management. Advertisements.

01595

Chartered Institute of Plumbing and Heating Engineering
CIPHE

64 Sta. Ln., Essex, Hornchurch, RM12 6NB, UK
Tel: 01708 472791
Fax: 01708 448987
Email: info@ciphe.org.uk
Website: http://www.ciphe.org.uk
Members: 12000
Staff: 15
Contact: Reg James, Chm.
Fee: £10
Membership Type: trainee
Fee: £15
Membership Type: affiliate

Description: Promotes professionalism in the plumbing industry.
Formerly: Absorbed, Registered Plumbers Association
Publication: Newsletter
Publication title: Plumbing

01596

Chartered Institute of Public Finance and Accountancy
CIPFA

3 Robert St., London, WC2N 6RL, UK
Tel: 020 75435600
Fax: 020 75435700
Email: info@cipfa.org.uk
Website: http://www.cipfa.org.uk
Members: 13500
Staff: 250
Contact: Steve Freer, Chief Exec.
Fee: £280
Membership Type: full, overseas
Fee: £140
Membership Type: career break, partially retired
Description: Members manage finances across all sectors of the public services, in the health service, local and national government; National Audit; gas, electricity and water companies, education, and housing associations. Also in accountancy firms, in public audit sections. Provides education and training in accountancy and financial management, and sets and monitors professional standards. Professional qualification is high quality, relevant and practical, and is supported by a range of other products and services.
Publication: Magazine
Publication title: Public Finance

01597

Chartered Institute of Public Relations
CIPR

CIPR Public Relations Centre, 52-53 Russell Sq., London, WC1B 4HP, UK
Tel: 020 76316900
Fax: 020 76316944
Email: info@cipr.co.uk
Website: http://www.cipr.co.uk
Members: 9000
Staff: 17
Contact: Jay O'Connor, Pres.
Fee: £210
Membership Type: fellow
Fee: £175
Membership Type: associate
Description: Employees of local and central governments, consulting and industrial firms, and voluntary organizations in 40 countries. Promotes the development, recognition, and understanding of the public relations field. Encourages members to attain professional academic qualifications and to comply with standards of professional conduct. Maintains vocational committees and special interest groups. Provides placement services. Sponsors competitions. Compiles statistics.
Library Subject: public relations
Library Type: reference
Formerly: Formerly, Institute of Public Relations
Publication: Magazine
Publication title: Profile. Advertisements.
Meetings/Conventions: Freshly Squeezed – periodic breakfast

01598

Chartered Institute of Purchasing and Supply
CIPS

Easton House, Easton on the Hill, Stamford, PE9 3NZ, UK
Tel: 01780 756777
Fax: 01780 751610
Email: info@cips.org
Website: http://www.cips.org
Members: 40000
Staff: 90
Contact: David Noble, Chief Exec.
Fee: £140
Membership Type: full, affiliate, associate
Fee: £100
Membership Type: student
Description: Represents the interests of individuals involved in the purchasing and supply management professions. Serves as the professional body for purchasing, supply and materials management staff in the public and private sectors of industry, local and central government. Offers a degree level qualification leading to the accreditation MCIPS. Also offers training courses, seminars and workshops.
Publication: Journal
Publication title: CPO Agenda. Advertisements.

01599

Chartered Institute of Taxation
CIOT

1st Fl., 11-19 Artillery Row, London, SW1P 1RT, UK
Tel: 020 73400550
Fax: 08445 796701
Email: post@ciot.org.uk
Website: http://www.tax.org.uk
Members: 14000
Staff: 40
Contact: Bob A. Dommett, Sec. Gen.
Fee: £290
Membership Type: fellow
Fee: £275
Membership Type: associate
Description: Membership consists of tax advisers, most of whom are in practice, providing the widest range of taxation services to the public. Also includes accountants and solicitors who work in commerce and industry or are self employed. Members are known by the title "chartered tax advisor". Promotes the study of the administration and practice of taxation. Makes recommendations to improve or simplify tax law and practice. Holds examinations throughout the UK twice a year and runs residential conferences, one-day courses and, through branches, technical meetings and social activities.
Publication: Newsletter
Publication title: CTA News

01600

Chartered Institution of Building Services Engineers - England
CIBSE

222 Balham High Rd., London, SW12 9BS, UK
Tel: 020 86755211
Fax: 020 86755449
Email: smatthews@cibse.org
Website: http://www.cibse.org
Staff: 34
Contact: Stephen Matthews, Chief Exec./Sec.
Fee: £217
Membership Type: fellow
Fee: £198
Membership Type: regular
Description: Professional engineers and other interested individuals. Promotes the art, science, and practice of building services engineering and the advancement of education and research. Organizes educational and training courses. Sponsors charitable programs.
Formerly: Absorbed, Illuminating Engineering Society
Publication: Journal
Publication title: Building Services Engineering Research and Technology. Advertisements.
Meetings/Conventions: Lighting Conference – biennial conference – Exhibits.

01601

Chartered Institution of Civil Engineering Surveyors
CICES

Dominion House, Sibson Rd., Cheshire, Sale, M33 7PP, UK
Tel: 0161 9723100
Fax: 0161 9723118
Email: president@cices.org
Website: http://www.cices.org
Members: 4242
Staff: 11
Contact: Ken Hall, Pres.
Fee: £147
Membership Type: technical
Fee: £192
Membership Type: member
Description: Land/engineering and quantity surveyors within the civil engineering industry. Entry is subject to qualifications, approved training and examination. Works for the continuing development and promotion of the institution as a centre of excellence in the art and science of civil engineering surveying to serve the public benefit and satisfy the needs of industry.
Library Type: reference
Publication: Survey
Publication title: Civil Engineering Surveyor. Advertisements.

01602

Chartered Institution of Highways and Transportation
CIHT

119 Britannia Walk, London, N1 7JE, UK
Tel: 020 73361555
Fax: 020 73361556
Email: info@ciht.org.uk
Website: http://www.ciht.org.uk
Members: 10500
Staff: 19
Contact: Mary Lewis, Chief Exec.
Fee: £163
Membership Type: fellow (UK direct)
Fee: £122
Membership Type: individual (UK direct)
Description: Professionals working in the highways and transportation sector. Aims to be a learned multi-modal transport institution relevant to all sectors of the industry for the benefit of society. Provides services that meet the needs of its members. Aims to be a leading body in the award of transportation related qualifications.
Library Subject: road infrastructure
Library Type: open to the public
Formerly: Formerly, Institution of Highways and Transportation
Publication: Journal
Publication title: HET. Advertisements.

01603

Chartered Institution of Wastes Management CIWM

9 Saxon Ct., St. Peter's Gardens, Marefair, Northampton, NN1 1SX, UK
Tel: 01604 620426
Fax: 01604 621339
Email: membership@ciwm.co.uk
Website: http://www.iwm.co.uk
Members: 7300
Staff: 45
Contact: Steve Lee, Chief Exec.
Fee: £186
Membership Type: fellow (in UK)
Fee: £181
Membership Type: fellow (overseas)
Description: Qualified professional and technical persons experienced in all aspects of the management of wastes.
Publication: Proceedings
Publication title: Scientific and Technical Review

01604

Chartered Institution of Water and Environmental Management CIWEM

15 John St., London, WC1N 2EB, UK
Tel: 020 78313110
Fax: 020 74054967
Email: admin@ciwem.org
Website: http://www.ciwem.org
Staff: 20
Contact: Nick Reeves, Exec. Dir.
Fee: £221
Membership Type: fellow
Fee: £216
Membership Type: regular
Description: Engineers, chemists, biologists, geologists, hydrologists, and individuals engaged in water and environmental management issues in 100 countries. Advances the science and practice of water and environmental management, including the treatment and the distribution of drinking water and the treatment and disposal of domestic and industrial waste waters. Conducts symposia; sponsors study tours and competitions for young members.
Publication: Directory
Publication title: International Directory

01605

Chartered Insurance Institute CII

42-48 High Rd., S Woodford, London, E18 2JP, UK
Tel: 020 89898464
Fax: 020 85303052
Email: customer.serv@cii.co.uk
Website: http://www.cii.co.uk/cii.aspx
Members: 90000
Staff: 150
Contact: Barry Smith, Pres.
Description: Persons employed or engaged in insurance or financial services. Plays a vital role in insurance and financial services promoting the highest standards of professionalism through education and training.
Publication: Journal
Publication title: The Journal. Advertisements.

01606

Chartered Quality Institute CQI

12 Grosvenor Crescent, London, SW1X 7EE, UK
Tel: 020 72456722
Fax: 020 72456788
Email: info@thecqi.org
Website: http://www.thecqi.org
Members: 13600
Staff: 50
Contact: David Brown, Pres.
Fee: £41
Membership Type: student
Fee: £101
Membership Type: associate
Description: Those involved with the attainment and improvement of quality in any product or service. Concerned with the promotion and advancement of quality management and practices, together with the promotion of education, training and professional development of those involved in quality assurance and quality management.
Library Type: by appointment only
Formerly: Formerly, Institute of Quality Assurance
Publication: Magazine
Publication title: Quality World. Advertisements.

01607

Chartered Society of Designers CSD

1 Cedar Ct., Bermondsey St., Royal Oak Yard, London, SE1 3GA, UK
Tel: 020 73578088
Email: info@csd.org.uk
Website: http://www.csd.org.uk
Members: 3000
Staff: 10
Fee: £20
Membership Type: student
Fee: £60
Membership Type: graduate
Description: Represents interests of designers in U.K. Promotes high standards of design, fosters professionalism, and emphasizes designers' responsibilities to society.
Library Subject: design disciplines
Library Type: reference
Formerly: Formerly, Society of Industrial Artists and Designers
Publication: Newsletter
Publication title: Business and Design

01608

Chartered Society of Physiotherapy CSP

14 Bedford Row, London, WC1R 4ED, UK
Tel: 020 73066666
Email: enquiries@csp.org.uk
Website: http://www.csp.org.uk
Members: 47000
Staff: 130
Contact: Ann Green, Chair
Fee: £294
Membership Type: qualified individual (working)
Fee: £219.84
Membership Type: qualified individual in higher education
Description: Serves as the professional association, educational body and trade union of the United Kingdom's 39,000 chartered psychotherapists, physical students and assistants. Aims to protect member's interests and help them to achieve the best possible patient care.
Library Subject: physiotherapy, health management
Library Type: not open to the public
Publication: Magazine
Publication title: Frontline. Advertisements.

01609

Chatham House

Chatham House, 10 St. James Sq., London, SW1Y 4LE, UK
Tel: 020 79575700
Fax: 020 79575710
Email: contact@chathamhouse.org.uk
Website: http://www.chathamhouse.org.uk
Members: 3385
Staff: 73
Contact: Robin Niblett, Dir.
Fee: £290
Membership Type: individual
Fee: £2600
Membership Type: corporate
Description: Members come from the fields of politics, academia, the media and business, and usually active in, or have special knowledge of, international issues. Promotes the study and understanding of international affairs. Operates ten research areas in: Europe; Russia and Eurasia; International Economics; International Security; Asia; Middle East; Energy, Environment and Development; Africa; International Law; Americas.
Library Subject: international relations, politics, economics, law, energy and environment
Library Type: reference
Formerly: Formerly, Royal Institute of International Affairs
Publication: Journal
Publication title: International Affairs

01610

Chemical and Industrial Consultants Association CICA

19 St. Annes Dr., Morda, Shropshire, Oswestry, SY10 9LU, UK
Tel: 01691 679967
Fax: 01691 679967
Email: secretary@chemical-consultants.co.uk
Website: http://www.chemical-consultants.co.uk
Members: 40
Contact: B. Whitehouse, Chm.
Description: Network of consultants based in the UK, members are prepared to undertake projects anywhere in the world. Provides innovation solutions to client's problems; offers advice based on experience; carries out tasks for companies and individuals in the chemical and related industries.

01611

Chemical Business Association CBA

Lyme Bldg., Westmere Dr., Crewe Business Park, Cheshire, Crewe, CW1 6ZD, UK
Tel: 01270 258200
Fax: 01270 258444
Email: cba@chemical.org.uk
Website: http://www.chemical.org.uk/home.asp
Members: 114
Staff: 6
Contact: Peter J.C. Newport, Dir.

Description: Chemical distributors, traders and merchants. Aims to promote and protect the interests of chemical distributors, traders and merchants in the UK.
Formerly: Formerly, British Chemical Distributors and Traders Association

01612
Chemical Hazards Communication Society
CHCS
PO Box 222, Lymington, SO42 7GY, UK
Tel: 0844 6362427
Fax: 0844 6362428
Email: chcs@chcs.org.uk
Website: http://www.chcs.org.uk
Members: 400
Contact: Desmond C. Waight, Consultant
Fee: £56.4
Membership Type: individual
Description: Aims to provide information and training guidance to as many individuals as possible, regardless of whether they work in small or large companies, for associations or for government involved with the ever-increasing complexity of chemical hazards regulations and international codes.
Library Subject: hazard communication
Library Type: not open to the public

01613
Chemical Industries Association
CIA
King's Bldg., Smith Sq., London, SW1P 3JJ, UK
Tel: 020 78343399
Fax: 020 78344469
Email: enquiries@cia.org.uk
Website: http://www.cia.org.uk
Members: 170
Staff: 65
Contact: Steve Elliott, Chief Exec.
Description: Assists members to secure sustainable profitability and improved recognition of contributions to society; works to influence relevant people and policies by stimulating and helping towards appropriate internal action.
Formerly: Formerly, Association of British Chemical Manufacturers
Publication: Report
Publication title: Basic International Chemical Industry Statistics
Meetings/Conventions: Business Outlook Conference – annual conference

01614
Chief Cultural and Leisure Officers Association
CLOA
Park Farm, Hethersett, Norfolk, NR9 3DL, UK
Tel: 01603 813700
Fax: 07902 811792
Email: davidalbutt@cloa.org.uk
Website: http://www.cloa.org.uk
Members: 300
Contact: David Albutt, Policy Off.
Fee: £120
Membership Type: chief officer/chief executive
Fee: £360
Membership Type: public sector
Description: Directors and Chief Officers in Local Government Authorities (England and Wales) responsible for range of services including arts, sports, amenities, libraries, museums, countryside, economic development etc. Represents the views and interests of its members in discussion with those who determine national policies in the leisure arena and who influence the resourcing of those policies. Provides a forum and a network for the exchange of knowledge and the practical application of that knowledge.
Publication: Newsletter
Publication title: CLOA News. Advertisements.

01615
Child Action Nepal
PO Box 39679, London, W2 6YP, UK
Tel: 07773 277647
Email: info@childactionnepal.org.uk
Website: http://www.childactionnepal.org.uk
Contact: Florence Krief, Contact
Description: Provides support to orphanages in Nepal along with education and healthcare.

01616
Child Rights Information Network
CRIN
East Studio, 2, Pontypool Pl., London, SE1 8QF, UK
Tel: 020 74012257
Email: info@crin.org
Website: http://www.crin.org
Members: 2000
Staff: 3
Contact: Peter Newell, Chm.
Description: Global network of organizations sharing their information on children's rights. Supports and promotes the implementation of the United Nations Convention on the Rights of the Child.
Publication: Newsletter

01617
Childhood Eye Cancer Trust
CHECT
The Royal London Hospital, Whitechapel Rd., London, E1 1BB, UK
Tel: 020 73775578
Fax: 020 73770740
Email: info@chect.org.uk
Website: http://www.chect.org.uk
Members: 730
Staff: 3
Contact: Libby Halford, Chief Exec.
Description: Children with retinoblastoma (eye cancer) and their families; other interested individuals. Provides support and information to families affected at the point of diagnosis, during treatment and later in life as required. Raises awareness of the condition with health professionals and the general public. Promotes and funds retinoblastoma related research.
Formerly: Formerly, Retinoblastoma Society
Publication: Newsletter
Publication title: Infocus. Advertisements.

01618
Children England
Unit 25, Angel Gate, 1st Fl., City Rd., London, EC1V 2PT, UK
Tel: 020 78333319
Fax: 020 78338637
Email: info@childrenengland.org.uk
Website: http://www.childrenengland.org.uk/index.php?pageID=398
Members: 108
Staff: 10
Contact: Maggie Jones, Chief Exec.
Fee: £120
Membership Type: full, subscriber
Fee: £60
Membership Type: associate, regional
Description: Voluntary organizations providing childcare or supporting childcare work throughout England. Aims to be an independent, identifiable member-led organization maintaining the distinctive voice of voluntary child care; promotes and sustains the voluntary sector's contribution to the provision of services for children and families.
Formerly: Formerly, National Council of Voluntary Child Care Organisations
Publication: Bulletin
Publication title: Magnet. Advertisements.

01619
Children in Northern Ireland
CiNI
40 Montgomery Rd., Unit 9, Belfast, BT6 9HL, UK
Tel: 028 90401290
Fax: 028 90709418
Email: info@ci-ni.org.uk
Website: http://www.ci-ni.org.uk
Members: 100
Contact: Pauline Leeson, Dir.
Fee: £50-250
Membership Type: organization (based on turnover)
Fee: £150
Membership Type: associate
Description: Acts as umbrella organization for the children's voluntary sector in Northern Ireland; facilitates networking and creates a single point of contact for voluntary sector childcare bodies. Offers support and coordinates efforts to develop the voluntary sector by providing services.
Publication: Newsletter
Publication title: CiniTalk

01620
Children in Scotland
Princes House, 5 Shandwick Pl., Edinburgh, EH2 4RG, UK
Tel: 0131 2288484
Fax: 0131 2288585
Email: info@childreninscotland.org.uk
Website: http://www.childreninscotland.org.uk
Members: 400
Staff: 17
Contact: Bronwen Cohen, Chief Exec.
Fee: £85-950
Membership Type: voluntary organization, professional associations (based on income)
Fee: £60
Membership Type: individual
Description: Represents the united voice of over 300 voluntary, statutory and professional organizations and individuals working with children and families throughout Scotland. Involved in fair policy development for children. Offers a wide range of courses, seminars, and workshops; established Scotland-wide networks on specific policy areas regarding children, special needs, and HIV.
Formerly: Formerly, Scottish Child and Family Alliance
Publication: Magazine

01621

Children in Wales

25 Windsor Pl., Cardiff, CF10 3BZ, UK
Tel: 029 20342434
Fax: 029 20343134
Email: info@childreninwales.org.uk
Website: http://www.childreninwales.org.uk/index.html
Contact: Catriona Williams, Chief Exec.
Fee: £8.4
Membership Type: local authority, local health board
Fee: £300
Membership Type: government unit
Description: Acts as national umbrella organization for children's organizations in Wales; seeks to improve services to children; disseminates information on policy, research and best practices.

01622

Children Living with Inherited Metabolic Diseases CLIMB

Climb Bldg., 176 Nantwich Rd., Crewe, CW2 6BG, UK
Tel: 0800 6523181
Fax: 0870 2412174
Email: info@climb.org.uk
Website: http://www.climb.org.uk
Members: 1000
Staff: 11
Contact: Steve Hannigan, Exec. Dir.
Fee: £24
Membership Type: adult
Fee: £36
Membership Type: family
Description: Aims to alleviate the suffering of children and young adults affected by metabolic diseases through research, awareness, and support. Funds research and facilitates medical treatment. Provides information, advice, and support to families and professionals. Supports families through grants to help meet equipment and other medical costs.
Publication: Magazine
Publication title: Climb Update

01623

Children of the Andes COTA

56-64 Leonard St., London, EC2A 4LT, UK
Tel: 020 75490225
Fax: 020 75490226
Email: info@childrenoftheandes.org
Website: http://www.childrenoftheandes.org
Contact: Rachel Joseph, Exec. Dir.
Description: Seeks to provide relief to children and their families in Colombia with social and economic issues.

01624

Children's HIV Association of UK and Ireland CHIVA

Mediscript Ltd., 1 Mountview Ct., 310 Friern Barnet Ln., London, N20 0LD, UK
Tel: 020 84468898
Fax: 020 84469194
Email: chiva@chiva.org.uk
Website: http://www.chiva.org.uk
Members: 200
Contact: Paddy McMaster, Chm.
Fee: £40
Membership Type: non-consultant
Fee: £60
Membership Type: consultant
Description: Promotes issues relevant to children infected or affected by HIV, including perinatal mother-to-infant transmission of HIV. Develops and regularly updates standards of care for children and families with HIV, recognizing and promoting the multi-disciplinary support that is required. Highlights the needs of adolescents with HIV and promotes good practice for transitional care to adult services.

01625

Children's Hospices UK

4th Fl., Bridge House, 48-52 Baldwin St., Bristol, BS1 1QB, UK
Tel: 0117 9897820
Fax: 0117 9291999
Email: info@childhospice.org.uk
Website: http://www.childhospice.org.uk
Members: 40
Contact: Barbara Gelb, Chief Exec.
Description: Represent children's hospice services in the UK. Raises public and professional awareness of the services offered by children's hospices throughout the UK. Provides training, education, networking and research to members. Provides information and advice to individuals and organizations working in children's palliative care, both national and international. Raises funds on a national basis for children's hospices through the Corporate Funding Scheme.
Formerly: Formerly, Association of Children's Hospices

01626

Children's International Summer Villages - England

MEA House, Ellison Pl., Newcastle upon Tyne, NE1 8XS, UK
Tel: 0191 2324998
Fax: 0191 2614710
Email: international@cisv.org
Website: http://www.cisv.org
Description: Works with children and youth to promote peace and understanding.

01627

Children's Legal Centre CLC

University of Essex, Wivenhoe Park, Colchester, C04 3SQ, UK
Tel: 01206 877910
Fax: 01206 877963
Email: clc@essex.ac.uk
Website: http://www.childrenslegalcentre.com
Staff: 60
Contact: Carolyn Hamilton, Dir.
Description: Promotes children's rights in the United Kingdom. Monitors policy and legislation affecting children. Asserts the rights of children to exert influence on the policies and laws that affect them. Offers confidential legal advice and information services; as well as an education advocacy unit. Works to: make policy-makers accountable to young people; make young people more independent; improve health services; provide young people with freedom of information and privacy; make available to children adequate opportunities for education and employment.
Publication: Journal
Publication title: childRIGHT

01628

Children's Rights Alliance for England CRAE

94 White Lion St., London, N1 9PF, UK
Tel: 020 72788222
Email: info@crae.org.uk
Website: http://www.crae.org.uk
Contact: Carolyne Willow, Natl. Coor.
Fee: £25
Membership Type: individual (over 18 years old)
Fee: £35-70
Membership Type: voluntary sector (based on number of staff)
Description: Promotes children's human rights worldwide; advocates for laws and policies to be fully compatible with the Convention on the Rights of the Child; disseminates information to professionals and the public.
Publication: Booklet
Publication title: Case for a Children's Rights Commissioner

01629

Chilled Food Association CFA

PO Box 6434, Kettering, NN15 5XT, UK
Tel: 01536 514365
Fax: 01536 515395
Email: cfa@chilledfood.org
Website: http://www.chilledfood.org
Members: 29
Contact: Kaarin Goodburn, Sec. Gen.
Description: Promotes food safety and hygiene standards in chilled food manufacture and the chill chain.
Library Type: not open to the public
Publication: Newsletter
Publication title: CFA News

01630

Chilterns American Women's Club CAWC

PO Box 445, Gerrards Cross, SL9 8YU, UK
Tel: 07523 699460
Email: membership@cawc.co.uk
Website: http://www.cawc.co.uk
Members: 200
Fee: £50
Membership Type: full, associate, honorary
Description: Promotes friendship and cooperation among members. Provides financial support to several local philanthropies.

01631
China-Britain Business Council
CBBC
3rd Fl. Portland House, Bressenden Pl., London, SW1E 5BH, UK
Tel: 020 78022000
Fax: 020 78022029
Email: enquiries@cbbc.org
Website: http://www.cbbc.org
Members: 900
Staff: 50
Contact: David Brewer, Chm.
Fee: £2875
Membership Type: corporate (large enterprise)
Fee: £1437.5
Membership Type: corporate (medium enterprise)
Description: British companies doing business in China. Promotes British trade in China. Acts as a liaison between the British and Chinese governments and member companies.
Library Subject: China economy, United Kingdom-China business
Library Type: open to the public
Publication: Magazine
Publication title: China-Britain Business Review. Advertisements.

01632
Choice in Personal Safety
CIPS
Mt. House, Urra, Chop Gate, Middlesborough, TS9 7HZ, UK
Tel: 01642 778302
Website: http://individualist.org.uk/cipsframe.htm
Contact: Gordon Read, Chm.
Description: Evaluates road safety measures. Promotes responsible personal behavior and use of personal safety devices.

01633
Choir Schools' Association
CSA
Wolvesey, College St., Hants, Winchester, S023 9ND, UK
Tel: 01962 890530
Email: csamds@tiscali.co.uk
Website: http://www.choirschools.org.uk
Members: 47
Contact: Susan Rees, Admin.
Description: Head teachers of schools regularly singing public services attached to cathedrals, colleges and churches. Exists to promote the interests of schools where choristers who sing regular public services in cathedrals, churches and college chapels, are educated. Also runs a bursary trust to help families with insufficient funds.
Publication title: Choir Schools Today

01634
Christian Aid
35 Lower Marsh, Waterloo, London, SE1 7RL, UK
Tel: 020 76204444
Email: info@christian-aid.org
Website: http://povertyover.christianaid.org.uk
Staff: 279
Contact: Loreta Minghella, Dir.
Description: Aid and development arm of the Council of Churches for Britain and Ireland. Supports community development programs designed to help some of the world's poorest people. Works in partnership with other organizations in 70 countries throughout the world. Seeks to combat the causes of poverty through advocacy, campaigns, and public education.
Publication: Magazine
Publication title: Christian Aid News

01635
Christian Blind Mission International - UK
CBM UK
Vision House, 7/8 Oakington Business Park, Dry Drayton Rd., Oakington, Cambridge, CB24 3DQ, UK
Tel: 01223 484700
Fax: 01223 484701
Email: info@cbmuk.org.uk
Website: http://www.cbmuk.org.uk
Contact: Bill McAllister, Natl. Dir.
Description: Works to cure and prevent blindness, deafness and other disabilities. Provides medical intervention, education and rehabilitation. Gives emergency relief services. Supports community based rehabilitation programmes.

01636
Christian Engineers in Development
CED
c/o Mr. Graeme Addison, Admin.
10 Monteath St., Perthshire, Crieff, PH7 3BQ, UK
Tel: 01764 653350
Email: admin@ced.org.uk
Website: http://www.ced.org.uk
Members: 60
Staff: 2
Contact: Barbara Brighouse, Sec.
Fee: £50
Membership Type: full (over the age of 30)
Description: Represents Christian engineers and other professionals interested in equitable and sustainable development of economically underdeveloped areas worldwide. Seeks to apply engineering principles to the design and implementation of economic development programs; makes available technical assistance to local programs sharing similar goals. Promotes environmental protection and the development of indigenous leadership to guide local development.
Publication: Newsletter
Publication title: CED Newsletter

01637
Chromatographic Society
ChromSoc
c/o Meeting Makers
Jordanhill Campus, 76 S Brae Dr., Glasgow, G13 1PP, UK
Tel: 0141 4341500
Fax: 0141 4341519
Email: chromsoc@meetingmakers.co.uk
Website: http://www.chromsoc.com
Members: 400
Staff: 1
Fee: £42
Membership Type: fellow
Fee: £37
Membership Type: individual
Description: Promotes chromatography and separation techniques.
Publication title: Chromatography Abstracts

01638
Chronic Lymphocytic Leukaemia Support Association
CLLSA
39/40 Eagle St., London, WC1R 4TH, UK
Tel: 020 76443052
Email: info@cllsupport.org.uk
Website: http://www.cllsupport.org.uk
Contact: Jane Barnard, Chair
Description: Aims to provide help and support for patients with CLL (Chronic Lymphocytic Leukaemia) and other related conditions. Advances public education of CLL. Promotes and supports scientific research into the treatment and care of CLL patients.

01639
Church Monuments Society
CMS
55, Bowden Park Rd., Crownhill, Plymouth, PL6 5NG, UK
Tel: 01752 773634
Email: churchmonuments@aol.com
Website: http://www.churchmonumentssociety.org
Members: 500
Contact: Clive Easter, Membership Sec.
Fee: £20
Membership Type: ordinary
Fee: £15
Membership Type: student
Description: Art historians and historians of dress and armor, religion, and society; archaeologists, genealogists, geologists, heralds, masons, sculptors, and stone conservators in several countries. Promotes the study, care, and conservation of funerary monuments and related art of all periods and countries, including sculpture with its architectural framework, flat memorials, stained glass, and wall painting associated with burials. Visits sites; advises on all aspects of care and conservation of church monuments, including fundraising. Sponsors study days and lectures.
Publication: Journal
Publication title: Journal of Church Monuments Society

01640
Churchill Society London
Ivy House, 18 Grove Ln., Suffolk, Ipswich, IP4 1NR, UK
Tel: 01473 413533
Fax: 01473 413533
Email: secretary@churchill-society-london.org.uk
Website: http://www.churchill-society-london.org.uk/Webmap.html
Members: 2800
Staff: 6
Contact: Pamela Timms, Chair
Fee: £20
Membership Type: regular, in UK
Fee: £38
Membership Type: regular, in U.S.
Description: Educational society for schools and young people; promotes the life and accomplishments of Churchill.

01641
CILT - The National Centre for Languages
111 Westminster Bridge Rd., London, SE1 7HR, UK
Tel: 020 76333300
Email: info@cilt.org.uk
Website: http://www.cilt.org.uk
Staff: 45
Contact: Kathryn Board, Chief Exec.
Description: Aims to promote greater national capability in languages. Services cover language teaching in all education sectors from primary to university as well as language training and languages in employment. The library is a reference collection open to researchers, teachers and others. An information service is also provided.
Formerly: Formerly, Centre for Information on Language Teaching and Research

01642
CIMTECH
University of Hertfordshire, College Ln., Hatfield, AL10 9AB, UK
Tel: 01707 281060
Fax: 01707 281061
Email: c.cimtech@herts.ac.uk
Website: http://www.cimtech.co.uk
Members: 1000
Staff: 10
Contact: Tony Hendley, Managing Dir.
Fee: £200
Membership Type: corporate
Fee: £235
Membership Type: corporate, overseas
Description: Publishers and consultants; private and public companies; educational institutions; records management and management service departments. Provides information about media and methods for originating, distributing, storing, and retrieving information. Covers such topics as: computer assisted retrieval; document imaging; records management; optical character recognition; information processing. Conducts sponsored research projects. Offers educational courses. Provides consulting services in electronic content, document and records management.
Library Type: not open to the public
Formerly: Formerly, National Reprographic Centre for Documentation
Publication: Journal
Publication title: Information Management & Technology. Advertisements.

01643
Cinema Theatre Association
CTA
128 Gloucester Terr., London, W2 6HP, UK
Email: taylor@homecall.co.uk
Website: http://www.cinema-theatre.org.uk
Members: 1500
Contact: Neville Taylor, Membership Sec.-Treas.
Fee: £22
Membership Type: in UK
Fee: £15
Membership Type: in UK under 25 years of age
Description: Represents individuals interested in the architectural and technical history of cinema buildings. Campaigns for the preservation and continued use of cinemas and theatres for their original purpose, organises visits to cinemas and theatre of interest; lectures and film shows are held from time to time, archive holding of related material.
Publication: Magazine
Publication title: Picture House

01644
Circle of Wine Writers
CWW
c/o Jim Budd
34 Frobisher Ct., Sydenham Rise, London, SE23 3XH, UK
Tel: 020 86992473
Fax: 020 86993173
Email: editor@winewriters.org
Website: http://www.winewriters.org
Members: 281
Staff: 1
Contact: Steven Spurrier, Pres.
Fee: £50
Membership Type: regular
Description: Provides members with a strong voice to express views and a forum for the exchange of information. Improves the standard of communication about wines, spirits and beers. Conducts programme of workshops, meetings, talks and tasting.
Publication: Newsletter
Publication title: Circle Update

01645
CIRIA
Classic House, 174-180 Old St., London, EC1V 9BP, UK
Tel: 020 75493300
Fax: 020 72530523
Email: enquiries@ciria.org
Website: http://www.ciria.org
Members: 700
Contact: Peter Gammie, Chief Exec.
Description: Works to identify the research needs of the construction industry. Formulates research projects; arranges funding; assigns research contracts; assists in technology transfer; disseminates information. Research interests include structural design, civil engineering, earthworks and foundations, management, building design and construction, water engineering, environmental management, and quality management.
Formerly: Formerly, CIRIA: Construction Industry Research and Information Association
Publication: Newsletter
Publication title: CIRIA News
Meetings/Conventions: Contaminated Land Conference – annual conference – Exhibits.

01646
CISV International
MEA House, Ellison Pl., Newcastle upon Tyne, NE1 8XS, UK
Tel: 0191 2324998
Fax: 0191 2614710
Email: international@cisv.org
Website: http://www.cisv.org
Members: 48000
Staff: 5
Fee: £9
Membership Type: regular
Fee: £75
Membership Type: life
Description: Unites children from all over the world through summer camps. Seeks to further the education of children in international understanding without distinction of race, religion or politics. Fosters among the youth knowledge and understanding of the various customs of different countries. Encourages friendships in the hope of achieving peaceful solutions to worldwide problems.
Formerly: Formerly, International Association of Children's International Simmer Villages
Publication: Annual Report
Publication title: CISV Annual Report. Advertisements.

01647
City and Guilds of London Institute
1 Giltspur St., London, EC1A 9DD, UK
Tel: 084 475430000
Fax: 020 72942400
Email: enquiry@city-and-guilds.co.uk
Website: http://www.cityandguilds.com/int-home.html
Contact: Michael Howell, Chm.
Description: Provides training and accreditation to individuals seeking professional enrichment. Promotes the importance of an educated workforce to company prosperity. Develops in-house training programs for companies. Offers resources that aid in program completion.

01648
City Women's Network
CWN
PO Box 353, Uxbridge, UB10 0UN, UK
Tel: 01895 272178
Fax: 01895 272178
Email: admin@citywomen.org
Website: http://www.citywomen.org
Members: 250
Contact: India Gary-Martin, Pres.
Fee: £260
Membership Type: full
Description: Senior executive and professional businesswomen. Provides a forum for members to share common professional and social interests and experiences.
Publication: Newsletter
Publication title: Connections. Advertisements.

01649
Civil Engineering Contractors Association
CECA
1 Birdcage Walk, London, SW1H 9JJ, UK
Tel: 020 73400450
Fax: 020 72227514
Email: rosemarybeales@ceca.co.uk
Website: http://www.ceca.co.uk
Members: 350
Contact: Rosemary Beales, Dir.
Description: Represents British civil engineering contractors as an integral part of the economy.
Publication: Newsletter
Publication title: CECA Communicates
Meetings/Conventions: Council Meeting – meeting

01650
Clarinet and Saxophone Society of Great Britain
CASS
15 Springwell, Ingleton, County Durham, Darlington, DL2 3JJ, UK
Website: http://www.cassgb.org
Members: 1225
Contact: David Campbell, Chm.
Fee: £20
Membership Type: student, senior citizen
Fee: £300

Membership Type: life
Description: Promotes the playing of the instruments, clarinets and saxophones.
Publication: Magazine
Publication title: Clarinet and Saxophone. Advertisements.

01651
Clarsach Society
CS
Blue Drill Hall, Studio G43, 36 Dalmeny St., Edinburgh, EH6 8RG, UK
Tel: 0131 6674645
Email: clarsach.society@hotmail.co.uk
Website: http://www.clarsachsociety.co.uk
Members: 950
Staff: 2
Contact: Mary Scott, Hon. Sec.
Fee: £20
Membership Type: adult
Fee: £25
Membership Type: family
Description: Promotes and encourages the playing of the clarsach (Scottish harp). Collects music, organizes performances and sponsors competitions. Holds concerts and festivals.
Publication title: Harp Music Folios

01652
Clay Pipe Development Association
CPDA
Copsham House, 53 Broad St., Buckinghamshire, Chesham, HP5 3EA, UK
Tel: 01494 791456
Fax: 01494 792378
Email: cpda@aol.com
Description: Represents all companies producing vitrified clay drainage and sewerage pipes and clay flue liners cable ducts in United Kingdom; represents the industry on British, European and international standards works and to government bodies as necessary. Organizes research work, writes technical literature, gives direct advice on design and construction issues and provides troubleshooting services. Conducts lectures to professional and educational organizations and to individual companies.
Publication: Booklet
Publication title: Bedding Construction and Flow Capacity of Vitrified Clay Pipelines

01653
Clay Roof Tile Council
CRTC
British Ceramic Confederation, Federation House, Station Rd., Stoke-on-Trent, ST4 2SA, UK
Tel: 01782 744631
Fax: 01782 744102
Email: chrish@ceramfed.co.uk
Website: http://www.clayroof.co.uk
Members: 6
Staff: 2
Contact: Chris Hall, Sec.
Description: Promotes the use of Clay Roof Tiles in the interest of members. Promotes, supports and improves technical education, knowledge and research in the field of Clay Roof Tiles.

01654
Cleaning and Hygiene Suppliers' Association
CHSA
PO Box 770, Buckinghamshire, Marlow, SL7 2SH, UK
Tel: 01628 478273
Fax: 01628 478286
Email: secretary@chsa.co.uk
Website: http://www.chsa.co.uk
Members: 200
Staff: 1
Contact: Jeff Bell, Chm.
Fee: £285
Membership Type: associate
Fee: £395-1850
Membership Type: manufacturer (based on turnover)
Description: Suppliers and distributors of cleaning and hygiene materials and equipment. Works with raising industry standards, information and guidance to members on regulatory issues, warehousing and transport safety and environmental protection.

01655
Cleaning and Support Services Association
CSSA
Warnford Ct., 29 Throgmorton St., London, EC2N 2AT, UK
Tel: 020 79209632
Fax: 020 72569360
Email: alarge@cleaningassoc.org
Website: http://www.cleaningindustry.org/home
Contact: Andrew Large, Chief Exec.
Description: Cleaning and support industries in the Europe. Promotes cleaning and maintenance industry. Conducts research programs; compiles statistics.
Library Type: reference
Publication: Report
Publication title: Labor Market Survey

01656
Cleft Lip and Palate Association
CLAPA
Green Man Tower, 1st Fl., 332B Goswell Rd., London, EC1V 7LQ, UK
Tel: 020 78334883
Fax: 020 78335999
Email: info@clapa.com
Website: http://www.clapa.com
Contact: Rosanna Preston, Chief Exec.
Description: Local groups comprising parents of children with cleft lips or palates and health care professionals. Seeks to improve treatment of cleft lips and palates; promotes an improved quality of life for children with cleft lips and palates. Provides support to children with cleft lips and palates and their parents; supports research into the causes and treatment of cleft lips and palates; conducts educational programs; undertakes fundraising campaigns. Maintains specialist service for parents having difficulty feeding children with cleft lips or palates.

01657
CLIC Sargent
Mercantile Chambers, 5th Fl., 53 Bothwell St., Glasgow, G2 6TS, UK
Tel: 0141 5725700
Email: mediarelations@clicsargent.org.uk
Website: http://www.clicsargent.org.uk/Home
Contact: Lorraine Clifton, CEO
Description: Provides care for children and young adults experiencing cancer and their families and works closely within the hospital multi-disciplinary team. Provides supported short breaks for families.

01658
Clinical Dental Technicians Association
CDTA
12, Upper St. N, New Ash Green, Kent, Longfield, DA3 8JR, UK
Tel: 01474 879430
Fax: 01474 872086
Email: ednarogers@btinternet.com
Website: http://www.cdta.org.uk
Contact: Christopher Allen, Chief Exec.
Description: Dental technicians seeking legal status in the United Kingdom to train and qualify to make and fit dentures directly with the public under Act of Parliament. Works closely with other professions complementary to dentistry to ensure that the proposals and legislation are fair, equitable and in the interest of dental patients.
Library Subject: dental technology
Library Type: open to the public
Formerly: Formerly, Association for Denture Prosthesis
Publication: Newsletter
Publication title: The Denturist

01659
Clinical Genetics Society
CGS
Clinical Genetics Unit, Birmingham Women's Hospital, Edgbaston, Birmingham, B15 2TG, UK
Tel: 0121 6272634
Fax: 0121 6236971
Email: cgs@bshg.org.uk
Website: http://www.bshg.org.uk
Contact: Ruth Cole, Exec. Off.
Fee: £70
Membership Type: individual
Description: Seeks to advance and promote the science and practice of clinical genetics. Promotes and facilitates education for the genetics community and other health care professionals. Encourages high standards of training. Facilitates research into basic human genetics and genetic disorders. Maintains links with patient groups.

01660
Clinical Pathology Accreditation
CPA
45 Rutland Park, Botanical Gardens, Sheffield, S10 2PB, UK
Tel: 0114 2515800
Fax: 0114 2515801
Email: office@cpa-uk.co.uk
Website: http://www.cpa-uk.co.uk
Contact: Cheryl Blair, Exec. Mgr.
Description: Provides a means to accredit clinical pathology services, including external audits and peer review.

01661
Clothworkers' Company
Dunster Ct., Mincing Ln., London, EC3R 7AH, UK
Tel: 020 76237041
Fax: 020 73970107

Website: http://www.clothworkers.co.uk
Description: Supports the textile industry of which some members are still involved. Organizes charitable work and provides educational grants.
Publication: Book
Publication title: The Golden Ram. A Narrative History of The Clothworkers' Company (1958)

01662
Clubs for Young People CYP
371 Kennington Ln., London, SE11 5QY, UK
Tel: 020 77930787
Fax: 020 78209815
Email: office@clubsforyoungpeople.org.uk
Website: http://www.clubsforyoungpeople.org.uk
Members: 400000
Staff: 24
Contact: Simon Antrobus, Chief Exec.
Description: Aims to enable young people to develop spiritually, morally, culturally, mentally and physically, thereby helping them to prepare for life and adult responsibility.
Formerly: Formerly, NACYP - Clubs for Young People

01663
Clwyd Welsh Pony and Cob Association
c/o Mrs. Audrey Weaver, Sec.
Morwyn Stud, Bryn Meibion, Clawddnewydd, Denbighshire, Ruthin, LL15 2NL, UK
Tel: 01824 750256
Email: morwynponies@aol.com
Website: http://www.clwydwpca.com
Members: 400
Contact: Dilwyn Roberts, Chm.
Fee: £10
Membership Type: individual
Fee: £12
Membership Type: dual
Description: Records the breeding details of Welsh ponies and cobs. Seeks to improve the breed and promote its excellence.

01664
Co-operative Women's Guild
4 Freeman Close, Myland, Essex, Colchester, CO4 5FJ, UK
Tel: 01206 752237
Email: coopwomensguild4@btconnect.com
Website: http://www.coopwomensguild.co.uk
Members: 2500
Staff: 2
Contact: Claire Morgan, Gen. Sec.
Description: Promotes equal opportunities for complete and free development. Educates women on principles and practices of cooperation so that they may participate in the women's movement. Works towards improving the status of women and encouraging their participation in community, national, and international affairs. Promotes world peace. Provides social, cultural, and recreational activities.

01665
Coach Operators Federation COF
64 Brookside, Paulton, Bristol, BS39 7YR, UK
Tel: 01761 415456
Fax: 01761 415456
Email: somerbus@tinyworld.co.uk
Website: http://www.cofed.net
Members: 85
Contact: Tim Jennings, Treas.
Description: Represents the coach operators in UK. Aims to improve the coach industry.

01666
Coachmakers' and Coach Harness Makers' Company
Elm Tree Cottage, Bottom House Farm Ln., Buckinghamshire, Chalfont St. Giles, UK
Tel: 07971 017255
Website: http://www.coachmakers.co.uk
Contact: Michael Davis, Master
Description: Promotes excellence in the modern automotive, aerospace and rail industries.

01667
Coal Merchants' Federation - England CMF
7 Swanwick Ct., Derbyshire, Alfreton, DE55 7AS, UK
Tel: 01773 835400
Fax: 01773 834351
Email: cmf@solidfuel.co.uk
Website: http://www.coalmerchants.co.uk
Members: 1150
Staff: 5
Description: Coal merchants who fulfill prescribed standards for quality of products and services. Concerned with retail distribution of solid fuel.
Publication title: Coal Trader

01668
Coalition for Quality in Care
c/o Counsel and Care
Twymann House, 16 Bonny St., London, NW1 9PG, UK
Tel: 020 72418521
Fax: 020 72676877
Email: general@coalitionforqualitycare.org.uk
Website: http://www.coalitionforqualitycare.org.uk
Contact: Donna Peart, Contact
Fee: £75
Membership Type: organization
Fee: £10
Membership Type: individual
Description: Brings together a wide range of organizations and individuals with a common concern for the well-being of older people receiving long-term care in different settings and different circumstances. Aims to raise awareness of the needs, rights and aspirations of all older people in long term care, particularly those who are most vulnerable. seeks to promote good practice and vigilance in the face of pressures from many quarters to compromise on the important issues which ensure quality of care, funding, the legislative framework, training, ageism and social exclusion.

01669
Coalition to Stop the Use of Child Soldiers
9 Marshalsea Rd., 4th Fl., London, SE1 1EP, UK
Tel: 020 73674110
Fax: 020 73674129
Email: info@child-soldiers.org
Website: http://www.child-soldiers.org
Staff: 9
Contact: Victoria Forbes Adam, Dir.
Description: Eliminates the recruitment of young boys and girls as soldiers. Aims to secure children's demobilization. Promotes their integration in community through research and monitoring, advocacy and public education.

01670
Cobalt Development Institute CDI
167 High St., Surrey, Guildford, GU1 3AJ, UK
Tel: 01483 578877
Fax: 01483 573873
Email: info@thecdi.com
Website: http://www.thecdi.com
Members: 44
Staff: 4
Contact: David Weight, Gen. Mgr.
Fee: £11600
Membership Type: full
Fee: £1900
Membership Type: industrial, associate
Description: Cobalt producers and users in 14 countries; research organizations. Aims to develop and promote uses for cobalt in industry, medicine, and science; consults with governments, research organizations, and ecological groups on environmental and other questions connected with the utilization of cobalt and its compounds; provides members with information regarding legislation and regulations affecting the cobalt industry; arranges for the exchange of information relevant to the cobalt industry; encourages cooperation between members and other international organizations. Compiles statistics.
Library Subject: cobalt and its applications
Library Type: reference
Publication: Magazine
Publication title: Cobalt News

01671
Cochrane Collaboration
Summertown Pavilion, 18-24 Middle Way, Oxford, OX2 7LG, UK
Tel: 01865 310138
Fax: 01865 316023
Email: secretariat@cochrane.org
Website: http://www.cochrane.org
Contact: Nick Royle, CEO
Description: Provides up-to-date and accurate information about the effects of health care readily available worldwide. Produces and disseminates systematic reviews of health care interventions. Promotes the search for evidence in the form of clinical trials and other studies of interventions.
Publication: Report
Publication title: Cochrane Database of Systematic Reviews

01672

Coeliac UK
CUK

Apollo Ctr., 3rd Fl., Desborough Rd., High Wycombe, HP11 2QW, UK
Tel: 01494 437278
Fax: 01494 474349
Website: http://www.coeliac.org.uk
Members: 80800
Staff: 29
Contact: Sarah Sleet, Chief Exec.
Fee: £20
Membership Type: individual
Fee: £10
Membership Type: concessionary
Description: Supports people with coeliac disease and dermatitis herpetiformis. Seeks to improve the lives of people living with the condition through support, campaign and research.
Formerly: Formerly, Coeliac Society of the United Kingdom
Publication: Magazine
Publication title: Crossedgrain

01673

Coffee Trade Federation
CTF

Blackfriars Foundry, 156 Blackfriars Rd., London, SE1 8EN, UK
Tel: 020 73285222
Fax: 020 73285444
Email: secretariat@coffeetradefederation.org.uk
Website: http://www.coffeetradefederation.org.uk
Contact: Angus Kerr, Chm.
Description: Protects the interests of the UK coffee trade.

01674

College of Operating Department Practitioners
CODP

1 Mabledon Pl., London, WC1H 9AJ, UK
Tel: 0870 7460984
Fax: 0870 7460985
Email: office@codp.org.uk
Website: http://www.codp.org.uk
Members: 7500
Fee: £25
Membership Type: student
Description: Seeks to maintain quality standards among operating department practitioners.
Formerly: Absorbed, Association of Operating Department Practitioners
Publication: Journal
Publication title: Technic. Advertisements.

01675

College of Optometrists

42 Craven St., London, WC2N 5NG, UK
Tel: 020 78396000
Fax: 020 78396800
Email: optometry@college-optometrists.org
Website: http://www.college-optometrists.org
Members: 13000
Staff: 21
Contact: Bryony Pawinska, Chief Exec.
Fee: £293.73
Membership Type: individual in UK
Fee: £164.98
Membership Type: individual outside UK
Description: Consists of Fellows and Members, both home and overseas, Associate Members who do not hold full qualifications, non-practising Fellows, Honorary and Life Fellows. Concerned with the improvement and conservation of human vision, advancement for the public benefit of the study of and research into optometry and publication of the results, promotion of the science and practice of optometry and encouragement of the highest possible standards of professional competence and conduct for the public benefit.
Library Subject: optometry and vision
Library Type: reference
Formerly: Formerly, British College of Optometrists
Publication: Journal
Publication title: Ophthalmic and Physiological Optics

01676

College of Piping

16-24 Otago St., Glasgow, G12 8JH, UK
Tel: 0141 3343587
Fax: 0141 3376068
Email: college@college-of-piping.co.uk
Website: http://www.college-of-piping.co.uk
Contact: Robert Wallace, Contact
Fee: £30
Membership Type: individual
Fee: £200
Membership Type: life
Description: Promotes interest in great Highland bagpipe and music.

01677

College of Teachers
CoT

20 Bedford Way, London, WC1H 0AL, UK
Tel: 020 79115536
Fax: 020 76314865
Website: http://www.collegeofteachers.ac.uk
Members: 2000
Staff: 4
Contact: Alma Harris, Pres.
Fee: £72
Membership Type: fellow
Fee: £68
Membership Type: full
Description: Teachers united to promote sound learning and advance the interests of education. Makes available programs and facilities enabling teachers to expand their knowledge and professional capabilities. Establishes in-service qualifications for teachers; conducts lectures and seminars.
Publication: Journal
Publication title: Education Today

01678

Combined Edible Nut Trade Association
CENTA

18 Lichfield Rd., Essex, Woodford, IG8 9ST, UK
Tel: 020 85062391
Fax: 020 85062391
Email: treenuts@centa.uk.com
Website: http://www.centa.uk.com
Members: 45
Contact: D.G. Sunderland, Sec.
Fee: £520
Membership Type: in UK
Description: Aims to circulate members on topical issues relating to the nut trade; to discuss, debate all matters appertaining to the trade; to maintain arbitration rules and up to date trading terms on which contracts may be based; to have representation in Europe through membership of FRUCOM.
Publication: Brochure
Publication title: Terms and Conditions of Trading and Rules

01679

Combined Heat and Power Association
CHPA

Grosvenor Gardens House, 35-37 Grosvenor Gardens, London, SW1W 0BS, UK
Tel: 020 78284077
Fax: 020 78280310
Email: info@chpa.co.uk
Website: http://www.chpa.co.uk
Members: 106
Staff: 8
Contact: Graham Meeks, Dir.
Fee: £18250
Membership Type: supporting
Fee: £12100
Membership Type: full
Description: Major energy suppliers, local authorities, CHP users, equipment suppliers, etc. Promotes the wider use of CHP and community heating.
Library Subject: community heating, power
Library Type: by appointment only

01680

Comic Relief

5th Fl., 89 Albert Embankment, London, SE1 7TP, UK
Tel: 020 78205555
Fax: 020 78205500
Email: info@comicrelief.com
Website: http://www.comicrelief.com
Contact: Peter Bennett-Jones, Chm.
Description: Aims to alleviate poverty and social injustice in the UK and in the poorest countries in the world by raising money from the general public through the red nose day fundraising event. Uses comedy and laughter in raising awareness, educating, and promoting social change in areas where poverty exists. Seeks the assistance of renowned comedians to get their message to the public.

01681

Comics Creators Guild
CCG

22 St. James Mansions, W End Ln., London, NW6 2AA, UK
Email: webmaster@comicscreatorsguild.co.uk
Website: http://www.comicscreatorsguild.co.uk
Members: 163
Contact: Win Wiacek, Contact
Fee: £40
Membership Type: regular
Description: Represents the comics professionals in UK. Aims to raise public awareness of comics art and industry and to establish better communication among its members through social meetings and networking.

Comite Europeen de Liaison des Importateurs de Machines-Outils
see European Liaison Committee of Machine Tool Importers

Comite International pour la Protection des Cables Sous-marins
see International Cable Protection Committee

Comite International Radio-Maritime
see International Association for Marine Electronics Companies

Comite Mundial de Consulta de los Amigos
see Friends World Committee for Consultation - United Kingdom

01682

Commercial Boat Operators Association CBOA
PO Box 38479, London, SE16 4WX, UK
Tel: 020 72316247
Email: j.dodwell@cboa.org.uk
Website: http://www.cboa.org.uk
Contact: John Dodwell, Chm.
Fee: £15
Membership Type: associate
Fee: £350
Membership Type: firm (with more than 5 craft)
Description: Operators of boats or freight facilities are traders; other individuals who support the aims of the association are associates. Promotes increased use of British canals and other inland waterways for transportation of freight and as vacation destinations. Conducts promotional activities to increase public awareness of vacation opportunities associated with Britain's inland waterways and the environmental friendliness and economic efficiency of transporting freight by canal barge.

01683

Commercial Horticultural Association CHA
Stoneleigh Park, Warwickshire, Kenilworth, CV8 2LG, UK
Tel: 024 76692291
Fax: 01959 565885
Email: info@cha-hort.com
Website: http://www.cha-hort.com
Members: 110
Staff: 4
Contact: Pat Flynn, Chair
Fee: £419.75
Membership Type: individual
Description: Manufacturers and suppliers of equipment, products and services for the commercial horticultural industry worldwide. Trade association looking after interests of members; is particularly active in the area of exhibitions and regional shows covering commercial and amenity horticulture in UK and overseas.
Publication: Booklet
Publication title: Buyers Guide. Advertisements.

01684

Commercial Trailer Association CTA
Society of Motor Manufacturers and Traders Ltd., Forbes House, Halkin St., London, SW1X 7DS, UK
Tel: 020 72357000
Fax: 020 72357112
Email: ctaweb@smmt.co.uk
Website: http://www.smmt.co.uk/home.cfm
Members: 12
Contact: Paul Everitt, Chief Exec.
Description: Gives a forum for the informal exchange of views on issues about the trailer business in UK. Provides essential technical information and regulatory advice to the industry.

01685

Commission for Local Administration in England
10th Fl., Millbank Tower, Millbank, London, SW1P 4QP, UK
Tel: 020 72174620
Fax: 020 72174621
Website: http://www.lgo.org.uk
Members: 4
Staff: 210
Contact: Tony Redmond, Ombudsman
Description: Provides independent, impartial and prompt investigation and resolution of complaints of injustice caused by maladministration by local authorities and certain other bodies. Offers guidance intended to promote fair and effective administration in local government.

01686

Commission for Racial Equality CRE
St. Dunstan's House, 201-211 Borough High St., London, SE1 1GZ, UK
Tel: 020 79390000
Fax: 020 79390001
Email: info@cre.gov.uk
Website: http://83.137.212.42/sitearchive/cre/index.html
Staff: 200
Contact: Kay Hampton, Chair
Description: Works to eliminate discrimination based on race. Promotes equal opportunity among persons of different races.

Commission Internationale de la Microflore du Paleozoique
see International Commission of the Palaeozoic Microflora

Commission Internationale de Nomenclature Zoologique
see International Commission on Zoological Nomenclature

Commission Internationale des Oeufs
see International Egg Commission

Commission Internationale pour l'Unification des Methodes d'Analyse du Sucre
see International Commission for Uniform Methods of Sugar Analysis

Committee Internationale pour la Definition des Caracteristiques Microbiologiques des Aliments
see International Commission on Microbiological Specifications for Foods

01687

Committee of Advertising Practice CAP
Mid City Pl., 71 High Holborn, London, WC1V 6QT, UK
Tel: 020 74922222
Fax: 020 72423696
Email: enquiries@cap.org.uk
Website: http://www.cap.org.uk
Contact: Andrew Brown, Chm.
Description: Executive and policy-making body responsible for the advertising industry's system of self-regulation. Devises codes for marketing communications, which are independently supervised by the Advertising Standards Authority.

01688

Committee of Scottish Clearing Bankers CSCB
38B Drumsheugh Gardens, Edinburgh, EH3 7SW, UK
Tel: 0131 4737770
Fax: 0131 4737799
Email: info@scotbanks.org.uk
Website: http://www.scotbanks.org.uk
Members: 4
Staff: 4
Contact: Gordon Fenton, Contact
Description: Trade association of Scottish clearing banks.

01689

Commons, Open Spaces and Footpaths Preservation Society
25 A Bell St., Henley-on-Thames, RG9 2BA, UK
Tel: 01491 573535
Fax: 01491 573051
Email: hq@oss.org.uk
Website: http://www.oss.org.uk
Members: 2400
Staff: 5
Contact: Kate Ashbrook, Gen. Sec.
Fee: £600
Membership Type: life
Fee: £30
Membership Type: single
Description: Seeks to conserve and protect common land, village greens, open spaces and public rights of way in England and Wales.
Publication: Magazine
Publication title: Open Space. Advertisements.

01690

Commonwealth Association of Architects
CAA

PO Box 508, London, HA8 9XZ, UK
Tel: 020 89510550
Fax: 020 89510550
Email: info@comarchitect.org
Website: http://comarchitect.org
Members: 39
Staff: 2
Contact: Mubasshar Hussain, Pres.
Description: National architectural institutes and associations in 39 Commonwealth countries. Seeks to: act as a clearinghouse for architects and architectural institutes, teachers, research workers, and students; promote the field of architecture and encourage professionalism; foster social, intellectual, artistic, scientific, and professional exchange; represent architectural interests before governmental bodies; evaluate the quality and standards of courses in architecture against set criteria and maintains a list of recognized courses in architecture.
Library Type: reference
Formerly: Absorbed, Commonwealth Board of Architectural Education
Publication: Journal
Publication title: CAA Newsnet

01691

Commonwealth Association of Planners
CAP

c/o Royal Town Planning Institute in Scotland
57 Melville St., Edinburgh, EH3 7HL, UK
Tel: 0131 2261959
Fax: 0131 2261909
Email: annette.odonnell@rtpi.org.uk
Website: http://www.commonwealth-planners.org
Members: 25300
Contact: Annette O'Donnell, Sec.
Fee: £1
Membership Type: individual
Description: Nationally recognized planning organizations or groups; professional physical planners in 50 countries. Promotes physical planning as a professional activity and a function of government. Fosters cooperation among British Commonwealth organizations and individuals in order to achieve the optimum social and environmental contribution of planners; encourages Commonwealth countries to improve the scale and quality of their planning service. Seeks to improve communication among planners in countries having no national organization. Works to develop adequate research and educational facilities; encourages standards promoting free movement of planners, coordinated rights of professional practice, and reciprocity of qualifications. Assists in the exchange of professional, educational, research, and technical information; fosters liaison and collaboration among planners, other related professions, the Commonwealth, and international bodies. Holds regional seminars and workshops.
Publication: Newsletter
Publication title: Planners Newsletter

01692

Commonwealth Association of Science, Technology and Mathematics Educators
CASTME

University of Winchester, Faculty of Education, Winchester, SO22 4NR, UK
Email: bridget.egan@winchester.ac.uk
Website: http://www.castme.org
Members: 290
Staff: 1
Contact: Bridget Egan, Chair
Fee: £11
Membership Type: individual
Fee: £40
Membership Type: institutional
Description: Teachers of science, technology, and mathematics. Provides social, cultural, human and economic context in the teaching of science technology and mathematics. Provides assistance to national and local teachers' organizations pursuing similar goals; conducts research and educational programs.
Publication: Journal
Publication title: CASTME Journal
Meetings/Conventions: Science Technology and Mathematics Education for Human Development – triennial conference – Exhibits.

01693

Commonwealth Association of Surveying and Land Economy
CASLE

University of the West of England, School of the Built and Natural Environment, Coldharbour Ln., Bristol, BS16 1QY, UK
Tel: 0117 3283036
Fax: 0117 3283036
Email: susan.spedding@uwe.ac.uk
Website: http://www.casle.org
Members: 40
Contact: Susan Spedding, Admin. Sec.
Fee: £25
Membership Type: associate (individual)
Fee: £50
Membership Type: full
Description: Represents national professional societies concerned with land economy, land surveying, and quantity surveying. Aims to: provide Commonwealth countries with high quality surveying services; encourage the establishment of research and technical information services; strengthen relations among Commonwealth countries; and encourage the interchange of relevant information among societies. Maintains Education Advisory Service that assists the evaluation of existing courses in surveying and land economy and in establishing new courses in the field. Appoints correspondents in countries having no surveying organization.
Formerly: Absorbed, Commonwealth Board of Surveying Education
Publication: Report
Publication title: Built Environment professionals and the Habitat agenda

01694

Commonwealth Association of Tax Administrators
CATA

c/o COMSEC
Marlborough House, Pall Mall, London, SW1Y 5HX, UK
Tel: 020 77476473
Fax: 020 77476225
Email: cata@commonwealth.int
Website: http://www.catatax.org
Members: 47
Staff: 8
Contact: Zahir Kaleem, Exec. Dir.
Description: Government departments concerned with direct and indirect taxes and represented by senior tax officials. Works to improve all aspects of tax administration in 47 countries. Organizes annual management and technical training programs and assistance programs.
Publication: Reports
Publication title: Survey Reports

01695

Commonwealth Broadcasting Association
CBA

17 Fleet St., London, EC4Y 1AA, UK
Tel: 020 75835550
Fax: 020 75835549
Email: elizabeth@cba.org.uk
Website: http://www.cba.org.uk
Members: 102
Contact: Elizabeth Smith, Sec. Gen.
Description: Broadcasting organizations and groups of such organization. Aims to secure funds for training of developing commonwealth countries; fosters freedom of expression and the right to communicate; furthers the concept of public service and broadcasting and provides contact and a forum for discussion.
Publication: Magazine
Publication title: Commonwealth Broadcaster. Advertisements.

01696

Commonwealth Countries League
CCL

37 Priory Ave., Middlesex, Sudbury, HA0 2SB, UK
Tel: 01923821364
Email: info@ccl-int.org
Website: http://www.ccl-int.org
Members: 400
Description: Societies of men and women interested in the British Commonwealth; spouses of High Commissioners in London, England; women members of Parliament. Strives to secure equality of liberties, status, and opportunities for women and men in the Commonwealth. Promotes and funds secondary education for girls based on ability and financial need. Sponsors annual fundraising Commonwealth Fair.
Publication: Newsletter
Publication title: CCL News Update

01697

Commonwealth Dental Association
CDA

64 Wimpole St., London, W1G 8YS, UK
Tel: 020 75634133
Fax: 020 75634556
Email: administrator@cdauk.com
Website: http://www.cdauk.com
Members: 44
Staff: 1
Contact: Ulrike Matthesius, Admin.
Description: Local dental associations. Serves as a forum for discussion of matters of interest to members; works to coordinate members' activities. Promotes dental hygiene and oral health. Develops primary preventive dental strategies; conducts training programs for dental

health workers; provides technical support to members in implementing programs. Holds educational courses.
Publication: Newsletter
Publication title: CDA Bulletin. Advertisements.
Meetings/Conventions: triennial general assembly August 30 to September 2, 2012. Cape Town Republic of South Africa

01698
Commonwealth Forestry Association
CFA
The Crib, Dinchope, Shropshire, Craven Arms, SY7 9JJ, UK
Tel: 01588 672868
Fax: 0870 0116645
Email: cfa@cfa-international.org
Website: http://www.cfa-international.org
Contact: Jim Ball, Pres.
Fee: £15-30
Membership Type: student
Fee: £15-75
Membership Type: ordinary
Description: Organizations and individuals in 108 countries including foresters, forest and wood scientists, timber merchants, ecologists and resource managers, and conservationists interested in worldwide forestry; libraries. Seeks to unite all those concerned with forest conservation, development, and management.
Formerly: Formerly, Empire Forestry Association
Publication: Newsletter
Publication title: CFA Newsletter

01699
Commonwealth Foundation
CF
Marlborough House, Pall Mall, London, SW1Y 5HY, UK
Tel: 020 79303783
Fax: 020 78398157
Email: geninfo@commonwealth.int
Website: http://www.commonwealthfoundation.com
Members: 46
Contact: Mark Collins, Dir.
Description: An intergovernmental organisation with a mandate to support the work of the non-governmental sector in the Commonwealth. Funding is provided by Commonwealth governments. Supports professional development, training opportunities, and the sharing of skills, experience and information among the people of the 54 Commonwealth member countries through the provision of specific awards. Provides programmes and grants benefit to non-governmental organisations (NGOs), professional associations and cultural bodies. Encourages activities that facilitate co-operation between developing countries in priority areas including the eradication of poverty, rural development, health, non-formal education, community enterprise, gender and development, disability and the arts and culture.
Publication: Magazine
Publication title: Commonwealth People

01700
Commonwealth Fund for Technical Co-Operation
CFTC
Commonwealth Secretariat, Marlborough House, Pall Mall, London, SW1Y 5HX, UK
Tel: 020 77476500
Fax: 020 79300827
Email: info@commonwealth.int
Website: http://www.thecommonwealth.org
Members: 54
Staff: 200
Contact: Kamalesh Sharma, Sec. Gen.
Description: A fund of the Commonwealth Secretariat. Provides technical assistance by offering experts, training, in-house consultancy services and best practice guides to developing Commonwealth countries in areas of comparative advantage such as debt management, trade capacity building, export development, small and medium enterprise development, public sector reform, governance and democracy, sustainable development of natural resource sector: petroleum, gas and minerals, and capacity and institutional development in areas of priority for member countries.
Publication: Book
Publication title: Skills for Development

01701
Commonwealth Hansard Editors Association
CHEA
House of Commons, Department of Official Report, Westminster, London, SW1 0AA, UK
Email: sutherlandl@parliament.uk
Website: http://www.hansard-westminster.co.uk/chea
Members: 60
Contact: Lorraine Sutherland, Ed.
Description: Editors of Hansard (the body of reports containing verbatim parliamentary proceedings). Works to enhance the service provided by editors to their parliaments through the sharing of information.
Publication: Report
Publication title: Report of Meetings

01702
Commonwealth Human Ecology Council
CHEC
Church House, Newton Rd., London, W2 5LS, UK
Tel: 0020 77925934
Fax: 0020 77925948
Email: chec@btopenworld.com
Website: http://www.checinternational.org
Members: 95
Staff: 2
Contact: Zena Daysh, Exec. Vice Chair
Fee: £20
Membership Type: retired
Fee: £60
Membership Type: corporate
Description: Governmental departments, academicians and universities, ecological associations, and interested individuals in 41 countries. Seeks to make the human ecology field a major component in national planning and policy and to increase awareness and improve programs concerned with the interrelationship of humans in the total environment; works for creation of human ecology institutions in Commonwealth countries. Conducts courses, seminars, and workshops.
Publication: Journal
Publication title: CHEC Journal. Advertisements.

01703
Commonwealth Lawyers' Association
CLA
17 Russell Sq., London, WC1B 5DR, UK
Tel: 020 78628824
Fax: 020 78628816
Email: cla@sas.ac.uk
Website: http://www.commonwealthlawyers.com
Members: 880
Staff: 1
Contact: Mohamed Husain, Pres.
Fee: £40
Membership Type: individual
Fee: £100-500
Membership Type: institution (499-2500 employees)
Description: Lawyers, bar associations, and law societies in Commonwealth countries. Works to raise and maintain the standard of legal services in the Commonwealth. Protects members' interests; conducts workshops and professional development programs. Seeks to stimulate a reappraisal of values, institutions, and methodologies among members of the legal profession. Facilitates the exchange of information among members concerning developments relevant to the organization and useful to legal professionals.
Publication: Newsletter
Publication title: Clarion

01704
Commonwealth Magistrates and Judges' Association
CMJA
c/o Uganda House
58-59 Trafalgar Sq., London, WC2N 5DX, UK
Tel: 020 79761007
Fax: 020 79762394
Email: info@cmja.org
Website: http://cmja.org
Members: 1000
Staff: 2
Contact: Karen Brewer, Sec. Gen.
Fee: £30
Membership Type: associate
Fee: £500
Membership Type: associate (life)
Description: Associations of magistrates, judges, and legal officers in Commonwealth countries. Advances the administration of the law by the promotion of judiciary independence. Fosters education in the law, administration of justice, treatment for offenders, and prevention of crime within the Commonwealth. Disseminates information concerning the legal process within Commonwealth countries. Compiles statistics. Conducts seminars, study groups, and workshops. Sponsors charitable programs.
Publication: Journal
Publication title: Commonwealth Judicial Journal

01705
Commonwealth Nurses Federation
CNF
c/o Royal College of Nursing
20 Cavendish Sq., London, W1G 0RN, UK
Tel: 061 438647252
Fax: 020 76473413
Email: jill@commonwealthnurses.org
Website: http://www.commonwealthnurses.org
Contact: Susie Kong, Pres.
Description: Exists to influence health policy throughout the Commonwealth; develop nursing networks; enhance nursing education; improve nursing standards and competence; and strengthen nursing leadership. Makes a constructive and influential contribution to the work of the Commonwealth Steering Committee for Nursing and Midwifery. Fosters active participatory membership and

collaborates with international organisations such as the International Council of Nurses, the World Health Organisation and regional nursing organisations.
Publication: Newsletter
Publication title: CNF Newsletter. Advertisements.

01706
Commonwealth Parliamentary Association
CPA
Westminster House, Ste. 700, 7 Millbank, London, SW1P 3JA, UK
Tel: 020 77991460
Fax: 020 72226073
Email: pirc@cpahq.org
Website: http://www.cpahq.org
Members: 15000
Staff: 14
Contact: William F. Shija, Sec. Gen.
Description: Members in more than 170 national, state, provincial, and territorial Commonwealth Parliaments. Objectives are to: provide for understanding, cooperation, and regular consultation among Commonwealth parliamentarians; promote study of the theory and practice of parliamentary democracy; act as clearinghouse on parliamentary subjects and political events. Sponsors topical study groups with senior parliamentarians; conducts exchange visits for delegations, parliament officials, and parliamentary librarians; holds seminars on parliamentary practice and procedure.
Publication: Journal
Publication title: The Parliamentarian. Advertisements.

01707
Commonwealth Partnership for Technology Management
CPTM
63 Catherine Pl., London, SW1E 6DY, UK
Tel: 020 77982500
Fax: 020 77982525
Email: smart.partnership@cptm.org
Website: http://www.cptm.org
Members: 400
Staff: 8
Contact: Mihaela Y. Smith, CEO
Description: Public and private sector organizations. Seeks "to enhance national capabilities for the creation and participation in wealth through sound management of technology, using public/private sector partnerships." Operates: Country Task Programme, which develops and implements a "portfolio of projects to be implemented in Commonwealth countries; and the National, Regional, and International Smart Partnership Dialogue Programme, which brings public, private, and labor organizations together to facilitate a cooperative approach to the management of macroeconomic development".
Formerly: Formerly, Commonwealth Consultative Group on Technology Management
Meetings/Conventions: Interactive Dialogue – periodic seminar

01708
Commonwealth Pharmaceutical Association
CPA
1 Lambeth High St., London, SE1 7JN, UK
Tel: 020 77522364
Fax: 020 77522508
Email: admin@commonwealthpharmacy.org
Website: http://www.commonwealthpharmacy.org/site
Members: 1200
Contact: Ivan Kotze, Pres.
Description: Pharmaceutical organizations in 40 Commonwealth countries; pharmacists. Aims to: maintain the honor and traditions of the profession and promote high standards of conduct, practice, and education at all levels; encourage close links among members in the profession and facilitate personal contacts between pharmacists and students; disseminate information about the professional practice of pharmacy and the pharmaceutical sciences.

01709
Commonwealth Secretariat
COMSEC
Marlborough House, Pall Mall, London, SW1Y 5HX, UK
Tel: 020 77476500
Fax: 020 79300827
Email: info@commonwealth.int
Website: http://www.thecommonwealth.org
Members: 53
Staff: 266
Contact: Kamalesh Sharma, Sec. Gen.
Description: Central body of 53 independent sovereign states organized to coordinate consultations and programs for the Commonwealth. Conducts cooperative technical projects, programs, services committees, and international conferences. Focuses on training, technical assistance, economics, industry, agriculture, food production, education, law, science, youth, health, human rights, and women and development. Areas of interest include: post-apartheid South Africa; recognition of democratically elected leaders; environmental protection and sustainable development; measures to counter international drug trafficking; alleviation of poverty; combating AIDS; international economic issues. Administers the Commonwealth Fund for Technical Cooperation, the Commonwealth Science Council, and the Commonwealth Youth Programme.
Publication: Report
Publication title: An Agenda for the Development Round of Trade Negotiations in the Aftermath of Cancun

01710
Commonwealth Society for Deaf
CSD
34 Buckingham Palace Rd., London, SW1W 0RE, UK
Tel: 020 72335700
Email: admin@sound-seekers.org.uk
Website: http://www.sound-seekers.org.uk
Contact: JK Fincham, Chm.
Description: Works for the deaf, especially children, in developing Commonwealth countries. In conjunction with governmental and voluntary organizations, deploys working parties of ENT Surgeons/Audiologists who are volunteers; trains technicians to support audiologists, and to maintain and repair electronic equipment; provides equipment for use by schools for the deaf. Conducts research into the prevention of deafness and compiles statistics on such research; has studied the incidence and causes of deafness in Gambia, Nigeria, and Botswana. Maintains contact with and disseminates information about schools, societies, and government councils for the deaf throughout the Commonwealth.
Formerly: Also Known As, Sound Seekers
Publication: Newsletter

01711
Commonwealth Telecommunications Organisation
CTO
64-66 Glenthorne Rd., Hammersmith, London, W6 0LR, UK
Tel: 0208 6003800
Fax: 0208 6003819
Email: info@cto.int
Website: http://www.cto.int
Members: 37
Staff: 22
Contact: Ekwow Spio-Garbrah, CEO
Fee: £20000
Membership Type: commonwealth country/industry
Fee: £5000
Membership Type: small nation of less than 100,000 population
Description: Represents inter-governmental development partnership of Commonwealth and non-Commonwealth countries, business organizations and civil society organizations. Provides assistance to members in enabling ICTs for development. Aims to achieve socio-economic development by bridging the digital divide and by delivering to developing countries unique knowledge-sharing programmes in the areas of telecommunications, IT, broadcasting and the Internet. Maintains Commonwealth Telecommunications Council and Commonwealth Telecommunications Headquarters.
Formerly: Formerly, Commonwealth Telecommunications Board
Publication: Newsletter
Publication title: CTO Update
Meetings/Conventions: annual conference

01712
Commonwealth Youth Exchange Council
CYEC
7 Lion Yard, Tremadoc Rd., London, SW4 7NQ, UK
Tel: 020 74986151
Fax: 020 76224365
Website: http://www.cyec.org.uk
Members: 222
Staff: 4
Contact: Vic Craggs, Chief Exec.
Fee: £50-500
Membership Type: organization
Description: International youth exchange organizations; individuals and institutions with an interest in international exchange. Promotes international and intercultural understanding through supporting UK groups undertaking youth exchange with the Commonwealth. Facilitates international educational visits; gathers and disseminates information. Promotes forums for young people across the Commonwealth.
Publication: Newsletter
Publication title: Citizen

01713

Communication Workers Union of England
CWU

150 The Broadway, Wimbledon, London, SW19 1RX, UK
Tel: 020 89717200
Fax: 020 89717300
Email: info@cwu.org
Website: http://www.cwu.org
Members: 250000
Staff: 150
Contact: Billy Hayes, Gen. Sec.
Description: British Telecom, the Post Office, Alliance Leicester related technologies and industries. Represents members employed in postal, telecommunications, information technology and related industries, and is committed to improving general working conditions, protecting individual employees, and increasing the influence of the union with employers and other bodies.
Publication: Journal
Publication title: CWU Voice. Advertisements.

01714

Communication Workers' Union
CWU

150 The Broadway, Wimbledon, London, SW19 1RX, UK
Tel: 020 89717200
Fax: 020 89717300
Email: info@cwu.org
Website: http://www.cwu.org
Members: 250000
Contact: Billy Hayes, Gen. Sec.
Description: Represents the communications industry in the UK. Assures security of employment to its members and protect their interests.

01715

Communication, Advertising, and Marketing Education Foundation
CAM

Moor Hall, Cookham, Berkshire, Maidenhead, SL6 9QH, UK
Tel: 01628 427120
Fax: 01628 427158
Email: cam@cim.co.uk
Website: http://www.camfoundation.com
Description: Maintains an examinations board that serves the communications industry.
Publication title: Prospectus

01716

Communications Management Association
CMA

1st Fl., Block D, North Star House, North Star Ave., Swindon, SN2 1FA, UK
Tel: 01372 361234
Email: cma@thecma.com
Website: http://www.thecma.com
Contact: Carolyn Kimber, Chair
Fee: £625
Membership Type: corporate (plus VAT)
Fee: £125.22
Membership Type: individual (plus VAT)
Description: Represents corporate enterprises and individual professionals. Fosters the knowledge and expertise of its members in networking. Promotes the quality use of technologies.

01717

Community and District Nursing Association
CDNA

367 Chiswick High Rd., London, W4 4AG, UK
Tel: 020 87478944
Fax: 020 87478883
Email: info@cdnaonline.org
Website: http://www.cdna-online.org.uk
Fee: £119.5
Membership Type: full
Fee: £74.28
Membership Type: HCA/auxiliary
Description: Unites to represent those nurses who work in the community, making highly skilled decisions on a daily basis in primary care.
Publication: Journal
Publication title: PNC. Advertisements.

01718

Community Development Finance Association
CDFA

Rm. 101, Hatton Sq. Business Ctre., 16/16a Baldwins Gardens, London, EC1N 7RJ, UK
Tel: 020 74300222
Fax: 020 74302112
Email: info@cdfa.org.uk
Website: http://www.cdfa.org.uk
Contact: Bernie Morgan, Chief Exec.
Fee: £275-825
Membership Type: charter (based on annual turnover)
Fee: £275
Membership Type: associate
Description: Represents independent financial institutions that provide support and capital to disadvantaged communities or underserved markets. Supports development and strengthens the community development finance sector. Promotes the sector to government and stakeholder.

01719

Community Foundation Network
CFN

12 Angel Gate, 320-326 City Rd., London, EC1V 2PT, UK
Tel: 020 77139326
Fax: 020 72789068
Email: network@communityfoundations.org.uk
Website: http://www.communityfoundations.org.uk
Members: 66
Staff: 11
Contact: John Weston, Pres.
Description: Support organization for community foundations. Seeks to advance the community foundation movement in the United Kingdom. Provides educational support and technical assistance to community trusts and foundations; organizes staff exchanges between members and their counterparts abroad.
Formerly: Formerly, Association of Community Trusts and Foundations

01720

Community Hospitals Association
CHA

Meadow Brow, Broadway Rd., Ilminster, TA19 9RG, UK
Tel: 01460 55951
Fax: 01460 53207
Email: commhosp@gxn.co.uk
Website: http://www.communityhospitals.org.uk
Contact: Barbara Moore, Chief Exec.
Fee: £100
Membership Type: full, corporate
Fee: £25
Membership Type: individual
Description: Community hospitals within and outside the NHS. Works towards developing the range and continuing improvement of services provided by community hospitals. Gathers and disseminates information on all aspects of work carried out in community hospitals; gives help and advice to members in furthering the interests of community hospitals.

01721

Community Matters: The National Federation of Community Organisations

12-20 Baron St., London, N1 9LL, UK
Tel: 020 78377887
Fax: 020 72789253
Email: info@communitymatters.org.uk
Website: http://www.communitymatters.org.uk
Members: 1180
Staff: 13
Contact: David Tyler, Chief Exec.
Fee: £22
Membership Type: category A
Fee: £74.5
Membership Type: category B
Description: National federation of local community organizations in the United Kingdom. Promotes and supports action by local communities, community development. Supports member organizations in response to leisure, recreational educational and social needs in their communities. Designs, develops, and delivers training in the development and management of community buildings and management committees. Represents members' interests to central government and other agencies.
Formerly: Formerly, National Federation of Community Organizations
Publication: Magazine
Publication title: Community. Advertisements.

01722

Community Pharmacy Scotland

42 Queen St., Edinburgh, EH2 3NH, UK
Tel: 0131 4677766
Fax: 0131 4677767
Email: enquiries@communitypharmacyscotland.org.uk
Website: http://www.communitypharmacyscotland.org.uk
Staff: 19
Contact: Harry McQuillan, CEO
Description: Body recognised by Secretary of State for Scotland as representing the interests of the general body of chemist contractors in Scotland. Concerned with all NHS matters, which affect retail pharmacy in Scotland.
Formerly: Formerly, Scottish Pharmaceutical General Council

01723

Community Transport Association CTA

Highbank, Halton St., Hyde, SK14 2NY, UK
Tel: 0161 3511475
Fax: 0161 3517221
Email: info@ctauk.org
Website: http://www.ctauk.org
Members: 1500
Staff: 35
Contact: Dai Powell, Chm.
Fee: £24
Membership Type: community
Fee: £75-195
Membership Type: full (based on annual turnover)
Description: Operators of voluntary sector, non-profit and accessible transport services, and their supporters. Exists to promote good practice in the community transport sector, and to provide services to operators, including advice; publications; training; representation; annual conference and trade exhibition.
Publication: Magazine
Publication title: Community Transport Magazine

01724

Community: The Union for Life

Covent Garden, 67/68 Long Acre, London, WC2E 9FA, UK
Tel: 020 74204000
Email: info@community-tu.org
Website: http://www.community-tu.org
Members: 16000
Contact: Michael Leahy, Gen. Sec.
Fee: £1.45
Description: Trade union for workers in knitwear, textiles, lace, dyeing and finishing, footwear, leather, gloving, made-up leather goods. Regulates the relations between members and their employers; and seeks the social, educational, economic and political advancement of members. Provides members with advice and representation (including legal) in connection with issues arising out of their employment.
Formerly: Formerly, Iron and Steel Trades Confederation
Publication: Journal
Publication title: KFAT News. Advertisements.

01725

Company Chemists Association CCA

Garden Studios, 11-15 Betterton St., Covent Garden, London, WC2H 9BP, UK
Tel: 0207 4708775
Email: rob.darracott@thecca.org.uk
Website: http://www.thecca.org.uk
Members: 9
Contact: Rob Darracott, Chief Exec.
Description: Aims to work in the interests of community pharmacy and, particularly, to represent the interests of, and add value to, nationally represented UK multiple community pharmacy.

01726

Compassion in World Farming CIWF

River Ct., Mill Ln., Surrey, Godalming, GU7 1EZ, UK
Tel: 01483 521953
Email: compassion@ciwf.co.uk
Website: http://www.ciwf.co.uk
Contact: Philip Lymbery, CEO
Fee: £24
Membership Type: single
Fee: £36
Membership Type: family
Description: Campaigns against factory farming through peaceful protests and lobbying. Seeks to raise awareness of animal welfare.
Publication: Magazine
Publication title: Farm Animal Voice

01727

Competition Law Association CLA

Brick Court Chambers, 7-8 Essex St., London, WC2R 3LD, UK
Tel: 020 73793550
Fax: 020 73793558
Email: sharonmehorwitz@yahoo.co.uk
Website: http://www.competitionlawassociation.org.uk
Contact: James Flynn, Chm.
Fee: £35
Membership Type: full-time academic
Fee: £55
Membership Type: full
Description: Promotes the study and discussion of the law and commercial practices affecting competition both national and international.

01728

Computer Aid International CAI

Unit 10, Brunswick Industrial Park, Brunswick Way, London, N11 1JL, UK
Tel: 0208 3615540
Fax: 0208 3617051
Email: info@computeraid.org
Website: http://www.computeraid.org
Contact: Tony Roberts, CEO
Description: Provides used IT equipment and computers overseas. Increases the number of refurbished computers being re-used. Offers training and work experience in computer repair to people from socially excluded communities.

01729

Computer Conservation Society CCS

25 Comet Close, Ash Vale, Hampshire, Aldershot, GU12 5SG, UK
Email: david.hartley@clare.cam.ac.uk
Website: http://www.computerconservationsociety.org
Members: 750
Contact: David Hatley, Chm.
Description: Seeks to preserve and restore computer hardware. Builds and maintains working original and replica examples. Preserves historic software, including operating systems, and emulates them on current machines. Maintains register of private and public collections. Seeks to find suitable homes for historic equipment becoming available for conservation, preferably in a major collection.
Library Subject: computer hardware
Library Type: reference
Publication: Journal
Publication title: Computer Resurrection

01730

Computer Education Management Association - Europe CEDMA-EUROPE

Hale Partnership Ltd., 7 Manor Courtyard, Hughenden Ave., High Wycombe, HP13 5RE, UK
Tel: 07766 704342
Email: info@cedma-europe.org
Website: http://www.cedma-europe.org
Contact: Mike Dowsey, Exec. Dir.
Fee: £1300
Membership Type: corporate
Description: Raises the profile and the understanding of computer education management. Serves as a source of information and expertise and contributes to the development of high standards in the IT training industry. Provides a forum for its members to meet and exchange ideas and information and to discuss and resolve issues relating to computer education management.

01731

Computer-Aided Learning in Veterinary Education CLIVE

c/o Learning Technology Section
University of Edinburgh, College of Medicine and Veterinary Medicine, Hugh Robson Bldg., 15 George Sq., Edinburgh, EH8 9XD, UK
Tel: 0131 6508384
Fax: 0131 6503011
Email: clive@ed.ac.uk
Website: http://www.clive.ed.ac.uk
Description: Veterinary schools working to make computer-assisted learning an established part of veterinary undergraduate education.

Comunn na Clarsaich

see Clarsach Society

01732

Conchological Society of Great Britain and Ireland

c/o Rosemary E. Hill, Honorary Gen. Sec.
447B Wokingham Rd., Earley, Reading, RG6 7EL, UK
Email: secretary@conchsoc.org
Website: http://www.conchsoc.org
Contact: Bas Payne, Pres.
Fee: £33
Membership Type: ordinary
Fee: £35
Membership Type: family, joint
Description: Promotes the study and conservation of molluscs.
Publication: Journal
Publication title: Journal of Conchology

01733

Concord Video and Film Council CVFC

22 Hines Rd., Ipswich, IP3 9BG, UK
Tel: 01473 726012
Fax: 01473 274531
Email: sales@concordmedia.org.uk
Website: http://www.concordvideo.co.uk
Members: 5

Staff: 5
Description: Provides educational videocassettes and 16mm films on social issues including illiteracy, mental health, race relations, medical topics, unemployment, and world poverty, as well as other topics such as the arts, education, theatre, and youth.
Publication: Catalog
Publication title: Catalogue and Supplements

01734
Concordia - Youth Service Volunteers
CYSV
19 North St., Portslade, Brighton, BN41 1DH, UK
Tel: 01273 422218
Fax: 01273 421182
Email: info@concordiavolunteers.org.uk
Website: http://www.concordiavolunteers.org.uk
Contact: Rob Orme, Exec. Dir.
Description: Operates a youth agricultural work program that unites young people worldwide in an effort to help them gain insight into their own and other cultures. Places youth volunteers with fruit and other crop growers in Britain for a short period during harvest time. Also organizes short international voluntary work camps in the U.K. in summer, particularly in the field of nature conservation.

01735
Concrete Block Association
CBA
60 Charles St., Leicester, LE1 1FB, UK
Tel: 0116 2536161
Fax: 0116 2534568
Email: enquiries@cba-blocks.org.uk
Website: http://www.cba-blocks.org.uk
Members: 64
Contact: Chris Hudson, Chm.
Description: Block manufacturers and suppliers to the industry. Aims to promote the interests of the precast concrete block industry in expanding its markets; to act as the recognized trade association for the aggregate block industry; to undertake all necessary action with regulatory and similar bodies and especially in regard to European harmonization, to ensure that the interests of the industry are protected.
Publication: Newsletter
Publication title: CBA Update

01736
Concrete Pipeline Systems Association
CPSA
60 Charles St., Leicester, LE1 1FB, UK
Tel: 0116 2536161
Fax: 0116 2514568
Email: mail@concretepipes.co.uk
Website: http://www.concretepipes.co.uk
Members: 9
Contact: Andy Goring, Chm.
Description: Promotes technical, commercial, and environmental benefits of precast concrete pipeline systems and maximize their use in the construction industry.
Formerly: Formerly, Concrete Pipe Association
Publication: Newsletter
Publication title: CPSA Pipelines

01737
Concrete Repair Association
CRA
Kingsley House, Ganders Business Park, Kingsley, Bordon, GU35 9LU, UK
Tel: 01420 471615
Email: admin@cra.org.uk
Website: http://cra.associationhouse.org.uk/cra_index.htm
Members: 40
Staff: 5
Contact: J. Farley, Sec.
Description: Contractors utilizing concrete repair methods, manufacturers of materials and plant. Promotes and develops the practice of concrete repair. Aims to advance education and technical training in concrete repair and to improve liaison with professional bodies, authorities and specifiers.
Publication: Journal
Publication title: Cracking Matters

01738
Concrete Society
Riverside House, 4 Meadows Business Park, Station Approach Blackwater, Surrey, Camberley, GU17 9AB, UK
Tel: 01276 607140
Fax: 01276 607141
Email: membership@concrete.org.uk
Website: http://www.concrete.org.uk
Members: 7000
Staff: 21
Fee: £115.15
Membership Type: personal
Fee: £246.75
Membership Type: individual (sole trader)
Description: All the disciplines within the construction industry, including contractors, engineers and architects. Brings together all those with an interest in concrete and provides information and advice on its uses.
Publication: Magazine
Publication title: Concrete. Advertisements.

Confederation Europeene des Relations Publiques
see European Public Relations Confederation

Confederation Mondiale pour la Therapie Physique
see World Confederation for Physical Therapy

01739
Confederation of Aerial Industries
CAI
Communications House, 41a Market St., Hertfordshire, Watford, WD18 0PN, UK
Tel: 019 23803030
Fax: 019 23803203
Email: office@cai.org.uk
Website: http://www.cai.org.uk
Members: 750
Staff: 6
Contact: David Hodges, Chm.
Fee: £294-1765
Membership Type: domestic
Fee: £452-1933
Membership Type: system
Description: Members are contractors, manufacturers, retailers or wholesalers of domestic TV, FM and satellite including entryphones, warden call or other communication systems. Aims to raise standards within the industry; to represent its members to government, local authorities, nationalised bodies, etc. to unite the industry on its common aims; to keep abreast of technological change.
Publication: Journal
Publication title: Codes of Practice. Advertisements.
Meetings/Conventions: annual trade show – Exhibits.

01740
Confederation of British Industry
CBI
Centre Point, 103 New Oxford St., London, WC1A 1DU, UK
Tel: 020 73797400
Email: bourne@cbi.org.uk
Website: http://www.cbi.org.uk/ndbs/staticpages.nsf/StaticPages/home.html/?OpenDocument
Members: 15000
Staff: 220
Contact: Nigel Bourne, Dir.
Description: Works to ensure that the government understands the intentions, needs, and problems of British business.
Publication: Magazine
Publication title: Business Voice

01741
Confederation of British Wool Textiles
CBWT
Textile House, Red Dolores Ln., Huddersfield, HD2 1YF, UK
Tel: 01484 346500
Fax: 01484 346501
Email: info@cbwt.co.uk
Website: http://www.cbwt.co.uk
Members: 150
Staff: 12
Contact: John Lambert, Dir. Gen.
Description: Manufacturers of wool yarns and fabrics, textile dyers and finishers, dealers in, and processors of, raw wool and textile waste. Promotes and protects the interests of the British wool textile industry, and provides to member firms a wide range of services in the fields of employment law, health and safety, environmental issues and training.

01742
Confederation of Dental Employers
CODE
Elm Tree House, Bodmin St., Devon, Holsworthy, EX22 6BB, UK
Tel: 01409 254354
Fax: 01409 254364
Email: info@codeuk.com
Website: http://www.codeuk.com
Members: 700
Staff: 10
Contact: Paul Mendlesohn, Chief Exec.
Fee: £385
Membership Type: regular
Description: Owners of dental practices. Promotes success of dental businesses; seeks to advance the profession of dentistry. Develops codes of business ethics and standards of professional practice for members;

conducts research and advises members on business issues including taxation, business management, and the law. Implements discount care schemes for promotional use by members.
Publication: Magazine
Publication title: Dentistry Opportunities. Advertisements.

01743
Confederation of Forest Industries
ConFor
59 George St., Edinburgh, EH2 2JG, UK
Tel: 0131 2401410
Fax: 0131 2401411
Email: mail@confor.org.uk
Website: http://www.confor.org.uk
Members: 2300
Staff: 5
Contact: Chris Inglis, Exec. Dir./Sec.
Fee: £60-70
Membership Type: woodland owner
Fee: £70-540
Membership Type: corporate, sawmiller, wood user
Description: Woodland owners, forestry contractors, managers, and consultants; manufacturers and suppliers of equipment; nurseries and others who earn their living through forestry. It endeavors to promote and contribute to the future of employment in the home-based forest industry. Represents members' interests to government, statutory bodies and other organizations, as well as to Europe through the Union of European Foresters. Provides support and information services; makes recommendations and comments on issues such as health and safety and forest policy. Through the Education and Provident Funds (reg. charity), small discretionary grants are available to members of more than one year, for assistance in education and training; or in cases of hardship (respectively). International visits and exchanges are arranged worldwide.
Formerly: Formerly, Association of Professional Foresters
Publication: Catalogs
Publication title: Exhibition. Advertisements.

01744
Confederation of Indian Industry - United Kingdom
c/o Confederation of British Industry
Centre Point, 103 New Oxford St., London, WC1A 1DU, UK
Tel: 020 78364121
Fax: 020 78361972
Email: gunveena.chadha@cii.in
Website: http://www.cii.co.uk
Contact: Gunveena Chadha, Dir.
Description: Works to create and sustain an environment conducive to growth of the Indian industry. Links the industry and the government through advisory and consultative process. Serves as a reference point for the Indian industry and the international business community.

01745
Confederation of Paper Industries
CPI
1 Rivenhall Rd., Wiltshire, Swindon, SN5 7BD, UK
Tel: 01793 889600
Fax: 01793 878700
Email: cpi@paper.org.uk
Website: http://www.paper.org.uk
Contact: David Workman, Dir. Gen.
Description: Works to ensure the efficient utilization of human, technological and financial resources for mutual benefit of all member companies.

01746
Confederation of Passenger Transport - UK
CPT
Drury House, 34-43 Russell St., London, WC2B 5HA, UK
Tel: 020 72403131
Fax: 020 72406565
Email: admin@cpt-uk.org
Website: http://www.cpt-uk.org
Members: 1200
Staff: 22
Contact: Simon Posner, Chief Exec.
Description: Corporate members are operators of the UK's buses, coaches and fixed track systems. Associate members are those companies who supply services to the industry ranging from chassis manufacturers and bodybuilders to tourist attractions and hotels. Acts as a forum for the industry representing the interests of its members to local, national and international government, and other external bodies related to the industry. Helps to shape the direction and future of the industry.
Publication: Newsletter
Publication title: Newsline

01747
Confederation of Roofing Contractors
CRC
Association House, 22d Victoria Pl., Brightlingsea, Essex, Colchester, CO7 0BX, UK
Tel: 01206 306600
Fax: 01206 306200
Email: enquiries@corc.co.uk
Website: http://www.corc.co.uk
Members: 600
Staff: 5
Contact: Mike Wolfe, Membership Coor.
Fee: £320
Membership Type: full, associate
Description: Protects the general public against unscrupulous roofing contractors; provides roofing services to all market sectors.
Publication: Magazine
Publication title: Roofing Trades Journal. Advertisements.

Conference Internationale pour les Bateaux de Sauvetage
see International Maritime Rescue Federation

01748
Conference of Drama Schools
CDS
PO Box 34252, London, NW5 1XJ, UK
Email: info@cds.drama.ac.uk
Website: http://www.drama.ac.uk
Members: 22
Staff: 1
Contact: Saul Hyman, Exec. Sec.
Fee: £4000
Membership Type: regular
Description: Representatives from 21 schools, which are concerned with the training of actors' stage managers and theatre related professionals. Strengthens the voice of member schools in order to develop and encourage the highest standards in training for both actors and stage managers.
Publication: Directory
Publication title: Official Guide to U.K. Drama Training. Advertisements.

01749
Conference of European Rabbis
CER
87 Hodford Rd., London, NW11 8NH, UK
Tel: 020 84559960
Fax: 020 84554968
Email: spgrf@free.fr
Website: http://www.cer-online.org/en/index.asp
Members: 750
Staff: 4
Contact: Joseph Sitruk, Pres.
Description: European rabbis. Promotes reconstruction and organization of Jewish communal life in Europe. Serves as a forum for the exchange of information among members; sponsors educational, social, and religious services.
Publication: Journal
Publication title: Sridim. Advertisements.
Meetings/Conventions: semiannual meeting

01750
Conflict Research Society
CRS
28 Severn Dr., Newport Pagnell, MK16 9DQ, UK
Email: gordonjburt@gmail.com
Website: http://www.conflictresearchsociety.org.uk
Members: 60
Contact: Gordon Burt, Ed.
Fee: £15
Membership Type: full
Fee: £5
Membership Type: student, unwaged
Description: Provides contact with experts in the field of conflict resolution or management.

01751
Congleton Chamber of Commerce and Enterprise
CCCE
Sandbach Enterprise Cte., Wesley Ave., Cheshire, Sandbach, CW11 1DG, UK
Tel: 01270 752120
Email: peter.whiers@sece.co.uk
Website: http://www.congletonchamber.co.uk
Members: 240
Staff: 7
Contact: Peter Wheirs, Chief Exec.
Fee: £99.88-470
Membership Type: company (based on number of employees)
Description: Represents members across Congleton at local, regional and national level on matters concerning trade, commerce and industry and lobbying. Facilitates networking, forums and events to enable members to exchange ideas, information, views and business practice.
Library Subject: business
Library Type: reference
Publication: Directory
Publication title: South East Cheshire Enterprise Business Directory. Advertisements.

Congres Mondiaux du Petrole
see World Petroleum Council

01752
CONNECT: The Union for Professionals in Communications
30 St. George's Rd., Wimbledon, London, SW19 4BD, UK
Tel: 020 89716000
Fax: 020 89716002
Email: union@connectuk.org
Website: http://www.connectuk.org
Members: 18000
Staff: 45
Contact: Leslie Manasseh, Deputy Gen. Sec.
Fee: £15.95
Membership Type: general
Description: Managers and professionals in communications industry. Represents the interests of members; works to negotiate their terms and conditions; provides a range of individual benefits.
Formerly: Formerly, Society of Telecom Executives
Publication: Magazine
Publication title: The Review

Conseil du Commonwealth pour l'Ecologie Humaine
see Commonwealth Human Ecology Council

Conseil International des Associations des Industries Nautiques
see International Council of Marine Industry Associations

Conseil International des Cereales
see International Grains Council

Conseil International des Normes Comptables
see International Accounting Standards Board

Conseil International des Tanneurs
see International Council of Tanners

Conseil Mondial de l'Energie
see World Energy Council - England

01753
Conservation Foundation
1 Kensington Gore, London, SW7 2AR, UK
Tel: 020 75913111
Fax: 020 75913110
Email: info@conservationfoundation.co.uk
Website: http://www.conservationfoundation.co.uk
Staff: 4
Contact: David Shreeve, Dir./Co-Founder
Description: Creates and manages environmental programmes many of which are sponsored by commercial organizations. Covers all environmental interests in the United Kingdom, Europe, and internationally. Operates as a registered charity housed at the headquarters of the Royal Geographical Society.

01754
Conservation Volunteers Northern Ireland
CVNI
Beech House, 159 Ravenhill Rd., Belfast, BT6 0BP, UK
Tel: 02890 645169
Fax: 02890 644409
Email: cvni@btcv.org.uk
Website: http://www.cvni.org
Contact: Barbara Boardman, Dir.
Description: Offers training events to anyone who wants to improve their local environment. Delivers outreach programmes.
Publication: Book
Publication title: Our Remarkable Trees

01755
Conservative Future
CF
30 Millbank, London, SW1P 4DP, UK
Tel: 020 72229000
Email: michael.rock@conservativefuture.com
Website: http://www.conservativefuture.com
Members: 20000
Staff: 1
Contact: Michael Rock, Chm.
Fee: £5
Membership Type: youth
Fee: £25
Membership Type: standard
Description: Serves as official youth wing of the Conservative and Unionist Party of the United Kingdom.

01756
Conservative Future Scotland
CFS
c/o Scottish Conservative Central Office
83 Princes St., Edinburgh, EH2 2ER, UK
Tel: 0131 2476890
Fax: 0131 2476891
Email: keelan.carr@scottishconservatives.com
Website: http://www.scottishconservatives.com/future
Members: 1500
Staff: 1
Contact: David Ritchie, Pres.
Description: Promotes and represents the interests of young people within the Scottish Conservative and Unionist Party.
Formerly: Formerly, Young Unionists

01757
Conservative Party Central Office
30 Millbank, London, SW1P 4DP, UK
Tel: 020 72229000
Email: camerond@parliament.uk
Website: http://www.conservatives.com
Contact: David Cameron, Leader
Description: Conservative political party in England. Supports strengthened defense, free enterprise, decentralization, and aid to those in need.
Formerly: Formerly, Conservative Party

01758
Consortium of European Building Control
CEBC
53 Goodwood Close, Ipswich, IP1 6SY, UK
Tel: 01473 748182
Fax: 01473 741881
Email: david.smith@cebc.eu
Website: http://www.cebc.eu
Members: 50
Contact: David Smith, Chm.
Description: Representatives of building control organizations and health and safety organizations. Provides a forum for discussing technical and legal building issues. Conducts research.
Publication: Newsletter
Publication title: CEBC News. Advertisements.

01759
Consortium of European Research Libraries
CERL
40 Bowling Green Ln., Clerkenwell, London, EC1R 0NE, UK
Tel: 020 74157134
Fax: 020 79705643
Email: secretariat@cerl.org
Website: http://www.cerl.org
Members: 91
Staff: 3
Contact: Cristina Dondi, Sec.
Fee: £8000
Membership Type: full/group
Fee: £1000
Membership Type: special
Description: Brings together information about the written heritage of Europe in a single historical, central resource in support of scholarship, interdisciplinary research, intercultural study and cultural enrichment; aims to offer a connected range of tools for all who work in the field of interpreting European cultural heritage with books written or printed before the mid-19th Century.

01760
Consortium on AIDS and International Development
28 Charles Sq., Grayston Ctre., London, N1 6HT, UK
Tel: 020 73244780
Email: info@aidsconsortium.org.uk
Website: http://www.aidsconsortium.org.uk
Contact: Richard Walker, Communications Mgr.
Description: Promotes an effective global response to HIV and AIDS that contributes to sustainable development. Encourages, initiates and supports collaborative action by civil society to contribute to and influence the global response to HIV and AIDS.
Publication: Report
Publication title: HIV and AIDS in China

01761
Construction Confederation
CC
55 Tufton St., Westminster, London, SW1P 3QL, UK
Tel: 0870 8989090
Fax: 0870 8989095
Email: enquiries@thecc.org.uk

Website: http://www.thecc.org.uk
Members: 5500
Contact: Kurt Calder, Contact
Description: Building and civil engineering contractors. Seeks to advance the building industries. Represents members' common interests before national and European government agencies. Negotiates agreements on members' behalf with pan-industry bodies; provides information and advice to members; conducts promotional campaigns.

01762

Construction Employers' Federation
CEF

143 Malone Rd., Belfast, BT9 6SU, UK
Tel: 028 90877143
Fax: 028 90877155
Email: mail@cefni.co.uk
Website: http://www.cefni.co.uk/CMS/DefaultCMS.aspx
Members: 500
Staff: 20
Contact: John Armstrong, Managing Dir.
Description: Employers in the NI Construction Industry. Protects and promotes the interests of member firms in the NI construction industry.

01763

Construction Equipment Association
CEA

Airport House, Purley Way, Croydon, CR0 0XZ, UK
Tel: 020 82534502
Fax: 020 82534510
Email: cea@admin.co.uk
Website: http://www.coneq.org.uk
Members: 100
Contact: Rob Oliver, Chief Exec.
Description: Represents construction equipment manufacturers, their component and accessory suppliers and service providers.
Formerly: Formerly, Federation of Manufacturers of Construction Equipment and Cranes
Publication: Directory
Publication title: Business Tracker

01764

Construction Fixings Association
CFA

65 Deans St., Oakham, LE15 6AF, UK
Tel: 01664 823687
Fax: 01664 823687
Email: info@fixingscfa.co.uk
Website: http://www.fixingscfa.co.uk
Members: 6
Contact: Pietro Grandesso, Chm.
Description: Represents the interests of major UK suppliers of construction fixings. Offers variety of information on the use of fixings including series of free guidance notes being directly involved in the development of the Guidelines for European Technical Approval of anchors for safety critical applications. Supports specific industries in the development of guidelines for their use of fixings. Offers support in the training of contractors in the correct installation of construction fixings. Publishes articles for members and other individuals. Provides anchoring products with comprehensive technical support services including performance data, applications advice, on-site testing and training in the correct use of their products.

01765

Construction History Society
CHS

The Chartered Institute of Bldg., Englemere, Kings Ride, Ascot, SL5 7TB, UK
Email: secretary@constructionhistory.co.uk
Website: http://www.constructionhistory.co.uk
Members: 300
Contact: James Campbell, Chm.
Fee: £25
Membership Type: individual
Description: Disseminates research and information about historical buildings and construction techniques; encourages today's industry to pay greater care to the safe keeping of its records. Demonstrates the fascination of construction history studies through an active programme of visits and lectures.
Library Subject: construction history, construction techniques and materials, company histories
Library Type: by appointment only
Publication: Journal
Publication title: Construction History

01766

Construction Industry Council
CIC

26 Store St., London, WC1E 7BT, UK
Tel: 020 73997400
Fax: 020 73997425
Email: info@cic.org.uk
Website: http://www.cic.org.uk
Members: 500000
Contact: Graham Watts, CEO
Fee: £250
Membership Type: affiliate
Description: Unites to serve society by promoting quality and sustainability in the built environment and to give leadership to the construction industry.

01767

Construction Industry Trade Alliance
CITA

PO Box 97, Carmarthen, SA31 1WT, UK
Tel: 0845 2504390
Fax: 0845 2504391
Email: enquiries@cita.co.uk
Website: http://www.cita.co.uk
Description: Builders, roofing contractors, painters and decorators, plumbers, electricians, and other building industry contractors and workers. Promotes the interests of the building trade in Britain.

01768

Construction Plant-hire Association
CPA

27/28 Newbury St., Barbican, London, EC1A 7HU, UK
Tel: 020 77963366
Fax: 020 77963399
Email: enquiries@cpa.uk.net
Website: http://www.cpa.uk.net/p/Home-Page
Members: 1400
Staff: 8
Contact: Colin Wood, Chief Exec.
Fee: £163-3610
Membership Type: company (based on total annual turnover)
Fee: £858
Membership Type: non-plant hire corporate
Description: Represents the interests of plant hirers.

01769

Construction Products Association
CPA

26 Store St., London, WC1E 7BT, UK
Tel: 020 73233770
Fax: 020 73230307
Email: enquiries@constructionproducts.org.uk
Website: http://www.constructionproducts.org.uk
Members: 66
Staff: 10
Contact: Michael Ankers, Chief Exec.
Fee: £2680
Membership Type: trade association
Fee: £1625
Membership Type: affiliate, associate
Description: Acts as a single voice for the producers and suppliers of construction projects in the UK. Seeks to build a growing, profitable, and sustainable future for the construction products industry by conducting activities that focus in four specific areas: increasing investment in the built environment; developing a positive regulatory and fiscal framework; improving industry performance; and responding to the environmental challenge.
Library Subject: statistics, forecasts, sector information
Library Type: reference
Formerly: Formerly, National Council of Building Material Producers
Publication title: Construction Industry Forecasts

01770

Consultant Quantity Surveyors Association
CQSA

Freshfields, Off the Pound, Berkshire, Cookham, SL6 9QD, UK
Email: secretary@cqsa.co.uk
Website: http://www.cqsa.co.uk
Members: 50
Contact: Tony Wood, Honorary Sec.
Description: Consists of senior owners of quantity surveying consultancy businesses ranging from sole practitioners to larger organizations. Promotes the business interests of its members.

01771

Consumer Credit Trade Association CCTA

The Wave, 1 View Croft Rd., Ste. 4, Shipley, BD17 7DU, UK
Tel: 0127 4714959
Fax: 0845 2571199
Email: chris.oakes@ccta.co.uk
Website: http://www.ccta.co.uk
Members: 500
Staff: 6
Contact: Chris Oakes, Chief Exec.
Fee: £5465.8
Membership Type: credit grantor
Fee: £3100.79
Membership Type: credit broker (based on gross)
Description: Credit grantors of many types who offer credit to consumers. Includes finance companies, retailers, some building societies, other lenders and suppliers of ancillary services. Represents to government, the media and EC authorities the interests of companies providing and operating credit, leasing and rental facilities. Offers a range of services to members including advice, courses and seminars, standard agreement forms, Short Guides on legislation, magazine and discussion groups and forums.
Publication: Newsletter

01772

Consumer Focus

Artillery House, 4th Fl., Artillery Row, London, SW1P 1RT, UK
Tel: 020 77997900
Fax: 020 77997901
Email: contact@consumerfocus.org.uk
Website: http://www.consumerfocus.org.uk
Staff: 170
Contact: Mike O'Connor, Chief Exec.
Description: Works for interests of all gas users in the UK. Offers free independent advice, information and complaint handling services to all gas and electricity consumers.
Formerly: Formerly, EnergyWatch and Postwatch
Publication: Report
Publication title: From Feast to Famine

01773

Consumers International - England CI

24 Highbury Crescent, London, N5 1RX, UK
Tel: 020 72266663
Fax: 020 73540607
Email: consint@consint.org
Website: http://www.consumersinternational.org
Members: 220
Staff: 70
Contact: Joost Martens, Dir. Gen.
Fee: £50-4000
Membership Type: affiliate
Fee: £300-3000
Membership Type: government
Description: Global association for consumers' organizations from more than 100 countries. Aims to support the formation and development of strong and effective consumer organizations; foster international cooperation amongst consumer organizations and other supporting bodies; pursue an agenda for international action to protect consumers, especially the poor, the marginalized and the disadvantaged; and establish an authoritative and influential presence in global and regional policy making bodies. Works on such issues as sustainable consumption, food and technical standards, health concerns and international trade. Works closely with the United Nations agencies and other international decision-making bodies. Helped found and works closely with Health Action International, Pesticides Action Network, and International Baby Food Action Network.
Formerly: Formerly, International Organization of Consumers Unions

01774

Contaminated Land: Applications in Real Environments CL:AIRE

1 Great Cumberland Pl., 7th Fl., London, W1H 7AL, UK
Tel: 020 72585321
Fax: 020 72585322
Email: enquiries@claire.co.uk
Website: http://www.claire.co.uk
Contact: Jane Garrett, Chief Exec.
Fee: £40-70
Membership Type: company (based on relevant members)
Description: Stimulates the regeneration of contaminated land. Raises awareness of sustainable remediation technologies. Increases the uptake and development of innovative and practical solutions to the remediation of contaminated land. Provides a unique system of independent appraisals for technologies, monitoring and site investigation techniques.

01775

Contemporary Art Society CAS

11/15 Emerald St., London, WC1N 3QL, UK
Tel: 020 78311243
Fax: 020 78311214
Email: info@contemporaryartsociety.org
Website: http://www.contemporaryartsociety.org
Members: 1700
Staff: 6
Contact: Alison Myners, Chair
Fee: £50
Membership Type: blood (student)
Fee: £95
Membership Type: blood
Description: Purchases works of art by living artists and gives them to UK museums and galleries. Funding is obtained from arts council and other grants, membership dues and profits from the Contemporary Art Society Projects.

01776

Contemporary Glass Society CGS

c/o Broadfield House Glass Museum
Compton Dr., West Midlands, Kingswinford, DY6 9NS, UK
Tel: 01603 507737
Fax: 01603 507737
Email: admin@cgs.org.uk
Website: http://www.cgs.org.uk/view.aspx?id=121
Contact: Pam Reekie, Gen. Admin.
Fee: £30
Membership Type: professional (individual), concession (student/senior/registered disabled citizen individual plus partner)
Fee: £45
Membership Type: professional (individual plus partner)
Description: Represents artist, academics, suppliers, collectors, galleries and enthusiasts in contemporary glass. Encourages excellence in glass as a creative medium and develops awareness of contemporary glass worldwide.
Publication: Newsletter
Publication title: Glass Network

01777

Contract Flooring Association CFA

4C St. Mary's Pl., The Lace Market, Nottingham, NG1 1PH, UK
Tel: 0115 9411126
Fax: 0115 9412238
Email: info@cfa.org.uk
Website: http://www.cfa.org.uk
Members: 460
Staff: 4
Contact: John Butler, Pres.
Description: Manufacturers, contractors, distributors and consultants of carpets, vinyls, timber, rubber, cork linoleum etc. Promotes standards within the flooring industry and provides advice and guidance to members.
Publication: Journal
Publication title: Contracts Flooring Journal

01778

Convention of Scottish Local Authorities COSLA

Rosebery House, 9 Haymarket Terr., Edinburgh, EH12 5XZ, UK
Tel: 0131 4749200
Fax: 0131 4749292
Email: enquiries@cosla.gov.uk
Website: http://www.cosla.gov.uk
Members: 29
Staff: 35
Contact: Rory Mair, Chief Exec.
Description: Local authorities in Scotland. Considers legislation before Parliament; represents the interests of local authorities to the central government. Disseminates information on local government in Scotland. Serves as an employers' association for member councils; advises on salaries and conditions of service; assists in negotiations. Offers training courses.
Publication: Directory
Publication title: Scottish Local Government

01779

Cooltan Arts

Unit B 237 Walworth Rd., London, SE17 1RL, UK
Tel: 020 77012696
Fax: 020 77012696
Email: info@cooltanarts.org.uk
Website: http://cooltanarts.org.uk
Contact: Michelle Baharier, Chief Exec.
Description: Works as a resource for individuals with disabilities, both artists and non-artists, to work together to create an inclusive environment.

01780

Coopers' Company

Coopers' Hall, 13 Devonshire Sq., London, EC2M 4TH, UK
Tel: 020 72479577
Fax: 020 73778061
Email: clerk@coopers-hall.co.uk

Website: http://www.coopers-hall.co.uk/coopers/index.htm
Description: Promotes the livery industry in London.
Publication: Magazine
Publication title: The Cooper

01781

Copper Development Association
CDA

5 Grovelands Business Ctre., Boundary Way, Hemel Hempstead, HP2 7TE, UK
Tel: 01442 275705
Fax: 01442 275716
Email: mail@copperdev.co.uk
Website: http://www.copperinfo.co.uk
Members: 15
Staff: 6
Contact: Angela Vessey, Dir.
Description: Provides technical advice and information about the use of copper and copper alloys.
Publication: Video
Publication title: Domestic Heating Systems

01782

Copper Development Association - United Kingdom
CDA

5 Grovelands Business Cte., Boundary Way, Hemel Hempstead, HP2 7TE, UK
Tel: 01442 275705
Fax: 01442 275716
Email: mail@copperdev.co.uk
Website: http://www.copperinfo.co.uk
Contact: Carol Godfrey, Exec. Sec.
Fee: £3400-6800
Membership Type: semi-fabricator
Fee: £1700-3400
Membership Type: other industrial company
Description: International copper producers and national copper fabricators. Encourages the use of copper and copper alloys and promotes correct and efficient application.

01783

Copyright Licensing Agency
CLA

Saffron House, 6-10 Kirby St., London, EC1N 8TS, UK
Tel: 020 74003100
Fax: 020 74003101
Email: cla@cla.co.uk
Website: http://www.cla.co.uk
Members: 2
Staff: 54
Contact: Kevin Fitzgerald, Chief Exec.
Description: Authors' Licensing and Collecting Society and the Publishers Licensing Society on whose behalf CLA acts as agent. Administers collectively photocopying and other copying rights that it is uneconomic for writers and publishers to administer for themselves. Issues collective and transactional licenses, and the fees it collects, after the deduction of costs, are distributed at regular intervals to authors and publishers via their respective societies.
Publication: Newsletter
Publication title: CLArion Newsletter

01784

Cordwainers' Company

Clothworkers' Hall, Dunster Ct., Mincing Ln., London, EC3R 7AH, UK
Tel: 020 79291121
Fax: 020 79291124
Email: office@cordwainers.org
Website: http://www.cordwainers.org
Members: 120
Contact: John Miller, Contact
Description: Aims to support the education and training in the design and production of footwear and associated leather accessories and the promotion of the footwear industry.

01785

CORE

3 St. Andrews Pl., London, NW1 4LB, UK
Tel: 020 74860341
Email: info@corecharity.org.uk
Website: http://www.corecharity.org.uk
Staff: 3
Contact: John Bennett, Chm.
Description: Aims to raise money for research of digestive disorders and diseases.
Formerly: Formerly, Digestive Disorders Foundation
Publication title: Annual Review

01786

Cork Industry Federation
CIF

13 Felton Lea, Kent, Sidcup, DA14 6BA, UK
Tel: 020 83024801
Fax: 020 83024801
Email: info@cork-products.co.uk
Website: http://www.cork-products.co.uk
Members: 14
Description: The majority of firms involved in the import, manufacture and distribution of cork in the UK and export markets. Exists to monitor and uphold quality standards within the industry and to promote the use of cork in a host of different applications, closures (bottle stoppers), floor and wall tiles, industrial uses.

01787

Cornwall Archaeological Society
CAS

16 Cross St., Padstow, PL28 8AT, UK
Email: membership@cornisharchaeology.org.uk
Website: http://www.cornisharchaeology.org.uk
Members: 600
Staff: 9
Contact: Jenny Beale, Membership Sec.
Fee: £25
Membership Type: single
Fee: £32.5
Membership Type: 2 at one address (with journal)
Description: Represents a group of enthusiasts who study archaeology. Organizes county walks led by local experts and holds winter lecture programs with speakers.
Publication: Journal
Publication title: Cornish Archaeology

01788

Corona Worldwide

S Bank House, Black Prince Rd., London, SE1 7SJ, UK
Tel: 0207 7934020
Fax: 0207 7934020
Email: corona@coronaworldwide.org
Website: http://www.coronaworldwide.org
Members: 4000
Staff: 1
Contact: Pam Cowan, Pres.
Fee: £18
Membership Type: full
Fee: £16
Membership Type: concession
Description: Assists women and families who live and work overseas from their native country. Strives to spread friendship and understanding between people. Works to make living in different cultures a stimulating and an enjoyable experience for the whole family. Disseminates practical information on resettlement. Conducts educational and research programs.
Publication: Magazine
Publication title: Corona News

01789

Coronary Artery Disease Research Association
CORDA

Chelsea Sq., London, SW3 6NP, UK
Tel: 020 73498686
Fax: 020 73499414
Email: info@corda.org.uk
Website: http://www.corda.org.uk
Staff: 1
Contact: Richard Hunting, Chm.
Description: Supports clinical research into the prevention and diagnosis of heart diseases and strokes through non-invasive techniques.

01790

Corps of Drums Society

c/o Christine Fairfax, Sec.
103 Clare Ln., E Malling, Maidstone, Kent, ME19 6JB, UK
Email: info@corpsofdrums.com
Website: http://www.corpsofdrums.com
Members: 469
Contact: Richard Holmes, Pres.
Fee: £10
Membership Type: individual
Fee: £25
Membership Type: group
Description: Persons making or supporting drum and flute music based on the traditions of the British Army. Concerned with the presentation and promotion of the concept and traditions of the drum and flute Corps of Drums based on British Army practice.
Publication: Journal
Publication title: The Drummer's Call. Advertisements.

01791

Corrugated Sector of the Confederation of Paper Industries

1 Rivenhall Rd., Wiltshire, Swindon, SN5 7BD, UK
Tel: 01793 889600
Fax: 01793 878700
Email: cpi@paper.org.uk
Website: http://www.corrugated.org.uk
Members: 110
Staff: 5

Contact: Andrew Barnetson, Contact
Description: Trade association.
Formerly: Formerly, British Fibreboard Packaging Association

01792
Cosmetic, Toiletry, and Perfumery Association - England
CTPA
Josaron House, 5-7 John Princes St., London, W1G 0JN, UK
Tel: 0207 4918891
Fax: 0207 4938061
Email: info@ctpa.org.uk
Website: http://www.ctpa.org.uk
Contact: Joyce Traylen, Contact
Description: Manufacturers, raw material suppliers and contract services to the cosmetic toiletry and perfumery industry in the UK. Aims to provide a legislative and technical information service to members. Represents members' interests to UK Government, EC Commission and other opinion forums.
Publication: Annual Report

01793
COTREL
Beama Power Ltd., Westminster Tower, 3 Albert Embankment, London, SE1 7SL, UK
Tel: 020 77933042
Fax: 020 77933003
Email: ngrant@beama.org.uk
Website: http://www.cotrel.com
Contact: Nigel Grant, Gen. Sec.
Description: Manufacturers of transformers. Seeks to advance the transformer and related electronics industries. Facilitates communication and cooperation among members; represents members before labor, industrial, and international trade organizations, government agencies, and the public.

01794
Council for Aluminium in Building
CAB
Bank House, Bonds Mill, Gloucestershire, Stonehouse, GL10 3RF, UK
Tel: 01453 828851
Fax: 01453 828861
Email: enquiries@c-a-b.org.uk
Website: http://www.c-a-b.org.uk
Members: 120
Contact: Justin Ratcliffe, Chief Exec.
Fee: £1700-3399
Membership Type: company (plus VAT)
Fee: £1133
Membership Type: consultant, architect (plus VAT)
Description: Aims to support the interests of the architectural aluminium industry by encouraging the increasing use of aluminium products in buildings and the construction industry as a whole; to provide technical information to specifiers, architects, industry and end users.

01795
Council for British Archaeology
CBA
St. Mary's House, 66 Bootham, York, YO30 7BZ, UK
Tel: 01904 671417
Fax: 01904 671384
Website: http://www.britarch.ac.uk
Contact: Mike Heyworth, Dir.
Fee: £21
Membership Type: student
Fee: £29
Membership Type: individual
Description: Societies, museums, universities, national and local government services, archaeological units and trusts, and other conservation bodies with mutual interests, as well as a large number of individuals, both professional and amateur. Promotes the study and safeguarding of Britain's historic environment, provides a forum for archaeological opinion, and improves public knowledge of Britain's past.
Library Subject: British archaeology
Library Type: open to the public
Publication: Bibliography
Publication title: British and Irish Archaeological Bibliography

01796
Council for British Archaeology I Society for Church Archaeology
SCA
St. Mary's House, 66 Bootham, York, YO30 7BZ, UK
Email: kevin.booth@english-heritage.org.uk
Website: http://www.britarch.ac.uk/socchurcharchaeol
Contact: Kevin Booth, Sec.
Fee: £25
Membership Type: individual (waged)
Fee: £12
Membership Type: unwaged, retired, student
Description: Promotes the study of churches and other places of worship, along with their associated monuments and landscapes. Provides a focus for all who are interested in promoting the care, conservation and study of the ecclesiastical buildings and landscapes of Britain and Ireland. Works to ensure recognition of archaeological aspects of church conservation. Contributes to the preservation and management of sites and buildings.
Publication: Journal
Publication title: Church Archaeology

01797
Council for Dance Education and Training - UK
CDET
Old Brewer's Yard, 17-19 Neal St., Covent Garden, London, WC2H 9UY, UK
Tel: 020 72405703
Fax: 020 72402547
Email: info@cdet.org.uk
Website: http://www.cdet.org.uk
Members: 70
Staff: 3
Contact: Sean Williams, Dir.
Description: Dance teaching associations, dance training institutions and related dance professional bodies. Aims to maintain and improve standards of dance education and training at all levels throughout the country; advises, cooperates with and makes representation to government departments, local authorities and other interested bodies.
Publication title: Code of Professional Conduct and Practice for Teachers of Dance

01798
Council for Education in the Commonwealth
CEC
Commonwealth House, 7 Lion Yard, Tremadoc Rd., London, SW4 7NQ, UK
Tel: 01277 212357
Email: membership@cecomm.org.uk
Website: http://www.cecomm.org.uk/home
Members: 250
Contact: Valerie Davey, Exec. Chair
Fee: £30
Membership Type: individual
Fee: £15
Membership Type: student
Description: An organization based in the British parliament with academic institutions, corporations, non-governmental organizations and interested individuals as supporters. Encourages discussion on problems in education and training in the Commonwealth, particularly in developing countries, and the role that Great Britain should play in the solution of these problems. Promotes educational cooperation; works to influence public opinion. Promotes a series of public meetings in the UK and recommendations to the Commonwealth Secretariat, British Government, Commonwealth governments and other bodies. Initiates studies and research on particular educational issues in the Commonwealth.
Publication: Reprint
Publication title: Islam and the Education of Women and Girls in the Commonwealth

01799
Council for Environmental Education
CEE
94 London St., Reading, RG1 4SJ, UK
Tel: 0118 9502550
Fax: 0118 9591955
Email: info@cee.org.uk
Website: http://www.cee.org.uk
Members: 73
Staff: 11
Contact: Libby Grundy, Dir.
Description: Serves as the umbrella body for environmental and sustainable development education in England.

01800
Council for Hospitality Management Education
CHME
University of Bournemouth, Dorset House, Talbot Campus, Fern Barrow, Dorset, BH12 5BB, UK
Email: igrebliunaite@bournemouth.ac.uk
Website: http://www.chme.co.uk
Members: 50
Contact: Ina Grebliunaite, Honorary Sec.
Fee: £300
Membership Type: institutional, affiliate
Fee: £85
Membership Type: individual
Description: Universities and colleges which offer degree and/or HND courses in hospitality management. Represents member institutions' interests in the field of hospitality management education at HE level, EC, government, industry and professional levels. Promotes hospitality management education in general, as well as specialist levels, e.g. industrial placement, research, access to courses, etc.

01801

Council for Independent Archaeology CIA

2 The Watermeadows, Swarkestone, Derby, DE73 7FX, UK
Tel: 01332 704148
Email: skfoster@btinternet.com
Website: http://www.independents.org.uk
Members: 460
Contact: Kevan Fadden, Honorary Treas.
Fee: £10
Membership Type: regular
Description: Amateur archeologists and other individuals with an interest in archeology. Promotes participation in archeological activities by independent individuals. Serves as a forum for the exchange of information among members. Provides support to independent archeology projects; initiated development of resistivity meter.

01802

Council for Music in Hospitals

Case House, 85-89 High St., Walton-on-Thames, KT12 5LW, UK
Tel: 01932 260810
Fax: 01932 224123
Email: info@music-in-hospitals.org.uk
Website: http://www.music-in-hospitals.org.uk
Contact: Diana Greenman, Chief Exec.
Description: Provides live, professional concerts in hospitals, homes, hospices and day centres.

01803

Council for Registered Gas Installers CORGI

1 Elmwood, Chineham Park, Crockford Ln., Basingstoke, RG24 8WG, UK
Tel: 0870 4012200
Fax: 0870 4012600
Email: answers@trustcorgi.com
Website: http://www.trustcorgi.com/Pages/index.html
Contact: Mike Thompson, Chm./CEO
Description: Works as National Watchdog for Gas Safety in the United Kingdom; promotes and enhances gas safety, standards and quality.
Publication: Manual
Publication title: Essential Guide to Gas Safety

01804

Council for the Advancement of Arab-British Understanding CAABU

1 Gough Sq., London, EC4A 3DE, UK
Tel: 020 78321321
Fax: 020 78321329
Website: http://www.caabu.org
Members: 900
Staff: 4
Contact: Chris Doyle, Dir.
Fee: £25
Membership Type: overseas
Fee: £5
Membership Type: student/unwaged
Description: Individuals united to promote mutual cultural appreciation between the peoples of Britain and the Arab World. Advocates social policies tending to increase beneficial interaction between British and Arab peoples.
Publication: Newsletter
Publication title: Campaign Bulletin

01805

Council for the Registration of Schools Teaching Dyslexic Pupils CRESTED

Greygarth, Littleworth, Winchcombe, Gloucestershire, Cheltenham, GL54 5BT, UK
Tel: 01242 604852
Email: crested@crested.org.uk
Website: http://www.crested.org.uk
Contact: Christine Hancock, Admin.
Description: Offers guidance to parents seeking a school for their dyslexic child. Provides a list of schools approved for their dyslexia provision.

01806

Council of Academic and Professional Publishers CAPP

c/o Publishers Association
29 B Montague St., London, WC1B 5BW, UK
Tel: 020 76919191
Fax: 020 76919199
Email: gtaylor@publishers.org.uk
Website: http://www.publishers.org.uk
Members: 90
Staff: 2
Contact: Graham Taylor, Dir.
Description: Academic/professional publishing companies specializing in books and journals. A subscription organization covering the following areas of activity on behalf of academic/professional publishers: representation to Government; collective marketing/promotion; specialist publishing services; copyright/licensing; information/statistical services.
Formerly: Formerly, University College Professional Publishers Council
Publication: Newsletter
Publication title: CAPP Bnef
Meetings/Conventions: annual seminar

01807

Council of Mortgage Lenders CML

Bush House, NW Wing, Aldwych, London, WC2B 4PJ, UK
Tel: 0845 3736771
Fax: 0845 3736778
Email: web.enquiries@cml.org.uk
Website: http://www.cml.org.uk/cml/home
Members: 157
Contact: Michael J. Coogan, Dir. Gen.
Fee: £6610
Membership Type: associate
Description: Mortgage lending institutions, including building societies, clearing banks, insurance companies and their subsidiaries, finance houses and centralized lenders. Works; to be a central representative body; to be a research and statistical centre; to be a technical centre; to be a forum for the exchange of information; and to be a focus of media relations, in relation to residential mortgage lending in the UK.
Publication: Newsletter
Publication title: CML News & Views

01808

Council of National Beekeeping Associations in the United Kingdom CONBA-UK

11 Coach Rd., Warton, Lancashire, Carnforth, LA5 9PP, UK
Tel: 01542 730451
Email: martintovey@hotmail.co.uk
Website: http://www.britishbee.org.uk/articles/conba-uk.php
Members: 11000
Contact: Martin Tovey, Treas.
Description: Promotes the aims and objectives of the national beekeeping associations of England, Scotland, Ulster, and Wales.

01809

Council of Occupational Therapists for the European Countries COTEC

106-114 Borough High St., London, SE1 1LB, UK
Tel: 020 74502353
Fax: 020 74502350
Email: beryl.steeden@cot.co.uk
Website: http://www.cotec-europe.org
Members: 27
Contact: Anu Soderstrom, Pres.
Fee: £30
Membership Type: regular
Description: Works to enable national associations in European countries to develop, harmonize, and improve standards of professional practice and education, as well as to advance the theory of occupational therapy throughout Europe.
Meetings/Conventions: Occupation Diversity for the Future – quadrennial congress – Exhibits. May 24 to 27, 2012. Stockholm Sweden

01810

Counselling and Psychotherapy in Scotland COSCA

16 Melville Terr., Stirling, FK8 2NE, UK
Tel: 01786 475140
Fax: 01786 446207
Email: info@cosca.org.uk
Website: http://www.cosca.org.uk
Contact: Brian Magee, Chief Exec.
Fee: £28
Membership Type: student
Fee: £38
Membership Type: associate
Description: Acts as the professional body for counseling and psychotherapy in Scotland; seeks to advance all forms of counseling and psychotherapy and the use of counseling skills.

01811

Country Land and Business Association CLA

16 Belgrave Sq., London, SW1X 8PQ, UK
Tel: 020 72350511
Fax: 020 72354696
Email: mail@cla.org.uk
Website: http://www.cla.org.uk
Members: 49400
Staff: 77
Contact: Henry Aubrey-Fletcher, Pres.
Fee: £385
Membership Type: business/professional
Fee: £165
Membership Type: individual
Description: Members are owners of rural land. Promotes and safeguards the legitimate interests of owners of rural land; safeguards and develops the capital invested in the ownership of agricultural and other rural land and secures an appropriate return from these assets.
Formerly: Formerly, Country Landowners Association
Publication title: CLA in Wales

01812

Countryside Alliance CA

The Old Town Hall, 367 Kennington Rd., London, SE11 4PT, UK
Tel: 0207 8409200
Website: http://www.countryside-alliance.org.uk
Members: 107000
Contact: Kate Hoey, Chair
Fee: £28
Membership Type: full single
Fee: £43
Membership Type: full joint, trade
Description: Individuals interested in the countryside and the preservation of rural areas of the United Kingdom. Seeks to "preserve the freedoms of country people and their way of life" and "champion the countryside, country sports and the rural way of life". Conducts lobbying and advocacy campaigns to raise the awareness of rural issues among legislators at all levels of government; works on behalf of animal welfare and conservation programs; develops educational programs to improve public understanding of rural lifestyles and issues; sponsors research to develop solutions to problems facing rural areas.
Publication: Newsletter
Publication title: Update

01813

Countryside Council for Wales CCW

Maes-y-Ffynnon, Penrhosgarnedd, Gwynedd, Bangor, LL57 2DW, UK
Tel: 0845 1306229
Fax: 01248 355782
Email: enquiries@ccw.gov.uk
Website: http://www.ccw.gov.uk/Splash.aspx
Members: 12
Staff: 511
Contact: Morgan Parry, Chm.
Description: Advises government agencies on "sustaining natural beauty, wildlife, and the opportunity for outdoor enjoyment throughout Wales and its inshore waters". Cooperates with similar organizations in England and Scotland and at the international level.

01814

Coventry and Warwickshire Chamber of Commerce

Oak Tree Ct., Binley Business Park, Harry Weston Rd., Coventry, CV3 2UN, UK
Tel: 024 76654321
Fax: 024 76450242
Email: info@cw-chamber.co.uk
Website: http://www.cw-chamber.co.uk/homeTemplate.aspx/Home
Members: 1728
Staff: 194
Contact: Louise Bennett, Chief Exec.
Fee: £206.8
Membership Type: general (self only, no staff)
Fee: £3174.85
Membership Type: general (maximum; based on the number of full time employees)
Description: Promotes business and commerce.

01815

Craft Guild of Chefs

1 Victoria Parade, 331 Sandycombe Rd., Surrey, Richmond, TW9 3NB, UK
Tel: 0208 9483870
Fax: 0208 9483944
Email: sbarshall@craftguildofchefs.org
Website: http://craftguildofchefs.org
Contact: Suzanne Barshall, Sec.
Fee: £19.98
Membership Type: student, trainee
Fee: £52.88
Membership Type: master, regular, associate
Description: Working cooks and chefs, catering teachers and trainees; members of the food and beverage industries, waiters, hotel managers. Aims to promote and develop the art and technology of cookery and supervisory and management skills related to cookery and associated professions, to foster and provide training and education especially for the young.
Library Subject: food
Library Type: reference
Formerly: Formerly, Cookery and Food Association
Publication: Magazine
Publication title: Stockpot

01816

Craft Potters Association of Great Britain

25 Foubert's Pl., London, W1F 7QF, UK
Tel: 020 74377601
Fax: 020 72879954
Email: admin@cpaceramics.co.uk
Website: http://www.cpaceramics.co.uk
Members: 850
Staff: 4
Contact: Karen Bunting, Chair
Description: Aims to give support and encouragement to members. It has three companies Ceramic Review, Craft Potters Trading Company Limited (which sells work of its members) and the Craft Potters Association.
Publication: Magazine
Publication title: Ceramic Review

01817

Crafts Council

44a Pentonville Rd., Islington, London, N1 9BY, UK
Tel: 020 78062500
Fax: 020 78376891
Website: http://www.craftscouncil.org.uk
Staff: 49
Contact: Joanna Foster, Chair
Description: National organization for contemporary crafts in Great Britain offering exhibition and educational programmes. Maintains picture and book libraries, a collection of contemporary craft, and runs a gallery shop and an outlet at the V&A Museum. Offers start-up grants to makers.
Publication: Magazine
Publication title: Crafts. Advertisements.

01818

Craniosacral Therapy Association of the UK

Monomark House, 27 Old Gloucester St., London, WC1N 3XX, UK
Tel: 07000 784735
Email: office@craniosacral.co.uk
Website: http://www.craniosacral.co.uk
Members: 450
Contact: Roger James, Contact
Description: Represents craniosacral therapy practitioners in the United Kingdom.
Publication: Journal
Publication title: The Fulcrum

01819

Credit Protection Association CPA

CPA House, 350 King St., London, W6 0RX, UK
Tel: 0208 8460000
Fax: 0208 7417459
Email: sales@cpa.co.uk
Website: http://www.cpa.co.uk
Contact: David S. Baber, Managing Dir.
Description: Businesses and other organizations that offer their customers credit. Promotes prompt and effective action in cases of late or overdue payments. Provides support and advice to members attempting to collect on past due accounts; maintains nationwide network to screen potential credit recipients. Group claims to resolve 84% of overdue account situations within days by using interactive technologies that can track missing persons or corporations, and access legal and financial advice and business status reports.

01820

Cremation Society of Great Britain CSGB

Brecon House, 1st Fl., 16/16A Albion Pl., Kent, Maidstone, ME14 5DZ, UK
Tel: 01622 688292
Fax: 01622 686698
Email: info@cremation.org.uk
Website: http://www.cremation.org.uk
Staff: 3
Contact: Roger N. Arber, Sec.
Description: Promotes the practice of cremation in the U.K. Compiles statistics and provides information on all aspects of cremation.
Publication: Directory
Publication title: Directory of Crematoria
Meetings/Conventions: Cremation Conference – annual conference – Exhibits.

01821

Cromwell Association
CA

c/o David Hall
33 Cheyne Ave., South Woodford, London, E18 2DP, UK
Email: cromwellmuseum@cambridgeshire.gov.uk
Website: http://www.olivercromwell.org
Fee: £20
Membership Type: adult, individual under 23 (overseas)
Fee: £15
Membership Type: individual (under 23)
Description: Students and admirers of Oliver Cromwell (1599-1658), English statesman who directed English government from 1653 to 1658; individuals interested in the history of the period. Works to preserve the memory of Oliver Cromwell and to encourage study of the history of the Civil War, Commonwealth, and Protectorate. Organizes competitions, organized conferences and day schools. Supports the Cromwell Museum. Maintains speakers' bureau.
Publication: Journal
Publication title: Cromwelliana. Advertisements.
Meetings/Conventions: Cromwell Day – annual meeting

01822

Crop Protection Association
CPA

2 Swan Ct., Cygnet Pk., Hampton, Peterborough, PE7 8GX, UK
Tel: 01733 355370
Fax: 01733 355371
Email: info@cropprotection.org.uk
Website: http://www.cropprotection.org.uk
Members: 56
Staff: 14
Contact: Dominic Dyer, Chief Exec.
Description: Companies with manufacturing or technical control of the manufacture of pesticides in UK or which are substantial distributors of pesticides marketed under their own name. Supports and promotes the interests of major distributors and manufacturers of crop protection, amenity and garden products in the United Kingdom. Represents the views of its members in any forum.
Formerly: Formerly, British Agrochemicals Association
Publication: Handbook
Publication title: Annual Review and Handbook

01823

Croydon Chamber of Commerce and Industry

The Lansdowne Bldg., 2 Lansdowne Rd., Croydon, Surrey, CR9 2ER, UK
Tel: 020 82632345
Fax: 020 82632352
Email: info@croydonchamber.org.uk
Website: http://www.croydonchamber.org.uk
Members: 3500
Staff: 16
Contact: Matthew Sims, Gen. Mgr.
Fee: £266-998
Membership Type: local (based on number of employees)
Fee: £443-3811
Membership Type: premier plus (based on number of employees)
Description: Promotes business and commerce.

01824

Cruse Bereavement Care Scotland
CBCS

Riverview House, Friarton Rd., Perth, PH2 8DF, UK
Tel: 01738 444178
Fax: 01738 444807
Email: info@crusescotland.org.uk
Website: http://www.crusescotland.org.uk
Contact: Colin Murray Parkes, Pres.
Description: Individuals and organizations. Seeks to improve the quality of life of people who have lost a loved one. Provides support and services to bereaved individuals; conducts research and educational programs; makes available children's services; participates in charitable initiatives; compiles statistics.

01825

Cumbria and North Lancs Campaign for Nuclear Disarmament

13 E Rd., Lancaster, LA1 3EE, UK
Tel: 01524 33991
Email: r.allwright@lancaster.ac.uk
Website: http://www.cnduk.org/index.php/regional-groups/cumbria-and-north-lancs-cnd.html
Description: Aims to eliminate British nuclear weapons and other weapons of mass destruction.

01826

Customer Contact Association
CCA

20 Newton Pl., Glasgow, G3 7PY, UK
Tel: 0141 5649010
Fax: 0141 5649011
Email: cca@cca.org.uk
Website: http://www.cca-global.com
Members: 800
Staff: 14
Contact: Anne Marie Forsyth, Chief Exec.
Description: Acts as professional body for the call and contact centre industry; seeks to improve standards from both the user and employee perspective.
Library Subject: call and contact, e-commerce, technology, staffing
Library Type: not open to the public
Formerly: Formerly, Call Centre Association
Publication: Handbook
Publication title: Centrecalls

01827

Cutlery and Allied Trades Research Association
CATRA

Henry St., Sheffield, S3 7EQ, UK
Tel: 0114 2769736
Fax: 0114 2722151
Email: info@catra.org
Website: http://www.catra.org
Staff: 20
Description: Promotes and carries out research, development, testing and consultancy into the cutlery and allied trades association, including knives, tools, cookware, surgical blades, razor blades, and machine and industrial blades.

01828

Cybernetics Society

3 Willow Grove, Hertfordshire, Welwyn Garden City, AL8 7NA, UK
Fax: 08707 627076
Website: http://www.cybsoc.org
Contact: Martin Smith, Pres.
Fee: £20
Membership Type: individual
Description: Promotes the advancement of pure and applied cybernetics. Supports the continuing professional development of its members. Maintains a list of consultants. Lists recommended books and journals. Provides a web archive on Cybernetics. Holds regular lecture meetings and conferences.

01829

Cyclamen Society

Little Orchard, Church Rd., Kent, Sevenoaks, TN15 6LG, UK
Email: info@cyclamen.org
Website: http://www.cyclamen.org
Members: 1600
Contact: Arthur Nicholls, Membership Sec.
Fee: £10
Membership Type: single adult in UK
Fee: £12
Membership Type: family in UK
Description: Encourages cultivation and conservation of the genus Cyclamen and its species, forms, and cultivars. The genus Cyclamen contains 20 species of plants, which are part of the Primrose family.

Cymdeithas Cerddoriaeth Cymru
see Welsh Music Guild

Cymdeithas Ddrama Cymru
see Drama Association of Wales

Cymdeithas Gwartheg Duon Cymreig
see Welsh Black Cattle Society

Cyngor Cefn Gwlad Cymru
see Countryside Council for Wales

Cyngor Celfyddydau Cymru (CCC)
see Arts Council of Wales

Cyngor Llyfrau Cymru
see Welsh Books Council

01830

Cystic Fibrosis Trust

11 London Rd., Kent, Bromley, BR1 1BY, UK
Tel: 020 84647211
Fax: 020 83130472
Email: enquiries@cftrust.org.uk
Website: http://www.cftrust.org.uk
Members: 62500
Staff: 64

Contact: Rosie Barnes, Chief Exec.
Description: Represents individuals affected by Cystic Fibrosis.
Publication: Magazine
Publication title: CF Talk
Meetings/Conventions: quarterly meeting

01831

Dairy Council - United Kingdom

93 Baker St., London, W1U 6QQ, UK
Tel: 020 74672629
Fax: 020 79353920
Email: info@dairycouncil.org.uk
Website: http://www.milk.co.uk
Staff: 5
Contact: Sandy Wilkie, Chm.
Description: Coordinates the dairy industry's generic information and promotion activities. Represents dairy farmers, dairy processors and manufacturers. Aims to strengthen public perception of the quality and nutritional value of milk and dairy products.
Publication: Booklet
Publication title: Animal Welfare Dairy Cows

01832

Dairy UK

93 Baker St., London, W1U 6QQ, UK
Tel: 020 74867244
Fax: 020 74874734
Email: info@dairyuk.org
Website: http://www.dairyuk.org
Members: 60
Staff: 17
Contact: Mark Allen, Chm.
Description: Trade association representing processors, manufacturers, wholesalers and retailers of milk and milk products.
Formerly: Formerly, Dairy Industry Association
Publication: Newsletter
Publication title: Dairy UK News

01833

Daiwa Anglo-Japanese Foundation

Daiwa Foundation Japan House, 13/14 Cornwall Terr., London, NW1 4QP, UK
Tel: 0020 74864348
Fax: 0020 74862914
Email: office@dajf.org.uk
Website: http://www.dajf.org.uk
Contact: Marie Conte-Helm, Gen. Dir.
Description: To enhance the UK and Japan's understanding of each other's people and culture. To enable British and Japanese students and academics to further their education through exchange and cooperation.

01834

Danish-UK Chamber of Commerce
DUCC

55 Sloane St., London, SW1X 9SR, UK
Tel: 020 72596795
Email: info@ducc.co.uk
Website: http://www.ducc.co.uk
Members: 140
Staff: 3
Contact: Per Troen, Chm.
Fee: £450
Membership Type: large corporate
Fee: £200
Membership Type: small corporate
Description: Works to promote trade and investment between Denmark and Britain.
Publication: Newsletter
Publication title: DUCC Red Letter

01835

Dartmoor Sheep Breeders' Association
DSBA

c/o Lower Stockadon Farm
St. Mellion, Cornwall, Saltash, PL12 6QF, UK
Tel: 01579 350920
Email: info@greyface-dartmoor.org.uk
Website: http://www.greyface-dartmoor.org.uk
Members: 200
Contact: Patrick Aubrey-Fletcher, Sec.
Fee: £18
Membership Type: general
Description: Promotes the Greyface Dartmoor Sheep.
Publication: Book
Publication title: Flock Book

01836

Data Publishers Association
DPA

Queens House, 28 Kingsway, London, WC2B 6JR, UK
Tel: 020 74050836
Fax: 020 74044167
Email: info@dpa.org.uk
Website: http://www.dpa.org.uk
Members: 80
Staff: 1
Contact: Jerry Gosney, Exec. Dir.
Fee: £490-2570
Membership Type: full
Fee: £595-995
Membership Type: UK and overseas associate
Description: Directory and data publishers in the UK and overseas. Seeks to: maintain a professional practice code; raise professional standards; promote business directories as an ideal advertising medium; promote and protect the trade's legal interests; foster common interests and provide for exchange of technical, commercial, and managerial information.
Formerly: Formerly, Association of British Directory Publishers
Publication: Newsletter
Publication title: DPA News

01837

Davis Dyslexia Association - UK
DDA - UK

Unit 3A, Slaney Pl., Headcorn Rd., Staplehurst, Kent, TN12 0DT, UK
Tel: 01580 892928
Fax: 01580 893429
Email: info@davislearningfoundation.org.uk
Website: http://www.davistraining.co.uk
Contact: Richard Whitehead, Dir.
Description: Provides public awareness of dyslexia. Helps children and adults correct problems with reading, spelling, mathematics, handwriting, coordination and attention focus. Offers training programs for those seeking a deeper understanding of dyslexia and the Davis techniques.

01838

Daycare Trust

2nd Floor, Novas Contemporary Urban Centre, 73-81 Southwark Bridge Road, London, SE1 0NQ, UK

Tel: 020 79407510

Fax: 020 79407515

Email: info@daycaretrust.org.uk

Website: http://www.daycaretrust.org.uk

Staff: 20

Contact: Severine Njock, Exec. PA/Personnel

Fee: £40

Membership Type: policy supporter

Fee: £150

Membership Type: nursery chain, college/universitie

Description: Daycare Trust, the national childcare charity, is campaigning for quality, accessible, affordable childcare for all and raising the voices of children, parents and carers. We lead the national childcare campaign by producing high quality research, developing credible policy recommendations through publications and the media, and by working with others. Our advice and information on childcare assists parents and carers, providers, employers and trade unions and policymakers.

Formerly: Formerly, National Childcare Campaign/Daycare Trust

Publication: Pamphlet

Publication title: Childwise

01839

DBA - The Barge Association
DBA

Cormorant, Spade Oak Reach, Cookham, Maidenhead, SL6 9RQ, UK

Tel: 0303 6660636

Email: info@barges.org

Website: http://www.barges.org

Members: 1500

Contact: Andy Soper, Chm.

Fee: £35

Membership Type: single (domestic)

Fee: £40

Membership Type: single (overseas)

Description: Aims to bring together people interested in barges and barging. Establishes and maintains contact with other relevant societies and clubs, navigation authorities and trade associations. Represents the interests of barge owners in areas such as moorings rights, navigation permits and charges, provision and maintenance of barge navigations and navigation safety regulations.

Publication: Magazine

Publication title: Blue Flag

01840

Deaf Education Through Listening and Talking
DELTA

Con Powell Centre, Alfa House, Molesey Rd., Surrey, KT12 3PD, UK
Tel: 0845 1081437
Fax: 0193 2243018
Email: enquiries@deafeducation.org.uk
Website: http://www.deafeducation.org.uk
Members: 800
Staff: 4
Contact: Margaret Glasgow, Chair
Fee: £15
Membership Type: concession
Fee: £30
Membership Type: individual
Description: Parents and teachers of children with hearing impairment and adults with hearing impairment. Promotes the development of natural and effective spoken language among children with profound hearing impairment. Advocates the use of the natural aural approach in teaching children with profound hearing impairment to use spoken language. Conducts workshops for teachers and families of children with profound hearing impairment. Makes available teaching resources, sponsors research and provides children's services.
Formerly: Formerly, National Aural Group
Publication: Newsletter
Publication title: Chat

01841

Deafblind Scotland

21 Alexandra Ave., Lenzie, Glasgow, G66 5BG, UK
Tel: 0141 7776111
Fax: 0141 7753311
Email: info@deafblindscotland.org.uk
Website: http://www.deafblindscotland.org.uk
Members: 500
Staff: 11
Contact: Bob Nolan, Chm.
Description: Assists the deaf-blind or dual sensory impaired people to cope with their disability. Helps with accessing benefits, health and social services for the deaf and blind.
Publication: Report
Publication title: Guide Communicator

01842

Deafblind UK

c/o National Centre for Deafblindness
John and Lucille van Geest Pl., Cygnet Rd., Hampton, Peterborough, PE7 8FD, UK
Tel: 01733 358100
Fax: 01733 358356
Email: info@deafblinduk.org.uk
Website: http://www.deafblind.org.uk
Contact: Jeff Skipp, Chief Exec.
Description: Deafblind persons. Helps alleviate the isolation felt by those with dual sensory loss. Negotiates with government to secure better services and facilities for individuals with visual and hearing impairments. Conducts public service programs. Offers advice and financial consultation and some housing assistance. Organizes conferences, seminars, and communication courses.

01843

DEBRA European

Debra House, 13 Wellington Business Park, Duke's Ride, Crowthorne, RG45 6LS, UK
Tel: 01344 771961
Fax: 01344 762661
Email: debra@debra.org.uk
Website: http://www.debra-international.org/index.php?id=52
Members: 20
Staff: 1
Contact: Anna Kemble-Welch, Pres.
Description: Serves as patient support groups for people whose lives have been affected by Epidemidysis Bullosa (EB). Offers peer support, workshops and dissemination of research findings.
Formerly: Formerly, EUR Network of EB Support Groups

01844

Deer Commission for Scotland
DCS

Great Glen House, Leachkin Rd., Inverness, IV3 5LH, UK
Tel: 01463 725000
Fax: 01463 725048
Email: enquiries@dcs.gov.uk
Website: http://www.dcs.gov.uk/default.aspx
Contact: Nick Halfhide, Dir.
Description: Works for the conservation, control and sustainable management of all species of wild deer in Scotland. Commissions' research projects and conducts deer counts. Reviews all matters relating to wild deer.

01845

Defence Manufacturers Association of Great Britain
DMA

Marlborough House, Headley Rd., Grayshott, Surrey, GU26 6LG, UK
Tel: 01428 607788
Fax: 01428 604567
Email: salzmann@the-dma.org.uk
Website: http://www.the-dma.org.uk
Members: 500
Staff: 28
Contact: Ian Godden, Chm.
Description: UK companies, large or small, concerned with selling products or services to government defense agencies and main defense contractors in the UK or overseas. Represents the views and needs of its members to government and the MOD.
Publication: Membership Directory
Publication title: Register of Members

01846

Delius Society
DS

c/o Delius Trust
7-11 Britannia St., London, WC1X 9JS, UK
Tel: 020 72399143
Email: thedeliussociety@aol.com
Website: http://www.delius.org.uk/aboutus.htm
Members: 400
Contact: Martin Lee-Browne, Chm.
Fee: £28
Membership Type: in UK and Europe
Fee: £55
Membership Type: in U.S. and Canada
Description: Works for wider knowledge and appreciation of Frederick Delius (1862-1934), English composer. Objectives are: to share interest in Delius with others to promote performance, broadcasting, recording, and publishing of his works; to sustain isolated devotees. Sponsors lectures, discussions, and concert and opera visits.
Publication: Journal
Publication title: Delius Society Journal

Democratiaid Rhyddfrydol Cymru
see Welsh Liberal Democrats

01847

Dental Anxiety and Phobia Association
DAPA

11 The South Border, Purley, Surrey, CR8 3LL, UK
Tel: 020 86604723
Email: drmpoynter@aol.com
Website: http://www.healthyteeth.com
Contact: Marylyn Poynter, Founder
Description: Aims to help dental patients who developed fear and anxiety of the dental procedure. Encourages self help groups among members and promotes awareness within the dental profession for the need of appropriate empathy.

01848

Dental Laboratories Association
DLA

44-46 Wollaton Rd., Beeston, Nottingham, NG9 2NR, UK
Tel: 0115 9254888
Fax: 0115 9254800
Email: info@dla.org.uk
Website: http://www.dla.org.uk
Members: 1000
Staff: 8
Contact: Trevor Dundee, Chm.
Fee: £600-1100
Membership Type: affiliate (based on number of members)
Fee: £350
Membership Type: education affiliate
Description: Seeks to advance the study, teaching, and practice of dental technology and the dental sciences. Represents members' commercial and professional interests; facilitates communication and cooperation among members; sponsors research and educational programs.
Publication: Journal
Publication title: Dental Laboratory. Advertisements.
Meetings/Conventions: Dental Technology Show – biennial conference – Exhibits.

01849

Dental Practitioners Association
DPA

61 Harley St., London, W1G 8QU, UK
Tel: 0207 6361072
Fax: 0207 6361086
Email: info@uk-dentistry.org
Website: http://www.uk-dentistry.org
Members: 700
Staff: 3
Contact: Derek Watson, Chief Exec.
Fee: £199
Membership Type: associate/performer

Fee: £299
Membership Type: practice (any number of dentists at a single practice location)
Description: Represents UK dentists. Provides support, advice and representation at all levels.
Formerly: Formerly, General Dental Practitioners Association
Publication: Magazine
Publication title: The GDP. Advertisements.

01850

Department for International Development
DFID

1 Palace St., London, SW1E 5HE, UK
Tel: 0135 5843132
Fax: 0135 5843632
Email: enquiry@dfid.gov.uk
Website: http://www.dfid.gov.uk
Staff: 1449
Description: Government department responsible for all aspects of international development policy. Administers the UK development programme, promotes more coherent UK and international policies in support of sustainable development.
Formerly: Formerly, Overseas Development Administration
Publication: Magazine
Publication title: Developments. Advertisements.

01851

Depression Alliance
DA

20 Great Dover St., London, SE1 4LX, UK
Tel: 0845 1232320
Email: information@depressionalliance.org
Website: http://www.depressionalliance.org
Members: 3500
Staff: 8
Contact: Alison Lawrence, Chair
Fee: £24
Membership Type: regular
Description: Provides information and support to anyone affected by depression. Promotes services that include self-help groups, correspondence schemes, and a unique range of literature.
Library Subject: depression
Library Type: reference
Publication: Newsletter
Publication title: A Single Step

01852

Derbyshire Conservation Volunteers
DCV

21 Nesfield Close, Alvaston, Derby, DE24 0QT, UK
Tel: 01332 733871
Email: chair@derby-cv.org.uk
Website: http://www.derby-cv.org.uk
Contact: Sue Weston, Chair
Description: Works to conserve and enhance the wildlife potential of rural and urban sites in the county of Derbyshire through practical outdoor tasks. Conducts hedgelaying, dry stone walling, woodland management, pond digging, fencing, tree planting and footpath maintenance.

01853

Design and Artists Copyright Society
DACS

33 Great Sutton St., London, EC1V 0DX, UK
Tel: 020 73368811
Fax: 020 73368822
Email: info@dacs.org.uk
Website: http://www.dacs.org.uk
Staff: 12
Contact: Gilane Tawadros, Chief Exec.
Description: Represents the copyright interests of artists, photographers, illustrators, craftspeople, cartoonists, architects, animators, designers, and visual creators in the UK and around the world. Serves copyright consumers seeking to license the individual rights of an artist. Also administers the Artist's Resale Right.
Publication: Annual Report
Publication title: Annual Review

01854

Design and Technology Association
D&T

16 Wellesbourne House, Walton Rd., Wellesbourne, Warwick, CV35 9JB, UK
Tel: 01789 470007
Fax: 01789 841955
Email: info@data.org.uk
Website: http://www.data.org.uk
Members: 8000
Staff: 13
Contact: Richard Green, Chief Exec.
Fee: £35
Membership Type: primary
Fee: £65
Membership Type: secondary
Description: Represents individuals involved in delivering design and technology in the national curriculum. Aims to uphold high standards of teaching and learning. Promotes and disseminates good practice and act as catalyst for well-planned change and development.
Publication: Newsletter
Publication title: D&T News. Advertisements.

01855

Design Business Association
DBA

35-39 Old St., London, EC1V 9HX, UK
Tel: 020 72519229
Fax: 020 72519221
Email: deborah.dawton@dba.org.uk
Website: http://www.dba.org.uk
Contact: Deborah Dawton, Chief Exec.
Fee: £1040-5200
Membership Type: full (based on number of employees)
Description: Promotes professional excellence through productive partnerships between commerce and the design industry. Fosters effective design to improve the quality of people's lives.

01856

Design Council

34 Bow St., London, WC2E 7DL, UK
Tel: 020 74205200
Fax: 020 74205300
Email: info@designcouncil.org.uk
Website: http://www.designcouncil.org.uk
Staff: 200
Contact: David Kester, CEO
Description: Organized to improve the design of British products by researching and communicating the benefits of design to government departments, agencies, companies, financial and educational institutions, medical practices, consultant groups, and industrial designers. Promotes improvements in design education. Organized to advise the government on national design policy, with particular reference to education curriculum developments.
Publication: Newsletter
Publication title: BusinessInnovation

01857

Design History Society
DHS

c/o Paula Thomson
Oxford University Press, Great Clarendon St., Oxford, OX2 6DP, UK
Email: d.bhagat@londonmet.ac.uk
Website: http://www.designhistorysociety.org
Members: 225
Contact: Dipti Bhagat, Chm.
Fee: £46
Membership Type: individual
Fee: £164
Membership Type: institutional
Description: Promotes the study of and research into design history.

01858

Despatch Association
DA

Lamb's End House, 36 Church Rd., Magdalen, Norfolk, King's Lynn, PE34 3DG, UK
Tel: 01553 813479
Fax: 01553 813479
Email: phil@despatch.co.uk
Website: http://www.despatch.co.uk
Members: 250
Staff: 1
Contact: Phillip Stone, CEO
Fee: £200
Membership Type: corporate
Fee: £50
Membership Type: joining
Description: Express delivery services in UK. Represents the despatch industry, protects the interests of members, sets and maintains standards within the industry, improves the public image of the industry and improves safety standards within the industry.
Publication: Magazine
Publication title: Despatches Magazine. Advertisements.

Deutsch-Britische Industrie-und Handelskammer

see German-British Chamber of Industry and Commerce

Deutsch-Britische Juristenvereinigung

see British - German Jurists Association

Deutsch-Britische Stiftung

see Anglo-German Foundation for the Study of Industrial Society

01859

Developing Technologies
DT

City University, Tait Bldg., Rm. CG54, Northampton Sq., London, EC1V 0HB, UK
Tel: 020 70408109
Email: info@developingtechnologies.org
Website: http://www.developingtechnologies.org
Description: Small NGOs, development workers and indigenous communities committed to bringing together the skills of engineers with development agencies and workers to empower people in developing countries.

01860

Development Education Association
DEA

CAN Mezzanine, 32-36 Loman St., London, SE1 0EH, UK
Tel: 020 79227930
Fax: 020 79227929
Email: dea@dea.org.uk
Website: http://www.dea.org.uk
Members: 250
Staff: 14
Contact: Hetan Shah, Chief Exec.
Fee: £40-500
Membership Type: organisation (based on annual budget)
Fee: £20
Membership Type: individual
Description: National umbrella body which aims to support and promote organizations and individuals working to raise awareness and understanding of global and development issues in the United Kingdom.
Formerly: Absorbed, NADEC and Inter-Agencies Group
Publication: Journal
Publication title: DEA Journal. Advertisements.

01861

Development Planning Unit
DPU

University College London, 34 Tavistock Sq., London, WC1H 9EZ, UK
Tel: 020 76791111
Fax: 020 76791112
Email: dpu@ucl.ac.uk
Website: http://www.ucl.ac.uk/dpu
Contact: Caren Levy, Dir.
Description: An international centre specializing in academic teaching, practical training, research and consultancy in the field of urban and regional development, planning and management. It is concerned with understanding the process of rapid urbanisation and the policy, planning and management responses to the economic and social development of both urban and rural areas. The full time academic staff of the DPU is a multidisciplinary group of 17 professionals and academics (embracing 11 different nationalities), all with extensive and ongoing research and professional experience in various fields of urban and institutional development throughout the world. Annually, some 100 participants from more than 30 countries undertake courses or research degrees at the DPU.
Publication: Magazine
Publication title: DPUNEWS

01862

Development Studies Association
DSA

PO Box 108, Devon, Bideford, EX39 6ZQ, UK
Tel: 0845 5193372
Email: admin@devstud.org.uk
Website: http://www.devstud.org.uk
Members: 700
Staff: 1
Contact: Frances Hill, Exec. Dir.
Fee: £30
Membership Type: individual
Fee: £15
Membership Type: concessionary
Description: Scholars with an interest in international economic development. Promotes the "advancement of knowledge on international development". Serves as a clearinghouse on international development and international development studies; encourages research; facilitates interdisciplinary exchange and cooperation in the field of development studies.
Publication: Newsletter
Publication title: Forum. Advertisements.
Meetings/Conventions: Policy Workshop – periodic workshop

01863

Development Trusts Association
DTA

33 Corsham St., London, N1 6DR, UK
Tel: 0845 4588336
Fax: 0845 4588337
Email: info@dta.org.uk
Website: http://www.dta.org.uk
Contact: Steve Wyler, Dir.
Fee: £50-500
Membership Type: full
Fee: £30
Membership Type: individual (unwaged)
Description: Represents the community enterprise movement. Supports and promotes local organizations that use enterprising methods. Encourages exchange of information and good practice. Conducts research and promotes the work of development trusts. Advocates and contributes to public policy developments.

01864

Diabetes UK

Macleod House, 10 Pkwy., London, NW1 7AA, UK
Tel: 020 74241000
Fax: 020 74241001
Email: info@diabetes.org.uk
Website: http://www.diabetes.org.uk
Members: 165000
Description: Improves the lives of people with diabetes and works towards a future without diabetes. Funds research, campaigns and helps people with diabetes in UK.
Publication: Magazine
Publication title: Balance. Advertisements.

01865

Dickens Fellowship

48 Doughty St., London, WC1N 2LX, UK
Email: postbox@dickens.fellowship.org
Website: http://www.dickensfellowship.org
Members: 4000
Contact: Grahame Smith, Pres.
Fee: £8
Membership Type: regular
Description: Charles Dickens enthusiasts, scholars, professors, and literary and Victorian specialists in 23 countries. Seeks to create a common bond of friendship between admirers of English novelist Charles Dickens (1812-70) and preserve properties associated with Charles Dickens and his works.
Publication: Journal
Publication title: The Dickensian. Advertisements.

01866

Digital and Screen Printing Association
DSPA

Innovation Way, South Yorkshire, Barnsley, S75 1JL, UK
Tel: 01226 321202
Fax: 01226 294797
Email: info@prismuk.org
Website: http://www.prismuk.org
Members: 220
Staff: 1
Contact: John Keith, Bus. Mgr.
Fee: £1186.8
Membership Type: full
Fee: £386.4
Membership Type: inplant
Description: Producers, suppliers, and trade houses involved in the screen-printing and digital printing industry. Promotes the screen-printing industry in the United Kingdom; represents members' interests. Fosters technical exchange among members; disseminates information. Conducts educational programs; maintains apprenticeship project. Provides placement service.
Formerly: Formerly, Display Producers and Screen Printers Association

01867

Digital TV Group
DTG

1 Nine Elms Ln., Vauxhall, London, SW8 5NQ, UK
Tel: 020 75014300
Email: office@dtg.org.uk
Website: http://www.dtg.org.uk
Contact: Richard Lindsay Davies, Dir. Gen.
Fee: £10000
Membership Type: full
Fee: £20000
Membership Type: principal
Description: Represents individuals involved in the development and marketing of digital television. Facilitates the introduction of digital terrestrial TV. Focuses on digital switchover and on the delivery of leading television and media products and services.
Publication: Book
Publication title: D-Book

01868

Dignity in Dying

181 Oxford St., London, W1D 2JT, UK
Tel: 020 74797730
Email: info@dignityindying.org.uk
Website: http://www.dignityindying.org.uk
Members: 15000
Contact: Sarah Wootton, Chief Exec.
Fee: £25
Membership Type: individual
Fee: £35
Membership Type: joint

Description: Represents doctors, lawyers and clergymen dedicated to legalizing euthanasia for competent adults suffering from terminal illnesses wanting to die.
Formerly: Formerly, Voluntary Euthanasia Society

01869
Dinosaur Society
Gnoll House, 15 Forster Rd., Surrey, Guildford, GU2 9AE, UK
Email: editor@dinosaursociety.com
Website: http://www.dinosaursociety.com
Contact: Richard Moody, Trustee
Description: Dedicated to supporting the work of individuals engaged in advancing the science of palaeontology, dinosaurs, and earth science in general.
Publication: Book
Publication title: If Dinosaurs Were Alive Today

01870
Direct Marketing Association DMA
DMA House, 70 Margaret St., London, W1W 8SS, UK
Tel: 0207 2913300
Fax: 0207 3234426
Email: info@dma.org.uk
Website: http://www.dma.org.uk
Contact: David Metcalfe, Chm.
Description: Maximizes value for members. Maintains and enhances consumers' trust and confidence in direct marketing. Works for the protection and development of the UK direct marketing industry. Promotes best practice and raises industry standards through the DM Code of Practice, best practice guidelines and the DMA Awards.

01871
Direct Marketing Association - United Kingdom DMA
DMA House, 70 Margaret St., London, W1W 8SS, UK
Tel: 020 72913300
Fax: 020 73234426
Email: info@dma.org.uk
Website: http://www.dma.org.uk
Members: 830
Staff: 51
Contact: David Metcalfe, Chm.
Fee: £985
Membership Type: associate (special)
Fee: £755
Membership Type: charity (special)
Description: Direct marketing agencies, advertisers, and service suppliers in the United Kingdom. Represents members' interests and promotes self-regulations and public awareness. Compiles statistics. Conducts seminars and training programs.
Library Subject: direct marketing media
Library Type: open to the public
Publication: Newsletter
Publication title: Weekly Fax

01872
Direct Selling Association - United Kingdom DSA
29 Floral St., London, WC2E 9DP, UK
Tel: 020 74971234
Fax: 020 74973144
Email: info@dsa.org.uk
Website: http://www.dsa.org.uk
Members: 66
Staff: 3
Contact: Richard Berry, Dir.
Fee: £500
Membership Type: associate (business with sales under 1 million)
Fee: £1000
Membership Type: associate (business with sales over 1 million)
Description: Maintains high standards in the direct selling of consumer goods and services in the U.K. Represents members' interests before government agencies and consumer bodies; lobbies for favorable legislation. Disseminates market data and information concerning direct selling.
Library Subject: direct selling
Library Type: by appointment only
Publication: Book
Publication title: Direct Selling - From Door To Door to Network Marketing
Meetings/Conventions: Bridging the World – congress – Exhibits.

01873
Directors Guild of Great Britain DGGB
4 Windmill St., London, W1T 2HZ, UK
Tel: 020 75809131
Fax: 020 75809132
Email: info@dggb.org
Website: http://www.dggb.org
Members: 1000
Staff: 3
Contact: Peter Brook, Pres.
Fee: £65
Membership Type: associate
Fee: £25
Membership Type: student
Description: Represents directors across media. Develops policy to influence the future of the industry, advice for members in dispute and contractual issues.
Publication: Magazine
Publication title: Direct. Advertisements.

01874
Directors UK
Inigo Pl., 31-32 Bedford St., London, WC2E 9ED, UK
Tel: 020 72400009
Fax: 020 78459700
Email: info@directors.uk.com
Website: http://www.dprs.org
Members: 3500
Contact: Andrew Chowns, Chief Exec.
Description: Establishes and protects directors' rights in the UK and abroad. Assists directors and producers in reinforcing their rights in the industry. Improves the conditions and terms under which directors are employed. Collects and distributes money due to directors for the exploitation of their work.
Formerly: Formerly, Directors' and Producers' Rights Society

01875
Disability Alliance
Universal House, 89-94 Wentworth St., London, E1 7SA, UK
Tel: 020 72478776
Fax: 020 72478765
Email: office@disabilityalliance.org
Website: http://www.disabilityalliance.org
Members: 300
Staff: 9
Contact: Vanessa Stanislas, Chief Exec.
Description: Aims to break the link between poverty and disability in the UK, by providing information about UK social security benefits to disabled people, their carers, and advisers. Campaigns for improvements to the social security system and for increases in disability benefits so that entitlements reflect the costs of disability more accurately.
Formerly: Formerly, Disability Alliance Education and Research Association
Publication: Handbook
Publication title: Disability Rights Handbook. Advertisements.

01876
Disabled Birders Association DBA
18 St. Mildreds Rd., Kent, CT9 2LT, UK
Email: bo@disabledbirdersassociation.co.uk
Website: http://www.disabledbirdersassociation.co.uk
Contact: Bo Crombet-Beolens, Founder/Chm.
Description: Promotes universal access to all facilities, services and resources for bird watchers. Seeks to educate the general public and improve access for people with disabilities to reserves, facilities and services for birding.
Publication: Newsletter
Publication title: Update

01877
Disabled Living Foundation DLF
380-384 Harrow Rd., London, W9 2HU, UK
Tel: 020 72896111
Fax: 020 72662922
Email: info@dlf.org.uk
Website: http://www.dlf.org.uk
Staff: 35
Contact: Margaret McKinlay, Chair
Description: Provides impartial information on disability equipment for daily living.

01878
Disabled Motorists Federation DMF
Chester-le-Street and District, CVS Volunteer Centre, Clarence Terr., Chester-Le-Street, DH3 3DQ, UK
Tel: 0191 4163172
Email: jkillick2214@yahoo.co.uk
Website: http://www.dmfed.org.uk
Members: 2500
Contact: J. Killick, Sec.
Fee: £45
Membership Type: affiliated club
Fee: £14
Membership Type: affiliated individual
Description: Represents the interests of affiliated motor clubs and affiliated members.
Publication: Magazine
Publication title: The Way Ahead. Advertisements.

01879
Disabled Photographers' Society
DPS
PO Box 85, Kent, DA3 9BA, UK
Email: enquiries@disabledphotographers.co.uk
Website: http://www.disabledphotographers.co.uk
Members: 300
Contact: Mike Birbeck, Pres.
Fee: £10
Membership Type: full
Fee: £25
Membership Type: group
Description: Disabled and handicapped persons involved in photography. Provides photographic equipment for disabled use, together with ancillary equipment, such as wheelchair supports etc. Holds annual exhibition.
Publication: Magazine
Publication title: In Focus

01880
Disasters Emergency Committee
DEC
43 Chalton St., 1st Fl., London, NW1 1DU, UK
Tel: 020 73870200
Fax: 020 73872050
Email: info@dec.org.uk
Website: http://www.dec.org.uk
Members: 13
Description: Provides assistance to disaster victims. Aims to raise the standard of humanitarian response.
Publication: Handbook
Publication title: DEC Policy

01881
Disinfected Mail Study Circle
DMSC
25 Sinclair Grove, London, NW11 9JH, UK
Email: vdvpratique@aol.com
Website: http://www.stampcircuit.com/Societies/Dmsc
Members: 140
Contact: V. Denis Vandervelde, Contact
Fee: £15
Membership Type: within UK
Fee: £18
Membership Type: in Europe
Description: Represents postal historians, doctors, researchers, libraries, and research foundations in 25 countries. Studies the historic treatment of mail so as to prevent the spread of contagious diseases. Works on the research study of the late Dr. K. F. Meyer and his associates, which have been extended to include health certificates and passports, quarantine ephemera, anti-vaccination postal propaganda, and related subjects. Maintains speakers' bureau. Conducts research programs.
Publication: Journal
Publication title: Cumulative Indexes. Advertisements.
Meetings/Conventions: annual conference – Exhibits.

01882
Ditchley Foundation
Ditchley Park, Enstone, Oxfordshire, Chipping Norton, OX7 4ER, UK
Tel: 01608 677346
Fax: 01608 677399
Email: info@ditchley.co.uk
Website: http://www.ditchley.co.uk
Staff: 9
Contact: Jeremy Greenstock, Dir.
Description: Interested individuals united to promote, carry out, or advance any charitable activities, particularly in the sphere of education for the benefit to British or American citizens. Provides forum for individuals from the United States, the European Union, Japan, Canada, and elsewhere to discuss issues facing each country. Provides facilities for appropriate conferences sponsored by other groups.
Publication: Proceedings
Publication title: Ditchley Conference Reports

Doctors of the World UK
see Medecins du Monde UK

01883
Doctors Worldwide
DWW
134 Wellington Rd. N, Stockport, SK4 2LL, UK
Tel: 01612925788
Fax: 01612925776
Email: info@doctorsworldwide.org
Website: http://www.doctorsworldwide.org
Description: Provides medical relief and aid to victims of poverty, famine, diseases, disasters, and wars. Works with other organizations to minimize costs and maximize the efficiency of relief operations.

01884
Dog Assistance in Disability
DOG AID
43 Sir Alfred's Way, Sutton Coldfield, Birmingham, B76 1ET, UK
Tel: 01743 891314
Email: clanfraser33@hotmail.com
Website: http://www.dogaid.org.uk
Contact: Sandra Fraser, Contact
Description: Provides access to dog training for persons with physical disabilities, enabling them to train pets in general obedience and specialized tasks to help them better manage their disability in everyday life.

01885
Dogs Trust
17 Wakley St., London, EC1V 7RQ, UK
Tel: 020 78370006
Email: customerservices@dogstrust.org.uk
Website: http://www.dogstrust.org.uk
Members: 20000
Staff: 380
Contact: Clarissa Baldwin, CEO
Description: Dedicated to the rescue and rehoming of stray and abandoned dogs.
Formerly: Formerly, National Canine Defence League
Publication: Magazine
Publication title: Wag

01886
Domestic Appliance Service Association
DASA
2nd Fl., 145-157 St. John St., London, EC1V 4PY, UK
Tel: 0870 2240343
Fax: 0870 2240358
Email: dasa@dasa.org.uk
Website: http://www.dasa.org.uk
Members: 180
Staff: 1
Contact: Walter Russel, Chm.
Fee: £130-260
Membership Type: regular/provisional (depending on the number of engineers)
Fee: £260
Membership Type: associate
Description: Represents independent electrical and electronics service organizations. Aims to promote good service, efficiency and courtesy to all members of the public. Encourages communication between independent repairers, consults them on national issues and represents their interests within the trade. Sets national standards of competence and service quality.
Publication: Newsletter
Publication title: ORBIT Newsletter. Advertisements.

01887
Doncaster Chamber
ICON, First Point, Balby Carr Bank, Doncaster, DN4 5JQ, UK
Tel: 01302 341000
Fax: 01302 328382
Email: chamber@doncaster-chamber.co.uk
Website: http://www.doncaster-chamber.co.uk
Members: 1050
Staff: 43
Contact: Stephen Shore, Chief Exec.
Fee: £125
Membership Type: sole trader
Fee: £1760.74
Membership Type: company (based on number of employees of 2 - over 1500)
Description: Promotes business and commerce.

01888
Donizetti Society
146 Bordesley Rd., Morden, SM4 5LT, UK
Tel: 020 86489364
Email: info@donizettisociety.com
Website: http://www.donizettisociety.com
Members: 150
Contact: Alexander Weatherson, Chm.
Fee: £65
Membership Type: outside UK
Fee: £50
Membership Type: in UK
Description: Promotes the interest, understanding and learning in the works of Gaetano Donizetti, his teacher Giovanni Mayr and the operatic life of their times. Offers informational services to all opera companies performing Italian and French operas of this period.
Publication: Newsletter

01889
Donkey Breed Society
DBS
The Hermitage, Pootings, Edenbridge, TN8 6SD, UK
Tel: 01732 864414
Fax: 01732 864414
Email: societysecretary@donkeybreedsociety.co.uk
Website: http://www.donkeybreedsociety.co.uk/Page.aspx?TagName=HomePage
Contact: Carol Morse, Sec.
Fee: £25
Membership Type: adult, single
Fee: £40
Membership Type: adult, joint
Description: Committed to the use, well-being and protection of donkeys and the breeding of quality stock; aims to improve the quality and conformation of donkeys.

Publication: Newsletter
Publication title: Bray Talk

01890

Donkey Sanctuary

Slade House Farm, Devon, Sidmouth, EX10 0NU, UK
Tel: 01395 578222
Fax: 01395 579266
Website: http://drupal.thedonkeysanctuary.org.uk
Staff: 280
Contact: Jim Duncan, Emeritus
Description: Seeks to prevent the suffering of donkeys worldwide through the provision of high quality, professional advice, training and support on donkey welfare. In the UK and Ireland permanent sanctuary is provided to any donkey in need of refuge.

01891

Door and Hardware Federation DHF

42 Heath St., Staffordshire, Tamworth, B79 7JH, UK
Tel: 01827 52337
Fax: 01827 310827
Email: info@dhfonline.org.uk
Website: http://www.dhfonline.org.uk
Members: 120
Staff: 7
Contact: Bob Perry, Chm.
Fee: £425-4550
Membership Type: company (based upon the annual turnover)
Description: Manufacturers of industrial and commercial metal doors, garage doors and shutters. Encourages the continual advancement of design, operational techniques, efficiency and safety standards throughout the metal door industry; participates in the preparation and finalization of technical, trading and contractual standards involving metal door products, both on a national and international basis. Provides a forum for discussion on matters of common interest.
Formerly: Formerly, Door and Shutter Manufacturers Association and Association of Building Hardware Manufacturers

01892

Dorothy L. Sayers Society DLS

Rose Cottage, Malthouse Ln., Hurstpierpoint, West Sussex, Hassocks, BN6 9JY, UK
Tel: 01273 833444
Fax: 01273 835988
Email: info@sayers.org.uk
Website: http://www.sayers.org.uk
Members: 500
Contact: Christopher J. Dean, Chm.
Fee: £15
Membership Type: single
Fee: £20
Membership Type: family (rest of the world)
Description: Detective fiction enthusiasts, and students of religious philosophy; those interested in medieval French and Italian literature. Promotes the study of the life and works of Dorothy Leigh Sayers (1893-1957), British dramatist, poet, novelist, essayist, and scholar of medieval French and Italian literature. Encourages the performance of Sayers' plays and the publication of books by and about her. Seeks to preserve original materials. Encourages study and research into Sayers' life and works. Acts as forum and information center on the author; operates speakers' bureau; Sponsors competitions.
Library Subject: Dorothy L. Sayers life and works
Library Type: reference
Publication: Journal
Publication title: Sidelights on Sayers

01893

Dorset Business, The Chamber of Commerce and Industry

Chamber House, Acorn Office Park, Ling Rd., Poole, BH12 4NZ, UK
Tel: 01202 714800
Fax: 01202 747862
Email: contact@dcci.co.uk
Website: http://www.dorsetbusiness.net
Members: 1004
Staff: 10
Contact: Peter Scott, Chief Exec.
Fee: £175
Membership Type: sole trader
Fee: £1740
Membership Type: company (maximum; based on the number of employees)
Description: Promotes business and commerce.
Formerly: Formerly, Dorset Chamber of Commerce and Industry
Publication: Magazine
Publication title: Dorset Business Magazine. Advertisements.

01894

Dorset Horn and Poll Dorset Sheep Breeders Association

Agriculture House, Acland Rd., Dorchester, Dorset, London, DT1 1EF, UK
Tel: 01305 262126
Fax: 01305 262126
Email: mail@dorsetsheep.org
Website: http://www.dorsetsheep.org
Contact: Phillip Baker, Pres.
Description: Encourages Dorset Horn sheep breeding in the UK and abroad. Maintains the purity of sheep breeding.

01895

Dorset Natural History and Archaeological Society

Dorset County Museum, High West St., Dorchester, DT1 1XA, UK
Tel: 01305 262735
Email: enquiries@dorsetcountymuseum.co.uk
Website: http://80.68.95.48/~dcmresearch/index.html
Fee: £32
Membership Type: full
Fee: £43
Membership Type: joint
Description: Works to preserve and promote history. Ensures the highest-quality expressions of state and local history in publications, exhibitions, and public programs through diverse services.

01896

Down Syndrome Association DSA

Langdon Down Centre, 2a Langdon Park, Teddington, TW11 9PS, UK
Tel: 0845 2300372
Fax: 0845 2300373
Email: info@downs-syndrome.org.uk
Website: http://www.downs-syndrome.org.uk
Members: 20000
Contact: Carol Boys, Chief Exec.
Membership Type: parent/caregiver
Fee: £30
Membership Type: overseas parent/caregiver
Description: Provides information, advice, and support in England, Wales, and Northern Ireland on Down's Syndrome. Does this through its information service and helpline, regional offices, and parent-led local branches. Works toward creating the conditions whereby individuals with Down's Syndrome can receive necessary medical, educational, social, and financial support to develop to their full potential.
Publication: Newsletter
Meetings/Conventions: annual conference

01897

Drama Association of Wales DAW

The Old Library, Singleton Rd., Splott, Cardiff, CF24 2ET, UK
Tel: 029 20452200
Fax: 029 20452277
Email: aled.daw@virgin.net
Website: http://www.dramawales.org.uk
Contact: Aled-Rhys Jones, Dir.
Fee: £20
Membership Type: individual
Fee: £20-22
Membership Type: group, corporate
Description: Provides information and networking services to the whole range of participatory drama. Offers wide range of services to Community Drama. Provides help and advice on current legislative policy governing good practice within the voluntary arts.
Publication: Magazine
Publication title: Dawn

01898

Draught Proofing Advisory Association DPAA

PO Box 12, Haslemere, GU27 3AH, UK
Tel: 01428 654011
Fax: 01428 651401
Email: dpaaassociation@aol.com
Website: http://www.dpaa-association.org.uk
Staff: 6
Description: Manufacturers, contractors. Aims to promote the advantages of fitting high quality draught excluders, together with their good installation, and as original equipment by window and door manufacturers. Adopts a Code of Professional Practice, by which all members agree to abide. Furthers good technical and ethical practice, particularly in relation to the selling and installing of draught proofing products.
Publication: Pamphlet

01899

Drilling and Sawing Association DSA

Unit 3, Brand St., Nottingham, NG2 3GW, UK
Tel: 0115 9867029
Fax: 0115 9850341
Email: dsa@drillandsaw.org.uk
Website: http://www.drillandsaw.org.uk
Members: 110
Description: Specialist contractors for the drilling, sawing and cutting of concrete and other construction materials using diamond cutting equipment. Also suppliers and distributors of the specialized machines and accessories. Aims to provide skilled experienced operatives on a contract basis and to raise standards of work through training and safety awareness, together with the provision of the appropriate specialist equipment.
Publication: Journal
Publication title: Concrete Cutter

01900

Driving Instructors Association DIA

Safety House, Beddington Farm Rd., Croydon, CR0 4XZ, UK
Tel: 0208 6655151
Fax: 0208 6655565
Email: dia@driving.org
Website: http://www.driving.org
Members: 10118
Staff: 11
Fee: £18.15
Membership Type: regular
Fee: £71.6
Membership Type: regular
Description: Aims to raise the standard of road user education, to create an increased awareness of road safety matters and to encourage and promote the interests and welfare of those engaged in professional driver training.
Publication: Newspaper
Publication title: Driving Instructor. Advertisements.

01901

DrugScope

Prince Consort House, Ste. 204, 109/111 Farringdon Rd., London, EC1R 3BW, UK
Tel: 020 75207550
Fax: 020 75207555
Email: info@drugscope.org.uk
Website: http://www.drugscope.org.uk
Members: 800
Staff: 20
Contact: Martin Barnes, Chief Exec.
Fee: £150
Membership Type: statutory/private sector organization
Fee: £90
Membership Type: voluntary group (with annual income above 250,000)
Description: Independent centre of expertise on drugs. Strives to inform policy development and reduce drug-related risk. Provides quality drug information. Conducts research at local, national, and international levels.
Formerly: Formed by Merger of, Institute for the Study of Drug Dependence
Publication: Magazine
Publication title: Druglink

01902

Dry Stone Walling Association of Great Britain DSWA

Westmorland County Showground, Lane Farm, Crooklands, Cumbria, Milnthorpe, LA7 7NH, UK
Tel: 01539 567953
Email: information@dswa.org.uk
Website: http://www.dswa.org.uk
Members: 1200
Staff: 1
Contact: Chris Stephens, Contact
Fee: £24
Membership Type: open
Fee: £60
Membership Type: professional
Description: Professional wallers, part-time wallers, amateur wallers and many others who wish to support the association. Seeks to ensure the best craftsmanship of the past is preserved and the craft has a thriving future.
Library Subject: dry stone walling
Library Type: by appointment only
Publication: Book
Publication title: Better Dry Stone Walling

Dualchas Nadair na h-Alba

see Scottish Natural Heritage

01903

Durrell Wildlife Conservation Trust

Les Augres Manor, La Profonde Rue, Trinity, Jersey, JE3 5BP, UK
Tel: 01534 860000
Fax: 01534 860001
Email: info@durrell.org
Website: http://www.durrell.org
Members: 12500
Staff: 75
Contact: Paul Masterton, CEO
Fee: £45
Membership Type: individual
Fee: £75
Membership Type: guest, joint
Description: Operates Species Recovery Programmes worldwide from Jersey to save acutely endangered species. Operates the International Training Centre for the Captive Breeding and Conservation of Endangered Species certificate and diploma levels. Offers summer school for the management of endangered species and the methods and goals of captive breeding.
Formerly: Formerly, Jersey Wildlife Preservation Trust
Publication: Bulletin
Publication title: Dodo Dispatch

01904

Dyfed Welsh Pony and Cob Association

6 Chalybeate St., Aberystwyth, Ceredigion, UK
Tel: 01970 617501
Fax: 01970 625401
Email: info@wpcs.uk.com
Website: http://www.wpcs.uk.com/society/areas.html
Contact: J. Pearce, Contact
Description: Records the breeding details of Welsh ponies and cobs. Seeks to improve the breed and promote its excellence.

01905

Dyslexia Action

Park House, Wick Rd., Surrey, Egham, TW20 0HH, UK
Tel: 01784 222300
Fax: 01784 222333
Email: info@dyslexiaaction.org.uk
Website: http://www.dyslexiaaction.org.uk
Staff: 300
Contact: Shirley Cramer, Chief Exec.
Description: Provides services and support for people with dyslexia and literacy difficulties. Specializes in assessment, teaching and training. Develops and distributes teaching materials and undertake research.
Formerly: Formerly, Dyslexia Institute
Publication: Newsletter
Publication title: As We See It

01906

Dyspraxia Foundation County Durham DFCD

PO Box 315, Durham, DH1 2GP, UK
Fax: 0191 3845858
Email: dfcd@btinternet.com
Website: http://www.durhamdyspraxia.org.uk
Contact: Tina Wilson, Coor.
Description: Supports families of children with Dyspraxia.
Publication: Newsletter
Publication title: Jumpstart
Meetings/Conventions: Jumpstart Kidz Club – monthly meeting

01907

Dystonia Society

89 Albert Embankment, Vauxhall, London, SE1 7TP, UK
Tel: 0845 4586211
Fax: 0845 4586311
Email: info@dystonia.org.uk
Website: http://www.dystonia.org.uk
Contact: Philip Eckstein, CEO
Fee: £12
Membership Type: individual
Fee: £18
Membership Type: family, professional
Description: Provides support to people affected by dystonia. Raises awareness of dystonia through education and research.
Publication: Video
Publication title: The Dystonia Society 1997 Conference

01908

Dystrophic Epidermolysis Bullosa Research Association - Europe DEBRA-Europe

Debra House, 13 Wellington Business Park, Dukes Ride, Berkshire, Crowthorne, RG45 6LS, UK
Tel: 01344 771961
Fax: 01344 762661
Email: debra@debra.org.uk
Website: http://www.debra.org.uk
Contact: Philip Evans, Chm.
Description: Provides financial support for medical research on Epidermolysis Bullosa (EB). Provides counseling and guidance on current legislation and governmental services available to EB families. Raises awareness of issues surrounding EB to the general public, healthcare professionals, schools, and other interested parties.

01909

E.F. Benson Society
EFBS

The Old Coach House, High St., Rye, TN31 7JF, UK
Tel: 01797 223114
Email: info@efbensonsociety.org
Website: http://www.efbensonsociety.org
Members: 200
Contact: Allan Downend, Sec.
Fee: £12
Membership Type: in United Kingdom, Europe
Fee: £20
Membership Type: overseas
Description: Individuals with an interest in the English novelist Edward Frederic Benson (1867-1940). Aims to further knowledge and appreciation of Benson and the Benson Family. Visits places of Benson interest and holds Benson exhibitions and talks.
Publication: Booklet
Publication title: Bensoniana. Advertisements.
Meetings/Conventions: Literary Evening – annual lecture

01910

Early English Text Society
EETS

c/o Prof. Vincent Gillespie, Exec. Sec.
Lady Margaret Hall, Oxford, OX2 6QA, UK
Email: vincent.gillespie@ell.ox.ac.uk
Website: http://www.eets.org.uk
Members: 871
Contact: Anne Hudson, Dir.
Fee: £20
Membership Type: individual/institution in UK
Fee: £40
Membership Type: individual/institution in Canada
Description: University teachers and other scholars; university and public libraries in 28 countries.

01911

Early Years - The Organisation for Young Children

6c Wildflower Way, Apollo Rd., Boucher Rd., Belfast, UK
Tel: 028 90662825
Fax: 028 90381270
Website: http://www.nippa.org
Members: 1000
Staff: 70
Contact: Siobhan Fitzpatrick, Chief Exec.
Fee: £67
Membership Type: organization
Fee: £22
Membership Type: individual
Description: Promotes the availability of childcare facilities for women with children under 5 years of age. Fosters children's educational and physical development.
Formerly: Formerly, Northern Ireland Pre-School Playgroups Association

01912

Earth Science Teachers' Association
ESTA

c/o Ros Todhunter, Sec.
81A Birches Ln., Northwich, CW9 7SN, UK
Tel: 001606 47539
Email: rostodhunter@aol.com
Website: http://www.esta-uk.org
Members: 800
Contact: Niki Witburn, Chair
Description: Teachers of earth sciences at all levels. Encourages and supports the teaching of earth sciences whether as a single subject such as geology, or as part of science or geography courses.

01913

Earth, Sea and Sky
ESS

PO Box 1063, Saxilby, Lincoln, LN1 2TN, UK
Tel: 0871 7115065
Email: yannis@earthseasky.org
Website: http://www.earthseasky.org
Contact: Yannis Vardakastanis, Founder/Dir.
Fee: £30
Membership Type: individual
Fee: £35
Membership Type: family
Description: Protects the endangered species of the Greek Ionian Islands. Provides material and financial support for educational, research and volunteer projects. Protects the nesting beaches of the loggerhead turtle and the natural habitats of all wildlife contained within the National Parks of Zakynthos.

01914

East Anglian Traditional Music Trust
EATMT

The Old Stables, Museum of East Anglian Life, Crowe St., Stowmarket, IP14 1DL, UK
Tel: 01449 771090
Email: info@eatmt.fsnet.co.uk
Website: http://www.eatmt.org.uk
Contact: Katie Howson, Artistic Dir./Gen. Mgr.
Description: Promotes the traditional music of the eastern region of England.

01915

East Midlands Campaign for Nuclear Disarmament

43 Cobden Rd., Chesterfield, S40 4TD, UK
Tel: 0124 6235723
Email: mathews@greenbee.net
Website: http://www.cnduk.org
Description: Aims to eliminate British nuclear weapons and other weapons of mass destruction.

01916

East Midlands Welsh Pony and Cob Association
EMWPCA

42 Hardwick Village, Clumber Park, Nottinghamshire, Worksop, S80 3PD, UK
Tel: 01909 485374
Email: emwpca@talktalk.net
Website: http://www.eastmidlandswpca.com
Contact: Jenny Chappell, Contact
Fee: £1.5
Membership Type: regular, junior (armband)
Fee: £1
Membership Type: junior (in conjunction with adult)
Description: Records the breeding details of Welsh ponies and cobs. Seeks to improve the breed and promote its excellence.
Publication: Newsletter

01917

Eastern Africa Association
EAA

2 Vincent St., London, SW1P 4LD, UK
Tel: 020 78285511
Fax: 020 78285251
Email: jcsmall@eaa-lon.co.uk
Website: http://www.eaa-lon.co.uk
Members: 300
Staff: 4
Contact: John C. Small, Chief Exec.
Description: Represents the interests of companies from Belgium, Denmark, France, Germany, Monaco, Netherlands, South Africa, Switzerland, Sweden, Hong Kong, the United Kingdom, and the United States with business interests in Eritrea, Ethiopia, Kenya, Madagascar, Mauritius, Seychelles, Tanzania and Uganda. Encourages foreign participation in the economic development of Eastern Africa. Works for the mutual benefit of Eastern African countries and foreign investors. Represents members' interests before governments; maintains a network of contacts; disseminates information.
Formerly: Formerly, The East African Association

01918

Eastern Welsh Pony and Cob Association

c/o Richard Eastwood, Sec.
Rosehill Farm, Downham Common, Little Downham, Cambridgeshire, Ely, CB6 2TY, UK
Tel: 01353 699112
Email: rwe99@hotmail.com
Website: http://www.ewpca.com
Contact: John Wilkinson, Pres.
Fee: £8
Membership Type: adult
Fee: £6
Membership Type: junior
Description: Records the breeding details of Welsh ponies and cobs. Seeks to improve the breed and promote its excellence.

01919

Economic and Social Research Council
ESRC

Polaris House, N Star Ave., Swindon, SN2 1UJ, UK
Tel: 01793 413000
Fax: 01793 413001
Email: sylvia.wratten@esrc.ac.uk
Website: http://www.esrcsocietytoday.ac.uk/ESRCInfoCentre/index.aspx
Contact: Sylvia Wratten, Exec. Office Mgr.
Description: Social science researchers. Conducts economic, social, demographic, and environmental studies. Focuses on current social and demographic trends in England and Scotland. Provides advisory services on data use. Offers courses and visiting fellowship program for researchers.
Publication: Bulletin
Publication title: Data Archive Bulletin

01920
Economic History Society
EHS
University of Glasgow, Department of Economic and Social History, Lilybank House, Bute Gardens, Glasgow, G12 8RT, UK
Tel: 0141 3304662
Fax: 0141 3304889
Email: ehsocsec@arts.gla.ac.uk
Website: http://www.ehs.org.uk
Members: 1300
Contact: Maureen Galbraith, Admin. Sec.
Fee: £21
Membership Type: ordinary, in Europe and rest of the world
Fee: £10.5
Membership Type: student in Europe and rest of the world
Description: Economic historians. Concerned with the promotion of study and publication in economic and social history.
Publication: Journal
Publication title: The Economic History Review. Advertisements.

01921
Economic Research Council
ERC
55 Tufton St., London, SW1P 3QL, UK
Tel: 020 73406016
Email: info@ercouncil.org
Website: http://www.ercouncil.org
Members: 300
Staff: 1
Contact: Damon de Laszlo, Chm.
Fee: £35
Membership Type: individual
Fee: £20
Membership Type: associate
Description: Economists, business executives, interested individuals. Promotes understanding of economics, particularly monetary practice. Encourages research and discussion among members; stimulates public interest in economic affairs; publicizes pertinent research findings. Maintains speakers' bureau.
Publication: Journal
Publication title: Britain & Overseas

01922
Economics and Business Education Association
EBEA
The Forum, 277 London Rd., W Sussex, Burgess Hill, RH15 9QU, UK
Tel: 01444 240150
Fax: 01444 240101
Email: office@ebea.org.uk
Website: http://www.ebea.org.uk/home
Members: 2500
Staff: 2
Contact: Claire Johnson, Admin.
Fee: £25
Membership Type: beginner teacher
Fee: £56
Membership Type: full
Description: Teachers of economics, business studies and related subjects in schools and colleges. Represents teachers of economics, business studies and related subjects in schools and colleges throughout the UK and provides its members with the professional support they need in the classroom. Aims to encourage and promote the teaching and study of economics and related subjects within a broadly based curriculum.
Publication: Magazine
Publication title: Teaching Business and Economics. Advertisements.

01923
Edexcel International
190 High Holborn, London, WC1V 7BH, UK
Tel: 01204 770696
Website: http://www.edexcel.com/Pages/home.aspx
Members: 800
Staff: 600
Contact: Jerry Jarvis, Managing Dir.
Description: Approves academic and work-related programmes of study including GNVQs, NVQs and GCSEs, A levels and A/S levels throughout England, Wales and Northern Ireland, and overseas and awards qualifications to students who successfully complete these and HND programmes.
Formerly: Formerly, University of London Examinations and Assessment Council

01924
Edinburgh Architectural Association
EAA
15 Rutland Sq., Edinburgh, EH1 2BE, UK
Tel: 0131 2297545
Fax: 0131 2282188
Email: mail@eaa.org.uk
Website: http://www.eaa.org.uk
Contact: Kenneth Ralston, Pres.
Description: Promotes the interests of members.

01925
Edinburgh Bibliographical Society
EBS
c/o Prof. David Finkelstein, Treas.
Queen Margaret University, School of Arts and Social Sciences, Edinburgh, EH21 6UU, UK
Email: i.mcgowan@btinternet.com
Website: http://mcs.qmuc.ac.uk/EBS
Contact: Ian McGowan, Pres.
Fee: £15
Membership Type: individual
Fee: £10
Membership Type: student
Description: Focuses on the bibliography of and in Scotland including the book trade, the history of libraries, scholarship and book collecting.

01926
Edinburgh Chamber of Commerce
Capital House, 2 Festival Sq., Edinburgh, EH3 9SU, UK
Tel: 0131 2212999
Fax: 0131 2211998
Website: http://www.edinburghchamber.co.uk
Members: 2000
Staff: 60
Contact: Ron Hewitt, Chief Exec.
Description: Promotes business and commerce.
Publication: Magazine
Publication title: Business Comment

01927
Edinburgh Geological Society
EGS
85 Grange Loan, Edinburgh, EH9 2ED, UK
Tel: 0131 6675429
Email: membership@edinburghgeolsoc.org
Website: http://www.edinburghgeolsoc.org
Contact: Christine L. Thompson, Membership Sec.
Fee: £20
Membership Type: ordinary fellow
Fee: £30
Membership Type: family fellow
Description: Stimulates public interests in geology and the advancement of geological knowledge.
Publication: Magazine
Publication title: The Edinburgh Geologist

01928
Edinburgh Mathematical Society
EMS
James Clerk Maxwell Bldg., Mayfield Rd., Edinburgh, EH9 3JZ, UK
Email: eedmathsoc@ed.ac.uk
Website: http://www.ems.ac.uk/wiki/tiki-index.php
Contact: Penny Davies, Pres.
Fee: £20
Membership Type: regular
Fee: £10
Membership Type: reciprocal
Description: Mathematicians employed by Scottish universities. Promotes "the mutual improvement of its members in the mathematical sciences, pure and applied". Facilitates cooperation and exchange of information among members; conducts research and educational programs. Provides support and assistance to schools offering mathematics courses and mathematics education programs operating in developing countries.
Library Subject: mathematics
Library Type: reference
Publication: Newsletter
Publication title: President's Newsletter

01929
Educational Development Association
EDA
PO Box 407, Keighley, BD20 5WN, UK
Fax: 01535 606032
Email: edasummerschool@aol.com
Website: http://www.edasummerschool.org.uk
Contact: Dave Shevill, Gen. Sec.
Description: Teachers who are members of various regional Branches of the EDA. Teachers' association for in-service training and provider of summer schools for teachers.

01930
Educational Institute of Scotland
EIS
46 Moray Pl., Edinburgh, EH3 6BH, UK
Tel: 0131 2256244
Fax: 0131 2203151
Email: enquiries@eis.org.uk
Website: http://www.eis.org.uk
Members: 59000
Contact: Helen Connor, Pres.

Description: Represents teachers and lecturers in nursery, primary, secondary, further and higher education in Scotland. Promotes sound learning and the interests and welfare of teachers and lecturers throughout Scotland. Disseminates information to members.
Publication: Magazine
Publication title: The Scottish Educational Journal. Advertisements.

01931

Educational Publishers Council EPC

The Publishers Association
29B Montague St., London, WC1B 5BW, UK
Tel: 020 76919191
Fax: 020 76919199
Email: nswann@publishers.org.uk
Website: http://www.publishers.org.uk/en/educational
Members: 50
Staff: 2
Contact: Graham Taylor, Dir.
Description: Members publish school books. Covers the following areas of activity on behalf of educational publishers: representation to Government; supply and market services; exhibitions and promotion; subject panels; copyright/licensing; information/statistical services.
Publication: Newsletter
Publication title: EPC Brief

01932

EEMA

PO Box 707, Worcester, WR7 4WP, UK
Tel: 01386 793028
Fax: 01386 792733
Email: roger.dean@eema.org
Website: http://www.eema.org
Members: 250
Staff: 12
Contact: Roger Dean, Exec. Dir.
Fee: £1500-4500
Membership Type: vendor or service supplier
Fee: £150-2100
Membership Type: user company/association/academic institution/government
Description: Promotes electronic business across Europe.
Library Subject: electronic business
Library Type: not open to the public
Formerly: Formerly, European Forum for Advanced Business Communication
Publication: Magazine
Publication title: EEMA Briefing. Advertisements.
Meetings/Conventions: Electronic Commerce Europe – conference – Exhibits.

01933

EFNARC EFNARC

Cobblers Cottage, Chester Rd, Daresbury, Warrington, WA4 4AJ, UK
Tel: 01925 740581
Fax: 01925 740581
Email: secretary@efnarc.org
Website: http://www.efnarc.org
Contact: Roland Harbron, Sec.
Description: European specialist contractors and materials suppliers, dealing with the repair and strengthening of all types of buildings and civil engineering structures. Acts as the technical, scientific and practical link between specialist contractors and material suppliers and the European construction repair and maintenance industry.
Formerly: Formerly, European Federation of National Associations Representing producers and applicators of specialist building products for Concrete

01934

Egypt Exploration Society EES

3 Doughty Mews, London, WC1N 2PG, UK
Tel: 0207 2421880
Fax: 0207 4046118
Email: contact@ees.ac.uk
Website: http://www.ees.ac.uk
Contact: Julian Horn-Smith, Pres.
Fee: £45
Membership Type: full
Fee: £60
Membership Type: joint
Description: Egyptologists and interested others organized to survey, explore, and excavate at archaeological sites in Egypt. Promotes the study of the history, religion, and culture of ancient Egypt. Makes records of the monuments of Egypt and the Sudan. Graeco-Roman Branch publishes Greek and Latin papyri of the Ptolemaic and Roman periods.
Library Subject: Egyptology
Library Type: reference
Formerly: Formerly, Egypt Exploration Fund
Publication: Bulletin
Publication title: Egyptian Archaeology. Advertisements.
Meetings/Conventions: British Egyptology – annual congress

01935

Electoral Reform Society ERS

6 Chancel St., London, SE1 0UU, UK
Tel: 020 79281622
Fax: 020 74017789
Email: ers@electoral-reform.org.uk
Website: http://www.electoral-reform.org.uk
Members: 2200
Staff: 15
Contact: Sam Younger, Interim Chief Exec.
Membership Type: regular
Fee: £5
Membership Type: underwaged
Description: Campaigns for the strengthening of democracy among members through changes to the voting system and electoral arrangements.
Publication: Bulletin
Publication title: Parliamentary Bulletin

01936

Electric Railway Society ERS

17 Catherine Dr., Sutton Coldfield, B73 6AX, UK
Email: iwfrew@tiscali.co.uk
Website: http://www.electric-rly-society.org.uk
Members: 370
Contact: Iain D.O. Frew, Contact
Fee: £15
Membership Type: UK resident
Description: Professionals in rail industry and enthusiasts in 14 countries interested in researching electric railways, traction motor design, and related equipment such as ticket machinery. Members visit electric railway installations.
Publication: Journal
Publication title: The Electric Railway. Advertisements.

01937

Electrical Contractors Association ECA

c/o ESCA House
34 Palace Ct., London, W2 4HY, UK
Tel: 020 73134800
Fax: 020 72217344
Email: info@eca.co.uk
Website: http://www.eca.co.uk
Members: 2000
Staff: 100
Contact: David Pollock, CEO
Description: Represents electrical engineering and building services installation companies in New England, Wales, and Northern Ireland.
Formerly: Formerly, Electrical Contractors Association - England
Publication title: Electrical Contractor

01938

Electrical Insulation Association EIA

PO Box 2462, Stafford, ST16 9AE, UK
Tel: 01785 661306
Email: jcgwheeler@tiscali.co.uk
Website: http://eiauk.org
Members: 17
Staff: 1
Contact: Jeremy C.G. Wheeler, Sec.
Description: Promotes the electrical insulation industry.
Publication: Proceedings
Publication title: INSUCON. Advertisements.

01939

Embroiderers' Guild

Hampton Ct. Palace, Apt. 41, Surrey, East Molesey, KT8 9AU, UK
Tel: 0208 9431229
Fax: 0208 9779882
Email: administrator@embroiderersguild.com
Website: http://www.embroiderersguild.com
Members: 25000
Staff: 18
Contact: Jane Sweet, Dir.
Fee: £10
Membership Type: young embroider 5-17
Fee: £8
Membership Type: additional family
Description: Aims to promote the art and craft of embroidery to highest standard, through workshops, lectures, conferences and exhibitions. Maintains Embroiderers' Development Scheme to help people with a high level of commitment to develop their skills at a professional and nationally recognized level.
Publication: Newsletter
Publication title: Contact

01940
Emergency Planning Society
EPS
The Media Ctre., Culverhouse Cross, Cardiff, CF5 6XJ, UK
Tel: 0845 6009587
Fax: 029 20590397
Email: opsman@the-eps.org
Website: http://www.the-eps.org
Members: 1435
Contact: Marc Beveridge, Chm.
Fee: £115
Membership Type: regular, associate, fellow (by direct debit)
Fee: £47
Membership Type: retired (by direct debit)
Description: Any person who is involved in a professional, managerial or operational capacity in emergency planning or management. Aims to promote effective emergency planning and management in the UK and to promote the professional interests of its members. Provides a forum for the study of the most effective means of planning and managing local emergency preparation and response, and disseminating good practice.

01941
EMILY'S List
11 Well House Rd., West Yorkshire, Leeds, LS8 4BS, UK
Email: contact@emilyslist.org.uk
Website: http://www.emilyslist.org.uk
Members: 600
Contact: Barbara Follett, Founder/Dir.
Description: Women members of the Labour Party. Conducts research and fundraising activities. Disseminates information.

01942
Employers Forum on Age
EFA
Fl. 3, Downstream, 1 London Bridge, London, SE1 9BG, UK
Tel: 0845 4562495
Fax: 020 77856536
Email: efa@efa.org.uk
Website: http://www.efa.org.uk
Members: 180
Staff: 4
Contact: Hamish Elvidge, Chair
Fee: £2000
Membership Type: corporate
Description: Supports member organizations in managing the skills and age mix of their workforces to obtain maximum business; removes barriers to achieving an age-balanced workforce by influencing key decision-makers, notably in government, education, training, recruitment, and the trade union movements; and informs all employers of the benefits of a mixed-age workforce.
Library Subject: age at work
Library Type: not open to the public
Publication: Report
Publication title: Attitude Not Age

01943
ENABLE Scotland
146 Argyle St., 2nd Fl., Glasgow, G2 8BL, UK
Tel: 0141 2264541
Fax: 0141 2044398
Email: enable@enable.org.uk
Website: http://www.enable.org.uk
Members: 4000
Staff: 1300
Contact: Mike Holmes, Dir.
Fee: £5
Membership Type: unwaged
Fee: £15
Membership Type: individual
Description: Campaigns for better rights and services for individuals with learning disabilities and their families in Scotland. Provides national information service, legal service and local advocacy projects. Offers jobs, training, respite and short breaks, day services, supported living for individuals with learning disabilities in different regions of Scotland.
Formerly: Formerly, Scottish Association for Parents of Handicapped Children
Publication: Newsletter
Publication title: Newslink. Advertisements.

01944
End Child Prostitution, Child Pornography and the Trafficking of Children for Sexual Purposes - UK
ECPAT UK
Grosvenor Gardens House, 35 - 37 Grosvenor Gardens, London, SW1W 0BS, UK
Tel: 020 723398087
Fax: 020 72339869
Email: info@ecpat.org.uk
Website: http://www.ecpat.org.uk
Members: 9
Staff: 3
Contact: Christine Beddoe, Dir.
Description: Individuals and organizations. Seeks to eradicate the commercial sexual exploitation of children worldwide, and to end "child sex tourism." Coordinates activities of British organizations working to end child prostitution; conducts educational programs to raise public awareness of sexual tourism; lobbies government agencies to insure British compliance with Article 34 of the United Nations Convention on the Rights of the Child. Works with governments worldwide to improve enforcement of laws banning the sexual exploitation of children. Campaigns on the issue of child trafficking for sexual purposes.
Publication: Report
Publication title: Cause for Concern: London Social Services and Child Trafficking. Advertisements.

01945
Endometriosis UK
50 Westminster Palace Gardens, Artillery Row, London, SW1P 1RR, UK
Tel: 020 72222781
Fax: 020 72222786
Email: enquiries@endometriosis-uk.org
Website: http://www.endometriosis-uk.org
Members: 1800
Staff: 5
Contact: Jeremy Payne, CEO
Fee: £20
Membership Type: UK resident
Fee: £35
Membership Type: health professional
Description: Supports women living with endometriosis. Provides services that enable those with endometriosis to understand their disease and to take control of their condition. Raises awareness of endometriosis, and the issues which affect people living with it, among healthcare professionals, people with endometriosis and their families and colleagues, the public and the media. Provides high quality information for people about endometriosis through events, leaflets, publications and on the internet.
Publication: Newsletter
Publication title: Endolink

01946
Energy Industries Council
EIC
89 Albert Embankment, London, SE1 7TP, UK
Tel: 020 70918600
Fax: 020 70918601
Email: info@the-eic.com
Website: http://www.the-eic.com
Members: 500
Contact: Mike Major, CEO
Description: Supplies capital goods and services to the energy industries worldwide. Supports its members and subscribers' efforts to market their products both at home and overseas. Organizes trade missions and attendance at major exhibitions, where members can meet and talk to influential figures from the major contractors, operators, and other end users.
Meetings/Conventions: annual dinner

01947
Energy Institute
EI
61 New Cavendish St., London, W1G 7AR, UK
Tel: 020 74677100
Fax: 020 72551472
Email: info@energyinst.org
Website: http://www.energyinst.org
Contact: Louise Kingham, Chief Exec.
Fee: £88
Membership Type: affiliate
Fee: £49
Membership Type: graduate
Description: Brings together individuals and organizations across the energy sectors of industry, academia, and government. Promotes topics about upstream and downstream oil, gas and other primary fuels and renewables, through power generation, transmission and distribution, to sustainable development, demand side management and energy efficiency. Holds conferences and courses. Maintains extensive library and information service.
Library Subject: oil, energy industry
Library Type: reference
Formerly: Formerly, Institute of Petroleum
Publication: Journal
Publication title: Energy World. Advertisements.
Meetings/Conventions: annual conference

01948
Energy Systems Trade Association
ESTA
PO Box 77, Benfleet, SS7 5EX, UK
Tel: 01268 569010
Fax: 01268 569737
Email: info@esta.org.uk
Website: http://www.esta.org.uk
Members: 110
Staff: 4
Contact: Alan Aldridge, Exec. Dir.
Description: Companies offering energy efficiency goods and services for industrial and commercial application. Aims to encourage good practice by the suppliers of

energy efficiency goods and services to the industrial, commercial and public sectors. Promotes awareness of the financial and environmental benefits of good energy management practice, and organizes up to 20 national and regional conferences for energy users.
Publication: Yearbook
Publication title: Energy Efficiency Yearbook
Meetings/Conventions: Meeting the Energy Challenge – annual seminar – Exhibits.

01949
Enforcement Services Association
ESA
Park House, 10 Park St., Bristol, BS1 5HX, UK
Tel: 0117 9074771
Fax: 0117 9154521
Email: enquiries@ensas.org.uk
Website: http://www.ensas.org.uk
Members: 106
Staff: 1
Contact: Simon Jacobs, Pres.
Description: Certificated bailiffs and enforcement agents in England and Wales. Promotes increased professionalism among the profession; represents members' interests. Encourages development of civil law enforcement; conducts certification examinations.
Formerly: Formerly, Certificated Bailiffs' Association
Publication: Newsletter
Publication title: Info. Advertisements.

01950
Engender
1a Haddington Pl., Edinburgh, EH7 4AE, UK
Tel: 0131 5589596
Email: info@engender.org.uk
Website: http://www.engender.org.uk
Members: 300
Staff: 3
Contact: Niki Kandirikirira, Exec. Dir.
Fee: £2
Membership Type: individual (waged)
Fee: £24
Membership Type: individual (low/unwaged)
Description: An information, research and networking organisation for women in Scotland. Works with other groups locally and internationally to improve women's lives and increase women's power and influence. Provides political skills training courses for women's groups so they can lobby and campaign more effectively.
Formerly: Formerly, The Scottish Women's Foundation
Publication: Annual Report

01951
Engineering and Physical Sciences Research Council
EPSRC
Polaris House, N Star Ave., Swindon, SN2 1ET, UK
Tel: 01793 444100
Email: infoline@epsrc.ac.uk
Website: http://www.epsrc.ac.uk/default.htm
Staff: 300
Contact: David Delpy, Chief Exec.
Description: Promotes and supports high quality basic, strategic and applied research and related postgraduate training in engineering and physical sciences. Advances knowledge and technology. Provides trained scientists and engineers, which meet the needs of users and beneficiaries thereby contributing to the economic competitiveness of UK and the quality of life.
Publication: Newsletter
Publication title: Connect

01952
Engineering Construction Industry Association
ECIA
Broadway House, 5th Fl., Tothill St., London, SW1H 9NS, UK
Tel: 020 77992000
Fax: 020 72331930
Email: ecia@ecia.co.uk
Website: http://www.ecia.co.uk/pages/index.cfm
Members: 300
Staff: 15
Contact: Michael Hockey, Managing Dir.
Fee: £2775
Membership Type: general
Fee: £10875
Membership Type: contractor, employment business
Description: Engineering construction firms. Represents the interests of member firms, with government departments, the NJC, the Training Board and other outside bodies. Provides services to members of advice, information and direct assistance on industrial relations, health and safety, training and commercial and economic matters.

01953
Engineering Council UK
ECUK
246 High Holborn, London, WC1V 7EX, UK
Tel: 020 32060500
Fax: 020 32060501
Email: aramsay@engc.org.uk
Website: http://www.engc.org.uk
Staff: 23
Contact: Kel Fidler, Chm.
Description: Regulates the UK's engineering profession, setting and maintaining standards of competence and ethics for engineers, technologist and technicians. Operates through 35 engineering institutions, which are licensed to assess members for inclusion on the UCUK Register of Engineers. Represents the interests of UK engineers abroad.
Publication: Newsletters
Publication title: Register News

01954
Engineering Employers' Federation
EEF
Broadway House, Tothill St., London, SW1H 9NQ, UK
Tel: 020 72227777
Fax: 020 72222782
Email: enquiries@eef-fed.org.uk
Website: http://www.eef.org.uk
Members: 6000
Staff: 55
Contact: Martin Temple, Dir. Gen.
Description: Members include manufacturing, engineering and technology-based companies. Represents the interests of manufacturing companies at all levels of government. Working through a strong network of regional associations. Provides support and services to its member companies through HR and legal; health and safety; environmental services; training and development; policy and representation; and information and research.
Publication title: EEF Annual Review

01955
Engineering Equipment and Materials Users Association
EEMUA
10-12 Lovat Ln., London, EC3R 8DN, UK
Tel: 020 76210011
Fax: 020 76210022
Email: info@eemua.org
Website: http://www.eemua.org
Members: 26
Staff: 6
Contact: Clive Tayler, Exec. Dir.
Description: Represents companies that own or operate industrial facilities. Aims to improve the safety, environmental and operating performance of industrial facilities. Facilitates sharing of engineering experiences and expertise.
Library Subject: engineering, industrial, asset, management, inspection, maintenance
Library Type: reference

01956
Engineering Industries Association - England
EIA
62 Bayswater Rd., London, W2 3PS, UK
Tel: 020 72986455
Fax: 020 72986456
Email: head.office@eia.co.uk
Website: http://www.eia.co.uk
Members: 200
Staff: 3
Contact: Ronald Halstead, Pres.
Fee: £125-750
Membership Type: employee (based on number of employees)
Description: Represents the interests and aspirations of the United Kingdom engineering and manufacturing sector; provides advice, government lobbying, and business opportunities through overseas exhibitions and trade leads.
Publication: Directory
Publication title: Engineering Buyers Guide and Directory

01957
Engineering Integrity Society
EIS
18 Oak Close, Bedworth, Warwickshire, CV12 9AJ, UK
Tel: 02476 730126
Fax: 02476 730126
Email: lmansfield@e-i-s.org.uk
Website: http://www.e-i-s.org.uk
Staff: 1
Contact: Peter Watson, Pres.
Fee: £25
Membership Type: personal
Fee: £30
Membership Type: overseas
Description: Stimulates the exchange of ideas and information between engineers and technologists.
Publication: Journal
Publication title: Engineering Integrity. Advertisements.

01958

Engineers' Company

c/o Air Vice Marshal Graham Skinner, RAF, Clerk
Wax Chandlers Hall, 6 Gresham St., London, EC2V 7AD, UK
Tel: 020 77264830
Fax: 020 77264820
Email: clerk@engineerscompany.org.uk
Website: http://www.engineerscompany.org.uk
Members: 310
Contact: John H. Robinson, Master
Description: Aims to afford the means of professional and social intercourse and mutual information among its members.

01959

English Amateur Dancesport Association EADA

4 Winds, Old Potbridge Rd., Winchfield, RG27 8BT, UK
Fax: 01252 843887
Email: membership@eada.org.uk
Website: http://cms.eada.org.uk
Members: 3500
Contact: David Corfield, Pres.
Fee: £12
Membership Type: juvenile
Fee: £15
Membership Type: junior
Description: Amateur Dancesport governing body covering all Amateur competitors in England. Provides training for top Squads, selects couples and teams for international events.

01960

English Association EA

University of Leicester, University Rd., Leicester, LE1 7RH, UK
Tel: 0116 2297622
Fax: 0116 2297618
Email: engassoc@le.ac.uk
Website: http://www.le.ac.uk/engassoc
Members: 3000
Staff: 2
Contact: Helen Lucas, Chief Exec.
Fee: £23
Membership Type: basic
Fee: £116
Membership Type: ordinary
Description: University and public libraries, schools, and individuals in 75 countries. Promotes appreciation and knowledge of English language and literature.
Publication: Journal
Publication title: English. Advertisements.

01961

English Centre of International PEN English PEN

60 Farringdon Rd., London, EC1R 3GA, UK
Tel: 020 73242535
Email: enquiries@englishpen.org
Website: http://www.englishpen.org
Contact: Lisa Appignanesi, Pres.
Fee: £50
Membership Type: in London, overseas
Fee: £45
Membership Type: outside London (by cheque)
Description: Promotes and protects literature, literacy and freedom of expression.

01962

English Folk Dance and Song Society EFDSS

Cecil Sharp House, 2 Regents Park Rd., London, NW1 7AY, UK
Tel: 020 74852206
Fax: 020 72840534
Email: info@efdss.org
Website: http://www.efdss.org
Members: 5500
Staff: 16
Contact: Katy Spicer, Chief Exec.
Fee: £38
Membership Type: individual, joint senior
Fee: £58
Membership Type: joint individual
Description: Individual members, corporate members and affiliated groups, clubs and local societies who share the aims of the society. Aims to preserve and make known English folk dances, songs and music and to encourage their practice by means of classes, demonstrations and festivals. Promotes and encourages collection and research into the development and traditional practice of English folk dances, songs and music.
Publication: Magazine
Publication title: English Dance and Song. Advertisements.

01963

English Place-Name Society/Institute for Name Studies EPNS

c/o School of English Studies
University of Nottingham, Nottingham, NG7 2RD, UK
Tel: 0115 9515919
Fax: 0115 8467526
Email: name-studies@nottingham.ac.uk
Website: http://www.nottingham.ac.uk/english/ins/epns
Members: 650
Staff: 3
Contact: R.A. Coates, Contact
Fee: £35
Membership Type: full
Fee: £12
Membership Type: associate within UK
Description: Carries out the Survey of English Place-Names and undertakes research in the field of name studies.
Publication: Journal
Publication title: EPNS Journal

01964

English Poetry and Song Society EPSS

76 Lower Oldfield Park, Surrey, BA2 3HP, UK
Tel: 01225 313531
Email: menistral@yahoo.co.uk
Website: http://www.musicair.co.uk/english_poetry_and_song.html
Members: 70
Contact: Richard Carder, Chm.
Fee: £12
Membership Type: individual
Fee: £15
Membership Type: international, joint
Description: Composers, singers, pianists and anyone interested. Concerned with the promotion of English art songs, through recordings and publication; concerts and competitions for composers.
Library Type: reference

01965

English UK

219 St. John St., London, EC1V 4LY, UK
Tel: 020 76087960
Fax: 020 76087961
Email: info@englishuk.com
Website: http://www.englishuk.com
Members: 430
Staff: 16
Contact: Tony Millns, Chief Exec.
Fee: £800
Membership Type: full (accredited centre)
Description: Offers a wide range of English language courses, with many specializations and optional extras. Aims to develop professionalism among members and to protect and promote their business and interests.
Formerly: Formerly, Association of Recognised English Language Services
Publication: Bulletin
Publication title: Newsflash

01966

English Westerners Society EWS

130 The Keep, Kingston Upon Thames, KT2 5UE, UK
Email: keg.cagb@btinternet.com
Website: http://www.english-westerners-society.org.uk
Members: 200
Contact: Kevin Galvin, Sec.
Fee: £12.5
Membership Type: UK resident
Fee: £20
Membership Type: associate (overseas)
Description: Publishes research materials on the American West on behalf of its members.
Publication: Journal
Publication title: Tally Sheet. Advertisements.

01967

Entertainment and Leisure Software Publishers Association ELSPA

167 Wardour St., London, W1F 8WL, UK
Tel: 020 75340580
Fax: 020 75340581
Email: info@elspa.com
Website: http://www.elspa.com
Members: 95
Staff: 19
Contact: Michael Rawlinson, Dir. Gen.
Fee: £2500
Membership Type: associate
Fee: £50000
Membership Type: full (based on the turnover)
Description: Aims to protect, promote, and provide for members' interests in the interactive leisure software industry. Collects and disseminates retail sales statistics; undertakes consumer research in respect to computer and video games; operates anti-piracy crime unit; conducts legislative lobbying with UK and EU governments; supports higher education sector to provide relevant courses and industry input.
Meetings/Conventions: Games Summit – annual conference

01968
Entomological Livestock Group
ELG
50 Burns Rd., Dinnington, Sheffield, S25 2LN, UK
Email: pwbelg@clara.co.uk
Website: http://www.pwbelg.clara.net
Members: 600
Contact: Paul W. Batty, Contact
Fee: £17
Membership Type: in UK and Europe
Fee: £21
Membership Type: in U.S., Canada, and rest of the world
Description: Promotes butterfly and insect breeders; works as entomological livestock exchange.

01969
Environment and Development Group
EDG
41 Walton Crescent, Oxford, OX1 2JQ, UK
Tel: 01865 318180
Fax: 01865 318188
Email: admin@edg.org.uk
Website: http://www.edg.org.uk
Staff: 20
Contact: Stephen Cobb, Dir./Founder
Description: Promotes environmental protection and wise use of natural resources worldwide. Works with global corporation, governments and NGOs throughout the developing world, creating practical solutions that meet the social, environmental and economic aspirations of clients.

01970
Environmental Industries Commission
EIC
45 Weymouth St., London, W1G 8ND, UK
Tel: 020 79351675
Fax: 020 74863455
Website: http://www.eic-uk.co.uk
Members: 330
Contact: Adrian Wilkes, Chm.
Description: Provides environmental technology equipment and services suppliers with a strong and effective voice to influence the debate on the future of the industry among policy makers in Westminster, Whitehall and Brussels. Promotes constructive cooperation between the regulated, the regulators and the UK's environmental technology suppliers.

01971
Environmental Protection UK
44 Grand Parade, Brighton, BN2 9QA, UK
Tel: 01273 878770
Fax: 01273 606626
Email: admin@environmental-protection.org.uk
Website: http://www.environmental-protection.org.uk
Members: 800
Staff: 10
Contact: James Grugeon, Chief Exec.
Fee: £2750
Membership Type: corporate (gold)
Fee: £300
Membership Type: individual (gold)
Description: Local authority, industry, academic, and individuals. Secures environmental improvement by promoting clean air through the reduction of air pollution, noise and other contaminants while having due regard for other aspects of the environment. Brings together pollution expertise from industry; local and central government; technical, academic and institutional bodies.
Formerly: Formerly, National Society for Clean Air and Environmental Protection
Publication: Newsletter
Publication title: Briefing

01972
Environmental Services Association
ESA
154 Buckingham Palace Rd., London, SW1W 9TR, UK
Tel: 020 78248882
Fax: 020 78248753
Email: info@esauk.org
Website: http://www.esauk.org
Members: 290
Staff: 14
Contact: Dirk Hazell, Chief Exec.
Description: Represents the waste management and secondary resources industry in the UK.
Publication: Newsletter
Publication title: ESA Briefing

01973
Environmental Transport Association
ETA
68 High St., Surrey, Weybridge, KT13 8RS, UK
Tel: 0845 3891010
Fax: 0845 3891015
Email: eta@eta.co.uk
Website: http://www.eta.co.uk
Members: 20000
Staff: 12
Contact: Yannick Read, Contact
Description: Environmentally aware motorists. Provides roadside rescue and other great services with a real difference. Aims to raise awareness of the impact of excessive car use and to help individuals and organizations to make positive changes in their travel habits. Other services include cycle insurance, cycle rescue, motor insurance, travel insurance and house insurance.
Publication: Magazine
Publication title: Going Green. Advertisements.

Epilepsi Cymru
see Epilepsy Wales

01974
Epilepsy Scotland
48 Govan Rd., Glasgow, G51 1JL, UK
Tel: 0141 4274911
Fax: 0141 4191709
Email: enquiries@epilepsyscotland.org.uk
Website: http://www.epilepsyscotland.org.uk
Members: 600
Staff: 31
Contact: Lesslie Young, Chief Exec.
Fee: £5
Membership Type: unwaged, aged 16-18
Fee: £10
Membership Type: individual
Description: Works to enable people with epilepsy to maximize their choices in life. Lobbies for better services to meet local needs and campaigns against the stigma of epilepsy by raising public awareness.
Library Subject: epilepsy
Library Type: reference
Formerly: Formerly, Epilepsy Association of Scotland
Publication: Newsletter
Publication title: Epilepsy News. Advertisements.

01975
Epilepsy Wales
PO Box 4168, Cardiff, CF14 0WZ, UK
Fax: 029 20755515
Email: admin@epilepsy-wales.co.uk
Website: http://www.epilepsy-wales.co.uk
Description: Improves the quality of life of people with epilepsy through advocacy, services, support and information. Raises public awareness and understanding of epilepsy.

01976
Epping Forest Conservation Volunteers
EFCV
86 Larkswood Rd., Chingford, London, E4 9DU, UK
Email: kjm86larks@bun.com
Website: http://www.efcv.co.uk
Contact: Kevin Mason, Membership Sec.
Fee: £5
Membership Type: individual
Description: Works in the conservation and management of Epping Forest. Conducts hedgelaying, woodland management, pond digging, fencing, tree planting and shrub clearance.
Publication: Newsletter
Publication title: Forest Leaves

01977
Equality Commission for Northern Ireland
ECNI
Equality House, 7-9 Shaftesbury Sq., Belfast, BT2 7DP, UK
Tel: 02890 500600
Fax: 02890 248687
Email: information@equalityni.org
Website: http://www.equalityni.org/site/default.asp?secid=home
Staff: 143
Contact: Evelyn Collins, Chief Exec.
Description: Works to combat discrimination and promotes equality of opportunity through advice, promotion and enforcement.
Formerly: Formerly, Equal Opportunities Commission - Northern Ireland

01978
Equitoy
Somers Mounts Hill, Benenden, Cranbrook, TN17 4ET, UK
Tel: 01580 240819
Fax: 01580 241109
Email: info@equitoy.com
Website: http://www.equitoy.com
Members: 100
Contact: Alan Milne, Sec.
Fee: £550
Membership Type: general
Description: Members import and distribute the majority of quality toys and components on sale in the UK and

Republic of Ireland. Safeguards and promotes the interests of members by keeping fully informed of matters affecting trade. Advises on safety matters and quality assurance and the Safety Adviser ensures that the Association is given the opportunity to comment on new developments in safety legislation. Owner of Toycred Accreditation scheme.
Formerly: Formerly, British Toy Importers and Distributors Association

01979

Equity

Guild House, Upper St. Martins Ln., London, WC2H 9EG, UK
Tel: 0207 3796000
Fax: 0207 3797001
Email: info@equity.org.uk
Website: http://www.equity.org.uk
Members: 37000
Staff: 50
Contact: Christine Payne, Gen. Sec.
Fee: £133-349
Membership Type: full (based on annual gross income)
Fee: £15.5
Membership Type: student
Description: United Kingdom trade union representing actors, club and circus performers, stage managers, theatre designers, directors, choreographers, dancers, stunt performers and singers. Works to "secure the best possible terms and conditions for its members through collective bargaining". Makes representations to government and authorities on matters of policy relating to the performing arts. Negotiates terms of employment in all sections of entertainment including theatre, television, film, radio, and recording. Makes casting agreements with employers to encourage artists who are not already members to join the union. Offers legal counsel to members involved in disputes. Operates advisory service on insurance, pension, and investment matters.
Formerly: Formerly, British Actors' Equity Association
Publication: Annual Report
Publication title: Equity Annual Report

Esperanto-Asocio de Skotlando
see Scottish Esperanto Association

01980

Essex Chamber of Commerce

8/9 St. Peters Ct., Essex, Colchester, CO1 1WD, UK
Tel: 01206 765277
Fax: 01206 578073
Email: enquiries@essexchambers.co.uk
Website: http://www.essexchambers.co.uk
Members: 2500
Staff: 28
Fee: £1075.13
Membership Type: firm/company (maximum; based on number of employees)
Description: Promotes business and commerce.
Publication: Magazine
Publication title: Business Leader

01981

EURISOL, The UK Mineral Wool Association

PO Box 35084, London, NW1 4XE, UK
Tel: 020 79358532
Fax: 0700 6065950
Email: eurisol@live.com
Website: http://www.eurisol.com
Members: 4
Staff: 1
Contact: Crispin Dunn-Meynell, Sec. Gen.
Description: Large manufacturers of insulation materials. Aims to further the cause of energy conservation in the UK by promoting the benefits of mineral wool products in achieving effective solutions to better standards of thermal and acoustic insulation and fire protection in building, industry and commerce.

01982

Eurocentres Business Institute

56 Eccleston Sq., London, SW1V 1PH, UK
Tel: 0208 2971488
Fax: 0208 3189057
Email: info@eurocentres.com
Website: http://www.eurocentres.com
Members: 2
Staff: 3
Description: Members teach English to managers from abroad. Provides language training (English and foreign languages) for executives, managers, and professional people. Provides language training services (courses, materials, language audits) for corporate clients as well as specialized courses such as legal English.

01983

European Academy of Design
EAD

Lancaster University, Lancaster Institute for the Contemporary Arts, Lancaster, LA1 4YD, UK
Tel: 01524 592982
Email: n.sarjent@lancaster.ac.uk
Website: http://www.europeanacademyofdesign.org.uk
Members: 250
Contact: Nicky Sarjent, Contact
Description: Promotes the publication and dissemination of research in design.
Publication: Journal
Publication title: Design

01984

European Actuarial Consultative Group

Napier House, 4 Worcester St., Oxford, OX1 2AW, UK
Tel: 01865 268218
Fax: 01865 268244
Email: mlucas@gcactuaries.org
Website: http://www.gcactuaries.org
Members: 33
Contact: Michael Lucas, Sec.
Description: Actuarial associations in Europe. Responds to requests for opinions on matters of interest to the actuarial profession by institutions of the European Union. Maintains contact with the International Actuarial Association. Acts as a forum for all actuarial associations in Europe.
Publication: Book
Publication title: Glossary of Pensions Terminology
Meetings/Conventions: annual meeting October 21, 2011. Prague Czech Republic

01985

European and Mediterranean Cereal Rusts Foundation
EMCRF

Cereal Research Department, John Innes Centre, Colney Ln., Norwich, NR4 7UH, UK
Email: james.brown@bbsrc.ac.uk
Website: http://www.crpmb.org
Contact: James K.M. Brown, Chm.
Description: Participants in the conference come from research and breeding institutes in 35 countries interested in cereal grains and cereal grain diseases. Promotes international cooperation in scientific research regarding rust and powdery mildew diseases of cereals; seeks to further practical application of scientific results, with special reference to Europe and the Mediterranean area.
Publication: Bulletin
Publication title: Cereal Rust and Powdery Mildews Bulletin. Advertisements.
Meetings/Conventions: quadrennial conference – Exhibits.

01986

European Aspirin Foundation
AF

PO Box 223, Haslemere, GU27 3ZJ, UK
Tel: 01428 641119
Fax: 01428 641927
Email: aspirin@healthcom.eu.com
Website: http://www.aspirin-foundation.com
Contact: G.N. Henderson, Exec. Dir.
Description: Provides information to consumers, health professionals, and journalists on scientific and general aspects of aspirin usage. Supports medical and scientific studies.

01987

European Association for Cancer Research
EACR

University of Nottingham, School of Pharmacy, Nottingham, NG7 2RD, UK
Tel: 0115 9515116
Fax: 0115 9515115
Email: eacr@nottingham.ac.uk
Website: http://www.eacr.org
Members: 7000
Staff: 3
Contact: Richard Marais, Sec. Gen.
Fee: £30
Membership Type: active
Description: Persons who have worked actively in cancer research for at least 2 years and who have an academic degree or the equivalent; membership in 40 countries. Seeks to advance cancer research by facilitating communication among research workers, particularly by organizing meetings.
Publication: Journal
Publication title: European Journal of Cancer

01988

European Association for Cardio-Thoracic Surgery
EACTS

3 Park St., Berkshire, Windsor, SL4 1LU, UK
Tel: 01753 832166
Fax: 01753 620407

Email: info@eacts.co.uk
Website: http://www.eacts.org
Members: 2000
Contact: Pascal R. Vouhe, Pres.
Fee: £198
Membership Type: resident
Fee: £50
Membership Type: trainee
Description: Aims to advance education in the field of cardio-thoracic surgery. Promotes research into thoracic physiology, pathology and therapy.
Publication: Journal
Publication title: European Journal of Cardio-Thoracic Surgery

01989

European Association for Chemical and Molecular Sciences
EUCHEMS

Royal Society of Chemistry, Burlington House, Piccadilly, London, W1J 0BA, UK
Tel: 020 74403303
Fax: 020 74378883
Email: mcewane@rsc.org
Website: http://www.euchems.org
Members: 50
Contact: Evelyn K. McEwan, Gen. Sec.
Description: National societies throughout Europe representing 200,000 chemists. Fosters cooperation among member societies. Encourages discussion in all fields of chemistry.
Formerly: Formerly, Federation of European Chemical Societies - England
Publication: Manual
Publication title: Guide for Museums with collections on History of Chemistry and of Pharmacy
Meetings/Conventions: Chemistry for Life Sciences – annual conference

01990

European Association for Comparative Economic Studies
EACES

University of Brighton, Brighton Business School, Mithras House, Lewes Rd., Brighton, BN2 4AT, UK
Email: j.holscher@bton.ac.uk
Website: http://www.eaces.net
Contact: Jens Holscher, Pres.
Fee: £30
Membership Type: individual (Western)
Fee: £20
Membership Type: junior (Western, Eastern)
Description: Works to advance theoretical and applied knowledge in the field of comparative study of real economic systems, including German tax law.

01991

European Association for Cranio-Maxillofacial Surgery
EACMFS

PO Box 85, Midhurst, GU29 9WS, UK
Tel: 01730 810951
Fax: 01730 812042
Email: secretariat@eacmfs.org
Website: http://www.eurofaces.com
Members: 800
Contact: Jill McFarland, Sec. Gen.
Fee: £50
Membership Type: trainee, retired
Fee: £150
Membership Type: active, associate
Description: Surgeons involved in oral and cranio-maxillofacial surgery. Encourages discussion and conducts medical courses on subjects such as orthognathic and temporomandibular joint surgery and plastic and aesthetic surgery. Maintains speakers' bureau.
Publication: Journal
Publication title: Journal of Cranio-Maxillofacial Surgery. Advertisements.
Meetings/Conventions: semiannual congress – Exhibits. September 11 to 15, 2012. Dubrovnik Croatia

01992

European Association for Forensic Child and Adolescent Psychiatry, Psychology and Other Involved Professionals
EFCAP

c/o Dr. Susan Bailey, Sec.
Bury New Rd., Prestwich, Manchester, M25 3BL, UK
Email: t.doreleijers@debascule.com
Website: http://www.efcap.org
Contact: Theo A.H. Doreleijers, Chm.
Description: Aims to improve the assessment and treatment of children and young people who find themselves in the justice system. Promotes interdisciplinary training and education. Facilitates joint international scientific research. Raises awareness of the need for constant change in the criminal and civil justice systems.

01993

European Association for Jewish Studies
EAJS

European Centre for the University of Teaching of Jewish Civilization, Yarnton Manor, Yarnton, Oxford, OX5 1PY, UK
Tel: 01865 377946
Email: admin@eurojewishstudies.org
Website: http://www.eurojewishstudies.org
Members: 450
Staff: 2
Contact: Mauro Perani, Pres.
Fee: £15
Membership Type: full/associate
Description: Provides encouragement and support of the teaching of Jewish studies at university level in Europe; seeks to further an understanding of the importance of Jewish culture and civilization and the impact it has had on European cultures over many centuries.
Publication: Directory
Publication title: Directory of Jewish Studies in Europe

01994

European Association for Passive Fire Protection
EAPFP

Kingsley House, Ganders Business Park, Hampshire, Bordon, GU35 9LU, UK
Tel: 01420 471616
Fax: 01420 471611
Email: katherine.gitsham@eapfp.com
Website: http://www.eapfp.com
Members: 10
Staff: 5
Contact: Katherine Gitsham, Contact
Fee: £1800
Membership Type: full
Fee: £650
Membership Type: associate
Description: European manufacturers and contractors involved in passive fire protection, including steelwork, timber and other specialist applications. Promotes high industry standards.

01995

European Association for Philanthropy and Giving
EAPG

Central House, 5th Fl., 14 Upper Woburn Pl., London, WC1H 0AE, UK
Tel: 020 73875459
Email: info@eapg.org.uk
Website: http://www.eapg.org.uk
Members: 300
Staff: 4
Contact: James K. Myers, Founder/Pres.
Fee: £1250
Membership Type: for profit
Fee: £295
Membership Type: not-for-profit/charity
Description: Brings together nonprofit fundraisers and their professional advisors involved in charitable giving. Aims to advance the development of planned giving in Europe through roundtable meetings, seminars, publications and other media addressing major gift fundraising and the associated cross-border tax and legal issues that arise.
Formerly: Formerly, European Association for Planned Giving
Publication: Bulletin
Publication title: EAPG Bulletin

01996

European Association for the History of Medicine and Health
EAHMH

c/o Dr. Alex Mold, Sec.
Centre for History in Public Health, London School of Hygiene and Tropical Medicine, Keppel St., London, WC1E 7HT, UK
Tel: 020 79272166
Email: alex.mold@lshtm.ac.uk
Website: http://www.eahmh.net
Contact: Frank Huisman, Pres.
Fee: £25
Membership Type: regular
Description: Fosters research and education in the history of medicine and health; encourages scientific cooperation.
Meetings/Conventions: biennial meeting September 1 to 4, 2011. Utrecht Netherlands

01997
European Association for the Treatment of Addiction - U.K. EATA

1st Fl., 1 Regent Terr., Rita Rd., London, SW8 1AW, UK
Tel: 020 78208130
Fax: 020 78200055
Email: sharoncarson@eata.org.uk
Website: http://www.eata.org.uk
Members: 120
Staff: 2
Contact: Sharon Carson, Chief Exec.
Fee: £225-1000
Membership Type: full (based on total running costs)
Fee: £50
Membership Type: associate (individual)
Description: Substance abuse treatment centers, health care, and other professionals with an interest in the treatment of people who abuse substances. Seeks to advance the treatment of people with substance abuse problems. Promotes increased understanding of the scientific, psychological, and medical aspects of substance abuse. Facilitates communication and cooperation among members. Facilitates research and educational programs.
Publication: Reports

01998
European Association of Chinese Studies EACS

University of Cambridge, Department of E Asian Studies, Sidgwick Ave., Cambridge, CB3 9DA, UK
Tel: 01223 335137
Fax: 01223 335110
Email: rs10009@cam.ac.uk
Website: http://www.soas.ac.uk/eacs
Contact: Brunhild Staiger, Pres.
Fee: £20
Membership Type: individual, corporate
Fee: £10
Membership Type: student
Description: Promotes and fosters all scholarly activities related to Chinese studies in Europe.

01999
European Association of Fibre Drum Manufacturers

PO Box 110, North Yorkshire, Knaresborough, HG5 8ZX, UK
Tel: 07770 633320
Fax: 01423 867098
Email: seffi@theipa.co.uk
Website: http://www.seffi.org
Members: 20
Contact: P.D. Pease, Sec.
Description: Works to develop useful product standards. Conducts activities to broaden the industry's markets. Creates wider appreciation and acceptance of its products and services.

02000
European Association of Geographers EUROGEO

19 Blackwood Ave., Liverpool, L25 4RN, UK
Tel: 0151 2913042
Email: donertk@hope.ac.uk
Website: http://www.eurogeography.eu
Members: 100
Contact: Karl Donert, Pres.
Fee: £100
Membership Type: regular
Description: National organizations of European geography teachers. Promotes geographical education; encourages development of geographic awareness. Conducts research and educational programs.
Formerly: Formerly, European Network of Geography Teachers' Association

02001
European Association of Neurosurgical Societies EANS

c/o Susie Hide, Admin. Dir.
18 The St., Martson Meysey, Wiltshire, SN6 6LQ, UK
Tel: 01285 810921
Fax: 07967 458028
Email: susie.hide@btinternet.com
Website: http://www.eans.org
Contact: Johannes Schramm, Pres.
Fee: £200
Membership Type: full, associate
Fee: £125
Membership Type: junior, senior
Description: National European neurosurgical societies in 32 countries. Sponsors two training courses per year with various other activities and research projects.
Publication: Journal
Publication title: Acta Neurochirurgica
Meetings/Conventions: European Neurosurgical Congress – quadrennial conference – Exhibits.

02002
European Association of Science Editors EASE

PO Box 6159, Reading, RG19 9DE, UK
Email: secretary@ease.org.uk
Website: http://www.ease.org.uk
Members: 600
Contact: Sheila Evered, Sec.
Fee: £70
Membership Type: individual
Fee: £202
Membership Type: corporate (3 people)
Description: Editors of serial and other scientific publications in 50 countries; others responsible for editing or managing such a publication; individuals representing scientific publications or publishing bodies. Promotes improved communication in science by encouraging cooperation among editors in all disciplines of science. Assists in the efficient operation of publications in the field. Encourages discussion on topics including: finding and keeping authors, editors, readers, publishers, and printers; strives to produce publications quickly and economically; keeping up with modern technology in editing and printing; intellectual and practical problems in the transfer of scientific information.
Formerly: Formerly, European Association of Earth Science Editors
Publication: Journal
Publication title: European Science Editing. Advertisements.
Meetings/Conventions: Integrity in Science Communication – triennial conference – Exhibits.

02003
European Association of Social Anthropologists EASA

Univ. of Bristol, Dept. of Archaeology and Anthropology, 43 Woodland Rd., Bristol, B58 1UU, UK
Email: thomas.fillitz@univie.ac.at
Website: http://www.easaonline.org
Contact: Thomas Fillitz, Sec.
Fee: £50-100
Membership Type: ordinary (varies according to the income)
Fee: £30
Membership Type: student
Description: Encourages understanding and development of social anthropology through professional communication.
Publication: Journal
Publication title: Social Anthropology

02004
European Association of Teachers - UK Section

8 Staplegrove, Shoeburyness, SS3 8AQ, UK
Tel: 01702 586622
Fax: 01702 586622
Email: eat_uk@tiscali.co.uk
Website: http://www.aede.eu
Members: 70
Staff: 1
Contact: Brian Sandford, Sec.
Description: Aims to broaden children's knowledge and understanding of Europe through the provision of materials and information to members, support for teachers, and the organization of Tests in European Knowledge (Levels 1 and 2).
Publication: Journal
Publication title: The European Teacher

02005
European Beer Consumers' Union EBCU

230 Hatfield Rd., St. Albans, AL1 4LW, UK
Tel: 01727 867201
Email: ebcu@ebcu.org
Website: http://www.ebcu.org
Members: 125000
Contact: Terry Lock, Chm.
Description: National beer consumers' unions. Seeks to protect the economic and aesthetic rights of beer buyers. Represents members before brewery operators and consumer protection agencies; facilitates communication and good fellowship among beer consumers.

02006
European Biological Rhythms Society EBRS

John Radcliffe Hospital, Headley Way, Oxford, OX3 9DU, UK
Tel: 01865 234777
Email: russell.foster@eye.ox.ac.uk
Website: http://www.ebrs.info
Contact: Russell Foster, Pres.
Fee: £30
Membership Type: general
Fee: £300

Membership Type: life
Description: Promotes research on the pineal organ in its broadest.
Formerly: Formerly, European Pineal and Biological Rhythm Society

02007

European Biomedical Research Association
EBRA

25 Shaftesbury Ave., London, W1D 7EG, UK
Email: matfield@ecbr.eu
Website: http://www.ebra.org
Fee: £50
Membership Type: individual
Description: Promotes the best practices in animal research and high standards of laboratory animal welfare.

02008

European Board and College of Obstetrics and Gynaecology
EBCOG

c/o Charlotte Mercer, Admin.
7 Killeaton Park, Dunmurry, Belfast, BT17 9HE, UK
Tel: 028 90610559
Fax: 028 90610584
Email: charlotte.mercer@btinternet.com
Website: http://www.ebcog.org
Members: 66
Staff: 1
Contact: Peter Hornnes, Pres.
Description: Enhances the health of women and babies by promoting the highest possible standards of care in all European countries.
Publication: Journal
Publication title: European Clinics in Obstetrics and Gynaecology

02009

European Board of Plastic, Reconstructive and Aesthetic Surgery
EBOPRAS

Queen Victoria Hospital, Holtye Rd., West Sussex, East Grinstead, RH19 3DZ, UK
Tel: 01342 414276
Email: john@boorman.myzen.co.uk
Website: http://www.ebopras.org
Members: 42
Staff: 8
Contact: John Boorman, Pres.
Description: Promotes high standards of care in the field of plastic surgery. Organizes the harmonization of standards in EU and UEMS member countries.

02010

European Botanical and Horticultural Libraries Group
EBHL

Library, Art and Archives, Royal Botanic Gardens, Kew, Richmond, TW9 3AE, UK
Tel: 020 83325422
Fax: 020 83325430
Email: f.ainsworth@kew.org
Website: http://www.kew.org/ebhl/home.htm
Contact: Fiona Ainsworth, Sec.
Fee: £20
Membership Type: personal
Fee: £30
Membership Type: institutional
Description: Promotes botanical and horticultural libraries in Europe.

02011

European Calcified Tissue Society
ECTS

PO Box 337, Bristol, BS32 4ZR, UK
Tel: 01454 610255
Fax: 01454 610255
Email: sales@portlandpress.com
Website: http://www.ectsoc.org
Contact: Roland Baron, Pres.
Fee: £42
Membership Type: full
Fee: £30
Membership Type: student
Description: Represents the interests of researchers and clinicians working in calcified tissues and related fields. Advances clinical research and scientific knowledge of the structure and function of calcified tissues and related subjects.
Publication: Journal
Publication title: Calcified Tissue International
Meetings/Conventions: Bone Research Society/British Orthopaedic Research Society Joint Meeting – quarterly meeting

02012

European Central Council of Homeopaths
ECCH

School House, Market Pl., Norfolk, Kenninghall, NR16 2AH, UK
Tel: 01953 888163
Fax: 01953 888163
Email: ecch@gn.apc.org
Website: http://www.homeopathy-ecch.eu
Members: 7000
Staff: 2
Contact: Stephen Gordon, Gen. Sec.
Description: Promotes the development of the highest standards of practice among the homeopathic profession in Europe for the benefit of patients.
Formerly: Formerly, European Council for Classical Homeopathy
Meetings/Conventions: Crossing Bridges – annual conference

02013

European Centre for Medium-Range Weather Forecasts
ECMWF

Shinfield Park, Berkshire, Reading, RG2 9AX, UK
Tel: 0118 9869450
Fax: 0118 9869450
Email: ecmwf-director@ecmwf.int
Website: http://www.ecmwf.int
Members: 18
Staff: 162
Contact: Gianpaolo Balsamo, Contact
Description: National weather services and organizations. Promotes the development of numerical methods for medium-range weather forecasting. Prepares medium-range weather forecasts for distribution to members; conducts scientific and technical research to improve weather forecasting; gathers and disseminates meteorological data. Assists in the implementation of the programs of the World Meteorological Organisation; provides advanced training to the scientific staff of national weather services; assists members conducting meteorological research. Produces and distributes weather forecasting products. Compiles data reception statistics.
Library Subject: meteorology
Library Type: reference
Publication: Newsletter

02014

European Centre for Occupational Health, Safety and the Environment
ECOHSE

Adam Smith Bldg., University of Glasgow, Glasgow, G12 8QQ, UK
Tel: 0141 3304665
Fax: 0141 3304665
Email: ecohse@socsci.gla.ac.uk
Contact: Charles Woolfson, Dir.
Description: Promotes the exchange of academic, policy and practitioner experience in the fields of industrial relations and workplace health, safety and the environment.
Publication: Book
Publication title: Lethal Work: A History of the Asbestos Tragedy in Scotland

02015

European Chilled Food Federation
ECFF

PO Box 6434, Kettering, NN15 5XT, UK
Tel: 01536 514365
Fax: 01536 515395
Email: cfa@chilledfood.org
Website: http://www.ecff.net
Members: 9
Description: Promotes the chilled food industry in Europe.

02016

European Coalition to End Animal Experiments
ECEAE

16A Crane Grove, London, N7 8NN, UK
Tel: 020 77004888
Fax: 020 77000252
Email: info@eceae.org
Website: http://www.eceae.org
Description: Animal protection groups in the European Union. Works to eliminate animal experiments.

02017

European Coastal Association for Science and Technology
EUROCOAST

PO Box 914, Cardiff, CF10 3YE, UK
Tel: 029 20874830
Fax: 029 20874326
Email: eurocoast@cardiff.ac.uk
Website: http://www.eurocoast.org
Contact: Rhoda Ballinger, Treas.

Description: Scientists, engineers, and decision makers in the European community. Promotes protection, development and management of the coastal zone. Fosters research; disseminates information.

02018

European College of Hypnotherapy ECH

5 Schroder Ct., Northcroft Rd., Egham, Surrey, TW20 0EH, UK
Tel: 01784 479930
Website: http://www.european-college.co.uk
Contact: Keith Hearne, Contact
Description: Promotes the development of new techniques in hypnotherapy, including the conversion of nightmares into pleasant dreams, externalizing hypnotic imagery, new pain-control procedures, and the concept of the virtual self.

02019

European College of Veterinary Pathologists ECVP

University of Liverpool, Veterinary Pathology, Crown St., Liverpool, L69 7ZJ, UK
Tel: 0151 7944258
Fax: 0151 7944268
Email: ecvpjf@liverpool.ac.uk
Website: http://www.ecvpath.org
Members: 272
Contact: Anja Kipar, Sec.
Description: Represents veterinary pathologists in Europe.

02020

European Consortium for Political Research ECPR

University of Essex, Wivenhoe Park, Colchester, CO4 3SQ, UK
Tel: 01206 872501
Fax: 01206 872500
Email: ecpr@essex.ac.uk
Website: http://www.ecprnet.eu
Members: 300
Contact: Clare Dekker, Admin. Dir.
Description: Supports and encourages the training, research and cross-national cooperation of approximately 8000 political scientists in over 300 institutions throughout Europe and beyond. Organizes workshops, round tables, conferences and summer schools.
Publication: Directory
Publication title: Directory of European Political Scientists
Meetings/Conventions: biennial conference September 5 to 7, 2013. Bordeaux France

02021

European Construction Institute ECI

c/o Steve Rothwell, Admin.
Loughborough University, Sir Frank Gibb Annex, West Park, Loughborough, LE11 3TU, UK
Tel: 01509 223526
Fax: 01509 260118
Email: eci@lboro.ac.uk
Website: http://www.eci-online.org
Staff: 17
Contact: Michel Virlogeux, Pres.
Fee: £7700
Membership Type: company
Fee: £3850
Membership Type: education, non-profit
Description: Construction client, contractor, and project support organizations in Europe. Aligns the major contributors in the business to collectively devise techniques and practices to improve performance and share experiences on implementation.
Library Subject: best practices in engineering construction
Library Type: not open to the public
Publication: Manual
Publication title: Construction Health and Safety in Developing Countries

02022

European Council for Cardiovascular Research ECCR

c/o Mrs. Gerry McCarthy, Sec.
Hampton Medical Conferences Ltd., 113-119 High St., Hampton Hill, Middlesex, London, TW12 1NJ, UK
Tel: 020 89798300
Fax: 020 89796700
Email: eccr@hamptonmedical.com
Website: http://www.eccr.org
Members: 220
Contact: Michael Mulvany, Pres.
Description: Promotes clinical and experimental research in hypertension and cardiovascular disease in Europe.

02023

European Council for High Ability ECHA

c/o Johanna Raffan, Sec.
PO Box 242, Oxford, OX2 9FR, UK
Tel: 01865 861879
Fax: 01865 861880
Website: http://www.echa.info
Members: 280
Contact: Kirsi Tirri, Pres.
Description: Educators, psychologists, students, and parents. Promotes intellectual research, accomplishment, and high achievement. Fosters exchange of information among people interested in high ability. Seeks to advance the study and development of potential excellence in people.
Publication: Newsletter
Publication title: ECHA News

02024

European Council for Steiner Waldorf Education ECSWE

Steiner Waldorf Schools Fellowship, Kidbrooke Park, East Sussex, Forest Row, RH18 5JB, UK
Tel: 01342 822115
Email: ecswe@waldorf.net
Website: http://www.steinerwaldorfeurope.org
Members: 800
Contact: Christopher Clouder, Dir.
Description: Works to strengthen and develop the Steiner education method.

02025

European Council for the Village and Small Town ECOVAST

59 Bodycoats Rd., Chandlers Ford, Hampshire, Eastleigh, SO53 2HA, UK
Tel: 02380 275153
Fax: 01962 622508
Email: pam.moore59@ntlworld.com
Website: http://www.ecovast.org
Members: 500
Contact: Pam Moore, Sec. Gen.
Fee: £42
Membership Type: full
Fee: £21
Membership Type: student, pensioner, unwaged
Description: Fosters the economic, social and cultural vitality and the administrative identity of rural communities throughout Europe; safeguards and promotes a renewal of these areas which is both innovative and adapted to the heritage of the architectural and natural environment.

02026

European Council of International Schools ECIS

21B Lavant St., Hampshire, Petersfield, GU32 3EL, UK
Tel: 01730 268244
Fax: 01730 267914
Email: ecis@ecis.org
Website: http://www.ecis.org
Members: 1800
Staff: 25
Contact: Jean Vahey, Exec. Dir.
Fee: £100
Membership Type: individual
Fee: £117.5
Membership Type: individual living in EU
Description: Members include international schools, colleges, and institutions involved in the field of education worldwide; manufacturers of educational equipment and publishers; individuals interested in international education. Represents members' interests and serves as a liaison between member-schools and institutions of higher learning throughout the world. Evaluates and accredits schools according to standards set by international educational agencies. Provides guidance to schools regarding educational programs, teaching methods, and organizational questions. Assists schools in the recruitment of directors and teaching staff. Conducts research and gathers information of interest to members. Holds training courses on education in an international setting. Compiles statistics; operates placement service.
Publication: Directory
Publication title: ECIS International Schools Directory. Advertisements.
Meetings/Conventions: Administrators' Conference – conference

02027

European Council on Chiropractic Education ECCE

1 Spinnaker View, Bedhampton, Hants, Havant, PO9 3JD, UK
Tel: 02392 480887
Email: info@cce-europe.org

Website: http://www.cce-europe.com
Contact: Timothy Raven, Pres.
Description: Works to assure the quality of chiropractic undergraduate education and training primarily in Europe and Africa against a set of educational standards.

02028

European Council on Eating Disorders
ECED

St. George's University of London Medical School, Division of Mental Health, Cranmer Terr., London, SW17 0RE, UK
Tel: 020 87255528
Fax: 020 87253538
Email: hlacey@sgul.ac.uk
Website: http://www.eced.co.uk
Members: 500
Contact: J. Hubert Lacey, Admin.
Description: European medical clinicians and researchers with an interest in eating disorders. Seeks to advance the diagnosis and medical treatment of eating disorders. Facilitates exchange of information and clinical skills among members.

02029

European Council on Refugees and Exiles
ECRE

153-157 Commercial Rd., 4th Fl., London, E1 2DA, UK
Tel: 020 77902954
Fax: 020 77904610
Email: ecre@ecre.org
Website: http://www.ecre.org
Members: 74
Staff: 15
Contact: Bjarte Vandvik, Sec. Gen.
Description: Aims to address the needs of individuals seeking refuge and protection within Europe. Promotes the protection and integration of refugees based on the values of human dignity, human rights and an ethic of solidarity. Facilitates the exchange of policy information; serves as a forum for discussion of legal issues among attorneys and other professionals. Conducts research and educational programs on refugees and international law. Works to enhance the capacities of non-governmental organizations working with displaced people in central and eastern Europe.
Formerly: Formerly, European Consultation on Refugees and Exiles

02030

European Dystonia Federation
EDF

69 E King St., Helensburgh, G84 7RE, UK
Tel: 0143 6678799
Fax: 0143 6678799
Email: alistair@newton1.co.uk
Website: http://www.dystonia-europe.org
Members: 19
Staff: 67
Contact: Alistair Newton, Exec. Dir.
Description: Promotes awareness and understanding of the public and the medical profession on dystonia.

02031

European Federation for Psychoanalytic Psychotherapy
EFPP

5 Windsor Rd., Finchley, London, N3 3SN, UK
Tel: 02083 499873
Fax: 02083 433197
Email: joycepiper@googlemail.com
Website: http://www.efpp.org
Contact: Joyce Piper, Financial Admin.
Description: Umbrella organization that links together national networks of adult, child, and adolescent and group psychoanalytic psychotherapists, and psychoanalysts involved in public sector services.

02032

European Federation of Associations of Insulation Contractors

c/o Thermal Insulation Contractors Association
Tica House, Allington Way, Yarm Road Business Park, Durham, DL1 4QB, UK
Tel: 01325 466704
Fax: 01325 487691
Email: ralphbradley@tica-acad.co.uk
Website: http://www.insulation.org/links/fesi.cfm
Members: 15
Contact: Ralph Bradley, Chief Exec.
Description: Represents groups representing firms involved in thermal, soundproof, and fireproof insulation. Facilitates contacts among members; addresses questions concerning the industry; defends members' interests before international bodies.
Meetings/Conventions: World Insulation and Acoustic Congress – biennial general assembly

02033

European Federation of Campingsite Organisations and Holiday Park Associations
EFCO&HPA

6 Pullman Ct., Great Western Rd., Gloucester, GL1 3ND, UK
Tel: 01452 526911
Fax: 01452 508508
Email: efco@bhhpa.org.uk
Website: http://www.campingeurope.com
Contact: Ros Pritchard, Sec. Gen.
Description: Represents camping and caravanning industry in Europe. Promotes and defends the interests of the industry. Aims to ensure the exchange of expertise among professionals. Facilitates operation in the single market.

02034

European Federation of Foundation Contractors
EFFC

c/o Dianne Jennings, Sec.
Forum Ct., 83 Copers Cope Rd., Kent, Beckenham, BR3 1NR, UK
Tel: 020 86630948
Fax: 020 86630949
Email: fionamcw@googlemail.com
Website: http://www.foundationworld.org.uk
Members: 450
Staff: 2
Contact: Peter Maurice Bottiau, Pres.
Description: Represents specialist foundation contractors from all European and East European countries engaged in the construction of specialist foundations and ground improvement techniques.
Publication: Magazine
Publication title: European Foundations. Advertisements.

02035

European Federation of Hereditary Ataxias
Euro-ATAXIA

Lincoln House, Kennington Park, 1-3 Brixton Rd., London, SW9 6DE, UK
Tel: 0207 5821444
Email: marco.meinders@euro-ataxia.eu
Website: http://www.euro-ataxia.eu
Members: 5000
Contact: Sue Millman, Sec.-Gen.
Description: Aims to widen the scope of research initiatives about hereditary ataxia. Coordinates with other research groups and gathers funds to support both researches and people with hereditary ataxia.

02036

European Federation of Road Traffic Victims
FEVR

PO Box 53318, London, NW10 3WT, UK
Email: president@fevr.org
Website: http://www.fevr.org
Members: 25
Staff: 25
Contact: Marcel Haegi, Pres.
Description: Victims of traffic accidents and their families and friends. Seeks to prevent road accidents. Lobbies for more effective traffic safety laws and regulations; provides assistance to road accident victims and their families.

02037

European Federation of Sexology
EFS

Porterbrook Clinic, 75 Osborne Rd., Sheffield, S11 9BF, UK
Email: info@europeansexology.com
Website: http://www.europeansexology.com
Contact: Kevan Wylie, Gen. Sec.-Treas.
Fee: £85-130
Membership Type: society
Description: Coordinates associations working in the field of sexology by encouraging research projects at a European level.
Publication: Journal
Publication title: Sexologies

02038

European Federation of Societies for Ultrasound in Medicine and Biology
EFSUMB

36 Portland Pl., London, W1B 1LS, UK
Tel: 020 70997140
Fax: 020 74367934
Email: efsumb@efsumb.org
Website: http://www.efsumb.org/intro/home.asp
Members: 19344
Staff: 1
Contact: Lynne Rudd, Gen. Sec.
Description: Serves as interdisciplinary national organizations and subgroups of bodies representing 26 countries. Promotes the application of ultrasound in biology and medicine or engage in research and development in the field. Proposes standards for ultrasound use and interpretation; arranges congresses and study and development meetings; promotes the exchange of information on ultrasound as applied to biology and medicine. Represents the European national societies in the World Federation of Societies for Ultrasound in Medicine and Biology.
Publication: Journal
Publication title: European Journal of Ultrasound. Advertisements.
Meetings/Conventions: annual congress – Exhibits.

02039

European Federation of Statisticians in the Pharmaceutical Industry
EFSPI

2nd Fl., Pacific House, Imperial Way, Worton Grange, Reading, RG2 0TD, UK
Tel: 0118 9181070
Fax: 0118 9181001
Email: howittnigel@praintl.com
Website: http://www.efspi.org
Members: 11
Contact: Nigel Howitt, Pres.
Description: Represents national groups of statisticians working in or for the pharmaceutical industry; promotes all aspects of research, development, production, and surveillance of drugs and medical devices.

02040

European Federation of the Contact Lens Industry
EFCLIN

108 Stortford Hall Park, Bishops Stortford, Herts, Chelmsford, CM23 5AN, UK
Tel: 01279 659235
Email: steve@efclin.com
Website: http://www.efclin.com
Members: 110
Staff: 3
Contact: Steve Wheeler, Exec. Dir.
Fee: £400-900
Membership Type: regular
Description: Represents the interests of contact lens and IOL industry.
Library Subject: contact lens manufacturing
Library Type: reference

02041

European Fishing Tackle Trade Association
EFTTA

Unit 2i Ashley Works, 25 Ashley Rd., Tottenham Hale, London, N17 9LJ, UK
Tel: 0208 3650405
Fax: 0208 4937220
Email: info@eftta.com
Website: http://www.eftta.com/english/index.html?cart=125211230115257966
Members: 280
Staff: 5
Contact: Kathleen Glausch, Membership Mgr./Deputy Gen. Mgr.
Fee: £531
Membership Type: in UK
Fee: £750
Membership Type: in Europe
Description: Promotes and protects the interests of European manufacturers, wholesalers, and distributors of fishing tackle and accessories in over 30 countries. Encourages the exchange of views on matters of concern, such as the environment, within the European industry. Develops and monitors specifications and standards for fishing tackle. Sponsors market research.
Publication: Newsletter
Publication title: EFTTA Newsline
Meetings/Conventions: European Fishing Tackle Trade Exhibition – annual trade show – Exhibits.

02042

European Flexographic Technical Association - UK
EFTA

4/5 Bridge Barns, Langport Rd., Somerset, Long Sutton, TA10 9PZ, UK
Tel: 01458 241455
Fax: 01458 241684
Email: hiding@efia.uk.com
Website: http://www.efia.uk.com
Members: 420
Staff: 4
Contact: Lesley Hide, Managing Dir.
Fee: £210
Membership Type: company in UK (with 1-10 employees)
Fee: £350
Membership Type: company in UK (with 11-49 employees)
Description: Companies concerned with flexographic printing process. All technical and training aspects of the flexographic printing process.

02043

European General Galvanizers Association
EGGA

Maybrook House, Godstone Rd., Caterham, CR3 6RE, UK
Tel: 0188 3331277
Fax: 0188 3331287
Email: mail@egga.com
Website: http://www.egga.com
Members: 13
Staff: 2
Contact: Frances Holmes, Sec.
Description: European galvanizing associations. Promotes the practice and technical development of hot-dip galvanizing of fabricated steel products. Arranges conferences, meetings, and study tours for members.
Publication: Proceedings
Publication title: International Conferences
Meetings/Conventions: International Galvanizing Conference – triennial conference – Exhibits.

02044

European Glaucoma Society
EGS

Western Eye Hospital, Marylebone Rd., London, NW1 5YE, UK
Email: secretary1@eugs.org
Website: http://www.eugs.org
Contact: Clive Migdal, Sec.
Description: Aims to improve the mutual understanding of the glaucoma. Provides a rational approach to the diagnosis and management of glaucoma.
Publication: Book
Publication title: Terminology and Guidelines for Glaucoma

02045

European Hair Research Society
EHRS

40 Court Ln., Stevington, MK43 7QT, UK
Tel: 01234 823888
Fax: 01234 252035
Email: secretariat@ehrs.org
Website: http://www.ehrs.org
Members: 129
Contact: Gill Westgate, Sec.
Description: Represents scientists, dermatologists, and professionals interested in hair biology and hair disease in Europe.

02046

European Health Psychology Society
EHPS

University of Aberdeen, School of Psychology, Colorado of Life Sciences and Medicine, King's College, William Guild Bldg., Aberdeen, AB24 2UB, UK
Email: f.sniehotta@abdn.ac.uk
Website: http://www.ehps.net
Contact: Falko F. Sniehotta, Pres.-Elect
Fee: £90
Membership Type: full
Fee: £25
Membership Type: student
Description: Promotes empirical and theoretical research in health psychology in Europe, in particular the study of behavior, health, illness and health care.

02047

European Historical Economics Society
EHES

c/o Elvira Ryan, Membership Sec.
Latin American Ctre., St. Anthony's College, Oxford, OX2 6JF, UK
Tel: 046 2227476
Email: enquiries@latin-american-centre.oxford.ac.uk
Website: http://www.ekh.lu.se/ehes
Contact: Lennart Schon, Pres.
Fee: £27
Membership Type: regular
Fee: £39.5
Membership Type: joint
Description: Organizes conferences and summer schools.

02048
European Human Resource Forum
EHRF
Bakers Ln., Lower Langford, Bristol, BS40 5HT, UK
Tel: 01934 863331
Fax: 01934 863220
Email: office@ehrf.org
Website: http://www.ehrf.org
Description: Provides a forum for those involved in human resource development, including companies, consultancies, other organizations, independent consultants, and academics.
Meetings/Conventions: Lugano Forum – annual retreat

02049
European Information Association
EIA
PO Box 28, Flintshire, Mold, CH7 6FE, UK
Tel: 01352 700051
Email: paul@eia.org.uk
Website: http://www.eia.org.uk
Members: 500
Staff: 2
Contact: Paul Clarke, Chm.
Fee: £105
Membership Type: corporate
Fee: £28
Membership Type: personal
Description: Information intermediaries and others who provide European information services. Concerned with the development, coordination and improvement of the provision of information on the European Union and related matters. Regular events and training courses allow members to develop skills, exchange experience and make new contacts. Also plays a major role in improving EU information through lobbying and publications.
Publication: Newsletter
Publication title: Focus. Advertisements.

02050
European Institute of Golf Course Architects
EIGCA
Meadow View House, Tannery Ln., Bramley, Surrey, GU5 0AJ, UK
Tel: 01428 891831
Fax: 01428 891846
Email: info@eigca.org
Website: http://www.eigca.org
Members: 130
Staff: 3
Contact: David Krause, Pres.
Description: Represents the majority of qualified and experienced golf course architects throughout Europe. Aims to enhance the professional status of the profession, developing the role of education and increasing the opportunities for members to practice in countries throughout the world. Acts as the authoritative voice on all related matters, being recognized by the Royal and Ancient Golf Club of St. Andrews.
Library Subject: golf course architecture and maintenance
Library Type: lending
Publication: Handbook
Publication title: The Positive Face of Golf Development

02051
European Investment Casters' Federation
EICF
c/o Mrs. Julie Boyce, Sec.
Holly Cottage, Gorcott Hill, Beoley, Worcestershire, Redditch, B98 9EW, UK
Tel: 01564 742603
Fax: 01564 742080
Email: julieboyce@eicf.org
Website: http://www.eicf.org
Members: 61
Contact: D.A. Ford, Sec. Gen.
Fee: £385
Membership Type: regular
Description: Aims to publicise the advantages of the Investment Casting as a precision manufacturing process and to improve the process capability through the sponsorship of research and development.
Publication: Journal
Publication title: Foundry Trade Journal

02052
European Liaison Committee of Machine Tool Importers
CELIMO
c/o MTA
62 Bayswater Rd., London, W2 3PS, UK
Tel: 020 72986400
Fax: 020 72986430
Email: celimo@mta.org.uk
Website: http://www.celimo.com
Members: 13
Contact: Geoff Noon, Sec.
Description: Promotes the machine tool market throughout Europe.
Publication: Newsletter
Publication title: CQ News

02053
European Lupus Erythematosus Federation
ELEF
27-43 Eastern Rd., St. James House, Essex, Romford, RM1 3NH, UK
Tel: 01708 731251
Fax: 01708 731252
Email: elef@rheumanet.org
Website: http://www.elef.rheumanet.org
Contact: Yvonne Norton, Chair
Description: Promotes research and improves the knowledge of systematic Lupus Erythematosus.
Publication: Newsletter
Publication title: Caring and Sharing

02054
European Medical Writers Association
EMWA
Durford Mill, Hampshire, Petersfield, GU31 5AZ, UK
Tel: 01730 715216
Fax: 0870 4429940
Email: info@emwa.org
Website: http://www.emwa.org
Members: 300
Contact: Laurence Auffret, Pres.
Fee: £120
Membership Type: regular (within Europe)
Fee: £140
Membership Type: regular (outside Europe)
Description: Promotes standards of excellence in medical writing.
Publication: Journal
Publication title: The Write Stuff. Advertisements.

02055
European Microscopy Society
EMS
University of Cambridge, Dept. of Materials Science and Metallurgy, Pembroke St., Cambridge, GCB2 3QZ, UK
Tel: 01223 334561
Fax: 01223 334567
Email: pam33@cam.ac.uk
Website: http://www.eurmicsoc.org
Members: 3000
Contact: Paul Midgley, Pres.
Fee: £200-500
Membership Type: corporate
Fee: £25
Membership Type: individual
Description: Promotes the development of microscopy in all its aspects by supporting activities and stimulating new ones.

02056
European Movement
7 Graphite Sq., Vauxhall Walk, London, SE11 5EE, UK
Tel: 020 31760543
Email: emoffice@euromove.org.uk
Website: http://www.euromove.org.uk
Members: 1500
Contact: Charles Kennedy, Pres.
Fee: £25
Membership Type: single
Fee: £5
Membership Type: youth (unwaged)
Description: Serves as pro-Europe pressure group.

02057
European Orthodontic Society
EOS
49 Hallam St., Flat 20, London, W1W 6JN, UK
Tel: 020 76370367
Fax: 020 73230410
Email: eoslondon@aol.com
Website: http://www.eoseurope.org
Members: 2700
Staff: 2
Contact: Nejat Erverdi, Pres.
Fee: £82
Membership Type: active, associate
Fee: £24
Membership Type: post graduate
Description: Represents orthodontists in 78 countries promoting the science of orthodontics.
Formerly: Formerly, European Orthodontia Society
Publication: Journal
Publication title: European Journal of Orthodontics. Advertisements.

02058
European Paediatric Neurology Society
EPNS
Bridge House, Harrow Rd., Bolton, BL1 4NH, UK
Tel: 01204 492888
Fax: 01204 492888
Email: info@epns.info
Website: http://www.epns.info
Contact: Sue Hargreaves, Membership Sec.
Fee: £150
Membership Type: regular
Description: Promotes development of knowledge in child neurology.

02059
European Palm Society
EPS
c/o The Palm Centre, Ham Central Nursery
Ham St., Ham, Surrey, Richmond, TW10 7HA, UK
Tel: 020 82556191
Fax: 020 82556192
Email: info@palmsociety.org
Website: http://www.palmsociety.org.uk
Members: 800
Fee: £5
Membership Type: standard
Description: Provides information on cold hardy palms and other exotics.
Publication: Journal
Publication title: Chamaerops Magazine

02060
European Parkinson's Disease Association
EPDA
4 Golding Rd., Sevenoaks, Kent, TN13 3NJ, UK
Tel: 01732 457683
Fax: 01732 457683
Email: lizzie@epda.eu.com
Website: http://www.epda.eu.com
Members: 43
Staff: 4
Contact: Lizzie Graham, Sec. Gen.
Description: Works for the health and welfare of people living with Parkinson's disease and their families. Collaborates with European patient and neurological organizations, European Commission, World Health Organization, World Federation of Neurology, and treatment industry to QoL research projects, education materials and multidisciplinary conferences.

02061
European Personal Construct Association
EPCA
School of Business and Management, Queen Mary University of London, Mile End Rd., London, E1 4NS, UK
Tel: 020 78827440
Fax: 020 78823615
Email: info@epca-net.org
Website: http://www.epca-net.org
Fee: £10
Membership Type: student
Fee: £17
Membership Type: full
Description: Promotes awareness into personal construct psychology and applications among Europeans.
Publication: Newsletter

02062
European Phenolic Foam Association
EPFA
Kingsley House, Ganders Business Park, Kingsley, Hampshire, Bordon, GU35 9LU, UK
Tel: 01420 471617
Fax: 01420 471611
Email: admin@epfa.org.uk
Website: http://www.epfa.org.uk
Members: 6
Staff: 2
Description: Members are either producers of phenolic foam insulation or are closely linked with the industry through the provision of raw materials. Aims to promote an awareness of the benefits of phenolic foam in insulation applications and consequently to increase use.

02063
European Piano Teachers Association
EPTA
c/o Nadia Lasserson
28 Emperor's Gate, London, SW7 4HS, UK
Tel: 020 72476821
Fax: 020 77375015
Email: carogrindea@yahoo.com
Website: http://www.epta-europe.org
Contact: Carola Grindea, Founder
Fee: £21
Membership Type: associate (airmail)
Fee: £17
Membership Type: associate (surface)
Description: Promotes human and artistic values linked to musical activity.

02064
European Policy Forum
EPF
49 Whitehall, London, SW1A 2BX, UK
Tel: 0203 1743197
Fax: 0203 1372040
Email: info@epfltd.org
Website: http://www.epfltd.org
Staff: 5
Contact: Graham Mather, Pres.
Description: Promotes improved understanding of economic, regulatory, and constitutional issues facing the European Union. Serves as a clearinghouse on European public policies; sponsors educational programs; conducts policy studies.

02065
European Powder Metallurgy Association
EPMA
Talbot House, 2nd Fl., Market St., Shrewsbury, SY1 1LG, UK
Tel: 01743 248899
Fax: 01743 362968
Email: info@epma.com
Website: http://www.epma.com
Contact: Ingo Cremer, Pres.
Fee: £3395
Membership Type: full
Fee: £880
Membership Type: affiliate
Description: Represents and promotes the powder metallurgy industry in Europe, from component, metal powder, and equipment producers to end users, research centers, universities, and individuals interested in powder metallurgy.
Publication: Booklet
Publication title: Introduction to Powder Metallurgy-The Process and its Products

02066
European Prosthodontic Association
EPA
c/o Dr. Trevor Coward

Kings College Dental School and Hospital, Dept. of Prosthetic Dentistry, Bessemer Rd., London, SE5 9RS, UK

Tel: 020 73463584

Email: trevor.coward@kcl.ac.uk

Website: http://www.epadental.org

Members: 554

Contact: Ingrid Grunert, Pres.

Fee: £20

Membership Type: individual

Description: Prosthodontists. Seeks to advance the speciality of prosthodontics within the profession of dentistry; promotes continuing professional development of members. Serves as a forum for the exchange of information among European prosthodontists; sponsors research and educational programs.

Library Subject: prosthodontics

Library Type: not open to the public

02067
European Public Relations Confederation
CERP
Chartered Institute of Public Relations, Public Relations Cte., 32 St., James Sq., London, SW1Y 4JR, UK

Tel: 0207 7663333

Fax: 0207 7663344

Email: colinf@cipr.co.uk

Website: http://www.cerp.org

Members: 15

Contact: Colin Farrington, Sec. Gen.

Description: Promotes the public relations industry in the European Community. Represents members' interests. Compiles statistics.

02068
European Regions Airline Association
ERA

The Baker Ste., Fairoaks Airport, Chobham, Surrey, Woking, GU24 8HX, UK
Tel: 01276 856495
Fax: 01276 857038
Email: info@eraa.org
Website: http://www.eraa.org
Members: 252
Staff: 15
Contact: Mike A. Ambrose, Dir. Gen.
Description: Seeks to be the principal body representing the interests of organizations involved in air transport in Europe's regions. Provides expert advice and support on any issue affecting the aviation industry. Facilitates the communication of topical and relevant information to members.
Formerly: Formerly, European Regional Airlines Organisation
Publication: Handbook
Publication title: ERA Emergency Planning Handbook
Meetings/Conventions: Crisis Management Workshop – annual workshop

02069
European Relocation Association
EURA

PO Box 189, Diss, IP22 1PE, UK
Tel: 08700 726727
Fax: 01379 641940
Email: enquiries@eura-relocation.com
Website: http://www.eura-relocation.com
Contact: Tad Zurlinden, Sec. Gen.
Fee: £600
Membership Type: full, associate
Fee: £700
Membership Type: affiliate, worldwide
Description: Promotes professionalism and service and the concept of relocation. Encourages the development of professional relocation qualifications. Tracks industry trends and disseminates relocation industry information. Provides support, advice and training to relocation professionals.
Publication: Bulletin
Publication title: EURA Bulletin

02070
European Resin Manufacturers' Association
ERMA

14 Castle Mews, High St., Hampton, Middlesex, London, TW12 2NP, UK
Tel: 020 84870859
Fax: 020 84870801
Email: info@erma.org.uk
Website: http://www.erma.org.uk
Members: 36
Staff: 2
Contact: R. Kennedy, Sec.
Fee: £3715
Membership Type: regular
Fee: £1856
Membership Type: associate
Description: Provides ongoing corporate platform to represent the legitimate interests of resin manufacturers.

02071
European Sales and Marketing Association
ESMA

Barley View House, 1 Barely View, Buckinghamshire, Prestwood, HP16 9BW, UK
Tel: 01 8903760
Fax: 01 9619203
Email: info@esma.org
Website: http://www.esma.org
Members: 120
Contact: Klaus Smuda, CEO
Description: Bona fide food brokerage companies in 25 European countries. Applicants for membership must be in business for at least three years before applying for membership. Holds an annual conference in different countries for its members. Conferences held in country of current ESMA president, who serves for one year from June to July annually. Conference usually held in June.
Library Type: not open to the public
Publication: Newsletter
Publication title: News & Views

02072
European Scientific Cooperative on Phytotherapy
ESCOP

Argyle House, Gandy St., Devon, Exeter, EX4 3LS, UK
Tel: 01392 424626
Fax: 01392 424864
Email: secretariat@escop.com
Website: http://www.escop.com
Members: 11
Contact: Simon Mills, Sec.
Description: Seeks to advance the scientific status of phytomedicines; works as an umbrella organization representing national phytotherapy associations in Europe, especially in discussions with European medicines regulators.
Publication: Newsletter
Publication title: The European Phytojournal

02073
European Sealing Association
ESA

Tegfryn, Gwynedd, Tregarth, LL57 4PL, UK
Tel: 01248 600250
Fax: 01248 600250
Email: bse@europeansealing.com
Website: http://www.europeansealing.com
Contact: David Mitchell, Chm.
Fee: £3850
Membership Type: regular
Fee: £1500
Membership Type: regular, new
Description: Promotes the sealing technology industry concerned with the safe containment of fluids.

02074
European Snacks Association
ESA

6 Catherine St., London, WC2B 5JJ, UK
Tel: 020 74207220
Fax: 020 74207221
Email: esa@esa.org.uk
Website: http://www.esa.org.uk
Members: 200
Staff: 5
Contact: Steve Chandler, Sec. Gen.
Fee: £1300-45000
Membership Type: business
Fee: £1000-3400
Membership Type: associate
Description: Promotes the production of potato chips, edible nuts, and other savoury snack products in Europe. Promotes high quality standards for the industry. Represents members' interests; sponsors technical research. Promotes cooperation and the exchange of information among members.
Library Subject: food industry
Library Type: reference
Formerly: Formerly, European Chips and Snacks Association
Publication: Magazine
Publication title: The Snacks Magazine. Advertisements.
Meetings/Conventions: Snackex – biennial trade show – Exhibits.

02075
European Social Network
ESN

Victoria House, 125 Queens Rd., Brighton, BN1 3WB, UK
Tel: 01273 739039
Fax: 01273 739239
Email: info@esn-eu.org
Website: http://www.esn-eu.org
Contact: Lars-Goran Jansson, Chm.
Fee: £1855
Membership Type: regular
Fee: £930
Membership Type: associate
Description: Promotes social justice, inclusion, equality, and anti-poverty in Europe through development of quality public social services.

02076
European Society for Biomaterials
ESB

GKT Dental Inst., Guy's Tower, 17th Fl., London Bridge, London, SE1 9RT, UK
Tel: 020 7955 4923
Fax: 020 7955 2963
Email: lucy.di_silvio@kcl.ac.uk
Website: http://www.esbiomaterials.eu
Members: 600
Contact: Lucy Di Silvio, Sec.
Fee: £144
Membership Type: full
Fee: £26
Membership Type: junior
Description: Promotes progress in the field of biomaterials, including research, teaching and clinical applications.
Publication: Journal
Publication title: Journal of Materials Science: Materials in Medicine

02077
European Society for Mass Spectrometry
ESMS

The University of Edinburgh, Dept. of Chemistry, King's Bldgs., W Mains Rd., Edinburgh, EH9 3JJ, UK
Tel: 0131 6504710
Fax: 0131 6506453
Email: john.monaghan@ed.ac.uk

Website: http://www.bmb.leeds.ac.uk/esms
Contact: John J. Monaghan, Pres.
Description: Disseminates information about mass spectrometry and its related subjects. Aims to improve communication and collaboration through the mass spectrometry community in Europe.

02078

European Society for Movement Analysis for Adults and Children ESMAC

Nuffield Orthopaedic Ctre., Windmill Rd., Headington, OX3 7LD, UK
Email: administration@esmac.org
Website: http://www.esmac.org
Members: 97
Contact: Malgorzata Syczewska, Sec.-Treas.
Fee: £65
Membership Type: ordinary (with gait and posture issues)
Fee: £25
Membership Type: ordinary (without gait and posture issues)
Description: Orthopedists and other health care professionals, researchers, and scientists with an interest in human gait and posture and their impact on overall health. Works to advance scientific knowledge in the field of movement analysis; promotes continuing professional development of members. Facilitates communication and cooperation among members; conducts educational programs and courses.

02079

European Society for Oceanists ESfO

University of St. Andrews, Department of Social Anthropology, Fife, St. Andrews, KY16 9AL, UK
Email: tony.crook@st-andrews.ac.uk
Website: http://cc.joensuu.fi/esfo
Contact: Tony Crook, Chm.
Description: Conducts research on the island cultures of the central, west and south Pacific Ocean.

02080

European Society for Organ Transplantation ESOT

Royal Infirmary of Edinburgh, Little France Crescent, Transplant Unit, Rm. S3316, Edinburgh, EH16 5SA, UK
Tel: 0131 2421715
Fax: 0131 2421739
Email: secretariat@esot.org
Website: http://www.esot.org
Contact: J.L.R. Forsythe, Sec.
Fee: £100
Membership Type: regular, international
Fee: £50
Membership Type: trainee
Description: Represents medical professionals in the field of organ transplantation in Europe.
Publication: Journal
Publication title: Transplant International
Meetings/Conventions: biennial congress September 4 to 7, 2011. Glasgow United Kingdom

02081

European Society for Paediatric Endocrinology ESPE

c/o Joanne Fox-Evans
BioScientifica, Euro House, 22 Apex Ct., Woodlands, Bristol, BS32 4JT, UK
Tel: 01454 642246
Fax: 01454 642222
Email: espe@eurospe.org
Website: http://www.eurospe.org
Contact: Franco Chiarelli, Sec. Gen.
Fee: £120
Membership Type: ordinary, developing country
Fee: £60
Membership Type: retired (non-mandatory)
Description: Promotes research on paediatric endocrinology including metabolism, haematology, immunology, molecular biology, growth and development, nephrology, electrolytes and water metabolism.
Publication: Journal
Publication title: Hormone Research

02082

European Society for Philosophy and Psychology ESPP

University of Edinburgh, Dept. of Philosophy, David Hume Tower, George Sq., Edinburgh, EH8 9JX, UK
Tel: 0131 6503651
Email: matthew.nudds@ed.ac.uk
Website: http://www.eurospp.org
Contact: Matthew Nudds, Treas.
Fee: £25
Membership Type: full
Fee: £5
Membership Type: student
Description: Promotes interaction between philosophers and psychologists on issues of common concern. Encourages professionals to report experimental, theoretical and clinical work that they judge to have philosophical significance.

02083

European Society for Precision Engineering and Nanotechnology EUSPEN

Cranfield University Campus, Bldg. 70, Bedford, MK43 0AL, UK
Tel: 01234 754024
Fax: 01234 754080
Email: theresa-burke@euspen.com
Website: http://www.euspen.eu
Members: 640
Staff: 4
Contact: Theresa Burke, CEO
Description: Composed of industrialists and researchers. Conducts research on the development of nanotechnology. Disseminates information to its members through training and education.

02084

European Society for Rural Sociology ESRS

The University of Exeter, The Queen's Dr., Devon, Exeter, EX4 4QJ, UK
Tel: 01392 263351
Fax: 01392 263342
Email: j.k.little@exeter.ac.uk
Website: http://www.ruralsociology.eu
Members: 300
Contact: Jo Little, Pres.
Fee: £81
Membership Type: ordinary (in Europe)
Fee: £28
Membership Type: ordinary (in non-European CEE country)
Description: Sociologists and other individual interested in rural sociological issues. Promotes study of rural societies and development of strategies for insuring their continued viability. Facilitates communication among members; works to improve methods of rural sociological training and study; serves as a forum for discussion of issues affecting rural societies and their development.
Publication: Newsletter
Publication title: Rural Sociology News

02085

European Society of Agricultural Engineers EurAgEng

The Bullock Bldg., University Way, Cranfield, Bedford, MK43 0GH, UK
Tel: 01234 750876
Fax: 01234 751319
Website: http://www.eurageng.net
Members: 2300
Staff: 1
Contact: David Tinker, Sec. Gen.
Fee: £250
Membership Type: regular (en-bloc)
Fee: £65
Membership Type: regular (individual)
Description: Agricultural engineers and agricultural engineering societies in Europe. Seeks to advance the study, teaching, and practice of agricultural engineering. Represents the commercial and professional interests of agricultural engineers before European Union agencies. Holds an international conference on agricultural engineering every two years in Europe.
Publication: Journal
Publication title: Biosystems Engineering. Advertisements.
Meetings/Conventions: biennial conference

02086

European Society of Association Executives ESAE

1 Queen Anne's Gate, London, SW1H 9BT, UK
Tel: 020 72273590
Fax: 020 72224440
Email: info@esae.org
Website: http://www.esae.org
Members: 200
Staff: 20
Contact: Luc Maene, Pres.
Fee: £250
Membership Type: individual
Fee: £1200
Membership Type: corporate
Description: Develops, endorses and promotes training, qualification, education, networking opportunities and resources for its members and for the wider sector. Provides opportunities for professional development and networking for members.
Publication: Magazine
Publication title: Headquarters

02087
European Society of Coloproctology
ESCP
c/o Integrity International Events Ltd.
7 St. Alban's Rd., Edinburgh, EH8 9PA, UK
Tel: 0131 6246040
Fax: 0131 6246045
Email: info@escp.eu.com
Website: http://www.escp.eu.com
Contact: Freddy Penninckx, Pres.
Fee: £90
Membership Type: full
Fee: £60
Membership Type: trainee, affiliate
Description: Represents medical practitioners, scientists, technicians or nurses working in the field of coloproctology. Conducts multidisciplinary research into the diseases of the colon, rectum and anus (coloproctology), especially with respect to prevention, diagnosis and treatment. Promotes coloproctology as a medical speciality in Europe.

02088
European Society of Endocrinology
ESE
Euro House, 22 Apex Ct., Woodlands, Bradley Stoke, Bristol, BS32 4JT, UK
Tel: 01454 642247
Fax: 01454 642222
Email: info@euro-endo.org
Website: http://www.euro-endo.org
Contact: Eberhand Nieschlag, Pres.
Fee: £35
Membership Type: ordinary (reduced)
Fee: £70
Membership Type: ordinary (country that has high income)
Description: Promotes endocrinology in Europe. Seeks to advance research and education in endocrinology. Organizes postgraduate courses.
Formerly: Formerly, European Federation of Endocrine Societies
Publication: Journal
Publication title: European Journal of Endocrinology

02089
European Society of Feline Medicine
ESFM
c/o Feline Advisory Bureau
Taeselbury, High St., Tisbury, SP3 6LD, UK
Tel: 01747 871872
Fax: 01747 871873
Email: information@fabcats.org
Website: http://www.fabcats.org/esfm/index.php
Contact: Angie Hibbert, Contact
Fee: £110
Membership Type: individual (in United Kingdom)
Fee: £135
Membership Type: joint (in United Kingdom)
Description: Veterinarians with an interest in feline medicine. Seeks to advance the medical treatment of cats; promotes continuing professional development of members. Facilitates exchange of information among veterinarians and researchers working in the field of feline medicine; sponsors educational courses.
Publication: Journal
Publication title: FAB
Meetings/Conventions: semiannual conference

02090
European Society of Nematologists
ESN
Applied Plant Science Div., Agri-Food and Biosciences Institute, Newforge Ln., Belfast, BT9 5PX, UK
Tel: 028 90255280
Fax: 028 90255380
Email: sue.turner@afbini.gov.uk
Website: http://www.ifns.org/membership/esn.html
Contact: Sue Turner, Sec.-Treas.
Fee: £20
Membership Type: full
Fee: £10
Membership Type: student
Description: Individuals and groups in 75 countries working or interested in the field of nematology. (Nematology is the study of nematodes, which are elongated, cylindrical worms that are parasitic to animals and plants or free-living in soil and water.) Fosters collaboration among nematologists. Operates placement service.
Formerly: Formerly, Society of European Nematologists
Publication: Newsletter
Publication title: Nematology News
Meetings/Conventions: International Congress of Nematology – biennial symposium – Exhibits.

02091
European Society of Paediatric Radiology
ESPR
Great Ormond Street Hospital for Children, Department of Imaging, London, WC1N 3JH, UK
Email: secretary@espr.org
Website: http://www.espr.org
Members: 282
Contact: Catherine M. Owens, Gen. Sec.
Fee: £220
Membership Type: full
Description: Radiologists involved or interested in pediatric radiology. Seeks to contribute to the advancement of the clinical and scientific aspects of pediatric radiology in European countries through educational activities. Conducts annual postgraduate courses and sponsors research programs.
Publication: Journal
Publication title: Pediatric Radiology

02092
European Society of Pathology
ESP
University of Sheffield Medical School, Academic Unit of Pathology, Beech Hill Rd., Sheffield, S10 2RX, UK
Tel: 0114 2712397
Fax: 0114 2261464
Email: m.wells@sheffield.ac.uk
Website: http://esp-pathology.org
Members: 1352
Contact: Michael Wells, Pres.
Description: Pathologists and other medical doctors in 49 countries with an interest in pathology. Fosters communication among pathologists; promotes publication of works on pathology and the development of a European school of pathology.
Publication: Newsletter
Publication title: European Pathology Newsletter
Meetings/Conventions: European Congress of Pathology – biennial congress – Exhibits.

02093
European Society of Thoracic Surgeons
ESTS
PO Box 159, Exeter, EX2 4SH, UK
Tel: 01392 430671
Fax: 01392 430671
Email: sue@ests.org.uk
Website: http://www.ests.org
Members: 720
Contact: Sue Hesford, Admin. Sec.
Fee: £210
Membership Type: full, ordinary (high income countries)
Fee: £150
Membership Type: full, ordinary (high middle income countries)
Description: Represents thoracic surgeons in Europe. Seeks to improve the study and practice of thoracic surgery.

02094
European Society of Veterinary Dermatology
ESVD
c/o Ian Mason, Treas. /Membership Sec.
Abbey Veterinary Services, 89 Queen St., Devon, Newton Abbot, TQ12 2BG, UK
Fax: 01626 335135
Email: president@esvd.org
Website: http://www.esvd.org
Members: 550
Staff: 6
Contact: Luc Beco, Pres.
Fee: £105
Membership Type: affiliate, associate, full, honored
Fee: £120
Membership Type: non-European
Description: Fosters exchange of information with veterinary dermatologists; promotes veterinary dermatology in Europe.
Library Subject: dermatology
Library Type: not open to the public
Publication: Journal
Publication title: Veterinary Dermatology. Advertisements.

02095
European Society of Veterinary Neurology
ESVN
Veterinary Companion Animal Sciences, Faculty of Veterinary Medicine, 464 Bearsden Rd., Glasgow, G61 1QH, UK
Tel: 0141 330 5739
Fax: 0141 330 5729
Email: treasurer@ecvn.org
Website: http://www.ecvn.org/index.htm
Contact: Cheryl Marshall, Treas.
Fee: £45
Membership Type: regular
Description: Works as a forum for all individuals interested in all aspects of the animal nervous system; promotes training programs in veterinary neurology.

02096

European Sponsorship Association ESA

Claremont House, Ste. 1, 22-24 Claremont Rd., Surrey, Surbiton, KT6 4QU, UK
Tel: 0208 3903311
Fax: 0208 3900055
Email: enquiries@sponsorship.org
Website: http://www.sponsorship.org
Members: 200
Staff: 3
Contact: Karen Earl, Chair
Fee: £2000
Membership Type: platinum
Fee: £1200
Membership Type: gold
Description: Consultancy companies who specialize in sponsorship consultancy and event management, audits and PR/promotions in connection with sponsored events/activities/persons. Serves as an independent neutral and authoritative body comprising professional sponsorship consultants. Aims to set and maintain standards within the sponsorship industry, and both to lobby on legislative and other matters relating to sponsorship as well as to act as a valuable independent reference point for current and first-time sponsors. Organizes major international congress annually for the professionals in the sponsorship industry; conferences, seminars, educational meetings, and socials for its members; and educational/training courses for students of universities/colleges and individuals from the commercial sector.
Formerly: Formerly, Institute of Sports Sponsorship
Publication: Directory
Publication title: Consultants Register
Meetings/Conventions: annual general assembly

02097

European String Teachers Association ESTA

c/o Anja Josefsberg, Membership Sec.
61 Worlds End Ln., Buckinghamshire, Weston Turville, HP22 5RX, UK
Tel: 0845 2412198
Email: anja@estastrings.org.uk
Website: http://www.estaweb.org.uk
Members: 1250
Staff: 2
Contact: Tasmin Little, Pres.
Fee: £48
Membership Type: standard individual
Fee: £24
Membership Type: student
Description: Represents violin, viola, cello and double-bass teachers, players and all interested in improving the quality of music education.
Publication: Magazine
Publication title: News and Views. Advertisements.

02098

European Suzuki Association ESA

Stour House, E Bergholt, Colchester, CO7 6TF, UK
Tel: 01206 299448
Fax: 01206 298490
Email: esa@europeansuzuki.org
Website: http://www.europeansuzuki.org
Members: 5800
Staff: 8
Contact: Koen Rens, Chm.
Description: Music teachers, specialized educators, parents, and interested individuals. Promotes musical education among children using the educational philosophy and ideas of Shinichi Suzuki, a Japanese musician. Methods include the "mother tongue" method which involves children learning music in the same way they learned their own native language. Conducts certification examinations for instructors.

02099

European Tour Operators Association ETOA

6 Weighouse St., London, W1K 5LT, UK
Tel: 020 74994412
Fax: 020 74994413
Email: info@etoa.org
Website: http://www.etoa.org
Members: 360
Contact: Jack Coronna, Pres.
Fee: £1490-3600
Membership Type: tour operator (based on volume of passengers)
Fee: £1000-1650
Membership Type: associate
Description: Provides individual companies with representation at European level, providing members with the opportunity to make their case heard directly. Promotes greater awareness of the benefits provided by the group travel industry in Europe particularly the increased income and employment.

02100

European Training and Simulation Association ETSA

Denvilles House, 33 Emsworth Rd., Hampshire, Havant, PO9 2SN, UK
Tel: 02392 484488
Fax: 02392 454848
Email: etsa@andrich.com
Website: http://www.etsaweb.org
Contact: Lorna Katon, Contact
Fee: £2000
Membership Type: government or user
Fee: £96
Membership Type: individual
Description: Represents the European training and simulation community. Provides an environment for users and suppliers to exchange opportunities, ideas, information and strategies on training and simulation technology and methodology. Brings together all those who have a professional interest in improving the effectiveness of training and training related interoperability, standards and codes of practice.

02101

European Union for Responsible Incineration and Treatment of Special Waste EURITS

Church House, Great Smith St., London, SW1P 3AZ, UK
Tel: 020 72221265
Fax: 020 72221250
Email: admin@eurits.org
Website: http://www.incineration.info/home
Members: 27
Contact: Axel Korn, Pres.
Description: Aims to conduct hazardous waste incineration in a safe, legal qualitative and responsible way; adheres to the priority philosophy of waste management, including waste avoidance; waste re-use, recycling, recuperation; waste incineration with energy recovery; waste incineration without energy recovery; and waste landfills.

02102

European Union of Agreement EUA

c/o British Board of Agreement
Bucknalls Ln., Garston, Herts, Watford, WD25 9BA, UK
Tel: 01923 665300
Fax: 01923 665301
Email: mail@ueatc.com
Website: http://www.ueatc.com
Staff: 1
Description: National organizations certifying procedure and product innovations in the construction field. Issues agreement certification which verifies the durability of materials and building techniques, purpose of construction, and safety. Promotes mutual recognition of agreement certification among member states.
Publication: Magazine
Publication title: UEATC Information

02103

European Union Youth Orchestra EUYO

6A Pont St., London, SW1X 9EL, UK
Tel: 020 72357671
Fax: 020 72357370
Email: info@euyo.org.uk
Website: http://www.euyo.org.uk
Members: 140
Staff: 4
Contact: Joy Bryer, Co-Founder/Sec. Gen.
Description: Musicians between the ages of 14 to 23 representing Belgium, Denmark, France, Germany, Greece, Italy, Luxembourg, Netherlands, Portugal, Republic of Ireland, Spain, Austria, Sweden, Finland, and the United Kingdom. Promotes orchestral music among young musicians and to help them launch their professional careers.
Formerly: Formerly, European Community Youth Orchestra
Publication: Brochure
Publication title: Tour Brochure. Advertisements.

02104

European Venous Forum EVF

c/o Beaumont Associates
PO Box 172, Greenford, UB6 9ZN, UK
Tel: 020 85757044
Fax: 020 85757044
Email: evenousforum@aol.com
Website: http://www.europeanvenousforum.org
Members: 260
Staff: 1
Contact: Anne Taft, Exec. Sec.
Fee: £55
Description: Develops scientific knowledge, research, clinical expertise, training and education and aims to establish standards in the fields of venous disease; promotes collaboration between phlebological and vascular societies, health agencies and authorities at national and European levels.
Publication: Journal
Publication title: Phlebology

02105

European Veterinary Dental College
EVDC

Chess Veterinary Clinic, 97 Uxbridge Rd., Herts, Rickmansworth, WD3 7DJ, UK
Email: secretary@evdc.org
Website: http://www.evdc.info
Contact: Simone Kirby, Sec.
Description: Promotes the advancement of veterinary dentistry, odonto-stomatology and oral surgery.
Meetings/Conventions: ANN – meeting

02106

European Veterinary Dental Society
EVDS

21 Station Rd., Warwickshire, Studley, B80 7HR, UK
Tel: 01527 853304
Fax: 01527 853688
Email: treasurer@evds.org
Website: http://www.evds.info
Contact: Pete Haseler, Treas.
Fee: £140
Membership Type: regular (with journal)
Fee: £90
Membership Type: regular (without journal)
Description: Supports education in and promotion of clinical excellence in veterinary dentistry.
Publication: Newsletter
Publication title: EVDS Forum

02107

European Young Bar Association
EYBA

105 St. Peter St., St. Albans, AL1 3EJ, UK
Tel: 0207 3397043
Fax: 39 432 402630
Email: info@eyba.org
Website: http://www.eyba.org
Contact: Gabriella Geatti, Pres.
Fee: £125
Membership Type: individual
Fee: £500
Membership Type: group
Description: Represents the interests of young lawyers in Europe. Promotes the welfare of and encourages links among young lawyers. Facilitates interaction and networking activities.

02108

Events Industry Alliance
EIA

119 High St., Berkhamsted, HP4 2DJ, UK
Tel: 01442 873331
Fax: 01442 875551
Email: info@aeo.org.uk
Website: http://www.eventsindustryalliance.com
Contact: Austen Hawkins, CEO
Description: Promotes the live events industry. Provides an association secretariat service. Increases the resources for event industry and the professionalism and knowledge of member companies. Educates the business community about the value of event marketing.

02109

Executives Association of Great Britain
EAGB

Kent Innovation Centre, Thanet Research Business Park, Millennium Way, Kent, Broadstairs, CT10 2QQ, UK
Tel: 07957 151787
Email: jo@eagb.biz
Website: http://www.eagb.biz
Contact: Jo Gideon, Dir. of Operations
Description: Executives of businesses in the United Kingdom. Provides a forum for the exchange of information between members.
Publication: Directory
Publication title: Membership List. Advertisements.

02110

EXIT

17 Hart St., Edinburgh, EH1 3RN, UK
Tel: 0131 5564404
Email: exit@euthanasia.cc
Website: http://www.euthanasia.cc
Contact: Chris Docker, Dir.
Fee: £50
Membership Type: supporter
Fee: £100
Membership Type: supporter (overseas)
Description: Aims to make dying with dignity an option available to anyone. Protects patients and doctors in upholding the humanity of dying well. Seeks legal reform, where necessary and introduces safeguards regarding voluntary euthanasia.
Formerly: Formerly, Voluntary Euthanasia Society of Scotland

02111

Exmoor Horn Sheep Breeders Society

Kitridge Farm, Somerset, Withypool, TA24 7RY, UK
Tel: 01643 831593
Email: info@exmoorhornbreeders.co.uk
Website: http://www.exmoorhornbreeders.co.uk/contactus.htm
Members: 180
Staff: 1
Contact: Gina Rawle, Sec.
Description: Seeks to promote improvement of sheep breeding.

02112

Experimental Psychology Society
EPS

Department of Experimental Psychology, University of Bristol, 12a Priory Rd., Bristol, BS8 1TU, UK
Website: http://www.eps.ac.uk
Members: 720
Contact: Chris Jarrold, Hon. Sec.
Description: Aims to further scientific enquiry within the field of psychology and cognate subjects. Disseminates information and educational material made available as a consequence of psychological research.
Publication: Journal
Publication title: Quarterly Journal of Experimental Psychology

02113

Eyecare Trust

PO Box 804, Aylesbury, HP20 9DF, UK
Tel: 0845 1295001
Fax: 0845 1295002
Email: info@eyecaretrust.org.uk
Website: http://www.eyecaretrust.org.uk
Staff: 1
Contact: Iain Anderson, Chm.
Fee: £250
Membership Type: regular
Description: Acts as an independent source of information on all eye-related issues, with key task of raising public awareness about the importance of regular eye care, as well as the enjoyment and benefits from using quality eye wear. Seeks to increase understanding about the work of the ophthalmic profession, communicating with the public via the media, including local and national newspapers, general and special interest magazine and national and local radio and television.
Formerly: Formerly, Eyecare Information Service

02114

Faculty of Actuaries

Maclaurin House, 18 Dublin St., Edinburgh, EH1 3PP, UK
Tel: 020 76322100
Fax: 0131 2401313
Email: faculty@actuaries.org.uk
Website: http://www.actuaries.org.uk
Members: 1870
Staff: 10
Contact: Richard Maconachie, Sec.
Description: Aims to develop the role and enhance the reputation of the actuarial profession on providing expert and relevant solutions to financial and business problems especially those involving uncertain future events.
Library Subject: actuarial science, pensions, insurance, mortality, probability statistics, investment
Library Type: not open to the public
Publication: Journal
Publication title: British Actuarial Journal

02115

Faculty of Advocates

Parliament House, Advocates Library, Edinburgh, EH1 1RF, UK
Tel: 0131 2265071
Fax: 0131 2253642
Email: clerkoffaculty@advocates.org.uk
Website: http://www.advocates.org.uk
Members: 698
Contact: Bruce McKain, Dir. of Public Affairs
Description: All members of the Scottish Bar. Concerned with the provision of specialist advocacy before courts, tribunals, inquiries, arbitrations and similar bodies; the provision of legal advice on both litigious and non litigious matters.

02116

Faculty of Dental Surgery
FDS

c/o The Royal College of Surgeons of England
35-43 Lincoln's Inn Fields, London, WC2A 3PE, UK
Tel: 020 78696810
Fax: 020 78696816
Email: fds@rcseng.ac.uk
Website: http://www.rcseng.ac.uk/fds
Members: 2500
Staff: 20

Contact: Derrick Willmot, Chm.
Description: Provides useful information for specialists and trainees in the dental specialties.

02117
Faculty of Homeopathy
Hahnemann House, 29 Park St. W, Luton, LU1 3BE, UK
Tel: 01582 408680
Fax: 01582 723032
Email: info@trusthomeopathy.org
Website: http://www.facultyofhomeopathy.org
Members: 1400
Staff: 8
Contact: Sara Eames, Pres.
Fee: £100
Membership Type: associate
Fee: £120
Membership Type: licensed
Description: Professional body responsible for regulating the education, training and practice of homeopathy by medically qualified doctors, veterinary surgeons, dentists, pharmacists and other statutorily registered health care professionals. Accredited post-graduate training courses lead to the LFHom qualification and, for doctors and vets, medical/veterinary membership of the faculty.
Library Subject: homeopathic references
Library Type: reference
Publication: Journal
Publication title: Homeopathy. Advertisements.
Meetings/Conventions: British Homeopathic Congress – biennial congress

02118
Faculty of Occupational Medicine
FOM
c/o Royal College of Physicians
New Derwent House, 3rd Fl., 69-73 Theobalds Rd., London, WC1X 8TA, UK
Tel: 020 73175890
Website: http://www.facoccmed.ac.uk
Contact: David Coggon, Pres.
Description: Provides professional and academic body empowered to develop and maintain high standards of training, competence, and professional integrity in occupational medicine.
Library Type: reference

02119
Faculty of Public Health
FPH
4 St. Andrews Pl., London, NW1 4LB, UK
Tel: 020 79350243
Fax: 020 72246973
Email: enquiries@fph.org.uk
Website: http://www.fph.org.uk
Members: 3000
Staff: 20
Contact: Paul Scourfield, Chief Exec.
Description: Principally trainees and consultants in public health medicine. Aims to promote, for the public benefit, the advancement of education in the field of public health medicine; and to develop public health medicine with a view to maintaining the highest possible standards of professional competence and practice, and act as an authoritative body for the purpose of consultation in matters of education or public interest concerning public health medicine.
Publication: Journal
Publication title: Journal of Public Health Medicine
Meetings/Conventions: Public Health – annual conference

02120
Faculty of Royal Designers for Industry
RDI
c/o Royal Society for the Encouragement of Arts, Manufactures and Commerce
8 John Adam St., London, WC2N 6EZ, UK
Tel: 020 79305115
Fax: 020 74516981
Email: melanie.andrews@rsa.org.uk
Website: http://www.thersa.org/projects/design/rdi
Members: 172
Contact: Matthew Taylor, CEO
Description: Works to encourage a high standard of industrial design and enhance the status of designers.

02121
Fair Organ Preservation Society
FOPS
Gaythorpe, Blacketts Wood Dr., Chorleywood, WD3 5QQ, UK
Tel: 01923 284441
Fax: 01923 490128
Email: membership@fops.org
Website: http://www.fops.org
Members: 900
Contact: Norman Rogers, Membership Sec.
Fee: £21
Membership Type: single (overseas)
Fee: £15
Membership Type: senior citizen (UK)
Description: Persons in 15 countries interested in fair organs, street organs, band organs, and dance organs united to promote interest in mechanical musical instruments. Promotes and encourage all forms of interest in and the preservation of fairground organs and mechanical musical instruments. Makes available technical assistance to members.
Publication: Journal
Publication title: The Key Frame. Advertisements.

02122
Fair Play for Children Association
32 Longford Rd., W Sussex, Bognor Regis, PO21 1AG, UK
Tel: 0845 3307635
Email: fairplay@arunet.co.uk
Website: http://www.fairplayforchildren.org
Members: 450
Staff: 2
Contact: Jan Cosgrove, Natl. Sec.
Fee: £24
Membership Type: local group
Fee: £15
Membership Type: individual
Description: Provides campaigns for the child's right to play. Gives support to membership organisations.
Library Subject: children's play, children's rights, child's health, child's protection, youth, youth justice, charity and voluntary
Library Type: reference
Publication: Magazine
Publication title: Play Action. Advertisements.

02123
Fairground Society
PO Box 549, Telford, TF7 5WA, UK
Email: simonjharris@btinternet.com
Website: http://www.fairgroundsociety.co.uk
Members: 450
Contact: Simon Harris, Membership Sec.
Fee: £10
Membership Type: regular
Fee: £16
Membership Type: family
Description: Caters to anyone interested in fairgrounds past or present.
Publication: Magazine
Publication title: Platform. Advertisements.

02124
Families Need Fathers
FNF
134 Curtain Rd., London, EC2A 3AR, UK
Tel: 020 76135060
Fax: 020 77393410
Email: fnf@fnf.org.uk
Website: http://www.fnf.org.uk
Staff: 10
Contact: Craig Pickering, CEO
Fee: £39
Membership Type: full
Fee: £750
Membership Type: life
Description: Provides information and support to parents about maintaining a child's relationship with both parents during and after family breakdown. Works to increase awareness of the problems of family breakdown.
Publication: Newsletter
Publication title: McKenzie

02125
Family Education Trust
FET
Jubilee House, 19-21 High St., Whitton, Twickenham, TW2 7LB, UK
Tel: 020 88942525
Fax: 020 88943535
Email: info@famyouth.org.uk
Website: http://www.famyouth.org.uk
Staff: 3
Contact: Norman Wells, Dir.
Description: Conducts research into the "social, psychological, and cultural consequences of sexual behavior and family breakdown".
Formerly: Also Known As, Family and Youth Concern
Publication: Newsletter
Publication title: Family Bulletin

02126
Family Planning Association of the United Kingdom
FPA
50 Featherstone St., London, EC1Y 8QU, UK
Tel: 020 76085240
Fax: 0845 1232349
Email: membership@fpa.org.uk
Website: http://www.fpa.org.uk/Homepage
Contact: Julie Bentley, Chief Exec.
Fee: £30
Membership Type: individual
Fee: £90
Membership Type: corporate
Description: Improves the sexual health and reproductive rights of all people throughout the UK.

02127
Fan Circle International
FCI
Cronk-y-Voddy, Rectory Rd., Coltishall, Norwich, NR12 7HF, UK
Email: fans@coltishall.freeserve.co.uk
Website: http://www.fancircleinternational.org
Members: 300
Fee: £53
Membership Type: in U.S.
Fee: £24
Membership Type: individual (domestic)
Description: Museums, art galleries, auction houses, and private collectors in 20 countries with an artistic, historical, or general interest in fans. Promotes interest in and knowledge of the fan in all aspects. Sponsors competitions. Organizes exhibitions; offers advice on preservation and repairs; arranges contacts among members for those traveling and wishing to view collections. Compiles statistics.
Publication: Bulletin
Publication title: Fans. Advertisements.

02128
Fan Makers' Company
Skinners Hall, 8 Dowgate Hill, London, EC4R 2SP, UK
Tel: 020 73294633
Email: clerk@fanmakers.com
Website: http://www.fanmakers.com
Contact: Martin Davies, Clerk
Description: Promotes the fan industry. Aims to retain the interest in maintaining and conserving the collection of fans.

02129
Fastener Engineering and Research Association
FERA
National Metalforming Centre, 47 Birmingham Rd., West Bromwich, B70 6PY, UK
Tel: 0121 6016350
Fax: 0121 6016373
Email: generalsec@fera.org.uk
Website: http://www.fera.org.uk
Fee: £70
Membership Type: individual
Fee: £110
Membership Type: corporate
Description: Represents engineers and designers involved in the specification of fasteners, installation of mechanical fasteners and the use of adhesives and involvement in application joint design. Aims to further the development of fastener industry. Promotes the knowledge and understanding of fastener technology.

02130
Fauna and Flora International
FFI
Jupiter House, 4th Fl., Station Rd., Cambridge, CB1 2JD, UK
Tel: 01223 571000
Fax: 01223 461481
Email: info@fauna-flora.org
Website: http://www.fauna-flora.org
Members: 4000
Staff: 20
Contact: Mark Rose, CEO
Fee: £35
Membership Type: supporter
Fee: £75
Membership Type: oryx
Description: Individuals, libraries, universities, natural history societies, other wildlife conservation organizations, and governmental departments responsible for wildlife, national parks, and tourism in 80 countries. Purpose is to prevent the extinction of species of wild animals and plants by promoting the conservation of wildlife, the establishment of new national parks, the enactment and enforcement of laws to protect wildlife, and the education of governments and individuals in the value of world wildlife as a non-renewable natural resource. Conducts research relating to endangered species.
Formerly: Formerly, Fauna and Flora Preservation Society
Publication: Magazine
Publication title: Fauna & Flora

02131
Fawcett Society
1-3 Berry St., London, EC1V 0AA, UK
Tel: 020 72532598
Fax: 020 72532599
Email: info@fawcettsociety.org.uk
Website: http://www.fawcettsociety.org.uk
Members: 2000
Staff: 10
Contact: Geri Goddard, Chief Exec.
Fee: £5
Membership Type: general
Description: Campaigns for equality between men and women. Seeks to abolish all sex discrimination. Strives for new attitudes towards gender relationships in society. Conducts lobbying activities including equal value, equal pay, and equal partners campaign.
Formerly: Formerly, London Society of Obtaining Political Rights for Women
Publication: Newsletter
Publication title: Towards Equality

02132
FDA
8 Leake St., London, SE1 7NN, UK
Tel: 084 54701111
Email: info@fda.org.uk
Website: http://www.fda.org.uk
Members: 18000
Staff: 24
Contact: Oliver Rowe, Contact
Description: Represents the interests of senior civil servants, public sector and NHS managers.
Publication: Magazine
Publication title: Public Service Magazine. Advertisements.

Federacion International de Juventudes Liberales y Radicales
see International Federation of Liberal and Radical Youth

02133
Federation Against Software Theft
FAST
York House, 18 York Rd., Maidenhead, SL6 1SF, UK
Tel: 0845 5218630
Fax: 0845 5218625
Email: info@fastiis.org
Website: http://www.fastiis.org
Members: 500
Contact: Philip Keown, Chm.
Description: Represents the interests of software publishers and end users. Advocates for the protection of copyright law for software programs. Provides consultancy services to businessman.

Federation des Employeurs Europeens
see Federation of European Employers

Federation du Commerce des Cacaos
see Federation of Cocoa Commerce

Federation Europeenne des Syndicats d'Entreprises d'Isolation
see European Federation of Associations of Insulation Contractors

Federation Europeenne des Victimes de la Route
see European Federation of Road Traffic Victims

Federation Internationale d'Ingegnerie Municipal
see International Federation of Municipal Engineering

Federation Internationale de Gynecologie et d'Obstetrique
see International Federation of Gynecology and Obstetrics

Federation Internationale de la Presse Periodique
see International Federation of the Periodical Press

Federation Internationale de Navigabilite Aerospatiale
see International Federation of Airworthiness

Federation Internationale des Armateurs
see International Shipping Federation

Federation Internationale des Associations Contre la Lepre
see International Federation of Anti-Leprosy Associations

Federation Internationale des Associations de Patrons de Navires

see International Federation of Shipmasters' Associations

Federation Internationale des Associations de Pilotes de Ligne

see International Federation of Air Line Pilots Associations

Federation Internationale des Ouvriers du Transport

see International Transport Workers' Federation

Federation Internationale des Services des Espaces Verts et de la Recreation

see International Federation of Park and Recreation Administration

Federation Internationale des Societes d'Ingenieurs des Techniques de l' Automobile

see International Federation of Automotive Engineering Societies

Federation Internationale pour la Planification Familiale

see International Planned Parenthood Federation - United Kingdom

Federation Internationale Pour La Recherche En Histoire Des Femmes

see International Federation for Research in Women's History

Federation Internationale pour la Recherche Theatrale

see International Federation for Theatre Research

Federation Mondiale des Societes d'Anesthesiologistes

see World Federation of Societies of Anaesthesiologists

02134

Federation of Bakers
FOB

6 Catherine St., London, WC2B 5JW, UK
Tel: 020 74207190
Fax: 020 73790542
Email: info@bakersfederation.org.uk
Website: http://www.bakersfederation.org.uk/home.aspx
Members: 70
Staff: 5
Contact: Gordon Polson, Dir.
Fee: £13.24
Membership Type: full (per 1000 weekly net turnover)
Fee: £500
Membership Type: associate
Description: Large-scale plant bakers - predominantly wholesale. Promotes and maintains the economic stability of the bread industry; represents members' interests within the United Kingdom and Europe in areas of legislation, media and in co-operation with other organizations and associations; provides a forum for members to pursue common interests and resolve problems; provides statistics as required by members.
Publication: Booklet
Publication title: Bread is Good for You

02135

Federation of British Artists
FBA

c/o Mall Galleries
17 Carlton House Terr., London, SW1Y 5BD, UK
Tel: 020 79306844
Fax: 020 78397830
Email: info@mallgalleries.com
Website: http://www.mallgalleries.org.uk
Members: 614
Staff: 8
Contact: Lewis McNaught, Dir.
Description: Umbrella organization for the U.K.'s nine top art societies which run the Mall Galleries in London, offering open exhibitions and competitions. Works of art are for sale or on commission; the galleries are used as a venue and educational activities.

02136

Federation of British Hand Tool Manufacturers
FBHTM

c/o The Manufacturing Technologies Association
62 Bayswater Rd., London, W2 3PS, UK
Tel: 020 72986400
Fax: 020 72986430
Email: info@britishtools.co.uk
Website: http://www.mta.org.uk/trade-associations/FBHTM
Members: 48
Staff: 9
Contact: Nick Stamp, Sec.
Description: Works to further the interests of all hand tool manufacturers; aims to establish suitable technical standards in conjunction with BSI, CEN and ISO.

02137

Federation of Children's Book Groups

2 Bridge Wood View, Horsforth, West Yorkshire, Leeds, LS18 5PE, UK
Tel: 0113 2588910
Email: info@fcbg.org.uk
Website: http://www.fcbg.org.uk
Members: 500
Contact: Adam Lancaster, Chm.
Fee: £30
Membership Type: individual
Fee: £50
Membership Type: individual overseas
Description: Parents, teachers, librarians, publishers and schools. Fosters the education of children by the provision of books, National Share-a-Story Month, and local group events.

02138

Federation of City Farms and Community Gardens
FCFCG

c/o The GreenHouse
Hereford St., Bristol, BS3 4NA, UK
Tel: 0117 9231800
Fax: 0117 9231900
Email: admin@farmgarden.org.uk
Website: http://www.farmgarden.org.uk
Members: 210
Staff: 15
Contact: Jeremy Iles, Chief Exec.
Description: Network organization coordinating community farm and garden groups in city environments throughout the UK. Promotes and supports sustainable regeneration through community managed farming and gardening.
Formerly: Formerly, National Federation of City Farms
Publication: Newsletter
Publication title: Growing Places

02139

Federation of Clothing Designers and Executives
FCDE

c/o Fashion Design Technology
London College of Fashion, 100 Curtain Rd., London, EC2A 3AA, UK
Website: http://www.fcde.org.uk
Members: 287
Contact: Alan Cannon Jones, Sec.
Description: Clothing designers, fashion designers, stylists, pattern technologists, clothing company executives, senior production controllers, technicians, senior quality controllers. Affiliate members are senior clothing college lecturers, clothing technicians in allied trades, after two years total involvement they can apply for membership.

02140

Federation of Cocoa Commerce
FCC

Cannon Bridge House, 1 Cousin Ln., London, EC4R 3XX, UK
Tel: 020 73792884
Fax: 020 73792389
Email: fcc@liffe.com
Website: http://www.cocoafederation.com
Members: 102
Staff: 2
Contact: Philip M. Sigley, Chief Exec.
Fee: £1200
Membership Type: non-voting
Fee: £2500
Membership Type: voting

Description: Aims to protect and promote interests of those engaged in physical cocoa trade.
Publication: Newsletter
Publication title: Cocoa News

02141
Federation of Communication Services
FCS
Provident House, Burrell Row, Kent, Beckenham, BR3 1AT, UK
Tel: 0208 2496363
Fax: 0844 8705927
Email: fcs@fcs.org.uk
Website: http://www.fcs.org.uk/Home.aspx
Members: 300
Staff: 7
Contact: Jacqui Brookes, CEO/Exec. Dir.
Fee: £350-2265
Membership Type: corporate
Description: Represents the mobile and telecommunication services industry including network operators, service providers, equipment manufacturers and suppliers, dealers in GSM, PMR, Public Access Mobile Radio-Tetra, paging, fixed telephony, and all supporting businesses.
Library Type: not open to the public
Publication: Bulletin
Publication title: FCS Bulletin. Advertisements.
Meetings/Conventions: Business Radio Future – annual seminar – Exhibits.

02142
Federation of Crafts and Commerce
FCC
4, 5 and 6 Quaypoint, Northarbour Rd., Portsmouth, Hampshire, PO6 3TD, UK
Tel: 0844 3716757
Fax: 0844 3759609
Email: mail@fcc.org.uk
Website: http://www.fcc.org.uk
Members: 10000
Description: Aims to reduce the impact of problems that can otherwise so often damage, or even destroy, a valuable enterprise. Provides a unique package of practical support services which can be accessed easily and quickly by its members.

02143
Federation of Drug and Alcohol Professionals
FDAP
95 Wilton Rd., Unit 84, London, SW1V 1BZ, UK
Tel: 0163 6612590
Email: office@fdap.org.uk
Website: http://www.fdap.org.uk
Contact: Carole Sharma, Chief Exec.
Fee: £70
Membership Type: standard
Fee: £200
Membership Type: affiliate (not-for-profit, less than 10 practitioners)
Description: Represents practitioners in the substance use field.

02144
Federation of Engine Re-Manufacturers
FER
59 Mewstone Ave., Wembury, Plymouth, PL9 0JT, UK
Tel: 01752 863681
Email: enquiries@fer.co.uk
Website: http://www.fer.co.uk/fer/portal/main/HomePage.asp
Members: 200
Staff: 1
Description: Promotes the reconstruction of gasoline and diesel engines and the sale and exchange of such engines. Sponsors technical lectures and work visits.
Publication: Journal
Publication title: FER News. Advertisements.

02145
Federation of Environmental Trade Associations
FETA
2 Waltham Ct., Milley Ln., Hare Hatch, Berkshire, Reading, RG10 9TH, UK
Tel: 0118 9403416
Fax: 0118 9406258
Email: info@feta.co.uk
Website: http://www.feta.co.uk
Members: 250
Staff: 5
Contact: Cedric Sloan, Dir. Gen.
Description: Members are manufacturers, distributors and contractors serving the heating, ventilating, air conditioning, refrigeration, chimney and flues industries. Serves the interests of the heating, ventilating, air conditioning and refrigeration industries and the users of HVACR equipment.

02146
Federation of European Employers
FedEE
Adam House, 7-10 Adam St., The Strand, London, WC2N 6AA, UK
Tel: 020 75209264
Fax: 020 75209265
Email: info@fedee.com
Website: http://www.fedee.com
Contact: Robin E.J. Chater, Sec. Gen.
Fee: £995-1495
Membership Type: corporate (based on number of employees)
Description: Supports and represents the interests of employers operating in Europe.

02147
Federation of European Ergonomics Society
FEES
The Old Forge, 4 High St., Bedford, MK45 4AB, UK
Tel: 01525 860164
Fax: 07816 559611
Email: doneillassoc@yahoo.co.uk
Website: http://www.fees-network.org
Contact: Pieter Rookmaaker, Pres.
Fee: £1000-5000
Membership Type: sustaining (based on categories)
Description: Promotes ergonomics as a tool for economic development, high quality of life, health and safety at work, as well as for social progress of European countries.
Publication: Brochures
Meetings/Conventions: Meeting Diversity in Ergonomics – periodic congress

02148
Federation of European Laboratory Animal Science Associations
FELASA
PO Box 3993, Staffs, Tamworth, B78 3QU, UK
Email: felasaeu@felasa.eu
Website: http://www.felasa.eu/index.php
Contact: Patri Vergara, Chm.
Description: Acts as a forum for information exchange; promotes recognition as the specialist organization in the field.

02149
Federation of European Nurses in Diabetes
FEND
24 Holmesdale Ave., London, SW14 7BQ, UK
Tel: 020 88766122
Email: info@fend.org
Website: http://www.fend.org
Contact: Anne-Marie Felton, Pres.
Description: Promotes the delivery of evidence-based care for people with diabetes throughout Europe. Aims to: develop and promote the professional role of the diabetes nurse in Europe; influence European health care policy relevant to diabetes care and research; promote acceptable standards and equity of care for people with diabetes throughout Europe; cooperate and collaborate with national and international health care organizations.
Publication: Journal
Publication title: European Journal of Diabetes Nursing. Advertisements.
Meetings/Conventions: annual conference – Exhibits.

02150
Federation of Independent Practitioner Organisations
FIPO
14 Queen Anne's Gate, London, SW1H 9AA, UK
Tel: 020 72220975
Website: http://www.fipo.org.uk
Contact: Linda Hulks, Contact
Description: Aims to preserve and promote the highest standards of clinical care. Works with all independent hospital providers and the private medical insurance industry. Advances the cause of independent healthcare in Britain. Maintains the independence of the consultant and the freedom of choice for patients and doctors. Provides a forum for the representatives of independent practitioners to agree to a common policy relating to medical practice.

02151

Federation of Master Builders FMB

Gordon Fisher House, 14-15 Great James St., London, WC1N 3DP, UK
Tel: 020 72427583
Fax: 020 74040296
Website: http://www.fmb.org.uk
Members: 13000
Staff: 58
Contact: Richard Diment, Dir. Gen.
Fee: £45
Membership Type: regular, MasterBond
Description: Members may be self-employed, in partnership or limited companies. Strives to organize, represent and promote the interests of employers in the building industry on a national basis. Warranty scheme provides insurance-backed cover for the customer for a period of 2 years or 5 years on major structural alterations.
Library Subject: buildings, employment law
Library Type: open to the public
Publication title: BATJIC Working Rule Agreement

02152

Federation of National Associations of Shipbrokers and Agents FONASBA

85, Gracechurch St., Ground Fl. N, London, EC3V 0AA, UK
Tel: 020 76233113
Fax: 020 76233113
Email: generalmanager@fonasba.com
Website: http://www.fonasba.com
Members: 51
Staff: 2
Contact: Jonathan C. Williams, Gen. Mgr.
Description: National associations of shipbrokers and ship's agents united in promotion of fair and equitable practices within the profession. Seeks recognition and acceptance of the traditional role of shipbrokers and agents as intermediaries and advisers to ship owners and merchants. Coordinates efforts to improve, modernize, simplify, and standardize shipping contracts and documents. Cooperates with and represents members' interests before other national and international bodies, authorities, and organizations. Conducts lectures and conferences.
Publication: Newsletter
Publication title: The New Horizon

02153

Federation of Oils, Seeds, and Fats Associations FOSFA

20 St. Dunstan's Hill, London, EC3R 8NQ, UK
Tel: 020 72835511
Fax: 020 76231310
Email: membership@fosfa.org
Website: http://www.fosfa.org
Members: 850
Staff: 10
Fee: £675-1250
Membership Type: trading (based on annual turnover)
Fee: £500
Membership Type: full broker
Description: Trade association primarily involved with contacts for the international trade in oils and fats, oilseeds, and selected groundnuts.
Library Subject: trade
Library Type: not open to the public
Publication: Newsletter

02154

Federation of Ophthalmic and Dispensing Opticians FODO

199 Gloucester Terr., London, W2 6LD, UK
Tel: 020 72985151
Fax: 020 72985111
Email: optics@fodo.com
Website: http://www.fodo.com
Contact: David Hewlett, Chief Exec.
Fee: £102.5
Membership Type: full
Description: Represents registered opticians in United Kingdom. Seeks to influence government and policy makers by demonstrating an inclusive and united approach across the optical sector. Promotes professional excellence through involvement in and support for education programs. Works with optical partners to take joint action wherever possible and to present a united voice for the profession.

02155

Federation of Petroleum Suppliers FPS

6 Royal Ct., Tatton St., Cheshire, Knutsford, WA16 6EN, UK
Tel: 01565 631313
Fax: 01565 631314
Email: info@fpsonline.co.uk
Website: http://www.fpsonline.co.uk
Members: 280
Staff: 5
Contact: Susan Hancock, Chief Exec.
Fee: £150-813
Membership Type: category A to C (1-14 vehicles in UK)
Fee: £948-1209
Membership Type: category D to F (15 to more than 30 vehicles in UK)
Description: Represents distributors of petroleum products.
Publication: Journal
Publication title: Downstream. Advertisements.

02156

Federation of Piling Specialists FPS

c/o Forum Court
83 Copers Cope Rd., Kent, Beckenham, BR3 1NR, UK
Tel: 020 86630947
Fax: 020 86630949
Email: fps@fps.org.uk
Website: http://www.fps.org.uk
Members: 18
Staff: 2
Contact: Dianne Jennings, Sec.
Description: Specialist contractors offering all types of foundation, earth retaining and soil improving techniques.

02157

Federation of Plastering and Drywall Contractors FPDC

4th Fl., 61 Cheapside, London, EC2V 6AX, UK
Tel: 020 76349480
Fax: 020 72483685
Email: donna.rickaby@fpdc.org
Website: http://www.fpdc.org
Members: 200
Staff: 5
Contact: Gavin Colclough, Pres.
Description: Represents contractor members' interests. Provides membership with services and opportunities that create a meaningful competitive advantage. Acts as a forum for the people in the plastering and drywall sector to discuss issues of mutual interest and concern. Looks to actively develop and advance the standards of plastering and drywall trades.
Publication: Magazine
Publication title: Specialist Building Finishes

02158

Federation of Private Residents' Associations FPRA

PO Box 10271, Epping, CM16 9DB, UK
Tel: 0871 2003324
Email: info@fpra.org.uk
Website: http://www.fpra.org.uk
Members: 3000
Staff: 19
Contact: Robert Levene, Chief Exec.
Fee: £70-250
Membership Type: regular (depends on block size 25-151 flats)
Fee: £50
Membership Type: joining
Description: Residents' associations in England and UK. For those holding long leases on their properties or who have purchased the freehold. Offers assistance in setting up residents' associations; advice given on legal matters in connection with landlords, agents, purchase of freehold, maintenance of blocks of flats.
Publication: Newsletter
Publication title: FPRA Newsletter

02159

Federation of Recorded Music Societies FRMS

18 Albany Rd., Hartshill, Stoke-on-Trent, ST4 6BB, UK
Tel: 01782 251460
Email: frms.sec@tiscali.co.uk
Website: http://www.thefrms.co.uk
Members: 235
Contact: Tony Baines, Sec.
Description: Musical organizations. Promotes the appreciation of all types of music; sponsors lectures and recitals.

02160

Federation of Small Businesses FSB

c/o Sir Frank Whittle Way
Blackpool Business Park, Blackpool, FY4 2FE, UK
Tel: 01253 336000

Fax: 01253 348046
Website: http://www.fsb.org.uk
Members: 215000
Contact: John Wright, Natl. Chm.
Fee: £120-870
Membership Type: general (based on number of employees)
Description: Lobby organization representing the interests of small business and the self-employed. Provides benefits to members, does not provide grants.
Publication: Magazine
Publication title: Business Network

02161

Federation of Sports and Play Associations
FSPA

Federation House, Stoneleigh Park, Warwickshire, Kenilworth, CV8 2RF, UK
Tel: 024 76414999
Fax: 024 76414990
Email: admin@sportsandplay.com
Website: http://www.sportslife.org.uk
Members: 650
Staff: 11
Contact: David Pomfret, Operations Dir.
Description: Manufacturers of sporting goods and clothing. Serves as a forum for discussion of industry issues among members; represents members' interests before government agencies and international organizations. Promotes export of members' products; works to increase public participation in athletics.
Formerly: Formerly, The Sports Industries Federation
Publication: Newsletter
Publication title: Sportslife. Advertisements.
Meetings/Conventions: Eurogolf – annual trade show – Exhibits.

02162

Federation of the Retail Licensed Trade
FRLT

91 University St., Belfast, BT7 1HP, UK
Tel: 028 90327578
Fax: 028 90327578
Email: margaret.scott@ulsterpubs.com
Website: http://www.ulsterpubs.com/opencontent/default.asp
Members: 1200
Staff: 5
Contact: Colin Neill, Chief Exec.
Fee: £250
Membership Type: associate
Fee: £170
Membership Type: individual
Description: Promotes trade protection and development.
Publication: Magazine
Publication title: Catering and Licensing Review. Advertisements.

02163

Federation of Tour Operators
FTO

30 Park St., London, SE1 9EQ, UK
Tel: 020 31170590
Fax: 020 31170581
Email: info@fto.co.uk
Website: http://www.fto.co.uk
Members: 12
Staff: 5
Contact: Andrew Cooper, Dir. Gen.
Description: Aims to improve conditions for tourists from the UK. Promotes the professional and positive image of the industry in UK and to overseas destination countries.

02164

Federation of Worker Writers and Community Publishers
FWWCP

Burslem School of Art, Queen St., Staffordshire, Stoke-on-Trent, ST6 3EJ, UK
Tel: 01782 822327
Email: fwwcp@tiscali.co.uk
Website: http://www.fedonline.org.uk/fed
Members: 70
Fee: £40
Membership Type: full, funded
Fee: £20
Membership Type: full, unfunded
Description: Independent writers' groups, community publishers, and adult literacy and literature development organizations. Creates and supports a national community of writers and publishers; offers people greater access to developing skills in participatory writing and publishing activities; encourages people to write and read creatively, especially those who may be socially excluded. Hosts creative writing events and performances; provides training in organizational and management skills; offers advice and information.

02165

Feline Advisory Bureau
FAB

Taeselbury, High St., Wilshire, Salisbury, SP3 6LD, UK
Tel: 01747 871872
Fax: 01747 871873
Email: information@fabcats.org
Website: http://www.fabcats.org
Members: 3000
Staff: 5
Contact: Claire Bessant, Chief Exec.
Fee: £30
Membership Type: individual within UK
Fee: £40
Membership Type: individual outside UK, affiliate
Description: Veterinary surgeons, cat breeders, and pet owners. Promotes humane behavior toward cats and provides information on feline health and care. Raises funds for feline clinical research. Provides cat boarding information service.
Library Type: not open to the public
Publication: Manual
Publication title: Boarding Cattery Manual
Meetings/Conventions: monthly conference – Exhibits.

02166

Fell Pony Society

Fell Pony Society Office, Ion House, Great Asby, Appleby, Cumbria, CA16 6HD, UK
Tel: 01768 353100
Fax: 01768 353100
Email: fellponysocietysecretary@hotmail.co.uk
Website: http://www.fellponysociety.org
Contact: Elizabeth Parkin, Sec.
Fee: £25
Membership Type: full
Fee: £30
Membership Type: full (overseas)
Description: Aims to foster and keep pure the old breed of pony, which has roamed the northern fells for years. Circulates knowledge and general information about the pony breed.

02167

Fellowship of Makers and Researchers of Historical Instruments
FoMRHI

Southside Cottage, Brook Hill, Albury, Guildford, GU5 9DJ, UK
Tel: 01483 202159
Fax: 01483 203088
Email: lutesoc@aol.com
Website: http://www.nrinstruments.demon.co.uk/fomrhi.html
Members: 500
Contact: Chris Goodwin, Sec./Ed.
Description: Makers and researchers of historical musical instruments and interested others in 33 countries. Promotes the preservation, reconstruction and use of historical musical instruments; upholds standards of authenticity.
Publication: Journal
Publication title: FoMRHI Quarterly

02168

Fellowship of St. Nicholas
FSN

St. Nicholas Centre, 66 London Rd., East Sussex, St. Leonards-on-Sea, TN37 6AS, UK
Tel: 01424 423683
Website: http://www.fsncharity.co.uk
Staff: 10
Contact: Christine Brosnan, Exec. Asst.
Description: Provides mobile projects; operates after-school care and day care for preschool children. Works to protect children from exploitation.

Femmes sous lois musulmanes
see Women Living Under Muslim Laws

02169

Fencing Contractors Association
FCA

Warren Rd., Trellech, Monmouth, NP25 4PQ, UK
Tel: 07000 560722
Fax: 01600 860888
Email: info@fencingcontractors.org
Website: http://www.fencingcontractors.org
Members: 214
Staff: 4
Contact: Wendy Baker, CEO
Fee: £295-945
Membership Type: full (based on annual turnover)
Fee: £325
Membership Type: associate (for turnover up to 75,000)
Description: Trade association for the fencing industry, including contractors, suppliers and manufacturers.
Publication: Newsletter
Publication title: FCA News Update

02170
Feng Shui Society
123, Mashiters Walk, Essex, Romford, RM1 4BU, UK
Email: joan@fengshuisociety.org.uk
Website: http://www.fengshuisociety.org.uk
Contact: Joan Vine, Admin. Sec.
Fee: £20
Membership Type: friend (in UK)
Fee: £30
Membership Type: friend (overseas)
Description: Promotes the highest standards of feng shui practice. Advances the teaching and use of feng shui. Increases public awareness and understanding of feng shui.
Publication: Journal
Publication title: Feng Shui News. Advertisements.

02171
FeRFA Resin Flooring Association FeRFA
16 Edward Rd., Surrey, Farnham, GU9 8NP, UK
Tel: 01252 714250
Email: lisa@ferfa.org.uk
Website: http://www.ferfa.org.uk/html
Members: 73
Staff: 5
Contact: Helen McGachie, CEO
Fee: £900
Membership Type: contractor/associate
Fee: £2215
Membership Type: manufacturer
Description: Represents manufacturers, contractors and associate companies in the resin flooring industry. Sets and maintains high standards of product quality, health and safety, technical competence and application capability. Promotes and develops understanding and knowledge of the benefits of resin flooring.
Formerly: Formerly, Federation for the Repair and Protection of Structures
Publication: Newsletter
Publication title: FeRFA Newsletter

Ffederasiwn Cerddoriaeth Amatur Cymru
see Welsh Amateur Music Federation

02172
FIABCI - United Kingdom
45 Bridge St., Hereford, HR4 9DG, UK
Tel: 01432 344779
Fax: 01432 352229
Email: info@jiprop.com
Website: http://www.fiabci.co.uk
Contact: Bill Jackson, Pres.
Fee: £295
Membership Type: full
Fee: £155
Membership Type: young (under 35)
Description: Represents professionals involved in the property industry. Gives members access to information on real estate markets all over the world. Disseminates general and technical information and recommends solutions to problems facing the real estate profession. Provides assistance to members whenever the rules of the profession are called into question. Encourages private property ownership.

02173
Fibreoptic Industry Association FIA
The Manor House, Buntingford, SG9 9AB, UK
Tel: 01763 273039
Fax: 01763 273255
Email: secretary@fia-online.co.uk
Website: http://www.fia-online.co.uk
Members: 220
Staff: 1
Contact: Paul Bateson, Chm.
Fee: £335-945
Membership Type: corporate (depending on relevant turnover)
Fee: £175
Membership Type: associate
Description: Represents installers, manufacturers, distributors, consultants and educational establishments associated with fibre optic communications. Aims to improve professional standards of manufacture, installation and training throughout the fibre optics industry.
Library Subject: communications
Library Type: not open to the public
Publication title: Cable Selection Guide

02174
Field Studies Council FSC
Preston Montford, Montford Bridge, Shropshire, Shrewsbury, SY4 1HW, UK
Tel: 01743 852100
Fax: 01743 852101
Email: enquiries@field-studies-council.org
Website: http://www.field-studies-council.org
Members: 3800
Contact: Rob Lucas, Chief Exec.
Fee: £15
Membership Type: individual
Fee: £25
Membership Type: family
Description: Educational charity committed to raising awareness about the natural world. Works through a network of 17 residential and day centers in the U.K. providing courses for schools and colleges at all levels. A programme of leisure learning and professional development courses is offered in the U.K. and overseas. Provides outreach education, training and consultancy, publishes many titles to support work.
Publication: Journal
Publication title: Field Studies

02175
Fife Chamber of Commerce and Enterprise
Wemyssfield House, Wemyssfield, Kirkcaldy, KY1 1XN, UK
Tel: 01592 201932
Fax: 01592 641187
Email: info@fifechamber.co.uk
Website: http://www.fifechamber.co.uk
Members: 350
Staff: 6
Contact: Bob Garmory, Pres.
Fee: £199-799
Membership Type: firm/company (based on number of employees)
Fee: £120
Membership Type: new business start-up
Description: Facilitates business opportunities and offers business representation information and advice.
Formerly: Formerly, Fife Chamber of Commerce and Industry

02176
Fight Against Animal Cruelty in Europe FAACE
29 Shakespeare St., Merseyside, Southport, PR8 5AB, UK
Tel: 01704 535922
Email: action@faace.co.uk
Website: http://www.faace.co.uk
Contact: Vicki Moore, Co-Founder
Fee: £25
Membership Type: family
Fee: £15
Membership Type: individual
Description: Aims to end cruelty to all animals; campaigns to stop the torture and death of animals for entertainment, especially bullfighting, blood fiestas, and hare coursing.

02177
Film Artistes Association FAA
373-377 Clapham Rd., London, SW9 9BT, UK
Tel: 020 73460900
Fax: 020 73460901
Email: info@bectu.org.uk
Website: http://www.bectu.org.uk/home
Members: 600
Contact: Spencer MacDonald, Contact
Fee: £60
Description: Comprised of supporting artistes, stand-ins and doubles employed in the film and television industry.
Formerly: Absorbed, Film Artistes Association

02178
Film Distributors' Association FDA
22 Golden Sq., London, W1F 9JW, UK
Fax: 020 77340912
Email: info@fda.uk.net
Website: http://www.launchingfilms.com
Members: 14
Description: Includes all major distribution companies and several independent companies. Promotes members' generic interests and co-operates with all other organizations and agencies where distribution interests are involved.
Formerly: Formerly, Society of Film Distribution
Publication: Yearbook
Publication title: FDA YearBook

02179
Filtration Society FS
19 Clyst Valley Rd., Winslade Park, Clyst St. Mary, Exeter, EX5 1DD, UK
Tel: 01392 874398
Fax: 01392 874398
Email: richard.wakeman@lineone.net
Website: http://www.filtsoc.org
Contact: Richard Wakeman, Sec.
Fee: £98
Membership Type: individual
Fee: £49
Membership Type: student/retired
Description: Users of filtration and separation technology and equipment; research scientists and engineers in government establishments, universities, and technical

colleges; manufacturers and designers of equipment. Promotes knowledge of filtration and separation in all industries; has established award fund to stimulate research and innovation in the field. Organizes and sponsors conferences, symposia, and laboratory and industrial visits.
Publication: Journal
Publication title: Filtration. Advertisements.

02180
Finance and Leasing Association
FLA
Imperial House, 2nd Fl., 15-19 Kingsway, London, WC2B 6UN, UK
Tel: 020 78366511
Fax: 020 74209600
Email: info@fla.org.uk
Website: http://www.fla.org.uk
Contact: Stephen Sklaroff, Dir. Gen.
Description: Trade association representing the UK asset, consumer, and motor finance sectors. Provides high-level representation and lobbying at both national and EU levels, supported by technical information and industry statistics. Complies with the association's code of conduct, which is supported by their conciliation and arbitration schemes. Provides a focus and forum for the industry, and has a high level of member involvement in its many working groups. Organizes conferences, workshops, and training courses.
Formerly: Formerly, Finance Houses Association
Publication: Annual Report
Publication title: Annual Review
Meetings/Conventions: monthly convention

02181
Financial Services Authority
FSA
25 The N Colonnade, Canary Wharf, London, E14 5HS, UK
Tel: 020 70661000
Fax: 020 70669870
Website: http://www.fsa.gov.uk
Members: 1400
Staff: 260
Contact: Adair Turner, Chm.
Description: Investment businesses that deal on the organized City markets e.g. stockbrokers, market makers, investment banks, futures dealers and brokers. The regulatory body for dealers and advisers in securities, bonds, financial futures and options commodity futures and corporate finance.
Library Type: reference
Formerly: Formerly, Securities and Futures Authority
Publication: Book
Publication title: Rule Book

02182
Find Your Feet
FYF
Unit 316, Bon Marche Ctre., 241-251 Ferndale Rd., London, SW9 8BJ, UK
Tel: 020 73264464
Fax: 020 77338848
Email: fyf@fyf.org.uk
Website: http://www.find-your-feet.org
Staff: 5
Contact: Koy Thomson, Chm.
Description: Works in partnership with NGOs in Southern Africa and South Asia in long-term development programs promoting sustainable livelihoods. Helping to break the cycle of poverty by providing investment to enable people to increase their income and achieve long-term food security.

02183
Findhorn Foundation
The Park, Findhorn, Forres, IV36 3TZ, UK
Tel: 01309 690311
Fax: 01309 691301
Email: enquiries@findhorn.org
Website: http://www.findhorn.org/index.php
Members: 150
Staff: 70
Contact: Yvonne Cuneo, Communications Mgr.
Description: Serves as a community, ecovillage and centre for holistic education, helping to build a sustainable and positive future, today. Its services include courses in personal development, sustainable development, conflict resolution, and environmental issues; management and organisational consultancy; Universal Hall venue for performing arts and conferences; ecological building techniques; sustainable energy systems; and organic food production. Committed to teaching and demonstrating intrinsic values necessary for creating a culture that is peaceful, inclusive and sustainable. Offers a range of residential programmes encouraging the acquisition of new skills and awareness to bring about constructive and compassionate change.
Publication: Newsletters
Publication title: Findhorn Foundation and Community Network News. Advertisements.

02184
Fine Art Trade Guild
16-18 Empress Pl., London, SW6 1TT, UK
Tel: 020 73816616
Fax: 020 73812596
Website: http://www.fineart.co.uk
Members: 1800
Staff: 10
Contact: Paul Cumberland, Treas.
Fee: £257.2
Membership Type: gallery, artists' agent, artist, picture/frame restorer, other retail
Fee: £524.1
Membership Type: picture wholesaler/distributor, publisher, fine art printer, framing material/equipment supplier, framer/picture manufacturer
Description: Art dealers; fine art printers and publishers; framing materials suppliers; art galleries; picture framers; artists; agents. Association for all those involved in the picture industry. Aims to help members develop their businesses via consumer marketing, retail and craft training and testing, setting of industry standards, financial savings and information services.
Publication: Magazine
Publication title: Art Business Today. Advertisements.

02185
Fingerprint Society
FPS
Derbyshire Constabulary, Scientific Support Unit, Butterley Hall, Derbyshire, Ripley, DE5 3RS, UK
Email: karen.stow.9864@derbyshire.pnn.police.uk
Website: http://www.fpsociety.org.uk
Members: 1000
Contact: Karen Stow, Pres.
Fee: £39
Membership Type: fellow/associate (in UK and Australia)
Fee: £80
Membership Type: fellow/associate in U.S.
Description: Fingerprint and scene of the crime officers employed by police, civilian, or military organizations in 74 countries. Purpose is to further the study of fingerprints. Facilitates communication and cooperation among members and others interested in the field of personal identification.
Publication: Handbook
Publication title: The Fingerprint Society Handbook
Meetings/Conventions: annual conference – Exhibits.

02186
Fire Brigades Union
FBU
Bradley House, 68 Coombe Rd., Surrey, Kingston upon Thames, KT2 7AE, UK
Tel: 020 85411765
Fax: 020 85465187
Email: office@fbu.org.uk
Website: http://www.fbu.org.uk
Members: 50000
Staff: 25
Contact: Matt Wrack, Gen. Sec.
Description: Uniformed members of local authority fire brigades in the United Kingdom. Serves its members by winning for them the best possible conditions, and to serve the community by encouraging its members to be skilled at their craft.
Publication: Newsletter
Publication title: CARe

02187
Fire Industry Association
FIA
Tudor House, Kingsway Business Park, Oldfield Rd., Hampton, TW12 2HD, UK
Tel: 020 31665002
Fax: 020 89410972
Email: info@fia.uk.com
Website: http://www.fia.uk.com
Members: 80
Staff: 12
Contact: Martin Duggan, Gen. Mgr.
Description: Is committed to upholding and where appropriate, to raising the standards of performance and reliability of portable firefighting equipment and fitting and fire hoses manufactured and/or maintained by its members.
Formerly: Formerly, Fire Extinguishing Trades Association
Publication: Newsletter
Publication title: FETA News

02188
Fire Protection Association - England
FPA
London Rd., Moreton-in-Marsh, GL56 0RH, UK
Tel: 01608 812500
Fax: 01608 812501
Email: fpa@thefpa.co.uk
Website: http://www.thefpa.co.uk
Members: 5850
Staff: 25
Contact: Jonathan O'Neill, Managing Dir.
Fee: £150
Membership Type: bronze
Fee: £350
Membership Type: silver

Description: Insurers, brokers, loss adjusters, industrial, commercial and private sector companies/organizations, fire brigades, fire liaison panels, Industrial Fire Protection Association and local FPAs, engineers, architects and fire safety specialists/consultants. Identifying and drawing attention to fire dangers, and the means by which their potential for loss can be minimized, services are designed to assist fire, security and safety managers and their professional advisors, achieve and maintain the highest standards of fire safety within its premises.
Library Subject: fire safety, loss prevention, related subjects
Library Type: not open to the public
Formerly: See parent group for further info, Loss Prevention Council
Publication: Video
Publication title: Extinguishing Fires in the Workplace

02189

First Person Plural
FPP

PO Box 2537, Wolverhampton, WV4 4ZL, UK
Email: fpp@firstpersonplural.org.uk
Website: http://www.firstpersonplural.org.uk
Contact: Kathryn Livingston, Treas.
Fee: £10
Membership Type: full, associate
Fee: £20
Membership Type: international
Description: Supports individuals who experience dissociative distress and encourages the public to accept and understand them. Promotes awareness of dissociative distress to health and social care professionals.
Publication: Newsletter
Publication title: Rainbow's End

02190

First Steps to Freedom

PO Box 476, Newquay, TR7 1WQ, UK
Tel: 0845 8410619
Email: first.steps@btconnect.com
Website: http://www.first-steps.org
Contact: Jeffrey M. Schwartz, Pres.
Fee: £10
Membership Type: regular
Description: People who suffer from phobias, panic attacks, general anxiety, obsessive compulsive disorders, and tranquilizer withdrawal. Makes available telephone helpline, support groups, relaxation audiotapes. Conducts educational programs.

02191

Fitness Industry Association
FIA

Castlewood House, 77-91 New Oxford St., London, WC1A 1PX, UK
Tel: 020 74208560
Fax: 020 74208561
Email: info@fia.org.uk
Website: http://www.fia.org.uk
Members: 2000
Staff: 20
Contact: David Stalker, Exec. Dir.
Description: Represents operators, suppliers, educational establishments, and professionals in the fitness industry. Aims to raise standards, promote and represent the health and fitness industry in pursuit of a more physically active and healthier nation.
Library Subject: fitness club retention and attention, health and safety, business excellence
Library Type: reference
Publication: Magazine
Publication title: Club Business International. Advertisements.
Meetings/Conventions: Leisure Industry Week – annual convention – Exhibits.

02192

Flag Institute

38 Hill St., Mayfair, London, W1J 5NS, UK
Tel: 01932 240820
Email: info@flaginstitute.org
Website: http://www.flaginstitute.org
Members: 504
Staff: 1
Contact: Mike Kearsley, Sec.
Fee: £25
Membership Type: individual
Fee: £30
Membership Type: individual (non-UK)
Description: Individual, trade, group, and junior. Serves as a documentation and resource centre to which trade members, national libraries, government departments and museums subscribe, together with a body of individual members. Offers advice, information, guidelines and publications on all aspects of flags.
Publication: Journal
Publication title: Flagmaster
Meetings/Conventions: semiannual meeting

02193

Fleet Air Arm Officers Association
FAAOA

4 St. James's Sq., London, SW1Y 4JU, UK
Tel: 020 79307722
Fax: 020 79307728
Email: faaoa@fleetairarmoa.org
Website: http://www.fleetairarmoa.org
Contact: S. Lidbetter, Chm.
Fee: £35
Membership Type: full, associate
Description: Serves as a focal point for all who are professionally and socially bound together by their common interest and vocation in Naval Aviation.
Publication: Book
Publication title: Broadsheet

02194

Fletchers' Company

49 Sheen Rd., Surrey, Richmond upon Thames, TW9 1AJ, UK
Tel: 020 34906389
Email: clerk@fletchers.org.uk
Website: http://www.fletchers.org.uk
Members: 1371
Contact: Georgina Butler, Clerk
Description: Organizes charitable work for people with disabilities. Provides networking events for members to meet and socialize.
Publication: Newsletter
Publication title: La Fleche

02195

Flour Advisory Bureau
FAB

21 Arlington St., London, SW1A 1RN, UK
Tel: 020 74932521
Email: fab@nabim.org.uk
Website: http://www.fabflour.co.uk
Members: 68
Staff: 2
Description: Acts as the promotional arm of the National Association of British and Irish Millers which provides information on wheat, flour and bread.

02196

Flowers and Plants Association
F&PA

266-270 Flower Market, New Covent Garden Market, London, SW8 5NB, UK
Tel: 020 77388044
Fax: 020 77388083
Email: info@flowers.org.uk
Website: http://www.flowers.org.uk
Members: 220
Staff: 4
Fee: £125
Membership Type: full (UK company)
Fee: £1000
Membership Type: research
Description: Growers, wholesalers, importers, retailers, colleges, and associated companies. Encourages the sales of cut flowers and indoor plants and educates consumers about these products through promotional campaigns, advertising, information service, and press office offering statistics, facts, advice, and spokespersons.

02197

FOCAL International

Pentax House, S Hill Ave., South Harrow, HA2 0DU, UK
Tel: 020 84235853
Fax: 020 89334826
Email: info@focalint.org
Website: http://www.focalint.org
Members: 300
Staff: 2
Contact: Anne Johnson, Commercial Mgr.
Fee: £90
Membership Type: individual
Fee: £550
Membership Type: company
Description: Footage, stills and sound libraries; film and stills researchers; production companies and producers; research companies; facility companies. Promotes the use of library footage, stills and sound in programming, advertising, multimedia, corporate videos etc. Holds seminars and meetings.
Formerly: Formerly, Federation of Commercial Audio Visual Libraries International
Publication title: Members Guide

02198

FolkArts England
FAE

PO Box 296, Derbyshire, Matlock, DE4 3XU, UK
Tel: 01629 827014
Fax: 01629 821874
Email: info@folkarts-england.org
Website: http://www.folkarts-england.org
Contact: Richard Carver, Contact

Fee: £60
Membership Type: organization
Fee: £90
Membership Type: associate
Description: Promotes the growth, accessibility and development of folk arts in England. Provides information, publishing, education, training, communication and marketing to its members.

02199
Folklore Society
FLS
c/o The Warburg Institute
Woburn Sq., London, WC1H 0AB, UK
Tel: 020 78628564
Email: enquiries@folklore-society.com
Website: http://www.folklore-society.com
Members: 950
Staff: 2
Contact: Eddie Cass, Pres.
Fee: £50
Membership Type: household
Fee: £45
Membership Type: individual
Description: Includes the collection and study of popular custom and belief; traditional narrative, drama, music, song and dance; foodways; language; arts and crafts; and children's folklore. Interests also extend to the related areas of oral history and popular culture.
Publication: Book
Publication title: FLS Library Publications

02200
Folkus
55 The Strand, Fleetwood, FY7 8NP, UK
Tel: 01253 872317
Fax: 01253 878382
Email: alanbell@fylde-folk-fest.demon.co.uk
Website: http://www.folkus.co.uk
Contact: Alan Bell, Chm.
Description: Provides a folk arts network in and around Lancashire. Strives to link together music and dance from the different cultures and to share techniques, styles, instruments and artists.

Fondos Internacionales de Indemnizacion de Danos Debidos a la Contaminacion por Hidrocarburos
see International Oil Pollution Compensation Funds

02201
Food Additives and Ingredients Association
FAIA
10 Whitchurch Close, Kent, Maidstone, MEI6 8UR, UK
Email: info@faia.org.uk
Website: http://www.faia.org.uk
Members: 26
Description: Company membership comprising manufacturers, blenders and distributors of food additives and ingredients. Represents the interests of the UK food additives and ingredients industry by promoting a better understanding of the importance of food additives and ingredients among food manufacturers, legislators and consumers, providing a centre of expertise on food additives and ingredients technology and safe use and making representation to relevant authorities on all aspects of food additives and ingredients legislation.
Formerly: Formerly, Food Additives Industry Association
Publication: Booklet
Publication title: The Chemistry On Your Table

02202
Food and Drink Federation - England
FDF
6 Catherine St., London, WC2B 5JJ, UK
Tel: 020 78362460
Fax: 020 78360580
Email: generalenquiries@fdf.org.uk
Website: http://www.fdf.org.uk
Staff: 60
Contact: Melanie Leech, Dir. Gen.
Fee: £1150
Membership Type: affiliate
Fee: £240
Membership Type: full
Description: Represents the interests of the U.K. food and drink manufacturers.
Library Type: not open to the public

02203
Food for the Hungry - UK
47 Burgess Wood Rd. S, Beaconsfield, HP9 1EL, UK
Tel: 01494 674898
Email: uk@fhi.net
Website: http://www.uk.fhi.net
Staff: 1
Contact: Paul Cornelius, Contact
Description: Christian relief and development organisation, seeking to feed both spiritual and physical hunger. Primary emphasis is on long-term development among the extremely poor, recognizing their dignity, creativity and ability to solve their own problems. Programmes are designed to strengthen and empower the local churches, leaders and families, to move their communities toward their God-given potential. Part of the International FHI Partnership, with operations in 25 nations in Africa, Central and South America, and eastern Europe. Key activities include food production, land reclamation and agro-forestry, primary health care, education, water development for drinking and irrigation, emergency relief and rehabilitation and micro-enterprise development.

02204
Food Storage and Distribution Federation
FSDF
Unit 7, Diddenham Ct., Lamb Wood Hill, Grazeley, Reading, RG7 1JS, UK
Tel: 0118 9884468
Fax: 0118 9887035
Email: info@csdf.org.uk
Website: http://www.fsdf.org.uk
Contact: Hayley Bruwer, Sec.
Description: Provides services and representation for temperature controlled storage and distribution industry in United Kingdom.
Formerly: Formerly, Cold Storage and Distribution Federation
Publication: Directory

02205
FoodService Packaging Association
FPA
The Old Rectory, Bletchingdon, Oxon, OX5 3DH, UK
Tel: 01869 351139
Fax: 01869 350231
Email: admin@foodservicepackaging.org.uk
Website: http://www.foodservicepackaging.org.uk
Members: 50
Staff: 1
Contact: Greg Fitchett, Chm.
Fee: £600
Membership Type: manufacturer, distributor (national)
Fee: £500
Membership Type: distributor (multi site)
Description: Manufacturers, stockists, distributors and importers of catering disposables.
Formerly: Formerly, British Disposable Products Association

02206
Ford Madox Ford Society
165 Fleet St., HSBC, 6th Fl., London, EC4A 2DY, UK
Email: s.j.haslam@open.ac.uk
Website: http://www.open.ac.uk/Arts/fordmadoxford-society
Members: 100
Contact: Sara Haslam, Chair
Fee: £15-20
Membership Type: individual
Fee: £8.5
Membership Type: concession
Description: Promotes knowledge of and interest in the life and works of Ford Madox Ford. Facilitates exchange of information pertaining to Ford Madox Ford and his literary works. Fosters communication and cooperation among members.

02207
Forecourt Equipment Federation
FEF
PO Box 35084, London, NW1 4XE, UK
Tel: 020 79358532
Fax: 070 06065950
Email: office@fef.org.uk
Website: http://www.fef.org.uk
Members: 14
Description: Forecourt equipment manufacturing companies in the UK. Represents the interest of forecourt equipment in the UK.
Formerly: Formerly, Petrol Pump Manufacturers Association

02208
Foreign Press Association in London
FPA
25 Northumberland Ave., London, WC2N 5AP, UK
Tel: 020 79300445
Email: christopherwyld@foreign-press.org.uk
Website: http://www.foreign-press.org.uk
Members: 700
Staff: 3
Contact: Christoph Wyld, Dir.
Fee: £200
Membership Type: full
Fee: £265

Membership Type: associate
Description: Mainly foreign journalists representing overseas media covering UK news. Membership is also open to freelance/British press and Embassy press attaches, and PR executives. Facilitates the work of UK based foreign correspondents covering British news.

02209
Forensic Science Society FSSOC
Clarke House, 18A Mt. Parade, N Yorkshire, Harrogate, HG1 1BX, UK
Tel: 01423 506068
Fax: 01423 566391
Email: info@forensic-science-society.org.uk
Website: http://www.forensic-science-society.org.uk
Members: 2500
Staff: 5
Contact: Ann Priston, Pres.
Description: Forensic scientists, lawyers, pathologists, police officers, odontologists and police surgeons in UK and the Republic of Ireland. Promotes the study, application and stand of forensic science. Facilitates cooperation among persons interested in forensic science throughout the world.
Publication: Newsletter
Publication title: INTERfaces

02210
Forest Peoples Programme FPP
1c Fosseway Business Centre, Stratford Rd., Moreton-in-Marsh, GL56 9NQ, UK
Tel: 01608 652893
Fax: 01608 652878
Email: info@forestpeoples.org
Website: http://www.forestpeoples.org
Staff: 23
Contact: Marcus Colchester, Dir.
Description: Citizen's groups. Promotes protection of rainforests and the people and wildlife that inhabit them worldwide. Campaigns for the defense of the civil and human rights of people indigenous to the rainforest. Provides support and assistance to environmental protection organizations operating in rainforests.
Formerly: Formerly, World Rainforest Movement

02211
Forest School Camps FSC
c/o Sue Brearley
PO Box 3185, London, SW18 3JG, UK
Email: children@fsc.org.uk
Website: http://www.fsc.org.uk
Members: 2000
Staff: 600
Contact: Daphne Carre, Chair
Description: Educational youth camps and youth leaders. Promotes the healthy physical and spiritual development of youth through woodcraft and increased understanding of nature. Maintains forest camps providing young people with the opportunity to develop improved self-esteem while learning woodcraft skills. Conducts woodcraft and environmental education programs; sponsors recreational activities; makes available children's services.

02212
Fork Lift Truck Association FLTA
Manor Farm Bldg., Lasham, Alton, GU34 5SL, UK
Tel: 01256 381441
Fax: 01256 381735
Email: mail@fork-truck.org.uk
Website: http://www.fork-truck.org.uk
Members: 200
Staff: 2
Contact: David Ellison, Chief Exec.
Description: Manufacturers, dealers and associated members offering the hire and supply of fork truck services and services to other members in the UK and Europe. Aims to ensure the highest standards of quality and service. Ensures the safe, reliable hiring of fork trucks for both casual and contract hire. Promotes the virtues of hire as a means of funding the acquisition of capital plant.
Publication: Manual
Publication title: Health and Safety Manual

02213
Fortress Study Group FSG
c/o Michael Clark, Membership Sec.
Brookfield, Rectory Dr., Staplegrove, Somerset, TA2 6AP, UK
Email: membership@fsgfort.com
Website: http://www.fsgfort.com
Members: 700
Contact: Bill Clements, Chm.
Fee: £25
Membership Type: in UK, Europe
Fee: £35
Membership Type: outside Europe
Description: Societies, libraries, and individuals in 34 countries. Studies fortification as developed since the introduction of gunpowder and artillery. Organizes annual trips to places of interest.
Publication: Newsletter
Publication title: Casemate

02214
Forum for the Built Environment FBE
35 Hayworth Rd., Sandiacre, Nottingham, NG10 5LL, UK
Tel: 0845 0096810
Fax: 015 9491664
Email: simon.hudson@fbe.org.co.uk
Website: http://www.fbe-org.co.uk
Members: 4250
Contact: Simon Hudson, Contact
Fee: £116
Membership Type: technician, regular (minimum age 21)
Fee: £53
Membership Type: regular (under the age of 30), technician (minimum age 18)
Description: Promotes unity and understanding through networking, social activity and the interaction of the diverse disciplines of the construction industry. Improves the exchange and furtherance of knowledge through technical forum, conferences, discussion and lectures.
Formerly: Formerly, Faculty of Building

Forum Maritime International des Compagnies Petrolieres
see Oil Companies International Marine Forum

02215
FOSFA International
20 St. Dunstan's Hill, London, EC3R 8NQ, UK
Tel: 020 72835511
Fax: 020 76231310
Email: membership@fosfa.org
Website: http://www.fosfa.org
Members: 850
Fee: £675-1250
Membership Type: trading (based on annual turnover)
Fee: £200
Membership Type: non-trading
Description: Supports the world trade of oilseeds, fats and edible nuts. Aims to provide standard forms of contract and a well-established system for resolving disputes.
Publication: Newsletter

02216
Fostering Network
87 Blackfriars Rd., London, SE1 8HA, UK
Tel: 020 76206400
Fax: 020 76206401
Email: info@fostering.net
Website: http://www.fostering.net
Members: 50000
Staff: 80
Contact: Robert Tapsfield, Chief Exec.
Fee: £45
Membership Type: household
Description: Foster care workers, social workers, and advisors. Promotes good foster care practice and supports carers in their work. Offers training for foster care service; conducts educational and research programs; disseminates information on changes in child care policy.
Library Subject: foster care, child development
Library Type: by appointment only
Formerly: Formerly, National Foster Care Association
Publication: Magazine
Publication title: Foster Care

02217
Foundation for International Environmental Law and Development FIELD
3 Endsleigh St., London, WC1H 0DD, UK
Tel: 0207 8727200
Fax: 0207 3882826
Email: field@field.org.uk
Website: http://www.field.org.uk
Members: 12
Staff: 16
Contact: Joy Hyvarinen, Dir.
Description: Attorneys, jurists, and other individuals with an interest in environmental law. Promotes environmental protection through legal action and reform. Provides consulting services to legal and governmental agencies with an interest in environmental protection.
Publication: Newsletter
Publication title: FIELD in Brief

02218

Foundation for the Study of Infant Deaths FSID

11 Belgrave Rd., London, SW1V 1RB, UK
Tel: 020 78023200
Email: office@fsid.org.uk
Website: http://fsid.org.uk
Staff: 34
Contact: Joyce Epstein, Dir.
Description: Works to prevent Sudden Infant Death Syndrome (SIDS) and to promote infant health. Offers emotional support services to families who have suffered the loss of a child to SIDS. Provides networking and a forum for discussion and support among bereaved parents. Disseminates information about infant death and infant care to families, health professionals, the media, and government agencies.

02219

Foundation for Women's Health Research and Development FORWARD

8 Scrubs Ln., Ste. 2.1, Chandelier Bldg., 2nd Fl., London, NW10 6RB, UK
Tel: 020 89604000
Fax: 020 89604014
Email: forward@forwarduk.org.uk
Website: http://www.forwarduk.org.uk
Members: 951
Staff: 4
Contact: Efua Dorkenoo, Founder
Fee: £25
Membership Type: student
Fee: £15
Membership Type: student, unwaged
Description: Promotes the studies of women's health research and development throughout Europe and other western countries and Africa. Supports the rights of women and children. Promotes the prevention of early childhood marriage that contributes to VVF and RVF. Protects women and children from becoming victims of abuse. Opposes and fights for the elimination of the practice of genital mutilation of young girls. Disseminates information. Conducts training programs.
Publication: Video
Publication title: Another Form of Physical Abuse: Prevention of Female Genital Mutilation in the United Kingdom

02220

Foundry Equipment and Supplies Association FESA

National Metalforming Centre, 47 Birmingham Rd., West Midlands, West Bromwich, B70 6PY, UK
Tel: 0121 6016976
Fax: 01544 340332
Email: secretary@fesa.org.uk
Website: http://www.fesa.org.uk
Members: 41
Staff: 1
Description: Promotes the industry of foundry equipment and supplies.

02221

Fountain Society

c/o Ian Hay-Campbell, Honorary Sec.
High House, Bucknell, SY7 0AA, UK
Website: http://www.fountainsoc.org.uk
Members: 200
Contact: Peter M. Brown, Chm.
Fee: £25
Membership Type: individual (UK)
Fee: £35
Membership Type: overseas, couple
Description: Seeks for the conservation and restoration of fountains, cascades, and waterfalls of aesthetic merit for public and domestic enjoyment; also promotes the provision and restoration of cascades, waterfalls and other water features for public enjoyment. Offers advice on the design, construction, sighting and maintenance of fountains.

02222

FPA

50 Featherstone St., London, EC1Y 8QU, UK
Tel: 020 76085240
Fax: 0845 1232349
Email: fpadirect@fpa.org.uk
Website: http://www.fpa.org.uk/Homepage
Members: 2000
Staff: 8
Contact: Julie Bentley, Chief Exec.
Fee: £30
Membership Type: individual
Fee: £90
Membership Type: corporate
Description: Promotes family planning and sexual health in England. Conducts training for professionals. Provides helpline, reference library, and publications for consumers and professionals.
Formerly: Formerly, Family Planning Association
Publication: Newsletter
Publication title: In Brief

02223

Fragile X Society

Rood End House, 6 Stortford Rd., Essex, Great Dunmow, CM6 1DA, UK
Tel: 01371 875100
Fax: 01371 859915
Email: info@fragilex.org.uk
Website: http://www.fragilex.org.uk/default.aspx
Members: 1679
Contact: Tim Potter, Managing Dir.
Fee: £30
Membership Type: overseas
Description: Aims to provide support and comprehensive information to families whose children and adult relatives have fragile X syndrome. Raises awareness of fragile X and encourages research.
Library Subject: learning disabilities, children and adults, genetics, fragile X syndrome
Library Type: reference

02224

Franco-British Lawyers Society FBLS

Victoria Chambers, 16-18 Strutton Ground, London, SW1 2HP, UK
Tel: 020 72223860
Fax: 020 72223870
Email: secretary-england@fbls.org
Website: http://www.franco-british-law.org
Contact: Marie-Blanche Camps, Admin.
Membership Type: student
Fee: £50-70
Membership Type: individual
Description: Advances public education and training in the practice of French, Scottish and English law. Works to improve relations and exchanges between French, Scottish and English lawyers.

02225

Franco-British Society

3 Dovedale Studios, 465 Battersea Park Rd., London, SW11 4LR, UK
Tel: 020 79243511
Email: francobritish@googlemail.com
Website: http://www.francobritishsociety.org.uk
Contact: Kate Brayn, Exec. Sec.
Fee: £18
Membership Type: single
Fee: £25
Membership Type: joint
Description: Focuses on individuals who aspire to keep in touch with the culture, history and current affairs of France.

02226

Free Tibet Campaign

28 Charles Sq., London, N1 6HT, UK
Tel: 020 73244605
Fax: 020 73244606
Email: mail@freetibet.org
Website: http://www.freetibet.org
Members: 17000
Contact: Stephanie Brigden, Dir.
Fee: £23
Membership Type: individual
Fee: £30
Membership Type: family, overseas
Description: Aims to end the Chinese occupation of Tibet. Runs public campaigns, coordinates direct actions, and raises awareness through education and publicity. Initiates press and TV reportage and organizes exhibitions, seminars, and other events.
Publication: Magazine
Publication title: Free Tibet

02227

Freedom Organisation for the Right to Enjoy Smoking Tobacco FOREST

33 Margaret St., 6th Fl., London, W1G 0JD, UK
Tel: 07071 766537
Email: contact@forestonline.org
Website: http://www.forestonline.org/output/home.aspx
Members: 5000
Staff: 3
Contact: Simon Clark, Dir.
Fee: £20
Membership Type: individual
Fee: £1000
Membership Type: corporate
Description: Defends the freedom of choice of adults to smoke. Works to counter campaigns launched by smoking and tobacco prohibitionists. Maintains that it is not the role of the state to restrict smoking rights. Sponsors representatives attending debates and discussions on the topic and appearing on television and radio shows to advocate smoking rights.

02228

Freight Transport Association FTA

Hermes House, St. John's Rd., Tunbridge Wells, TN4 9UZ, UK
Tel: 01892 526171
Fax: 01892 534989
Email: membership@fta.co.uk
Website: http://www.fta.co.uk
Members: 14121
Staff: 470
Contact: Stewart Oades, Pres.
Description: Companies with a transport interest whether by road, rail, sea or air. Represents the transport interests of British industry.
Library Subject: transport
Library Type: not open to the public
Publication: Book
Publication title: Designing for Deliveries
Meetings/Conventions: Freight Summit – annual conference

02229

French Chamber of Commerce in Great Britain FCCGB

Lincoln House, 4th Fl., 300 High Holborn, London, WC1H 7JH, UK
Tel: 020 70926600
Fax: 020 70926601
Email: mail@ccfgb.co.uk
Website: http://www.ccfgb.co.uk
Members: 610
Staff: 25
Contact: Florence Gomez, Managing Dir.
Fee: £585
Membership Type: active
Fee: £1975
Membership Type: corporate
Description: Works to develop and promote trade and investments between Great Britain and France.
Library Subject: Franco-British trade
Library Type: reference
Publication: Directory
Publication title: Franco British Trade Directory

02230

Fresh Produce Consortium - UK FPC

Minerva House, Minerva Business Park, Lynch Wood, Peterborough, PE2 6FT, UK
Tel: 01733 237117
Fax: 01733 237118
Email: info@freshproduce.org.uk
Website: http://www.freshproduce.org.uk
Members: 1200
Staff: 12
Contact: Nigel Jenney, CEO
Fee: £130-6755
Membership Type: full (based on annual turnover)
Fee: £130
Membership Type: associate, non-trade individual
Description: Growers, producers, importers, retailers (independent and multiple), marketing organizations, wholesalers, pre-packers of fresh produce and flowers/plants. Represents the industry in negotiations, consultations and with DEFRA, EU Commission, NFU and National Association of British Market Authorities, and Freshfel.
Publication title: Code of Practice for Pesticide Controls

02231

Freshwater Biological Association FBA

The Ferry Landing, Far Sawrey, Ambleside, Cumbria, LA22 0LP, UK
Tel: 015394 42468
Fax: 015394 46914
Email: info@fba.org.uk
Website: http://www.fba.org.uk
Members: 1750
Staff: 5
Contact: Michael Dobson, Dir.
Fee: £35
Membership Type: ordinary
Fee: £20
Membership Type: student
Description: Promotes freshwater science through an innovative research programme, an active membership organization, and by providing sound, independent scientific opinion.
Library Subject: freshwater biology
Library Type: reference
Publication: Newsletter
Publication title: FBA News. Advertisements.

02232

Friends of Falun Gong Europe

33 Exeter Rd., Rayners Ln., Middlesex, Harrow, HA2 9PW, UK
Tel: 020 84227789
Email: johndee@fofg-europe.net
Website: http://www.fofg-europe.net
Contact: John Dee, Vice Chm.
Description: Works to discover the truth about reported persecution of practitioners of Falun Gong in China. Aims to bring justice and to protect the human rights of Falun Gong practitioners.

02233

Friends of the Earth - England, Wales, and Northern Ireland

26-28 Underwood St., London, N1 7JQ, UK
Tel: 020 74901555
Fax: 020 74900881
Website: http://www.foe.co.uk
Members: 100000
Staff: 120
Contact: Andrew McMurray, Dir.
Fee: £36
Membership Type: individual
Fee: £40
Membership Type: family, overseas
Description: Operates as an environmental pressure group, campaigning on a wide range of issues including climate change corporate accountability, resource use, transport, energy, waste, habitats, forests, and sustainable development. Exists to protect and improve the environment, now and for the future, through changing political policies and business practices, empowering individuals and communities to take personal and political action, and stimulating wide and intelligent public debate on sustainability issues.

02234

Friends of the Earth - Scotland FoE

Thorn House, 5 Rose St., Edinburgh, EH2 2PR, UK
Tel: 0131 2432700
Fax: 0131 2432725
Email: info@foe-scotland.org.uk
Website: http://www.foe-scotland.org.uk
Members: 4500
Staff: 14
Contact: Duncan McLaren, Chief Exec.
Fee: £3
Membership Type: support
Description: Represents individuals campaigning for environmental justice.
Publication: Newsletter
Publication title: What On Earth. Advertisements.

02235

Friends of the National Libraries

The British Library, Department of Manuscripts, 96 Euston Rd., London, NW1 2DB, UK
Tel: 020 74127559
Email: secretary@fnlmail.org.uk
Website: http://www.friendsofnationallibraries.org.uk
Members: 750
Contact: Michael Borrie, Honorary Sec.
Fee: £25
Membership Type: ordinary
Fee: £40
Membership Type: corporate
Description: Assists British libraries and record offices in acquiring printed books, manuscripts and archives by eliciting donations and sponsorship.
Publication: Annual Report

02236

Friends World Committee for Consultation - United Kingdom FWCC

c/o Harry Albright, Membership Sec.
173 Euston Rd., London, NW1 2AX, UK
Tel: 020 76631199
Fax: 020 76631189
Email: world@friendsworldoffice.org
Website: http://fwccworld.org
Members: 340000
Staff: 16
Contact: Nancy Irving, Gen. Sec.
Description: Works to encourage and strengthen the worldwide character and spiritual life of the Religious Society of Friends Quakers. Promotes understanding between Friends and members of other religious denominations throughout the world. Sponsors intervisitation among Friends of differing nationalities and cultures. Conducts studies. Represents concerns of Quakers at the United Nations on peace, disarmament, economic justice, human rights, and sustainable development. Disseminates information concerning United Nations affairs.
Publication title: Friends World News

02237

Fuellers' Company

26 Merrick Sq., London, SE1 4JB, UK
Email: clerk@fuellers.co.uk
Website: http://www.fuellers.co.uk/html/466.html
Contact: John Bainbridge, Master
Description: Represents all of the energy industries, originating from the coal industry with roots dating back to the ancient Woodmongers. Fosters the business of persons involved in providing energy for the home, industry, commerce and export. Provides social intercourse and mutual information between members.
Publication: Magazine
Publication title: The Fueller

02238

Funeral Furnishing Manufacturers Association FFMA

c/o Sue Bullock, Sec.
11 Fentham Rd., Hampton in Arden, West Midlands, Solihull, B92 0BE, UK
Tel: 0167 5443718
Email: bullocksue@aol.com
Website: http://www.ffma.co.uk
Members: 40
Staff: 1
Contact: David Crampton, Pres.
Description: Represents manufacturing and supply companies in the funeral industry. Ensures that quality goods are produced and high standards are maintained within the industry.

02239

Furniture History Society FHS

1 Mercedes Cottages, St. John's Rd., Haywards Heath, RH16 4EH, UK
Tel: 01444 413845
Fax: 01444 413845
Email: furniturehistorysociety@hotmail.com
Website: http://www.furniturehistorysociety.org
Members: 1700
Contact: Brian Austen, Membership Sec.
Fee: £30
Membership Type: in UK
Fee: £35
Membership Type: overseas
Description: Libraries and museums, antique dealers, furniture historians, and others in 28 countries interested in the study of furniture. Sponsors visits to important furniture collections; organizes seminars, lectures, and international tours.
Publication: Journal
Publication title: Furniture History

02240

Furniture Industry Research Association FIRA

Maxwell Rd., Stevenage, SG1 2EW, UK
Tel: 01438 777700
Fax: 01438 777800
Email: info@fira.co.uk
Website: http://www.fira.co.uk
Staff: 75
Contact: Emma Delea, Contact
Fee: £600-12000
Membership Type: furniture manufacturer
Fee: £1100
Membership Type: retailer, supplier to the furniture industry
Description: Manufacturers, suppliers, purchasers and businessmen engaged in furniture business. Conducts research, testing and consultancy of furniture.
Publication: Report
Publication title: Statistical Digest

02241

Futures and Options Association FOA

36-38 Botolph Ln., 2nd Fl., London, EC3R 8DE, UK
Tel: 020 79290081
Fax: 020 76210223
Email: belchambersa@foa.co.uk
Website: http://www.foa.co.uk
Members: 200
Staff: 9
Contact: Steve Sparke, Chm.
Description: Banks and other financial institutions, commodity trade houses, brokerage houses, fund managers, corporate users of the markets, exchanges, clearing houses and specialist firms of lawyers and accountants. Monitors and responds to regulatory and tax developments likely to affect the carrying on of members' business; provides training programmes; heightens product and market awareness and promotes the business of members.

02242

Galloway Cattle Society of Great Britain and Ireland

15 New Market St., Castle Douglas, DG7 1HY, UK
Tel: 01556 502753
Fax: 01556 502753
Email: info@gallowaycattlesociety.co.uk
Website: http://www.gallowaycattlesociety.co.uk
Members: 560
Staff: 2
Fee: £20
Membership Type: regular
Fee: £400
Membership Type: life
Description: Aims to maintain the purity of the breed of cattle known as Calloway Cattle and to promote the breeding of these cattle.
Publication: Journal
Publication title: The Galloway Journal

02243

Galpin Society GS

37 Townsend Dr., St. Albans, AL3 5RF, UK
Email: administrator@galpinsociety.org
Website: http://www.galpinsociety.org
Members: 950
Contact: Maggie Kilbey, Admin.
Fee: £25
Membership Type: individual in United Kingdom
Fee: £36
Membership Type: individual outside Europe
Description: Individuals, libraries, and institutions in 33 countries. Formed for the publication of original research into the history, construction, development, and use of musical instruments. Commemorates the late Canon F.W. Galpin, a pioneer in this field. Conducts symposia, holds exhibitions and organizes visits to major collections worldwide.
Publication: Journal

02244

Galvanizers Association GA

Wren's Ct., 56 Victoria Rd., W Midlands, Sutton Coldfield, B72 1SY, UK
Tel: 0121 3558838
Fax: 0121 3558727
Email: ga@hdg.org.uk
Website: http://www.hdg.org.uk
Members: 50
Staff: 8
Description: Firms engaged in hot dip galvanizing in the United Kingdom and the Republic of Ireland. Promotes the use of hot dip galvanized steel and provides authoritative information and advice to users and potential users.
Publication: Handbook
Publication title: The Engineers & Architects' Guide to Hot Dip Galvanizing

02245

GAMBICA, Association for Instrumentation, Control, Automation and Laboratory Technology

Broadwall House, 21 Broadwall, London, SE1 9PL, UK
Tel: 020 76428080
Fax: 020 76428096
Email: assoc@gambica.org.uk
Website: http://www.gambica.org.uk
Members: 300
Staff: 14
Contact: Geoff Young, Chief Exec.
Description: Associates in instrumentation, control, laboratory technology, and automation industry in the UK. Represents the interests of members.
Formerly: Formerly, Gambica Association for the Instrumentation, Control and Automation Industry in the United Kingdom
Publication: Directory
Publication title: Product Guides

02246

Game and Wildlife Conservation Trust GWCT

Burgate Manor, Fordingbridge, SP6 1EF, UK
Tel: 01425 652381
Fax: 01425 655848
Email: info@gwct.org.uk
Website: http://www.gct.org.uk
Members: 22000
Staff: 102
Contact: Stephen Tapper, Dir. of Policy and Public Affairs
Fee: £2.5
Membership Type: individual (retired)
Fee: £5
Membership Type: joint/family (full)
Description: Research is undertaken on all aspects of game and the environment with a view to the development of practical management plans for landowners and farmers.
Formerly: Formerly, Game Conservancy Trust
Publication: Article
Publication title: Game & Wildlife Conservation Review. Advertisements.

02247

Garage Equipment Association GEA

2-3 Church Walk, Daventry, NN11 4BL, UK
Tel: 01327 312616
Fax: 01327 312606
Email: info@gea.co.uk

Website: http://www.gea.co.uk
Members: 143
Description: Manufacturers, distributors, importers, service and installation technicians, and other interested individuals of the garage equipment industry. Strives to produce and maintain quality garage equipment. Promotes high standards in the technical and economic aspects of garage equipment.
Library Subject: automotive
Library Type: reference
Publication: Book
Publication title: Auto-Solve Diagnostic Assistance
Meetings/Conventions: bimonthly meeting

02248
Garden Centre Association
GCA

Leafield Technical Centre, Leafield, Witney, OX29 9EF, UK
Tel: 01993 871000
Fax: 01993 871458
Email: info@gca.org.uk
Website: http://www.gca.org.uk
Members: 350
Staff: 3
Description: Represents the interests of Britain's leading independent garden centres. Maintains standards by annual inspection.
Meetings/Conventions: annual conference

02249
Garden History Society
GHS

70 Cowcross St., London, EC1M 6EJ, UK
Tel: 020 76082409
Fax: 020 74902974
Email: enquiries@gardenhistorysociety.org
Website: http://www.gardenhistorysociety.org
Members: 1500
Staff: 4
Contact: Richard Carew Pole, VP
Fee: £10
Membership Type: young (24 or under)
Fee: £35
Membership Type: single (in UK)
Description: Strives to study and protect historic gardens by promoting landscape gardening, horticulture, conservation of historic park gardens and encouraging new structures of parks, gardens and landscapes.
Publication: Journal
Publication title: Garden History. Advertisements.

02250
Garden Industry Manufacturers Association
GIMA

225 Bristol Rd., Edgbaston, Birmingham, B5 7UB, UK
Tel: 0121 4465213
Fax: 0121 4465215
Email: info@gima.org.uk
Website: http://www.gima.org.uk
Members: 150
Staff: 2
Contact: Rebecca Abbott, Sec.
Fee: £495
Membership Type: full
Fee: £250
Membership Type: associate
Description: Suppliers of garden products for use by consumers. Provides an opportunity to exchange views and for co-operation between members on matters of importance to garden industry. Represents their opinions and views to other bodies, associations, the media, government and trade generally. Organizes a calendar of events that are of business value to member companies.
Library Type: open to the public

02251
GARDENEX: Federation of Garden and Leisure Manufacturers

The White House, High St., Kent, Brasted, TN16 1JE, UK
Tel: 01959 565995
Fax: 01959 565885
Email: info@gardenex.com
Website: http://www.gardenex.com/index.html
Members: 185
Staff: 9
Contact: Amanda Sizer Barrett, Dir. Gen.
Description: Promotes and expands the exports of British garden and leisure products. Membership is comprised of British garden and leisure product manufacturers who export products; associate member category open to companies who supply services to exporters. Services to members include: regular export leads; joint ventures to overseas exhibitions; a product sourcing service for the use of overseas buyers; discounts on a wide range of business services; organizing inward and outward trade missions; publicizing members' garden products worldwide.
Library Subject: gardening market information worldwide, export procedure information
Library Type: by appointment only
Publication: Directory
Publication title: British Garden Products and Services Guide for International Buyers. Advertisements.
Meetings/Conventions: Growing Worldwide – annual conference – Exhibits.

02252
Gas Forum

Centurion House, 7th Fl., 10 Fenchurch St., London, EC3M 3BE, UK
Tel: 020 70901030
Fax: 020 70901001
Email: gasforum@gemserv.co.uk
Website: http://www.gasforum.co.uk
Contact: Frank Neel, Chm.
Description: Comprises virtually every significant UK gas shipper and gas supplier. Leads in formulating the rules for governance of the retail side of the gas industry by initiating and supporting the work that has culminated in the draft Supply Point. Serves as a forum in which to exchange views with industry peers whilst complying with Competition Law.

02253
Gasket Cutters Association
GCA

105 St. Peter's St., Hertfordshire, St. Albans, AL1 3EJ, UK
Tel: 01727 896084
Fax: 01727 896026
Email: info@gcassociation.co.uk
Website: http://www.gcassociation.co.uk
Fee: £485
Membership Type: regular
Fee: £585
Membership Type: associate, affiliate
Description: Companies engaged in the conversion of materials into gaskets for all types of industrial use. Furthers and protects the commercial interests of members.

02254
Gauchers Association
GA

3 Bull Pitch, Dursley, Gloucestershire, Gloucester, GL11 4NG, UK
Tel: 01453 549231
Fax: 01453 549231
Email: ga@gaucher.org.uk
Website: http://www.gaucher.org.uk
Contact: Tanya Collin-Histed, Exec. Dir.
Fee: £15
Membership Type: full voting, associate
Fee: £25
Membership Type: overseas
Description: Individuals with Gaucher's disease. (Gaucher's disease is a genetic disorder resulting in enzyme deficiency, producing symptoms including anemia, fatigue, bone pain and degeneration, easy bruising, and a tendency to bleed. The rare Type 2 and Type 3 forms of Gaucher's disease can also cause various neurological problems.) Seeks to improve the quality of life of people with Gaucher's disease; encourages medical research on the diagnosis, prevention, and treatment of the disease. Serves as a support group for people with Gaucher's disease; works to increase the availability of enzyme treatments; facilitates contact among the families of people with Gaucher's disease in the UK.

02255
Gauge and Tool Makers' Association
GTMA

3 Forge House, Summerleys Rd., Princes Risborough, HP27 9DT, UK
Tel: 01844 274222
Fax: 01844 274227
Email: gtma@gtma.co.uk
Website: http://www.gtma.co.uk/default.asp?folder=0&home=1
Members: 310
Staff: 7
Contact: Julia Moore, Chief Exec.
Description: Gauge and tool making companies. Concerned with jigs, fixtures, press tools, moulds and dies, measuring equipment, special tooling and precision machining.
Publication: Directory
Publication title: Buyer's Guide

02256
Gay Police Association
GPA

BM GPA, London, WC1N 3XX, UK
Tel: 07092 700212
Fax: 07092 700100
Email: info@gpa.police.uk
Website: http://www.gay.police.uk
Contact: Paul M. Cahill, Chm.
Description: Works towards equal opportunities for lesbian and gay police service employees. Offers advice and support to lesbian and gay police service employees. Promotes better relations between the police service and the lesbian and gay community.

02257

Gemmological Association and Gem Testing Laboratory of Great Britain
Gem-A

27 Greville St., London, EC1N 8TN, UK
Tel: 020 74043334
Fax: 020 74048843
Email: information@gem-a.com
Website: http://www.gem-a.info
Members: 3500
Staff: 19
Contact: Jack Ogden, Chief Exec.
Fee: £72.5
Membership Type: fellow/diamond/associate in UK
Fee: £80
Membership Type: fellow/diamond/associate in Europe
Description: Ordinary - those members who have not passed exams; laboratory mainly trade for use of testing and identifying stones; Fellow - those members who have passed exams. Lectures for members/non-members throughout the year. Takes exams and issues results. Sells Gemological instruments. Tests gemstones for members and trade. Attends various jewelry trade shows throughout the year.
Publication: Newsletter
Publication title: Gem and Jewellery News

02258

Gender and Science and Technology Association
GASAT

University of Brighton, School of Education, M108 Mayfield House, Falmer, Brighton, BN1 9PH, UK
Email: y.ramma@mieonline.org
Website: http://www.gasat-international.org
Contact: Yashwant Ramma, Sec.
Description: Focuses on issues arising from interactions between gender and science and technology. Promotes the inclusion of science and technology in areas where gender is concerned. Increases the knowledge and skills of women about science and technology.

02259

General Chiropractic Council
GCC

44 Wicklow St., London, WC1X 9HL, UK
Tel: 020 77135155
Fax: 020 77135844
Email: enquiries@gcc-uk.org
Website: http://www.gcc-uk.org
Staff: 14
Contact: Margaret Coats, Chief Exec./Registrar
Description: Aims to protect the public by regulating chiropractors. Sets standards of chiropractic education, practice and conduct.
Publication: Newsletter
Publication title: News from the GCC

02260

General Council and Register of Naturopaths
GCRN

Goswell House, 2 Goswell Rd., Street, BA16 0JG, UK
Tel: 08707 456984
Fax: 08707 456985
Email: admin@naturopathy.org.uk
Website: http://www.naturopathy.org.uk
Members: 300
Staff: 3
Contact: Linda Goodman, Pres.
Fee: £150
Membership Type: full, overseas
Fee: £100
Membership Type: not in practice
Description: Fully qualified naturopathic practitioners. Maintains educational, professional and ethical standards and the safe practice of naturopathy for the benefit and protection of the public.
Publication: Journal
Publication title: British Naturopatyhic

02261

General Council of the Bar

289-293 High Holborn, London, WC1V 7HZ, UK
Tel: 020 72420082
Fax: 020 78319217
Email: chairman@barcouncil.org.uk
Website: http://www.barcouncil.org.uk
Members: 16000
Staff: 85
Contact: Nicholas Green, Chm.
Description: Serves as professional and governing body for barristers.
Formerly: Also Known As, Bar Council
Publication: Annual Report

02262

General Council of the Bar of Northern Ireland

The Bar Library, 91 Chichester St., Belfast, BT1 3JQ, UK
Tel: 02890 562349
Fax: 02890 562350
Email: chief.executive@barcouncil-ni.org.uk
Website: http://www.barlibrary.com
Members: 600
Staff: 36
Contact: Brendan Garland, Contact
Description: Professional body representing all barristers in Northern Ireland.

02263

General Dental Council
GDC

37 Wimpole St., London, W1G 8DQ, UK
Tel: 020 78873800
Fax: 020 72243294
Email: information@gdc-uk.org
Website: http://www.gdc-uk.org
Members: 29
Staff: 120
Contact: Alison Lockyer, Chair
Fee: £300
Membership Type: dentist
Fee: £250
Membership Type: orthodontic
Description: Regulates the dental profession in the UK.
Publication: Book
Publication title: Dentists Register

02264

General Federation of Trade Unions
GFTU

Headland House, 308-312 Grays Inn Rd., 4th Fl., London, WC1H 0HY, UK
Tel: 020 75208340
Fax: 020 75208350
Email: gftuhq@gftu.org.uk
Website: http://www.gftu.org.uk
Members: 225687
Contact: Mike Bradley, Gen. Sec.
Description: Specialist trade unions. Provides members with education courses, research facilities, training, technology and information.
Publication title: Federation News

02265

General Hypnotherapy Register
GHR

PO Box 204, Lymington, SO41 6WP, UK
Tel: 01590 683770
Email: admin@general-hypnotherapy-register.com
Website: http://www.general-hypnotherapy-register.com
Members: 1800
Staff: 2
Contact: William Broom, Sec.
Description: Counselors and therapists, mainly offering short-term treatment in private practice. Most members offer hypnotherapy as their main method of treatment. Represents and protects the interests of independent therapists and hypnotherapists. Provides referrals lists of practitioners in which the public may have full confidence by maintaining high standards of practice and conduct among members. Provides register of practitioners.
Formerly: Formerly, National Council of Psychotherapists and Hypnotherapy Register

02266

General Medical Council
GMC

Regent's Pl., 350 Euston Rd., London, NW1 3JN, UK
Tel: 0161 9236602
Email: gmc@gmc-uk.org
Website: http://www.gmc-uk.org
Members: 102
Staff: 180
Contact: Niall Dickson, Chief Exec.
Description: Protects the public by overseeing medical education. Keeps a registry of qualified doctors. Takes action where doctor's fitness to practice is in doubt.
Publication title: Duties of a Doctor - Guidance on Professional Ethics

02267

General Optical Council
GOC

41 Harley St., London, W1G 8DJ, UK
Tel: 020 75803898
Fax: 020 73073939
Email: goc@optical.org
Website: http://www.optical.org
Members: 23500
Staff: 32
Contact: Dian Taylor, Chief Exec./Registrar
Fee: £219
Membership Type: ordinary
Description: Represents optometrists, dispensing opticians, student opticians and optical businesses. Serves

as the regulator for the optical professions in UK. Aims to protect the public by promoting high standards of education, performance and conduct amongst opticians.

02268

General Osteopathic Council GOsC

Osteopathy House, 176 Tower Bridge Rd., London, SE1 3LU, UK
Tel: 070 3576655
Fax: 070 3570011
Email: info@osteopathy.org.uk
Website: http://www.osteopathy.org.uk
Members: 4000
Staff: 21
Contact: Sonia van Heerden, Contact
Description: Regulates, promotes and develops the profession of osteopathy and maintains a statutory register of those entitled to practice osteopathy.
Publication: Journal
Publication title: The Osteopath. Advertisements.

02269

General Teaching Council for Scotland GTCS

Clerwood House, 96 Clermiston Rd., Edinburgh, EH12 6UT, UK
Tel: 0131 3146000
Email: gtcs@gtcs.org.uk
Website: http://www.gtcs.org.uk
Members: 50
Staff: 51
Contact: Anthony Finn, Chief Exec./Registrar
Fee: £30
Membership Type: teacher
Description: Acts as regulatory body for members of the teaching profession in Scotland. Registration is a mandatory requirement for teaching in education authority schools in Scotland; keeps standards of teacher education and fitness to teach under review. Makes recommendations when necessary to Scotland's First Minister on the supply of teachers and on the continuing professional development and staff development review of teachers. Maintains a register of teachers eligible to teach in education authority and self-governing schools in Scotland. Oversees the probationary service of new entrants to the profession.

02270

Genetic Alliance UK

Unit 4D, Leroy House, 436 Essex Rd., London, N1 3QP, UK
Tel: 020 77043141
Fax: 020 73591447
Email: mail@geneticalliance.org.uk
Website: http://www.geneticalliance.org.uk
Members: 130
Contact: Alastair Kent, Dir.
Fee: £25
Membership Type: individual
Fee: £50-17500
Membership Type: full (based on income)
Description: Seeks to educate and raise awareness among opinion formers, people of influence, and the public about human genetics and genetic disorders. Focuses on issues of policy and keeps active watch on developments within the UK and Europe that influence the effective transfer of knowledge and understanding into products and services for families that are supported by the organization's member groups.
Formerly: Formerly, Genetic Interest Group

02271

Genetics Society GS

Roslin BioCentre, Wallace Bldg., Roslin, Midlothian, EH25 9PS, UK
Tel: 0131 2006392
Fax: 0131 2006394
Email: mail@genetics.org.uk
Website: http://www.genetics.org.uk
Members: 2000
Staff: 2
Contact: Veronica van Heyningen, Pres.
Fee: £25
Membership Type: full
Fee: £15
Membership Type: postgraduate student
Description: Individuals with an interest in genetical research, or in the practical breeding of plants and animals. Promotes the study of the mechanisms of inheritance.
Publication: Journal
Publication title: Genes & Development
Meetings/Conventions: annual meeting – Exhibits.

02272

Genito-Urinary Nurses Association GUNA

Nurse Metrosexual Health Limited/SohoBoyz, Unit FF15 Base Station, Saga Ctre., 326 Kensal Rd., London, W10 5BZ, UK
Tel: 020 82640143
Fax: 020 89683409
Email: justin.gaffney@metrosexual.co.uk
Website: http://www.guna.org.uk
Contact: Justin Gaffney, Chm.
Fee: £10
Membership Type: student, health support worker, retired
Fee: £20
Membership Type: practitioner
Description: Promotes the sciences and arts that comprise genito-urinary medicine (GU medicine) nursing. Ensures better education and training of GU nurses in order to improve the efficiency of their work. Holds regional meetings to allow the exchange of information and purchase and sale of books, papers, reports and other communications.

02273

Geographical Association of England GA

160 Solly St., Sheffield, S1 4BF, UK
Tel: 0114 2960088
Fax: 0114 2967176
Email: info@geography.org.uk
Website: http://www.geography.org.uk
Members: 6000
Staff: 21
Contact: JW Halocha, Pres.
Fee: £28.5
Membership Type: general
Fee: £57
Membership Type: full
Description: Corporations and individuals. Works to promote the study of geography at all educational levels. Represents its members in national and international matters. Conducts educational programs. Maintains working groups and speakers' bureau.
Publication: Magazine
Publication title: GA Magazine
Meetings/Conventions: annual conference – Exhibits.

02274

Geological Society of Glasgow

Gregory Bldg., Univ. of Glasgow, Department of Geographical and Earth Sciences, Glasgow, G12 8QQ, UK
Email: gsgmemsec@ntlworld.com
Website: http://www.geologyglasgow.org.uk
Members: 450
Contact: Iain Allison, Hon. Sec.
Fee: £20
Membership Type: ordinary
Fee: £10
Membership Type: associate, junior with journal supplement
Description: Dedicated to promoting understanding of geology, the science of the Earth, especially the study of geology in Scotland.

02275

Geological Society of London GSL

Burlington House, Piccadilly, London, W1J 0BG, UK
Tel: 020 74349944
Fax: 020 74398975
Email: enquiries@geolsoc.org.uk
Website: http://www.geolsoc.org.uk
Members: 9000
Staff: 32
Contact: Edmund Nickless, Exec. Sec.
Fee: £52
Membership Type: joint fellowship
Fee: £31-178
Membership Type: fellow
Description: Geologists, geophysicists, geotechnical engineers, students, and interested individuals. Promotes the study and practice of geology and allied disciplines. Holds scientific and technical meetings at its Piccadilly headquarters and its regional branches. Bestows the title of Chartered Geologist to candidates with the appropriate academic qualifications, practical training, and professional responsibility.
Library Subject: geological sciences
Library Type: open to the public
Formerly: Absorbed, Institution of Geologists
Publication: Journal
Publication title: Engineering Geology and Hydrogeology. Advertisements.

02276

Geologists' Association GA

Burlington House, Piccadilly, London, W1J 0DU, UK
Tel: 020 74349298
Fax: 020 72870280
Email: geol.assoc@btinternet.com
Website: http://www.geologists.org.uk
Members: 2500
Staff: 1
Contact: Danielle Schreve, Pres.
Fee: £40
Membership Type: regular
Fee: £58
Membership Type: joint
Description: Amateur and professional geologists. Serves the interests of amateur geologists.
Publication: Magazine
Publication title: Magazine of the Geologists' Association

02277
George MacDonald Society
GMS
10 Appian Ct., Parnell Rd., London, E3 2RS, UK
Email: macdonald-society@britishlibrary.net
Website: http://www.george-macdonald.com
Members: 170
Contact: Roger Bardet, Treas./Membership Sec.
Fee: £10
Membership Type: individual
Fee: £13
Membership Type: joint
Description: Individuals devoted to the study of the life and works of George MacDonald (1824-1905), Scottish novelist and lecturer remembered primarily for his fairy tales and adult fantasies. Aims to expose modern generations to the writings and religious views of MacDonald and establish biographical archives. Sponsors discussions.
Publication: Journal
Publication title: North Wind. Advertisements.

02278
German History Society
GHS
Open Univ., Dept. of History, Walton Hall, Milton Keynes, MK7 6AA, UK
Email: a.mombauer@open.ac.uk
Website: http://www.germanhistorysociety.org
Members: 300
Contact: Annika Mombauer, Sec.
Description: Professional association for historians of the German-speaking world.
Publication: Journal
Publication title: German History

02279
German Industry UK
Ymwlch Isaf, Criccieth, LL52 0PW, UK
Tel: 020 1766523113
Email: info@gi-uk.co.uk
Website: http://www.gi-uk.co.uk
Members: 100
Contact: Bernd Atenstaedt, Chief Exec.
Fee: £300
Membership Type: general
Fee: £1000
Membership Type: sustaining
Description: Works to provide forum for the discussion and exchange of experience and views on subjects relating to industry, economy and politics. Provides sales opportunities for members.
Formerly: Formerly, German Industry Association - UK Chapter

02280
German-British Chamber of Industry and Commerce
Mecklenburg House, 16 Buckingham Gate, London, SW1E 6LB, UK
Tel: 020 79764100
Fax: 020 79764101
Email: mail@ahk-london.co.uk
Website: http://grossbritannien.ahk.de/en/home
Members: 1000
Staff: 31
Contact: Nigel Broomfield, Pres.
Fee: £2300
Membership Type: sustaining (in UK)
Fee: £680
Membership Type: corporate (in UK)
Description: Businesses and individuals. Promotes trade and investment between Germany and the U.K. Disseminates information on import and export requirements, and wholesale, distribution, and retail companies. Offers advice on legal matters, management and marketing problems, tax and VAT matters, debt collection, and purchasing. Organizes seminars, lectures, and market research and analysis programs.
Library Type: not open to the public
Publication: Book
Publication title: Employing Staff in Germany

02281
Ghost Club
GC
PO Box 910, Ipswich, IP1 9PT, UK
Email: chairman@ghostclub.org.uk
Website: http://www.ghostclub.org.uk
Contact: Alan Murdie, Chm.
Fee: £15-30
Membership Type: single
Fee: £22-45
Membership Type: joint
Description: Membership by invitation only. Investigates and researches "all subjects not yet fully understood or accepted by science". Focuses on both spontaneous and induced psychic phenomena. Compiles statistics.
Library Subject: paranormal research, ghosts, haunting
Library Type: reference
Publication: Newsletter

02282
Giftware Association
GA
Federation House, 10 Vyse St., Birmingham, B18 6LT, UK
Tel: 0121 2362657
Fax: 0121 2363921
Email: enquiries@ga-uk.org
Website: http://www.ga-uk.org
Members: 1500
Staff: 5
Contact: Isabel Martinson, Chief Exec.
Description: Manufacturers, importers, distributors, wholesalers and retailers of giftware. Services offered by the Association include Code of Practice, discounts-trade fairs, healthcare, hotels, export assistance, free legal advice, copyright assistance, training, seminars, credit management services, newsletters.
Publication: Newsletter
Publication title: Newsline. Advertisements.

02283
Gilbert and Sullivan Society
G&S
7 Mace Walk, Essex, CM1 2GE, UK
Email: stuart.box@burningsuit.co.uk
Website: http://www.gilbertandsullivansociety.org.uk
Members: 450
Contact: Stuart Box, Hon. Sec.
Fee: £20
Membership Type: in UK
Fee: £25
Membership Type: outside UK
Description: Encourages interest in the Gilbert and Sullivan operas and enables members to develop their knowledge of all aspects appertaining to the operas and their authors.
Publication: Magazine
Publication title: Gilbert & Sullivan News. Advertisements.

02284
Gin and Vodka Association
GVA
Cross Keys House, Queen St., Salisbury, SP1 1EY, UK
Tel: 01722 415892
Fax: 01722 415840
Email: gva@ginvodka.org.uk
Website: http://www.ginvodka.org
Members: 25
Staff: 3
Contact: Edwin Atkinson, Dir. Gen.
Description: Producers, brand owners and importers of gin and/or vodka. Protects and promotes the interests of the UK gin and vodka trades at home and abroad and aims to prevent malpractice or abuses within the trade. Puts the trade's views to UK Government and to EC bodies and informs members of relevant developments and of business opportunities.
Formerly: Formerly, Gin Rectifiers and Distillers Association

02285
Gingerbread
255 Kentish Town Rd., London, NW5 2LX, UK
Tel: 020 74285400
Fax: 020 74854851
Email: info@gingerbread.org.uk
Website: http://www.gingerbread.org.uk/portal/page/portal/Website
Members: 11000
Staff: 21
Contact: Fiona Weir, Chief Exec.
Description: Offers assistance to lone parents and their children. Helps to counter the effects of childhood poverty through holidays, discount vouchers, outings and other activities.
Publication: Newsletter
Publication title: Ginger Junior

02286
Girl Guiding Scotland
16 Coates Crescent, Edinburgh, EH3 7AH, UK
Tel: 0131 2264511
Fax: 0131 2204828
Website: http://www.girlguidingscotland.org.uk
Members: 658915
Staff: 50
Contact: Dinah Faulds, Chief Commissioner
Description: Girls aged 5 to 18; adult leaders. Promotes healthy physical and social development of girls and young women. Conducts social, educational, and recreational activities, with an emphasis on camping and other outdoor pursuits.
Formerly: Formerly, Guide Association Scotland

02287
Girlguiding UK
17-19 Buckingham Palace Rd., London, SW1W 0PT, UK
Tel: 020 78346242
Fax: 020 78288317
Email: chq@girlguiding.org.uk
Website: http://www.girlguiding.org.uk
Members: 650000
Staff: 170
Contact: Denise King, Chief Exec.
Description: Assists the emotional, spiritual, mental, and physical development of girls and young women in the United Kingdom. Promotes the development of self-awareness, self-respect, and self-confidence; teaches teamwork and leadership skills. Promotes the

protection of the environment. Fosters the ideals of multicultural youth work.
Formerly: Formerly, Girl Guides Association
Publication: Magazine
Publication title: Brownie. Advertisements.

02288
Girls Friendly Society - United Kingdom - GFS Platform
GFS
Unit 2, Angel Gate, 326 City Rd., London, EC1V 2PT, UK
Tel: 020 78379669
Email: info@gfsplatform.org.uk
Website: http://www.gfsplatform.org.uk
Members: 2000
Staff: 70
Description: Girls and women over the ages of 6. Conducts recreational and training activities for young women. Offers low-cost, secure housing for women. Provides guidance and support to troubled young women.
Publication: Newsletter
Publication title: Platform News

02289
Girls' Schools Association
GSA
130 Regent Rd., Leicester, LE1 7PG, UK
Tel: 0116 2541619
Fax: 0116 2553792
Email: office@gsa.uk.com
Website: http://www.gsa.uk.com
Staff: 4
Contact: Sheila Cooper, Exec. Dir.
Description: Works to inform and influence national educational debate; to raise awareness of the benefits of single sex education for girls; to promote high standard of education for girls and support members through the provision of a broad range of services.

02290
Glasgow Archaeological Society
GAS
University of Glasgow, Department of Archaeology, Glasgow, G12 8QQ, UK
Email: s.driscoll@archaeology.gla.ac.uk
Website: http://www.glasarchsoc.org.uk/page.php?1
Contact: Stephen T. Driscoll, Contact
Fee: £20
Membership Type: full
Fee: £10
Membership Type: associate, student
Description: Supports archaeological work by both professionals and amateurs throughout Scotland. Fosters public awareness of the importance of archaeology.
Publication: Journal
Publication title: Scottish Archaeological Journal

02291
Glasgow Chamber of Commerce
30 George Sq., Glasgow, G2 1EQ, UK
Tel: 0141 2042121
Fax: 0141 2212336
Email: chamber@glasgowchamber.org
Website: http://www.glasgowchamber.org
Members: 1516
Staff: 14
Contact: Stuart Patrick, Chief Exec.
Fee: £196
Membership Type: sole trader/charity
Fee: £383
Membership Type: association
Description: Promotes business and commerce.
Publication: Newsletter
Publication title: Business Update

02292
Glasgow Mathematical Association
GMA
University of Glasgow, Mathematics Dept., Glasgow, G12 8QW, UK
Tel: 0141 3305176
Fax: 0141 3304111
Email: fhg@maths.gla.ac.uk
Website: http://www.maths.gla.ac.uk/~fhg/gma
Members: 60
Contact: Frances Goldman, Treas.
Fee: £7
Membership Type: individual
Fee: £3
Membership Type: student, retired, unwaged
Description: Aims to arrange talks and provide a meeting place for anyone interested in mathematics and its applications.

02293
Glasgow Natural History Society
GNHS
c/o Zoology Museum
University of Glasgow, Graham Kerr Bldg., Glasgow, G12 8QQ, UK
Tel: 0141 3391343
Email: info@glasgownaturalhistory.org.uk
Website: http://www.glasgownaturalhistory.org.uk
Contact: Mary Child, Sec.
Fee: £23
Membership Type: ordinary
Fee: £16
Membership Type: student
Description: Encourages the study of the wildlife of West Central Scotland.
Library Subject: natural history
Library Type: not open to the public
Publication: Journal
Publication title: Glasgow Naturalist

02294
Glasgow Women's Aid
30 Bell St., 4th Fl., Glasgow, G1 1LG, UK
Tel: 0141 5532022
Fax: 0141 5530592
Email: admin@glasgowwomensaid.org.uk
Website: http://www.scottishwomensaid.org.uk
Staff: 35
Contact: Susan Jack, Contact
Description: Offers support, information, and temporary accommodations for women and their children who are physically, emotionally, or sexually abused. Disseminates information on law and housing. Encourages women to determine their own future. Conducts community education programs.

02295
Glass and Glazing Federation
GGF
54 Ayres St., London, SE1 1EU, UK
Tel: 020 79399100
Fax: 020 73577458
Email: info@ggf.org.uk
Website: http://www.ggf.org.uk
Members: 580
Staff: 20
Contact: Robert Aitken, Pres.
Description: Promotes the flat glass industry.
Formerly: Also Known As, Glass and Glazing Federation Conservatory Association
Publication: Newsletter
Publication title: Glasseye. Advertisements.

02296
Global Ideas Bank
GIB
12a Blackstock Mews, Blackstock Rd., London, N4 2BT, UK
Tel: 020 73598391
Fax: 020 73543831
Email: glidbk@hotmail.com
Website: http://www.globalideasbank.org
Staff: 3
Contact: Nick Temple, Dir.
Fee: £15
Membership Type: individual
Description: Seeks to gather and disseminate ideas for improving the quality of life worldwide. Maintains registry of socially innovative ideas and projects contributed by interested individuals worldwide.

02297
Global Lung Cancer Coalition
GLCC
c/o The Roy Castle Lung Cancer Foundation
134 Douglas St., Glasgow, G2 4HF, UK
Fax: 0141 3310590
Email: glcc@roycastle.liv.ac.uk
Website: http://www.lungcancercoalition.org
Description: Promotes the understanding of lung cancer and the right of patients to effective early detection, better treatment and supportive care. Seeks to change public perception and lessen the stigma of lung cancer. Influences legislative or regulatory policies to optimize treatment and care of lung cancer.

02298
Global Organisation for Lysosomal Diseases
GOLD
3 Albion Rd., Chalfont St. Giles, HP8 4EW, UK
Fax: 01494 870708
Email: enquiries@goldinfo.org
Website: http://www.goldinfo.org
Contact: Rhonda P. Buyers, Exec. Dir.
Description: Strives to improves the lives of all patients with lysosomal diseases. Clarifies the importance of early diagnosis in bringing patients to therapy while there is still a chance for change. Builds a collaboration for patient databanks, including specimen and tissue banks.

02299

Global Vision International
GVI

3 High St., St. Albans, AL4 4ED, UK
Tel: 0172 7250250
Fax: 0172 7840666
Email: info@gvi.co.uk
Website: http://www.gvi.co.uk
Staff: 150
Contact: Richard Walton, Dir.
Description: Promotes sustainable solutions to international charities, nonprofit, and governmental agencies supporting conservation and humanitarian projects worldwide.

02300

Global Witness

Buchanan House, 6th Fl., 30 Holborn, London, EC1N 2HS, UK
Tel: 020 74925820
Fax: 020 74925821
Email: mail@globalwitness.org
Website: http://www.globalwitness.org
Contact: Naomi Love, Contact
Description: Works to stop environmentally destructive trade in areas of the world that has a financing conflict.

02301

Glosa Education Organisation
GEO

PO Box 18, Richmond, TW9 2GE, UK
Email: m001@glosa.org
Website: http://www.glosa.org
Members: 400
Staff: 2
Contact: Wendy Ashby, Contact
Fee: £28
Membership Type: regular
Description: Promotes the teaching and use of Glosa (a language having no grammar and a vocabulary based on Latin and Greek root words) in 20 countries for international communications, particularly between Third World workers and representatives of industrialized nations. Encourages the publication of scientific and technical papers in Glosa; provides consultative services and educational programs; sponsors courses; discussions; speakers; sample talks.

02302

Glued Laminated Timber Association
GLTA

Chiltern House, Stocking Ln., Buckinghamshire, High Wycombe, HP14 4ND, UK
Tel: 01494 565180
Fax: 01494 565487
Email: sales@glulam.co.uk
Website: http://www.glulam.co.uk
Members: 6
Description: Manufacturers and suppliers of glued laminated timber. Focuses on the promotion and seeks awareness of glued laminated timber.

02303

GMB

22-24 Worple Rd., London, SW19 4DD, UK
Tel: 020 89473131
Fax: 020 89446552
Email: info@gmb.org.uk
Website: http://www.gmb.org.uk
Members: 604000
Contact: Paul Kenny, Gen. Sec.
Fee: £11.05
Membership Type: full time
Fee: £6.2
Membership Type: part time, under 18
Description: Advances the economic and social interests of working people. Regulates relations between members and their employers. Promotes favorable legislation. Provides employment assistance and legal aid. Offers educational programs covering shop standards, staff representatives, pensions, negotiations, and health and safety. Conducts research into work injuries and health and safety.
Formerly: Formerly, Association of Professional, Executive, Clerical, and Computer Staff and GMB

02304

Goat Veterinary Society
GVS

29 Winfield, Gloucestershire, Newent, GL18 1QB, UK
Tel: 01531 820074
Email: nickclayton2@mac.com
Website: http://www.goatvetsoc.co.uk
Contact: Nick Clayton, Hon. Sec.
Fee: £30
Membership Type: full/associate, overseas
Fee: £10
Membership Type: student
Description: Works to improve knowledge about goats in the veterinary profession.
Publication: Journal
Publication title: The Goat Veterinary Society Journal

02305

Gold and Silver Wyre Drawers' Company
GSWD

9a Prince of Wales Mansions, Prince of Wales Dr., London, SW11 4BG, UK
Tel: 020 74980590
Fax: 020 74980590
Email: clerk@gswd.co.uk
Website: http://www.gswd.org.uk
Members: 306
Staff: 1
Contact: Robin House, Clerk
Description: Makes charitable grants and donations, prizes for schools and Royal Ballet School. Provides bursary for apprenticeship at Royal School of Needlework and for an opera student at the Guildhall School of Music and Drama.
Publication: Report
Publication title: Master's Report to the Livery

02306

Goldsmiths' Company

Goldsmiths' Hall, Foster Ln., London, EC2V 6BN, UK
Tel: 020 76067010
Fax: 020 76061511
Email: the.clerk@thegoldsmiths.co.uk
Website: http://www.thegoldsmiths.co.uk/welcome
Members: 1900
Staff: 100
Description: Serves retired members of the silversmithing, jewellery and allied trades, but includes members from many other professions. Operates the London Assay Office and promotes excellence in design and craftsmanship for modern silverware and jewellery.
Library Subject: hallmarks, silver and jewellery
Library Type: by appointment only
Publication: Magazine
Publication title: Goldsmiths Review

02307

Grace and Compassion Benedictines

Grace & Compassion Convent, 57 Surrenden Rd., Brighton, BN1 6PQ, UK
Tel: 01273 502129
Fax: 01273 552540
Email: osb@graceandcompassion.co.uk
Website: http://www.graceandcompassionbenedictines.org.uk
Members: 201
Staff: 20
Contact: Kathy Yeeles, Contact
Description: Benedictine congregation providing long-term care facilities for the elderly. Seeks to improve the quality of life of elderly people requiring residential care and other living assistance. Maintains network of nursing homes, group residences, and shelters for the frail elderly.
Publication: Newsletter
Publication title: Our Lady's Newsletter

02308

Grain and Feed Trade Association
GAFTA

9 Lincoln's Inn Fields, London, WC2A 3BP, UK
Tel: 020 78149666
Fax: 020 78148383
Email: post@gafta.com
Website: http://www.gafta.com
Members: 1000
Staff: 16
Contact: Pamela Kirby Johnson, Dir. Gen.
Fee: £1500
Membership Type: trader
Fee: £220
Membership Type: branch
Description: Promotes international trade in grain, animal feeding stuffs, pulses and rice and to protect the interests of members worldwide, providing support and international contacts.

02309

Greater London Industrial Archaeology Society
GLIAS

c/o Sue Hayton, Membership Sec.
31 The High St., Farnborough Village, Kent, Orpington, BR6 7BQ, UK
Tel: 0168 9852186
Email: membership@glias.org.uk
Website: http://www.glias.org.uk
Members: 600
Contact: Denis Smith, Chm./VP
Fee: £10
Membership Type: ordinary
Fee: £12

Membership Type: family
Description: Is concerned with recording and, where applicable, conserving London's industrial past and bringing this to the notice of general public.
Publication: Newsletter

02310

Greater Manchester and District Campaign for Nuclear Disarmament GMDCND

Bridge 5 Mill, 22a Beswick St., Manchester, M4 7HR, UK
Tel: 0161 2738283
Fax: 0161 2738293
Email: gmdcnd@gn.apc.org
Website: http://www.gmdcnd.org.uk
Staff: 1
Description: Aims to eliminate British nuclear weapons and other weapons of mass destruction. Organizes meetings, events, demonstrations, petitions, and leafleting.
Publication: Newsletter
Publication title: Nuclear Alert

02311

Greek Animal Rescue GAR

69 Great North Way, Hendon, London, NW4 1PT, UK
Tel: 020 82031956
Email: info@greekanimalrescue.com
Website: http://www.greekanimalrescue.com
Contact: Vesna Jones, Founder
Fee: £14
Membership Type: regular
Fee: £7
Membership Type: concession
Description: Seeks to expand rescue work through shelters; provide needy animals necessary treatment and care; re-home animals; spay and neuter dogs and cats. Seeks to advance public education in all aspects of animal care and protection.

02312

Green Organisation

The Mill House, Mill Ln., Earls Barton, Northampton, NN6 0NR, UK
Tel: 01604 810507
Email: rogerwolens@btconnect.com
Website: http://www.thegreenorganisation.info
Members: 150
Staff: 2
Contact: Roger Wolens, Contact
Fee: £250
Membership Type: individual
Fee: £350
Membership Type: small business
Description: Represents individuals interested in environmental protection and the conservation of natural resources. Assists companies wishing to become environmentally responsible, and to be recognized as such by the public.
Publication: Newsletter
Publication title: Eco Echo
Meetings/Conventions: Environmental Best Practice – annual seminar

02313

Green Space

Cavernsham Ct., Church Rd., Reading, RG4 7AD, UK
Tel: 0118 9469060
Fax: 0118 9469061
Email: info@green-space.org.uk
Website: http://www.green-space.org.uk
Staff: 16
Contact: Paul Bramhill, Chief Exec.
Fee: £295
Membership Type: non-local authority, large local authority
Fee: £175
Membership Type: small local authority
Description: Strives to conserve, restore and improve the parks, gardens and green spaces. Promotes the concept of a single parks or green space system. Provides network for the exchange of expertise and information about sustainable planning, landscape and ecological needs, purposes and values of the communities that use them.
Publication: Magazine
Publication title: Spaces and Places

02314

GreenNet

Development House, 56-64 Leonard St., London, EC2A 4LT, UK
Tel: 0845 0554011
Fax: 020 70650936
Email: info@gn.apc.org
Website: http://www.gn.apc.org
Members: 1500
Staff: 7
Fee: £29.38
Membership Type: organization
Fee: £7.05
Membership Type: home/active
Description: Computer network seeking to bring together, and provide ISP services to, individuals interested in issues of global concern, particularly environmental protection and human rights. Gathers and disseminates information; conducts charitable and educational programs.
Publication: Newsletter
Publication title: GreenNet News

02315

Greenpeace UK

Canonbury Villas, London, N1 2PN, UK
Tel: 020 78658100
Fax: 020 78658200
Email: info@uk.greenpeace.org
Website: http://www.greenpeace.org.uk
Members: 20
Staff: 100
Contact: John Sauven, Exec. Dir.
Fee: £19.5
Membership Type: individual
Fee: £24.5
Membership Type: family
Description: Individuals interested in environmental protection and peace issues. Greenpeace campaigns on global issues such as climate change, forests, oceans, toxic pollution, nuclear, genetic engineering and peace.

02316

Greeting Card Association GCA

United House, North Rd., London, N7 9DP, UK
Tel: 020 76190396
Email: gca@max-publishing.co.uk
Website: http://greetingcardassociation.org.uk/home
Members: 360
Staff: 1
Contact: Sharon Little, Gen. Mgr.
Fee: £75-2100
Membership Type: company (based on turnover)
Description: Publishers of greeting cards and related products. Represents, promotes and protects the greeting card industry in the United Kingdom.
Publication: Magazine
Publication title: Progressive Greetings. Advertisements.

02317

Greyhound Awareness League GAL

PO Box 7577, Glasgow, G42 2EB, UK
Tel: 0870 8887277
Email: memberships@gal.org.uk
Website: http://www.gal.org.uk
Members: 350
Fee: £18
Membership Type: single
Fee: £28
Membership Type: joint
Description: Rescues ex-racing, ex-working or abandoned greyhounds and lurchers in Scotland and provides new homes for them.

02318

Greyhounds in NEED GIN

33 High St., Middlesex, Wraysbury, TW19 5DA, UK
Tel: 01784 483206
Fax: 01784 482501
Email: info@greyhoundsinneed.co.uk
Website: http://www.greyhoundsinneed.co.uk
Contact: Carolyn Davenport, Gen. Mgr.
Fee: £10
Membership Type: general
Fee: £5
Membership Type: non-wage earner
Description: Seeks to improve the quality of life for greyhounds and galgos.

02319

Group-Analytic Society GAS

102 Belsize Ln., London, NW3 5BB, UK
Tel: 020 74356611
Fax: 020 74339576
Email: office@groupanalyticsociety.co.uk
Website: http://www.groupanalyticsociety.co.uk
Members: 600
Staff: 3
Contact: Gerda Winther, Pres.
Fee: £165
Membership Type: full
Fee: £150
Membership Type: associate
Description: Group-analysts, doctors, psychiatrists, professors, educationalists, caring professions. Receives and administers funds to be used for the promotion and development of group analysis as a treatment, prophylaxis

and science; its advancement through study, research and teaching, and the provision of advisory services, lectures and publications.
Publication: Journal
Publication title: Group Analysis

Groupe Consultatif Actuariel Europeen

see European Actuarial Consultative Group

02320

GS1 UK

Staple Ct., 11 Staple Inn Bldgs., London, WC1V 7QH, UK
Tel: 020 70923500
Fax: 020 76812290
Email: support@gs1uk.org
Website: http://www.gs1uk.org
Members: 19000
Staff: 40
Contact: James Spittle, Chm.
Fee: £102-2471
Membership Type: user
Fee: £119-2818
Membership Type: association
Description: Business association that works to improve supply chain efficiency through the widespread adoption of e-business.
Library Type: not open to the public
Formerly: Formerly, Electronic Commerce Association
Publication: Manuals
Publication title: EDI Manuals
Meetings/Conventions: periodic conference

02321

GSM Association
GSMA

5 New St. Sq., 7th Fl., New Fetter Ln., London, EC4A 3BF, UK
Tel: 020 73560600
Fax: 020 73560601
Email: webmaster@gsm.org
Website: http://www.gsmworld.com
Members: 924
Contact: Alexander Izosimov, Chm.
Description: Represents and promotes the interests of GSM (Global System for Mobile Communications) mobile operators throughout the world. Aims to accelerate the implementation of collectively identified, commercially prioritized operator requirements.

02322

Guernsey Chamber of Commerce

16 Glategny Esplanande, Ste. 1, St. Peter Port, Guernsey, GY1 1WN, UK
Tel: 01481 727483
Fax: 01481 710755
Email: office@guernseychamber.com
Website: http://www.guernseychamber.com
Members: 700
Staff: 4
Contact: Julian Winser, Pres.
Description: Represents members across Guernsey at local, regional and national level on matters concerning trade, commerce and industry and lobbying. Facilitates networking, forums and events to enable members to exchange ideas, information, views and business practice.
Publication: Magazine
Publication title: Contact. Advertisements.

02323

Guide Dogs for the Blind Association

Hillfields, Burghfield Common, Reading, RG7 3YG, UK
Tel: 0118 9835555
Fax: 0118 9835433
Email: guidedogs@guidedogs.org.uk
Website: http://www.guidedogs.org.uk
Contact: Bridget Warr, Chief Exec.
Description: Provides mobility and freedom to blind and partially sighted people. Campaigns for the rights of those with visual impairments. Educates the public about eye care. Conducts eye disease research.
Publication: Magazine
Publication title: Forward
Meetings/Conventions: annual meeting

02324

Guild of Agricultural Journalists
GAJ

c/o Liz Snaith, Membership Sec.
62 Percy St., Shrewsbury, SY1 2QG, UK
Tel: 01743 344986
Email: lizsnaith@btopenworld.com
Website: http://www.gaj.org.uk/contextra/TemplateParser.asp?sId=1
Members: 600
Contact: Stephen Howe, Chm.
Description: Agricultural and horticultural journalists (full members); and those in the agricultural/horticultural industry with media connections (PRs, etc.) (associate members). Aims to promote a high professional standard among journalists who specialize in agriculture, horticulture and allied subjects; to represent members' interests; to provide a forum, through business meetings and social activities, to maintain contact with associations of agricultural journalists overseas and to promote schemes for the education of members of the Guild.
Publication: Yearbook
Publication title: GAJ Yearbook

02325

Guild of Air Pilots and Air Navigators
GAPAN

Cobham House, 9 Warwick Ct., Gray's Inn, London, WC1R 5DJ, UK
Tel: 020 74044032
Fax: 020 74044035
Email: gapan@gapan.org
Website: http://www.gapan.org
Members: 1650
Staff: 5
Contact: Paul Tacon, Clerk
Fee: £37
Membership Type: associate
Fee: £155
Membership Type: freeman (UK resident)
Description: Professional, civil and military, and private pilots and navigators covering lighter than air, fixed and rotary wing aircraft. Aims to maintain the highest standards of air safety; to enhance the knowledge and status of air pilots and air navigators; to advise, consult and facilitate the exchange of information; to assist air pilots and air navigators and their dependents in need through a Benevolent Fund.
Library Subject: aviation
Library Type: by appointment only
Publication: Newsletter
Publication title: Guild News
Meetings/Conventions: Sir Alan Cobham Presentation – annual general assembly

02326

Guild of Air Traffic Control Officers
GATCO

4 St. Mary's Rd., Nottinghamshire, Bingham, NG13 8DW, UK
Tel: 01949 876405
Fax: 01949 876405
Email: caf@gatco.org
Website: http://www.gatco.org
Members: 2200
Staff: 1
Contact: Steve Brindley, Pres./CEO
Fee: £84
Membership Type: regular
Fee: £60
Membership Type: associate operational, full member abroad
Description: Promotes members' interests.
Library Subject: aviation
Library Type: not open to the public
Publication: Journal
Publication title: Transmit. Advertisements.

02327

Guild of Antique Dealers and Restorers
GADAR

2 Willow Cottages, Hereford Rd., Shropshire, Shrewsbury, SY3 7QL, UK
Tel: 01743 271852
Website: http://www.gadar.co.uk
Members: 300
Staff: 3
Contact: Maureen Edmondson, Sec.
Fee: £40
Membership Type: antique dealer, restorer
Description: Promotes the image and standards of the Guild, thus creating public awareness of the trade. Represents members' views wherever their interests are involved. Assists members with information to benefit them in their day-to-day trading.
Library Subject: antiques, architecture, restoration
Library Type: not open to the public

02328

Guild of Architectural Ironmongers
GAI

8 Stepney Green, London, E1 3JU, UK
Tel: 0207 7903431
Fax: 0207 7908517
Email: info@gai.org.uk
Website: http://www.gai.org.uk
Members: 525
Staff: 3
Contact: Andrew Hall, Pres.
Description: Architectural ironmongers and manufacturers of architectural ironmongery products are corporate members; individual members are those who have passed the guilds examination. Serves to further all aspects of architectural ironmongery, promotes the interchange of information to encourage better product design and high professional standards of ironmongery scheduling and specification. Operates a four-year programme leading to the GAI Diploma, an industry recognized qualification.

Publication: Journal
Publication title: Architectural Ironmongery Journal. Advertisements.

02329
Guild of Aviation Artists
Trenchard House, 85 Farnborough Rd., Farnborough, GU14 6TF, UK
Tel: 01252 513123
Fax: 01252 510505
Email: admin@gava.org.uk
Website: http://www.gava.org.uk
Members: 500
Contact: Michael Turner, Pres.
Fee: £25
Membership Type: friend
Fee: £45
Membership Type: associate
Description: Professional artists, part time amateur artists and non painting supporters. Encouragement of aviation art in all its forms.

02330
Guild of British Camera Technicians
GBCT
Metropolitan Ctre., Bristol Rd., Greenford, UB6 8GD, UK
Tel: 0208 8131999
Fax: 0208 8132111
Email: admin@gbct.org
Website: http://www.gbct.org
Members: 541
Staff: 4
Contact: Jamie Harcourt, Chm.
Fee: £185
Membership Type: full
Fee: £120
Membership Type: overseas
Description: All qualified freelance camera technicians.

02331
Guild of Drama Adjudicators
GoDA
25 The Drive, Bengeo, Hertford, SG14 3DE, UK
Tel: 01992 581993
Email: crossley@bengeo25.freeserve.co.uk
Website: http://amdram.co.uk/goda
Members: 135
Contact: Joan Crossley, Hon. Sec.
Description: Persons with knowledge of the stage and drama especially those who have had some experience of adjudication at drama festivals, verse-speaking and can lecture on drama and theatrical art. Aims to improve the standards of adjudication of amateur drama by establishing recognised principles of practice to which members must adhere.

02332
Guild of Experienced Motorists
GEM
Station Rd., East Sussex, Forest Row, RH18 5EN, UK
Tel: 01342 825676
Fax: 01342 824847
Email: info@motoringassist.com
Website: http://www.motoringassist.com/home.aspx
Members: 60000
Staff: 13
Contact: David Williams, Chief Exec.
Fee: £18.5
Membership Type: individual, joint
Description: Membership is available to all motorists who have not been disqualified from driving during the previous five years; members are encouraged to drive showing care, courtesy, and concentration at all times.
Formerly: Formerly, The Company of Veteran Motorists
Publication: Magazine
Publication title: Good Motoring. Advertisements.

02333
Guild of Fine Food Retailers
Station Rd., Somerset, Wincanton, BA9 9FE, UK
Tel: 01963 824464
Fax: 01963 824651
Email: info@finefoodworld.co.uk
Website: http://www.finefoodworld.co.uk
Members: 700
Staff: 5
Contact: Linda Farrand, Contact
Fee: £103.5
Membership Type: accredited supplier (for turnover below 1 million)
Fee: £230
Membership Type: accredited supplier (for turnover of 1 million and above)
Description: Fine food retailers.
Publication: Magazine
Publication title: Artisan. Advertisements.
Meetings/Conventions: Specialty and Fine Food Fairs – trade show – Exhibits.

02334
Guild of Food Writers
255 Kent House Rd., Kent, Beckenham, BR3 1JQ, UK
Tel: 020 86590422
Email: guild@gfw.co.uk
Website: http://www.gfw.co.uk
Members: 350
Staff: 1
Contact: Jonathan Woods, Admin.
Fee: £85
Membership Type: regular
Description: Brings together professional food writers including journalists, broadcasters and authors. Prints and issues an annual list of members; extends the range of members' knowledge and experience; contributes to the growth of the public's interest in, and knowledge of, the subject of food.

02335
Guild of International Butler Administrators and Personal Assistants
GIBAPA
12 Little Bornes, Dulwich, London, SE21 8SE, UK
Tel: 020 86705585
Fax: 020 86700055
Website: http://www.ivorspencer.com
Members: 75
Staff: 3
Contact: Ivor Spencer, Pres.
Description: Butlers are trained in the Ivor Spencer International School for Butler Administrators and Personal Assistants. Provides a forum for discussion of professional problems and concerns. Encourages the highest standards among British-trained butlers throughout the world. Seeks to keep members informed of current methods of operating a household. Provides consultancy services to film and television companies regarding British-trained butlers. Maintains speakers' bureau and placement service.
Formerly: Formerly, Guild of British Butlers

02336
Guild of International Professional Toastmasters
12 Little Bornes, London, SE21 8SE, UK
Tel: 020 86705585
Fax: 020 86700055
Email: ivor@ivorspencer.com
Website: http://www.ivorspencer.com
Members: 20
Staff: 2
Contact: Ivor Spencer, Pres./Founder
Description: A toastmaster is accepted into the Guild when he has had 5 years experience in the UK's top hotels and livery companies or have received a Diploma from the Ivor Spencer School for Professional Toastmasters. Aims to meet and to discuss ways of keeping professional standards as high as possible. Acts as advisers to firms of repute and promotes special traditional banquets with authentic ceremonies worldwide.

02337
Guild of International Songwriters and Composers
Sovereign House, 12 Trewartha Rd., Praa Sands, Penzance, TR20 9ST, UK
Tel: 01736 762826
Fax: 01736 763328
Email: songmag@aol.com
Website: http://www.songwriters-guild.co.uk
Members: 8000
Staff: 9
Contact: Carole A. Jones, Gen. Sec.
Fee: £55
Membership Type: regular
Description: Songwriters, composers, publishers, record companies, management companies, recording studios, musicians, singers, lyricists, producers. Advises and assists with the needs of its members in the many aspects of the music industry. Members vary from amateur to professional songwriters, composers, lyricists, poets, musicians, music publishers, record companies, managers, etc. Membership is open to all persons throughout the world. Free songwriters' news magazine available on request with S.A.E./International Reply Coupons.
Publication title: Songsearch

02338
Guild of Master Craftsmen
GMC
166 High St., East Sussex, Lewes, BN7 1XU, UK
Tel: 01273 478449
Fax: 01273 478606
Website: http://www.guildmc.com/consumer
Members: 15000
Staff: 58
Contact: Jonathan Phillips, Sec.
Description: Trade association for skilled craftspeople. Aims to protect the public by instilling among members a greater sense of responsibility and by encouraging members always to strive for excellence. Runs a helpline and provides selective lists of skilled craftsmen and women, across the country.

02339
Guild of Motoring Writers
40 Baring Rd., Bournemouth, BH6 4DT, UK
Tel: 01202 422424
Email: generalsec@gomw.co.uk
Website: http://www.gomw.co.uk/home/welcome
Members: 420
Contact: Patricia Lodge, Gen. Sec.
Fee: £95
Membership Type: general
Fee: £50
Membership Type: journalist, photographer, broadcaster (under 30 years old)
Description: Members may be of any nationality, whose occupation has been for at least two years, that of a journalist, author, artist, photographer, broadcaster or film maker whose work is either wholly concerned with motoring or concerned to a significant degree with motoring topics. Activities include training days for new journalists and several social functions for members.
Publication: Yearbook
Publication title: Who's Who in the Motor Industry/The Guild of Motoring Writers Yearbook

02340
Guild of Psychotherapists
47 Nelson Sq., Blackfriars Rd., London, SE1 0QA, UK
Tel: 020 74013260
Fax: 020 74013472
Email: admin@guildofpsychotherapists.org.uk
Website: http://www.guildofpsychotherapists.org.uk
Members: 250
Staff: 2
Description: Qualified and registered psychoanalytic psychotherapists practising in London and all parts of the country. Aims to train psychoanalytic psychotherapists and to offer a clinical referral service with qualified psychotherapists in all areas of the country. Reduced fees available.
Meetings/Conventions: Study Days – annual meeting

02341
Guild of Railway Artists
GRA
c/o John Hughes
17 Manor Rd., Alcombe, Somerset, Minehead, TA24 6EH, UK
Tel: 01643 708026
Email: frank.hodges@virgin.net
Website: http://www.railart.co.uk
Members: 190
Contact: Frank Hodges, CEO
Description: Artists who depict railway as one of their subject matters. Provides a tangible link between artists depicting the heritage and the modern practices of the railway scene.
Publication: Book
Publication title: A Century of Railways

02342
Guild of Taxidermists
14 Lawnsfield Walk, Parkside, Stafford, ST16 1TS, UK
Tel: 01785 223215
Website: http://www.taxidermy.org.uk
Members: 200
Contact: Adrian Sailor, Contact
Fee: £30
Membership Type: regular
Fee: £10
Membership Type: under 18 years old
Description: Amateur, museum, commercial taxidermists and individuals interested in the subject from historical side. Represents the interests of taxidermists to government bodies.

02343
Guild of Television Cameramen
GTC
1, Churchill Rd., Whitchurch, Tavistock, Devon, PL19 9BU, UK
Tel: 01822 614405
Email: administration.07@gtc.org.uk
Website: http://www.gtc.org.uk
Members: 1200
Contact: Graeme McAlpine, Chm.
Fee: £65
Membership Type: full, affiliate
Fee: £40
Membership Type: associate
Description: Television cameramen united to ensure the professional status of the art. Activities include meetings, discussions, demonstrations of new equipment, and cooperation with similar groups in other countries.
Publication: Newsletter
Publication title: GTC in Focus. Advertisements.

02344
Guild of Travel Management Companies
GTMC
85 Tottenham Court Rd., London, W1T 4TQ, UK
Tel: 020 72683540
Fax: 020 72683105
Email: info@gtmc.org
Website: http://www.gtmc.org
Members: 38
Contact: Anne Godfrey, Chief Exec.
Description: Represents the interests and requirements of the business travel market.
Formerly: Formerly, Guild of Business Travel Agents

02345
Guild of Vision Mixers
GVM
85 Oliphant St., Queens Park, London, W10 4EE, UK
Email: contact@visionmixers.tv
Website: http://www.guildofvisionmixers.co.uk
Members: 100
Contact: Peter Turl, Contact
Fee: £20
Membership Type: associate, full (without directory listing)
Fee: £30
Membership Type: full (with directory listing)
Description: Represents the interests of vision mixes working in television production; provides a directory of freelance vision mixers available to companies free of charge.

02346
GuildHE
Woburn House, 3rd Fl., 20 Tavistock Sq., London, WC1H 9HB, UK
Tel: 020 73877711
Fax: 020 73877712
Email: alice.hynes@guildhe.ac.uk
Website: http://www.guildhe.ac.uk
Members: 37
Staff: 5
Contact: Alice Hynes, CEO
Description: Eligible membership is available to heads of institutions with over 55% HE. Associate membership is at the discretion of the Council of Management. Exists to further the interests of these members in dialogue with government and other bodies and in providing other services to its members. Provides a forum in which the executive heads of the institutions are able to consider and take action on matters of common concern. Shows concern on national planning and debate on higher education.
Formerly: Formerly, Standing Conference of Principals
Publication: Pamphlet
Publication title: Higher Destinations - Go To College

02347
Gun Trade Association
GTA
PO Box 43, Tewkesbury, GL20 5ZE, UK
Tel: 01684 291868
Fax: 01684 291864
Email: enquiries@gtaltd.co.uk
Website: http://www.guntradeassociation.co.uk
Members: 700
Staff: 3
Contact: John Batley, Dir.
Fee: £25
Membership Type: regular
Fee: £138
Membership Type: full, probationary (individual trader)
Description: Manufactures (gun makers etc.), distributors and retailers of firearms, ammunition and related components and accessories, and those who offer a service related to the production, maintenance and legitimate use of such items. Represents the interests of those involved in all aspects of the legitimate trade in firearms, ammunition and related items in the United Kingdom and offers associate membership to those based outside the United Kingdom.
Publication: Newsletter
Publication title: GTA Newsletter. Advertisements.

02348
Gwent Area Welsh Pony and Cob Association
Pen Y Fan Fach Farm, Aberbeeg, Blaenau Gwent, NP13 2DT, UK
Tel: 01495 214810
Fax: 01495 214810
Email: secretary@gwentwpca.com
Website: http://www.gwentwpca.com
Contact: Jan Woodland, Sec.
Fee: £5
Membership Type: adult
Fee: £1.5
Membership Type: junior
Description: Records the breeding details of Welsh ponies and cobs. Seeks to improve the breed and promote its excellence.

02349
Gypsum Products Development Association
GPDA
PO Box 35084, London, NW1 4XE, UK
Tel: 020 79358532
Fax: 020 79358532
Email: admin@gpda.com

Website: http://www.gpda.com
Members: 4
Contact: Crispin Dunn-Meynell, Contact
Description: Gypsum product manufacturers in the U.K. and Ireland. Promotes, encourages and develops the use of gypsum products.

02350
H.G. Wells Society
HGWS
c/o Paul Allen
1 Nackington Rd., Kent, Canterbury, CT1 3NU, UK
Email: juststruckone@hotmail.com
Website: http://hgwellsusa.50megs.com
Members: 200
Contact: P. Nymadawa, Pres.
Fee: £18
Membership Type: individual (in UK and Europe)
Fee: £21
Membership Type: individual (outside Europe), couple
Description: Individual members are students, scholars, and other interested persons; corporate members are universities, libraries, and institutes. Aims to encourage and promote an active interest in and an appreciation of the life, work, and thought of H.G. Wells (1866-1946), British novelist, sociological writer, and historian. Provides book service, information service, and speakers' panel.
Publication: Bibliography
Publication title: H.G. Wells Bibliography

02351
Haberdashers' Company
Haberdasher's Hall, 18 W Smithfield, London, EC1A 9HQ, UK
Tel: 020 72469988
Fax: 020 72469989
Email: enquiries@haberdashers.co.uk
Website: http://www.haberdashers.co.uk
Contact: David Evans, Contact
Description: Haberdashers. Works to provide highest quality governance and to promote common values in Haberdasher schools.

02352
Habitat for Humanity - Eastbourne
PO Box 2853, Eastbourne, BN20 8WU, UK
Tel: 01323 438527
Website: http://web.ukonline.co.uk/christianityonline/habitatforhumanity.htm
Contact: Chris Savile, Chm.
Description: Works in partnership with volunteers from all faiths who are committed to its goal of eliminating poverty housing. Brings families and communities in need together with volunteers and resources to build decent shelter sold with no profit.

02353
Habitat for Humanity - Great Britain
46 W Bar St., Banbury, OX16 9RZ, UK
Tel: 01295 264240
Fax: 01295 264230
Email: supporterservices@habitatforhumanity.org.uk
Website: http://www.habitatforhumanity.org.uk
Contact: Michael Kirkwood, Chm.
Description: Works in partnership with volunteers from all faiths who are committed to its goal of eliminating poverty housing. Brings families and communities in need together with volunteers and resources to build decent shelter sold with no profit.

02354
Habitat for Humanity - Northern Ireland
HFHNI
638 Springfield Rd., Belfast, BT12 7DY, UK
Tel: 028 90243686
Fax: 028 90331878
Email: enquiries@habitatni.co.uk
Website: http://www.habitatni.co.uk
Contact: Angus Beck, Chm.
Description: Works in partnership with volunteers from all faiths who are committed to the goal of eliminating poverty housing. Brings families and communities in need together with volunteers and resources to build decent shelter sold with no profit.

02355
Haemophilia Society
1st Fl., Petersham House, 57a Hatton Garden, London, EC1N 8JG, UK
Tel: 0207 8311020
Fax: 0207 4054824
Email: info@haemophilia.org.uk
Website: http://www.haemophilia.org.uk
Members: 2000
Contact: Christopher James, Chief Exec.
Fee: £25
Membership Type: overseas
Description: Provides information, advice and support services to people with haemophilia and other bleeding disorders. Advocates and campaigns to secure the best possible care and treatment through lobbying and raising public awareness. Provides services for people with haemophilia affected by HIV and Hepatitis C.
Publication: Newsletter
Publication title: HQ News

02356
Hairdressing Council
HC
30 Sydenham Rd., Croydon, CR0 2EF, UK
Tel: 020 87607010
Email: registrar@haircouncil.org.uk
Website: http://www.haircouncil.org.uk
Members: 18000
Staff: 5
Description: Hairdressers trained and qualified to a prescribed standard may apply to become State Registered Hairdressers. Acts as the statutory authority for hairdressing. Provides the administration for the Hairdressing Industry Coordinating Committee, the industry umbrella body, and is the contact point for the government, European Commission and other areas of officialdom.
Publication: Magazine
Publication title: State Registered Hairdresser. Advertisements.

02357
Hakluyt Society - England
HS
c/o Map Library
The British Library, 96 Euston Rd., London, NW1 2DB, UK
Tel: 01428 641850
Fax: 01428 641933
Email: office@hakluyt.com
Website: http://www.hakluyt.com
Members: 2300
Staff: 1
Contact: Will Ryan, Pres.
Fee: £60
Membership Type: regular (domestic and elsewhere)
Fee: £110
Membership Type: in U.S.
Description: Individuals in 64 countries interested in the literature of geographical discovery and travel. Publishes original and rare narratives of notable voyages and naval expeditions (in addition to other geographical materials) in order to educate and enlighten the public; such published volumes currently number more than 300. Society is named after Richard Hakluyt.
Publication: Directory
Publication title: List of Publications in Print

02358
Hampshire Conservation Volunteers
HCV
PO Box 146, Romsey, SO51 6XW, UK
Tel: 01252 547508
Email: alan@hcv.org.uk
Website: http://www.hcv.hampshire.org.uk
Contact: Alan Thurbon, Contact
Fee: £6.5
Membership Type: individual
Fee: £3.5
Membership Type: student, unemployed
Description: Works to make a practical contribution to nature conservation in Hampshire. Conducts woodland management, heath and downland management, pond restoration, fencing and path work.
Publication: Booklet
Publication title: Introduction to Conservation

02359
Handbell Ringers of Great Britain
HRGB
1A Glover Rd., Totley Rise, Sheffield, S17 4HN, UK
Tel: 0114 2362286
Email: alan@hrgb.org.uk
Website: http://www.hrgb.org.uk
Members: 3000
Contact: Allan Hartley, Natl. Chm.
Fee: £10
Membership Type: adult
Fee: £4
Membership Type: junior
Description: Handbell tune ringing teams throughout the UK. Caters for active ringers, ringers of handchimes and belleplates and also those with merely an interest in ringing. Aims to promote the art of handbell tune ringing, through rallies, workshops, concerts, etc. that are mostly arranged by the eight regional branches. Provides advice and information to the members.
Publication: Magazine
Publication title: Reverberations. Advertisements.

02360
Handicap International - UK
HI
Can Mezzanine, 32-36 Loman St., London, SE1 0EH, UK
Tel: 0870 7743737

Fax: 0870 7743738
Email: info@hi-uk.org
Website: http://www.handicap-international.org.uk
Staff: 6
Description: Supports people with disabilities. Raises awareness of disability and landmine issues.
Publication: Newsletter
Publication title: Positive Progress

02361

Hansard Society

40-43 Chancery Ln., London, WC2A 1JA, UK
Tel: 020 74381222
Fax: 020 74381229
Email: hansard@hansard.lse.ac.uk
Website: http://www.hansardsociety.org.uk
Members: 400
Staff: 7
Contact: Fiona Booth, Chief Exec.
Fee: £20
Membership Type: basic
Fee: £35
Membership Type: individual (in UK/Europe)
Description: Promotes knowledge of and interest in parliamentary governments and procedures. Conducts research, educational programs, and training courses for companies and teachers; sponsors international student exchange programs. Organizes academic competitions and lobbying seminars.
Publication: Book
Publication title: Parliament at Work

02362

Harris Tweed Authority

6 Garden Rd., Isle of Lewis, Stornoway, HS1 2QJ, UK
Tel: 01851 702269
Fax: 01851 702600
Email: enquiries@harristweed.org
Website: http://www.harristweed.org
Members: 10
Staff: 5
Contact: Lorna Macaulay, Chief Exec.
Description: Concerns with the promotion, protection, certification and authentication of Harris Tweed.

02363

Harrow Association of Disabled People
HAD

Ground Fl., Bentley House, Headstone Dr., Wealdstone, Harrow, HA3 5QX, UK
Tel: 020 88619920
Fax: 020 88619926
Email: general@had.org.uk
Website: http://www.had.org.uk
Contact: Ann Groves, Chair
Description: Offers support services to disabled people residing and working in the London Borough of Harrow.

02364

Hartlepool Special Needs Support Group
HSNSG

109 Park Rd., Hartlepool, TS26 9HR, UK
Tel: 01429 863766
Email: info@hsnsg.org.uk
Website: http://www.hsnsg.org.uk
Contact: Loraine Potts, Chair
Description: Works to relieve the needs and advance the education of children and young people with various physical/mental disabilities and to support families and friends.

02365

Havergal Brian Society
HBS

37 Leylands, Viewfield Rd., London, SW18 1NF, UK
Email: hbswebmaster@mbecker.fsnet.co.uk
Website: http://www.havergalbrian.org/society.htm
Members: 230
Contact: John Grimshaw, Chm.
Fee: £12
Membership Type: in U.K.
Fee: £16
Membership Type: in Europe, worldwide (newsletters sent by surface mail)
Description: Individuals in 15 countries interested in the work of English composer Havergal Brian (1876-1972). Provides information about Brian and his music; gathers information on the location of Brian's missing scores. Advises and assists prospective performers of Brian's music; arranges and sponsors recitals, recordings, and concerts.
Publication: Book
Publication title: Brian's Complete Music for Solo Piano

02366

Hawk and Owl Trust
HOT

PO Box 400, Taunton, TA4 2WX, UK
Tel: 0844 9842824
Email: enquiries@hawkandowl.org
Website: http://www.hawkandowl.org
Contact: Chris Packham, Pres.
Fee: £22
Membership Type: individual
Fee: £14
Membership Type: student (under 21)
Description: Works to protect and conserve all wild birds of prey and their habitats through creative conservation, practical research and imaginative education.
Publication: Newsletter
Publication title: Peregrine

02367

Headmasters' and Headmistresses' Conference
HMC

12, The Point, Rockingham Rd., Market Harborough, Leicester, LE16 7QU, UK
Tel: 0185 8469059
Email: hmc@hmc.org.uk
Website: http://www.hmc.org.uk
Members: 243
Staff: 4
Contact: Geoff Lucas, Sec.
Description: Heads of major independent boys and co-educational schools. Responds to any major government initiatives, like those on the curriculum, examinations, teacher training and children's welfare. Provides professional training, inspection of schools and general advice on educational matters.
Formerly: Formerly, Headmasters' Conference
Publication: Newsletter
Publication title: NCCA Newsletter. Advertisements.

02368

Headway - The Brain Injury Association

Bradbury House, 190 Bagnall Rd., Old Basford, Nottinghamshire, Nottingham, NG6 8SF, UK
Tel: 0115 9240800
Fax: 0115 9584446
Email: enquiries@headway.org.uk
Website: http://www.headway.org.uk
Contact: Peter McCabe, Chief Exec.
Fee: £25
Membership Type: individual
Fee: £250-500
Membership Type: corporate
Description: Promotes understanding of all aspects of head injury. Provides information, support and services to people with head injury, their families and carers.
Publication: Magazine
Publication title: Headway News

02369

Health Food Manufacturers' Association
HFMA

1 Wolsey Rd., E Moleysey, Surrey, KT8 9EL, UK
Tel: 020 84817100
Fax: 020 84817101
Email: hfma@hfma.co.uk
Website: http://www.hfma.co.uk
Staff: 6
Contact: Graham Keen, Exec. Dir.
Description: Trade association covering manufacturers, distributors and suppliers of specialist health products including foods, supplements, natural medicines and cosmetics. Covers legislation, training and education, standards and ethics and the dissemination of information; also involved in the more commercial aspects of export and trade exhibitions but primarily it is concerned with providing a safe and expanding marketing arena within which its members can increase sales and influence.
Publication title: Nutrition Research
Meetings/Conventions: monthly meeting

02370

Health in Prisons Project
HIPP

Department of Health, 110 Wellington House, 133-155 Waterloo St., London, SE1 8UG, UK
Tel: 07867 538391
Email: richard.bradshaw@dh.gsi.gov.uk
Website: http://www.euro.who.int
Members: 200
Contact: Richard Bradshaw, Dir.
Description: Medical and health care professionals; associate members are administrators of prison health care agencies. Promotes discussion among prison health professionals. Strives to improve health care worldwide; encourages postgraduate training for doctors working in prison settings.
Publication: Newsletter
Publication title: HIP News
Meetings/Conventions: periodic congress

02371

Healthcare Financial Management Association

HFMA

Albert House, Ste. 32, 111 Victoria St., Bristol, BS1 6AX, UK
Tel: 0117 9294789
Fax: 0117 9294844
Email: info@hfma.org.uk
Website: http://www.hfma.org.uk
Members: 3000
Staff: 20
Contact: Paul Assinder, Pres.
Fee: £65
Membership Type: ordinary
Fee: £40
Membership Type: abated, retired
Description: Any qualified accountant and/or financial employee working in the NHS. Promotes professional standards of financial practice in the management and audit of the NHS.
Publication title: NHS Health Authorities
Meetings/Conventions: annual conference – Exhibits.

02372

Healthcare People Management Association

HPMA

Gothic House, 3 The Green, Richmond, TW9 1PL, UK
Tel: 020 83344530
Fax: 020 83344531
Email: admin@hpma.org.uk
Website: http://www.hpma.org.uk
Contact: Kelvin Cheatle, Pres.
Fee: £20-45
Membership Type: individual
Fee: £350-450
Membership Type: corporate (based on the turnover)
Description: Represents individuals in the field of people management. Raises the profile of human resource practitioners. Promotes excellence in workforce management, development and leadership within healthcare services. Influences policy-makers in national issues related to human resource management.
Publication: Newsletter
Publication title: Network

02373

Healthlink Worldwide

The Grayston Centre, 28 Charles Sq., London, N1 6HT, UK
Tel: 020 72506950
Fax: 020 73244600
Email: info@healthlink.org.uk
Website: http://www.healthlink.org.uk
Members: 70
Staff: 18
Contact: Andrew Chetley, Exec. Dir.
Description: Provides innovative applications of communication in the health sector. Collaborates with a network of over 50 partnerships across 30 developing countries to improve the health and well-being of vulnerable and disadvantaged communities. Works on the major health issues such as HIV/AIDS, TB, Malaria, polio, leprosy, and children and women's health. Works at community, national and international levels with academic and government institutions and civil society organizations, through grant-funded programmes and consultancy services. Aims to strengthen the communication skills of the most marginalized people to enable their active participation in their societies.
Library Subject: primary health care in developing countries
Library Type: reference
Formerly: Formerly, Appropriate Health Resources and Technologies Action Group

02374

Hearing Concern LINK

19 Hartfield Rd., East Sussex, Eastbourne, BN21 2AR, UK
Tel: 01323 638230
Fax: 01323 642968
Email: info@hearingconcernlink.org
Website: http://www.hearingconcernlink.org
Members: 3000
Staff: 6
Contact: Stewart Simpson, Chm.
Fee: £18
Membership Type: individual
Fee: £21
Membership Type: couple
Description: Works to improve the quality of life for those who are hard of hearing. Provides advice, information and support, as well as communication access, and raises public and professional awareness of the issues associated with hearing loss.
Formerly: Formerly, Hearing Concern, British Association of the Hard of Hearing
Meetings/Conventions: annual conference – Exhibits.

02375

Heartland Conservation Society

HCS

PO Box 109, Surrey, Camberley, GU15 4ZF, UK
Tel: 01276 507122
Email: information@heathland-conservation-society.org
Website: http://www.heathland-conservation-society.org
Description: Protects and preserves Heartland from damage and misuse. Works to carry out valuable conservation work.

02376

Heating and Ventilating Contractors' Association

HVCA

ESCA House, 34 Palace Ct., London, W2 4JG, UK
Tel: 0207 3134900
Fax: 0207 7279268
Email: contact@hvca.org.uk
Website: http://www.hvca.org.uk
Members: 1400
Staff: 42
Contact: Martin Burton, Pres.
Description: Contractors involved in heating, ventilating, air conditioning, refrigeration, duct work and related work. Aims to provide a range of services to the membership. Represents, promotes and protects their interests in the broadest possible sense and at the highest possible levels.
Publication: Magazine
Publication title: The Specifier. Advertisements.
Meetings/Conventions: annual conference

02377

Heating, Ventilating and Air Conditioning Manufacturers' Association

HEVAC

Federation of Environmental Trade Associations, Milley Ln., 2 Waltham C., Berkshire, Reading, RG10 9TH, UK
Tel: 0118 9403416
Fax: 0118 9406258
Email: info@feta.co.uk
Website: http://www.feta.co.uk
Members: 130
Staff: 5
Contact: Cedric Sloan, Dir. Gen.
Description: Manufacturers and distributors of heating, ventilating and air conditioning equipment. Serves the interests of manufacturers and users of heating, ventilating and air conditioning equipment.

02378

Hebe Society

c/o Mr. Val Haywood, Treas.
1 Woodpecker Dr., East Sussex, Hailsham, BN27 3EZ, UK
Website: http://www.hebesoc.org
Members: 300
Contact: Tony Hayter, Sec.
Fee: £8
Membership Type: individual
Fee: £10
Membership Type: joint
Description: Aims to encourage, improve, conserve and extend the cultivation of Hebe, parahebe and all New Zealand native plants.
Publication: Magazine
Publication title: Hebe News. Advertisements.

02379

Helicopter Club of Great Britain

HCGB

Ryelands House, Aynho, Banbury, OX17 3AT, UK
Email: jeremy@ryelands.net
Website: http://www.britishhelicopterteam.co.uk/default.asp?id=385736
Members: 500
Fee: £55
Membership Type: individual
Description: Promotes safe and considerate flying. Organizes helicopter events throughout the year including the British Helicopter Championships.

02380

HelpAge International

PO Box 32832, London, N1 9ZN, UK
Tel: 020 72787778
Fax: 020 77137993
Website: http://www.helpage.org/Home
Members: 65
Staff: 178
Contact: Eric M. Kimani, Chm.
Description: Works with and for disadvantaged older people worldwide, to achieve lasting improvement in the quality of their lives. Supports the development of "grass roots" activity and the growth of local organisations working with older people. Projects focus on health, social services, residential, community and home care, income generation, advocacy, training and organisational development.
Publication: Newsletter
Publication title: Ageways

02381
Henry Doubleday Research Association
HDRA
Garden Organic Ryton, Warwickshire, Coventry, CV8 3LG, UK
Tel: 024 76303517
Fax: 024 76639229
Email: enquiry@gardenorganic.org.uk
Website: http://www.gardenorganic.org.uk
Members: 30000
Staff: 100
Contact: Jackie Gear, Gen. Mgr.
Fee: £28
Membership Type: individual
Fee: £36
Membership Type: family
Description: Provides research and advice on all aspects of organic horticulture, primarily on a small or garden scale. Examines the problem of peasant agriculture in developing countries.
Formerly: Also Known As, Garden Organic
Publication: Magazine
Publication title: The Organic Way

02382
Henry Williamson Society
16 Doran Dr., Red Hill, Surrey, RH1 6AX, UK
Website: http://www.henrywilliamson.co.uk
Members: 540
Contact: Margaret Murphy, Membership Sec.
Fee: £15
Membership Type: individual
Fee: £5
Membership Type: student
Description: Aims to encourage interest in and a deeper understanding of the life and work of the writer Henry Williamson.

02383
Herb Society
Sulgrave Manor, PO Box 946, Northampton, NN3 0BN, UK
Tel: 01295 768899
Email: info@herbsociety.org.uk
Website: http://www.herbsociety.org.uk
Members: 2000
Staff: 1
Contact: Anne McIntyre, Pres.
Fee: £25
Membership Type: full
Fee: £22.5
Membership Type: concessionary
Description: Aims to disseminate information on all aspects of herbs.
Publication: Journal
Publication title: Herbs. Advertisements.

02384
Heritage Railway Association
HRA
2 Littlestone Rd., Kent, New Romney, TN28 8PL, UK
Email: hradw@globalnet.co.uk
Website: http://ukhrail.uel.ac.uk
Members: 250
Contact: Dame Margaret Weston, Pres.
Fee: £17.25
Membership Type: friend
Description: Open to Railway Preservation Organizations World Wide and individuals. Co-ordinates the activities of railway preservation societies and groups, and represents the membership in matters of relevant legislation, and regulations, e.g., The Health and Safety Executive. Also publishes lists and details of preserved railway activities in UK and Eire. Manages by an elected council. Officers' function in a voluntary capacity as staff.
Formerly: Formerly, Association of Independent Railways and Preservation Societies
Publication: Journal
Publication title: Heritage Railways Journal

02385
Herpes Viruses Association
HVA
41 N Rd., London, N7 9DP, UK
Tel: 0845 1232305
Email: info@herpes.org.uk
Website: http://www.herpes.org.uk
Members: 1500
Staff: 3
Contact: Marian Nicholson, Dir.
Fee: £25
Membership Type: regular
Description: Provides accurate information on herpes simplex virus (to counteract the "herpes hype"), to the media, health professionals and the public.
Library Subject: herpes viruses
Library Type: reference
Publication: Journal
Publication title: Sphere. Advertisements.

02386
Hertfordshire Chamber of Commerce and Industry
HCCI
4 Bishops Sq., Business Park, Hatfield, AL10 9NE, UK
Tel: 01707 398400
Fax: 01707 398430
Email: enquiries@hertschamber.com
Website: http://www.hertschamber.com
Members: 1450
Staff: 9
Contact: Tim Hutchings, Chief Exec.
Fee: £1586.25
Membership Type: firm/company (maximum; based on number of employees)
Fee: £94
Membership Type: school/registered charity
Description: Promotes business and commerce.
Publication: Newsletter
Publication title: Chamber News

02387
Higher Education Funding Council for England
HEFCE
Northavon House, Coldharbour Ln., Bristol, BS16 1QD, UK
Tel: 0117 9317317
Fax: 0117 9317203
Email: hefce@hefce.ac.uk
Website: http://www.hefce.ac.uk
Contact: Ed Smith, Chm.
Description: Non-departmental public body set up under the Further and Higher Education Act of 1992. Distributes public funding for teaching and research to universities and colleges. In doing so, it aims to promote high quality education and research, within a financially healthy sector. The Council also plays a key role in ensuring accountability and promoting good practice.

02388
Highland Cattle Society
Stirling Agricultural Ctre., Stirling, FK9 4RN, UK
Tel: 01786 446866
Fax: 01786 446022
Email: info@highlandcattlesociety.com
Website: http://www.highlandcattlesociety.com
Members: 1200
Staff: 3
Contact: Ian Bowie, Pres.
Fee: £12.55
Membership Type: junior, associate
Fee: £1569
Membership Type: life
Description: Promotes the breeding of highland cattle in Scotland.

02389
Highland Railway Society
Ringmarsh Cottage, Horsington Marsh, Somerset, Templecombe, BA8 0EL, UK
Tel: 01963 370697
Email: secretary@hrsoc.org.uk
Website: http://www.hrsoc.org.uk
Members: 300
Contact: John Roake, Treas.
Fee: £12.5
Membership Type: full
Fee: £10
Membership Type: age under 18 or over 65
Description: Studies the Highland railway, its constituents, and successors.
Library Subject: Highland railway
Library Type: not open to the public
Publication: Journal
Publication title: Highland Railway Journal

02390
Hire Association Europe
HAE
2450 Regents Ct., Birmingham Business Park, Solihull, B37 7YE, UK
Tel: 0121 3804600
Fax: 0121 3334109
Email: mail@hae.org.uk
Website: http://www.hae.org.uk/pages/index.cfm
Members: 1100
Staff: 16
Contact: Kevin McGuinness, Chm.
Fee: £436-4370
Membership Type: full (based on turnover)
Fee: £475.15
Membership Type: supplier in UK
Description: Companies which hire out equipment and vehicles including tools, audio-visual equipment catering and leisure equipment, portable toilets and access equipment, boats, trailers and recreational vehicles. Aims to represent, promote and enhance the hire industry for the benefit of its members and their customers.
Publication title: Focus

02391
Historic Houses Association
HHA
2 Chester St., London, SW1X 7BB, UK
Tel: 020 72595688
Fax: 020 72595590
Email: info@hha.org.uk
Website: http://www.hha.org.uk
Members: 1600
Staff: 7
Contact: Peter Sinclair, Asst. Dir. of Operations
Fee: £37
Membership Type: friend (single)
Fee: £60
Membership Type: friend (double)
Description: Owners of privately owned historic houses and gardens around 300 of which are open regularly, to the public. Represents the owners of historic houses, parks and gardens in private ownership in Britain. Provides practical advice and services to owners and seeks to establish a fiscal, political and economic climate in which owners can maintain Britain's historic houses for the benefit of the nation. Operates a friends scheme for people who support the aims and enjoy visiting houses, which are open to the public. Friends have free access to around 280 HHA members' properties.
Publication: Journal
Publication title: Historic House. Advertisements.

02392
Historical Association
HA
59a Kennington Park Rd., London, SE11 4JH, UK
Tel: 020 77353901
Fax: 020 75824989
Email: enquiry@history.org.uk
Website: http://www.history.org.uk
Members: 6000
Staff: 10
Contact: Anne Curry, Pres.
Fee: £24
Membership Type: regular
Description: Promotes the study and teaching of history at all educational levels; organizes lectures, study tours, and vacation history courses.
Publication: Magazine
Publication title: Historian. Advertisements.
Meetings/Conventions: annual conference

02393
Historical Diving Society
HDS
Little Gatton Lodge, 25 Gatton Rd., Reigate, RH2 0HD, UK
Tel: 01737 249961
Fax: 01384 896079
Email: enquiries@thehds.com
Website: http://www.thehds.com
Contact: John Bevan, Chm.
Fee: £40
Membership Type: individual (in UK)
Fee: £45
Membership Type: individual (overseas)
Description: Individuals with an interest in diving and the history of underwater exploration. Seeks to identify, protect, and preserve artifacts and archival materials pertaining to the history of diving. Serves as a forum for the exchange of information among members; encourages public awareness of diving and its history; provides support and assistance in the maintenance of working diving equipment. Maintains profile and historical equipment registries.

02394
Historical Manuscripts Commission
HMC
National Archives, Kew, Surrey, Richmond, TW9 4DU, UK
Tel: 020 88763444
Website: http://www.nationalarchives.gov.uk
Staff: 24
Description: Functions as the U.K.'s central coordinating and advisory body on all matters relating to manuscript sources for British history. Maintains the National Register of Archives and the Manorial Documents Register.

02395
Historical Metallurgy Society
HMS
267 Kells Ln., Gateshead, NE9 5HU, UK
Tel: 0191 4821037
Email: hon-sec@hist-met.org
Website: http://hist-met.org
Members: 700
Contact: David Cranstone, Honorary Gen. Sec.
Fee: £20
Membership Type: ordinary individual/institutional, overseas
Fee: £22
Membership Type: family (UK)
Description: International organization of institutions, families, individuals, academies, libraries, museums, University departments, and archaeological and other societies. Encourages and records the preservation and study of all aspects of metallurgical history including: the extraction of ores and minerals; the melting and working of metals; the examination and analysis of metal artifacts; the preservation of archaeological and historical sites and objects.
Library Subject: out-of-date metallurgy
Library Type: by appointment only
Publication: Journal
Publication title: Historical Metallurgy

02396
HIV Pharmacy Association
HIVPA
43 Raymond Rd., Langley, SL3 8LN, UK
Tel: 01753 543611
Fax: 0870 4215611
Email: info@hivpa.org
Website: http://www.hivpa.org
Contact: Sharon Byrne, Chair
Fee: £30
Membership Type: pharmacist, technician, industry associate
Fee: £10
Membership Type: international
Description: Represents pharmacists and pharmacy technicians working with HIV. Improves the personal and professional development of HIV pharmacists. Offers education and networking opportunities to members.

02397
Home Counties Welsh Pony and Cob Association
HCWPCA
58 The Pastures, Chells Manor, Herts, Stevenage, SG2 7DZ, UK
Tel: 01604 864184
Email: hcwpca04@yahoo.co.uk
Website: http://www.hcwpca.com
Contact: Louise Davies, Membership Sec.
Fee: £10
Membership Type: single
Fee: £15
Membership Type: family
Description: Records the breeding details of Welsh ponies and cobs. Seeks to improve the breed and promote its excellence.
Publication: Newsletter

02398
Home for Unwanted and Lost Animals
HULA
Glebe Farm, Salford Rd., Aspley Guise, Milton Keynes, MK17 8HZ, UK
Tel: 01908 584000
Fax: 01908 282020
Email: hularescue@tiscali.co.uk
Website: http://www.hularescue.org
Fee: £15
Membership Type: full
Fee: £10
Membership Type: youth, senior citizen
Description: Provides sanctuary for dogs, cats, rabbits, and other domestic animals until new homes can be found; cares for resident, retired animals including goats, pigs, sheep, cows, ponies, donkeys; operates 17-acre site for the animals.

02399
Home Laundering Consultative Council
HLCC
5 Portland Pl., London, W1N 3AA, UK
Tel: 020 76367788
Email: labelling@5portlandplace.org.uk
Website: http://www.care-labelling.co.uk
Members: 40
Fee: £695
Membership Type: regular
Description: Aims to develop and promote the use of International Care Labelling code in the United Kingdom.

02400
Home-Start North and Mid Beds
Broadway House, 4-6 The Broadway, Bedford, MK40 2TE, UK
Tel: 01234 270601
Email: wendie@homestartnmb.co.uk
Website: http://www.homestartnmb.co.uk
Contact: Wendie Lovatt, Scheme Mgr.
Description: Promotes stable family life for healthy child development; supports parents struggling to cope with stresses and difficulties; works with parents in crises situations.

02401

Homeless Children International - United Kingdom HCI-UK

Clifton Hall Centre, Clifton Rd., West Sussex, Worthing, BN11 4DP, UK
Tel: 01903 267283
Fax: 01903 267283
Email: hciuk@hotmail.com
Website: http://homelesskids.org/uk
Contact: John Venner, Contact
Description: Cares for the physical and emotional needs of homeless children. Promotes programs that support their needs at different stages in their lives. Provides rehabilitation, education and leadership services to children.

02402

Homes for Scotland

5 New Mart Pl., Edinburgh, EH14 1RW, UK
Tel: 0131 4558350
Fax: 0131 4558360
Email: info@homesforscotland.com
Website: http://www.homesforscotland.com/Home.aspx
Contact: Jonathan Fair, Chief Exec.
Fee: £325-525
Membership Type: full (based on building turnover)
Fee: £1650
Membership Type: associate (contracting and supply)
Description: Represents major homebuilders and home companies in Scotland. Liaises with authorities and policy makers and provides strategic and practical support to its members.

02403

Homoeopathic Medical Association HMA

7 Darnley Rd., Kent, Gravesend, DA11 0RU, UK
Tel: 01474 560336
Fax: 01474 327431
Email: info@the-hma.org
Website: http://www.the-hma.org
Members: 300
Fee: £55
Membership Type: student
Fee: £70
Membership Type: homeopath
Description: Develops, supports and encourages the practice of homeopathic medicine in the UK and in other countries. Increases public awareness and acceptance of homeopathy.
Publication: Journal
Publication title: Homeopathy International

02404

Hong Kong Trade Development Council - London Office HKTDC

16 Upper Grosvenor St., London, W1K 7PL, UK
Tel: 020 76169500
Fax: 020 76169510
Email: london.office@hktdc.org
Website: http://www.hktdc.com/info/ms/uk/United-Kingdom.ht
Contact: David Marsden, Dir.
Description: Promotes the value of Hong Kong as a business center for China and Asian region to international firms. Helps small and medium sizes enterprises in overseas markets.

02405

Honourable Company of Master Mariners HCMM

Temple Stairs, Victoria Embankment, London, WC2R 2PN, UK
Tel: 020 78368179
Fax: 020 72403082
Email: info@hcmm.org.uk
Website: http://www.hcmm.org.uk
Members: 800
Staff: 6
Contact: Malcolm W. Parrott, Sr. Warden
Fee: £160
Membership Type: liveryman (direct debit)
Fee: £60-221
Membership Type: associate (direct debit)
Description: Promotes the efficiency of the Merchant Navy. Administers charitable trusts; supports the Corporation and City of London; maintains a small museum and library; develops interaction and dialogue between members and other maritime organizations.
Library Subject: maritime
Library Type: by appointment only

02406

HOPE for Children

Hope House, 14a Queensway, Hemel Hempstead, HP1 1RL, UK
Tel: 0844 7799774
Fax: 0845 0099628
Email: hope@hope4c.org
Website: http://www.hope-for-children.org
Contact: Simon Jackman, Chief Exec.
Description: Seeks to improve the quality of life and advances the rights of children. Assists handicapped, orphaned, poor and exploited children in developing countries.

02407

Horticultural Trades Association HTA

c/o Horticulture House
19 High St., Theale, Reading, RG7 5AH, UK
Tel: 0118 9303132
Fax: 0118 9323453
Email: info@the-hta.org.uk
Website: http://www.the-hta.org.uk
Members: 3000
Staff: 30
Description: Trade association; supports the needs of United Kingdom horticulture, including garden centers, retail, wholesale nurseries, landscapers, manufacturers and suppliers, and service-providing associate members.
Publication: Magazine
Publication title: HTA News

02408

Hospital Caterers Association HCA

c/o Mr. Martin Cantor, Asst. Natl. Sec.
Royal Wolverhampton Hospital NHS Trust, New Cross Hospital, Wednesfield Rd., Wolverhampton, WV10 0QP, UK
Tel: 01902 695028
Fax: 01902 695614
Email: sewellyn.douglass-james@worcsmhp.nhs.uk
Website: http://www.hospitalcaterers.org
Members: 400
Contact: Sewellyn Douglass-James, Natl. Sec.
Fee: £43
Membership Type: full/associate
Fee: £43
Membership Type: life, retired
Description: Improves the standards of catering in hospitals and health care establishments in Great Britain, Northern Ireland and elsewhere. Promotes the education and training of persons in health care catering services, and the provision and improvement of the professional interests and status of people engaged in health care catering services.
Publication: Journal
Publication title: Hospital Caterer

02409

Hospital Consultants and Specialists Association HCSA

1 Kingsclere Rd., Overton, Hampshire, Basingstoke, RG25 3JA, UK
Tel: 01256 771777
Fax: 01256 770999
Email: conspec@hcsa.com
Website: http://www.hcsa.com
Contact: Stephen Campion, Chief Exec.
Fee: £200
Membership Type: consultant, associate specialist
Fee: £17.35
Membership Type: consultant, associate specialist
Description: Membership is open to hospital consultants, associate specialists, senior registrars, and staff grade doctors working in the National Health Service. Works with the interests of senior hospital doctors and their patients. Aims to improve the conditions of service of members, informing them on matters affecting their practice and endeavoring to ensure that key health decisions are taken with due regard to their views.
Publication title: The Consultant

02410

Hospital Infection Society HIS

162 Kings Cross Rd., London, WC1X 9DH, UK
Tel: 020 77130273
Fax: 020 77130255
Email: tim.hogan@his.org.uk
Website: http://www.his.org.uk
Members: 800
Contact: Tim Hogan, Chief Exec.
Fee: £55
Membership Type: ordinary, associate
Fee: £25
Membership Type: trainee
Description: Furthers medical knowledge and disseminates information on the subject of hospital associated infection.
Publication: Journal
Publication title: Journal of Hospital Infection

02411

Hostelling International
HI

2nd Fl., Gate House, Fretherne Rd., Welwyn Garden City, AL8 6RD, UK
Tel: 01707 324170
Fax: 01707 323980
Email: info@hihostels.com
Website: http://www.hihostels.com
Members: 90
Staff: 28
Description: National youth hostel associations in 60 countries representing 4 million members. Encourages cooperation among national youth hostel associations and seeks to educate young people of all nations by promoting youth tourism and an appreciation of travel. Provides low-cost accommodation and programs on outdoor education, recreation, and touring. Carries out development projects in Asia and Latin America. Conducts research and compiles statistics. Maintains numerous committees.
Formerly: Formerly, International Youth Hostel Federation
Publication: Book
Publication title: Guide to Budget Accommodation

02412

Hostelling International Northern Island
HINI

22-32 Donegall Rd., Belfast, BT12 5JN, UK
Tel: 028 90324733
Fax: 028 90315889
Email: info@hini.org.uk
Website: http://www.hini.org.uk
Fee: £10
Membership Type: under 25 years of age
Fee: £15
Membership Type: over 25 years of age, family (1 parent)
Description: Seeks to educate people by promoting tourism to increase appreciation of nature and culture. Provides low-cost accommodations and programs on outdoor education, recreation and touring. Facilitates networking among members. Conducts educational programs, leader courses, environmental walks and tree plantings.

02413

House Builders Federation
HBF

1st Fl., Byron House, 7-9 St. James St., London, SW1A 1EE, UK
Tel: 020 79601600
Fax: 020 79601601
Email: info@hbf.co.uk
Website: http://www.hbf.co.uk
Members: 350
Staff: 35
Contact: Stewart Baseley, Exec. Chm.
Description: Represents and promotes the political, land use planning and economic interests of residential house builders in the United Kingdom. Conducts lobbying and advocacy campaigns. Gathers and disseminates industry information.
Publication: Magazine
Publication title: Designing Homes for Life

02414

Housman Society
HS

80 New Rd., Worcs, Bromsgrove, B60 2LA, UK
Tel: 01527 878586
Email: info@housman-society.co.uk
Website: http://www.housman-society.co.uk
Members: 300
Contact: Jim Page, Chm.
Description: Aims to bring together all those interested in the lives and works of members of the Housman family, particularly the poet Alfred Edward (1859-1936), his brother Laurence (1865-1959), and his sister Clemence (1861-1955). Collects and preserves letters, manuscripts, personal belongings, and published works of the Housmans; supports, develops, and collates research; preserves Housman family graves and monuments.
Publication title: A.E. Housman Poet and Scholar

02415

Howard League for Penal Reform
HLPL

1 Ardleigh Rd., London, N1 4HS, UK
Tel: 020 72497373
Fax: 020 72497788
Email: info@howardleague.org
Website: http://www.howardleague.org
Members: 1700
Staff: 8
Contact: Frances Crook, Dir.
Fee: £42
Membership Type: individual
Fee: £84
Membership Type: overseas individual
Description: Lawyers, judges, and other practitioners in the criminal justice system; academics; prisoners and their families; interested individuals. Aim is to increase professional and public awareness of issues relating to criminal justice. Encourages discussion and analysis, and makes recommendations for change. Believes that "prison is the severest penalty on the statute book, and to use it more than can be shown to be the minimum necessary to protect the public is wrong in principle, besides being ineffective and costly." Undertakes research; offers training programs; holds seminars; operates speakers' bureau.
Publication: Journal
Publication title: Howard Journal of Criminal Justice

02416

HR Society

1-5 Stud Offices, Redenham Park Farm, Redenham, Hampshire, SP11 9AQ, UK
Tel: 01264 774004
Fax: 01264 774009
Email: lararoberts@hrsociety.co.uk
Website: http://www.hrsociety.co.uk
Members: 400
Contact: Chris Nutt, VP
Fee: £625
Membership Type: corporate
Fee: £150
Membership Type: individual
Description: Encourages excellence at the "Hard Edge" of HR across the private and public sectors. Works to build a network of people involved in the hard edge of people issues. Disseminates knowledge to relevant bodies. Facilitates research. Holds events to facilitate the sharing of knowledge.
Formerly: Formerly, Manpower Society
Meetings/Conventions: periodic seminar

02417

Hull and Humber Chamber of Commerce, Industry and Shipping

34/38 Beverley Rd., Hull, HU3 1YE, UK
Tel: 01482 324976
Fax: 01482 213962
Email: info@hull-humber-chamber.co.uk
Website: http://www.hull-humber-chamber.co.uk
Members: 1600
Staff: 35
Contact: Ian Kelly, Chief Exec.
Fee: £99
Membership Type: general
Description: Promotes business and commerce.
Publication: Magazine
Publication title: Business Intelligence. Advertisements.

02418

Human Appeal International
HAI

Victoria Ct., 376 Wilmslow Rd., Fallowfield, Manchester, M14 6AX, UK
Tel: 0161 2250225
Fax: 0161 2250226
Email: help@humanappeal.org.uk
Website: http://humanappeal.org.uk
Description: Aims to improve the quality of life of the underprivileged communities through education, health and social development. Provides relief to victims of natural disasters, wars and social hardships.

02419

Human Writes

Old Hall, Rectory Hill, East Bergholt, Colchester, CO7 6TG, UK
Email: humanwritesuk@yahoo.co.uk
Website: http://www.humanwrites.org
Members: 1300
Contact: Kay Murphy, Contact
Fee: £18
Membership Type: waged
Fee: £10
Membership Type: unwaged/low income
Description: Represents the interests of individuals who oppose the death penalty. Reaches out to all people on Death Row in the USA. Provides emotional and practical support to inmates through letter writing.

02420

Humane Slaughter Association
HSA

The Old School, Brewhouse Hill, Wheathampstead, AL4 8AN, UK
Tel: 01582 831919
Fax: 01582 831414
Email: info@hsa.org.uk
Website: http://www.hsa.org.uk
Staff: 9
Contact: James K. Kirkwood, Chief Exec./Scientific Dir.
Fee: £15
Membership Type: individual
Fee: £5
Membership Type: student
Description: Promotes humane methods of slaughter and the introduction of reforms in livestock markets, including transport facilities.
Formerly: Formerly, Council of Justice to Animals and Humane Slaughter Association
Publication: Video
Publication title: Humane Slaughter of Livestock

02421
Hunt Saboteurs Association
HSA
BM HSA, London, WC1N 3XX, UK
Tel: 0845 4500727
Email: info@huntsabs.org.uk
Website: http://www.huntsabs.org.uk
Contact: Nathan Brown, Press Off.
Fee: £15
Membership Type: regular
Description: Seeks to ban bloodsports and sabotages organized hunts in the UK. Employs non-violent tactics to save the lives of hunted animals. Operates in the fields where the hunts are taking place.
Publication: Magazine
Publication title: Howl

02422
Hunter Archaeological Society
Royd Farm, Carr Rd., Deepcar, Sheffield, S36 2NR, UK
Tel: 0114 2361471
Email: amjballfca@blueyonder.co.uk
Website: http://www.shef.ac.uk/archaeology/hunter
Contact: Ruth A. Morgan, Honorary Sec.
Fee: £20
Membership Type: individual
Description: Promotes history and archaeology of South Yorkshire and North Derbyshire.
Publication: Journal
Publication title: Transactions of the Hunter Archaeological Society

02423
Hunterian Society
11 Chandos St., Lettsom House, London, W19 9EB, UK
Tel: 020 74367363
Email: info@hunteriansociety.org.uk
Website: http://www.hunteriansociety.org.uk
Contact: Betty Smallwood, Gen. Admin.
Description: Devotes activities to the pursuit of medical knowledge and learning in the broadest sense.

02424
Huntington Disease Association
HDA
Neurosupport Centre, Norton St., Liverpool, L3 8LR, UK
Tel: 015 12983298
Fax: 015 12989440
Email: info@hda.org.uk
Website: http://www.hda.org.uk
Contact: Karen Crowder, Admin.
Fee: £10
Membership Type: professional
Fee: £50
Membership Type: life
Description: Individuals united to provide assistance, treatment, and information on the effects of Huntington's Disease, a hereditary nervous disorder causing terminal physical and mental disability. Provides counseling program designed for families and involved professionals; network of regional advisers and local groups throughout the country; confidential telephone and correspondence service; financial assistance; aid to patients undergoing presymptomatic tests or brain tissue donations. Encourages research on the medical and social effects of Huntington's Disease. Raises funds.
Formerly: Formerly, Association to Combat Huntington's Disease
Publication: Book
Publication title: Genes and Generations
Meetings/Conventions: biennial congress

02425
Hymn Society of Great Britain and Ireland
99 Barton Rd., Lancaster, LA1 4EN, UK
Tel: 01524 66740
Fax: 01524 66740
Email: robcanham@haystacks.fsnet.co.uk
Website: http://www.hymnsocietygbi.org.uk
Members: 500
Contact: Robert A. Canham, Sec.
Description: Promotes the study and research in the field of hymnody. Promotes good standards of hymn singing. Encourages the discerning use of hymns and songs in worship. Sponsors relevant publications.

02426
Hypnotherapy Association
14 Crown St., Chorley, PR7 1DX, UK
Tel: 01257 262124
Fax: 01257 262124
Email: theha@tiscali.co.uk
Website: http://www.thehypnotherapyassociation.co.uk
Members: 483
Staff: 2
Contact: Josephine Teague, Chair
Fee: £60
Membership Type: full, associate, licentiate
Description: Practitioners with at least 4 years post graduate of training in psychotherapy and hypnotherapy who comply with the Association's code of competence and ethics. Concerned with professional standards in the treatment of nervous disorders by trained psychotherapists who use hypnosis when appropriate to facilitate recall by the patient, as well as using other methods proven by research into long-term results. Referrals, research, lectures, broadcasts, talks, papers, articles, books and seminars arranged.
Publication: Journal
Publication title: The Hypnotherapist. Advertisements.

02427
I CAN
8 Wakley St., London, EC1V 7QE, UK
Tel: 0845 2254073
Fax: 0845 2254072
Email: info@ican.org.uk
Website: http://www.ican.org.uk
Staff: 250
Contact: Virginia Beardshaw, Chief Exec.
Description: Works as charity helping children with speech and language difficulties across the U.K. Provides a combination of specialist therapy and education for children, information for parents, and training and advice for teachers and other professionals.

02428
IA
Peverill House, 1-5 Mill Rd., County Antrim, Ballyclare, BT39 9DR, UK
Tel: 028 93344043
Fax: 028 93324606
Email: info@iasupport.org
Website: http://www.iasupport.org
Members: 9636
Staff: 1
Fee: £12
Membership Type: under 60 years old
Fee: £8
Membership Type: 60 years old and over
Description: Aims to help people who have had or are about to have their colon removed, to return to a fully active and normal life as soon as possible. Includes activities such as: hospital and home visiting, members' meetings, equipment exhibitions, medical research, stoma-care clinics, advisory services, lectures and demonstrations.
Publication: Journal
Publication title: IA Journal. Advertisements.

02429
ICC Commercial Crime Services
ICC-CCS
Cinnabar Wharf, 26 Wapping High St., London, E1W 1NG, UK
Tel: 0207 4236960
Fax: 0207 4236961
Email: ccs@icc-ccs.org
Website: http://www.icc-ccs.org
Contact: P. Mukundan, Chief Exec.
Fee: £1550-3200
Membership Type: International Maritime Bureau
Fee: £1400
Membership Type: level one (Financial Investigation Bureau)
Description: Works to combat commercial fraud. Maintains ICC Counterfeiting Intelligence Bureau, ICC International Maritime Bureau, and CC Commercial Crime Bureau.

02430
ICC Counterfeiting Intelligence Bureau
CIB
Cinnabar Wharf, 26 Wapping High St., London, E1W 1NG, UK
Tel: 020 74236960
Fax: 020 74236961
Email: ccs@icc-ccs.org
Website: http://www.icc-ccs.org
Contact: Peter Lowe, Dir.
Description: Specialized division of the International Chamber of Commerce. Manufacturers and trade associations in 23 countries; staff members include former officers of commercial police fraud squads with international investigative experience, experts in the detection and analysis of forged documents, and consultants from industries affected by counterfeiting. Serves as a focal point for industries to combat economic crime by investigating and seeking to prevent counterfeiting of trademarked goods and trade dress, patents, copyrights, and industrial designs and models. Gathers information on activities of product counterfeiters and disseminates findings to members. Conducts international inquiries on the sources and distribution of counterfeit products, thereby enabling law enforcement agencies worldwide to make arrests and seize counterfeit goods. Provides investigative services to members.

02431

ICC International Maritime Bureau ICC-IMB

Cinnabar Wharf, 26 Wapping High St., London, E1W 1NG, UK
Tel: 020 74236960
Fax: 020 74236961
Email: imb@icc-ccs.org
Website: http://www.icc-ccs.org
Contact: Michael Howlett, Asst. Dir.
Fee: £1550
Membership Type: level 1
Fee: £3200
Membership Type: level 2
Description: Works to prevent and investigate combat maritime and trading crime.
Publication: Bulletin
Publication title: Confidential Bulletin

02432

Ice Cream Alliance ICA

3 Melbourne Ct., Pride Park, Derby, DE24 8LZ, UK
Tel: 01332 203333
Fax: 01332 203420
Email: info@ice-cream.org
Website: http://www.ice-cream.org
Members: 800
Staff: 4
Contact: Andrew Caldwell, Pres.
Fee: £144
Membership Type: standard
Fee: £399
Membership Type: supply house corporate, manufacturing/mobiling corporate
Description: Companies and individuals connected with the ice cream industry in the UK. Aims to promote the UK ice-cream industry, protect individuals who work within it and encourage good practice within the industry. Holds annual conference and exhibition. Serves as an information point via the Ice Cream Information Service.
Publication: Magazine
Publication title: Ice Cream. Advertisements.

02433

ICHCA International Limited IIL

Ste. 2, 85 Western Rd., Essex, Romford, RM1 3LS, UK
Tel: 01708 735295
Fax: 01708 735225
Email: info@ichca.com
Website: http://www.ichcainternational.co.uk
Members: 900
Staff: 8
Contact: John Strang, Intl. Chm.
Description: Individuals and organizations in 84 countries with interests in international handling and transport of goods. Works to increase efficiency and economy in the handling and movement of goods from origin to destination by all modes and at all phases of transportation. Maintains information service and expert committees; sponsors research programs, and intergovernmental representation (NGO).
Library Subject: cargo handling, international transportation
Library Type: reference
Formerly: Formerly, International Cargo Handling Coordination Association
Publication: Magazine
Publication title: Cargo Today. Advertisements.
Meetings/Conventions: biennial conference – Exhibits.

02434

ICOM Energy Association

Camden House, Warwick Rd., Warwickshire, Kenilworth, CV8 1TH, UK
Tel: 01926 513748
Fax: 01926 855017
Email: peter.mccree@icomenergyassociation.org.uk
Website: http://www.icomenergyassociation.org.uk
Members: 50
Staff: 2
Contact: Peter McCree, Dir./Chief Exec.
Description: Manufacturers and suppliers of commercial and industrial combustion equipment. Promotes and assists in the preparation of British, European and international standards in order to ensure optimum levels of equipment and performance and safety. Seeks to provide other technical and commercial support to members as required.
Formerly: Formerly, British Combustion Equipment Manufacturers Association

02435

IFS School of Finance

Peninsular House, 8th Fl., 36 Monument St., London, EC3R 8LJ, UK
Tel: 0207 4447111
Fax: 0207 4447115
Email: customerservices@ifslearning.ac.uk
Website: http://www.ifslearning.ac.uk
Contact: Bruce Carnegie-Brown, Chm.
Fee: £515
Membership Type: small company (with less than 500 employees)
Fee: £1495
Membership Type: standard (company)
Description: Develops and delivers life long career support services and a range of appropriate qualifications to the wider financial services community, for which the CIB acts as an examining and awarding body. Gives provision to targeted services like specialist educational programs to particular sectors, including the areas of Banking and Finance, E-commerce and Technology, and Regulatory and Retail.
Library Subject: financial services
Library Type: reference
Formerly: Formerly, Chartered Institute of Bankers - England
Publication: Magazine
Publication title: CIB News. Advertisements.

02436

IMAGO - European Federation of Cinematographers IMAGO

29 Boscombe Rd., London, W12 9HT, UK
Email: waltatbush@aol.com
Website: http://www.imago.org
Contact: Nigel Walters, Pres.
Description: Advocates for high standards of excellence in European cinematography. Supports professional film and cinematographic festivals in Europe. Provides opportunities for members to learn more about the art of cinematography.

02437

Immigration Advisory Service IAS

County House, 190 Great Dover St., London, SE1 4YB, UK
Tel: 0844 9744000
Fax: 0207 3780665
Website: http://www.iasuk.org/home.aspx
Description: Provides independent and confidential advice, assistance, and representation to persons subject to immigration control.
Formerly: Formerly, United Kingdom Immigrants' Advisory Service
Publication: Book
Publication title: Immigration Law Update

02438

Imperial Society of Teachers of Dancing ISTD

22/26 Paul St., London, EC2A 4QE, UK
Tel: 020 73771577
Fax: 020 76558829
Email: membership@istd.org
Website: http://www.istd.org
Members: 10000
Contact: Peggy Spencer, Pres.
Fee: £42
Membership Type: student
Fee: £67
Membership Type: non-active professional
Description: Seeks to educate the public in the art of dancing in all forms; promotes knowledge of dance; works to maintain and improve teaching standards; provides techniques to train dancers for professions; offers courses; covers the full spectrum of dance examinations worldwide.
Publication: Magazine
Publication title: Dance

02439

Imported Tyre Manufacturers' Association ITMA

5A Pindock Mews, London, W9 2PY, UK
Tel: 020 72891043
Fax: 020 72869859
Email: prt@itma-europe.com
Website: http://www.itma-europe.com
Members: 16
Contact: Peter Taylor, Dir.
Description: Tire manufacturers and importers. Provides information, help, and a promotion forum for overseas tire manufacturers and their brands in the UK and the European Union.
Library Subject: tire manufacturing, tire recycling, statistics
Library Type: not open to the public

02440

Inclusion International

II

c/o The Rix Centre
University of East London, Docklands Campus, 4-6 University Way, London, E16 2RD, UK
Tel: 020 82237709
Fax: 020 82236081
Email: info@inclusion-international.org
Website: http://www.inclusion-international.org
Members: 200
Staff: 5
Contact: Diane Richler, Pres.
Description: Grassroots human rights organization of families, self-advocates and committed citizens. Aims to protect and promote the rights of persons with intellectual disabilities and to help them live in the mainstream of society. Improves public attitudes towards persons with mental disabilities.
Formerly: Formerly, International League of Societies for Persons with Mental Handicap
Meetings/Conventions: International Conference on Intellectual Disability/Mental Retardation – international conference

02441

Incorporated Association of Organists

IAO

19 The Poplars, Gosforth, Newcastle upon Tyne, NE3 4AE, UK
Tel: 0191 2857303
Email: pvc1@btinternet.com
Website: http://www.iao.org.uk
Members: 6000
Contact: John Chatfield, Gen. Sec.
Description: Lovers of (classical) organ music, players and listeners alike. Many are church organists and choirmasters. Most are members of local organists' associations affiliated to the IAO. An educational charity. It arranges an annual week-long Organ Festival that includes concerts, recitals, lectures, tuition and master-classes with international artists such as lovers of (classical) organ music, players and listeners alike. Promotes and sponsors educational events in London and the provinces.
Publication title: Organists' Review. Advertisements.

02442

Incorporated Society of British Advertisers

ISBA

Langham House, 1b, Portland Pl., London, W1B 1PN, UK
Tel: 020 72919020
Fax: 020 72919030
Email: answers@isba.org.uk
Website: http://www.isba.org.uk/isba/home
Members: 380
Staff: 15
Contact: Mike Hughes, Dir. Gen.
Description: Major UK advertising companies. Represents the interests of the majority of British advertisers on everything connected with advertising and communication.

02443

Incorporated Society of Musicians

ISM

10 Stratford Pl., London, W1C 1AA, UK
Tel: 020 76294413
Fax: 020 74081538
Email: membership@ism.org
Website: http://www.ism.org/home.php
Members: 5000
Staff: 10
Contact: Gavin Henderson, Pres./Treas.
Fee: £150
Membership Type: full (professional)
Fee: £75
Membership Type: associate (amateur)
Description: All professional musicians - performers, composers, conductors, lecturers, schoolteachers and private teachers. Protects the interests of everyone who works with music; promotes higher standards through codes of conduct and by professional development and training schemes; offers members comprehensive legal, financial and technical services, as well as careers advice, publications, discounts and insurances.
Publication: Booklet
Publication title: Careers with Music. Advertisements.

02444

Incorporated Society of Organ Builders - England

ISOB

c/o Smithy Steads Farm
Cragg Vale, West Yorkshire, Hebden Bridge, HX7 5SQ, UK
Tel: 0870 1393645
Fax: 0870 1393645
Email: admin1@isob.co.uk
Website: http://www.isob.co.uk
Members: 200
Contact: Robert G. Ince, Pres.
Fee: £63.5
Membership Type: fellow, counsellor
Fee: £55
Membership Type: associate
Description: Students, ordinary members, associates, fellows and counsellors. Advances the science and practice of organ building, by discussion, inquiry, research, experiment and other means and aims to diffuse knowledge regarding organ building by means of lectures, publications and exchange of information.

02445

Independent Association of Preparatory Schools

IAPS

11 Waterloo Pl., Leamington Spa, CV32 5LA, UK
Tel: 01926 887833
Fax: 01926 888014
Email: iaps@iaps.org.uk
Website: http://www.iaps.org.uk
Members: 600
Staff: 14
Contact: David Hanson, Chief Exec.
Description: Heads of independent preparatory schools. Fosters the interchange of experience and ideas on education between Heads of preparatory schools, promoting collective views and providing a channel of communication with senior independent schools and other bodies concerned with education. A wide variety of services and a broad range of training courses are offered to members and their staff.
Publication: Magazine
Publication title: Attain. Advertisements.

02446

Independent Footwear Retailers' Association

IFRA

PO Box 123, Oxfordshire, Banbury, OX15 6WB, UK
Tel: 01295 738726
Fax: 01295 738725
Email: ifra@shoeshop.org.uk
Website: http://www.shoeshop.org.uk
Members: 306
Staff: 2
Contact: Nigel Hamilton, Pres.
Description: Independent footwear retailers.
Publication: Magazine
Publication title: Footprint. Advertisements.

02447

Independent Midwives UK

PO Box 539, Abingdon, OX14 9DF, UK
Tel: 0845 4600105
Email: information@independentmidwives.org.uk
Website: http://www.independentmidwives.org.uk
Members: 60
Contact: Liz Nightingale, Sec.
Description: Midwives practicing in England. Promotes the involvement of midwives in childbirth, doing mainly home births. Promotes education in midwifery. Represents members' interests.
Formerly: Formerly, Independent Midwives Association

02448

Independent Print Industries Association

IPIA

Unit 9, Business Innovation centre, Technology Park, Beaconside, Stafforshire, Stafford, ST18 0AR, UK
Tel: 0844 9020214
Fax: 0844 9020215
Email: info@ipia.org.uk
Website: http://www.ipia.org.uk
Contact: Andrew Pearce, Chief Exec.
Fee: £395-2550
Membership Type: group
Description: Promotes the highest standards within the independent sector of the UK printing industry. Aims to improve the quality and performance in production, sales, marketing, financial and managerial activities. Supports the independent print sector in providing solutions to common industry problems.
Publication: Magazine
Publication title: Innovation in Print. Advertisements.

02449

Independent Publishers Guild

IPG

PO Box 12, Llain, Whitland, SA34 0WU, UK
Tel: 01437 563335
Fax: 01437 562071
Email: info@ipg.uk.com
Website: http://www.ipg.uk.com
Members: 430
Staff: 2
Contact: Andrew Johnston, Chm.
Fee: £199-675
Membership Type: company (based on turnover)
Description: Independent publishing companies, book packagers, and publishing suppliers. Offers a forum for the exchange of ideas and information in the changing

world of publishing. Activities include open meetings, training seminars, an annual conference and corporate stands at major book fairs.

02450
Independent Schools Council
ISC

St. Vincent House, 30 Orange St., London, WC2H 7HH, UK
Tel: 020 77667070
Fax: 020 77667071
Email: information@isc.co.uk
Website: http://www.isc.co.uk
Members: 1273
Staff: 23
Contact: David Lyscom, Chief Exec.
Description: Serves independent schools in the UK.
Publication: Bulletin
Publication title: ISC Bulletin

02451
Independent Schools Council Information Service
ISCIS

St. Vincent House, 30 Orange St., London, WC2H 7HH, UK
Tel: 020 77667070
Fax: 020 77667071
Email: office@isc.co.uk
Website: http://www.isc.co.uk
Members: 1300
Staff: 13
Contact: David Lyscom, Chief Exec.
Description: Promotes Information and PR and Press services for independent schools.
Publication: Survey
Publication title: ISC Census

02452
Independent Television Association
ITV

200 Gray's Inn Rd., London, WC1X 8HF, UK
Email: itvihelp@itv.com
Website: http://www.itv.com
Members: 15
Description: Contributes to the UK's culture, economy and communities through broadcasting.

02453
Independent Theatre Council
ITC

12 The Leathermarket, Weston St., London, SE1 3ER, UK
Tel: 020 74031727
Fax: 020 74031745
Email: admin@itc-arts.org
Website: http://www.itc-arts.org/page69.aspx
Members: 600
Staff: 10
Contact: Charlotte Jones, Chief Exec.
Fee: £282-1645
Membership Type: organization (based on turnover)
Fee: £240
Membership Type: independent
Description: Represents touring theatre and performing arts companies or venues.

02454
Indonesia Human Rights Campaign
TAPOL

111 Northwood Rd., Surrey, Thornton Heath, CR7 8HW, UK
Tel: 020 87712904
Fax: 020 86530322
Email: tapol@gn.apc.org
Website: http://tapol.gn.apc.org
Contact: Carmel Budiardjo, Founder
Description: Informs individuals worldwide about human rights violations in Indonesia, East Timor, and West Papua. Obtains the assistance of British and other governments to pressure the Indonesian military government to change. Stops all British arms sales to Indonesia. Cooperates with British and other peace organizations in order to further human rights concerns.
Publication: Bulletin
Publication title: Tapol Bulletin

02455
Industrial Cleaning Machine Manufacturers' Association
ICMMA

480 Salisbury House, Ste. 478, London Wall, London, EC2M 5QQ, UK
Tel: 0207 9209638
Fax: 0207 6386990
Website: http://www.icmma.org.uk
Members: 12
Contact: Andrew Large, Sec.
Description: Represents manufacturers of cleaning machinery in the entire spectrum of industrial cleaning technology from floor and carpet maintenance through to fixed installation cleaning systems and mechanised sweeping. Liaises with departments of the government. Drafts national and international standards for the industry.
Publication title: Product Guide to Member Companies

02456
Industry Council for Electronic Equipment Recycling
ICER

6 Bath Pl., Rivington St., London, EC2A 3JE, UK
Tel: 020 77294766
Fax: 020 77299121
Email: ws03@icer.org.uk
Website: http://www.icer.org.uk
Members: 100
Contact: Claire Snow, Dir.
Description: Members are drawn from all who have a stake in the electronic and electrical product chain. Includes raw material suppliers, manufacturers, distributors, retailers, waste management companies, local authorities, and recyclers. Aims to develop industry-led solutions to management of end-of-life products - solutions which are both environmentally sound and commercially realistic. Works with government - UK and EC to put those solutions into practice.
Publication title: ICER Design

02457
Industry Council for Packaging and the Environment
INCPEN

6-8 Market Pl., Berkshire, Reading, RG1 2EG, UK
Tel: 0118 9255991
Fax: 0118 9255993
Email: info@incpen.org
Website: http://www.incpen.org
Members: 60
Staff: 6
Contact: Vicki Procko, Contact
Description: Members are major British and international corporations with an active interest in minimizing the impact of packaging on the environment and involved in the manufacture of packaging and its use for packaged goods. Brings together all sectors of industry involved in the manufacture of packaging and the manufacture and retailing of packaged goods; leads in the rational debate on packaging and the environment, promotes the positive social and environmental benefits of packaging. Encourages environmentally responsible industrial practices for packaging and tries to ensure that balanced environmentally effective legislation on packaging is effected.
Publication: Journal
Publication title: The Pen

02458
Industry for Turnaround
IFT

The Bridge, 12-16 Clerkenwell Rd., London, EC1M 5PQ, UK
Tel: 0207 3246244
Fax: 0207 2535029
Email: info@instituteforturnaround.com
Website: http://www.instituteforturnaround.com
Contact: Christine Elliot, Chief Exec.
Fee: £525
Membership Type: full
Description: Raises the profile of turnaround professionals and its culture. Encourages intervention into underperforming businesses. Promotes turnaround knowledge among business community. Encourages high standards of ethics, behavior and quality of turnaround practitioners.
Formerly: Formerly, Society of Turnaround Professionals

02459
Industry Technology Facilitator
ITF

Enterprise Centre, Aberdeen Science and Energy Park, Exploration Dr., Aberdeen, AB23 8GX, UK
Tel: 01224 222410
Email: itf@oil-itf.com
Website: http://www.oil-itf.com
Staff: 11
Contact: Max Rowe, Chm./Dir.
Description: Fosters new technology for the oil and gas industry. Connects technology developers with end users and sources of funding to develop joint industry projects. Provides an independent project brokering and technology delivery services.

02460
Infection Control Nurses' Association
ICNA
c/o FitwiseMananagement Ltd.
Drumcross Hall, Bathgate, EH48 4JT, UK
Tel: 01506 811077
Email: lynne@fitwise.co.uk
Website: http://www.ips.uk.net
Members: 1400
Staff: 1
Contact: Phil Pugh, Honorary Sec.
Fee: £70
Membership Type: full
Fee: £60
Membership Type: associate
Description: Represents infection control nurses and allied professionals. Concerned with the education of public and health care staff in infection.
Publication: Journal
Publication title: British Journal of Infection Control. Advertisements.

02461
Infertility Network UK
INUK
Charter House, 43 St. Leonards Rd., East Sussex, Bexhill-on-Sea, TN40 1JA, UK
Tel: 08701 188088
Fax: 01424 731858
Email: admin@infertilitynetworkuk.com
Website: http://www.infertilitynetworkuk.com
Members: 6000
Staff: 5
Contact: Susan Seenan, Communications Off.
Fee: £20
Membership Type: regular
Description: Infertile women and men. Disseminates information and provides support and offers telephone counseling to infertile individuals on all aspects of infertility.
Formerly: Formerly, ISSUE, the National Fertility Association and CHILD
Publication: Magazine
Publication title: ISSUE

02462
Information for School and College Governors
ISCG
PO Box 3934, Gerrards Cross, SL9 1AG, UK
Tel: 01483 300280
Email: iscg@governors.uk.com
Website: http://www.governors.uk.com
Staff: 6
Description: Provides a unique independent research and information service for governors and LEAs.
Formerly: Formerly, Institution for School and College Governors

02463
Inland Waterways Advisory Council
IWAC
City Rd. Lock, 38 Graham St., London, N1 8JX, UK
Tel: 020 72531745
Fax: 020 74907656
Email: iwac@iwac.gsi.gov.uk
Website: http://www.iwac.org.uk
Members: 14
Staff: 2
Contact: Diana Wray, Office Mgr.
Description: Provides strategic advice to government, navigation authorities and other interested persons on Britain's inland waterways.
Formerly: Formerly, Inland Waterways Amenity Advisory Council

02464
Inland Waterways Association of England
IWA
Island House, Moor Rd., Chesham, HP5 1WA, UK
Tel: 01494 783453
Email: iwa@waterways.org.uk
Website: http://www.waterways.org.uk
Members: 18000
Staff: 14
Contact: Neil Edwards, Chief Exec.
Fee: £27
Membership Type: single
Fee: £34
Membership Type: family/joint
Description: Campaigns for the restoration, conservation, retention, and development of inland waterways for commercial and recreational use.
Publication: Magazine
Publication title: Waterways. Advertisements.

02465
Inn Sign Society
9 Denmead Dr., Wednesfield, Wolverhampton, WV11 2QS, UK
Tel: 01902 721808
Email: info@innsignsociety.com
Website: http://www.innsignsociety.com
Members: 400
Contact: Alan Rose, Contact
Fee: £15
Membership Type: inside UK
Fee: £20
Membership Type: outside UK
Description: Dedicated to investigating information about inns, their names and their signs.
Publication: Journal
Publication title: At The Sign Of

02466
Innholders' Company
Innholders Hall, 30 College St., London, EC4R 2RH, UK
Tel: 020 72366703
Fax: 020 72360059
Email: mail@innholders.co.uk
Website: http://www.innholders.co.uk
Contact: Robert Finch, Master
Description: Represents the hospitality industry in the City of London, UK. Organizes charitable events and projects as part of its main activities.

02467
Insol International
II
6-7 Queen St., London, EC4N 1SP, UK
Tel: 020 72483333
Fax: 020 72483384
Email: heather@insol.ision.co.uk
Website: http://www.insol.org
Members: 40
Staff: 3
Contact: Claire Broughton, Exec. Dir.
Description: Organizations representing 7,300 insolvency practitioners from 62 countries worldwide. Seeks international professional recognition of insolvency practitioners. Works to improve communication and cooperation among members; facilitates the exchange of information; establishes working committees to examine international issues of insolvency practice. Is developing a bibliographic database of insolvency publications.
Publication: Membership Directory
Publication title: INSOL International Membership

02468
Insolvency Practitioners Association
IPA
Valiant House, 4-10 Heneage Ln., London, EC3A 5DQ, UK
Tel: 020 76235108
Fax: 020 76235127
Email: secretariat@insolvency-practitioners.org.uk
Website: http://www.insolvency-practitioners.org.uk
Members: 1500
Contact: Carl Faulds, Pres.
Fee: £152-182
Membership Type: student
Fee: £210
Membership Type: affiliate
Description: Individuals licensed to act as insolvency practitioners in England, Wales, Scotland and Northern Ireland. Represents members' interests and indirectly the public.
Publication: Magazine
Publication title: Index of Members

Institut Africain International
see International African Institute

Institut de l'Horticulture
see Institute of Horticulture

Institut des Sciences de l'Environnement
see Institution of Environmental Sciences

Institut International d'Aluminium
see International Aluminium Institute

Institut International d'Etudes Strategiques
see International Institute for Strategic Studies

Institut International des Communications

see International Institute of Communications

02469

Institute for Animal Health

IAH

Compton Laboratory, Compton, Berks, Newbury, RG20 7NN, UK
Tel: 01635 578411
Fax: 01483 232448
Email: iah@bbsrc.ac.uk
Website: http://www.iah.bbsrc.ac.uk
Staff: 480
Contact: Martin Shirley, Dir.
Description: Aims to understand the pathogenesis of infectious diseases from which knowledge disease control methods will emerge.

02470

Institute for Complementary and Natural Medicine

ICNM

Can-Mezzanine, 32-36 Loman St., London, SE1 0EH, UK
Tel: 020 79227980
Fax: 020 79227981
Email: info@icnm.org.uk
Website: http://www.i-c-m.org.uk
Contact: Beverly Martin, Chair
Description: Registered charity of individuals united to promote the practice of alternative medicine. Seeks to establish educational standards for practitioners and to establish ties between therapy groups, organizations, teachers, and practitioners. Cooperates with the British government to develop natural therapy curricula. Maintains British Register of Complementary Practitioners. Conducts research; disseminates information. Advises groups establishing healing practices on legal, organizational, and practical matters.
Library Type: reference
Formerly: Absorbed, Healing Research Trust
Publication: Journal
Publication title: Journal for Complementary Medicine

02471

Institute for Development Policy and Management

IDPM

PO Box 88, Manchester, M60 1QD, UK
Tel: 0161 2750969
Fax: 0161 2750421
Email: idpm@manchester.ac.uk
Website: http://www.sed.manchester.ac.uk/idpm/index.htm
Staff: 60
Contact: Philip Woodhouse, Sr. Lecturer
Description: Development professionals. Promotes appropriate and sustainable economic and community development worldwide. Provides technical support and consulting services to development organizations and government agencies regulating development; sponsors research and educational programs.

02472

Institute for European Environmental Policy

IEEP

15 Queen Anne's Gate, London, SW1H 9BU, UK
Tel: 020 77992244
Fax: 020 77992600
Email: central@ieep.eu
Website: http://www.ieep.eu
Staff: 31
Contact: David Baldock, Exec. Dir.
Description: Undertakes research, analysis, and consultancy on the European dimension of environmental protection with a main focus placed on the development, implementation, and evaluation of EU environmental policy. Encompasses several other EU policies of environmental significance, including agriculture, transport, regional development, and fisheries. Seeks both to increase awareness of the European dimension of environmental protection and to advance European policy-making in this field.
Publication: Newsletter
Publication title: Rural Areas Newslink

02473

Institute for Fiscal Studies

IFS

7 Ridgmount St., 3rd Fl., London, WC1E 7AE, UK
Tel: 0207 2914800
Fax: 0207 3234780
Email: mailbox@ifs.org.uk
Website: http://www.ifs.org.uk
Members: 1300
Staff: 35
Contact: Rachel Lomax, Pres.
Fee: £50
Membership Type: individual
Fee: £125
Membership Type: institution
Description: Academics, civil servants, financiers, industrialists, accountants, solicitors, industry, professions, trade unions, universities, civil service. Looks at public policy with particular reference to taxation.
Publication: Journal
Publication title: Fiscal Studies. Advertisements.

02474

Institute for Jewish Policy Research

JPR

7-8 Market Pl., London, W1W 8AG, UK
Tel: 020 74361553
Fax: 020 74367262
Email: jpr@jpr.org.uk
Website: http://www.jpr.org.uk
Contact: Jonathan Boyd, Exec. Dir.
Description: Works to assist Jewish communities understand themselves better, determine their priorities and achieve their objectives. Provides a forum for all segments of the Jewish community to discuss critical issues of common concern.

02475

Institute for Manufacturing

IfM

17 Charles Babbage Rd., Cambridge, CB3 0FS, UK
Tel: 01223 766141
Fax: 01223 464217
Email: ifm-enquiries@eng.cam.ac.uk
Website: http://www.ifm.eng.cam.ac.uk/default.html
Contact: Mike Gregory, Hd.
Description: Aims to assist companies to grow and to increase competitiveness across the business cycle, thereby helping industry to create wealth more effectively.

02476

Institute for Outdoor Learning

IOL

Warwick Mill Business Centre, Warwick Bridge, Carlisle, Cumbria, CA4 8RR, UK
Tel: 01228 564580
Fax: 01228 564581
Email: institute@outdoor-learning.org
Website: http://www.outdoor-learning.org
Members: 1100
Staff: 2
Contact: Chris Millet, Dir.
Fee: £40
Membership Type: individual (in United Kingdom)
Fee: £115-285
Membership Type: organization (based on number of staffs)
Description: Supports, develops and promotes learning through outdoor experiences.
Formerly: Formerly, Association for Outdoor Education
Publication: Magazine
Publication title: Horizons. Advertisements.

02477

Institute for Sport, Parks and Leisure

ISPAL

Abbey Business Ctre., 1650 Arlington Business Park, Theale, Berkshire, Reading, RG7 4SA, UK
Tel: 0118 9298350
Fax: 0118 9298001
Email: infocentre@ispal.org.uk
Website: http://www.ispal.org.uk
Staff: 50
Contact: Sue Sutton, Chief Exec.
Description: Managers working in art and entertainment complexes, health and fitness clubs, museums, parks and playgrounds, and sports centers in the United Kingdom and the Republic of Ireland. Aims to: promote high standards in the field of leisure management; encourage cooperation and information exchange; represent the interests of members in legislative matters; promote professional development and improved management methods and skills; encourage research in the field of leisure management. Provides career and course advisory services and contract arbitration services. Offers training courses and seminars; grants certificates and diplomas.
Publication: Magazine
Publication title: INFORM

02478

Institute for the Management of Information Systems
IMIS

5 Kingfisher House, New Mill Rd., Orpington, BR5 3QG, UK
Tel: 070 00023456
Fax: 070 00023023
Email: central@imis.org.uk
Website: http://www.imis.org.uk
Members: 12000
Contact: Ian M. Rickwood, Chief Exec.
Fee: £143
Membership Type: fellow
Fee: £110
Membership Type: full
Description: Professional and student information systems practitioners in 56 countries. Seeks to advance the interests of the information systems profession, set professional standards, and recognize practitioners meeting these standards. Serves as an examining body for IMIS students.
Formerly: Formerly, Data Processing Management Association
Publication: Journal

02479

Institute of +Refrigeration
IOR

Kelvin House, 76 Mill Ln., Surrey, Carshalton, SM5 2JR, UK
Tel: 020 86477033
Fax: 020 87730165
Email: ior@ior.org.uk
Website: http://www.ior.org.uk
Members: 2000
Staff: 6
Contact: Andy Pearson, Pres.
Fee: £63-68
Membership Type: regular
Fee: £63
Membership Type: affiliate
Description: Represents individuals engaged in the science and practice of refrigeration. Works for the promotion and development of science and practice of refrigeration and air conditioning.
Library Subject: refrigeration, air conditioning
Library Type: not open to the public

02480

Institute of Acoustics
IOA

77A St. Peter's St., Hertfordshire, St. Albans, AL1 3BN, UK
Tel: 01727 848195
Fax: 01727 850553
Email: ioa@ioa.org.uk
Website: http://www.ioa.org.uk
Members: 2500
Staff: 5
Contact: Kevin Macan-Lind, Chief Exec.
Description: Membership covers all aspects of acoustics.
Publication: Magazine
Publication title: Acoustics Bulletin. Advertisements.

02481

Institute of Actuaries - United Kingdom

Staple Inn Hall, High Holborn, London, WC1V 7QJ, UK
Tel: 0207 6322100
Fax: 0207 6322111
Email: institute@actuaries.org.uk
Website: http://www.actuaries.org.uk
Members: 15369
Staff: 85
Contact: Caroline Instance, Chief Exec.
Description: Controlled by the Institute of Actuaries in London and the Faculty of Actuaries in Edinburgh; seeks to develop the role and standing of the actuarial profession and to enhance its reputation for serving the public interest. Together, the Faculty and Institute sets examinations, continuing professional development, professional codes and disciplinary standards; issues technical guidance and runs Boards and Committees to develop actuarial techniques in various business areas.
Library Subject: actuarial sciences, life assurance, general insurance, pensions, employee benefits, friendly societies, social security, investment, demography, mortality, probability, risk theory, histories of insurance companies
Library Type: by appointment only
Publication: Journal
Publication title: Annals of Actuarial Science

02482

Institute of Administrative Management
IAM

6 Graphite Sq., Vauxhall Walk, London, SE11 5EE, UK
Tel: 020 70912600
Fax: 020 70912619
Email: info@instam.org
Website: http://www.instam.org
Members: 10000
Staff: 20
Contact: Jenny Hewell, Chief Exec.
Fee: £75
Membership Type: general
Description: Seeks to promote and develop, for the public benefit, the science of administrative management in all branches; encourage the attainment of professional academic qualifications. Provides the latest techniques and developments in the field of administrative management via conferences, seminars, meetings and publications.
Library Subject: management
Library Type: reference
Publication: Journal
Publication title: British Manager, Journal of Administrative Management. Advertisements.

02483

Institute of Advanced Motorists
IAM

c/o IAM House
510 Chiswick High Rd., London, W4 5RG, UK
Tel: 020 89969600
Fax: 020 89969601
Website: http://www.iam.org.uk
Members: 112000
Staff: 37
Contact: Nigel Mansell, Pres.
Description: Individuals who have passed the Advanced Driving Test or who have recognised standards for exemption. Aims to enhance road safety through improved driving standards; conducts advanced driving tests (for cars, motorcycles, minibuses and commercial vehicles); provides commercial fleet driver training through IAM Fleet Training Limited.

02484

Institute of Agricultural Secretaries and Administrators
IAGSA

National Agricultural Ctre., Stoneleigh Park, Kenilworth, CV8 2LG, UK
Tel: 02476 696592
Email: iagsa@iagsa.co.uk
Website: http://www.iagsa.co.uk
Members: 900
Contact: Tim Cartwright, Chm.
Fee: £50
Membership Type: affiliate, member
Fee: £25
Membership Type: student
Description: Represents secretaries and managers employed within the agricultural industry. Supports farm and rural administrators employed within the agricultural industry. Offers support to all practicing agricultural secretaries and administrators, advises student members on education and training, helps the new entrant to the profession, and maintains close links with all relevant education bodies.
Meetings/Conventions: annual conference – Exhibits.

02485

Institute of Animal Technology
IAT

5 S Parade, Summertown, Oxford, OX2 7JL, UK
Tel: 0800 854380
Email: admin@iat.org.uk
Website: http://www.iat.org.uk
Members: 2200
Fee: £40
Membership Type: affiliate, associate, corporate
Fee: £50
Membership Type: overseas
Description: Promotes high ethical standards in technology and the practice of laboratory animal care and welfare.
Publication: Journal
Publication title: Animal Technology and Welfare

02486

Institute of Archaeo-Metallurgical Studies
IAMS

University College London, Institute of Archaeology, 31-34 Gordon Sq., London, WC1H 0PY, UK
Tel: 020 76794918
Email: b.rothenberg@ucl.ac.uk
Website: http://www.ucl.ac.uk/iams
Contact: Beno Rothenberg, Dir.
Description: Fosters research into the origins of metallurgy.
Publication: Journal

02487

Institute of Association Management
IofAM

Venture House, 6 Silver Ct., Hertfordshire, Welwyn Garden City, AL7 1TS, UK
Tel: 08456 590704
Email: info@iofam.co.uk
Website: http://www.iofam.org.uk
Members: 500
Contact: Hazel Morley, Pres.
Description: Executives of associations and association suppliers in the United Kingdom. Provides a forum for the exchange of information between members.
Formerly: Formerly, Society of Association Executives
Publication: Newsletter
Publication title: Association

02488

Institute of Automotive Engineer Assessors
IAEA

Brooke House, 24 Dam St., Staffordshire, Lichfield, WS13 6AB, UK
Tel: 01543 266906
Fax: 01543 257848
Website: http://guideto.iaea.org.uk
Members: 1500
Description: Automotive engineer assessors in England. Promotes and protects members' interests.

02489

Institute of Biomedical Science
IBMS

12 Coldbath Sq., London, EC1R 5HL, UK
Tel: 020 77130214
Fax: 020 78379658
Email: mail@ibms.org
Website: http://www.ibms.org
Members: 19000
Staff: 30
Contact: Kenny Rae, Pres.
Fee: £43
Membership Type: associate
Fee: £142
Membership Type: fellow
Description: Biomedical scientists (medical laboratory scientists) and related staff in the National Health Service, private sector, commercial sector and overseas. Promotes the study and development of biomedical science and maintains high standards of professional education and practice.
Library Subject: biomedical science
Library Type: not open to the public
Publication: Magazine
Publication title: Biomedical Scientist. Advertisements.
Meetings/Conventions: biennial congress – Exhibits.

02490

Institute of British Foundrymen

Natl. Metalforming Ctre., 47 Birmingham Rd., W Bromwich, West Midlands, B70 6PY, UK
Tel: 0121 6016979
Fax: 0121 6016981
Email: info@icme.org.uk
Website: http://www.icme.org.uk
Members: 1200
Staff: 5
Contact: Pam Murrell, Dir.
Description: Represents individuals' employed in the Cast Metals industry and related industries. Provides education, training and professional membership.
Library Type: by appointment only
Formerly: Also Known As, Institute of Cast Metals Engineers

02491

Institute of Business Consulting
IBC

2 Savoy Ct., 4th Fl., Strand, London, WC2R 0EZ, UK
Tel: 020 74970580
Fax: 020 74970463
Email: ibc@ibconsulting.org.uk
Website: http://www.ibconsulting.org.uk
Members: 2100
Staff: 8
Contact: Alan Warr, Contact
Fee: £50
Membership Type: student
Fee: £75
Membership Type: affiliate
Description: Represents professional, independent business advisers, business counsellors, business mentors, trainers and support staff in a wide range of business support organizations. Responsible for the accreditation of independent business advisers. Provides services to small and medium size businesses through Business Links, local Enterprise Agencies and Training and Enterprise Councils (Technologies) or Local Enterprise Companies (LECs).
Formerly: Formerly, Institute of Business Advisers and Institute of Management Consultancy
Publication: Journal
Publication title: Business Adviser

02492

Institute of Career Guidance
ICG

Copthall House, 3rd Fl., 1 New Rd., Stourbridge, DY8 1PH, UK
Tel: 01384 376464
Email: linda.hills@icg-uk.org
Website: http://www.icg-uk.org
Members: 4200
Staff: 6
Contact: Chris Evans, Exec. Dir.
Fee: £106
Membership Type: full
Fee: £72
Membership Type: full (low income)
Description: Careers guidance practitioners, including those employed by careers services. Professional body for those engaged in careers advisory work.
Library Subject: career guidance
Library Type: reference
Publication: Journal
Publication title: Career Guidance Today. Advertisements.

02493

Institute of Carpenters
IOC

Carpenters' Hall, 3rd Fl. D, 1 Throgmorton Ave., London, EC2N 2BY, UK
Tel: 020 72562700
Fax: 020 72562701
Email: info@instituteofcarpenters.com
Website: http://www.instituteofcarpenters.com
Members: 2200
Contact: William Avery, Pres.
Fee: £100
Membership Type: fellow
Fee: £88
Membership Type: regular
Description: Oversees training for carpenters and joiners in an effort to maintain standards.
Publication: Magazine
Publication title: The Cutting Edge

02494

Institute of Cast Metals Engineers
ICME

47 Birmingham Rd., West Bromwich, B70 6PY, UK
Tel: 0121 6016979
Fax: 0121 6016981
Email: info@icme.org.uk
Website: http://www.icme.org.uk
Members: 1500
Staff: 4
Contact: Patrick Helly, Natl. Pres.
Fee: £112
Membership Type: fellow
Fee: £88
Membership Type: professor
Description: Workers in the cast metals industry. Offers educational, research, and public service programs. Offers placement service.
Library Subject: cast metals, pattern making
Library Type: reference
Formerly: Formerly, Institute of British Foundrymen
Publication: Journal
Publication title: Foundry Trade. Advertisements.

02495

Institute of Chartered Accountants in England and Wales
ICAEW

Chartered Accountants' Hall, PO Box 433, London, EC2P 2BJ, UK
Tel: 020 79208100
Fax: 020 79200547
Email: information.centre@icaew.com
Website: http://www.icaew.com
Members: 130000
Contact: Michael Izza, Chief Exec.
Description: Serves as an accountancy body with over 130,000 members working in business and public practice in 160 different countries. Maintains standard professional business qualifications. Entitles members to the description chartered accountant and to the designatory letters ACA or FCA. Undertakes or facilitates a range of professional activities including education and training of students, continuing professional development for members, maintenance of professional and ethical standards, cutting-edge work on technical accounting issues, and provision of advice and services to members.
Publication: Membership Directory
Publication title: Complete List of Members

02496

Institute of Chartered Accountants in Ireland
ICAI

The Linenhall, 32-38 Linenhall St., Belfast, BT2 8BG, UK
Tel: 028 90321600
Fax: 028 90230071

Email: ca@icai.ie
Website: http://www.icai.ie
Members: 17000
Contact: Jim Aiken, Pres.
Description: Chartered accountants in Ireland.
Publication: Newsletter
Publication title: Business Matters

02497

Institute of Chartered Accountants of Scotland
ICAS

CA House, 21 Haymarket Yards, Edinburgh, EH12 5BH, UK
Tel: 0131 3470100
Fax: 0131 3470105
Email: enquiries@icas.org.uk
Website: http://www.icas.org.uk
Members: 15000
Staff: 140
Contact: Alan Thompson, Pres.
Description: Chartered accountants. Provides the following: accountancy services, education, business courses, information technology services, computer consultancy, business publishing, printing, information service. Authorized to grant permits under the Insolvency Act 1986, authorization under the Financial Services Act 2000n for Investment Business and Registration under the Companies Act 1989.
Publication: Magazine
Publication title: CA Magazine. Advertisements.

02498

Institute of Chartered Foresters
ICF

59 George St., Edinburgh, EH2 2JG, UK
Tel: 0131 2401425
Fax: 0131 2401424
Email: icf@charteredforesters.org
Website: http://www.charteredforesters.org
Members: 1200
Staff: 4
Contact: Shireen Chambers, Exec. Dir.
Fee: £342
Membership Type: fellow
Fee: £239
Membership Type: professional
Description: Provides services to members including support and promotion of the work of foresters and arboriculturists; information and guidance to the public and industry; and training and educational advice to students and professionals looking to build upon their experience. Regulates the standards of entry to the profession and offer examinations for professional qualifications.
Library Subject: forestry
Library Type: reference
Formerly: Formerly, Institute of Foresters
Publication: Magazine
Publication title: Chartered Forester Magazine. Advertisements.
Meetings/Conventions: Study Tour – annual meeting

02499

Institute of Chartered Secretaries and Administrators - United Kingdom
ICSA

16 Park Crescent, London, W1B 1AH, UK
Tel: 020 75804741
Fax: 020 73231132
Email: info@icsa.org.uk
Website: http://www.icsa.org.uk/home?c=1
Members: 73000
Contact: David Wilson, Chief Exec.
Description: Chartered secretaries and administrators in England.
Publication: Magazine
Publication title: Chartered Secretary

02500

Institute of Chartered Shipbrokers - England
ICS

85 Gracechurch St., London, EC3V 0AA, UK
Tel: 020 76231111
Fax: 020 76238118
Email: admin@ics.org.uk
Website: http://www.ics.org.uk
Members: 3500
Staff: 10
Contact: George Greenwood, Pres.
Fee: £135
Membership Type: fellowship
Fee: £100
Membership Type: individual
Description: Professional, qualified Chartered Shipbrokers. Education and examination - qualification for shipping personnel. Guidance and promotion of company members' interests.
Library Subject: maritime economics
Library Type: reference
Publication: Journal
Publication title: Shipbroker. Advertisements.

02501

Institute of Chiropodists and Podiatrists
IOCP

27 Wright St., Merseyside, Southport, PR9 0TL, UK
Tel: 01704 546141
Fax: 01704 500477
Email: secretary@iocp.org.uk
Website: http://www.iocp.org.uk
Members: 2500
Staff: 4
Fee: £190
Membership Type: regular
Description: Chiropodists, podiatrists and foot health practitioners. Members governed by strict code of ethics. Third party surgery risks insurance provided for members.
Formerly: Formerly, Institute of Chiropodists
Publication: Journal
Publication title: Podiatry Review. Advertisements.
Meetings/Conventions: annual conference – Exhibits.

02502

Institute of Civil Protection and Emergency Management
ICPEM

PO Box 596, Eastleigh, SO50 0HQ, UK
Email: admin@icpem.net
Website: http://www.icpem.net
Contact: Tim Cross, Pres.
Fee: £30
Membership Type: student
Fee: £40
Membership Type: regular
Description: Seeks to raise public awareness and civil protection in the event of war, through training, educational and disaster mitigation research. Implements emergency response procedures. Encourages co-operation.

02503

Institute of Clerks of Works and Construction Inspectorate of Great Britain

Equinox, 28 Commerce Rd., Lynch Wood, Peterborough, PE2 6LR, UK
Tel: 01733 405160
Fax: 01733 405161
Email: info@icwci.org
Website: http://www.icwci.org
Members: 2000
Staff: 3
Contact: Rachel Morris, Gen. Sec.
Fee: £150
Membership Type: regular, licentiate
Fee: £145
Membership Type: fellow
Description: Qualified clerks of works working to ensure the client obtains value for money in all areas of the construction industry - civil engineering, building, M and E and landscape. Recognized as the authoritative organization for Clerks of Works, has 24 UK meeting centres and a Hong Kong branch. Arranges an annual residential seminar and regional CPD events, offers guidance on employment matters, publishes a number of guides and leaflets and provides annual examinations worldwide to corporate membership.
Publication: Journal
Publication title: Site Recorder. Advertisements.
Meetings/Conventions: annual conference – Exhibits.

02504

Institute of Clinical Research
ICR

Institute House, Boston Dr., Buckinghamshire, Bourne End, SL8 5YS, UK
Tel: 0845 5210056
Fax: 01628 530641
Email: info@icr-global.org
Website: http://www.icr-global.org
Members: 5500
Staff: 20
Contact: Janette Benaddi, Chair
Fee: £56
Membership Type: affiliate
Fee: £84
Membership Type: registered
Description: Individuals engaged in the design, organization or conduct of clinical trials for the pharmaceutical industry. Aims to establish and maintain the professional identity of members; to facilitate communications between members of clinical research departments in the industry; to provide a forum for discussion and to foster good relations with other professional groups. Maintains resource center.
Formerly: Formerly, Association of Clinical Research for the Pharmaceutical Industry
Publication: Journal
Publication title: Clinical Research Focus. Advertisements.

02505

Institute of Commercial Management
ICM

ICM House, Castleman Way, Hampshire, Ringwood, BH24 3BA, UK
Tel: 01202 490555
Fax: 01202 490666
Email: info@icm.ac.uk
Website: http://www.icm.ac.uk/home
Members: 249000
Staff: 34
Contact: Derek C. Gladwell, Pres.
Fee: £55
Membership Type: associate
Fee: £95
Membership Type: regular
Description: Managers/supervisors in industry and commerce. Consists of examining body for business and management students providing a range of recognized qualifications. Seeks to provide a range of high quality global education, training, and consulting services which raise performance standards for business and enhance the professional status of individuals. Offers certification programs.
Publication title: ICM Review

02506

Institute of Commonwealth Studies

University of London, School of Advanced Studies, Senate House, Malet St., London, WC1E 7HU, UK
Tel: 0207 8628844
Fax: 0207 8628813
Email: ics@sas.ac.uk
Website: http://commonwealth.sas.ac.uk
Members: 2000
Staff: 20
Contact: Philip Murphy, Dir.
Fee: £65
Membership Type: board
Fee: £30
Membership Type: unwaged
Description: Academics, educators, students, and other individuals with an interest in the history of the British Commonwealth and its component countries. Promotes interest in and study of the economic, social, and cultural aspects of the Commonwealth. Conducts research and educational programs.

02507

Institute of Concrete Technology
ICT

Riverside House, 4, Meadows Business Park, Station Approach, Blackwater, Camberley, GU17 9AB, UK
Tel: 01276 607140
Fax: 01276 607141
Website: http://ict.concrete.org.uk
Members: 600
Staff: 1
Contact: Peter Hewlett, Pres.
Fee: £12
Membership Type: graduate
Fee: £52
Membership Type: associate
Description: Professionally qualified concrete technologists (UK and overseas). Promotes concrete technology through technical meetings; representation on national technical committees; newsletter and technical information to members.
Publication: Yearbook
Publication title: ICT Yearbook. Advertisements.

02508

Institute of Consumer Affairs
ICA

134 Trinity Rd., London, SW17 7HS, UK
Tel: 020 87676887
Email: secretary@icanet.org.uk
Website: http://www.icanet.org.uk
Members: 150
Contact: Jacqui King, Membership Sec.
Fee: £14
Membership Type: unwaged
Fee: £35
Membership Type: full
Description: People who are employed as consumer advisers within Consumer Advice Centres, those who manage a Consumer Advice Centre at any level or people who are involved in consumer education or information at any level. Aims to protect the status of consumer advisers and encourage, maintain and improve standards of consumer service.

02509

Institute of Contemporary Arts
ICA

c/o Industry of Contemporary Arts
12 Carlton House Terr., London, SW1Y 5AH, UK
Tel: 020 79300493
Website: http://www.ica.org.uk
Members: 7000
Staff: 50
Contact: Ekow Eshun, Dir.
Fee: £35
Membership Type: individual
Description: Available to all people with an interest in live and contemporary art, including artists, young people and students (concessions available). Aims to encourage debate around central issues of contemporary art. Provides a forum for young people to display their work.

02510

Institute of Corrosion
ICorr

Corrosion House, 7b High St. Mews, Leighton Buzzard, LU7 1FG, UK
Tel: 01525 851771
Fax: 01525 376690
Email: admin@icorr.org
Website: http://www.icorr.org
Members: 1550
Staff: 2
Contact: Cerri Sweet, Contact
Fee: £17
Membership Type: student
Fee: £64
Membership Type: ordinary
Description: Corrosion engineers, technologists and scientists interested in corrosion prevention and control. Aims to advance the understanding of the science of corrosion and the technology of corrosion prevention and control, and to encourage the exchange of information and ideas of these subjects for the public benefit.
Publication: Magazine
Publication title: Corrosion Management. Advertisements.

02511

Institute of Credit Management
ICM

Station Rd., The Water Mill, Leicestershire, South Luffenham, LE15 8NB, UK
Tel: 01780 722900
Fax: 01780 721333
Email: info@icm.org.uk
Website: http://www.icm.org.uk
Members: 9000
Staff: 24
Contact: Philip King, Chief Exec.
Fee: £105
Membership Type: fellow
Fee: £96
Membership Type: vocational, graduate
Description: Individuals working in credit management and its ancillary services. Serves as the central reference point in the UK on all matters relating to credit management. Raises professional standards through the provision of examinations, seminars, conferences and publications. Courses are offered at local colleges, by the Rapid Results Correspondence College and by distance learning.
Library Subject: credit management
Library Type: not open to the public
Publication: Journal
Publication title: Credit Management. Advertisements.

02512

Institute of Cultural Affairs United Kingdom
ICA-UK

41 Old Birley St., Unit 14, Manchester, M15 5RF, UK
Tel: 0845 4500305
Email: ica@ica-uk.org.uk
Website: http://www.ica-uk.org.uk
Members: 130
Contact: Clare Vermes, Admin.
Fee: £15
Membership Type: family
Fee: £10
Membership Type: individual
Description: Seeks to facilitate a social network fostering personal growth in order to strengthen the society worldwide.
Publication: Newsletter
Publication title: ICA: UK Network News

02513

Institute of Decontamination Sciences
IDSc

c/o Fitwise Management Ltd.
Drumcross Hall, West Lothian, Bathgate, EH48 4JT, UK
Tel: 01506 811077
Fax: 01506 811477
Email: idsc@fitwise.co.uk
Website: http://www.idsc-uk.co.uk
Contact: Robert C. Spencer, Pres.
Description: Different grades of membership - fellow, member, student member, associate, corporate, honorary, associate technician. Aims to organise and initiate training programmes for members/students, with the object of achieving high professional standards; provides a forum for members through regional branches to consider and discuss matters relating to sterilization and disinfection and promotes and encourages research and development in the world of sterile service.

Formerly: Formerly, Institute of Sterile Services Management
Publication: Journal
Publication title: The ISSM Journal. Advertisements.

02514
Institute of Development Studies
IDS
University of Sussex, Brighton, BN1 9RE, UK
Tel: 01273 606261
Fax: 01273 621202
Email: ids@ids.ac.uk
Website: http://www.ids.ac.uk/go/home
Staff: 135
Contact: Lawrence Haddad, Dir.
Description: Research and teaching institute seeking to reduce poverty and create economies capable of providing secure livelihoods to individuals worldwide. Aims to influence development policies; through research, training, and post-graduate teaching.
Publication: Journal
Publication title: IDS Bulletin. Advertisements.

02515
Institute of Directors - England
IoD
116 Pall Mall, London, SW1Y 5ED, UK
Tel: 020 78391233
Fax: 020 77668833
Email: enquiries@iod.com
Website: http://www.iod.com/Home
Members: 55000
Staff: 225
Contact: Neville Bain, Chm.
Fee: £313
Membership Type: full, associate
Description: Represents company directors and other people holding a similar position in industry, commerce, the professions or government organizations. Aims to advance company directors' interests and foster free enterprise. Includes services to members: branch network, professional development activities and conferences, information and advisory services. Provides meeting rooms and restaurant facilities to its members.
Publication: Magazine
Publication title: Director

02516
Institute of Domestic Heating and Environmental Engineers
IDHEE
New Forest Enterprise Centre, Unit 35A, Chapel Ln., Totton, Southampton, SO40 9LA, UK
Tel: 02380 668900
Fax: 02380 660888
Email: admin@idhee.org.uk
Website: http://www.idhee.org.uk
Contact: Chris Laughton, Chm.
Fee: £75
Membership Type: regular, technical sales
Fee: £62
Membership Type: associate, technician, domestic energy assessor
Description: Aims to promote energy efficient domestic central heating components and the installation of safe and energy efficient systems.

02517
Institute of Ecology and Environmental Management
IEEM
43 Southgate St., Winchester, SO23 9EH, UK
Tel: 01962 868626
Fax: 01962 868625
Email: enquiries@ieem.net
Website: http://www.ieem.net
Members: 1800
Contact: Jim Thompson, Exec. Dir.
Fee: £130
Membership Type: full, fellowship
Fee: £95
Membership Type: associate
Description: Individuals working in local authorities, government departments and agencies, environmental consultants; ecologists and environmental managers in industry, conservation bodies (voluntary and public), academic and research institutes. Concerned to raise the profile of the profession of ecology and environmental management, to establish, maintain and enhance professional standards and to promote an ethic of environmental care within the profession and to clients and employers of the members.
Publication: Journal
Publication title: In Practice. Advertisements.

02518
Institute of Economic Affairs
IEA
2 Lord North St., Westminster, London, SW1P 3LB, UK
Tel: 020 77998900
Fax: 020 77992137
Email: iea@iea.org.uk
Website: http://www.iea.org.uk
Contact: Mark Littlewood, Dir. Gen.
Description: Works to improve public understanding of the fundamental institutions of a free society through publishing, conferences, seminars and lectures and outreach to educational institutions.
Publication: Journal
Publication title: Economic Affairs

02519
Institute of Ecotechnics
IE
24 Old Gloucester St., London, WC1N 3AL, UK
Tel: 020 74051824
Fax: 020 74051851
Email: info@ecotechnics.edu
Website: http://www.ecotechnics.edu
Members: 30
Contact: Mark Nelson, Chm.
Description: Council members only. Aims to develop a conceptual model for ecosystem management which includes human cultures, techniques, and decision-making populations. These dynamic factors together with studies of soil, plant and animal interactions, energy flows and material cycles, facilitate a total systems approach to complex environmental issues. Serves as a consultant to a number of demonstration projects in West Australia, New Mexico, Puerto Rico, France, and the UK.

02520
Institute of Employment Rights
IER
The People's Centre, 50-54 Mt. Pleasant, Liverpool, L3 5SD, UK
Tel: 0151 7026925
Fax: 0151 7026935
Email: office@ier.org.uk
Website: http://www.ier.org.uk
Members: 800
Staff: 3
Contact: Carolyn Jones, Dir.
Fee: £165
Membership Type: commercial
Fee: £170
Membership Type: international commercial
Description: Trade union general secretaries, academics and legal practitioners. Aims to analyze, discuss and promote issues relating to employment law. Wide network of experts - legal practitioners, academics and trade unionists - to develop an alternative legal agenda for the future through publications and seminars.

02521
Institute of Ergonomics and Human Factors
IEHF
Elms Ct., Elms Grove, Loughborough, LE11 1RG, UK
Tel: 01509 234904
Fax: 01509 235666
Email: d.oneill@ergonomics.org.uk
Website: http://www.ergonomics.org.uk
Members: 1363
Staff: 5
Contact: David O'Neill, Chief Exec.
Fee: £20
Membership Type: student
Fee: £57-68
Membership Type: graduate
Description: Academic and practitioners in ergonomics and allied fields. Furthers the discipline of ergonomics through publications, conferences, professional standards and educational material.
Formerly: Formerly, Ergonomics Society - England
Publication: Journal
Publication title: Applied Ergonomics

02522
Institute of Estuarine and Coastal Studies
IECS
University of Hull, Rother Bldg., Hull, HU6 7RX, UK
Tel: 01482 464120
Fax: 01482 464130
Email: iecs@hull.ac.uk
Website: http://www.hull.ac.uk/iecs
Staff: 14
Contact: Mike Elliott, Dir.
Description: Covers the entire range of coastal studies, from fundamental scientific research to the preparation of management plans and environmental impact assessment. Focuses on field measurement and monitoring both of physical and biological systems and using a variety of surveying and instrumental techniques.
Library Subject: estuarine, coastal science and management
Library Type: by appointment only
Meetings/Conventions: International Symposium on Estuarine and Lagoon Fish and Fisheries – periodic symposium

02523
Institute of Explosives Engineers
IExpE
Cranfield University, Wellington Hall 289, Defence Academy of the UK, Shrivenham, Swindon, SN6 8LA, UK
Tel: 01793 785322
Fax: 01793 785772
Email: iexpe@cranfield.ac.uk
Website: http://www.iexpe.org
Members: 1000
Staff: 1
Fee: £500
Membership Type: company (within UK and EEC)
Fee: £510
Membership Type: company (all other country)
Description: Civil and Military engineers, academics and scientists engaged in the development and/or manufacture of explosives/munitions. Aims to promote the profession of explosive engineering and to achieve professional standing so that the Institute takes its place alongside other specialized Engineering bodies and provides technical consultative facilities for government departments and other external agencies within its field.
Publication: Journal
Publication title: Explosives Engineering. Advertisements.

02524
Institute of Export
IoE
Minerva Business Park, Lynch Wood, Cambridgeshire, Peterborough, PE2 6FT, UK
Tel: 01733 404400
Fax: 01733 404444
Email: institute@export.org.uk
Website: http://www.export.org.uk
Members: 3000
Staff: 7
Contact: Lesley Batchelor, Natl. Chair
Fee: £67.5
Membership Type: individual (minimum), affiliate
Fee: £97.5
Membership Type: individual (maximum), institute (graduate)
Description: Professionally Qualified Exporters. Enhances and promotes the UK's international trade and the support of the professional exporter in both the corporate and personal context. Sets and maintains the standards for professional education and training in international trade.
Publication: Magazine
Publication title: Exporting World

02525
Institute of Field Archaeologists
IFA
University of Reading, PO Box 227, Whiteknights, Reading, RG6 6AB, UK
Tel: 0118 3786446
Fax: 0118 3786448
Email: admin@archaeologists.net
Website: http://www.archaeologists.net
Members: 2500
Staff: 6
Contact: Peter Hinton, Chief Exec.
Fee: £5
Membership Type: affiliate
Fee: £10
Membership Type: practitioner
Description: Provides an active professional organization, involving and offering appropriate services to its membership; develops proper professional guidelines and standards for the execution of archaeological work and establishes these guidelines and standards by promoting membership of the institute to all those practicing field of archaeology.
Publication: Magazine
Publication title: The Archaeologist. Advertisements.

02526
Institute of Financial Accountants
IFA
Burford House, 44 London Rd., Sevenoaks, TN13 1AS, UK
Tel: 01732 458080
Fax: 01732 455848
Email: mail@ifa.org.uk
Website: http://www.ifa.org.uk
Members: 8000
Staff: 15
Contact: Eric Anstee, Chm.
Description: Financial accountants and controllers, finance directors, lecturers, secretaries, and teachers in 80 countries engaged in commerce, industry, and public service. Promotes and protects the status and high standards of members. Administers examinations. Operates speakers' bureau. Compiles statistics. Conducts seminars.
Publication: Journal
Publication title: Financial Accountant

02527
Institute of Financial Planning
IFP
Lewins Mead, Whitefriars Centre, Bristol, BS1 2NT, UK
Tel: 0117 9452470
Fax: 0117 9292214
Email: enquiries@financialplanning.org.uk
Website: http://www.financialplanning.org.uk
Members: 1000
Staff: 11
Contact: Nick Cann, CEO
Fee: £25
Membership Type: associate, fellow, ordinary (25 years and above)
Fee: £150
Membership Type: associate, fellow, ordinary
Description: Members provide holistic financial planning objectively to members of the public and to companies. Membership includes IFAs, accountants, solicitors, bankers and tax-consultants. Intends to continue to promote the profession and practice of financial planning, to increase public awareness of the need for financial planning and to ensure high professional and ethical standards amongst its members. Shares knowledge and skills with other professionals for the benefit of mutual clients is of paramount importance. Confers certified financial planner license to qualified individuals. Affiliated to Certified Financial Planner Board of Standards.
Formerly: Absorbed, Financial Planning Association
Publication: Journal
Publication title: Financial Planning. Advertisements.

02528
Institute of Fisheries Management
IFM
22 Rushworth Ave., West Bridgford, Nottingham, NG2 7LF, UK
Tel: 0115 9822317
Fax: 0115 9826150
Email: info@ifm.org.uk
Website: http://www.ifm.org.uk
Members: 1400
Contact: Ian Dolben, Chm.
Fee: £60
Membership Type: registered
Fee: £75-150
Membership Type: corporate
Description: Mainly professional people who are interested in fisheries management. Aims to promote the advancement of fisheries management in all or any of its branches, to improve and elevate the technical and general knowledge and efficiency of persons engaged in, or about to engage in, fisheries management so as to advance the standing of the profession.
Publication: Magazine
Publication title: Fish. Advertisements.
Meetings/Conventions: annual conference – Exhibits.

02529
Institute of Food Science and Technology - UK
IFST
5 Cambridge Ct., 210 Shepherds Bush Rd., London, W6 7NJ, UK
Tel: 020 76036316
Fax: 020 76029936
Email: info@ifst.org
Website: http://www.ifst.org
Members: 3100
Staff: 5
Contact: Jon Poole, Chief Exec.
Fee: £79
Membership Type: associate
Fee: £17
Membership Type: student
Description: Food scientists and technologists. Professional qualifying body for food scientists and technologists. Educational charity. Advances the standing of food science and technology both as a subject and as a profession.
Publication: Journal
Publication title: Food Science and Technology. Advertisements.
Meetings/Conventions: annual conference – Exhibits.

02530
Institute of Fundraising
Park Pl., 12 Lawn Ln., London, SW8 1UD, UK
Tel: 020 78401000
Fax: 020 78401001
Website: http://www.institute-of-fundraising.org.uk
Members: 4000
Staff: 20
Contact: Paul Amadi, Chm.
Fee: £80
Membership Type: associate
Fee: £90
Membership Type: full, fellow
Description: Individuals working as fundraisers, or in support of fundraising activities in the UK. Exists to promote the highest standards of fundraising. Regional groups organize networking and training meetings at a local level.
Formerly: Formerly, Institute of Charity Fundraising Managers
Publication: Handbook
Publication title: The Fundraisers

02531

Institute of Gerontology
IoG

King's College London, Rm. 6.27, The Strand Bldg., London, WC2R 2LS, UK
Tel: 020 78482735
Fax: 020 78481866
Email: gerontology@kcl.ac.uk
Website: http://www.kcl.ac.uk/schools/sspp/geront
Members: 20
Contact: Simon Biggs, Dir.
Description: Scientists, health and social care professionals with an interest in the aging process and policy; the lives of older people and the biological, psychological and social challenges of the later life. Works to ensure high standards of research and practice in gerontology. Conducts research and educational activities.
Formerly: Formerly, British Society of Gerontology

02532

Institute of Grocery Distribution
IGD

Grange Ln., Letchmore Heath, Hertfordshire, Watford, WD25 8GD, UK
Tel: 01923 857141
Fax: 01923 852531
Email: igd@igd.com
Website: http://www.igd.com/index.asp?id=0
Members: 665
Contact: Joanne Denney-Finch, Chief Exec.
Fee: £1975
Membership Type: company
Description: Provides information, research, and education for the food and grocery industry. Focuses on the whole food and grocery chain from the consumer, retailing and foodservice, to manufacturing, wholesaling, distribution, and farming.
Publication: Newsletter
Publication title: Convenience Update

02533

Institute of Groundsmanship
IOG

28 Stratford Office Village, Walker Ave., Wolverton Mill E, Milton Keynes, MK12 5TW, UK
Tel: 01908 312511
Fax: 01908 311140
Email: iog@iog.org
Website: http://www.iog.org
Members: 8000
Staff: 4
Contact: Geoff Webb, Chief Exec.
Fee: £104
Membership Type: associate
Fee: £47
Membership Type: individual
Description: From all sectors of the sports and leisure management and maintenance industry. Disseminates information and enhances the training of groundsmen. Organizes training in UK and Europe on Sportsturf management. Runs the trade exhibition (SALTEX) annually for the Sport and Leisure maintenance industry. Organizes a conference each year and runs a consultancy service on all aspects of turf management.
Library Subject: grounds management
Library Type: not open to the public
Publication: Magazine
Publication title: Groundsman. Advertisements.
Meetings/Conventions: annual meeting – Exhibits.

02534

Institute of Group Analysis
IGA

1 Daleham Gardens, London, NW3 5BY, UK
Tel: 020 74312693
Fax: 020 74317246
Email: iga@igalondon.org.uk
Website: http://www.groupanalysis.org
Members: 350
Staff: 5
Contact: Elizabeth Rimmer, Exec. Dir.
Fee: £300
Membership Type: IGA-qualified group analyst
Description: Counselors, social workers, psychologists, psychiatrists, caring professionals, probation officers. Responsible for the establishment of a widely recognized professional qualification in group-analytic psychotherapy. The principal aim is to promote and forward the selection, education and training of persons in order to qualify them for the conduct and study of group analysis and related forms of psychotherapy.
Library Subject: group analysis, psychotherapy, psychiatry
Library Type: not open to the public
Publication: Newsletter
Publication title: Dialogue

02535

Institute of Health Promotion and Education
IHPE

c/o Helen Draper, Sec.
University of Manchester, School of Dentistry, Higher Cambridge St., Manchester, M15 6FH, UK
Email: honsec@ihpe.org.uk
Website: http://www.ihpe.org.uk/home/index.htm
Members: 1000
Contact: C. Choudhury, Pres.
Fee: £36
Membership Type: regular
Fee: £31.5
Membership Type: associate
Description: Represents individuals concerned with the promotion of health and the prevention of illness in all sections of the community at home, school, work and leisure.
Publication: Journal
Publication title: International Journal of Health Promotion and Education. Advertisements.

02536

Institute of Healthcare Engineering and Estate Management
IHEEM

2 Abingdon House, Cumberland Business Ctre., Northumberland Rd., Hants, Portsmouth, PO5 1DS, UK
Tel: 023 92823186
Fax: 023 92815927
Email: office@iheem.org.uk
Website: http://www.iheem.org.uk
Members: 2500
Staff: 4
Contact: John Long, Chief Exec.
Fee: £40
Membership Type: fellow, regular, associate, affiliate
Description: Individuals involved in hospital engineering in 24 countries; hospital engineering and estate management students. Works to enhance the education and training of hospital engineers and other professionals working in estate management. Sponsors qualified members for registration as chartered engineer, incorporated engineer, and engineering technician.
Library Type: reference
Formerly: Formerly, Institute of Hospital Engineering
Publication: Journal
Publication title: Health Estate Journal. Advertisements.

02537

Institute of Healthcare Management - United Kingdom
IHM

18-21 Morley St., London, SE1 7QZ, UK
Tel: 020 76201030
Fax: 020 76201040
Email: enquiries@ihm.org.uk
Website: http://www.ihm.org.uk
Members: 7000
Staff: 12
Contact: Susan Hodgetts, CEO
Fee: £176
Membership Type: full
Fee: £132
Membership Type: associate
Description: Individuals involved in the management and administration of health care. Aims to promote excellence in health services management and the development of good managers, to affect health services policy and its implementation and to create and sustain a professional community of health services managers. Serves as a forum, network and management development association for individuals both inside and outside the NHS.
Formerly: Formerly, Institute of Health Services Management
Publication: Magazine
Publication title: Health Management. Advertisements.

02538

Institute of Highway Incorporated Engineers
IHIE

De Morgan House, 58 Russell Sq., London, WC1B 4HS, UK
Tel: 020 74367487
Fax: 020 74367488
Email: secretary@ihie.org
Website: http://www.ihie.org.uk
Members: 3000
Staff: 4
Contact: Judith M. Walker, Sec.
Fee: £110
Membership Type: fellow
Fee: £89
Membership Type: ordinary
Description: Engineers and technicians in highway and traffic engineering and transportation; students. Promotes professionalism among members. Conducts educational and training programs; offers certification testing. Determines qualifications for incorporated engineers and engineering technicians.
Formerly: Formerly, Highway and Traffic Technicians Association
Publication: Magazine
Publication title: Highways

02539

Institute of Horticulture

IoH

Capel Manor College, Bullsmoor Ln., Middlesex, Enfield, EN1 4RQ, UK
Tel: 019 92707025
Email: heather-b-m@waitrose.com
Website: http://www.horticulture.org.uk
Members: 2010
Staff: 3
Contact: Heather Barrett-Mold, Pres.
Fee: £96
Membership Type: regular
Fee: £121
Membership Type: fellow
Description: Professional horticulturists. Aims to promote and encourage good horticultural practice by the dissemination of information, consultation with governments and other bodies, promoting educational and training opportunities, and conferring status upon professionally qualified horticulturists. (There are various categories of membership, each requiring specific entry qualifications).
Publication: Journal
Publication title: The Horticulturist. Advertisements.

02540

Institute of Hospitality

Trinity Ct., 34 West St., Surrey, Sutton, SM1 1SH, UK
Tel: 020 86614900
Fax: 020 86614901
Website: http://www.instituteofhospitality.org
Members: 23000
Staff: 34
Contact: Peter Lederer, Pres.
Description: Managers and potential managers in the hospitality/foodservice industry. Concerns itself with the setting of standards by the development and provision of hotel and catering management education and the collation and dissemination of industry and technical information. Works with government, industry and education sectors. Plans seminars and conferences.
Library Subject: hospitality industry
Library Type: open to the public
Formerly: Formerly, Hotel and Catering International Management Association
Publication: Magazine
Publication title: Hospitality
Meetings/Conventions: Presidents Conference and Diner – annual conference – Exhibits.

02541

Institute of Insurance Brokers

IIB

Higham Business Centre, Midland Rd., Northamptonshire, Higham Ferrers, NN10 8DW, UK
Tel: 01933 410003
Fax: 01933 410020
Email: inst.ins.brokers@iib-uk.com
Website: http://iib-uk.com
Members: 1100
Staff: 12
Contact: John Greenway, Pres.
Fee: £648
Membership Type: band A (1 to 5 employees)
Fee: £780
Membership Type: band B (6 to 12 employees)
Description: Promotes and represents brokers in the insurance industry.
Library Subject: insurance, finance, law
Library Type: not open to the public

02542

Institute of Internal Auditors - UK and Ireland

IIA

13 Abbeville Mews, 88 Clapham Park Rd., London, SW4 7BX, UK
Tel: 020 74980101
Fax: 020 79782492
Email: membership@iia.org.uk
Website: http://www.iia.org.uk
Contact: Ian Peters, CEO
Fee: £190
Membership Type: voting
Fee: £145
Membership Type: affiliate
Description: Provides membership services for internal auditors in the U.K. and Ireland, including information, qualifications, training courses, a monthly magazine, bookstore and online knowledge centre.
Publication: Magazine
Publication title: Internal Auditing & Business Risk. Advertisements.
Meetings/Conventions: annual conference – Exhibits.

02543

Institute of Internal Communication

IoIC

Oak House, Ste. GA2, Woodlands Business Park, Linford Wood, Milton Keynes, MK14 6EY, UK
Tel: 01908 313755
Fax: 01908 313661
Email: enquiries@ioic.org.uk
Website: http://www.ioic.org.uk
Members: 1000
Staff: 1
Contact: Kathie Jones, Chief Exec.
Fee: £194.12
Membership Type: individual
Fee: £28.22
Membership Type: student
Description: Directors, managers, editors, and assistants involved in the management, editing, and production of corporate communication media. Represents members' interests; fosters information exchange among members. Conducts educational courses.
Formerly: Formerly, British Association of Industrial Editors
Publication: Newsletter
Publication title: CIB News

02544

Institute of International Licensing Practitioners

IILP

28 Main St., Milton Keynes, MK17 0RT, UK
Tel: 01296 728136
Fax: 01296 720070
Email: enquiries@iilp.net
Website: http://www.iilp.net
Staff: 7
Fee: £95
Membership Type: fellow, associate
Fee: £85
Membership Type: affiliate
Description: Aims to set, promote, and maintain the highest standards of professional practice and technical expertise amongst those providing consultancy services for commercializing invention and licensing intellectual property. Fellows are bound by a strict professional Code of Conduct; membership is by election only. Circulates licensing enquiries to fellows; provides speakers for training seminars and conferences, TV, radio and other media events. Judges for technology fairs. Provides services as expert witnesses and mediators.
Publication: Directory
Publication title: Directory of Fellows and Associates

02545

Institute of Inventors

19-21-23 Fosse Way, Ealing, London, W13 0BZ, UK
Tel: 020 89983540
Email: mikinvent@aol.com
Website: http://instituteofinventors.com
Contact: Michael V. Rodrigues, Pres.
Fee: £120
Membership Type: regular
Fee: £40
Membership Type: renewal
Description: Private inventors, professional inventors, business members. Voluntary inventor's club, to help inventors at all stages of invention -appraisal, patent searches, patent drafting, licensing agreements, business consultations/funding advice.
Library Subject: science, technology, innovation
Library Type: not open to the public

02546

Institute of Leadership and Management

ILM

Stowe House, Netherstowe, Staffordshire, Lichfield, WS13 6TJ, UK
Tel: 01543 266886
Fax: 01543 266893
Email: customer@i-l-m.com
Website: http://www.i-l-m.com
Members: 24000
Staff: 40
Contact: Ralph Bauer, Chm.
Fee: £95
Membership Type: affiliate, associate
Fee: £125
Membership Type: fellow
Description: Fellows, Members and Associates - Corporate grades; Affiliates and Students - Non-corporate grades. Aims to encourage and develop the science and practice of management and gain recognition of management as a profession.
Library Subject: management, training
Library Type: reference
Formerly: Formerly, Institute of Supervisory Management
Publication: Journal

02547
Institute of Legal Cashiers and Administrators
ILCA
Marlowe House, 2nd Fl., 109 Station Rd., Sidcup, Kent, DA15 7ET, UK
Tel: 020 83022867
Fax: 020 83027481
Email: info@ilca.org.uk
Website: http://www.ilca.org.uk
Contact: Dawn Chapman, Chm.
Fee: £81.56
Membership Type: ordinary, affiliate
Description: Legal-cashiers, administrators, partnership secretaries, financial controllers, office managers, some legal executives and solicitors. Dedicated to the education, support and promotion of specialist financial and administrative personnel working within the legal community.
Formerly: Absorbed, Institute of Legal Cashiers
Publication: Journal
Publication title: Legal Abacus. Advertisements.

02548
Institute of Legal Executives
ILEX
Kempston Manor, Bedfordshire, Kempston, MK42 7AB, UK
Tel: 01234 841000
Fax: 01234 840373
Email: info@ilex.org.uk
Website: http://www.ilex.org.uk
Members: 22000
Contact: David McGrady, Pres.
Fee: £50
Membership Type: student
Fee: £100
Membership Type: affiliate
Description: Members are staff working in solicitors' offices, legal departments, or who are studying for a career in the law. Functions as the professional and examining body representing Legal Executives in England and Wales. A Legal Executive is a trained, qualified and experienced lawyer working in a law firm, private company or government department.
Publication: Journal
Publication title: Legal Executive Journal. Advertisements.

02549
Institute of Management
2 Savoy Ct., 3rd Fl., Strand, London, WC2R 0EZ, UK
Tel: 020 74970580
Fax: 020 74970463
Email: enquiries@managers.org.uk
Website: http://www.managers.org.uk
Members: 80000
Staff: 150
Contact: David Howard, Pres.
Fee: £50
Membership Type: student
Fee: £88
Membership Type: affiliate
Description: Promotes the development, exercise and recognition of professional management. Provides services in the areas of management development, management advice, management information and management networks.
Library Subject: management
Library Type: open to the public

02550
Institute of Management Services
IMS
Brooke House, 24 Dam St., Staffordshire, Lichfield, WS13 6AA, UK
Tel: 01543 266909
Fax: 01543 257848
Website: http://www.ims-productivity.com
Contact: John Lucey, Treas.
Fee: £240
Membership Type: life - UK/EU
Fee: £125
Membership Type: regular
Description: Represents industry, commerce and the public sector including armed services and police. Serves as professional, qualifying body whose main activities are to provide qualifications and education and to disseminate knowledge in the field of management services. Investigates, advises and carries out solutions to management and organizational problems.
Publication: Journal
Publication title: Management Services. Advertisements.

02551
Institute of Marine Engineering, Science and Technology
IMarEST
80 Coleman St., London, EC2R 5BJ, UK
Tel: 020 73822600
Fax: 020 73822670
Email: info@imarest.org
Website: http://www.imarest.org
Members: 17000
Staff: 50
Contact: C. G. Hodge, Chm.
Fee: £185
Membership Type: fellow
Fee: £165
Membership Type: regular
Description: Represents professionals in 43 countries involved in marine engineering, naval architecture, and offshore and subsea engineering. Promotes the development of all branches of marine engineering and advances the professional status of the engineer; facilitates advancement in the field. Sponsors seminars, symposia, and technical meetings. Serves as a forum for the exchange of information among members; disseminates information.
Library Subject: marine engineering
Library Type: reference
Publication: Journal
Publication title: Journal of Offshore Technology. Advertisements.

02552
Institute of Masters of Wine
IMW
2/3 Philpot Ln., London, EC3M 8AN, UK
Tel: 020 76212830
Fax: 020 79292302
Email: sturner@mastersofwine.org
Website: http://www.mastersofwine.org
Members: 278
Staff: 5
Contact: Siobhan Turner, Exec. Dir.
Description: Members of the wine industry who have passed the Master of Wine Examination.
Publication: Journal
Publication title: Journal of Wine Research

02553
Institute of Materials, Minerals, and Mining
IOM3
1 Carlton House Terr., London, SW1Y 5DB, UK
Tel: 020 74517300
Fax: 020 78391702
Email: bernie.rickinson@iom3.org
Website: http://www.iom3.org
Members: 20000
Staff: 16
Contact: Bernie Rickinson, Chief Exec.
Description: Metallurgists, geologists, mining engineers, and petroleum engineers. Promotes and develops all aspects of materials science and engineering, geology, mining and associated technologies, mineral and petroleum engineering and extraction metallurgy. Serves as the professional body for the international materials, minerals, and mining community. Provides information and library services, conferences, workshops, publications, and various educational resources.
Library Subject: minerals industry
Library Type: reference
Formerly: Absorbed, Institution of Mining and Metallurgy
Publication: Magazine
Publication title: Materials World. Advertisements.

02554
Institute of Mathematics and its Applications
IMA
c/o Catherine Richards' House
16 Nelson St., Southend-on-Sea, Essex, SS1 1EF, UK
Tel: 01702 354020
Fax: 01702 354111
Email: post@ima.org.uk
Website: http://www.ima.org.uk
Members: 5000
Contact: David Youdan, Exec. Dir.
Fee: £23
Membership Type: chartered scientist
Fee: £16
Membership Type: chartered mathematician
Description: Promotes and supports the understanding, teaching, research, and application of mathematics.
Publication: Journal
Publication title: IMA Journal of Numerical Analysis

02555
Institute of Measurement and Control
INSTMC
87 Gower St., London, WC1E 6AF, UK
Tel: 020 73874949
Fax: 020 73888431
Website: http://www.instmc.org.uk
Members: 4750
Staff: 8
Contact: Bill Bardo, Pres.
Fee: £182.3
Membership Type: fellow
Fee: £177.7
Membership Type: regular
Description: Measurement and control technology practitioners in manufacturing and user companies and in research and academic establishments. Advances the science and practice of measurement and control technology. Maintains seven technical committees.
Publication: Newsletter
Publication title: Interface

02556

Institute of Metal Finishing
IMF

Exeter House, 48 Holloway Head, Birmingham, B1 1NQ, UK
Tel: 0121 6227387
Fax: 0121 6666316
Email: exeterhouse@instituteofmetalfinishing.org
Website: http://www.uk-finishing.org.uk
Contact: R.S. Briggs, Pres.
Fee: £60
Membership Type: affiliate
Fee: £65
Membership Type: associate
Description: Professional people working in surface engineering industry. Metal finishing process include electro-plating, organic (paint) finishing, anodizing, printed circuitry and ancillary methods of surface treatment.
Publication: Newsletter
Publication title: IMFormation. Advertisements.
Meetings/Conventions: annual conference – Exhibits.

02557

Institute of Musical Instrument Technology
IMIT

Northfield House, 11 Kendal Ave. S, Sanderstead, Surrey, Croydon, CR2 0QR, UK
Website: http://www.imit.org.uk
Contact: Malcolm Dalton, Hon. Sec.
Fee: £53
Membership Type: fellow
Fee: £20.5
Membership Type: graduate, retired
Description: Seeks to advance musical instrument technology through the exchange of information and ideas. Promotes the professional status of members engaged in musical instrument design manufacture or repair.
Library Subject: musical instrument manufacture and repair
Library Type: not open to the public

02558

Institute of Occupational Medicine
IOM

Research Ave. N, Riccarton, Edinburgh, EH14 4AP, UK
Tel: 0131 4498000
Fax: 0131 4498084
Email: info@iom-world.org
Website: http://www.iom-world.org
Contact: Philip Woodhead, CEO
Description: Major independent centre of scientific excellence in the fields of occupational and environmental health, hygiene and safety. Aims to provide quality research, consultancy and training to help ensure that people's health is not damaged by conditions at work or in the environment.
Library Subject: occupational medicine, health, safety, hygiene, toxicology, environmental health, ergonomics
Library Type: not open to the public

02559

Institute of Operations Management
IOM

Earlstrees Ct., Earlstrees Rd., Northants, Corby, NN17 4AX, UK
Tel: 01536 740105
Fax: 01536 740101
Email: info@iomnet.org.uk
Website: http://www.iomnet.org.uk
Members: 3000
Staff: 6
Contact: Catherine Milner, Chair
Fee: £120
Membership Type: fellow
Fee: £99
Membership Type: associate, individual
Description: Directors, senior, middle and junior management of manufacturing and service companies who are actively engaged in the fields of operations management, production and inventory control, logistics, materials and supply chain management and related activities. Aims to assist British industry to compete more effectively in the world market by improving the knowledge and skill base of operations management professionals through the provision of events, publications and qualifications appropriate to their needs.
Library Subject: operations management, supply chain management, production control, inventory management
Library Type: reference
Formerly: Formerly, British Production and Inventory Control Society
Publication: Journal
Publication title: Operations Management. Advertisements.

02560

Institute of Ophthalmology
IOO

11-43 Bath St., London, EC1V 9EL, UK
Tel: 020 76086800
Email: p.luthert@ucl.ac.uk
Website: http://www.ucl.ac.uk/ioo
Contact: Phil Luthert, Dir.
Description: Promotes research into eye diseases and other causes of blindness.

02561

Institute of Paper

83 Guildford St., Surrey, Chertsey, KT16 9AS, UK
Tel: 01932 569896
Fax: 01932 569749
Website: http://www.instituteofpaper.com
Staff: 6
Description: Represents individuals employed in, or associated with, the paper industry.

02562

Institute of Patentees and Inventors
IPI

PO Box 39296, London, SE3 7WH, UK
Tel: 0871 2262091
Fax: 0208 2935920
Email: ipi@invent.org.uk
Website: http://www.invent.org.uk
Members: 1000
Staff: 1
Fee: £70
Membership Type: personal (associate grade)
Fee: £110-320
Membership Type: company (based on number of employees)
Description: Inventors who have applied for or received a patent, aspiring inventors who have product ideas but are unaware of the patent application process and companies wishing to stimulate innovation are members; elected members who submit an accepted thesis are fellows. Seeks to further the interests of individual and employee patentees and inventors; serves as a clearinghouse for members in all areas pertaining to the inventive process. Makes recommendations to government agencies regarding changes to patent laws.

02563

Institute of Payroll Professionals
IPP

PO Box 13514, Solihull, B90 9BP, UK
Tel: 0121 7121000
Fax: 0121 7121001
Email: info@payrollprofession.org
Website: http://www.payrollprofession.org
Members: 5000
Staff: 50
Contact: Karen Thomson, Assoc. Dir.
Fee: £176
Membership Type: full (overseas)
Fee: £149
Membership Type: full (in UK)
Description: Aims to promote excellence in the payroll and pensions professions. Fosters awareness of developments in payroll and pensions. Identifies training needs and provides national and regional exchange of information. Makes available advisory, recruitment and consultancy services.
Formerly: Formerly, Association of Payroll and Superannuation Administrators
Publication: Magazine
Publication title: PAYadvice. Advertisements.

02564

Institute of Pharmacy Management International
IPMI

14 Coronation Way, Bearsden, Glasgow, G61 1DA, UK
Email: howard.mcnulty@ntlworld.com
Website: http://www.ipmi.org.uk
Contact: Howard McNulty, Gen. Sec.
Fee: £70
Membership Type: associate, fellow, regular
Fee: £42
Membership Type: retiree
Description: Members are pharmaceutical chemists, and managers in the hospitals and pharmaceutical industry. Provides research and study of management within the pharmaceutical industry and profession of pharmacy in hospital and community practice with particular reference to the National Health Service pharmaceutical service; sales and marketing activities in connection with OTC medicines and allied healthcare products. Hosts twice in a year conferences on management subjects.
Publication: Journal
Publication title: IPMI Focus

02565

Institute of Physics
IOP

76 Portland Pl., London, W1B 1NT, UK
Tel: 020 74704800
Fax: 020 74704848
Email: physics@iop.org
Website: http://www.iop.org
Members: 36000
Staff: 220
Contact: Dame Jocelyn Bell-Bernell, Pres.
Description: International learned society and professional body for physicists. Chartered by a royal charter to "promote the advancement and dissemination of knowledge and education in the science of pure and applied physics". Represents the physics community to government and other legislative or policy-making bodies. Sets and supports professional standards and qualifications.
Formerly: Formerly, Institute of Physics
Publication: Journal
Publication title: Classical and Quantum Gravity

02566

Institute of Physics and Engineering in Medicine
IPEM

Fairmount House, 230 Tadcaster Rd., York, YO24 1ES, UK
Tel: 01904 610821
Fax: 01904 612279
Email: office@ipem.ac.uk
Website: http://www.ipem.org.uk
Members: 2200
Staff: 5
Contact: C.J. Gibson, Pres.
Description: Works to promote to the public the benefit and the advancement of physics and engineering applied to medicine and biology and to advance public education in the field.
Formerly: Formerly, Biological Engineering Society
Publication: Journal
Publication title: Medical Engineering and Physics
Meetings/Conventions: bimonthly meeting – Exhibits.

02567

Institute of Physics I Women in Physics Group
WIPG

76 Portland Pl., London, W1B 1NT, UK
Tel: 0207 4704800
Fax: 0207 4704848
Website: http://www.iop.org
Members: 34000
Contact: Robert Kirby-Harris, CEO
Description: Open to all female members (including student members) of Institute of Physics. Strives to increase the number of girls studying physics and to raise the status of professional women physicists. Promotes physics as a viable career choice for women in Britain. Encourages networking among members. Disseminates information.
Formerly: Formerly, Women in Physics
Publication: Magazine
Publication title: Compound Semiconductor

02568

Institute of Practitioners in Advertising
IPA

44 Belgrave Sq., London, SW1X 8QS, UK
Tel: 020 7235 7020
Fax: 020 7245 9904
Email: web@ipa.co.uk
Website: http://www.ipa.co.uk
Members: 18665
Staff: 55
Contact: Hamish Pringle, Dir. Gen.
Description: Represents advertising agencies and individuals in Britain. Provides programs in: training, leadership, legal advising, marketing, and public relations. Represents members' interests to government agencies, media, and advertising-related organizations. Conducts research and educational programs.
Formerly: Formerly, Association of British Advertising Agents
Publication: Directory
Publication title: IPA Member Companies List

02569

Institute of Professional Administrators
IPA

6 Graphite Sq., Vauxhall Walk, London, SE11 5EE, UK
Tel: 020 70912606
Fax: 020 70917340
Email: info@inprad.org
Website: http://www.inprad.org
Members: 2000
Staff: 2
Contact: Jenny Hewell, Chief Exec.
Fee: £60
Membership Type: individual
Description: Represents and promotes secretaries, personal assistants, administrators and lecturers. Facilitates and encourages training and continuing professional development of secretaries, to raise the profile of the profession, encourage networking, promote the attainment of excellent standards of secretarial performance and to liaise with secretarial associations worldwide, the media, government, business and educational organizations.
Library Subject: training and development
Library Type: not open to the public
Formerly: Formerly, Institute of Qualified Private Secretaries
Publication: Magazine
Publication title: Career Secretary. Advertisements.

02570

Institute of Professional Soil Scientists
IPSS

Cranfield University, Institute of Professional Soil Scientists, Bldg. 53, Bedfordshire, Cranfield, MK43 0AL, UK
Tel: 01234 752983
Fax: 01234 752970
Email: admin@soils.org.uk
Website: http://www.soilscientist.org
Contact: Rob Askew, Chm.
Fee: £65
Membership Type: fellow
Fee: £60
Membership Type: regular
Description: Professional soil scientists and associated disciplines operating as private consultants or as employees working in a variety of organizations and fields of work. Aims to advance the practice of soil science and allied disciplines within industry and the environment. Members offer services covering soil survey and evaluation; agricultural, horticultural and forestry extension; environmental monitoring, protection and management; soil and water management; research and development; education; overseas assignments and expert witness. Prescribes professional standards and advances the scientific/technical competence of members. Provides an authoritative voice on all matters of interest to its members and the profession.
Publication: Newsletter
Publication title: IPSS Newsletter

02571

Institute of Psychiatry
IOP

c/o Kings College London
De Crespigny Park, Denmark Hill, London, SE5 8AF, UK
Tel: 020 78481000
Email: pr@kcl.ac.uk
Website: http://www.iop.kcl.ac.uk
Staff: 525
Description: Promotes excellence in the research, development and teaching of psychiatry and its allied subjects and to apply and disseminate this knowledge through the development of treatment for the relief of suffering.
Library Type: not open to the public

02572

Institute of Psychosexual Medicine
IPM

12 Chandos St., Cavendish Sq., London, W1G 9DR, UK
Tel: 020 75800631
Email: admin@ipm.org.uk
Website: http://www.ipm.org.uk
Contact: Claudine Domoney, Chair
Description: Medical practitioners only. Seeks to promote the study and practice of psychosexual medicine through seminar training and research.

02573

Institute of Public Loss Assessors

Hill House, 10 Ye Corner, Watford, Bushey, WD19 4BS, UK
Tel: 01923 225201
Fax: 01923 818657
Website: http://www.lossassessors.org
Members: 100
Description: Represents professionals actively engaged in Loss Assessing.

02574

Institute of Quarrying - England

7 Regent St., Nottingham, NG1 5BS, UK
Tel: 0115 9453880
Fax: 0115 9484035
Email: mail@quarrying.org
Website: http://www.quarrying.org
Members: 3000
Contact: David Sharman, Pres.
Fee: £80
Membership Type: fellow
Fee: £75
Membership Type: associate, individual

Description: Individuals in 70 countries employed in the quarrying and related industries. Promotes education and training in order to improve all aspects of quarry operation and business management. Works to enhance recognition of professional managers in the quarrying industry. Organizes courses and field trips to factories, plants, and quarries and occasional international study tours. Conducts examinations.
Publication: Newsletter
Publication title: Quarry Management. Advertisements.
Meetings/Conventions: annual conference – Exhibits.

02575
Institute of Race Relations
IRR
2-6 Leeke St., London, WC1X 9HS, UK
Tel: 020 78370041
Fax: 020 72780623
Email: info@irr.org.uk
Website: http://www.irr.org.uk
Members: 200
Staff: 5
Contact: Colin Prescod, Chm.
Description: Promotes good race relations. Encourages research and educational work. Supports solidarity committees; services organizations opposing racism.
Publication: Bulletin
Publication title: European Race

02576
Institute of Revenues, Rating and Valuation
IRRV
41 Doughty St., London, WC1N 2LF, UK
Tel: 020 76918973
Fax: 020 78312048
Email: membership@irrv.org.uk
Website: http://www.irrv.net/index.ASP
Members: 5000
Staff: 31
Contact: David Magor, CEO
Description: Local government revenues, rating, benefit and valuation officers in local government, valuation office officials and private practice valuers. To develop the knowledge of professionals involved in the levying, collection and administration of local revenues, the valuation of property etc. Organizes national and international conferences. Advises its members on technical matters and responds to government proposals in its sphere of interest.
Publication: Books
Publication title: Distress Law and Practice

02577
Institute of Risk Management
IRM
6 Lloyd's Ave., London, EC3N 3AX, UK
Tel: 020 77099808
Fax: 020 77090716
Email: enquiries@theirm.org
Website: http://www.theirm.org
Members: 2000
Staff: 13
Contact: Steve Fowler, CEO
Fee: £85
Membership Type: diploma student, affiliate, specialist (with low GDP)
Description: Serves as the risk management industry's professional body. Seeks to provide flexible routes to professional qualifications and training in risk management. Strives to provide opportunities to gain an internationally recognized qualification while allowing people to develop skills at their own place and at their own pace. Promotes technical and ethical good practice.
Library Subject: business organization and finance, risk analysis, risk control, corporate risk management, risk financing, occupational health and safety, insurance liability exposures, health sector risk management, local authority risk management
Library Type: reference
Publication: Magazine
Publication title: InfoRM. Advertisements.

02578
Institute of Road Safety Officers
IRSO
Pin Point, Rosslyn Crescent, Horrow, HA1 2SU, UK
Tel: 0870 0104442
Fax: 0870 3337772
Email: irso@dbda.co.uk
Website: http://www.irso.org.uk
Members: 570
Contact: Emma Norton, Membership Off.
Fee: £55
Membership Type: regular
Fee: £44
Membership Type: associate
Description: Provides recognition of the professional standing of road safety officers by accrediting qualification courses and being involved in vocational training. Provides an open forum for all members to discuss road safety matters.
Publication: Journal
Publication title: Inroads. Advertisements.

02579
Institute of Roofing
IOR
Roofing House, 31 Worship St., London, EC2A 2DX, UK
Tel: 020 74483858
Fax: 020 74483195
Email: info@instituteofroofing.org
Website: http://www.instituteofroofing.org
Members: 1100
Staff: 2
Contact: Mike Harris, Chm.
Description: Professional qualifications for all sectors of the roofing industry namely contracting, manufacturing, and stocking, by examination or assessed vocational experience. Promotes and stimulates the improvement of the technical and general knowledge of individuals engaged in management in the roofing industry; confers a recognized status on individuals in the industry and conducts training by the management of courses, seminars, lectures work visits, study tours.
Publication: Magazine
Publication title: Bulletin
Meetings/Conventions: periodic seminar

02580
Institute of Sales and Marketing Management
ISMM
1 Harrier Ct., Lower Woodside, Bedfordshire, Luton, LU1 4DQ, UK
Tel: 01582 840001
Fax: 01582 849142
Email: sales@ismm.co.uk
Website: http://www.ismm.co.uk
Members: 12000
Staff: 12
Contact: Susan Challenger, Contact
Fee: £27
Membership Type: direct debit
Fee: £98
Membership Type: direct debit
Description: Open to all sales and marketing professionals, from students to main board directors. Promotes the prestige and integrity of the sales and marketing professions. Makes legal, recruitment and consultancy services available to its members and, through publications, supplies market intelligence and sales information.
Publication: Magazine
Publication title: Sales & Marketing Professional. Advertisements.
Meetings/Conventions: Successful Selling – annual convention – Exhibits.

02581
Institute of Science and Technology
IST
Kingfisher House, 90 Rockingham St., Sheffield, S1 4EB, UK
Tel: 0114 2763197
Fax: 0114 2726354
Email: office@istonline.org.uk
Website: http://www.istonline.org.uk
Members: 1500
Contact: John D. Robinson, Chm.
Fee: £50
Membership Type: fellow
Fee: £39
Membership Type: regular
Description: Fellows, Members (Corporate Grades) Associates, affiliates. Grades awarded by examination standard and experience and thesis. Works in education or research, e.g., universities, colleges of further education, schools, hospitals, agricultural establishments with a few in industry. Provides own qualifications in analytical chemistry techniques, biochemical techniques, microbiological techniques, animal sciences techniques HPLC and gas chromatography. Makes available training support packages for science technicians.

02582
Institute of Scientific and Technical Communicators
ISTC
Airport House, Purley Way, Croydon, CR0 0XZ, UK
Tel: 020 82534506
Fax: 020 82534510
Email: istc@istc.org.uk
Website: http://www.istc.org.uk
Members: 1500
Staff: 1
Contact: Simon Butler, Pres.
Fee: £84
Membership Type: fellow
Fee: £63
Membership Type: associate, junior
Description: Technical authors, technical editors, illustrators, publication managers, freelance and contract technical writers. Maintains professional codes of practice for members, who are employed in all branches of scientific and technical communication throughout industry, commerce, IT, finance, education and the

public sector. Provides a forum for exchange of views and disseminates information through local meetings, publications, an annual conference and lectures.
Publication: Journal
Publication title: Communicator. Advertisements.

02583
Institute of Sheet Metal Engineering
ISME
c/o Bill Pinfold, Honorary Sec.
102 Richmond Dr., Perton, Wolverhampton, WV6 6EU, UK
Tel: 07891 499146
Email: ismesec@gmail.com
Website: http://www.isme.org.uk
Contact: Dilwyn Gurney, Chm.
Fee: £85
Membership Type: fellow
Fee: £60
Membership Type: individual
Description: Aims to promote the science of working and using sheet metal. Provides opportunities for people to exchange ideas and information. Develops closer co-operation between industries, universities and research establishments. Encourages the development of sheet metal working skills through the annual Sheet Metal Skills Competition.
Publication: Newsletter
Publication title: Oracle

02584
Institute of Sport and Recreation Management
ISRM
Sir John Beckwith Center for Sport, Loughborough University, 3 Oakwood Dr., Loughborough, LE11 3QF, UK
Tel: 01509 226474
Fax: 01509 226475
Email: info@isrm.co.uk
Website: http://www.isrm.co.uk
Members: 4900
Staff: 15
Contact: Sean Holt, Chief Exec.
Fee: £110
Membership Type: fellow, diploma, full, associate
Fee: £245
Membership Type: corporate affiliate
Description: Full membership for those who have passed the Sport and Recreation Management Certificate. Diploma membership for those members who pass the Diploma Examination. Provides approved industry led education and training programmes leading to recognised qualifications in the management and operation of sports and recreation facilities. Associated activities include annual conference and exhibition, advisory and consultancy services, and publications.
Publication: Reports
Publication title: The Business of Swimming

02585
Institute of Spring Technology
IST
Henry St., Sheffield, S3 7EQ, UK
Tel: 0114 2760771
Fax: 0114 2527997
Email: ist@ist.org.uk
Website: http://www.ist.org.uk
Contact: Julie Bull, Contact
Fee: £740
Membership Type: spring user
Fee: £780
Membership Type: machinery/consumable supplier
Description: Manufacturers of testing and special purpose equipment to the spring industry. Promotes the industry and its products through information and technical support. Maintains accredited testing laboratory.
Formerly: Formerly, Spring Research Association

02586
Institute of the Motor Industry
IMI
Fanshaws, Brickendon, Hertford, SG13 8PQ, UK
Tel: 01992 511521
Fax: 01992 511548
Email: imi@motor.org.uk
Website: http://www.motor.org.uk
Members: 25000
Staff: 38
Contact: Steve Nash, Pres.
Fee: £102
Membership Type: fellow
Fee: £68.8
Membership Type: individual
Description: Professional body for individuals employed in the motor industry and associated sectors. Performs the role of promoting and recognizing professionalism in the motor industry. Also acts as an awarding body for a wide variety of qualifications including National Vocational qualifications (NVQ), learning programmes, and sales and management qualifications.
Publication: Magazine
Publication title: Motor Industry Management. Advertisements.

02587
Institute of Trade Mark Attorneys
ITMA
c/o Canterbury House
2-6 Sydenham Rd., Surrey, Croydon, CR0 9XE, UK
Tel: 020 86862052
Fax: 020 86805723
Email: tm@itma.org.uk
Website: http://www.itma.org.uk
Members: 1700
Staff: 8
Contact: Gillian Deas, Pres.
Fee: £194
Membership Type: student
Fee: £270
Membership Type: affiliate
Description: Exists to protect the interests of its members, and, by extension those of trade mark proprietors; it acts as an information exchange, and arranges meetings and conferences on subjects of interest to all those concerned with trade marks. Lobbies for changes in trademark law.

02588
Institute of Transactional Analysis
ITA
Broadway House, 149-151 St. Neots Rd., Hardwick, Cambridge, CB23 7QJ, UK
Tel: 01954 212468
Fax: 01954 212468
Email: admin@ita.org.uk
Website: http://www.ita.org.uk
Staff: 1
Contact: Judith Macroff, Admin.
Fee: £47
Membership Type: regular
Fee: £64
Membership Type: student
Description: Professional members, qualified to teach and supervise the practice of TA. Certified TA analysts and trainee TA analysts. Also those interested in TA. Promotes and maintains the practice of TA, sets and maintains standards of professional practice and training.
Publication: Newsletter
Publication title: ITA News

02589
Institute of Translation and Interpreting
ITI
Fortuna House, S 5th St., Milton Keynes, MK9 2PQ, UK
Tel: 01908 325250
Fax: 01908 325259
Email: info@iti.org.uk
Website: http://www.iti.org.uk
Members: 2800
Staff: 6
Contact: Pamela Mayorcas, Chair
Fee: £216
Membership Type: qualified - MITI, corporate (education)
Fee: £76
Membership Type: associate
Description: Professional translators and interpreters; translation companies; universities; commercial firms (translation and interpreting services buyers); students; lecturers. Promotes professional standards, offers guidance and training to those wishing to enter the profession, and advice to users of translation and interpreting services. Primary aim is to promote the profession and thereby ensure improved conditions of work.
Library Subject: languages
Library Type: not open to the public
Publication: Proceedings
Publication title: Conference Proceedings - Online

02590
Institute of Transport Administration
IoTA
The Old Studio, 25 Greenfield Rd., Bedfordshire, Westoning, MK45 5JD, UK
Tel: 01525 634940
Fax: 01525 750016
Email: director@iota.org.uk
Website: http://www.iota.org.uk
Contact: Alan Whittington, Deputy Pres.
Fee: £36.25
Membership Type: associate (overseas)
Fee: £15
Membership Type: student (UK and overseas)
Description: Persons engaged in transportation management and administration of transportation via air, land, rail, or sea in 25 countries. Works to formulate standards of training, education, and experience required for proper administration and registration within the transportation industry. Encourages exchange of information among members. Offers educational programs; grants diplomas by examination. Compiles statistics.
Library Subject: general transportation
Library Type: reference
Publication: Book
Publication title: Rule
Meetings/Conventions: annual conference – Exhibits.

02591

Institute of Travel and Tourism

ITT

PO Box 217, Hertfordshire, Ware, SG12 8WY, UK
Tel: 0844 4995653
Fax: 0844 4995654
Email: enquiries@itt.co.uk
Website: http://www.itt.co.uk
Members: 3125
Staff: 7
Contact: Steven Freudmann, Chm.
Fee: £145
Membership Type: fellow
Fee: £125
Membership Type: ordinary
Description: Represents senior personnel in the travel industry. Serves as the professional body for the travel and tourism industry. Offers membership to appropriately qualified individuals.

02592

Institute of Trichologists

IT

24 Langroyd Rd., London, SW17 7PL, UK
Tel: 0845 6044657
Fax: 01722 741380
Email: admin@trichologists.org.uk
Website: http://www.trichologists.org.uk
Members: 240
Staff: 2
Contact: Marilyn Sherlock, Chair
Description: Promotes study, research, and application in the treatment and care of human scalp and hair. Provides scientific training of individuals qualified to advise and offer treatment of hair and scalp disorders and serves as an examining body for students of trichology. Provides centers for clinical study. Maintains Scalp and Hair Hospital where students conduct clinical observations and gain practical experience. Sponsors charitable program; maintains speakers' bureau.

02593

Institute of Vehicle Recovery

IVR

Bignell House, Top Fl., Horton Rd., Middlesex, West Drayton, UB7 8EJ, UK
Tel: 01895 436426
Fax: 01895 436412
Email: mail@theivr.com
Website: http://www.theivr.com
Members: 431
Contact: Mac Hobbs, Chm.
Fee: £49
Membership Type: regular
Description: Persons normally active in vehicle recovery work. Promotes training and professionalism in the vehicle recovery industry.

02594

Institute of Vitreous Enamellers

IVE

39 Sweetbriar Way, Heath Hayes, Staffordshire, Cannock, WS12 2US, UK
Tel: 01543 450596
Fax: 08700 941237
Email: info@ive.org.uk
Website: http://www.ive.org.uk
Members: 112
Staff: 1
Contact: M.A. Collins, Pres.
Fee: £67
Membership Type: individual
Fee: £545
Membership Type: company
Description: Promotes the vitreous enameller industry. Provides publication, technical support, education and training.
Library Subject: vitreous enamel
Library Type: reference
Publication: Book
Publication title: Atlas of Enamel Defects

02595

Institute of Water

4 Carlton Ct., Team Valley, Gateshead, NE11 0AZ, UK
Tel: 0191 4220088
Fax: 0191 4220087
Email: info@instituteofwater.org.uk
Website: http://www.instituteofwater.org.uk
Members: 2000
Staff: 4
Contact: Louise Wright, Office Mgr.
Fee: £85
Membership Type: associate
Fee: £95
Membership Type: corporate
Description: Offers members the opportunity to attend seminars, conferences, technical visits and weekend schools. Provides registration as Chartered Engineer, Incorporate Engineer, Chartered Environmentalist and Engineering Technician.
Publication: Journal
Publication title: Institute of Water Journal. Advertisements.

02596

Institute of Welfare

Newland House, 2nd Fl., PO Box 5570, Stourbridge, DY8 9BA, UK
Tel: 020 88669787
Email: info@instituteofwelfare.co.uk
Website: http://www.instituteofwelfare.co.uk
Members: 3000
Staff: 5
Contact: Cary L. Cooper, Pres.
Fee: £50
Membership Type: regular
Fee: £25
Membership Type: retired
Description: Registered Professional Welfare Officers and others engaged in the provision of Welfare Services and students studying the Certificate and Diploma in Welfare Studies UK wide. Aims to promote education and training for persons desirous of attaining a career in welfare and its related issues. Maintains and promotes professional standards among practitioners and students. Registers professional Welfare Officers.
Formerly: Formerly, Institute of Welfare Officers
Publication: Newspaper
Publication title: Welfare World. Advertisements.

02597

Institute of Wood Science

IWSc

Carpenters' Hall, 3rd Fl. D, 1 Throgmorton Ave., London, EC2N 2BY, UK
Tel: 07256 2700
Fax: 07256 2701
Email: info@iwsc.org.uk
Website: http://www.iwsc.org.uk
Members: 1735
Staff: 1
Contact: Jim Lumsden, Contact
Fee: £83
Membership Type: fellow
Fee: £47
Membership Type: affiliate
Description: Fellows, associates, members, certificated members, student members. Works to advance and encourage the scientific, technical, practical and general knowledge of timber and wood-based materials.
Library Subject: timber technology
Library Type: not open to the public
Publication: Journal
Publication title: Journal of the Institute of Wood Science

02598

Institution of Agricultural Engineers

IAgrE

The Bullock Bldg., University Way, Cranfield, Bedford, MK45 4FH, UK
Tel: 01234 750876
Fax: 01234 751319
Email: secretary@iagre.org
Website: http://www.iagre.org
Members: 2000
Staff: 5
Contact: Christopher R. Whetnall, Chief Exec./Sec.
Fee: £108
Membership Type: regular
Fee: £40-84
Membership Type: associate (based on membership)
Description: Represents scientists, technologists, engineers, managers and students working in the land-based sector.
Library Subject: biosystems engineering
Library Type: by appointment only
Publication: Journal
Publication title: Landwards. Advertisements.
Meetings/Conventions: meeting

02599

Institution of Analysts and Programmers

IAP

Charles House, 36 Culmington Rd., London, W13 9NH, UK
Tel: 020 85672118
Website: http://www.iap.org.uk
Members: 3000
Contact: Michael Ryan, Dir. Gen.
Fee: £60
Membership Type: licentiate
Fee: £70
Membership Type: graduate
Description: Consists of professionals engaged in computer programming or systems analysis for commerce, industry or the public service. Aims to assist members to advance in their profession, and to secure public recognition of their professional status. Has four grades of membership, and members are entitled to use designatory letters as a public assurance of their experience and professional status.

02600

Institution of Chemical Engineers IChemE

Davis Bldg., Railway Terr., Rugby, CV21 3HQ, UK
Tel: 01788 578214
Fax: 01788 560833
Email: onlineassistance@icheme.org
Website: http://cms.icheme.org
Members: 27000
Staff: 85
Contact: Desmond King, Pres.
Fee: £20
Membership Type: undergraduate student
Fee: £40
Membership Type: professional
Description: Chemical engineers united to promote and develop the science of chemical engineering and to further scientific and economic development and application of manufacturing processes in which chemical and physical changes of materials are involved. Promotes research into chemical engineering and communicates with governments on behalf of industry; compiles statistics.
Library Subject: chemical engineering
Library Type: reference
Publication: Magazine
Publication title: The Chemical Engineer. Advertisements.

02601

Institution of Civil Engineers ICE

One Great George St., Westminster, London, SW1P 3AA, UK
Tel: 020 72227722
Email: secretariat@ice.org.uk
Website: http://www.ice.org.uk/homepage/index.asp
Members: 80000
Contact: Paul Jowitt, Pres.
Fee: £325
Membership Type: fellow (resident within UK)
Fee: £250
Membership Type: regular, companion, associate (resident within UK)
Description: Professional organization of chartered civil engineers in England. Sponsors competitions. Promotes civil engineering.
Library Subject: civil engineering, related sciences
Library Type: reference
Formerly: Absorbed, Society of Civil Engineering Technicians
Publication: Journal
Publication title: Civil Engineering. Advertisements.

02602

Institution of Diagnostic Engineers IDE

16 Thistlewood Rd., Wakefield, WF1 3HH, UK
Tel: 0192 4821000
Fax: 0192 4821200
Email: admin@diagnosticengineers.org
Website: http://www.diagnosticengineers.org
Members: 9164
Contact: Karen Seiles, Office Mgr./Admin.
Fee: £45
Membership Type: individual
Fee: £18.5
Membership Type: retired
Description: Aims to be of direct, immediate and positive assistance to all who are concerned with the servicing and maintenance of machines and structures, or who have a concern for the well-being and whole-life effectiveness of all industrial systems.
Publication: Journal
Publication title: Diagnostic Engineering. Advertisements.

02603

Institution of Diesel and Gas Turbine Engineers IDGTE

Bedford Heights, Manton Ln., Bedford, MK41 7PH, UK
Tel: 01234 214340
Fax: 01234 355493
Email: enquiries@idgte.org
Website: http://www.idgte.org
Members: 700
Staff: 4
Contact: Peter Tottman, Dir. Gen.
Fee: £31
Membership Type: student (UK & Europe)
Fee: £79
Membership Type: associate (UK & Europe)
Description: Diesel and gas turbine engineers, manufacturers, consultants and operators. Provides a forum for exchanging information on gas turbines, diesel, gas, and dual-fuel reciprocating engines CHP technologies and practices. Regular discussion meetings are arranged and the paper's subsequent oral and written contributions are published in the transactions of the institution. Seminars, conferences and exhibitions are also arranged.
Library Type: open to the public
Formerly: Formerly, Diesel Engineers and Users Association
Publication: Journal
Publication title: Power Engineer. Advertisements.

02604

Institution of Economic Development IED

PO Box 796, Northampton, NN4 9TS, UK
Tel: 01604 874613
Fax: 01604 705359
Email: info@ied.co.uk
Website: http://www.ied.co.uk
Members: 1000
Contact: John Lockett, Business Development Dir.
Fee: £125
Membership Type: fellow
Fee: £110
Membership Type: full
Description: Economic development practitioners in both public and private sector organizations. Committed to demonstrating the value of economic development work for local and regional communities and to the pursuit of best practice in economic development and to the attainment of the highest standards of professional training and competence.
Publication: Journal

02605

Institution of Engineering and Technology IET

Michael Faraday House, Herts, Stevenage, SG1 2AY, UK
Tel: 01438 313311
Fax: 01438 765526
Email: postmaster@theiet.org
Website: http://www.theiet.org
Members: 150000
Staff: 450
Contact: Nigel Fine, Chief Exec./Sec.
Fee: £127
Membership Type: fellow
Fee: £117
Membership Type: associate
Description: Individuals in 121 countries united to promote the advancement of electrical and electronic science and engineering. Represents the profession of electrical and electronic engineering and related sciences; sets qualification standards for electrical, electronics, and software engineers; accredits industrial training schemes and courses at universities, polytechnics, and colleges; assists in the formulation of safety standards for the installation of electrical and electronic equipment. Operates schools liaison service, providing information and advice to young people; provides career information and advice to members. Conducts lectures, meetings, conferences, and residential vacation schools; sponsors competitions and bestows scholarships, grants, and prizes.
Library Subject: technical and commercial aspects of electrotechnology, computer science, control
Library Type: reference
Formerly: Formerly, Institution of Electronic and Radio Engineers
Publication: Magazine
Publication title: Computing and Control Engineering. Advertisements.

02606

Institution of Engineering Designers IED

Courtleigh, Westbury Leigh, Wiltshire, Westbury, BA13 3TA, UK
Tel: 01373 822801
Fax: 01373 858085
Email: libby@ied.org.uk
Website: http://www.ied.org.uk
Members: 5500
Staff: 7
Contact: Libby Brodhurst, Sec./Chief Exec.
Fee: £136
Membership Type: fellow
Fee: £121
Membership Type: ordinary, graduate, diplomate (six years from graduation)
Description: Persons working in the field of engineering design as designers, managers or educators. fellows (FIED), members (MIED), are corporate members, Associates (AIED) and Competent Design Associates (CDAIED) are non-corporate, while students and diplomates may join as affiliate members. Acts as a professional body for designers who operate in widely diverse fields of engineering practice, including product, domestic appliance, jog and tool, special purpose machine, electro-mechanical, piping, design etc., in industry, in consultative practice and in education.
Library Subject: engineering design, engineering
Library Type: not open to the public
Publication: Journal
Publication title: Engineering Designer. Advertisements.

02607

Institution of Environmental Sciences IES

34 Grosvenor Gardens, 2nd Fl., London, SW1W 0DH, UK
Tel: 020 77305516
Fax: 020 77305519
Email: enquiries@ies-uk.org.uk
Website: http://www.ies-uk.org.uk
Members: 800
Contact: Phil Holmes, Honorary Sec.
Fee: £65
Membership Type: associate
Fee: £95
Membership Type: fellowship
Description: Professional and educational institutions, industrial companies, environmental consultants and agencies and college and graduate students (overseas members from many countries). Seeks to increase public interest, awareness, and involvement in the problems of world environment and environmental sciences. Promotes interdisciplinary studies of the environment and educational research in related sciences. Provides advisory services to schools, agencies, libraries, and the public on environmental matters. Conducts seminars.
Publication: Journal
Publication title: The Environmental Scientist. Advertisements.

02608

Institution of Fire Engineers - England IFE

London Rd., Gloucestershire, Moreton-in-Marsh, GL56 0RH, UK
Tel: 01608 812580
Fax: 01608 812581
Email: info@ife.org.uk
Website: http://www.ife.org.uk
Members: 11000
Staff: 8
Contact: Louise Craig, CEO
Fee: £126
Membership Type: fellow
Fee: £82
Membership Type: ordinary
Description: Members are involved in all areas of the fire world operating in both the public and private sectors. Aims to promote and improve the science and practice of fire extinction, fire prevention and fire engineering.
Publication: Journal
Publication title: Fire Risk Management. Advertisements.

02609

Institution of Gas Engineers and Managers IGEM

IGEM House, High St., Derbyshire, Kegworth, DE74 2DA, UK
Fax: 01509 678198
Email: general@igem.org.uk
Website: http://www.igem.org.uk
Members: 5000
Staff: 12
Contact: Jeremy Bending, Pres.
Fee: £195
Membership Type: fellow
Fee: £179
Membership Type: chartered
Description: Provides technical and managerial foundation for a safe and efficient gas industry.
Library Subject: gas engineering and technology from the 19th century onward
Library Type: open to the public
Publication: Journal
Publication title: Gas International, Engineering and Management. Advertisements.

02610

Institution of Lighting Engineers ILE

Regent House, Regent Pl., Rugby, CV21 2PN, UK
Tel: 01788 576492
Fax: 01788 540145
Email: info@ile.org.uk
Website: http://www.ile.org.uk
Members: 2200
Contact: Chris Hardy, Pres.
Fee: £149
Membership Type: fellow
Fee: £125
Membership Type: regular
Description: Promotes advancements in the science and art of efficient lighting. Facilitates the exchange of information and ideas.
Library Subject: all forms of lighting
Library Type: reference
Publication: Journal
Publication title: Lighting Journal. Advertisements.

02611

Institution of Mechanical Engineers IMechE

1 Birdcage Walk, Westminster, London, SW1H 9JJ, UK
Tel: 020 72227899
Fax: 020 72224557
Email: enquiries@imeche.org
Website: http://www.imeche.org
Members: 80000
Staff: 180
Contact: Stephen Tetlow, Chief Exec.
Fee: £176.5
Membership Type: individual
Fee: £210
Membership Type: fellow
Description: Mechanical and mechanical related engineers working in industry, academia, government departments, research associations and representative of all levels of responsibility from chief executive to student. Involved in the education, training and professional development of engineers, acting as an international centre for technology transfer in mechanical engineering. It is active in professional ethics and representation, collaborative activities with government and industry, provision of services to its members and provision for the future of the profession.
Library Subject: mechanical engineering, automotive, rail, power, manufacturing, mathematics, bioengineering, tribology, and aerospace
Library Type: open to the public
Publication: Magazine
Publication title: Automotive Engineer. Advertisements.

02612

Institution of Occupational Safety and Health IOSH

The Grange, Highfield Dr., Leicestershire, Wigston, LE18 1NN, UK
Tel: 0116 2573100
Fax: 0116 2573101
Email: enquiries@iosh.co.uk
Website: http://www.iosh.co.uk
Members: 35000
Staff: 85
Contact: John Holden, Pres.
Fee: £78
Membership Type: affiliate
Fee: £94
Membership Type: graduate, technician
Description: Represents safety and health professionals. Promotes excellence in the discipline and practice of occupational safety and health; supports members by providing facilities to maintain and enhance professional skills and knowledge; offers a range of certified health and safety, risk management and environmental management training, designed to be delivered by members.
Publication: Journal
Publication title: Policy and Practice in Health and Safety

02613

Institution of Railway Signal Engineers IRSE

4th Fl., 1 Birdcage Walk, Westminster, London, SW1H 9JJ, UK
Tel: 020 78081180
Fax: 020 78081196
Email: hq@irse.org
Website: http://www.irse.org
Members: 3900
Staff: 8
Contact: Colin Porter, Chief Exec./Sec.
Fee: £83
Membership Type: accredited technician, associate, student, ordinary (all ages)
Fee: £41.5
Membership Type: accredited technician, associate, student, ordinary (concession)
Description: Membership from railways and manufacturers of railway signaling and telecommunications apparatus worldwide. Encourages the advancement of the science and practice of railway signaling and telecommunications by means of discussion enquiry research and experiments. The diffusion of knowledge, regarding railway signaling by means of lectures, publications and otherwise.
Library Subject: railway signal engineering and control systems
Library Type: not open to the public
Publication: Reports
Publication title: Technical Reports

02614
Institution of Structural Engineers
IStructE

11 Upper Belgrave St., London, SW1X 8BH, UK
Tel: 020 72354535
Fax: 020 72354294
Website: http://www.istructe.org/Pages/Default.aspx
Members: 21000
Contact: Martin Powell, Chief Exec.
Fee: £44-133
Membership Type: student
Fee: £268
Membership Type: chartered
Description: Represents structural engineers in 105 countries. Promotes the advancement of structural engineering through continuing professional and technical development programs. Holds charitable programs; sponsors competitions. Maintains committees and task groups.
Library Subject: structural engineering
Library Type: lending
Formerly: Formerly, Concrete Institute
Publication: Journal
Publication title: Structural Engineer. Advertisements.
Meetings/Conventions: periodic conference

02615
Insulated Render and Cladding Association
INCA

Royal London House, 22-25 Finsbury Sq., London, EC2A 1DX, UK
Tel: 0844 2490040
Fax: 0844 2490042
Email: info@inca-ltd.org.uk
Website: http://www.inca-ltd.org.uk
Members: 57
Staff: 10
Fee: £3150
Membership Type: system designer
Fee: £1050
Membership Type: associate
Description: System designers, component manufacturers, contractors and others with an interest in external wall insulation. Aims to establish good technical, ethical and legal standards for the industry; to give impartial advice and to promote the concept and advantages of external wall insulation, as designed and applied by recognized member companies; and to represent the industry when liaising with government, local authorities and other bodies.
Formerly: Formerly, External Wall Insulation Association
Publication: Handbook
Publication title: Andy Swan Awards Yearbook. Advertisements.

02616
Insurance Institute of London
IIL

20 Aldermanbury, 5th Fl., London, EC2V 7HY, UK
Tel: 0207 6001343
Fax: 0207 6006857
Email: iil.london@cii.co.uk
Website: http://www.iilondon.co.uk
Members: 15000
Contact: Grahame Millwater, Pres.
Description: Professional men and women in the insurance industry in London. Aims to raise the levels of professional knowledge of those working in insurance in London and to assist members in their career development and to support and reinforce the role and work of the Chartered Insurance Institute.
Publication: Journal
Publication title: New London Journal
Meetings/Conventions: Lecture Programme – weekly lecture

02617
Insurers' Company

Insurers Hall, 20 Aldermanbury, London, EC2V 7HY, UK
Tel: 020 76004006
Fax: 020 79720153
Email: enquiries@wci.org.uk
Website: http://www.wci.org.uk
Contact: Graeme King, Master
Description: Provides social intercourse and mutual information among members of the business.

02618
Intellect

Russell Square House, 10-12 Russell Sq., London, WC1B 5EE, UK
Tel: 020 73312000
Fax: 020 73312040
Email: info@intellectuk.org
Website: http://www.intellectuk.org
Members: 800
Staff: 60
Contact: John Higgins, Dir. Gen.
Description: Covers manufacturers of radio and television receivers, video recorders, and all consumer electronic products. Aims to promote, encourage, foster, develop and protect the radio and electronic equipment manufacturing industry and all ancillary and allied trades in the United Kingdom.
Formerly: Formerly, British Radio and Electronic Equipment Manufacturers' Association
Publication: Newsletter
Publication title: The Bulletin

02619
Intelligent Building Group
IBG

Riverside Bldg., County Hall, London, SE1 7PB, UK
Tel: 020 79289150
Fax: 0845 3307267
Email: administrator@ibgroup.org.uk
Website: http://www.ibgroup.org.uk
Members: 145
Fee: £100
Membership Type: associate
Description: Represents leading professionals from all sectors of the industry that aims to increase contacts, share knowledge and propose solutions for the sustainable advancement of the built environment.
Formerly: Formerly, European Intelligent Building Group
Publication title: IB Focus

02620
Intelligent Transport Systems - Arab

2nd Fl., 145-157 St. John St., London, EC1V 4PY, UK
Tel: 0207 5537103
Fax: 0207 1609388
Email: mail@its-arab.org
Website: http://www.itsarab.org
Contact: Abdullah Al-Mogbel, Pres.
Fee: £500
Membership Type: individual
Fee: £7000
Membership Type: organization, corporate
Description: Promotes partnership between transport professionals, decision makers, research/academic institutions and industry. Facilitates the deployment and development of Intelligent Transport System (ITS) technologies. Enhances the safety, security and sustainability of transport environments. Analyzes the current state of transport systems and develops a long-term ITS strategy plan.

02621
Intelligent Transport Systems - United Kingdom

Ste. 312, Tower Bridge Business Centre, 46-48 E Smithfield, London, E1W 1AW, UK
Tel: 020 77093003
Fax: 020 77093007
Email: mailbox@its-uk.org.uk
Website: http://www.its-uk.org.uk
Contact: Jennie Martin, Sec. Gen.
Fee: £450
Membership Type: associate
Fee: £1350
Membership Type: corporate
Description: Promotes the benefits of Intelligent Transport Systems (ITS). Encourages mutual understanding and increases knowledge and awareness of ITS. Provides a forum to discuss issues, standards, legislation and new technology in transportation systems.

02622
Intensive Care Society
ICS

Churchill House, 35 Red Lion Sq., London, WC1R 4SG, UK
Tel: 020 72804350
Fax: 020 72804369
Email: pauline@ics.ac.uk
Website: http://www.ics.ac.uk
Members: 2400
Staff: 3
Contact: Pauline Kemp, Hd. Sec.
Fee: £100
Membership Type: ordinary, trainee (inside UK)
Fee: £85
Membership Type: overseas
Description: Represents medical and scientific specialists in the field of intensive care. Seeks to provide the scientific and professional basis necessary for the research activities related to intensive care issues, and to make advice and information available to interested parties. Promotes communication among related organizations.
Publication: Journal
Publication title: Journal of the Intensive Care Society. Advertisements.

02623
Interact Worldwide

Studio 325, Highgate Studios, 5-7 Cranwood St., London, EC1V 9LH, UK
Tel: 0300 7778500
Fax: 0300 7779778
Email: volunteer@interactworldwide.org
Website: http://www.interactworldwide.org
Staff: 20
Contact: Marie Staunton, Chief Exec.

Description: Works to build support for and implement programmes which enable marginalized people to exercise their right to sexual and reproductive health.
Formerly: Formerly, Population Countdown

02624
Interights, the International Centre for the Legal Protection of Human Rights
Lancaster House, 33 Islington High St., London, N1 9LH, UK
Tel: 020 72783230
Fax: 020 72784334
Email: ir@interights.org
Website: http://www.interights.org
Staff: 23
Contact: Jeremy McBride, Chm.
Description: Attorneys and other individuals with an interest in human rights. Seeks to protect and expand the rights of the individual by strengthening their statutory underpinning worldwide. Drafts model human rights legislation and statutes; provides legal representation for individuals and groups appearing before international human rights tribunals; sponsors public education programs.
Publication: Report
Publication title: Commonwealth Human Rights Law Digest

02625
Interim Management Association IMA
15 Welbeck St., London, W1G 9XT, UK
Email: scott.pendry@rec.uk.com
Website: http://www.interimmanagement.uk.com
Members: 27
Contact: James Fallan, Treas.
Description: Recruitment consultancies specializing in interim managers for industry and commerce at senior level.
Formerly: Formerly, Association of Temporary and Interim Executive Secretaries
Publication: Directory
Publication title: Annual Guide

Internacional Socialista
see Socialist International

02626
International Academy of Matrimonial Lawyers IAML
2 Yew Tree Close, Hatfield Peverel, Chelmsford, Essex, CM3 2SG, UK
Tel: 01245 380010
Fax: 01245 550397
Email: donna.goddard@iaml.org
Website: http://www.iaml.org
Members: 560
Contact: Donna Goddard, Exec. Dir.
Fee: £210
Membership Type: regular
Fee: £375
Membership Type: regular
Description: Works to improve international family law practice worldwide.
Publication title: Certified List

02627
International Accounting Standards Board IASB
c/o IFRS Foundation
30 Cannon St., London, EC4M 6XH, UK
Tel: 020 72466410
Fax: 020 72466411
Email: info@ifrs.org
Website: http://www.ifrs.org
Members: 143
Staff: 21
Contact: Tommaso Padoa-Schioppa, Chm.
Description: Professional accountancy bodies representing more than 2,000,000 accountants in 104 countries. Aims to formulate and publish, in the public interest, International Accounting Standards to be observed in the presentation of audited financial statements and to promote their worldwide acceptance and observance. (International Accounting Standards are statements regulating the representation and disclosure of figures within financial statements; such standards do not nullify local laws and may not be in accordance with local legislature.) Works for the improvement and harmonization of regulations, accounting standards, and procedures relating to the presentation of financial statements. Provides standards developed in response to the needs and problems of both developed and developing nations. Provides liaison between members and stock exchanges, representative bodies of accountants, industry groups, and other international organizations. Operates several technical committees to research current programs; maintains consultative group of representatives from banks, business, labor, law, securities commissions, stock exchanges, and international governmental organizations who offer advice on the process of setting International Accounting Standards.
Library Type: reference
Publication: Booklet
Publication title: A Briefing for Chief Executives, Audit Committees and Board of Directors

02628
International Action Network on Small Arms IANSA
Development House, 56-64 Leonard St., London, EC2A 4JX, UK
Tel: 020 70650870
Fax: 020 70650871
Email: contact@iansa.org
Website: http://www.iansa.org
Members: 700
Contact: Rebecca Peters, Dir.
Description: Works to stop the proliferation and misuse of small arms and light weapons.

02629
International Advertising Festival
Greater London House, Hampstead Rd., London, NW1 7EJ, UK
Tel: 020 77284040
Fax: 020 77284044
Email: terrys@canneslions.com
Website: http://www.canneslions.com
Members: 44
Staff: 10
Contact: Terry Savage, Chm.
Description: Film, television, and print advertisers. Sponsors International Advertising Festival in Cannes, France. Encourages exchange among members. Sponsors competitions.
Publication: Newsletter
Publication title: EuroBest

02630
International African Institute IAI
SOAS, Thornhaugh St., Russell Sq., London, WC1H 0XG, UK
Tel: 020 78984420
Fax: 020 78984419
Email: iai@soas.ac.uk
Website: http://www.internationalafricaninstitute.org
Members: 22
Staff: 4
Contact: Philip Burnham, Honorary Dir.
Description: Engages in encouraging the study of African society and disseminating the results of research. Aims to facilitate communications between scholars within the continent and Africans throughout the world on issues that are of direct relevance to the peoples of this region. Achieves this through its publication programme which embraces the journal Africa, monographs, ethnographic and linguistic surveys, directories, bibliographies, and other reference works; seminars which bring together African and non-African scholars; and projects, which, are concerned with the infrastructure for learning and research in Africa.
Formerly: Formerly, International Institute of African Languages and Cultures
Publication: Journal
Publication title: Africa

02631
International Agency for the Prevention of Blindness IAPB
London School of Hygiene & Tropical Medicine, Keppel St., London, WC1E 7HT, UK
Tel: 0207 9272974
Email: office@v2020.org
Website: http://www.vision2020.org/main.cfm?type=IAPBORGHOME
Staff: 1
Contact: Peter Ackland, CEO
Fee: £1545
Membership Type: level C
Fee: £16480
Membership Type: level B
Description: Ophthalmic societies and societies for the prevention of blindness whose members include ophthalmologists, public health officers, nutritionists, geneticists, and other health workers. Coordinates international research into the causes of impaired vision or blindness; promotes measures calculated to eliminate such causes; disseminates knowledge worldwide on preventing blindness and on matters pertaining to care of the eyes. Cooperates with the World Health Organization, United Nations Children's Fund, and other international agencies.
Publication: Proceedings
Publication title: IAPB Fifth General Assembly

02632

International Air Rail Organisation IARO

50 Eastbourne Terr., 6th Fl., London, W2 6LX, UK
Tel: 020 87506632
Fax: 020 87506615
Email: enquiries@iaro.com
Website: http://www.iaro.com
Members: 60
Contact: Andrew Sharp, Dir. Gen.
Fee: £2000
Membership Type: organisation/company
Description: Committed to the planning, developing, building, and operating of rail air links, or integrated air-rail intermodality.
Publication: Yearbook

02633

International Alliance of ALS/MND Associations

PO Box 246, Northampton, NN1 2PR, UK
Tel: 01604 611821
Fax: 01604 624726
Email: alliance@alsmndalliance.org
Website: http://www.alsmndalliance.org
Members: 57
Staff: 1
Contact: Gudjon Sigurdsson, Chm.
Fee: £50
Membership Type: full, associate
Description: Serves as umbrella organization for Amyotrophic Lateral Sclerosis (ALS) and Motor Neurone Disease (MND) associations. Provides a forum for support and exchange of information for ALS and MND associations worldwide.
Formerly: Formerly, International Association of ALS/MND Associations

02634

International Alliance of Law Firms

Waverley House, 7-12 Noel St., London, W1F 8GQ, UK
Tel: 020 73397000
Fax: 020 73070240
Email: alliance@jgrlaw.co.uk
Website: http://www.ialawfirms.co.uk
Contact: Monica Fitzgerald Oathout, Pres.
Description: Represents the interests of and encourages interactions among law firms. Promotes the professional excellence and high standards of ethics of law firms. Provides clients with practical solutions and legal services.
Publication: Newsletter

02635

International Alliance of Patients' Organizations IAPO

703 The Chandlery, 50 Westminster Bridge Rd., London, SE1 7QY, UK
Tel: 020 77217508
Fax: 020 77217596
Email: info@patientsorganizations.org
Website: http://www.patientsorganizations.org
Contact: Joanna Groves, CEO
Description: Promotes Patient-Centered Healthcare and patient participation worldwide across all diseases.

02636

International Aluminium Institute IAI

New Zealand House, 8th Fl., Haymarket, London, SW1Y 4TE, UK
Tel: 0207 9300528
Fax: 0207 3210183
Email: iai@world-aluminium.org
Website: http://www.world-aluminium.org
Members: 27
Staff: 8
Contact: Ron Knapp, Sec. Gen.
Description: Producers of primary aluminum from 23 countries. Seeks to increase world understanding of the aluminum industry and to develop additional uses of primary aluminum. Provides a forum for the exchange of information and the discussion of developments affecting the industry; conducts studies on problem areas affecting the industry including energy, the environment, and health and safety; collects and disseminates information.
Formerly: Formerly, International Primary Aluminum Institute
Publication: Paper
Publication title: Aluminium Applications and Society

02637

International Animal Rescue - UK IAR

Lime House, Regency Close, E Sussex, Uckfield, TN22 1DS, UK
Tel: 01825 767688
Email: info@internationalanimalrescue.org
Website: http://www.iar.org.uk
Contact: Alan Knight, Chief Exec.
Description: Aims to rescue and rehabilitate suffering animals.
Publication: Magazine
Publication title: Animal Tracks

02638

International Artist Managers' Association IAMA

23 Garrick St., Covent Garden, London, WC2E 9BN, UK
Tel: 020 73797336
Fax: 020 73797338
Email: info@iamaworld.com
Website: http://www.iamaworld.com
Members: 220
Staff: 3
Contact: John Willan, Chm.
Fee: £464-3054
Membership Type: full
Fee: £238-323
Membership Type: affiliate
Description: Represents the interests of classical music artist managers and concert agents. Affiliate membership includes other professionals in related areas of the classical music business.
Formerly: Formerly, British Association of Concert Agents
Publication: Directory
Publication title: Classical Music Artists - Who Represents Whom. Advertisements.

02639

International Asclepiad Society IAS

17 High St., Norfolk, Wells, Wighton, NR23 1AL, UK
Email: plantsman@tiscali.co.uk
Website: http://www.asclepiad-international.org
Members: 400
Contact: Tim Marshall, Membership Sec.
Fee: £15
Membership Type: within UK
Fee: £15
Membership Type: Europe (airmail)
Description: Promotes the study and knowledge of plants of the Asclepiadaceae family, commonly known as ascleps, or milkweeds in the United States.
Publication: Journal
Publication title: Asklepios

02640

International Association Against Painful Experiments on Animals IAAPEA

PO Box 14, Hampshire, Hayling Island, PO11 9BF, UK
Tel: 02392463738
Email: iaapea@hotmail.com
Website: http://www.iaapea.com
Members: 60
Contact: Brian Gunn, Sec. Gen.
Description: Animal welfare organizations in 30 countries united to abolish painful experiments on animals. Supports the campaign against the exploitation of animals and encourages the development of research techniques that would replace experiments on animals. Established World Day for Laboratory Animals (April 24) to draw attention to the plight of animals in laboratories throughout the world. Provides assistance to societies and individuals working to eliminate laboratory experiments on animals. Operates an international photo agency to provide the media with photographs of animal experiments; produces documentary films; organizes seminars.
Publication title: International Animal Action

02641

International Association for Citizenship Social and Economics Education IACSEE

11 Eldon St., Glasgow, G3 6NH, UK
Tel: 0141 3303011
Email: c.fagan@educ.gla.ac.uk
Website: http://www.iacsee.org
Members: 130
Staff: 5
Contact: Catherine Fagan, Chair
Description: Teachers of 3-14 year olds, teacher educators, researchers, and individuals working in support services or networks. Promotes the advancement of theoretical and practical knowledge about children in the areas of citizenship education, social studies and economics education and understanding.
Publication: Journal
Publication title: Children's Social and Economics Education

02642

International Association for Educational and Vocational Guidance IAEVG

South London Connexions Ltd., Canius House, 1, Scarbrook Rd., Croydon, CR0 1SQ, UK
Tel: 020 89294707
Email: lindataylor@connexions-southlondon.org.uk
Website: http://www.iaevg.org/IAEVG
Members: 300
Staff: 1
Contact: Linda Taylor, Sec. Gen.
Description: Individuals, institutions, and national associations in 54 countries concerned with educational and vocational guidance. Collects and distributes information pertaining to educational and vocational guidance; promotes professional training and encourages research by granting scholarships for study and travel. Collaborates with international organizations, governmental and non-governmental, and individuals involved in educational and vocational guidance and related matters; participates in activities relating to educational and vocational guidance in research as well as in practical application. Organizes seminars, colloquia, conferences, workshops, and study tours in conjunction with related organizations. Advises government and national and international organizations on the development of guidance systems.
Publication: Book
Publication title: Glossary of Educational and Vocational Guidance Terms in English, French, German, and Spanish

02643

International Association for Forensic Psychotherapy IAFP

c/o Ms. Anne Aiyegbusi, Sec.
West London Mental Health NHS Trust, 3 Bridges Unit, St. Bernard's, Southall, London, UB1 3EU, UK
Email: info@forensicpsychotherapy.com
Website: http://forensicpsychotherapy.com
Members: 200
Contact: Tilman Kluttig, Pres.
Fee: £40
Membership Type: regular
Description: Promotes scientific research into causes and prevention of crime; establishes observation centres and clinics for diagnosis and treatment of delinquency and crime; secures cooperation between all bodies engaged in similar work.
Publication: Directory

02644

International Association for Identification - Great Britain

Forensic Science Service, Metropolitan Laboratory, 109 Lambeth Rd., London, SE1 7LP, UK
Website: http://www.theiai.org/divisions/reps.php
Contact: Paul Chamberlain, Regional Rep.
Description: Organizes people in the profession of forensic identification, investigation and scientific examination of physical evidence. Provides education, training and research. Encourages research in scientific crime detection.

02645

International Association for Jungian Studies IAJS

30 Dorset House, Gloucester Pl., London, NW1 5AD, UK
Fax: 020 86090347
Email: leslieann@ukonline.co.uk
Website: http://www.jungianstudies.org
Contact: Leslie Gardner, Membership Sec.
Fee: £27.5
Membership Type: individual (no income)
Fee: £47
Membership Type: individual (waged)
Description: Seeks to promote and develop Jungian and post-Jungian studies and scholarship. Encourages exploration and exchange of views about all aspects of Jung's work and the history of analytical psychology. Advances the understanding of contemporary cultural trends and the history of psychological and cultural tendencies.
Publication: Journal
Publication title: International Journal for Jungian Studies

02646

International Association for Lichenology IAL

University of Nottingham, School of Biology, Biology Bldg., University Park, Nottingham, NG7 2RD, UK
Email: cliff@hawaii.edu
Website: http://www.botany.hawaii.edu/cpsu/ial.htm
Contact: Peter D. Crittenden, Pres.
Fee: £30
Membership Type: regular
Description: Promotes and encourages communication among those interested in the study of lichens.
Publication: Newsletter
Publication title: International Lichenological Newsletter

02647

International Association for Marine Electronics Companies

Southbank House, Black Prince Rd., London, SE1 7SJ, UK
Tel: 020 75871245
Fax: 020 75871436
Email: secgen@cirm.org
Website: http://www.cirm.org
Members: 75
Contact: Michael Rambaut, Sec. Gen.
Description: Represents marine electronics and radio communications companies from 23 nations. Promotes the application of electronic technology to the safety of life and efficient conduct of vessels at sea, and represents the industry at IMO, ITU and IEC, providing technical advice in the development of international standards. Sponsors technical committee and working groups.

02648

International Association for Media and Communication Research IAMCR

University of London, School of Oriental and African Studies, Centre for Media and Film Studies, Russell Sq., London, WC1 0XG, UK
Tel: 020 78984422
Fax: 020 63398919
Email: iamcr@lse.ac.uk
Website: http://www.iamcr.org
Members: 2500
Staff: 2
Contact: Annabelle Sreberny, Pres.
Fee: £130
Membership Type: high income (regular)
Fee: £500
Membership Type: high income (institutional)
Description: Individuals, institutes, universities, research groups, and other organizations in the field of media and communication.
Publication: Newsletter

02649

International Association for Media and Communications Research IAMCR

University of London, School of Oriental & African Studies, Centre for Media and Film Studies, Russell Sq., London, WC1 0XG, UK
Tel: 020 78984422
Email: membership@iamcr.org
Website: http://www.iamcr.org
Members: 1500
Contact: Annabelle Sreberny, Pres.
Fee: £130
Membership Type: individual (wealthy country)
Fee: £40
Membership Type: individual (low income country)
Description: Promotes the interests of the professional community of communication researchers in terms of occupational security, career development, and freedom of academic thought and expression. Encourages research and exchange of information on practices and conditions that impede communication and communication research.
Library Subject: all aspects of media and communications research
Library Type: not open to the public
Formerly: Formerly, International Association for Mass Communication Research
Publication: Newsletters
Publication title: IAMCR Newsletter. Advertisements.
Meetings/Conventions: annual conference – Exhibits.

02650

International Association for Religious Freedom IARF

Essex Hall, 1-6 Essex St., London, WC2R 3HY, UK
Email: hq@iarf.net
Website: http://www.iarf.net
Contact: Geoffrey Usher, Treas.
Description: Represents religious groups in 30 countries subscribing to the principles of openness. Collaborates in worldwide efforts to liberate religion from exclusionary tendencies. Conducts religious freedom awareness freedom programmes and interreligious/intercultural encounters. Maintains consultative status at the United Nations.
Publication: Proceedings
Publication title: Congress Proceedings

02651

International Association for Research on Epstein Barr Virus and Associated Diseases

University of Birmingham Medical School, Birmingham, B15 2TT, UK
Tel: 0121 4146876
Fax: 0121 4145376
Email: l.s.young@bham.ac.uk
Website: http://www.bcm.edu/ebvassociation
Contact: Lawrence Young, Pres.
Fee: £120
Membership Type: full
Fee: £35
Membership Type: student
Description: Aims to promote and stimulate the exchange of ideas, knowledge and research materials among research workers throughout the world who study the Epstein-Barr virus (EBV) and related diseases. Encourages cooperative activities between institutions, organizations and societies that have interests in common relating to basic and applied research on EBV and associated diseases. Organizes and conducts international symposium on EBV research.

02652

International Association for the Exchange of Students for Technical Experience IAESTE

PO Box 102, Banbridge, BT32 4WY, UK
Email: general.secretary@iaeste.org
Website: http://www.iaeste.org
Members: 84
Staff: 1
Contact: Pauline Ferguson, Gen. Sec.
Description: National committees (65) and cooperating institutions (19). Represents academic, industrial, and student interests in the organization of technical exchange programs supplementing university and college education. Promotes international understanding by providing students with technical experience abroad. Maintains placement service; active in 84 countries.

02653

International Association for the Exchange of Students for Technical Experience - United Kingdom IAESTE

British Council, 10 Spring Gardens, London, SW1A 2BN, UK
Tel: 020 73894114
Fax: 020 73894426
Email: united_kingdom@iaeste.org
Website: http://www.iaeste.org/countries
Description: Provides students in higher education with technical experience abroad relevant to studies. Offers employers well-qualified and motivated international trainees. Serves as a source of cultural enrichment for trainees and host communities.
Publication: Newsletter
Publication title: Directions

02654

International Association for the Scientific Study of Intellectual Disabilities IASSID

University of Kent, Tizard Centre, Kent, Canterbury, CT2 7LZ, UK
Tel: 01227 823960
Fax: 01227 763674
Email: g.h.murphy@kent.ac.uk
Website: http://www.iassid.org
Contact: Glynis Murphy, Pres.
Description: National associations, research centers and individuals representing scientists and clinicians in 40 countries working in the field of intellectual disabilities. Encourages research in the field of intellectual disabilities, including its causes, prevention, diagnosis, evaluation, therapy, and rehabilitation, management, education, and social inclusion.
Formerly: Formerly, International Association for the Scientific Study of Mental Deficiency
Publication: Journal
Publication title: JIDR - Journal of Intellectual Disability Research. Advertisements.
Meetings/Conventions: New Millennium: From Research to Practice – biennial conference – Exhibits.

02655

International Association for the Scientific Study of Intellectual Disabilities - Ireland IASSID

University of Kent, Tizard Centre, Canterbury, K7M 8A6, UK
Email: g.h.murphy@kent.ac.uk
Website: http://www.iassid.org
Members: 430
Contact: Glynis Murphy, Pres.
Fee: £120
Membership Type: full (with one journal)
Fee: £30
Membership Type: student, pensioner
Description: Scientific study of mental deficiency by means of a multidisciplinary approach.
Publication: Journal
Publication title: Journal of Intellectual Disability Research

02656

International Association for the Study of Forced Migration IASFM

c/o Refugee Studies Centre
3 Worcester St., Oxford, OX1 2PZ, UK
Tel: 01865 270728
Fax: 01865 270721
Email: secretariat@iasfm.org
Website: http://www.iasfm.org
Contact: Susan Martin, Pres.
Fee: £150
Membership Type: full
Fee: £25
Membership Type: student associate
Description: Promotes knowledge and understanding of appropriate practice related to forced migration.

02657

International Association for the Study of German Politics ASGP

University of Sussex, Department of Politics and Contemporary European Studies, Falmer, Brighton, BN1 9SN, UK
Tel: 01273 877648
Email: d.t.hough@sussex.ac.uk
Website: http://www.iasgp.org
Contact: Dan Hough, Sec.
Fee: £30
Membership Type: full
Fee: £15
Membership Type: postgraduate
Description: Scholars with an interest in the politics and societies of German-speaking countries. Promotes study and teaching in the field of German studies "in the widest possible context". Facilitates exchange of information among members; maintains liaison network of graduate students engaged in German studies.
Publication: Journal
Publication title: German Politics

02658

International Association for the Study of Maritime Mission IASMM

c/o Stephen Friend, Sec.
School of Education and Theology, York St. John College, Lord Mayor's Walk, York, YO31 7EX, UK
Tel: 01904 716861
Fax: 01904 612512
Email: s.friend@yorksj.ac.uk
Website: http://www.freewebz.com/iasmm
Members: 200
Contact: Stephen Friend, Sec.
Fee: £20
Membership Type: individual
Fee: £25
Membership Type: organization
Description: Individuals and organizations involved in chaplaincy work in ports worldwide, and in education, social, pastoral, and medical work among seafarers. Promotes the preservation, cataloging, and publicizing of sources for research in maritime mission and encourages maritime mission studies in places of learning.
Publication: Journal
Publication title: Maritime Mission Studies

02659

International Association for the Study of Obesity IASO

28 Portland Pl., London, W1B 1LY, UK
Tel: 020 74679610
Fax: 020 76369258
Email: enquiries@iaso.org
Website: http://www.iaso.org
Contact: Philip James, Pres.
Description: Improves prevention, management and treatment of obesity worldwide by promoting medical research, extending and disseminating knowledge, facilitating contact between investigators and promoting public education.
Publication: Journal
Publication title: International Journal of Obesity

02660

International Association for Time Use Research IATUR

c/o Dr. Kimberly Fisher, Sec.-Treas.
University of Oxford, Department of Sociology, Manor Road Bldg., Manor Rd., Oxford, OX1 3UQ, UK
Email: kimberly.fisher@sociology.ox.ac.uk
Website: http://www.stmarys.ca/partners/iatur
Members: 114
Contact: Michael Bittman, Pres.
Description: Professional statisticians, academics and others interested in how time is used. Facilitates communication and exchange of information among members; works to establish international standards for time use studies. Promotes continued professional advancement of members.
Library Subject: time use, unpaid work, leisure time, women's work, work time
Library Type: by appointment only
Formerly: Formerly, International Research Group on Time Budgets and Social Activities
Publication: Proceedings
Publication title: Fifteenth Reunion of the International Association for Time Use Research Amsterdam

02661

International Association of Air Travel Couriers - UK IAATC

The Old Cottage, Tidenham, Chepstow, NP16 7JL, UK
Tel: 01291 625656
Email: info@aircourier.co.uk
Website: http://www.aircourier.co.uk
Contact: David Sands, Mgr.
Fee: £32
Description: Keeps track of every courier company in the world that requires air couriers and regularly distributes this information to members.
Publication: Magazine
Publication title: Travel Guide International

02662

International Association of Airport and Seaport Police IAASP

ACPO/Ports Policing, 8th Fl., 10 Victoria St., Westminster, London, SW1H ONN, UK
Tel: 0207 0848550
Email: kimsey@iaspolice.org
Website: http://www.iaasp.net
Members: 160
Staff: 2
Contact: Tim Kimsey, Sec.
Fee: £200
Membership Type: individual
Fee: £150
Membership Type: retired
Description: Law enforcement officers; associate members are senior management personnel connected with airports and seaports. Works to prevent and detect crime at air and sea ports, to study methods of investigation and detection, and to exchange information.
Meetings/Conventions: annual meeting

02663

International Association of Assay Offices IAAO

Goldsmiths' Hall, Foster Ln., London, EC2V 6BN, UK
Tel: 020 73679006
Fax: 020 73679005
Email: info@assayofficelondon.co.uk
Website: http://www.theiaao.com
Members: 37
Staff: 2
Contact: Robert Organ, Sec.
Description: National and regional mineral assay offices and precious metal laboratories. Promotes international standardization of assay procedures. Serves as a forum for the discussion of international assay standards.
Formerly: Formerly, Association of European Assay Offices
Meetings/Conventions: semiannual meeting

02664

International Association of Book-Keepers IAB

40 Churchill Sq., Ste. 30, Kings Hill, Kent, West Malling, ME19 4YU, UK
Tel: 01732 897750
Fax: 01732 897751
Email: mail@iab.org.uk
Website: http://www.iab.org.uk
Members: 1275
Staff: 12
Contact: Fabian Hamilton, Pres.
Fee: £60
Membership Type: associate
Fee: £75
Membership Type: regular
Description: Associated with the Institute of Financial Accountants. Professionals in the field of bookkeeping in 55 countries. Aims to bring together members of the profession and administers professional examinations.
Publication: Journal
Publication title: International Book Keeper. Advertisements.

02665

International Association of Broadcasting Manufacturers IABM

PO Box 2264, Berkshire, Reading, RG31 6WA, UK
Tel: 0118 9418620
Fax: 0118 9418630
Email: info@theiabm.org
Website: http://www.theiabm.org
Members: 250
Contact: Peter White, Dir. Gen.
Fee: £390-1300
Membership Type: corporate (based on number of employees)
Fee: £130
Membership Type: associate
Description: Represents the broadcast manufacturing industry; acts as liaison with manufacturers of professional audio and video equipment on a number of topics including engineering, technical, legislative, commercial and training issues. Contributes to technical standards, advises members on relevant legislative changes, maintains contact with exhibition organizers and has a formal presence at NAB, Broadcast Asia and IBC.
Publication: Newsletter
Publication title: Broadcast and Media Technology eNews

02666

International Association of Classification Societies IACS

IACS Ltd., 6th Fl., 36 Broadway, London, SW1H 0BH, UK
Tel: 020 79760660
Fax: 020 78081100
Email: permsec@iacs.org.uk
Website: http://www.iacs.org.uk
Members: 10
Contact: Derek Hodgson, Sec.
Description: Classification societies. Objectives are to: work towards the improvement of standards of safety at sea and of marine environment pollution prevention; coordinate technical requirements; promote a uniform interpretation of international maritime conventions; consult and cooperate with maritime organizations and marine industries of the world.
Formerly: Formerly, European Association of Classification Societies

02667

International Association of Dry Cargo Shipowners INTERCARGO

9th Fl., St. Clare House, 30-33 Minories, London, EC3N 1DD, UK
Tel: 0207 9777030
Fax: 0207 9777011
Email: info@intercargo.org
Website: http://www.intercargo.org
Members: 120
Staff: 3
Contact: Rob Lomas, Sec. Gen.
Fee: £4150-21000
Membership Type: full (based on number of ships)
Fee: £1045
Membership Type: associate
Description: Promotes and protects the interests of its members, exchange views, frames policies, especially in the areas of safety and freedom of navigation, and cooperates with other bodies avoiding duplication where possible. Is a consultative member of I.M.O.
Publication: Journal
Publication title: Intercargo Annual Review

02668

International Association of Entertainment Lawyers - France IAEL

DLA Piper UK LLP, 3 Noble St., London, EC2V 7EE, UK
Tel: 08700 111111
Email: duncan.calow@dlapiper.com
Website: http://www.iael.org
Members: 200
Contact: Duncan Calow, Sec.
Fee: £300
Membership Type: full
Fee: £75
Membership Type: associate
Description: Lawyers and individuals in 25 countries who are directly or indirectly concerned with entertainment law and practice. Promotes studies to increase knowledge in the law, rules, and regulations governing entertainment. Organizes meetings between lawyers and other professionals concerned with entertainment law and practice.

02669

International Association of Entertainment Lawyers - United Kingdom
IAEL

DLA Piper Rudnick Gray Cary UK LLP, 3 Noble St., London, EC2V 7EE, UK
Tel: 08700 111111
Email: iael@dentonwildesapte.com
Website: http://www.iael.org
Members: 200
Contact: Duncan Calow, Sec.
Fee: £300
Membership Type: full
Fee: £75
Membership Type: associate
Description: Represents lawyers with expertise in entertainment law. Provides international forum for members to discuss current issues relevant to their practice.
Publication: Report
Publication title: The IAEL Report

02670

International Association of Hydrogeologists - United Kingdom

Environment Agency, Kings Meadow House, Kings Meadow Rd., Reading, RG1 8QT, UK
Tel: 07717 432960
Email: jdottridge@btinternet.com
Website: http://www.iah.org/about_chapters.asp
Contact: Jane Dottridge, Chair
Description: Advances the science of hydrogeology worldwide. Promotes research and awareness of proper management and protection of groundwater. Facilitates the international exchange of information on groundwater.

02671

International Association of Language Centres
IALC

Lombard House Business Centre, 12/17 Upper Bridge St., Canterbury, CT1 2NF, UK
Tel: 01227 769007
Fax: 01227 769014
Email: info@ialc.org
Website: http://www.ialc.org
Members: 90
Staff: 4
Contact: Jan Capper, Exec. Dir.
Description: Serves as an accreditation and a professional and marketing network for independent language schools teaching the official language(s) of their country. Provides language programmes for different levels, ages and needs, from short and long-term courses to work experience and vocational training. Services include counselling and placement, local accommodation, examinations, cultural and social activities, practical help and support and advice on continuing education.

02672

International Association of Maritime Institutions
IAMI

South Tyneside College, St. George's Ave., Tyne and Wear, South Shields, NE34 6ET, UK
Tel: 0191 4273568
Email: mmeng@stc.ac.uk
Website: http://www.iami.info
Contact: Gary Hindmarch, Sec.
Fee: £740
Membership Type: full
Fee: £270
Membership Type: associate
Description: Maritime institutions. Works to further marine education and training.

02673

International Association of Music Libraries, Archives and Documentation Centres - United Kingdom and Ireland
IAML UK&IrL

Royal Northern College of Music Library, 124 Oxford Rd., Manchester, M13 9RD, UK
Tel: 0161 9075245
Fax: 0161 2737611
Email: general_secretary@iaml-uk-irl.org
Website: http://www.iaml.info/organization/national_branches/uk_and_ireland
Members: 300
Contact: Geoff Thomason, Gen. Sec.
Fee: £62
Membership Type: institutional (domestic)
Fee: £92
Membership Type: institutional (international)
Description: Members working in or have an interest in music librarianship. Promotes the interests of music librarians and libraries in UK and Ireland.
Publication: Journal
Publication title: BRIO. Advertisements.
Meetings/Conventions: annual international conference – Exhibits.

02674

International Association of Practising Accountants
IAPA

Old Chambers, 93-94 West St., Surrey, Farnham, GU9 7EB, UK
Tel: 01252 720810
Fax: 01252 720820
Email: admin@iapa.net
Website: http://www.iapa.net
Members: 230
Contact: Juan Carlos Ronco Corsi, Chm.
Fee: £1995
Membership Type: firm
Fee: £340
Membership Type: additional branch
Description: Medium sized firms of chartered accountants. Seeks to promote and advance the interests of medium sized firms of chartered accountants by means of discussion, publicity, cooperation and exchange of information.
Publication: Booklet
Publication title: Becoming A Chartered Accountant - Training With A Medium Sized Firm

02675

International Association of Professional Congress Organizers
IAPCO

Brambles House, Colwell Rd., Freshwater, PO40 9SL, UK
Fax: 01983 755546
Email: info@iapco.org
Website: http://www.iapco.org
Members: 100
Contact: Sarah Storie-Pugh, Admin.
Description: Represents professional congress organizers. Promotes high professional standards in the organization and administration of international congresses, conferences, and meetings. Encourages the study of theoretical and practical aspects of international congresses through international and national training programs. Seeks to further the recognition of the profession of congress organizations.
Publication: Book
Publication title: Meeting Industry Terminology Dictionary
Meetings/Conventions: Wolfsberg Platform for Executive and Business Development – annual seminar

02676

International Association of Sanskrit Studies
IASS

University of Edinburgh, School of Asian Studies, 7-8 Buccleuch Pl., Edinburgh, EH8 9LW, UK
Email: j.l.brockington@ed.ac.uk
Website: http://www.sanskrit.nic.in/IASS/HOME_page.htm
Contact: John L. Brockington, Sec. Gen.
Description: Aims to gather together scholars in Sanskrit and related disciplines from all parts of the world at triennial World Sanskrit Conferences and to promote Sanskrit Studies generally.

02677

International Association of Teachers of English as a Foreign Language
IATEFL

Darwin Coll., University of Kent, Canterbury, Kent, CT2 7NY, UK
Tel: 01227 824430
Fax: 01227 824431
Email: generalenquiries@iatefl.org
Website: http://www.iatefl.org
Members: 3500
Contact: Glenda Smart, Exec. Off.
Fee: £46
Membership Type: individual
Fee: £29.5
Membership Type: retired, student
Description: Teachers of English as a foreign or second language; educational institutions. Aim is to exchange experience, views, and information among members in 112 countries so that the teaching of English might be improved at all age levels and in all countries.
Publication: Book
Publication title: IATEFL Conference Selections. Advertisements.

02678

International Association of Tour Managers IATM

397 Walworth Rd., London, SE17 2AW, UK
Tel: 020 77039154
Fax: 020 77030358
Email: iatm@iatm.co.uk
Website: http://www.iatm.co.uk
Members: 1500
Staff: 3
Fee: £110
Membership Type: individual
Fee: £75
Membership Type: individual associate
Description: Active members are professional tour managers. Allied and Associate members are companies involved with group tourism. Promotes the highest standards of professional competence and improves the status and welfare of tour managers. Represents the interests of tour managers within the industry and to all governmental and non-governmental organisations concerned with group tourism.
Publication: Newsletter
Publication title: IATM Newsletter

02679

International Association of Tour Managers - France IATM - FRA

19 Cheval Pl., Ste. 5010, London, SW7 1EW, UK
Tel: 020 77039154
Fax: 020 77030358
Email: venetg@voila.fr
Website: http://www.iatm.co.uk
Contact: Gerard Venet, Contact
Description: Promotes and maintains the highest standards of competence, integrity and professional conduct. Protects and improves the status and welfare of tour managers.

02680

International Association of Tour Managers - Spain IATM - SP

c/o IATM Central Office
397 Walworth Rd., London, SE17 2AW, UK
Tel: 020 77039154
Fax: 020 77030358
Email: iatm@iatm.co.uk
Website: http://www.iatm.co.uk
Members: 1000
Staff: 2
Description: Promotes and maintains the highest standards of competence, integrity and professional conduct of tour managers.

02681

International Association of Women Police

British Transport Police, 25 Camden Rd., London, NW1 9LN, UK
Tel: 07900 578615
Email: janetownsley.iawp@blueyonder.co.uk
Website: http://www.iawp.org
Contact: Jane Townsley, Pres.
Description: Open to all women and men in the criminal-justice field, regardless of rank, assignment, or department affiliation. Strengthens, unite and raise the profile of women in criminal justice internationally. Hosts an annual training conference.

02682

International Association of Wool Textile Laboratories INTERWOOLLABS

Wool House, Roydsdale Way, West Yorkshire, Huddersfield, BD4 6SE, UK
Tel: 01274 688666
Fax: 01274 652233
Email: info@interwoollabs.org
Website: http://www.interwoollabs.org
Members: 106
Contact: J.M. Lambert, Sec. Gen.
Fee: £689
Membership Type: regular
Description: Wool textile laboratories in 35 countries. Seeks to ensure correct and uniform application of measuring and sampling methods among member laboratories in order to obtain consistent test results. Aids member laboratories in settling disputes resulting from measurement discrepancies. Conducts research.

02683

International Autistic Research Organization IARO

49 Orchard Ave., Shirley, Croydon, CR0 7NE, UK
Tel: 020 87770095
Fax: 020 87762362
Email: iaro@autismresearch.wanadoo.co.uk
Website: http://www.iaro.org.uk
Members: 300
Staff: 3
Contact: Gerda I.M. McCarthy, Founder
Description: Provides information about scientific research in autism.

02684

International Bar Association IBA

1 Stephen St., 10th Fl., London, W1T 1AT, UK
Tel: 020 76916868
Fax: 020 76916544
Email: member@int-bar.org
Website: http://www.ibanet.org
Members: 30000
Contact: Fernando Pelaez-Pier, Pres.
Fee: £215
Membership Type: full
Fee: £110
Membership Type: general
Description: National bar associations and individual members of the legal profession working in the field of international law in 183 countries. Works to advance the science of jurisprudence; promotes uniformity in related legal fields and administration of justice under law. Seeks to establish and maintain friendly relations among members of the legal profession worldwide. Supports the legal principles and aims of the United Nations.
Publication title: Business Law International

02685

International Bee Research Association IBRA

16 N Rd., Cardiff, CF10 3DY, UK
Tel: 029 20372409
Fax: 05601 135640
Email: mail@ibra.org.uk
Website: http://www.ibra.org.uk
Members: 800
Staff: 6
Contact: Richard Jones, Dir.
Fee: £30
Membership Type: institutional, personal
Description: Individuals, beekeeping societies, and research organizations in 130 countries. Promotes and coordinates bee research work and research on pollination. Provides worldwide information service through publications, correspondence, and journals. Aids beekeepers and promotes beekeeping as a sustainable activity in developing countries.
Formerly: Formerly, Bee Research Association
Publication: Journal
Publication title: Apicultural Abstracts. Advertisements.

02686

International Behavioural and Neural Genetics Society IBANGS

Institute of Psychiatry, Psychological Medicine and Psychiatry, PO 82, De Crespigny Park, London, SE5 8AF, UK
Email: c.fernandes@iop.kcl.ac.uk
Website: http://www.ibangs.org
Members: 250
Contact: Cathy Fernandes, Treas.
Fee: £135
Membership Type: regular
Fee: £45
Membership Type: student
Description: Scientists and students in the field of behavioural neurogenetics. Promotes excellence in the field of neurobehavioral genetics.
Publication: Journal
Publication title: Genes, Brain and Behavior
Meetings/Conventions: annual meeting

02687

International Bioacoustics Council IBAC

The British Library Sound Archive, 96 Euston Rd., London, NW1 2DB, UK
Email: ibac@ibac.info
Website: http://www.ibac.info
Contact: Cheryl Tipp, Sec.
Description: Fosters international participation in the scientific study of biological sounds.

02688

International Biodeterioration and Biodegradation Society
IBBS

Thor Specialties, Wincham Ave., Wincham, Northwich, CW9 6GB, UK
Tel: 01606 818869
Email: johng@thor.uk.com
Website: http://www.ibbsonline.org
Members: 300
Contact: John Gillatt, Honorary Sec.
Fee: £70
Membership Type: ordinary (with journal)
Fee: £55
Membership Type: student (with journal)
Description: Academics, representatives of the biocide industry, and research scientists from industry and government organizations. Promotes the sciences of biodeterioration and biodegradation. Sponsors symposia; conducts the Bunker Memorial Lecture.
Meetings/Conventions: Latin American Biodegradation and Biodeterioration Symposium – triennial symposium

02689

International Boundaries Research Unit
IBRU

University of Durham, Dept. of Geography, South Rd., Durham, DH1 3LE, UK
Tel: 0191 3341961
Fax: 0191 3341962
Email: ibru@durham.ac.uk
Website: http://www.dur.ac.uk/ibru
Members: 4
Staff: 4
Contact: Martin Pratt, Dir. of Research
Description: Seeks to enhance the resources available for the peaceful resolution of problems associated with international boundaries on land and at sea around the world. Conducts research.
Library Subject: cartography, border disputes
Library Type: open to the public
Publication: Newsletter
Publication title: Borderlines

02690

International Brain Tumour Alliance
IBTA

PO Box 244, Tadworth, KT20 5WQ, UK
Email: kathy@theibta.org
Website: http://www.theibta.org
Contact: Kathy Oliver, Co-Dir.
Description: Provides support, advocacy and information for brain tumour patients and carers. Promotes research of the causes and treatment of brain tumours. Advocates for improved access to palliative care, rehabilitation and psychosocial support of people living with brain tumours and their families.

02691

International Bunker Industry Association
IBIA

Ground Fl., Latimer House, 5-7 Cumberland Pl., Southampton, SO15 2BH, UK
Tel: 023 80226555
Fax: 023 80221777
Email: ian.adams@ibia.net
Website: http://www.ibia.net
Members: 480
Staff: 2
Contact: Ian Adams, CEO
Fee: £550
Membership Type: corporate
Fee: £110
Membership Type: individual
Description: Anyone who has an interest in bunkering including ship owners, charterers, managers, bunker suppliers, traders, brokers, barging companies, storage companies, surveyors, port authorities, credit reporting companies, lawyers, equipment manufacturers, shipping journalists and marine consultants. Aims to provide an international forum to address the concerns of all sectors of the bunker industry.

02692

International Cable Protection Committee
ICPC

PO Box 150, Lymington, SO41 6WA, UK
Tel: 01590 681673
Fax: 0870 4327761
Email: secretary@iscpc.org
Website: http://www.iscpc.org
Members: 76
Staff: 1
Contact: Graham Marle, Sec.
Fee: £1200
Membership Type: full, provisional
Description: Represents governmental administrations and commercial companies in 44 countries that own or operate submarine telecommunications cables as well as commercial companies that own or operate submarine power cables. Promotes the safeguarding of submarine telecommunications cables against man-made and natural hazards. Serves as a forum for the exchange of technical and legal information pertaining to submarine cable protection methods and programmes.
Publication: Video
Publication title: Fishing and Submarine Cables - Sharing the Seabed

02693

International Cartographic Association
ICA

Newcastle University, School of Civil Engineering and Geosciences, Newcastle upon Tyne, NE1 7RU, UK
Tel: 0191 2226353
Fax: 0191 2228691
Email: dave.fairbairn@newcastle.ac.uk
Website: http://icaci.org
Contact: David Fairbairn, Sec. Gen./Treas.
Description: National societies and committees for cartography and geographic information science. Works to advance the study of gathering, visualization and analysis of geospatial data for decision-making and geographic information science; coordinates cartographic and GIScience research involving international cooperation.
Formerly: Formerly, International Cartographic Association - The International Society for Cartography and Geographical
Publication: Newsletter
Publication title: ICA News. Advertisements.
Meetings/Conventions: International Cartographic Conference – biennial conference – Exhibits.

02694

International Centre for Island Technology
ICIT

Heriot-Watt University, Old Academy, Back Rd., Orkney Islands, Stromness, KW16 3AW, UK
Tel: 01856 850605
Fax: 01856 851349
Email: e.mackay@hw.ac.uk
Website: http://www.icit.hw.ac.uk
Contact: Jonathan Side, Dir.
Description: Carries out advanced research, post-graduate training and consultancy in marine resource management and related issues.
Publication: Book
Publication title: Abandonment of Offshore Installattions

02695

International Chamber of Commerce - UK
ICC UK

12 Grosvenor Pl., London, SW1X 7HH, UK
Tel: 020 78389363
Fax: 020 72355447
Email: taniabaumann@iccorg.co.uk
Website: http://www.iccuk.net
Members: 350
Staff: 4
Contact: Tania Baumann, Acting Dir.
Description: Small, medium and large companies; multinationals; trade associations; chambers of commerce; academic institutions; law firms; banks. Promotes trade and investment and the free market system. Practical services to business include the ICC International Court of Arbitration; the ICC Institute of International Business Law. Has conferences and triennial congress that are held in cities throughout the world.

02696

International Chamber of Shipping
ICS

12 Carthusian St., London, EC1M 6EZ, UK
Tel: 020 74178844
Fax: 020 74178877
Email: post@marisec.org
Website: http://www.marisec.org
Members: 45
Contact: Peter Hinchliffe, Sec. Gen.
Description: International trade association for national associations of ship owners. Promotes interests of members worldwide in shipping matters such as documentation, insurance, marine safety, maritime law, navigation, and pollution control. Facilitates exchange of information and ideas. Represents members' concerns before governments and intergovernmental organizations throughout the world in an effort to formulate policies for national and international application. Produces a number of operational guides on safety and pollution prevention for the shipping industry. Maintains consultative status with the International Maritime Organization and other agencies of the United Nations; participates in the work of international organizations with common interests.
Formerly: Formerly, International Shipping Conference
Publication: Manual
Publication title: Assessment and Development of Safety Management Systems

02697

International Clematis Society
ICIS

3 Cuthberts Close, Waltham Cross, EN7 5RB, UK
Tel: 01992 636524
Email: clematis@clematisinternational.com
Website: http://www.clematisinternational.com
Members: 275
Contact: Fiona Woolfenden, Sec.
Fee: £30
Membership Type: single
Description: Individuals worldwide who cultivate, research, or share an interest in the Clematis flower. Seeks to improve and extend the cultivation of Clematis; disseminate knowledge; stimulate scientific research and international cooperation and exchange. Provides a seed exchange program.
Publication: Journal
Publication title: Clematis International. Advertisements.

02698

International Cocoa Organization
ICCO

Commonwealth House, 1-19 New Oxford St., London, WC1A 1NU, UK
Tel: 020 74005050
Fax: 020 74215500
Email: info@icco.org
Website: http://www.icco.org
Contact: Tony Fofie, Chm.
Description: Works as international organization of cocoa exporting and importing countries established to implement the International Cocoa Agreement which was first negotiated in 1972 to bring stability to the world cocoa market by preventing excessive fluctuation in the price of cocoa, which adversely affects the long-term interests of producers and consumers. Acts as a center for the collection and distribution of information on all aspects of the world cocoa economy. Compiles and publishes statistics.
Library Subject: cocoa-related material
Library Type: by appointment only
Publication: Bulletin
Publication title: Quarterly Bulletin of Cocoa Statistics

02699

International Coffee Organization
ICO

22 Berners St., London, W1T 3DD, UK
Tel: 020 76120600
Fax: 020 76120630
Email: info@ico.org
Website: http://www.ico.org
Members: 77
Staff: 30
Contact: Nestor Osorio, Exec. Dir.
Description: Countries that export and import coffee. Seeks to further international cooperation among coffee-exporting and coffee-importing countries and to achieve fair prices for consumers and producers. Promotes economic development of coffee-producing countries. Seeks to bring supply and demand into reasonable balance to avoid excessive fluctuation in coffee prices. Aims to increase the consumption of coffee.
Library Subject: coffee, commodity trade, development issues
Library Type: by appointment only
Publication: Newsletter
Publication title: Coffee Newsletter

02700

International Commission for Uniform Methods of Sugar Analysis
ICUMSA

British Sugar plc, Sugar Way, Peterborough, PE2 9AY, UK
Tel: 017 33563171
Fax: 017 33422487
Email: president@icumsa.org
Website: http://www.icumsa.org
Contact: Geoff Parkin, Pres.
Description: Represents about 250 active members from 34 countries that are organized in 29 national committees. Provides an international forum for all matters pertaining to the science of sugar analysis. Encourages scientific research relating to the analysis of sugars and sugar products. Provides for the interchange of information between the different countries. Publishes international recommendations for uniform methods of sugar analysis.
Publication: Newsletter
Publication title: ICUMSA News

02701

International Commission of the Palaeozoic Microflora

Fugro Robertson Ltd., Llandudno, LL30 1SA, UK
Email: gary.mullins@fugro-robertson.com
Website: http://www.cimp.ulg.ac.be
Contact: Gary Mullins, Sec. Gen.
Fee: £10
Membership Type: professional
Description: Supports collaboration in the field of palaeozoic palynology.
Publication: Newsletters
Publication title: CIMP Newsletter

02702

International Commission on Biological Effects of Noise
ICBEN

c/o Prof. Stephen A. Stansfeld, PhD, Chm.
Queen Mary's School of Medicine and Dentistry, Charterhouse Sq., London, EC1M 6BQ, UK
Tel: 020 78822031
Fax: 020 78825728
Email: s.a.stansfeld@qmul.ac.uk
Website: http://www.icben.org
Members: 500
Staff: 23
Contact: Mathias Basner, Sec.
Description: Encourages international cooperation in the study of the biological effects of noise; promotes communication among research scientists, governmental agencies, industrial workers and managers, and other parties and entities concerned with noise effects.

02703

International Commission on Irrigation and Drainage - England
ICID UK

c/o Institution of Civil Engineers
1 Great George St., Westminster, London, SW1P 3AA, UK
Tel: 020 86652234
Fax: 020 87991325
Email: tim.fuller@ice.org.uk
Website: http://www.icid.org.uk
Members: 200
Contact: Tim Fuller, Sec.
Fee: £50
Membership Type: individual
Fee: £250
Membership Type: corporate
Description: Organizes a regular programme of meetings and events; periodic meetings for the presentation and discussion of technical papers; an annual weekend symposium; field events; an annual memorial lecture.
Publication: Journal
Publication title: Irrigation and Drainage

02704

International Commission on Microbiological Specifications for Foods
ICMSF

c/o Prof. Leon G.M. Gorris, Sec.
Safety & Environmental Assurance Ctr., Unilever, Colworth House, Bedford, Sharnbrook, MK44 1LQ, UK
Tel: 01234 264798
Fax: 01234 264929
Email: leon.gorris@unilever.com
Website: http://www.icmsf.iit.edu/main/home.html
Members: 17
Contact: Martin Cole, Chm.
Description: Food microbiologists employed by governments, industries, universities, research institutes, and hospitals. Studies, recommends, and provides information on the microbiology of foods and food safety. Seeks to establish comparable standards of microbiological judgment among countries; foster safe movement of foods in international commerce; overcome difficulties caused by differing microbiological standards. Maintains Latin American, Balkan-Danubian, subcommissions to handle problems peculiar to these regions.
Publication: Proceedings
Publication title: International Commission on Microbiological Specifications for Foods–Proceedings of the General Conference

02705

International Commission on Zoological Nomenclature
ICZN

Natural History Museum, Cromwell Rd., London, SW7 5BD, UK
Tel: 020 79425653
Email: iczn-em@nhm.ac.uk
Website: http://iczn.org
Members: 28
Staff: 3
Contact: Ellinor Michel, Exec. Sec.
Description: Zoologists, paleozoologists, scientists, and others interested in zoological nomenclature in 19 countries. Serves as a bureau to assist zoologists worldwide with problems in zoological nomenclature.
Library Type: reference
Publication: Bulletin
Publication title: Bulletin of Zoological Nomenclature

02706
International Committee on Seafarer's Welfare
ICSW
Gresham House, 53 Clarendon Rd., Hertfordshire, Watford, WD17 1LA, UK
Tel: 01923 222653
Fax: 01923 222663
Email: icsw@icsw.org.uk
Website: http://www.seafarerswelfare.org
Members: 37
Staff: 2
Contact: Rosemary Hendry, Admin.
Description: National agencies and international organizations in 14 countries concerned with maritime welfare. Promotes and fosters the provision of welfare services at sea and ashore for seafarers of all nationalities, races, colours, and creeds in line with the International Labour Organisation (ILO) instruments concerning seafarers' welfare. Provides advice and assistance to international, national, municipal and port authorities and agencies, shipowners, seafarers, welfare organizations, and other interested bodies. Maintains close working relationships with the ILO and acts as an advisory body to the ILO regarding the objectives of the ILO instruments concerning seafarers' welfare.
Publication: Directory
Publication title: Port of the Seven Seas Directory 2000/2001

02707
International Continence Society
ICS
19 Portland Sq., Bristol, BS2 8SJ, UK
Tel: 0117 9444881
Fax: 0117 9444882
Email: info@icsoffice.org
Website: http://www.icsoffice.org/Home.aspx
Members: 3000
Staff: 5
Contact: Avicia Burchill, Admin. Mgr.
Fee: £50
Membership Type: regular
Description: Promotes the study of the storage and voiding function of the lower urinary tract, its diagnosis, and the management of lower urinary tract dysfunction to its members (urologists, gynecologists, physicians, surgeons, nurses, physicists, physiotherapists, bioengineers and scientists). Encourages research into pathophysiology, diagnostic techniques, and treatment.
Library Subject: incontinence
Library Type: not open to the public
Publication: Journal
Publication title: Neurourology and Urodynamics
Meetings/Conventions: annual meeting

02708
International Cooperative and Mutual Insurance Federation
ICMIF
Denzell House, Denzell Gardens, Dunham Rd., Bowdon, WA14 4PD, UK
Tel: 0161 9295090
Fax: 0161 9295163
Email: shaun@icmif.org
Website: http://www.icmif.org
Members: 216
Staff: 20
Contact: Shaun Tarbuck, Chief Exec.
Description: Promotes co-operation and collaboration between members; provides technical and financial assistance for the information and development of insurance organizations; conducts collaborative research projects; offers training in reinsurance; organizes technical seminars, workshops and study visits; publishes research reports, training manuals and regular newsletters; facilitates personnel exchanges; fosters alliances with related external organizations.
Library Type: reference
Publication: Journal
Publication title: Shiftkey
Meetings/Conventions: biennial conference – Exhibits. October 26 to 28, 2011. Tokyo Japan

02709
International Corrections and Prisons Association
ICPA
PO Box 17369, Edinburgh, EH12 1GE, UK
Tel: 0131 2448773
Fax: 0131 2445964
Email: edwozniak@icpa.ca
Website: http://www.icpa.ca
Contact: Ed Wozniak, Exec. Dir.
Fee: £50
Membership Type: individual
Fee: £1000
Membership Type: bronze
Description: Provides a forum for criminal justice professionals to join in a dialogue and to share ideas and practices aimed at advancing professional corrections.

02710
International Council for Archaeozoology
ICAZ
c/o Umberto Albarella, Sec.
University of Sheffield, Dept. of Archaeology, Northgate House, West St., Sheffield, S1 4ET, UK
Email: icaz@alexandriaarchive.org
Website: http://www.alexandriaarchive.org/icaz
Members: 330
Contact: Umberto Albarella, Sec.
Fee: £20
Membership Type: individual, institution
Fee: £10
Membership Type: student, retired, unwaged
Description: Seeks to develop and stimulate archaeozoological research; strengthen cooperation among archaeozoologists; foster cooperation with archaeologists and scientists working in other fields; and promote high ethical and scientific standards. Standardizes data recording, nomenclature, measurements, and policies relating to archaeology and archaeozoology.

02711
International Council of Marine Industry Associations
ICOMIA
Marine House, Thorpe Lea Rd., Surrey, Egham, TW20 8BF, UK
Tel: 01784 223702
Fax: 01784 223705
Email: info@icomia.com
Website: http://www.icomia.com
Members: 29
Contact: Lorenzo Selva, Pres.
Description: Marine industry associations united to remove trade barriers and promote boating as an international recreational activity by establishing a medium for the exchange of information on common matters such as safety, service, quality, and marinas, in order to stimulate the sale and usage of boats and their equipment. Compiles statistics.
Publication: Book
Publication title: Boating Industry Statistics

02712
International Council of Tanners
ICT
Leather Trade House, Kings Park Rd., Moulton Park, Northampton, NN3 6JD, UK
Tel: 01604 679917
Fax: 01604 679998
Email: sec@tannerscouncilict.org
Website: http://www.tannerscouncilict.org
Members: 33
Staff: 2
Contact: Bulent Hazer, Pres.
Description: Represents leather trade associations united to promote the leather industry throughout the world. Fosters research and development in the industry.
Publication: Newsletter
Publication title: ICT Update

02713
International Council on Mining and Metals
ICMM
35/38 Portman Sq., London, W1H 6LR, UK
Tel: 020 74675070
Fax: 020 74675071
Email: info@icmm.com
Website: http://www.icmm.com
Members: 38
Staff: 12
Contact: Richard Adkerson, Chm.
Description: Promotes environmentally responsible production and disposal of metals and increased use of recycling in the metal-producing industries. Disseminates information on environmentally sustainable mining and metal production.
Formerly: Formerly, International Council on Metals and the Environment
Publication: Newsletter

02714
International Cultural Youth Exchange - United Kingdom
ICYE UK
Latin America House, Kingsgate Pl., London, NW6 4TA, UK
Tel: 020 76810983
Fax: 020 79161246
Email: info@icye.org.uk
Website: http://www.icye.co.uk
Members: 26
Contact: Cat Udal, Contact
Fee: £4495
Membership Type: participant
Description: Promotes intercultural understanding, equality of opportunity, tolerance and peace. Provides challenging intercultural learning experiences for young people. Enhances social and personal development through international volunteer programs.

02715
International Dance Teachers' Association
IDTA

International House, 76 Bennett Rd., E Sussex, Brighton, BN2 5JL, UK
Tel: 01273 685652
Fax: 01273 674388
Email: info@idta.co.uk
Website: http://www.idta.co.uk
Members: 6000
Staff: 32
Contact: Yvonne Gout, Pres.-Elect
Description: Represents dance schools and commercial dance instructors who pass a qualifying examination in the United Kingdom. Strives to uphold the highest ideals of the dance profession. Organizes and grants the right to organize certified theatre dance championship competitions. Formulates and administers amateur grade and medal tests to measure students' progress. Offers low-cost equipment and services to support members' educational activities; sponsors competitions. Produces media advertisements promoting participation in dance programs.
Formerly: Formerly, IDMA
Publication: Magazine
Publication title: Dance International
Meetings/Conventions: Ballroom and Theatre Seminar – annual congress

02716
International Egg Commission
IEC

89 Charterhouse St., 2nd Fl., London, EC1M 6HR, UK
Tel: 020 74903493
Fax: 020 74903495
Website: http://www.internationalegg.com
Contact: Julian Madeley, Dir. Gen.
Fee: £635
Membership Type: producer-packer/egg processor international
Fee: £920
Membership Type: allied industry
Description: National organizations of commercial egg producers in 55 countries. Works to improve egg statistics. Estimates import-export trends. Maintains cooperation with authorities in importing-exporting countries. Examines means of increasing consumption. Seeks to improve marketing techniques. Aims to standardize egg products and dispose of surpluses.
Meetings/Conventions: Production and Marketing Conference – annual conference

02717
International Exhibition Logistics Associates
IELA

119 High St., Hertfordshire, Berkhamsted, HP4 1DJ, UK
Tel: 0845 0714395
Fax: 01442 869090
Email: adminiela@iela.org
Website: http://www.iela.org
Contact: Declan Gane, Exec. Dir.
Description: Associations in 43 countries involved in organization of international exhibitions. Creates guidelines and implements existing standards. Fosters communication among members. Maintains charitable program. Compiles statistics. Contributes to educational foundation of the International Exhibitors Association.

02718
International Farm Management Association
IFMA

38 W End Whittlesford, Cambridge, CB22 4LX, UK
Tel: 01223 839707
Email: honsecretary@ifmaonline.org
Website: http://www.ifmaonline.org
Members: 1000
Staff: 1
Contact: Tony King, Sec.
Fee: £25
Membership Type: full
Fee: £67.5
Membership Type: corporate
Description: Farmers, extension workers, academics, resource use planners, and managers in 68 countries concerned with the planning, production, and marketing in agriculture. Furthers the knowledge and understanding of farm business management and fosters the exchange of ideas and information about farm management theory and practice worldwide.
Publication: Proceedings
Publication title: Congress Proceedings

02719
International Federation for Heat Treatment and Surface Engineering
IFHTSE

1 Carlton House Terr., London, SW1Y 5DB, UK
Email: ifhtwood@aol.com
Website: http://www.ifhtse.org
Members: 32
Staff: 2
Contact: Robert B. Wood, Sec. Gen.
Description: Federation of scientific and technological societies and associations worldwide. Promotes the study and development of the science, practice, and application of heat treating and surface engineering.
Publication: Bulletin
Publication title: IFHTSE Bulletin

02720
International Federation for Research in Women's History
IFRWH

Sheffield Hallam University, City Campus, Howard St., Sheffield, S1WB, UK
Email: c.c.midgley@shu.ac.uk
Website: http://www.ifrwh.com
Contact: Clare Midgley, Pres.
Description: Promotes research into women's history worldwide. Fosters communication among members.

02721
International Federation for Theatre Research
IFTR

Lancaster University, Lancaster, LA1 4YN, UK
Email: d.whitton@lancaster.ac.uk
Website: http://www.firt-iftr.org
Members: 400
Contact: David Whitton, Sec. Gen.
Fee: £185
Membership Type: institutional
Fee: £75
Membership Type: individual
Description: Public and private organizations in over 40 countries devoting all or part of their activity to theatre research; individual researchers and other interested persons. Promotes and coordinates the study of theatre history; disseminates scholarly, technical, and other important works on theatre research; assists in the preservation of historic theatre buildings and theatre material. Aids theatrical researchers in obtaining facilities in libraries and museums; helps members obtain research grants. Promotes relations with other historical and artistic studies departments.
Publication: Bulletin
Publication title: News Bulletin

02722
International Federation of Air Line Pilots Associations
IFALPA

Interpilot House, Gogmore Ln., Surrey, Chertsey, KT16 9AP, UK
Tel: 01932 571711
Fax: 01932 570920
Email: ifalpa@ifalpa.org
Website: http://www.ifalpa.org
Members: 100
Staff: 19
Contact: Carlos Limon, Pres.
Description: National pilot associations representing more than 100,000 pilots. Promotes the development of a safe and orderly system of air transportation and the protection of the interests of airline pilots. Activities include: the regular exchange of information and ideas; examination of common problems; coordination of policies. Maintains team of accident investigation experts to assist pilots involved in accidents. Works to standardize legislation concerning hijacking. Conducts surveys. Maintains liaison with the International Civil Aviation Organization and the International Air Transport Association.
Publication: Newsletter
Publication title: IFALFA News

02723
International Federation of Airworthiness
IFA

14 Railway Approach, West Sussex, East Grinstead, RH19 1BP, UK
Tel: 01342 301788
Fax: 01342 317808
Email: sec@ifairworthy.org
Website: http://www.ifairworthy.com
Members: 122
Staff: 6
Contact: John W. Saull, Exec. Dir.
Fee: £1000
Membership Type: corporate
Fee: £400
Membership Type: university/college, professional society/organization
Description: Aerospace manufacturers, airlines, aircraft engineering and service facilities, international flight safety associations, professional aeronautical societies, and airworthiness authorities in 47 countries. Provides a forum for the exchange of experience and ideas on all areas of airworthiness including maintenance, design, and operations. Encourages mutual understanding between airlines and airworthiness authorities. Organizes

working parties to investigate specific problems in the aerospace industry.
Formerly: Formerly, International Federation of Airworthiness Technology and Engineering
Publication: Annual Report
Publication title: Annual Report of Accounts
Meetings/Conventions: annual conference – Exhibits.

02724

International Federation of Anti-Leprosy Associations ILEP

234 Blythe Rd., London, W14 0HJ, UK
Tel: 020 76026925
Fax: 020 73711621
Email: ilep@ilep.org.uk
Website: http://www.ilep.org.uk
Members: 14
Staff: 5
Contact: Rene Staheli, Pres.
Description: International federation of autonomous non-governmental anti-leprosy organizations, most of which generate their income by raising funds from private donors to support more than a thousand projects in more than 90 countries. Supports medical, scientific, social, and humanitarian activities throughout the world to cure and rehabilitate people affected by leprosy and to prevent and eventually eradicate the disease. Facilitates the coordination of activities and cooperation between its members while recognizing their autonomy.

02725

International Federation of Automotive Engineering Societies

30 Percy St., London, W1T 2DB, UK
Tel: 020 72996630
Fax: 020 72996633
Email: info@fisita.com
Website: http://www.fisita.com
Members: 175000
Contact: Ian Dickie, Chief Exec.
Description: Helps create efficient, affordable, safe and sustainable automotive transportation by providing a global forum involving engineers together with representatives from industry, government, academia and standardization bodies. Makes sure that everyone concerned with automotive transportation is working together towards the development of cleaner, safer, more sustainable vehicles.
Library Type: open to the public
Publication: Magazine
Publication title: Auto Technology. Advertisements.
Meetings/Conventions: World Automotive Congress – biennial congress

02726

International Federation of Boat Show Organisers IFBSO

22 St. Johns Rd., Surrey, Woking, GU21 7SA, UK
Tel: 01483 751506
Fax: 01483 751021
Email: info@ifbso.com
Website: http://www.ifbso.com
Members: 51
Contact: Tom Willis, Sec. Gen.
Fee: £1250
Membership Type: individual
Description: Promotes the interests of organizers of international boat shows. Helps to maintain or improve the recreational marine industry.

02727

International Federation of Essential Oils and Aroma Trades IFEAT

9 Lincolns Inn Fields, London, WC2A 3BP, UK
Tel: 020 77295904
Fax: 020 78148383
Email: secretariat@ifeat.org
Website: http://www.ifeat.org
Members: 250
Staff: 2
Contact: Alastair Hitchen, Chm.
Fee: £380
Membership Type: regular
Description: Producers, compounders, and traders of fragrance and flavor materials. Purpose is to promote and advance commercial interests of members of the aroma chemicals and essential oils industry throughout the world. Awards diplomas in perfumery to students completing one-year correspondence course offered by Plymouth University (UK).
Publication: Newsletter
Publication title: IFEAT Newsletter
Meetings/Conventions: The Industry in India: Naturals and Aroma Chemicals - Production and Markets – annual conference – Exhibits.

02728

International Federation of Gynecology and Obstetrics

FIGO House, 10 Theed St., Ste. 3, Waterloo Ct., London, SE1 8ST, UK
Tel: 020 79281166
Fax: 020 79287099
Email: figo@figo.org
Website: http://www.figo.org
Members: 124
Staff: 11
Contact: Bryan Thomas, Admin. Dir.
Description: Promotes and assists in the development of scientific and research work relating to all facets of gynecology and obstetrics; improves the physical and mental health of women, mothers, and their children; provides an exchange of information and ideas; improves teaching standards; promotes international cooperation among medical bodies. Acts as liaison with World Health Organization and other international organizations.
Publication: Journal
Publication title: International Journal of Gynecology and Obstetrics

02729

International Federation of Hardware and Housewares Associations IHA

Millbridge House, Chaddesdley Corbett, Worcestershire, Kidderminster, DY10 4PR, UK
Tel: 01562 777268
Email: jonathanswift10@btinternet.com
Website: http://www.ihaworldwide.org
Members: 22
Staff: 1
Contact: Jonathan Swift, Sec. Gen
Fee: £239-2334
Membership Type: national trade association
Description: National associations in 21 countries representing 75,000 firms dealing with wholesale and retail trade of hardware and household goods. Promotes exchange of information among members; establishes special committees on technical questions; coordinates advertising and sales promotions; furthers professional training and development. Performs market and motivation research and supports an international student exchange. Compiles statistics; operates placement service.
Library Type: reference
Formerly: Formerly, International Federation of Ironmongers and Iron Merchants Association
Meetings/Conventions: International Congress – biennial general assembly – Exhibits.

02730

International Federation of Health Plans IFHP

Grosvenor Gardens House, Ste. 196, 35-37 Grosvenor Gardens, London, SW1W 0BS, UK
Tel: 020 76305656
Fax: 020 76305040
Email: maria@ifhp.com
Website: http://www.ifhp.com
Members: 100
Staff: 3
Contact: George C. Halvorson, Chm./CEO
Description: Executes independent health care finance (100). Consists of associations of health funds (11) and individuals (26) in 20 countries. Promotes the study and development of independent health care services. Encourages research and the exchange of information. Shares information to a network of member health funds. Offers study tours and educational programs.
Formerly: Formerly, International Federation of Voluntary Health Service Funds
Publication: Proceedings
Publication title: Conference Proceedings
Meetings/Conventions: biennial conference – Exhibits.

02731

International Federation of Hydrographic Societies IFHS

PO Box 103, Plymouth, PL4 7YP, UK
Tel: 01752 223512
Fax: 01752 223512
Email: helen@hydrographicsociety.org
Website: http://www.hydrographicsociety.org
Members: 1500
Staff: 1
Contact: Helen Atkinson, Operations and Publications Mgr.
Description: Hydrographers and persons in approximately 70 countries working in associated academic, business, commercial, engineering, and professional disciplines. Promotes the science of surveying at sea and related sciences and encourages the exchange of information between technologists and others engaged in hydrography and related disciplines. Conducts workshops and international symposia. Maintains an educational fund for those starting a career in hydrography and allied sciences.
Formerly: Formerly, Hydrographic Society
Publication: Journal
Publication title: Hydrographic Journal. Advertisements.

02732

International Federation of Infection Control IFIC

c/o Ms. Pamela Allen
47 Wentworth Green, County Armagh, Portadown, BT62 3WG, UK
Tel: 028 38612555
Email: info@theific.org
Website: http://www.theific.org
Members: 66
Contact: Michael A. Borg, Chm.
Fee: £25
Membership Type: associate
Description: Serves as the umbrella organization for societies and organizations seeking to reduce or minimize nosocomial infections worldwide. Aims to develop network of infection control organizations. Promotes education and training programs and serves as liaison with the World Health Organization and other organizations.
Publication: Booklet
Publication title: Educational Programme for Infection Control Basic Concepts and Training
Meetings/Conventions: Education Conference – annual conference

02733

International Federation of Liberal and Radical Youth IFLRY

1 Whitehall Pl., London, SW1A 2HD, UK
Tel: 020 78710940
Fax: 020 71008159
Email: office@iflry.org
Website: http://iflry.org/Default.aspx
Members: 85
Staff: 1
Contact: Sarah Wong, Exec. Dir.
Description: International youth organizations representing 1,500,000 individuals in 52 countries. Strives to foster peace, freedom, justice, and international unity. Stages political pressure campaigns to denounce racism and xenophobia worldwide. Supports continued democratization of Eastern Europe.
Formerly: Formerly, European Federation of Liberal and Radical Youth

02734

International Federation of Municipal Engineering IFME

1 Great George St., Westminster, London, SW1P 3AA, UK
Tel: 02 72227722
Email: neilbuchan1@tiscali.co.uk
Website: http://www.ifme.info
Contact: Neil Buchan, Sec. Gen.
Description: Municipal engineers, public works directors, consultants, and educators in 17 countries. Seeks to improve cultural relations and promotes the sharing of municipal engineering papers and knowledge among affiliated organizations and members.
Formerly: Formerly, Institution of Civil Engineers

02735

International Federation of Park and Recreation Administration IFPRA

Globe House, Crispin Close, Caversham, Reading, RG4 7JS, UK
Tel: 0118 9461680
Fax: 0118 9461680
Email: ifpraworld@aol.com
Website: http://www.ifpra.org
Members: 456
Contact: Rob Small, Pres.
Fee: £25
Membership Type: retired, student
Fee: £45
Membership Type: professional or supporting
Description: Individuals from the fields of parks, recreation, amenity, leisure, and related services; government departments, municipal and public authorities, universities, and scientific and educational institutions; national allied professional associations are affiliates. Aims to: establish a world-coordinating center; collect and disseminate general and statistical information to members; promote the establishment of national associations for affiliation with the federation. Attempts to facilitate the exchange of students and professionals between countries and to adopt internationally acceptable training and qualification standards. Establishes special committees to study matters of professional interest; studies matters of professional interest; promotes research.
Publication: Bulletin
Publication title: IFPRA Bulletin. Advertisements.

02736

International Federation of Professional Aromatherapists IFPA

82 Ashby Rd., Leicestershire, Hinckley, LE10 1SN, UK
Tel: 01455 637987
Fax: 01455 890956
Email: admin@ifparoma.org
Website: http://www.ifparoma.org
Members: 2700
Staff: 3
Contact: Kerry Payne, Office Admin.
Description: Various categories of membership, the main group of which has trained with or meet the high standards required by IFPA accredited schools. Works to develop and stimulate high professional standards through qualification and practice. Provides accredited schools across the country, and local practitioner lists and public hot-line service.
Formerly: Formerly, International Society of Professional Aromatherapists
Publication: Journal
Publication title: Aromatherapy World. Advertisements.

02737

International Federation of Shipmasters' Associations IFSMA

202 Lambeth Rd., London, SE1 7JY, UK
Tel: 020 72610450
Fax: 020 79289030
Email: hq@ifsma.org
Website: http://www.ifsma.org
Members: 11000
Contact: Rodger M. MacDonald, Sec. Gen.
Fee: £45
Membership Type: individual
Fee: £5
Membership Type: joining
Description: National associations of qualified seagoing master mariners and shipmasters in 44 countries. Promotes safety at sea and serves as professional representative at meetings of the International Maritime Organization.
Publication: Newsletter
Publication title: IFSMA Newsletter - The International Shipmasters Link

02738

International Federation of Societies of Cosmetic Chemists IFSCC

Langham House E, Ste. 6, Mill St., Beds, Luton, LU1 2NA, UK
Tel: 01582 726661
Fax: 01582 405217
Email: enquiries@ifscc.org
Website: http://www.ifscc.org
Members: 14000
Staff: 2
Contact: Gavin Greenoak, Pres.
Description: National societies representing over 14,000 cosmetic chemists or cosmetic scientists throughout the world. Fosters advancement in cosmetic science by encouraging fundamental research in industry and academia. Provides information and documentation. Works to develop standardized procedures for analyses of raw materials and finished products and for estimating efficiency of products.
Publication: Monographs
Publication title: Scientific Monographs

02739

International Federation of the Periodical Press

Queens House, 55-56 Lincoln's Inn Fields, London, WC2A 3LJ, UK
Tel: 020 74044169
Fax: 020 74044170
Email: info@fipp.com
Website: http://www.fipp.com
Members: 800
Contact: Chris Llewellyn, Pres./CEO
Fee: £1250-3950
Membership Type: individual (associate)
Fee: £1370-7250
Membership Type: publisher
Description: National associations of periodical publishers (42) and individual periodical publishing companies (120) in 42 countries. Supports press freedom. Protects and represents the interests of its members before international bodies. Compiles and distributes information internationally. Promotes the image of the periodical press as an advertising medium. Encourages the adoption of uniform standards. Maintains liaison with United Nations Educational, Scientific and Cultural Organization, International Chamber of Commerce, and Universal Postal Union.
Library Subject: all aspects of periodical publishing
Library Type: open to the public
Publication: Report
Publication title: Global Research Update
Meetings/Conventions: World Magazine Congress – biennial congress – Exhibits.

02740

International Federation of the Phonographic Industry - England
IFPI

10 Piccadilly, London, W1J 0DD, UK
Tel: 020 78787900
Fax: 020 78787950
Email: info@ifpi.org
Website: http://www.ifpi.org
Members: 1400
Contact: Frances Moore, CEO
Fee: £2800
Membership Type: major producer of phonograms or music videos
Fee: £1400
Membership Type: medium-sized producer of phonograms or music videos
Description: Producers and distributors of phonograms and videograms in 75 countries. Promotes the interests of members through the use of statutes, case law, contracts, and agreements. Represents members on national and international copyright issues; coordinates anti-piracy actions. Compiles statistical information on the international recording industry. Provides industry contacts and advisory services.
Library Subject: copyright and other intellectual property matters
Library Type: reference
Publication title: Annual Review

02741

International Feed Industry Federation
IFIF

7 St. George's Terr., Gloucestershire, Cheltenham, GL50 3PT, UK
Tel: 01242 267702
Fax: 01242 267701
Email: membership@ifif.org
Website: http://www.ifif.org
Contact: Roger Gilbert, Sec. Gen.
Fee: £1000-20000
Membership Type: national feed association (based on annual national production)
Fee: £10000
Membership Type: corporate
Description: Feed companies, industry associations and federations, financial institutions, and suppliers to the feed industry. Promotes growth and development of the global feed industry. Gathers and disseminates information on the feed industries; represents members' interests before government agencies, industrial, and international trade organizations. Compiles statistics.
Publication: Newsletter
Publication title: IFIF News

02742

International Fellowship of Reconciliation - England

19 Paradise St., Oxford, OX1 1LD, UK
Tel: 01865 250781
Email: office@for.org.uk
Website: http://www.ifor.org
Contact: John Johansen-Berg, Chm.
Description: Represents the interests of men and women who are committed in political, social and economic transformation through non-violent ways. Promotes programs and activities for international understanding and cooperation.

02743

International Fellowship of Reconciliation - Wales

3, Tai Minffordd, Rhostryfan, Gwynedd, Caernarfon, LL54 7NF, UK
Tel: 01286 830913
Email: cymdeithasycymod@btinternet.com
Website: http://www.ifor.org
Description: Represents the interests of men and women who are committed in political, social and economic transformation through non-violent ways. Promotes programs and activities for international understanding and cooperation.

02744

International Fertiliser Society - England
IFS

PO Box 4, York, YO32 5YS, UK
Tel: 01904 492700
Fax: 01904 492700
Email: secretary@fertiliser-society.org
Website: http://www.fertiliser-society.org
Members: 450
Contact: Hans Reuvers, Pres.
Fee: £65
Membership Type: ordinary
Description: Agronomists, environmentalists, chemists, engineers, journalists, equipment manufacturers, contractors, marketing and purchasing managers. Provides a medium for the discussion of scientific, technical, economic and environmental aspects of production, use and application of fertilisers.
Formerly: Formerly, Fertiliser Society - England
Publication: Proceedings
Publication title: Proceedings of the International Fertiliser Society

02745

International Fishmeal and Fish Oil Organisation
IFFO

2 College Yard, Lower Dagnall St., Hertfordshire, St. Albans, AL3 4PA, UK
Tel: 01727 842844
Fax: 01727 842866
Email: secretariat@iffo.net
Website: http://www.iffo.net
Members: 200
Contact: Jonathan Shepherd, Dir. Gen.
Fee: £5000
Membership Type: producer
Fee: £2250
Membership Type: associate
Description: National fish meal and oil producing organizations and companies in 18 countries. Organizes and finances the interchange of production and trade statistics. Conducts research and promotes development. Acts as a network for technical and scientific information. Represents the industry before international organizations and users of fish meal and oil.
Formerly: Formerly, International Fish Meal and Oil Manufacturer Association
Publication: Bulletin
Publication title: Technical Bulletin

02746

International Food Information Service
IFIS

Lane End House, Shinfield Rd., Shinfield, Reading, RG2 9BB, UK
Tel: 0118 9883895
Fax: 0118 9885065
Email: ifis@ifis.org
Website: http://www.foodsciencecentral.com
Staff: 30
Contact: Luke Davies, Account Mgr.
Description: Publishes food science, food technology and food-related human nutrition information.
Publication: Journal
Publication title: Food Manufacturing Efficiency

02747

International Foundation for Dermatology
IFD

Willan House, 4 Fitzroy Sq., London, W1T 5HQ, UK
Fax: 020 73885263
Email: roderick.hay@ifd.org
Website: http://www.ifd.org
Contact: Roderick J. Hay, Chm.
Description: Seeks to improve dermatologic care in rural areas of developing countries.

02748

International Fur Trade Federation
IFTF

PO Box 495, Surrey, Weybridge, KT13 8WD, UK
Tel: 01932 850033
Email: pressoffice@iftf.com
Website: http://www.iftf.com
Members: 39
Contact: Andreas Lenhart, Chm.
Description: Represents für trade interests in 30 countries. Seeks to protect für trade interests. Promotes innovation, high standards and positive factual image of für and the für industry.

02749

International General Produce Association
IGPA

Gafta House, 6 Chapel Pl., Rivington St., London, EC2A 3SH, UK
Tel: 020 78149666
Fax: 020 78148383
Email: igpa@gafta.com
Website: http://www.igpa.com
Members: 100
Staff: 16
Contact: Pamela Kirby Johnson, Dir. Gen.
Fee: £450
Membership Type: full
Fee: £200
Membership Type: trade associate
Description: Traders in general produce.

02750

International Glaciological Society
IGS

Scott Polar Research Institute, Lensfield Rd., Cambridge, CB2 1ER, UK
Tel: 01223 355974
Fax: 01223 354931
Email: igsoc@igsoc.org
Website: http://www.igsoc.org
Members: 850
Staff: 5
Contact: E. Brun, Pres.
Fee: £79
Membership Type: ordinary
Fee: £40
Membership Type: junior (under the age of 30), student
Description: Persons with a scientific, practical, or general interest in any aspect of ice and snow study; membership comprises scientists and others from 33 countries in such fields as physics, meteorology, oceanography, geology, geography, engineering, and chemistry. The society also has 1000 libraries as subscribers. Aims to stimulate research and interest in the practical and scientific problems of snow and ice. Conducts symposia, discussions, and meetings.
Library Subject: glaciology
Library Type: not open to the public
Formerly: Formerly, British Glaciological Society
Publication: Journal
Publication title: Annals of Glaciology
Meetings/Conventions: Earth and Planetary Ice-Volcano Interactions – symposium

02751

International Glaucoma Association
IGA

15A Highpoint Business Village, Woodcote House, Henwood, Kent, Ashford, TN24 8DH, UK
Tel: 01233 648170
Fax: 01233 648179
Email: info@iga.org.uk
Website: http://www.glaucoma-association.com
Contact: David Wright, Chief Exec.
Fee: £17.5
Membership Type: friend
Fee: £250
Membership Type: life
Description: Glaucoma patients. Seeks to educate the public about glaucoma, its causes, detection, and treatment. Provides patients, doctors, opticians, optometrists, and others a forum for the exchange of ideas on glaucoma. Supports research; conducts surveys; disseminates information.
Formerly: Formerly, Glaucoma Association
Publication: Booklet
Publication title: Glaucoma - A Greater Understanding

02752

International Grains Council
IGC

1 Canada Sq., Canary Wharf, London, E14 5AE, UK
Tel: 020 75131122
Fax: 020 75130630
Email: igc@igc.int
Website: http://www.igc.org.uk/en/Default.aspx
Members: 26
Staff: 17
Description: Administers the Grains Trade Convention (1995), which is part of the International Grains Agreement (1995), an intergovernmental agreement whose main objectives are international cooperation in all aspects of grains, the expansion of grains trade and its freest possible flow, stability of international grains markets and enhanced food security. Provides a forum for the exchange of information and discussion of members' concerns regarding grains.
Formerly: Formerly, International Wheat Council
Publication: Report
Publication title: Grain Market Report
Meetings/Conventions: Grains Conference – annual conference

02753

International Grains Council I Food Aid Committee
FAC

1 Canada Sq., Canary Wharf, London, E14 5AE, UK
Tel: 020 75131122
Fax: 020 75130630
Email: igc@igc.int
Website: http://www.igc.org.uk/en/aboutus/default.aspx
Members: 33
Staff: 17
Description: Implements the Food Aid Convention 1999 (FAC), which is part of the International Grains Agreement, 1995.
Publication: Report
Publication title: Food Aid Shipments

02754

International Guild of Artists
IGA

Briargate, 2 The Brambles, Victoria Dr., Ilkley, LS29 9DH, UK
Tel: 01943 609075
Fax: 01943 603753
Email: info@britpaint.co.uk
Website: http://www.britpaint.co.uk
Members: 150
Contact: Margaret Simpson, Dir.
Fee: £100
Membership Type: selected artist
Description: Professional artists. Provides assistance and support to members. Operates a telephone helpline to answer members' art questions. Fosters communication among members.

02755

International Harbour Masters' Association
IHMA

PO Box 314, Fareham, PO17 5XZ, UK
Tel: 01329 832771
Fax: 01329 834975
Email: secretary.ihma@harbourmaster.org
Website: http://www.harbourmaster.org
Members: 236
Staff: 1
Contact: Michael Hadley, Sec.
Fee: £165
Membership Type: full
Fee: £80
Membership Type: associate
Description: Harbour masters from ports large and small, publicly and privately owned. Provides up-to-date, hands-on expertise in a range of maritime operations, including: safety of navigation, vessel traffic services, shipping movements, port management, protection of the marine environment, the ship/port interface, cargo handling, safety management and training, security, and the good practice of seamanship in port and harbour environs.
Publication: Newsletter
Publication title: Harbour Master. Advertisements.

02756

International Harm Reduction Association
IHRA

Unit 701-The Chandlery, 50 Westminster Bridge Rd., London 3051, UK
Tel: 020 79537412
Fax: 020 79537404
Email: info@ihra.net
Website: http://www.ihra.net
Contact: Rick Lines, Exec. Dir.
Fee: £80
Membership Type: premium
Fee: £20
Membership Type: individual
Description: Assists individuals and communities in improving health outcomes and in protecting human rights. Fosters collaboration and communication among individuals involved in harm reduction. Promotes best practices of reducing drug use and its prevention and treatment strategies. Provides education, training and research on harm reduction.

02757

International Headache Society
IHS

41 Welbeck St., London, W1G 8EA, UK
Email: carol.taylor@i-h-s.org
Website: http://www.i-h-s.org
Members: 1200
Staff: 1
Contact: Carol Taylor, Admin.
Fee: £195
Membership Type: ordinary
Fee: £60
Membership Type: clinical trainee, full-time student
Description: Conducts research into the causes, mechanisms, treatment and other aspects of headache.
Publication: Journal
Publication title: Cephalagia
Meetings/Conventions: biennial congress – Exhibits.

02758

International Hologram Manufacturers Association
IHMA

4 Windmill Business Village, Sunbury-on-Thames, TW16 7DY, UK
Tel: 01932 785680
Fax: 01932 780790
Email: info@ihma.org
Website: http://www.ihma.org
Contact: Ian M. Lancaster, Gen. Sec.
Fee: £1575-2200
Membership Type: full
Description: Represents and promotes the interests of hologram manufacturers worldwide.
Publication: Booklet
Publication title: Hologram Copyright Guidelines

02759
International Humanist and Ethical Union
IHEU
1 Gower St., London, WC1E 6HD, UK
Tel: 0870 2887631
Fax: 0870 2887631
Email: office@iheyo.org
Website: http://www.iheu.org
Members: 4000000
Staff: 3
Contact: Sonja Eggerickx, Pres.
Fee: £1518
Membership Type: full
Fee: £759
Membership Type: specialist
Description: Members of humanist and ethical organizations in 37 countries, which work against authoritarian traditions and encourage activities in the interest of a more humane world. Working parties coordinate activities in the field of moral education and human rights. Maintains an active part in issues of education, racism, pollution, mental health, and human rights through its relations with the Council of Europe, the United Nations Educational, Scientific and Cultural Organization, UNICEF, and the United Nations. Engages in development work in various parts of the world including Africa, Asia, the European Union, and Latin America through the Humanistic Institute for Cooperation with Developing Countries.
Publication: Magazine
Publication title: International Humanist News

02760
International Institute for Conservation of Historic and Artistic Works
IIC
6 Buckingham St., London, WC2N 6BA, UK
Tel: 020 78395975
Fax: 020 79761564
Email: iic@iiconservation.org
Website: http://www.iiconservation.org
Members: 4000
Staff: 2
Contact: Graham Voce, Exec. Sec.
Fee: £50
Membership Type: individual
Fee: £180
Membership Type: institution
Description: Restorers and conservators in private or museum practice, scientists, educators, and collection managers; supporting institutions include museums, galleries, libraries, universities, and research establishments. Provides a permanent organization for coordinating and improving the knowledge, methods, and working standards needed to protect and preserve historic and artistic works.
Publication: Articles
Publication title: Reviews in Conservation

02761
International Institute for Environment and Development
IIED
3 Endsleigh St., London, WC1H 0DD, UK
Tel: 020 73882117
Fax: 020 73882826
Email: info@iied.org
Website: http://www.iied.org
Staff: 55
Contact: Maureen O'Neil, Chair
Description: Aims to provide expertise and leadership in researching and achieving sustainable development at local, national, regional, and global levels. In alliance with others, seeks to help shape a future that ends global poverty and delivers and sustains efficient and equitable management of the world's natural resources.
Formerly: Formerly, International Institute for Environmental Affairs

02762
International Institute for Strategic Studies
IISS
Arundel House, 13-15 Arundel St., Temple Pl., London, WC2R 3DX, UK
Tel: 020 73797676
Fax: 020 78363108
Website: http://www.iiss.org
Members: 2500
Staff: 50
Contact: John Chipman, Dir. Gen./Chief Exec.
Fee: £25000
Membership Type: executive corporate
Fee: £10000
Membership Type: premier corporate
Description: Journalists, politicians, businesspersons, academic personnel, retired service officers, economists, and interested others in 80 countries; associate members are active service officers and government officials; corporate members are newspapers, universities, television stations, embassies and government ministries, service colleges, and other corporate entities. Prepares studies on topical strategic subjects.

02763
International Institute of Communications
IIC
Regent House, 24-25 Nutford Pl., London, W1H 5YN, UK
Tel: 020 77237210
Fax: 020 77236982
Email: j.grimshaw@iicom.org
Website: http://www.iicom.org
Members: 1500
Staff: 8
Contact: Fabio Colasanti, Pres.
Fee: £95
Membership Type: individual
Fee: £3700
Membership Type: institutional
Description: Broadcasters, academics, professionals, technologists, journalists and others; broadcasting organizations, telecommunications, computer and electronic firms, news agencies, corporations, foundations, and universities. Objectives are the provision of an independent forum for those concerned with present use and future development of communication and the promotion and dissemination of research and policy studies concerned with the impact of electronic media on society and with the economic, social, legal, and political implications of contemporary communication technology. Examines issues such as ownership, control of the media, cultural ecology, international telecommunications structures, communications, and development.
Publication: Journal
Publication title: Intermedia

02764
International Institute of Peace Studies and Global Philosophy
IIPSGP
Rhos y Gallt, Llanerfyl, Wales, Powys, SY21 0ER, UK
Tel: 01938 820586
Email: iipsgp@educationaid.net
Website: http://www.educationaid.net
Staff: 4
Contact: Thomas Clough Daffern, Dir.
Description: Promotes peace, education, interfaith, dialogue, comparative philosophy, educational research, and academic work.
Publication: Journal
Publication title: The Muses Journal

02765
International Institute of Reflexology
IIR
3 Ashley Ln., Sheffield, S21 1AB, UK
Tel: 01142 471725
Fax: 01142 471725
Email: info@reflexology-uk.net
Website: http://www.reflexology-uk.net/site
Contact: Dwight C. Byers, Pres.
Description: Dedicated to professional standards in reflexology based on the Ingham Method of Foot Reflexology.

02766
International Institute of Risk and Safety Management
IIRSM
Ste. 7a, 77 Fulham Palace Rd., London, W6 8JA, UK
Tel: 020 87419100
Fax: 020 87411349
Email: info@iirsm.org
Website: http://www.iirsm.org
Members: 8000
Staff: 5
Contact: Keith Scott, Chm.
Fee: £63
Membership Type: student
Fee: £107
Membership Type: affiliate
Description: Membership in various grades, is open to all individuals who have interest in occupational health, safety, and risk management. Benefits include newsletters and magazines. Designatory letters (where qualified). Conducts health and safety information services, seminars, and other events.
Publication: Newsletter
Publication title: Health and Safety Managers Newsletter

02767
International Institute of Tropical Agriculture - United Kingdom
IITA
Carolyn House, 26 Dingwall Rd., Croydon, CR9 3EE, UK
Tel: 020 86869031
Fax: 020 86808583
Email: hartmann@cgiar.org
Website: http://www.iita.org
Contact: Peter Hartmann, Dir. Gen.
Description: Works for the development of sustainable production systems in the humid tropics. Conducts

research to increase agricultural production, improve food systems and sustainable management of natural resources.

02768
International ISBN Agency
c/o EDItEUR
39-41 N Rd., London, N7 9DP, UK
Tel: 0207 5036418
Fax: 0207 5036418
Email: info@isbn-international.org
Website: http://www.isbn-international.org
Staff: 4
Contact: Brian Green, Exec. Dir.
Description: Promotes, coordinates and supervises the use of the International Standard Book Number (ISBN), a unique machine-readable identification number, which marks any book unmistakably and is defined by ISO standard 2108. The international agency approves the definition and structure of national ISBN agencies advising on their establishment and function while assigning them with group identifiers.
Publication: Handbook
Publication title: International ISBN Users' Manual

02769
International Labour Organization Office for the United Kingdom and Republic of Ireland
PO Box 54890, London, SW1P 9HL, UK
Tel: 020 77985681
Email: london@ilo.org
Website: http://www.ilo.org/public/english/region/eurpro/london_r/index.htm
Contact: Bill Brett, Dir.
Description: Formulates international labour standards in the form of conventions and recommendations setting minimum standards of basic human rights. Provides technical assistance primarily in the fields of vocational training and vocational rehabilitation, employment policy, labour administration, labour law and industrial relations. Promotes the development of independent employers' organizations. Promotes work and represents the interests of the International Labour Organization (ILO) in the United Kingdom and the Republic of Ireland.

02770
International Law Association
ILA
Charles Clore House, 17 Russell Sq., London, WC1B 5DR, UK
Tel: 020 73232978
Fax: 020 73233580
Email: info@ila-hq.org
Website: http://www.ila-hq.org
Members: 3700
Staff: 1
Contact: David J.C. Wyld, Sec. Gen.
Fee: £30
Membership Type: basic
Description: Lawyers and representatives in 85 countries active in the shipping, commercial, and banking industries. Fosters interest in the study, advancement and unification of international public and private law and comparative law, and in resolving legal conflicts. Conducts seminars.
Publication: Proceedings
Publication title: Conference Reports

02771
International Lead Association
ILA
17a Welbeck Way, London, W1G 9YJ, UK
Tel: 020 74998422
Fax: 020 74931555
Email: enq@ila-lead.org
Website: http://www.ila-lead.org
Members: 40
Staff: 6
Contact: Maura McDermott, Exec. Asst.
Description: Mining companies, metal producers, semi-fabricators, associations, and user groups in 10 countries. Promotes use of lead in all forms; represents the lead industry at national and international levels. Provides promotional and technical information concerning lead to developing countries. Organizes seminars on technical and environmental aspects of the production and use of lead. Conducts market surveys.
Library Type: reference
Meetings/Conventions: European Lead Battery Conference – biennial conference – Exhibits.

02772
International League Against Epilepsy of United Kingdom
ILAE UK
c/o Juliet Solomon, Membership Sec.
Institute of Neurology, 6th Fl., Department of Clinical Neurology, Queen Sq., London, WC1N 3BG, UK
Email: j.solomon@ion.ucl.ac.uk
Website: http://www.ilae-uk.org.uk
Contact: John Duncan, Pres.
Fee: £25
Membership Type: ordinary
Description: Seeks to advance and disseminate knowledge about Epilepsy. Aims to improve services and care for patients. Strives to increase public awareness of Epilepsy as a treatable brain disorder. Fosters the development of and cooperation among associations with common interests.

02773
International Marine Contractors Association
IMCA
52 Grosvenor Gardens, London, SW1W 0AU, UK
Tel: 020 78245520
Fax: 020 78245521
Email: imca@imca-int.com
Website: http://www.imca-int.com
Members: 130
Staff: 6
Contact: Hugh Williams, Chief Exec.
Fee: £2265
Membership Type: international or national contractor, vessel owner
Fee: £1135
Membership Type: supplier of equipment or services
Description: Companies active in the offshore marine contracting industry, including vessel owners/operators, and marine and underwater contractors. Represents members on an international basis with particular reference to improvements in safety standards.
Formerly: Absorbed, The AODC

02774
International Maritime Industries Forum
IMIF
c/o The Baltic Exchange
38 St. Mary Axe, London, EC3A 8BH, UK
Tel: 020 79296429
Fax: 020 79296430
Email: imif@btconnect.com
Website: http://web.ukonline.co.uk/imif
Contact: J.G. Davis, Chm.
Description: Shipowners and builders, shipbreakers, oil companies, insurance companies, classification societies, and bankers in 25 countries. Seeks to: maintain a healthy commercial and financial climate for all sectors of shipping, including ownership, operation, construction, and international trade; encourage discussions of mutual interest; foster change and stimulate action to benefit the maritime industry. Strives to upgrade the standards of ships, port state control and to establish shipbreaking plants in the Third World to promote its large market for rerolled and recycled ship scrap.

02775
International Maritime Organization
IMO
4, Albert Embankment, London, SE1 7SR, UK
Tel: 020 77357611
Fax: 020 75873210
Email: info@imo.org
Website: http://www.imo.org
Members: 169
Staff: 300
Contact: Efthimios E. Mitropoulos, Sec. Gen.
Description: Governments involved in promoting the safety and security of international merchant shipping and preventing pollution at sea caused by ships.
Library Subject: maritime, shipping
Library Type: reference
Formerly: Formerly, Intergovernmental Maritime Consultative Organization
Publication: Magazine
Publication title: IMO News. Advertisements.
Meetings/Conventions: Assembly – biennial assembly

02776
International Maritime Pilots' Association
IMPA
HQS Wellington, Temple Stairs, Victoria Embankment, London, WC2R 2PN, UK
Tel: 020 72403973
Fax: 020 72403518
Email: office@impahq.org
Website: http://www.impahq.org
Members: 8000
Contact: Nick Cutmore, Sec. Gen.
Description: Associations of maritime pilots in 40 countries. Disseminates information on matters of mutual interest to members.
Publication: Newsletter
Publication title: International Pilot. Advertisements.

02777

International Maritime Rescue Federation

IMRF

W Quay Rd., Poole, BH15 1HZ, UK
Tel: 01202 663398
Fax: 01202 663399
Email: info@international-maritime-rescue.org
Website: http://www.international-maritime-rescue.org
Members: 89
Staff: 2
Contact: Gerry Keeling, CEO
Description: Government-organized and voluntary lifeboat services. Activities include the design and operation of lifeboats, search and rescue at sea, communications, and medical, financial, and training programs. Demonstrates boats and equipment. Exchanges information regarding new methods of rescue.
Formerly: Formerly, International Lifeboat Federation
Publication: Proceedings
Publication title: Conference Report

02778

International Maritime Satellite Organisation

Inmarsat

99 City Rd., London, EC1Y 1AX, UK
Tel: 020 77281777
Fax: 020 77281142
Email: customer_care@inmarsat.com
Website: http://www.inmarsat.com
Members: 67
Description: Aims to pursue a range of new data opportunities at the convergence of information technology, telecoms and mobility, while continuing to serve traditional maritime, aeronautical, land-mobile and remote-area markets.
Publication: Magazine
Publication title: Via Inmarsat incorporating Ocean Voice

02779

International Masonry Society

IMS

6 Church Rd., Surrey, Whyteleafe, CR3 0AR, UK
Tel: 020 86603633
Fax: 020 86686983
Email: secretary@masonry.org.uk
Website: http://www.masonry.org.uk
Contact: Kenneth Fisher, Sec.
Description: Promotes discussion and advancement of the science and practice of masonry as allied to its constituent materials, and to all aspects of the design and use of masonry and the construction process. Aims to provide a means of contact for all those involved in masonry science, design and industry, generating published papers having an international circulation.
Formerly: Formerly, British Masonry Society
Publication: Journal
Publication title: Masonry International

02780

International Menopause Society

IMS

PO Box 687, Wray, Lancaster, LA2 8WY, UK
Tel: 015242 21190
Fax: 015242 22596
Email: jwright.ims@btopenworld.com
Website: http://www.imsociety.org
Members: 800
Contact: Jean Wright, Exec. Dir.
Fee: £175
Membership Type: regular
Description: Medical doctors, sociologists, psychologists, anthropologists, and others in 42 countries interested in basic research and clinical work in the field of menopause and climacteric. Objectives are to promote study of medical, sociological, and psychological aspects of the climacteric, or menopausal stage in men and women and to advance international exchange of information and research plans. Studies subjects such as anatomy, gynecology, biochemistry, cardiology, etc. and psychology as they relate to the aging process; examines methods of management, preventive measures, and therapeutic problems related to aging.
Library Subject: menopause
Library Type: not open to the public
Publication: Journal
Publication title: Climacteric. Advertisements.
Meetings/Conventions: World Congress on the Menopause – triennial congress – Exhibits.

02781

International Mobile Satellite Organization

IMSO

99 City Rd., London, EC1Y 1AX, UK
Tel: 020 77281249
Fax: 020 77281172
Email: info@imso.org
Website: http://www.imso.org
Members: 88
Contact: Esteban Pacha-Vicente, Dir. Gen.
Description: Supports links for phone, fax and data communications to more than 287,000 ship, vehicle, aircraft and other mobile users.

02782

International Molybdenum Association

IMOA

4 Healthfield Terr., London, W4 4JE, UK
Tel: 0207 8711580
Fax: 0208 9946067
Email: info@imoa.info
Website: http://www.imoa.info
Contact: Tim Outteridge, Sec. Gen.
Fee: £7800
Membership Type: general
Description: Promotes the use of molybdenum in architecture, building and construction. Develops and disseminates toxicity and ecotoxicity data to regulatory authorities.

02783

International Musculoskeletal Laser Society

IMLAS

Office Block 1, Southlink Business Park, Hamilton St., Oldham, OL4 1DE, UK
Tel: 0161 6281394
Fax: 0161 6281394
Email: imlas@imlas.org
Website: http://www.imlas.org
Members: 350
Staff: 1
Contact: Martin Knight, Gen. Sec.
Fee: £150
Membership Type: physician fellow, physician-associate, technical
Fee: £50
Membership Type: student
Description: Advances the development of medical laser techniques, mainly in the musculoskeletal system.

02784

International Network for Contemporary Iraqi Artists

INCIA

c/o Ayagallery
15 Fulham High St., London, SW6 3JH, UK
Tel: 020 73718080
Email: info@incia.co.uk
Website: http://www.incia.co.uk
Contact: Maysaloun Faraj, Founder/Chair
Description: Seeks to advance and educate the public about Iraqi art. Assists in the provision of exhibitions, literature, workshops and advocacy related to Iraqi art.

02785

International Network for the Availability of Scientific Publications

INASP

60 St. Aldates, Oxford, OX1 1ST, UK
Tel: 01865 249909
Fax: 01865 251060
Email: inasp@inasp.info
Website: http://www.inasp.info
Staff: 15
Contact: Tag McEntegart, Exec. Dir.
Description: Promotes the enhancement in the flow of information within and between countries, especially those with less developed systems of publication and dissemination. Encourages access to and dissemination of scientific and scholarly information and knowledge.
Publication: Annual Report
Publication title: INASP Annual Report

02786

International Network of Liberal Women

INLW

1 Whitehall Pl., London, SW1A 2HD, UK
Email: inlw@inlw.org
Website: http://www.inlw.org/default.asp?id_cat=19
Members: 1800
Contact: Joaquima Alemany, Pres.
Fee: £10
Membership Type: individual
Fee: £150
Membership Type: group
Description: Comprises of women representatives of parties and groups within Liberal International.

02787

International NGO Training and Research Centre INTRAC

Oxbridge Ct., Osney Mead, Oxford, OX2 0ES, UK
Tel: 01865 201851
Fax: 01865 201852
Email: info@intrac.org
Website: http://www.intrac.org
Staff: 20
Contact: Geof Wood, Chm.
Description: Provides specialist training, consultancy, and research services to international relief and development organizations. Focuses on key areas such as North/South NGO relations, strategic policy issues, performance assessment, small enterprise development, and strengthening Southern NGOs and training centres. Works to improve the effectiveness and performance of Northern and Southern NGOs.
Publication: Book
Publication title: Measuring the Process: Guidelines for Evaluating Social Development

02788

International Oil Pollution Compensation Funds IOPC Funds

23rd Fl., Portland House, Bressenden Pl., London, SW1E 5PN, UK
Tel: 0207 5927100
Fax: 0207 5927111
Email: info@iopcfund.org
Website: http://www.iopcfund.org
Members: 103
Staff: 26
Contact: Willem Oosterveen, Dir.
Description: Provides compensation for oil pollution damage resulting from spills of persistent oil from tankers.
Publication: Manual
Publication title: Claims Manual

02789

International Opticians Association IOA

c/o Association of British Dispensing Opticians
199 Gloucester Terr., London, W2 6LD, UK
Tel: 020 72985100
Fax: 020 72985111
Email: general@abdo.org.uk
Website: http://www.abdo.org.uk
Members: 7
Staff: 2
Contact: Don Smith, Pres.
Description: Companies engaged in the business of retail opticians which are optical employers. Represents the interests of optical employers, in legislation, relating with the Department of Health, with the General Optical Council and other optical bodies. Issues advice and guidance to members and is involved in European matters through the Joint Optical Committee on the EC.
Formerly: Formerly, Federation of Ophthalmic and Dispensing Opticians

02790

International Organ Festival at St. Albans

PO Box 80, St. Albans, AL3 4HR, UK
Tel: 01727 844765
Fax: 01727 868941
Email: info@organfestival.com
Website: http://www.organfestival.com
Members: 550
Contact: Peter Hurford, Founder/Pres.
Fee: £25
Membership Type: ordinary
Fee: £40
Membership Type: joint
Description: Musicians, musicologists, and others interested in the study of the organ and organ music of the baroque, romantic, and 20th century styles. Promotes exchange and cooperation between members in 28 countries. Holds organ, choral, vocal, orchestral, and instrumental performances. Produces children's events. Organizes master classes. Promotes student interest in and study of baroque organ music and performance.
Publication: Newsletter
Publication title: IOF Newsletter. Advertisements.

02791

International Organization for Migration - United Kingdom IOM

21 Westminster Palace Gardens, Artillery Row, London, SW1P 1RR, UK
Tel: 020 72330001
Fax: 020 72333001
Email: iomuk@iom.int
Website: http://www.iomlondon.org
Description: Carries out operational assistance programs for migrants. Encourages social and economic development through migration. Prevents trafficking and smuggling of persons. Fosters orderly and planned migration of refugees, displaced persons and other individuals to countries offering resettlement opportunities. Upholds the human dignity and well-being of migrants.
Publication: Newsletter
Publication title: IOM in the UK

02792

International Organization for Succulent Plant Study IOS

The Manse, Chapel Ln., Milborne Port, Sherborne, DT9 5DL, UK
Email: secretariat@iosweb.org
Website: http://www.iosweb.org
Contact: David Hunt, Sec.
Description: Professional botanists and horticulturists in more than 30 countries who are interested in research, conservation, and cultivation of water-retaining plants, such as cacti. Promotes the study of succulent and allied plants and encourages cooperation between national and international organizations.
Library Subject: succulent plants
Library Type: reference
Publication: Bulletin
Publication title: IOS Bulletin

02793

International Orthoptic Association IOA

Moorfields Eye Hospital, City Rd., London, EC1V 2PD, UK
Email: secretary@internationalorthoptics.org
Website: http://www.internationalorthoptics.org
Members: 4000
Contact: Elizabeth Caines, Pres.
Description: Represents orthoptists in 22 countries certified to treat defects in binocular vision, faulty visual habits, and low visual acuity.
Library Type: reference
Publication: Journal
Publication title: Abstracts of Congress. Advertisements.
Meetings/Conventions: International Orthoptic Congress – quadrennial congress – Exhibits.

02794

International Otter Survival Fund IOSF

7, Black Park, Isle of Skye, Broadford, IV49 9DE, UK
Tel: 01471 822487
Fax: 01471 822487
Email: info@otter.org
Website: http://www.otter.org
Contact: Paul Yoxon, Hd. of Operations
Description: Dedicated to protecting all 13 species of otters worldwide and supports people working in rescue and rehabilitation, education and practical conservation.
Publication: Journal
Publication title: Journal of the International Otter Survival Fund

02795

International P.E.N. - England

50-51 High Holborn, Brownlow House, London, WC1V 6ER, UK
Tel: 020 74050338
Fax: 020 74050339
Email: info@internationalpen.org.uk
Website: http://www.internationalpen.org.uk
Members: 14000
Staff: 5
Contact: John Ralston Saul, Pres.
Description: Poets, playwrights, essayists, novelists, editors, translators, radio and television scriptwriters, historians, and other types of writers from 96 countries. Promotes intellectual exchange, friendship, and goodwill among writers internationally. Supports freedom of expression. Promotes freedom for the exchange of literature among all countries regardless of political situations. Informs publishers, editors, librarians, and university departments about literature in languages of lesser currency. Defends writers suffering from governmental harassment, imprisonment, or other forms of oppression. Holds special subject conferences and literary sessions.
Formerly: Formerly, Federation Internationale des P.E.N. Clubs
Publication: Magazine
Publication title: Pen International

02796

International P.E.N. - Scottish Centre

c/o The Writers' Museum
Lady Stairs' Close, Lawnmarket, Edinburgh, EH1 2PA, UK
Email: info@scottishpen.org
Website: http://www.scottishpen.org
Members: 250
Contact: John Ralston Saul, Pres.
Fee: £25
Membership Type: regular
Description: Writers and editors united to: encourage and support writing in Scotland, encourage and support among countries; provide for the "unhampered transmission of thought" within and between nations; combat the suppression of freedom of expression;

oppose arbitrary censorship and the "evils" that often accompany a free press, such as deceptive publication and deliberate falsifications for political or personal gain.

02797

International P.E.N., Writers in Prison Committee WIPC

Brownlow House, 50/51 High Holborn, London, WC1V 6ER, UK
Tel: 020 74050338
Fax: 020 74050339
Email: info@internationalpen.org.uk
Website: http://www.internationalpen.org.uk
Members: 45
Staff: 3
Contact: Caroline McCormick, Exec. Dir.
Description: A committee of International P.E.N. Seeks to secure the release from prison, house arrest, or confinement in a psychiatric institution of writers, journalists, translators, and publishers worldwide who have been detained for their writings or opinions. Works to ensure that imprisoned writers are treated well and given prompt, fair trials. Conducts letter-writing campaigns directed at authorities responsible for the imprisonment of writers; sends delegations to visit imprisoned writers; encourages members to "adopt" an imprisoned writer, work for their release and publish and distribute their works. Conducts research.
Publication: Report
Publication title: Writers in Prison Committee Report

02798

International Patient Association for Primary Immunodeficiencies IPOPI

Firstside, Main Rd., Downderry, Cornwall, PL11 3LE, UK
Tel: 01503 250668
Fax: 01503 250961
Email: info@ipopi.org
Website: http://www.ipopi.org
Contact: David Watters, Exec. Dir.
Description: Represent the interests of the primary immune deficiency community. Improves the quality of life of people with primary immunodeficiencies. Promotes access to early diagnosis and optimal treatment of primary immunodeficiencies.
Publication: Newsletter
Publication title: e-Update

02799

International PEN Writers Association

Brownlow House, 50/51 High Holborn, London, WC1V 6ER, UK
Tel: 020 74050338
Fax: 020 74050339
Email: info@internationalpen.org.uk
Website: http://www.internationalpen.org.uk
Members: 15000
Staff: 7
Contact: John Ralston Saul, International Pres.
Description: Works for international cooperation and the maintenance of the free exchange of ideas between writers of all nations; operates for freedom of expression.
Publication: Magazine
Publication title: PEN International

02800

International Permafrost Association - United Kingdom

University of Sussex, Dept. of Geography, Brighton, BN1 9QJ, UK
Tel: 01273 678293
Fax: 01273 677196
Email: j.b.murton@sussex.ac.uk
Website: http://ipa.arcticportal.org
Contact: Julian Murton, Contact
Description: Fosters the dissemination of knowledge concerning permafrost and promotes the cooperation of persons and national or international organizations engaged in scientific investigations and engineering work on permafrost. Conducts theoretical, basic, and applied frozen ground research (including permafrost, seasonal frost, artificial freezing, and periglacial phenomena).

02801

International Petroleum Industry Environmental Conservation Association IPIECA

209-215 Blackfriars Rd., 5th Fl., London, SE1 8NL, UK
Tel: 020 76332388
Fax: 020 76332389
Email: info@ipieca.org
Website: http://www.ipieca.org
Members: 35
Staff: 6
Contact: Richard Sykes, Exec. Sec.
Description: Represents 52% of worldwide oil and gas production drawn from 26 private and state-owned companies as well as 12 national, regional, international associations. Represents both upstream and downstream of the oil and gas industry on key global environmental issues, including oil spill preparedness and response, global climate change, health, fuel quality, biodiversity and social responsibility.

02802

International Planned Parenthood Federation - United Kingdom IPPF

4 Newhams Row, London, SE1 3UZ, UK
Tel: 020 79398200
Fax: 020 79398300
Email: info@ippf.org
Website: http://www.ippf.org/en
Members: 180
Staff: 248
Contact: Gill Greer, Dir. Gen.
Description: Initiates and supports worldwide sexual and reproductive health services, including family planning, HIV prevention, care, and support programs.
Publication: Handbook
Publication title: Family Planning Handbook for Health Professionals

02803

International Police Association IPA

Intl. Administration Ctre., 1 Fox Rd., West Bridgford, Nottingham, NG2 6AJ, UK
Tel: 0115 9455985
Fax: 0115 9822578
Email: isg@ipa-iac.org
Website: http://www.ipa-iac.org
Members: 390500
Staff: 2
Contact: Georgios Karsaropoulos, International Sec. Gen.
Description: Members of the police service, either in employment or retired. Seeks to unite all active and retired members of the police service to establish ties of friendship and mutual aid among them. Organizes exchange holidays, pen-friendships, and group visits; encourages and stimulates public service to promote respect for law and the maintenance of order among members of the police service in all countries. Engages in social and cultural activities; Works to establish a correspondence service. NGO (special status) with UN, the council of Europe and UNESCO.
Publication: Newsletter
Publication title: ISG Newsletter

02804

International Powered Access Federation IPAF

Moss End Business Village, Crooklands, LA7 7NU, UK
Tel: 015395 66700
Fax: 015395 66084
Email: info@ipaf.org
Website: http://www.ipaf.org
Contact: Tim Whiteman, Managing Dir.
Description: Represents manufacturers, owners, hirers and users of all types of powered access equipment through direct international involvement in legislation and safety standards affecting powered access users. Promotes and extends use of members' products; takes action on matters of interest to powered access equipment industry; encourages high standards of safety and good trading by members; promotes safety for operators; represents industry at government level in user countries; liaises with other trade associations; encourages technical efficiency by cooperation in the establishment of standards and discussion of common issues.
Formerly: Formerly, International Work Platform Association
Publication: Magazine
Publication title: Access International. Advertisements.
Meetings/Conventions: IPAF Summit – annual conference

02805

International Press Telecommunications Council IPTC

20 Garrick St., London, WC2E 9BT, UK
Tel: 020 31784922
Fax: 020 76647878
Email: office@iptc.org
Website: http://www.iptc.org
Members: 70
Contact: Michael Steidl, Managing Dir.
Description: Develops and publishes news industry standards for the interchange of news data. Seeks representation on national and international organisations or committees dealing with telecommunications matters.
Publication: Newsletter
Publication title: Mirror

02806

International Private Practitioners Association
IPPA

Worcester Park Physiotherapy Clinic, 9 Worcester Gardens, Worcester Park, Worcester, UK
Tel: 0208 3304204
Fax: 0208 3371650
Email: jean.kelly@physiofit.org.uk
Website: http://www.ippaworld.org
Contact: Jean Kelly, Chair
Fee: £250-650
Membership Type: full (based on the number of individual members registered with the private organization)
Fee: £250
Membership Type: associate
Description: Fosters cooperation between physical therapists in independent practice throughout the world. Encourages improved standards of independent practice by physical therapists. Advances independent practice by communication and exchange of information.

02807

International Professional Security Association - England
IPSA

Northumberland House, 11, The Pavement, Popes Ln., Ealing, London, W5 4NG, UK
Tel: 020 88327417
Fax: 020 88327418
Email: post@ipsamail.org.uk
Website: http://www.ipsa.org.uk
Members: 550
Staff: 6
Contact: Patrick J. Somerville, Intl. Chm.
Fee: £64.32
Membership Type: individual (ordinary)
Fee: £128.64
Membership Type: individual (management, associate, trainer)
Description: Employers and employees in the field of industrial and commercial security. Works to improve the status of the industry by organizing educational activities for security staff, including lectures, seminars, and training courses.
Library Subject: security
Library Type: reference
Publication: Book
Publication title: 1001 Things To Know About Security

02808

International Psychoanalytical Association
IPA

Broomhills, Woodside Ln., London, N12 8UD, UK
Tel: 020 84468324
Fax: 020 84454729
Email: ipa@ipa.org.uk
Website: http://www.ipa.org.uk
Members: 10700
Staff: 8
Contact: Charles M.T. Hanly, Pres.
Description: Organizations in 30 countries involved in psychoanalysis. Encourages communication among members and promotes high educational standards. Organizes training programs, conferences, and gives research grants.
Publication: Booklet
Publication title: Information Booklet
Meetings/Conventions: Psychoanalysis: Working at the Frontiers – biennial congress – Exhibits.

02809

International Public Relations Association
IPRA

12 Dunley Hill Ct., Ranmore Common, Surrey, Dorking, RH5 6SX, UK
Tel: 01483 280130
Fax: 01483 280131
Email: info@ipra.org
Website: http://www.ipra.org
Members: 1000
Staff: 3
Contact: Elizabeth Ananto, Pres.
Fee: £200
Membership Type: regular
Description: Senior public relations practitioners in over 95 countries worldwide. Provides for exchange and dissemination of professional information, standards, and education. Supports the International Foundation for Public Relations Research and Education. Compiles statistics.
Publication: Journal
Publication title: Frontline. Advertisements.
Meetings/Conventions: annual conference

02810

International Records Management Trust
IRMT

88-90 Hatton Garden, Ste. 14/15 2nd Fl., London, EC1 8PN, UK
Tel: 020 78314101
Fax: 020 78316303
Email: info@irmt.org
Website: http://www.irmt.org
Staff: 7
Contact: Anne Thurston, Dir.
Description: Provides records and archive management services. Supports developing countries to preserve official records. Gives technical consultancy, educational projects and research projects.
Library Subject: public sector records, human resource records management, financial records management, legal and judicial records management, freedom of information, Africa, Asia
Library Type: not open to the public

02811

International Salvage Union
ISU

St. Clare House, 2nd Fl., 30-33 Minories, London, EC3N 1BP, UK
Tel: 020 31799222
Fax: 020 31799224
Email: isu@marine-salvage.com
Website: http://www.marine-salvage.com
Members: 52
Contact: Michael Lacey, Sec. Gen.
Fee: £950
Membership Type: associate
Description: Represents the marine salvage industry. Fosters a wider understanding of the industry's contribution to environmental protection and the recovery of property.
Publication: Magazine
Publication title: Bulletin 23

02812

International Seismological Centre
ISC

Pipers Ln., Berkshire, Thatcham, RG19 4NS, UK
Tel: 01635 861022
Fax: 01635 872351
Email: admin@isc.ac.uk
Website: http://www.isc.ac.uk
Members: 64
Staff: 9
Contact: Dmitry Storchak, Dir.
Fee: £2100
Membership Type: general
Description: National seismological academies of science, research institutes, and government departments (45); reinsurance companies, engineering consultancies, and oil and instrument companies requiring earthquake information are associate members (19). Objectives are to: collect, analyze, and disseminate information on earthquakes worldwide; continually refine information on earthquake times and positions; act as an international source for information on earthquake locations and statistics; search for undetected earthquakes. Collects earthquake readings from 2000 seismograph stations. Conducts consulting services; maintains collection of computer programs and files.
Library Type: reference

02813

International SGML/XML Users' Group
ISUG

Copse House, 15 Upton Close, Wilts, Swindon, SN25 4UL, UK
Fax: 01793 721106
Email: info@isgmlug.org
Website: http://www.isgmlug.org
Members: 1100
Contact: Yvonne Vine, Sec.
Fee: £62
Membership Type: individual
Fee: £125
Membership Type: corporate
Description: Users of SGML/XML computer software worldwide. Promotes efficient use of this program and full exploitation of its capabilities. Serves as a forum for discussion of matters of common interest to members.
Publication: Newsletter
Publication title: InterChange. Advertisements.

02814

International Ship Electrical and Engineering Service Association
ISES

Studio 204, Mill Studio, Crane Mead, Hertfordshire, Ware, SG12 9PY, UK
Tel: 01920 444005
Fax: 01920 444006
Email: secretariat@isesassociation.com
Website: http://www.isesassociation.com
Contact: Thomas S. Cash, Sec. Gen.
Fee: £950
Membership Type: new
Fee: £1950
Membership Type: regular
Description: Repair and service companies. Provides quality electrical, electronic, and specialized marine services, either in port or during a voyage.
Formerly: Formerly, International Ship Electric Service Association
Publication title: ISES Marine Service Guide

02815

International Ship Suppliers and Services Association ISSA

The Baltic Exchange, 38 St. Mary Axe, London, EC3A 8BH, UK
Tel: 020 76266236
Fax: 020 76266234
Email: secretariat@shipsupply.org
Website: http://www.shipsupply.org
Members: 1620
Staff: 1
Contact: Jens Olsen, Pres.
Description: Companies in 87 countries engaged in the supplying of merchant and naval shipping with ship stores. Aims to promote, maintain and protect the economic interests of ship suppliers; represents the industry at international level; promotes relationships with ship owners and managers; encourages members to abide by Code of Ethics.
Library Type: reference
Publication: Directory
Publication title: International Ship Suppliers Register
Meetings/Conventions: annual convention – Exhibits.

02816

International Shipping Federation ISF

12 Carthusian St., London, EC1M 6EZ, UK
Tel: 020 74178844
Fax: 020 74178877
Email: isf@marisec.org
Website: http://www.marisec.org
Members: 35
Staff: 4
Contact: Spyros Polemis, Pres.
Description: National shipowners' associations and maritime employers' federations in 30 countries. Monitors and disseminates information on all aspects of maritime employment and social affairs; proposes and coordinates international shipowners' positions concerning employment and other public issues; represents members before governments and unions, particularly before the international bodies concerned with these issues. Promotes the exchange of views and policies among members on questions pertaining to the employment of seamen, such as pay conditions and benefits of officers and ratings at the national level, relations with unions, developments in manning organization on board, the role of management in ship operations, safe working practices, and maritime training.
Publication: Book
Publication title: Guidelines on Good Employment Practice

02817

International Skin Care Nursing Group ISNG

21 Tower St., Covent Garden, London, WC2H 9NS, UK
Tel: 020 73951924
Email: secretariat@isng.org
Website: http://www.isng.org
Contact: Steven Ersser, Chm.
Description: Promotes healthy skin care.
Publication: Pamphlet
Publication title: Lymphatic Filariasis Leaflet

02818

International Society for Anthrozoology ISAZ

c/o Dr. Anthony L. Podberscek, Ed.
University of Cambridge, Dept. of Veterinary Medicine, Madingley Rd., Cambridge, CB3 0ES, UK
Email: secretary@isaz.net
Website: http://www.isaz.net
Contact: Erika Friedmann, Pres.
Fee: £53
Membership Type: individual, society affiliate
Fee: £26.5
Membership Type: student affiliate
Description: Aims to promote the study of all aspects of human-animal relationships. Activities include publishing research, holding public meetings, and dissemination information to support objectives.
Meetings/Conventions: Human-Animal Interaction: Impacting Multiple Species – annual conference

02819

International Society for Clinical Electrophysiology of Vision ISCEV

Dept. of Vision Sciences, Glasgow Caledonian Univ., Cowcaddens Rd., Glasgow, G4 0BA, UK
Tel: 0141 3313388
Fax: 0141 3313387
Email: dlmc@gcal.ac.uk
Website: http://www.iscev.org
Members: 500
Staff: 25
Contact: Daphne L. McCulloch, Sec. Gen.
Fee: £135
Membership Type: regular, corporate
Fee: £270
Membership Type: regular, corporate
Description: Ophthalmologists, vision scientists, and other individuals interested in the electrophysiology of vision. Seeks to advance understanding of the mechanics of vision; promotes development of new ophthalmologic techniques and technologies; facilitates cooperation and communication among workers in the field of the clinical and basic electrophysiology of vision; formulates standards of terminology, research, and practice in the field.
Library Type: reference
Publication: Newsletter
Publication title: Documents of Ophthalmology

02820

International Society for Ecology and Culture ISEC

Foxhole, Devon, Darlington, TQ9 6EB, UK
Tel: 01803 868650
Fax: 01803 868651
Email: infouk@isec.org.uk
Website: http://www.isec.org.uk
Contact: Kristen Steele, Contact
Description: Promotes locally-based alternatives to the global consumer culture.
Publication: Book
Publication title: Ancient Futures: Learning from Ladakh

02821

International Society for Eighteenth-Century Studies ISECS

c/o Voltaire Foundation
99 Banbury Rd., Oxford, OX2 6JX, UK
Email: admin@isecs.org
Website: http://www.isecs.org
Members: 9000
Contact: Keith Baker, Pres.
Description: Individuals interested in 18th century culture; libraries, associations, and institutes concerned with 18th century studies are corporate members. Objectives are to promote growth, development, and cooperation in studies and research related to the 18th century and to advance communication and circulation of information.

02822

International Society for Endocrinology ISE

c/o Ms. Carol Kenny, Sec.
University of Birmingham, Institute of Biomedical Research, Dept. of Medicine, Wolfson Dr., Edgbaston, Birmingham, B15 2TT, UK
Tel: 0121 4147075
Email: info@endosociety.com
Website: http://www.endosociety.com
Members: 63
Contact: Hannah van Oudheusden, Exec. Off.
Description: Federation of national endocrinology societies with 15,000 individual members. Disseminates information on endocrinology and facilitates collaboration between national endocrinological societies and persons interested in the field.
Publication: Newsletter
Publication title: Abstracts of Congresses

02823

International Society for Heart Research ISHR

Cardiovascular Division, King's College London, Rayne Institute, St. Thomas Hospital, London, SE1 7EH, UK
Tel: 020 71883899
Fax: 020 71880970
Email: metin.avkiran@kcl.ac.uk
Website: http://www.ishrworld.org
Members: 3000
Contact: Metin Avkiran, Sec. Gen.
Fee: £55
Membership Type: in Australia
Fee: £44
Membership Type: full-time graduate student in Australia
Description: Professionals and investigators in the field of experimental cardiology united to foster multidisciplinary approaches for finding solutions to the problems of heart disease. Conducts research in cardiac metabolism.
Formerly: Formerly, International Society for Cardiovascular Research
Publication: Journal
Publication title: Advances in Myocardiology

02824
International Society for Prosthetics and Orthotics - United Kingdom
ISPO

c/o Irene Cameron
PO Box 2781, Glasgow, G61 3YL, UK
Tel: 0141 5604092
Fax: 0141 5604092
Email: info@ispo.org.uk
Website: http://www.ispo.org.uk
Contact: Paul Charlton, Chm.
Fee: £85
Membership Type: full
Fee: £27
Membership Type: student
Description: Encourages a high level of clinical practice around the world through research, education and training. Facilitates exchange of ideas and information among members.

02825
International Society for Soil Mechanics and Geotechnical Engineering
ISSMGE

City University, Northampton Sq., London, EC1V 0HB, UK
Tel: 020 70408154
Email: secretariat@issmge.org
Website: http://www.issmge.org/web/page.aspx
Members: 76
Staff: 2
Contact: R.N. Taylor, Sec. Gen.
Description: National societies of engineers in soil mechanics and related areas representing 17,000 individuals. Fosters international fellowship and cooperation among engineers and scientists for the advancement of knowledge in the field of geotechnics and its engineering applications. Facilitates exchange of information among member societies. Maintains 29 technical committees.
Publication: Proceedings
Publication title: Conference Proceedings

02826
International Society for Spelaeological Art
ISSA

49 Grove Meadows, Cleobury Mortimer, Worcestershire, Kidderminster, DY14 8AG, UK
Email: crazeechris@hotmail.co.uk
Website: http://www.issa.org.uk
Contact: Chris Day, Contact
Fee: £25
Membership Type: full
Fee: £20
Membership Type: associate
Description: Promotes the appreciation and conservation of caves and mines through artistic expression. Encourages members to improve their techniques and styles through workshops and exhibitions. Provides its members the opportunity to expand their knowledge and ways of depicting landscapes and the enjoyment of cave explorations.

02827
International Society for the Philosophy of Chemistry
ISPC

c/o Michael Akeroyd
Bradford and Ilkley College, Great Horton Rd., Bradford, BD7 1AY, UK
Email: m.akeroyd@bradfordcollege.ac.uk
Website: http://ispc.sas.upenn.edu
Contact: Rom Harre, Pres.
Fee: £10
Membership Type: in U.S.
Fee: £5
Membership Type: in UK
Description: Facilitates exchange of ideas between chemists, biochemists, philosophers, historians, sociologist and educators around the world. Focuses on the philosophical foundations of chemical sciences and other related fields.
Publication: Journal
Publication title: Foundations of Chemistry

02828
International Society for the Study of Tension in Performance
ISSTIP

6 Jonathans, Dene Rd., Northwood, Middlesex, HA6 2AD, UK
Tel: 020 71937037
Email: isstip@gmail.org
Website: http://www.isstip.org
Members: 360
Staff: 3
Contact: Hara Trouli, Chm.
Fee: £5
Membership Type: student
Fee: £20
Membership Type: full
Description: Musicians, actors, dancers, medical practitioners, consultants, psychologists, physiotherapists, Alexander Technique, yoga, Feldenkrais disciplines teachers and practitioners and others interested in the subject and in the problems created by muscular and nervous tensions, and physical injuries, among instrumentalists. Aims to collect and disseminate information regarding the debilitating effects of excess anxiety and tensions experienced by musicians, actors, dancers, public speakers, sportsmen, etc; to foster research and related activities; to provide advisory service for members and to assist performers with their physical or psychological problems offering free consultations.
Library Type: not open to the public
Meetings/Conventions: Performing Arts Clinic – annual conference – Exhibits.

02829
International Society for the Systems Sciences
ISSS

47 Southfield Rd., Pocklington, York, YO42 2XE, UK
Tel: 01759 302718
Fax: 01759 302718
Email: isssoffice@dsl.pipex.com
Website: http://isss.org/world/index.php
Members: 300
Contact: Allena Leonard, Pres.
Fee: £115
Membership Type: regular
Fee: £60
Membership Type: student
Description: Mathematicians, physical scientists, engineers, psychologists, social scientists, psychiatrists, medical researchers, and others interested in general systems research. Encourages development of theoretical systems that are applicable to more than one of the traditional departments of knowledge. Investigates the isomorphy of concepts, laws, and models in various fields and help in useful transfers from one field to another. Encourages the development of adequate theoretical models in fields which lack them. Seeks to minimize the duplication of theoretical effort in different fields. Promotes unity of science by improving communication among scientists. Maintains speakers' bureau.
Formerly: Formerly, Society for the Advancement of General Systems Theory
Publication: Newsletter
Publication title: General Systems Bulletin

02830
International Society for Trenchless Technology
ISTT

15 Belgrave Sq., London, SW1X 8PS, UK
Email: info@istt.co.uk
Website: http://www.istt.com
Members: 3500
Staff: 2
Contact: Dec Downey, Chm.
Fee: £70
Membership Type: corporate
Fee: £30
Membership Type: individual
Description: Promotes the use of trenchless methods of installing, renovating and replacing underground utilities.
Library Subject: trenchless technology
Library Type: not open to the public
Publication: Magazine
Publication title: Trenchless Technology International. Advertisements.
Meetings/Conventions: International No-Dig – international conference – Exhibits.

02831
International Society for Tropical Root Crops
ISTRC

Natural Resources Institute, University of Greenwich, Central Ave., Chatham, ME4 4TB, UK
Tel: 01634 883478
Fax: 01634 883714
Email: a.westby@gre.ac.uk
Website: http://www.istrc.org
Members: 250
Contact: Andrew Westby, Pres.
Fee: £90
Membership Type: ordinary
Fee: £45
Membership Type: student
Description: Studies tropical crops through its agricultural scientists and other interested individuals. Seeks to increase understanding of the cultivation and utilization of root crops in tropical regions. Serves as a forum for the exchange of information among members; conducts research to develop new varieties, improve crop management and on post-harvest utilization.

02832
International Society for Utilitarian Studies
ISUS
Bentham Project, University College London, Bentham House, Endsleigh Gardens, London, WC1H 0EG, UK
Tel: 020 76793610
Email: i.nicoll@ucl.ac.uk
Website: http://www.ucl.ac.uk/Bentham-Project/isus/isus
Members: 200
Contact: Philip Schofield, Honorable Sec.
Description: Historians, lawyers, political scientists, and philosophers interested in the teachings of Jeremy Bentham (1748-1832), English author, philosopher, and developer of utilitarianism (a doctrine maintaining that the propriety of an action depends on its tendency to promote the greatest happiness of the greatest number). Encourages study of utilitarian ideas and serves as a liaison for scholars working in the field. Organizes activities to raise funds for publication of a new scholarly edition of Bentham's books and literary treatises; conducts seminars.
Formerly: Formerly, International Bentham Society
Publication: Journal
Publication title: Utilitas. Advertisements.

02833
International Society of Acoustic Remote Sensing of the Atmosphere and Oceans
ISARS
High Cross, Madingley Rd., Cambridge, CB3 0ET, UK
Tel: 01223 221489
Fax: 01223 221489
Email: philip.s.anderson@bas.ac.uk
Website: http://www.boku.ac.at/imp/isars/isars.html
Contact: Philip Anderson, Chm.
Description: Aims to promote and provide information regarding remote sensing of the atmosphere and oceans.

02834
International Society of Arboriculture - United Kingdom and Ireland
ISA-UKI
148 Hydes Rd., Wednesbury, WS10 0DR, UK
Tel: 0121 5568302
Fax: 0121 5568302
Email: enquiries@isa-arboriculture.org
Website: http://www.isa-arboriculture.org
Contact: Jean McDermott, Office Mgr.
Fee: £95
Membership Type: professional
Fee: £303
Membership Type: sustaining
Description: Represents UK based professional arborists. Fosters greater appreciation for trees. Promotes research, technology and the professional practice of arboriculture. Provides a platform for the advancement of the science of arboriculture.
Publication: Magazine
Publication title: Treeline. Advertisements.

02835
International Society of Chemotherapy
ISC
Medical Microbiology, Aberdeen Royal Infirmary, Aberdeen, AB25 2ZN, UK
Tel: 01224 552127
Fax: 01224 550632
Email: isc@abdn.ac.uk
Website: http://www.ischemo.org
Members: 65
Staff: 1
Contact: Fiona MacKenzie, Exec. Dir.
Description: Societies or specialized groups within societies that are concerned with chemotherapy; scientists and clinicians working in chemotherapy. (Chemotherapy is the use of chemical agents in the treatment or control of infectious and neoplastic diseases and immunological disorder.) Promotes the development of chemotherapy through scientific and educational means. Encourages cooperation between members and scientists in related fields. Urges formation of new societies in countries where such groups do not exist. Promotes and/or sponsors formation of international working groups and training projects in the field of antimicrobial, antiparasitic, and antineoplastic chemotherapy; coordinates their activities. Appoints commissions for special activities.
Library Subject: antimicrobial therapy
Library Type: open to the public
Publication: Newsletter
Publication title: Antibiotics Chemotherapy. Advertisements.
Meetings/Conventions: International Congress of Chemotherapy – biennial lecture

02836
International Society of Hypertension - United Kingdom
c/o Hampton Medical Conferences Ltd.
113-119 High St., Hampton Hill, TW12 1NJ, UK
Tel: 020 8979 8300
Fax: 020 8979 6700
Email: secretariat@ish-world.com
Website: http://www.ish-world.com/default.aspx?Home
Contact: AM Heagerty, Pres.
Description: Membership is open to those who work in the field of hypertension and heart disease, with recommendations from two society members and a list of academic degrees, professional positions and a list of five best and five most recent publications relating to hypertension or allied fields. The society is committed to promoting and encouraging the advancement of scientific research and knowledge and its application to the prevention and management of heart disease and stroke in hypertension and related cardiovascular diseases around the world. Hosts workshops and seminars.

02837
International Society of Magnetic Resonance in Medicine - British Chapter
ISMRM
Cancer Research UK Clinical Magnetic Resonance Research Group, Institute of Cancer Research, Royal Marsden NHS Trust, Downs Rd., Sutton, SM2 5PT, UK
Tel: 020 86613338
Email: martin@icr.ac.uk
Website: http://www.ismrm.org.uk
Contact: Martin Leach, Chm.
Fee: £20
Membership Type: full
Description: Promotes communication, research, development, applications and availability of information on magnetic resonance in medicine and biology and other related topics.

02838
International Society of Neuropathology
ISN
University of Bristol, Dept. of Neuropathology, Frenchay Hospital, Bristol, BS16 1LE, UK
Fax: 0117 9753765
Email: seth.love@bristol.ac.uk
Website: http://www.intsocneuropathol.com
Contact: Seth Love, Sec. Gen.
Description: Aims to further the science of neuropathology. Initiates and maintains permanent cooperation between national and regional societies of neuropathology. Fosters the formation of national and regional societies of neuropathology. Initiates international congresses, meetings, colloquia, symposia and research projects in the field of neuropathology. Encourages the exchange of information and the publication of matters relevant to the science of neuropathology in its official journal and other publications.
Publication: Journal
Publication title: Brain Pathology. Advertisements.

02839
International Society of Protozoologists
ISOP
c/o David Montagnes, VP
University of Liverpool, School of Biological Science, Crown St., Liverpool, L69 7ZB, UK
Tel: 0151 7954400
Email: dmontag@liverpool.ac.uk
Website: http://www.uga.edu/protozoa
Members: 302
Staff: 2
Contact: Robert W. Sanders, Pres.
Description: Protozoologists who specialize in general, medical, or veterinary protozoology. Promotes member interests and provides exchange of information and research.
Library Subject: all areas in the field of protozoology
Library Type: open to the public
Formerly: Formerly, Society of Protozoologists
Publication: Journal
Publication title: Protistology

02840
International Society of Radiographers and Radiological Technologists
ISRRT
c/o Dr. Alexander Yule, CEO/Sec. Gen.
143 Bryn Pinwydden, Cardiff, CF23 7DG, UK
Email: isrrt.yule@btopenworld.com
Website: http://www.isrrt.org/isrrt/Default_EN.asp
Members: 80
Staff: 1
Contact: Robert George, Pres.
Fee: £2000

Membership Type: platinum
Fee: £1000
Membership Type: gold
Description: National radiographic societies and other organizations having radiographers as members. Objectives are to: advance the science and practice of radiography, radiotherapy, and allied subjects by promoting improved standards of training and research in technical aspects of radiation medicine and protection; make results of research and experience available to practitioners; raise funds to further these objectives. Compiles statistics and maintains museum. Has established educational trust fund. Conducts teachers' seminars.
Library Subject: radiation medicine technology
Library Type: reference
Formerly: Formerly, International Society of Radiographers and Radiological Technicians
Publication: Newsletter

02841
International Society of Typographic Designers ISTD
PO Box 725, Somerset, Taunton, TA2 8WE, UK
Tel: 020 74360984
Fax: 020 76377352
Email: mail@istd.org.uk
Website: http://www.istd.org.uk
Members: 630
Staff: 1
Contact: Freda Sack, Pres.
Fee: £100
Membership Type: ordinary, fellow
Fee: £250
Membership Type: corporate
Description: Promotes professionalism among typographic designers. Offers annual student assessment; conducts lectures.
Publication: Journal
Publication title: Typographic
Meetings/Conventions: monthly meeting – Exhibits.

02842
International Society of Ultrasound in Obstetrics and Gynecology ISUOG
Unit 4, Blythe Mews, Blythe Rd., London, W14 OHW, UK
Tel: 020 74719955
Fax: 020 74719959
Email: info@isuog.org
Website: http://www.isuog.org
Members: 3300
Staff: 2
Contact: Gianluigi Pilu, Pres.
Fee: £135
Membership Type: full
Description: Healthcare practitioners in the field of ultrasound in obstetrics and gynecology. Fosters scientific and educational advancements in ultrasound technology in obstetrics and gynecology. Conducts training programs.
Publication: Journal
Publication title: Ultrasound in Obstetrics and Gynecology

02843
International Society on General Relativity and Gravitation ICGRG
Queen Mary, University of London, School of Mathematical Sciences, Mile End Rd., London, E1 4NS, UK
Tel: 020 78825445
Fax: 020 89819587
Email: m.a.h.maccallum@qmul.ac.uk
Website: http://grg.maths.qmul.ac.uk/grgsoc
Contact: Malcolm A.H. MacCallum, Pres.
Description: Fosters the study of general relativity and gravitation (GRG).
Publication: Journal
Publication title: General Relativity & Gravitation

02844
International Spinal Cord Society ISCoS
Stoke Mandeville Hospital, National Spinal Injuries Centre, Aylesbury, HP21 8AL, UK
Tel: 01296 315866
Fax: 01296 315870
Email: admin@iscos.org.uk
Website: http://www.iscos.org.uk
Members: 1200
Staff: 2
Contact: Marianne Bint, Exec. Admin.
Fee: £60
Membership Type: full
Fee: £10
Membership Type: associate
Description: Qualified medical practitioners with an interest and activity in research or treatment and rehabilitation of spinal cord afflictions. Studies all problems concerning traumatic and non-traumatic problems of the spinal cord. Advances research, treatment and prevention and social integration of paraplegics. Encourages medical services throughout the world especially in developing countries. Sponsors young specialists to attend annual scientific meetings and undertake research work.
Formerly: Formerly, International Medical Society of Paraplegia
Publication: Journal
Publication title: Spinal Cord. Advertisements.

02845
International Spinal Research Trust ISRT
Bramley Business Centre, Station Rd., Bramley, Surrey, Guildford, GU5 0AZ, UK
Tel: 01483 898786
Fax: 01483 898763
Email: fundraising@spinal-research.org
Website: http://www.spinal-research.org
Contact: John Hick, Chm.
Description: Aims to establish a world free of the permanence paralysis caused by spinal cord injury. Promotes collaboration between organizations concerned with spinal cord injury paralysis through membership of the ICCP (International Campaign for Cures of Spinal Injury Paralysis).
Formerly: Also Known As, Spinal Research

02846
International Sports Engineering Association ISEA
University of Sheffield, Dept. of Mechanical Engineering, Mappin St., Sheffield, S1 3JD, UK
Tel: 0114 2227755
Fax: 0114 2227890
Email: r.kaye@sheffield.ac.uk
Website: http://www.sportsengineering.org
Members: 142
Contact: Kim B. Blair, Pres.
Fee: £110
Membership Type: regular
Fee: £20
Membership Type: student
Description: Promotes sports engineering.
Publication: Journal
Publication title: Sports Engineering

02847
International Steel Trade Association ISTA
Broadway House, Tothill St., London, SW1H 9NQ, UK
Tel: 020 77992662
Fax: 020 77992468
Email: hbailey@steeltrade.co.uk
Website: http://www.steeltrade.co.uk
Members: 100
Contact: Hugh W. Bailey, Dir.
Fee: £325
Membership Type: regular
Description: International steel traders of iron and steel. Assists members in manner determined by Executive Committee.

02848
International Stress Management Association UK ISMA UK
PO Box 491, Bradley Stoke, Bristol, BS34 9AH, UK
Tel: 0117 9697284
Email: info@isma.org.uk
Website: http://www.isma.org.uk
Contact: Cary Cooper, Pres.
Fee: £45
Membership Type: student
Fee: £75
Membership Type: associate
Description: Promotes sound knowledge and best practice in the prevention and reduction of human stress. Sets professional standards for the benefit of individuals and organizations by applying criteria for acceptance into full membership as well as validating stress management trainers and coaches; promoting continuing professional development and providing and maintaining a code of conduct.
Publication: Journal
Publication title: Stress News

02849

International Study Association for Teachers and Teaching
ISATT

University of Reading, PO Box 220, Reading, RG6 6AF, UK
Tel: 0118 3786959
Fax: 0118 9314404
Email: d.hotolean@reading.ac.uk
Website: http://www.isatt.org
Contact: Daniela Hotolean, Admin.
Fee: £70
Membership Type: new
Fee: £50
Membership Type: student
Description: Teacher-researchers worldwide at every academic level from a range of disciplines. Promotes, presents, discusses, and disseminates research on teachers and teaching, with a focus on the way teachers understand teaching and their roles in it.
Publication: Journal
Publication title: Teachers and Teaching - Theory and Practice

02850

International Substance Abuse and Addiction Coalition
ISAAC

PO Box 6149, Reading, RG19 9BS, UK
Tel: 0118 9836684
Fax: 0870 0940563
Email: info@isaac-international.org
Website: http://www.isaac-international.org
Members: 350
Description: Works to prevent and reduce the problems related to substance abuse and addiction. Encourages its members to share information, training and expertise. Undertakes researches and educational campaigns to reduce drug and alcohol related harm.

02851

International Sugar Organization
ISO

1 Canada Sq., Canary Wharf, London, E14 5AA, UK
Tel: 020 75131144
Fax: 020 75131146
Email: info@isosugar.org
Website: http://www.isosugar.org
Members: 84
Staff: 11
Contact: Peter Baron, Exec. Dir.
Description: Represents governments of sugar exporting and importing countries. Administers the 1992 International Sugar Agreement. Promotes the sugar industry.
Publication: Articles
Publication title: ISO Studies. Advertisements.

02852

International Tank Container Organisation
ITCO

Ste. 34, Isabel House, 46 Victoria Rd., Surbiton, KT6 4JL, UK
Tel: 02 83900000
Fax: 0870 7620434
Email: secretary@itco.be
Website: http://www.itco.be
Contact: Patrick Hicks, Sec.
Fee: £2000
Membership Type: general
Description: Promotes the interests of the tank container industry. Represents the tank container industry to the public and governmental bodies. Promotes the tank container concept and the development of the tank container industry worldwide. Establishes industry codes of practice. Deals with issues including safety, the use of technology in the industry and raising the profile of the use of tank containers.

02853

International Tanker Owners Pollution Federation
ITOPF

1 Oliver's Yard, 55 City Rd., London, EC1Y 1HQ, UK
Tel: 020 75666999
Fax: 020 75666950
Email: central@itopf.com
Website: http://www.itopf.com
Members: 5400
Staff: 25
Contact: Karen Purnell, Managing Dir.
Description: Tanker owners, bareboat charterers, and other ship owners. Responds to spills from all types of vessels; offers advice on clean-up, investigates the impact of spills, and assesses the technical merits of subsequent claims for compensation for clean-up costs and damage. Undertakes contingency planning and training assignments and maintains various databases, including oil spills from tankers.

02854

International Tax Planning Association
ITPA

PO Box 1508, St. Helier, Channel Islands, Jersey, JE4 2YE, UK
Tel: 01534 855488
Fax: 01534 855488
Email: singleton@itpa.org
Website: http://www.itpa.org
Contact: David Singleton, Registrar
Fee: £510
Membership Type: full
Fee: £160
Membership Type: library
Description: Aims to disseminate and exchange information about international tax planning.

02855

International Tea Committee
ITC

1 Carlton House Terr., London, SW1Y 5DB, UK
Tel: 0207 8395090
Email: info@inttea.com
Website: http://www.inttea.com
Members: 38
Contact: Rumi Ali, Exec. Asst.
Fee: £490
Membership Type: associate, corporate
Description: Tea-producing and consuming governments and associations. Collects and disseminates information and statistics on tea.
Publication: Report
Publication title: Statistical Summary

02856

International Tourism Trade Fairs Association
ITTFA

1 Old Forge Cottage, Carrington Rd., Richmond, TW10 5AA, UK
Tel: 0208 9399000
Email: info@ittfa.org
Website: http://www.ittfa.org
Contact: Tom Nutley, Chm.
Description: Travel trade fairs. Seeks to "enhance the quality and effectiveness of participation in travel trade fairs". Represents members before industrial organizations and the public; serves as a forum for the exchange of information among members.

02857

International Transport Workers' Federation
ITF

49-60 Borough Rd., London, SE1 1DR, UK
Tel: 020 74032733
Fax: 020 73577871
Email: mail@itf.org.uk
Website: http://www.itfglobal.org/language-selector.cfm
Members: 759
Staff: 90
Contact: David Cockroft, Gen. Sec.
Description: Trade unions representing 5 million workers in railways, road transport, inland navigation, ports and docks, shipping, fisheries, civil aviation, tourism services and a special seafarers' department for the promotion of fair practices in the maritime industry. Promotes and defends the economic and social interests of transport workers internationally.
Publication: Proceedings
Publication title: Congress Proceedings

02858

International Travel Catering Association
ITCA

Guardian House, The Maple Ste., Borough Rd., Surrey, Godalming, GU7 2AE, UK
Tel: 01483 419449
Fax: 01483 419780
Website: http://www.itcanet.com
Members: 690
Contact: David Young, Chm.
Fee: £400
Membership Type: first year
Fee: £250
Membership Type: regular
Description: Represents virtually all major airlines and larger regional carriers, and in flight catering companies world-wide. Works to improve the hospitality service provided by the transportation industry to the traveler.
Formerly: Formerly, International Flight Catering Association
Publication: Book
Publication title: Flight Catering

02859

International Tree Foundation

Sandy Ln., W Sussex, Crawley Down, RH10 4HS, UK
Tel: 01342 717300
Fax: 01342 718282
Email: info@internationaltreefoundation.org
Website: http://internationaltreefoundation.org
Members: 3000
Staff: 4
Contact: Spencer Keys, Chm.
Description: Works to plant and protect the trees at home and abroad. Offers advice on all aspects of tree care. Provides support to well-researched planting projects in the Third World.
Formerly: Formerly, Men of the Trees
Publication: Journal
Publication title: Trees

02860

International Trombone Association
ITA

1 Broomfied Rd., Coventry, CV5 6JW, UK
Tel: 0870 0052113
Fax: 0870 0052114
Email: accounts@trombone.net
Website: http://www.ita-web.org
Members: 4500
Staff: 1
Contact: Magnus Nilsson, Exec. Dir.
Fee: £30
Membership Type: student
Fee: £33
Membership Type: retired
Description: Professional trombonists, teachers, students, composers, libraries, instrument manufacturers, music publishers, and trombone enthusiasts. Is dedicated to the artistic advancement of trombone teaching, performance, and literature. Maintains library and biographical archives; grants commissions to composers of new titles. Sponsors composition contests and performance competitions. Compiles statistics.

02861

International Tube Association
ITA

46 Holly Walk, Leamington Spa, CV32 4HY, UK
Tel: 01926 834681
Fax: 01926 314755
Email: info@itatube.org
Website: http://www.itatube.org
Contact: Phillip G. Knight, Exec. Sec.
Fee: £95
Membership Type: personal
Fee: £98
Membership Type: personal
Description: Professional association of tube and pipe engineers in 71 countries. Promotes and organizes exhibitions, conferences and seminars covering all aspects of tube production and processing. Industry partner to Tube Dusseldorf.

02862

International Tungsten Industry Association
ITIA

4 Heathfield Terr., London, W4 4JE, UK
Tel: 020 89962221
Fax: 020 89948728
Email: info@itia.info
Website: http://www.itia.info
Contact: Michael Maby, Sec. Gen.
Fee: £8000
Description: Organizations and companies engaged in the production, processing, and consumption of tungsten; trading companies; assayers. Promotes cooperation among members in research, production, processing, and use of tungsten. Protects the common interests of members in technical, environmental, and health matters. Collects and disseminates information; compiles statistics.
Formerly: Supersedes, Primary Tungsten Association

02863

International Tyre, Rubber, and Plastics Federation
ITRPF

c/o Pelmar Engineering UK
Hastingwood Industrial Park, Wood Ln., Erdington, Birmingham, B24 9QR, UK
Tel: 0121 3866675
Fax: 0121 3866795
Email: info@itrpf.org
Website: http://www.itrpf.org
Members: 70
Staff: 1
Description: Represents tire dealers, and plastics and rubber manufacturers. Promotes trade between members; offers advice on pertinent legislation. Works to solve the problem of disposal and recycling of tires.

02864

International Underwriting Association of London
IUA

London Underwriting Ctre., 3 Minster Ct., Mincing Ln., London, EC3R 7DD, UK
Tel: 020 76174444
Fax: 020 76174440
Email: info@iua.co.uk
Website: http://www.iua.co.uk/AM/Template.cfm?Section=Home
Members: 180
Staff: 30
Contact: Dave J. Matcham, Chief Exec.
Description: Insurance and reinsurance companies across all classes, central accounting and policy checking firms. Provides central accounting and processing services for ordinary members; representational activities and information and research services for all members.
Formerly: Formerly, Institute of London Underwriters
Meetings/Conventions: monthly meeting – Exhibits.

02865

International Union Against Sexually Transmitted Infections - United Kingdom
IUSTI

Royal South Hants Hospital, Brintons Terr., Southampton, SO14 0YG, UK
Tel: 023 80825152
Fax: 023 80825122
Email: treasurer@iusti.org
Website: http://www.iusti.org
Contact: Raj Patel, Pres.-Elect/Treas.
Fee: £40
Membership Type: full
Fee: £200
Membership Type: organization
Description: Promotes international cooperation in the control of sexually transmitted diseases, including HIV infection, with an emphasis on the medical, social, and epidemiological aspects.
Meetings/Conventions: annual congress November 2 to 5, 2011. New Delhi Delhi India

02866

International Union for Land Value Taxation and Free Trade
theIU

Studio 5, St. Oswald's Studios, 82 Sedlescombe Rd., London, SW6 1RH, UK
Tel: 020 73865277
Email: office@theiu.org
Website: http://www.theiu.org
Members: 300
Staff: 1
Contact: Megan Campbell, Gen. Sec.
Description: Concerned persons in 32 countries. Works to gain worldwide support for permanent peace and prosperity for all peoples, which the union believes is achievable through the progressive removal of the basic economic causes of poverty and war as demonstrated in the writings of Henry George (1839-97), American economist. (George developed the single tax theory, according to which only the rental value of land should be taxed.) George meant free trade (la Libre-Echange) in a market emancipated from monopolies, privileges, and from taxation of labor and investments. Encourages the raising of public revenues by land value taxation (apart from improvements) in order to secure economic rent for the community and promotes abolition of taxes, tariffs, or imposts that interfere with free production and exchange of wealth.
Publication: Journal
Publication title: Georgist Journal

02867

International Union for Vacuum Science, Technique and Applications
IUVSTA

84 Oldfield Dr., Vicars Cross, Chester, CH3 5LW, UK
Tel: 01244 342675
Fax: 07005 860135
Email: iuvsta.secretary.general@ronreid.me.uk
Website: http://www.iuvsta.org
Members: 31
Contact: Ron J. Reid, Sec. Gen.
Description: National vacuum science and engineering organizations. Purposes are to: promote and develop vacuum science, technique, and applications in all countries; coordinate activities of members; establish international working groups to study areas such as standardization and training of specialists; develop and instigate exchanges, meetings, and communications in vacuum science in cooperation with members and other associations.
Publication: Bulletin
Publication title: News Bulletin
Meetings/Conventions: International Conference on Solid Surfaces – triennial congress – Exhibits. September 9 to 13, 2013. Paris France

02868

International Union of Air Pollution Prevention and Environmental Protection Associations

IUAPPA

Oakwood House, 11 Wingle Tye Rd., Burgess Hill, RH15 9HR, UK
Tel: 01444 236848
Fax: 01444 236848
Email: iuappa@btinternet.com
Website: http://www.iuappa.com
Members: 38
Staff: 5
Contact: Alan Gertler, Pres.
Description: National air pollution prevention and environmental protection associations in 36 countries. Promotes global public education relating to the importance of clean air and methods and results of pollution control. Facilitates the exchange of information and publications; encourages the use of uniform scientific and technical terminology; promotes uniform methods of measurement and monitoring. Acts as liaison with other international and national scientific and technical organizations. Maintains information service.
Formerly: Formerly, International Union of Air Pollution Prevention Associations
Publication: Book
Publication title: Clean Air Around the World
Meetings/Conventions: World Clean Air Congress and Exhibition – triennial congress – Exhibits.

02869

International Union of Aviation Insurers

IUAI

141 Fenchurch St., London, EC3M 6BL, UK
Tel: 020 76265314
Fax: 020 79293534
Website: http://www.iuai.org/iuai/index.htm
Members: 56
Contact: David Gasson, Sec. Gen.
Description: Serves as a focal point for international aviation insurance interests. Provides a forum for members to discuss aviation and space risks insurance matters. Offers a central office for the circulation of information between members. Assists in providing better understanding and conduct of international aviation and space insurance.
Publication: Handbook
Publication title: Aviation Statistical Handbook
Meetings/Conventions: annual meeting

02870

International Union of Credit and Investment Insurers/The Berne Union

1st Fl., 27-29 Cursitor St., London, EC4A 1LT, UK
Tel: 0207 8411110
Fax: 0207 4300375
Email: bu-sec@berneunion.org.uk
Website: http://www.berneunion.org.uk
Members: 51
Staff: 5
Contact: Angus Armour, Pres.
Description: Organizations insuring or guaranteeing export credit insurance transactions and/or foreign investments; organizations whose activities are related to export credit insurance. Seeks to: promote international cooperation in fostering a favorable investment climate; develop and maintain sound principles of export credit insurance; establish and sustain discipline in the terms of credit for international trade. Facilitates exchange of information, continuing consultation, and close co-operation among members. Acts as liaison between members and other international institutions. Maintains technical and ad hoc sub-committees, groups, and working parties to study specific problems and issues.
Publication: Yearbook
Publication title: Berne Union Yearbook. Advertisements.

02871

International Union of Crystallography

IUCr

2 Abbey Sq., Chester, CH1 2HU, UK
Tel: 01244 345431
Fax: 01244 344843
Email: execsec@iucr.org
Website: http://www.iucr.org
Members: 40
Staff: 21
Contact: Sine Larsen, Pres.
Description: National academies, national research councils, scientific societies, and similar bodies in 40 countries. Objectives are to: promote international cooperation in crystallography (the study of crystal form, structure, and modes of aggregation); contribute to all aspects of its advancement including related topics concerning the non-crystalline states; facilitate international standardization of methods used such as units, nomenclature, and symbols; form a focus for the relations of crystallography to other sciences. Organizes training schools on various aspects of crystallography; publishes seven journals. Maintains 18 commissions.
Publication: Journal
Publication title: Acta Crystallographica Section A. Advertisements.

02872

International Union of Physiological Sciences

IUPS

Oxford University, Department of Physiology, Anatomy and Genetics, Parks Rd., Oxford, OX1 3PT, UK
Tel: 01865 272528
Email: denis.noble@dpag.ox.ac.uk
Website: http://www.iups.org
Members: 54
Staff: 1
Contact: Denis Noble, Pres.
Description: Physiological societies united to exchange scientific information. Aims to increase mankind's understanding of the functions of cells, tissues, organs and organ systems of animals and humans. Encourages the advancement of the physiological sciences. Promotes measures that will contribute to the development of physiological sciences in developing countries.
Publication: Journal
Publication title: Physiology
Meetings/Conventions: International Congress of Physiological Sciences – quadrennial congress – Exhibits.

02873

International Union of Sex Workers

IUSW

Thorne House, 152 Brent St., London, NW4 2DP, UK
Tel: 0777 2638748
Email: branch.secretary@iusw.org
Website: http://www.iusw.org
Fee: £10.84
Membership Type: full time
Fee: £71.76
Membership Type: part time
Description: Advocates for the protection of sex workers and prostitutes around the world. Seeks the abolition of all forms of discrimination on all aspects of sex work involving consenting adults. Provides legal assistance and support to sex workers who want to sue those who exploit their labor. Seeks equal opportunity, health access, and professionalization of the career.

02874

International Union of Soil Sciences

IUSS

PO Box 233, Reading, RG6 6DW, UK
Tel: 0118 3786559
Email: iuss@reading.ac.uk
Website: http://www.iuss.org
Members: 45000
Staff: 1
Contact: Stephen Nortcliff, Sec. Gen.
Description: Promotes contacts among scientists; stimulates scientific research to further the application of soil research.
Library Type: reference
Formerly: Formerly, International Society of Soil Science
Publication: Bulletin
Publication title: Bulletin of the IUSS. Advertisements.
Meetings/Conventions: World Congress of Soil Science – quadrennial meeting – Exhibits.

02875

International Vegetarian Union

IVU

Parkdale, Dunham Rd., Cheshire, Altrincham, WA14 4QG, UK
Fax: 0161 9269182
Email: chair@ivu.org
Website: http://www.ivu.org
Members: 300
Staff: 1
Contact: John Davis, Mgr.
Fee: £12
Membership Type: full, associate, individual
Fee: £25
Membership Type: business
Description: Union of societies from 40 countries whose members live on a diet of cereals, vegetables, fruit, pulses, nuts, and herbs, with or without the addition of eggs and dairy products, but excluding animal flesh whether meat, fish, fowl or their derivatives. Seeks to coordinate the work of all affiliated and associated member societies. Sponsors information service on vegetarian/vegan accommodation, restaurants, and health food stores in the world. Conducts and continuously reviews world census of vegetarian/vegan organizations. Promotes the publication of leaflets on horticulture, balanced vegetarian recipes, lectures, and articles. Compiles statistics.
Publication: Magazine
Publication title: IVU Magazine. Advertisements.
Meetings/Conventions: periodic congress

02876

International Visual Communications Association
IVCA

1st Fl., 23 Golden Sq., London, W1F 9JP, UK
Tel: 020 72871002
Fax: 020 72872651
Email: info@ivca.org
Website: http://www.ivca.org
Members: 2500
Staff: 7
Contact: Marco Forgione, CEO
Fee: £1290
Membership Type: patron
Fee: £399-1220
Membership Type: production company, in-house team, service provider or facility (based on annual turnover)
Description: Patrons, corporate commissioner/user, corporate supplier, institutional/non profit making, individual, student/trainee. Represents the users and suppliers of visual communication. Strives to advance the standing and recognition of the industry and its practitioners and provides a comprehensive range of membership services. Assumes a proactive role in marketing visual communications to potential users.
Publication: Newsletter
Publication title: IVCA Update

02877

International Voluntary Service
IVS

5 Rose St., Edinburgh, EH2 2PR, UK
Tel: 0131 2432745
Fax: 0131 2432747
Email: info@ivsgb.org
Website: http://ivsgb.org/info
Members: 920
Staff: 1
Fee: £35
Membership Type: employed
Fee: £45
Membership Type: family
Description: Aims to increase international understanding and cooperation through voluntary work. Brings together volunteers from different countries to work on short term volunteer projects, on local community projects throughout Great Britain and the world. Organizes a variety of projects fulfilling specific sustainable development needs. Assistance provided includes: helping refugees; services for children, the disabled and the disadvantaged; arts and culture; conservation and environmental projects, "Anti-Racist Work".
Formerly: Formerly, International Voluntary Service - Scotland
Publication title: Annual Review. Advertisements.

02878

International Water Association, United Kingdom
IWA

Alliance House, 12 Caxton St., London, SW1H 0QS, UK
Tel: 020 76545500
Fax: 020 76545555
Email: water@iwahq.org
Website: http://www.iwahq.org/Home
Members: 10400
Staff: 17
Contact: Paul Reiter, Exec. Dir.
Fee: £64
Membership Type: individual (high income country)
Fee: £29
Membership Type: student, retired (high income country), individual (low income country)
Description: Individuals, national organizations, municipal authorities, pollution control agencies, government departments, research institutes, and commercial concerns in 120 countries. Objectives are to: contribute to the advancement of research, development, and applications in drinking water treatment and supply, wastewater treatment, water pollution control and water quality management; encourage communication and a better understanding among those engaged in the solution of water quality problems and water quality management. Promotes the exchange of information on drinking water treatment and supply, wastewater treatment, water pollution control, water quality management, and its practical application.
Formerly: Formerly, International Association on Water Pollution Research and Control
Publication: Yearbook
Publication title: IAWQ Yearbook. Advertisements.

02879

International Well Control Forum
IWCF

Inchbraoch House, South Quay, Angus, Montrose, DD10 9UA, UK
Tel: 01674 678120
Fax: 01674 678125
Email: admin@iwcf.org
Website: http://www.iwcf.org
Members: 145
Contact: David Price, CEO
Fee: £300
Membership Type: associate
Description: Companies or persons employed in the oil industry with an interest in the development of well control skills. Develops and administers well control examination programmes for personnel employed in oil well drilling and well intervention operations.

02880

International Whaling Commission
IWC

The Red House, 135 Station Rd., Impington, Cambridge, CB24 9NP, UK
Tel: 01223 233971
Fax: 01223 232876
Email: secretariat@iwcoffice.org
Website: http://www.iwcoffice.org
Members: 88
Staff: 17
Contact: Simon Brockington, Sec.
Description: Commissioners represent member countries. Aims to provide for the proper conservation of whale stocks in order to allow the orderly development of the whaling industry. Encourages, coordinates, and funds whale research, publishes the results of scientific research and promotes studies into related matters such as the humaneness of the killing operations and environmental concerns. Collects and publishes whaling statistics previously compiled by Norway's Bureau of International Whaling Statistics.
Library Subject: conservation, whales, whaling, intergovernmental reports, scientific reports
Library Type: reference
Publication: Annual Report
Publication title: Annual Report of the International Whaling Commission

02881

International Wire and Machinery Association
IWMA

46 Holly Walk, Warwickshire, Leamington Spa, CV32 4HY, UK
Tel: 01926 834680
Fax: 01926 314755
Email: info@iwma.org
Website: http://www.iwma.org
Members: 300
Staff: 2
Contact: Phillip Knight, Exec. Sec.
Fee: £280
Membership Type: basic
Description: Serves as a trade association for manufacturers of wire, cable, and fibre optic machinery and products and suppliers of related production and process machinery in 52 countries. Promotes the exchange of technology and standards and seeks to advance quality control among industries internationally.
Library Subject: technical information
Library Type: reference
Publication: Newsletter
Publication title: Wire Cable Newsletter
Meetings/Conventions: annual show

02882

International Wrought Copper Council
IWCC

55 Bryanston St., London, W1H 7AJ, UK
Tel: 020 78688930
Fax: 020 78688819
Email: iwcc@coppercouncil.org
Website: http://www.coppercouncil.org
Contact: Heiner Otten, Chm.
Description: Represents national trade associations of the copper and copper alloy fabricating industries. Promotes information exchange and cooperation within the industry; conducts promotional activities.
Publication: Survey
Publication title: Survey Capacities of Copper Mines, Smelters, Refineries and Copper Wire Rod Plants

02883

International Young Democrat Union
IYDU

1st Fl., 100 Pall Mall, London, SW1Y 5HP, UK
Email: iydu@iydu.com
Website: http://www.iydu.org
Members: 60
Contact: Tim Dier, Chm.
Description: Organizations comprising students and young people with center-right political viewpoints. Promotes freedom and democracy worldwide. Conducts research and educational programs in areas including government policies and human rights.

Internationale des Resistants a la Guerre

see War Resisters' International

Internationale Liberale

see Liberal International

Internationale Organisation für Sukkulenten-Forschung

see International Organization for Succulent Plant Study

Internationale Socialiste des Femmes

see Socialist International Women

Internationale Vereinigung für Schul-und Berufsberatung

see International Association for Educational and Vocational Guidance

Internationaler Draht- und Maschinenverband

see International Wire and Machinery Association

02884

Internet Advertising Bureau IAB

14 Macklin St., London, WC2B 5NF, UK
Tel: 020 70506969
Fax: 020 72429928
Email: info@iabuk.net
Website: http://www.iabuk.net/en/1/home.html
Contact: Guy Phillipson, CEO
Fee: £1000-10000
Membership Type: associate (based on total turnover)
Fee: £1000-32000
Membership Type: full (based on advertising revenue)
Description: Represents the interests of companies with online business. Helps marketers build their brands. Provides its members the tools to stay ahead in the industry.
Library Subject: marketing
Library Type: reference
Publication: Newsletter
Publication title: Byte Size

02885

Internet Telephony Services Providers' Association ITSPA

111 Buckingham Palace Rd., London, SW1W 0SR, UK
Tel: 020 73408733
Fax: 020 73408747
Email: admin@itspa.org.uk
Website: http://www.itspa.org.uk
Contact: Eli Katz, Chair
Fee: £500-750
Membership Type: small sized company
Fee: £1500-2000
Membership Type: medium sized company
Description: Represents UK-based network operators, service providers and other businesses involved with the supply of VoIP services. Aims to promote competition and self-regulation in VoIP services. Encourages development and innovation of the Internet Telephony industry.

02886

InterNICHE

42 S Knighton Rd., Leicester, LE2 3LP, UK
Tel: 0116 2109652
Fax: 0116 2109652
Email: coordinator@interniche.org
Website: http://www.interniche.org
Contact: Nick Jukes, Coor.
Description: Promotes high quality and fully humane education in biological science, veterinary and human medicine. Supports progressive science teaching and the replacement of animal experiments. Works with teachers to introduce alternatives, and with students to support freedom of conscience.
Publication: Video
Publication title: Alternatives in Education Video: New Approaches for a New Millennium
Meetings/Conventions: InterNICHE Conference – conference – Exhibits.

02887

INTERPAVE

60 Charles St., Leicester, LE1 1FB, UK
Tel: 0116 2536161
Fax: 0116 2514568
Email: info@paving.org.uk
Website: http://www.paving.org.uk
Members: 6
Staff: 2
Description: Represents manufacturers of precast concrete block and flag paving and kerbs. Promotes research to develop improved product application.
Formerly: Formerly, Precast Concrete Paving and Kerb Association
Publication: Handbook
Publication title: The Design

02888

Investment Management Association IMA

65 Kingsway, London, WC2B 6TD, UK
Tel: 020 78310898
Fax: 020 78319975
Email: ima@investmentuk.org
Website: http://www.investmentuk.org
Members: 200
Staff: 40
Contact: Richard Saunders, Chief Exec.
Description: Represents the interests of unit trust and investment fund management companies. Aims to improve the regulatory, fiscal and legal environment for unit trusts and investment funds; to increase public awareness of collective investments; to provide information, guidance, assistance and other services to its members.
Formerly: Formerly, Association of Unit Trusts and Investment Funds

02889

Investor Relations Society IRS

3 Bedford St., Bedford House, London, WC2E 9HD, UK
Tel: 020 73791763
Fax: 020 72401320
Email: enquiries@irs.org.uk
Website: http://www.ir-soc.org.uk
Members: 700
Staff: 6
Contact: Michael Mitchell, Gen. Mgr.
Fee: £550
Membership Type: standard plus rate (full and associate)
Fee: £385
Membership Type: standard rate (full and associate)
Description: UK's professional body for investor relations practitioners. Seeks to promote excellence in investor relations and enhance corporate value through effective communication. Contributes proposals for regulatory change and legislation, represents its members on relevant working parties and committees, and promotes education and training at all levels of investor relations. Is also a founder member of the International Investor Relations Federation and maintains contact with fellow organizations in Europe, the Americas and the Far East.
Publication: Journal
Publication title: Informed. Advertisements.
Meetings/Conventions: annual conference – Exhibits.

02890

Involvement and Participation Association IPA

42 Colebrooke Row, London, N1 8AF, UK
Tel: 020 73548040
Fax: 020 73548041
Email: involve@ipa-involve.com
Website: http://www.ipa-involve.com
Members: 210
Staff: 8
Contact: Bill Connor, Pres.
Description: All organizations, private and public, who want to release the full potential of their employees. Promotes employee involvement and participation at work.
Publication: Magazine
Publication title: IPA Magazine

02891

IoP: The Packaging Society

Springfield House, Springfield Business Pk., Grantham, NG31 7BG, UK
Tel: 01476 514590
Fax: 01476 514591
Email: heather.kendle@incadigital.com
Website: http://www.iom3.org/packaging
Contact: Heather Kendle, Chm.
Fee: £75
Membership Type: full, associate, fellow
Fee: £30
Membership Type: student
Description: Serves as the only UK professional and qualifying body for individuals working in or with the packaging industry.
Library Subject: packaging
Library Type: by appointment only
Formerly: Formerly, Institute of Materials, Minerals and Mining and Institute of Packaging - United Kingdom
Publication: Magazine
Publication title: The Packaging Professional. Advertisements.

02892

IP Federation

63-66 Hatton Garden, 5th Fl., London, EC1N 8LE, UK
Tel: 020 72423923
Fax: 020 72423924
Email: admin@ipfederation.com
Website: http://www.ipfederation.com
Members: 40
Staff: 2
Description: Trade association representing industrial and commercial companies with interests in intellectual property. Aims to promote and secure cooperation in all matters relating to trade marks, patents, designs and other intellectual property rights; through considering developments in intellectual property, expressing views and trying to influence decisions and holding open conferences.
Formerly: Formerly, Trade Marks Patents and Designs Federation
Publication: Newsletter
Publication title: INPACT

02893

Iraq Occupation Focus

PO Box 44680, London, N16 7XX, UK
Email: iraqfocus@riseup.net
Website: http://www.iraqoccupationfocus.org.uk
Fee: £15
Membership Type: individual
Fee: £3
Membership Type: unwaged
Description: Campaigns to end the occupation of Iraq. Disseminates information and provides coverage about the realities of the occupation. Develops and publicizes the arguments for ending the occupation. Provides research and highlights the reasons for British involvement.
Publication: Newsletter

02894

Iraqi Association
iA

Palingswick House, 241 King St., London, W6 9LP, UK
Tel: 020 87415491
Fax: 020 87489010
Email: info@iraqiassociation.org
Website: http://www.iraqiassociation.org
Contact: Noaman Muna, Chm.
Description: Seeks to enable Iraqis to settle in the United Kingdom with rights to express their culture. Provides volunteerism, advice, public health support, counseling, training, employment guidance, and information services. Promotes awareness about relevant events in Iraq and how they are related to those in the United Kingdom.
Publication: Annual Report

02895

Irish Heritage

10 Brackley Rd., Manchester, M30 9LG, UK
Email: irish.heritage1@googlemail.com
Website: http://www.irishheritage.co.uk
Contact: Niall Gallagher, Chm.
Fee: £30
Membership Type: individual
Fee: £50
Membership Type: family
Description: Promotes Irish and Anglo-Irish music and literature.

02896

Irish Moiled Cattle Society

7 The Terrace, Martinstown, Dorset, Dorchester, DT2 9JY, UK
Tel: 01305 889828
Email: mandjlight@moilies.plus.com
Website: http://www.irishmoiledcattlesociety.com
Members: 140
Contact: Jane Light, Sec.
Fee: £30
Membership Type: individual
Description: Committed to development and improvement of the moiled cattle breed; introduced a DNA testing program to ensure validity of pedigrees and integrity of the breed gene pool.

02897

Irish Pattern Recognition and Classification Society
IPRCS

University of Ulster, Coleraine Campus, Cromore Rd., Londonberry, Coleraine, BT52 1SA, UK
Tel: 028 70124637
Email: pj.morrow@ulster.ac.uk
Website: http://elm.eeng.dcu.ie/~iprcs
Members: 38
Contact: Philip Morrow, Sec.
Description: Promotes pattern recognition and the allied branches of engineering together with its related arts and sciences. Stimulates research, development and the application of pattern recognition in science and human activity.

02898

Irish Texts Society
ITS

c/o Sean Hutton, Hon. Sec.
69a, Balfour St., London, SE17 1PL, UK
Email: hon.secretary@irishtextssociety.org
Website: http://www.irishtextssociety.org
Members: 500
Contact: Padraig O Riain, Pres.
Fee: £15
Membership Type: individual
Description: Individuals in 13 countries. Strives to advance public education by promoting the study of Irish literature.
Publication: Book
Publication title: Irish-English Dictionary

02899

Ironmongers' Company

c/o Ironmongers' Hall
Shaftesbury Pl., Barbican, London, EC2Y 8AA, UK
Tel: 020 77762304
Fax: 020 76003519
Email: clerk@ironhall.co.uk
Website: http://www.ironhall.co.uk
Members: 230
Staff: 12
Contact: Hamon Massey, Clerk
Description: City of London Livery Company administering charitable trusts for the care of the elderly, education and the relief of needy people. No longer involved in the trade of its name but makes grants towards iron-related projects. Tudor-style Hall is available for public use.

02900

ISCO Careerscope

St. George's House, Knoll Rd., Surrey, Camberley, GU15 3SY, UK
Tel: 01276 687525
Website: http://www.isco.org.uk
Members: 80373
Staff: 60
Contact: Andy Airey, Chief Exec.
Description: Individual - children enrolled in Student Scheme. Corporate Independent Schools in subscription paying membership from where the individual membership arises. Aims to advise and assist careers and other staff in its member schools, to advise individual students and their parents on all careers and higher education matters and to advise and assist employers in contacts with independent schools and vice versa.
Publication: Directory
Publication title: Directory of Independent Further Education

02901

Islamic Texts Society
ITS

Miller's House, Kings Mill Ln., Great Shelford, Cambridge, CB22 5EN, UK
Tel: 01 223842425
Fax: 01 223842425
Email: info@its.org.uk
Website: http://www.its.org.uk
Staff: 3
Description: Serves as educational charity registered in the UK and specializing in the publication of works of traditional importance to the Islamic faith and culture including translations of heritage titles.

02902

Isle of Man Chamber of Commerce

17 Drinkwater St., Douglas, IM1 1PP, UK
Tel: 01624 674941
Fax: 01624 663367
Email: enquiries@iomchamber.org.im
Website: http://www.iomchamber.org.im
Members: 380
Contact: Mike Hennessy, Chief Exec.
Description: Promotes business and commerce.

02903

Isle of Wight Chamber of Commerce

Mill Ct., Furrlongs, Newport, PO30 2AA, UK
Tel: 01983 520777
Fax: 01983 554555
Email: chamber@iwchamber.co.uk
Website: http://www.iwchamber.co.uk
Members: 418
Staff: 3
Contact: Kevin Smith, Chief Exec.
Description: Promotes business and commerce.
Publication: Magazine
Publication title: Island Business Magazine

02904

ISTD Dance Examinations Board

Imperial House, 22/26 Paul St., London, EC2A 4QE, UK
Tel: 020 73771577
Fax: 020 76558829
Email: chiefexecutive@istd.org
Website: http://www.istd.org
Members: 10000
Staff: 27
Contact: Peter Kyle, Chm.
Fee: £41
Membership Type: student (UK & EU)
Fee: £66
Membership Type: non-active professional (UK & EU)
Description: Teachers of dancing by examination at three levels. A qualifying body for many forms of dance providing grade examinations and medal tests for children and adults. Courses, congresses, and competitions are provided for professional teachers and the public.
Formerly: Formerly, Imperial Society of Teachers of Dancing
Publication: Magazine
Publication title: Dance. Advertisements.

02905

Italian Chamber of Commerce and Industry for the UK

1 Princes St., London, W1B 2AY, UK
Tel: 020 74958191
Fax: 020 74958194
Email: info@italchamind.org.uk
Website: http://www.italchamind.org.uk
Contact: Leonardo Simonelli Santi, Pres.
Fee: £75
Membership Type: ordinary
Fee: £110
Membership Type: corporate
Description: Works to promote and extend business relations between the UK and Italy.
Publication: Newsletter
Publication title: Italy/UK Highlights

02906

ITRI Innovation

Unit 3, Curo Park, Frogmore, St. Albans, AL2 2DD, UK
Tel: 01727 875544
Fax: 01727 871341
Email: info@itri.co.uk
Website: http://www.tintechnology.com
Staff: 30
Contact: Mark Berrisford, Contact
Description: Develops the use of tin based on the scientific and technical study of its alloys and compounds and the industrial processes that would make use of tin or may provide future markets for it. Offers a comprehensive range of analytical techniques providing solutions to diverse issues and problems. Maintains a well-equipped chemical and metallurgical analysis laboratory.
Library Subject: tin, tin alloys, compounds, coatings, properties and uses
Library Type: reference
Formerly: Formerly, International Tin Research Council

02907

Jacob Sheep Society

Oaktree Farm, Buttermilk Ln., Yarningale Common, Claverdon, Warwickshire, Warwick, CV35 8HP, UK
Tel: 01926 843434
Fax: 01926 843434
Email: secretary@jacobsheep.org.uk
Website: http://www.jacobsheepsociety.co.uk
Members: 800
Staff: 1
Contact: Louise Smith, Sec.
Fee: £25
Membership Type: regular (inside UK and Europe)
Fee: £34.5
Membership Type: regular (outside UK and Europe)
Description: Small flock owners and large breeders of Jacob sheep. Saves and promotes the Jacob sheep breed and encourages and supports members. Registers pedigree sheep in flock book.
Publication: Journal
Publication title: Jacob Journal

02908

Jane Austen Society of the United Kingdom
JAS

22 Belmont Grove, Hampshire, Havant, PO9 3PU, UK
Tel: 023 92475855
Email: hq@jasoc.org.uk
Website: http://www.janeaustensociety.org.uk
Members: 2050
Contact: Rosemary Culley, Membership Sec.
Fee: £20
Membership Type: individual, regular
Fee: £10
Membership Type: student
Description: Individuals worldwide interested in the life and works of Jane Austen (1775-1817), English novelist. Acts as a clearinghouse for information on Jane Austen.
Formerly: Formerly, Jane Austen Society - England
Publication: Report
Publication title: Collected Reports. Advertisements.

02909

JANET

Lumen House, Library Ave., Didcot, OX11 0SG, UK
Tel: 01235 822200
Fax: 01235 822399
Email: service@ja.net
Website: http://www.ja.net
Contact: Tim Marshall, CEO
Description: Committed to research, development and provision of advanced electronic communication facilities for community and industry, thus facilitating the extension of many classes of trade through community links with industry.
Formerly: Formerly, United Kingdom Education and Research Networking Association

02910

Japan Society - United Kingdom

Swire House, 59 Buckingham Gate, London, SW1E 6AJ, UK
Tel: 020 7828 6330
Fax: 020 7828 6331
Email: info@japansociety.org.uk
Website: http://www.japansociety.org.uk
Contact: Heidi Potter, Chief Exec.
Description: Open to all individuals and organizations. Enhances links between the United Kingdom and Japan, with the aim of providing a better mutual understanding of the cultures, societies and businesses of both countries. Hosts luncheons, workshops and lectures.

02911

Japanese Shipowners Association - United Kingdom

Dexter House, Royal Mint Ct., London, EC3N 4JR, UK
Tel: 020 74880899
Fax: 020 74883167
Email: office@jsaldn.org.uk
Website: http://www.jsanet.or.jp
Members: 107
Description: Promotes fair and free business activities in the shipping industry in the UK. Aims to contribute to the healthy development of shipping industry.

02912

Jennifer Trust for Spinal Muscular Atrophy
JTSMA

Elta House, Birmingham Rd., Warwickshire, Stratford-upon-Avon, CV37 0AQ, UK
Tel: 01789 267520
Fax: 01789 268371
Email: jennifer@jtsma.org.uk
Website: http://www.jtsma.org.uk
Members: 1500
Staff: 7
Contact: Heather Brown, Gen. Mgr.
Description: Offers support information and advice to people whose lives have been affected by Spinal Muscular Atrophy (SMA).
Library Type: lending
Publication: Newsletter
Publication title: Holding Hands

02913

Jerome K. Jerome Society

c/o Peter J. Wilson, Membership Sec.
45 Chetwynd Rd., Edgmond, Shropshire, Newport, TF10 8AD, UK
Email: peter.wilson@jeromekjerome.com
Website: http://www.jeromekjerome.com
Members: 200
Contact: Tony Gray, Honorable Sec.
Fee: £12
Membership Type: single
Fee: £8
Membership Type: student, OAP
Description: Promotes the life and works of Jerome K. Jerome and funds the birthplace museum in Bradford Street, Walsall. Hosts an annual dinner in May, a Christmas Concert, and a trip to the Black Forest to celebrate the 100th anniversary of the publication Three Men on the Bummel.
Publication: Book
Publication title: Idle Thoughts on Jerome K. Jerome

02914

Jersey Chamber of Commerce and Industry

Chamber House, 25 Pier Rd., St. Helier, Jersey, JE1 4HF, UK
Tel: 01534 724536
Fax: 01534 734942
Email: admin@jerseychamber.com
Website: http://www.jerseychamber.com
Members: 640
Staff: 2
Contact: Ray Shead, Pres.
Description: Promotes business, trade, commerce industry and navigation.

Publication: Newsletter
Publication title: Chamber Online. Advertisements.

02915
Jewellery and Allied Industries Training Council
JAITC

c/o British Jewellers' Association
10 Vyse St., Birmingham, B18 6LT, UK
Website: http://www.jaitc.org.uk
Contact: Geoff Field, Chm.
Description: Represents jewellery manufacturers, silversmiths, pewterers and cutlers in public affairs. Provides training and education to help maintain the standards of the industry.

02916
Jewellery Distributors' Association of the United Kingdom
JDA

Federation House, 10 Vyse St., Birmingham, B18 4BR, UK
Tel: 0121 2362657
Fax: 0121 2363921
Email: secretariat@jda.org.uk
Website: http://www.jda.org.uk
Members: 100
Staff: 1
Contact: Lynn B. Snead, Mgr.
Fee: £230-855
Membership Type: full (based on number of employees)
Fee: £230
Membership Type: overseas
Description: Wholesalers, distributors and importers in the gold and silver jewellery, fashion jewellery and allied trades. Offers trade protection, export services, debt collection. Discounts are available at certain trade fairs and source information is available to promote business opportunities to members; represents the industry to government and other bodies to provide a forum for discussion on topics of concern to the industry.
Publication: Newsletter
Publication title: The Distributer. Advertisements.
Meetings/Conventions: National Committee Meeting – quarterly meeting

02917
Jewish Historical Society of England
JHSE

33 Seymour Pl., London, W1H 5AP, UK
Tel: 020 77235852
Fax: 020 77235852
Email: info@jhse.org
Website: http://www.jhse.org
Members: 700
Staff: 1
Contact: Ada Rapoport-Albert, Pres.
Fee: £40
Membership Type: regular
Description: Libraries and other institutions; academics, amateur historians, students and other interested persons. Works to research and promote Jewish and Anglo-Jewish history and literature. Encourages research; sponsors lecture program.

02918
Jewish Socialists Group
JSG

BM 3725, London, WC1N 3XX, UK
Tel: 0870 1629244
Fax: 0870 1629244
Email: thebigfish@redherringclub.com
Website: http://www.jewishsocialist.org.uk
Fee: £12
Membership Type: waged
Fee: £6
Membership Type: unwaged
Description: Campaigns for Jewish rights and the rights of all oppressed minorities in building a socialist future. Encourages minorities to express and develop historical and cultural identities that will liberate ordinary people of all communities from poverty, racism, sexism, oppression, and war.
Publication: Magazine
Publication title: Jewish Socialist

02919
Jockey Club

75 High Holborn, London, WC1V 6LS, UK
Tel: 020 71893800
Email: info@thejockeyclub.co.uk
Website: http://www.thejockeyclub.co.uk
Contact: Cedric Burton, Chief Exec.
Description: Responsible for the regulation of the conduct of British horse racing.

02920
John Clare Society

c/o Sue Holgate, Membership Sec.
9 The Chase, Ely, CB6 3DR, UK
Tel: 01353 668438
Email: sueholgate@hotmail.co.uk
Website: http://www.johnclare.org.uk
Members: 550
Contact: Linda Curry, Chair
Fee: £12
Membership Type: individual, joint retired
Fee: £15
Membership Type: joint, group
Description: Promotes the work of John Clare, the 19th Century Northamptonshire peasant poet.
Publication: Journal
Publication title: John Clare Society Journal. Advertisements.

02921
John Hampden Society

Little Hampden, Cryers Hill, Buckinghamshire, High Wycombe, HP15 6JS, UK
Tel: 07543 054335
Email: thesecretary@johnhampden.org
Website: http://www.johnhampden.org
Members: 150
Contact: Samuel Hearn, Chm.
Fee: £10
Membership Type: adult - local
Fee: £15
Membership Type: joint - local
Description: Works to make the character and achievements of John Hampden better known, to stimulate research into his life and times, and encourage and assist the preservation and/or renovation of the monument and artifacts associated with him. Provides access to compiled information.
Publication: Newsletter
Publication title: The Patriot

02922
John Innes Manufacturers Association
JIMA

Horticulture House, 19 High St., Theale, Reading, RG7 5AH, UK
Tel: 01423 879208
Fax: 01423 870025
Email: john.innes@the-hta.org.uk
Website: http://www.johninnes.info
Members: 10
Staff: 4
Fee: £500
Membership Type: full
Description: Manufacturers of John Innes loam-based potting mixes for both amateur gardeners and professional growers. Represents the leading UK manufacturers of traditional loam-based John Innes potting mixes, who all use the associations' seal of approval on the packaging.
Library Type: not open to the public
Publication: Brochure
Publication title: Brochure and Technical Data Sheets

02923
Johnson Society - Lichfield
JS

Johnson Birthplace Museum, Breadmarket St., Lichfield, WS13 6LG, UK
Email: info@thejohnsonsociety.org.uk
Website: http://www.thejohnsonsociety.org.uk
Members: 800
Contact: Barbara Hattersley, Gen. Sec.
Fee: £10
Membership Type: individual
Fee: £15
Membership Type: joint
Description: Individuals in 6 countries interested in the life and works of Dr. Samuel Johnson (1709-84), English author and lexicographer. Fosters interest in Johnson and preserves the writer's birthplace as well as objects associated with him. Organizes tours.
Publication title: Transactions. Advertisements.

02924
Johnson Society of London
JSL

c/o Christopher T.W. Ogden, Membership Sec.
16 Laurier Rd., London, NW5 1SG, UK
Website: http://www.johnsonsocietyoflondon.org
Members: 200
Contact: Lord Harmsworth, Pres.
Fee: £15
Membership Type: student
Fee: £25
Membership Type: joint
Description: Individuals in 8 countries interested in the study of the 18th century and Dr. Samuel Johnson (1709-84), English author and lexicographer.
Publication: Journal
Publication title: The New Rambler. Advertisements.

02925
Joiners' and Ceilers' Company

75 Meadway Dr., Horsell, Surrey, Woking, GU21 4TF, UK
Fax: 01483 720098
Email: info@joinersandceilers.co.uk
Website: http://www.joinersandceilers.co.uk

Contact: A.L. Jackson, Clerk
Description: Represents the guild members and is associated with all types of heavy woodwork and carving. Organizes events (black tie or white tie) for members to meet and gather together.

02926

Joint Association of Classical Teachers
JACT

Senate House, Malet St., London, WC1E 7HU, UK
Tel: 020 78628719
Fax: 020 72552297
Email: office@jact.org
Website: http://www.jact.org
Members: 1500
Staff: 1
Contact: Bettany Hughes, Pres.
Fee: £40
Membership Type: full
Fee: £16
Membership Type: student
Description: Teachers of classics in schools and universities. Promotes classic teaching in general (includes popular Summer Schools in Ancient Greek, Latin, Classical Civilization/Ancient History).
Publication: Magazine
Publication title: Omnibus

02927

Joint Council for the Welfare of Immigrants
JCWI

115 Old St., London, EC1V 9RT, UK
Tel: 020 72518708
Fax: 020 72518707
Email: info@jcwi.org.uk
Website: http://www.jcwi.org.uk
Members: 1000
Staff: 15
Contact: Habib Rahman, Chief Exec.
Fee: £20
Membership Type: unwaged
Fee: £70-150
Membership Type: commercial organization (based on annual turnover)
Description: Independent national organization which exists to campaign for justice in immigration, nationality, refugee law, and policy. Undertakes strategic casework and acts as an expert training resource for others who work in this field. Eliminates discrimination in this sphere.
Publication: Handbook
Publication title: Immigration, Nationality & Refugee Law Handbook

02928

Joint Information Systems Committee
JISC

c/o HEFCE
Northavon House, Coldharbour Ln., Bristol, BS16 1QD, UK
Tel: 0117 9317403
Fax: 0117 9317255
Email: info@jisc.ac.uk
Website: http://www.jisc.ac.uk
Contact: Malcolm Read, Exec. Sec.
Description: Provides strategic guidance, advice, and opportunities to use ICT to support teaching, learning, research, and administration.
Publication: Manual
Publication title: Advice and Guidance

02929

Joint Nature Conservation Committee
JNCC

Monkstone House, City Rd., Peterborough, PE1 1JY, UK
Tel: 01733 562626
Fax: 01733 555948
Email: comment@jncc.gov.uk
Website: http://www.jncc.gov.uk
Staff: 112
Contact: Peter Bridgewater, Chm.
Description: Serves as a forum through which the three country nature conservation agencies, the Countryside Council for Wales, English Nature, and Scottish Natural Heritage, deliver their statutory responsibilities as a whole and internationally. Contributes to sustaining and enriching biological diversity, enhancing geological features and sustaining natural systems. Advises a minister on the development of policies. Establishes common standards throughout Great Britain for the monitoring of nature conservation and for research. Commissions or supports research which the Committee deems relevant.

02930

Joint Radio Co.
JRC

Dean Bradley House, 6th Fl., 52 Horseferry Rd., London, SW1P 2AF, UK
Tel: 020 77065199
Email: info@jrc.co.uk
Website: http://www.jrc.co.uk
Members: 35
Contact: David Smith, Chm.
Description: Manages the block allocation of spectrum for the gas and electricity industries in order that this scarce natural resource is used efficiently and in a way amenable to use by the utilities.
Formerly: Formerly, Joint Radio Committee for the Nationalised Fuel and Power Industries

02931

Joint University Council
JUC

Nottingham Trent University, College of Business, Law and Social Sciences, Rm. 517 Victoria House, Nottingham, NG1 4BU, UK
Tel: 0115 8488117
Fax: 0115 8486808
Email: sandra.odell@ntu.ac.uk
Website: http://www.juc.ac.uk/default.aspx
Members: 100
Staff: 1
Contact: Sandra Odell, Sec.
Description: Academic institutions with up to 3 academic representatives in each institution representing the Council's Public Administration, Social Policy and Social Work Education Committees. Co-ordinates and develops the work of universities, university colleges and other relevant centers teaching the applied social sciences to degree level.
Publication: Journal
Publication title: Public Policy and Administration. Advertisements.

02932

Jubilee Action - UK

Carroll House, 11 Quarry St., Guildford, GU1 3UY, UK
Tel: 01483 230250
Fax: 01483 546035
Email: info@jubileeaction.co.uk
Website: http://www.jubileeaction.co.uk
Staff: 9
Description: Serves to protect the lives of children at risk of abuse worldwide and combating poverty.
Publication: Magazine
Publication title: Just Right

02933

Jubilee Research

3 Jonathan St., London, SE11 5NH, UK
Tel: 0207 8206350
Fax: 0207 8206301
Email: info.jubilee@neweconomics.org
Website: http://www.jubileeresearch.org
Contact: Ann Pettifor, Coor.
Description: Individuals and organizations concerned about international debt among developing countries. Seeks to secure forgiveness of the international debts of developing nations by the year 2000. Serves as a clearinghouse on international debt; conducts lobbying and advocacy campaigns.
Formerly: Formerly, Jubilee 2000

02934

Junior Chamber International United Kingdom
JCI UK

PO Box 6638, Grantham, NG31 9BX, UK
Tel: 01476 404005
Fax: 01476 404006
Email: head-office@jciuk.org.uk
Website: http://www.jciuk.org.uk
Contact: Lesley Young, Pres.
Description: Provides opportunities for young people to develop leadership skills, responsibility, fellowship and entrepreneurship. Conducts individual development courses. Conducts charitable programs and sponsors competitions.

02935

Justices' Clerks' Society
JCS

Port of Liverpool Bldg., 2nd Fl., Pier Head, Liverpool, L3 1BY, UK
Tel: 0151 2550790
Fax: 0151 2364458
Email: secretariat@jc-society.co.uk
Website: http://www.jc-society.com
Members: 367
Staff: 5
Contact: Sid Brighton, Chief Exec./Sec.
Description: Clerks and chief executives of justices. Promotes communication and cooperation among members.
Publication: Manual
Publication title: Legal Adviser Manual, Criminal Law

02936

Karg-Elert Archive

3 Cunnery Terr., Cunnery Rd., Church Stretton, SY6 6AL, UK
Email: anthony@caldicott247.fslife.co.uk
Website: http://www.karg-elert-archive.org.uk
Members: 55
Staff: 4
Contact: Anthony Caldicott, Chm.
Fee: £8
Membership Type: ordinary
Fee: £12
Membership Type: international
Description: Encourages and implements the recording performance, publications and study of the music and writings of Sigfrid Karg-Elert.
Publication: Newsletter
Publication title: Karg-Elert Archive Newsletter

02937

Karuna Trust
KT

72 Holloway Rd., London, N7 8JG, UK
Tel: 020 77003434
Fax: 020 77003535
Email: info@karuna.org
Website: http://www.karuna.org
Staff: 8
Contact: Ulla Brown, Chair
Description: Buddhist charity. Coordinates and supports health, education, and employment projects that promote self-reliance for individuals in India.
Publication title: A Peaceful Revolution

02938

Keep Britain Tidy

The Pier, Elizabeth House, Wigan, WN3 4EX, UK
Tel: 01942 612621
Fax: 01942 824778
Email: applications@keepbritaintidy.org
Website: http://www.keepbritaintidy.org
Members: 2000
Staff: 109
Contact: Mike Phillips, Chm.
Description: Works to improve local environments, from streets to town centres, local parks, rural areas, beaches and rivers. Partly funded by Government, through Defra (Department for Environment, Food and Rural Affairs), works closely with other government departments such as the Office of the Deputy Prime Minister, and the Anti-Social Behaviour Unit in the Home Office. Additional funding is received through private sector backing or via consultancy work with local authorities and others.
Formerly: Formerly, ENCAMS
Publication: Book
Publication title: Britain in Bloom

02939

Kidney Cancer UK
KCUK

PO Box 2473, Staffordshire, Uttoxeter, ST14 8WZ, UK
Tel: 01889 565801
Email: julienash@kcuk.org
Website: http://www.kcuk.org
Contact: Julie Nash, Admin. Off.
Fee: £24
Membership Type: full
Fee: £16
Membership Type: unwaged, student
Description: Raises public awareness of kidney cancer and its treatment. Brings patients and carers together to share their experiences and discuss common problems. Works with the medical profession to improve standards of care.
Publication: Magazine
Publication title: Insight

02940

Kilvert Society

30 Bromley Heath Ave., Downend, Bristol, BS16 6JP, UK
Website: http://www.communigate.co.uk/here/kilvertsociety
Members: 667
Staff: 7
Contact: Alan Brimson, Honorary Sec.
Fee: £12
Membership Type: individual
Fee: £15
Membership Type: joint
Description: Aims to foster an interest in the Rev. Francis Kilvert, his work, his diary and the countryside.
Publication: Journal
Publication title: Journal of the Kilvert Society

02941

Kipling Society

6 Clifton Rd., London, W9 1SS, UK
Email: jmkeskar@btinternet.com
Website: http://www.kipling.org.uk
Members: 600
Contact: Jane Keskar, Hon. Sec.
Fee: £24
Membership Type: general (over 28)
Fee: £12
Membership Type: general (under 28)
Description: Individuals, universities and libraries from 25 countries interested in the life and works of English poet and prose writer Rudyard Kipling (1865-1936). Promotes exchange and discussion among members. Maintains a library and archive at City University London, and a Kipling exhibition in Rottingdean, Brighton, Sussex, England.
Library Subject: Rudyard Kipling
Library Type: reference
Publication: Journal
Publication title: Kipling Journal. Advertisements.
Meetings/Conventions: annual luncheon

02942

Kiribati and Tungaru Association
KTA

47 Chelsea Pk., Easton, Bristol, BS5 6AH, UK
Tel: 01179 553959
Email: beta_tentoa@yahoo.co.uk
Website: http://www.ktaweb.org.uk
Contact: Nei Beta Turpin, Chair
Fee: £10
Membership Type: ordinary
Fee: £5
Membership Type: student, visitor
Description: Aims to foster good relations between Kiribati families and friends in Europe. Offers assistance and hospitality to I-Kiribati friends visiting the United Kingdom, Ireland and continental Europe. Teaches the young generation about the cultures and traditions of Kiribati through dialogue and dance.
Publication: Newsletter
Publication title: Te Buu

02943

Kitchen, Bathroom, Bedroom Specialists Association
KBSA

Pleasley Vale Business Park, Unit L4A, Mill 3, Nottinghamshire, Mansfield, NG19 8RL, UK
Tel: 01623 818808
Fax: 01623 818805
Email: ruthward@kbsa.org.uk
Website: http://www.kbsa.org.uk
Members: 400
Staff: 3
Contact: Ruth Ward, Sales/Marketing Dir.
Description: Members design, supply or install fitted kitchens, bedrooms, bathrooms. Recognized body for the professional kitchen, bedroom and bathroom supplier who can prove to the consumer the design, supply and installation services they provide. Consumercare scheme protects consumer deposits and marketing message enforces and reinforces that security to the general public.
Formerly: Formerly, Kitchen Specialists Association
Publication: Magazine
Publication title: The Specialist. Advertisements.

02944

Knitting Industries' Federation
KIF

c/o Knitting Together
Leicester City Museums Service, 12th Fl., A Block, New Walk Ctre., Welford Pl., Leicester, LE1 5XY, UK
Tel: 0116 2527322
Fax: 0116 2556084
Email: knittingtogether.museums@leicester.gov.uk
Website: http://www.knittingtogether.org.uk/doc.asp?doc=14063&cat=670
Members: 250
Staff: 3
Fee: £300-30000
Description: Knitting manufacturers in UK, including dyers and finishers. Provides a service of representation, advice and information to members both as knitting manufacturers and employers, nationally and internationally.

02945

Kurdish Human Rights Project
KHRP

11 Guilford St., London, WC1N 1DH, UK
Tel: 020 74053835
Fax: 020 74049088
Email: khrp@khrp.org
Website: http://www.khrp.org
Contact: Kerim Yildiz, Chief Exec.
Description: Works to protect the human rights of all persons within the Kurdish regions, irrespective of race, religion, sex, political persuasion and other beliefs or opinions.
Publication: Newsletter
Publication title: Newsline

L'Organisation Internationale du Cafe

see International Coffee Organization

L'Organisation Pour La Conservation Du Saumon De l'Atlantique Nord

see North Atlantic Salmon Conservation Organization

L'Union Internationale pour la Taxatione sur la Valeur de la Terre et la Libre-Echange

see International Union for Land Value Taxation and Free Trade

02946

La Societe Guernesiaise

Candie Gardens, St. Peter Port, Guernsey, GY1 1UG, UK
Tel: 01481 725093
Fax: 01481 726248
Email: societe@cwgsy.net
Website: http://www.societe.org.gg
Members: 1500
Contact: Lawney Martin, Sec.
Fee: £22
Membership Type: single (in UK)
Fee: £20
Membership Type: single, double (overseas)
Description: Encourages the study of the history, natural history, geography and geology of the Bailiwick of Guernsey, the conservation of the Bailiwick's natural environment and the preservation of its historic buildings and monuments.
Publication title: Annual Transactions

02947

Laban Guild
LG

c/o Janet Harrison, Membership Sec.
11 Sherborne Rd., Basingstoke, RG21 5TH, UK
Email: janeteharrison@aol.com
Website: http://www.labanguild.f9.co.uk
Members: 450
Contact: Anna Carlisle, Pres.
Fee: £25
Membership Type: individual (full)
Fee: £30
Membership Type: affiliated group
Description: Individuals who work in the fields of movement analysis and professional and recreational dance in education, industry, and therapy. Founded by Rudolf von Laban and his pupils in order to ensure the development of his studies. (Laban, 1879-1958, was a German innovator in the fields of modern dance and the analysis of human movement.) The influence of Laban's work has been felt in theatrical dance and drama, in educational dance and kinetography (movement notation), and in industry and therapy. Offers tutorial service; provides training scheme for leaders of community dance groups.
Publication: Magazine
Publication title: Movement and Dance. Advertisements.

02948

Laboratory Animal Science Association
LASA

PO Box 524, Hull, HU9 9HE, UK
Tel: 08456 711956
Fax: 08456 711957
Email: info@lasa.co.uk
Website: http://www.lasa.co.uk
Contact: David Smith, Pres.
Fee: £51
Membership Type: individual
Fee: £235
Membership Type: institution
Description: Advances the knowledge of the care and welfare of laboratory animals and promotes refinement of scientific procedures.
Publication: Newsletter

02949

Labour Party - Britain

Eldon House, Regent Ctre., Newcastle upon Tyne, NE3 3PW, UK
Tel: 08705 900200
Website: http://www.labour.org.uk
Members: 375000
Staff: 200
Contact: Gordon Brown, Leader
Description: British centre/left political party.

02950

Labour Women's Network
LWN

11 Well House Rd., West Yorkshire, Leeds, LS8 4BS, UK
Email: contact@lwn.org.uk
Website: http://www.lwn.org.uk
Members: 500
Contact: Harriet Harman, Contact
Fee: £15
Membership Type: waged
Fee: £10
Membership Type: unwaged, low
Description: Supports and advises women in the Labour Party who are seeking selection for public office.

02951

Lace Guild

The Hollies, 53 Audnam, West Midlands, Stourbridge, DY8 4AE, UK
Tel: 01384 390739
Fax: 01384 444415
Email: hollies@laceguild.org
Website: http://www.laceguild.demon.co.uk
Members: 5000
Staff: 3
Contact: Sue Dane, Honorary Chm.
Fee: £26
Membership Type: full, UK
Fee: £30.5
Membership Type: full, rest of Europe
Description: Worldwide; adult and junior; amateur and professional; all abilities. Promotes the craft of lace making, its history and use, and with these objects in mind, organizes courses and workshops, lace study days, exhibitions and events.
Publication: Magazine
Publication title: Lace. Advertisements.

02952

Ladder Association

PO Box 26970, Glasgow, G3 9DS, UK
Tel: 0845 2601048
Fax: 0845 2601049
Email: info@ladderassociation.org.uk
Website: http://ladderassociation.org.uk
Members: 20
Contact: Chris Ball, Chm.
Fee: £375
Membership Type: regular
Description: Represents companies ranging from blue chips to small privately owned manufacturers of access equipment.
Formerly: Formerly, British Ladder Manufacturers Association

02953

Lancashire Welsh Pony and Cob Association
LWPCA

Corran Stud, Hinds Ln., Radcliffe, Manchester, M26 2XY, UK
Tel: 0161 7645303
Fax: 0161 7645303
Email: corranstud@btinternet.com
Website: http://www.lancashirewelshponycob.org.uk
Members: 200
Contact: Corran Stud, Gen. Sec.
Fee: £10
Membership Type: single
Fee: £15
Membership Type: family
Description: Promotes the breeding and ownership of Welsh ponies and cobs. Seeks to improve the breed and promote its excellence.

02954

Lancaster District Chamber of Commerce, Trade and Industry

Commerce House, Fenton St., Lancanshire, Lancaster, LA1 1AB, UK
Tel: 01524 381331
Email: info@lancaster-chamber.org.uk
Website: http://www.lancaster-chamber.org.uk
Members: 353
Staff: 28
Contact: Ann Morris, Chief Exec.
Fee: £938.83
Membership Type: firm/company (maximum; based on number of employees)
Description: Represents members across Lancaster at local, regional and national level on matters concerning trade, commerce and industry and lobbying. Facilitates networking, forums and events to enable members to exchange ideas, information, views and business practice.
Publication: Newsletter
Publication title: Businessmatters

02955

Landex - The Association for Land Based Colleges

10 Mount Dr., Nantwich, CW5 6JF, UK
Tel: 007876 488336
Email: vic.croxson@btinternet.com
Website: http://www.landex.org.uk
Members: 36

Staff: 2
Contact: Vic Croxson, Chief Exec.
Description: Represents land based colleges in England, Wales, Scotland, and Northern Ireland.
Formerly: Formerly, National Association of Principal Agricultural Education Officers

02956

Landscape Institute
LI

33 Great Portland St., London, W1W 8QG, UK
Tel: 020 72994500
Fax: 020 72994501
Email: mail@landscapeinstitute.org
Website: http://www.landscapeinstitute.org
Members: 5000
Staff: 26
Contact: Jo Watkins, Pres.
Fee: £24
Membership Type: student
Fee: £80
Membership Type: affiliate
Description: Professional body for chartered landscape architects in the United Kingdom. Aims to protect, conserve and enhance the natural and built environment for the benefit of the public.
Library Subject: landscape architecture
Library Type: reference
Publication: Directory
Publication title: Directory of Registered Landscape Practices

02957

Landscape Research Group
LRG

The University of Sheffield, Department of Landscape, Arts Tower, 3rd Fl., Western Bank, Sheffield, S10 2TN, UK
Tel: 0114 2220605
Email: e.lange@sheffield.ac.uk
Website: http://lrg.ethz.ch/lrg_main.html
Members: 650
Staff: 1
Contact: Eckart Lange, Hd.
Description: Individuals and corporations in 30 countries with a professional, academic or practical interest in the landscape. Promotes education and research; encourages exchange of information for public benefit in the field of landscaping and related subjects. Conducts symposia and seminars on landscape research.
Publication: Journal
Publication title: Landscape Research. Advertisements.

02958

Law Society

113 Chancery Ln., London, WC2A 1PL, UK
Tel: 020 72421222
Fax: 020 78310344
Email: contact@lawsociety.org.uk
Website: http://www.lawsociety.org.uk/home.law
Contact: Linda Lee, Pres.
Description: Solicitors in England and Wales. Provides services and support for members; sets standards for the legal profession. Works to improve access to the law by the general public.

02959

Law Society of England

113 Chancery Ln., London, WC2A 1PL, UK
Tel: 020 72421222
Fax: 020 78310344
Email: editorialteam@lawsociety.org.uk
Website: http://www.lawsociety.org.uk/home.law
Members: 120000
Contact: Des Hudson, Chief Exec.
Description: Members of the Law Society are solicitors in England and Wales. Represents solicitors and provides services to support them.
Publication: Magazine
Publication title: Law Society Gazette. Advertisements.

02960

Law Society of Northern Ireland

96 Victoria St., Belfast, BT1 3GN, UK
Tel: 028 90231614
Fax: 028 90232606
Email: info@lawsoc-ni.org
Website: http://www.lawsoc-ni.org
Contact: Alan Hunter, Chief Exec.
Description: Solicitors working to regulate the solicitors' profession in Northern Ireland to maintain the independence, ethical standards, professional competence and quality of services offered to the public.

02961

Law Society of Scotland

26 Drumsheugh Gardens, Edinburgh, EH3 7YR, UK
Tel: 0131 2267411
Fax: 0131 2252934
Email: lawscot@lawscot.org.uk
Website: http://www.lawscot.org.uk
Members: 9000
Staff: 103
Contact: Lorna Jack, Chief Exec.
Description: Scottish solicitors. Statutory duties to promote the profession of Scottish solicitors and the interests of the public in relation to that profession. Activities include legal education, client relations, law reform, practice development, and international law.
Publication: Journal
Publication title: Journal of the Law Society of Scotland. Advertisements.

02962

Lead Contractors Association
LCA

Centurion House, 36 London Rd., East Grinstead, RH19 1AB, UK
Tel: 01342 317888
Fax: 01342 303200
Email: info@lca.gb.com
Website: http://www.leadcontractorsassociation.com
Members: 115
Contact: Dave Martin, Chm.
Description: Contracting firms which provide leadworking services to the construction industry in the United Kingdom. Promotes the use of lead in construction. Protects members' interests. Sponsors competitions.
Publication: Membership Directory
Publication title: Directory of Specialist Leadworking Contractors. Advertisements.
Meetings/Conventions: annual seminar

02963

LEAD International - United Kingdom

Sundial House, 2nd Fl., 114 Kensington High St., London, W8 4NP, UK
Tel: 020 79388700
Fax: 020 79388710
Email: nina@lead.org
Website: http://www.lead.org
Members: 1600
Staff: 18
Contact: Simon Lyster, Chief Exec.
Description: Facilitates sharing of knowledge, skills and expertise on sustainable development issues. Provides the public with training and leadership skills on sustainable development.

02964

LEAD International: Leadership for Environment and Development

Sundial House, 114 Kensington High St., London, W8 4NP, UK
Tel: 020 79388700
Fax: 020 79388710
Email: nina@lead.org
Website: http://www.lead.org
Members: 1600
Contact: Nina Keleher, Admin.
Description: Supports networks of people and institutions promoting change towards sustainable development that is economically sound, environmentally responsible, and socially equitable.
Publication: Handbook
Publication title: Training Across Cultures

02965

Lead Sheet Association
LSA

Unit 10 Archers Park, Branbridges Rd., E Peckham, Kent, Tonbridge, TN12 5HP, UK
Tel: 01622 872432
Fax: 01622 871649
Email: info@leadsheetassociation.org.uk
Website: http://www.leadsheetassociation.org.uk
Members: 4
Staff: 6
Description: Represents manufacturers of lead sheet. Promotes and encourages the use of rolled lead sheet in building applications throughout the UK. Provides a technical advisory service and operates a national network of educational centers and a mobile training unit.
Publication: Manual
Publication title: Rolled Lead Sheet

02966

League for the Exchange of Commonwealth Teachers
LECT

60 Queens Rd., Reading, RG1 4BS, UK
Tel: 0118 9021171
Email: info@lect.org.uk
Website: http://www.lect.org.uk/home.aspx
Members: 3000
Staff: 10
Contact: Anna Tomlinson, Dir.

Description: Participating schools in Australia, Bahamas, Bangladesh, Barbados, Bermuda, Canada, India, Jamaica, Kenya, New Zealand, Sierra Leone, Singapore, South Africa, Trinidad and Tobago, and other countries. Conducts 12-month teacher exchanges among Commonwealth countries to enhance professional growth while providing exposure to diverse cultures and educational systems. Seeks to foster professional adaptability through participation in teacher exchanges at all academic levels. Collects information through study projects. Provides grants for air fare, conferences, dependent children, and personal allowance. Offers in-service training.
Publication title: The Story of the League 1901-1991

02967
League of Jewish Women
LJW
6 Bloomsbury Sq., London, WC1A 2LP, UK
Tel: 020 72428300
Fax: 020 72428313
Email: office@theljw.org
Website: http://www.theljw.org
Members: 3000
Contact: Marilyn Brummer, Pres.
Fee: £10
Membership Type: regular
Fee: £7
Membership Type: above 70 years old, LADS member
Description: Promotes friendly relations, understanding, and mutual support among Jewish women. Seeks to: improve the status of women in the Jewish and general communities; "intensify in each Jewish woman her sense of Jewish consciousness"; and encourage solidarity among members.
Publication: Magazine
Publication title: In Contact

02968
Learn to Care
c/o Selly Wick House
59 - 61 Selly Wick Rd., Selly Park, Birmingham, B29 7JE, UK
Tel: 0121 4156805
Fax: 0121 4156806
Email: info@learntocare.org.uk
Website: http://www.learntocare.org.uk
Contact: Trevor Hewitt, Vice Chm.
Description: Aims to promote workforce development, particularly those who deliver services or support the social care industry. Works with other professional bodies in order to their professional development. Promotes the professional interests of members. Strengthens links with all regional and national organisations involved in learning and workforce development.
Formerly: Formerly, National Association of Training Officers in Personal Social Services

02969
Learning and Teaching Scotland
LTS
The Optima, 58 Robertson St., Glasgow, G2 8DU, UK
Tel: 0141 2825000
Fax: 0141 2825050
Email: enquiries@ltscotland.org.uk
Website: http://www.ltscotland.org.uk
Staff: 220
Contact: Bernard McLeary, Chief Exec.
Description: Provides advice, support, resources and staff development to enhance the quality of learning and teaching in Scotland, combining expertise in the curriculum 3 to 18 with advice on the use of ICT in education. Works in close partnership with the Scottish Executive, HMIE, the SQA, ADES, COSLA, education authorities, schools and with a range of professional associations, playing a key role in the drive to improve learning and teaching.
Formerly: Formerly, Scottish Consultative Council on the Curriculum
Publication: Journal
Publication title: Connected

02970
Leatherhead Food International
LFI
Randalls Rd., Surrey, Leatherhead, KT22 7RY, UK
Tel: 01372 376761
Fax: 01372 386228
Email: help@leatherheadfood.com
Website: http://www.leatherheadfood.com
Members: 1000
Staff: 200
Contact: Paul Berryman, Chief Exec.
Description: Manufacturers and suppliers of food products. Seeks to advance members' commercial interests. Provides national and international support and services to food products manufacturers and suppliers.
Library Subject: food science technology, market information
Library Type: not open to the public
Publication: Manual
Publication title: European Legislation Manual
Meetings/Conventions: weekly conference – Exhibits.

02971
Leeds Chamber of Commerce
White Rose House, 28a York Pl., Leeds, LS1 2EZ, UK
Tel: 0113 2470000
Email: info@leedschamber.co.uk
Website: http://www.leedschamber.co.uk
Members: 1456
Staff: 60
Contact: Gary Williamson, Chief Exec.
Fee: £1610
Membership Type: firm/company (based on number of employees)
Description: Represents members across Leeds at local, regional and national level on matters concerning trade, commerce and industry and lobbying. Facilitates networking, forums and events to enable members to exchange ideas, information, views and business practice.

02972
Leeds Philosophical and Literary Society
Leeds City Museum, 7th Fl. W, Cookridge St., Leeds, LS2 8BH, UK
Email: bjbcjh@aol.com
Website: http://www.leedsphilandlit.org.uk
Contact: John Lydon, Sec.
Fee: £18
Membership Type: general
Description: Promotes the advancement of science, literature and the arts in the City of Leeds.

02973
Legal Software Suppliers Association
LSSA
River Cottage, Water Ln., N Witham, Grantham, NG33 5LJ, UK
Tel: 01476 860417
Fax: 07768 737449
Email: roger@number-one.org.uk
Website: http://www.lssa.co.uk
Contact: Roger Hancock, Sec.
Description: Serves as an industry body for legal system developers and vendors. Represents legal software suppliers in UK. Aims to set and maintain professional standards within the industry. Facilitates communication between lawyers and software providers.

02974
Legal Technology Insider
Oak Lodge, Darrow Green Rd., Denton, Norfolk, Harleston, IP20 0AY, UK
Tel: 01986 788666
Fax: 01986 788808
Email: news@legaltechnology.com
Website: http://www.legaltechnology.com
Description: Provides a regulatory body to legal software suppliers in England.
Publication: Newsletter

02975
Leicestershire Chamber of Commerce and Industry
1 Mill Ln., Leicester, LE2 7HU, UK
Tel: 0116 2471800
Fax: 0116 2470430
Email: leics@chamberofcommerce.co.uk
Website: http://www.chamberofcommerce.co.uk
Members: 1930
Staff: 40
Contact: Martin Traynor, Managing Dir.
Fee: £1157.62
Membership Type: firm, company
Fee: £173
Membership Type: charity
Description: Promotes business and commerce.

02976
Leisure and Outdoor Furniture Association
LOFA
113 Worcester Rd., Chichester, PO19 5EE, UK
Tel: 01243 839593
Fax: 01243 839467
Email: info@lofa.com
Website: http://www.lofa.com
Members: 65
Contact: Richard Plowman, Sec.
Description: Manufacturers and distributors of garden furniture and barbecues. Works to represent and promote members' interests and products.

02977

Leisure Studies Association
LSA

c/o Mrs. Myrene L. McFee
University of Brighton, The Chelsea School, Eastbourne, BN20 7SP, UK
Tel: 01323 640357
Fax: 01323 644641
Email: myrene.mcfee@leisure-studies-association.info
Website: http://www.leisure-studies-association.info/LSAWEB/Index.html
Members: 200
Staff: 1
Contact: Karl Spracklen, Chm.
Fee: £80
Membership Type: corporate
Fee: £40
Membership Type: individual
Description: Researchers, planners, policy-makers, administrators and practitioners involved in leisure studies/research. Covers sociology, geography, psychology, management, planning, government, tourism, media, environment, education, economics, leisure industries. Themes - culture, politics, sport, social history, unemployment, consumerism, aging, gender, arts, etc.
Publication: Journal
Publication title: Leisure Studies
Meetings/Conventions: Journeys in Leisure: Current and Future Alliances – annual conference

02978

Leonard Cheshire International
LCI

66 S Lambeth Rd., London, SW8 1RL, UK
Tel: 020 32420200
Fax: 020 32420250
Email: info@lcdisability.org
Website: http://www.lcdisability.org
Staff: 10
Contact: Fionna McConnon, International Coor. Mgr.
Description: Locally operated programs for people with disabilities and their families in 54 countries. Seeks to improve the quality of life of people with disabilities. Maintains rehabilitation centers, skills training centers, support for employment and education programs, independent living programs, community-based support and residential services.
Publication: Magazine
Publication title: COMPASS

02979

Leopold Stokowski Society
LSS

12 Market St., Deal, CT14 6HS, UK
Email: edward.johnson5@btopenworld.com
Members: 1250
Staff: 5
Contact: Christine A. Ducrotoy, Contact
Fee: £20
Membership Type: individual in United Kingdom
Fee: £40
Membership Type: individual in U.S.
Description: Individuals dedicated to celebrating the life and works of Leopold Stokowski (1882-1977), American conductor, composer, and founder of the American Symphony Orchestra. Strives to ensure that his works remain available for pleasure and study; advocates the release on digital disc of important Stokowski recordings; transfers old recordings onto records. Assists members in the acquisition of recordings. Sponsors lectures, discussions, and concert and opera outings. Operates speakers' bureau.
Publication: Magazine
Publication title: List of Available Recordings. Advertisements.

02980

LEPRA - England

28 Middleborough, Colchester, CO1 1TG, UK
Tel: 01206 216700
Fax: 01206 762151
Email: lepra@leprahealthinaction.org
Website: http://www.lepra.org.uk
Description: Seeks to eradicate leprosy throughout the world. Operates training programs for medical personnel. Supports research for the development of leprosy drugs and vaccines, and research projects of the World Health Organization. Concentrates efforts in Africa, Asia, and Brazil. Maintains special children's, eye, and hand remobilization funds. Investigates potential for treatment of leprosy in conjunction with that of other diseases. Sponsors competitions.
Library Subject: leprosy, TB, HIV
Library Type: reference
Publication: Journal
Publication title: Leprosy Review. Advertisements.

02981

Leprosy Relief Association
LEPRA

28 Middleborough, Essex, Colchester, CO1 1TG, UK
Tel: 01206 216700
Fax: 01206 762151
Email: lepra@leprahealthinaction.org
Website: http://www.lepra.org.uk
Staff: 470
Contact: Terry Vasey, Chief Exec.
Description: Works as a medical development charity restoring health, hope and dignity to people affected by leprosy and other diseases of poverty.
Publication: Newsletter
Publication title: LEPRA News

02982

Leukaemia CARE
LC

One Birch Ct., Blackpole E, Worcester, WR3 8SG, UK
Tel: 0190 5755977
Fax: 0190 5755166
Email: care@leukaemiacare.org.uk
Website: http://leukaemiacare.org.uk
Members: 6000
Contact: Eve Martin, Deputy Chief Exec.
Description: Provides care and support for the sufferers of leukemia, Hodgkin's and other lymphomas, myelodysplasia, myeloproliferative disorders, Myeloma and aplastic anemia. Promotes awareness of leukemia and other allied blood disorders.

02983

Lewis Carroll Society
LCS

50 Lauderdale Mansions, Lauderdale Rd., London, W9 1NE, UK
Email: alanwhite@tesco.net
Website: http://lewiscarrollsociety.org.uk
Members: 400
Contact: Mark Richards, Chm.
Fee: £20
Membership Type: individual (full)
Fee: £18
Membership Type: individual (retired)
Description: Admirers of British author Lewis Carroll (1832-98), whose works include *Alice's Adventures in Wonderland* and *Through the Looking Glass*. Promotes appreciation of Carroll's works.
Publication: Journal
Publication title: The Carrollian

02984

Liberal International
LI

1 Whitehall Pl., London, SW1A 2HD, UK
Tel: 020 78395905
Fax: 020 79252685
Email: all@liberal-international.org
Website: http://www.liberal-international.org
Members: 102
Staff: 5
Contact: Emil Kirjas, Sec. Gen.
Description: National liberal political parties and groups. Promotes: the welfare and protection of economic, racial, political, and ethnic minorities; the respect of human rights; decentralization of political and economic power; individual liberty and tolerance; conflict resolution by peaceful means. Monitors national elections. Coordinates international activities of liberal parties; conducts study visits. Cooperates with liberal forces in the developing world and cultural and research institutions.
Publication: Magazine
Publication title: Liberal Matters. Advertisements.

02985

Liberal Youth

c/o Liberal Democrats
4 Cowley St., London, SW1P 3NB, UK
Tel: 020 72271387
Email: liberalyouthadmin@libdems.org.uk
Website: http://liberalyouth.org
Members: 3000
Staff: 1
Contact: Alan Belmore, Acting Chm.
Description: Youth and student organization of the Liberal Democrats.
Formerly: Formerly, Liberal Democrat Youth and Students - UK
Publication: Magazine
Publication title: Free Radical. Advertisements.

02986

Libertarian Alliance
LA

2 Landsdowne Row, Ste. 35, London, W1J 6HL, UK
Tel: 020 7956472199
Email: tim@libertarian.co.uk
Website: http://www.libertarian.co.uk
Contact: Tim Evans, Pres.
Description: Members in 10 countries. Promotes libertarian ideas through activities including publishing, maintaining a speakers' bureau, and holding seminars.
Formerly: Formerly, Radical Libertarian Alliance
Publication title: Foreign Policy Perspectives

02987

Liberty

21 Tabard St., London, SE1 4LA, UK
Tel: 020 74033888
Email: info@liberty-human-rights.org.uk
Website: http://www.liberty-human-rights.org.uk
Members: 7000
Staff: 23
Contact: Shami Chakrabarti, Dir.
Fee: £30
Membership Type: individual
Fee: £12
Membership Type: unwaged
Description: Individuals committed to the defense and extension of civil liberties in the United Kingdom. Campaigns for: a Bill of Rights, protection against inhumane or degrading punishment; equality before the law; freedom from discrimination on grounds of disability, political opinion, race, religion, sex, or sexual orientation; protection from arbitrary arrest and unnecessary detention and for fair hearings and associated legal rights; freedom of thought and belief, speech and publication, and peaceful assembly and association; free movement, privacy, and the right of access to official information. Lobbies Parliament; takes important test cases to court; advises people on legal rights. Commissions research.
Formerly: Formerly, Liberty National Council for Civil Liberties
Publication: Book
Publication title: Your Rights

02988

Library and Information Research Group LIRG

c/o CILIP
7 Ridgmount St., London, WC1E 7AE, UK
Tel: 020 72550500
Fax: 020 72550501
Email: christine.irving8@googlemail.com
Website: http://www.cilip.org.uk/specialinterestgroups/bysubject/research
Contact: Christine Irving, Honorary Sec.
Description: Promotes awareness of the need for library and information research. Bridges the gap between library research and practice.
Publication: Journal
Publication title: Library and Information Research News

02989

Licensed Taxi Drivers Association LTDA

LTDA Taxi House, Woodfield Rd., London, W9 2BA, UK
Tel: 020 72861046
Fax: 020 72862494
Website: http://www.ltda.co.uk
Members: 6500
Staff: 10
Description: Licensed taxi drivers. Represents members in consultation with government, local and international authorities and organizations in matters affecting the taxi trade.

02990

Licensing Executives Society Britain and Ireland LES B&I

c/o Northern Networking Events Ltd.
Glenfinnan Ste., Braeview House, 9-11 Braeview Pl., East Kilbride, G74 3XH, UK
Tel: 01355 244966
Fax: 01355 249959
Email: les@northernnetworking.co.uk
Website: http://www.les-bi.org
Members: 750
Contact: Mark Wilson, Pres.
Fee: £80
Membership Type: general
Description: Businessmen, financiers, academics, scientists, engineers, lawyers and other professionals, united by a common interest in the successful commercialisation of technology and intellectual property rights by licensing or assignment. Membership is open to all who have an interest in technology transfer and are prepared to abide by proper professional standards.

02991

LIFE

Life House, 1 Mill St., Leamington Spa, CV31 1ES, UK
Tel: 01926 421587
Fax: 01926 336497
Email: info@lifecharity.org.uk
Website: http://www.lifecharity.org.uk
Members: 35000
Staff: 50
Contact: Michaela Aston, Contact
Fee: £5
Membership Type: unwaged
Fee: £15
Membership Type: waged
Description: Individuals dedicated to the abolition of abortion in the United Kingdom. Seeks to increase knowledge of the potential health risks involved in abortion. Operates 120 pregnancy care centers offering free pregnancy counseling, abortion counseling and counseling after abortion, free testing, welfare advice, and provision of baby and maternity clothes and equipment. Maintains 40 Life houses providing shelter and aid to impoverished pregnant women. Offers speakers' bureau.

02992

Life Academy

9 Chesham Rd., Surrey, Guildford, GU1 3LS, UK
Tel: 01483 301170
Fax: 01483 300981
Email: info@life-academy.co.uk
Website: http://www.life-academy.co.uk
Members: 404
Staff: 7
Contact: Stuart Royston, Chief Exec.
Description: People with associated interests in a personal or professional capacity and companies willing to be associated with the development of retirement/redundancy advice/mid life planning. Promotes awareness of the needs of all those preparing for retirement. Provides education, planning and support services that relate to the successful management of transitional changes from an increasing diversity of employment patterns. Runs a course leading to a certificate in pre-retirement education with life planning.
Formerly: Formerly, Pre-Retirement Association of Great Britain and Northern Ireland
Publication: Newsletter
Publication title: Life Academy News

02993

Lift and Escalator Industry Association LEIA

33/34 Devonshire St., London, W1G 6PY, UK
Tel: 020 79353013
Fax: 020 79353321
Email: enquiries@leia.co.uk
Website: http://www.leia.co.uk
Members: 135
Staff: 6
Description: Manufacturers. Covers the manufacture, installation, service and repair, also provision of components for lifts, escalators and passenger conveyors. Maintains the LEIA Educational Trust, a registered charity for the furtherance of education and training in the lift industry.
Formerly: Formerly, National Association of Lift Makers
Publication: Book
Publication title: LEIA Review - Industry in Focus

02994

Lifting Equipment Engineers Association LEEA

3, Osprey Ct., Kingfisher Way, Hinchingbrooke Business Park, Huntingdon, PE29 6FN, UK
Tel: 01480 432801
Fax: 01480 436314
Website: http://www.leea.co.uk
Members: 370
Staff: 8
Contact: Geoff Holden, Chief Exec.
Fee: £925
Membership Type: full, associate
Fee: £820
Membership Type: overseas associate
Description: Companies that supply, service, or use lifting equipment in the United Kingdom. Promotes the use of lifting equipment. Maintains standards for the industry. Conducts educational programs. Provides a forum for the exchange of information between members in order to increase product quality and efficiency.
Library Type: reference
Publication: Handbook
Publication title: A User's Pocket Guide

02995

Light Music Society LMS

19a Eshton Terr., Lancashire, Clitheroe, BB7 1BQ, UK
Tel: 01200 427066
Email: hilary.ashton@talk21.com
Website: http://www.lightmusicsociety.com
Members: 400
Staff: 1
Contact: Hilary Ashton, Sec.
Fee: £18
Membership Type: individual (in UK)
Fee: £22
Membership Type: individual (in Europe)
Description: Acts as the backing organization for the Library of Light Orchestral Music, an archive of light-orchestral performance material from the 1850s to the present.
Library Subject: music orchestral sets
Library Type: not open to the public
Publication: Newsletter
Publication title: Light Music Society Newsletter. Advertisements.

02996
Light Rail Transit Association
LRTA
138 Radnor Ave., Welling, DA16 2BY, UK
Tel: 01179 517785
Fax: 01179 517785
Email: office@lrta.org
Website: http://www.lrta.org
Members: 4000
Contact: Geoffrey Claydon, Pres.
Fee: £53.83
Membership Type: in UK
Fee: £68.08
Membership Type: in Europe
Description: Professionals, firms, and libraries involved in public transport and light rail systems. (Light rail transit is a flexible form of electric railway which can, where appropriate, mix with motor traffic or pedestrians.) Encourages the development of light rail transit worldwide, particularly in the United Kingdom. Advocates the reduction of motor traffic, improvement of public transport, and energy conservation through the utilization of light rail systems. Promotes the exchange of information concerning light rail transit and its historical aspects. Organizes study tours; collects data on tramways and light rail systems.
Library Subject: trainways, light rail transit
Library Type: not open to the public
Publication: Magazine
Publication title: Tramway Review

02997
Lighting Association
LA
Stafford Park 7, Shropshire, Telford, TF3 3BQ, UK
Tel: 01952 290905
Fax: 01952 290906
Email: enquiries@lightingassociation.com
Website: http://www.lightingassociation.com
Members: 230
Staff: 25
Contact: Jonathan Lucas, Pres.
Fee: £524-3485
Membership Type: full (based on turnover)
Description: Represents manufacturers, importers and wholesalers of lighting, lighting accessories and components. Across all sectors of the market. Provides technical advice, manufacturing and retail training courses. Supplies product safety labels. Offers full test laboratory facilities for luminaries.
Publication: Catalog
Publication title: Buyers' Guide. Advertisements.
Meetings/Conventions: Lighting Show – annual show – Exhibits.

02998
Lighting Industry Federation
LIF
Westminster Tower, Ground Fl., 3 Albert Embankment, London, SE1 7SL, UK
Tel: 020 77933020
Email: info@lif.co.uk
Website: http://www.lif.co.uk
Members: 90
Staff: 7
Contact: Eddie Taylor, Chief Exec.
Description: Manufacturers of lighting equipment. Promotes the United Kingdom's lighting industry.

02999
Lightmongers' Company
Crown Wharf, 11A Coldharbour, Blackwall Reach, London, E14 9NS, UK
Tel: 020 75159055
Fax: 020 75385466
Website: http://www.lightmongers.org.uk
Contact: Hugh Ogus, Master
Description: Fosters the art and science of lighting by bringing together those practising in the many different skilled involved in the art. Promotes goodwill in the industry.

Ligue des Pays du Commonwealth
see Commonwealth Countries League

03000
Limbless Association
LA
Queen Mary's Hospital, Roehampton Ln., London, SW15 5PN, UK
Tel: 020 87881777
Fax: 020 87883444
Email: enquiries@limbless-association.org
Website: http://www.limbless-association.org
Members: 5000
Staff: 7
Contact: Ray Edwards, CEO
Fee: £17
Membership Type: full (in UK, normal)
Fee: £15
Membership Type: full (in UK, online)
Description: Provides information and advice to people who have had amputations or who have been born without upper or lower limbs. Through a nationwide network of volunteer representatives who are all amputees themselves, offers support and encouragement to prospective amputees, careers, and those already trying to come to terms with limb loss or deficiency.

03001
LIMRA Europe
2nd Fl., Cardinal Point, Park Rd., Hetfordshire, Rickmansworth, WD3 1RE, UK
Tel: 01923 437685
Fax: 01923 432814
Email: philip.green@limraeurope.com
Website: http://www.limra.com
Members: 145
Staff: 18
Contact: Philip Green, CEO
Description: Financial services companies with an interest in long term business. Aims to enhance the marketing function of member companies through industry supported research, products and services.
Library Subject: life insurance, pensions, health insurance
Library Type: not open to the public
Formerly: Formerly, Life Insurance Marketing and Research Association
Publication: Magazine
Publication title: Market Facts. Advertisements.

03002
Lincolnshire Chamber of Commerce and Industry
LCCI
Commerce House, Outer Circle Rd., Lincolnshire, Lincoln, LN2 4HY, UK
Tel: 01522 523333
Fax: 01522 546667
Email: enquiries@lincs-chamber.co.uk
Website: http://www.lincs-chamber.co.uk
Members: 1190
Staff: 17
Contact: Simon Beardsley, Chief Exec.
Fee: £138
Membership Type: sole proprietor
Fee: £189.75
Membership Type: firm/company (minimum; based on number of employees)
Description: Represents members across Lincolnshire at local, regional and national level on matters concerning trade, commerce and industry and lobbying. Facilitates networking, forums and events to enable members to exchange ideas, information, views and business practice.
Publication: Magazine
Publication title: Chamber Matters

03003
Linguistic Society of Europe
University of Lancaster, Dept. of Linguistic and English Language, Lancaster, LA1 4YT, UK
Tel: 015 2464975
Fax: 015 24843085
Email: d.bakker@uva.nl
Website: http://www.societaslinguistica.eu
Members: 850
Contact: Ruth Wodak, Pres.
Fee: £30
Membership Type: individual
Fee: £15
Membership Type: student
Description: Represents the interests of linguists in 50 countries. Advances the field of linguistics in European and non-European countries.
Publication: Bulletin
Publication title: Bulletin SLE

03004
Linguistics Association of Great Britain
LAGB
c/o Dr. David Willis, Honorary Sec.
Dept. of Linguistics, Selwyn College, Grange Rd., Cambridge, CB3 9DQ, UK
Tel: 01223 335885
Fax: 01223 335053
Email: dwew2@cam.ac.uk
Website: http://www.lagb.org.uk
Contact: Kersti Borjars, Pres.
Fee: £20
Membership Type: waged
Fee: £44
Membership Type: waged (with journal)
Description: Acts as bridge between language education and academic linguistics. Represents linguists and linguistics in matters related to research funding and quality assessment.
Publication: Journal
Publication title: Journal of Linguistics

03005

Linnean Society of London

LSL

Burlington House, Piccadilly, London, W1J 0BF, UK
Tel: 020 74344479
Fax: 020 72879364
Email: info@linnean.org
Website: http://www.linnean.org
Members: 2000
Staff: 7
Contact: Ruth Temple, Exec. Sec.
Fee: £45
Membership Type: standard fellowship
Fee: £10
Membership Type: student (18-23 years old)
Description: Professional scientists and others interested in natural sciences. Promotes study in all disciplines of pure biology such as agriculture, anatomy, biochemistry, genetics, medicine, and paleobiology while focusing on evolution, ecology, and systematics. Organization is named for Swedish naturalist Carl Linnaeus (1707-78), who is credited with classifying and naming over 9,000 plants, 828 shells, 2,100 insects, and 477 fish using a method of binomial nomenclature for species and plants (fundamentals of which are still used today).
Library Subject: biology
Library Type: open to the public
Publication: Journal
Publication title: Biological Journal

03006

Little Theatre Guild of Great Britain

Satley House, Bishop Auckland, DL13 4HU, UK
Tel: 01388 730042
Website: http://www.littletheatreguild.org.uk
Members: 95
Contact: Caroline Chapman, Sec.
Description: Independent and self-governing theatre companies, non-commercial in character and controlling and established theatre. Aims to extend close cooperation between members in all areas of theatre; to organize national and regional conferences and seminars; to act as a coordinating body for the development of little theatres, and to lobby on their behalf on matters of national interest, such as taxation, charitable status, licensing, sponsorship, insurance and royalties.

03007

Liverpool Chamber of Commerce and Industry

LCCI

1 Old Hall St., Liverpool, L3 9HG, UK
Tel: 0151 2271234
Fax: 0151 2360121
Email: chamber@liverpoolchamber.org.uk
Website: http://www.liverpoolchamber.org.uk
Members: 2100
Staff: 80
Contact: Jack Stopforth, Chief Exec.
Fee: £140-1498
Membership Type: organization/firm (based on number of employees)
Fee: £95
Membership Type: individual
Description: Represents members across Liverpool at local, regional and national level on matters concerning trade, commerce and industry and lobbying. Facilitates networking, forums and events to enable members to exchange ideas, information, views and business practice.
Publication: Newsletter

03008

Livestock Auctioneers' Association

LAA

Cobblethwaite, Wreay, Carlisle, CA4 0RZ, UK
Tel: 016974 75433
Fax: 016974 75423
Email: chris.dodds@laa.co.uk
Website: http://www.laa.co.uk
Members: 165
Staff: 2
Contact: Christoper W. Dodds, Exec. Sec.
Description: Open to companies operating livestock auction markets in England and Wales. Membership dependent on recommendation from local Livestock Auctioneers Association. All matters affecting the marketing of cattle, sheep and pigs.

03009

Living Streets

Universal House, 4th Fl., 88-94 Wentworth St., London, E1 7SA, UK
Tel: 0207 3774900
Email: info@livingstreets.org.uk
Website: http://www.livingstreets.org.uk
Members: 1200
Staff: 7
Contact: Tony Armstrong, Chief Exec.
Description: Seeks to make roads safer for all users, particularly pedestrians. Works to insure that public walkways are both safe and scenic; promotes establishment of pedestrians only areas cities; lobbies for strict observance and enforcement of speed limits, and for the rights of pedestrians at crosswalks and intersections. Maintains Walkways advice service to assist local communities with traffic problems; makes available Walk Talk environmental education program.
Formerly: Formerly, Pedestrians' Association
Publication: Journal
Publication title: WALK. Advertisements.

03010

Local Authorities Coordinators of Regulatory Services

LACORS

Local Govt. House, Smith Sq., London, SW1P 3HZ, UK
Tel: 020 76653888
Fax: 020 76653887
Email: info@lacors.gov.uk
Website: http://www.lacors.gov.uk/lacors/home.aspx
Members: 500
Staff: 22
Contact: Paul Bettison, Chm.
Description: Local authorities in England, Wales, Scotland and Northern Ireland. Aims to provide a uniform interpretation of legislation and be a centre for conciliation and exchange of information. Promotes good enforcement practice, maintains a register of overloading convictions and liaises with trade and consumer organizations; advises government and European institutions. Develops contacts with enforcement practitioners overseas.

03011

Local Authorities Research and Intelligence Association

LARIA

1 Henderson Close, Great Sankey, Warrington, WA5 3JJ, UK
Tel: 01925 723539
Email: admin@laria.gov.uk
Website: http://www.laria.gov.uk/laria/core/page.do?pageId=1
Members: 1100
Staff: 1
Contact: Doris Besford, Admin.
Fee: £10
Membership Type: full
Fee: £80
Membership Type: corporate
Description: Mainly research officers in local government, health service, academia and central government. Promotes the further development of research practices and to encourage communication between those engaged in research and intelligence in local government by providing a national forum for the sharing of technical knowledge and research methods.
Publication: Newsletter
Publication title: Laria News. Advertisements.

03012

Local Authority Caterers Association

LACA

Bourne House, Horsell Park, Surrey, Woking, GU21 4LY, UK
Tel: 01483 766777
Fax: 01483 751991
Email: info@laca.co.uk
Website: http://www.laca.co.uk
Members: 1052
Staff: 2
Contact: Beverley Baker, Chair
Fee: £73.72
Membership Type: individual
Fee: £334.36
Membership Type: corporate (with 5 members)
Description: Qualified catering managers in local authority departments. Promotes the professionalism of local authority caterers by running annual national conferences and exhibitions for national members. Regional seminars and training programmers. Also lobbies MPs on concerns of members.
Formerly: Formerly, National Association of Senior Meals Organizers

03013

Local Authority Recycling Advisory Committee

LARAC

PO Box 28, Knighton, LD8 2WA, UK
Tel: 01544 267860
Fax: 01544 267860
Email: larac@btinternet.com
Website: http://www.larac.org.uk
Members: 404
Staff: 6
Contact: Colin Kirkby, Exec. Off.
Fee: £250
Membership Type: regular
Description: Aims to exchange information on waste reduction within local government and with other organizations; provides expert response to national, European and private sector recycling initiatives; assists others with technical information and advice to promote best practice; produces training and educational materials and publications on waste reduction and recycling.
Publication: Bulletin
Publication title: LARAC OnLine

03014
Locomotive and Carriage Institution
LCI
c/o Peter Lindop, Membership Sec.
1 Woodlands Ct., Woodlands Rd., Harrow, Middlesex, HA1 2RU, UK
Email: membership.sec@lococarriage.org.uk
Website: http://www.lococarriage.org.uk
Members: 295
Contact: Nick Agnew, Pres.
Fee: £13
Membership Type: working
Fee: £6
Membership Type: retired (over 55)
Description: Employees of rail transport administrations or associated industries. Aims to promote knowledge concerning all aspects of the railway industry. Enables members to meet and facilitate the exchange of ideas and information and to discuss technical developments. Also arranges speakers from the industry to address meetings. Visits to railway installations and those of the associated industries as well as visits abroad are arranged.
Formerly: Formerly, Loco & Carr Inst
Publication: Newsletter
Meetings/Conventions: general assembly

03015
London and Middlesex Archaeological Society
LAMAS
c/o The Museum of London
150 London Wall, London, EC2Y 5HN, UK
Tel: 020 78145734
Fax: 020 76001058
Email: jkeily@museumoflondon.org.uk
Website: http://www.lamas.org.uk
Members: 654
Contact: Jackie Keily, Honorary Sec.
Fee: £15
Membership Type: individual
Fee: £17
Membership Type: joint
Description: Encourages the study of and interest in the archaeology local history and historic buildings of the London area.
Publication: Journal
Publication title: Transactions

03016
London Association of Primal Psychotherapists
LAPP
West Hill House, 6 Swains Ln., London, N6 6QS, UK
Tel: 020 72679616
Fax: 020 74820858
Email: info@lapp.org
Website: http://www.lapp.org
Members: 55
Staff: 5
Contact: Sue Cowan Jenssen, Contact
Description: Student membership open to trainees; associate membership open to people with an interest in the field of psychotherapy; full membership open to those qualified to work as primal psychotherapists. Aims to refine and develop primal psychotherapy. Runs a training programme that is recognized by the United Kingdom Council for Psychotherapy. Administers a trust fund that is devoted to working with people facing life threatening illnesses.

03017
London Chamber of Commerce and Industry
33 Queen St., London, EC4R 1AP, UK
Tel: 020 72484444
Fax: 020 74890391
Email: lc@londonchamber.co.uk
Website: http://www.londonchamber.co.uk
Members: 3100
Staff: 100
Contact: Willie Walsh, Pres.
Fee: £461-3971
Membership Type: company (based on number of employees)
Fee: £189.18
Membership Type: overseas
Description: Promotes business and commerce.
Publication: Magazine
Publication title: Business Matters

03018
London Councils
59 1/2 Southwark St., London, SE1 OAL, UK
Tel: 020 79349999
Email: info@londoncouncils.gov.uk
Website: http://www.londoncouncils.gov.uk
Members: 33
Staff: 160
Contact: John O'Brien, Chief Exec.
Description: Open to all London boroughs and City of London. Acts as a voice for London boroughs in negotiations and consultations with central government. Central government consults member authorities through the ALG on a wide range of issues. Also coordinates a number of London wide initiatives and projects on behalf of London borough.
Publication: Annual Report
Publication title: ALG Annual Report

03019
London International Financial Futures and Options Exchange
LIFFE
Cannon Bridge House, 1 Cousin Ln., London, EC4R 3XX, UK
Tel: 020 76230444
Fax: 020 79293278
Email: membership@liffe.com
Website: http://www.euronext.com/landing/indexMarket-18812-EN.html
Members: 200
Staff: 500
Contact: Hugh Freedberg, CEO
Description: Represents variety of sectors and geographical areas of the international financial community.
Library Type: by appointment only

03020
London Mathematical Society
LMS
De Morgan House, 57-58 Russell Sq., London, WC1B 4HS, UK
Tel: 020 76373686
Fax: 020 73233655
Email: lms@lms.ac.uk
Website: http://www.lms.ac.uk
Members: 2400
Staff: 12
Contact: A.J. Macintyre, Pres.
Fee: £49
Membership Type: ordinary
Fee: £24.5
Membership Type: reciprocity
Description: Works for the promotion and extension of mathematical knowledge and education.
Publication: Journal
Publication title: LMS Bulletin

03021
London Natural History Society
LNHS
c/o Robin Blades
32 Ashfield Rd., London, N14 7JY, UK
Email: david.howdon@virgin.net
Website: http://www.lnhs.org.uk
Members: 1400
Contact: David Howden, Sec.
Fee: £20
Membership Type: ordinary, corporate
Fee: £5
Membership Type: student
Description: Promotes natural history within 20 miles of central London, through scientific investigations, nature conservation and publication.
Library Subject: natural history
Library Type: open to the public
Publication: Journal
Publication title: The London Bird Report

03022
London Record Society
PO Box 691, Exeter, EX1 9PH, UK
Email: londonrecordsoc@btinternet.com
Website: http://www.londonrecordsociety.org.uk
Members: 339
Contact: Stephanie Hovland, Honorable Sec.
Fee: £18
Membership Type: individual
Fee: £23
Membership Type: institutional
Description: Publishes transcripts, abstracts and lists of primary sources for the history of London, and generally stimulates interest in archives related to London.

03023
London Region Campaign for Nuclear Disarmament
Mordechai Vanunu House, 162 Holloway Rd., London, N7 8DQ, UK
Tel: 0207 6072302
Fax: 0207 7002357
Email: david.lrcnd@cnduk.org
Website: http://www.cnduk.org/index.php/regional-groups/london-region-cnd.html
Contact: David Polden, Contact
Description: Aims to eliminate British nuclear weapons and other weapons of mass destruction.

03024
London Society
LS
Mortimer Wheeler House, 46, Eagle Wharf Rd., London, N1 7ED, UK
Tel: 020 72539400
Email: info@londonsociety.org.uk
Website: http://www.londonsociety.org.uk/index.php
Contact: Frank Kelsall, Chm.
Fee: £20
Membership Type: ordinary, corporate
Fee: £25
Membership Type: overseas (air mail)
Description: Individuals and organizations with an interest in the growth and development of the city of London. Promotes economically and environmentally sustainable urban growth. Provides advice and assistance to city planning and development organizations and corporations; represents the environmental interests of local inhabitants when new developments are proposed. Conducts architectural tours.
Publication: Journal
Publication title: Journal of the London Society
Meetings/Conventions: Christmas Party – annual party

03025
London Swing Dance Society
LSDS
22 Bessingby Rd., Ruislip, Middlesex, HA4 9BX, UK
Tel: 01895 613703
Email: swinguk@zetnet.co.uk
Website: http://www.swingdanceuk.com
Members: 2000
Staff: 2
Contact: Simon Selmon, Contact
Fee: £1
Membership Type: regular
Description: Supports and promotes swing dance events, classes and performances. Performs as "Sugarfoot Stompers".

03026
London Topographical Society
Southgate, 7 Linden Ave., Dorchester, DT1 1EJ, UK
Tel: 01305 261 548
Email: patfrazer@yahoo.co.uk
Website: http://www.topsoc.org
Members: 1100
Contact: Patrick Frazer, Hon.Sec.
Fee: £20
Membership Type: regular (inside UK)
Fee: £25
Membership Type: regular (outside UK)
Description: Individuals and institutions interested in maps and the history of London. Publishes reproductions of maps, prints, and views of London. Promotes original research into London's history and topography.
Publication: Book
Publication title: Annual publication

03027
London Transport Users Committee
LTUC
6 Middle St., London, EC1A 7JA, UK
Tel: 020 75059000
Fax: 020 75059003
Email: enquiries@londontravelwatch.org.uk
Website: http://www.londontravelwatch.org.uk
Members: 26
Staff: 23
Contact: Janet Cooke, Chief Exec.
Description: Members are appointed by the Greater London Assembly. Represents the interests of users of London Transport's bus network, the Underground, Heathrow Express, Eurostar, and the national railways in and around London.
Formerly: Also Known As, London TravelWatch

03028
Londonderry Chamber of Commerce
1 St. Columb's Ct., Bishop St., Londonderry, BT48 6PT, UK
Tel: 028 71262379
Fax: 028 71286789
Email: info@londonderrychamber.co.uk
Website: http://www.londonderrychamber.co.uk
Contact: Sinead McLaughlin, Chief Exec.
Fee: £838.7
Membership Type: corporate (based on number of employees)
Fee: £90
Membership Type: individual
Description: Promotes commerce and industry in Londonderry, Northern Ireland.

03029
Longhorn Cattle Society
3, Eastgate, Stoneleigh Park, Warwickshire, Stoneleigh, CV8 2LG, UK
Tel: 0845 0171027
Fax: 0845 0171027
Email: secretary@longhorncattlesociety.com
Website: http://www.longhorncattlesociety.com
Members: 450
Staff: 1
Contact: Debbie Dann, Sec.
Fee: £30
Membership Type: full
Fee: £15
Membership Type: associate
Description: Seeks to maintain, conserve and promote the British Longhorn breed of cattle.

03030
Lotteries Council
LC
c/o Mrs. Tina Sandford, Exec. Off.
31 Lingen Close, Shrewsbury, SY1 2UN, UK
Email: tina@lotteriescouncil.org.uk
Website: http://lotteriescouncil.org.uk
Members: 170
Contact: John Greenway, Pres.
Fee: £175
Membership Type: regular
Description: Presents a strong and unified voice for lottery fundraising. Represents the interests of Society Lotteries from a mixture of sectors including charities, sports, community and the arts, which use lottery devices to generate funds.

03031
Low Impact Living Initiative
LILI
Redfield Community, Buckingham Rd., Winslow, MK18 3LZ, UK
Tel: 01296 714184
Fax: 01296 714184
Email: lili@lowimpact.org
Website: http://www.lowimpact.org
Contact: Dave Darby, Dir.
Description: Offers practical activities that individuals can do to reduce impact on the environment: residential weekend courses, information sheets, manuals and books, online shop and related events.

03032
Lute Society
LS
Southside Cottage, Brook Hill, Albury, Guildford, GU5 9DJ, UK
Tel: 01483 202159
Fax: 01483 203088
Email: lutesoc@aol.com
Website: http://www.lutesoc.co.uk
Members: 730
Staff: 1
Contact: Christopher Goodwin, Sec.
Fee: £35
Membership Type: full
Fee: £17
Membership Type: student
Description: Individuals and university libraries in 23 countries interested in the lute and associated instruments. Promotes appreciation of lute playing and knowledge of lute history, technique, and construction. Maintains picture collection.
Publication: Journal
Publication title: The Lute. Advertisements.

03033
Lymphoma Association
PO Box 386, Aylesbury, HP20 2GA, UK
Tel: 01296 619400
Email: information@lymphomas.org.uk
Website: http://www.lymphomas.org.uk
Members: 2000
Staff: 20
Contact: David Barnett, Contact
Fee: £5
Membership Type: individual
Description: Provides information and emotional support for anyone affected by lymphoma. Provides a Help line; telephone links to helpers with similar experience of lymphoma; and a network of regional support groups.
Library Subject: lymphomas, living with cancer, treatments
Library Type: lending
Publication: Newsletter
Publication title: Fundraising News

03034
Macclesfield Chamber of Commerce and Enterprise
Churchill Chambers, Churchill Way, Cheshire, Macclesfield, SK11 6AS, UK
Tel: 01625 665940
Fax: 01625 665941
Email: info@macclesfieldchamber.co.uk
Website: http://www.macclesfieldchamber.co.uk
Members: 660

Staff: 14

Description: Represents members across Macclesfield at local, regional and national level on matters concerning trade, commerce and industry and lobbying. Facilitates networking, forums and events to enable members to exchange ideas, information, views and business practice.

Library Type: open to the public

03035

Macular Disease Society
MDS

PO Box 1870, Andover, SP10 9AD, UK

Tel: 01264 350551

Fax: 01264 350558

Email: info@maculardisease.org

Website: http://www.maculardisease.org

Members: 17000

Staff: 7

Contact: Helen Jackman, Chief Exec.

Fee: £15

Membership Type: regular, ophthalmologist, optometrist, nurse, local society for the blind

Fee: £25

Membership Type: overseas (Europe)

Description: Aims to provide information, fellowship and support to those with macular disease.

03036

Magistrates' Association of England and Wales

28 Fitzroy Sq., London, W1T 6DD, UK

Tel: 020 73872353

Fax: 020 73834020

Email: information@magistrates-association.org.uk

Website: http://www.magistrates-association-temp.org.uk

Members: 29000

Staff: 11

Contact: Patrick Cracroft-Brennan, Exec. Dir./Sec.

Description: Magistrates.

Publication: Journal

Publication title: The Magistrate. Advertisements.

03037

Mail Order Traders' Association
MOTA

PO Box 51909, London, SW99 0WZ, UK

Tel: 0208 3303333

Email: mota@mota.org.uk

Website: http://www.mota.org.uk

Members: 7

Staff: 2

Description: Serves as the large general catalogue mail order companies and firms trading in the United Kingdom. Protects and enhances the interests of its membership, deals with queries and complaints made by members of the public including the supervision and enforcement of the Association's Code of Practice. Responds to points raised by Central government, the European Commission, the Parliament of Westminster and the European Parliament.

03038

Mail Users' Association
MUA

70 Main Rd., Hampshire, Emsworth, PO10 8AX, UK

Email: jeremypartridge@mailusers.co.uk

Website: http://www.mailusers.co.uk

Members: 100

Contact: Jeremy Partridge, Exec. Dir.

Description: Open to any business, large or small, wishing to support the aims of the organization. Business sectors currently represented include financial services, publishing, communications, print distribution, direct marketing, banking and charities. Aims to strive for the improvement of postal services to/from all addresses in terms of reliability, security, choice and value. Its activities revolve around bringing pressure to bear upon the Post Office and government to achieve its goals. Funded by membership subscriptions.

03039

Major Energy Users Council
MEUC

PO Box 30, London, W5 3ZT, UK

Tel: 020 89973854

Email: enquiries@meuc.co.uk

Website: http://www.meuc.co.uk

Contact: Andrew Bainbridge, Dir. Gen.

Fee: £3210

Membership Type: regular

Description: Works to help organizations to save money on their energy and utilities purchasing and to achieve improved contract terms from suppliers.

03040

Making Music

2-4 Great Eastern St., London, EC2A 3NW, UK

Tel: 020 74228280

Fax: 020 74228299

Email: info@makingmusic.org.uk

Website: http://www.makingmusic.org.uk

Members: 2500

Staff: 8

Contact: Robin Osterley, Chief Exec.

Fee: £53.55

Membership Type: group

Description: Members belong to amateur music clubs, choral and orchestral societies.

Formerly: Formerly, National Federation of Music Societies

Publication: Newsletter

Publication title: NFMS News. Advertisements.

03041

Malacological Society of London

Canterbury Christ Church University, Kent, CT1 1QU, UK

Tel: 02075 942949

Email: webmanager@malacsoc.org.uk

Website: http://www.malacsoc.org.uk/index.html

Members: 280

Contact: Mark Davies, Pres.

Fee: £45

Membership Type: ordinary

Fee: £25

Membership Type: student

Description: Promotes members' interests.

Publication: Journal

Publication title: Journal of Molluscan Studies

03042

Malawi Association of Christian Support
MACS

Sweech Cottage, Preston Ln., Preston, Canterbury, CT3 1EY, UK

Tel: 01227 728310

Email: richardgbarton@yahoo.co.uk

Website: http://www.malawimacs.org

Contact: Richard Barton, Chm.

Description: Aims to support the communities and improve the quality of life for local people in Malawi. Supports self help initiatives that promote Christian religion, education and health of Malawi community.

Publication: Newsletter

Publication title: Nkhani

03043

Malone Society
MS

Institute of English Studies, Senate House, Malet St., London, WC1E 7HU, UK

Tel: 020 78628679

Fax: 020 78628720

Email: conor.wyer@sas.ac.uk

Website: http://ies.sas.ac.uk/malone

Members: 650

Contact: Sonia Massai, Contact

Fee: £20

Membership Type: regular

Description: Individuals worldwide interested in English Renaissance drama; libraries. Prints 1 or 2 volumes each year of edited texts of early English dramatic works, particularly rare and inaccessible texts of Renaissance plays, and of documents relating to the drama.

Publication: Book

Publication title: Malone Society Reprints

03044

Maltsters Association of Great Britain
MAGB

31B Castlegate, Newark, NG24 1AZ, UK

Tel: 01636 700781

Fax: 01636 701836

Website: http://www.ukmalt.com

Members: 14

Staff: 3

Contact: Colin West, Exec. Dir.

Description: Sales maltsters, selling malt on the open market, and brewer and distiller maltsters, who make malt for brewing and distilling in-house. Works to promote the interests of the trade, and to keep a watch on all legislation, litigation, and public proceedings which may affect the trade; secures the benefits of co-operation to members in aspects of training, health, safety, etc.

03045

Mammal Society
MS

3 The Carronades, New Rd., Southampton, SO14 0AA, UK

Tel: 023 80237874

Fax: 023 80634726

Email: enquiries@mammal.org.uk

Website: http://www.mammal.org.uk

Members: 2000

Staff: 3
Contact: Derek Yalden, Pres.
Fee: £20
Membership Type: unwaged, student with Mammal Review
Fee: £12.5
Membership Type: unwaged, student
Description: Individuals interested in the study of mammals. Promotes the conservation and study of British mammals. Organizes conservation projects, surveys, and symposia.
Publication: Journal
Publication title: Mammal Review

03046
Management Consultancies Association
MCA
60 Trafalgar Sq., London, WC2N 5DS, UK
Tel: 020 73213990
Fax: 020 73213991
Email: info@mca.org.uk
Website: http://www.mca.org.uk/home
Members: 65
Staff: 5
Contact: Alan Leaman, Chief Exec.
Description: Enhances the consultancy management profession. Furthers the collective objectives and interests of its members. Acts as a focal point for individuals wishing to seek advice on management consultancy. Serves as a forum for members to discuss matters of current interest and future policy.
Library Subject: management consultancy
Library Type: not open to the public

03047
Manchester Chamber of Commerce and Industry
MCCI
c/o Greater Manchester Chamber of Commerce
Churchgate House, 56 Oxford St., Manchester, M60 7HJ, UK
Tel: 0161 2363210
Email: info@gmchamber.co.uk
Website: http://www.gmchamber.co.uk
Members: 5000
Staff: 12
Contact: Angie Robinson, Chief Exec.
Fee: £1232.58
Membership Type: regular (based on number of employees)
Description: Businesses, professionals, and interested individuals. Promotes the commercial and industrial interests of businesses throughout England. Facilitates the development of national and international trade by providing traders and investors with information and advice on new markets and products. Services offered include research and information gathering on trade opportunities, educational programs, and consumer and business assistance.
Publication: Newsletter
Publication title: The Business
Meetings/Conventions: New Members Evening – monthly dinner

03048
Manchester Geological Association
MGA
c/o Fred Owen, Membership Sec.
29 Westage Ln., Great Budworth, Northwich, CW9 6HJ, UK
Tel: 01606 892690
Email: info@mangeolassoc.org.uk
Website: http://www.mangeolassoc.org.uk
Contact: Tony Adams, Pres.
Fee: £13
Membership Type: full
Fee: £2
Membership Type: associate
Description: Provides a network to professional and amateur geologists in Manchester. Conducts lectures on conservation of geological sites, evolution, rocks, minerals, fossils, and other related areas of interests.

03049
Manorial Society of Great Britain
MSGB
104 Kennington Rd., London, SE11 6RE, UK
Tel: 0207 7356633
Fax: 0207 5827022
Email: manorial@msgb.co.uk
Website: http://www.msgb.co.uk
Members: 1900
Staff: 5
Contact: Robert Smith, Exec. Chm.
Fee: £50
Membership Type: individual
Fee: £500
Membership Type: life
Description: Aristocrats, gentry, landowners, lawyers, and real estate agents in Europe and the United States; others interested in British manors. Provides legal and estate advice; gathers historical information concerning manors in the United Kingdom. Sponsors research and educational programs. Organizes annual exhibitions, auctions, receptions, and dinners.
Publication: Bulletin
Publication title: Bulletin of the Manorial Society of Great Britain. Advertisements.

03050
Manufacturers' Agents' Association of Great Britain and Ireland
MAA
Unit 16, Thrales End, Herts, Harpenden, AL5 3NS, UK
Tel: 01582 767618
Fax: 01582 766092
Email: info@themaa.co.uk
Website: http://www.themaa.co.uk
Members: 400
Description: Self-employed professional sales agents. Promotes the interests of manufacturers' agents.
Publication: Magazine
Publication title: Agents News. Advertisements.

03051
Manufacturing Technologies Association
MTA
62 Bayswater Rd., London, W2 3PS, UK
Tel: 020 72986400
Fax: 020 72986430
Email: info@mta.org.uk
Website: http://www.mta.org.uk/home
Members: 250
Staff: 19
Contact: Bob Hunt, Pres.
Description: Represents manufacturers and suppliers of machine tools and related equipment in the United Kingdom. Promotes the development of the machine tool industry. Represents members' interests before government agencies. Conducts research and compiles statistics. Sponsors competitions. Organizes exhibitions.
Library Type: not open to the public
Formerly: Formerly, Machine Tool Technologies Association
Publication: Newsletter
Publication title: MTA Update
Meetings/Conventions: MACH Exhibition – biennial trade show – Exhibits.

03052
Manufacturing Technologies Association I British Hardmetal and Engineers' Cutting Tools Association
BHECTA
62 Bayswater Rd., London, W2 3PS, UK
Tel: 020 72986400
Fax: 020 72986430
Email: bhecta@mta.org.uk
Website: http://www.mta.org.uk/home
Contact: N. Stamp, Sec.
Description: Represents manufacturers of engineers' cutting tools including twist drills, reamers, milling cutters, tool bits and thread cutting tools.
Formerly: Formerly, The British Hardmetal Association and British Engineers' Cutting Tool Association

03053
Marce Society
105 St. Peters St., St. Albans, AL1 3EJ, UK
Tel: 017 27896088
Email: info@marcesociety.com
Website: http://www.marcesociety.com
Contact: Katherine L. Wisner, Pres.
Description: Promotes the understanding prevention and treatment of mental illness related to childbearing. Facilitates research into all aspects of the mental health of women, their infants and partners around the time of childbirth.

03054
Marfan Association UK
Rochester House, 5, Aldershot Rd., Hampshire, Fleet, GU51 3NG, UK
Tel: 01252 810472
Fax: 01252 810473
Email: marfan@tinyonline.co.uk
Website: http://www.marfanworld.org/members.htm#UnitedKingdom
Contact: Diane Rust, Contact
Fee: £15
Membership Type: regular
Fee: £22
Membership Type: overseas
Description: Disseminates information regarding Marfan syndrome and facilitates international communication

among medical professionals and the general public. Fosters research and facilitates communication with research centers. Establishes standards for diagnosis and treatment of the Marfan syndrome.

03055

Margarine and Spreads Association MSA

6 Catherine St., London, WC2B 5JJ, UK
Tel: 020 78362460
Fax: 020 73795735
Email: info@margarine.org.uk
Website: http://www.margarine.org.uk
Contact: Caroline Lynch, Contact
Description: Works as margarine and spreads Association in England. Represents members' interests; disseminates information. Seeks to maintain the best possible operating environment for its members.
Formerly: Formerly, Margarine and Shortening Manufacturers Association

03056

Margery Allingham Society

28 Parkfield Ave., Bucks, Amersham, HP6 6BE, UK
Tel: 01494 721012
Email: honsec@margeryallingham.org.uk
Website: http://www.margeryallingham.org.uk
Members: 86
Contact: Josephine Hesslewood, Hon. Sec.
Fee: £14
Membership Type: individual
Fee: £20
Membership Type: joint (two members at the same address)
Description: Aims to celebrate the life and work of Margery Allingham. Preserves and promotes the author's literary work and reputation through meetings and social events.
Publication: Journal
Publication title: The Bottle Street Gazette

03057

Marie Curie Cancer Care MCCC

89 Albert Embankment, London, SE1 7TP, UK
Tel: 020 75997777
Email: info@mariecurie.org.uk
Website: http://www.mariecurie.org.uk
Contact: Thomas Hughes-Hallett, Chief Exec.
Description: Health care professionals working with people who have cancer. Seeks to improve the quality of life of people with cancer and to promote increased availability and effectiveness of cancer care. Operates nationwide network of Marie Curie Nurses in the community and operates ten hospices across England, Scotland, Wales, and Northern Ireland. Provides specialist care for people with cancer. Conducts cancer research and educational programs.
Publication: Newsletter
Publication title: Marie Curie News

03058

Marie Stopes International - United Kingdom MSI

1 Conway St., Fitzroy Sq., London, W1T 6LP, UK
Tel: 0207 6366200
Fax: 0207 0342370
Email: services@mariestopes.org.uk
Website: http://www.mariestopes.org.uk
Members: 5000
Contact: Dana Hovig, CEO
Description: Provides a wide range of maternal health and family planning services. Programs conducted include: contraceptive social marketing; male oriented services. Specializes in working with indigenous personnel to develop clinical family planning services and social marketing programs.

03059

Marine Biological Association of the United Kingdom MBAUK

The Laboratory, Citadel Hill, Devon, Plymouth, PL1 2PB, UK
Tel: 01752 633207
Fax: 01752 633102
Email: sec@mba.ac.uk
Website: http://www.mba.ac.uk
Members: 1200
Staff: 26
Contact: Geoffrey Holland, Pres.
Description: Marine biologists, botanists, and scientists. Encourages cooperation among members; disseminates information on latest research; studies living resources of the seas. Assists cooperative research programs; organizes scientific meetings.
Library Subject: marine sciences
Library Type: reference

03060

Marine Connection

PO Box 2404, London, W2 3WG, UK
Tel: 079 31366352
Email: info@marineconnection.org
Website: http://www.marineconnection.org
Contact: Margaux Dodds, Dir./Co-Founder
Fee: £30
Membership Type: regular (UK)
Fee: £35
Membership Type: regular (overseas)
Description: Promotes the importance of protecting the marine environment through programs such as "Adopt a Dolphin". Strives to make a positive contribution towards a world that understands and respects the ocean and its marine life.
Publication: Book
Publication title: Dolphins

03061

Marine Conservation Society MCS

Wolf Business Park, Unit 3, Alton Rd., Ross-on-Wye, HR9 5NB, UK
Tel: 01989 566017
Fax: 01989 567815
Email: info@mcsuk.org
Website: http://www.mcsuk.org
Members: 5000
Staff: 16
Contact: Richard Harrington, Communications Mgr.
Fee: £25
Membership Type: in UK
Fee: £30
Membership Type: outside UK
Description: Individuals and organizations concerned with and interested in marine conservation. Protects the marine environment for wildlife and future generations.
Publication: Book
Publication title: Good Fish Guide

03062

Marine Society

202 Lambeth Rd., London, SE1 7JW, UK
Tel: 020 76547000
Fax: 020 79288914
Email: info@ms-sc.org
Website: http://www.ms-sc.org
Members: 300
Staff: 30
Contact: Mike Cornish, CEO
Description: Governors who subscribe annually or are life governors support the society and elect its council. The training, education and general welfare of professional seafarers (both RN and MN) and the support of those intending to make a career at sea, or who have been professional seafarers, and their dependents. Activities include Seafarers Library Service, College of the Sea, Training Ships and financial support for the education and training of seafarers.
Publication: Magazine
Publication title: Seafarer. Advertisements.

03063

Marine Society and Sea Cadets MSSC

202 Lambeth Rd., London, SE1 7JW, UK
Tel: 020 76547000
Fax: 020 79288914
Email: info@ms-sc.org
Website: http://www.ms-sc.org
Members: 850
Staff: 50
Contact: Mike Cornish, CEO
Fee: £25
Membership Type: general
Fee: £650
Membership Type: life
Description: Charity and Company limited by guarantee. Exists to jointly sponsor the Sea Cadet Corps, which seeks to develop leadership qualities in youth through sports and boating activities. Offers research and educational programs for cadets (boys and girls ages 10 to 18, enrolled in program) and leaders. Sponsors internal competitions.
Formerly: Formerly, Navy League

03064

Marine Stewardship Council MSC

Mountbarrow House, 3rd Fl., 6-20 Elizabeth St., London, SW1W 9RB, UK
Tel: 020 78113300
Fax: 020 78113301
Email: info@msc.org
Website: http://www.msc.org
Staff: 29
Contact: Will Martin, Chm.
Description: Promotes responsible fishing practices through sustainable marine fisheries; promotes responsible, environmentally appropriate, socially beneficial and economically viable fisheries practices while maintaining biodiversity, productivity and ecological processes of the marine environment.
Publication: Bulletin
Publication title: Fish4Thought

03065

Maritime Information Association MIA

c/o Stephen Grace, Membership Sec.
40 Frobisher Pl., London, SE15 2EQ, UK
Email: michael@mpnaxton.fsnet.co.uk
Website: http://www.maritime-information.net
Members: 120
Contact: Michael Naxton, Chm.
Fee: £15
Membership Type: full
Fee: £10
Membership Type: part time, unemployed
Description: Librarians and information officers from 11 countries who are concerned with maritime and nautical subjects. Promotes contact and cooperation among marine librarians and information officers and the development of a body of professional expertise on relevant literature and information sources. Acts as a forum for exchange of problems and information.
Formerly: Formerly, Marine Librarians Association
Publication: Proceedings
Publication title: Conference Proceedings

03066

Market Research Society of the United Kingdom MRS

15 Northburgh St., London, EC1V 0JR, UK
Tel: 020 74904911
Fax: 020 74900608
Email: info@mrs.org.uk
Website: http://www.mrs.org.uk
Members: 8000
Staff: 40
Contact: Jeremy Bullmore, Pres.
Fee: £111.5
Membership Type: full, associate, affiliate
Description: Represents providers and users of market, social, and opinion research, and business intelligence. Offers training and professional development; conferences, seminars and other events, and networking opportunities.
Library Subject: market research methodology
Library Type: not open to the public
Publication: Journal
Publication title: International Journal of Market Research

03067

Marketing Society - United Kingdom

1 Park Rd., Middlesex, Teddington, TW11 0AR, UK
Tel: 020 89731700
Fax: 020 89731701
Email: hugh@marketingsociety.co.uk
Website: http://www.marketing-society.org.uk
Members: 2600
Contact: Hugh Burkitt, Chief Exec.
Fee: £423
Membership Type: executive
Fee: £473
Membership Type: business leader
Description: Provides members with access to a network for leading edge ideas and practices. Encourages debate and contact between members. Organises a nationwide series of conferences, seminars, workshops, and lectures where speakers address the topical and urgent issues of the day.

03068

Marlowe Society

10 Lindum Rd., Middlesex, Teddington, TW11 9DR, UK
Tel: 020 89779706
Email: bruce.young@marlowe-society.org
Website: http://www.marlowe-society.org
Members: 150
Staff: 12
Contact: Bruce Young, Treas.
Fee: £15
Membership Type: standard
Fee: £10
Membership Type: concessionary
Description: Presents Christopher Marlowe in "his true light as a great poet and dramatist".
Publication: Journal
Publication title: Research Journal

03069

MARQUES - Association of European Trademark Owners

840 Melton Rd., Thurmaston, Leicester, LE4 8BN, UK
Tel: 0116 2640080
Fax: 0116 2640141
Email: info@marques.org
Website: http://www.marques.org
Members: 500
Staff: 6
Contact: Guido Baumgartner, Chm.
Fee: £335
Membership Type: corporate
Fee: £590
Membership Type: expert
Description: Assists European-based brand owners in the selection, management, and protection of their trademarks. Protects members' interests. Acts as an information exchange.
Meetings/Conventions: annual conference September 13 to 16, 2011. Baveno Italy

03070

Mars Society

16/7 Easter Dairy Rd., Lothian, Edinburgh, EH11 2TS, UK
Email: info@marssociety.org.uk
Website: http://www.marssociety.org.uk
Members: 700
Contact: Bo Maxwell, Pres.
Fee: £10
Membership Type: student/retired
Fee: £20
Membership Type: individual
Description: Committed to a vision of pioneering the planet Mars. Special interests include space exploration, the exploration of Mars and the generation of an international space effort.
Publication: Book
Publication title: A Man on the Moon: The Voyages of the Apollo Astronauts

03071

Masons' Company

22 Cannon Hill, Southgate, London, N14 6LG, UK
Tel: 020 88829520
Fax: 020 88829520
Website: http://www.masonslivery.co.uk
Contact: Heather Rowell, Clerk
Description: Supports the craft of stonemasonry through charities. Awards educational assistance to stonemasonry students and recognitions to masons for excellence in making new buildings or restorations made.

03072

Master Carvers Association MCA

c/o Paul Ferguson, Sec.
Unit 2, 15b Vandyke Rd., Leighton Buzzard, LU7 3HG, UK
Tel: 01525 851594
Email: info@mastercarvers.co.uk
Website: http://www.mastercarvers.co.uk
Members: 40
Contact: Ben Harms, Pres.
Description: Represents companies and employers of wood and/or stone carvers and self employed wood/stone carvers.

03073

Master Locksmiths Association MLA

5D Great Central Way, Woodford Halse, Daventry, NN11 3PZ, UK
Tel: 01327 262255
Fax: 01327 262539
Email: enquiries@locksmiths.co.uk
Website: http://www.locksmiths.co.uk
Members: 1550
Staff: 4
Description: Membership is divided into four divisions: British Locksmiths Institute (professional body); MLA Trade Division (trade association); MLA Affiliate Division (manufacturers, wholesalers, etc.); Guild of Keycutters. Concerned with promoting the interests of those in the locksmithing industry, advancing the education and training of persons preparing to enter or engaged in the trade, encouraging the issue of standards by members, and ensuring high standards are maintained for the protection of the public.
Publication: Magazine
Publication title: Keyways. Advertisements.
Meetings/Conventions: biennial convention – Exhibits.

03074

Master Photographers Association MPA

Jubilee House, 1 Chancery Ln., County Durham, Darlington, DL1 5QP, UK
Tel: 01325 356555
Fax: 01325 357813
Email: general@mpauk.com
Website: http://www.thempa.com
Members: 2000
Staff: 5
Contact: Colin Buck, Chief Exec.
Description: Photographers practising full time may be accepted into membership.
Publication: Magazine
Publication title: Master Photographers. Advertisements.

03075

Mastic Asphalt Council MAC

PO Box 77, Hastings, TN35 4WL, UK
Tel: 01424 814400
Fax: 01424 814446
Email: masphaltco@aol.com
Website: http://www.masticasphaltcouncil.co.uk
Members: 90
Staff: 2
Contact: John K. Blowers, Dir./Sec.
Description: Mastic asphalt contractors. Supports member contractors with free technical advisory service for

potential specifiers. Conducts technical seminars and presentations.
Formerly: Formerly, Mastic Asphalt Council and Employer's Federation

03076
Materials Handling Engineers Association
MHEA
2B Hills Ln., Cambridgeshire, Ely, CB6 1AY, UK
Tel: 01353 666298
Fax: 07006 072242
Email: pw@mhea.co.uk
Website: http://www.mhea.co.uk
Members: 44
Staff: 1
Contact: Peter Webster, Sec.
Fee: £850
Membership Type: general
Description: Aims to further the commercial interests of companies supplying the bulk and continuous handling industries, mineral extraction, tunneling and solids handling, such as mining, quarrying, sand and gravel production, ports handling and loose materials handling.
Publication: Newsletters
Publication title: MHEA Matters. Advertisements.

03077
Mathematical Association
MA
259 London Rd., Leicester, LE2 3BE, UK
Tel: 0116 2210013
Fax: 0116 2122835
Email: office@m-a.org.uk
Website: http://www.m-a.org.uk
Members: 5000
Staff: 6
Contact: David Acheson, Pres.
Fee: £48.5
Membership Type: institutional (minimum)
Fee: £39.5
Membership Type: personal (minimum)
Description: Students, teachers, lecturers, advisers/inspectors across all age ranges. Represents all major national bodies concerned with mathematics education. Works to help teachers through its publications, support networks and branches, national conferences, developing mathematical thinking, and giving ideas for the classroom.
Library Subject: mathematics and mathematics education
Library Type: not open to the public
Publication: Magazine
Publication title: Equals. Advertisements.
Meetings/Conventions: Sailing Through Mathematics – annual conference – Exhibits.

03078
McLibel Support Campaign - UK
MSC UK
5 Caledonian Rd., London, N1 9DX, UK
Tel: 0171 7131269
Fax: 0171 7131269
Email: mclibel@globalnet.co.uk
Website: http://www.mcspotlight.org/campaigns/current/msc.html
Description: Organized to generate solidarity and financial support for campaigners involved in GreenPeace (London) being sued for libel in the United Kingdom by the McDonald's restaurant chain. Conducts campaigns against McDonald's; advocates an end to the exploitation of people, animals, and the environment by multinational companies and others.

03079
Mechanical and Metal Trades Confederation
METCOM
Mirren Ct. (One), 119 Renfrew Rd., Paisley, PA3 4EA, UK
Tel: 0141 8471265
Fax: 0141 8474747
Website: http://www.metcom.org.uk
Members: 36
Fee: £750
Membership Type: regular
Description: Represents the interests of the mechanical and metalworking industries.

03080
MEDACT
The Grayston Centre, 28 Charles Sq., London, N1 6HT, UK
Tel: 020 73244739
Fax: 020 73244734
Email: info@medact.org
Website: http://www.medact.org
Staff: 6
Contact: Jane Young, Office Mgr.
Fee: £15-75
Membership Type: individual (based on annual income)
Description: Educates and updates physicians and the general public on ecological problems impinging health and safety of individuals. Promotes human health through the protection and restoration of the environment.
Publication: Magazine
Publication title: Communique

03081
Medau Movement
1 Grove House, Foundry Ln., Horsham, RH13 5PL, UK
Tel: 01403 266000
Fax: 01403 266111
Email: office@emdp.org
Website: http://www.medau.org.uk
Members: 2000
Staff: 2
Contact: Daran Bennett, Chief Exec.
Description: Trains and supports movement teachers. Maintains a national register of Medau Movement classes and runs recreational courses.

03082
Medecins du Monde UK
MdM-UK
14 Heron Quays, London, E14 4JB, UK
Tel: 020 75157534
Fax: 020 75157560
Email: info@medecinsdumonde.org.uk
Website: http://www.mdmuk.org.uk
Contact: Susan Wright, Dir.
Description: Provides medical assistance to vulnerable populations, whether in emergency situations arising from political or natural disasters, or from the long-term effects of economic and political development or marginality.
Meetings/Conventions: Sahara Trek Challenge – competition

03083
Medecins Sans Frontieres - UK
MSF-UK
67-74 Saffron Hill, London, EC1N 8QX, UK
Tel: 020 74046600
Fax: 020 74044466
Email: office-ldn@london.msf.org
Website: http://www.msf.org.uk
Contact: Marc DuBois, Exec. Dir.
Description: Provides emergency humanitarian and medical assistance to people affected by disaster or natural calamities around the world regardless of creed or affiliation. Recruits medical and logistical personnel in the UK for relief and medical aid operations around the world.
Publication: Handbook
Publication title: Blood Transfusions in Remote Areas

03084
Mediawatch - UK
3 Willow House, Kennington Rd., Kent, Ashford, TN24 0NR, UK
Tel: 01233 633936
Fax: 01233 633836
Email: info@mediawatchuk.org
Website: http://www.mediawatchuk.org
Members: 7000
Staff: 2
Contact: John C. Beyer, Dir.
Fee: £15
Membership Type: general
Description: Campaigns for better standards of taste and decency in broadcasting and media generally.
Formerly: Formerly, National Viewers and Listeners Association
Publication: Newsletter
Publication title: Mediawatch-UK Newsbrief

03085
Medical Defence Union
MDU
230 Blackfriars Rd., London, SE1 8PJ, UK
Tel: 020 72021500
Fax: 020 72021666
Email: mdu@the-mdu.com
Website: http://www.the-mdu.com
Description: Represents the interests of doctors, dentists and other healthcare professionals. Supports the medico-legal needs and reputations of members throughout their professional lives.

03086
Medical Foundation for AIDS and Sexual Health
MedFASH
BMA House, Tavistock Sq., London, WC1H 9JP, UK
Tel: 020 73836345
Fax: 0870 4421792
Email: enquiries@medfash.bma.org.uk
Website: http://www.medfash.org.uk
Staff: 3
Contact: Ruth Lowbury, CEO
Description: Works with policy-makers and health professional to promote excellence in the prevention and management of HIV and other sexually transmitted infections. Develops materials to support health professionals.
Publication: Book
Publication title: HIV in Primary Care

03087

Medical Journalists' Association MJA

54 Overdrive Rd., London, TN21 0SH, UK
Tel: 01435 868786
Email: secretary@mja-uk.org
Website: http://www.mja-uk.org
Members: 420
Contact: Maya Anaokar, Mem. Sec.
Fee: £40
Membership Type: full
Fee: £30
Membership Type: associate
Description: Supports and encourages its members and enables them to work efficiently at high levels of accuracy. Serves as the natural point of contact for anyone wanting to employ a writer with specific expertise, or alert medical journalists of events or achievements that deserve publicity. Conducts educational meetings, debates and networking events.
Publication: Newsletter
Publication title: MJA News. Advertisements.

03088

Medical Officers of Schools Association MOSA

c/o Dr. Neil D. Arnott, Honorary Sec.
Amherst Medical Practice, 21 St. Botolphs Rd., Kent, Sevenoaks, TN13 3AQ, UK
Tel: 01732 459255
Fax: 01732 450751
Email: honorary.secretary@mosa.org.uk
Website: http://www.mosa.org.uk
Members: 440
Staff: 2
Contact: Rosalind Wilmot, Pres.
Fee: £140
Membership Type: regular
Description: School doctors and doctors with an interest in the health of the school child. Aims to represent school doctors and doctors with an interest in the health of the school child; to provide an advisory service for members, and non-members, on any aspect of school medicine.
Publication: Handbook
Publication title: Handbook of School Health. Advertisements.

03089

Medical Protection Society MPS

33 Cavendish Sq., London, W1G 0PS, UK
Tel: 020 73991300
Fax: 020 73991301
Email: info@mps.org.uk
Website: http://www.medicalprotection.org
Members: 250000
Contact: Shelley McNicol, Hd. of Communication
Fee: £10
Membership Type: regular
Description: Aims to help doctors with legal problems that arise from their clinical practice.
Publication: Journal
Publication title: Casebook. Advertisements.

03090

Medical Research Society MRS

Dialysis Ctre., Box 118, Addenbrooke's Hospital, Hills Rd., Cambridge, CB2 2QQ, UK
Fax: 07092 388555
Website: http://www.medres.org.uk
Members: 1300
Contact: Afzal Chaudhry, Academic Sec.
Fee: £25
Membership Type: ordinary
Fee: £5
Membership Type: training fellowship
Description: Individuals engaged in basic and clinical medical research. Facilitates interdisciplinary exchange of information and provides a forum for data presentations by biomedical researchers.
Publication: Journal
Publication title: Clinical Science

03091

Medical Women's Federation MWF

Tavistock House N, Tavistock Sq., London, WC1H 9HX, UK
Tel: 020 73877765
Fax: 020 73889216
Email: admin.mwf@btconnect.com
Website: http://www.medicalwomensfederation.org.uk
Members: 1500
Staff: 3
Contact: Clarissa Fabre, Pres.
Fee: £50-110
Membership Type: individual (based on annual income of below 20,000-40,000)
Fee: £36
Membership Type: permanently retired
Description: Aims to advance the personal and professional development of women in medicine, to change discriminatory attitudes and practices, and to work on behalf of patients.
Publication: Bulletin
Publication title: Medical Woman. Advertisements.

03092

Mediterranean Association to Save the Sea Turtles - United Kingdom MEDASSET

24 Park Towers, 2 Brick St., London, W1J 7DD, UK
Tel: 020 76290654
Fax: 020 76290654
Email: medasset@medasset.org
Website: http://www.medasset.org/cms/index.php
Members: 80
Staff: 4
Contact: Lily Venizelos, Pres.
Fee: £15
Membership Type: friend, supporter
Fee: £30
Membership Type: regular
Description: Promotes the preservation and conservation of all species of sea turtles, their natural environment, and associated biotope in the Mediterranean, and other international waters. Promotes the formulation of protective legislation and its enforcement. Supports scientific research and assessment projects and education, public awareness, publicity, and political liaison activities. Works as an observer-member of the Bern Convention standing committee, an NGO partner to the UNEP/MP (Barcelona Convention).
Publication: Brochures
Publication title: Public Awareness

03093

Meet A Mum Association MAMA

54 Lilington Rd., Norton Radstock, BA3 3NR, UK
Tel: 0845 1206162
Email: meet_a_mum.assoc@btinternet.com
Website: http://www.mama.co.uk
Contact: Esther Rantzen, Pres.
Fee: £5
Membership Type: general
Description: Provides friendship and support to mothers suffering from postnatal depression.
Publication: Booklet
Publication title: Behind the Painted Smile - An Insight into Postnatal Depression

03094

Mensa International MI

Saint John's House, Saint John's Sq., Wolverhampton, WV2 4AH, UK
Tel: 01902 772771
Fax: 01902 392500
Website: http://www.mensa.org
Members: 100000
Description: Individuals from 100 countries whose intelligence, as measured by standardized tests, is within the top 2 percent of the general population. Aims to promote: social contact among intelligent people; research in psychology and the social sciences; the identification and development of human intelligence. Maintains no religious or political affiliations and is open to all who meet the intelligence criterion. Conducts research on public opinions and sociological potential of the highly intelligent. Provides volunteers for research workers requiring a high I.Q. group. Sponsors projects to foster intelligence and provides educational facilities. Sponsors periodic competitions; maintains speakers' bureau. Offers children's services and charitable program.
Publication: Journal
Publication title: International Journal

03095

Mental Health Foundation MHF

20 Upper Ground, Sea Containers House, 9th Fl., London, SE1 9QB, UK
Tel: 020 78031101
Fax: 020 78031111
Email: mhf@mhf.org.uk
Website: http://www.mentalhealth.org.uk
Contact: William Utting, Pres.
Description: Plays a vital role in pioneering new approaches to prevention, treatment and care. Allocates grants for research and community projects, contributes to public debate and strives to reduce the stigma attached to mental illness and learning disabilities.

03096

Mercers' Company

Mercer's Hall, Ironmonger Ln., London, EC2V 8HE, UK
Tel: 020 77264991
Fax: 020 76001158
Email: mail@mercers.co.uk
Website: http://www.mercers.co.uk
Members: 300
Contact: D.H Hodson, Chm.
Description: Administers large programme of charitable grant making. Provides housing for the elderly. Supports education. Acts as a fraternity for its members.

03097

Merchant Taylors' Company

Merchant Taylors' Hall, 30 Threadneedle St., London, EC2R 8JB, UK
Tel: 0207 4504440
Fax: 0207 5882776
Website: http://www.merchanttaylors.co.uk
Description: Protects the interests of merchant tailors.

03098

Mercy Universal

PO Box 81, Greenford, UB6 9YW, UK
Tel: 020 85755999
Fax: 020 85753666
Email: info@mercyuniversal.com
Website: http://www.mercyuniversal.com
Description: Provides humanitarian relief in the UK. Responds to emergencies around the world by rushing much needed relief to victims of wars and natural disasters. Aims to eradicate the root causes of poverty. Promotes self reliance, vocational training and income generation schemes. Provides assistance for shelter and house repair. Runs a sponsorship program for orphans and poor children.

03099

Merseyside Campaign for Nuclear Disarmament
MCND

50/4 Mt. Pleasant, Liverpool, L3 5SD, UK
Tel: 0151 7093995
Email: mcnd@care4free.net
Website: http://www.mcnd.org.uk
Description: Aims to eliminate British nuclear weapons and other weapons of mass destruction.
Publication: Newsletter
Publication title: Merseyside CND

03100

Metal Packaging Manufacturers Association
MPMA

The Stables, Tintagel Farm, Sandhurst Rd., Berkshire, Wokingham, RG40 3JD, UK
Tel: 0118 9788433
Email: enquiries@mpma.org.uk
Website: http://www.mpma.org.uk
Members: 41
Staff: 3
Contact: Nick Mullen, Dir.
Description: Represents companies involved in the manufacture of light metal containers, closures and components. Aims to promote common interests and protect members through debate with government.

03101

Metalforming Machinery Makers' Association
MMMA

The Cottage, Down End, Hook Norton, Oxfordshire, Hook Norton, OX15 5LW, UK
Tel: 01608 737129
Fax: 01295 253333
Email: enquiries@mmma.org.uk
Website: http://www.mmma.org.uk/page.asp?node=1&dec=Home
Members: 34
Staff: 1
Contact: Ian Kimberley, Chm.
Fee: £368
Membership Type: corporate
Description: Represents and promotes the interests of British-based manufacturers and distributors of metalforming machinery and ancillary products in the UK. When purchasing metalforming machinery or ancillary products, always specify a member to be guaranteed: first class products; first class product support; and first class customer service.
Publication: Handbook
Publication title: Member's Handbook

03102

Metamorphic Association

159 Bembrook Rd., East Sussex, Hastings, TN34 3PD, UK
Tel: 01424 432566
Email: secretary@metamorphicassociation.org
Website: http://www.metamorphicassociation.org
Members: 500
Contact: Keith Moore, Membership Sec.
Fee: £60
Membership Type: practitioner
Fee: £100
Membership Type: teacher
Description: Promotes good health and well-being through awareness, understanding and use of Metamorphic Technique in the UK and internationally, and upholds standards and procedures and teaching the technique.
Publication: Newsletter
Publication title: The Programme

03103

Micro and Anophthalmic Childrens Society
MACS

22 Lower Park St., Isle of Anglesey, North Wales, Holyhead, LL65 1DU, UK
Tel: 0800 1698088
Email: enquiries@macs.org.uk
Website: http://www.macs.org.uk
Contact: Lynda Rhodes, Sec.
Description: Aims to enhance the quality of life for children and families of children with anophthalmia, microphthalmia, and coloboma. Provides support and information to parents and professionals in the UK and around the world. Fosters research in anophthalmia, microphthalmia, coloboma and other related conditions.

03104

Microwave Technologies Association
MTA

c/o Lewis Napleton
5 Lincoln Close, Bembridge, Isle of Wight, PO35 5RP, UK
Tel: 01983 874008
Email: lewisnapleton@btinternet.com
Website: http://www.microwaveassociation.org.uk
Members: 38
Contact: Jennipher Marshall-Jenkinson, Chair
Fee: £50
Membership Type: individual (home economist, consultant and technician), educational (university, college and special interest)
Fee: £300
Membership Type: corporate
Description: Companies, producers, colleges, universities and individuals who are involved in the microwave and attendant food industries and wish to exchange technical and general information as well as to ensure users are informed of the best way to prepare food safely and well. Runs an annual conference and periodic seminars at educational establishments and a number of public exhibitions and demonstration are held in a year. Takes part in major food/equipment exhibitions. Works closely with MAFF on the voluntary labeling scheme for microwaves and microwave foods and sits on the UK Microwave Working Group.
Formerly: Formerly, Microwave Association
Publication: Book
Publication title: Microwave Magic - The Art of 21st Century Cooking. Advertisements.

03105

Mid Somerset Campaign for Nuclear Disarmament

12 Neales Way, Evercreech, Somerset, Shepton Mallet, BA4 6LA, UK
Tel: 01749 830741
Fax: 01749 830741
Email: msomcnd@aol.com
Website: http://www.cnduk.org/index.php/regional-groups/mid-somerset-cnd.html
Description: Aims to eliminate British nuclear weapons and other weapons of mass destruction.

03106

Middle East Association
MEA

Bury House, 33 Bury St., St. James, London, SW1Y 6AX, UK
Tel: 020 78392137
Fax: 020 78396121
Email: charles@the-mea.co.uk
Website: http://www.the-mea.co.uk
Members: 400
Staff: 12
Contact: Charles Hollis, Dir. Gen.
Description: Firms in the United Kingdom doing business with companies in the Middle East, Iran, Turkey and Afghanistan. Promotes trade and business between the United Kingdom and the Middle East. Advises new exporters/companies regarding all aspects of trade in the Middle East.
Library Subject: Middle East trade, politics, economy, society
Library Type: open to the public
Publication: Newsletter
Publication title: Information Digest. Advertisements.
Meetings/Conventions: Discussion Group Meeting – periodic meeting

03107

Midwives Information and Resource Service
MIDIRS

9 Elmdale Rd., Clifton, Bristol, BS8 1SL, UK
Tel: 0117 9251791
Fax: 0117 9251792
Email: sales@midirs.org
Website: http://www.midirs.org
Contact: Sue Penn, Contact
Description: Provides information for midwives and nurses who want to keep up-to-date with contemporary knowledge and thinking in the world of midwifery care,

women's health, and care of newborns. Offers articles, books, and other information concerning midwifery. Conducts educational programs.
Library Subject: midwifery, maternity services, maternal health, neonatal care, pregnancy, labour, care of the infant up to 1 year of age
Library Type: by appointment only
Publication: Newsletter
Publication title: Essence. Advertisements.

03108

Migraine Action
MA

27 East St., Leicester, LE1 6NB, UK
Tel: 01162 758317
Fax: 01162 542023
Email: info@migraine.org.uk
Website: http://www.migraine.org.uk
Members: 6000
Staff: 8
Contact: Lee Tomkins, Dir.
Fee: £12.5
Membership Type: standard
Fee: £17.5
Membership Type: enhanced
Description: Migraine sufferers, their families and friends, or anyone else who is interested, including medical professionals. Support for research into aspects of migraine, grants, information, understanding and encouragement to migraine sufferers.
Formerly: Formerly, British Migraine Association
Publication: Newsletter
Publication title: Challenging Migraine

03109

Military Heraldry Society

8 Green Acres, Eythorne, Kent, Dover, CT15 4LX, UK
Email: info@militaryheraldrysociety.com
Website: http://www.militaryheraldrysociety.com
Members: 320
Staff: 8
Contact: Michael Elsey, Contact
Fee: £15
Membership Type: ordinary
Description: Collectors and others interested in cloth military insignia worldwide.
Library Subject: militaria
Library Type: lending
Publication: Journal
Publication title: Formation Sign. Advertisements.

03110

Milton Keynes and North Buckinghamshire Chamber of Commerce

9 Rillaton Walk, Milton Keynes, MK9 2FZ, UK
Tel: 01908 259000
Fax: 01908 246799
Email: enquiry@mk-chamber.co.uk
Website: http://www.mk-chamber.co.uk
Members: 1375
Staff: 130
Contact: Silvia Vitiello, Pres.
Fee: £296-1727
Membership Type: firm/company (based on number of employees)
Fee: £240.58
Membership Type: sole trader
Description: Represents members across Milton Keynes and North Buckinghamshire at local, regional and national level on matters concerning trade, commerce and industry and lobbying. Facilitates networking, forums and events to enable members to exchange ideas, information, views and business practice.

03111

Mind - National Association for Mental Health

15-19 Broadway, London, E15 4BQ, UK
Tel: 020 85192122
Fax: 020 85221725
Email: contact@mind.org.uk
Website: http://www.mind.org.uk
Members: 2100
Staff: 105
Contact: Paul Farmer, Chief Exec.
Fee: £15
Membership Type: full
Fee: £5
Membership Type: unwaged
Description: Promotes mental health and encourages a better understanding of mental health problems. Seeks to eliminate the stigma associated with mental illness. Conducts research; disseminates information. Offers legal referral services. Sponsors charitable program. Maintains information service. Conducts training and educational courses and seminars.
Library Subject: mental health
Library Type: reference
Publication: Magazine
Publication title: OpenMIND. Advertisements.
Meetings/Conventions: annual conference – Exhibits.

03112

Mineral Industry Research Organisation
MIRO

Concorde House, Trinity Park, Solihull, Birmingham, B37 7UQ, UK
Tel: 0121 6355225
Fax: 0121 6355226
Email: mail@miro.co.uk
Website: http://www.miro.co.uk
Members: 60
Staff: 9
Contact: Alan Gibbon, Dir.
Fee: £2180
Membership Type: industrial company, national association
Fee: £1595
Membership Type: SME, research institute, laboratory, consultant
Description: Companies or organisations that are involved in the exploration, mining, extraction or processing of primary and secondary raw materials. Technology brokerage that identifies, promotes and manages new technology research projects for its members. Aims, wherever possible, to obtain co-funding from European, national or regional agencies. Studies are contracted to either universities or independent research laboratories.
Library Subject: technical, statistical, research output related to mineral industry
Library Type: not open to the public
Publication: Bulletin
Publication title: MIRO Bulletin
Meetings/Conventions: annual meeting – Exhibits.

03113

Mineral Products Association
MPA

Gillingham House, 38-44 Gillingham St., London, SW1V 1HU, UK
Tel: 020 79638000
Fax: 020 79638001
Email: info@mineralproducts.org
Website: http://www.mineralproducts.org
Members: 130
Staff: 20
Contact: Patrick O'Shea, Chm.
Fee: £650
Membership Type: associate
Description: Represents the interests of aggregates, asphalt, surfacing, ready-mixed concrete, silica sand, and mortar industries. Constitutes 90% of crushed rock and sand and gravel production in the UK.
Formerly: Formerly, British Ready Mixed Concrete Association
Publication: Magazine
Publication title: Quarrying Today

03114

Mineralogical Society

12 Baylis Mews, Amyand Park Rd., Middlesex, Twickenham, TW1 3HQ, UK
Tel: 020 88916600
Fax: 020 88916599
Email: info@minersoc.org
Website: http://www.minersoc.org
Contact: Kevin B. Murphy, Exec. Dir.
Fee: £33
Membership Type: individual/fellow
Fee: £10
Membership Type: student
Description: Museum and research scientists, research organizations, students, and university staff involved in mineralogical studies in 57 countries. Aims to advance the knowledge of crystallography, geochemistry and petrology, and mineralogy through scientific gatherings and publications.
Formerly: Formerly, Mineralogical Society of Great Britain and Ireland
Publication: Book
Publication title: Environmental Mineralogy

03115

Minerals Engineering Society
MES

2 Ryton Close, Blyth, Nottinghamshire, Worksop, S81 8DN, UK
Tel: 01909 591787
Fax: 01909 591940
Email: secretary@mineralsengineering.org
Website: http://www.mineralsengineering.org
Members: 450
Contact: Andrew W. Howells, Natl. Sec./Treas.
Fee: £20
Membership Type: fellow
Fee: £16
Membership Type: individual
Description: Learned society to promote minerals engineering.
Publication: Journal
Publication title: Mine, Quarry & Recycling

03116

Mining Institute of Scotland

10 Woodhill Grove, Crossford, Dunfermline, KY12 8YG, UK
Tel: 01383 432856
Fax: 01383 432856
Email: d.seath@btinternet.com
Website: http://www.mining-scotland.org
Members: 478
Contact: David Seath, Honorable Sec.
Description: Represents the interests of colliery managers, assistant managers, undermanagers, mining engineers, agents, proprietors and others interested in minerals and mining. Promotes and develops every aspect of minerals and mining science, and engineering and technology by providing information and related services. Holds regular meetings and conducts interviews of applicants for UK Chartered Engineer, Incorporated Engineer and Engineering Technician status.

03117

Minor Metals Trade Association MMTA

Angel Gate, 326A City Rd., London, EC1V 2PT, UK
Tel: 0207 8330237
Fax: 0207 1839933
Email: secretary@mmta.co.uk
Website: http://www.mmta.co.uk/home
Members: 68
Staff: 3
Contact: Charles Swindon, Chm.
Fee: £1000
Membership Type: general
Description: UK and overseas traders in minor metals. Also associate non-trading members. Encourages, participates in and fosters the activities of traders in minor metals in order to maintain good trade practices and healthy competition on the basis of sound commercial principles.
Formerly: Formerly, Minor Metals Traders Association

03118

Minority Rights Group International MRG

54 Commercial St., London, E1 6LT, UK
Tel: 020 74224200
Fax: 020 74224201
Email: minority.rights@mrgmail.org
Website: http://www.minorityrights.org
Staff: 27
Contact: Kevin Boyle, Chm.
Description: Obtains justice for minority and indigenous groups. Aims to enhance awareness of groups suffering discrimination. Attends meetings of the United Nations. Maintains nongovernmental organization and consultative status with the Economic and Social Council. Conducts research.
Publication: Newsletter
Publication title: Outsider

03119

MIRA

Watling St., Warwickshire, Nuneaton, CV10 0TU, UK
Tel: 024 76355000
Fax: 024 76355355
Email: enquiries@mira.co.uk
Website: http://www.mira.co.uk
Members: 100
Staff: 540
Description: Serves as a contract research organization for the automotive and wider transport industries. Has a substantial number of laboratories and test facilities at its 700-acre technology center and proving ground. Operates on behalf of customers in virtually every aspect of design and development of vehicles and components, safety and legislation.
Library Subject: vehicle design, development engineering, general motor industry
Library Type: reference
Formerly: Formerly, Motor Industry Research Association
Publication: Newsletter
Publication title: Automotive Business News

03120

Miscarriage Association

c/o Clayton Hospital
Northgate, W Yorkshire, Wakefield, WF1 3JS, UK
Tel: 01924 200799
Fax: 01924 298834
Email: info@miscarriageassociation.org.uk
Website: http://www.miscarriageassociation.org.uk
Members: 1400
Staff: 6
Contact: Ruth Bender Atik, Natl. Dir.
Fee: £20
Membership Type: individual/couple in UK
Fee: £5
Membership Type: individual/couple in UK (unwaged)
Description: Provides support and information for all on the subject of pregnancy loss. Gathers information about causes and treatments and promote good practice in the way pregnancy loss is managed in hospitals and in the community.

03121

Mission to Seafarers

St. Michael Paternoster Royal, College Hill, London, EC4R 2RL, UK
Tel: 020 72485202
Fax: 020 72485202
Website: http://www.missiontoseafarers.org
Members: 3000
Staff: 125
Contact: Tom Heffer, Sec. Gen.
Description: Charity of the Anglican Church concerned with the well-being of merchant seafarers of all races in ports throughout the world. Maintains fully staffed seafarers' clubs in over 100 ports and part-time chaplains in 200 others.
Formerly: Formerly, Missions to Seamen
Publication: Newspaper
Publication title: Flying Angel News

03122

Mission Without Borders - United Kingdom

175 Tower Bridge Rd., London, SE1 2AG, UK
Tel: 020 79401370
Fax: 020 74037348
Email: info_uk@mwbi.org
Website: http://www.mwbuk.org
Contact: Harry Graham, CEO
Description: Serves the physical, material and spiritual needs of people living in poverty or suffering persecution. Provides support and assistance to families and children.

03123

Mobile Data Association MDA

PO Box 9347, Sleaford, NG34 4DA, UK
Tel: 0870 2255632
Email: mda@themda.org
Website: http://www.themda.org
Contact: Mike Short, Honorary Pres.
Fee: £600-3500
Membership Type: company (based on number of employees)
Description: Works to increase awareness of mobile data among users and advisors; promotes the uses and benefits of wireless value added services.
Publication: Newsletter
Publication title: MDA News
Meetings/Conventions: Member Forums – quarterly meeting

03124

Mobile Operators Association MOA

Russell Sq. House, 10-12 Russell Sq., London, WC1B 5EE, UK
Tel: 020 73312015
Fax: 020 73312047
Email: info@ukmoa.org
Website: http://www.mobilemastinfo.com
Members: 5
Contact: Christine Jude, Chief Press Off.
Description: Represents the five UK mobile phone network operators on radio frequency health and planning issues. Cooperates with interested parties such as local planners, elected counselors, resident groups in sharing information relevant to both the operators and the public.
Publication: Brochure
Publication title: Mobile Phone Networks

03125

Modern Humanities Research Association MHRA

1 Carlton House Terr., London, SW1Y 5AF, UK
Email: mail@mhra.org.uk
Website: http://www.mhra.org.uk
Members: 500
Contact: Barry Nisbet, Pres.
Description: Scholars working in the area of modern European languages and literatures; university graduates interested in the humanities. Encourages study and research in modern European languages and literatures; promotes academic diversity. Recognizes accomplishments in the humanities.
Publication: Bulletin
Publication title: Annual Bulletin of the Modern Humanities Research Association

03126

Modular and Portable Building Association MPBA

PO Box 99, Caersws, SY17 5WR, UK
Tel: 0870 2417687
Fax: 0870 2417687
Email: mpba@mpba.biz
Website: http://mpba.biz
Members: 1
Staff: 2
Contact: Jackie Maginnis, Chief Exec.
Fee: £1530
Membership Type: associate - maximum (based on number of employees)
Fee: £1425
Membership Type: full - maximum (based on number of employees)
Description: Large and small companies in the prefabricated building industry may qualify by experience and practice for full membership. Associate membership also available for companies and individuals with an interest in the industry. Promotion and marketing of prefabricated buildings. Members make, sell and hire buildings, many of which are relocatable and some portable. Government, commerce, leisure and domestic requirements are covered. Standards are set, codes of practice and model terms of business produced. Market surveys are conducted.
Formerly: Formerly, National Prefabricated Building Association

Mondiale ORT
see World ORT

03127

Money Advice Scotland MAS

Pentagon Centre, Ste. 410, 36 Washington St., Glasgow, G3 8AZ, UK
Tel: 0141 5720237
Fax: 0141 5720428
Email: info@moneyadvicescotland.org.uk
Website: http://www.moneyadvicescotland.org.uk
Members: 130
Staff: 7
Contact: Yvonne Gallacher, Chief Exec.
Fee: £187-624
Membership Type: local authority (based on number of advisers)
Fee: £101-150
Membership Type: local voluntary organization (based on number of advisers)
Description: Individuals, organizations, companies, and public agencies involved in the provision debt counseling services. Promotes availability of money management advice to people of all economic strata and seeks to insure effectiveness of financial planning and debt counseling services. Represents members' interests, facilitates communication and cooperation among members. Conducts training programs for financial planning counselors.
Library Subject: financial planning, debt counseling
Library Type: by appointment only

03128

Monumental Brass Society MBS

Lowe Hill House, Stratford St. Mary, Suffolk, CO7 6JX, UK
Email: mgtharris@btinternet.com
Website: http://www.mbs-brasses.co.uk
Members: 500
Contact: H.M. Stuchfield, VP
Fee: £25
Membership Type: individual, overseas, institutional
Fee: £35
Membership Type: family
Description: Libraries, schools, and interested individuals. Promotes the preservation and study of monumental brasses and incised slabs as well as the study of indents of lost brasses.
Publication: Bulletin
Publication title: MBS Bulletin

03129

Mortar Industry Association MIA

Gillingham House, 38-44 Gillingham St., London, SW1V 1HU, UK
Tel: 020 79638000
Fax: 020 79638001
Email: mia@mineralproducts.org
Website: http://www.mortar.org.uk
Members: 26
Contact: Brian James, Contact
Description: Represents the interests of the companies involved in the factory production of mortars.
Publication: Manual
Publication title: Data Sheets

03130

Mothers' Union - England MU

Mary Sumner House, 24 Tufton St., London, SW1P 3RB, UK
Tel: 020 72225533
Fax: 020 72279737
Email: mu@themothersunion.org
Website: http://www.themothersunion.org
Members: 1000000
Staff: 45
Contact: Reg Bailey, Chief Exec.
Description: An Anglican organization, which promotes the well-being of families worldwide.
Publication: Magazine
Publication title: Home and Family. Advertisements.

03131

Motor Neurone Disease Association of the United Kingdom MNDA

PO Box 246, Northampton, NN1 2PR, UK
Tel: 01604 250505
Fax: 01604 638289
Email: enquiries@mndassotciation.org
Website: http://www.mndassociation.org
Members: 7000
Staff: 100
Contact: Sarah Fitzgerald, Hd. of PR/Media
Fee: £12
Membership Type: individual, health and social care professional
Fee: £18
Membership Type: family
Description: Aims to ensure that people affected by MND can secure the care and support needed; funds research into the disease. Provides services that include a national telephone helpline, literature on all aspects of living with MND, free loan of specialist equipment, network of Regional Care Advisors, support groups and limited financial support to those with the disease.
Library Subject: motor neurone disease
Library Type: not open to the public
Publication: Magazine
Publication title: Thumb Print. Advertisements.

03132

Motor Schools Association of Great Britain MSA

101 Wellington Rd. N, Cheshire, Stockport, SK4 2LP, UK
Tel: 0161 4299669
Fax: 0161 4299779
Email: mail@msagb.co.uk
Website: http://www.msagb.com/home/home.asp
Members: 7500
Staff: 4
Contact: John Lepine, Gen. Mgr.
Fee: £72
Description: Department of Transport approved driving instructors. Keeps members informed on any matters of practical interest to them and sets standards of professional and ethical behavior for teachers of driving. Also prides itself on the information and representation available to its members. Most of the information passed on to members is contained in organization's national and regional publications.
Publication: Newspaper
Publication title: MSA Newslink

03133

Motor Vehicle Dismantlers' Association of Great Britain MVDA

33 Market St., Lichfield, WS13 6LA, UK
Tel: 01543 254254
Fax: 01543 254274
Email: enquiries@mvda.org.uk
Website: http://www.mvda.org.uk
Members: 500
Contact: John Allen, Chm.
Description: Represents the vehicle dismantlers and their customers in UK and Ireland. Promotes safety and ensures recycling and reuse of ELV's.

03134

Motorcycle Industry Association MCI

1 Rye Hill Office Park, Birmingham Rd., Allesley, Coventry, CV5 9AB, UK
Tel: 024 76408000
Fax: 024 76408001
Website: http://www.mcia.co.uk
Members: 146
Staff: 24
Contact: Steve Kenward, CEO
Fee: £1120
Membership Type: service provider, associate
Fee: £565-7020
Membership Type: motorcycle industry (based on annual turnover)

Description: Works for the benefit of its members and motorcycling in general. Represents members' interests; organizes exhibitions.
Library Type: reference
Formerly: Formerly, MCIA
Publication: Booklet
Publication title: Statistics Booklet
Meetings/Conventions: International Motorcycle and Scooter Show – annual show

03135

Motorsport Industry Association
MIA

Federation House, Stoneleigh Park, Warwickshire, Stoneleigh, CV8 2RF, UK
Tel: 024 76692600
Fax: 024 76692601
Email: info@the-mia.com
Website: http://www.the-mia.com
Contact: Chris Aylett, CEO
Fee: £695-6795
Membership Type: corporate/international (based on annual turnover)
Fee: £955
Membership Type: associate
Description: Provides business support service and advice to companies in the motorsport industry. Offers information, assistance and encouragement to members in all aspects of business development. Promotes the achievements of members and industry to the business and general media sectors.

03136

Movement for Compassionate Living the Vegan Way
MCL

105 Cyfyng Rd., Ystalyfera, Swansea, SA9 2BT, UK
Tel: 01639 841223
Email: mcl@gciow.freeserve.co.uk
Website: http://www.mclveganway.org.uk
Members: 800
Contact: Alan Garrett, Contact
Description: Individuals in 32 countries. Promotes a way of life that is free of the exploitation and slaughter of sentient beings, that is possible for all the world's people and that is sustainable within the recourses of the planet.
Publication: Journal
Publication title: New Leaves

03137

Mozambique News Agency

26 Withdean Crescent, Brighton, BN1 6WH, UK
Tel: 01273 7941890630
Email: aim@tvcabo.co.mz
Website: http://www.poptel.org.uk/mozambique-news
Staff: 55
Description: Journalists and staff involved in news operations in Mozambique. Provides feature and photographic services.
Publication: Magazine
Publication title: Mozambiquefile. Advertisements.

03138

Multi-Faith Group for Healthcare Chaplaincy
MFGHC

PO Box 2261, Salisbury, SP3 6WE, UK
Email: chief.officer@mfghc.com
Website: http://www.mfghc.com
Contact: Manhar Mehta, Chm.
Description: Seeks to advance the multi-faith healthcare chaplaincy in England and Wales. Facilitates a common understanding and support for healthcare chaplaincy amongst faith groups, chaplaincy bodies and users. Provides a means for consultation between the faiths about healthcare chaplaincy. Cooperates with healthcare and chaplaincy organizations, bodies and authorities.
Publication: Bulletin

03139

Multiple Sclerosis International Federation
MSIF

3rd Fl., Skyline House, 200 Union St., London, SE1 0LX, UK
Tel: 020 76201911
Fax: 020 76201922
Email: info@msif.org
Website: http://www.msif.org/language_choice.html
Contact: Peer Baneke, CEO
Description: Aims to stimulate scientific research at a global scale, disseminate information internationally, assist the development of national MS societies, and encourage full integration and participation of all people affected by MS.
Library Subject: multiple sclerosis
Library Type: reference
Formerly: Formerly, International Federation of Multiple Sclerosis Societies
Publication: Annual Report
Publication title: Annual Review

03140

Multiple Sclerosis Society of the United Kingdom
MS

MS National Centre, 372 Edgware Rd., London, NW2 6ND, UK
Tel: 020 84380700
Fax: 020 84380701
Email: helpline@mssociety.org.uk
Website: http://www.mssociety.org.uk
Members: 45000
Staff: 110
Contact: Tony Kennan, Chm.
Fee: £5
Membership Type: regular
Description: Dedicated to support everyone whose life is touched by Multiple Sclerosis. Provides respite care, a freephone MS helpline, grants for home adaptations and mobility aids, education and training, specialist MS nurses and a wide range of information. Maintains local branches which cater to all ages and interests and are run by individuals with direct experience of MS.
Library Subject: multiple sclerosis
Library Type: open to the public
Publication: Magazine
Publication title: MS Matters. Advertisements.

03141

Multiple Sclerosis South Africa
MSSA

372 Edgware Rd., London, NW2 6ND, UK
Tel: 020 87380700
Fax: 020 87380701
Email: info@mssociety.org.uk
Website: http://www.mssociety.org.uk/about_us
Members: 1900
Staff: 2
Contact: Tony Kennan, Chm.
Fee: £5
Membership Type: regular
Description: MS patients, families and professionals. Seeks to improve the quality of life for persons with multiple sclerosis and their families.

03142

MultiService Association
MSA

PO Box 9378, Newark, NG24 9FE, UK
Tel: 01400 281298
Fax: 01400 282326
Email: info@msauk.biz
Website: http://www.msauk.biz
Members: 280
Contact: Martyn Harvey, CEO
Fee: £120
Membership Type: regular
Description: Shoe repairers. Trade association for shoe repairers throughout the UK.
Library Type: reference
Formerly: Absorbed, British Shoe Repair Association
Publication: Magazine
Publication title: Shoe Service. Advertisements.

03143

Museums Association - England
MA

24 Calvin St., London, E1 6NW, UK
Tel: 020 74266910
Fax: 020 74266961
Email: info@museumsassociation.org
Website: http://www.museumsassociation.org
Members: 5850
Staff: 27
Contact: Mark Taylor, Dir.
Fee: £63-203
Membership Type: individual (based on annual income)
Fee: £49
Membership Type: retired, full-time student, museum governing body, unwaged, volunteer
Description: Museums and people working in the museums. Represents the interests of museum employees, museums, and collections.
Publication: Journal
Publication title: Museums Journal

03144

Music Education Council
MEC

54 Elm Rd., Hale, Cheshire, Altrincham, WA15 9QP, UK
Tel: 0161 9283085
Fax: 0161 9299648
Email: ahassan@easynet.co.uk
Website: http://www.mec.org.uk
Members: 250
Staff: 1

Contact: Anna Hassan, Admin.
Fee: £115-367
Membership Type: organization (based on annual turnover)
Fee: £115
Membership Type: music department (within institution)
Description: Organizations, institutions, and individuals involved in music education. Represents members' interest to central government. Offers advice concerning music education and training in Great Britain to domestic and international enquirers.

03145

Music Industries Association - England
MIA

Ivy Cottage Offices, Finch's Yard, Eastwick Rd., Great Bookham, Surrey, KT23 4BA, UK
Tel: 01372 750600
Fax: 01372 750515
Email: enquiries@mia.org.uk
Website: http://www.mia.org.uk
Members: 370
Staff: 5
Contact: Paul McManus, Chief Exec.
Fee: £350
Membership Type: allied trade
Fee: £150-630
Membership Type: retailer (based on UK sales of music products)
Description: Manufacturers, distributors and retailers of musical instruments and accessories. Gives active support to members in the marketing and promotion of musical instruments and accessories; promotes the making of music as an enjoyable and worthwhile activity in work, leisure and education.
Publication: Survey
Publication title: Attitudes to Music in the UK
Meetings/Conventions: London International Music Show – annual show – Exhibits.

03146

Music Managers Forum
MMF

c/o British Music House
26 Berners St., London, W1T 3LR, UK
Tel: 020 73064888
Email: info@themmf.net
Website: http://www.themmf.net
Contact: Jon Webster, CEO
Fee: £440
Membership Type: company
Fee: £240
Membership Type: full
Description: Represents the interests of managers in the music industry. Runs comprehensive training courses throughout the country and has international chapters across the globe.
Formerly: Formerly, International Managers Forum

03147

Music Masters' and Mistresses' Association
MMA

8 The Crescent, Storey's Way, Cambridge, CB3 0AZ, UK
Website: http://www.mma-online.org.uk
Members: 950
Contact: Sophie Kirk, Membership Sec.
Fee: £51
Membership Type: full
Fee: £27
Membership Type: retired, associate
Description: Music educators. Aims to further all aspects of music in schools. Annual conferences are held at a different school every year, courses and regional meetings are held throughout the year.

03148

Music Producers Guild
MPG

PO Box 38134, London, W10 6XL, UK
Tel: 020 32397606
Email: sue@whitenoisepr.co.uk
Website: http://www.mpg.org.uk/home
Members: 220
Contact: Steve Levine, Chm.
Fee: £120
Membership Type: full
Fee: £55
Membership Type: associate
Description: Record producers and engineers in the UK and overseas.
Formerly: Formerly, Guild of Recording Producers, Directors and Engineers
Publication title: A & R Guidelines
Meetings/Conventions: V and A Show – annual show – Exhibits.

03149

Music Publishers Association
MPA

6th Fl., British Music House, 26 Berners St., London, W1T 3LR, UK
Tel: 020 75800126
Fax: 020 76373929
Email: info@mpaonline.org.uk
Website: http://www.mpaonline.org.uk
Members: 200
Staff: 5
Contact: Stephen Navin, Chief Exec.
Description: Represents and promotes the interests of its music publisher members to government, within the music industry and generally.
Publication: Catalog
Publication title: Catalogue of Printed Music

03150

Musical Box Society of Great Britain
MBSGB

PO Box 373, Welwyn, AL6 0WY, UK
Website: http://www.mbsgb.org.uk
Members: 500
Fee: £24
Membership Type: in UK, in Europe
Fee: £75
Membership Type: in U.S.
Description: Aims to further the interest in an appreciation of all forms of mechanical music.
Publication: Journal
Publication title: Music Box. Advertisements.

03151

Musicians Union
MU

60-62 Clapham Rd., London, SW9 0JJ, UK
Tel: 020 75825566
Fax: 020 75829805
Email: info@musicianunion.org.uk
Website: http://www.musiciansunion.org.uk
Members: 31000
Staff: 48
Contact: John F. Smith, Gen. Sec.
Fee: £155-275
Membership Type: individual (based on previous year's gross earnings for music)
Fee: £75
Membership Type: student
Description: Performers engaged in the music profession including music writers and instrumental music teachers and instructors. Secures the organization of members for mutual protection and advancement; improves the status and remuneration of members and provides assistance when needed.
Publication: Magazine
Publication title: Musician. Advertisements.

03152

MUTA

3 Priory Ct., Pilgrim St., London, EC4V 6DR, UK
Tel: 0207 6189196
Fax: 0207 3297301
Email: info@muta.org.uk
Website: http://www.muta.org.uk
Members: 283
Contact: Dan Wilson Craw, Sec.
Fee: £210-652
Membership Type: company (based on number of employees)
Fee: £410
Membership Type: supplier, overseas associate
Description: Companies engaged in the manufacture and processing of tarpaulins, marquees, tents, awnings, sails flags, inflatables, reusable healthcare textiles and banners. Represents the interests of companies which manufacture and process heavy textiles. Represents its members in international, European and national standards organizations and by lobbying government departments in London and Brussels. MUTA members use their collective expertise to develop codes of practice for the industry and to initiate research in relevant technologies.
Formerly: Formerly, Made Up Textiles Association
Meetings/Conventions: MUTA Trade Fair – semiannual conference – Exhibits.

03153

Muzzle Loaders Association of Great Britain
MLAGB

c/o Louise Ward, Membership Mgr.
7 Olympus Ct., Tachbrook Park, Warwick, CV34 6RZ, UK
Tel: 01926 458198
Email: membership@mlagb.com
Website: http://www.mlagb.com
Members: 2000
Staff: 2
Contact: Ken Hocking, Chm.
Fee: £44
Membership Type: full, affiliated
Fee: £33.5
Membership Type: senior citizen, family/shooting

Description: Collectors, students, shooters of antique muzzle loading firearms and replicas thereof. Concerned with the use and study of antique firearms, particularly the safe and effective use of muzzle loading rifles, pistols and shotguns together with safeguarding of the rights of members to own and use them.
Publication: Newsletter
Publication title: Black Powder Newsletter. Advertisements.

03154

Myasthenia Gravis Association MGA

The College Business Centre, Uttoxeter New Rd., Derby, DE23 6UQ, UK
Tel: 01332 290219
Fax: 01332 293641
Email: mg@mga-charity.org
Website: http://www.mga-charity.org
Members: 1125
Staff: 18
Description: Supports research in management and cure of Myasthenia.
Publication: Magazine
Publication title: MGA News

03155

MYCCI

Lockwood Hall, Lockwood Park, Brewery Dr., Huddersfield, HD4 6EN, UK
Email: info@mycci.co.uk
Website: http://www.mycci.co.uk
Members: 1800
Staff: 400
Contact: Andrew Choi, Exec. Dir.
Fee: £12.99
Membership Type: sole trader
Fee: £19.99
Membership Type: professional
Description: Represents members across Mid-Yorkshire at local, regional and national level on matters concerning trade, commerce and industry and lobbying. Facilitates networking, forums and events to enable members to exchange ideas, information, views and business practice.

03156

NACE International - United Kingdom Section

CMC Ltd., 48 Lexham Gardens, Ste. 5, London, W8 5JA, UK
Tel: 0207 4609408
Email: p.sidky@cmc.ltd.uk
Website: http://web.nace.org/Departments/Membership/Chapters
Contact: Paulette Sidky, Contact
Description: Promotes public safety by advancing the knowledge of corrosion engineering and science. Works to raise awareness of corrosion control and prevention technology among government agencies and legislators, businesses, professional societies and the general public.

03157

Nacro

Park Pl., 10-12 Lawn Ln., London, SW8 1UD, UK
Tel: 020 78407200
Fax: 020 78407240
Email: helpline@nacro.org.uk
Website: http://www.nacro.org.uk
Staff: 1500
Contact: Matthew Litobarski, Chm.
Description: Individuals and organizations in sympathy with organization's aims; organizations actively concerned with after-care or the prevention of crime. Helps people who have been in trouble with the law and those at risk of becoming so to deal with the problems they face and to be reaccepted into society without stigma. Promotes a more humane and constructive criminal justice system and to prevent crime.
Formerly: Formerly, National Association for the Care and Resettlement of Offenders
Publication: Catalog
Publication title: Publications Catalogue

03158

Napoleonic Association NA

c/o Chrissy Wisken
7 Fair Oak, Wokingham, RG41 1LX, UK
Tel: 0118 9783006
Email: enquiries@napoleonicassociation.org
Website: http://www.napoleonicassociation.org
Members: 750
Staff: 6
Contact: Lesley Stene, Membership Sec.
Fee: £22
Membership Type: individual
Fee: £29
Membership Type: family
Description: Members of the armed forces, civil servants, film and stage professionals, historians, academics, and others interested in the study of battles fought by European armies from 1796 to 1815 and known as the Napoleonic Wars. Studies and recreates, for public entertainment and instruction, the uniforms, equipment, and tactics of the European armies during the Napoleonic Wars and periods of the French Empire. Performs drills and battle maneuvers of the period including wargames and re-enactments. Provides drill groups and live firing for film and television work; makes available to members collections of memoirs, orders of battles, and drill manuals. Compiles statistics.

03159

NARA: The Association of Property and Fixed Charge Receivers

PO Box 629, Oldham, OL1 9HH, UK
Tel: 0870 6001925
Email: admin@nara.org.uk
Website: http://www.nara.org.uk
Contact: Carolyn Hirst, Admin.
Fee: £176.25
Membership Type: fellowship
Fee: £195
Membership Type: associate
Description: Represents professionals from the property, legal, and insolvency disciplines. Fosters relationships between lenders and non-administrative receivers as well as members and the providers of Registered Property Receivers Practicing Licenses. Provides education and training to maintain the highest standards in the profession.
Formerly: Formerly, Non-Administrative Receivers Association
Publication: Newsletter
Publication title: Narator

03160

Narcolepsy Association United Kingdom UKAN

PO Box 13842, Penicuik, EH26 8WX, UK
Tel: 0845 4500394
Fax: 0870 7773039
Email: info@narcolepsy.org.uk
Website: http://www.narcolepsy.org.uk
Members: 700
Fee: £10
Membership Type: ordinary (domestic)
Fee: £15
Membership Type: ordinary (overseas)
Description: Narcoleptics, their relatives, and others interested in improving the lives of those afflicted with narcolepsy. Promotes awareness of narcolepsy and provides authoritative information about it to narcoleptics, the medical profession, and to the public. Supports the establishment of local self-help groups; encourages research; cooperates with narcolepsy associations overseas.
Publication: Newsletter
Publication title: Catnap

03161

Narcotics Anonymous UK Region UKNA

202 City Rd., London, EC1V 2PH, UK
Tel: 020 72514007
Fax: 020 72514006
Email: ukso@ukna.org
Website: http://www.ukna.org
Description: Provides a recovery process and support network for drug addicts. Facilitates and stabilizes the recovery of the members. Uses 12-step program adapted from Alcoholics Anonymous to aid in the recovery process.

03162

NASEN

Nasen House, 4/5 Amber Business Village, Amber Close, Amington, Tamworth, B77 4RP, UK
Tel: 01827 311500
Fax: 01827 313005
Email: welcome@nasen.org.uk
Website: http://www.nasen.org.uk
Members: 5000
Staff: 7
Contact: Lorraine Petersen, CEO
Fee: £68
Membership Type: individual - in UK
Fee: £88
Membership Type: small school (maximum of 140 pupils)
Description: Mainly teachers and other practitioners in special education, also lectures in further and higher education, LEA staff, HMI and those from the caring professions. Promotes the development of children and young people with special educational needs, wherever they are located, and supports those who work with them. Details of course, conferences, and publications may be obtained.
Formerly: Formerly, National Association for Special Educational Needs
Publication: Journal
Publication title: British Journal of Special Education. Advertisements.

03163
National Acrylic Painters' Association
NAPA
134 Rake Ln., Wirral, Merseyside, Wallasey, CH45 1JW, UK
Tel: 0151 6392980
Fax: 0151 6392980
Email: alan.edwards420@ntlworld.com
Website: http://www.napauk.org
Members: 433
Contact: Alan Edwards, Sec.
Fee: £30
Membership Type: regular
Description: Promotes usage and understanding of the need for acrylic paints.
Library Subject: acrylics
Library Type: reference
Publication: Newspaper
Publication title: International NAPA Newspaper

03164
National AIDS Trust
NAT
New City Cloisters, 196 Old St., London, EC1V 9FR, UK
Tel: 020 78146767
Fax: 020 72160111
Email: info@nat.org.uk
Website: http://www.nat.org.uk
Staff: 19
Contact: Deborah Jack, Chief Exec.
Description: Aims to transform society's response to HIV. Provides fresh thinking, expert advice and practical resources. Campaigns for change, shaping attitudes, challenging injustice and changing lives.
Publication: Reports
Publication title: Commissioning HIV Prevention Activities in England

03165
National Animal Welfare Trust
Tyler's Way, Watford-By-Pass, Watford, WD25 8WT, UK
Tel: 020 89500177
Fax: 020 84204454
Email: d.warner@nawt.org.uk
Website: http://www.nawt.org.uk/headquarters/index.asp
Contact: David Warner, Chief Exec.
Description: Provides rescue for ill-treated and abandoned animals and birds.

03166
National Ankylosing Spondylitis Society
NASS
One Victoria Villas, Unit 2, Surrey, Richmond, TW9 2GW, UK
Tel: 020 89489117
Fax: 020 89407736
Email: admin@nass.co.uk
Website: http://www.nass.co.uk
Members: 6000
Staff: 5
Contact: Jane Skerrett, Dir.
Fee: £20
Membership Type: standard (UK only)
Fee: £6
Membership Type: concession (UK only)
Description: Patients, doctors and physiotherapists of ankylosing spondylitis. Promotes patient education in the medical and social aspects of ankylosing spondylitis. Provides support through local UK groups for supervised physiotherapy one evening per week.
Library Type: not open to the public
Publication: Newsletter

03167
National Anti-Vivisection Society
NAVS
Millbank Tower, Millbank, London, SW1P 4QP, UK
Tel: 020 76303340
Fax: 020 78282179
Website: http://www.navs.org.uk/home
Members: 30000
Staff: 25
Contact: Jan Creamer, Chief Exec.
Description: Campaigns to end all animal experiments. Aims to educate parliament and the public about the dangers of relying upon animal research.

03168
National Assembly of Women
NAW
92 Wansbeck Ave., Tyne and Wear, Cullercoats, NE30 3DJ, UK
Tel: 0191 2520961
Email: naw@sisters.org.uk
Website: http://www.sisters.org.uk
Members: 1000
Contact: Dona Feltham, Pres.
Fee: £15
Membership Type: individual
Fee: £30
Membership Type: affiliate (regional)
Description: Women of all classes, intellectual and physical description, color, race, sexual orientation and religion. Works to raise the economic, social, and legal status of women. Campaigns for international peace and understanding. Organizes educational and campaign meetings for both members and nonmembers.
Publication: Pamphlet
Publication title: A Short History of the National Assembly of Women

03169
National Association Agricultural Contractors
NAAC
The Old Cart Shed, Easton Lodge Farm, Old Oundle Rd., Wansford, Peterborough, PE8 6NP, UK
Tel: 08456 448750
Fax: 01780 784933
Email: jill.hewitt@naac.co.uk
Website: http://www.naac.co.uk
Members: 400
Staff: 3
Contact: Jill Hewitt, Chief Exec.
Description: Represents agricultural and amenity contractors in United Kingdom and their commercial and regulatory interests at the national level.
Publication: Newsletter
Publication title: Contractors Bulletin. Advertisements.

03170
National Association for Areas of Outstanding Natural Beauty
NAAONB
Fosse Way, Gloucestershire, Northleach, GL54 3JH, UK
Tel: 01451 862007
Fax: 01451 862001
Email: jill.smith@cotswoldsaonb.org.uk
Website: http://www.aonb.org.uk
Contact: Jill Smith, Communications and Development Mgr.
Description: Represents individuals responsible and involved in the management of all protected landscape areas of international importance in the UK. Promotes the awareness and commitment to Areas of Outstanding Natural Beauty (AONB). Acts as a focus for technical information and expertise on the protection and management of AONBs.
Publication: Newsletter
Publication title: AONB News

03171
National Association for Educational Guidance for Adults
NAEGA
c/o SAS Event Management
The Old George Brewery, Rollestone St., Wiltshire, SP1 1DX, UK
Tel: 01722 415154
Email: admin@naega.org.uk
Website: http://www.naega.org.uk
Members: 1000
Contact: Ann Ruthven, Chair
Fee: £50
Membership Type: personal
Fee: £25
Membership Type: associate, student
Description: Members include individuals and organisations who are involved in adult guidance. Aims to promote the provision of adult guidance services, encourage high standards of practice, promote equal access to learning and work opportunities for adults in the UK.

03172
National Association for Environmental Education
NAEE
University of Wolverhampton, Walsall Campus, Gorway Rd., Walsall, WS1 3BD, UK
Tel: 01922 631200
Fax: 01922 631200
Email: info@naee.org.uk
Website: http://www.naee.org.uk
Members: 1000
Staff: 16
Contact: Sue Fenoughty, Sec.
Fee: £25
Membership Type: institutional
Fee: £40
Membership Type: Europe
Description: Represents teachers, lecturers and others concerned with education and the environment. Works in all types of schools, colleges, polytechnics and universities. Produces a timely journal and a series of practical guides for promoting environmental education in schools.
Publication: Journal
Publication title: Environmental Education. Advertisements.

03173
National Association for Gifted Children
NAGC

Challenge House, Ste. 14, Sherwood Dr., Bletchley, Milton Keynes, MK3 6DP, UK
Tel: 0845 4500295
Fax: 0870 7703219
Email: amazingchildren@nagcbritain.org.uk
Website: http://www.nagcbritain.org.uk
Members: 2000
Staff: 10
Contact: Denise Yates, Chief Exec.
Fee: £35
Membership Type: family
Fee: £40-60
Membership Type: organization
Description: Institutions, families, and individuals. Seeks to enable gifted children to fulfill their potential and to render parents, health visitors, and persons who care for very young children more aware of the special needs of gifted children. Provides parents of gifted children with confidential counselling and support as well as opportunities for exchange of ideas and information. Works to improve the provision of the school system for gifted children.
Publication: Book
Publication title: A Bright Start

03174
National Association for Literature Development
NALD

PO Box 243, Ilkley, LS29 7ET, UK
Email: director@nald.org
Website: http://www.nald.org
Contact: Steve Dearden, Dir.
Fee: £30
Membership Type: basic
Description: Represents developing writers and readers of literature. Disseminates knowledge and skills relating to literature. Provides professional development and training.

03175
National Association for Pastoral Care in Education
NAPCE

PO Box 4997, Coventry, CV4 0FD, UK
Tel: 07531 453670
Email: base@napce.org.uk
Website: http://www.napce.org.uk
Members: 1000
Staff: 2
Contact: Jill Robson, Chair
Fee: £66
Membership Type: group
Fee: £44
Membership Type: individual
Description: Supports individuals that have professional concern for pastoral care. Promotes the theoretical study of pastoral care in education and disseminates good practice in pastoral care in education. Also aims to promote the education, training and development of those engaged in pastoral care and to laities with other organizations having similar objects.
Publication: Journal
Publication title: Pastoral Care in Education. Advertisements.

03176
National Association for Pre-Paid Funeral Plans
NAPFP

15 Riverside Dr., West Midlands, Solihull, B91 3HH, UK
Tel: 0121 7055133
Email: burtonnr@btinternet.com
Website: http://www.napfp.co.uk
Members: 7
Description: Represents the majority of funeral plan companies in the United Kingdom.

03177
National Association for Premenstrual Syndrome
NAPS

41 Old Rd., East Peckham, Kent, TN12 5AP, UK
Tel: 0844 8157311
Email: contact@pms.org.uk
Website: http://www.pms.org.uk
Members: 1000
Staff: 7
Contact: Nicholas Panay, Chm.
Fee: £25
Membership Type: standard
Fee: £50
Membership Type: professional
Description: Provides advice and support to those affected by and treating PMS and postnatal depression. Undertakes research, clinical trials, professional development and provides clinical advice.
Library Subject: understanding PMS, dietary guidelines for PMS
Library Type: reference
Publication: Newsletter
Publication title: NAPS News

03178
National Association for Primary Education
NAPE

University of Leicester, Moulton College, Moulton, Northampton, NN3 7RR, UK
Tel: 01604 647646
Fax: 01604 647660
Email: nationaloffice@nape.org.uk
Website: http://www.nape.org.uk
Members: 1500
Staff: 1
Contact: Pady Powell, Chm.
Fee: £20
Membership Type: individual
Fee: £30
Membership Type: school
Description: Membership includes teachers, school communities, parents and all interested in the primary phase of schooling and child development. Works so that all children should enjoy access to full educational opportunity. Believes that the primary phase of education should receive equal resourcing per pupil to every other phase and that the education of children is a partnership between parents, schools and other concerned groups and that good practice is a matter of continual debate.
Publication: Newsletter
Publication title: Newsbrief. Advertisements.

03179
National Association for Professional Inspectors and Testers
NAPIT

4th Fl., Mill 3, Pleasley Vale Business Park, Mansfield, NG19 8RL, UK
Tel: 0845 5430330
Fax: 0845 5430332
Email: info@napit.org.uk
Website: http://www.napit.org.uk
Contact: John Andrews, Chief Exec.
Fee: £399.5
Membership Type: full
Description: Represents electrical, plumbing, heating and ventilation professionals. Sets standards for the inspecting and testing industry. Carries out equipment testing and electrical installation, as well as testing in commercial and industrial sectors.

03180
National Association for Small Schools
NASS

Cloudshill, High St., Shutford, Banbury, OX15 6PQ, UK
Tel: 01295 780225
Fax: 01295 780308
Email: mbenford@bigfoot.com
Website: http://www.smallschools.org.uk
Members: 300
Contact: Mervyn Benford, Information Off.
Fee: £10
Membership Type: individual
Fee: £15
Membership Type: school
Description: Parish councils, rural community councils, governing bodies, schools, parents' and friends' groups, charities, Diocesan boards of education and individuals interested in supporting village schools. Aims to provide a voice and a link for those who believe that small schools, particularly in rural areas, have educational and social roles to perform, too precious to lose. Provides advice and assistance to schools facing closure proposals.

03181
National Association for Teaching English and other Community Languages to Adults
NATECLA

Rm. HA205, South Birmingham College, Hall Green Campus, Cole Bank Rd., Hall Green, Birmingham, B28 8ES, UK
Tel: 0121 6888121
Fax: 0121 6945062
Email: co-ordinator@natecla.fsnet.co.uk
Website: http://www.natecla.org.uk
Members: 600
Staff: 2
Contact: Patricia Sullivan, Co-Chair
Fee: £35
Membership Type: paid teacher/organizer over 18.5 hours per week
Fee: £20
Membership Type: paid teacher/organizer 4.5-18.5 hours per week
Description: Individual teachers, volunteers and community workers using English or community languages

with multilingual groups; colleges and adult education institutions and organisations providing vocational training as associate members. A forum for ESOL and community language tutors, and others working with multilingual people settled in the UK. Its publications include practical ideas and reviews. Expertise is shared through conferences and training events; new initiatives in the field may be developed through working parties.
Formerly: Formerly, NATESLA
Publication: Journal
Publication title: Language Issues. Advertisements.

03182
National Association for the Teaching of English
NATE
50 Broadfield Rd., S Yorkshire, Sheffield, S8 0XJ, UK
Tel: 0114 2555419
Fax: 0114 2555296
Email: info@nate.org.uk
Website: http://www.nate.org.uk
Members: 3000
Staff: 8
Contact: Ian McNeilly, Dir.
Fee: £90
Membership Type: institution
Fee: £75
Membership Type: individual
Description: Individuals, school departments, colleges, university libraries, advisers in English. Aims to support the teaching of English at all levels by publishing books for and by teachers, organizing conferences and INSET courses and a network of local branches. Gives English teachers a forum for discussion and a national voice.
Publication: Newsletter
Publication title: NATENews

03183
National Association for Voluntary and Community Action
NAVCA
The Tower, 2 Furnival Sq., Sheffield, S1 4QL, UK
Tel: 0114 2786636
Fax: 0114 2787004
Email: navca@navca.org.uk
Website: http://www.navca.org.uk
Contact: Kevin Curley, Chief Exec.
Fee: £339.6
Membership Type: local infrastructure organization (based on annual income), affiliate (based on annual income)
Fee: £30-250
Membership Type: friend (individual, corporate)
Description: Promotes and supports the local voluntary and community action. Provides information, advice, networking and learning opportunities to members. Helps to combat poverty and discrimination.
Publication: Newsletter
Publication title: Circulation

03184
National Association of British and Irish Millers
NABIM
21 Arlington St., London, SW1A 1RN, UK
Tel: 020 74932521
Fax: 020 74936785
Email: info@nabim.org.uk
Website: http://www.nabim.org.uk
Members: 32
Staff: 14
Contact: Alexander Waugh, Dir. Gen.
Description: Acts as a trade association for UK flour milling industry.

03185
National Association of Catering Butchers
NACB
224 Central Markets, London, EC1A 9LH, UK
Tel: 020 72481896
Fax: 020 73290658
Email: info@nacb.co.uk
Website: http://www.nacb.co.uk
Members: 90
Staff: 3
Contact: Peter Allen, Chm.
Description: Catering butchers whose premises have been inspected and approved by the Plant Evaluation Committee and who maintain the required standard. Seeks to raise the standards of catering butchery throughout the UK; aims to promote through the catering press so as to ensure a greater volume of business for members and to protect the interests of its members through negotiations with the authorities in London and Brussels.

03186
National Association of Chimney Engineers
NACE
PO Box 849, Metheringham, Lincoln, LN4 3WU, UK
Tel: 01526 322555
Fax: 01526 323181
Email: info@nace.org.uk
Website: http://www.nace.org.uk
Contact: Michael Carr, Sec.
Description: Aims to ensure the safety of all fuel users who depend upon a chimney or flue for the operation of a heating appliance by providing a register of competent and qualified chimney engineers for all types of chimney work.
Formerly: Formerly, National Association of Chimney Lining Engineers

03187
National Association of Chimney Sweeps
NACS
Unit 15, Emerald Way, Stone Business Park, Staffordshire, Stone, ST15 0SR, UK
Tel: 01785 811732
Fax: 01785 811712
Email: nacs@chimneyworks.co.uk
Website: http://www.nacs.org.uk
Members: 300
Staff: 2
Contact: Martin P. Glynn, Pres./Dir./Sec.
Description: Represents individual chimney sweeps and allied suppliers. Encourages regular sweeping of flues for safety and environmental reasons. Aims to raise the standard of professional work through training and qualifications.
Meetings/Conventions: Chimney Works – annual trade show – Exhibits.

03188
National Association of Choirs
NAC
Wollaton Park, 35 Hawton Crescent, Nottingham, NG8 1BZ, UK
Tel: 0115 9788847
Email: general.secretary@nationalassociationofchoirs.org.uk
Website: http://www.nationalassociationofchoirs.org.uk
Members: 520
Contact: Frank Rhodes, VP
Fee: £34
Membership Type: corporate
Fee: £17
Membership Type: individual, youth choir
Description: Promotes, develops, and maintains public education and appreciation of the art and science of choral music. Provides comprehensive services to choirs including Annual Year Book, trimestrial magazine, music loan/search, festivals information, insurance, charity registration and banking, organization of group choral activities and annual conference/concert.
Publication: Newsletter
Publication title: News and Views. Advertisements.

03189
National Association of Citizens Advice Bureaux
CAB
Myddleton House, 115-123 Pentonville Rd., London, N1 9LZ, UK
Tel: 020 78332181
Fax: 020 78334371
Website: http://www.citizensadvice.org.uk
Contact: David Harker, CEO
Description: Delivers quality advice and information from Citizens Advice Bureaux across England, Wales and Northern Ireland, as well as by telephone, internet and media; advice provided is free, independent, confidential, impartial and open to everybody. Coordinates social policy, media, publicity and parliamentary work.
Formerly: Also Known As, Citizens Advice

03190
National Association of Colitis and Crohn's Disease
NACC
4 Beaumont House, Sutton Rd., St. Albans, AL1 5HH, UK
Tel: 01727 830038
Email: nacc@nacc.org.uk
Website: http://www.nacc.org.uk/content/home.asp
Members: 30000
Staff: 16
Contact: Richard Driscoll, Dir.
Fee: £12
Membership Type: regular
Fee: £15
Membership Type: overseas
Description: Patients, relatives, health professionals, and anyone interested in colitis and Crohn's disease. Provides support and information for patients and families living with these conditions.

03191

National Association of Commercial Finance Brokers NACFB

3 Silverdown Office Park, Fair Oak Close, Devon, Exeter, EX5 2UX, UK
Tel: 01392 440040
Fax: 01392 363931
Email: admin@nacfb.org.uk
Website: http://www.nacfb.org
Contact: Adam Tyler, Chief Exec.
Fee: £120
Membership Type: associate
Fee: £220
Membership Type: full
Description: Seeks to protect consumer from fraud and malpractice in the commercial finance industry. Raises professional standards of commercial finance brokers. Provides training, education and information.
Publication: Newsletter
Meetings/Conventions: Commercial Finance Expo – annual conference – Exhibits.

03192

National Association of Counsellors, Hypnotherapists and Psychotherapists NACHP

PO Box 719, Burwell, Cambridge, CB5 0NX, UK
Tel: 0870 8505383
Email: mail@nachp.org
Website: http://www.nachp.org
Members: 105
Staff: 4
Contact: James Hammond, Chm.
Description: Works as a registered charity for accrediting, training of therapists, and educating and protecting the general public about therapy.

03193

National Association of Cytologists NAC

Southmead Hospital, Cytology Training Centre, Bristol, BS10 5NB, UK
Tel: 0117 3235649
Fax: 0117 3235640
Email: mike.rowell@virgin.net
Website: http://www.nac.org.uk
Contact: Mike Rowell, Pres.
Fee: £30
Membership Type: regular
Fee: £10
Membership Type: trainee
Description: Seeks to advance the cytology profession through research and information gathering from members and different professional groups.
Publication: Journal
Publication title: SCAN

03194

National Association of Deafened People NADP

PO Box 50, Amersham, HP6 6XB, UK
Tel: 0845 559663
Fax: 01305 262591
Email: enquiries@nadp.org.uk
Website: http://www.nadp.org.uk
Members: 500
Contact: Ross Trotter, Chm.
Description: People with acquired profound hearing loss and professionals associated with them. Aims to work for improvements in the quality of life of deafened people, by providing a support service of information and advice and promoting an improvement in education, training and rehabilitation opportunities available. Increases public awareness of the needs and problems of deafened people, and to support research.
Publication: Booklet
Publication title: An Introduction to Cochlear Implants

03195

National Association of Decorative and Fine Arts Societies NADFAS

NADFAS House, 8 Guilford St., London, WC1N 1DA, UK
Tel: 020 74300730
Fax: 020 72420686
Email: enquiries@nadfas.org.uk
Website: http://www.nadfas.org.uk
Members: 90000
Staff: 14
Contact: David Bell, Chief Exec.
Description: Membership is through local societies. There are no qualifications for membership other than an interest in the decorative and fine arts. Works to promote and advance the aesthetic education of the public, the cultivation, appreciation and study of the decorative and fine arts and the giving of aid to the preservation of the national artistic heritage for the benefit of the public.
Publication: Magazine
Publication title: NADFAS Review. Advertisements.

03196

National Association of Estate Agents NAEA

Arbon House, 6 Tournament Ct., Edgehill Dr., Warwick, CV34 6LG, UK
Tel: 01926 496800
Fax: 01926 808182
Email: info@naea.co.uk
Website: http://www.naea.co.uk
Members: 10000
Fee: £175
Membership Type: regular, fellow
Fee: £115
Membership Type: student
Description: Estate agents in the United Kingdom. Promotes the use of estate agents. Sets standards for members.
Formerly: Absorbed, Federation of Overseas Property Developers, Agents and Consultants

03197

National Association of Farriers, Blacksmiths and Agricultural Engineers NAFBAE

The Forge, Ave. B, 10th St., Stoneleigh Park, Warwikshire, Kenilworth, CV8 2LG, UK
Tel: 024 76696595
Fax: 024 76696708
Email: nafbaehq@nafbae.org
Website: http://www.forgemagazine.co.uk
Members: 1000
Staff: 2
Contact: Craig D'Arcy, Pres.
Description: Farriers, blacksmiths and trade suppliers. Association for the craft of farriers and blacksmiths. Provides insurance, pension funds and healthcare plan services to farriers, blacksmiths and trade supplier members.
Publication: Magazine
Publication title: Forge. Advertisements.

03198

National Association of Flower Arrangement Societies NAFAS

Osborne House, 12 Devonshire Sq., London, EC2M 4TE, UK
Tel: 020 72475567
Fax: 020 72477232
Email: flowers@nafas.org.uk
Members: 70000
Staff: 4
Contact: Valerie Best, Natl. Chair/CEO
Fee: £35
Membership Type: individual affiliate
Description: Dedicated amateur flower arrangers. Aims to advance public education in the art of flower arranging and related subjects; to encourage the love of flowers and to demonstrate their decorative value; to instruct, train and qualify judges, demonstrators, teachers and speakers in order to raise the standard of work throughout the Country.
Publication: Magazine
Publication title: The Flower Arranger. Advertisements.

03199

National Association of Funeral Directors NAFD

618 Warwick Rd., Solihull, B91 1AA, UK
Tel: 0121 7111343
Fax: 0121 7111351
Email: info@nafd.org.uk
Website: http://www.nafd.org.uk/funeral-advice/funeral-advice-home.aspx
Members: 3266
Staff: 11
Contact: Alan Slater, CEO
Description: Funeral director firms and suppliers within the UK and overseas. Represents funeral service interests to government departments, local authorities, etc. Protects and assists the rights of members.
Library Type: reference
Publication: Magazine
Publication title: Funeral Director Monthly. Advertisements.
Meetings/Conventions: annual conference

03200

National Association of Goldsmiths NAG

78a Luke St., London, EC2A 4XG, UK
Tel: 020 76134445
Email: michael@jewellers-online.org
Website: http://www.jewellers-online.org/pages/home.php
Members: 1500
Contact: Michael Hoare, Chief Exec.
Fee: £195-650
Membership Type: ordinary (based on number of persons)

Fee: £52-63
Membership Type: additional branch (1-99)
Description: Represents the retail jewellers in Great Britain and Ireland. Promotes the industry and provides its members with services to achieve high standards in the profession.
Publication: Book
Publication title: Photoatlas of Inclusions in Gemstones

03201

National Association of Head Teachers NAHT

1 Heath Sq., Boltro Rd., W Sussex, Haywards Heath, RH16 1BL, UK
Tel: 01444 472472
Email: info@naht.org.uk
Website: http://www.naht.org.uk
Members: 28000
Staff: 33
Contact: Mick Brookes, Gen. Sec.
Description: Heads/principals, deputy heads/vice-principals of schools and colleges. Provides a ready means of communication for all members; renders help to all members in cases of professional difficulty; furthers the cause of education generally; upholds a high standard of professional conduct among members and to regulate relations between members and their employers.
Publication: Magazine
Publication title: Head Teachers Review

03202

National Association of Hospital Fire Officers NAHFO

c/o David Cox, Treas.
University Hospital of Wales, Cardiff and Vales NHS Trust, Health Park, Cardiff, CF14 4XW, UK
Tel: 029 20744646
Fax: 029 20744789
Website: http://www.nahfo.org
Members: 350
Description: Hospital fire prevention officers throughout the UK. Promotes and encourages the furtherance of the highest standards of fire safety in health service premises.
Meetings/Conventions: annual conference – Exhibits.

03203

National Association of Language Advisers NALA

c/o Adrian Finbow, Treas.
8 Linden Close, Edenfield, Lancashire, BL0 0LN, UK
Tel: 01706 825569
Email: j.mcelwee@btinternet.com
Website: http://www.nala.org.uk
Members: 210
Contact: J. McElwee, Honorary Sec.
Fee: £50
Membership Type: ordinary
Description: Advisers, inspectors, and consultants in modern languages in education. Supports modern language professionals in their work.

03204

National Association of Laryngectomee Clubs NALC

Lower Ground Fl., 152 Buckingham Palace Rd., London, SW1W 9TR, UK
Tel: 020 77308585
Fax: 020 77308584
Website: http://www.laryngectomy.org.uk
Members: 4000
Staff: 2
Contact: Marilyn Jones, Pres.
Description: Promotes the welfare of laryngectomees by providing literature to them, their friends and their families and also the relevant professionals. Membership is via a club only.

03205

National Association of Licensed Paralegals NALP

3.08 Canterbury Ct., 1-3 Brixton Rd., London, SW9 6DE, UK
Tel: 020 31760900
Email: info@nationalparalegals.co.uk
Website: http://www.nationalparalegals.com
Members: 5000
Staff: 7
Contact: Shane Wood, Business Development Mgr.
Fee: £30
Membership Type: student
Fee: £40
Membership Type: associate, fellow, graduate
Description: Works to supervise the system of self-regulation and licensing of Paralegals. Seeks to reinforce and constantly increase its position as the leading professional body catering solely for the needs of the Para-Legal. Strives to ensure the proper recognition of its members by the auditing of its qualifications, professional development and standards of behavior laid down for its members. Encourages and develops the role and practice of the Para-Legal and represents the interests of its members.
Formerly: Formerly, National Association of Paralegals

03206

National Association of Local Councils NALC

109 Great Russell St., London, WC1B 3LD, UK
Tel: 020 76371865
Fax: 020 74367451
Email: nalc@nalc.gov.uk
Website: http://www.nalc.gov.uk
Members: 10000
Staff: 21
Contact: John Findlay, Chief Exec.
Description: Parish, town, and community councils in England and Wales. Represents the national interests generally of member councils and gives advice and guidance to individual member councils normally supplied through the 48 county associations (addresses available on request).
Publication: Newsletter
Publication title: Direct Information Service

03207

National Association of Master Bakers - England NAMB

21 Baldock St., Ware, SG12 9DH, UK
Tel: 01920 468061
Fax: 01920 461632
Email: namb@masterbakers.co.uk
Website: http://www.masterbakers.co.uk
Members: 2050
Staff: 11
Contact: Ian Storey, Pres.
Description: Small and medium bakery and confectionery businesses in England and Wales. Protects and promotes the interests of master bakers throughout England and Wales.

03208

National Association of Mathematics Advisers NAMA

PO Box 51, Wotton-under-Edge, Gloucestershire, GL12 7XA, UK
Email: info@nama.org.uk
Website: http://www.nama.org.uk
Members: 365
Staff: 1
Contact: Lynn Churchman, Chair
Fee: £35
Membership Type: regular
Description: Members are mathematics inspectors, advisers and consultants. Aims to ensure that inspection, advice and support, individually and collectively, make an effective contribution to and provide information on mathematics education.

03209

National Association of Memorial Masons NAMM

1 Castle Mews, Warwickshire, Rugby, CV21 2XL, UK
Tel: 01788 542264
Fax: 01788 542276
Email: enquiries@namm.org.uk
Website: http://www.namm.org.uk
Members: 400
Staff: 4
Contact: Gerald Priestman, Chm.
Description: Retail and wholesale memorial masonry companies throughout the UK and suppliers of ancillary products (Associate Members). Also some overseas companies interested in the UK market. Employers organization for the memorial masonry trade. Concerned with liaison with burial authorities; drawing up Codes of Practice and technical information; running a Conciliation and Arbitration Service; training; disseminating memorialisation information; organizing trade and public exhibitions and negotiating wages for the industry.
Library Subject: memorial masonry and related topics
Library Type: not open to the public
Formerly: Formerly, National Association of Master Monumental Masons
Publication: Journal
Publication title: Review

03210

National Association of Mining History Organisations NAMHO

c/o Peak District Mining Museum
The Pavilion, Matlock Bath, Derbyshire, Matlock, DE4 3NR, UK
Tel: 01629 583834
Website: http://www.namho.org
Members: 80
Contact: Kevin Baker, Chm.
Fee: £15
Membership Type: organization
Description: Mining museums, mining history societies and other organizations interested in mining history. Representation of member organizations and furtherance of mining history. Serves as a contact point for enquiries about any aspect of mining history or exploration of disused mines.
Publication: Book
Publication title: Mining History Heritage Guide. Advertisements.

03211

National Association of Music Educators NAME

Gordon Lodge, Snitterton Rd., Matlock, DE4 3LZ, UK
Tel: 01629 760791
Email: lis.mccullough@ukonline.co.uk
Website: http://www.name2.org.uk
Members: 580
Staff: 1
Contact: Lis McCullough, Chair
Fee: £28-93
Membership Type: individual
Fee: £111
Membership Type: associate corporate
Description: A broad cross-section of music educators. Presses for the continued supply of well qualified music educators in schools and colleges; promotes professional dialogue and research and acts as a forum for exchange of good practice.
Formerly: Absorbed, Association for the Advancement of Teacher Education in Music

03212

National Association of Official Prison Visitors NAOPV

Azure House, 10 Imperial Ave., Westcliff-on-Sea, SS0 8NE, UK
Email: info@naopv.com
Website: http://www.naopv.com
Members: 800
Staff: 1
Contact: Ian Currie, Membership Sec.
Fee: £10
Description: Aims to befriend prisoners whilst in prison in England and Wales.

03213

National Association of Ovulation Method Instructors UK NAOMI

c/o The Billings Method Centre
4 Southgate Dr., West Sussex, Crawley, RH10 6RP, UK
Tel: 01444 881744
Fax: 01444 881744
Website: http://www.billingsnaomi.org
Description: Provides information on the Billings Ovulation Method of natural family planning; provides training for instructors. Enables couples to plan their families as they wish through the guidelines against conception.
Publication title: Resource List

03214

National Association of Paper Merchants NAPM

PO Box 2850, Nottingham, NG5 2WW, UK
Tel: 0115 8412129
Fax: 0115 8410831
Email: info@napm.org.uk
Website: http://www.napm.org.uk
Members: 40
Staff: 6
Contact: Tim Bowler, Dir.
Description: Trade association representing the interests of UK paper merchants.
Publication: Magazine
Publication title: Distribute

03215

National Association of Pension Funds NAPF

NIOC House, 138 Cheapside, London, EC2V 6AE, UK
Tel: 020 76011700
Fax: 020 76011799
Email: napf@napf.co.uk
Website: http://www.napf.co.uk
Members: 1300
Contact: Joanne Segars, Chief Exec.
Fee: £222-5000
Membership Type: fund
Fee: £450-9000
Membership Type: business
Description: Firms in the United Kingdom offering pensions. Provides a forum for the exchange of information between members. Promotes the availability of pensions.

03216

National Association of Percussion Teachers NAPT

11 Mallard Close, Kempshott, Basingstoke, RG22 5JP, UK
Email: natter@napt.org.uk
Website: http://www.napt.org.uk
Members: 181
Contact: Wendy Harding, Sec.
Fee: £25
Membership Type: individual
Fee: £85
Membership Type: corporate
Description: Percussion teachers. Brings together percussion teachers to share views and improve the quality of percussion teaching. Organizes an annual October conference.

03217

National Association of Press Agencies NAPA

c/o Mercury Press Agency
Contemporary Urban Centre, 2nd Fl., 41-51 Greenland St., Liverpool, L1 0BS, UK
Tel: 0870 6091935
Email: enquires@napa.org.uk
Website: http://www.napa.org.uk
Members: 50
Description: Members include some of Britain's major news and picture agencies, established correspondents for all leading newspapers, magazines, TV and broadcasting outlets. Concerned with safeguarding and promoting members' interests, with agencies covering most of Britain.

03218

National Association of Primary Care NAPC

Lettsom House, 11 Chandos St., Cavendish Sq., London, W1G 9DP, UK
Tel: 020 76367228
Fax: 020 76361601
Email: napc@napc.co.uk
Website: http://www.napc.co.uk
Members: 1000
Staff: 2
Contact: Johnny Marshall, Chm.
Fee: £1200
Membership Type: private sector
Description: GP fundholding practices in England, Scotland, Wales and Northern Ireland. Aims to promote good communication amongst fundholding practices; develop and extend the scope of services to patients offered by fundholding practices; encourage education research for and within fundholding practices; maintain and promote the highest ethical standards on the part of practitioners in fundholding practices; and encourage the creation of new fundholding practices.
Formerly: Formerly, National Association of Fundholding Practices

03219

National Association of Private Ambulance Services NAPAS

21 Bassenhally Rd., Whittlesey, Peterborough, PE7 1RN, UK
Tel: 01733 350916
Fax: 01733 350916
Email: napas@ambulanceservices.co.uk
Website: http://www.ambulanceservices.co.uk
Members: 63
Staff: 450
Contact: Peter A. Littledyke, Dir.
Description: Provides self-regulation for private and professional ambulance service throughout the U.K. and Ireland.
Library Subject: ambulance service all sections
Library Type: reference

03220
National Association of Probation Officers
NAPO
4 Chivalry Rd., London, SW11 1HT, UK
Tel: 020 72234887
Fax: 020 72233503
Email: info@napo.org.uk
Website: http://www.napo.org.uk
Members: 7500
Staff: 20
Contact: Jonathan Ledger, Gen. Sec.
Fee: £15
Membership Type: retired
Fee: £50
Membership Type: life - retired
Description: Probation officers and other grades of staff in the Probation Service in England, Wales, and Northern Ireland. Salaries and conditions of service. Probation practice issues. Campaigning on wide range of legal, penal and social issues and the promotion of anti-discriminatory practice in probation and the criminal justice system.
Publication: Newsletter
Publication title: NAPO News. Advertisements.

03221
National Association of Professionals with Language Impairment in Children
NAPLIC
29 Franklands Dr., Rowtown, Surrey, Addlestone, KT15 1EG, UK
Email: information@naplic.org.uk
Website: http://www.naplic.org.uk
Contact: John Parrott, Chm.
Fee: £20
Membership Type: general
Fee: £30
Membership Type: group, school
Description: Increases the awareness and understanding of children and young people with speech, language and communication needs. Promotes collaborative practice through professional discussion, cooperation and networking.
Publication: Journal
Publication title: Child Language and Teaching Therapy

03222
National Association of Schoolmasters and Union of Women Teachers
NASUWT
Rose Hill, Rednal, Birmingham, B45 8RS, UK
Tel: 0121 4536150
Fax: 0121 4576208
Email: nasuwt@mail.nasuwt.org.uk
Website: http://www.nasuwt.org.uk/index.htm
Members: 212000
Staff: 260
Contact: Chris Keates, Gen. Sec.
Description: Represents teachers in all sectors of education in UK; campaigns on issues of teacher workload and bureaucracy, induction of fair and transparent pay structure and pupil discipline.
Formerly: Formerly, National Association of Schoolmasters
Publication: Journal
Publication title: Career Teacher. Advertisements.

03223
National Association of Shopfitters
NAS
NAS House, 411 Limpsfield Rd., Warlingham, CR6 9HA, UK
Tel: 01883 624961
Fax: 01883 626841
Email: enquiries@shopfitters.org
Website: http://www.shopfitters.org
Members: 175
Staff: 3
Contact: Richard Easton, Pres.
Description: Bespoke shopfitting and interior contractors. Represents the major shopfitting companies throughout Great Britain. Work carried out by member companies covers interiors of all kinds, including shops, bars, offices, banks, public buildings, hotels and restaurants.
Publication: Newsletter
Publication title: Nastalk

03224
National Association of Steel Stockholders
NASS
The Citadel, 1st Fl., 190 Corporation St., Birmingham, B4 6QD, UK
Tel: 0121 2002288
Fax: 0121 2367444
Email: info@nass.org.uk
Website: http://www.nass.org.uk
Members: 70
Staff: 3
Contact: Bryan Holden, Contact
Fee: £750
Membership Type: full
Fee: £1000
Membership Type: associate
Description: Steel stockholders, processors, and firms providing services to steel stockholders. Represents members' interests before governmental and European Community agencies; encourages exchange of ideas and information between members. Organizes training courses; compiles statistics.
Library Subject: United Kingdom, European, world steel industry, stockholding
Library Type: not open to the public
Publication: Video
Publication title: Beating the Odds - Safety in Steel Stockholding
Meetings/Conventions: Steel Industry Dinner – annual dinner

03225
National Association of Street Entertainers
NASE
c/o John Arno, Sec.
8 Hartfield Ave., Brighton, BN1 8AE, UK
Tel: 07754 2951
Email: arno100@hotmail.com
Website: http://www.nase.org.uk
Members: 130
Staff: 1
Contact: Peter Moore, Chm.
Description: Street performers, festival and corporate acts.

03226
National Association of Student Employment Services
NASES
Centre for Lifelong Learning, University of Liverpool, 150 Mt. Pleasant, Liverpool, L69 3GD, UK
Tel: 0151 7944629
Fax: 0151 7945871
Email: nases@liv.ac.uk
Website: http://www.nases.org.uk
Contact: Alison Clark, Dir.
Fee: £150
Membership Type: HE institution
Fee: £500
Membership Type: corporate
Description: Represents the student employment service sector. Aims to facilitate continuing development and encourage interaction between practitioners of student employment services.
Publication: Book
Publication title: The Guide for Student Employment

03227
National Association of the Launderette Industry
NALI
33 Buckland Ave., Berkshire, SL3 7PJ, UK
Tel: 017 53521463
Website: http://www.nali.co.uk
Members: 1000
Staff: 2
Contact: A.R. Duckworth, Pres.
Fee: £60
Membership Type: regular
Description: Aims to unite launderette owners and their service providers (suppliers of equipment, consumer products and specialist business services).
Publication: Journal
Publication title: Launderette and Cleaning World. Advertisements.

03228
National Association of Women Pharmacists
NAWP
c/o Mrs. Ann Munday, Registrar
60 Riplingham Rd., East Yorks, Kirk Ella, HU10 7TR, UK
Email: enquiries@nawp.org.uk
Website: http://www.nawp.org.uk
Members: 300
Contact: Virginia Watson, Pres.
Fee: £30
Membership Type: full-time pharmacist
Fee: £20
Membership Type: part-time pharmacist
Description: Women pharmacists. Promotes the careers of women in pharmacy and the role of women pharmacists in public life. Encourages continuing education and career development for women pharmacists. Maintains communication with pharmacists who have left the Register of the Royal Pharmaceutical Society of Great Britain (RPSGB) during a career break. Works with other women's organizations. Conducts courses and lectures, provides mentoring for members.
Publication: Book
Publication title: Careers in Pharmacy
Meetings/Conventions: Recent Developments In Cancer Therapies – annual conference – Exhibits.

03229

National Association of Writers in Education
NAWE

PO Box 1, Sheriff Hutton, York, YO60 7YU, UK
Tel: 0165 3618429
Email: paul@nawe.co.uk
Website: http://www.nawe.co.uk/metadot/index.pl/NAWE
Members: 500
Contact: Paul Munden, Dir.
Fee: £20
Membership Type: student/associate
Fee: £75
Membership Type: institutional
Description: Open to all, including writers, teachers, arts advisers, students and librarians. Supports writers and creative writing of all genres in all educational settings throughout the United Kingdom. Maintains an online directory of extensive details on over 1000 writers. Produces Writing in Education magazine that is sent free to members three times per year.

03230

National Association of Youth Orchestras
NAYO

Central Hall, West Tollcross, Edinburgh, EH3 9BP, UK
Tel: 0131 2211927
Email: information@nayo.org.uk
Website: http://www.nayo.org.uk
Members: 140
Staff: 4
Contact: David Marcou, Acting Chief Exec.
Fee: £55
Membership Type: patron
Fee: £73
Membership Type: independent orchestra/ensemble, international youth orchestra, student orchestra/societies
Description: Youth orchestras. Represents members' collective interests; fosters development of young musicians; facilitates exchange of ideas and information among members. Organizes annual European Youth Music Week, held alternately in Britain and Germany, enabling young musicians to play modern compositions not normally included in concert programs. Annual Festival of British Youth Orchestras in Edinburgh and Glasgow, in August, concurrent with Edinburgh Festival, with guests from abroad.
Publication: Directory
Publication title: Directory of Youth Orchestras & Ensembles

03231

National Association of Youth Theatres
NAYT

Arts Ctre., Vane Terr., Darlington, DL3 7AX, UK
Tel: 01325 363330
Fax: 01325 363313
Email: nayt@btconnect.com
Website: http://www.nayt.org.uk
Staff: 5
Contact: Jill Adamson, Chief Exec.
Description: Promotes youth theatre practice in England; supports the development of youth theatre through programmes of training, advocacy and participation.
Publication: Manual
Publication title: The Big Youth Theatre Manual

03232

National Auricula and Primula Society
NAPS

9 Church St., Belton, Leicestershire, Loughborough, LE12 9UG, UK
Email: david.tarver@btinternet.com
Website: http://www.auriculaandprimula.org.uk
Members: 400
Contact: David Tarver, Honorary Sec.
Fee: £8
Membership Type: single, family
Fee: £10
Membership Type: overseas
Description: Promotes the interest of individuals who raise and show Auriculas, Gold Laced Polyanthus and other primulas, some rare and difficult to grow and others well known and easily recognizable as garden and wild plants.

03233

National Auricula and Primula Society Midland and West Section

9 Church St., Belton, Leics, Loughborough, LE12 9UG, UK
Fax: 01530 222458
Email: david.tarver@btinternet.com
Website: http://www.auriculaandprimula.org.uk
Contact: David Tarver, Honorary Sec.
Fee: £8
Membership Type: family, single
Fee: £10
Membership Type: family, single (overseas)
Description: Works to promote the cultivation and plantation of flowers, particularly the members of the primula family.
Publication: Yearbook
Publication title: Argus

03234

National Autistic Society
NAS

393 City Rd., London, EC1V 1NG, UK
Tel: 020 78332299
Fax: 020 78339666
Email: nas@nas.org.uk
Website: http://www.autism.org.uk
Members: 17000
Staff: 1900
Contact: Mark Lever, Chief Exec.
Fee: £20
Membership Type: individual
Fee: £25
Membership Type: joint
Description: Parents of people with autism; professionals; caregivers. Exists to champion the rights and interests of all people with autism and to ensure that they and their families receive quality services appropriate to their needs. Develops a range of educational and support services; runs schools and adult centres; offers families and carers information, advice and support; works to improve awareness of autism; offers a diagnostic and assessment service; and provides training and promotes research.
Library Subject: Autism, Asperger's syndrome
Library Type: reference
Publication: Newsletter
Publication title: Asperger United

03235

National Bed Federation
NBF

High Corn Mill, Chapel Hill, North Yorkshire, Skipton, BD23 1NL, UK
Tel: 0845 0556406
Fax: 0845 0556407
Email: info@bedfed.org.uk
Website: http://www.bedfed.org.uk
Members: 112
Staff: 2
Contact: Jessica Alexander, Exec. Dir.
Description: Bed manufacturers and manufacturers engaged in trade allied to bed manufacture. Represents bed manufacturers and their suppliers.

03236

National Begonia Society
NBS

c/o John Taylor, Membership Sec.
3 Rose Close, N Luffenham, Rutland, Oakham, LE15 8JJ, UK
Tel: 01780 721597
Email: j79taylor@btinternet.com
Website: http://www.national-begonia-society.co.uk
Members: 800
Contact: Alan Harris, Sec.
Fee: £6
Membership Type: new (single, joint)
Description: Promotes the growing and cultivation of begonias.

03237

National Black Police Association - UK
NBPA

Ground Fl., 24 Laburnam Rd., West Yorkshire, Wakefield, WF1 3QP, UK
Tel: 079 71162821
Fax: 019 24292127
Email: nbpa@nationalbpa.com
Website: http://www.nbpa.co.uk
Contact: Charles Crichlow, Pres.
Description: Promotes good race relations and equality of opportunity within the police service. Seeks to improve the working environment and protect the rights of black staff employed in police service. Enhances the racial harmony and quality of service to the black community.

03238

National Blind Children's Society
NBCS

Shawton House, 792 Hagley Rd., Quinton, Birmingham, B68 0PJ, UK
Tel: 01278 764770
Fax: 01278 764790
Email: enquiries@nbcs.org.uk
Website: http://www.nbcs.org.uk
Contact: Carolyn Fullard, Chief Exec.
Description: Enables blind and partially sighted children and young people to achieve their educational and recreational goals. Provides support and educational advocacy advice to blind and partially sighted children and their families.

03239

National Campaign for Real Nursery Education NCRNE

Tachbrook Nursery School, Aylesford St., London, SW1V 3RN, UK
Email: ncrne@yahoo.co.uk
Website: http://www.ncne.co.uk
Contact: Tess Robson, Membership Sec.
Fee: £50
Membership Type: organization
Fee: £20
Membership Type: school
Description: Advocates for the rights of every three and four year old child to a state-funded nursery education place; works for a rapid increase in nursery education provision.

03240

National Caravan Council NCC

Catherine House, Victoria Rd., Hampshire, Aldershot, GU11 1SS, UK
Tel: 01252 318251
Fax: 01252 322596
Email: info@nationalcaravan.co.uk
Website: http://www.nationalcaravan.co.uk
Members: 800
Staff: 20
Contact: John Lally, Dir. Gen.
Description: Manufacturers, distributors, park operators and suppliers of components, accessories and services. Acts as the trade association for all aspects of the caravan industry in the UK. Includes touring caravans, motorhomes, caravan holiday-homes and park homes.
Publication: Magazine
Publication title: The Business. Advertisements.

03241

National Childbirth Trust NCT

Alexandra House, Oldham Terr., Acton, London, W3 6NH, UK
Tel: 0870 7703236
Email: ceo@nct.org.uk
Website: http://www.nct.org.uk/home
Members: 96000
Staff: 50
Contact: Belinda Phipps, CEO
Fee: £39
Membership Type: standard
Fee: £29
Membership Type: renewal
Description: Provides information regarding pregnancy, childbirth, and parenting to interested individuals. Sponsors support groups for disabled parents and parents who have experienced miscarriage. Disseminates information.
Publication: Journal
Publication title: New Digest

03242

National Childminding Association NCMA

Royal Ct., 81 Tweedy Rd., Kent, Bromley, BR1 1TG, UK
Tel: 0845 8800044
Email: info@ncma.org.uk
Website: http://www.ncma.org.uk
Members: 50000
Staff: 400
Contact: Dame Gillian Pugh, Pres.
Fee: £65
Membership Type: childminder
Fee: £60
Membership Type: group
Description: Child care professionals, parents, and interested individuals. Promotes quality day care, recreation, and education for young children and seeks to advance the education of child care professionals. Offers seminars; conducts research.
Publication: Magazine
Publication title: Who Minds

03243

National Children's Bureau NCB

8 Wakley St., London, EC1V 7QE, UK
Tel: 020 78436000
Fax: 020 72789512
Email: websupport@ncb.org.uk
Website: http://www.ncb.org.uk
Members: 2800
Staff: 150
Contact: Nicola Hilliard, Hd. of Library and Information Service
Fee: £100
Membership Type: education sector, care and service provider
Fee: £350
Membership Type: district council, government
Description: Professionals and policy makers from health education and social services; parents and individuals from many different organizations. Identifies and promotes the interests of all children and young people and improves their status in a diverse society.
Publication: Journal
Publication title: Children and Society

03244

National Childrenswear Association NCWA

3 Queen Sq., Bloomsbury, London, WC1N 3AR, UK
Tel: 020 78439488
Fax: 020 78439478
Email: enquiries@ncwa.co.uk
Website: http://www.ncwa.co.uk
Contact: David Burgess, Chm.
Fee: £85
Membership Type: regular
Description: Promotes the welfare of all those engaged in the British children's wear industry. Monitors legislation and defends the rights and interests of members.
Publication: Magazine

03245

National Chrysanthemum Society NCS

317 Plessey Rd., Northumberland, Blyth, NE24 3LJ, UK
Tel: 01670 353580
Email: peter@fpeter.fsnet.co.uk
Website: http://www.nationalchrysanthemumsociety.org.uk
Members: 5000
Staff: 3
Contact: Terry Porter, Pres.
Fee: £15
Membership Type: fellow
Fee: £25
Membership Type: patron
Description: Promotes the growing of chrysanthemums.
Formerly: Formerly, State Capital Law Firm Group

03246

National Coalition of Anti-Deportation Campaigns NCADC

110 Hamstead Rd., Birmingham, B20 2QS, UK
Tel: 01479 841770
Email: ncadc-north@ncadc.org.uk
Website: http://www.ncadc.org.uk
Staff: 4
Contact: Michael Collins, Contact
Description: Families and individuals facing deportation and organizations that defend asylum seekers and economic migrants. Seeks to prevent the deportation of families and individuals seeking asylum and economic migrants in the United Kingdom. Publicizes the cases of anyone facing deportation; works to reform statutes governing immigration and asylum.

03247

National Cochlear Implant Users Association NCIUA

7 Elridge Close, Dorset, Dorchester, DT1 2JS, UK
Tel: 01305 262591
Email: enquiries@nciua.org.uk
Website: http://www.nciua.org.uk/index.php
Contact: Paul Tomlinson, Treas.
Fee: £10
Membership Type: individual
Fee: £25
Membership Type: corporate, affiliate
Description: Represents cochlear implant users in the United Kingdom. Provides support to families and friends of cochlear implant users. Increases public awareness of the benefits of cochlear implants. Advances public education in the use and benefits of cochlear implants.
Publication: Booklet
Publication title: Cochlear Implants

03248

National College of Hypnosis and Psychotherapy NCHP

PO Box 5779, Loughborough, LE12 5ZF, UK
Tel: 0845 2578735
Email: enquiries@nchp.org.uk
Website: http://www.hypnotherapyuk.net
Members: 200
Staff: 11
Contact: Fiona Biddle, Managing Dir.
Description: Mature students seeking a reputable, externally accredited (by the British Accreditation Council) training with a view to running their own practices, for interest or to augment their existing professional skills. Concerned with training in hypnotherapy/psychotherapy/counseling on part-time basis to appropriate, suitably motivated, mature students in London, Liverpool, Glasgow, Leeds and Oxford. Courses are held at regular intervals throughout the year. Member of United Kingdom Council for Psychotherapy and European Association for Hypnopsychotherapy.

Higher Education. Courses are held at regular intervals throughout the year. Member of United Kingdom Council for Psychotherapy.

03249

National Council for Drama Training
NCDT

249 Tooley St., London, SE1 2JX, UK
Tel: 020 74073686
Email: info@ncdt.co.uk
Website: http://www.ncdt.co.uk
Staff: 3
Contact: Hilary Strong, Dir.
Description: Promotes drama industry employers, equity and vocational drama schools. Ensures the professional relevance of training and good practice.
Publication: Handbook
Publication title: A Practical Guide to Vocational Training in Dance and Drama

03250

National Council for Graduate Entrepreneurship
NCGE

Baskerville House, Centenary Sq., Broad St., Birmingham, B1 2ND, UK
Tel: 0121 5032233
Email: ian.robertson@ncge.org.uk
Website: http://www.ncge.com
Contact: Ian Robertson, Chief Exec.
Description: Aims to raise the profile of entrepreneurship and the option of starting a business as a career choice among students and graduates. Increases the number of students and graduates who give serious thought to self employment or business start-up. Provides research, education and facilitation.

03251

National Council for Palliative Care
NCPC

The Fitzpatrick Bldg., 188-194 York Way, London, N7 9AS, UK
Tel: 020 76971520
Fax: 020 76971530
Email: enquiries@ncpc.org.uk
Website: http://www.ncpc.org.uk
Members: 35
Staff: 4
Contact: Eve Richardson, Chief Exec.
Fee: £160-450
Membership Type: acute trust, palliative care unit
Fee: £120-210
Membership Type: not-for-profit organization
Description: Members are nominated by national charities and professional organizations or elected by regional hospice and palliative care units. Represents the views and interests of hospice and palliative care services to ministers, civil servants, MPs, the media and statutory and other agencies. Provides advice to hospice and specialist palliative care services in relations with health authorities, local authorities and other agencies.
Formerly: Formerly, National Council for Hospice and Specialist Palliative Care Services
Publication: Magazine
Publication title: Information Exchange

03252

National Council for the Conservation of Plants and Gardens
NCCPG

12 Home Farm, Loseley Park, Guildford, GU3 1HS, UK
Tel: 01483 447540
Fax: 01483 458933
Email: info@plantheritage.org.uk
Website: http://www.nccpg.com
Staff: 8
Contact: Genevieve Melbourne Webb, Exec. Off.
Fee: £25
Membership Type: national (individual)
Fee: £15
Membership Type: student (up to 25 in full time education)
Description: Consists of gardeners, amateur and professional horticulturists and botanists. Aims to conserve garden plants for future generations through a network of local groups of supporters and 650 national plant collection holders.
Formerly: Formerly, NCCPG
Publication: Directory
Publication title: Directory of The National Plant Collection. Advertisements.

03253

National Council for the Training of Journalists
NCTJ

The New Granary, Station Rd., Newport, Essex, Saffron Walden, CB11 3PL, UK
Tel: 01799 544014
Fax: 01799 544015
Email: info@nctj.com
Website: http://www.nctj.com
Members: 6
Staff: 10
Contact: Joanne Butcher, Chief Exec.
Description: Representatives of the newspaper employers, Editors Guild, national trade unions throughout UK. Aims to advance the education and training of trainee journalists including press photographers.
Publication: Video
Publication title: Interviewing Techniques

03254

National Council for Voluntary Organisations
NCVO

Regent's Wharf, 8 All Saints St., London, N1 9RL, UK
Tel: 020 77136161
Fax: 020 77136300
Email: ncvo@ncvo-vol.org.uk
Website: http://www.ncvo-vol.org.uk
Members: 7000
Staff: 80
Contact: Stuart Etherington, Chief Exec.
Description: Voluntary organizations, professional associations, and government bodies in Britain. Promotes and protects members' interests. Encourages the formation of voluntary and charitable organizations. Offers advisory services; acts as a liaison between members and government authorities; works with national and international government bodies.
Formerly: Formerly, National Council of Social Service
Publication: Magazine
Publication title: Engage. Advertisements.

03255

National Council of Resistance of Iran
NCRI

PO Box 2516, London, NW4 2DD, UK
Email: info@ncr-iran.org
Website: http://www.iranncr.org
Members: 560
Contact: Maryam Rajavi, Pres.
Description: Coalition of organizations opposed to the Ayatollah Ruhollah Khomeini's regime in Iran. Aims to replace the rule of Khomeini's remnants with a democratic government. Works to organize opposition to the Khomeini regime through diplomatic activities worldwide and through demonstrations and strikes conducted in Iran.

03256

National Courier Association
NCA

NCA House, 30 Woodhall Croft, Pudsey, LS28 7TU, UK
Tel: 0845 6037813
Email: theadministrator@thenca.co.uk
Website: http://www.thenca.co.uk
Members: 110
Description: Same-day courier companies. Seeks to "allow members to inter-trade and provide customers with same-day collection and delivery services". Screens courier companies and confers membership upon qualifying services; facilitates communication and cooperation among members. Represents members' interests before government agencies, labor and industrial organizations, and the public. Plans to establish courier services in the Republic of Ireland as associate members.
Formerly: Formerly, National Network of Courier Companies

03257

National Day Nurseries Association
NDNA

National Early Years Enterprise Centre, Longbow Close, West Yorkshire, Huddersfield, HD2 1GQ, UK
Tel: 0148 4407070
Fax: 0148 4407060
Email: info@ndna.org.uk
Website: http://www.ndna.org.uk
Members: 3000
Staff: 60
Contact: Purnima Tanuku, Chief Exec.
Fee: £148
Membership Type: early years provider (based on the number of sites/places)
Fee: £51
Membership Type: additional site
Description: Aims to enhance the development and education of children in their early years through the provision of support services to members. Conducts training courses for members. Campaigns on key issues to the government both nationally and locally.
Publication: Magazine
Publication title: Nursery News. Advertisements.

03258
National Deaf Children's Society
NDCS
15 Dufferin St., London, EC1Y 8UR, UK
Tel: 020 74908656
Fax: 020 72515020
Email: ndcs@ndcs.org.uk
Website: http://www.ndcs.org.uk
Members: 9000
Staff: 64
Contact: Andy Ford, Chm.
Description: Supports families and young deaf people, chiefly through providing information and advice on education, state benefits, audiology and equipment.
Library Subject: deafness
Library Type: not open to the public
Publication: Pamphlet
Publication title: Communication Tips and Terms

03259
National Disabled Police Association
NDPA
PO Box 215, Ashford, TN23 9FL, UK
Tel: 07983 458859
Email: scott.westbrook@met.police.uk
Website: http://www.ndpa.info
Contact: Scott Westbrook, Chm.
Fee: £12
Membership Type: individual
Fee: £350
Membership Type: associate
Description: Promotes disability rights and the equality of opportunity within the police services. Improves recruitment, induction, training, retention and progression of staff with disabilities. Assists police service in the development of new and existing policies. Influences policies concerning equality issues and anti-discrimination within the police service and wider criminal justice system.

03260
National Dog Warden Association
NDWA
Haffield Lodge, Gloucester Rd., Staunton, Gloucester, GL19 3RA, UK
Email: sbell@ndwa.co.uk
Website: http://www.ndwa.co.uk
Members: 300
Contact: Sue Bell, Pres.
Fee: £55
Membership Type: associate
Fee: £40
Membership Type: full
Description: Promotes the compassionate enforcement of animal welfare, both statutory and voluntary at the local government level.
Publication: Magazine
Publication title: Dog Warden News

03261
National Dried Fruit Trade Association
NDFTA
18 Lichfield Rd., Essex, IG8 9ST, UK
Tel: 020 85062379
Fax: 020 85062379
Email: cathy@ndfta.co.uk
Website: http://www.driedfruit-info.com
Members: 48
Contact: Cathy Grant, Sec. Gen.
Fee: £400
Membership Type: associate
Fee: £1325
Membership Type: overseas
Description: Dried fruit importers and packers. Protects the interests of the dried fruit trade.

03262
National Eczema Society
NES
Hill House, Highgate Hill, London, N19 5NA, UK
Tel: 020 72813553
Email: info@eczema.org
Website: http://www.eczema.org
Members: 7000
Staff: 6
Fee: £20
Membership Type: regular
Fee: £40
Membership Type: overseas
Description: People with eczema, dermatitis, and sensitive skin. Seeks to improve the quality of life of people with eczema; promotes advancement of the diagnosis and treatment of eczema and related disorders. Provides information and support to those affected by the condition. Conducts information days to raise public awareness of eczema; raises funds to support dermatological research; represents the interests of people with eczema before pertinent government agencies and health care organizations.
Publication: Journal
Publication title: Exchange. Advertisements.

03263
National Energy Foundation
NEF
Davy Ave., Knowlhill, Milton Keynes, MK5 8NG, UK
Tel: 01908 665555
Fax: 01908 665577
Email: info@nef.org.uk
Website: http://www.nef.org.uk
Contact: Mary Archer, Pres.
Description: Promotes energy efficiency and safe renewable energy.

03264
National Farmers' Union - England
NFU
Agriculture House, Stoneleigh Park, Warwickshire, Stoneleigh, CV8 2TZ, UK
Tel: 024 76858500
Fax: 024 76858501
Email: membership@nfu.org.uk
Website: http://www.nfuonline.com
Members: 100000
Staff: 650
Contact: Peter Kendall, Pres.
Fee: £210
Membership Type: professional
Fee: £41.5
Membership Type: countryside
Description: Membership is restricted to working farmers. Represents farmers and growers of England and Wales.
Publication: Bulletin
Publication title: NFU Bulletin

03265
National Federation of Builders
NFB
B and CE Bldg., Manor Royal, West Sussex, Crawley, RH10 9QP, UK
Tel: 08450 578160
Fax: 08450 578161
Website: http://www.builders.org.uk
Members: 2500
Staff: 35
Contact: June Davis, Training and Membership Services Mgr.
Description: Acts as the principal focus for the views of small and medium sized general building contractors in England and Wales. Presents views to government, clients, etc. and generally promotes the role of the general contractor. Also advises and assists individual member with legal, technical, tax and employment problems.
Formerly: Formerly, Building Contractors Federation

03266
National Federation of Cemetery Friends
NFCF
42 Chestnut Grove, South Croydon, CR2 7LH, UK
Email: secretary@cemeteryfriends.org.uk
Website: http://www.cemeteryfriends.org.uk
Members: 40
Contact: Arthur Tait, Chm.
Description: Acts as a link for voluntary groups who aim to conserve and preserve cemeteries and encourage public use for educational and recreational purpose.

03267
National Federation of Demolition Contractors
NFDC
Resurgam House, Paradise, Herts, Hemel Hempstead, HP2 4TF, UK
Tel: 01442 217144
Fax: 01442 218268
Email: info@demolition-nfdc.com
Website: http://www.demolition-nfdc.com
Members: 201
Staff: 3
Contact: David Darsey, Pres.
Fee: £1985.75
Membership Type: corporate
Fee: £1386.5
Membership Type: associate
Description: Contractors that provide demolition services to the building and construction industry in the United Kingdom. Represents and protects members' interests.
Publication: Magazine
Publication title: Demolition and Dismantling. Advertisements.

03268

National Federation of Enterprise Agencies
NFEA

12 Stephenson Ct., Fraser Rd., Priory Business Park, Bedford, MK44 3WJ, UK
Tel: 01234 831623
Fax: 01234 831625
Email: enquiries@nfea.com
Website: http://www.nfea.com
Members: 135
Staff: 9
Description: Aims to influence government, the EU and other key decision makers in the development of effective strategies that will assist small businesses to sustain themselves and, ultimately, to prosper.
Publication: Newsletter
Publication title: Enterprise in Action

03269

National Federation of Fish Friers
NFFF

4 Greenwood Mt., Leeds, LS6 4LQ, UK
Tel: 0113 2307044
Fax: 0113 2307010
Email: mail@federationoffishfriers.co.uk
Website: http://www.federationoffishfriers.co.uk
Members: 2300
Staff: 3
Contact: Bill Crook, Pres.
Fee: £132.18
Membership Type: standard
Fee: £260
Membership Type: associate
Description: Represents bona fide fish and chip shop proprietors. Offers three day trade training courses from own training school monthly, specially designed for new and prospective entrants to the trade.
Publication: Magazine
Publication title: Fish Friers Review. Advertisements.

03270

National Federation of Fishermen's Organisations
NFFO

30 Monkgate, York, YO31 7PF, UK
Tel: 01904 635430
Fax: 01904 635431
Email: nffo@nffo.org.uk
Website: http://www.nffo.org.uk
Members: 2500
Staff: 7
Contact: Fred Normandale, Pres.
Fee: £1.05
Membership Type: vessel capacity unit
Description: Fishermen's associations in England and Wales. Represents and promotes the interests of commercial fishermen. Compiles statistics.
Publication: Yearbook
Publication title: Official Yearbook

03271

National Federation of Fishmongers
NFF

PO Box 9639, Colchester, CO5 9WR, UK
Tel: 01376 571391
Email: info@fishmongersfederation.co.uk
Website: http://www.fishmongersfederation.co.uk
Members: 9000
Contact: Gary Hooper, Pres.
Fee: £69
Membership Type: company (first outlet)
Fee: £35
Membership Type: additional outlet
Description: Retail fishmongers. Represents fishmongers to government departments and other statutory bodies and the press. Annual competition and conference organised.

03272

National Federation of Meat and Food Traders
NFMFT

1 Belgrove, Tunbridge Wells, TN1 1YW, UK
Tel: 01892 541412
Fax: 01892 535462
Email: info@nfmft.co.uk
Website: http://www.beabutcher.com
Members: 2000
Staff: 7
Contact: Graham Bidston, Chief Exec.
Fee: £250
Membership Type: full
Fee: £350
Membership Type: corporate
Description: Independent retail butchers, slaughterhouse operators, bacon curers, meat manufacturers and wholesale distributors.
Publication: Handbook
Publication title: Essential Business Guide

03273

National Federation of Plus Areas of Great Britain

210 Commerce House, High St., Sutton Coldfield, B72 1AB, UK
Tel: 0870 8747587
Email: chairman@18plus.org.uk
Website: http://www.plusgroups.org.uk/plus
Members: 1000
Staff: 2
Contact: Adrian Barnard, Natl. Chm.
Fee: £18.75
Membership Type: associate
Fee: £25
Membership Type: full
Description: Represents volunteers 18-35 years old engaged in social activities. Offers training.
Formerly: Formerly, National Federation of 18 Plus Groups
Publication: Magazine
Publication title: Plus News

03274

National Federation of Retail Newsagents
NFRN

Yeoman House, Sekforde St., London, EC1R 0HF, UK
Tel: 020 72534225
Fax: 020 72500927
Email: service@nfrnonline.com
Website: http://www.nfrnonline.com
Members: 25000
Staff: 104
Contact: Paul Chambers, Gen. Mgr.
Fee: £4.5
Membership Type: full
Description: Independent retail newsagents with some managers of multiple newsagents. Improves the conditions and raises the status of the independent newsagent, trade and business, and protects their interests. Provides legal aid and constant advice, with a wide ranging benefits package for fee paying members. Maintains two limited companies which negotiate commercial deals on behalf of members and publish and distribute promotional materials.
Library Type: reference
Publication: Magazine
Publication title: The Fed

03275

National Federation of Roofing Contractors
NFRC

Roofing House, 31 Worship St., London, EC2A 2DY, UK
Tel: 020 76387663
Fax: 020 72562125
Email: info@nfrc.co.uk
Website: http://www.nfrc.co.uk
Members: 785
Contact: Gary Simcock, Sec./Gen. Mgr.
Description: Roofing contractors and manufacturers of roofing products and equipment in the United Kingdom. Promotes the interests of members.
Publication: Bulletin
Publication title: Technical Bulletin

03276

National Federation of SubPostmasters
NFSP

Evelyn House, 22 Windlesham Gardens, West Sussex, Shoreham-by-Sea, BN43 5AZ, UK
Tel: 01273 452324
Fax: 01273 465403
Email: admin@nfsp.org.uk
Website: http://www.nfsp.org.uk
Staff: 6
Contact: George Thomson, Gen. Sec.
Fee: £191.16
Membership Type: office (with salary of 8,498 or above)
Fee: £54.84
Membership Type: office (with salary of 8,498 or below)
Description: Represents the interests of subpostmasters. Seeks to achieve a thriving, successful post office network. Ensures that all rural and urban communities throughout the country are able to access post office services.
Publication: Journal
Publication title: The Subpostmaster

03277

National Federation of Terrazzo, Marble and Mosaic Specialists

PO Box 2843, London, W1A 5PG, UK
Tel: 0845 6090050
Fax: 0845 6078610
Email: info@nftmms.co.uk
Website: http://www.nftmms.co.uk
Members: 50
Staff: 1
Contact: Brian James, Sec.
Description: Firms engaged in supplying and fixing terrazzo, marble, mosaic and other stone products. Provides technical and other information to architects and

other specifiers in the building industry, together with a service of inspection and report on works involving their materials, and is represented on British and European Standards Committees relevant to the trades.

03278

National Federation of Women's Institutes NFWI

104 New Kings Rd., London, SW6 4LY, UK
Tel: 020 73719300
Fax: 020 77363652
Email: hg@nfwi.org.uk
Website: http://www.thewi.org.uk
Members: 205000
Contact: Jana Osborne, Gen. Sec.
Fee: £29.5
Membership Type: individual
Fee: £40
Membership Type: associate
Description: Offers a wide range of activities for women, like conferences, trainings, arts and crafts and other social events. Campaigns for issues that affect women and the communities.

03279

National Federation of Young Farmers' Clubs NFYFC

c/o YFC Centre, NAC
Stoneleigh Park, 10th St., Warwickshire, Kenilworth, CV8 2LG, UK
Tel: 024 76857200
Fax: 024 76857229
Email: post@nfyfc.org.uk
Website: http://www.nfyfc.org.uk
Members: 27000
Staff: 21
Contact: Chris Lloyd, Chm.
Description: Clubs representing 27,000 rural young people. Seeks to develop self-reliance and responsibility in members and to increase knowledge of agriculture, home crafts, and country life. Offers courses and competitions. Raise funds for UK charities. Participates in farming unions. Operates exchange service. Cooperates with branches of government promoting agricultural skills.
Publication title: International Competitions

03280

National Fireplace Association NFA

PO Box 583, High Wycombe, HP15 6XT, UK
Tel: 0845 6431901
Website: http://www.fireplace.co.uk/ind01.htm
Members: 250
Staff: 1
Description: Retail showrooms, manufacturers of fireplaces, appliances, flues, chimneys and accessories, fuel suppliers and other fireplace industry trade associations or bodies. Aims to unite all who have an interest in fires, fireplaces, fuels, chimneys and associated products, and promote their businesses. Works closely with other organizations and trade associations, and with its diversity of membership, represents the whole fire and fireplace industry as well as specialist groups within it, caring for their interests at home and abroad.
Publication: Yearbook
Publication title: Fireplace. Advertisements.

03281

National Foundation for Educational Research NFER

The Mere, Upton Park, Berkshire, Slough, SL1 2DQ, UK
Tel: 01753 574123
Fax: 01753 691632
Email: enquiries@nfer.ac.uk
Website: http://www.nfer.ac.uk/index.cfm
Contact: Sue Rossiter, Chief Exec.
Description: Represents education and children's services research organization working to improve education, children's services and training, nationally and internationally through research and development and dissemination activities.
Publication: Survey
Publication title: Annual Survey of Trends in Primary Education

03282

National Hairdressers' Federation NHF

Priory Business Park, 1 Abbey Ct., Fraser Rd., Bedford, MK44 3WH, UK
Tel: 0845 3456500
Fax: 01234 838875
Email: enquiries@nhf.info
Members: 7000
Staff: 4
Fee: £222
Membership Type: single salon
Fee: £110
Membership Type: sub group salon
Description: Hairdressing and/or beauty salon owners. Offers support, advice, a comprehensive legal advisory service, industrial tribunal representation, a tax advisory and protection service, a commercial property emergency service, management and artistic seminars, and many other benefits to assist salon owners with the conduct of their business and to stimulate their artistic talents.
Publication: Newsletter
Publication title: Headline News

03283

National Harmonica League NHL

112 Hag Hill Rise, Taplow, Maidenhead, SL6 OLT, UK
Tel: 01628 604069
Email: nhl@harmonica.co.uk
Website: http://harmonica.co.uk
Contact: Roger Trobridge, Chm.
Fee: £20
Membership Type: inside the United Kingdom
Fee: £22
Membership Type: inside Europe
Description: Members range from beginners to virtuoso amateurs and professionals, and include non players with an interest, collectors, traders, etc. Concerned with the presentation and advancement of the harmonica. Encourages amateur participation at national events, which also include inspiring virtuosos. Competitions inspire many to reach high standards of musical attainment. Social events provide for enthusiasts at all levels from raw beginners upwards. Teaching material is also available.
Publication: Magazine
Publication title: Harmonica World. Advertisements.

03284

National Heart Forum NHF

Entrance D, Tavistock House S, Tavistock Sq., London, WC1H 9LG, UK
Tel: 020 73837638
Fax: 020 73872799
Email: nhf-post@heartforum.org.uk
Website: http://www.heartforum.org.uk
Contact: Alexander Macara, Pres.
Description: Works to prevent disability and death from coronary heart disease in the United Kingdom. Provides a forum for members for the exchange of information, ideas and initiatives on coronary heart disease prevention.
Publication: Newsletter
Publication title: Heart To Heart

03285

National Hedgelaying Society NHLS

88 Manor Rd., Bedfordshire, Toddington, LU5 6AJ, UK
Tel: 0525 873795
Email: nhls.enquiries@googlemail.com
Website: http://www.hedgelaying.org.uk
Members: 250
Staff: 3
Contact: Robin Dale, Chm.
Fee: £10
Membership Type: senior citizen
Fee: £30
Membership Type: professional
Description: Works to encourage the craft of hedgelaying and to maintain local styles.
Publication: Book
Publication title: Hedgelaying Explained
Meetings/Conventions: National Hedgelating Championships – annual competition – Exhibits.

03286

National HIV Nurses Association NHIVNA

Mediscript, 1 Mountview Ct., 310 Friern Barnet Ln., London, N20 OLD, UK
Tel: 020 84468898
Fax: 020 84469194
Email: nhivna@mediscript.ltd.uk
Website: http://www.nhivna.org
Contact: Jacqueline English, Sec./Mgr.
Fee: £55
Membership Type: consultant nurse, manager, matron, doctor (UK)
Fee: £65
Membership Type: overseas
Description: Represents nurses who are working in the field of HIV/sexual health. Provides an academic and educational forum for the dissemination of original nursing research in the field of HIV/AIDS. Addresses the communication and support needs of nurses working with HIV/AIDS patients.

03287

National Home Improvement Council
NHIC

31 Worship St., London, EC2A 2DY, UK
Tel: 020 74483853
Fax: 020 72562125
Email: info@nhic.org.uk
Website: http://www.nhic.org.uk
Members: 35
Staff: 2
Contact: Andrew Leech, Exec. Dir.
Description: Manufacturers, distributors, contractors and trade associations involved in all aspects of home improvement, repair and maintenance. Aims to increase awareness of the benefits of home improvement and proper presentation of existing homes; to ensure co-operation between private manufacturers, distributors etc. and Housing Associations and Local Authorities to achieve the most effective level of improvement; to ensure Government and MPs are kept abreast of the industry's issues.
Publication title: Home Improvement Progress

03288

National House-Building Council
NHBC

Buildmark House, Chiltern Ave., Amersham, HP6 5AP, UK
Tel: 0844 6331000
Fax: 01494 735201
Email: cssupport@nhbc.co.uk
Website: http://www.nhbc.co.uk
Members: 181000
Staff: 1000
Contact: Imtiaz Farookhi, Chief Exec.
Description: Registers housebuilders and developers across the UK. Sets the standards for house-building, inspects homes built to those standards, and then provides its 'Buildmark' insurance cover on around 85% of all private sector new homes in the UK.
Publication title: NHBC Technical Standards

03289

National Household Hazardous Waste Forum
NHHWF

Munro House, 3rd Fl., Duke St., Leeds, LS9 8AG, UK
Tel: 0113 2467584
Fax: 0113 2344222
Email: enquiry@nhhwf.org.uk
Website: http://www.nhhwf.org.uk
Members: 160
Staff: 3
Contact: Roy Watkinson, Chm.
Fee: £130-600
Description: Manufacturers, trade associations, packaging manufacturers, equipment suppliers, retailers, local authorities, local authority institutions, waste management companies, research institutes and voluntary organizations. Seeks practical solutions to the many problems associated with the collection, recycling and safe disposal of household hazardous waste and its packaging.
Publication: Manual
Publication title: Good Practice Guide

03290

National Illumination Committee of Great Britain

9 Bishops Dr., Salisbury, SP2 8NZ, UK
Email: mrpointer@btinternet.com
Website: http://www.cie-uk.org.uk
Members: 52
Contact: Mike Pointer, Exec. Sec.
Description: Organizations, companies, universities, and government departments. Aims to provide an international forum for the discussion of all matters relating to the science, technology and art in the fields of light and lighting and for the interchange of information in these fields between countries.

03291

National Inspection Council for Electrical Installation Contracting
NICEIC

Warwick House, Houghton Hall Park, Houghton Regis, Dunstable, LU5 5ZX, UK
Tel: 0870 130382
Fax: 01582 539090
Email: enquiries@niceic.com
Website: http://niceic.org.uk
Staff: 80
Contact: Jim Speirs, Exec. Chm.
Description: Devoted to the protection of consumers against the hazards of unsafe and unsound electrical installations.
Publication title: The Roll

03292

National Institute for Biological Standards and Control
NIBSC

Blanche Ln., South Mimms, Hertfordshire, Potters Bar, EN6 3QG, UK
Tel: 01707 641000
Fax: 01707 641050
Email: enquiries@nibsc.hpa.org.uk
Website: http://www.nibsc.ac.uk
Staff: 260
Contact: Janet Darbyshire, Contact
Description: Research institution and national control laboratory for biological used in medicine.
Library Subject: vaccines, blood products, AIDS, biochemistry, hematology, virology, microbiology, immunology, endocrinology
Library Type: by appointment only
Publication: Catalog
Publication title: Catalogue of Biological Standards and Reference Materials

03293

National Institute of Adult Continuing Education
NIACE

Renaissance House, 20 Princess Rd. W, Leicester, LE1 6TP, UK
Tel: 0116 2044200
Fax: 0116 2854514
Email: enquiries@niace.org.uk
Website: http://www.niace.org.uk
Members: 700
Staff: 200
Contact: Clare Newton, Contact
Fee: £60
Membership Type: individual
Fee: £510
Membership Type: corporate
Description: Government departments, local education authorities, voluntary sector agencies, educational institutions, broadcasts, universities, and individuals. Promotes the study and general advancement of the education of adults. Offers a means of consultation and cooperation for all those interested in the education of adults.
Publication: Yearbook
Publication title: Adult Learning Yearbook

03294

National Institute of Agricultural Botany
NIAB

Huntingdon Rd., Cambridge, CB3 0LE, UK
Tel: 01223 342200
Fax: 01223 277602
Email: info@niab.com
Website: http://www.niab.com
Members: 4000
Staff: 252
Contact: Tina Barsby, CEO
Description: Farmers, seed trade, agrochemical, plant breeders, universities and colleges, consultants and advisers, individuals. Promotes the improvement of existing varieties of seed, plants and crops and aids the introduction or distribution of new varieties.
Library Type: not open to the public
Publication: Handbook
Publication title: Cereal Variety

03295

National Institute of Carpet and Floorlayers
NICF

4c St. Mary's Pl., The Lace Market, Nottingham, NG1 1PH, UK
Tel: 0115 9583077
Fax: 0115 9412238
Email: info@nicfltd.org.uk
Website: http://www.nicfltd.org.uk
Members: 415
Description: Individual installers of carpets with some manufacturers corporate patron members. Aims to promote standards within the carpet industry and provide advice and guidance to members.
Formerly: Formerly, National Institute of Carpet Fitters
Publication: Directory
Publication title: Directory of NICF Members

03296

National Institute of Economic and Social Research
NIESR

2 Dean Trench St., Smith Sq., London, SW1P 3HE, UK
Tel: 020 72227665
Fax: 020 76541900
Email: enquiries@niesr.ac.uk
Website: http://www.niesr.ac.uk
Staff: 40
Contact: Gill Clisham, Sec.
Description: Promotes economic and social research.
Publication: Journal
Publication title: National Institute Economic Review. Advertisements.

03297

National Institute of Medical Herbalists NIMH

Elm House, 54 Mary Arches St., Exeter, EX4 3BA, UK
Tel: 01392 426022
Fax: 01392 498963
Email: info@nimh.org.uk
Website: http://www.nimh.org.uk
Members: 700
Staff: 2
Description: Practitioners of herbal medicine. Promotes the benefits of herbal medicine.
Publication: Directory
Publication title: Register of Members

03298

National Insulation Association NIA

2 Vimy Ct., Vimy Rd., Beds, Leighton Buzzard, LU7 1FG, UK
Tel: 01525 383313
Fax: 01525 854918
Website: http://www.nationalinsulationassociation.org.uk
Members: 120
Staff: 10
Contact: Neil Marshall, Chief Exec.
Description: Manufacturers and contractors. Aims to raise and maintain high standards of competence and conduct in the business of cavity wall insulation, loft insulation, draught proofing, and insulated thermal linings to ensure a good service to the specifier, the public and to industry.
Formerly: Formerly, National Cavity Insulation Association
Publication: Pamphlet

03299

National Landlords Association NLA

22-26 Albert Embankment, London, SE1 7TJ, UK
Tel: 020 78408900
Fax: 0871 2477535
Email: info@landlords.org.uk
Website: http://www.landlords.org.uk
Members: 13000
Staff: 40
Contact: David Salusbury, Chm./Interim Chief Exec.
Fee: £80
Membership Type: individual
Fee: £120
Membership Type: local authority, council
Description: Private landlords of residential property in the United Kingdom. Exists to protect and promote the interests of landlords in the private rented sector. Offers discounts on insurance, tax advice, building materials and paints, legal stationery and computer software.
Formerly: Absorbed, National Federation of Residential Landlords
Publication: Magazine
Publication title: UK Landlord. Advertisements.

03300

National Market Traders' Federation NMTF

Hampton House, Hawshaw Ln., Hoyland, Barnsley, S74 0HA, UK
Tel: 01226 749021
Fax: 01226 740329
Email: joe.harrison@nmtf.co.uk
Website: http://www.nmtf.co.uk
Members: 26854
Staff: 13
Contact: Joe Harrison, CEO
Fee: £88
Membership Type: single/sole trader
Fee: £132
Membership Type: dual trader
Description: Market traders and licensed street traders. Promotes and protects markets and market traders. Represents its members' interests to the EC and national and local government.
Publication: Newsletter
Publication title: Conference Supplement

03301

National Metalforming Centre I Aluminium Powder and Paste Association

47 Birmingham Rd., W Bromwich, W Midlands, Birmingham, B70 6PY, UK
Tel: 0121 6016363
Fax: 0870 1389714
Email: alfed@alfed.org.uk
Website: http://www.alfed.org.uk/page.asp?node=1&dec=Home
Members: 4
Contact: Will Savage, CEO
Description: Represents companies that produces aluminium products and user of aluminium products. Aims to expand the market for aluminium products in UK and to promote the interests of the members. Promotes technical cooperation and information exchange within the aluminium industry.

03302

National Metalforming Centre I Aluminium Primary Producers Association APPA

47 Birmingham Rd., West Bromwich, B70 6PY, UK
Tel: 0121 6016363
Fax: 0121 1389714
Email: alfed@alfed.org.uk
Website: http://www.alfed.org.uk/page.asp?node=1&dec=Home
Members: 2
Contact: Will Savage, CEO
Description: Represents producers of primary based wrought alloys for rolling and extrusion. Produces primary aluminium ingot.
Library Type: not open to the public

03303

National Metalforming Centre I Aluminium Rolled Products Manufacturers Association ARPMA

47 Birmingham Rd., West Bromwich, B70 6PY, UK
Tel: 0121 6016363
Fax: 0870 1389714
Email: alfed@alfed.org.uk
Website: http://www.alfed.org.uk/page.asp?node=1&dec=Home
Contact: Will Savage, Chief Exec.
Description: Represents the interests of the producers of rolled aluminium products for construction, automotive, packaging and general engineering use.

03304

National Metalforming Centre I Aluminium Stockholders Association ASA

47 Birmingham Rd., West Bromwich, Birmingham, B70 6PY, UK
Tel: 0121 6016716
Fax: 0121 6016375
Email: asa@alfed.org.uk
Website: http://www.asauk.co.uk
Members: 37
Contact: Karl Weston, Chm.
Description: Trade association of companies and independent organizations.
Publication title: Review

03305

National Metalforming Centre I British Industrial Furnace Constructors Association BIFCA

47 Birmingham Rd., West Midlands, West Bromwich, B70 6PY, UK
Tel: 0121 6016350
Fax: 0121 6016387
Email: enquiry@bifca.org.uk
Website: http://www.bifca.org.uk
Members: 20
Description: Industrial furnace constructors and ancillary equipment suppliers.
Meetings/Conventions: Advances in Furnace Technology – annual conference

03306

National Metalforming Centre I Confederation of British Metalforming CBM

47 Birmingham Rd., W Midlands, West Bromwich, B70 6PY, UK
Tel: 0121 6016350
Fax: 0121 6016373
Email: info@britishmetalforming.com
Website: http://www.britishmetalforming.com
Staff: 11
Contact: John Houseman, Dir. Gen.
Fee: £690
Membership Type: company (based on annual turnover)
Description: Companies involved in the forging industry in Great Britain. Represents members' interests.
Formerly: Formerly, British Forging Industry Association
Publication: Directory
Publication title: Membership List: Buyers Guide

03307

National Music Council of The United Kingdom NMC

60/62 Clapham Rd., London, SW9 0JJ, UK
Tel: 020 74228297
Fax: 0870 7065329
Email: info@nationalmusiccouncil.org.uk
Website: http://www.nationalmusiccouncil.org.uk
Members: 30
Staff: 1
Contact: Dame Cleo Laine, Pres.
Description: Musical societies and related organizations. Aims to represent and promote the interests of the music industry in the United Kingdom.

03308

National Operatic and Dramatic Association NODA

NODA House, 58-60 Lincoln Rd., Peterborough, PE1 2RZ, UK
Tel: 01733 865790
Fax: 01733 319506
Email: info@noda.org.uk
Website: http://www.noda.org.uk
Members: 5000
Staff: 8
Contact: Tony Gibbs, Chief Exec.
Fee: £30.6
Membership Type: joint
Fee: £25.5
Membership Type: individual
Description: Opera and drama societies (2,500) and interested individuals (2,500). Encourages information exchange and mutual assistance among members dedicated to amateur stage performances. Offers consulting services. Sponsors competitions. Operates a summer school for one week each year covering all aspects of theater.
Publication: Magazine
Publication title: NODA Theatre Business. Advertisements.

03309

National Organization of Restoring Men - UK NORM-UK

PO Box 71, Stone, ST15 0SF, UK
Tel: 01785 814044
Email: info@norm-uk.org
Website: http://www.norm-uk.org
Contact: John Warren, Chm.
Fee: £15
Membership Type: donation
Fee: £20
Membership Type: donation (overseas)
Description: Advocates education of the public in all matters relating to circumcision and other forms of surgical alteration of the genitals, including alternative treatments.
Publication: Booklet
Publication title: Alternatives to Circumcision

03310

National Osteoporosis Society NOS

Camerton, Bath, BA2 0PJ, UK
Tel: 0845 1303076
Email: info@nos.org.uk
Website: http://www.nos.org.uk/NetCommunity
Members: 27000
Staff: 50
Contact: Claire Severgnini, Chief Exec.
Fee: £15
Membership Type: standard
Fee: £25
Membership Type: professional
Description: Improves the diagnosis, prevention and treatment of osteoporosis. Works with health care professionals to facilitate greater understanding of the needs of individuals with the disease. Offers support to people with osteoporosis and their families through a range of detailed information booklets, a national telephone helpline and a network of regional support groups throughout the UK. Raises funds for research to increase understanding of the disease and improve treatment options and patient care. Raises awareness of the disease and campaigns to promote bone health.
Publication: Magazine
Publication title: Osteoporosis News

03311

National Outdoor Events Association NOEA

PO Box 4495, Wells, BA5 9AS, UK
Tel: 01749 674531
Email: secretary@noea.org.uk
Website: http://www.noea.org.uk
Members: 350
Staff: 2
Contact: Susan Tanner, Gen. Sec.
Fee: £175
Membership Type: full
Fee: £78
Membership Type: associate
Description: Local authorities, show organizers, suppliers of equipment and services and general practitioners for the outdoor events industry. Forum between suppliers of equipment and the clientele - show organizers, local authorities etc. Initiates meetings between various organizations for the benefit of industry; promotes technical standards at outdoor events and various Codes of Practice. Members must adhere to Code of Professional Practice.
Formerly: Absorbed, National Entertainment Agents Council
Publication: Newsletter
Publication title: Outdoor

03312

National Parrot Sanctuary NPS

Dickonhill Rd., Friskney, PE22 8PP, UK
Tel: 0871 3841130
Fax: 01754 820406
Email: contact@parrotzoo.co.uk
Website: http://www.parrotsanctuary.co.uk
Contact: Steve Nichols, Founder/Chief Exec.
Description: Provides rescue and rehabilitation for neglected and unwanted parrots and parrot-type birds, and on rehabilitation to re-home as many as possible to good homes; also provides sanctuary to birds that cannot live as a pet; seeks to further study of Psittacine psychology and behavior to advance help and minimize future neglect to parrots; provides free psychological and behavioral assistance to owners of problem birds.

03313

National Pawnbrokers Association NPA

Chiltern Ct., 37 St. Peters Ave., Caversham, Reading, RG4 7DH, UK
Tel: 08456 120640
Fax: 08450 175180
Email: des.milligan@thenpa.com
Website: http://www.thenpa.com
Members: 250
Staff: 3
Fee: £395
Membership Type: head office
Fee: £100-195
Membership Type: branch
Description: Pawnbrokers. Provides a robust platform to represent the interests of Pawnbroking members nationwide.
Publication: Newsletter
Publication title: NPA Times

03314

National Pest Technicians Association NPTA

NPTA House, Hall Ln., Kinoulton, Nottingham, NG12 3EF, UK
Tel: 01949 81133
Fax: 01949 823905
Email: officenpta@aol.com
Website: http://www.npta.org.uk
Description: Represents all those who are employed within the pest control industry. Keeps members up-to-date with the latest pest control techniques. Conducts pest control training and other programs.
Publication: Survey
Publication title: Rodent Report

03315

National Pharmacy Association NPA

Mallinson House, 38-42 St. Peter's St., Hertfordshire, St. Albans, AL1 3NP, UK
Tel: 01727 858687
Fax: 01727 795934
Email: npa@npa.co.uk
Website: http://www.npa.co.uk
Members: 7000
Staff: 122
Contact: Ian Facer, Chm.
Description: Represents 7,000 pharmacy owners in UK, who collectively own 12,000 retail pharmacies. Provides members with legal and financial services; insurance; defense and indemnity; training; publications; public relations; business services and pharmacy planning.
Formerly: Formerly, National Pharmaceutical Association
Publication: Journal
Publication title: Professional Practice Notes

03316

National Pony Society
NPS

c/o Willingdon House
7, The Windmill, Turk St., Hants, Alton, GU34 1EF, UK
Tel: 01420 88333
Fax: 01420 80599
Email: secretary@nationalponysociety.org.uk
Website: http://www.nationalponysociety.org.uk
Members: 3000
Staff: 3
Contact: Angela Pretious, Membership Sec.
Fee: £35
Membership Type: standard
Fee: £15
Membership Type: junior, associate, judge, performance
Description: Pony owners, breeders, exhibitors, competitors, equine students, people with general interest in pony matters. Encourages the breeding, registration and improvement of British riding ponies and mountain and moorland ponies and to foster the welfare of ponies in general.
Publication title: The National Pony Society Review
Meetings/Conventions: periodic meeting

03317

National Register of Hypnotherapists and Psychotherapists
NRHP

18 Carr Rd., Nelson, BB9 7JS, UK
Tel: 01282 716839
Email: admin@nrhp.co.uk
Website: http://www.nrhp.co.uk
Members: 390
Staff: 2
Contact: Jon Beilby, Exec. Off.
Description: Therapists who have graduated from the National College of Hypnosis and Psychotherapy or equivalent trainings. Promotes and protects the professional status, standards, ethics and interest of its members and also promotes the interests of those members of the public who seek professional help, and for whom it provides a nationwide referral service. Member of the United Kingdom Council for Psychotherapy.
Publication: Directory
Publication title: Directory of Practitioners

03318

National Register of Personal Trainers
NRPT

PO Box 870, Northamptonshire, Sywell, NN6 0ZB, UK
Tel: 0844 8484644
Email: info@nrpt.co.uk
Website: http://www.nrpt.co.uk
Members: 1000
Staff: 5
Contact: Ann Morgan, Contact
Fee: £99
Membership Type: individual
Description: Qualified fitness instructors available for one to one personal training throughout the UK. Representative and advisory body for personal fitness trainers in UK. Acts as a referral service for the general public when looking for a personal trainer; provides networking and secures the best possible services and products for personal trainers to enhance their professionalism.
Formerly: Formerly, National Register of Personal Fitness Trainers
Publication: Newsletter
Publication title: One to One. Advertisements.

03319

National Register of Warranted Builders

Gordon Fisher House, 14-15 Great James St., London, WC1N 3DP, UK
Tel: 020 72427583
Fax: 020 74040296
Website: http://www.fmb.org.uk
Members: 3000
Staff: 5
Contact: Richard Diment, Dir. Gen.
Description: Small to medium size building companies and allied trades. Provision of insurance backed warranties on building work.
Publication: Magazine
Publication title: Master Builder. Advertisements.

03320

National Rheumatoid Arthritis Society
NRAS

Unit B4, Westacott Business Centre, Westacott Way, Littlewick Green, Berkshire, Maidenhead, SL6 3RT, UK
Tel: 0845 4583969
Fax: 0845 4583971
Email: enquiries@nras.org.uk
Website: http://www.rheumatoid.org.uk
Contact: Ailsa Bosworth, Chief Exec./Founder
Fee: £17.5
Membership Type: full
Fee: £25
Membership Type: international
Description: Provides information, education, advocacy and support for people with Rheumatoid Arthritis (RA), their families, and health professionals with an interest in RA. Raises public and government awareness of RA. Facilitates the networking of people with RA and encourages self-help.
Publication: Newsletter

03321

National Secular Society
NSS

25 Red Lion Sq., London, WC1R 4RL, UK
Tel: 020 74043126
Fax: 0870 7628971
Email: enquiries@secularism.org.uk
Website: http://www.secularism.org.uk
Contact: Keith Porteous Wood, Exec. Dir.
Fee: £29
Membership Type: individual in UK (over 18 years old), group (affiliated to the NSS)
Fee: £45
Membership Type: joint
Description: Campaigns against religious privilege in the UK and the EU.
Publication: Newsletter
Publication title: Newsline

03322

National Security Inspectorate
NSI

Sentinel House, 5 Reform Rd., Berkshire, Maidenhead, SL6 8BY, UK
Tel: 01628 637512
Email: nsi@nsi.org.uk
Website: http://www.nsi.org.uk
Members: 800
Staff: 50
Description: Represents companies in the security and fire sectors. Applies groups of standards: Technical Standards, Business Standards, Codes of Practice, and Quality Management.
Publication: Newsletter
Publication title: Network

03323

National Sewerage Association
NSA

42 Menor Dr. N, New Malden, KT3 5NY, UK
Tel: 020 83300123
Fax: 020 83300123
Email: nsa@sewerage.org
Website: http://www.sewerage.org
Members: 30
Staff: 2
Contact: Val Gibbens, Sec.-Treas.
Description: Companies engaged in the survey, operation, renovation, and maintenance of sewers, drains, and pipelines. Promotes adherence to high standards of ethics and practice by members. Works with external bodies to monitor and advance technical and technological capabilities in the sewerage and pipeline industries.
Formerly: Absorbed, Association of Flow Survey Contractors
Publication: Directory
Publication title: Directory of Members. Advertisements.

03324

National Sheep Association
NSA

The Sheep Centre, Worcestershire, Malvern, WR13 6PH, UK
Tel: 01684 892661
Fax: 01684 892663
Email: membership@nationalsheep.org.uk
Website: http://www.nationalsheep.org.uk
Members: 24000
Staff: 6
Contact: Lord Plumb, Pres.
Fee: £50
Membership Type: in UK
Fee: £55
Membership Type: outside UK
Description: Almost entirely sheep farmers in UK and some 35 other countries. Represents the sheep industry in discussions with all bodies influencing the industry. Researches, compiles and publishes a diverse array of publications and holds technical conferences.
Publication: Book
Publication title: British Sheep. Advertisements.

03325

National Society for Education in Art and Design
NSEAD

3 Mason's Wharf, Patley Ln., Wiltshire, Corsham, SN13 0BZ, UK
Tel: 01225 810134
Fax: 01225 812730
Email: johnsteers@nsead.org
Website: http://www.nsead.org/home/index.aspx
Members: 2500
Staff: 6
Contact: John Steers, Gen. Sec.
Fee: £164
Membership Type: full
Fee: £90
Membership Type: associate
Description: Instructors, students, and individuals interested in art, craft, and design education. Aims to strengthen the role of the arts in general education and promote high professional standards in art education. Provides legal advice and insurance benefits to members.
Formerly: Formerly, National Society for Art Education
Publication: Journal
Publication title: International Journal of Art and Design Education. Advertisements.

03326

National Society for Epilepsy
NSE

Chesham Ln., Chalfont St. Peter, Bucks, Aylesbury, SL9 0RJ, UK
Tel: 01494 601400
Fax: 01494 871927
Website: http://www.epilepsynse.org.uk
Members: 2000
Staff: 450
Contact: Earl Howe, Pres.
Fee: £50
Membership Type: research associate
Fee: £17.5
Membership Type: associate
Description: Individuals with an interest in epilepsy who wish to support epilepsy education and research. Provides assessment, treatment, rehabilitation, long term and respite care for adults with epilepsy. The education department provides support and information, produces educational resources and runs conferences and seminars. Coordinates a national network of trained volunteers offering information services.
Library Subject: epilepsy
Library Type: open to the public
Publication: Magazine
Publication title: Epilepsy Review

03327

National Society for Phenylketonuria
NSPKU

PO Box 26642, London, N14 4ZF, UK
Tel: 020 83643010
Fax: 0845 48341
Email: info@nspku.org
Website: http://www.nspku.org
Contact: Dave Stening, Chm./Webmaster
Fee: £17
Membership Type: family (in UK)
Fee: £23
Membership Type: family (non-UK)
Description: Helps and supports people with phenylketonuria, their families and careers. Promotes the care and treatment of PKU's and works closely with medical professionals in the UK.
Publication: Newsletter
Publication title: News and Views

03328

National Society for Research into Allergy
NSRA

PO Box 45, Hinckley, LE10 1JY, UK
Tel: 01455 250715
Email: eunicerose@onetel.com
Website: http://web.onetel.com/~eunicerose
Members: 1000
Description: Aims to educate the populace on the devastating effects of allergy/intolerance and to see effective treatment in all teaching hospitals. Offers elimination diet and recipe books as well as counseling, advice on all types of allergy/intolerance/hyperventilation and the tests and treatments for same.

03329

National Society for the Prevention of Cruelty to Children
NSPCC

Weston House, 42 Curtain Rd., London, EC2A 3NH, UK
Tel: 020 78252500
Fax: 020 78252525
Email: info@nspcc.org.uk
Website: http://www.nspcc.org.uk
Staff: 2500
Contact: Andrew Flanagan, Chief Exec.
Description: Exists to prevent children suffering from significant harm as a result of ill treatment. Helps and protects children who are at risk from such harm. Help abused children to overcome the effects of abuse and works to protect abused children from further harm. Works on 180 community based projects for children, young people and families, and provides a helpline available 24 hours a day, 7 days a week for people to with their concerns about the welfare of a child.

03330

National Society of Allied and Independent Funeral Directors

SAIF Business Centre, 3 Bullfields, Sawbridgeworth, CM21 9DB, UK
Tel: 0845 2306777
Fax: 0127 9726300
Email: info@saif.org.uk
Website: http://www.saif.org.uk
Contact: Peter O'Neill, CEO
Description: Represents independent, family-owned and operated funeral homes. Seeks to promote and protect the future of the independent funeral director. Maintains a strict code of practice to which members must adhere; monitors members' services and certifies qualifying homes.
Publication: Magazine
Publication title: Saiflink. Advertisements.

03331

National Society of Master Thatchers
NSMT

13 Parkers Hill, Tetsworth, Oxfordshire, Thame, OX9 7AQ, UK
Tel: 01844 281208
Fax: 01844 281208
Email: marjoriesanders@btinternet.com
Website: http://www.nsmtltd.co.uk
Members: 95
Staff: 1
Contact: Marjorie Sanders, Sec.
Description: Represents all member thatchers and negotiates on their behalf with official and other bodies. Aims to promote, encourage and uphold high standard of craftsmanship, and to regulate the needs of the craft.

03332

National Specialist Contractors Council
NSCC

Royal London House, 22-25 Finsbury Sq., London, EC2A 1DX, UK
Tel: 0844 2495351
Fax: 0844 2495352
Email: enquiries@nscc.org.uk
Website: http://www.nscc.org.uk
Members: 28
Staff: 6
Contact: Suzannah Nichol, Chief Exec.
Description: Represents the specialists in the United Kingdom construction industry. Promotes the use of trade association members and the role of Specialist Contractors.
Publication: Newsletter
Publication title: Newsline

03333

National Taxi Association
NTA

60 Chesterholm, Carlisle, CA2 7XX, UK
Tel: 01228 598740
Email: secretary@national-taxi-association.co.uk
Website: http://www.national-taxi-association.co.uk
Members: 100
Staff: 2
Fee: £36.5
Membership Type: individual
Fee: £200
Membership Type: full
Description: Taxi associations in the United Kingdom, excluding Scotland. Aims to carry on important activities in the common interest of all its members, to cultivate acquaintance, fellowship, co-operation, goodwill and a professional spirit among them; to facilitate the exchange of ideas and methods; to recognize and honor their exceptional services and achievements.
Formerly: Formerly, National Federation of Taxicab Associations

03334

National Trust

PO Box 39, Warrington, WA5 7WD, UK
Tel: 0800 8001895
Fax: 0800 8004642
Email: enquiries@thenationaltrust.org.uk
Website: http://www.nationaltrust.org.uk/main

Members: 3500000
Contact: Simon Jenkins, Chm.
Fee: £47.5
Membership Type: individual
Fee: £32
Membership Type: additional (family)
Description: Seeks to preserve places of historic interest or natural beauty for the enjoyment of everyone in the nation. Protects and keeps open to the public over 200 historic houses and 49 monuments and mills. Seeks to protect farms, forests, woods, archaeological remains and natural reserves.

03335

National Trust for Scotland
NTS

Wemyss House, 28 Charlotte Sq., Edinburgh, EH2 4ET, UK
Tel: 0844 4932100
Fax: 0844 4932102
Email: information@nts.org.uk
Website: http://www.nts.org.uk/Home
Members: 310000
Staff: 500
Contact: Dick Balharry, Chm.
Fee: £5
Membership Type: family
Fee: £3
Membership Type: individual
Description: Individuals and organizations with an interest in Scottish history and countryside conservation. Promotes preservation and restoration of historic sites. Provides voluntary assistance to site maintenance, restoration, and preservation projects; sponsors educational programs; participates in charitable activities. Runs conservation working holidays for volunteers from March to October.
Publication: Handbook
Publication title: Scotland for You

03336

National Trust, Central Volunteering Team

Heelis, Kemble Dr., Swindon, SN2 2NA, UK
Tel: 01793 817632
Fax: 01793 817401
Email: volunteers@nationaltrust.org.uk
Website: http://www.nationaltrust.org.uk/main/w-trust/w-volunteering.htm
Members: 3500000
Staff: 5000
Description: Works to preserve places of historic interest or natural beauty in England, Wales and Northern Ireland, permanently for the benefit of the nation. Volunteers (52,000) give their time to help restore and preserve properties owned by the National Trust.
Formerly: Formerly, National Trust Volunteering and Community Involvement Office

03337

National Tyre Distributors Association
NTDA

8 Temple Sq., Bucks, Aylesbury, HP20 2QH, UK
Tel: 0870 9000600
Fax: 0870 9000610
Email: info@ntda.co.uk
Website: http://www.ntdamain.orchardhostings7.co.uk/cms
Members: 2000
Staff: 5
Contact: Richard Edy, Dir.
Description: Companies in tyre specialist and fast-fit trade. UK Trade Association for tyre specialist companies and fast fit business.

03338

National Union of Journalists - England
NUJ

Headland House, 308-312 Gray's Inn Rd., London, WC1X 8DP, UK
Tel: 020 72787916
Fax: 020 78378143
Email: info@nuj.org.uk
Website: http://www.nuj.org.uk
Members: 38000
Staff: 40
Contact: Jeremy Dear, Gen. Sec.
Fee: £12.84
Membership Type: new media personnel (provincial newspapers, magazines outside London, independent local radio, employees outside UK and Ireland)
Fee: £16.27
Membership Type: new media personnel (press and public relations, magazines, freelances and advertising copywriters)
Description: Trade union of journalists in the United Kingdom and the Republic of Ireland. Defends members' interests.
Publication: Magazine
Publication title: The Journalist. Advertisements.

03339

National Union of Mineworkers - United Kingdom
NUM

2 Huddersfield Rd., Barnsley, S70 2LS, UK
Tel: 01226 215555
Website: http://www.num.org.uk
Members: 32947
Contact: C. Kitchen, Sec.
Description: Represents the interests of miners, past and present, working and retired and supports their extended families. Assists miners who are suffering chest diseases and other injuries caused by the negligence of the coal industry employers.

03340

National Union of Rail, Maritime and Transport Workers
RMT

39 Chalton St., London, NW1 1JD, UK
Tel: 020 73874771
Fax: 020 73874123
Email: info@rmt.org.uk
Website: http://www.rmt.org.uk
Members: 80000
Staff: 60
Contact: Bob Crow, Gen. Sec.
Description: Represents sector of the transport industry, from mainline and underground rail to shipping, buses and road-freight.
Publication: Magazine
Publication title: RMT News. Advertisements.

03341

National Union of Students - United Kingdom
NUS

Centro 3, 19 Mandela St., London, NW1 0DU, UK
Tel: 0207 3806600
Email: nusuk@nus.org.uk
Website: http://www.nus.org.uk
Members: 600
Staff: 40
Contact: Matt Hyde, Chief Exec.
Description: Students and student organizations. Seeks to advance the educational, social, and cultural interests of students.

03342

National Vegetable Society
NVS

14 Dronley Rd., Birkhill, Dundee, DD2 5QD, UK
Tel: 001382 580394
Email: peter.cranfield@care4free.net
Website: http://www.nvsuk.org.uk/index.php
Members: 2500
Contact: David Thornton, Sec.
Fee: £18.5
Membership Type: ordinary
Fee: £23.5
Membership Type: married couple, society
Description: Promotes members' interests in the cultivation and improvement of vegetables.

03343

National Voices

202 Hatton Sq., 16 Baldwins Gardens, London, EC1N 7RJ, UK
Tel: 020 31760738
Email: info@nationalvoices.org.uk
Website: http://www.nationalvoices.org.uk
Members: 115
Staff: 8
Contact: Jeremy Hughes, Chm.
Description: Works with member organizations towards better lives for people with long-term health conditions. Aims to gain recognition of people's needs and ensure resources are available to meet them, to campaign to achieve change in areas of common concern, to develop effective partnerships between service providers and service users, and to promote participation by individuals in their own care and treatment.
Formerly: Formerly, Long-term Medical Conditions Alliance

03344

National Youth Agency
NYA

Eastgate House, 19-23 Humberstone Rd., Leicester, LE5 3GJ, UK
Tel: 0116 2427350
Fax: 0116 2427444
Email: nya@nya.org.uk
Website: http://www.nya.org.uk
Contact: Fiona Blacke, Chief Exec.
Description: Promotes the personal and social development of youth through leadership training and other advocacy works. Encourages youth participation in public policy, governance, design development, and evaluation of services.
Publication: Newspaper
Publication title: The Edge

03345

Nationwide Caterers Association NCASS

Association House, 89 Mappleborough Rd., Shirley, Solihull, B90 1AG, UK
Tel: 0121 6032524
Fax: 0121 4743938
Email: enq@ncass.org.uk
Website: http://www.ncass.org.uk
Members: 850
Staff: 2
Contact: Bob Fox, Contact
Fee: £100
Membership Type: franchisee, retail, licensed pitch
Fee: £164
Membership Type: fixed site
Description: Mobile and outside caterers and suppliers to the trade. Acts as a voice for the industry, discourages inexperienced and unscrupulous operators, maintains high quality standards and practices. Encourages all members in professional activities only. Close liaison with other organizations and Government Departments. Hygiene training and due diligence systems adopted code of practice.
Formerly: Formerly, Mobile and Outside Caterers Association (Great Britain)
Publication: Book
Publication title: Getting Started. Advertisements.
Meetings/Conventions: Food on the Move – annual trade show – Exhibits.

03346

Natural England

1 E Parade, Sheffield, SE1 2ET, UK
Tel: 0845 6003078
Fax: 0300 0601622
Email: enquiries@naturalengland.org.uk
Website: http://www.naturalengland.org.uk
Staff: 850
Contact: Helen Phillips, Chief Exec.
Description: Promotes wildlife conservation and wise land use in England. Selects, establishes, and manages wildlife and marine reserves; designates sites of special scientific interest; supports and conducts conservation research. Seeks to increase public awareness of the dangers posed to wildlife by loss of habitat.

03347

Nautical Archaeology Society NAS

Ft. Cumberland Rd., Portsmouth, PO4 9LD, UK
Tel: 023 92818419
Fax: 023 92818419
Email: nas@nauticalarchaeologysociety.org
Website: http://www.nauticalarchaeologysociety.org
Contact: George Lambrick, Chm.
Fee: £50
Membership Type: full
Fee: £40
Membership Type: affiliate, concessionary
Description: Promotes the preservation of nautical heritage in the area; provides training courses, awareness courses; publishes international journals and additional volumes.
Publication: Journal
Publication title: International Journal of Nautical Archaeology

03348

Nautical Institute NI

202 Lambeth Rd., London, SE1 7LQ, UK
Tel: 020 79281351
Fax: 020 74012817
Email: sec@nautinst.org
Website: http://www.nautinst.org
Members: 7000
Staff: 15
Contact: Philip Wake, Chief Exec.
Fee: £165
Membership Type: regular, associate fellow
Fee: £135
Membership Type: associate
Description: Qualified mariners in navies and the merchant marine; membership represents 70 countries. Promotes high standards of knowledge and competence among those operating sea-going vessels. Conducts research and educational programs. Sponsors competitions.
Publication: Journal
Publication title: Seaways

03349

Nautilus International

Oceanair House, 750-760 High Rd., Leytonstone, London, E11 3BB, UK
Tel: 020 89896677
Fax: 020 85301015
Email: enquiries@nautilusint.org
Website: http://www.nautilusint.org
Members: 25000
Contact: Mark Dickinson, Gen. Sec.
Description: Merchant navy and all related areas. Recruits and retains members from maritime, maritime related, and other sectors by providing a high quality, cost-effective service covering their professional, industrial, legal, financial welfare and trade union needs.
Formerly: Formerly, National Union of Marine, Aviation and Shipping Transport Officers
Publication: Newspaper
Publication title: Telegraph. Advertisements.

03350

NEIGHBOURS

Grove Rd. Christian Centre, Grove Rd., London, N11 1LX, UK
Tel: 020 813616100
Fax: 020 813616100
Website: http://www.muswell-hill.com/muswell/organisations/neighbours.htm
Contact: Garry French, Coor.
Description: Committed to alleviating the problems of elderly and vulnerable people living alone in order for them to maintain a quality of life in their own homes.

03351

Netherlands British Chamber of Commerce NBCC

Imperial House, 15-19 Kingsway, London, WC2B 6UN, UK
Tel: 020 75397960
Fax: 020 78366988
Email: info@nbcc.co.uk
Website: http://www.nbcc.co.uk
Contact: Henk Lafebre, Chm.
Fee: £215
Membership Type: ordinary
Fee: £615
Membership Type: donating
Description: Works to promote business and commerce in UK and Netherlands.

03352

Network

18 Langley Ave., Burnhope, Durham, DH7 0AG, UK
Tel: 01207 520710
Email: administrator@national-womens-network.co.uk
Website: http://national-womens-network.co.uk
Members: 800
Contact: Janice Ross, Admin.
Fee: £50
Membership Type: individual
Description: Professional women in England. Seeks to enhance the status of women. Provides a forum for women to develop social and professional contacts.

03353

Network for Education and Academic Rights NEAR

London South Bank University, 90 London Rd., London, SE1 9LN, UK
Tel: 020 9027700
Fax: 020 70210881
Email: contact@nearinternational.org
Website: http://www.nearinternational.org
Contact: John Akker, Exec. Dir.
Description: Represents independent, non-governmental organizations that have interests that promotes academic freedom and/or human rights in education. Facilitates international collaboration between organizations active in issues of academic freedom and educational rights. Establishes a clearinghouse of information on academic freedom and education rights and facilitates joint action.

03354

Network Myanmar

PO Box 1080, Guildford, GU1 9HT, UK
Tel: 01483 233576
Fax: 01483 233161
Email: info@networkmyanmar.org
Website: http://networkmyanmar.org
Contact: Derek Tonkin, Chm.
Description: Supports the individuals, organizations and associations in Britain and overseas that promote the rights, liberties, security and prosperity of the Burmese people. Assists in the process of reconciliation and rehabilitation in Myanmar. Fosters contact and interaction among Burmese people.

03355

Network of Government Library and Information Specialists

King Charles St., London, SW1A 2AH, UK
Tel: 020 70082659
Fax: 020 70083270
Email: diane.murgatroyd@fco.gov.uk
Website: http://www.nglis.org.uk
Members: 500
Contact: Diane Murgatroyd, Vice Chair
Fee: £10
Membership Type: regular
Description: Aims to stimulate interest in the cost effective management of information. Promotes cooperation

among staff in government and allied library and information services. Organizes training courses and visits to libraries and other places of interest; holds annual conference.
Formerly: Formerly, Circle of State Librarians
Publication: Journal
Publication title: Network

03356
Neurofibromatosis Association of the United Kingdom
NFAUK
Quayside House, 38 High St., Kingston Upon Thames, KT1 1HL, UK
Tel: 0208 4391234
Fax: 0208 4391200
Email: info@nfauk.org
Website: http://www.nfauk.org
Members: 1870
Staff: 21
Contact: Melanie Hammerton, Office Mgr.
Fee: £15
Membership Type: individual
Fee: £22
Membership Type: family
Description: Seeks to establish and maintain a network of family support workers who are able to support and offer practical help and advice to those affected by Neurofibromatosis and their families. Neurofibromatosis is a genetic disorder of the nerve tissue, the characteristics of which include six or more coffee colored marks on the skin in the first two years of life and nodules on or just below the surface of the skin, or tumors on both acoustical nerves. Fosters research; disseminates information.

03357
New Economics Foundation
NEF
3 Jonathan St., London, SE11 5NH, UK
Tel: 020 78206300
Fax: 020 78206301
Email: info@neweconomics.org
Website: http://neweconomics.org
Contact: Stewart Wallis, Exec. Dir.
Description: Promotes innovative solutions that challenge mainstream thinking on economic, environment, and social issues that lead to improvement of quality of life. Works in partnership with civil societies, government, individuals, businesses, and academia to create more understanding and effective strategies that will put the planet first in all economic and social agenda.
Publication: Report
Publication title: The Inner City 100: Impacts and Influences

03358
New English Art Club
NEAC
36a Abercorn Pl., St. John's Wood, London, NW8 9XP, UK
Email: friends@neac.co.uk
Website: http://www.newenglishartclub.co.uk
Members: 45
Contact: Charlotte Halliday, Contact
Fee: £30
Membership Type: regular
Description: Promotes excellence in drawing and painting. Organizes annual exhibits and sales.
Publication: Catalog
Publication title: Annual Exhibition Catalogue. Advertisements.

03359
New Forest Pony Breeding and Cattle Society
NFPB&CS
The Corner House, Ringwood Rd., Hampshire, Bransgore, BH23 8AA, UK
Tel: 01425 672775
Fax: 01425 672775
Email: info@newforestpony.com
Website: http://www.newforestpony.com
Members: 1100
Staff: 1
Contact: Jane Murray, Honorable Sec.
Fee: £15
Membership Type: ordinary
Fee: £22.5
Membership Type: joint
Description: Owners and breeders of New Forest ponies. Strives for the conservation and preservation of New Forest ponies. Sponsors point to point races; encourages breed registration; compiles and distributes sales lists.
Publication: Book
Publication title: Forest Pony Stud Book

03360
New Producers Alliance
NPA
NPA Film Ctre., 7.03, Tea Bldg., 56 Shoreditch High St., London, E1 6JJ, UK
Tel: 020 76130440
Fax: 020 77291852
Email: queries@npa.org.uk
Website: http://www.npa.org.uk
Members: 1000
Staff: 3
Contact: David Pope, CEO
Fee: £65
Membership Type: unemployed, student, OAP
Fee: £95
Membership Type: individual, international
Description: Membership organization for first and second time filmmakers. Affiliate membership for entertainment lawyers, accountants, etc. is also available. Educates and informs film producers in the UK. Promotes the role of the film producer. Shares information and experience and seeks creative partnerships with producers worldwide.
Library Subject: coproduction treaties, form contracts
Library Type: reference
Publication: Newsletter
Publication title: Ezine

03361
Newcomen Society for the Study of the History of Engineering and Technology
NSSHET
The Science Museum, London, SW7 2DD, UK
Tel: 0207 73714445
Fax: 0207 73714445
Email: office@newcomen.com
Website: http://www.newcomen.com
Members: 1100
Staff: 1
Contact: Tim Crichton, Exec. Sec.
Fee: £33
Membership Type: individual in UK without transaction
Fee: £36
Membership Type: individual outside UK without transaction
Description: Institutions (120) and individuals (1,000) in 28 countries. Promotes study of the history of engineering, industry, and technology. Disseminates information.
Publication: Proceedings
Publication title: History of Thermionic Valves

03362
Newspaper Conference
The Newspaper Soc., St. Andrew's House, 18-20 St. Andrew St., 8th Fl., London, EC4A 3AY, UK
Tel: 020 76327400
Fax: 020 76327401
Email: ns@newspapersoc.org.uk
Website: http://www.newspapersoc.org.uk
Members: 25
Contact: Georgina Harvey, Pres.
Description: Comprises London editors and political correspondents of newspapers in membership of the Newspaper Society. Revolves around a series of lunch meetings, at which senior politicians are invited to address the members and answer questions relevant to regional newspapers. Gives its members the opportunity to address MPs directly and raise issues of regional and national concern.

03363
Newspaper Society
NS
St. Andrew's House, 8th Fl., 18-20 St. Andrew St., London, EC4A 3AY, UK
Tel: 020 76327400
Fax: 020 76327401
Email: ns@newspapersoc.org.uk
Website: http://www.newspapersoc.org.uk
Members: 142
Staff: 40
Contact: David Newell, Dir.
Description: Represents regional and local press in the United Kingdom. Covers an immense range of activities, from individual advertisement control advice to lobbying in Brussels, Westminster and Whitehall on all political and legislative issues of concern to publishers. Provides marketing services and promotes the regional press and national advertisers.
Formerly: Formerly, Newspaper Society of England
Publication: Newsletter
Publication title: Commercial Update

03364
NFSH The Healing Trust
NFSH THT
21 York Rd., Northampton, NN1 5QG, UK
Tel: 01604 603247
Fax: 01604 603534
Email: office@thehealingtrust.org.uk
Website: http://www.thehealingtrust.org.uk
Members: 3600
Staff: 7
Contact: Paula Docksey, Contact
Fee: £20
Membership Type: friend
Fee: £30
Membership Type: associate
Description: Spiritual Healers. Promotes research into healing.
Publication: Magazine
Publication title: Healing Today. Advertisements.

03365
NHS Blood and Transplant
NHSBT
c/o Organ Donation and Transplantation Directorate
Fox Den Rd., Stoke Gifford, Bristol, BS34 8RR, UK
Tel: 0117 9757575
Fax: 0117 9757577
Email: enquiries@nhsbt.nhs.uk
Website: http://www.uktransplant.org.uk/ukt/default.jsp
Description: Provides support to transplantation services across the UK. Ensures that donated organs are matched, organised nationally and allocated in a fair and unbiased way for patients that are in need of organ transplant, particularly in the case of kidneys.
Publication: Handbook
Publication title: Freedom of Information Act 2000

03366
NHS Consultants Association
NHSCA
Hill House, Great Bourton, Banbury, Oxon, OX17 1QH, UK
Tel: 01295 750407
Fax: 01295 750407
Email: nhsca@pop3.poptel.org.uk
Website: http://www.nhsca.org.uk
Members: 600
Contact: Paul Evans, Dir.
Fee: £50
Membership Type: standard
Fee: £30
Membership Type: retired
Description: Senior doctors committed to the NHS and the basic principles on which it was founded. Acts as a pressure group lobbying politicians and others concerned with health.
Formerly: Formerly, National Health Service Consultants Association

03367
Nicaragua Solidarity Campaign
NSC
86 Durham Rd., London, N7 7DT, UK
Tel: 020 75614836
Email: nsc@nicaraguasc.org.uk
Website: http://www.nicaraguasc.org.uk
Members: 700
Staff: 4
Contact: Helen Yuill, Contact
Fee: £25
Membership Type: waged individual, household
Fee: £7.5
Membership Type: unwaged individual
Description: Campaigning organization concerned with political solidarity work for Nicaragua. Promotes support in the United Kingdom for grass roots organizations. Aims to channel material and financial support to Nicaragua and to publicize political and social developments. Maintains speakers' bureau.
Publication: Journal
Publication title: Central America Report

03368
Nickel Institute - UK
European Technical Information Centre, The Holloway, Alvechurch, Birmingham, B48 7QA, UK
Tel: 01527 584777
Fax: 01527 585562
Email: ni_birmingham_uk@nickelinstitute.org
Website: http://www.nickelinstitute.org
Members: 11
Staff: 3
Contact: C. Peter Cutler, Technical Dir.
Description: Represents primary nickel producers. Serves as the market development organization of the primary nickel industry. Defends and promotes the appropriate use of nickel. Carries out market development research and provides technical service and advice to nickel and nickel alloy users worldwide.
Library Type: not open to the public
Formerly: Formerly, Nickel Development Institute - UK
Publication: Magazine
Publication title: Nickel

03369
Noctis
5 Waterloo Rd., Cheshire, Stockport, SK1 3BD, UK
Tel: 0161 4768381
Fax: 0161 4297214
Email: info@noctisuk.org
Website: http://noctis.net-genie.co.uk
Members: 1600
Contact: Paul Smith, Exec. Dir.
Fee: £250-5000
Membership Type: night bar/music venue (based on company turnover)
Fee: £250-500
Membership Type: associate trade
Description: Works to represent the interests of late night operators across the UK. Gives support on issues such as transition to the Licensing Act 2003 and the roll out of the Security Industry Authority registration scheme, offers practical advice, updates on timings and information provision in a variety of formats.
Formerly: Formerly, Bar Entertainment and Dance Association
Publication: Magazine
Publication title: Night

03370
NOF Energy
1/F Thames House, Mandale Business Park, Belmolnt Industrial Estate, Durham, DH1 1TH, UK
Tel: 0191 3846464
Fax: 0191 3846611
Email: business@nofenergy.co.uk
Website: http://www.nofenergy.co.uk
Members: 300
Contact: George Rafferty, Chief Exec.
Fee: £405-1275
Membership Type: full, maximum (based on annual turnover)
Description: Assists member companies to become competitive in the national and international marketplace. Assists with the development of members' capabilities in response to changing demands of the industry. Provides consultancy, financial assistance, and support for innovation and training initiatives. Gathers and disseminates information.
Formerly: Formerly, Northern Offshore Federation

03371
Non-Executive Directors Association
NEDA
Crowthorne Enterprise Centre, Crowthorne Business Estate, Old Wokingham Rd., Berkshire, RG45 6AW, UK
Tel: 01344 751672
Email: info@nedaglobal.com
Website: http://www.nedaglobal.com
Contact: Graham Durgan, Chm.
Fee: £195
Membership Type: individual
Fee: £500
Membership Type: corporate
Description: Represents non-executive directors. Promotes the professional development and training of non-executive directors. Increases understanding of business and corporate governance.
Publication: Handbook
Publication title: Non-Executive Directors Handbook

03372
Norfolk Chamber of Commerce and Industry
9 Norwich Business Park, Whiting Rd., Norfolk, Norwich, NR4 6DJ, UK
Tel: 01603 625977
Email: membership@norfolkchamber.co.uk
Website: http://www.norfolkchamber.co.uk/default.aspx
Members: 2000
Staff: 20
Contact: Caroline Williams, Chief Exec.
Fee: £224-629
Membership Type: company (0-100 employees)
Fee: £975-1669
Membership Type: company (101-750 employees)
Description: Represents members across Norfolk at local, regional and national level on matters concerning trade, commerce and industry and lobbying. Facilitates networking, forums and events to enable members to exchange ideas, information, views and business practice.

03373
North American Connection
NAC
PO Box 10543, Solihull, B93 8ZY, UK
Tel: 0870 7200663
Website: http://www.naconnect.com
Members: 80
Fee: £25
Membership Type: regular
Fee: £18
Membership Type: senior
Description: Strives to understand the needs of new expatriates and to help bridge their transition into British culture. Provides friendship and support, as well as social, educational and philanthropic activities for members.

03374
North Atlantic Salmon Conservation Organization
NASCO
11 Rutland Sq., Edinburgh, EH1 2AS, UK
Tel: 0131 2282551
Fax: 0131 2284384
Email: hq@nasco.int
Website: http://www.nasco.int
Members: 7
Staff: 4
Contact: Malcolm Windsor, Sec.
Description: Promotes the conservation, restoration, enhancement, and rational management of salmon stocks in the North Atlantic, taking into account the best available scientific evidence.
Publication: Annual Report
Publication title: Annual Report of the Council

03375
North East Chamber of Commerce
NECC

Aykley Heads Business Centre, Aykley Heads, Durham, DH1 5TS, UK
Tel: 0191 3861133
Fax: 0191 3861144
Email: enquiries@necc.co.uk
Website: http://www.necc.co.uk
Members: 5000
Staff: 252
Contact: James Ramsbotham, Chief Exec.
Fee: £240-6000
Membership Type: business (based on number of employees)
Description: Promotes business and commerce.
Publication: Magazine
Publication title: Contact. Advertisements.

03376
North Eastern Counties Welsh Pony and Cob Association
NECWPCA

Ave. Farm, The Avenue, Coxhoe, Durham, DH6 4AF, UK
Tel: 0191 3771928
Email: margaretrandall3@hotmail.com
Website: http://www.welshponyandcob.com/necwpca
Contact: Margaret Randall, Sec.
Description: Records the breeding details of Welsh ponies and cobs. Seeks to improve the breed and promote its excellence.

03377
North Hampshire Chamber of Commerce and Industry
NHCC&I

Business Support Centre, Deanes Bldg., London Rd., Hampshire, Basingstoke, RG21 7YP, UK
Tel: 01256 352275
Fax: 01256 479391
Email: office@nhcci.co.uk
Website: http://www.nhcci.co.uk
Contact: John Harrocks, Chief Exec.
Fee: £185-265
Membership Type: company (1-10 staff)
Fee: £434-881
Membership Type: company (11-250 staff)
Description: Promotes business and commerce.
Publication: Magazine
Publication title: Chamber News. Advertisements.

03378
North of England Institute of Mining and Mechanical Engineers
NEIMME

Neville Hall, Westgate Rd., Newcastle upon Tyne, NE1 1SE, UK
Tel: 0191 2322201
Fax: 0191 2322201
Email: office@mininginstitute.org.uk
Website: http://www.mininginstitute.org.uk
Contact: Malcolm Richard Tilley, Pres.
Fee: £30
Membership Type: corporate
Fee: £25
Membership Type: associate, student
Description: Works to publicize mining and mechanical engineering through education, young engineers' programme, and preservation of historically important works.
Library Subject: mining, geology
Library Type: open to the public

03379
North of England Zoological Society
NEZS

c/o Chester Zoo
Cedar House, Caughall Rd., Upton-by-Chester, Chester, CH2 1LH, UK
Tel: 01244 380280
Fax: 01244 371273
Email: info@chesterzoo.org
Website: http://www.chesterzoo.org
Contact: Gordon McGregor Reid, Dir. Gen.
Description: Promotes conservation by breeding rare and endangered animals, by excellent welfare, high quality public service, recreation and science.

03380
North Staffordshire Chamber of Commerce and Industry
NSCCI

Commerce House, Festival Park, Staffordshire, Stoke-on-Trent, ST1 5BE, UK
Tel: 01782 202222
Fax: 01782 202448
Website: http://www.nscci.co.uk
Members: 1000
Staff: 27
Contact: Mike Herbert, Deputy Pres.
Fee: £150-1545
Membership Type: company/unincorporated firm (based on number of employees)
Description: Promotes business and commerce.
Publication: Bulletin
Publication title: Business Bulletin

03381
North West England and North Wales Narcotics Anonymous
NW NA

PO Box 57, Manchester, M60 1HP, UK
Email: info@nwna.info
Website: http://www.nwe-ukna.co.uk
Description: Provides a recovery process and support network for drug addicts. Facilitates and stabilizes the recovery of the members. Uses 12-step program adapted from Alcoholics Anonymous to aid in the recovery process.

03382
North Yorkshire AIDS Action
NYAA

11 St., Saviour's Pl., York, YO1 7PJ, UK
Tel: 01904 640024
Email: info@nyaa.org.uk
Website: http://www.northyorkshireaidsaction.co.uk
Description: Provides help and active support to people with HIV/AIDS and their families, friends and carers. Informs and educates people about issues concerning HIV/AIDS.

03383
North-East Atlantic Fisheries Commission
NEAFC

22 Berners St., London, W1T 3DY, UK
Tel: 0207 6310016
Fax: 0207 6369225
Email: info@neafc.org
Website: http://www.neafc.org
Members: 6
Staff: 3
Contact: Kjartan Hoydal, Sec.
Description: Government representatives from Denmark (representing Greenland and the Faroe Islands), European Union, Iceland, Norway, Poland, Estonia, and the Russian Federation contracting parties. Promotes the conservation and optimum utilization of the fish resources of the North East Atlantic area. Encourages international cooperation and discussion on fish stock management. The Commission has no regulatory powers over waters within member states' jurisdiction, unless the relevant member states agree.

03384
Northamptonshire Chamber of Commerce

Opus House, Anglia Way, Moulton Park, Northampton, NN3 6JA, UK
Tel: 01604 490490
Fax: 01604 670362
Email: info@northants-chamber.co.uk
Website: http://www.northants-chamber.co.uk
Members: 1550
Staff: 132
Contact: Paul Griffiths, Chief Exec.
Description: Represents members across Northamptonshire at local, regional and national level on matters concerning trade, commerce and industry and lobbying. Facilitates networking, forums and events to enable members to exchange ideas, information, views and business practice.
Formerly: Formerly, Northhamptonshire Chamber of Commerce, Training and Enterprise
Publication: Magazine
Publication title: In Business

03385
Northern Ireland Association for Mental Health
NIAMH

80 University St., Belfast, BT7 1HE, UK
Tel: 028 90328474
Email: info@niamhwellbeing.org
Website: http://www.niamh.co.uk
Members: 280
Staff: 145
Contact: Graeme McDonald, Chm.
Fee: £10
Membership Type: regular
Description: Promotes dignity, choice, integration and participation for those with mental health needs living in the community. Aims to offer services of the highest standard to people with mental health needs; inform and educate the public about mental health; and press for high standards in the provision of mental health services.
Publication title: Mental Health Matters. Advertisements.

03386

Northern Ireland Bat Group
NIBG

33 Glebe Manor, Antrim, Newtownabbey, BT36 6HF, UK
Tel: 07989 354592
Email: ni.bats@gmail.com
Website: http://www.bats-ni.org.uk
Members: 50
Contact: James McCrory, Honorary Sec.
Fee: £10
Membership Type: individual
Fee: £5
Membership Type: unwaged
Description: Coordinates bat conservation and research activities in Northern Ireland. Sponsors public education programs to encourage protection of bats and roosting sites.

03387

Northern Ireland Chamber of Commerce and Industry
NICCI

22 Great Victoria St., Belfast, BT2 7BJ, UK
Tel: 028 90244113
Fax: 028 90247024
Email: mail@northernirelandchamber.com
Website: http://www.nicci.co.uk
Members: 1200
Staff: 11
Contact: Ann McGregor, Chief Exec.
Fee: £185-1221
Membership Type: firm/company (based on number of employees)
Description: Represents members across Northern Ireland at local, regional and national level on matters concerning trade, commerce and industry and lobbying. Facilitates networking, forums and events to enable members to exchange ideas, information, views and business practice.
Publication: Magazine
Publication title: Business First

03388

Northern Ireland Chest Heart and Stroke Association
NICHSA

21 Dublin Rd., Belfast, BT2 7HB, UK
Tel: 028 90320184
Fax: 028 90333487
Email: mail@nichsa.com
Website: http://www.nichsa.com
Staff: 106
Contact: Andrew Dougal, Chief Exec.
Description: Promotes the prevention of, and alleviate the suffering resulting from chest, heart, and stroke illnesses in Northern Ireland. Supports rehabilitation facilities; offers subsidized vacations for families affected by these diseases; provides nebulizers for asthmatic children and adults; provides help and advice; provides grants for people with low incomes; funds research.
Publication: Journal
Publication title: CHS News

03389

Northern Ireland Federation of Housing Associations
NIFHA

6c Citylink Business Park, Albert St., Belfast, BT12 4HB, UK
Tel: 028 90230446
Fax: 028 90238057
Email: info@nifha.org
Website: http://www.nifha.org
Members: 43
Staff: 8
Contact: Chris Williamson, Chief Exec.
Description: Supports housing associations in their provision of affordable housing for the benefit of the community in Northern Ireland.

03390

Northern Ireland Food and Drink Association
NIFDA

Belfast Mills, 71-75 Percy St., Belfast, BT13 2HW, UK
Tel: 028 90241010
Fax: 028 90240500
Email: info@nifda.co.uk
Website: http://www.nifda.co.uk
Staff: 3
Contact: Michael Bell, Exec. Dir.
Description: Companies involved in all sectors of the food and drink industry. Represents and promotes member interests to improve the competitiveness of the industry in Northern Ireland.
Publication: Newsletter
Publication title: NIFDA News

03391

Northern Ireland Grain Trade Association
NIGTA

Cuinne an Chaireil, 27 Berwick View, Moira, BT67 0SX, UK
Tel: 028 92611044
Fax: 028 92611979
Email: info@nigta.co.uk
Website: http://www.nigta.co.uk
Contact: Doris Leenan, Exec. Sec.
Description: Represents the main suppliers to the agricultural industry that includes importers of raw materials for animal feed, manufacturers of animal feed and supplements, specialist nutritional consultants and agricultural merchants.

03392

Northern Ireland Hotels Federation
NIHF

The McCune Bldg., 1 Shore Rd., Belfast, BT15 3PG, UK
Tel: 028 90776635
Fax: 028 90771899
Email: office@nihf.co.uk
Website: http://www.nihf.co.uk
Members: 170
Staff: 2
Contact: Janice Gault, Chief Exec.
Description: Hotel, guesthouse and trade members. Represents members in discussion with government, tourist boards, and other representative bodies. Coordinates information and advisory function for members.
Formerly: Formerly, Northern Ireland Hotels and Caterers Association
Publication: Newsletter
Publication title: Hotplate

03393

Northern Ireland Human Rights Commission
NIHRC

Temple Ct., 39 North St., Belfast, BT1 1NA, UK
Tel: 028 90243987
Fax: 028 90247844
Website: http://www.nihrc.org
Members: 9
Staff: 16
Contact: Peter O'Neill, Chief Exec.
Description: Aims to promote and protect the human rights of everyone in Northern Ireland. Established by the Belfast (Good Friday) Agreement 1998.

03394

Northern Ireland Local Government Association
NILGA

Unit 5B Castlereagh Business Park, 478 Castlereagh Rd., Belfast, BT5 6BQ, UK
Tel: 02890 798972
Fax: 02890 791248
Email: n.winder@nilga.org
Website: http://www.nilga.org/home.asp
Members: 26
Staff: 2
Contact: Nora Winder, Acting Chief Exec.
Description: Open to all district councils in Northern Ireland. Promotes and protects the interests of district councils.
Formerly: Formerly, Association of Local Authorities of Northern Ireland
Publication: Handbook
Publication title: Councilor's Handbook

03395

Northern Ireland Meat Exporters Association
NIMEA

Lissue House, 31 Ballinderry Rd., Lisburn, BT28 2SL, UK
Tel: 028 92622510
Email: info@nimea.co.uk
Website: http://www.nimea.co.uk
Description: Major beef and lamb EC approved slaughtering and cutting companies. Promotes the interests of meat processors and exporters in Northern Ireland.

03396

Northern Ireland Mixed Marriage Association
NIMMA

28 Bedford St., Belfast, BT2 7FE, UK
Tel: 028 90235444
Fax: 028 90434544
Email: nimma@nireland.com
Website: http://www.nimma.org.uk
Members: 70
Staff: 2
Fee: £10

Membership Type: couple/individual
Description: Seeks to provide mutual help and support for people involved in or about to be involved in mixed marriages in Northern Ireland.
Publication: Newsletter
Publication title: NIMMA Update

03397
Northern Ireland Public Service Alliance
NIPSA
Harkin House, 54 Wellington Park, Belfast, BT9 6DP, UK
Tel: 028 90661831
Fax: 028 90665847
Email: info@nipsa.org.uk
Website: http://www.nipsa.org.uk/Home
Members: 45000
Staff: 51
Contact: Brian Campfield, Gen. Sec.
Description: Civil and public servants in Northern Ireland. Promotes and protects members' interests. Acts as a liaison between members and their employers. Offers legal assistance; sponsors courses.
Formerly: Absorbed, Civil Service Group
Publication title: NIPSA News

03398
Norwich Campaign for Nuclear Disarmament
258 Earlham Rd., Norwich, NR2 3RH, UK
Tel: 01603 453530
Email: jean.davis@talk21.com
Website: http://www.cnduk.org/index.php/regional-groups/norwich-cnd.html
Description: Aims to eliminate British nuclear weapons and other weapons of mass destruction.

03399
Nuclear Institute
Allan House, 1 Penerley Rd., London, SE6 2LQ, UK
Tel: 020 86958220
Fax: 020 86958229
Email: admin@nuclearinst.com
Website: http://www.nuclearinst.com/ibis/Nuclear%20Institute/Home
Members: 1400
Staff: 1
Contact: Mark Askew, Exec. Sec.
Fee: £150
Membership Type: fellow
Fee: £123
Membership Type: regular
Description: Represents all persons interested in the Nuclear Sector.
Library Type: not open to the public
Formerly: Formerly, British Nuclear Energy Society
Publication: Journal
Publication title: Nuclear Future. Advertisements.

03400
Nuffield Council on Bioethics
28 Bedford Sq., London, WC1B 3JS, UK
Tel: 020 76819619
Fax: 020 73236203
Email: cjoynson@nuffieldbioethics.org
Website: http://nuffieldbioethics.org
Members: 17
Staff: 8
Contact: Hugh Whittall, Dir.
Description: Philosophers, scientists, lawyers, theologians, clinicians and scientists. Aims to identify, examine, and report on ethical questions raised by recent advances in biological and medical research. Seeks to play a role in policymaking and in stimulating debate on bioethics. Publishes eight major reports on the ethical issues associated with genetic screening, ownership of tissue, xenotransplantation, genetics and mental disorders, genetically modified crops, the ethics of research related to healthcare in developing countries, behavioural genetics and pharmacogenetics.
Library Subject: bioethics
Library Type: by appointment only
Publication: Report
Publication title: Animal-to-Human Transplantation: The Ethics of Xenotransplantation
Meetings/Conventions: Ethical Issue of Clinical Research in Developing Countries – annual workshop

03401
Nurses' Hypertension Association
NHA
c/o Wendy Callister, Sec.
Peart-Rose Clinic, 59-61 N Wharf Rd., London, W2 1LA, UK
Email: nha_email@yahoo.co.uk
Website: http://www.nha.uk.net
Contact: Naomi Stetson, Chair
Fee: £40
Membership Type: regular
Description: Promotes the advancement and dissemination of information concerning hypertension findings and related vascular disease. Provides an international forum for education, communication and research development among nurses taking an active interest in hypertension.

03402
Nutrition Society
NS
10 Cambridge Ct., 210 Shepherds Bush Rd., London, W6 7NJ, UK
Tel: 020 76020228
Fax: 020 76021756
Email: office@nutsoc.org.uk
Website: http://www.nutritionsociety.org
Members: 2400
Staff: 11
Contact: J.J. Strain, Pres.
Fee: £75.2
Membership Type: full
Fee: £20.07
Membership Type: graduate, low income, retired, unwaged
Description: Persons involved in nutrition research or in health maintenance organized to promote the scientific study of nutrition. Maintains special regional groups; disseminates information via journals.
Publication: Journal
Publication title: British Journal of Nutrition
Meetings/Conventions: annual conference

03403
Oasis
The Oasis Centre, 75 Westminster Bridge Rd., Lambeth, London, SE1 7HS, UK
Tel: 020 79214200
Fax: 020 79214201
Email: enquiries@oasisuk.org
Website: http://www.oasisuk.org
Staff: 400
Contact: Steve Chalke, Founder
Description: Delivers educational, health and housing services. Aims to serve people and transform communities by confronting injustice and promoting inclusion.
Formerly: Formerly, AIDS Care and Education Training
Publication: Newsletter
Publication title: ACET Newsletter

03404
Obstetric Anaesthetists' Association
OAA
PO Box 3219, Barnes, London, SW13 9XR, UK
Tel: 0208 7411311
Fax: 0208 7410611
Website: http://www.oaa-anaes.ac.uk/content.asp?ContentID=1
Members: 2000
Contact: Paul Howell, Pres.
Fee: £110
Membership Type: consultant, staff, associate specialist
Fee: £90
Membership Type: trainee
Description: Promotes the highest standards of anaesthetic practice in the care of the mother and baby. Provides a focus for all anaesthetists who want to improve the care and safety of women in childbirth.
Publication: Booklet
Publication title: Guidelines for Obstetric Anaesthesia Services
Meetings/Conventions: Obstetric Anaesthesia – annual international conference – Exhibits.

03405
Ocean Youth Trust Scotland
OYTS
Victoria House, 5 E Blackhall St., Greenock, PA15 1HD, UK
Tel: 01475 722722
Fax: 01475 727977
Email: office@oytscotland.org.uk
Website: http://www.oytscotland.org.uk
Members: 180
Staff: 10
Contact: Nick Fleming, Chief Exec.
Description: Youths; adult leaders. Promotes healthy physical and social development of young people "through the spirit of adventure under sail." Conducts sailing trips; sponsors educational programs.
Formerly: Formerly, Ocean Youth Club Scotland
Publication: Magazine
Publication title: Scotmates. Advertisements.

03406
Ockenden International - England
OI
PO Box 1275, Woking, GU22 2FT, UK
Website: http://www.ockenden.org.uk
Members: 40
Staff: 120
Contact: Kofi Annan, Sec. Gen.
Description: Promotes self-reliance for displaced people in eight countries in Asia and Africa; establishes skills training courses and micro credit systems; establishes and maintains schools.

03407
Office of Health Economics
OHE
12 Whitehall, London, SW1A 2DY, UK
Tel: 020 77478850
Fax: 020 77478851
Email: ohegeneral@ohe.org
Website: http://www.ohe.org/page/index.cfm
Staff: 7
Contact: Adrian Towse, Dir.
Description: Undertakes research on the economic aspects of medical care, with particular reference to the pharmaceutical industry.

03408
Offshore Contractors Association
OCA
Heritage House, Grandholm Crescent, Aberdeen, AB22 8BH, UK
Tel: 01224 707545
Fax: 01224 706400
Email: info@ocainternet.com
Website: http://www.ocainternet.com/Default.aspx?id=1&mid=1
Members: 73
Staff: 5
Contact: Bill Murray, Chief Exec.
Fee: £540
Membership Type: associate (small and medium company)
Fee: £5000
Membership Type: full
Description: Works as lead representative for contractors and suppliers, including mechanical, electrical and allied services, construction, modifications and maintenance work, design and project engineering, fabrication and decommissioning.
Publication: Newsletter
Publication title: Guidance Notes of Good Contracting Practice Within the Oil and Gas Industry: Hand/Arm Vibration Syndrome

03409
Offshore Pollution Liability Association
OPOL
29 High St., Surrey, Ewell, KT17 1SB, UK
Tel: 020 87863640
Fax: 020 87863641
Email: info@opol.org.uk
Website: http://www.opol.org.uk
Members: 76
Staff: 1
Contact: Roger Segal, Managing Dir.
Description: European offshore oil company operators in European Union, Norway, Isle of Man, Faroe Islands. Aims to administer the OPOL Agreement which relates to the settlement of claims made against offshore oil companies as a result of oil spills.

03410
Oil and Colour Chemists' Association
OCCA
3 Eden Ct., 1st Fl., Eden Way, Leighton Buzzard, LU7 4FY, UK
Tel: 01525 372530
Fax: 01525 372600
Email: membership@occa.org.uk
Website: http://www.occa.org.uk
Members: 2500
Staff: 5
Contact: Chris Pacey-Day, Gen. Sec.
Fee: £65
Membership Type: ordinary in UK/overseas
Description: Learned society/professional body for technical staff employed in surface coatings industries. Organizes exhibitions, technical and social meetings.
Publication: Bulletin
Publication title: Surface Coatings International Bulletin

03411
Oil Companies International Marine Forum
OCIMF
29 Queen Anne's Gate, London, SW1H 9BU, UK
Tel: 020 76541200
Fax: 020 76541205
Email: enquiries@ocimf.com
Website: http://www.ocimf.com
Members: 82
Contact: Jan Kopernicki, Chm.
Description: Oil companies worldwide united to promote safety in the transportation and storage of crude oil and its products, including gas and petrochemicals, and to prevent pollution from tankers and at terminals. Works to establish guidelines for equipment at terminals and offshore moorings, and for tanker and gas carrier manifolds. Conducts studies and research projects on such projects as effects of wind and currents, safe terminal moorings of large ships, tanker salvage, and the handling of disabled ships. Is involved with other organizations in the consideration of governmental and industrial contingency plans to handle spills. Participates in work of the International Maritime Organization in areas of carriage of bulk chemicals and gases, equipment, fire protection, navigation safety, ship design, standards of training, and watchkeeping. Works with governments represented by IMO and provides information and assistance. Cooperates with other industry organizations, including the International Chamber of Shipping and the Society of International Gas Tanker and Terminal Operators, on the operation of tankers and gas carriers such as the ship to ship transfer for oil tankers and gas carriers, and planned passage in the Malacca/Singapore Straits.
Library Type: reference
Publication: Book
Publication title: International Safety Guide for Oil Tankers and Terminals

03412
Oil Firing Technical Association for the Petroleum Industry
OFTEC
Foxwood House, Dobbs Ln., Kesgrave, Ipswich, IP5 2QQ, UK
Tel: 0845 6585080
Fax: 0845 6585181
Email: enquiries@oftec.org
Website: http://www.oftec.co.uk
Description: Promotes members' interests.
Library Subject: oil central heating, oil distribution
Library Type: reference

03413
OISTAT Centre of Great Britain
ABTT
Association of British Theatre Technicians, 55 Farringdon Rd., London, EC1M 3JB, UK
Tel: 020 72429200
Fax: 020 72429303
Email: info@abtt.org.uk
Website: http://www.abtt.org.uk
Members: 1700
Contact: Mark White, Chm.
Description: National office of the Organisation Internationale des Scenographes, Techniciens, et Architectes de Theatre. Facilitates exchange of ideas and information among professional theatrical technicians. Gathers and disseminates information on subjects relating to technical installations with theatrical applications.

03414
Omnibus Society
OS
100-102 Sandwell St., Walsall, WS1 3EB, UK
Website: http://www.omnibussoc.org
Members: 950
Contact: Mark Howarth, Pres.
Description: Individuals in 15 countries interested in preserving the history of bus, coach, trolleybus, and tramway vehicles and records. Facilitates exchange of information and discussion of traffic and engineering matters. Organizes field trips and study tours. Maintains news and historical service, photographic register, route recording scheme, ticket and timetable collection.
Library Subject: road passenger transport
Library Type: reference
Publication: Magazine
Publication title: Omnibus Magazine

03415
One Parent Families Scotland
OPFS
13 Gayfield Sq., Edinburgh, EH1 3NX, UK
Tel: 0131 5563899
Email: info@opfs.org.uk
Website: http://www.opfs.org.uk
Members: 300
Staff: 71
Contact: Rachael Gibbins, Sec.
Description: Provides support and information to single parents in Scotland. Also organizes conferences and workshops and offers training to agencies which help single parents.
Formerly: Formerly, Scottish Council for the Unmarried Mother and Her Child
Publication: Book
Publication title: Lone Parent Rights Guide

03416
One Village
OV
Charlbury, Chipping Norton, OX7 3SQ, UK
Tel: 01608 811811
Fax: 01608 811911
Email: progress@onevillage.org
Website: http://www.onevillage.org
Description: Campaigns to enhance public understanding of global interdependence and encourages community action to increase the well-being of communities and the worldwide community. Operates with workers'

cooperatives and community associations involved in craft production in Africa, Asia, and Central and South America.

03417

One World Action
OWA

Bradley's Close, 74-77 White Lion St., London, N1 9PF, UK
Tel: 020 78334075
Fax: 020 78334102
Email: info@oneworldaction.org
Website: http://www.oneworldaction.org
Staff: 12
Contact: Andy Rutherford, Acting Dir.
Description: Works in Europe and with partner organizations in poor countries to defeat poverty and to promote democracy and respect for human rights.
Publication: Newsletter
Publication title: A Partnership for Change

03418

Open and Distance Learning Quality Council
ODL QC

44 Bedford Row, London, WC1R 4LL, UK
Tel: 020 74472543
Email: info@odlqc.org.uk
Website: http://www.odlqc.org.uk
Members: 55
Staff: 3
Contact: John Ainsworth, Chm.
Description: Organisations awarded accreditation. Aims to raise standards in distance education and training, protect the interests of learners and increase awareness of the work of ODLQC and its accredited organisations.
Formerly: Formerly, Council for the Accreditation of Correspondence Colleges
Publication: Brochure
Publication title: Buyers Guide to Distance Learning

03419

Open Spaces Society
OSS

25 A Bell St., Henley-on-Thames, RG9 2BA, UK
Tel: 01491 573535
Fax: 01491 573051
Email: hq@oss.org.uk
Website: http://www.oss.org.uk
Members: 2400
Staff: 5
Contact: Kate Ashbrook, Gen. Sec.
Fee: £30
Membership Type: individual
Fee: £600
Membership Type: life
Description: Individuals' groups, parish councils, national organizations, local authorities. Campaigns to create and conserve common land, village greens, open spaces, and public paths and country in England and Wales.
Publication: Book
Publication title: Getting Greens Registered-A Guide to Law and Procedure for Town and Village Greens

03420

Operation Smile - United Kingdom

4th Fl., Horatio House, 77 Fulham Palace Rd., London, W6 8JA, UK
Tel: 0208 5765660
Fax: 020 85765601
Email: info@operationsmile.org.uk
Website: http://www.operationsmile.org/countries/uk
Contact: Manoj Badale, Chm.
Description: Works to increase the availability of cosmetic and reconstructive surgery among impoverished children. Performs free reconstructive surgery on needy children. Conducts training programs for surgeons. Distributes medical equipment and supplies to indigenous health care centers.

03421

Operational Research Society of the United Kingdom

Seymour House, 12 Edward St., Birmingham, B1 2RX, UK
Tel: 0121 2339300
Fax: 0121 2330321
Email: email@theorsociety.com
Website: http://www.theorsociety.com
Members: 3080
Staff: 7
Contact: Gavin Blackett, Sec./Gen. Mgr.
Fee: £69
Membership Type: full
Fee: £23
Membership Type: student
Description: Membership Practitioners and academics in operational research, decision support systems, business research, management science, decision science. Purpose Aims to further knowledge and good practice in the use of scientific, analytic, systematic, and structured, approaches to assist in planning and decision-making in industry, commerce, government at all levels and in public and private services.
Library Subject: operational research
Library Type: open to the public
Publication: Journal
Publication title: European Journal of Information Systems

03422

Optimum Population Trust
OPT

12 Meadowgate, Urmston, Manchester, M41 9LB, UK
Tel: 0208 81239166
Email: info@optimumpopulation.org
Website: http://www.optimumpopulation.org
Members: 1400
Staff: 3
Contact: Roger Martin, Chm.
Fee: £20
Membership Type: supporter
Description: Seeks to achieve what the group feels are optimum population levels worldwide. Conducts research and educational programs.
Publication: Journal
Publication title: OPT Journal

03423

Oral History Society
OHS

PO Box 464, Berkhamsted, Hertfordshire, CO4 3SQ, UK
Tel: 01442 879097
Fax: 01442 872279
Email: oralhistory@webscribe.info
Website: http://www.ohs.org.uk
Members: 1000
Contact: Robert Perks, Sec.
Fee: £20
Membership Type: individual (in UK)
Fee: £30
Membership Type: institution (in UK)
Description: Historians and other individuals with an interest in oral history. Promotes recording and preservation of oral histories as a method of historical research. Provides practical support to individuals wishing to record oral histories; serves as a clearinghouse on oral history; conducts research and educational programs.
Publication: Journal
Publication title: Oral History Journal. Advertisements.

Orchestre des Jeunes de l'Union Europeenne

see European Union Youth Orchestra

03424

Orders and Medals Research Society
OMRS

PO Box 1233, High Wycombe, HP11 9BW, UK
Tel: 01494 441207
Email: generalsecretary@omrs.org.uk
Website: http://www.omrs.org.uk
Members: 2500
Contact: Peter Helmore, Gen. Sec.
Fee: £20
Membership Type: in United Kingdom
Fee: £28
Membership Type: outside United Kingdom
Description: Individuals (2700); firms and military museums (50). Objectives are: to promote and foster interest in the study of orders, decorations, and medals, and all related material; to assist collectors and students in their research; to advance the interests of members as collectors. Organizes lectures.
Publication title: The Miscellany of Honours

03425

Organic Food Federation
OFF

Eco-Tech Business Park, 31 Turbine Way, Norfolk, Swaffham, PE37 7XD, UK
Tel: 01760 720444
Fax: 01760 720790
Email: info@orgfoodfed.com
Website: http://www.orgfoodfed.com
Members: 350
Staff: 5
Description: Manufacturers, processors, importers and producers of organic foods or ingredients. Provides organic certification. Represents manufacturers' and importers' interests on governmental and other bodies. Disseminates information on organic food and ingredients and relevant matters to members. It is the focal point for organic manufacturers, distributors, and importers to establish contact and meet regularly.
Meetings/Conventions: Certification and Management Committee – meeting

03426

Organisation for Professionals in Regulatory Affairs
TOPRA

Bellerive House, 3 Muirfield Crescent, London, E14 9SZ, UK
Tel: 0207 5102560
Fax: 0207 5372003
Email: info@topra.org
Website: http://www.topra.org
Members: 3076
Staff: 11
Contact: Lynda Wight, Exec. Dir.
Fee: £75
Membership Type: fellow, registered
Fee: £37.5
Membership Type: concession, retired fellow
Description: Professionals active in the field of regulatory affairs. Seeks to increase understanding of the affects of national and international manufacturing and trade regulations on business, with particular emphasis on the development and production of pharmaceutical products. Promotes professional advancement of members. Serves as a forum for the sharing of experience and knowledge among members; sponsors educational and training programs.
Formerly: Formerly, European Society of Regulatory Affairs
Publication: Journal
Publication title: Regulatory Rapporteur. Advertisements.

Organisation Maritime Internationale
see International Maritime Organization

Organisation Mondiale pour la Systemique et la Cybernetique
see World Organisation of Systems and Cybernetics

Organizacion Internacional del Azucar
see International Sugar Organization

Organizacion Internationale del Cacao
see International Cocoa Organization

03427

Oriental Ceramic Society
OCS

PO Box 517, Cambridge, CB21 5BE, UK
Tel: 01223 881328
Email: ocslondon@btinternet.com
Website: http://www.ocs-london.com
Members: 1100
Staff: 1
Contact: Mary Painter, Contact
Fee: £55
Membership Type: inside U.K.
Fee: £50
Membership Type: outside U.K.
Description: Individuals, museums, and libraries. Increases knowledge of Eastern ceramics and other arts. Organizes loan exhibitions of objects from members' private collections and museums.
Publication: Journal
Publication title: Transactions of the Oriental Ceramic Society. Advertisements.

03428

Ornamental Aquatic Trade Association
OATA

Wessex House, 40 Station Rd., Wiltshire, Westbury, BA13 3JN, UK
Tel: 01373 301353
Fax: 01373 301236
Email: info@ornamentalfish.org
Website: http://www.ornamentalfish.org
Members: 750
Contact: Keith Davenport, Sec.
Fee: £107.66
Membership Type: retailer, association, college
Fee: £2357.5
Membership Type: breeder, dry goods distributor, glass aquaria manufacturer (based on turnover)
Description: Represents the interests of ornamental fish importers, breeders, wholesalers, retailers and manufacturers of glass aquaria. Promotes responsible pet ownership by informing the public of the proper ways of maintaining a pet fish or how to transport pets from one place to another. Provides individual and industry member training through the organization's distance learning packages.
Publication: Report
Publication title: Koi Herpes Virus

03429

Ornithological Society of the Middle East
OSME

Bedfordshire, Sandy, SG19 2DL, UK
Email: secretary@osme.org
Website: http://www.osme.org
Members: 1000
Contact: Owen Roberts, Membership/Recruitment Sec.
Fee: £20
Membership Type: individual in UK
Fee: £25
Membership Type: family in UK, individual in Europe
Description: Individuals and organizations in 50 countries interested in birds of the Middle East. Encourages knowledge and conservation of Middle Eastern birds. Collects and collates ornithological data. Seeks to develop working relationships with environmental, conservation, and natural history societies concerned with the Middle East.
Library Subject: ornithology in the Middle East
Library Type: reference
Publication: Journal
Publication title: Sandgrouse. Advertisements.

03430

OSPAR Commission

New Ct., 48 Carey St., London, WC2A 2JQ, UK
Tel: 020 74305200
Fax: 020 74305225
Email: secretariat@ospar.org
Website: http://www.ospar.org
Members: 16
Staff: 12
Description: Represents governments of Belgium, Denmark, Germany, Finland, France, Iceland, Luxembourg, Netherlands, Norway, Portugal, Republic of Ireland, Spain, Sweden, Switzerland, the United Kingdom and the Commission of European Communities.

03431

Outdoor Advertising Association of Great Britain
OAA

Summit House, 27 Sale Pl., London, W2 1YR, UK
Tel: 020 79730315
Fax: 020 79730318
Email: enquiries@oaa.org.uk
Website: http://www.oaa.org.uk
Members: 50
Staff: 3
Contact: Mike Baker, Chief Exec.
Description: Represents outdoor media owners.

03432

Outdoor Industries Association
OIA

c/o Louise Ramsay
EICA-Ratho, South Platt Hill, Newbridge, Edinburgh, EH28 8AA, UK
Tel: 0131 3334414
Email: info@outdoorindustriesassociation.co.uk
Website: http://www.outdoorindustriesassociation.co.uk
Members: 310
Staff: 4
Contact: Chris Bonington, Pres.
Description: Trade association representing manufacturers, retailers, wholesalers, importers and distributors of outdoor leisure equipment and accessories. Provides an organization for the promotion and development of the outdoor leisure and camping trades.
Formerly: Formerly, Camping and Outdoor Leisure Association
Publication: Newsletter
Publication title: Go Outdoors Bulletin
Meetings/Conventions: Go Outdoors – annual trade show – Exhibits.

03433

Outdoor Writers and Photographers Guild
OWPG

1 Waterside Close, Garstang, Preston, PR3 1HJ, UK
Tel: 01995 605340
Email: secretary@owg.org.uk
Website: http://www.owg.org.uk
Members: 160
Contact: Jon Sparks, Sec.
Description: Professional writers and journalists who write, film, photograph, broadcast, etc., about walking, climbing, mountaineering and similar outdoor activities, along with general travel. Aims to promote professional standards among writers specializing in outdoor writing; to represent members' interests; to provide a forum through meetings and social activities for members to meet colleagues and others in the outdoor leisure industry.
Publication: Journal
Publication title: Outdoor Focus. Advertisements.

03434
Overseas Development Institute
ODI
111 Westminster Bridge Rd., London, SE1 7JD, UK
Tel: 020 79220300
Fax: 020 79220399
Email: odi@odi.org.uk
Website: http://www.odi.org.uk
Staff: 168
Contact: Alexis Chapman, Dir.
Description: Serves as an independent non-governmental centre for development research and a forum for discussion of the problems facing developing countries. Has four main components on research programme: Natural Resources, Forestry, Human Security and Development, and International Economic Development. Has networks linking research to practitioners in Agricultural Research and Extension, rural Development Forestry and Relief and Rehabilitation.

03435
Overseas Press and Media Association
OPMA
15 Magrath Ave., Cambridge, CB4 3AH, UK
Tel: 01223 512631
Fax: 01223 512631
Email: contact@opma.co.uk
Website: http://www.opma.co.uk
Members: 150
Contact: Jackie Dunn, Contact
Fee: £135
Membership Type: full, one representative
Fee: £270
Membership Type: full, two representative
Description: Represents overseas media to market in the United Kingdom.
Publication: Book
Publication title: OPMA Guide

03436
Oxfam - U.K.
Oxfam House, John Smith Dr., Cowley, Oxford, OX4 2JY, UK
Tel: 01865 472602
Website: http://www.oxfam.org.uk
Staff: 1343
Contact: John Gaventa, Chm.
Description: Provides food and shelter to people in emergency situations. Assists people in their efforts to gain economic self-sufficiency. Believes in the fundamental dignity of people and their inherent ability to overcome obstacles imposed by geopolitical and socioeconomic hardships. Contends that the world's material resources can, if equitably distributed, satisfy the basic needs of all people. Administers charitable program. Maintains 50 field offices and operates over 2,900 relief and development projects in more than 70 countries. Conducts educational programs and campaigns in the United Kingdom and the Republic of Ireland. Supported by 180,000 financial donors and assisted by 30,000 volunteers.
Publication: Journal
Publication title: Development in Practice

03437
Packaging and Industrial Films Association
PIFA
Gothic House, 2nd Fl., Barker Gate, Nottingham, NG1 1JU, UK
Tel: 01159 598389
Fax: 01159 599326
Email: client-services@pr-principles.co.uk
Website: http://www.pafa.org.uk
Members: 150
Staff: 6
Contact: David Tyson, Chief Exec.
Description: Open to companies in the UK engaged in the manufacture, conversion and supply of plastic film. Associate Membership is open to those companies whose activities are closely related to the film industry. Acts as forum for developing industry consensus, a channel for information, advice and education, a regime for policing performance and quality standards, and a centre for trade statistics and a focus for representation.

03438
Packaging Federation
1 Warwick Row, London, SW1E 5ER, UK
Tel: 020 78087217
Fax: 020 78087218
Email: dicksearle@packagingfedn.co.uk
Website: http://www.packagingfedn.co.uk
Contact: Dick Searle, Chief Exec.
Description: Represents packaging companies in UK. Sponsors research and advances knowledge of packaging supply industry and user markets. Creates a better understanding of different requirements and challenges facing packaging industry.

03439
Painter-Stainers' Company
c/o Painters' Hall
9 Little Trinity Ln., London, EC4V 2AD, UK
Tel: 020 72366258
Email: beadle@painters-hall.co.uk
Website: http://www.painters-hall.co.uk
Members: 550
Staff: 5
Contact: Ernie Brocklehurst, Contact
Description: Livery company.

03440
Painting and Decorating Association of Great Britain
PDA
32 Coton Rd., Warwickshire, Nuneaton, CV11 5TW, UK
Tel: 02476 353776
Fax: 02476 354513
Email: info@paintingdecoratingassociation.co.uk
Website: http://www.paintingdecoratingassociation.co.uk
Members: 2500
Staff: 4
Contact: Paul Marsden, Chief Exec.
Description: Painters, decorators and decorating contractors. Aims to promote the continuous and progressive improvement of the painting and decorating industry, to advance the well-being and status of all connected with it. Also aims to federate the various regional and local associations, persons and companies engaged in the trade of painting and decorating and to act jointly by amalgamation, and to co-operate with any other associations, in promoting the objects of the Association.
Formerly: Formerly, British Decorators Association

Pairti Soisialta Daonlathach an Lucht Oibre
see Social Democratic and Labour Party

03441
Palaeontographical Society - United Kingdom
c/o Mr. F.W.J. Bryant, Marketing Mgr.
27 The Crescent, Berkshire, Maidenhead, SL6 6AA, UK
Email: jb014k3184@sky.com
Website: http://www.palaeosoc.org
Members: 289
Contact: P.M. Barrett, Co-Sec.
Fee: £17.5
Membership Type: student
Fee: £35
Membership Type: ordinary
Description: Professional and amateur paleontologists and libraries worldwide. Identifies and describes British fossils.
Publication: Monographs
Publication title: Monographs of the Palaeontographical Society

03442
Palaeontological Association
University of Wales-Aberstywyth, Institute of Geography and Earth Sciences, Ceredigion, Aberystwyth, SY23 3DB, UK
Email: palass@palass.org
Website: http://www.palass.org
Members: 1350
Staff: 2
Contact: Tim J. Palmer, Exec. Off.
Description: Professional and amateur palaeontologists. Covers topics from macropalaeontology, micropalaeontology, palaeobotany, vertebrate palaeotology, palaeoecology and biostratigraphy. Activities include up to two thematic review seminars each year and an annual conference, held in December, where a broad range of research is presented. Field trips to sites of palaeontological interest are led both within Britain and Europe.
Publication: Journal
Publication title: Palaeontology

03443
Panos Institute - London
9 White Lion St., London, N1 9PD, UK
Tel: 020 72781111
Fax: 020 72780345
Email: info@panos.org.uk
Website: http://www.panos.org.uk
Staff: 29
Contact: Mark Wilson, Exec. Dir.
Description: Promotes greater awareness of sustainable development; facilitates development journalism. Gathers and disseminates information on sustainable development; works with local organizations to conduct public education programs.
Library Subject: media development, communication for development, HIV/AIDS communication, oral testimonies, information society, globalization, environment
Library Type: reference
Publication: Report
Publication title: Panos Reports

03444
Paper Agents' Association
PAA
48 Courtmoor Ave., Hampshire, Fleet, GU52 7UE, UK
Tel: 01252 680449
Fax: 07092 386132
Email: info@paa.org.uk
Website: http://www.paa.org.uk
Members: 40
Staff: 1
Contact: John R. Paine, Dir.
Description: Paper agents and UK Sales offices of Overseas Paper and Board Mills. Represents overseas paper and board manufacturers in the UK.

03445
Paper Industry Technical Association
PITA
5 Frecheville Ct., Bury, BL9 0UF, UK
Tel: 0161 7645858
Fax: 0161 7645353
Email: info@pita.co.uk
Website: http://www.pita.co.uk
Staff: 3
Contact: Barry Read, Contact
Fee: £100
Membership Type: full, individual (plus 17.75 value added tax)
Fee: £35
Membership Type: junior (under 24 years old; plus 6.13 value added tax)
Description: An independent body. Stimulates discussion of technical matters to promote the cost effective application of new ideas and procedures. Promotes scientific and technical education. Cooperates with other scientific organizations. Maintains committees that organize paper presentations, annual meetings and programs, and field visits.
Publication: Book
Publication title: Essential Guide to Aqueous Coating of Paper and Board
Meetings/Conventions: biennial conference – Exhibits.

03446
Parentline Plus
520 Highgate Studios, 53-79 Highgate Rd., Kentish Town, London, NW5 1TL, UK
Tel: 020 72845500
Email: parentsupport@parentlineplus.org.uk
Website: http://www.parentlineplus.org.uk
Members: 600
Staff: 8
Contact: Jeremy Todd, Chief Exec.
Description: Provides information and advice and support services to parents. Supports research. Trains professionals.
Formerly: Absorbed, National Stepfamily Association
Publication: Magazine
Publication title: Changing Families

03447
Parents and Professionals and Autism Northern Ireland
PAPA
Donard House, Knockbracken Healthcare Park, Saintfield Rd., Belfast, BT8 8BH, UK
Tel: 028 90401729
Fax: 028 90403467
Email: info@autismni.org
Website: http://www.autismni.org
Members: 700
Staff: 6
Contact: Arlene Cassidy, Chief Exec.
Fee: £20
Membership Type: individual, family, organization
Fee: £5
Membership Type: student, unwaged
Description: Established by parents of autistic children and professionals that are concerned with autism in Northern Ireland. Seeks to ensure that people within the autistic spectrum and their caregivers have access to appropriate services, enabling people with autism to be valued members of their community. Provides resources, information, and advice on autism; encourages research and training; works in partnership with a range of voluntary, private, and statutory agencies; works to increase public awareness of autism.
Library Subject: autism
Library Type: open to the public
Publication: Newsletter
Publication title: Contact

03448
Parkinson's Disease Nurse Specialist Association
PDNSA
Nene House, Isebrook Hospital, Irthlingborough Rd., Wellingborough, NN8 1LP, UK
Email: richard.glasspool@northants.nhs.uk
Website: http://www.pdnsa.net
Contact: Richard Glasspool, Chm.
Fee: £20
Membership Type: full
Fee: £10
Membership Type: associate
Description: Acts as a national resource and network for nurses to share knowledge, expertise and best practice about Parkinson's disease and its management. Provides a forum for the discussion of professional issues where appropriate action can be taken to influence the development of nursing practice.
Publication: Newsletter
Publication title: Transmitter

03449
Parkinson's Disease Society of the United Kingdom
PDS
215 Vauxhall Bridge Rd., London, SV1V 1EJ, UK
Tel: 020 79318080
Fax: 020 72339908
Email: hello@parkinsons.org
Website: http://www.parkinsons.org.uk
Members: 30000
Staff: 160
Contact: Jane Asher, Pres.
Fee: £4
Membership Type: individual in UK
Fee: £15
Membership Type: individual overseas
Description: Promotes awareness of Parkinson's disease.
Library Subject: Parkinson's disease
Library Type: open to the public

03450
Parrot Society - U.K.
PS
92A High St., Hertfordshire, Berkhamsted, HP4 2BL, UK
Tel: 01442 872245
Fax: 01442 872245
Email: les.rance@theparrotsocietyuk.org
Website: http://www.theparrotsocietyuk.org
Members: 5000
Staff: 3
Contact: Leslie Rance, Sec.
Fee: £600
Membership Type: life
Fee: £20
Membership Type: family
Description: Zoos, bird gardens, traders, and individuals in the United Kingdom interested in the breeding and study of parrots. Disseminates information on parrots; advises pet owners. Conducts seminars; operates charitable program; compiles statistics.
Library Type: reference
Publication: Directory
Publication title: Breeding Register

03451
Partially Sighted Society
PSS
7/9 Bennetthorpe, Doncaster, DN2 6AA, UK
Tel: 0844 4774966
Fax: 0844 4774969
Email: info@partsight.org.uk
Website: http://www.partsight.org.uk
Members: 2000
Staff: 4
Description: Strives to improve social, medical, and domestic services available to the visually impaired in the United Kingdom and to increase educational and employment opportunities. Offers information and advice; provides visual aids and special printing and enlargement services. Operates 3 sight centers that offer vision assessment and training services. Arranges conferences, exhibitions, and displays.
Publication: Newsletter
Publication title: Oculus. Advertisements.

03452
Passenger Shipping Association
PSA
41/42 Eastcastle St., 1st Fl., London, W1W 8DU, UK
Tel: 020 74362449
Email: info@psa-ace.org
Website: http://www.the-psa.co.uk
Members: 50
Staff: 5
Contact: William Gibbons, Dir.
Description: Passenger shipping companies (cruising and ferry). Owners trade association for cruise lines and ferry operators. Provides market information to members as well as acting as contact body for wide ranging membership in consultation and liaison with UK government and industry bodies.

03453
Pastel Society
17 Carlton House Terr., London, SW1Y 5BD, UK
Tel: 020 79306844
Email: grambrus@gmail.com
Website: http://www.thepastelsociety.org.uk
Members: 56

Contact: Mark Leach, Pres.
Fee: £25
Membership Type: individual
Fee: £40
Membership Type: joint
Description: Professional artists specializing in dry medium. Organizes pastel exhibitions, helps to educate public in pastel medium through exhibitions and demonstrations.

03454

Pathological Society of Great Britain and Ireland

2 Carlton House Terr., London, SW1Y 5AF, UK
Tel: 020 79761260
Fax: 020 79302981
Email: admin@pathsoc.org
Website: http://www.pathsoc.org
Members: 1100
Staff: 2
Contact: Andrew H. Wyllie, Pres.
Fee: £53
Membership Type: regular
Fee: £112
Membership Type: regular (with journal)
Description: Individuals engaged in research or teaching in connection with pathology or allied science.
Publication: Journal
Publication title: Journal of Pathology
Meetings/Conventions: annual meeting

03455

Pattern, Model, and Mould Manufacturers Association PMMMA

National Metalforming Ctre., 47 Birmingham Rd., West Bromwich, B70 6PY, UK
Tel: 0121 6016976
Fax: 0154 4340332
Email: andrew@pmmma.co.uk
Website: http://www.pmmma.co.uk
Members: 43
Staff: 2
Contact: Andrew Turner, Contact
Fee: £100
Membership Type: regular (10 employees or below)
Fee: £200
Membership Type: regular (11 to 25 employees)
Description: Represents pattern, model and mould manufacturers.
Library Type: reference
Publication: Journal
Publication title: Patternmaking. Advertisements.

03456

Paviors' Company

3 Ridgemount Gardens, Enfield, EN2 8QL, UK
Tel: 020 83661566
Email: jlwhite@talk21.com
Website: http://www.paviors.org.uk
Contact: John White, Clerk
Description: Represents professionals in the field of construction, primarily with roads and pavements. Organizes social and charitable functions for its members.
Publication: Magazine
Publication title: The Pavior

03457

Pax Christi - Great Britain

Christian Peace Education Centre, St. Joseph's, Watford Way, Hendon, London, NW4 4TY, UK
Tel: 020 82034884
Fax: 020 82035234
Email: info@paxchristi.org.uk
Website: http://www.paxchristi.org.uk
Members: 1600
Staff: 2
Fee: £30
Membership Type: organisation
Fee: £22
Membership Type: family
Description: Purposes are to: work for peace while bearing witness to the peace of Christ; contribute to the construction of a more genuinely humane world, with respect for the life of each human being; collaborate with other Christian groups and peace movements; struggle against sources of injustice such as violence, war, hatred, and economic inequality. Condemns the arms race; urges arms control and disarmament. Stresses the importance of detente between the East and West, human rights, the Catholic Church's duty to emphasize peace, and the problems of the Third World.
Publication: Newsletter
Publication title: Justpeace

03458

Peace Brigades International - United Kingdom PBI

1b Waterlow Rd., London, N19 5NJ, UK
Tel: 020 72815370
Fax: 020 72815370
Website: http://www.peacebrigades.org.uk
Contact: Susi Bascon, Dir.
Description: Promotes non-violent transformation of conflicts and human rights protection worldwide. Facilitates protective accompaniment, peace education, independent observation and analysis of conflict situation. Spreads information on human rights and nonviolent struggle for peace and justice.
Publication: Newsletter
Publication title: PBI News

03459

Peace Child International PCI

White House, 46 High St., Buntingford, SG9 9AH, UK
Tel: 01763 274459
Fax: 01763 274460
Email: info@peacechild.org
Website: http://www.peacechild.org
Members: 500
Staff: 10
Contact: Rosey Simonds, Exec. Dir.
Description: Promotes sustainable development to young people.
Publication: Newsletter
Publication title: e-bulletin

03460

Peace Pledge Union PPU

1 Peace Passage, London, N7 0BT, UK
Tel: 020 74249444
Fax: 020 74826390
Website: http://www.ppu.org.uk
Members: 2000
Staff: 5
Contact: Jan Melichar, Contact
Description: Represents individuals who pledge to renounce war or aggressive action in order to achieve a world in which "justice and freedom are personal experiences and not abstract definitions." Furthers discussion of nonviolent approaches to problem solving and strives to develop conflict resolutions that satisfy pacifist aims. Focuses attention on societal influences on young people that encourage aggressive behavior. Campaigns for a voluntary ban on the sale of war toys and promotes development of cooperative play. Distributes educational materials on the causes of war and on alternative solutions. Sponsors speakers' bureau; compiles statistics on wars and war deaths.
Formerly: Formerly, Sheppard Peace Movement

03461

Penal Reform International PRI

60-62 Commercial St., London, E1 6LT, UK
Tel: 020 72476515
Fax: 020 73778711
Email: info@penalreform.org
Website: http://www.penalreform.org
Contact: Vivien Stern, Pres.
Description: Seeks to achieve penal reform, whilst recognizing diverse cultural contexts, by promoting: the development and implementation of international human rights instruments with regard to law enforcement, prison conditions and standards; the elimination of unfair and unethical discrimination in all penal measures; the abolition of the death penalty; the reduction in the use of imprisonment throughout the world; and the use of constructive non-custodial sanctions which encourage social reintegration whilst taking account of the interests of victims.

03462

Pensions Management Institute PMI

4/10 Artillery Ln., London, E1 7LS, UK
Tel: 020 72471452
Fax: 020 73750603
Email: membership@pensions-pmi.org.uk
Website: http://www.pensions-pmi.org.uk
Members: 5000
Contact: Vince Linnane, Chief Exec.
Fee: £90
Membership Type: student
Fee: £235
Membership Type: associate
Description: Works for the maintenance and further development of professional standards. Provides tuition and examination services leading to nationally recognized qualifications for managers, consultants, administrators, IFA, lawyers, accountants, trustees and support staff. Also provides a range of seminars, conferences and publications.
Publication: Newsletter
Publication title: PMI News. Advertisements.

03463
People and Dogs Society
PADS
45B Ashgap Ln., Normanton, WF6 2DT, UK
Email: pads@padsonline.org.uk
Website: http://www.padsonline.org
Members: 100
Contact: Kit Le Seelleur, Honorary Sec.
Fee: £10
Membership Type: adult
Fee: £20
Membership Type: affiliate
Description: Promotes responsible dog ownership. Offers free help and advice on dog care and ownership.
Publication: Newsletter
Publication title: Pawprints. Advertisements.

03464
People and Planet
P&P
51 Union St., Oxford, OX4 1JP, UK
Tel: 01865 245678
Fax: 01865 791927
Email: people@peopleandplanet.org
Website: http://peopleandplanet.org
Staff: 21
Contact: Ian Leggett, Dir.
Description: Dedicated to solving environmental and social justice issues, focusing on the impact of global economic relations and corporate behavior on people and the environment.

03465
People for the Ethical Treatment of Animals Europe
PETA
PO Box 36678, London, SE1 1YE, UK
Tel: 020 73579229
Fax: 020 73570901
Email: info@petauk.org
Website: http://www.peta.org.uk
Contact: Ingrid E. Newkirk, Pres.
Description: Believes that animals deserve the most basic rights. Considers the best interests of animals, regardless of whether animals are useful to humans. Seeks to educate policymakers and the public about cruelty to animals; promotes understanding of the right of all animals to be treated with respect.

03466
People In Aid
The Resource Centre, 356 Holloway Rd., London, N7 6PA, UK
Tel: 020 30953950
Fax: 020 76979580
Email: info@peopleinaid.org
Website: http://www.peopleinaid.org
Members: 122
Contact: Katja Pesari, Operations Mgr.
Fee: £150-700
Membership Type: agency in high income countries
Fee: £100-150
Membership Type: agency in all other countries
Description: Represents development and humanitarian assistance agencies. Seeks to advise organizations whose goal is to support the relief of poverty and suffering.
Publication title: Ahead of the Field

03467
People's Trust for Endangered Species
PTES
15 Cloisters House, 8 Battersea Park Rd., London, SW8 4BG, UK
Tel: 020 74984533
Fax: 020 74984459
Email: enquiries@ptes.org
Website: http://www.ptes.org
Staff: 14
Contact: Jill Nelson, Chief Exec.
Description: Aims to ensure a future for many species of endangered creatures worldwide. Committed to working in an effort to preserve species in their natural habitat for future generations to enjoy by funding scientific research whose results lead to the drawing up of effective conservation strategies.

03468
Peoples Dispensary for Sick Animals
PDSA
Whitechapel Way, Priorslee, Telford, TF2 9PQ, UK
Tel: 01952 290999
Fax: 01952 291035
Email: pr@pdsa.org.uk
Website: http://www.pdsa.org.uk
Contact: Freddie St. L. Bircher, Co-Chairman
Description: Seeks to care for the animals of needy people by providing free veterinary care to their sick and injured pets and by promoting responsible pet ownership.

03469
PERA
Nottingham Rd., Leicestershire, Melton Mowbray, LE13 0PB, UK
Tel: 01664 501501
Fax: 01664 501554
Email: innovation@pera.com
Website: http://www.pera.com
Members: 1200
Staff: 300
Contact: John Hill, Chief Exec.
Description: Technical and management consultancy and training organisation.

03470
Percy Grainger Society
6 Fairfax Crescent, Aylesbury, HP20 2ES, UK
Tel: 01296 428609
Fax: 01296 581185
Email: info@percygrainger.org.uk
Website: http://www.percygrainger.org.uk
Members: 500
Staff: 1
Contact: Leslie De'Ath, Contact
Fee: £14
Membership Type: regular
Fee: £100
Membership Type: life
Description: Promotes knowledge and understanding in the life and works of the Australian/British/American composer/pianist Percy Aldridge Grainger.
Library Type: reference
Formerly: Also Known As, Grainger Society
Publication: Journal
Publication title: Grainger Society Journal

03471
Performing Right Society
PRS
Copyright House, 29-33 Berners St., London, W1T 3AB, UK
Tel: 020 75805544
Fax: 020 73064455
Email: customerservice@prsformusic.com
Website: http://www.prsformusic.com
Contact: Ellis Rich, Chm.
Fee: £100
Membership Type: writer
Description: Composers, authors and/or music publishers. Works to license the public performance and broadcasting of copyright music on behalf of its composer, author and music publisher members. When music is used in public, e.g. in a pub, shop etc., a PRS license is required. Distributes the collected money as fairly as possible to composers, authors and publishers.
Publication: Newsletter
Publication title: PRS News

03472
Periodical Publishers Association
PPA
Queens House, 28 Kingsway, London, WC2B 6JR, UK
Tel: 020 74044166
Fax: 020 74044167
Email: barry.mcilheney@ppa.co.uk
Website: http://www.ppa.co.uk
Members: 400
Contact: Barry McIlheney, Chief Exec.
Fee: £895
Membership Type: publisher
Fee: £2500
Membership Type: associate
Description: Compiles statistics. Promotes and protects the magazine industry.
Library Type: reference
Publication: Newsletter
Publication title: Magazine News Member Briefing

03473
Permaculture Association
BCM Permaculture Association, London, WC1N 3XX, UK
Tel: 0845 4581805
Fax: 0845 4581092
Email: office@permaculture.org.uk
Website: http://www.permaculture.org.uk
Members: 1000
Staff: 4
Contact: Tomas Remiarz, Chm.
Fee: £24
Membership Type: individual
Fee: £15
Membership Type: concession
Description: Advanced design principles for food production and sustainable lifestyles, especially perennial crops and mixed plantings, water and energy conservation and permaculture design courses.
Publication: Newsletter
Publication title: Permaculture Works. Advertisements.

03474

Permanent Service for Mean Sea Level PSMSL

Proudman Oceanographic Laboratory, Joseph Proudman Bldg., 6 Brownlow St., Liverpool, L3 5DA, UK
Tel: 0151 7954800
Fax: 0151 7954801
Email: psmsl@pol.ac.uk
Website: http://www.psmsl.org
Staff: 4
Contact: Lesley J. Rickards, Dir.
Description: Member of the Federation of Astronomical and Geophysical Data Analysis Services. Collects, analyzes and publishes data regarding changes in global sea levels.

03475

Permanent Way Institution PWI

11 Caraway Pl., Meir Park, Stoke-on-Trent, ST3 7FE, UK
Tel: 01782 397880
Fax: 01782 397546
Email: john.linkin@larc-ltd.freeserve.co.uk
Website: http://www.permanentwayinstitution.com
Members: 4500
Contact: John Linkin, Sec.
Fee: £42.64
Membership Type: in UK (payment credit/debit card and cheque)
Fee: £40.64
Membership Type: in UK (payment by direct debit)
Description: Railway civil engineers, technical staff, supervisors, and trackmen in 46 countries. Seeks to advance the knowledge of railway permanent way and its exchange between the railway systems of the world.
Library Subject: railway civil engineering
Library Type: not open to the public
Publication: Book
Publication title: British Railway Track, 7th Ed. Advertisements.
Meetings/Conventions: Technical Seminar – annual conference – Exhibits.

03476

Personal Managers' Association PMA

PO Box 63819, London, N1P 1HL, UK
Tel: 0845 6027191
Email: info@thepma.com
Website: http://www.thepma.com
Members: 150
Contact: Fiona Williams, Chair
Fee: £350-650
Membership Type: agency (based on number of employees)
Description: Theatrical agents. For artists, technicians and writers in the entertainment industry.

03477

Pesticide Action Network UK PAN UK

Development House, 56-64 Leonard St., London, EC2A 4JX, UK
Tel: 020 70650905
Fax: 020 70650907
Email: admin@pan-uk.org
Website: http://www.pan-uk.org
Contact: Keith Tyrell, Dir.
Description: Groups and individuals concerned with health, environment, and development issues, focusing on the sustainable and ecological alternatives to chemical pest control.
Publication: Newsletter
Publication title: Greenfly

03478

Pet Care Trust

Bedford Business Centre, 170 Mile Rd., Bedford, MK42 9TW, UK
Tel: 01234 273933
Fax: 01234 273550
Email: info@petcare.org.uk
Website: http://www.petcare.org.uk
Members: 1600
Staff: 5
Contact: Janet Nunn, Chief Exec.
Fee: £91-6630
Membership Type: retailer
Fee: £89-159
Membership Type: groomer
Description: Represents professional dog groomers; retail pet stores; boarding kennels; manufacturers and distributors of livestock, pet foods, and accessories. Promotes the interests of the pet care industry. Encourages responsible pet ownership through education and training. Offers certificates in pet store management and dog grooming. Organizes the industry's annual conference.
Publication: Directory
Publication title: Buyers' Guide. Advertisements.
Meetings/Conventions: Petindex – annual trade show

03479

Pet Food Manufacturers' Association PFMA

6 Catherine St., 4th Fl., London, WC2B 5JJ, UK
Tel: 020 73799009
Fax: 020 78367409
Email: info@pfma.org.uk
Website: http://www.pfma.org.uk
Members: 56
Staff: 4
Contact: Michael Bellingham, Chief Exec.
Description: Represents the interests of manufacturers, packers, and importers for the prepared pet food industry. Promotes products that are safe, of sound nutrition, palatable, and offer value for money. Works to raise industry standards. Encourages responsible pet ownership.

03480

Peter Warlock Society PWS

c/o Malcolm Rudland, Honorary Sec.
31 Hammerfield House, Cale St., London, SW3 3SG, UK
Tel: 020 75899595
Fax: 020 75899595
Email: mrudland@talk21.com
Website: http://www.peterwarlock.org
Members: 300
Contact: Richard Rodney Bennett, Pres.
Fee: £15
Membership Type: full
Fee: £5
Membership Type: student
Description: Individuals in 14 countries who have an interest in the music of British composer Peter Warlock (1894-1930); Peter Warlock is a pseudonym for Philip Heseltine. Aims to act as a center of information concerning Warlock's music, and to arouse greater interest in this field. Sponsors competitions, concerts, and jaunts.

03481

Petroleum Exploration Society of Great Britain PESGB

5th Fl., 9 Berkeley St., London, W1J 8DW, UK
Tel: 020 74082000
Fax: 020 74082050
Email: pesgb@pesgb.org.uk
Website: http://www.pesgb.org.uk/pesgb/system/default.asp
Members: 5000
Staff: 4
Contact: Marian Scutt, Exec. Dir.
Fee: £40
Membership Type: active, associate
Fee: £20
Membership Type: student
Description: Promotes education in the scientific and technical aspects of petroleum exploration, for the benefit of the public.
Publication title: Tales of Early U.K. Oil Exploration

03482

Pharmaceutical and Healthcare Sciences Society PHSS

6a Kingsdown Orchard, Wiltshire, Swindon, SN2 7RR, UK
Tel: 01793 824254
Fax: 01793 832551
Email: info@phss.co.uk
Website: http://www.phss.co.uk
Members: 1250
Staff: 2
Contact: James Drinkwater, Chm.
Fee: £103.5
Membership Type: individual
Fee: £90
Membership Type: multiple (up to 6 individuals)
Description: Fosters the advancement in the interests of public health, the practice and science of parenteral therapy and to preserve and improve the integrity and standards of the parenteral and healthcare industry.
Formerly: Formerly, Parenteral Society

03483

Pharmaceutical Information and Pharmacovigilance Association PIPA

PO Box 254, Haslemere, GU27 9AF, UK
Tel: 07531 899537
Email: pipa@pipaonline.org
Website: http://www.pipaonline.org
Contact: Sarah Dunnett, Pres.
Fee: £60
Membership Type: regular
Fee: £75
Membership Type: overseas
Description: Supports and assists members in the development of their professional skills and responsibilities. Serves as the professional organization for individuals

who are involved in the provision and management of information and those involved in the fulfillment or regulatory requirements relating to drug safety.
Formerly: Formerly, Association of Information Officers in the Pharmaceutical Industry
Publication: Newsletter
Publication title: Pipeline

03484
Pharmaceutical Society of Northern Ireland
PSNI
73 University St., Belfast, BT7 1HL, UK
Tel: 028 90326927
Fax: 028 90439919
Email: complaints@psni.org.uk
Website: http://www.psni.org.uk
Members: 2000
Staff: 3
Contact: Trevor Patterson, Chief Exec.
Description: Registered pharmacists. Acts as a professional and registration body for pharmacists and pharmacies in Northern Ireland.

03485
Philip Larkin Society
PO Box 44, Hornsea, HU18 1WP, UK
Email: plschairman@philiplarkin.com
Website: http://www.philiplarkin.com
Contact: Edwin Dawes, Chm.
Description: Promotes awareness of the life and work of Philip Larkin and his literary contemporaries. Brings together all those who admire Larkin's work as poet, novelist, jazz critic and librarian.
Publication: Journal
Publication title: About Larkin

03486
Philological Society
Dept. of Africa, School of Oriental and African Studies, Thornhaugh St., London, WC1H 0XG, UK
Tel: 020 78984653
Fax: 020 78984399
Email: secretary@philsoc.org.uk
Website: http://www.philsoc.org.uk
Members: 600
Contact: Martin Orwin, Honorary Sec.
Fee: £10
Membership Type: individual
Fee: £2
Membership Type: student associate
Description: Individuals united to promote the study of the structure and history of languages.
Publication: Journal
Publication title: Transactions of the Philological Society. Advertisements.

03487
Photo Imaging Council
PIC
Airport House, Purley Way, Surrey, Croydon, CR0 0XZ, UK
Tel: 0208 2534507
Fax: 0208 2534510
Email: pic@admin.co.uk
Website: http://www.pic.uk.net
Members: 110
Staff: 4
Contact: Pam Hyde, Contact
Description: Represents and promotes the interests of companies in the photo and imaging industry in the United Kingdom to government, the media, external organizations, and the general public.

03488
Photo Marketing Association International
PMAI
Wisteria House, 28 Fulling Mill Ln., Hertfordshire, Welwyn Garden City, AL6 9NS, UK
Tel: 01438 840367
Fax: 01438 716572
Email: pmauk@pmai.org
Website: http://www.pmai.org
Members: 20000
Contact: Nigel McNaught, Dir.
Description: Promotes the growth of the photo marketing industry through cooperation. Strives to meet the needs of its diverse and widespread membership through the use of 21 territorial offices.
Publication: Magazine
Publication title: Photo Marketing

03489
Photoluminescent Safety Products Association
PSPA
PO Box 377, Surrey, RH1 2YZ, UK
Email: pspa@pspa.org.uk
Website: http://www.pspa.org.uk
Members: 28
Staff: 4
Fee: £900
Membership Type: full
Fee: £450
Membership Type: associate
Description: Promotes the use and knowledge of photo luminescent products in the field of safety applications.

03490
Physiological Society - UK
Peer House, Verulam St., London, WC1X 8LZ, UK
Tel: 020 72695710
Fax: 020 72695720
Email: membership@physoc.org
Website: http://www.physoc.org
Members: 2900
Staff: 26
Contact: Michael Collis, Chief Exec.
Description: Physiologists at senior levels in universities, research institutions, hospitals and relevant industries and government departments, about a third of who are resident overseas. Affiliation is now available for younger physiologists such as postgraduate students and postdoctoral workers. Aims to promote the advancement of physiology. Covers all areas of physiology. Main activities are Scientific publishing; organizing/funding scientific meetings, symposia, seminars, workshops, lectures for members, students, schoolteachers, sixthformers; school and university liaison; 25 special interest groups, plus 13 subcommittees.
Publication: Journal
Publication title: Experimental Physiology

03491
Phytochemical Society of Europe
PSE
c/o Dr. Deniz Tasdemir, Membership Sec.
University of London, School of Pharmacy, Centre for Pharmacognosy and Phytotherapy, 29-39 Brunswick Sq., London, WC1N 1AX, UK
Tel: 020 77535845
Fax: 020 77536000
Email: amstafford@hotmail.co.uk
Website: http://www.phytochemicalsociety.org
Members: 860
Contact: Angela Stafford, Gen. Sec.
Fee: £15
Membership Type: full
Fee: £10
Membership Type: student
Description: Scientists in 63 countries working in the field of plant chemistry, biochemistry, and molecular biology. Acts as a forum for specialists in plant chemistry, biochemistry, and biotechnology who are interested in applying their research findings to agriculture and industry.
Formerly: Formerly, Plant Phenolics Group
Publication: Journal
Publication title: Phytochemistry

03492
Phytochemical Society of Europe - United Kingdom
PSE
c/o Dr. Deniz Tasdemir, Membership Sec.
University of London, School of Pharmacy, Centre for Pharmacognosy, 29-39 Brunswick Sq., London, WC1N 1AX, UK
Tel: 020 77535845
Fax: 020 77535909
Email: deniz.tasdemir@pharmacy.ac.uk
Website: http://www.phytochemicalsociety.org
Members: 800
Contact: Angela Stafford, Gen. Sec.
Fee: £15
Membership Type: full
Fee: £10
Membership Type: student
Description: Promotes the advancement of knowledge about chemistry and biochemistry of plants for industry and agriculture.

03493
Pianoforte Tuners' Association
PTA
PO Box 1312, Woking, Lightwater, GU18 5UB, UK
Tel: 00845 6028796
Email: secretary@pianotuner.org.uk
Website: http://www.pianotuner.org.uk
Contact: Annette Summers, Hon. Gen. Sec.
Description: Piano tuners and technicians. Aims to bring together piano tuners and technicians for mutual protection and benefit; to educate the public on the need for regular and skilled tuning and servicing and to proclaim the importance of high professional standards; to provide the strength of association which is necessary to protect and represent the tuning profession.

03494

Picon

PO Box 300, Hitchin, SG4 8WJ, UK
Tel: 01438 832742
Fax: 01438 833812
Email: tim.webb@picon.co.uk
Website: http://www.picon.com
Members: 150
Staff: 7
Contact: Tim Webb, Exec. Dir.
Description: UK based companies manufacturing or supplying equipment and consumables for publishing, graphic arts, printing, paper-making and paper converting industries.
Formerly: Formerly, British Federation of Printing Machinery and Supplies
Publication: Paper
Publication title: Paper and Converting Machinery News

03495

Pigging Products and Services Association PPSA

PO Box 30, Ipswich, Kesgrave, GL6 8YB, UK
Tel: 01473 635863
Fax: 01473 353597
Email: ppsa@ppsa-online.com
Website: http://www.ppsa-online.com
Members: 90
Contact: Diane Cordell, Exec. Sec.
Fee: £1050
Membership Type: full
Fee: £470
Membership Type: associate
Description: Provides information and services for pipeline operators. Promotes knowledge of pigging and its related services. Pipeline pigs are devices that are inserted into and travel throughout the length of a pipeline driven by product flow.
Publication: Book
Publication title: An Introduction to Pipeline Pigging

03496

Pipe Jacking Association PJA

10 Greycoat Pl., London, SW1P 1SB, UK
Tel: 0845 0705201
Fax: 0845 0705202
Email: andrew.marshall@pipejacking.org
Website: http://www.pipejacking.org
Members: 18
Description: Companies or firms who specialise in carrying out, or supplying equipment and materials for, the process of pipe jacking and/or microtunnelling. Aims to promote the use of pipe jacking and microtunnelling as environmentally, socially and economically beneficial trenchless construction techniques; to promote the common interests of PJA members; to improve standards of workmanship; and to maintain high levels of technical competence and innovation.
Publication: Handbook
Publication title: An Introduction to Pipe Jacking and Microtunelling Design

03497

Pipeline Industries Guild

14/15 Belgrave Sq., London, SW1X 8PS, UK
Tel: 020 72357938
Fax: 020 72350074
Email: hqsec@pipeguild.co.uk
Website: http://www.pipeguild.com/Page.aspx?pid=191
Members: 1000
Staff: 4
Contact: Cheryl Burgess, Dir. Gen.
Fee: £88
Membership Type: individual
Fee: £1098-2196
Membership Type: corporate
Description: Engineers and representatives from pipeline owning companies, engineering companies, consultants, contractors, manufacturers and associated companies.
Publication: Directory
Publication title: Pipeline Industry Directory. Advertisements.

03498

PIRA International PIRAI

Cleeve Rd., Leatherhead, KT22 7RU, UK
Tel: 01372 802000
Fax: 01372 802079
Email: info@pira-international.com
Website: http://www.pira-international.com
Contact: Ciaran Little, Contact
Description: Provides consultancy and information services for the paper and board making, printing, publishing, and packaging industries. Disseminates information on these sectors, plus management, marketing, publishing, legislation, and technical and business developments. Services include literature searching, consulting, research, testing and referrals.
Library Subject: paper, packaging, printing, publishing
Library Type: by appointment only
Publication: Newsletter
Publication title: Active and Intelligent Pack News

03499

Pituitary Foundation

PO Box 1944, Bristol, BS99 2UB, UK
Tel: 0845 4500375
Fax: 0117 9330910
Email: helpline@pituitary.org.uk
Website: http://www.pituitary.org.uk
Contact: Kit Ashley, Exec. Dir.
Fee: £15
Membership Type: individual
Fee: £25
Membership Type: family (up to 3 adults residing at the same address)
Description: Provides assistance, information, and support to patients who are suffering from pituitary disorders. Helps raise awareness of the foundation and pituitary diseases in both the medical profession and general public.
Publication: Newsletter
Publication title: Pituitary News
Meetings/Conventions: conference

03500

Pizza, Pasta and Italian Food Association PAPA

Association House, 18c Moor St., Chepstow, NP16 5DB, UK
Tel: 01291 636338
Fax: 01291 630402
Email: jim@jandmgroup.co.uk
Website: http://www.papa.org.uk
Members: 687
Staff: 6
Contact: Jim Winship, Dir.
Fee: £650
Membership Type: retailer, restaurant, takeaway, delivery, supplier, manufacturer
Fee: £585
Membership Type: affiliated
Description: Trade body representing the pizza, pasta, and Italian food industries, including manufacturers, restaurants, pizzerias, pizza chains, distributors etc. Aims to set and maintain standards throughout the industry, in order to promote the reputation and growth of pizza, pasta, and Italian food products. It also encourages the interchange of knowledge amongst members to their mutual interest.
Formerly: Formerly, Pizza Association
Publication: Magazine
Publication title: Pizza, Pasta, and Italian Food Magazine. Advertisements.

03501

Plaid Cymru - The Party of Wales

c/o Ty Gwynfor
Marine Chambers, Anson Ct., Atlantic Wharf, Cardiff, CF10 4AL, UK
Tel: 029 20472272
Email: post@plaidcymru.org
Website: http://www.plaidcymru.org
Members: 10000
Staff: 10
Contact: Gwenllian Lansdown, Chief Exec.
Fee: £18
Membership Type: waged individual
Fee: £6
Membership Type: unwaged individual
Description: Political party in Wales. Advocates self-government for Wales.
Formerly: Formerly, Welsh National Party
Publication: Magazine
Publication title: CYMRU. Advertisements.

03502

Plan - United Kingdom

5-7 Cranwood St., London, EC1V 9LH, UK
Tel: 020 74829777
Fax: 020 74829778
Email: mail@plan-international.org.uk
Website: http://www.plan-uk.org
Contact: Sharon Goulds, Hd. of Communications
Description: Seeks to address the needs of children and families worldwide. Conducts services including: provision of health care, food, and clothing; educational programs for children and adults; community and individual skills development initiatives. Makes available emergency relief services to victims of natural and man-made disasters.

03503
Plan International
Chobham House, Christchurch Way, Surrey, Woking, GU21 6JG, UK
Tel: 01483 755155
Fax: 01483 756505
Email: info@plan-international.org
Website: http://plan-international.org
Staff: 7000
Contact: Paul Arlam, Chm.
Description: Aims to help children realize their full potentials in societies which respect people's rights and dignity. Works with children, their families and the wider community to make positive changes in their lives.
Publication: Report
Publication title: Growing Up in Asia

Plant Yng Nghymru
see Children in Wales

03504
Plastics Historical Society
PHS
PO Box Susan Lambert, Sec., Brick Hill, Berkshire, Burghclere, RG20 9HJ, UK
Email: memb.sec@plastiquarian.com
Website: http://www.plastiquarian.com
Members: 350
Contact: Susan Lambert, Sec.
Fee: £25
Membership Type: individual (in UK and Europe)
Fee: £35
Membership Type: family (in UK and Europe)
Description: Historians, collectors, and other individuals with an interest in the history of plastics. Encourages the study and preservation of all historical aspects of plastics and related materials. Promotes the recording of current developments for future generations; acts as an information center for collectors; maintains close contact with museums and galleries interested in conservation.
Library Subject: all areas concerned with polymeric materials
Library Type: reference
Publication: Newsletter
Publication title: PHS Newsletter. Advertisements.

03505
Plastics Window Federation
PWF
Federation House, 85-87 Wellington St., Luton, LU1 5AF, UK
Tel: 01582 456147
Fax: 01582 412215
Email: ins@pwfed.co.uk
Website: http://www.pwfed.co.uk
Members: 500
Staff: 20
Description: Companies engaged in the installation of PVC windows and doors. Provides survey, arbitration, commercial cover and sales staff licensing services. Offers total protection to purchasers of PVC-u products.
Publication: Newsletter
Publication title: Federation News

03506
Play Therapy International
PTI
The Coach House, Belmont Rd., East Sussex, Uckfield, TN22 1BP, UK
Tel: 01825 761143
Fax: 01825 769913
Email: ptukorg@aol.com
Website: http://www.playtherapy.org
Members: 1200
Staff: 4
Contact: Monika Jephcott, Pres.
Fee: £600
Membership Type: corporate
Fee: £150
Membership Type: regular
Description: Professional child psychotherapists and play therapists, students and other individuals with an interest in child psychology. Promotes advancement in the teaching, theory and practice of play therapy and child psychotherapy. Conducts examinations and makes available continuing professional advancement programs to members. Serves as a clearinghouse on play therapy; represents members within the psychological community and before public bodies. Sponsors research; provides children's services; maintains speakers' bureau.
Library Subject: child psychology, play therapy
Library Type: not open to the public
Meetings/Conventions: World Congress on Child and Play Therapy – annual convention

03507
Player Piano Group
PPG
Malcolm Billingsley, 7 Marion Grove, Woodford Green, Essex, IG8 9TA, UK
Email: membership@pianolasociety.com
Website: http://www.playerpianogroup.org.uk
Members: 300
Contact: Peter Katin, Pres.
Fee: £12
Membership Type: in United Kingdom
Fee: £15
Membership Type: international
Description: Persons in 8 countries with an interest in the mechanical and musical aspects of player pianos. Fosters sharing of information and experience concerning player pianos; provides a forum for selling, purchasing, repairing, and restoring player pianos and music rolls among members; promotes public concerts.
Publication: Bulletin
Publication title: The Player Piano Group Bulletin

03508
PLAYLINK
72 Albert Palace Mansions, Lurline Gardens, London, SW11 4DQ, UK
Tel: 020 7202452
Email: info@playlink.org
Website: http://www.playlink.org
Members: 30
Staff: 5
Contact: Bernard Spiegal, Principal
Description: Individuals, local voluntary organizations, local authorities, national and regional voluntary sector organizations with an interest in play services and playwork. Connects practical playwork experience to the broader policy issues affecting children's play and works with other organizations in support of children and their right to play. Provides services such as: advice, information, training design and build, safety inspections, and risk assessment.
Publication: Booklet
Publication title: A Playworkers Taxonomy of Play Types

03509
Plumbers' Company
Wax Chandlers' Hall, 6 Gresham St., London, EC2V 7AD, UK
Tel: 020 77962468
Fax: 020 77962468
Email: clerk@plumberscompany.org.uk
Website: http://www.plumberscompany.org
Members: 360
Staff: 3
Contact: Antony Paterson-Fox, Contact
Description: Promotes the craft of plumbing.

03510
Plunkett Foundation
The Quadrangle, Woodstock, Oxfordshire, Oxford, OX20 1LH, UK
Tel: 01993 810730
Fax: 01993 810849
Email: info@plunkett.co.uk
Website: http://www.plunkett.co.uk
Members: 120
Staff: 7
Contact: Peter Cleasby, Chm.
Fee: £24
Membership Type: individual
Fee: £100
Membership Type: corporate
Description: Supports the development of rural group enterprise worldwide. Draws on practical experience of working with partners from the public and private sectors to promote and implement economic self-help solutions to rural problems.
Publication: Newsletter
Publication title: Rural Connections

03511
Poetry Society
22 Betterton St., London, WC2H 9BX, UK
Tel: 020 74209880
Fax: 020 72404818
Email: info@poetrysociety.org.uk
Website: http://www.poetrysociety.org.uk
Members: 4000
Staff: 9
Contact: Jo Shapcott, Pres.
Fee: £40
Membership Type: full
Fee: £100
Membership Type: gold
Description: Readers and writers of poetry. Helps poets and poetry thrive in Britain; publishes poetry and acts as an advocate for contemporary poetry; provides information for schools.
Publication: Newsletter
Publication title: Poetry News. Advertisements.

03512
Police Federation of England and Wales
Federation House, Highbury Dr., Surrey, Leatherhead, KT22 7UY, UK
Tel: 01372 352000
Email: gensec@polfed.org

Website: http://www.polfed.org
Members: 132000
Staff: 60
Contact: Paul McKeever, Chm.
Description: Represents police officers from constable to chief inspector.
Publication: Magazine
Publication title: Police. Advertisements.

03513

Police History Society
PHS

c/o Leonard Woodley, Membership Sec.
37 S Lawne, Bletchley, MK3 6BU, UK
Email: info@policehistorysociety.co.uk
Website: http://www.policehistorysociety.co.uk
Members: 350
Contact: Denis O'Connor, Pres.
Fee: £10
Membership Type: personal, corporate
Description: Acts as a forum for those interested in the history of police and policing.
Publication: Journal

03514

Police Superintendents' Association of England and Wales
PSAEW

67A Reading Rd., Berkshire, Pangbourne, RG8 7JD, UK
Tel: 0118 9844005
Fax: 0118 9845642
Email: enquiries@policesupers.com
Website: http://www.policesupers.com
Members: 1550
Staff: 6
Contact: Derek Barnett, Pres.
Description: Superintending ranks of the British Police Service in England and Wales. Represents the interests of all superintending ranks in Home Office maintained police forces in England or Wales.
Publication: Journal
Publication title: The Superintendent

03515

Polish Underground Movement (1939-1945) Study Trust
PUMST

11 Leopold Rd., London, W5 3PB, UK
Tel: 0208 9926057
Fax: 0208 9926057
Email: info@spp-pumst.org
Website: http://www.spp-pumst.org
Staff: 23
Contact: Krzysztof Stolinski, Chm.
Description: Established to collect materials and conduct historical documentary research on the Polish Underground Movement, Polish Home Army, and Polish Secret State during World War II. Compiles statistics.
Formerly: Formerly, Polish Institute
Publication: Books
Publication title: Armia Krajowa w Dokumentach 1939-45

03516

Political Studies Association
PSA

University of Newcastle, Dept. of Politics, Newcastle upon Tyne, NE1 7RU, UK
Tel: 0191 2228021
Fax: 0191 2223499
Email: psa@ncl.ac.uk
Website: http://www.psa.ac.uk
Contact: Vicky Randall, Chair
Fee: £74
Membership Type: full (in UK/Europe)
Fee: £202
Membership Type: full (in North America)
Description: Political scientists and political science students and educators. Seeks to develop and promote the study of politics. Serves as a clearinghouse on politics and political science; facilitates communication and cooperation among members.
Publication: Journal
Publication title: Political Studies

03517

Polymer Machinery, Manufacturers and Distributors Association
PMMDA

PO Box 2539, Warwickshire, Rugby, CV23 9YF, UK
Tel: 0844 8111204
Fax: 0844 8111205
Email: pmmda@pmmda.org.uk
Website: http://www.pmmda.org.uk
Contact: Nikki Williams, Sec.
Description: Suppliers and manufacturers of processing machinery for the plastics industry in the United Kingdom and overseas. Promotes the plastics industry in the United Kingdom. Sets standards for the industry.
Library Subject: buyers guide, history
Library Type: not open to the public

03518

Ponies Association - UK
P(UK)

Chesham House, 56 Green End Rd., Sawtry, Huntingdon, PE28 5UY, UK
Tel: 01487 830278
Fax: 01487 832844
Email: info@poniesuk.org
Website: http://www.poniesuk.org
Members: 3000
Staff: 5
Contact: Davina Whiteman, Chair
Fee: £50
Membership Type: adult
Fee: £15
Membership Type: junior
Description: Promotes and improves standards of horse management and breeding.

03519

Portobello Antique Dealers Association
PADA

111 Portobello Rd., London, W11 2QB, UK
Tel: 020 72298354
Fax: 020 72433419
Email: info@portobelloroad.co.uk
Website: http://www.portobelloroad.co.uk
Contact: Costas Kleanthous, Chm.
Description: Promotes the antique shopping area in Portobello Road and Westbourne Grove. Encourages its members to follow the code of practice when dealing with customers.

03520

Portsmouth and South East Hampshire Chamber of Commerce and Industry

Regional Business Ctre., Harts Farm Way, Hampshire, Havant, PO9 1HR, UK
Tel: 02392 449449
Fax: 02392 449444
Email: sehants@chamber.org.uk
Website: http://www.chamber.org.uk
Members: 800
Staff: 12
Contact: Gary Jeffries, Pres.
Fee: £258.5
Membership Type: business (minimum; based on the number of employees)
Fee: £1468.75
Membership Type: business (maximum; based on the number of employees)
Description: Promotes business and commerce.
Library Subject: business, international business
Library Type: reference
Publication: Magazine
Publication title: Business News. Advertisements.

03521

Portuguese Chamber

11 Belgrave Sq., 4th Fl., London, SW1X 8PP, UK
Tel: 020 72016638
Fax: 020 72016637
Email: info@portuguese-chamber.org.uk
Website: http://www.portuguese-chamber.org.uk
Members: 320
Staff: 4
Contact: Philip Baker, Chm.
Description: Provides business services for bilateral business between Portugal/United Kingdom-Ireland.
Publication: Directory
Publication title: Directory Yearbook
Meetings/Conventions: meeting

03522

Portuguese Chamber of Commerce in Britain

11 Belgrave Sq., 4th Fl., London, SW1X 8PP, UK
Tel: 020 72016638
Fax: 020 72016637
Email: info@portuguese-chamber.org.uk
Website: http://www.portuguese-chamber.org.uk
Description: Promotes business and commerce.
Publication: Book
Publication title: Portugal - The Property Buyers' Guide

03523

Positively UK
PW

347-349 City Rd., London, EC1V 1LR, UK
Tel: 020 77130444
Email: info@positivelyuk.org
Website: http://www.positivelyuk.org
Staff: 20

Contact: Anjie Mailey, Admin.
Description: Offers peer support and self-help services to women with HIV and/or AIDS and their children. Provides information; maintains a resource facility.
Formerly: Formerly, Positively Women
Publication: Magazine
Publication title: Positively Women
Meetings/Conventions: semiweekly support group meeting

03524
Poverty Alliance
PA
162 Buchanan St., Glasgow, G1 2LL, UK
Tel: 0141 3530440
Fax: 0141 3530686
Email: admin@povertyalliance.org
Website: http://www.povertyalliance.org
Members: 100
Staff: 9
Contact: Peter Kelly, Dir.
Fee: £500
Membership Type: company
Fee: £200
Membership Type: associate (company)
Description: Local authorities, health boards, enterprise, and voluntary organizations working to alleviate poverty. Seeks to "combat poverty through collaborative action" by members. Develops partnerships and encourages cooperation among members; conducts educational programs to raise public awareness of poverty and related issues; empowers people in poverty to improve their own quality of life.
Publication: Newsletter
Publication title: Alliance News

03525
Power Fastenings Association
42 Heath St., Tamworth, Staffordshire, Birmingham, B79 7JH, UK
Tel: 01827 52337
Fax: 01827 310827
Email: enquiries@powerfastenings.org.uk
Website: http://www.powerfastenings.org.uk
Members: 9
Staff: 2
Contact: Jim Fleming, Chm.
Description: Manufacturers and suppliers of pneumatically operated nailing and stapling equipment. Aims to promote the safe use of pneumatic nailing and stapling equipment.

03526
Powys Society
PS
87 Ledbury Rd., Flat D, London, W11 2AG, UK
Tel: 020 72430168
Email: chris.d.thomas@hotmail.co.uk
Website: http://www.powys-society.org
Members: 250
Contact: Chris Thomas, Hon. Sec.
Fee: £18.5
Membership Type: in UK
Fee: £22
Membership Type: overseas
Description: Individuals, scholars, academics and general readers interested especially in the lives and works and literary achievements of John Cowper Powys (1872-1963), Theodore Francis Powys (1875-1953), and Llewelyn Powys (1884-1939) but also other members of the family. Authors of fiction, poetry, and criticism. Promotes the study and appreciation of the Powys family. Maintains collection and archive of original materials, manuscripts, letters and books and other documents relating to the Powys family. Organises regular meetings and an annual Conference.
Publication: Journal
Publication title: Powys Journal. Advertisements.

03527
PRA Coatings Technology Centre
14 Castle Mews, High St., Hampton, TW12 2NP, UK
Tel: 020 84870800
Fax: 020 84870801
Website: http://www.pra-world.com
Members: 200
Staff: 55
Contact: Susan Conyers, Membership Sec.
Description: Raw materials suppliers, all coating manufacturers including paints, inks and adhesives and users. Acts as an international centre for coatings technology, catering for manufacturers of coatings, its raw materials suppliers & users. Major activities are research, information, provision, testing, analysis, environmental and consultancy services and training.
Library Subject: paint and related technologies
Library Type: not open to the public
Formerly: Formerly, Paint Research Association
Publication: Journal
Publication title: Coatings Comet
Meetings/Conventions: Addcoat – semiannual conference – Exhibits.

03528
Practical Action
The Schumacher Centre for Technology and Development, Bourton-on-Dunsmore, Rugby, CV23 9QZ, UK
Tel: 01926 634400
Fax: 01926 634401
Email: practicalaction@practicalaction.org.uk
Website: http://practicalaction.org
Members: 7078000
Staff: 450
Contact: Simon Trace, Chief Exec.
Description: Organizations and interested individuals. Enables poor people in developing areas to acquire and use skills and technologies, which give them more control over their lives and which contribute to the sustainable development of their communities.
Formerly: Formerly, Intermediate Technology Development Group - England
Publication: Report
Publication title: Intermediate Technology Report

03529
Pre-Eclampsia Society
PETS
Rhianfa, Carmel, Gwynedd, Caernarfon, LL54 7RL, UK
Tel: 01286 882685
Email: dawnjames@clara.co.uk
Website: http://www.pre-eclampsia-society.org.uk
Members: 2000
Contact: Dawn James, Founder
Description: Provides self help and support groups for those suffering or having suffered from pre-eclampsia.
Library Subject: pre-eclampsia, pregnancy nutrition
Library Type: lending

03530
Pre-Raphaelite Society
PRS
18 Floyd Grove, Balsall Common, Coventry, CV7 7RP, UK
Email: info@pre-raphaelitesociety.org
Website: http://www.pre-raphaelitesociety.org
Members: 325
Staff: 10
Contact: Michael Wollaston, Contact
Fee: £14
Membership Type: individual
Fee: £22
Membership Type: corporate, overseas
Description: Promotes the art of the Pre-Raphaelite period.
Publication: Newsletter
Publication title: The Pre-Raphaelite Society Newsletter of the U.S. Advertisements.

03531
Pre-school Learning Alliance
The Fitzpatrick Bldg., 188 York Way, London, N7 9AD, UK
Tel: 020 76972500
Fax: 020 77000319
Email: info@pre-school.org.uk
Website: http://www.pre-school.org.uk
Members: 16000
Staff: 2000
Contact: Steve Alexander, Chief Exec.
Fee: £40
Membership Type: individual
Fee: £18
Membership Type: student
Description: Enhances the development and education of children under statutory school age by encouraging parents to understand and provide for the needs of their children through community pre-schools and nurseries.
Publication title: Under-Five Contact. Advertisements.

03532
Precast Flooring Federation
PFF
60 Charles St., Leicester, LE1 1FB, UK
Tel: 0116 2536161
Fax: 0116 2514568
Email: info@precastfloors.info
Website: http://www.precastfloors.info
Members: 15
Staff: 2
Contact: Norman E. Brown, Sec.
Description: Represents the interests of manufacturers of precast concrete flooring.
Publication: Book
Publication title: Code of Practice for Safe Erection of Precast Concrete Flooring

03533
Prehistoric Society
PS
University College London, Institute of Archaeology, 31-34 Gordon Sq., London, WC1H 0PY, UK
Email: prehistoric@ucl.ac.uk
Website: http://www.prehistoricsociety.org
Members: 2000
Contact: Alison Sheridan, Pres.
Fee: £35
Membership Type: ordinary
Fee: £50
Membership Type: institution

Description: Interested individuals in 30 countries concerned with the study of prehistory. Encourages prehistoric study and excavation. Conducts lectures and study tours.
Publication: Newsletter
Publication title: Past. Advertisements.

03534

Premenstrual Society
PMS

PO Box 429, Addlestone, KT15 1DZ, UK
Tel: 01932 872560
Website: http://www.patient.co.uk/showdoc/26739112
Members: 500
Staff: 4
Contact: M.G. Brush, Chm.
Fee: £10
Membership Type: ordinary
Fee: £5
Membership Type: student
Description: Seeks to provide advice and support for sufferers of premenstrual syndrome (PMS). Provides support for local groups and professionals in the field.
Library Subject: premenstrual syndrome, nutrition endocrinology
Library Type: not open to the public
Publication: Newsletter
Publication title: Premsol Newsletter

03535

Preoperative Association

21 Portland Pl., London, W1B 1PY, UK
Tel: 020 76318896
Fax: 020 76314352
Email: info@pre-op.org
Website: http://www.pre-op.org
Members: 700
Contact: Jane Jackson, Chair
Fee: £30
Membership Type: consultant doctor
Fee: £15
Membership Type: non-consultant doctor, pharmacist, nurse, administrative staff
Description: Exists to benefit the health and care of people who have surgery planned. Identifies preoperative services. Disseminates and ensures the proper implementation of this service.

03536

Press Complaints Commission
PCC

Halton House, 20/23 Holborn, London, EC1N 2JD, UK
Tel: 020 78310022
Fax: 020 78310025
Email: complaints@pcc.org.uk
Website: http://www.pcc.org.uk
Members: 16
Staff: 13
Contact: Tonia Milton, Information and Events Mgr.
Description: Sixteen members drawn from the lay public and the press; includes seven editors of national, regional and local newspapers and magazines. Non-press members are in the majority. Upholds a Code of Practice covering issues such as accuracy, harassment and invasion of privacy; deals with complaints about the editorial content of British newspapers and magazines and advises editors on journalistic ethics.
Publication title: Code of Practice

03537

Pressure Gauge and Dial Thermometer Association
PGDT

Heathcote House, 136 Hagley Rd., Edgbaston, Birmingham, B16 9PN, UK
Tel: 0121 4544141
Fax: 0121 4544949
Email: info@pgdt.org
Website: http://pgdt.org
Members: 15
Fee: £250
Description: Provides assistance for purchasers of pressure gauges and thermometers.

03538

Prestressed Concrete Association
PCA

60 Charles St., 4th Fl., Leicester, LE1 1FB, UK
Tel: 0116 2536161
Fax: 0116 2514568
Email: info@britishprecast.org
Website: http://www.britishprecast.org/associations/prestressed-concrete.php
Members: 2
Staff: 2
Description: Manufacturers of precast concrete bridge beams. Promotes growth and development of members' businesses. Represents members' interests before government agencies and labor and industrial organizations.
Publication: Book
Publication title: Integral Abutments for Prestressed Beam Bridges

03539

Primary Immunodeficiency Association
PIA

Alliance House, 12 Caxton St., London, SW1H 0QS, UK
Tel: 020 79767640
Fax: 020 79767641
Email: info@pia.org.uk
Website: http://www.pia.org.uk
Contact: Kate Ward, Membership/Admin. Coor.
Description: Immunologists, physicians, and others working to raise awareness of immunodeficiency. Conducts research; disseminates information.
Publication: Booklet
Publication title: Primary Immunodeficiency Disease

03540

Primate Society of Great Britain
PSGB

c/o Dr. Gillian Brown, Treas.
University of St. Andrews, School of Psychology, St. Andrews, KY16 9JP, UK
Email: treasurer@psgb.org
Website: http://www.psgb.org
Contact: Kim Bard, Pres.
Fee: £500
Membership Type: life (full, associate)
Fee: £30
Membership Type: institutional
Description: Promotes research in all aspects of primate biology, conservation and management.
Publication: Journal
Publication title: Primate Eye. Advertisements.

03541

Prince of Wales International Business Leaders Forum
IBLF

15-16 Cornwall Terr., Regent's Park, London, NW1 4QP, UK
Tel: 0207 4673600
Fax: 0207 4673610
Email: info@iblf.org
Website: http://www.iblf.org
Members: 60
Staff: 40
Contact: Adam Leach, CEO
Description: Business leaders in the United Kingdom. Promotes socially responsible business practices; seeks to achieve socially, economically, and environmentally responsible development worldwide.
Publication: Book
Publication title: Building Competitiveness and Communities

03542

Printing Historical Society
PHS

St. Bride Library, St. Bride Institute, Bride Ln., Fleet St., London, EC4Y 8EE, UK
Email: secretary@printinghistoricalsociety.org.uk
Website: http://www.printinghistoricalsociety.org.uk
Members: 700
Contact: Iain Bain, Pres.
Fee: £25
Membership Type: individual in UK, overseas
Fee: £30
Membership Type: institution in UK, overseas
Description: Printers, librarians, bibliographers, typographers, and graphic designers; libraries, printing firms, and learned societies. Aims: to foster interest in the history and traditions of printing and its methods, equipment, materials, and products; to preserve items of historical interest, including printing equipment and printed matter; to commemorate notable figures in the history of printing; to encourage study and discussion of such subjects in schools and among printers, designers, bibliophiles, and the public. Programs include: reading and discussion of papers on the history of printing and the allied trades; exhibitions and displays; visits to libraries, museums, and printing offices of historical interest.
Publication: Journal
Publication title: Index

03543

Prisoners Abroad

89-93 Fonthill Rd., Finsbury Park, London, N4 3JH, UK
Tel: 020 75616820
Fax: 020 75616821
Email: info@prisonersabroad.org.uk
Website: http://www.prisonersabroad.org.uk
Staff: 16
Contact: Pauline Crowe, Chief Exec.
Description: Provides support for British citizens in prison outside the UK and their families; information on foreign criminal justice systems, prison conditions and transfer, financial and practical assistance such as vitamin supplements and reading material; resettlement service for released prisoners returning to the UK.
Publication: Newsletter

03544
Privacy International
PI
265 Strand, London, WC2R 1BH, UK
Tel: 020 81237933
Email: privacyint@privacy.org
Website: http://www.privacyinternational.org
Members: 77
Staff: 3
Contact: Simon Davies, Dir.
Description: Represents human rights advocates, journalists, information technology experts, academics, and data protection experts. Works to protect personal privacy and monitor surveillance activities by governments and other organizations worldwide. Current activities include work on identity systems, biometrics, international cooperation, e-borders, freedom of information and data retention.

03545
Private Libraries Association
PLA
Ravelston, South View Rd., Pinner, Middlesex, HA5 3YD, UK
Email: dchambrs@aol.com
Website: http://plabooks.org
Members: 700
Contact: David Chambers, Hon. Chm.
Fee: £30
Membership Type: general
Fee: £55
Membership Type: general
Description: Individuals who collect or who are interested in books from an amateur or professional point of view, including collectors of rare books, fine books, single authors, reference books on special subjects, and individuals who collect books for the pleasure of reading and ownership. Encourages cooperation among book collectors. Sponsors Society of Private Printers, an informal group of owners of private presses who exchange ideas and printed specimens.
Publication: Newsletter
Publication title: Membership List

03546
Probation Boards' Association
PBA
83 Victoria St., London, SW1H 0HW, UK
Tel: 020 30087930
Fax: 020 30087931
Email: association@probationboards.co.uk
Website: http://probationassociation.co.uk
Members: 435
Staff: 12
Contact: Christine Lawrie, Chief Exec.
Description: Chief, deputy chief, assistant chief probation officers and other top managers in the 58 probation services of England, Wales, Northern Ireland, Jersey and Isle of Man. Promotes and co-ordinates the work of the probation services of England and Wales.
Formerly: Formerly, Association of Chief Officers of Probation

03547
Processed Vegetable Growers Association
PVGA
133 Eastgate, Lincolnshire, Louth, LN11 9QG, UK
Tel: 01507 602427
Fax: 01507 600689
Email: postbox@pvga.co.uk
Website: http://www.pvga.co.uk
Members: 1165
Staff: 8
Description: Represents growers of vegetables for processing.

03548
Processors' and Growers' Research Organisation
PGRO
The Research Station, Great North Rd., Thornhaugh, Peterborough, PE8 6HJ, UK
Tel: 01780 782585
Fax: 01780 783993
Email: info@pgro.org
Website: http://www.pgro.org
Members: 4750
Staff: 16
Contact: Salvador Potter, CEO
Description: Farmers, food processors, merchant seedsmen, agrochemical companies, higher education institutes and research stations. Provides research, evaluation and advice on the growing, harvesting and usage of different types of peas and beans. This includes the evaluation of new varieties, crop protection products and growing and harvesting techniques. Provides technical services including seed and soil testing and instrument calibration.

03549
Producers Alliance for Cinema and Television
PACT
Procter House, 3rd Fl., Fitzrovia St., 153-157 Cleveland St., London, W1T 6QW, UK
Tel: 020 73808230
Email: john@pact.co.uk
Website: http://www.pact.co.uk
Members: 1000
Staff: 19
Contact: John McVay, Chief Exec.
Fee: £500
Membership Type: film, digital media producer, digital facilitator
Fee: £350
Membership Type: affiliate
Description: Represents the commercial interests of independent feature film, television, animation, and interactive media companies.
Publication: Directory
Publication title: PACT Directory of British Film & Television Producers

03550
Producers and Composers of Applied Music
PCAM
Birchwood Hall, Storridge, Worcestershire, Malvern, WR13 5EZ, UK
Tel: 020 85638589
Email: info@pcam.co.uk
Website: http://www.pcam.co.uk
Members: 80
Staff: 1
Contact: Jonathan Goldstein, Chm.
Fee: £75
Membership Type: first year
Fee: £25
Membership Type: student
Description: Music production companies or individuals who produce and/or compose music for commercials, television programmes and audio-visual media generally. Aims to improve and regularise practices and conditions for the production of music in advertising, television and audio-visual media; to improve technical standards and practices in music production for these purposes and to increase the profile of music production companies within the advertising and television industries.
Formerly: Formerly, Society of Producers of Advertising Music, Society of Producers of Applied Music
Publication: Newsletter
Publication title: The Bugle

03551
Production Engineering Association
PEA
OTM Consulting Ltd., 44 Quarry St., Surrey, Guildford, GU1 3XQ, UK
Tel: 01483 598000
Fax: 01483 598010
Email: annie.hairsine@otmnet.com
Website: http://www.peajip.com
Members: 21
Contact: Annie Hairsine, Sec.
Fee: £3200
Membership Type: operator
Description: Companies concerned with all operations and equipment related to the production or injection of oil, water, gas from the reservoir to separation facilities. Identifies members' technology requirements and fosters a common view for the future of production technology. Promotes high industry standards.
Library Type: not open to the public

03552
Production Guild of Great Britain
Pinewood Rd., Iver Heath, Aylesbury, SL0 0NH, UK
Tel: 01753 651767
Fax: 01753 652803
Email: reception@productionguild.com
Website: http://fmu.useful.co.uk/productionguild
Members: 500
Staff: 2
Contact: David Martin, Chief Exec.
Fee: £275
Membership Type: full
Fee: £150
Membership Type: overseas, supplementary
Description: Represents senior production personnel in the UK's film, television and visual media industry.
Formerly: Formerly, Guild of Film Production Executives

03553
Production Managers Association
PMA
Ealing Studios, Ealing Green, Ealing, London, W5 5EP, UK
Tel: 020 87588699
Email: pma@pma.org.uk
Website: http://www.pma.org.uk
Members: 196
Staff: 2
Contact: Donall McCusker, Chm.

Fee: £190
Membership Type: regular
Fee: £95
Membership Type: associate
Description: Professional organization representing over 180 production managers working in film, television and multimedia.
Publication: Magazine
Publication title: The Bottom Line. Advertisements.

03554

Production Services Association
PSA

PO Box 2709, Bath, BA1 3YS, UK
Tel: 01225 332668
Fax: 01225 332701
Email: gm@psa.org.uk
Website: http://www.psa.org.uk
Members: 1100
Staff: 2
Contact: Andy Lenthall, Gen. Mgr.
Fee: £425
Membership Type: company, manufacturer, reseller
Fee: £212.5
Membership Type: small company (5 or less employees), school, college, charity
Description: Represents personnel and companies working in the production, design, touring, technical and support services in the live entertainment industry. Seeks to make representations to the government and EC Commission and other local national and overseas governmental bodies on legislation and other public matters and policies, which affect the business or professional interests of its members.
Publication: Newsletter
Publication title: Backstage. Advertisements.

03555

Professional Association of Alexander Teachers
PAAT

The Big Peg, Rm. 706, 120 Vyse St., Birmingham, B18 6NF, UK
Tel: 01743 236195
Email: info@paat.org.uk
Website: http://www.paat.org.uk
Contact: Mary Cox, Contact
Description: Aims to promote the principles of the Alexander Technique as laid down in the books of F.M. Alexander, and to provide help and support for members. Conducts a four-year training course in Birmingham for those wishing to become teachers of the Alexander Technique.

03556

Professional Boatman's Association
PBA

48 Loveys Rd., Yapton, BN18 0HG, UK
Tel: 01243 551927
Email: sec@pba.org.uk
Website: http://www.pba.org.uk
Contact: Daniel Parker, Sec.
Fee: £50
Description: Promotes safety and professionalism in the maritime industry; monitors legislation of interest to the industry.

03557

Professional Bodyguard Association
PBA

PO Box 532, Durham, DH1 9DW, UK
Tel: 0779 2607764
Email: info@professionalbodyguardassociation.co.uk
Website: http://www.probodyguardassociation.co.uk
Members: 1300
Contact: M.J. Tombs, Founder
Description: Represents bodyguards worldwide. All members must be trained up to PBA standards.
Library Subject: bodyguarding and surveillance
Library Type: reference

03558

Professional Computing Association
PCA

PO Box 48, Royston, SG8 6JS, UK
Tel: 0845 6349245
Fax: 0845 6349247
Email: admin@pcauk.org
Website: http://www.pcassociation.org
Members: 570
Staff: 6
Contact: Keith Warburton, CEO
Fee: £24-116
Membership Type: corporate (based on turnovers)
Fee: £59
Membership Type: individual
Description: Companies active in the UK computer channel. Members range from large multinationals to sole traders. Represents the interests of members and promotes the best practice within the computer industry via a Code of Practice. Organizes networking conferences, golf days and dinners throughout the year. Aims to keep the industry for as strong as possible for as long as possible. Works to lead, represent and deliver an outstanding level of service and support for members, so they and the industry as a whole develops and prosper in a rapidly changing environment.
Formerly: Absorbed, Personal Computer Direct Marketers' Association
Publication: Newsletter
Publication title: Interface. Advertisements.
Meetings/Conventions: semiannual conference – Exhibits.

03559

Professional Contractors Group
PCG

Heathrow Blvd., 280 Bath Rd., West Drayton, UB7 0DQ, UK
Tel: 020 88979970
Fax: 020 87591946
Website: http://www.pcg.org.uk/cms
Members: 18000
Contact: Chris Bryce, Chm.
Fee: £220
Membership Type: PCGPlus - single, OneStopPlus (bronze)
Fee: £310
Membership Type: PCGPlus (two companies)
Description: Protects and promotes the interests of freelance consultants and contractors. Promotes the positive benefits of independent workers to business, government and society. Provides full lifecycle support, information and protection to members.

03560

Professional Gardeners Guild
PGG

119 Campkin Rd., Cambridge, CB4 2NP, UK
Tel: 01223 335777
Email: chairman@pgg.org.uk
Website: http://www.pgg.org.uk
Members: 500
Contact: Tony Arnold, Chm.
Fee: £25
Membership Type: full
Fee: £23
Membership Type: retired/associate
Description: Promotes better management and maintenance of gardens and designed landscapes, especially those of historic, horticultural and botanic value.
Publication: Journal
Publication title: The Professional Gardener. Advertisements.

03561

Professional Lighting and Sound Association
PLASA

Redoubt House, 1 Edward Rd., Eastbourne, BN23 8AS, UK
Tel: 01323 524120
Fax: 01323 524121
Email: info@plasa.org
Website: http://www.plasa.org
Members: 500
Staff: 14
Contact: Ruth Rossington, Exec. Dir.
Fee: £645
Membership Type: business, premier
Fee: £390
Membership Type: business, standard
Description: Represents the interests of designers, manufacturers, suppliers and installers of sound, lighting and effects equipment for the entertainment and presentation industries. Also serves designers, consultants and students. Seeks to improve industry standards and influence business practices. Runs the PLASA Show.
Publication: Yearbook
Publication title: Industry Directory. Advertisements.
Meetings/Conventions: PLASA Show – trade show – Exhibits.

03562

Professional Photographic Laboratories Association
PPLA

Wisteria House, 28 Fulling Mill Ln., Herts, Welwyn Garden City, AL6 9NS, UK
Tel: 0870 2404542
Fax: 01438 716572
Email: pmauk@pmai.org
Website: http://www.pmai.org/content.aspx?id=4574
Members: 190
Staff: 1
Contact: Andrew J. Frith, Chm.
Description: Professional photographic imaging laboratories throughout the United Kingdom. Seeks to represent professional photographic processing laboratories exclusively. Committed to the highest standards of professionalism in laboratory work and therefore expects members to monitor carefully the standard of work carried out.
Library Subject: imaging issues
Library Type: reference
Publication: Newsletter

Publication title: PPLA Lablink. Advertisements.
Meetings/Conventions: annual trade show – Exhibits.

03563

Professional Plant Users Group

c/o Landscape Institute
33 Great Portland St., London, W1W 8QG, UK
Tel: 020 72994500
Fax: 020 72994501
Email: mail@landscapeinstitute.org
Website: http://www.landscapeinstitute.org
Members: 5
Contact: Neil Williamson, Pres.
Description: Landscape Institute; Institute of Leisure and Amenity Management; British Association of Landscape Industries; Institute of Horticulture; Arboricultural Association. Furthers the better use of plants in amenity landscapes, including plant selection, plant establishment and maintenance. Encourages research in all areas and informing members of constituent bodies through Plant User.
Publication: Newsletter
Publication title: Plant User

03564

Progress Educational Trust PET

140 Gray's Inn Rd., London, WC1X 8AX, UK
Tel: 020 72787870
Email: admin@progress.org.uk
Website: http://www.progress.org.uk
Members: 200
Staff: 4
Contact: Sarah Norcross, Dir.
Fee: £30
Membership Type: individual
Fee: £100
Membership Type: public sector
Description: Carries out public communication of reproductive and genetic science and facilitates discussion on their legal, ethical and social implications. Publishes a news, information and comment services.
Formerly: Formerly, Progress Campaign for Research into Human Reproduction

03565

Progressio

Unit 3, Canonbury Yard, 190a New North Rd., London, N1 7BJ, UK
Tel: 020 73540883
Fax: 020 73590017
Email: enquiries@progressio.org.uk
Website: http://www.ciir.org
Members: 3000
Staff: 39
Contact: Christine Allen, Exec. Dir.
Fee: £36
Membership Type: regular
Fee: £18
Membership Type: supporter
Description: Works to combine a heritage of radical Catholicism and secular thought. The values and goals include the eradication of poverty and exclusion through challenging unjust political, social and economic structures locally and globally; the full and active participation of the poorest groups in decision-making working to reduce vulnerability stemming from conflict, war and environmental degradation; and an equitable distribution of resources and power between men and women and communities and nations. Guatemala, Nicaragua, Yemen, Zimbabwe, Namibia, and Peru, providing skilled workers in agriculture, health, formal and non-formal education, and environment projects. Arranges forums providing resource material for members of British and European parliaments, policy-makers, and the media.
Formerly: Formerly, Sword of the Spirit

03566

Progressive Supranuclear Palsy Association - Europe

PSP House, 167 Watling St. W, Towcester, NN12 6BX, UK
Tel: 01327 322410
Fax: 01327 322412
Email: psp@pspeur.org
Website: http://www.pspeur.org
Contact: Michael Koe, Chm.
Fee: £25
Membership Type: individual (in Europe)
Fee: £40
Membership Type: individual (outside Europe)
Description: Promotes research into the cause, treatment and eventual cure of Progressive Supranuclear Palsy. Provides information and support to sufferers and their families. Promotes awareness of the disease among medical professionals and the general public within the UK.
Publication: Magazine
Publication title: PSP Matters

03567

Project Trust PT

The Hebridean Ctre., Argyll, Isle of Coll, PA78 6TE, UK
Tel: 01879 230444
Fax: 01879 230357
Email: info@projecttrust.org.uk
Website: http://www.projecttrust.org.uk
Staff: 14
Contact: Ingrid Emerson, Contact
Description: Individuals between 17 and 19 years old from member countries of the European Union. Seeks to develop responsibility and self-reliance in youth through volunteer work in Third World countries. Participants work as teachers' aides, assist in care of deprived and mentally handicapped children, and work in hospitals. Organizes training courses for volunteers; conducts annual debriefing course.
Publication: Newsletter
Publication title: Project Post

03568

Property Consultants Society

Basement Office, 1 Surrey St., West Sussex, Arundel, BN18 9DT, UK
Tel: 01903 883787
Fax: 01903 889590
Email: info@propertyconsultantssociety.org
Website: http://www.p-c-s.org.uk
Members: 650
Staff: 3
Contact: Carol C. Mortiboy, Pres.
Fee: £125
Membership Type: fellow
Fee: £115
Membership Type: associate
Description: Persons engaged in the property industry. Provides a central organization for persons engaged as consultants in the property business whether as principals or employees. Aims to advance members' interests and standing within the context of sound and professional advice.
Library Type: not open to the public

03569

Proprietary Association of Great Britain PAGB

Vernon House, Sicilian Ave., London, WC1A 2QS, UK
Tel: 020 72428331
Fax: 020 74057719
Email: info@pagb.co.uk
Website: http://www.pagb.co.uk
Members: 70
Staff: 15
Contact: Sheila Kelly, Exec. Dir.
Description: Trade association representing UK manufacturers of over-the-counter (OTC) medicines and food supplements. Promotes responsible consumers healthcare.
Library Type: not open to the public
Publication: Newsletter
Publication title: Member eNews
Meetings/Conventions: OTC Medicines Advertising Workshop – monthly workshop

03570

ProShare United Kingdom

8th Fl., Peninsular House, 36 Monument St., London, EC3R 8LJ, UK
Tel: 020 74447104
Fax: 020 74447115
Email: customerservices@ifslearning.ac.uk
Website: http://www.ifsproshare.org
Staff: 13
Contact: Anne Kiem, Chair
Description: Promotes responsible share based investment, including employee share ownership, through education and research.
Publication: Magazine
Publication title: Dividend. Advertisements.

03571

Prospect

New Prospect House, 8 Leake St., London, SE1 7NN, UK
Tel: 020 79026600
Fax: 020 79026667
Email: enquiries@prospect.org.uk
Website: http://www.prospect.org.uk
Members: 102000
Staff: 151
Contact: Catherine Donaldson, Contact
Description: Professional, technical engineering and scientific grades in the civil service, other government bodies and private sector organizations prospect members and branches are organized through professional sectors, such as agriculture, defence, health and safety, environment and energy, with additional sector bases in Scotland, Liverpool, Bristol, and Birmingham. Is concerned with the interests of members; to maintain and improve conditions of employment; to provide services for the benefit of members and personal assistance in time of need. Areas of representation include government departments and agencies, other public and private sector organizations such as CAA, British Energy, BNFL, AEA Technology, MLC, BAA, Unilever, etc.
Formerly: Formerly, Engineers and Managers Association

03572

Prostate Cancer Support Association
PSA

22 High St., Cheshire, SK1 1EG, UK
Tel: 061 4748222
Email: info@prostatecancersupport.info
Website: http://www.prostatecancersupport.info
Fee: £12
Membership Type: basic
Description: Relieves the physical or mental distress of persons with prostate cancer. Provides education and information about prostate cancer. Contributes to the provision of treatment and care of those affected by prostate cancer.

03573

Provincial Booksellers Fairs Association
PBFA

16 Melbourn St., Hertfordshire, Royston, SG8 7BZ, UK
Tel: 01763 248400
Fax: 01763 248921
Email: info@pbfa.org
Website: http://www.pbfa.org
Members: 600
Staff: 3
Contact: Becky Wears, Admin.
Fee: £148.94
Membership Type: regular
Description: Antiquarian and second-hand booksellers. Organizes book fairs throughout the country, with the Hotel Russell Fair in London the focal point of the British book trade. Aims to promote interest in the collection of antiquarian and secondhand books.
Publication: Book
Publication title: Book Collecting: A Guide to Antiquarian and Secondhand Books

03574

Provision Trade Federation
PTF

17 Clerkenwell Green, London, EC1R 0DP, UK
Tel: 020 72532114
Fax: 020 76081645
Email: secretray@ptbi.org.uk
Website: http://www.provtrade.co.uk
Members: 154
Staff: 5
Contact: Mette Barwick, Sec.
Description: Manufacturers, traders, importers, exporters, distributors, and retailers involved in trading dairy products, bacon and pig meat, chilled and processed meats, canned foods, and yogurt and short life dairy products in the UK. Represents, protects, and promotes the interests of members by negotiating with organizations and official bodies representing EU institutions, the UK government, trade associations, or local and regional authorities.
Formerly: Formerly, United Kingdom Provision Trade Federation

03575

Psoriasis and Psoriatic Arthritis Alliance
PAPAA

PO Box 111, St. Albans, AL2 3JQ, UK
Tel: 0192 3672837
Fax: 0192 3682606
Email: info@papaa.org
Website: http://www.papaa.org/tiki-custom_home.php
Contact: Julie Chandler, Founder
Fee: £12
Membership Type: full, within UK
Fee: £24
Membership Type: full, international
Description: Provides support to those affected by psoriasis and psoriatic arthritis. Disseminates information that has been approved by healthcare professionals or has been published as evidence. Advocates a signposting service to help people with psoriasis and psoriatic arthritis to make informed choices and understand how to deal with their condition.
Publication: Journal
Publication title: Skin 'n' Bones Connection

03576

Psoriasis Association

Dick Coles House, 2 Queensbridge, Northampton, NN4 7BF, UK
Tel: 0845 6760076
Fax: 01604 251621
Email: mail@psoriasis-association.org.uk
Website: http://www.timewarp.demon.co.uk/psoriasis.html
Members: 4000
Description: Provides up to date information and promotes self-help and support to people with psoriasis; works to raise standards of patient care and improves education about psoriasis with the public and healthcare professionals.
Publication: Magazine
Publication title: The Journal

03577

Public and Commercial Services Union
PCS

160 Falcon Rd., London, SW11 2LN, UK
Tel: 020 79242727
Fax: 020 79241847
Email: alexf@pcs.org.uk
Website: http://www.pcs.org.uk
Members: 300000
Contact: Alex Flynn, Natl. Press Off.
Description: Clerical, secretarial, computer support, and communications grades in the civil service, certain fringe organizations and public sector areas. Protects and promotes the interests of its members, regulates their relations with the employing body, and improves their employment conditions.
Formerly: Formerly, Civil and Public Services Association

03578

Public Monuments and Sculpture Association
PMSA

70 Cowcross St., London, EC1M 6EJ, UK
Tel: 020 74905001
Email: pmsa@btconnect.com
Website: http://www.pmsa.org.uk
Members: 230
Staff: 2
Contact: Peter Brown, Chm.
Fee: £35
Membership Type: ordinary
Fee: £27.5
Membership Type: student, retired/unemployed
Description: Aims to protect and promote public monuments and sculpture dating from post-medieval to tomorrow.
Publication: Newsletter
Publication title: Circumspice

03579

Public Relations Consultants Association
PRCA

Willow House, 17-23 Willow Pl., 1st Fl., London, SW1P 1JH, UK
Tel: 020 72336026
Fax: 020 78284797
Email: communications@prca.org.uk
Website: http://www.prca.org.uk
Members: 125
Contact: David Gallagher, Chm.
Description: Public relations consultants in England. Maintains professional standards in the field; promotes confidence in public relations consulting. Assists members with problems in financial management, industrial relations, and consulting practice, recruitment and training. Conducts research; compiles statistics. Operates referral system.
Publication: Book
Publication title: Managing Professional Communications Agencies

03580

Publicity Club of London
PCL

Sheraton House, 15-19 Great Chapel St., London, W1F 8FN, UK
Tel: 020 77345666
Fax: 020 77349666
Email: sue@ashcommunications.com
Website: http://www.thepcl.co.uk
Members: 340
Contact: Sue Ash, Chm.
Fee: £60
Membership Type: individual
Fee: £10
Membership Type: student
Description: Individuals from Advertising, Direct Marketing, Marketing, New Media, PR and the Media. Offers access to industry related events in the London calendar. Provides opportunities to meet like-minded people and to make invaluable personal and professional connections.

03581

Publishers Association
PA

29b Montague Street, London, WC1B 5BW, UK
Tel: 020 76919191
Fax: 020 76919199
Email: mail@publishers.org.uk
Website: http://www.publishers.org.uk/en/home
Members: 150
Staff: 15
Contact: Anita Desilva, Sec.
Fee: £4730-31505
Membership Type: individual (based on the turnover)
Description: Book, journal and electronic publishers. Promotes the publishing industry in the U.K. Provides industry information, market statistics, and notice of training opportunities.

03582
Publishers Licensing Society
PLS

37-41 Gower St., London, WC1E 6HH, UK
Tel: 020 72997730
Fax: 020 72997780
Email: pls@pls.org.uk
Website: http://www.pls.org.uk
Members: 1500
Staff: 4
Contact: Alicia Wise, CEO
Description: Represents and supports publishers.
Publication: Newsletter
Publication title: PLS Plus

03583
Publishers Publicity Circle
PPC

65 Airedale Ave., London, W4 2NN, UK
Tel: 020 89941881
Fax: 020 79381268
Email: ppc-@lineone.net
Website: http://www.publisherspublicitycircle.co.uk
Members: 280
Contact: Heather White, Sec.-Treas.
Fee: £75
Membership Type: regular
Description: People involved in book publicity at all levels in both publishing houses and independent PR companies. Monthly meetings provide a forum for press journalists, television and radio researchers and producers to meet publicists. The Circle enables publicists to meet and share information.

03584
Publishing Scotland

Scottish Book Centre, 137 Dundee St., Edinburgh, EH11 1BG, UK
Tel: 0131 2286866
Fax: 0131 2283220
Email: enquiries@publishingscotland.org
Website: http://www.publishingscotland.co.uk/Default.aspx?pid=1
Members: 80
Staff: 5
Contact: Caroline Gorham, Chair
Fee: £322-1505
Membership Type: full (based on annual turnover)
Fee: £322
Membership Type: associate
Description: Aims to help Scottish publishers to conduct their businesses in a professional manner, to market their output to the widest possible readership within Scotland, the UK and overseas, and to encourage the development of a literary culture in Scotland.
Formerly: Formerly, Scottish Publishers Association
Publication: Directory
Publication title: Directory of Publishing in Scotland. Advertisements.

03585
Pulmonary Hypertension Association - United Kingdom
PHA-UK

Unit 3A, Enterprise Ct., Fairfield Park, Manvers, South Yorkshire, Rotherham, S63 5DB, UK
Tel: 01709 761450
Fax: 01709 760265
Email: office@phassociation.uk.com
Website: http://www.phassociation.uk.com
Contact: Iain Armstrong, Chm./Trustee
Description: Seeks to improve the quality of life for individuals with pulmonary hypertension. Raises understanding and awareness of all aspects of pulmonary hypertension. Provides support and information for all those people whose lives are touched by pulmonary hypertension.
Publication: Newsletter
Publication title: Emphasis

03586
Pump Distributors Association
PDA

5 Chapelfield, Orford, Woodbridge, 1P12 2HW, UK
Tel: 01394 450181
Fax: 01394 450181
Email: pumps@the-pda.com
Website: http://www.the-pda.com
Members: 28
Staff: 1
Contact: Ian Castle, Dir.
Description: Pump distributors in the United Kingdom. Aims to be the representative body of the pump distributive industry of the UK and by setting and maintaining of proper standards for the professional conduct of its members to thereby protect and further enhance their reputation and interests.
Publication: Handbook
Meetings/Conventions: annual meeting

03587
Puppet Centre Trust
PCT

Battersea Arts Ctre., Lavender Hill, Battersea, London, SW11 5TN, UK
Tel: 020 72285335
Email: pct@puppetcentre.org.uk
Website: http://www.puppetcentre.org.uk
Staff: 1
Contact: Anthony Dean, Chm.
Description: Puppeteers, puppetry enthusiasts, teachers, students, bookers and funders of puppetry, arts boards and arts councils. Aims to further the arts of puppetry and animation, to service the needs of anyone involved in professional, amateur and educational puppetry. Seeks to evolve a more professional and scientific base for the development of the art form in partnership with funding bodies, community groups, local authorities, arts organizations and educational establishments.

03588
Quaker Peace and Social Witness
QPSW

Friends House, 173-177 Euston Rd., London, NW1 2BJ, UK
Tel: 020 76631000
Fax: 020 76631001
Email: qpsw@quaker.org.uk
Website: http://www.quaker.org.uk
Staff: 30
Contact: Nikolas Dadson, Contact
Description: Aims to build international peace and reduce violence. Seeks to advance social and economic change and reduce poverty and injustice in the world. Supports long term programs with experienced representatives in working on the tools of reconciliation at all levels, including the victims of wars or violence. Helps reconciliation work in Africa, Asia, the Middle East and Europe. Gives training in peacemaking skills, places workers with local service agencies and supports work in Britain which addresses the causes of economic injustice and violence.
Formerly: Formerly, Friends Peace and International Relations Council
Publication: Newsletter
Publication title: Opportunities for Action

03589
Qualifications and Curriculum Authority
QCA

83 Piccadilly, London, W1J 8QA, UK
Tel: 020 75095555
Email: info@qca.org.uk
Website: http://www.qcda.gov.uk
Members: 15
Staff: 200
Contact: Christopher Trinick, Chm.
Description: Teachers, educationalists and industrialists with expertise, experience and a direct interest in education. Keeps under review all aspects of the curriculum for maintained schools in England and all aspects of school examinations and assessment, and advises the Secretary of State on these curriculum examinations and assessment matters. Publishes and disseminates information relating to the curriculum, examinations, and assessment. Responsible for making arrangements for school-based assessments.
Formerly: Formerly, School Curriculum and Assessment Authority

03590
Quality Meat Scotland
QMS

Rural Centre, West Mains, Ingliston, Newbridge, Edinburgh, EH28 8NZ, UK
Tel: 0131 4724040
Fax: 0131 4724038
Email: info@qmscotland.co.uk
Website: http://www.qmscotland.co.uk
Staff: 18
Contact: Donald Biggar, Chm.
Description: Scotch livestock producers and marketers. Works on behalf of Scottish livestock farmers in the home and export markets to promote Scotch beef, lamb and pork with and through the wholesale, catering and retail sectors of the meat industry.
Library Type: reference
Formerly: Formerly, Scotch Quality Beef and Lamb Association

03591
Quality Scheme for Ready Mixed Concrete
QSRMC

1 Mt. Mews, High St., Hampton, TW12 2SH, UK
Tel: 020 89410273
Fax: 020 89794558
Email: enquiries@qsrmc.co.uk
Website: http://www.qsrmc.co.uk
Staff: 13
Contact: Collin Head, Sec.
Description: Provides a nationally accredited product conformity certification scheme for the supply and production of ready mixed concrete. Establishes and enforces prescribed standards for the industry that are

agreed between producers and customers. Promotes the development of new standards and specifications.
Publication: Directory
Publication title: QSRMC Directory of Quality Assured Suppliers of Ready Mixed Concrete and Certificated Plants

03592

Quaternary Research Association QRA

University of Wales, School of Ocean Sciences, Anglesey, Menai Bridge, LL59 5AB, UK
Email: oss048@bangor.ac.uk
Website: http://www.qra.org.uk
Members: 1000
Contact: James Scourse, Pres.
Fee: £20
Membership Type: individual
Fee: £10
Membership Type: student, retired, unwaged
Description: Archaeologists, botanists, civil engineers, geographers, geologists, soil scientists, zoologists and others interested in the problems of the Quaternary. Promotes the study of the Quaternary period of time.
Publication: Journal
Publication title: Journal of Quaternary Science

03593

Quekett Microscopical Club

90, The Fairway, Middlesex, South Ruislip, HA4 0SQ, UK
Email: president@quekett.org
Website: http://www.nhm.ac.uk/hosted_sites/quekett
Members: 450
Contact: Phil Greaves, Pres.
Fee: £31
Membership Type: in UK
Fee: £39
Membership Type: outside UK
Description: Encourages the study of every branch of microscopical science.
Library Subject: microscopy
Library Type: reference
Publication: Bulletin
Publication title: The Bulletin of the Quekett Microscopical Club

03594

Questscope for Social Development in the Middle East - United Kingdom

7-8 Grays Inn Sq., London, WC1R 5JQ, UK
Tel: 0207 6117988
Email: questscope@questscope.org
Website: http://www.questscope.org
Contact: Paul Martin, Chm.
Description: Seeks to help disadvantaged communities in the Hashemite Kingdom of Jordan to assist their most vulnerable members, especially street children, disadvantaged girls and women in poverty.

03595

Quilters' Guild of the British Isles

St. Anthony's Hall, Peasholme Green, York, YO1 7PW, UK
Tel: 01904 613242
Fax: 01904 632394
Email: info@quiltersguild.org.uk
Website: http://www.quiltersguild.org.uk
Members: 7000
Staff: 8
Contact: Margaret Hughes, Pres.
Fee: £37
Membership Type: adult
Fee: £45
Membership Type: international
Description: Quilters with varying experience and skills, collectors, traders, and teachers. Promotes the art, understanding, appreciation, technique and heritage of patchwork, quilting and applique.
Publication: Catalog
Publication title: The Nineties Catalogue

03596

Quit

63 St. Marys Axe, London, EC3A 8AA, UK
Tel: 020 74690400
Fax: 020 74690401
Email: info@quit.org.uk
Website: http://www.quit.org.uk
Staff: 100
Contact: Robin Rotherham, Chm.
Description: Offers information, advice and support to people who want to stop smoking.
Publication: Annual Report
Publication title: Celebrating Life

03597

Radio, Electrical and Television Retailers' Association RETRA

RETRA House, St. John's Terr., 1 Ampthill St., Bedford, MK42 9EY, UK
Tel: 01234 269110
Fax: 01234 269609
Email: retra@retra.co.uk
Website: http://www.retra.co.uk
Members: 1500
Staff: 8
Description: Independent and multiple electrical retailers, together with associate members (47). In addition to representing the views of its members, provides a host of time and cost saving services including free legal and business advice, business and consumer credit stationery, point of sale material, extended warranty insurance and subsidies on security equipment, shop insurance, workwear and credit referencing, discounts with HSBC, Barclaycard; operates Code of Practice; conducts useful surveys.
Publication: Magazine
Publication title: Alert. Advertisements.

03598

Radioactive Waste Management Advisory Committee RWMAC

Zone 4/E4, Ashdown House, 123 Victoria St., London, SWE1 6DE, UK
Tel: 020 70828483
Email: jeff.l.thompson@defra.gsi.gov.uk
Website: http://www.defra.gov.uk/rwmac
Members: 20
Staff: 4
Contact: Robert L. Jackson, Sec.
Description: Members appointed by the Secretary of State for the Environment, Food and Rural Affairs. Advises the Ministers in the Department for Environment Food and Rural Affairs, the Scottish Executive and the National Assembly for Wales on technical and environmental implications of major issues concerning the development and implementation of an overall policy for all aspects of the management of civil radioactive waste, including research and development, and on any other matters.

03599

Radionic Association RA

Baerlein House, Goose Green, Deddington, Oxon, Banbury, OX15 0SZ, UK
Tel: 01869 338852
Fax: 01869 338852
Email: enquiries@radionic.co.uk
Website: http://www.radionic.co.uk
Members: 501
Staff: 2
Fee: £25
Membership Type: associate (voting)
Fee: £30
Membership Type: associate (non-voting), retired
Description: Individuals who have trained in radionics and are qualified to practice professionally and laymen who are interested in radionics and wish to support the association. (Radionics is described as "a method of healing at a distance through the medium of a specially designed instrument using the faculty of extra-sensory perception".) Main objectives of the association are to promote knowledge and understanding of radionics and to maintain the highest standards of competence and conduct among its practicing members. Maintains School of Radionics that provides professional training.
Library Subject: medical
Library Type: reference
Publication: Book
Publication title: Horizons in Radionics

03600

Rail Freight Group RFG

Monticello House, 45 Russell Sq., London, WC1B 4JP, UK
Tel: 020 79074646
Fax: 020 79074684
Email: phillippa@rfg.org.uk
Website: http://www.rfg.org.uk
Members: 150
Contact: Phillippa O'Shea, Admin. Mgr.
Fee: £1449
Membership Type: full (includes VAT)
Description: Represents the rail freight industry comprise of suppliers, manufacturers, customers, operators and contractors. Works to increase the volume and market share of freight carried profitably by rail.
Meetings/Conventions: Christmas Lunch – annual luncheon

03601

Railfuture

c/o Mike Crowhurst, Chm.
33 Station Ct., Aberford Rd., Garforth, Leeds, LS25 2QQ, UK
Tel: 0113 2864844
Fax: 0113 2864844
Email: info@railfuture.org.uk
Website: http://www.railfuture.org.uk/tiki-page.php?pageName=RailFuture
Members: 3500
Staff: 5
Contact: Peter Lawrence, Pres.
Fee: £21
Membership Type: individual, family (plus 2/person)
Fee: £14
Membership Type: student
Description: Individuals, rail users' groups, local authorities, and companies interested in the objectives of the society. Aims to encourage development of a modern rail system fit for the next century, as a more environmentally friendly means of transport. Maintains intact the existing system, fight closures, encourage re-openings/opening of new lines and stations where justified.
Library Type: not open to the public
Formerly: Formerly, Railway Development Society
Publication: Book
Publication title: A-Z of Rail Re-openings (4th edition)

03602

Railway and Canal Historical Society
RCHS

3 West Ct., West St., Oxford, OX2 0NP, UK
Website: http://www.rchs.org.uk/trial/gwpf.php?wpage=home
Members: 780
Contact: Matthew Searle, Honorable Sec.
Fee: £15
Membership Type: ordinary
Fee: £18
Membership Type: joint
Description: Unites those interested in the history of transport, with particular reference to British railways and waterways. Promotes historical research and raises the standards of published history.
Publication: Journal
Publication title: R&CHS Journal

03603

Railway Children

1 The Commons, 1st Fl., Sandbach, Cheshire, CW11 1EG, UK
Tel: 01270 757596
Fax: 01270 763651
Email: enquiries@railwaychildren.org.uk
Website: http://www.railwaychildren.org.uk
Contact: Terina Keene, Chief Exec.
Description: Collaborates with local social welfare organizations to assists runaway and abandoned children around the world. Provides shelter, health care, education, training, protection, and friendship to street children.

03604

Railway Correspondence and Travel Society
RCTS

c/o Vron Cooke, Asst. Treas.
23 Haig Dr., Slough, SL1 9HA, UK
Website: http://www.rcts.org.uk
Members: 3500
Contact: Peter Davies, Sales Mgr.
Fee: £23
Membership Type: regular
Description: Promotes the interests of members in railway operation.
Library Subject: railways
Library Type: not open to the public
Publication: Magazine
Publication title: Railway Observer. Advertisements.

03605

Railway Industry Association
RIA

22 Headfort Pl., London, SW1X 7RY, UK
Tel: 020 72010777
Fax: 020 72355777
Email: ria@riagb.org.uk
Website: http://www.riagb.org.uk
Members: 140
Contact: Paul Johnson, Chm.
Fee: £1600
Membership Type: company (minimum)
Description: Works to supply the world's railways with equipment, services and consultancy. Promotes use and development of railroads.
Publication: Directory
Publication title: Members and Products

03606

Railway Preservation Society of Ireland
RPSI

PO Box 461, Newtownabbey, BT36 9BT, UK
Tel: 028 93373968
Email: rpsitrains@hotmail.com
Website: http://www.steamtrainsireland.com
Members: 1000
Staff: 5
Contact: Paul McCann, Sec.
Fee: £25
Membership Type: adult
Fee: £15
Membership Type: junior (under 18)
Description: Individuals working to promote interest in the railways of Ireland and their history. Promotes exchange of railway experience and knowledge among members. Seeks to restore, maintain, and operate steam locomotives and vintage rolling stock on the main line railways of Ireland.
Publication: Magazine
Publication title: Five Foot Three. Advertisements.

03607

RAPRA Technology

Shawbury, Shrewsbury, SY4 4NR, UK
Tel: 01939 250383
Fax: 01939 251118
Email: info@rapra.net
Website: http://www.rapra.net
Members: 190
Staff: 150
Fee: £600
Membership Type: small business
Fee: £1000
Membership Type: full
Description: Provides the rubber and plastics industry with technology, information, and consultancy on all aspects of rubber and plastics. Operates extensive processing, analytical, and testing laboratory facilities.
Library Subject: rubber, plastics, adhesives, polymer composites
Library Type: reference
Formerly: Formerly, Research Association of British Rubber Manufacturers
Publication: Journal
Publication title: Adhesives Abstracts

03608

Rating Surveyors' Association
RSA

c/o Sanderson Weatherall
25 Wellington St., Leeds, LS1 4WG, UK
Email: enquiries@ratingsurveyorsassociation.org
Website: http://www.ratingsurveyorsassociation.org
Members: 350
Contact: RGA Brown, Honorary Treas.
Fee: £25
Membership Type: individual, associate
Fee: £10
Membership Type: retired
Description: Persons practising or employed as rating surveyors. Upholds and improves the status of rating surveyors, regulates the customs and usages of the profession; encourages harmonious action between members; discusses matters or questions in connection with rating.

03609

Ray Society
RS

c/o Natural History Museum
Cromwell Rd., London, SW7 5BD, UK
Website: http://www.scientificbooks.co.uk
Contact: T. Ferrero, Honorary Sec.
Fee: £6
Membership Type: individual
Description: Individuals from 20 countries interested in natural history. Prints and promotes books and monographs on zoology and botany, with special but not exclusive relevance to British flora and fauna.
Publication: Annual Report
Publication title: Annual Report of the Council of the Ray Society

03610

Raynaud's and Scleroderma Association
RSA

112 Crewe Rd., Cheshire, Alsager, ST7 2JA, UK
Tel: 01270 872776
Fax: 01270 883556
Email: info@raynauds.org.uk
Website: http://www.raynauds.org.uk
Members: 6000
Staff: 4
Contact: Anne H. Mawdsley, CEO/Founder
Fee: £12
Membership Type: regular
Fee: £8

Membership Type: senior citizen
Description: Individuals afflicted with Raynaud's Disease or scleroderma; concerned medical professionals. Raynaud's Disease is marked by interruption of blood flow to the extremities, primarily the toes and fingers but can include the ears and nose, due to spasmodic contraction of small blood vessels; in severe cases this phenomenon is often noted in individual suffering from scleroderma, which affects the blood vessels, immune system and connective tissue. Encourages better communication among doctors and patients and provides mutual support among those with the condition. Strives to heighten public awareness on Raynaud's Disease and scleroderma. Conducts fundraising activities to help finance research.
Formerly: Formerly, Raynaud's Association Trust
Publication: Book
Publication title: Raynaud's and Scleroderma, A Journey of Discovery

03611

Re-Solv, the Society for the Prevention of Solvent and Volatile Substance Abuse RS

30A High St., Stone, ST15 8AW, UK
Tel: 01785 817885
Email: information@re-solv.org
Website: http://www.re-solv.org
Members: 300
Staff: 10
Contact: Steve Lambert, Dir.
Fee: £150
Membership Type: corporate
Fee: £75
Membership Type: public
Description: Promotes increased awareness on the part of parents, local authorities, retailers, and law enforcement officials of the problem of the "sniffing" of solvents and volatile substances. Acts as an information clearinghouse on solvent abuse. Liaises with other agencies, the Home Office, and other government bodies in the dissemination of information. Supports legislation that seeks to control solvent abuse. Provides videos and other materials for use in primary and secondary schools and by parents, teachers, doctors, social workers, retailers, and law enforcement personnel.
Publication: Video
Publication title: A Loaded Gun

03612

REACH Charity: Association for Children with Upper Limb Deficiency

PO Box 54, Helston, Cornwall, TR13 8WD, UK
Tel: 0845 1306225
Fax: 0845 1300262
Email: reach@reach.org.uk
Website: http://www.reach.org.uk/reachcms
Members: 1200
Staff: 1
Contact: Sue Stokes, COO
Fee: £25
Membership Type: full, overseas electronic
Fee: £35
Membership Type: overseas full
Description: Aims to offer support to families of children with upper limb deficiency.
Formerly: Formerly, REACH: Association for Children with Hand or Arm Deficiency
Publication: Newsletter
Publication title: Within Reach

03613

Records Management Society RMS

Benchmark Communications, 14 Blandford Sq., Newcastle upon Tyne, NE1 4HZ, UK
Tel: 0191 2442839
Fax: 0191 2453802
Email: info@rms-gb.org.uk
Website: http://www.rms-gb.org.uk
Members: 1017
Staff: 4
Contact: Paul Duller, Exec. Sec.
Fee: £13.8
Membership Type: student
Fee: £69
Membership Type: individual
Description: Represents individuals who are concerned with information management. Aims to improve the status of records management. Encourages the highest professional standards.
Publication: Journal
Publication title: Bulletin. Advertisements.

03614

Recruitment and Employment Confederation REC

15 Welbeck St., London, W1G 9XT, UK
Tel: 020 70092100
Fax: 020 79354112
Email: info@rec.uk.com
Website: http://www.rec.uk.com/home
Members: 14000
Staff: 60
Contact: Kevin Green, Chief Exec.
Description: Promotes the recruitment industry in Britain by supplying membership services, legal advice, education and training; represents members' interests before parliament and in Europe.
Formerly: Formerly, Institute of Employment Consultants
Publication: Journal
Publication title: Recruitment Matters. Advertisements.

03615

Recycling Association

Heritage House, Vicar Ln., Daventry, NN11 4GD, UK
Tel: 01327 703223
Fax: 01327 300612
Email: admin@iwppa.co.uk
Website: http://www.therecyclingassociation.com
Members: 100
Staff: 4
Description: Promotes independent waste paper merchants. Develops the interests of independent waste paper merchants. Works to ensure its members' views are represented to the relevant organisations.
Formerly: Formerly, Independent Waste Paper Processors Association

03616

Red Poll Cattle Society

1 Nabbott Rd., Essex, Chelmsford, CM1 2SW, UK
Tel: 01245 600032
Fax: 01245 600032
Email: secretary@redpoll.co.uk
Website: http://www.redpoll.org
Members: 393
Staff: 1
Contact: Ray Bowler, Sec.
Fee: £25
Membership Type: registering
Fee: £15
Membership Type: associate
Description: Promotes the Red Poll breed of cattle, a native British breed which is dual-purpose. It is long-lived, hardy and does well on low input systems.
Publication: Book
Publication title: Herd Book

03617

RedR International

Lower Beer, Uplowman, Tiverton, EX16 7PF, UK
Tel: 01884 821239
Email: redr.international@redr.org
Website: http://www.redr.org
Members: 2000
Contact: Robert Hodgson, Sec.
Description: Aims to relieve the suffering of victims of disasters. Provides sufficient, competent and effective relief personnel to front-line humanitarian agencies. Improves the competence of relief personnel through training and education. Works with other agencies to improve the availability and effectiveness of relief personnel.
Formerly: Also Known As, Registered Engineers for Disaster Relief

03618

RedR London - International Health Exchange RedR-IHE

1 Great George St., London, SW1P 3AA, UK
Tel: 020 72333116
Fax: 020 72333590
Website: http://www.redr.org.uk
Contact: Robert Hodgson, Chm.
Description: Provides humanitarian aid to those suffering from disasters.

03619

REDRESS

87 Vauxhall Walk, London, SE11 5HJ, UK
Tel: 020 77931777
Fax: 020 77931719
Email: info@redress.org
Website: http://www.redress.org
Contact: Carla Ferstman, Dir.
Description: Helps torture victims obtain justice and reparation by providing legal advice and access to the courts. Promotes the development and implementation of national and international standards that provide effective and enforceable civil and criminal remedies for torture. Assists in rebuilding the lives and livelihoods of torture survivors and their families.
Publication: Report
Publication title: The Reparation Report

03620
Refined Bitumen Association
RBA

Harrogate Business Centre, Hammerain House, Hookstone Ave., Harrogate, HG2 8ER, UK
Tel: 01423 876361
Fax: 01423 873999
Email: chris.southwell@ukrba.com
Website: http://www.bitumenuk.com
Contact: Chris Southwell, Technical Dir.
Description: Promotes the effective use of bituminous materials within the construction industry. Provides technical advice and information, and funds research into bituminous products.

03621
Refined Sugar Association
RSA

154, Bishopsgate, London, EC2M 4LN, UK
Tel: 020 73772113
Fax: 020 72472481
Email: durhamn@sugar-assoc.co.uk
Website: http://www.sugarassociation.co.uk
Members: 115
Contact: N. Durham, Sec.
Fee: £750
Membership Type: firm, company, organization
Description: Represents active traders in white sugar. Provides proper conduct of the international white sugar trade. Provides contract rules and arbitration services and looks after the interests of members in the white sugar trade.
Publication title: The Rules and Regulations

03622
Regency Foundation Networx

Gordon House, 6 Lissenden Gardens, London, NW5 1LX, UK
Tel: 020 74828809
Fax: 020 74828827
Email: info@regency.org
Website: http://www.regency.org
Description: Works with the United Nations and its agencies to develop programs related to people-centered sustainable development; encourages partnerships between the United Nations, governments, non-governmental organizations, institutional investors and the private sector; collaborates with educational authorities, national and international educational bodies, schools, colleges and universities. Supports the implementation of information and communication-related projects.
Publication: Book
Publication title: Human Rights - The New Consensus

03623
Regent Street Association
RSA

Linen Hall, Rm. 302, 162-168 Regent St., London, W1B 5TD, UK
Tel: 020 70383718
Fax: 020 70383708
Email: info@regentstreetonline.com
Website: http://www.regentstreetonline.com
Contact: Annie Walker, Dir./Exec. Off.
Fee: £105-630
Membership Type: office
Fee: £420
Membership Type: hotel, bar, restaurant
Description: Works to look after the interests of the retailers and businesses in the area. Builds constant communication and lobbies the local city councilors and officers on behalf of its members on crucial issues that affect the community.

03624
Regional Studies Association
RSA

PO Box 2058, Seaford, BN25 4QU, UK
Tel: 01323 899698
Fax: 01323 899798
Email: info@rsa-ls.ac.uk
Website: http://www.regional-studies-assoc.ac.uk
Contact: Sally Hardy, Chief Exec.
Fee: £101
Membership Type: individual (band A)
Fee: £205.5
Membership Type: corporate (band A)
Description: Individuals (550) and corporate groups (250) such as government departments, ministries, county councils, local authorities, research bodies, educational institutions, consultants' offices, geographers, economists, town planners, architects, and engineers interested in regional planning. Promotes education and research in the field of regional planning and development internationally; provides a forum for exchange of ideas and information; disseminates research results. Maintains European Regional Research Network, which produces reports, directories, surveys, and lists of contact addresses in Europe; promotes regional studies and research at European rather than national levels; develops contact among teachers and researchers throughout Europe.
Publication: Directory
Publication title: European Urban and Regional Research Directory

03625
Registered Nursing Home Association
RNHA

John Hewitt House, Tunnel Ln., Off Lifford Ln., Kings Norton, Birmingham, B30 3JN, UK
Tel: 0121 4511088
Fax: 0121 4863175
Email: info@rnha.co.uk
Website: http://www.rnha.co.uk/general.php?r=MANKY421443
Members: 1600
Staff: 8
Contact: Frank E. Ursell, CEO
Description: Nursing home owners who campaigns for high standards in nursing home care.
Publication: Magazine
Publication title: Nursing Home News. Advertisements.

03626
Relate

Herbert Gray College, Little Church St., Rugby, CV21 3AP, UK
Tel: 01788 573241
Fax: 01788 535007
Email: enquiries@relate.org.uk
Website: http://www.relate.org.uk
Members: 5500
Staff: 200
Contact: Angela Sibson, Chief Exec.
Description: Provides relationship counselling and sex therapy services to couples in England, Wales, and Northern Ireland.
Formerly: Formerly, National Marriage Guidance

03627
Relate Scotland

18 York Pl., Edinburgh, EH1 3EP, UK
Tel: 0845 1192020
Fax: 0845 1196089
Email: enquiries@relationships-scotland.org.uk
Website: http://www.relationships-scotland.org.uk
Members: 600
Staff: 14
Contact: Hilary Campbell, Chief Exec.
Fee: £50
Membership Type: local service, individual
Description: Offers counseling services to couples in intimate personal relationships. Trains volunteers as counselors. Also provides specialized training in psychosexual and divorce/separation counseling; and provides psychosexual therapy.
Formerly: Formerly, Marriage Counselling Scotland

03628
Relationships Scotland

18 York Pl., Edinburgh, EH1 3EP, UK
Tel: 0845 1192020
Fax: 0845 1196089
Email: enquiries@relationships-scotland.org.uk
Website: http://www.relationships-scotland.org.uk
Members: 12
Staff: 9
Contact: Elaine Smith, Contact
Description: Promotes the availability of family mediation services in Scotland. Works to maintain high standards for the qualifications and accreditation of mediators.
Formerly: Formerly, Scottish Association of Family Conciliation Services

03629
Relatives and Residents Association
R&RA

24 The Ivories, 6-18 Northampton St., London, N1 2HY, UK
Tel: 020 73598148
Fax: 020 72266603
Email: info@relres.org
Website: http://www.relres.org
Members: 2500
Staff: 12
Contact: Gillian Dalley, Chief Exec.
Fee: £15
Membership Type: individual
Fee: £60
Membership Type: corporate
Description: Provides advice and support to relatives and friends of older people in residential care homes, nursing homes and long stay hospitals. Offers training to homes in order to promote good practice through involvement of relatives.
Publication: Newsletter

03630

Remote Sensing and Photogrammetry Society
RSPSoc

Univ. of Nottingham, Dept. of Geography, University Park, Nottingham, NG7 2RD, UK
Tel: 0115 9515435
Fax: 0115 9515249
Email: rspsoc@rspsoc.org
Website: http://www.rspsoc.org
Members: 1000
Staff: 2
Contact: Samantha Lavender, Chm.
Fee: £22
Membership Type: concessionary
Fee: £40
Membership Type: corporate individual
Description: Seeks to promote the knowledge and understanding of remote sensing and photogrammetry.
Library Subject: remote sensing, photogrammetry
Library Type: reference
Formerly: Formerly, Remote Sensing Society
Publication: Journal
Publication title: International Journal of Remote Sensing. Advertisements.
Meetings/Conventions: RSPSoc – annual conference – Exhibits. September 13 to 15, 2011. Bournemouth United Kingdom

03631

Renaissance Universal

3A Cazenove Rd., London, N16 6PA, UK
Tel: 020 88064250
Email: newren@ru.org
Website: http://www.ru.org
Description: Works to bring about an intellectual renaissance to redesign major institutions, fosters individual growth and helps individuals to apply creative talents in a positive direction.

03632

Renal Association

Durford Mill, Hampshire, Petersfield, GU31 5AZ, UK
Tel: 0870 4584155
Fax: 0870 4429940
Email: renal@mci-group.com
Website: http://www.renal.org/pages
Members: 820
Staff: 1
Contact: Charlie Tompson, Pres.
Fee: £100
Membership Type: consultant
Fee: £50
Membership Type: non-consultant, trainee, staff, clinical lecturer
Description: Works as the professional body for nephrologists in the United Kingdom; promotes development of renal services within the U.K, including prevention and treatment of renal disorders.

03633

Renewable Energy Association
REA

Capital Tower, 91 Waterloo Rd., London, SE1 8RT, UK
Tel: 020 79253570
Fax: 020 79252715
Website: http://www.r-e-a.net
Contact: Gaynor Hartnell, CEO
Fee: £624
Membership Type: associate
Fee: £2400
Membership Type: medium corporate
Description: Promotes the UK renewable energy industry by representing the interests and viewpoint of producers of renewable energy.
Formerly: Formerly, Renewable Power Association
Publication: Newsletter
Meetings/Conventions: Solar and Micro Renewables – annual conference

03634

RenewableUK

Greencoat House, Francis St., London, SW1P 1DH, UK
Tel: 020 79013000
Fax: 020 79013001
Email: info@bwea.com
Website: http://www.renewable-uk.com
Members: 639
Staff: 35
Contact: Maria McCaffery, CEO
Fee: £780
Membership Type: correspondent
Fee: £1590
Membership Type: small company
Description: Trade and professional body for the UK wind energy industry. Members range from professional companies, organizations, engineers, scientists and others involved in the field of wind energy. Promotes the appropriate utilisation of the technology, through policy, development, and implementation. Acts as a central point of information for government, public, and the media.
Library Type: open to the public
Formerly: Formerly, British Wind Energy Association
Publication: Proceedings

03635

RESCARE

c/o Steven Jackson House
31 Buxton Rd., Heaviley, Cheshire, Stockport, SK2 6LS, UK
Tel: 0161 4747323
Email: office@rescare.org.uk
Website: http://www.rescare.org.uk
Members: 10000
Staff: 2
Contact: Richard S. Jackson, Honorary Chm.
Fee: £5
Membership Type: individual
Fee: £7.5
Membership Type: family
Description: Promotes the relief and welfare of children and adults with learning disabilities and their families. Raises awareness and provides information, advice and support through bulletins, newsletters, leaflets and personal contacts.

03636

Research and Development Society
R&D Society

6-9 Carlton House Terr., London, SW1Y 5AG, UK
Tel: 020 74512513
Fax: 020 79302170
Email: rdsociety@royalsociety.org
Website: http://www.rdsoc.org
Members: 450
Staff: 1
Contact: Richard Sykes, Pres.
Fee: £30
Membership Type: individual
Fee: £300
Membership Type: corporate
Description: Senior R&D personnel in industry, public sector and academic, private R&D consultants. Aims to promote and advance the better understanding of R&D and associated activities and to assist those concerned with its organization and management. Holds regular evening meetings, usually monthly from October to July, with high-profile speakers on R&D management; meetings are also open to non-members. Quarterly special interest group meetings on innovation and R&D Management Best Practice provide a workshop-format series of seminars for professional development.
Publication: Newsletter
Publication title: The R&D Society Newsletter. Advertisements.

03637

Resin Flooring Association
FeRFA

16 Edward Rd., Farnham, GU9 8NP, UK
Tel: 01252 714250
Website: http://www.ferfa.org.uk/html
Members: 60
Staff: 6
Contact: Lisa Hennessey, Contact
Fee: £900
Membership Type: contractor, associate
Fee: £2215
Membership Type: manufacturer
Description: Represents United Kingdom manufacturers, contractors and associated companies involved in industrial resin flooring systems. Publishes a range of useful guidance notes. Encourages the development of technically advanced products and processes in resin flooring.
Publication: Monograph
Publication title: Guide to the Selection of Synthetic Resin Flooring

03638

Resolution - First for Family Law

PO Box 302, Orpington, BR6 8QX, UK
Tel: 01689 820272
Fax: 01689 896972
Email: info@resolution.org.uk
Website: http://www.resolution.org.uk
Members: 5500
Fee: £157
Membership Type: full
Fee: £29
Membership Type: law student/member on parental leave/career break/long term sick leave/ retired solicitor/judge/law lecturer
Description: Solicitors engaged in the practice of family law. Seeks to reduce "the distress and anger that can arise when family relationships break down" and insure that members handle their cases so as to allow all the parties involved to preserve their dignity and reach agreement without conflict. Maintains and enforces a Code of Practice for family law practitioners; participates in legal reform initiatives; produces and distributes guidelines for effective family law practice.
Formerly: Formerly, Solicitors Family Law Association

03639

Restaurant Association
RA

c/o British Hospitality Association
Queens House, 55-56 Lincoln's Inn Fields, London, WC2A 3BH, UK
Tel: 020 74047744
Fax: 020 74047799
Email: bha@bha.org.uk
Website: http://www.bha.org.uk
Members: 10500
Staff: 6
Contact: Bob Walton, Pres.
Description: Trade association for independently owned and operated restaurants throughout the UK. Protects the interests and advances the views and opinions of independent and group restaurateurs.
Formerly: Formerly, Restaurateurs Association of Great Britain
Publication: Newsletter
Publication title: Digest

03640

Restless Development

2nd Fl., Faith House, 7 Tufton St., London, SW1P 3QB, UK
Tel: 020 79768070
Fax: 020 72330008
Email: info@restlessdevelopment.org
Website: http://www.restlessdevelopment.org
Members: 2000
Staff: 160
Contact: Beth Goodey, Contact
Description: Supports youth-led organizations and programmes to reach more than 420,000 young individuals across Africa and South Africa. Recognized by the World Bank, UNAIDS, UNICEF and other international institutions.
Formerly: Formerly, Students Partnership Worldwide - UK

03641

Restricted Growth Association
RGA

PO Box 15755, Solihull, B93 3FY, UK
Tel: 0300 1111970
Fax: 0300 1112454
Email: office@restrictedgrowth.co.uk
Website: http://www.restrictedgrowth.co.uk
Members: 700
Staff: 1
Contact: Michael Wright, Pres.
Fee: £20
Membership Type: full, associate (in the United Kingdom)
Fee: £24
Membership Type: family, joint (in the United Kingdom)
Description: Open to persons with restricted growth, families with a child with restricted growth, health professionals, and other interested persons. Aims to help reduce the distress and disadvantages of persons of restricted growth by trying to reduce social barriers, improve the quality of life and enhance their role in society. Offers counseling training, family support, medical information and other practical help. Works to support people and families with restricted growth conditions.
Publication: Magazine
Publication title: RGA Information Magazine. Advertisements.
Meetings/Conventions: meeting

03642

Results - United Kingdom

13 Maddox St., 2nd Fl., London, W1S 2QG, UK
Tel: 020 74998238
Email: info@results-uk.org
Website: http://www.results-uk.org
Contact: Louise Holly, Deputy Dir.
Fee: £15
Membership Type: individual
Fee: £30
Membership Type: organization
Description: Generates the public and political will to end hunger and poverty. Educates the public on hunger and poverty issues.

03643

Retail Motor Industry Federation
RMIF

201 Great Portland St., London, W1W 5AB, UK
Tel: 020 75809122
Fax: 020 75806376
Email: suerobinson@rmif.co.uk
Website: http://www.rmif.co.uk
Members: 10000
Contact: Sue Robinson, Dir.
Description: Serves and represents businesses concerned with the provision of motor industry products and services. Aims to assist, support and promote members in providing the highest standards of operation for the mutual benefit of themselves and their customers.
Publication: Magazine
Publication title: Forecourt

03644

Rethink

15th Fl., 89 Albert Embankment, London, SE1 7TP, UK
Tel: 0845 4560455
Email: info@rethink.org
Website: http://www.rethink.org
Members: 7102
Staff: 1400
Contact: Paul Jenkins, Chief Exec.
Fee: £24
Membership Type: regular
Description: Exists to improve the lives of everyone affected by Schizophrenia and other severe mental illnesses by providing quality support, services, and information and by influencing local, regional, and national policies.
Formerly: Formerly, National Schizophrenia Fellowship
Publication: Video
Publication title: A Meeting Of Minds - A Positive Response to Mental Disorder

03645

Retired Greyhound Trust
RGT

2nd Fl., Park House, Park Terrace, Worcester Park, KT4 7JZ, UK
Tel: 0844 8268424
Fax: 0844 8268425
Email: greyhounds@retiredgreyhounds.co.uk
Website: http://www.retiredgreyhounds.co.uk
Description: Committed to finding new homes for racing dogs.
Formerly: Formerly, Greyhound Trust

03646

Retread Manufacturers Association
RMA

PO Box 320, Cheshire, Crewe, CW2 6WY, UK
Tel: 01270 561014
Fax: 01270 668801
Email: rma@greentyres.com
Website: http://www.greentyres.com
Members: 60
Staff: 3
Contact: David Wilson, Dir.
Description: Consists of UK tyre retreaders, suppliers to the industry in machinery, equipment materials and casings. Processing members retread all categories of tyre from car to heavy commercial, earthmover, tractor etc. Represents the interests of the independent retreader and associated businesses and is the national body, recognized by government, the British Standards Institution, tyre manufacturers, press, and other trade associations.
Publication: Membership Directory

03647

Reunite - International Child Abduction Centre

PO Box 7124, Leicester, LE1 7XX, UK
Tel: 0116 2555345
Fax: 0116 2556370
Email: reunite@dircon.co.uk
Website: http://www.reunite.org
Staff: 5
Contact: Denise Carter, Dir.
Description: Offers support and information on the issue of child abduction. Advises lawyers and other interested professionals working in the area of child abduction. Provides a telephone advice line. Liaises with government organizations and similar associations. Conducts research on the legal issues of child custody and abduction.
Publication: Handbook
Publication title: Child Abduction Prevention Pack

03648

Rice Association

21 Arlington St., London, SW1A 1RN, UK
Tel: 020 74932521
Fax: 020 74936785
Email: info@riceassociation.org.uk
Website: http://www.riceassociation.org.uk
Description: Promotes interests of members in all areas pertaining to the import, preparation, processing, packaging, marketing and use of rice. Promotes public awareness and consumption of all types of rice in the United Kingdom.

03649

Richard Jefferies Society
RJS

Pear Tree Cottage, Oxon, Longcot, SN7 7SS, UK
Tel: 01793 783040
Email: info@richardjefferiessociety.co.uk
Website: http://richardjefferiessociety.co.uk
Members: 350
Contact: Margaret Evans, Membership Sec.
Fee: £7
Membership Type: single
Fee: £8
Membership Type: couple
Description: Conservationists, writers, academics, and other admirers of British writer, naturalist, and mystic Richard Jefferies (1848-87). Promotes knowledge of the life and works of Jefferies and maintains interest in places connected with him; is involved in the restoration of Jefferies' birthplace. Fosters fellowship among admirers of Jefferies. Circulates contemporary articles among readers, writers, lecturers, and students. Organizes trips to places related to Jefferies. Holds lectures, readings, and discussions. Maintains museum.
Publication: Newsletter
Publication title: Spring Newsletter
Meetings/Conventions: monthly meeting

03650

Rider Haggard Society
RHS

27 Deneholm, Whitley Bay, NE25 9AU, UK
Tel: 0191 2524516
Email: rb27allen@blueyonder.co.uk
Website: http://www.riderhaggardsociety.org.uk
Members: 100
Contact: Roger Allen, Sec.
Fee: £9
Membership Type: local
Fee: £11
Membership Type: outside Europe
Description: Works toward the dissemination of information on and enjoyment of the author. Sponsors a national meeting every 12 months.
Publication: Journal
Publication title: Rider Haggard Journal. Advertisements.

03651

Rights of Women
ROW

52-54 Featherstone St., London, EC1Y 8RT, UK
Tel: 020 72516577
Fax: 020 74905377
Email: info@row.org.uk
Website: http://www.rightsofwomen.org.uk
Members: 160
Staff: 7
Contact: Emma Scott, Dir.
Fee: £6
Membership Type: student
Fee: £10
Membership Type: low income individual
Description: Women's organizations, companies, and individuals. Informs women of their legal rights and promotes the interests of women through legal action. Provides legal advice for women regarding: relationship breakdown; sexual and domestic violence; lesbian parenting; housing; and immigration. Defends the rights of women. Operates an advice line offering legal advice and referrals to women solicitors. Organizes and sponsors talks, conferences, and training; undertakes research and policy work.
Publication: Bulletin
Publication title: Results of Women

03652

Road Emulsion Association Limited
REAL

September House, Plantation Way, Storrington, West Sussex, RH20 4JF, UK
Tel: 01903 746584
Fax: 01903 746584
Email: john@rea.org.uk
Website: http://www.rea.org.uk
Members: 6
Staff: 1
Contact: John Keayes, Consultant/Sec.
Description: Represents companies who supply or produce road emulsion products used in constructing and maintaining roads and footways.
Library Type: not open to the public
Publication title: Technical Data Sheets

03653

Road Haulage Association
RHA

Roadway House, 35 Monument Hill, Weybridge, KT13 8RN, UK
Tel: 01932 841515
Fax: 01932 838916
Email: kate.gibbs@rha.uk.net
Website: http://www.rha.uk.net
Members: 10000
Staff: 91
Contact: Andy Boyle, Natl. Chm.
Description: Training associations and licensing authorities in the British trucking industry. Promotes all aspects of the hire and reward transport in the U.K.; supports international operators.
Publication: Membership Directory
Publication title: National Directory of Haulers. Advertisements.
Meetings/Conventions: CV Show – annual trade show

03654

Road Operators' Safety Council
ROSCO

Osborn House, 20 High St. S, Buckinghamshire, Olney, MK46 4AA, UK
Tel: 01234 714420
Email: admin@rosco-uk.org
Website: http://www.rosco.org.uk
Members: 90
Contact: Peter Shipp, Chm.
Description: Bus and coach operators. Aims to promote among owners and operators of road transport vehicles, employees, measures to prevent accidents and encourage safety on the road.
Publication: Newsletter
Publication title: Safety First

03655

Road Surface Dressing Association
RSDA

Westwood Park, London Rd., Colchester, CO6 4BS, UK
Tel: 0120 6274052
Fax: 0120 6274053
Email: jbaxter@rsda-gb.co.uk
Website: http://www.rsda-gb.co.uk
Members: 38
Staff: 1
Contact: John Baxter, Consultant Dir./Sec.
Description: Contractors in the surface dressing industry. Represents contractors and suppliers of equipment and materials used in the surface dressing process. Concerned with the improvement in the quality of surface dressing carried out within the United Kingdom as well as the extended use of the process.
Publication: Book
Publication title: Advice Notes on Surface Dressing Binders, Racked-in Surface Dressing, Preparing Roads for Surface Dressing, Surface Dressing Aggregates, etc.

03656

Romantic Novelists' Association
RNA

c/o Nicola Cornick, Membership Sec.
North End Cottage, Kingston Winslow, Swindon, SN6 8NG, UK
Tel: 01793 710252
Email: ncornick@madasafish.com
Website: http://www.rna-uk.org
Members: 700
Contact: Diane Pearson, Chair
Fee: £40
Membership Type: full
Fee: £50
Membership Type: associate
Description: Full members: romantic novelists; associate members: agents, editors, publishers; new writers: unpublished romantic novelists. Aims to promote the prestige of the genre, professionalism of romantic novelists and to give mutual help.
Publication: Journal
Publication title: RNA News. Advertisements.

03657

Romany Society

62 Thornton Ave., Cheshire, Macclesfield, SK11 7XL, UK
Tel: 0161 7647078
Website: http://www.romanysociety.org.uk
Members: 300
Fee: £5
Membership Type: individual
Fee: £9
Membership Type: family
Description: Promotes and encourages the study and appreciation of Romany, his life and works.
Publication: Magazine
Publication title: Romany Magazine

03658

Ronald Stevenson Society
RSS

3 Chamberlain Rd., Edinburgh, EH10 4DL, UK
Fax: 0131 2299298
Email: info@ronaldstevensonsociety.org.uk
Website: http://www.ronaldstevensonsociety.org.uk
Members: 125
Staff: 3
Contact: Nick Davis, Vice Chm.
Fee: £15
Membership Type: ordinary
Description: Aims to publish the music of Ronald Stevenson and to promote and publish performances and recordings of the music.
Library Subject: music of Ronald Stevenson
Library Type: reference
Publication: Newsletter
Publication title: Ronald Stevenson Society Newsletter

03659

ROOMatRTPI

41 Botolph Ln., London, EC3R 8DL, UK
Tel: 020 79299494
Fax: 020 79299490
Email: online@rtpi.org.uk
Website: http://www.rtpi.org.uk
Members: 360
Contact: Janet O'Neil, Pres.
Description: Local authorities, housing associations, developers, building societies, housing and planning consultants, companies with housing and planning interests, public utilities, and individuals. Works to achieve better standards and conditions in housing, promote more effective town and country planning, and improve the built and natural environments. Aims to bring together people from a wide variety of backgrounds concerned with these issues.
Formerly: Formerly, ROOM, the National Council for Housing and Planning and Royal Town Planning Institute
Publication: Journal
Publication title: Axis, the Journal of Housing, Planning and Regeneration. Advertisements.

03660

Rotating Electrical Machines Association
REMA

Westminster Tower, 3 Albert Embankment, London, SE1 7SL, UK
Tel: 020 77933006
Fax: 020 77933000
Email: rema@beama.org.uk
Website: http://www.rema.uk.com
Members: 11
Staff: 2
Description: Manufacturers of rotating electrical machines. Represents members' interests.

03661

Rough Fell Sheep Breeders Association

High Newstead Farm, Jervaulx, Ripon, HG4 4PJ, UK
Tel: 077 4646794
Email: roughfell@fsmail.net
Website: http://www.roughfellsheep.co.uk
Members: 175
Contact: Amanda Croft, Sec.
Description: Maintains records of Rough Fell Rams.

03662

Royal Academy of Arts
RA

Burlington House, Picadilly, London, W1J 0BD, UK
Tel: 020 73005737
Fax: 020 73008032
Email: library@royalacademy.org.uk
Website: http://www.royalacademy.org.uk
Contact: Nicholas Grimshaw, Pres.
Description: Encourages the creation, enjoyment and appreciation of the visual arts through exhibitions, education and debate; mounts a continuous programme of internationally renowned loan exhibitions complemented by education events.

03663

Royal Academy of Dance
RAD

36 Battersea Sq., London, SW11 3RA, UK
Tel: 020 73268000
Email: info@rad.org.uk
Website: http://www.rad.org.uk
Members: 13000
Contact: Luke Rittner, Chief Exec.
Fee: £107
Membership Type: teaching
Fee: £65
Membership Type: full
Description: World's largest teaching and examining body for classical ballet, with ballet teachers in more than 75 countries. Strives to advance standards of classical ballet teaching and classical ballet performance throughout the world. Offers training programs for students, teachers, former professional dancers, notators leading to qualifications validated by the University of Durham. Provides students with a comprehensive range of courses and examinations. Sponsors special needs dance programs and competitions.
Formerly: Formerly, Association of Operatic Dancing of Great Britain
Publication: Magazine
Publication title: Dance Gazette. Advertisements.

03664

Royal Academy of Dramatic Art
RADA

62-64 Gower St., London, WC1E 6ED, UK
Tel: 020 76367076
Fax: 020 73233865
Email: enquiries@rada.ac.uk
Website: http://www.rada.org
Contact: Stephen Waley-Cohen, Chm.
Description: Serves as a vocational training establishment, which equips student actors, actresses, stage managers and technical craft specialists for careers in theatre, television, film and radio.

03665

Royal Academy of Engineering

3 Carlton House Terr., London, SW1Y 5DG, UK
Tel: 020 77660600
Fax: 020 79301549
Email: eva.culleton-oltay@raeng.org.uk
Website: http://www.raeng.org.uk
Members: 1196
Staff: 41
Contact: Philip Greenish, Chief Exec.
Description: Promotes the advancement of the science, art and practice of engineering for the benefit of the public.
Library Subject: engineering
Library Type: reference
Publication: Newsletter
Publication title: Higher Education News

03666

Royal Academy of Music

Marylebone Rd., London, NW1 5HT, UK
Tel: 020 78737373
Fax: 020 78737374
Email: go@ram.ac.uk
Website: http://www.ram.ac.uk/Pages/default.aspx
Contact: Jonathan Freeman-Attwood, Principal
Description: Works to prepare students for a successful career in music.

03667

Royal Aeronautical Society - United Kingdom
RAeS

4 Hamilton Pl., London, W1J 7BQ, UK
Tel: 020 76704300
Email: raes@aerosociety.com
Website: http://www.raes.org.uk
Members: 18000
Staff: 32
Contact: Graham Roe, Chief Exec.
Fee: £53-91
Membership Type: fellow/companion (retired under 65/over 65)
Fee: £290
Membership Type: fellow/companion (employed)
Description: All those professionally engaged in the aerospace industry. Founded in 1866 for the general advancement of aeronautical art, science and engineering. Stimulates research, debate and expert opinion. As a nominated body of the Engineering Council, the Society is the preferred route to registration for engineers working in the aerospace industry. Membership is open to all aerospace professionals; there are thirty-four branches in the United Kingdom and nine overseas in Cyprus, Dublin, Hong Kong, Malaysia, Munich, Northern Germany, Shannon, Toulouse and United Arab Emirates. Each branch has its own management committee and runs a program of events independently of the main Society. There are also five overseas divisions, in Australia, New Zealand, Pakistan, Southern Africa and Zimbabwe. These are larger organizations with more authority than branches.
Library Subject: aerospace science
Library Type: reference
Formerly: Absorbed, Institute of Aeronautical Engineers
Publication: Journal
Publication title: Aeronautical Journal. Advertisements.

03668

Royal African Society
RAS

36 Gordon Sq., London, WC1H 0PD, UK
Tel: 020 30738335
Fax: 020 30738340
Email: ras@soas.ac.uk
Website: http://www.royalafricansociety.org
Members: 850
Staff: 4
Contact: Gemma Haxby, Sec.
Fee: £48
Membership Type: individual
Fee: £20
Membership Type: student
Description: Individuals in 45 countries united to increase knowledge of peoples and countries of Africa and of encouraging interest in the continent.
Publication: Journal
Publication title: African Affairs. Advertisements.

03669

Royal Agricultural Society of England
RASE

Stoneleigh Park, Coventry, CV8 2LZ, UK
Tel: 024 76696969
Fax: 024 76696900
Email: info@rase.org.uk
Website: http://www.rase.org.uk
Members: 8000
Staff: 100
Contact: George watson, Pres.
Fee: £30
Membership Type: regular
Fee: £60
Membership Type: family
Description: Individuals and organizations. Promotes the "advancement of British agriculture through good science and the caring stewardship of land, animals, and people". Conducts educational programs; facilitates international agricultural programs and exchanges; maintains Arthur Rank Centre.

03670

Royal Agricultural Society of the Commonwealth
RASC

Royal Highland Centre, Ingliston, Edinburgh, EH28 8NF, UK
Tel: 0131 3356200
Fax: 0131 3356229
Email: rasc@commagshow.org
Website: http://www.commagshow.org
Members: 40
Staff: 3
Contact: William Yarr, Honorary Sec.
Description: Represents 50 agricultural show societies working in 20 Commonwealth countries. Aims to promote education in agriculture and forestry within the Commonwealth through agricultural shows. Supports the efficient utilization of land by encouraging conservation and sustainable development through the interchange of knowledge and experience in the practice and science of agriculture, forestry and aquaculture.
Formerly: Also Known As, RASC
Publication: Journal
Publication title: Conference Report

03671

Royal Anthropological Institute of Great Britain and Ireland
RAI

50 Fitzroy St., London, W1T 5BT, UK
Tel: 020 73870455
Fax: 020 73888817
Email: admin@therai.org.uk
Website: http://www.therai.org.uk
Members: 1500
Staff: 10
Contact: Roy Ellen, Pres.
Fee: £77
Membership Type: fellow
Fee: £68
Membership Type: fellow outside UK
Description: Acts as the learned society for anthropologists and interested laypeople worldwide. Maintains library at the Centre for Anthropology, British Museum and allows full access to members.
Publication title: Anthropological Index

03672

Royal Archaeological Institute

Society of Antiquaries of London, Pciiadilly, London, W1J 0BE, UK
Email: admin@royalarchaeolinst.org
Website: http://www.royalarchaeolinst.org
Members: 1550
Staff: 1
Contact: Britt Baillie, Admin.
Fee: £40
Membership Type: ordinary
Fee: £20
Membership Type: associate
Description: Honorary, ordinary and associate. Takes a leading part in stimulating interest in archaeology, assists in the preservation of national antiquities and in the field of architectural conservation. Maintains high standards of research and preservation, publishes materials on archaeology of all periods in the Archaeological Journal. Offers research grants and is represented on many committees and is in touch with local societies.
Publication: Journal
Publication title: The Archaeological Journal

03673

Royal Asiatic Society of Great Britain and Ireland

14 Stephenson Way, London, NW1 2HD, UK
Tel: 020 73884539
Fax: 020 73919429
Email: info@royalasiaticsociety.org
Website: http://www.royalasiaticsociety.org/site
Members: 900
Staff: 6
Contact: Anthony J. Stockwell, Pres.
Fee: £25
Membership Type: fellow residing in South or Central Asia
Fee: £55
Membership Type: fellow residing in British Isles
Description: Promotes the study of Asian science, literature, history, and arts. Provides a forum for communication and exchange among members.

03674

Royal Association for Deaf People
RAD

18 Westside Centre, London Rd., Stanway, Essex, Colchester, CO3 8PH, UK
Tel: 0845 6882525
Fax: 0845 6882526
Email: info@royaldeaf.org.uk
Website: http://www.royaldeaf.org.uk
Members: 80
Contact: Tom Fenton, Chief Exec.
Description: Meets the needs of profoundly deaf people.
Formerly: Formerly, Royal Association in Aid of Deaf People

03675

Royal Association for Disability and Rehabilitation
RADAR

12 City Forum, 250 City Rd., London, EC1V 8AF, UK
Tel: 020 72503222
Fax: 020 72500212
Email: radar@radar.org.uk
Website: http://www.radar.org.uk/radarwebsite
Members: 700
Staff: 40
Contact: Phil Friend, Chm.
Fee: £25
Membership Type: individual
Fee: £25-249
Membership Type: organisational (based on total income)
Description: Represents the rights and interests of disabled individuals in the United Kingdom. Strives to improve educational, health, and social services for disabled people and stresses their full integration and participation in community life. Seeks to eliminate barriers that impose restrictions on disabled people. Provides advice. UK Secretariat of Rehabilitation International.
Formerly: Formerly, British Council for Rehabilitation of the Disabled
Publication title: Holiday Guides

03676

Royal Association of British Dairy Farmers
RABDF

Dairy House, Unit 31, Stoneleigh Deer Park, Stareton, Warwickshire, Kenilworth, CV8 2LY, UK
Tel: 0845 4582711
Fax: 0845 4582755
Email: office@rabdf.co.uk
Website: http://www.rabdf.co.uk
Members: 3000
Staff: 3
Contact: Nick Everington, Chief Exec.
Fee: £20
Membership Type: young (18-27 years old)
Fee: £40
Membership Type: individual
Description: Dairy farmers and those associated with the dairy farming industry. Represents the interests of practical dairy farmers in the UK by representations, open days, conferences, published materials, and research. Organizes the UK's major specialist technical event for dairy farming and dairy farmers. The Dairy Event is held at the National Agricultural Centre, Stoneleigh, Warwickshire each September.
Publication: Newsletter
Publication title: RABDF News

03677

Royal Astronomical Society
RAS

Burlington House, Piccadilly, London, W1J 0BQ, UK
Tel: 020 77343307
Fax: 020 74940166
Email: webmaster@ras.org.uk
Website: http://www.ras.org.uk
Members: 3000
Staff: 15
Contact: R.L. Davies, Pres.
Fee: £24
Membership Type: ordinary fellow
Fee: £62
Membership Type: fellow (under 30 years of age)
Description: Professional astronomers and geophysicists. Encourages and promotes astronomy, geophysics, solar and solar-terrestrial physics and planetary sciences through publication of journals, scientific meetings, award of grants and prizes, educational outreach activities and the maintenance of a comprehensive reference library.
Library Subject: astronomy, geophysics
Library Type: lending
Publication: Journal
Publication title: Astronomy and Geophysics

03678

Royal Bath and West of England Society

The Show Ground, Shepton Mallet, BA4 6QN, UK
Tel: 01749 822200
Fax: 01749 823169
Email: info@bathandwest.co.uk
Website: http://www.bathandwest.com
Contact: Jane Guise, Chief Exec.
Fee: £60
Membership Type: adult
Fee: £90
Membership Type: joint
Description: Helps fund business proposals, opportunities, and income support. Encourages interest in agriculture, arts, manufacture, and commerce.

03679

Royal British Legion Women's Section RBLWS

Haig House, 199 Borough High St., London, SE1 1AA, UK
Tel: 0203 2072181
Email: women@britishlegion.org.uk
Website: http://www.womensbritishlegion.org.uk
Members: 52000
Staff: 14
Contact: Cecilia Harper, Natl. Chair
Description: Wives, widows, female dependents, and relatives of service and ex-service men and women. Promotes and defends the interests of those who have served or are serving in the military or Red Cross in Britain and their dependents. Raises funds.
Publication: Report
Publication title: Annual Report and Accounts Report

03680

Royal British Society of Sculptors RBS

108 Old Brompton Rd., London, SW7 3RA, UK
Tel: 020 73738615
Email: info@rbs.org.uk
Website: http://www.rbs.org.uk
Members: 450
Staff: 6
Description: Professional working sculptors. Aims to promote and advance the art of sculpture. Works to ensure the continued widespread debate on contemporary sculpture and promote the pursuit of excellence in the artform. Offers advice on technical, aesthetic and legal matters concerning the production of sculpture. Advocates good fair practice in the commissioning and exhibition of work.

03681

Royal Choral Society RCS

Studio 9, 92 Lots Rd., London, SW10 0QD, UK
Tel: 020 73763718
Fax: 020 73763719
Email: virginia@royalchoralsociety.co.uk
Website: http://www.royalchoralsociety.co.uk
Members: 200
Staff: 2
Contact: Virginia Edwyn-Jones, Admin.
Description: Individuals interested in singing choral music. Promotes performance of choral repertoire.

03682

Royal College of Anaesthetists RCoA

Churchill House, 35 Red Lion Sq., London, WC1R 4SG, UK
Tel: 020 70921500
Fax: 020 70921730
Email: info@rcoa.ac.uk
Website: http://www.rcoa.ac.uk
Members: 14000
Staff: 65
Contact: Kevin Storey, Chief Exec.
Description: Works to ensure the quality of patient care through the maintenance of standards in anesthesia, pain management and intensive care. Establishes standards for the training of anesthetists and other people practicing critical care and/or acute and chronic pain management. Administers examinations and provides continued medical education to all practicing anesthetists. Educates and informs the general public about anesthesia.
Publication: Bulletin
Publication title: RCoA Bulletin. Advertisements.

03683

Royal College of General Practitioners RCGP

1 Bow Churchyard, London, EC4M 9DQ, UK
Tel: 020 31887400
Fax: 020 31887401
Email: info@rcgp.org.uk
Website: http://www.rcgp.org.uk
Members: 22500
Staff: 130
Contact: Iona Heath, Pres.
Fee: £117.50-470
Membership Type: UK resident (based on annual gross income)
Fee: £117.50-235
Membership Type: resident overseas
Description: General practitioners. Responsible for the promotion of high quality general practice through education, research and standard setting.
Library Type: lending
Publication: Journal
Publication title: British Journal of General Practice. Advertisements.

03684

Royal College of Midwives RCM

15 Mansfield St., London, W1G 9NH, UK
Tel: 020 73123535
Email: membership@rcm.org
Website: http://www.rcm.org.uk
Members: 36000
Staff: 60
Fee: £230.16
Membership Type: full
Fee: £1.67
Membership Type: student
Description: Promotes the practice of midwifery, and works to maintain high standards in the field. Provides educational programs to midwives in the areas of maternity, child care, and personal development. Represents worker rights of midwives to national legal and political authorities. Encourages and supports research.
Library Subject: midwifery
Library Type: reference
Publication: Magazine
Publication title: Midwives

03685

Royal College of Nursing RCN

20 Cavendish Sq., London, W1G 0RN, UK
Tel: 020 74093333
Email: maura.buchanan.president@rcn.org.uk
Website: http://www.rcn.org.uk
Members: 360000
Staff: 620
Contact: Maura Buchanan, Pres.
Fee: £193
Membership Type: full
Fee: £96
Membership Type: full newly qualified, associate career break, RCN/RCM associate
Description: Nurses, midwives and health visitors. Represents nurses working at all levels of responsibility and in a wide variety of settings, from the NHS to the independent sector and from local government to private industry.
Library Subject: nursing
Library Type: open to the public
Publication: Journal
Publication title: Nursing Standard. Advertisements.

03686

Royal College of Obstetricians and Gynaecologists - United Kingdom RCOG

27 Sussex Pl., Regent's Park, London, NW1 4RG, UK
Tel: 020 77726200
Fax: 020 77230575
Email: examsadmin@rcog.org.uk
Website: http://www.rcog.org.uk
Members: 10324
Staff: 95
Contact: Sabaratnam Arulkumaran, Pres.
Description: Obstetricians and gynecologists, having completed a period of training recognised by the College and passed all components of the MRCOG examination. Encourages the study and improvement of the practice of obstetrics and gynaecology, by running examinations, postgraduate meetings, publications, committees and working parties.
Library Subject: obstetrics, gynaecology, closely related subjects
Library Type: reference
Publication: Journal
Publication title: BJOG: An International Journal of Obstetrics and Gynaecology. Advertisements.

03687

Royal College of Ophthalmologists RCOphth

17 Cornwall Terr., London, NW1 4QW, UK
Tel: 020 79350702
Fax: 020 79359838
Email: president@rcophth.ac.uk
Website: http://www.rcophth.ac.uk
Members: 3027
Staff: 20
Contact: Kathy Evans, Chief Exec.
Fee: £205
Membership Type: overseas fellow
Fee: £320
Membership Type: UK fellow (non-consultant)
Description: Medical practitioners (ophthalmologists). Advances the science and practice of ophthalmology. Educates medical practitioners in the science and practice of ophthalmology. Maintains proper standards in the practice of ophthalmology for the benefit of the public. Promotes study and research in ophthalmology and related subjects and publish the useful results of such study and research. Furthers instruction and training in ophthalmology both in the United Kingdom and overseas. Educates the general public in all matters relating to vision and the health of the human eye.
Publication: Journal
Publication title: EYE. Advertisements.
Meetings/Conventions: Scientific Congress – annual congress – Exhibits.

03688

Royal College of Organists RCO

PO Box 56357, London, SE16 7XL, UK
Tel: 05600 767208
Email: admin@rco.org.uk
Website: http://www.rco.org.uk
Members: 3100
Staff: 7
Contact: Kim Gilbert, Gen. Mgr.
Fee: £82
Membership Type: full
Fee: £43
Membership Type: student
Description: Open to all who take an interest in the work and profession of the organist and in organ music as well as to those who wish to gain the college's diplomas. Aims to promote the art of organ playing and choral directing, to hold examinations in these studies and related areas, to offer education at all levels in these studies, and to generate professional support to organists.
Publication: Newsletter
Publication title: RCO News. Advertisements.

03689

Royal College of Paediatrics and Child Health RCPCH

5-11 Theobalds Rd., London, WC1X 8SH, UK
Tel: 020 70926000
Fax: 020 70926001
Email: enquiries@rcpch.ac.uk
Website: http://www.rcpch.ac.uk
Members: 12000
Staff: 50
Contact: Terence Stephenson, Pres.
Fee: £437
Membership Type: fellow (in UK and Ireland)
Fee: £328
Membership Type: fellow (in rest of Europe and North America)
Description: Consultant paediatricians, community child health doctors, trainee paediatricians, research workers, general practitioners and other medical specialists who work with children. Aims to advance the understanding, treatment and prevention of disease in childhood, to further the study of child health and to promote excellence in paediatric practice.
Formerly: Formerly, British Paediatric Association
Publication: Journal
Publication title: Archives of Disease in Children

03690

Royal College of Pathologists - United Kingdom RCPath

2 Carlton House Terr., London, SW1Y 5AF, UK
Tel: 020 74516700
Fax: 020 74516701
Email: info@rcpath.org
Website: http://www.rcpath.org
Members: 7500
Staff: 25
Contact: Peter Furness, Pres.
Fee: £150
Membership Type: associate UK
Fee: £412
Membership Type: UK fellow
Description: Postgraduate medical and scientific graduates who have successfully completed all or part of the college's examinations following a specified period of approved training, or elected under specified college ordinances. Advances the science and practice of pathology, furthers public education, promotes study and research work in pathology and related subjects and publishes the results of such study and research.
Library Subject: pathology disciplines
Library Type: not open to the public
Publication: Magazine
Publication title: Colorado Bulletin. Advertisements.

03691

Royal College of Physicians RCP

11 St. Andrews Pl., Regent's Park, London, NW1 4LE, UK
Tel: 020 79351174
Fax: 020 74875218
Email: infocentre@rcplondon.ac.uk
Website: http://www.rcplondon.ac.uk/Pages/index.aspx
Members: 22000
Contact: Richard Thompson, Pres.
Fee: £105
Membership Type: associate
Fee: £140
Membership Type: affiliate/collegiate (in UK)
Description: Individuals in 64 countries. Is responsible for the postgraduate education and training of physicians in England, Wales, and Northern Ireland. Works to maintain the highest standards of medical practice. Advises the government, public, and members of the profession on health and medical issues. Conducts educational and training programs; organizes examinations; operates clinical effectiveness unit.
Library Subject: medical history
Library Type: open to the public
Publication: Journal
Publication title: Clinical Medicine. Advertisements.

03692

Royal College of Physicians and Surgeons of Glasgow RCPSG

232-242 St. Vincent St., Glasgow, G2 5RJ, UK
Tel: 0141 2216072
Fax: 0141 2211804
Email: sandra.clearie@rcpsg.ac.uk
Website: http://www.rcpsg.ac.uk/Pages/RCPSG_Welcome.aspx
Members: 8970
Staff: 65
Contact: Ian Anderson, Pres.
Fee: £60-360
Membership Type: fellow
Fee: £60-200
Membership Type: regular
Description: Physicians, surgeons, and dentists. Conducts educational and training programs.
Library Subject: medicine, surgery
Library Type: reference

03693

Royal College of Physicians of Edinburgh RCPE

9 Queen St., Edinburgh, EH2 1JQ, UK
Tel: 0131 2257324
Fax: 0131 2203939
Email: president@rcpe.ac.uk
Website: http://www.rcpe.ac.uk
Contact: Neil Dewhurst, Pres.
Description: Aims to develop and oversee an ongoing programme of medical examinations, education and training for qualified doctors who wish to undertake further (postgraduate) education and training to pursue a career in specialist (internal) medicine.
Library Subject: medicine, botany, science and travel
Library Type: lending
Publication: Journal

03694

Royal College of Psychiatrists

17 Belgrave Sq., London, SW1X 8PG, UK
Tel: 020 72352351
Fax: 020 72451231
Email: rcpsych@rcpsych.ac.uk
Website: http://www.rcpsych.ac.uk
Members: 10000
Staff: 100
Contact: Dinesh Bhugra, Pres.
Fee: £546
Membership Type: fellow (UK and Ireland)
Fee: £393
Membership Type: ordinary (UK and Ireland)
Description: Psychiatrists. Seeks to advance the profession of psychiatry. Aims to treat people suffering from mental health problems. Facilitates exchange of information among members; sponsors continuing professional education courses.
Library Type: reference
Publication: Journal
Publication title: British Journal of Psychiatry. Advertisements.

03695

Royal College of Radiologists - United Kingdom
RCR

38 Portland Pl., London, W1B 1JQ, UK
Tel: 020 76364432
Fax: 020 73233100
Email: enquiries@rcr.ac.uk
Website: http://www.rcr.ac.uk
Members: 7200
Contact: Andrew Hall, Chief Exec.
Fee: £131
Membership Type: junior (in UK)
Fee: £407
Membership Type: full (in UK)
Description: Represents diagnostic and interventional radiologists, nuclear medicine specialists, oncologists, radiotherapists, and ultrasound specialists. Works to advance the science and practice of radiological technology. Offers courses to further the education of practitioners. Establishes qualifications and examinations for fellowships and diplomas.
Formerly: Formerly, British Association of Radiologists
Publication: Journal
Publication title: Clinical Oncology
Meetings/Conventions: periodic meeting

03696

Royal College of Speech and Language Therapists
RCSLT

2 White Hart Yard, London, SE1 1NX, UK
Tel: 020 73781200
Email: info@rcslt.org
Website: http://www.rcslt.org
Members: 8500
Staff: 21
Contact: Kamini Gadhok, CEO
Fee: £199
Membership Type: practising
Fee: £70
Membership Type: associate
Description: Speech and language therapists, including practicing members, non-practicing and retired members. All members have a certificate to practice (or equivalent) issued by the college. Supports qualified speech and language therapists working for the relief of disorders of communication for both adults and children and the accreditation of courses leading to qualification as a speech and language therapist. Careers information available on request.
Formerly: Formerly, College of Speech Therapists
Publication: Bulletin
Publication title: Bulletin Supplement

03697

Royal College of Surgeons of Edinburgh
RCSE

Nicolson St., Edinburgh, EH8 9DW, UK
Tel: 0131 5271600
Fax: 0131 5576406
Email: enquiries@rcsed.ac.uk
Website: http://www.rcsed.ac.uk/site/0/default.aspx
Contact: A. Rooney, Chief Exec.
Fee: £368-375
Membership Type: surgical/dental inside UK and Ireland
Fee: £126-128
Membership Type: surgical/dental overseas
Description: Promotes the education, training and examination, and the raising of standards in surgical practice.

03698

Royal College of Surgeons of England
RCS Eng

35-43 Lincoln's Inn Fields, London, WC2A 3PE, UK
Tel: 020 74053474
Email: communications@rcseng.ac.uk
Website: http://www.rcseng.ac.uk
Contact: John Black, Pres.
Description: Surgeons and dental surgeons in the United Kingdom. Aims to promote and encourage the study and practice of surgery as an art and science. Maintains professional standards through examinations; establishes criteria for the qualification of consultant and dental surgeons in the National Health Service; advises government and other professional bodies on surgical matters; conducts research. Offers postgraduate courses in surgery and related subjects; sponsors seminars and workshops.
Library Subject: surgical procedures, medical history
Library Type: reference
Formerly: Supersedes, Company of Surgeons of London
Publication: Journal
Publication title: Annals of the Royal College of Surgeons of England. Advertisements.

03699

Royal College of Veterinary Surgeons
RCVS

Belgravia House, 62-64 Horseferry Rd., London, SW1P 2AF, UK
Tel: 020 72222001
Fax: 020 72222004
Email: admin@rcvs.org.uk
Website: http://www.rcvs.org.uk
Members: 21200
Staff: 50
Contact: Sandy Trees, Senior VP
Fee: £285
Membership Type: home - practising
Fee: £143
Membership Type: overseas - practising or postgraduate student
Description: Graduates possessing a veterinary degree, who intend to practice in the UK. Works as a statutory body governing the veterinary profession in the UK. Responsible for quality of veterinary undergraduate education at the UK veterinary schools. Provides membership examination and discipline of members. Establishes certificate and diploma examinations.
Library Subject: veterinary science
Library Type: open to the public
Publication: Directory
Publication title: Directory of Veterinary Practices. Advertisements.

03700

Royal Commonwealth Society
RCS

25 Northumberland Ave., London, WC2N 5AP, UK
Tel: 020 77669200
Fax: 020 79309705
Email: info@thercs.org
Website: http://www.thercs.org/society
Members: 10000
Staff: 40
Contact: Danny Sriskandarajah, Dir.
Fee: £290
Membership Type: full
Fee: £190
Membership Type: off peak
Description: Individuals and organizations worldwide with an interest in the nations and cultures of the Commonwealth. Aims to educate about the Commonwealth. Serves as a forum for the exchange of information on the peoples, nations, and cultures of the Commonwealth.

03701

Royal Economic Society
RES

University of St. Andrews, School of Economics and Finance, St. Andrews, Fife, KY16 9AL, UK
Tel: 013 34462479
Fax: 013 34462444
Email: royaleconsoc@st-andrews.ac.uk
Website: http://www.res.org.uk
Members: 3300
Contact: John Vickers, Pres.
Fee: £68
Membership Type: ordinary (Eurozone)
Fee: £34
Membership Type: developing country, retired (Eurozone)
Description: Represents professional economists in business, government service or higher education. Works to promote and encourage the study of economic science.
Library Type: reference
Publication: Journal
Publication title: Econometrics Journal

03702

Royal Entomological Society
RES

The Mansion House, Chriswell Green Ln., St. Albans, AL2 3NS, UK
Tel: 01727 899387
Fax: 01727 894797
Email: info@royensoc.co.uk
Website: http://www.royensoc.co.uk
Members: 2000
Staff: 6
Contact: Lin Field, Contact
Fee: £49
Membership Type: ordinary fellow
Fee: £44
Membership Type: individual
Description: An academic qualification is not required but must show genuine interest in entomology; Fellowships are open to those who have made a substantial contribution to entomology, through publications or other evidence of achievement. Concerned with the improvement and diffusion of entomological science. Holds meetings on all aspects of entomology, publishing the results of entomological research, supporting entomological expeditions. Generates discourse between entomologists.
Library Subject: entomology
Library Type: by appointment only
Publication: Journal
Publication title: Antenna. Advertisements.

03703

Royal Environmental Health Institute of Scotland
REHIS

3 Manor Pl., Edinburgh, EH3 7DH, UK
Tel: 0131 2256999
Fax: 0131 2282926
Email: contact@rehis.com
Website: http://www.royal-environmental-health.org.uk
Members: 1100
Staff: 10
Contact: Tom Bell, Chief Exec.
Description: Persons interested or engaged in any aspect of environmental health.
Library Type: open to the public
Publication: Journal
Publication title: Environmental Health Scotland

03704

Royal Forestry Society
RFS

102 High St., Hertfordshire, Tring, HP23 4AF, UK
Tel: 01442 822028
Fax: 01442 890395
Email: rfshq@rfs.org.uk
Website: http://www.rfs.org.uk
Members: 4200
Staff: 4
Contact: John Jackson, Chief Exec.
Fee: £48
Membership Type: individual
Fee: £24
Membership Type: full-time student
Description: Open - cosmopolitan. Encourages the positive management of Britain's woodlands so that they may be conserved, improved and expanded. Multi-purpose forestry; woodland, tree management; education; conservation; arboriculture; study tours; field meetings.
Library Subject: forestry
Library Type: open to the public
Publication: Journal
Publication title: Quarterly Journal of Forestry. Advertisements.

03705

Royal Geographical Society with the Institute of British Geographers
RGS-IBG

1 Kensington Gore, London, SW7 2AR, UK
Tel: 020 75913000
Fax: 020 75913001
Email: membership@rgs.org
Website: http://www.rgs.org/HomePage.htm
Members: 15000
Staff: 50
Contact: Michael Palin, Pres.
Fee: £107
Membership Type: regular
Fee: £87
Membership Type: fellow
Description: Businesses, schools, student exploration societies, university departments, and individuals in 45 countries interested in geography. Works to advance and improve geographical science by facilitating information exchange. Organizes overseas scientific projects; offers financial support for scientific expeditions; operates the Expedition Advisory Centre, offering advice and training to anyone planning an expedition. Conducts lectures, symposia, and exhibitions. Maintains museum. Active research groups in all aspects of geography in higher education. Advises on and responds to government and NGOs on geographical matters. Professional body and learned society for geography.
Library Subject: geography and related subjects
Library Type: reference
Formerly: Absorbed, African Association
Publication: Journal
Publication title: Area
Meetings/Conventions: Environmental Forum – annual conference – Exhibits.

03706

Royal Highland and Agricultural Society of Scotland
RHASS

Royal Highland Centre, Ingliston, Edinburgh, EH28 8NF, UK
Tel: 0131 3356200
Fax: 0131 3335236
Email: info@rhass.org.uk
Website: http://www.rhass.org.uk
Members: 13500
Staff: 35
Contact: Adele J. Thomson, Sec.
Fee: £180
Membership Type: junior term
Fee: £480
Membership Type: 10-year term
Description: Membership is open to everyone interested in the society and its work to promote the land-based and allied industries of Scotland, and create a wider public understanding of the management of the land and rural resources.
Publication: Magazine
Publication title: The Review. Advertisements.

03707

Royal Highland Education Trust
RHET

Royal Highland Centre, Ingliston, Edinburgh, EH28 8NB, UK
Tel: 0131 3356227
Fax: 0131 3335236
Email: rhetinfo@rhass.org.uk
Website: http://www.rhet.org.uk
Members: 108
Staff: 3
Contact: Denise Tyers, Admin.
Fee: £15
Membership Type: individual
Fee: £250
Membership Type: corporate
Description: Individuals, organizations, and corporations. Promotes increased understanding of farming and rural development issues. Serves as a clearinghouse for information on farming, rural development, and country life. Conducts educational programs; provides teaching aids to food and agricultural education courses; maintains educational center.
Formerly: Formerly, Scottish Farm and Countryside Educational Trust

03708

Royal Historical Society - United Kingdom

University College London, Gower St., London, WC1E 6BT, UK
Tel: 020 73877532
Fax: 020 73877532
Email: s.carr@ucl.ac.uk
Website: http://www.royalhistoricalsociety.org
Members: 2705
Staff: 2
Contact: Sue Carr, Exec. Sec.
Fee: £25
Membership Type: regular
Description: Promotes history and historical research, whether British or international history, through lectures, conferences and publications.

03709

Royal Horticultural Society
RHS

80 Vincent Sq., London, SW1P 2PE, UK
Tel: 0845 2605000
Email: info@rhs.org.uk
Website: http://www.rhs.org.uk
Members: 250000
Staff: 400
Contact: Elizabeth Banks, Pres.
Fee: £49
Membership Type: individual
Fee: £1000
Membership Type: life (single)
Description: Encourages horticulture in all its branches.
Publication: Magazine
Publication title: The Garden

03710

Royal Humane Society

50/51 Temple Chambers, 3/7 Temple Ave., London, EC4Y 2942, UK
Tel: 020 79362942
Fax: 020 79362942
Email: info@royalhumanesociety.org.uk
Website: http://www.royalhumanesociety.org.uk
Staff: 4
Contact: Richard Titley, Chm./Treas.
Description: Makes awards to those who were at risk to their own lives, saved or attempted to save a fellow citizen.

03711

Royal Incorporation of Architects in Scotland
RIAS

15 Rutland Sq., Edinburgh, EH1 2BE, UK
Tel: 0131 2297545
Fax: 0131 2282188
Email: info@rias.org.uk
Website: http://www.rias.org.uk/content
Members: 3900
Staff: 26
Contact: David Dunbar, Pres.
Fee: £135
Membership Type: associate
Fee: £460
Membership Type: fellow
Description: Professional body for around 3000 chartered architect members in Scotland working from 800 private and public across the country. Has charitable status and offers a wide range of services and products for architects, students of architecture, construction industry professionals and those interested in the built environment and the design process.
Library Subject: Scottish architecture
Library Type: by appointment only
Publication title: Architecture Guides to Scotland

03712

Royal Institute of British Architects RIBA

66 Portland Pl., London, W1B 1AD, UK
Tel: 020 75805533
Fax: 020 72551541
Email: info@inst.riba.org
Website: http://www.architecture.com
Members: 40500
Staff: 150
Contact: Harry Rich, Chief Exec.
Fee: £56
Membership Type: associate
Fee: £110-395
Membership Type: chartered (based on number of staff)
Description: Works to advance civil architecture. Seeks to promote and facilitate the acquirement of various arts and sciences connected with architecture. Aims to see that in meeting clients' requirements, architects have regard to the broader user and environmental implications of their work.
Library Type: open to the public

03713

Royal Institute of Navigation RIN

1 Kensington Gore, London, SW7 2AT, UK
Tel: 020 75913130
Fax: 020 75913131
Email: info@rin.org.uk
Website: http://www.rin.org.uk
Members: 3285
Staff: 6
Contact: David Barnes, Pres.
Fee: £10
Membership Type: junior associate
Fee: £15
Membership Type: student
Description: Fosters learning to society for those who have interest in all forms of navigation.
Publication: Newsletter
Publication title: IAIN Newsletter

03714

Royal Institute of Oil Painters ROI

17 Carlton House Terr., London, SW1Y 5BD, UK
Tel: 020 79306844
Fax: 020 78397830
Email: enquiries@theroi.org.uk
Website: http://www.mallgalleries.org.uk
Members: 73
Contact: Peter James Wileman, Pres.
Description: Professional painters in oils. Organizes the exhibition of oil paintings; sales and commissions of oil paintings; educating the public in oil paintings through its exhibitions; most work for sale at annual exhibition.
Publication: Catalog
Publication title: Annual Exhibition Catalogue. Advertisements.

03715

Royal Institute of Painters in Water Colours

17 Carlton House Terr., London, SW1Y 5BD, UK
Tel: 020 79306844
Fax: 020 78397830
Email: info@mallgalleries.com
Website: http://www.royalinstituteofpaintersinwatercolours.org.uk
Members: 56
Contact: Ronald Maddox, Pres.
Description: Professional water colour artists. Organises the exhibition of watercolour paintings, sales and commissions of watercolours, demonstrations of watercolour paintings. Educates the public about watercolour paintings through exhibitions and demonstrations.
Formerly: Also Known As, RI

03716

Royal Institute of Philosophy RIP

14 Gordon Sq., London, WC1H 0AG, UK
Tel: 020 73874130
Fax: 020 73834061
Email: j.garvey@royalinstitutephilosophy.org
Website: http://www.royalinstitutephilosophy.org
Members: 680
Contact: James Garvey, Sec.
Fee: £25
Membership Type: individual
Fee: £10
Membership Type: student, unemployed
Description: All those interested in philosophy. Promotes the study and discussion of philosophy and original work through its journal and by arranging and sponsoring programmes of lectures and conferences.
Publication: Journal
Publication title: Philosophy

03717

Royal Institute of Public Health RIPH

3rd Fl. Market Towers, 1 Nine Elms Ln., London, SW8 5NQ, UK
Tel: 020 31771600
Fax: 020 31771601
Website: http://www.rsph.org.uk
Members: 1700
Staff: 18
Contact: Selwyn Hodge, Chm.
Fee: £115
Membership Type: fellow
Fee: £82
Membership Type: regular
Description: Medical practitioners, dental practitioners, and environmental health officers from 19 countries. Seeks to advance public health and integrated health services. Provides a forum for information exchange among specialists. Reviews existing methodologies and proposes new practices. Serves as an advisory body to governmental and other organizations. Assists in developing continuing professional training for specialists in public health and preventive medicine. Conducts research.
Formerly: Formerly, Society of Public Health
Publication: Journal
Publication title: Health and Hygiene. Advertisements.

03718

Royal Institution of Chartered Surveyors RICS

Parliament Sq., London, SW1P 3AD, UK
Tel: 0870 3331600
Fax: 020 73343811
Email: contactrics@rics.org
Website: http://www.rics.org
Members: 140000
Staff: 350
Contact: John Armstrong, CEO
Description: Surveyors who seek to improve the surveying profession. Represents members' interests; organizes educational courses; administers examinations; offers placement service.
Library Subject: surveying and surveying history, valuation, construction economics, real estate, appraisal
Library Type: reference
Formerly: Absorbed, Institute of Quantity Surveyors
Publication: Magazine
Publication title: RICS Business

03719

Royal Institution of Great Britain RI

21 Albemarle St., London, W1S 4BS, UK
Tel: 020 74092992
Fax: 020 76702920
Email: ri@ri.ac.uk
Website: http://www.rigb.org
Members: 3100
Staff: 36
Contact: Alan Maries, Honorary Sec.
Fee: £95
Membership Type: full
Fee: £30
Membership Type: associate
Description: All who are interested in science with a remit of scientific research, communication and heritage. Concerned with the pursuit of independent scientific research, the popularization of science through activities and events and the custodianship of its historical collection and building.
Library Subject: science
Library Type: by appointment only
Publication title: Essays on Science and Technology

03720

Royal Institution of Naval Architects RINA

10 Upper Belgrave St., London, SW1X 8BQ, UK
Tel: 020 72354622
Fax: 020 72595912
Email: hq@rina.org.uk
Website: http://www.rina.org.uk
Contact: Trevor Blakeley, Chief Exec.
Fee: £48-158
Membership Type: fellow
Fee: £37-123
Membership Type: regular
Description: International professional institution whose members are involved in the design, construction, and repair of ships, boats, and maritime structures worldwide. Organizes an extensive programme of international conferences covering all aspects of naval architecture and maritime technology.
Library Subject: design, construction, maintenance and operation of commercial and naval vessels
Library Type: reference
Publication: Journal
Publication title: Naval Architect. Advertisements.

03721

Royal Isle of Wight Agricultural Society

Central House, 48/49 High St., Newport, PO30 1SE, UK
Tel: 01983 826275
Fax: 01983 826275
Email: riwas@aol.com
Website: http://www.riwas.org.uk
Contact: D.M. Groves, Pres.
Fee: £38
Membership Type: patron
Fee: £27
Membership Type: vice-patron
Description: Works for the improvement of agriculture.

03722

Royal Life Saving Society

River House, High St., Broom, Alcester, B50 4HN, UK
Tel: 01789 773994
Fax: 01789 773995
Email: lifesavers@rlss.org.uk
Website: http://www.lifesavers.org.uk
Members: 13000
Contact: Di Stanley, Chief Exec.
Fee: £22
Membership Type: individual
Fee: £9
Membership Type: youth
Description: Trains people in lifesaving, life support and water safety techniques.

03723

Royal Medical Society
RMS

Student Ctre., 5/5 Bristol Sq., Edinburgh, EH8 9AL, UK
Tel: 0131 6502672
Fax: 0131 6502672
Email: enquiries@royalmedical.co.uk
Website: http://www.royalmedical.co.uk
Members: 2500
Staff: 1
Contact: Andrew Brookes, Sen. Sec.
Description: Mainly medical students. Fellows and Life Members are medical graduates. An educational charity for medical students, run by medical students.
Publication: Journal
Publication title: Res Medica

03724

Royal Mencap Society
MENCAP

123 Golden Ln., London, EC1Y 0RT, UK
Tel: 020 74540454
Fax: 020 76083254
Email: information@mencap.org.uk
Website: http://www.mencap.org.uk
Description: Provides information and support for leisure, recreational services (Gateway Clubs), residential services and holidays.
Formerly: Formerly, Royal Society for Mentally Handicapped Children and Adults
Publication: Newspaper
Publication title: Viewpoint

03725

Royal Meteorological Society
RMetS

104 Oxford Rd., Reading, RG1 7LL, UK
Tel: 0118 9568500
Fax: 0118 9568571
Email: chiefexec@rmets.org
Website: http://www.rmets.org
Members: 3200
Staff: 10
Contact: Paul Hardaker, Chief Exec.
Fee: £64
Membership Type: fellow/associate
Fee: £32
Membership Type: associate fellow (full time student)
Description: Encourages research and information exchange on all aspects of meteorology and related sciences.
Publication: Journal
Publication title: International Journal of Climatology. Advertisements.
Meetings/Conventions: monthly meeting

03726

Royal Microscopical Society
RMS

37/38 St. Clements St., Oxford, OX4 1AJ, UK
Tel: 01865 254760
Fax: 01865 791237
Email: info@rms.org.uk
Website: http://www.rms.org.uk
Contact: Karen Lonsdale, Admin.
Fee: £59-159
Membership Type: fellow
Fee: £410-740
Membership Type: corporate
Description: Academic and industrial scientists; researchers and technicians using microscopes; university, industrial, and government research departments; microscope manufacturers. Promotes the advancement of microscopy. Fosters research into improved microscope construction and application. Offers training courses in basic and specialized microscopic techniques; conducts periodic scientific meetings and workshops. Has established undergraduate and postgraduate certificate programs in practical microscopy.
Formerly: Formerly, Microscopical Society of London
Publication: Journal
Publication title: Journal of Microscopy

03727

Royal Musical Association
RMA

4 Chandos Rd., Chorlton-cum-Hardy, Manchester, M21 0ST, UK
Fax: 0161 8617543
Email: jeffrey.dean@stingrayoffice.com
Website: http://www.rma.ac.uk
Members: 1025
Staff: 1
Contact: Jeffrey Dean, Exec. Off.
Fee: £48
Membership Type: ordinary
Fee: £24
Membership Type: student, senior
Description: Musicologists, music students, and interested amateurs. Promotes research and exchange of ideas in musicology.
Publication: Journal
Publication title: Journal of the Royal Musical Association. Advertisements.
Meetings/Conventions: annual conference – Exhibits.

03728

Royal National Institute for Deaf People
RNID

19-23 Featherstone St., London, EC1Y 8SL, UK
Tel: 020 72968000
Fax: 020 72968199
Email: informationline@rnid.org.uk
Website: http://www.rnid.org.uk
Members: 32000
Staff: 1500
Contact: John Low, Chief Exec.
Fee: £22
Membership Type: full-time employee
Fee: £15
Membership Type: retired, unwaged, full-time student
Description: Individual registered members. Provides the following quality services for the deaf, deaf blind and hard of hearing people: information, residential care, training (deaf awareness), specialist telephone services (Typetalk), assistive devices for sale from Sound Advantage, and Communication Support Units. All services are accessed through Regional offices, except Typetalk and Sound Advantage.
Library Subject: deafness, speech problems
Library Type: open to the public
Publication: Magazine
Publication title: One In Seven. Advertisements.

03729

Royal National Institute of Blind People - UK
RNIB

105 Judd St., London, WC1H 9NE, UK
Tel: 0207 3881266
Fax: 0207 3882034
Email: helpline@rnib.org.uk
Website: http://www.rnib.org.uk/xpedio/groups/public/documents/code/InternetHome.hcsp
Contact: Lesley-Anne Alexander, Chief Exec.
Fee: £15
Membership Type: individual (in UK)
Description: Represents blind or partially sighted people, their family or friends, and health care professionals. Wants a world in which blind and partially sighted people enjoy the same rights, freedoms, and responsibilities and quality of life as people who are fully sighted. Aims to challenge the disabling effects of blindness by providing services to help people determine their own lives. Challenges society's actions, attitudes, and assumptions. Works to dismantle barriers that are put into the path of the blind and partially sighted people. Works to prevent, cure, and alleviate blindness.
Publication: Catalog
Publication title: Publications Catalogue

03730

Royal Over-Seas League
ROSL

Over-Seas House, Park Pl., St. James's St., London, SW1A 1LR, UK
Tel: 020 74080214
Fax: 020 74996738
Email: info@rosl.org.uk
Website: http://www.rosl.org.uk
Members: 18000
Staff: 140
Contact: Robert F. Newell, Dir. Gen.
Fee: £270
Membership Type: individual

Fee: £80
Membership Type: student
Description: Offers clubhouse facilities to members. Organises Commonwealth art and music competitions and supports the Commonwealth through its own social, music, arts and welfare activities.
Publication: Journal
Publication title: Overseas

03731

Royal Pharmaceutical Society of Great Britain RPSGB

1 Lambeth High St., London, SE1 7JN, UK
Tel: 020 77359141
Fax: 020 77357629
Email: enquiries@rpsgb.org
Website: http://www.rpsgb.org.uk
Contact: Steve Churton, Pres.
Description: Pharmacists. Professional, statutory and regulatory body for practicing pharmacists in Great Britain.
Library Subject: pharmacy practice, history of pharmacy, pharmacology, pharmaceutics, pharmaceutical science, pharmacokinetics, therapeutics, drug development drug treatment, drug dosage and delivery, therapeutic guidelines, adverse drug reactions and drug interactions, herbal medicines, medical botany, specific drugs
Library Type: open to the public
Publication: Book
Publication title: Pharmaceutical Journal
Meetings/Conventions: British Pharmaceutical Conference – annual conference – Exhibits.

03732

Royal Philharmonic Society RPS

10 Stratford Pl., London, W1C 1BA, UK
Tel: 0207 4918110
Fax: 0207 4937463
Email: admin@royalphilharmonicsociety.org.uk
Website: http://www.royalphilharmonicsociety.org.uk
Members: 600
Staff: 2
Contact: John Gilhooly, Chm.
Fee: £30
Membership Type: general
Fee: £10
Membership Type: student
Description: Professional musicians and music lovers. Supports creativity, excellence, and understanding in music. Provides support for composers, new music, and young musicians.
Publication: Magazine
Publication title: Fanfare. Advertisements.
Meetings/Conventions: periodic competition

03733

Royal Philosophical Society of Glasgow

160 Bothwell St., Glasgow, G2 7EL, UK
Tel: 0141 5643841
Email: info@royalphil.org
Website: http://www.royalphil.org
Members: 420
Staff: 28
Contact: Roddy Macsween, Pres.
Fee: £25
Membership Type: full
Description: Seeks to aid the study, advancement, and development of the physical, natural, mental and moral sciences, arts of design, and applications; and to promote the diffusion of scientific knowledge. Holds public lectures.

03734

Royal Photographic Society of Great Britain RPS

Fenton House, 122 Wells Rd., Bath, BA2 3AH, UK
Tel: 01225 325733
Email: reception@rps.org
Website: http://www.rps.org
Members: 9500
Staff: 20
Contact: Stuart Blake, Dir. Gen.
Fee: £99
Membership Type: in UK
Fee: £84
Membership Type: overseas
Description: Individuals interested in the science and art of photography. Organizes international touring exhibitions. Conducts lectures, seminars, and conferences; offers children's services. Sponsors competitions. Maintains museum housing 19th and 20th century photography, photographic equipment, and journals.
Publication title: Imaging Abstracts
Meetings/Conventions: Touring Exhibitions – periodic meeting

03735

Royal Sailors' Rests RSR

Castaway House, 311 Twyford Ave., Hampshire, Portsmouth, PO2 8RN, UK
Tel: 023 92650505
Fax: 023 92652929
Email: admin@rsr.org.uk
Website: http://www.rsr.org.uk
Members: 3000
Staff: 60
Contact: Brian Deverson, Exec. Dir.
Description: Society of counseling centers proclaiming the Christian faith and preaching temperance to the men and women of the Royal Navy. Operates children's services and charitable programs.
Publication: Magazine
Publication title: Ashore and Afloat

03736

Royal Scottish Academy RSA

The Mound, Edinburgh, EH2 2EL, UK
Tel: 0131 2256671
Fax: 0131 2206016
Email: info@royalscottishacademy.org
Website: http://www.royalscottishacademy.org
Contact: Bill Scott, Pres.
Description: Promotes and supports the creation, understanding and enjoyment of visual arts.
Formerly: Formerly, Royal Scottish Academy of Painting, Sculpture and Architecture

03737

Royal Scottish Academy of Music and Drama RSAMD

100 Renfrew St., Glasgow, G2 3DB, UK
Tel: 0141 3324101
Fax: 0141 3328901
Website: http://www.rsamd.ac.uk
Members: 650
Staff: 500
Contact: John Wallace, Principal
Description: Provides an arts venue and conference venue.

03738

Royal Scottish Country Dance Society RSCDS

12 Coates Crescent, Edinburgh, EH3 7AF, UK
Tel: 0131 2253854
Fax: 0131 2257783
Email: info@rscds.org
Website: http://www.rscds.org
Members: 21000
Staff: 4
Contact: Alastair MacFadyen, Pres.
Description: Works to preserve the form and style of Scottish country-dance. Conducts research on the history of country-dance. Operates a summer training school; maintains a certification program for teachers of country-dance.
Publication: Magazine
Publication title: RSCDS Magazine

03739

Royal Scottish Forestry Society RSFS

4 Doonhill Way, Wigtownshire, Newton Stewart, DG8 6JF, UK
Tel: 01671 401591
Email: director@rsfs.org.uk
Website: http://www.rsfs.org.uk
Members: 1000
Staff: 1
Contact: Richard Kay, Dir.
Fee: £6
Membership Type: student
Fee: £38
Description: Individuals concerned with the advancement of forestry in Scotland. Fosters cooperation between industry professionals and conservationists. Encourages tree planting nationwide. Organizes excursions to sawmills and factories as well as parks and gardens. Sponsors education and training programs. Arranges forestry exhibits.
Publication: Journal
Publication title: Scottish Forestry. Advertisements.
Meetings/Conventions: Spring Excursion – annual meeting – Exhibits.

03740

Royal Scottish Geographical Society
RSGS

Lord John Murray House, 15-19 N Port, Perth, PH1 5LU, UK
Tel: 01738 455050
Email: enquiries@rsgs.org
Website: http://www.rsgs.org
Members: 2500
Staff: 6
Contact: Mike Robinson, Chief Exec.
Fee: £47
Membership Type: joint
Fee: £33
Membership Type: single
Description: Academic geographers and lay members interested in travel and travel lectures. Aims to further the science of geography, stimulate research into the nature and causes of change in human and physical environments on Earth and disseminate knowledge of these changes and their possible consequences.
Library Subject: geography, travel, environment
Library Type: reference
Formerly: Formerly, RSGS
Publication: Newsletter
Publication title: Geogscot. Advertisements.

03741

Royal Society
RS

6-9 Carlton House Terr., London, SW1Y 5AG, UK
Tel: 020 74512500
Fax: 020 79302170
Email: info@royalsoc.ac.uk
Website: http://royalsociety.org
Members: 1400
Staff: 125
Contact: Martin Rees, Pres.
Description: Recognizing excellence in science and its application, promoting authoritative advice, notably to government, on science and engineering-related matters; offers research fellowships and grants to individual scientists; disseminates the results of research through meetings, lectures and exhibitions; fosters public understanding of science; promotes science education and awareness; supports international scientific exchange and international scientific relations; provides resources for research into the history of science and acts as a forum and focus for discussion of issues relating to the wider scientific community.
Library Subject: history of science, scientific biography, and science policy
Library Type: reference
Publication: Book
Publication title: Biographical Memoirs of Fellows of the Royal Society
Meetings/Conventions: meeting

03742

Royal Society for Asian Affairs

2 Belgrave Sq., London, SW1X 8PJ, UK
Tel: 020 72355122
Fax: 020 72596771
Email: info@rsaa.org.uk
Website: http://www.rsaa.org.uk
Members: 1200
Staff: 4
Contact: Merilyn Hywel Jones, Sec.
Fee: £55
Membership Type: in London
Fee: £45
Membership Type: overseas
Description: Promotes greater knowledge and understanding of Asian countries. Conducts educational activities and tours. Maintains speakers' bureau.
Publication: Journal
Publication title: Asian Affairs. Advertisements.

03743

Royal Society for Public Health
RSPH

3rd Fl. Market Towers, 1 Nine Elms Lane, London, SW8 5NQ, UK
Tel: 020 31771600
Fax: 020 31771601
Email: rsph@rsph.org
Website: http://www.rsph.org.uk
Members: 6000
Staff: 23
Contact: Andrew E.J. Banfield, Pres.
Fee: £115
Membership Type: fellow
Fee: £82
Membership Type: regular
Description: **MBX** Members are drawn from a wide variety of professions and occupations with an interest in improving the health of the population. Membership includes architects, engineers, caterers, food scientists, and individuals from the health-related profession. <bd>/PPX</bd> Aims to improve the quality and dignity of human life worldwide and to promote the continuous improvement of health and safety through education communication and the encouragement of scientific research.
Formerly: Formerly, Royal Society of Health
Publication: Journal
Publication title: JRSH. Advertisements.

03744

Royal Society for the Encouragement of Arts, Manufactures, and Commerce
RSA

8 John Adam St., London, WC2N 6EZ, UK
Tel: 020 79305115
Fax: 020 78385805
Email: general@rsa.org.uk
Website: http://www.thersa.org
Members: 22500
Staff: 120
Contact: Matthew Taylor, Chief Exec.
Description: Individuals in 70 countries. Encourages the development of a principled, prosperous society through program of projects and events and with the support of a network of influential Fellows from every field and background.
Publication: Journal
Publication title: RSA Journal. Advertisements.

03745

Royal Society for the Prevention of Accidents
RoSPA

Edgbaston Park, 353 Bristol Rd., Edgbaston, Birmingham, B5 7ST, UK
Tel: 0121 2482000
Fax: 0121 2482001
Email: help@rospa.com
Website: http://www.rospa.com
Members: 6900
Staff: 120
Contact: Roger Vincent, Contact
Fee: £212
Membership Type: small organization
Fee: £360
Membership Type: large organization
Description: Companies, local authorities, road safety officers, schools, and leisure centres. Aims to enhance quality of life by exercising a powerful influence for accident prevention.
Publication: Journal
Publication title: Care on the Road. Advertisements.
Meetings/Conventions: Home Safety Conference – annual conference

03746

Royal Society for the Prevention of Cruelty to Animals National Headquarters
RSPCA

Wilberforce Way, Southwater, Horsham, RH13 9RS, UK
Tel: 0300 1234555
Fax: 0303 1230100
Website: http://www.rspca.org.uk
Members: 53754
Staff: 1600
Contact: Chris Reed, Information & Records Manager
Fee: £3
Membership Type: friend
Fee: £24
Membership Type: national
Description: Represents individuals and organizations concerned about the well-being of wild and domestic animals in the United Kingdom. Opposes: unnecessary animal experimentation; habitat destruction; factory farming; blood sports. Promotes: attitudes and behaviors.
Library Subject: Animal welfare
Library Type: reference
Publication: Magazine
Publication title: Animal Action. Advertisements.

03747

Royal Society for the Protection of Birds
RSPB

The Lodge, Potton Rd., Bedfordshire, Sandy, SG19 2DL, UK
Tel: 01767 680551
Email: membership@rspb.org.uk
Website: http://www.rspb.org.uk
Members: 1041000
Staff: 1300
Contact: Graham Wynne, CEO
Fee: £34
Membership Type: adult
Fee: £44
Membership Type: joint (adult)
Description: Voluntary wildlife conservation organization. Works to encourage better conservation and protection of wild birds. Promotes public interest and appreciation. Assists efforts to protect nesting grounds; purchases land for nature reserves. Conducts research and surveys; offers educational programs.
Publication: Magazine
Publication title: Bird Life. Advertisements.

03748

Royal Society of British Artists
RBA

17 Carlton House Terr., London, SW1Y 5BD, UK
Tel: 020 79306844
Fax: 020 78397830
Email: info@mallgalleries.com
Website: http://www.royalsocietyofbritishartists.org.uk
Members: 107
Contact: James Horton, Pres.
Description: Professional artists. Organizes art exhibitions of sculpture, watercolours, oils, drawings and prints, etc.; most work is for sale at annual exhibit.
Publication: Catalog
Publication title: Annual Exhibition Catalogue. Advertisements.

03749

Royal Society of Chemistry
RSC

Burlington House, Piccadilly, London, W1J 0BA, UK
Tel: 020 74378656
Fax: 020 74378883
Website: http://www.rsc.org
Members: 46000
Staff: 330
Contact: David Phillips, Pres.
Fee: £108
Membership Type: regular, fellow
Fee: £65
Membership Type: associate, affiliate
Description: Chemists and interested persons in most countries of the world. Fosters the growth and application of chemistry by disseminating information. Establishes standards of qualification and conduct for the profession. Seeks to serve the public in an advisory and consultative capacity in matters relating to science and chemistry; monitors developments in chemistry. Encourages communication and cooperation between higher education and industry; offers career guidance and continuing education courses; funds small research projects. Maintains the Benevolent Fund, which helps members, former members, and their dependents who are in need of aid and the Corday-Morgan Memorial Fund, which enables members to travel to developing countries to lecture and exchange information. Organizes symposia, conferences, scientific meetings, and exhibitions. Provides Schools Publications Service, offering subscriptions for schools in Canada, England, Ireland, and the United States. Compiles statistics; sponsors competitions.
Library Subject: chemistry
Library Type: reference
Formerly: Absorbed, Society for Analytical Chemistry
Publication: Journal
Publication title: Chemical Society Reviews

03750

Royal Society of Edinburgh
RSE

22-26 George St., Edinburgh, EH2 2PQ, UK
Tel: 0131 2405000
Fax: 0131 2405024
Website: http://www.royalsoced.org.uk
Members: 1503
Staff: 25
Contact: William Duncan, Chief Exec.
Description: Organizes events and promotes links between academia and industry.
Publication: Journal
Publication title: Proceedings of the Royal Society of Edinburgh: Mathematics

03751

Royal Society of Literature

Somerset House, Strand, London, WC2R 1LA, UK
Tel: 020 78454676
Fax: 020 78454679
Email: info@rslit.org
Website: http://www.rslit.org
Members: 860
Staff: 3
Contact: Maggie Fergusson, Sec.
Fee: £50
Membership Type: individual
Description: Individuals interested in literature. Seeks to sustain the best in English letters and encourages a Catholic appreciation of literature. Conducts monthly lectures and poetry readings.
Publication: Magazine
Publication title: The Royal Society of Literature Review

03752

Royal Society of Marine Artists
RSMA

17 Carlton House Terr., London, SW1Y 5BD, UK
Tel: 020 79306844
Fax: 020 78397830
Email: info@mallgalleries.com
Website: http://www.mallgalleries.org.uk/index.php?pid=120&subid=7
Members: 50
Contact: David Howell, Pres.
Description: Professional marine artists. Organizes the exhibition of original works of art by marine artists; sales and commissions of marine art; educates the public in marine art through exhibitions.
Publication: Catalog
Publication title: Exhibition Catalogue. Advertisements.

03753

Royal Society of Medicine
RSM

1 Wimpole St., London, W1G 0AE, UK
Tel: 0207 2902900
Fax: 0207 2902989
Email: membership@rsm.ac.uk
Website: http://www.rsm.ac.uk
Members: 23000
Staff: 160
Contact: Janice Liverseidge, Dir.
Fee: £390
Membership Type: london fellow
Fee: £318
Membership Type: regional fellow
Description: Doctors, dentists, vets and lay members with interest in medicine.
Library Subject: medicine
Library Type: reference
Publication: Journal
Publication title: International Journal of STD and AIDS

03754

Royal Society of Miniature Painters, Sculptors and Gravers

3 Briar Walk, Putney, London, SW15 6UD, UK
Tel: 0208 7852338
Email: tremrod@aol.com
Website: http://www.royal-miniature-society.org.uk
Members: 150
Staff: 1
Contact: Phyllis Rennell, Exec. Sec.
Description: Associate membership: candidates must have 5 works accepted 2 years running. Three years later they are eligible for election to full membership with six accepted works in election year. The council may invite to membership in special circumstances. Aims to achieve higher standard in the long-established fine art of miniature work and to present this for the instruction and enjoyment of the public.
Meetings/Conventions: annual specialty show – Exhibits.

03755

Royal Society of Musicians of Great Britain
RSMGB

10 Stratford Pl., London, WIN 9AE, UK
Tel: 0207 6296137
Email: ianp.tenor@blueyonder.co.uk
Website: http://www.ianpartridge.pwp.blueyonder.co.uk/rsminfo.html
Members: 1300
Contact: Ian Partridge, Chm.
Fee: £5
Membership Type: individual
Description: Provides immediate and vital aid for professional musicians and their families in distress due to accident, illness or old age.
Formerly: Absorbed, Royal Society of Female Musicians
Publication: Book
Publication title: History of the Royal Society of Musicians, 1738-1988

03756

Royal Society of Painter-Printmakers

Bankside Gallery, 48 Hopton St., London, SE1 9JH, UK
Tel: 0207 9287521
Fax: 0207 9282820
Email: info@banksidegallery.com
Website: http://www.banksidegallery.com/rehome.aspx
Members: 150
Staff: 5
Description: Artists, etchers, and engravers united to further the development of printmaking processes. Encourages public appreciation of prints; provides a forum for the presentation of original etchings and engravings. Organizes educational programs.
Publication: Magazine
Publication title: Bankside Bulletin. Advertisements.

03757

Royal Society of Portrait Painters
RP

Federation of British Artists, 17 Carlton House Terr., London, SW1Y 5BD, UK
Tel: 020 79306844
Fax: 020 78397830
Email: info@mallgalleries.com
Website: http://www.therp.co.uk
Members: 41
Contact: Alistair Adams, Pres.
Description: Represents professional portrait painters running a commission's service and annual exhibition of portraits by members and aspiring portrait painters; educates the public in portraiture through exhibitions and events; some work is sold at an annual auction.
Publication: Catalog
Meetings/Conventions: annual specialty show – Exhibits.

03758

Royal Society of Tropical Medicine and Hygiene
RSTMH

50 Bedford Sq., London, WC1B 3DP, UK
Tel: 020 75802127
Fax: 020 74361389
Email: info@rstmh.org
Website: http://www.rstmh.org
Members: 3000
Staff: 4
Contact: Hazel Dockrell, Pres.
Description: Medical and veterinary practitioners, scientists, and interested others representing 88 countries. Promotes health and seeks to advance the study, control, and prevention of tropical diseases in humans and animals. Encourages information exchange and facilitates discussion.
Publication: Newsletter
Publication title: The Bulletin

03759

Royal Society of Ulster Architects
RSUA

2 Mt. Charles, Belfast, BT7 1NZ, UK
Tel: 028 90323760
Fax: 028 90237313
Email: info@rsua.org.uk
Website: http://www.rsua.org.uk
Contact: Frank McCloskey, Dir.
Description: Works to provide additional support for architectural practices.
Publication: Magazine
Publication title: Perspective. Advertisements.

03760

Royal Society of Wildlife Trusts
RSWT

The Kiln Waterside, Mather Rd., Nottinghamshire, Newark, NG24 1WT, UK
Tel: 016 36677711
Fax: 016 36670001
Email: enquiry@wildlifetrusts.org
Website: http://www.rswt.org/welcome.php
Description: Promotes conservation and manages environmental funds.

03761

Royal Statistical Society
RSS

12 Errol St., London, EC1Y 8LX, UK
Tel: 020 76388998
Email: rss@rss.org.uk
Website: http://www.rss.org.uk/main.asp?page=0
Members: 7000
Staff: 33
Contact: Martin Dougherty, Exec. Dir.
Fee: £149
Membership Type: chartered statistician, standard
Fee: £75
Membership Type: chartered statistician, retired individual in economically developing area
Description: Statisticians. Promotes and protects the professional interests of members; encourages study among statisticians into the proper use of statistical techniques for the solution of practical problems. Advocates the training of persons in the principles of statistics so that statistics may be applied to problems of administration and research in industry, commerce, government, and all fields of applied science. Works to develop a syllabus of study in statistics and to ensure that students proficient in statistical theory also acquire adequate practical experience. Grants qualification for statisticians through the administration of an annual examination given worldwide; organizes seminars and courses.
Library Type: reference
Publication: Journal
Publication title: Journal of the Royal Statistical Society

03762

Royal Surgical Aid Society

47 Great Russell St., London, WC1B 3PB, UK
Tel: 020 76374577
Fax: 020 73236878
Email: enquiries@agecare.org.uk
Website: http://www.agecare.org.uk
Members: 17
Staff: 300
Contact: William Watson, Founder
Description: Seeks to improve the care and well being of older people who are physically frail or suffering from dementia, through a combination of continuous development of good practice in their own homes, seeking pre-eminence in education and training, supporting research and innovation, providing awards for excellence, and continuing in the exchange of knowledge and ideas.
Formerly: Also Known As, Age Care

03763

Royal Television Society
RTS

5th Fl., Kildare House, 3 Dorset Rise, London, EC4Y 8EN, UK
Tel: 0207 8222810
Fax: 0207 8222811
Email: info@rts.org.uk
Website: http://www.rts.org.uk
Members: 2000
Staff: 12
Contact: Simon Albury, Chief Exec.
Fee: £82
Membership Type: full
Fee: £10
Membership Type: student
Description: Provides a forum for discussion and debate on all aspects of the television community. Provides opportunities for learning and getting in contact with people at all levels across the television community. Organises regular dinners in central London, which are addressed by leaders in the world of television. Maintains 14 national and regional centres in the UK, each of which tailors an annual programme to meet the unique requirements of its members. Maintains an archive.
Library Type: open to the public
Meetings/Conventions: Cambridge Convention – biennial convention

03764

Royal Town Planning Institute
RTPI

41 Botolph Ln., London, EC3R 8DL, UK
Tel: 0207 9299494
Fax: 0207 9299490
Email: online@rtpi.org.uk
Website: http://www.rtpi.org.uk
Members: 18500
Contact: Ann Skippers, Pres.
Fee: £35
Membership Type: retired
Fee: £350
Membership Type: life (retired)
Description: Professional town planners in local government, private practice, central government, teaching and commerce. Exists to advance the science and art of town planning for the benefit of the public. Helps maintain high standards of professional education and training and promotes its members' expertise and competence. Provides a national voice for the profession and runs a free planning aid service.
Publication: Magazine
Publication title: Planning

03765

Royal Ulster Agricultural Society
RUAS

Balmoral, The King's Hall, Belfast, BT9 6GW, UK
Tel: 028 90665225
Fax: 028 90661264
Email: info@kingshall.co.uk
Website: http://www.balmoralshow.co.uk/content.aspx?page=ulster-agri-society.html
Contact: Margaret Armstrong, Membership Sec.
Fee: £32
Membership Type: full
Fee: £24
Membership Type: senior citizen (over 65 years old)
Description: Promotes agriculture in Northern Ireland by holding agricultural shows and giving agricultural instruction through exhibitions and lectures.

03766

Royal United Services Institute for Defence and Security Studies

Whitehall, London, SW1A 2ET, UK
Tel: 020 79305854
Email: membership@rusi.org
Website: http://www.rusi.org
Contact: Paul Lever, Chm.
Fee: £350
Membership Type: platinum individual
Fee: £340
Membership Type: standard (all-inclusive)
Description: Monitors national security and defense of the United Kingdom, with a recent focus on terrorism. Participates in military research and disseminates information via publications. Organizes conferences, workshops, and other meeting opportunities for those involved in national security and defense.

03767

Royal Watercolour Society
RWS

Bankside Gallery, 48 Hopton St., London, SE1 9JH, UK
Tel: 0207 9287521
Email: info@banksidegallery.com
Website: http://www.royalwatercoloursociety.co.uk
Members: 80
Staff: 4
Contact: David Paskett, Pres.
Description: Supports watercolor artists in order to make their works known to the public. Works to increase appreciation of watercolors through exhibitions. Sponsors the Adopt a Picture Campaign, which provides funding for preservation and restoration of the RWS Diploma

collection. Maintains permanent collection of works of present and past members. Organizes educational events including art days, demonstrations, studio visits, lectures, guided tours and international open painting competition for water-based media.
Publication: Bulletin
Publication title: Bankside Bulletin. Advertisements.

03768
Royal Welsh Agricultural Society
RWAS
Llanelwedd, Builth Wells, LD2 3SY, UK
Tel: 01982 553683
Fax: 01982 553563
Email: requests@rwas.co.uk
Website: http://www.rwas.co.uk/society
Fee: £25
Membership Type: junior (18 years and under)
Fee: £60
Membership Type: single
Description: Promotes agriculture, horticulture, and forestry in Wales.

03769
Royal Zoological Society of Scotland
RZSS
Edinburgh Zoo, 134 Corstorphine Rd., Edinburgh, EH12 6TS, UK
Tel: 0131 3349171
Fax: 0131 3140384
Email: info@rzss.org.uk
Website: http://www.edinburghzoo.org.uk
Members: 13000
Staff: 150
Contact: David Windmill, Chief Exec.
Fee: £56
Membership Type: adult
Fee: £90
Membership Type: joint
Description: Individuals, companies, schools, and outdoor groups in Scotland. Enhances knowledge of and interest in animal life. Provides environmental education programs. Conducts conservation breeding programs at Edinburgh Zoo and Highland Wildlife Park, Kincraig Inverness-shire.
Publication: Magazine
Publication title: Ark File

03770
Rubber Stamp Manufacturer's Guild
RSMG
Farringdon Point, 29-35 Farringdon Rd., London, EC1M 3JF, UK
Tel: 0845 4501565
Fax: 0207 4057784
Email: info@rsmg.org.uk
Website: http://www.rsmg.org.uk/page.asp?node=1
Members: 18
Contact: Philippa Morrell, Contact
Description: Works to provide a forum for the exchange of ideas, information and education and offers members the opportunity to keep up to date with emerging technologies and the development of new products.

03771
Runnymede Trust
RT
7 Plough Yard, Shoreditch, London, EC2A 3LP, UK
Tel: 020 73779222
Fax: 020 73776622
Email: info@runnymedetrust.org
Website: http://www.runnymedetrust.org
Staff: 9
Contact: Rob Berkeley, Dir.
Description: Seeks to eliminate all aspects of racism and discrimination in Great Britain and Europe. Conducts research and disseminates information on issues of race and immigration.
Publication: Journal
Publication title: Runnymede Bulletin

03772
Rural and Industrial Design and Building Association
RIDBA
5a The Maltings, Stowupland Rd., Suffolk, Stowmarket, IP14 5AG, UK
Tel: 01449 676049
Fax: 01449 770028
Email: secretary@ridba.org.uk
Website: http://www.ridba.org.uk
Members: 3004
Staff: 2
Contact: Tony Hutchinson, Natl. Sec.
Fee: £700
Membership Type: corporate business level 1
Fee: £175
Membership Type: college, business
Description: Works to represent the interest of members at a national level. Keeps members informed of impending changes to legislation, standards and regulations. Promotes good quality design and construction. Disseminates information relating to Rural and Industrial Buildings.
Formerly: Formerly, Rural Design and Building Association
Publication: Journal
Publication title: Countryside Building. Advertisements.
Meetings/Conventions: Agricultural Building Show – show

03773
Rural Crafts Association
Heights Cottage, Brook Rd., Wormley, Surrey, Godalming, GU8 5UA, UK
Tel: 01428 682292
Website: http://www.ruralcraftsassociation.co.uk
Members: 600
Staff: 8
Description: Mostly full time professional craftsmen and women who sell their work at the 50 shows a year the association organizes. Encourages men and women to make and sell their work and skills, to uphold the quality of work and to provide a vigorous forum for the sale of members' work, at a cost they can afford. Advisory service for crafts development and marketing for foreign governments.

03774
Russo-British Chamber of Commerce
RBCC
11 Belgrave Rd., London, SW1V 1RB, UK
Tel: 020 79316455
Fax: 020 72339736
Email: infolondon@rbcc.com
Website: http://www.rbcc.com
Members: 500
Staff: 20
Contact: Stephen Dalziel, Exec. Dir.
Description: Promotes business and commerce between Russia and the UK.
Publication: Bulletin

03775
Safety Assessment Federation
SAFed
70 S Lambeth Rd., Unit 4, 1st Fl., Vauxhall, London, SW8 1RL, UK
Tel: 020 75823208
Fax: 020 77350286
Email: info@safed.co.uk
Website: http://www.safed.co.uk
Staff: 4
Contact: Phil Moore, Chm.
Fee: £1000-5000
Membership Type: associate (based on the annual turnover)
Fee: £1250-65000
Membership Type: full (based on the annual turnover)
Description: Represents the interests of companies that undertake the independent safety inspection and certification of machinery plant and equipment.
Publication title: Fact Sheets

03776
Sailing Barge Association
SBA
c/o Frank P. Morris, Sec.
PO Box 5191, Bournemouth, BH1 3WZ, UK
Tel: 01202 552582
Email: sba@ffbs.co.uk
Website: http://www.sailingbargeassociation.co.uk
Contact: Peter Dodds, Chm.
Description: Works to preserve the Thames sailing barges heritage.

03777
Salers Cattle Society of the UK and Ireland
Brook House Farm, Norbury, Nr. Whitchurch, Shropshire, Shrewsbury, SY13 4HY, UK
Tel: 01948 667223
Fax: 01948 667448
Website: http://www.salers-cattle-society.co.uk
Contact: John Crowe, Sec.
Fee: £108
Membership Type: regular
Description: Represents individuals interested in the Salers Cattle breed in UK and Ireland. Seeks to advance the beef and cattle industries. Promotes and preserves the Salers breed.

03778
Salters' Company
Salters' Hall, 4 Fore St., London, EC2Y 5DE, UK
Tel: 020 75885216
Fax: 020 76383679
Email: info@salters.co.uk
Website: http://www.salters.co.uk
Members: 300
Staff: 18

Contact: Diane Bundock, Charities Admin.
Description: Salters. Activities are centered on charity and education. Hosts company events.
Library Type: reference
Publication: Newsletter
Publication title: Salters' Newsletter

03779
Salters' Institute
Salters' Hall, 4 Fore St., London, EC2Y 5DE, UK
Tel: 020 76285962
Fax: 020 76383679
Email: institute@salters.co.uk
Website: http://www.salters.co.uk/institute
Staff: 6
Contact: Audrey Strong, Institute Mgr.
Description: Aims to promote the appreciation of chemistry and related sciences among the young, and to encourage careers in the teaching of chemistry and in the UK chemical and allied industries.
Meetings/Conventions: Salters Teachers Conference – annual conference – Exhibits.

03780
Saltire Society
9 Fountain Close, 22 High St., Edinburgh, EH1 1TF, UK
Tel: 0131 5561836
Fax: 0131 5571675
Email: saltire@saltiresociety.org.uk
Website: http://www.saltiresociety.org.uk
Members: 1445
Staff: 2
Contact: Lord Cullen, Pres.
Fee: £30
Membership Type: ordinary
Fee: £96
Membership Type: benefactor (individual, family)
Description: All individuals and organizations who support the aims of the society. Seeks to preserve all that is best in Scotland and Scottish tradition and to encourage every new development which can strengthen and enrich the country's cultural life.
Publication: Magazine
Publication title: Saltire

03781
Salvation Army Home League - International
Salvation Army Intl. Heritage Ctr., House 14, The William Booth Coll., Denmark Hill, London, SE5 8BQ, UK
Tel: 020 77373327
Fax: 020 77374127
Email: heritage@salvationarmy.org
Website: http://www1.salvationarmy.org/heritage.nsf/titles/The_Home_League
Members: 396961
Contact: Israel L. Gaither, Contact
Description: Women over the age of 16 from 109 countries. Provides education, fellowship, service and worship.
Formerly: Formerly, Salvation Army Home League - England

03782
Salvation Army International Headquarters
SA IHQ
101 Queen Victoria St., London, EC4V 4EH, UK
Tel: 020 73320101
Fax: 020 72364681
Website: http://www.salvationarmy.org/ihq/www_sa.nsf
Members: 1100000
Staff: 125000
Contact: Robin Dunster, Chief of Staff
Description: Ordained ministers, volunteers, and others donating time to religious and social welfare activities in 110 countries and colonies. Christian church and charity; embraces Christian ideals and high moral standards; seeks to minister to the physical, spiritual, and emotional needs of mankind. Serves to propagate Christianity, provide education, relieve poverty, and establish charitable projects. Works for the betterment of the poor through evangelistic and social enterprises including alcohol and drug rehabilitation programs, hostels for the homeless, children's homes, schools, hospitals, clinics, and institutes for the blind and handicapped, HIV/AIDS prevention. Preaches the Christian Gospel and publishes in over 175 languages. Cooperates with international relief agencies and governments.
Publication: Newspaper
Publication title: Young Soldier

03783
Salvation Army UK and Ireland
101 Newington Causeway, London, SE1 6BN, UK
Tel: 020 73674500
Fax: 020 73674728
Email: info@salvationarmy.org.uk
Website: http://www2.salvationarmy.org.uk/uki/www_uki.nsf
Members: 46524
Staff: 15
Contact: Maureen Thomas, Sec.
Description: Encourages Christian ideals and good citizenship among young people.

03784
Samaritans - England
The Upper Mill, Kingston Rd., Surrey, Ewell, KT17 2AF, UK
Tel: 020 83948300
Fax: 020 83948301
Email: admin@samaritans.org
Website: http://www.samaritans.org
Members: 18300
Staff: 60
Contact: Chad Varah, Founder
Description: Provides confidential and emotional support to anyone in crisis, 24 hours a day, 365 days a year.
Publication title: Educational Materials

03785
Save the Children UK
SC UK
1 St. John's Ln., London, EC1M 4AR, UK
Tel: 020 70126400
Email: supporter.care@savethechildren.org.uk
Website: http://www.savethechildren.org.uk
Staff: 4600
Contact: Jasmine Whitbread, CEO
Description: Provides emergency relief and long-term development and prevention work to help children, their families, and communities to be self-sufficient. Part of the International Save the Children Alliance.
Publication: Magazine
Publication title: World's Children

03786
SBGI
Camden House, Warwick Rd., Warwickshire, Kenilworth, CV8 1TH, UK
Tel: 01926 513777
Fax: 01926 511926
Email: mail@sbgi.org.uk
Website: http://www.sbgi.org.uk/home
Members: 180
Staff: 16
Contact: John Stiggers, Chief Exec.
Description: Companies involved in all aspects of the gas industry, including shipping, supplying, transportation, pipe laying, distribution engineering, metering, utilization and installation and service. Represents the interests of contractors and suppliers of gas plant, gas appliances and equipment.
Publication: Journal
Publication title: Gas Business. Advertisements.

03787
School Journey Association
SJA
48 Cavendish Rd., London, SW12 0DH, UK
Tel: 0208 6756636
Fax: 0208 6738763
Email: thesja@btconnect.com
Website: http://www.sjatours.org
Members: 2029
Staff: 7
Description: Individual members form the Council which is responsible for the Association, which is managed by a Board of Management, assisted by some Tour Secretaries. Corporate members are those schools who use services. Assists schools with travel (UK and Europe), travel insurance. All tours are educational and oriented towards the classroom situation including National Curriculum.
Formerly: Formerly, Educational Travel Ltd.
Publication: Brochure
Publication title: SJA Tours. Advertisements.

03788
School Leaders Scotland
SLS
University of Strathclyde, Jordanhill Campus, Southbrae Dr., Glasgow, G13 1PP, UK
Tel: 0141 9503298
Email: sls@strath.ac.uk
Website: http://www.sls-scotland.org.uk
Members: 630
Staff: 6
Contact: Ken Cunningham, Gen. Sec.
Fee: £272
Membership Type: ordinary
Fee: £15
Membership Type: associate
Description: Headteachers, deputy, and assistant headteachers of secondary schools in Scotland. Aims to safeguard and promote the interests of headteachers, depute headteachers, and assistant headteachers in Scottish secondary schools and to promote education, particularly secondary education in Scotland.
Formerly: Formerly, Association of Head Teachers in Scotland

03789
School Library Association
SLA
Unit 2, Lotmead Business Village, Wanborough, Swindon, SN4 0UY, UK
Tel: 01793 791787
Fax: 01793 791786
Email: info@sla.org.uk
Website: http://www.sla.org.uk
Members: 3600
Staff: 6
Contact: Miranda McKearney, Pres.
Fee: £79.5
Membership Type: regular (includes 1 copy of journal)
Fee: £109.5
Membership Type: regular (includes 2 copies of journal)
Description: Schools, colleges, public library services, publishers, and individuals in the UK and overseas. Promotes the development of primary and secondary school libraries. Contributes to and reports on projects in education and librarianship. Works to assist in the development of training for school library work. Maintains advisory and information service. Lobbies for central role of the school library as essential in today's Information Society.
Publication: Bibliographies
Publication title: Books of Children's Fiction to Enjoy
Meetings/Conventions: annual conference – Exhibits.

03790
Schools Music Association
SMA
71 Margaret Rd., New Barnet, Herts, London, EN4 9NT, UK
Tel: 020 84406919
Fax: 020 84406919
Website: http://www.schoolsmusic.org.uk
Members: 400
Contact: Peter Maxwell Davies, Pres.
Fee: £35
Membership Type: individual
Fee: £12.5
Membership Type: retired, NQT start teaching Sept. 2005
Description: Teachers - primary, secondary, special, instrumental; lecturers and student teachers; inspectors, advisers, consultants; LEAs, local SMAs and Festivals; schools, colleges, music centers, libraries; the music trade -publishers, manufacturers, music shops. Promotes music education by providing opportunities for its members to learn about, discuss and evaluate developments in music education; organizing national and regional weekend conferences, day courses and workshops; providing opportunities for children to perform at major venues, such as the Royal Festival Hall; maintaining close contact with other organizations.

03791
Science Council of the United Kingdom
32-36 Loman St., Southwark, London, SE1 0EE, UK
Tel: 020 79227888
Fax: 020 79227879
Email: enquiries@sciencecouncil.org
Website: http://www.sciencecouncil.org
Members: 28
Staff: 2
Contact: Diana Garnham, Chief Exec.
Fee: £1000
Membership Type: organisation (minimum)
Description: Professional science bodies. Represents the members' views or acts in dealing with all those bodies that use the services of professionally qualified scientists and technologists, or who require advice on science and technology. Encourages and assists the adoption of common policies.
Formerly: Formerly, Council of Science and Technology Institutes

03792
Science Fiction Foundation
SFF
75 Rosslyn Ave., Harold Wood, Essex, Romford, RM3 0RG, UK
Email: sff.website@gmail.com
Website: http://www.sf-foundation.org
Contact: Roger Robinson, Contact
Fee: £18.5
Membership Type: individual (in UK and Ireland)
Fee: £40
Membership Type: institution
Description: Promotes the study of science fiction in education.
Publication: Journal
Publication title: Foundation: The International Review of Science Fiction. Advertisements.

03793
Scientific Committee on Antarctic Research
SCAR
Scott Polar Research Inst., Lensfield Rd., Cambridge, CB2 1ER, UK
Tel: 01223 336550
Fax: 01223 336549
Email: info@scar.org
Website: http://www.scar.org
Members: 44
Staff: 3
Contact: Mike Sparrow, Exec. Dir.
Description: A committee of the International Council of Scientific Unions. National organizations actively engaged in Antarctic research. Initiates, promotes, and coordinates, scientific research in the Antarctic and provides scientific advice to the Antarctic Treaty system.
Publication: Bulletin
Publication title: SCAR Bulletin
Meetings/Conventions: High Elevation Glaciers and Climate Records – annual symposium

03794
Scientific Exploration Society
SES
Motcombe, Expedition Base, Dorset, Shaftesbury, SP7 9PB, UK
Tel: 01747 853353
Email: base@ses-explore.org
Website: http://www.ses-explore.org
Members: 500
Staff: 6
Contact: John Blashford-Snell, Pres.
Fee: £35
Membership Type: full
Fee: £250
Membership Type: corporate, friend
Description: Encourages scientifically orientated expeditions.
Library Subject: expeditions
Library Type: open to the public
Publication: Magazine
Publication title: Sesame
Meetings/Conventions: monthly lecture

03795
Scoliosis Association
SAUK
4 Ivebury Ct., 323-327 Latimer Rd., London, W10 6RA, UK
Tel: 020 89645343
Fax: 020 89645343
Email: info@sauk.org.uk
Website: http://www.sauk.org.uk
Members: 3000
Staff: 5
Contact: Stephanie Clark, Chair
Description: Individuals affected by scoliosis; their parents and families. Seeks to increase knowledge and understanding of scoliosis (a lateral curvature of the spine) and emphasize the importance of early detection. Encourages contact between members; disseminates information to members and the public.
Publication: Booklet
Publication title: A Parents Guide to Scoliosis

03796
Scope
PO Box 833, Milton Keynes, MK12 5NY, UK
Tel: 0808 8003333
Fax: 01908 321051
Email: response@scope.org.uk
Website: http://www.scope.org.uk
Contact: Jon Sparkes, Chief Exec.
Fee: £10
Membership Type: individual
Description: People with cerebral palsy (CP), their families, and carers in England and Wales. Promotes equality for disabled people. Provides information on early years, education, work, and daily living. Provides advice and support on all aspects of cerebral palsy and disability.
Publication: Newspaper
Publication title: Disability Now

03797
Scotch Whisky Association
SWA
20 Atholl Crescent, Edinburgh, EH3 8HF, UK
Tel: 0131 2229200
Fax: 0131 2229237
Email: info@swa.org.uk
Website: http://www.scotch-whisky.org.uk
Members: 66
Staff: 38
Contact: Campbell Evans, Dir.
Description: Distillers, blenders, brokers and bottlers of Scotch Whisky. Works for the protection and promotion of Scotch Whisky at home and abroad.
Publication title: Distilleries Which Welcome Visitors

03798
ScotlandIS
Geddes House, Ste. 47, Kirkton N, Livingston, EH54 6GU, UK
Tel: 01506 472200
Fax: 01506 460615
Email: info@scotlandis.com
Website: http://www.scotlandis.com
Members: 350
Staff: 8
Contact: Polly Purvis, Exec. Dir.
Description: Represents the ICT industry involved in developing software, interactive media, e-commerce, and the Internet in Scotland.
Formerly: Formerly, Scotland Software Federation

03799
Scots Language Society
SLS
25 Buccleuch Pl., Edinburgh, Edinburgh, EH8 9LN, UK
Tel: 0131 6504149
Email: chris.robinson@ed.ac.uk
Website: http://www.lallans.co.uk
Contact: Christine Robinson, Pres.

Scots Leid Associe
see Scots Language Society

03800
Scottish Agricultural Organisation Society
SAOS
Rural Centre, West Mains, Ingliston, Newbridge, EH28 8NZ, UK
Tel: 0131 4724100
Fax: 0131 4724101
Email: saos@saos.co.uk
Website: http://www.saos.co.uk
Members: 82
Staff: 9
Contact: James Graham, Chief Exec.
Description: Co-operative Societies - Agricultural. Provides consultancy, advisory, and training services.

03801
Scottish Amateur Music Association
SAMA
18 Craigton Crescent, Clackmannanshire, Alva, FK12 5DS, UK
Email: secretary@sama.org.uk
Website: http://www.sama.org.uk
Contact: Margaret W. Simpson, Sec.
Description: Offers training courses to amateur musicians.
Publication title: Gentle Jacobite

03802
Scottish and Northern Ireland Plumbing Employers' Federation
SNIPEF
22 Hopetoun St., Edinburgh, EH7 4GH, UK
Tel: 0131 2252255
Fax: 0131 2267638
Email: info@snipef.org
Website: http://www.snipef.org
Members: 900
Staff: 26
Contact: Robert Burgon, Dir./Sec.
Fee: £260
Membership Type: regular
Description: Trade association for plumbing and heating firms.
Publication title: Plumb Heat

03803
Scottish and Northern Welsh Pony and Cob Association
SNWPCA
c/o Mrs. Sheila Henderson, Sec.
West Kyloe, Beal, Berwick-upon-Tweed, Northumberland, TD15 2PG, UK
Tel: 01289 381321
Email: secretary@snwpca.com
Website: http://www.snwpca.com
Contact: Elizabeth Russell, Pres.
Fee: £15
Membership Type: full
Fee: £6
Membership Type: junior (under 18)
Description: Records the breeding details of Welsh ponies and Cobs. Seeks to improve the breed and promote its excellence through breeding and performance enjoyed by all the family through all sections A B C D and part breeds.
Publication: Newsletter

03804
Scottish Arts Council
SAC
12 Manor Pl., Edinburgh, EH3 7DD, UK
Tel: 0131 2266051
Fax: 0131 2259833
Email: help.desk@scottisharts.org.uk
Website: http://www.scottisharts.org.uk
Staff: 90
Contact: Jim Tough, Chief Exec.
Description: Aims to celebrate artists and artistic excellence, encourage excellence and innovation and to invest in artists and creative environments. Seeks to improve the quality of life for all through the arts, strengthen communities through the arts, promote arts in education and lifelong learning, and to increase attendance and participation. Works to stimulate investment in the arts, promote the importance of the arts in social and economic policy and to increase openness and accountability.
Publication: Directory
Publication title: Information Directory: A Guide to Information, Advice and Services from the Scottish Arts Council

03805
Scottish Association for Marine Science
SAMS
c/o Dunstaffnage Marine Laboratory
Oban, Oban, PA37 1QA, UK
Tel: 01631 559000
Fax: 01631 559001
Email: info@sams.ac.uk
Website: http://www.sams.ac.uk
Members: 600
Staff: 150
Contact: Laurence Mee, Dir.
Description: Marine scientists and others interested in marine science, primarily in Scotland, but also a substantial number in other parts of the UK and overseas. Promotes and conducts research and education in marine science, particularly on issues relevant to Scotland. Encourages new marine research; develops a wide range of activities, including scientific meetings in different parts of Scotland and a programme for schools. Offers a BSC Marine Science degree course.
Library Type: by appointment only

03806
Scottish Association for Mental Health
SAMH
Cumbrae House, 15 Carlton Ct., Glasgow, G5 9JP, UK
Tel: 0141 5687000
Fax: 0141 5687001
Email: enquire@samh.org.uk
Website: http://www.samh.org.uk
Members: 239
Staff: 381
Contact: Billy Watson, Chief Exec.
Fee: £5
Membership Type: unwaged/student
Fee: £15
Membership Type: individual
Description: Health Boards, Regional Councils, District Councils, Psychiatric Hospitals, local and regional voluntary organizations, Trade Unions, Professional Bodies Universities, individuals, local associations for mental health. Campaigns for better hospital and community services; seeks to increase understanding of mental distress; provides direct services to people who have suffered from mental health problems, namely supported accommodation and training for employment on projects all over Scotland. Information, training and a development consultancy are also offered to local groups, professionals and affiliated local mental health associations.
Library Subject: mental health
Library Type: by appointment only
Publication: Magazine
Publication title: The Point

03807
Scottish Association for Public Transport
SAPT
11 Queens Crescent, Glasgow, G4 9BL, UK
Tel: 07760 381729
Email: mail@sapt.org.uk
Website: http://www.sapt.org.uk
Members: 140
Description: Campaigns for improved public passenger transport and the shift from lorries to rail and waterborne freight as part of sustainable, integrated, and inclusive transport policies for UK and Scotland.

03808
Scottish Association of Family History Societies
SAFHS
22 Spey Terr., Edinburgh, EH7 4PL, UK
Website: http://www.safhs.org.uk
Contact: Kenneth Nisbet, Sec.
Fee: £40
Membership Type: full
Fee: £30
Membership Type: associate
Description: Acts as the parent body for Scottish history societies.

03809

Scottish Association of Geography Teachers SAGT

21 Bankpark Crescent, Tranent, EH33 1AS, UK
Tel: 01875 612901
Email: liz@mcglashan.wanadoo.co.uk
Website: http://www.sagt.org.uk
Members: 700
Contact: Elizabeth McGlashan, Membership Sec.
Fee: £35
Membership Type: full
Fee: £20
Membership Type: probationer, retired, unwaged
Description: Mainly teachers of geography in Scottish schools: also College lecturers and University staff concerned with geography. Aims to further the teaching of geography in Scotland; to support teachers in developing new courses through publications, Annual Conference and Annual Field Excursion. Responds to proposals/publications related to geography, given by the Scottish Qualifications Authority. Comments annually to SQA re-examinations.
Publication: Newsletter
Publication title: SGN (Scottish Geographical News)

03810

Scottish Association of Health Councils SAHC

24A Palmerston Pl., Edinburgh, EH12 5AL, UK
Tel: 0131 2204101
Fax: 0131 2204108
Email: admin1@sahc.sol.co.uk
Website: http://www.sahc.scot.nhs.uk
Staff: 3
Contact: Patricia Dawson, Dir.
Description: Membership is open to all 15 health councils in Scotland. Provides information, training resources and development of public participation to all health related matters. The organization is the focal point between Local Health Councils, the Scottish Executive and Health Department and other national organizations, SAHC is voluntary and funded by LHC's subscriptions.
Library Subject: health, NHS, patients' issues
Library Type: reference

03811

Scottish Association of Master Bakers SAMB

Atholl House, 4 Torphichen St., Edinburgh, EH3 8JQ, UK
Tel: 0131 2291401
Fax: 0131 2298239
Email: master.bakers@samb.co.uk
Website: http://www.samb.co.uk
Members: 500
Staff: 11
Description: Bakers and manufacturers of bakery equipment and supplies in Scotland. Promotes the baked goods industry in Scotland. Protects members' interests.
Publication title: A History of the Baking Trade in Scotland

03812

Scottish Association of Meat Wholesalers SAMW

38 N Meggetland, Edinburgh, EH14 1XG, UK
Tel: 0131 4441715
Email: ianranderson@btinternet.com
Website: http://www.scottish-meat-wholesalers.org.uk
Members: 35
Contact: Ian Anderson, Exec. Mgr.
Description: Represents over 90 percent of the Scottish red meat slaughtering sector.

03813

Scottish Association of Sign Language Interpreters SASLI

Baltic Chambers, Ste. 404-408, 50 Wellington St., Glasgow, G2 6HJ, UK
Tel: 0141 2488159
Fax: 0141 2211693
Email: mail@sasli.org.uk
Website: http://www.sasli.org.uk
Contact: Helga McGilp, Dir.
Fee: £22.66
Membership Type: full
Fee: £19.06
Membership Type: associate
Description: Promotes sign language interpreting services. Enhances the communication skills of deaf and hearing people. Assists with the training and assessment of individuals wishing to develop their interpreting skills.

03814

Scottish Association of Young Farmers' Clubs SAYFC

c/o Fiona Bain, Natl. Sec.
Young Farmers' Ctre., Ingliston, Edinburgh, EH28 8NE, UK
Tel: 0131 3332445
Fax: 0131 3332488
Email: natsec@sayfc.org
Website: http://www.sayfc.org
Members: 5000
Contact: Penny Laird, Chief Exec.
Description: Individuals aged 14-26 who are interested in agriculture. Works to further the cultural education of youth; fosters knowledge and appreciation of country life. Encourages good citizenship and efficiency in agriculture. Seeks to make rural life more attractive to youth by providing social and recreational opportunities. Cooperates with colleges of agriculture, education authorities, and other organizations; promotes the formation of new clubs and international understanding through contact with similar organizations worldwide. Participates in international exchange programs with Australia, Canada, other European countries, New Zealand, and the United States. Promotes technical education through competitions, skills tests, leadership training, and discussion meetings. Sponsors seminars; organizes rallies and regional conferences. Offers pesticide application testing service. Sponsors competitions.

03815

Scottish Beekeepers' Association SBA

8 Mayfield Rd., Inverness, IV2 4AE, UK
Tel: 01463 226411
Email: teale@f2s.com
Website: http://www.scottishbeekeepers.org.uk
Members: 1200
Contact: Alan Teale, Pres.
Description: Represents Scottish beekeepers at the national and international level.
Publication: Magazine
Publication title: The Scottish Beekeeper. Advertisements.

03816

Scottish Building Contractors Association SBCA

c/o Norman J. Smith, Sec.
4 Woodside Pl., Glasgow, G3 7QF, UK
Tel: 0141 3535050
Fax: 0141 3322928
Email: sbca@btconnect.com
Website: http://www.scottishcontractors.com
Members: 40
Contact: Craig McKillop, Pres.
Description: Building contractors in Scotland.

03817

Scottish Building Federation

Crichton House, 4 Crichton's Close, Carrongrange Ave., Edinburgh, EH8 8DT, UK
Tel: 0131 5558866
Fax: 0131 5555247
Email: info@scottish-building.co.uk
Website: http://www.scottish-building.co.uk/pages/index_top.asp
Members: 20
Contact: Jamie Pert, Pres.
Description: Promotes the Scottish building industry; works to ensure the industry recruits, trains and retains a skilled workforce; maintains and develops standards and quality in the building industry.

03818

Scottish Campaign for Nuclear Disarmament SCND

15 Barrland St., Glasgow, G41 1QH, UK
Tel: 0141 4231222
Email: john.ainslie@banthebomb.org
Website: http://banthebomb.org/ne
Contact: John Ainslie, Coor.
Fee: £24
Membership Type: adult
Fee: £36
Membership Type: household
Description: Aims to eliminate British nuclear weapons and other weapons of mass destruction. Organizes regular protests and actively involved in wider peace issues.
Publication: Magazine
Publication title: Nuclear Free Scotland

03819

Scottish Catholic International Aid Fund SCIAF

19 Park Circus, Glasgow, G3 6BE, UK
Tel: 0141 3545555

Email: sciaf@sciaf.org.uk
Website: http://www.sciaf.org.uk
Contact: Paul Chitnis, Chief Exec.
Description: Seeks to ensure that international development benefits the economically disadvantaged worldwide. Provides financial, technical, and voluntary support to emergency relief and community development projects in Africa, Asia, and Latin America.
Publication: Magazine
Publication title: Review

03820
Scottish Childminding Association
SCMA
7 Melville Terr., Stirling, FK8 2ND, UK
Tel: 01786 445377
Fax: 01786 449062
Email: information@childminding.org
Website: http://www.childminding.org
Members: 5000
Contact: Maggie Simpson, Chief Exec.
Fee: £53.75
Membership Type: childminder
Description: Promotes childminding as a quality childcare service. Works to inform childminders, parents, employers, local authorities, and central government about good practice in childminding and ways to attain this.
Publication: Magazine
Publication title: Childminding. Advertisements.

03821
Scottish Church History Society
SCHS
16 Murrayburn Park, Edinburgh, EH14 2PX, UK
Tel: 0131 4423772
Email: enquiries@schs.org.uk
Website: http://www.schs.org.uk
Members: 293
Contact: Virginia Russell, Hon. Sec.
Description: Libraries, historians and interested individuals in 18 countries. Promotes the study of Scottish ecclesiastical history. Organizes symposia.

03822
Scottish Churches Housing Action
44 Hanover St., Edinburgh, EH2 2DR, UK
Tel: 0131 4774500
Fax: 0131 4772710
Email: scotchho@ednet.co.uk
Website: http://www.churches-housing.org
Members: 13
Staff: 5
Contact: Leslie Morrion, Chm.
Description: Churches. Supports the work of churches in Scotland; seeks to end homelessness in Scotland. Provides advice and other support to local groups through volunteering and community development approach to homelessness. Represents churches' views on homelessness to government. Promotes Homelessness Sunday in Scotland. Encourages churches to make property available for affordable housing.
Formerly: Formerly, Scottish Churches Housing Agency
Publication: Newsletter
Publication title: Our Homeless Neighbour

03823
Scottish Committee of Optometrists
SCO
5 St. Vincent St., Edinburgh, EH3 6SW, UK
Tel: 0131 2204542
Email: info@sco-online.org
Website: http://www.sco-online.org/index.html
Members: 760
Staff: 1
Contact: Neil Leslie, Chm.
Fee: £42.5
Membership Type: associate
Description: All optometrists in Scotland. Represents interests of independent optometrists in Scotland.
Publication: Newsletter
Publication title: Look North. Advertisements.

03824
Scottish Community Care Forum
SCCF
c/o West Dunbartonshire Community Care Forum
Benview, Strathleven Pl., Dumbarton, G82 1BA, UK
Tel: 01573 226969
Email: admin@bvccf.uk
Website: http://www.sccfonline.org.uk
Members: 47
Staff: 2
Description: Community care providers and organizations. Seeks to improve delivery and availability of community care and volunteer programs and services. Facilitates collaboration between users and providers of community care and related services; works to insure effective planning and practice among community care initiatives.

03825
Scottish Council for Development and Industry
SCDI
Campsie House, 17 Park Circus Pl., Glasgow, G3 6AH, UK
Tel: 0141 3329119
Fax: 0141 3330039
Email: enquiries@scdi.org.uk
Website: http://www.scdi.org.uk
Members: 1200
Staff: 23
Contact: Iain McTaggart, Gen. Mgr.
Description: Works to strengthen Scotland's competitiveness; lobbies for government policies that encourage sustainable economic growth.
Publication: Bulletin
Publication title: Indicator

03826
Scottish Council for International Arbitration
SCIA
Albany House, 58 Albany St., Edinburgh, EH1 3QR, UK
Tel: 0131 5571545
Fax: 0131 5258651
Email: jim.arnott@simpmar.com
Website: http://www.scia.co.uk
Members: 311
Contact: James M. Arnott, Dir./Sec.
Description: Individuals interested in promoting international arbitration in Scotland. Administers international arbitrations in Scotland and promotes arbitration as a method of resolving disputes.

03827
Scottish Council for Postgraduate Medical and Dental Education
SCPMDE
c/o NHS Education for Scotland
91 Haymarket Terr., Edinburgh, EH12 5HE, UK
Tel: 0131 3138000
Fax: 0131 3138001
Email: enquiries@nes.scot.nhs.uk
Website: http://www.nes.scot.nhs.uk
Contact: Malcolm Wright, Chief Exec.
Description: Directs, supports and commissions postgraduate studies in medical and dental education for approximately 4,700 doctors, dentists and clinical psychologists.

03828
Scottish Council for Research in Education
SCRE
University of Glasgow, St. Andrew's Bldg., 11 Eldon St., Glasgow, G3 6NH, UK
Tel: 0141 3303497
Email: h.eng@educ.gla.ac.uk
Website: http://www.gla.ac.uk/faculties/education/scre
Members: 26
Staff: 33
Contact: Joan Ballantine, Admin.
Description: Promotes the use and understanding of educational research throughout Scotland. Works to make teachers, administrators, researchers, parents, all these concerned with education aware of research ideas, findings and applications through a range of publications and meetings and through its information services.

03829
Scottish Council for Single Homeless
SCSH
Wellgate House, 200 Cowgate, Edinburgh, EH1 1NQ, UK
Tel: 0131 2264382
Fax: 0131 2254382
Email: admin@scsh.org.uk
Website: http://www.scsh.co.uk
Contact: Robert Aldridge, Chief Exec.
Fee: £150
Membership Type: representative
Fee: £25
Membership Type: individual
Description: Individuals and organizations. Promotes increased public awareness of the causes, nature and extent of single homelessness. Seeks to identify methods of preventing and alleviating homelessness. Gathers and disseminates information on single homelessness; advises policy makers and social workers on homelessness and related issues; serves as a forum for the public discussion of homelessness and its causes. Conducts research; collaborates in the implementation of policies designed to prevent and alleviate homelessness.
Publication: Newsletter
Publication title: In House

03830

Scottish Council for Voluntary Organisations SCVO

Mansfield Traquair Ctre., 15 Mansfield Pl., Edinburgh, EH3 6BB, UK
Tel: 0131 5563882
Fax: 0131 5560279
Email: enquiries@scvo.org.uk
Website: http://www.scvo.org.uk
Members: 1200
Staff: 140
Contact: Martin Sime, Chief Exec.
Fee: £125-500
Membership Type: full
Fee: £50-600
Membership Type: associate (based on organisation's annual income)
Description: Includes Scotland's major voluntary sector bodies. Works as a national coordinating body for the voluntary sector in Scotland. Represents and supports the interests of the voluntary sector at national level and provides a range of services to locally based groups.
Library Type: reference
Publication: Newspaper
Publication title: Third Force News. Advertisements.

03831

Scottish Council of Independent Schools SCIS

21 Melville St., Edinburgh, EH3 7PE, UK
Tel: 0131 2202106
Fax: 0131 2258594
Email: info@scis.org.uk
Website: http://www.scis.org.uk
Members: 75
Staff: 6
Contact: Anton Colella, Chm.
Description: Promotes and supports the contributions made by independent schools to education in Scotland.

03832

Scottish Council on Deafness SCoD

Central Chambers, Ste. 62, 93 Hope St., Glasgow, G2 6LD, UK
Tel: 0141 2482474
Fax: 0141 2482479
Email: admin@scod.org.uk
Website: http://www.scod.org.uk
Contact: Lilian Lawson, Dir.
Fee: £20
Membership Type: local, small deaf group
Fee: £30
Membership Type: organization (with annual gross income of less than 10000)
Description: Committed to addressing the needs of deaf, deafened, deafblind and hard of hearing individuals, their families and caregivers, and the professionals working with them. Works to improve the quality of life for all deaf people in Scotland.

03833

Scottish Council on Human Bioethics SCHB

15 Morningside Rd., Edinburgh, EH10 4DP, UK
Tel: 0131 4476394
Fax: 0131 4463348
Email: mail@schb.org.uk
Website: http://www.schb.org.uk
Contact: Anne Williams, Chair
Description: Doctors, lawyers, psychologists, ethicists and other professionals from disciplines associated with medical ethics whose principles are set out in the United Nations Universal Declaration of Human Rights. Works to collect and evaluate evidence and information relating to ethical issues to inform public debate; assist legislators, fellow professionals and other interested parties with ethical analysis and comment on issues; respond appropriately to the media.

03834

Scottish Crop Research Institute SCRI

Invergowrie, Dundee, DD2 5DA, UK
Tel: 01382 562731
Fax: 01382 562426
Email: info@scri.ac.uk
Website: http://www.scri.ac.uk
Contact: Peter Gregory, Dir./Chief Exec.
Description: Provides a link between the Scottish Crop Research Institute and farmers, processors and other interested bodies.
Publication: Annual Reports

03835

Scottish Daily Newspaper Society

21 Lansdowne Crescent, Edinburgh, EH12 5EH, UK
Tel: 0131 5351064
Email: info@sdns.org.uk
Members: 7
Staff: 1
Contact: J.B. Raeburn, Dir.
Description: Promotes and represents the interests of the publishers of Scottish daily and Sunday newspapers.

03836

Scottish Dance Teacher's Alliance SDTA

101 Park Rd., Glasgow, G4 9JE, UK
Tel: 0141 3398944
Fax: 0141 3574994
Email: info@thesdta.com
Website: http://www.thesdta.com/cgi-bin/index.pl
Members: 1600
Staff: 2
Contact: Andrew Cowan, Pres.
Description: Professional dance teachers, worldwide, who have passed an entrance examination. Seeks to: promote and encourage Scottish dance in all forms, particularly ballroom, ballet, Highland, theatre, rock 'n' roll, disco, and baton twirling; ensure that members are familiar with currently accepted techniques and principles; provide members with counsel and advice regarding the profession.

03837

Scottish Decorators Federation SDF

Castlecraig Business Park, Players Rd., Stirling, FK7 7SH, UK
Tel: 01786 448838
Fax: 01786 450541
Email: info@scottishdecorators.co.uk
Website: http://www.scottishdecorators.co.uk
Members: 250
Contact: James G. Hayes, Hon. Pres.
Description: Serves all types of firms involved in the decorating industry in Scotland. Offers a low cost Guarantee of Work Scheme under which all domestic work (within generous financial limits) is guaranteed to be undertaken to a satisfactory standard.
Publication: Newsletter

03838

Scottish Ecological Design Association SEDA

35/1 Granton Crescent, Edinburgh, EH5 1BN, UK
Email: info@seda.uk.net
Website: http://www.seda.uk.net
Members: 250
Staff: 1
Contact: Robin Baker, Chm.
Fee: £30
Membership Type: individual
Fee: £120
Membership Type: corporate large
Description: Open to all involved or interested in the design of the environment. Seeks to promote ecologically responsible design of products, environments and communities; awareness of ecological design and choice; interdisciplinary contacts; ecological principles in education and the training of designers; research and evaluation of materials, products and services.
Library Subject: ecological design
Library Type: reference
Publication: Magazine
Publication title: SEDA Magazine. Advertisements.

03839

Scottish Education and Action for Development SEAD

20 Graham St., Edinburgh, EH6 5QR, UK
Tel: 0131 5555550
Email: info@sead.org.uk
Website: http://www.sead.org.uk/index.php
Staff: 9
Fee: £15
Membership Type: individual
Fee: £6
Membership Type: unwaged
Description: Educates the people about pressing social and environmental issues, building solidarity between communities facing similar issues in Scotland and in developing countries. Works for peace and environmental and social justice.
Publication title: Living in the Real World: The International Role for Scotland's Parliament

03840
Scottish Engineering
105 W George St., Glasgow, G2 1QL, UK
Tel: 0141 2213181
Fax: 0141 2041202
Email: consult@scottishengineering.org.uk
Website: http://www.scottishengineering.org.uk
Members: 400
Staff: 18
Contact: Peter T. Hughes, Chief Exec.
Fee: £435-6790
Membership Type: basic (based on number of employees)
Description: Engineering employers - traditional heavy mechanical to micro electronics. Largest manufacturing employers' organization in Scotland. Strong representational role in dealings with central Government, European Commission, Scottish Office and Scottish Enterprise. Comprehensive employee relation's service, employment law and industrial tribunal management, health and safety and training including supervisor development courses. Quarterly Review of Scottish Engineering industry undertaken.
Publication title: Fortnightly Briefings

03841
Scottish Enterprise Energy Team
27 Albyn Pl., Aberdeen, AB10 1DB, UK
Tel: 01224 252000
Fax: 01224 213417
Email: energy.info@scotent.co.uk
Website: http://www.scottish-enterprise.com
Contact: Jim Davis, Mgr.
Description: Aims to improve competitiveness and diversification of companies in the oil and gas industry in Scotland. Works with small to medium sized enterprises in Scotland to enable them to respond positively to changes in markets and technology, thereby enabling them to compete internationally.
Formerly: Formerly, Scottish Enterprise Energy Group

03842
Scottish Esperanto Association
47 Airbles Crescent, Motherwell, ML1 3AP, UK
Tel: 01698 263199
Website: http://www.skotlando.org
Members: 100
Description: Promotes the international language Esperanto in Scotland. Aims to increase the language fluency of its members and encourage the use of Esperanto internationally.
Publication: Magazine
Publication title: Esperanto En Skotlando. Advertisements.

03843
Scottish Federation of Housing Associations
SFHA
Pegasus House, 375 W George St., Glasgow, G2 4LW, UK
Tel: 0141 3328113
Fax: 0141 3329684
Email: sfha@sfha.co.uk
Website: http://www.sfha.co.uk
Members: 400
Staff: 45
Contact: Mary Taylor, Chief Exec.
Description: Represents housing associations and cooperatives in negotiations on housing policy with government and other bodies, as well as campaigning on their behalf.
Publication: Magazine
Publication title: Federation Focus. Advertisements.

03844
Scottish Federation of Meat Traders Association
SFMTA
8-10 Needless Rd., Perth, PH2 0JW, UK
Tel: 01738 637472
Fax: 01738 441059
Email: enquiries@sfmta.co.uk
Website: http://www.sfmta.co.uk
Description: Meat trader associations in Scotland. Aims to promote best meat products and meat trading industry.
Publication: Newsletter
Publication title: Federation News

03845
Scottish Fishermen's Federation
SFF
24 Rubislaw Terr., Aberdeen, AB10 1XE, UK
Tel: 01224 646944
Fax: 01224 647058
Email: sff@sff.co.uk
Website: http://www.sff.co.uk
Members: 8
Staff: 6
Contact: Bertie Armstrong, Chief Exec.
Description: Associations of fishing vessel owners/share fishermen. Aims to promote and protect the interests of fishing vessel owners/share fishermen engaged in the Scottish fishing industry, through contact with government, parliament, the EU and the media.
Publication: Newsletter
Publication title: News

03846
Scottish Food and Drink Federation
SFDF
4a Torphichen St., Edinburgh, EH3 8JQ, UK
Tel: 0131 2299415
Fax: 0131 2299407
Email: generalenquiries@fdf.org.uk
Website: http://www.sfdf.org.uk/sfdf/sfdf_home.aspx
Staff: 2
Contact: Flora Mclean, Dir.
Fee: £240
Membership Type: full
Fee: £25.08
Membership Type: associate (based on sector turnover)
Description: Works to promote the interests of the food and drink manufacturing industry in Scotland, including issues related to legislation, economics, social or political.
Publication: Bulletin
Publication title: Update

03847
Scottish Further and Higher Education Funding Council
SFC
Donaldson House, 97 Haymarket Terr., Edinburgh, EH12 5HD, UK
Tel: 0131 3136500
Fax: 0131 3136501
Email: info@sfc.ac.uk
Website: http://www.sfc.ac.uk
Contact: John McClelland, Chm.
Description: Promotes and supports developments and innovations to benefit the Scottish higher education system.
Publication: Newsletter
Publication title: Highlight

03848
Scottish Grocers' Federation
SGF
222/224 Queensferry Rd., Edinburgh, EH4 2BN, UK
Tel: 0131 3433300
Fax: 0131 3436147
Email: info@scotgrocersfed.co.uk
Website: http://scottishshop.org.uk
Members: 298
Staff: 52
Contact: John Drummond, Chief Exec.
Description: Represents the interests of independent retail stores throughout Scotland; provides services such as training, buying, employment law, etc.

03849
Scottish History Society
SHS
University of St. Andrews, School of History, St. Andrews, KY16 9AL, UK
Email: katie.stevenson@st-andrews.ac.uk
Website: http://www.scottishhistorysociety.org
Members: 700
Contact: Ted Cowan, Pres.
Fee: £20
Membership Type: single
Fee: £25
Membership Type: joint
Description: Individuals (505) and libraries (195) interested in Scottish history. Seeks to print previously unpublished documents illustrative of the history of Scotland.

03850
Scottish Huntington's Association
SHA
St. James Business Ctre., Ste. 135, Linwood Rd., Paisley, PA3 3AT, UK
Tel: 0141 8480308
Fax: 0141 8876199
Email: sha-admin@hdscotland.org
Website: http://www.huntington-assoc.com
Staff: 35
Description: Promotes lay and professional education, individual and family support, clinical and biomedical research, and ethical and legal considerations related to Huntington's Disease. Cooperates with other voluntary health agencies and health organizations.
Publication: Booklet
Publication title: Living with Huntington's Disease: A guide to the early stages

03851
Scottish Inland Waterways Association
SIWA
c/o Andy Carnduff, Sec.
29 Hawkcraig Rd., Aberdour, Fife, KY3 0XB, UK
Tel: 01506 417685
Email: secretary@siwa.org.uk
Website: http://www.siwa.org.uk
Members: 25
Contact: Ann Street, Chair
Fee: £5
Membership Type: individual
Fee: £25
Membership Type: corporate
Description: Coordinates the Canal Societies in Scotland. Ensures the canals in Scotland are maintained in good order.

03852
Scottish Joint Industry Board for the Electrical Contracting Industry
SJIB
The Walled Garden, Bush Estate, Midlothian, EH26 0SB, UK
Tel: 0131 4459216
Fax: 0131 4455548
Email: employment.affairs@sjib.org.uk
Website: http://www.sjib.org.uk
Members: 550
Staff: 30
Contact: Fiona Harper, Sec.
Description: Membership is divided into two classes - employer and employee. Each employer and employee must be engaged in the electrical contracting industry and accepts to observe and to comply with decisions, regulations, agreements and the national working rules made by the national board. Provides a base for stable industrial relations to regulate and control employment and productive capacity within the industry and the level of skill and proficiency, safety, wages and welfare of persons concerned in the industry.
Library Subject: employment legislation
Library Type: not open to the public

03853
Scottish Language Dictionaries
SLD
27 George Sq., Edinburgh, EH8 9LD, UK
Tel: 0131 6504149
Fax: 0131 6504149
Email: mail@scotsdictionaries.org.uk
Website: http://www.scotsdictionaries.org.uk
Members: 130
Staff: 8
Contact: Christine Robinson, Dir.
Fee: £20
Membership Type: single
Fee: £30
Membership Type: joint
Description: Promotes research and publication of modern and historical Scots. Conducts outreach programs and educates people of all ages and backgrounds of cultural contribution of Scots to Scotland.
Library Type: by appointment only

03854
Scottish Law Agents Society
SLAS
166 Buchanan St., Glasgow, G1 2LW, UK
Tel: 0141 3524522
Fax: 0141 3533819
Email: secretary@slas.co.uk
Website: http://www.slas.co.uk
Members: 1800
Staff: 2
Contact: Michael Sheridan, Sec.
Fee: £70
Membership Type: solicitor
Fee: £35
Membership Type: retired, trainee, newly qualified
Description: Represents the interests of solicitors in Scotland.
Publication: Book
Publication title: Memorandum

03855
Scottish Licensed Trade Association
SLTA
10 Walker St., Edinburgh, EH13 7LA, UK
Tel: 0131 2255169
Fax: 0131 2204057
Email: theslta@aol.com
Website: http://www.slta.info/benefits.html
Members: 4500
Staff: 5
Contact: Colin A. Wilkinson, Sec.
Fee: £167.49
Membership Type: full (1 outlet)
Fee: £144
Membership Type: full (2-5 outlet)
Description: Licensees of hotels, public houses, off-sale. A federation of regional and local associations throughout Scotland. It is the recognized body for the Licensed Trade in Scotland and is consulted by government departments, national boards, press, radio and television, and other authorities when the interests of the trade are under consideration.
Publication: Newsletter
Publication title: The Scottish Licensee

03856
Scottish Local Authority Network of Physical Education
SLANOPE
Fife Council Education Service, Woodend Rd., Cardenden, Fife, KY5 0NE, UK
Tel: 01592 583373
Fax: 01592 583175
Email: david.maiden@fife.gov.uk
Members: 90
Contact: David Maiden, Service Mgr.
Fee: £50
Membership Type: local authority corporate
Description: Ensures that physical education makes its full contribution to formal and informal education and the health and well-being of the community. Promotes the continuing development and advancement of the teaching profession in the field of physical education.
Formerly: Formerly, Scottish Association Advisers of Physical Education

03857
Scottish Master Wrights and Builders Association
SMWBA
Blairtummock Lodge, Campsie Glen, Glasgow, G66 7AR, UK
Tel: 01360 770583
Fax: 01360 770583
Website: http://www.smwba.org.uk
Members: 49
Staff: 1
Contact: David C. Milliken, Sec.-Treas.
Description: Joiners and builders. Helps members and promotes the building industry.

03858
Scottish Microbiology Association
SMA
c/o Dr. Martin Connor, Membership Sec.
Dumfries and Galloway Royal Infirmary, Dept. of Microbiology, Bankhead Rd., Dumfries, UK
Email: martinconnor@nhs.net
Website: http://scottish-micro-assoc.org.uk
Contact: John Winning, Pres.
Fee: £10
Membership Type: general
Fee: £5
Membership Type: associate
Description: Represents the interests of professionals working in the field of medical microbiology. Promotes clinical and scientific interest in medical microbiology in Scotland.
Publication: Newsletter
Publication title: SMA Newsletter

03859
Scottish Microbiology Society
SMS
Section of Infection and Immunity, Level 9, University of Glasgow Dental School and Hospital, 378 Sauchiehall St., Glasgow, G2 3JZ, UK
Tel: 0141 2119752
Fax: 0141 2111593
Email: g.ramage@dental.gla.ac.uk
Website: http://www.scottish-microbiology.org.uk
Contact: Gordon Ramage, Sec.
Fee: £10
Membership Type: full
Fee: £5
Membership Type: student
Description: Provides a scientific and social forum for exchange of ideas and knowledge among microbiologists in Scotland.

03860

Scottish Motor Neurone Disease Association SMNDA

76 Firhill Rd., Glasgow, G20 7BA, UK
Tel: 0141 9451077
Fax: 0141 9452578
Email: info@mndscotland.org.uk
Website: http://www.mndscotland.org.uk
Members: 500
Staff: 8
Contact: Craig Stockton, Chief Exec.
Fee: £8
Membership Type: regular
Fee: £40
Membership Type: life
Description: Promotes interest in Motor Neurone Disease (MND) research among medical and scientific communities and the public in Scotland. Offers care and support services to MND patients in Scotland and their families. Offers an information center and equipment loan center; organizes study days for health professionals.
Library Subject: motor neurone disease, palliative care, bereavement, carers
Library Type: lending
Publication: Newsletter
Publication title: Aware. Advertisements.
Meetings/Conventions: annual conference

03861

Scottish Motor Trade Association SMTA

Palmerston House, 10 The Loan, S Queensferry, Edinburgh, EH30 9NS, UK
Tel: 0131 3315510
Fax: 0131 3314296
Email: info@smta.co.uk
Website: http://www.smta.co.uk
Members: 950
Staff: 11
Contact: Douglas Robertson, Chief Exec.
Description: Seeks to encourage, promote and protect the interests of its members.

03862

Scottish Museums Council SMC

Museums Galleries Scotland, 1 Papermill Wynd, McDonald Rd., Edinburgh, EH7 4QL, UK
Tel: 0131 5504100
Email: inform@museumsgalleriesscotland.org.uk
Website: http://www.museumsgalleriesscotland.org.uk
Members: 350
Staff: 25
Contact: Joanne Orr, CEO
Description: Museums or governing bodies of museums throughout Scotland: includes local authorities, universities and many independent charitable trusts. Aims to improve the quality of museum and gallery provision in Scotland. Represents the interests of museums and provides a wide range of services to its members.
Publication: Newsletter
Publication title: Museums and Galleries Quarterly

03863

Scottish National Council of YMCA's

11 Rutland St., Edinburgh, EH1 2DQ, UK
Tel: 0131 2281464
Fax: 0131 2285462
Email: info@ymcascotland.org
Website: http://www.ymcascotland.org
Description: Promotes the spiritual and physical development of the youth. Cooperates with the International YMCA network to attain organizational goals. Sponsors programs in areas covered including refugee assistance, housing and education. Provides facilities for the activity of members.

03864

Scottish National Party SNP

Gordon Lamb House, 3 Jackson's Entry, Edinburgh, EH8 8PJ, UK
Tel: 0131 5258900
Email: snp.hq@snp.org
Website: http://www.snp.org
Staff: 13
Contact: Nicola Sturgeon, Leader
Description: National political party. Seeks the independence of Scotland within the European Union.

03865

Scottish Natural Heritage SNH

Great Glen House, Leachkin Rd., Inverness, IV3 8NW, UK
Tel: 01463 725000
Fax: 01463 725067
Email: enquiries@snh.gov.uk
Website: http://www.snh.gov.uk
Staff: 798
Contact: Calum Macfarlane, Press/PR Mgr.
Description: Promotes wildlife conservation and wise land use in Scotland. Selects, establishes, and manages wildlife and marine reserves; designates sites of special scientific interest; supports and conducts conservation research. Conducts educational programs; seeks to increase public awareness of the dangers posed to wildlife by loss of habitat.
Library Subject: Climate, Earth Sciences, Ecology, Energy, Landscape, Natural History, Planning Issues, Protected Areas, Recreation and Access, Scottish Natural Heritage Technical Reports, Survey and Monitoring Techniques, Wildlife Conservation
Library Type: open to the public
Publication: Journal
Publication title: Earth Heritage Magazine

03866

Scottish Newspaper Publishers Association SNPA

108 Holyrood Rd., Edinburgh, EH8 8AS, UK
Tel: 0131 6208369
Fax: 0131 6208376
Email: info@snpa.org.uk
Website: http://www.snpa.org.uk
Members: 18
Staff: 7
Contact: Michael Johnston, Pres.
Description: Represents publishers of weekly, bi-weekly and free distribution newspapers. Concerned with marketing, relations with the Scottish Executive and UK government, representational work including self regulation of the press, employment relations and training.

03867

Scottish Official Board of Highland Dancing SOBHD

Heritage House, 32 Grange Loan, Edinburgh, EH9 2NR, UK
Tel: 0131 6683965
Fax: 0131 6620404
Email: admin@sobhd.net
Website: http://www.sobhd.net
Members: 30
Staff: 1
Contact: Helen Ford, Dir. of Admin.
Description: Teaching associations, independent members, competition organizer members, associations with an interest, either professional or otherwise, in highland dancing. Promotes fair play in both competition and judging, standardize highland dancing throughout the world and, as the world governing body, co-ordinates highland dancing on an international level.
Publication title: Highland Dancing

03868

Scottish Ornithologists' Club SOC

Waterston House, Aberlady, East Lothian, EH32 0PY, UK
Tel: 01875 871330
Fax: 01875 871035
Email: mail@the-soc.org.uk
Website: http://www.the-soc.org.uk
Members: 2400
Staff: 5
Contact: Wendy Hicks, Office Mgr.
Fee: £28
Membership Type: adult
Fee: £39
Membership Type: family
Description: Aims to document and study birds in Scotland. Organizes field meetings and winter programmes. Supports the Local Recorders' Network and Scottish Birds Records Committee.
Formerly: Formerly, Scottish Ornithologists' Club
Publication: Magazine
Publication title: Scottish Bird News

03869

Scottish Out of School Care Network SOSCN

Level 2, 100 Wellington St., Glasgow, G2 6DH, UK
Tel: 0141 5641284
Fax: 0141 5641286
Email: info@soscn.org
Website: http://www.soscn.org
Members: 400
Staff: 13
Contact: Irene Audain, Chief Exec.
Fee: £125
Membership Type: statutory organization
Fee: £20-50
Membership Type: other organization (based on income)
Description: Organizations and agencies engaged in out-of-school child care. Promotes increased availability of affordable, quality child care. Establishes partnerships

among members and between members and other organizations pursuing similar goals. Works to increase awareness of child care issues. Conducts research; makes available information about children's services; compiles statistics.
Publication: Newsletter
Publication title: Connections. Advertisements.

03870
Scottish Parent Teacher Council
SPTC
53 George St., Edinburgh, EH2 2HT, UK
Tel: 0131 2264378
Fax: 0131 2264378
Email: sptc@sptc.info
Website: http://www.sptc.info
Members: 1200
Staff: 3
Contact: Lynda Grant, Admin.
Fee: £65-98
Membership Type: ordinary (based on school's number of pupils)
Fee: £39
Membership Type: associate (without insurance)
Description: Parent and teacher groups. Promotes quality primary and secondary education. Facilitates communication and cooperation among members.
Publication: Newsletter
Publication title: Backchat

03871
Scottish Photographic Federation
SPF
34 Braemer Crescent, Carluke, ML8 4BH, UK
Tel: 01555 750737
Email: libby.neilsmith@btinternet.com
Website: http://www.scottish-photographic-federation.org
Contact: Neil Smith, Gen. Sec.
Description: Promotes photography in Scotland.

03872
Scottish Plant Owners Association
SPOA
302 St. Vincent St., Glasgow, G2 5RZ, UK
Tel: 0141 2483434
Fax: 0141 2211226
Email: info@spoa.org.uk
Website: http://www.spoa.org.uk
Members: 255
Contact: Gordon Bow, Pres.
Fee: £193.88
Membership Type: general
Description: Companies involved in the hiring out of plant and machinery. Aims to protect and further the interests of plant owners on all matters affecting plant ownership and plant usage; advises and offers guidance on terms and conditions relating to the hiring and taking on hire of plant.
Publication: Handbook
Publication title: Handbook and Schedule of Rates. Advertisements.
Meetings/Conventions: monthly executive committee meeting

03873
Scottish Police Federation
SPF
5 Woodside Pl., Glasgow, G3 7QF, UK
Tel: 0141 3325234
Fax: 0141 3312436
Email: gensec@spf.org.uk
Website: http://www.spf.org.uk
Members: 16500
Contact: Calum Steele, Gen. Sec.
Description: Represents police in Scotland.

03874
Scottish Pre-School Play Association
SPPA
21-23 Granville St., Glasgow, G3 7EE, UK
Tel: 0141 2214148
Fax: 0141 2216043
Email: info@sppa.org.uk
Website: http://www.sppa.org.uk
Members: 1924
Staff: 56
Contact: Ian McLaughlan, Chief Exec.
Description: Playgroups, toddler groups under fives groups, and interested organisations. Serves the needs of approximately 1,500 member playgroups and toddler groups in Scotland through a network of area teams; training courses covering child development, the value of play, committee and group work are held throughout the country. Distance learning courses are available for fieldworkers and playworkers.
Publication: Magazine
Publication title: First Five. Advertisements.

03875
Scottish Qualifications Authority
SQA
The Optima Bldg., 58 Robertson St., Glasgow, G2 8DQ, UK
Tel: 0845 2791000
Fax: 0845 2135000
Email: customer@sqa.org.uk
Website: http://www.sqa.org.uk
Staff: 750
Contact: Janet Brown, Chief Exec.
Description: Responsible for developing, awarding, and accrediting most qualifications in Scotland.
Formerly: Formerly, Scottish Vocational Education Council
Publication: Newsletter
Publication title: Core Skills Bulletin

03876
Scottish Railway Preservation Society
SRPS
Bo'ness Sta., Union St., Bo'ness, West Lothian, EH51 9AQ, UK
Tel: 01506 822298
Email: enquiries.railways@srps.org.uk
Website: http://www.srps.org.uk
Members: 1250
Staff: 3
Contact: John Evans, Chm.
Fee: £17
Membership Type: ordinary
Fee: £11.5
Membership Type: retired
Description: Aims to preserve, restore, display, and interpret Scotland's railway heritage. Owns and operates the Bo'ness and Kinneil Railway, the Scottish Railway Exhibition, and SRPS Railtours.
Publication: Magazine
Publication title: Blastpipe

03877
Scottish Refugee Council
SRC
5 Cadogan Sq., 170 Blythswood Ct., Glasgow, G2 7PH, UK
Tel: 0141 2489799
Fax: 0141 2432499
Email: info@scottishrefugeecouncil.org.uk
Website: http://www.scottishrefugeecouncil.org.uk
Contact: Davis Fraser, Chm.
Description: Provides advice and assistance to individuals forced to leave their country and seek protection in Scotland; dedicated to refugee and asylum issues.
Publication: Newsletter
Publication title: Finding Asylum

03878
Scottish Retail Consortium
SRC
PO Box 13737, Gullane, EH31 2WX, UK
Tel: 0870 6093631
Fax: 0870 6093631
Email: ian.shearer@brc.org.uk
Website: http://www.brc.org.uk/srcdefaultnew.asp
Contact: Fiona Moriarty, Dir.
Fee: £3565
Membership Type: associate (plus VAT)
Fee: £3462
Membership Type: trade (minimum)
Description: Represents the interests of the sector to the Scottish Parliament on the main issues affecting Scottish retailers. Seeks to ensure that the Scottish Parliament and Executive creates the right trading environment to allow for continuing investment, job creation and innovation by retailers.

03879
Scottish Rock Garden Club
SRGC
145 Stonehill Ave., Birstall, Leicester, LE4 4JG, UK
Email: info@srgc.org.uk
Website: http://www.srgc.org.uk
Members: 4500
Contact: Graham Bunkall, Membership Sec.
Fee: £16
Membership Type: single (in UK)
Fee: £19
Membership Type: family (in UK)
Description: Promotes the cultivation of alpine and rock garden plants and the interest of its members.
Publication: Journal
Publication title: The Rock Garden

03880
Scottish Rural Property and Business Association
SRPBA
Stuart House, Eskmills Business Park, Musselburgh, EH21 7PB, UK
Tel: 0131 6535400
Fax: 0131 6535401

Email: info@srpba.com
Website: http://www.srpba.com
Members: 3000
Staff: 12
Contact: Luke M. Borwick, Chm.
Description: Represents the interests of those involved with rural properties and businesses concerned with the land. Embodies a pro-active approach to rural property, rural business and rural enterprise.
Formerly: Formerly, Scottish Landowners Federation
Publication: Magazine
Publication title: Land Business

03881

Scottish Screen

249 W George St., Glasgow, G2 4QE, UK
Tel: 0845 3007300
Email: info@scottishscreen.com
Website: http://www.scottishscreen.com
Members: 15
Staff: 45
Contact: Ken Hay, Chief Exec.
Description: Funded by H.M. Government via the Scottish office. Promotes moving image culture throughout Scotland. Receives funding from the regional film theatre network, film societies. Conducts media education activities and industry development. Encompasses the Scottish Film & Television Archive.
Formerly: Formerly, Scottish Film Council
Publication: Newsletter
Publication title: Rough Cuts

03882

Scottish Secondary Teachers' Association
SSTA

W End House, 14 W End Pl., Edinburgh, EH11 2ED, UK
Tel: 0131 3137300
Fax: 0131 3468057
Email: info@ssta.org.uk
Website: http://www.ssta.org.uk/page.php?10
Members: 8500
Staff: 8
Contact: Peter Wright, Pres.
Fee: £14.9
Membership Type: full-time permanent teacher
Fee: £7.45
Membership Type: part-time, job-share, temporary, supply teacher
Description: Scottish secondary teachers trade union. Represents and negotiates on behalf of Scottish secondary teachers in professional matters. Recognized by all employing local authorities and by the Scottish Executive Education Department.

03883

Scottish Society for Autism

Hilton House, Alloa Business Park, Whins Rd., Alloa, FK10 3SA, UK
Tel: 01259 720044
Fax: 01259 720051
Email: ssapressoffice@autism-in-scotland.org.uk
Website: http://www.autism-in-scotland.org.uk
Members: 700
Staff: 430
Contact: Paul Prescott, Chm.
Description: Families affected by autism, Asperger syndrome, or related communication disorders, as well as professionals and caregivers in the field. Works to deliver a comprehensive range of expertise in care, support, and education for people with autism, their families, and caregivers in Scotland. Operates supported housing and units, outreach, respite care centers, and a school; provides family support visits and other advisory and information services.

03884

Scottish Society for Conservation and Restoration
SSCR

22-26 George St., Edinburgh, EH2 2PQ, UK
Tel: 0131 2405038
Email: scotland@icon.org.uk
Website: http://www.icon.org.uk/index.php?option=com_content&task=view&id=62
Members: 400
Staff: 1
Contact: Linda Ramsay, Chair
Fee: £145
Membership Type: accredited
Fee: £83
Membership Type: ordinary
Description: Individuals or institutions concerned with the conservation and restoration of Scotland's historic, scientific and artistic material, including conservators, restorers, architects, curators, archaeologists, historians and students. Exists to promote the conservation and restoration of Scotland's historic, scientific and artistic material. Seeks to maintain and improve standards by providing a forum for all those concerned with these objectives.

03885

Scottish Society for Contamination Control
S2C2

272 High St., Glasgow, G4 0QT, UK
Tel: 0844 8007809
Fax: 0844 8007810
Email: admin@s2c2.co.uk
Website: http://www.s2c2.co.uk
Members: 1000
Fee: £17
Membership Type: individual
Fee: £70
Membership Type: corporate
Description: Individuals and corporations with an interest in cleanrooms. Seeks to improve the design, maintenance, and function of facilities to contain biological contaminants. Represents members before national and international standards committees; serves as a clearinghouse on cleanrooms and related technologies, products, and services. Conducts educational courses.
Publication: Newsletter
Publication title: The Monitor

03886

Scottish Society for Psychical Research
SSPR

5 Church Wynd, Kingskettle, Fife, KY15 7PS, UK
Tel: 01337 830387
Fax: 01337 830387
Website: http://www.sspr.org.uk
Contact: Archie Lawrie, VP
Fee: £15
Membership Type: concessionary
Fee: £11
Membership Type: student
Description: Promotes psychical research in Scotland.
Publication: Magazine
Publication title: Psi Report

03887

Scottish Society for the Prevention of Cruelty to Animals
Scottish SPCA

Kingseat Rd., Halbeath, Dunfermline, KY11 8RY, UK
Tel: 03000 999999
Email: enquiries@scottishspca.org
Website: http://www.scottishspca.org
Members: 10500
Staff: 250
Contact: Stuart Earley, Chief Exec.
Fee: £375
Membership Type: life
Fee: £40
Membership Type: joint
Description: Provides treatment and offers food and shelter to sick, injured and neglected animals. Operates team of inspectors for responding emergency calls and for rescuing animals from cruel and abusive situations. Raises awareness of animal welfare. Offers education programs in schools and to community. Supports legislation that will improve the conditions of all animals.
Publication: Magazine
Publication title: Scottish SPCA News

03888

Scottish Society of the History of Medicine
SSHM

13 Craiglea Dr., Edinburgh, EH10 5PB, UK
Tel: 0131 4472572
Email: nigel@malcolm-smith43.wanadoo.co.uk
Website: http://www.st-andrews.ac.uk/~sshm
Members: 200
Contact: Nigel Malcolm-Smith, Sec.
Fee: £10
Membership Type: regular
Description: Aims to further the general history of medicine with particular attention to Scottish medicine.
Publication: Proceedings
Publication title: Report of Proceedings

03889

Scottish SPCA

Kingseat Rd., Halbeath, Dunfermline, KY11 8RY, UK
Email: enquiries@scottishspca.org
Website: http://www.scottishspca.org
Fee: £3
Membership Type: special friend
Fee: £25
Membership Type: individual
Description: Promotes animal welfare in Scotland; rescues and treats injured, abandoned or cruelly-treated animals; works to influence government legislation to improve animal welfare; provides education program to schools.
Publication: Magazine
Publication title: Scottish SPCA News

03890
Scottish Spina Bifida Association
SSBA
The Dan Young Bldg., 6 Craighalbert Way, Cumbernauld, G68 0LS, UK
Tel: 01236 794500
Fax: 01236 736435
Email: mail@ssba.org.uk
Website: http://www.ssba.org.uk
Members: 3000
Staff: 6
Contact: Andrew Wynd, Chief Exec.
Description: Seeks to increase public awareness and understanding of individuals with Spina Bifida/Hydrocephalus and allied disorders. Aims to secure provision for their special needs and those of their families.
Publication: Magazine
Publication title: talk:BACK

03891
Scottish Storytelling Forum
The Scottish Storytelling Centre, 43-45 High St., Edinburgh, EH1 1SR, UK
Tel: 0131 5569579
Fax: 0131 5575224
Email: reception@scottishstorytellingcentre.com
Website: http://www.scottishstorytellingcentre.co.uk
Contact: Donald Smith, Dir.
Description: Promotes the telling and sharing of stories across all ages and all sectors of Scotland.

03892
Scottish Text Society
STS
University of Nottingham, School of English, Nottingham, NG7 2RD, UK
Tel: 0115 5922
Email: editorialsecretary@scottishtextsociety.org
Website: http://www.scottishtextsociety.org
Members: 154
Staff: 1
Contact: Nicola Royan, Editorial Sec.
Fee: £20
Membership Type: individual
Fee: £30
Membership Type: institutional
Description: Aims to further the study and teaching of Scottish literature, its language and history, in particular by publishing editions of original texts.
Publication title: Annual Volume

03893
Scottish Timber Trade Association
STTA
John Player Bldg., Office 14, Stirling Enterprise Park, Springbank Rd., Stirling, FK7 7RP, UK
Tel: 01786 451623
Fax: 01786 473112
Email: mail@stta.org.uk
Website: http://www.stta.org.uk
Members: 37
Contact: David J. Sulman, Sec.
Description: Timber importers, merchants, sawmillers, agents and brokers. Represents the interests of Scottish Members of the Timber Trade Federation. Performs an educational role by ensuring its members are updated on relevant timber and trade matters.

03894
Scottish Urban Archaeological Trust
SUAT
55 S Methven St., Perth, PH1 5NX, UK
Tel: 01738 622393
Fax: 01738 631626
Email: director@suat.co.uk
Website: http://www.suat.co.uk
Members: 20
Staff: 11
Contact: David Bowler, Dir.
Description: Archaeologists and other individuals with an interest in the urban heritage and architecture of Scotland. Promotes public awareness of urban archeology and the development of Scottish towns. Conducts research and educational programs.

03895
Scottish Welsh Pony and Cob Association
SWPCA
7a Hospitland Dr., Lanark, ML11 7EJ, UK
Tel: 01555 666274
Email: jackiemcknight12@tiscali.co.uk
Website: http://www.swpca.com/indexm.htm
Contact: Jackie McKnight, Sec.
Fee: £15
Membership Type: adult
Fee: £10
Membership Type: junior
Description: Records the breeding details of Welsh ponies and cobs. Seeks to improve the breed and promote its excellence.
Publication: Newsletter

03896
Scottish Wild Land Group
SWLG
36 Mansfield Crescent, Clarkston, Glasgow, G76 7EB, UK
Tel: 0141 6382210
Email: enquiries@swlg.org.uk
Website: http://www.swlg.org.uk
Members: 500
Contact: Grant Cornwallis, Membership Sec.
Fee: £10
Membership Type: individual
Fee: £15
Membership Type: family
Description: Individuals interested in the protection of Scottish flora and fauna and their habitats. Promotes preservation and restoration of Scottish wild lands. Coordinates activities of conservation, environmental protection, and sustainable development organizations; conducts educational programs to raise public awareness of conservation issues; lobbies for legislation and policies supporting conservation initiatives.
Publication: Magazine
Publication title: Wild Land News

03897
Scottish Wildlife Trust
SWT
Cramond House, 3 Kirk Cramond, Edinburgh, EH4 6HZ, UK
Tel: 0131 3127765
Fax: 0131 3128705
Email: enquiries@swt.org.uk
Website: http://www.swt.org.uk
Contact: Allan Bantick, Chm.
Fee: £30
Membership Type: individual
Fee: £42
Membership Type: joint
Description: Aims to conserve wildlife in Scotland. Offers wildlife friendly incentives to farmers and helps in the development of legislation regarding the protection of wildlife.
Publication: Booklet
Publication title: Reserve

03898
Scottish Women's Aid
132 Rose St., 2nd Fl., Edinburgh, EH2 3JD, UK
Tel: 0131 2266606
Fax: 0131 2262996
Email: contact@scottishwomensaid.org.uk
Website: http://www.scottishwomensaid.org.uk
Members: 39
Staff: 10
Description: Serves as the national office of 39 Local women's aid groups. Offers information, counseling and support services, and refuge to abused women and their children. Monitors legislation to ensure that abused women's rights and well-being are protected. Campaigns to effect changes in legislation and societal attitudes to domestic violence.
Publication: Newsletter
Meetings/Conventions: annual conference

03899
Scottish Women's Rural Institutes
SWRI
42 Heriot Row, Edinburgh, EH3 6ES, UK
Tel: 0131 2251724
Fax: 0131 2258129
Email: swri@swri.demon.co.uk
Website: http://www.swri.org.uk
Members: 25000
Staff: 9
Contact: Marion Davidson, Chm.
Description: Promotes the interests of women living in rural areas in Scotland. Offers educational and recreational activities to women residing in the country or interested in country living. Encourages home-grown food production, home industry, and craftsmanship. Addresses issues of family welfare and community matters. Works to preserve the traditions of rural Scotland. Promotes peaceful living and understanding.
Publication: Magazine
Publication title: Scottish Home and Country. Advertisements.

03900
Scottish Youth Hostels Association
SYHA
7 Glebe Crescent, Stirling, FK8 2JA, UK
Tel: 01786 891400
Fax: 01786 891333
Email: info@syha.org.uk
Website: http://www.syha.org.uk/home.aspx
Fee: £8
Membership Type: senior
Fee: £10
Membership Type: adult
Description: Seeks to educate people by promoting tourism to increase appreciation of nature and culture. Provides low-cost accommodations and programs

on outdoor education, recreation and touring. Facilitates networking among members. Conducts educational programs, leader courses, environmental walks and tree plantings.

03901

Scout Association
SA

Scout Information Centre, Gilwell Park, Bury Rd., Chingford, London, E4 7QW, UK
Tel: 0845 3001818
Fax: 020 84337103
Email: info.centre@scout.org.uk
Website: http://www.scoutbase.org.uk
Members: 28000000
Staff: 210
Contact: Carmen Attard, Admin.
Description: Organization for Scouts in the United Kingdom. Promotes scouting and its ideals among youth.
Publication: Magazine
Publication title: Scouting Magazine. Advertisements.

03902

Screen Advertising World Association
SAWA

Pearl and Dean, 3 Waterhouse Sq., 138-142 Holborn, London, EC1N 2NY, UK
Tel: 020 78821100
Fax: 020 78821111
Email: rob.cooksey@pearlanddean.com
Website: http://www.sawa.com
Members: 75
Staff: 1
Contact: Rob Cooksey, Finance Mgr.
Description: All cinema (screen) contractors. Aims to promote and develop cinema screen advertising on an international basis.

03903

Seabird Group
SG

British Antarctic Survey, High Cross, Madingley Rd., Cambridge, CB3 0ET, UK
Email: notc@bas.ac.uk
Website: http://www.seabirdgroup.org.uk
Members: 250
Contact: Norman Ratcliffe, Chm.
Fee: £20
Membership Type: ordinary
Fee: £35
Membership Type: institution
Description: Represents amateur and professional ornithologists interested in seabirds. Seeks to promote knowledge of seabird biology, conservation, and ecology. Disseminates information; organizes and coordinates research activities.
Publication: Journal
Publication title: Atlantic Seabird

03904

Security Systems and Alarms Inspection Board
SSAIB

The Smoke Houses, Cliffords Ft., North Shields, NE30 1JE, UK
Tel: 0191 2963242
Fax: 0191 2962667
Email: joan@ssaib.co.uk
Website: http://www.ssaib.org
Description: Promotes and encourages high standards of service and ethics in the security industry.

03905

Seed Crushers' and Oil Processors' Association
SCOPA

c/o Lynda Simmons, Exec. Sec.
PO Box 259, Beckenham, BR3 3YA, UK
Tel: 020 83985955
Fax: 020 82495401
Email: lynda.simmons@scopa.org.uk
Website: http://www.scopa.org.uk
Contact: Angela Bowden, Sec. Gen.
Description: Encourages unity and cooperation in vegetable oils, marine oils and oil seed processing. Promotes research on scientific, technical and industrial issues. Represents the interests of members.

03906

Selden Society

Faculty of Laws, Queen Mary and Westfield College, Mile End Rd., London, E1 4NS, UK
Tel: 020 78825136
Fax: 020 89818733
Email: selden-society@qmul.ac.uk
Website: http://www.selden-society.qmw.ac.uk
Members: 1700
Contact: Victor Tunkel, Sec.
Fee: £30
Membership Type: individual in UK
Fee: £40
Membership Type: institution in UK
Description: Promotes the history of English law.

03907

SELECT

The Walled Garden, Bush Estate, Midlothian, EH26 0SB, UK
Tel: 0131 4455577
Fax: 0131 4455548
Email: admin@select.org.uk
Website: http://www.select.org.uk
Members: 800
Staff: 30
Contact: D. Geddes, Pres.
Fee: £220
Membership Type: regular
Fee: £120
Membership Type: associate representative
Description: Members range from large multi-national contractors to one man businesses. Provides a comprehensive package of services to membership covering industrial relations, training, contractual and legal, technical and marketing. Keeping members up to date on all issues and therefore fully qualified in every respect to carry out work ranging from large site installations to an extra socket in a kitchen.
Formerly: Formerly, Electrical Contractors Association of Scotland
Publication: Magazine
Publication title: Cabletalk. Advertisements.

03908

Self Help Africa

2nd Fl. Westgate House, Dickens Ct., Hills Ln., Shrewsbury, SY1 1QU, UK
Tel: 01743 277170
Website: http://www.selfhelpafrica.org/selfhelp/Main/Home.asp
Members: 1500
Staff: 5
Contact: Steve Langdon, Dir.
Description: Works in poor rural villages in Africa. Aims to raise the standards of farming, nutrition, and primary education in less-developed countries.
Publication: Newsletter
Publication title: Harvest Helper

03909

Self Storage Association of the United Kingdom
SSAUK

Priestley House, The Gullet, Nantwich, CW5 5SZ, UK
Tel: 01270 623150
Fax: 01270 623471
Email: admin@ssauk.com
Website: http://www.ssauk.com
Members: 200
Description: Encourages members, of the Self Storage Industry, to operate their storage facilities to a recommended minimum standard. Encourages prospective self-storage operators to carry out a full research of the Industry before opening their facilities. Preserves high standards of conduct in its members and in the industry. Promotes the industry to the general public.
Library Subject: self storage
Library Type: not open to the public

03910

SENSE

101 Pentonville Rd., London, N1 9LG, UK
Tel: 0845 1270060
Fax: 0845 1270061
Email: info@sense.org.uk
Website: http://www.sense.org.uk
Members: 650
Staff: 2000
Contact: Coman Kenny, Contact
Fee: £15
Membership Type: individual
Description: Families, professionals and interested individuals. Provides services for deafblind people, their families, carers and the professionals with whom they work. Campaigns for legislative support for deafblind people.
Library Subject: deafblind issues, associated disabilities
Library Type: not open to the public
Formerly: Formerly, National Deafblind and Rubella Association
Publication: Magazine
Publication title: Talking Sense. Advertisements.
Meetings/Conventions: periodic meeting

Service Permanent du Niveau Moyen des Mers

see Permanent Service for Mean Sea Level

03911

Severn Valley Welsh Pony and Cob Association

Bronheulog, Manafon, Powys, Welshpool, SY21 8BW, UK
Tel: 01686 650285
Email: secretary@svwpca.com
Website: http://www.svwpca.com
Contact: R.M. Andrew, Sec.
Description: Records the breeding details of Welsh ponies and cobs. Seeks to improve the breed and promote its excellence.

03912

Sexual Advice Association SDA

Emblem House, Ste. 301, London Bridge Hospital, 27 Tooley St., London, SE1 2PR, UK
Tel: 0207 4867262
Email: info@sexualadviceassociation.co.uk
Website: http://www.sda.uk.net
Members: 1300
Staff: 6
Contact: Graham Jackson, Chm.
Fee: £15
Membership Type: individual or couple
Fee: £20
Membership Type: health professional/overseas individual or couple
Description: Raises awareness among the public and health professionals on impotence. Offers free advice and information via a telephone hotline. Maintains up to date information on the causes and treatments available for impotence.
Formerly: Formerly, Impotence Association

03913

Shakespeare Birthplace Trust SBT

The Shakespeare Ctre., Henley St., Stratford-upon-Avon, Warwickshire, CV37 6QW, UK
Tel: 01789 204016
Fax: 01789 262073
Email: info@shakespeare.org.uk
Website: http://www.shakespeare.org.uk
Staff: 220
Contact: Helen Robson, Contact
Fee: £25
Membership Type: individual
Fee: £40
Membership Type: joint, family
Description: Purposes are: to honor William Shakespeare (1564-1616); to maintain Shakespeare's birthplace and other properties associated with Shakespeare; to further knowledge of Shakespeare's life and works. Maintains library, museum, and records office. Offers special educational services to schools and colleges and other groups. Produces a range of publications on Shakespeare and Stratford-upon-Avon.
Publication title: Shakespeare Houses

03914

Sharing Information and Experience for Safer Operations SIESO

7, Hardbarrow Woods, High Bar Ln., Thakeham, Pulborough, RH20 3ES, UK
Tel: 01798 712992
Email: sieso.mem@googlemail.com
Website: http://www.sieso.org.uk
Members: 400
Contact: Chris Pilgrim, Membership Sec.
Fee: £25
Membership Type: full (individual)
Description: Aims to reduce accidents in industrial and commercial operations. Provides information through seminars, workshops and other events that allows members to share ideas for ensuring the safety of industrial and commercial practices.
Publication: Magazine
Publication title: Industrial Safety Management. Advertisements.

03915

Sheffield Chamber of Commerce and Industry SCCI

Albion House, Savile St., Sheffield, S4 7UD, UK
Tel: 0114 2018888
Email: info@scci.org.uk
Website: http://www.scci.org.uk
Members: 2200
Staff: 60
Contact: Nigel Tomlinson, Chief Exec.
Fee: £145-1495
Membership Type: company (based on number of employees)
Fee: £10000
Membership Type: patronage
Description: Represents members across Sheffield at local, regional and national level on matters concerning trade, commerce and industry and lobbying. Facilitates networking, forums and events to enable members to exchange ideas, information, views and business practice.

03916

Sheffield Conservation Volunteers SCV

PO Box 510, Sheffield, S4 8XY, UK
Email: d.j.robson@sheffield.ac.uk
Website: http://www.sheffieldconservation.org
Contact: Dave Robson, Membership Sec.
Description: Provides opportunities for people to work in a supportive, friendly and relaxed atmosphere, while being involved in a practical conservation project. Conducts tree planting, stonewalling, hedgelaying, pond renovation, path laying and coppicing.

03917

Shellfish Association of Great Britain SAGB

Fishmongers' Hall, London Bridge, London, EC4R 9EL, UK
Tel: 0207 2838305
Email: sagb@shellfish.org.uk
Website: http://www.shellfish.org.uk
Members: 360
Staff: 4
Contact: Tom Pickerell, Dir.
Fee: £75
Membership Type: associate
Fee: £200
Membership Type: trading
Description: Cultivators and processors in the Shellfish Industry. Represents trade association for the shellfish industry, liaises direct with Governments, Local Authorities, Members of Parliament, and other bodies in the fishing industry. A market-orientated trade association used by embassies and other commercial groups as the contact point for developing new shellfish markets.

03918

Shetland Aquaculture

Shetland Seafood Ctre., Stewart Bldg., Shetland, Lerwick, ZE1 0LL, UK
Tel: 01595 695579
Fax: 01595 694494
Email: info@shetlandaquaculture.com
Website: http://www.shetlandaquaculture.com
Members: 46
Staff: 3
Contact: David Sandison, Gen. Mgr.
Description: Salmon farmers. Liaises with local and central government agencies and the EC; arranges marketing and promotion, and training. Gives advice to members.
Formerly: Formerly, Shetland Salmon Farmers' Association

03919

Shingles Support Society SSS

41 N Rd., London, N7 9DP, UK
Tel: 0845 1232305
Email: info@hinglessupport.org.uk
Website: http://www.shinglessupport.org
Staff: 2
Contact: Marian Nicholson, Dir.
Description: Individuals suffering from post-herpetic neuralgia and their families. Offers advice on self-help for post-herpetic neuralgia which can follow shingles. Provides information for primary care doctors by a consultant neurologist regarding drug treatment with dosage information.
Library Type: open to the public
Publication: Booklet
Publication title: Herpes Simplex-A Guide

03920

Shipbuilders and Shiprepairers Association SSA

Marine House, Meadlake Pl., Thorpe Lea Rd., Egham, TW20 8BF, UK
Tel: 0191 5678965
Email: office@ssa.org.uk
Website: http://www.ssa.org.uk
Members: 55
Staff: 7
Contact: Ash Sinha, Dir.
Description: UK private sector shipbuilding and ship repair companies and marine specialists. Monitors developments in health and safety and environmental matters as they affect members' interests. Promotes business performance improvement, research and development and innovation both in shipyards and supply chain companies. Provides a focal point for collaboration on environmental issues and technical matters including developments in the International Maritime Organisation (IMO). Sponsors collaborative research projects for the industry.

03921
Shop and Display Equipment Association SDEA

24 Croydon Rd., Caterham, CR3 6YR, UK
Tel: 01883 348911
Fax: 01883 343435
Email: enquiries@sdea.co.uk
Website: http://www.shopdisplay.org
Members: 200
Staff: 5
Contact: Lawrence Cutler, Dir.
Description: Suppliers of retail store fittings and equipment in the United Kingdom. Promotes the use of display equipment by retailers in the United Kingdom.
Publication: Directory
Publication title: SDEA Directory of Shopfittings and Display. Advertisements.

03922
Showmen's Guild of Great Britain

151A King St., Drighlington, BD11 1EJ, UK
Tel: 0113 2853341
Fax: 0113 2853329
Email: denise@showmensguild.com
Website: http://www.showmensguild.com
Members: 4500
Staff: 3
Contact: Denise Ablett, Sec.
Description: Individuals over the age of 18 who own and operate or propose to own and operate fairground equipment. Aims to secure the combination and organisation of all travelling showmen who regularly attend and carry on business at fairs and showgrounds and to regulate the conduct of all members.

03923
Shropshire Chamber of Commerce and Enterprise

Trevithick House, Stafford Park 4, Shropshire, Telford, TF3 3BA, UK
Tel: 01952 208200
Fax: 01952 208208
Email: enquiries@shropshire-chamber.co.uk
Website: http://www.shropshire-chamber.co.uk
Members: 1365
Staff: 70
Contact: Anthony D. Randall, Pres.
Fee: £180
Membership Type: company (1-10 employees)
Fee: £360
Membership Type: company (11-100 employees)
Description: Represents members across Shropshire at local, regional and national level on matters concerning trade, commerce and industry and lobbying. Facilitates networking, forums and events to enable members to exchange ideas, information, views and business practice.

03924
Sight Savers International - England

Grosvenor Hall, Bolnore Rd., Haywards Heath, RH16 4BX, UK
Tel: 01444 446600
Fax: 01444 446688
Email: info@sightsavers.org
Website: http://www.sightsavers.org/default.html
Members: 30
Staff: 88
Contact: Caroline Harper, Chief Exec.
Description: Works to prevent and cure blindness and also to provide education and rehabilitation for blind people in economically developing countries. Concentrates on comprehensive eye services that link the sectors together. Cooperates with indigenous government agencies and local leadership to develop and implement vision care programs. Conducts leadership development and educational programs to make projects sustainable using local resources and expertise.
Library Subject: eye care, education, rehabilitation, development, voluntary sector
Library Type: by appointment only
Publication: Newsletter
Publication title: Sight Savers News

03925
Signature-Durham

Mersey House, Mandale Business Park, Block 4, Stockton Rd., Durham, DH1 3UZ, UK
Tel: 0191 3831155
Fax: 0191 3837914
Email: durham@signature.org.uk
Website: http://www.signature.org.uk
Members: 1000
Staff: 23
Contact: Jim Edwards, Chief Exec.
Description: Aims to improve communication between deaf and hearing people by the development of curricula and examinations in communication skills. Offers certification in British Sign Language, Lipspeaking. Communicating with Deafblind people and Deaf Awareness, and carries out the selection, training, monitoring and registration of examiners.
Formerly: Formerly, Council for the Advancement of Communication with Deaf People

03926
Silica and Moulding Sands Association SAMSA

Gillingham House, 38-44 Gillingham St., London, SW1V 1HU, UK
Tel: 020 79638000
Fax: 020 79638001
Email: brian.james@mineralproducts.org
Website: http://www.samsa.org.uk
Members: 10
Staff: 2
Contact: Brian James, Dir.
Description: Producers and processors of industrial silica sand and associated products. Concerned with the promotion of the silica sand industry and its relationship with government departments, local authorities and the public. Ensures the continuity of essential supplies of indigenous industrial silica sands in the interests of consumer industries.

03927
Silk Association of Great Britain SAGB

5 Portland Pl., London, W1N 3AA, UK
Tel: 0171 6367788
Fax: 0171 6367515
Email: sagb@dial.pipex.com
Website: http://www.silk.org.uk
Members: 40
Staff: 1
Description: Trade associations and individuals. Seeks to further the aims of the UK silk industry. Promotes the use of silk. Offers educational services.
Formerly: Formerly, Silk Group of Silk and Man-Made Fibre Users Association
Publication: Newsletter
Publication title: Serica

03928
Single Ply Roofing Association SPRA

Roofing House, 31 Worship St., London, EC2A 2DY, UK
Tel: 0115 9144445
Fax: 0115 9749827
Email: enquiries@spra.co.uk
Website: http://www.spra.co.uk
Members: 63
Staff: 1
Contact: Phil Jarratt, Chm.
Description: Manufacturers and contractors of single ply roofing membrane. Promotes the benefits of single ply roofing, and the development of technical guidelines and codes of practice for the application of single layer roofing membranes.
Publication title: Technical Information Sheets

03929
Sir Arthur Sullivan Society SASS

c/o Mr. Stephen H. Turnbull, Sec.
Captain's Rest, The Old Rectory, Talland Hill, Polperro, Looe, PL13 2RY, UK
Tel: 01503 272874
Website: http://www.sullivansociety.org.uk
Members: 450
Contact: Charles Mackerras, Pres.
Fee: £15
Membership Type: individual
Fee: £25
Membership Type: individual (overseas)
Description: Aims to advance the knowledge of the public in and promote the performance of the music of Arthur Sullivan (1842-1900).

03930
Skillshare International

126 New Walk, Leicester, LE1 7JA, UK
Tel: 0116 2541862
Fax: 0116 2542614
Email: info@skillshare.org
Website: http://www.skillshare.org
Contact: Raul Pardinaz-Solis, Contact
Description: Works for sustainable development in partnership with the people and communities of Africa and Asia. Shares skills, facilitates organizational effectiveness, and supports organizational growth.
Formerly: Absorbed, Action Health - England

03931
Skinners' Company

Skinners' Hall, 8, Dowgate Hill, London, EC4R 2SP, UK
Tel: 020 72365629
Fax: 020 72366590
Email: beadle@skinners.org.uk
Website: http://www.skinnershall.co.uk
Members: 1000
Description: Provides charitable funds and grants and maintains several educational establishments. Offers its livery hall for use in receptions and gatherings.

03932
Small Electrical Appliance Marketing Association
SEAMA

Airport House, Purley Way, Surrey, Croydon, CR0 0XZ, UK
Tel: 020 82534508
Fax: 020 82534510
Email: seama@admin.co.uk
Website: http://www.seama.org.uk
Members: 11
Description: Serves as the trade association for manufacturers and importers of small electrical appliances. Represents 80% of the UK market. Products include irons, kettles, toasters, food preparation, electrical personal care etc. Offers a forum for the principal suppliers to the UK small electrical appliance market. Provides trade figures to members, lobbies government on key issues, support of service dealer network and annual trade dinner.

03933
Social Care Association
SCA

350 W Barnes Ln., Motspur Park, New Malden, Surrey, KT3 6NB, UK
Tel: 020 89495837
Fax: 020 89494384
Email: sca@socialcaring.co.uk
Website: http://www.socialcareassociation.co.uk
Members: 4100
Staff: 7
Contact: Diana Campbell, Ed.
Fee: £36-175
Membership Type: individual (depends upon the income rate)
Fee: £201.25
Membership Type: associate corporate
Description: Represents individuals involved in social care at all levels.

03934
Social Democratic and Labour Party
SDLP

121 Ormeau Rd., Belfast, BT7 1SH, UK
Tel: 028 90247700
Fax: 028 90236699
Email: info@sdlp.ie
Website: http://www.sdlp.ie
Staff: 7
Contact: Mark Durkan, Leader
Fee: £20
Membership Type: waged
Fee: £10
Membership Type: unwaged, student, retired
Description: Political party in Northern Ireland. Advocates European unity; encourages cooperation between Catholics and Protestants in Ireland; promotes social justice and human rights.
Publication: Newsletter
Publication title: SDLP Newsheet

03935
Social History Society
SHS

Furness Coll., Lancaster Univ., Bailrigg, Lancaster, LA1 4YG, UK
Tel: 01524 592547
Fax: 01524 846102
Email: l.persson@lancaster.ac.uk
Website: http://www.socialhistory.org.uk
Members: 500
Staff: 1
Contact: Linda Persson, Admin. Sec.
Fee: £40
Membership Type: ordinary
Fee: £15
Membership Type: student
Description: Consists of people interested in social history. Aims to keep people abreast with current work and developments in social history.
Publication: Journal
Publication title: Cultural and Social History. Advertisements.

03936
Social Policy Association
SPA

The Lavenham Group, Arbons House, Lavenham, Sudbury, 47 Water St., Suffolk, CO10 9RN, UK
Email: t.m.ridge@bath.ac.uk
Website: http://www.social-policy.com
Members: 580
Contact: Tess Ridge, Honorary Sec.
Description: Social policy academics, researchers, policymakers, policy officers, research officers and others with an interest in social policy. Encourages teaching, research and scholarship in social policy and administration. Represents members in government and other relevant policy-making bodies.
Publication: Journal
Publication title: Journal of Social Policy

03937
Social Research Association
SRA

24-32 Stephenson Way, London, NW1 2HX, UK
Tel: 020 73882391
Email: admin@the-sra.org.uk
Website: http://www.the-sra.org.uk
Members: 1000
Staff: 1
Contact: Barbara Doig, Chair
Fee: £84
Membership Type: full worker
Fee: £52.5
Membership Type: part time worker
Description: Membership open to anyone interested or involved in social research. It includes social researchers in central and local government, higher education, market research and other organisations as well as freelance consultants. Aims to provide a forum for discussion and communication about social research activity in all areas of employment; to encourage the development of social research methodology, standards of work and codes of practice and to review and monitor the organisation and funding of social research.
Publication: Book
Publication title: Commissioning Social Research: A Good Practice Guide, 2nd Ed.
Meetings/Conventions: Improving the Quality of Social Research – annual conference

03938
Social, Emotional and Behavioural Difficulties Association
SEBDA

Rm. 211, Triangle Exchange Sq., Manchester, M4 3TR, UK
Tel: 0161 2402418
Fax: 0161 8385601
Email: admin@sebda.org
Website: http://www.sebda.org
Members: 1100
Contact: Barbara Knowles, Exec. Dir.
Fee: £51
Membership Type: individual
Fee: £25
Membership Type: full-time student/retired/unwaged
Description: All professions involved in work with children and young people with emotional and behavioural difficulties and those who are involved in training. Seeks to meet the needs of children and young people with emotional and/or behavioural difficulties, in a variety of settings including education.
Formerly: Formerly, Association of Workers for Children with Emotional and Behavioural Difficulties
Publication: Journal
Publication title: Emotional and Behavioral Difficulties

03939
Socialist International
SI

Maritime House, Old Town, Clapham, London, SW4 0JW, UK
Tel: 020 76274449
Fax: 020 77204448
Email: secretariat@socialistinternational.org
Website: http://www.socialistinternational.org
Description: Represents socialist, democratic socialist, and labor parties worldwide.
Publication: Newsletter
Publication title: Socialist Affairs

03940
Socialist International Women
SIW

Maritime House, Old Town, London, SW4 0JW, UK
Tel: 020 77200568
Fax: 020 77204448
Email: socintwomen@gn.apc.org
Website: http://www.socintwomen.org
Contact: Marlene Haas, Sec. Gen.
Description: Promotes action programs to combat sex discrimination. Works for human rights, development, and peace.
Formerly: Formerly, Women's Conference of the Socialist International

03941
Socialist Party
SPGB

PO Box 24697, London, E11 1YD, UK
Tel: 0208 9888777
Email: info@socialistparty.org.uk
Website: http://www.socialistparty.org.uk/main/Home
Members: 600
Description: Seeks to establish a world social system based on human need instead of private or state profit. Propagates non-market socialist ideas, including common ownership and democratic control of all productive resources and means of distribution.

Formerly: Absorbed, World Socialist Party - Ireland
Publication: Pamphlet
Publication title: Ecology and Socialism, Ireland - Past, Present, and Future

Sociedad Anglo-Chilena
see Anglo Chilean Society

Societas Linguistica Europaea (SLE)
see Linguistic Society of Europe

Societe de Biologie Experimentale
see Society for Experimental Biology

Societe des Indexateurs
see Society of Indexers

Societe des Textes Anglais Anciens
see Early English Text Society

Societe H.G. Wells
see H.G. Wells Society

Societe Internationale d'Etude du XVIIIe Siecle (SIEDS)
see International Society for Eighteenth-Century Studies

Societe Internationale de Chimiotherapie
see International Society of Chemotherapy

Societe Internationale de Mecanique des Sols et de la Geotechnique
see International Society for Soil Mechanics and Geotechnical Engineering

Societe Internationale de Neuropathologie
see International Society of Neuropathology

Societe Internationale des Radiographes et Techniciens de Radiologie
see International Society of Radiographers and Radiological Technologists

Societe Kipling
see Kipling Society

Societe Mondiale pour la Protection des Animaux
see World Society for the Protection of Animals - England

03942

Society for Advanced Legal Studies
SALS

17 Russell Sq., London, WC1B 5DR, UK
Tel: 020 78625865
Fax: 020 78625855
Email: sals@sas.ac.uk
Website: http://ials.sas.ac.uk/SALS/society.htm
Members: 1000
Staff: 2
Fee: £75
Membership Type: regular
Fee: £600
Membership Type: regular
Description: Scholars, practitioners and those involved in the administration of justice from the UK and around the world.
Publication: Journal
Publication title: Amicus Curiae

03943

Society for All Artists
SAA

PO Box 50, Newark, NG23 5GY, UK
Tel: 01949 844050
Fax: 01949 844051
Email: info@saa.co.uk
Website: http://www.saa.co.uk
Members: 41900
Contact: John Hope-Hawkins, Chm.
Fee: £25
Membership Type: standard
Fee: £40
Membership Type: silver
Description: Promotes the interests of artists. Provides art tuition, step-by-step demonstrations, and free insurance for paintings.
Publication: Newsletter
Publication title: Paint

03944

Society for Anaerobic Microbiology
SAM

c/o Dr. Mark Wilks, Vice Chm./Honorary Treas.
Microbiology, Pathology and Pharmacy Bldg., 3rd Fl., 80 Newark St., London, E1 2ES, UK
Tel: 020 32460295
Email: m.wilks@qmul.ac.uk
Website: http://www.clostridia.net/SAM
Contact: Sheila Patrick, Chair
Description: Represents individuals interested in anaerobic microbiology.

03945

Society for Anglo-Chinese Understanding
SACU

PO Box 179, Barrow-in-Furness, LA14 9BQ, UK
Tel: 01229 472010
Website: http://www.sacu.org
Members: 700
Fee: £18
Membership Type: individual
Fee: £13
Membership Type: unwaged individual
Description: Individuals in Great Britain interested in promoting friendship and understanding between Great Britain and the People's Republic of China. Disseminates information on all aspects of contemporary China. Organizes Chinese language classes, cultural events, workshops, lectures, and seminars. Offers resources to schools.
Publication: Magazine
Publication title: China Eye. Advertisements.

03946

Society for Applied Microbiology
SFAM

Bedford Heights, Brickhill Dr., Bedford, MK41 7PH, UK
Tel: 01234 326661
Fax: 01234 326678
Email: pfwheat@sfam.org.uk
Website: http://www.sfam.org.uk
Staff: 6
Contact: Philip Wheat, CEO
Fee: £50
Membership Type: full
Fee: £25
Membership Type: full (student)
Description: Individuals involved in the study of microbiology. Seeks to promote and advance the study of microbiology, particularly bacteriology, in its application to agriculture, industry, and the environment. Studies genetic manipulation, microbial spoilage of fermented beverages, plant cleaning, preservatives in the food, pharmaceutical, and environmental industries, safety cabinets, and water management.
Formerly: Formerly, Society for Applied Bacteriology
Publication: Journal
Publication title: Environmental Microbiology
Meetings/Conventions: Summer – annual conference – Exhibits.

03947

Society for Applied Philosophy
SAP

University of Aberdeen, RIISS, Humanity Manse, 19 College Bounds, Aberdeen, AB24 3UG, UK
Tel: 01224 272343
Email: admin@appliedphil.org
Website: http://www.appliedphil.org
Contact: Jon Cameron, Admin.
Fee: £25
Membership Type: regular
Fee: £12.5
Membership Type: postgraduate
Description: Promotes philosophical study and research through workshops, conferences, and lecture programs.
Publication: Journal
Publication title: Journal of Applied Philosophy

03948

Society for Cardiological Science and Technology SCST

Executive Business Support (EBS), City Wharf, Davidson Rd., Staffordshire, Lichfield, WS14 9DZ, UK
Tel: 0845 8386037
Fax: 0121 3552420
Email: admin@scst.org.uk
Website: http://www.scst.org.uk
Members: 1300
Contact: Chris Eggett, Contact
Fee: £40
Membership Type: student, pre-enrolled
Fee: £45
Membership Type: regular, enrolled
Description: Persons whom the Council of the Society consider to be qualified to practice cardiography, technical cardiology and allied subjects. Aims to advance for the public benefit the science and practice of cardiography, technical cardiology and allied subjects by the promotion of improved standards of education and training and of research work therein and by making the results of such study and research available to practitioners and the general public.
Publication: Journal
Publication title: Journal of the Society for Cardiological Science and Technology. Advertisements.
Meetings/Conventions: semiannual meeting – Exhibits.

03949

Society for Cardiothoracic Surgery in Great Britain and Ireland

35-43 Lincoln's Inn Fields, London, WC2A 3PE, UK
Tel: 020 78696893
Fax: 020 78696890
Email: sctsadmin@scts.org
Website: http://www.scts.org
Members: 622
Staff: 1
Contact: Isabelle Ferner, Admin.
Fee: £245
Membership Type: consultant
Fee: £25
Membership Type: associate
Description: Cardiac and thoracic surgeons. Aims to study cardiothoracic disease.
Publication: Newsletter
Publication title: The Bulletin

03950

Society for Co-operation in Russian and Soviet Studies SCRSS

320 Brixton Rd., London, SW9 6AB, UK
Tel: 020 72742282
Fax: 020 72743230
Email: ruslibrary@scrss.org.uk
Website: http://www.scrss.org.uk
Members: 900
Staff: 2
Fee: £25
Membership Type: individual (London, home county, Europe)
Fee: £30
Membership Type: joint (London, home county), overseas
Description: Promotes research, historical and visual records of the F.S.U. Aims to promote knowledge of the culture, language and history of Russia and the former Soviet Union.
Publication: Newsletter
Publication title: SCR Information Digest

03951

Society for Companion Animal Studies SCAS

The Blue Cross, Shilton Rd., Burford, OX18 4PF, UK
Tel: 01993 825597
Fax: 01993 823083
Email: info@scas.org.uk
Website: http://www.scas.org.uk
Members: 500
Fee: £50
Membership Type: charity
Fee: £25
Membership Type: regular/overseas
Description: Academics, physicians, psychologists, veterinarians, and laypersons in 13 countries interested in the study of the relationship between people and companion animals. Examines the effects animals have on the emotional and physical well being of individuals. Studies and disseminates results on the benefits companion animals bring to the clients of health and social care professionals. Conducts surveys and research projects.
Library Subject: human-animal interaction
Library Type: reference
Publication: Book
Publication title: Companion Animal Death

03952

Society for Computers and Law SCL

10 Hurle Crescent, Clifton, Bristol, BS8 2TA, UK
Tel: 01179 237393
Fax: 01179 239305
Email: ruth.baker@scl.org
Website: http://www.scl.org/site.aspx?i=ho0
Members: 1500
Contact: Ruth Baker, Gen. Mgr.
Fee: £95
Membership Type: professional
Fee: £45
Membership Type: academic
Description: Academics, computer scientists, lawyers, librarians, and individuals in local government (2,700) in 34 countries. Promotes the use of high technology in law for the benefit of lawyers as well as the public. Studies the use of computers in legal research and practice. Seeks to advance education in the implications of computers applied to the law. Promotes the development of legal computer systems and legal information retrieval systems, monitoring their performance on behalf of the public and the legal profession. Collaborates with other organizations holding similar objectives.
Publication: Magazine
Publication title: Computers and Law. Advertisements.

03953

Society for Computing and Technology in Anaesthesia SCATA

Associates of Anaesthesia, 21 Portland Pl., London, W1B 1PY, UK
Tel: 01823 332860
Email: treasurer@scata.org.uk
Website: http://www.scata.org.uk
Members: 340
Contact: Anthony Madden, Honorary Pres.
Fee: £10
Membership Type: trainee/retired
Fee: £20
Membership Type: regular
Description: Anesthesiology associations in Europe concerned with coding, standards for medical devices, and development of medical information technology.

03954

Society for Court Studies SCS

PO Box 57089, London, EC1P 1RF, UK
Email: admin@courtstudies.org
Website: http://www.courtstudies.org
Contact: Simon Thurley, Pres.
Fee: £10
Membership Type: student/individual below 25 years old (in UK)
Fee: £45
Membership Type: institutional (in UK)
Description: Aims to stimulate and co-ordinate the study of courts from 1400 to the present. Conducts seminars and conferences.
Publication: Journal
Publication title: The Court Historian

03955

Society for Earthquake and Civil Engineering Dynamics SECED

c/o Institution of Civil Engineers
1 Great George St., Westminster, London, SW1P 3AA, UK
Tel: 020 72227722
Fax: 020 72227500
Email: secretary@seced.org.uk
Website: http://www.seced.org.uk
Members: 320
Staff: 1
Contact: Ahmed Elghazouli, Chm.
Fee: £29
Membership Type: individual
Fee: £10
Membership Type: retired
Description: Works for the advancement of knowledge in the fields of earthquake engineering and civil engineering dynamics.
Publication: Book
Publication title: Mallet-Milne Lecture
Meetings/Conventions: Informal Discussion – monthly seminar

03956

Society for Editors and Proofreaders SFEP

Erico House, 93-99 Upper Richmond Rd., Putney, London, SW15 2TG, UK
Tel: 0208 7855617
Fax: 0208 7855618
Email: administration@sfep.org.uk
Website: http://www.sfep.org.uk
Members: 1400
Contact: Sarah Price, Chair
Fee: £90
Membership Type: associate
Fee: £100
Membership Type: ordinary

Description: Aims to promote high editorial standards and achieve recognition of the professional status of its members.
Formerly: Formerly, Society of Freelance Editors and Proofreaders
Publication: Magazine
Publication title: Editing Matters. Advertisements.

03957

Society for Education, Music and Psychology Research
SEMPRE

University of London, Institute of Education, 20 Bedford Way, London, WC1H 0AL, UK
Tel: 0208 3923701
Email: e.turay@sempre.org.uk
Website: http://www.sempre.org.uk
Members: 612
Staff: 13
Contact: Graham F. Welch, Chm.
Fee: £30
Membership Type: full individual, institution
Fee: £12
Membership Type: student, unwaged
Description: Music educators and academics working in music departments, psychology departments, education departments and schools, and music teachers. Promotes and disseminates research in the psychology of music and music education, and explores the relationships between these two areas and with other related disciplines and practices, such as music therapy.
Formerly: Formerly, Society for Research in Psychology of Music and Music Education
Publication: Journal
Publication title: Psychology of Music

03958

Society for Endocrinology

22 Apex Ct., Woodlands, Bradley Stoke, Bristol, BS32 4JT, UK
Tel: 01454 642200
Fax: 01454 642222
Website: http://www.endocrinology.org
Members: 1900
Staff: 23
Contact: J.C. Buckingham, Chm.
Fee: £89
Membership Type: full
Fee: £34
Membership Type: associate, scientist-in-training
Description: Clinicians and scientists working within the field of hormones and hormone related disease. Undertakes scientific/medical publishing, conferences (including commercial exhibitions) and training courses.
Publication: Journal
Publication title: Clinical Endocrinology

03959

Society for Environmental Exploration
SEE

50-52 Rivington St., London, EC2A 3QP, UK
Tel: 020 76132422
Fax: 020 76132992
Email: info@frontier.ac.uk
Website: http://www.frontier.ac.uk
Staff: 42
Contact: Eibleis Fanning, Managing Dir.
Description: Promotes conservation and environmental protection. Conducts operations in areas including forest, protected areas, and coastal zone management, wildlife conservation, and artisanal fisheries research.
Library Subject: tropical biodiversity, tropical habitats, biodiversity conservation, tropical forests, rainforests, savannas, coastal, marine, coral reefs,
Library Type: reference
Formerly: Also Known As, Frontier
Publication: Reports
Publication title: Environmental Research Report Series

03960

Society for Existential Analysis
SEA

c/o Ursula Berghaus, Membership Sec.
70 Selhurst Close, London, SW14 6AZ, UK
Email: info@existentialanalysis.co.uk
Website: http://www.existentialanalysis.co.uk
Members: 350
Contact: Paul McGinley, Chm.
Fee: £50
Membership Type: standard (domestic)
Fee: £60
Membership Type: international
Description: Provides a forum for the expression of views and the exchange of ideas amongst those interested in the analysis of existence, from philosophical and psychological perspectives.
Publication: Journal
Publication title: Existential Analysis. Advertisements.

03961

Society for Experimental Biology
SEB

Charles Darwin House, 12 Roger St., London, WC1N 2JU, UK
Tel: 0207 6852600
Fax: 0207 6852601
Email: c.trimmer@sebiology.org
Website: http://www.sebiology.org
Members: 1900
Staff: 5
Contact: Chris Trimmer, CEO
Fee: £56
Membership Type: full
Fee: £225
Membership Type: full
Description: Experimental biologists, postgraduate, students; universities; scientific institutions. Disseminates information on recent advances in experimental biological research. Promotes research and discussion.
Library Subject: biological sciences
Library Type: not open to the public
Publication: Journal
Publication title: Journal of Experimental Botany

03962

Society for Folk Life Studies

Beamish Open Air Museum, Beamish, Durham, DH9 0RG, UK
Email: seblittlewood@beamish.org.uk
Website: http://www.folklifestudies.org.uk
Members: 400
Contact: Seb Littlewood, Membership Sec.
Fee: £20
Membership Type: individual, institutional (within UK and Ireland)
Fee: £21
Membership Type: individual, institutional (outside UK and Ireland)
Description: Deals with the interdisciplinary study of regional cultures and traditions within the British Isles.
Publication: Journal
Publication title: Folk Life

03963

Society for French Studies
SFS

French Dept., 17 Woodland Rd., Bristol, BS8 1TE, UK
Email: s.r.harrow@bristol.ac.uk
Website: http://www.sfs.ac.uk
Contact: Susan Harrow, Pres.
Description: Promotes French studies.

03964

Society for General Microbiology
SGM

Marlborough House, Basingstoke Rd., Spencers Wood, Reading, RG7 1AG, UK
Tel: 0118 9881800
Fax: 0118 9885656
Email: admin@sgm.ac.uk
Website: http://www.sgm.ac.uk
Members: 5500
Staff: 32
Contact: Ron S. Fraser, Chief Exec.
Fee: £55
Membership Type: ordinary
Fee: £25
Membership Type: associate
Description: Individuals interested in microbiology; students. Works to advance the study of general microbiology. Research interests include bacteria, viruses, micro-fungi, protozoa, and microscopic algae. Holds the biennial Marjory Stephenson Lecture and the biennial Fred Griffith and Colworth Lectures in alternating years, and the Fleming Lecture each year.
Publication: Journal
Publication title: International Journal of Systematic and Evolutionary Microbiology. Advertisements.

03965

Society for Italic Handwriting
SIH

11 Meynell House, Browns Green, Handsworth Wood, Birmingham, B20 1BE, UK
Email: nickthenibs@endwood.freeserve.co.uk
Website: http://www.quilljar.btinternet.co.uk/sih.html
Members: 1000
Staff: 1
Contact: Nicholas Caulkin, Sec.
Description: Individuals in 30 countries. Promotes the practice of italic script. Offers handwriting consultation service for members; sponsors workshops and competitions.
Publication: Newsletter
Publication title: Writing Matters

03966

Society for Latin American Studies
SLAS

PO Box 1269, Oxford, OX4 2ZE, UK
Tel: 01865 778171
Fax: 01865 471776
Email: membershipservices@oxon.blackwellpublishing.com
Website: http://www.slas.org.uk
Contact: Nicola Miller, Pres.
Fee: £38
Membership Type: ordinary (in Europe)/regular (rest of the world)
Fee: £36
Membership Type: ordinary (in U.S.)
Description: Represents academics, diplomats, journalists, and research analysts from business and non-governmental organizations with an interest in the study of Latin American affairs.
Publication: Journal
Publication title: The Bulletin of Latin American Research

03967

Society for Libyan Studies
SLS

Institute for Archaeology, 31-34 Gordon Sq., London, WC1H 0PY, UK
Email: shirleystrong@btconnect.com
Website: http://www.britac.ac.uk/institutes/libya
Members: 370
Staff: 1
Contact: S.K. Strong, Gen. Sec./VP
Fee: £30
Membership Type: ordinary, institutional
Description: Institutions (110) and individuals (260) interested in the study of Libya. Promotes academic research in all subjects concerning Libya. Current concentration of support is in archaeology. Sponsors British archaeological expeditions to Libya; conducts periodic colloquia and lectures. Maintains multilingual collection of books, pamphlets, and offprints.
Publication: Journal
Publication title: Libyan Studies

03968

Society for Lincolnshire History and Archaeology
SLHA

Jews' Ct., 2-3 Steep Hill, Lincoln, LN2 1LS, UK
Tel: 01522 521337
Fax: 01522 521337
Email: slha@lincolnshirepast.org.uk
Website: http://www.slha.org.uk
Fee: £13
Membership Type: full
Fee: £21
Membership Type: adult
Description: Increases awareness and knowledge of the history and heritage of Lincolnshire. Assists the discovery and recording of new and relevant information.

03969

Society for Low Temperature Biology
SLTB

Sustainability Research Institute, University of East London, 4-6 University Way, London, E16 2RD, UK
Tel: 020 81447332
Fax: 020 82232606
Email: j.e.green@uel.ac.uk
Website: http://www.sltb.info
Members: 250
Contact: Jon Green, Gen. Sec.
Fee: £20
Membership Type: individual
Fee: £15
Membership Type: student
Description: Scientists and others in 24 countries interested in the effects of low temperatures on living things. Firms manufacturing equipment for such studies. Fosters study in low temperature biology and the application of cryobiology in medicine, agriculture and industry for the good of the community.
Publication: Newsletter
Meetings/Conventions: annual meeting

03970

Society for Medicines Research
SMR

840 Melton Rd., Thurmaston, Leicester, LE4 8BN, UK
Tel: 0116 2691048
Fax: 0116 2640141
Email: secretariat@smr.org.uk
Website: http://www.smr.org.uk
Members: 520
Staff: 1
Contact: Phillip Cowley, Chm.
Fee: £25
Membership Type: ordinary, retired
Fee: £30
Membership Type: regular
Description: Researchers at academic institutions and in the pharmaceutical industry; other concerned individuals. Promotes advancement in the field of medicinal education and research in order to provide the public with proper information on drug usage for relief of sickness.
Formerly: Formerly, Society for Drug Research

03971

Society for Medieval Archaeology

Maney Publishing, Ste. 1C, Joseph's Well, Hanover Walk, Leeds, LS3 1AB, UK
Tel: 0114 2222900
Fax: 0114 2722563
Email: d.m.hadley@sheffield.ac.uk
Website: http://www.medievalarchaeology.co.uk
Members: 1500
Contact: Dawn Hadley, Honorary Sec.
Fee: £25
Membership Type: individual, family
Fee: £15
Membership Type: student
Description: Promotes the study of archaeology in the Medieval period 400-1500.

03972

Society for Mucopolysaccharide Diseases
MPS

MPS House, Repton Pl., White Lion Rd., Buckinghamshire, Amersham, HP7 9LP, UK
Tel: 0845 3899901
Fax: 0845 3899902
Email: mps@mpssociety.co.uk
Website: http://www.mpssociety.co.uk
Members: 2000
Staff: 10
Contact: Barry Wilson, Chm.
Description: Acts as a support group for individuals and their families worldwide afflicted with Mucopolysaccharide and related diseases. (MPS diseases, known individually as Hurler, Scheie, Hunter, Sanfilippo, Morquio, Maroteaux-Lamy, and Sly, and associated diseases called Mucolipidosis, Fucosidosis, Mannosidosis, Fabry and Sialic Acid Disease, are genetic diseases. Children born with MPS are unable to produce certain enzymes necessary for appropriate metabolism to take place; consequently complex sugars become stored in connective tissues, causing progressive damage, including physical and mental handicaps. In many cases, MPS patients die before reaching adulthood.) Encourages public awareness of MPS diseases and the international transmission of medical knowledge and techniques. Raises funds to further MPS research, including two research projects in biomarkers and looking at mechanisms to get enzymes into blood and brain using cell biology. Accepts donations to provide individual advocacy for MPS families. Sponsors research program on the natural history of MPS and the psychosocial problems of MPS children following bone marrow transplant.
Library Subject: MPSI, MPSII, MPSIII, MPSIV, MPSVI, MPSVII, MPSIX, Mannosidosis, Fucosidosis, Apartylglycosaminuria, Sialic Acid Disease, Mucolipidosis I, II, III, IV, Faby, Sialidosis, GMI-Gangliosidosis, Multiple Sulphatase Deficiency, Winchester
Library Type: by appointment only
Publication: Newsletters
Publication title: MPS Newsletter. Advertisements.

03973

Society for Music Analysis
SMA

c/o Dr. Edward Venn, Admin./Treas.
Lancaster University, Music (LICA), Lancaster, LA1 4YW, UK
Email: e.venn@lancaster.ac.uk
Website: http://www.lancs.ac.uk/sma
Contact: Michael Spitzer, Pres.
Fee: £36.5
Membership Type: individual (includes Music Analysis subscription)
Fee: £20
Membership Type: individual (without Music Analysis subscription)
Description: Advances the theory and practice of music analysis. Promotes the highest standards of musicianship. Encourages teaching, research and creativity in music analysis.
Publication: Journal
Publication title: Music Analysis
Meetings/Conventions: Study Days – semiannual meeting

03974

Society for Name Studies in Britain and Ireland
SNSBI

5 St. Edwards Dr., Gloucestershire, Stow-on-the-Wold, GL54 1AW, UK
Email: treasurer@snsbi.org.uk
Website: http://www.snsbi.org.uk
Members: 200
Contact: Julia Stanbridge, Membership Sec.
Fee: £20
Membership Type: individual, institutional
Fee: £5
Membership Type: student

Description: Professional scholars in name studies, philology, history, linguistics, etc., plus many individuals engaged in private study and research into place names. Conducts research into place names and personal names of Britain and Ireland.
Formerly: Formerly, Council for Name Studies in Great Britain and Ireland
Publication: Journal
Publication title: NOMINA

03975
Society for Nautical Research
SNR

The Lodge, The Drive, Hellingly, East Sussex, Hailsham, BN27 4EP, UK
Email: membership@snr.org.uk
Website: http://www.snr.org.uk
Members: 2000
Staff: 2
Contact: M.P.J. Garvey, Membership Sec.
Description: Libraries, maritime organizations, and individuals. Encourages research into nautical antiquities, current and historical seafaring and shipbuilding, the language and customs of the sea, and other subjects of nautical interest. Assists in archaeological expeditions and caretaking of historic ships; provides funds to the National Maritime Museum for the purchase of prints and drawings. Is preparing a nautical dictionary. Conducts lectures.
Publication: Newsletter
Publication title: Newsletter of the Society

03976
Society for Post-Medieval Archaeology
SPMA

46 Eagle Wharf Rd., London, N1 7ED, UK
Tel: 020 74908447
Email: gegan@museumoflondon.org.uk
Website: http://www.spma.org.uk
Contact: Geoff Egan, VP
Fee: £27
Membership Type: ordinary (25 years and older)
Fee: £32
Membership Type: joint (25 years and older)
Description: Professional archaeologists, historians, university libraries, institutions and interested individuals in 13 countries. Promotes the study of archaeology in the post-medieval period. Encourages the preservation of sites of archaeological importance, buildings, and artifacts. Strives to educate the public through the dissemination of information. Promotes archaeological research.
Publication: Journal
Publication title: Post Medieval Archaeology
Meetings/Conventions: semiannual conference

03977
Society for Psychical Research
SPR

49 Marloes Rd., Kensington, London, W8 6LA, UK
Tel: 020 79378984
Fax: 020 79378984
Website: http://www.spr.ac.uk/main
Members: 1000
Staff: 3
Contact: Deborah L. Delanoy, Pres.
Fee: £60
Membership Type: associate
Fee: £30
Membership Type: student
Description: Advances the understanding of events and abilities commonly described as "psychic" or "paranormal" without prejudice and in a scientific manner.
Library Subject: physical research
Library Type: lending
Publication: Journal
Publication title: Journal of the Society for Physical Research

03978
Society for Radiological Protection
SRP

76 Portland Pl., London, W1B 1NT, UK
Tel: 01364 644487
Fax: 01364 644492
Email: admin@srp-uk.org
Website: http://www.srp-uk.org
Members: 1100
Contact: Alan Marsh, Honorary Sec.
Fee: £60
Membership Type: fellow
Fee: £40
Membership Type: regular
Description: Open to those engaged professionally in radiation protection or allied fields for at least 3 years, age 25 or over and normally with a degree or equivalent. Aids in the development of scientific, technological, medical and legal aspects of radiological protection, including nuclear safety, and to promote and improve radiological protection as a profession. Achieves its objectives by meetings, publications and conferences with emphasis on subjects contributing to knowledge and practice of radiological protection.
Publication: Journal
Publication title: Journal of Radiological Protection

03979
Society for Renaissance Studies
SRS

Dept. of Art History, Lakeside Arts Centre, The University of Nottingham, Nottingham, NG7 2RD, UK
Email: gabriele.neher@nottingham.ac.uk
Website: http://www.rensoc.org.uk
Contact: Gabriele Neher, Honorary Sec.
Fee: £20
Membership Type: individual
Fee: £35
Membership Type: institutional
Description: Promotes the study of the renaissance.
Publication: Journal
Publication title: Renaissance Studies
Meetings/Conventions: annual conference July, 2012. Manchester United Kingdom

03980
Society for Research into Higher Education
SRHE

44 Bedford Row, London, WC1R 4LL, UK
Tel: 020 74472525
Fax: 020 74472526
Email: srheoffice@srhe.ac.uk
Website: http://www.srhe.ac.uk
Contact: Helen Perkins, Dir.
Fee: £100
Membership Type: standard
Fee: £40
Membership Type: retired
Description: Works to advance understanding of higher education, especially through the insights, perspectives and knowledge offered by systematic research and scholarship.

03981
Society for Research into Hydrocephalus and Spina Bifida
SRHSB

The James Cook University Hospital, Dept. of Neurosurgery, Marton Rd., Cleveland, Middlesborough, TS4 3BW, UK
Fax: 01642 282770
Email: info@srhsb.org
Website: http://www.srhsb.org
Members: 284
Contact: Roger Strachan, Honorable Treas.
Fee: £60
Membership Type: general
Description: Nursing, psychology, social work, scientific, and medical professionals from 29 countries with a common interest in hydrocephalus (an abnormal accumulation of fluid in the cranium) and spina bifida (a defect in the closing of the bony spinal canal). Aims to advance education and research on hydrocephalus and spina bifida. Brings together members to aid them in their endeavors to prevent, cure, and alleviate the conditions.
Publication: Proceedings
Publication title: Cerebrospinal Fluid Research
Meetings/Conventions: annual meeting – Exhibits.

03982
Society for Social Medicine
SSM

London School of Hygiene and Tropical Medicine, Keppel St., London, WC1E 7HT, UK
Tel: 020 79272229
Email: martin.mckee@lshtm.ac.uk
Website: http://www.socsocmed.org.uk
Members: 1300
Contact: Martin McKee, Chm.
Fee: £20
Membership Type: regular
Description: Aims to promote the development of scientific knowledge in social medicine.

03983
Society for Storytelling
SFS

PO Box 2344, Reading, RG6 7FG, UK
Tel: 0118 9351381
Email: admin@sfs.org.uk
Website: http://www.sfs.org.uk
Members: 580
Contact: Martin Manasse, Chm.
Fee: £25
Membership Type: individual
Fee: £35
Membership Type: couple
Description: Aims to provide a network for everyone interested in the exchange of knowledge regarding the art of storytelling. Provides information, increase public awareness, promotes exploration, advise and develop contacts, nationally and internationally, formally and informally.
Publication: Directory
Publication title: Directory of Storytellers

03984

Society for the Advancement of Anaesthesia in Dentistry SAAD

21 Portland Pl., London, W1B 1PY, UK
Tel: 020 76318893
Email: saad@aagbi.org
Website: http://www.saad.org.uk
Members: 4225
Staff: 1
Contact: Nigel Robb, Pres.
Fee: £15
Membership Type: nurse, hygienist
Fee: £25
Membership Type: dentist
Description: Dentists and physicians interested in dental anesthesia. Seeks to advance pain and anxiety control in dentistry. Offers courses on intravenous techniques and relative analgesia.
Library Subject: dental anesthesia and related topics
Library Type: reference
Publication: Book
Publication title: Dental Sedation and Anaesthesia

03985

Society for the History of Alchemy and Chemistry SHAC

19 Nethercote Rd., Tackley, Oxford, OX5 3AW, UK
Email: shacperkins@googlemail.com
Website: http://www.ambix.org
Members: 200
Contact: John Perkins, Honorary Treas.
Fee: £55
Membership Type: full
Fee: £31
Membership Type: student
Description: Seeks to study the history of chemical sciences. Encourages exchange among members.
Publication: Journal
Publication title: Ambix. Advertisements.

03986

Society for the History of Natural History SHNH

c/o The Natural History Museum
Cromwell Rd., London, SW7 5BD, UK
Email: info@shnh.org.uk
Website: http://www.shnh.org.uk
Contact: Geoff Moore, Pres.
Fee: £30
Membership Type: individual in UK
Fee: £35
Membership Type: individual (rest of the world)
Description: Archivists, bibliographers, book collectors, natural science historians, librarians, museum personnel, and university lecturers and professors. Provides a forum for the exchange of ideas and information on the history of botany, geology, and zoology and on artistic and literary expressions of the natural sciences.
Formerly: Formerly, Society for the Bibliography of Natural History
Publication: Journal
Publication title: Archives of Natural History

03987

Society for the Promotion of Byzantine Studies SPBS

University of Birmingham, College of Arts and Law, Birmingham, B15 2TT, UK
Email: mss714@bham.ac.uk
Website: http://www.byzantium.ac.uk
Members: 470
Staff: 1
Contact: Mike Saxby, Membership Sec.
Fee: £20
Membership Type: individual
Fee: £10
Membership Type: student
Description: Promotes Byzantine studies.
Publication: Bulletin
Publication title: Bulletin of British Byzantine Studies. Advertisements.

03988

Society for the Promotion of Hellenic Studies SPHS

Senate House, South Block, Rm. 245, Malet St., London, WC1E 7HU, UK
Tel: 0207 8628730
Fax: 0207 8628731
Email: office@hellenicsociety.org.uk
Website: http://www.hellenicsociety.org.uk
Members: 3500
Staff: 1
Contact: Malcolm Schofield, Pres.
Fee: £41
Membership Type: full
Fee: £60
Membership Type: institution, library, school
Description: Archaeologists, classicists, educators, numismatists, libraries, and museums worldwide. Promotes the study of the Greek language, literature, history, and art in the ancient, Byzantine, and modern periods. Maintains library jointly with the Society for the Promotion of Roman Studies.
Publication: Journal
Publication title: Archaeological Reports. Advertisements.

03989

Society for the Promotion of Roman Studies SPRS

c/o Senate House
Malet St., London, WC1E 7HU, UK
Tel: 0207 8628727
Fax: 0207 8628728
Email: office@romansociety.org
Website: http://www.romansociety.org
Members: 2800
Staff: 2
Contact: Andrew Burnett, Pres.
Fee: £46
Membership Type: individual
Fee: £100
Membership Type: institutional
Description: Academies, academic libraries, archaeologists and classicists in over 40 countries interested in the archaeology, art, literature and history of Italy and the Roman Empire until the year 700 A.D. Assists the British School in Rome, Italy.
Publication: Journal
Publication title: Britannia. Advertisements.

03990

Society for the Protection of Ancient Buildings SPAB

37 Spital Sq., London, E1 6DY, UK
Tel: 0207 3771644
Fax: 0207 2475296
Email: info@spab.org.uk
Website: http://www.spab.org.uk
Members: 7500
Staff: 14
Contact: Philip Venning, Sec.
Fee: £36
Membership Type: individual
Fee: £600
Membership Type: life
Description: Individuals united to preserve and protect ancient buildings. Gives advice and technical assistance on the treatment and repair of old structures. Investigates proposals that place historic buildings in jeopardy. Sponsors courses and training programs on the conservation of buildings.
Publication: Magazine
Publication title: Cornerstone

03991

Society for the Protection of Animals Abroad SPANA

14 John St., London, WC1N 2EB, UK
Tel: 020 78313999
Fax: 020 78315999
Email: enquiries@spana.org
Website: http://www.spana.org
Members: 165000
Staff: 15
Contact: Lord Newall, Pres.
Description: Charitable organization providing treatment for sick and injured working animals in many developing countries around the world. Maintains animal refuges and mobile clinics. Offers training for veterinary surgeons and an education program for children and animal owners.
Formerly: Formerly, Society for the Protection of Animals in North Africa
Publication: Magazine
Publication title: SPANA News

03992

Society for the Protection of Unborn Children SPUC

3 Whitacre Mews, Stannary St., London, SE11 4AB, UK
Tel: 020 70917091
Fax: 020 78203131
Email: information@spuc.org.uk
Website: http://www.spuc.org.uk
Members: 48000
Staff: 40
Contact: John Smeaton, Natl. Dir.
Fee: £250
Membership Type: life
Fee: £10
Membership Type: standard
Description: Education and lobbying on right to life (abortion, embryo abuse, euthanasia, population control). Promotes alternatives to abortion. Provides support and assistance to those suffering from post abortion

syndrome. Finances research into population disability and pre-natal development.
Publication: Newspaper
Publication title: Pro-Life Times

03993
Society for the Protection of Unborn Children - Scotland
SPUC

75 Bothwell St., Glasgow, G2 6TS, UK
Tel: 0141 2212094
Fax: 0141 2253696
Email: info@spucscotland.org
Website: http://www.spucscotland.org
Members: 5400
Staff: 4
Contact: Ian Murray, Dir.
Fee: £10
Membership Type: ordinary
Fee: £250
Membership Type: life
Description: Concerned with all pro-life issues including abortion, the treatment of embryos and euthanasia; involved in political lobbying at both Westminster and Holyrood; provides educational resources and speakers to schools and information to the general public; campaigns to raise awareness and support at the grassroots level for pro-life issues and concerns.
Publication: Journal
Publication title: Human Function

03994
Society for the Responsible Use of Resources in Agriculture and on the Land
RURAL

Chester House, Hillbury Rd., Alderholt, Fordingbridge, SP6 3BQ, UK
Tel: 01425 652035
Website: http://www.rural.org.uk
Staff: 1
Contact: John Hickman, Dir.
Description: Promotes policy studies on farming, food and countryside.

03995
Society for the Social History of Medicine
SSHM

Durham University, Ctre. for the History of Medicine and Disease, Queen's Campus, Wolfson Research Institute, University Blvd., Stockton-on-Tees, TS17 6BH, UK
Tel: 0191 3340702
Email: l.d.sauerteig@durham.ac.uk
Website: http://www.sshm.org
Contact: Lutz Sauerteig, Chair
Fee: £39
Membership Type: full
Fee: £20
Membership Type: student
Description: Professionals and interested amateurs in medical, historical, sociological, and related disciplines. Promotes the study of the social history of medicine as it relates to patients, doctors, disease, and health. Topics of interest include national health service, mental handicaps, occupational health, general practice, and health and town planning.
Publication: Journal
Publication title: Social History of Medicine. Advertisements.

03996
Society for the Study of Addiction to Alcohol and Other Drugs
SSA

c/o Graham Hunt
Leeds Addiction Unit, 19 Springfield Mt., Leeds, LS2 9NG, UK
Tel: 0113 2952787
Fax: 0113 2952787
Email: membership@addiction-ssa.org
Website: http://www.addiction-ssa.org
Members: 400
Staff: 4
Contact: Gillian Tober, Pres.
Fee: £85
Description: Medical and allied health professionals seeking to stimulate scientific study of alcohol and drug addiction. Conducts research and educational programs.
Library Subject: biographical
Library Type: reference
Publication: Journal
Publication title: Addiction. Advertisements.
Meetings/Conventions: annual symposium – Exhibits.

03997
Society for the Study of Human Biology
SSHB

Loughborough University, Dept. of Human Sciences, Leicestershire, Loughborough, LE11 3TU, UK
Tel: 01509 228486
Email: p.griffiths@lboro.ac.uk
Website: http://www.sshb.org
Contact: Paula Griffiths, Sec.
Fee: £42
Membership Type: regular in UK
Fee: £1
Membership Type: retired
Description: Professional human biologists in 45 countries. Aims to advance the study of the biology of human populations in all aspects, including human variability and genetics, human adaptability and ecology, and human evolution.
Publication: Journal
Publication title: Annals of Human Biology. Advertisements.

03998
Society for the Study of Labour History
SSLH

School of History, Univ. of Leeds, Leeds, LS2 9JT, UK
Email: m.s.chase@leeds.ac.uk
Website: http://www.sslh.org.uk
Members: 1000
Contact: Malcom Chase, Chm.
Fee: £18
Membership Type: individual
Fee: £20
Membership Type: institution
Description: Teachers, students, and others in 40 countries interested in the study, research, and teaching of labor history. Works to preserve labor archives. Provides the opportunity for researchers to publish papers of their recent work.

03999
Society for the Study of Medieval Languages and Literature
SSMLL

c/o History Faculty
George St., Oxford, OX1 2RL, UK
Email: ssmll@history.ox.ac.uk
Website: http://www.mod-langs.ox.ac.uk/ssmll/index.html
Members: 180
Contact: Anthony Lappin, Pres.
Description: Scholars, students, and others interested in medieval languages and literature. Encourages research in medieval literature and history, and medieval languages and linguistics, including Romance, Germanic, Latin, and English languages.
Publication: Monograph
Publication title: Medium Aevum Monographs

04000
Society for the Study of Normal Psychology

Colet House, 151 Talgarth Rd., London, W14 9DA, UK
Tel: 020 87489338
Fax: 020 85630551
Email: office@studysociety.org
Website: http://www.studysociety.com
Members: 270
Staff: 5
Fee: £50
Membership Type: regular
Description: Works to foster understanding of the nature of consciousness.
Library Type: not open to the public
Formerly: Also Known As, Study Society
Publication: Magazine
Publication title: Contact

04001
Society for Theatre Research
STR

PO Box 53971, London, SW15 6UL, UK
Email: contact@str.org.uk
Website: http://www.str.org.uk
Contact: Eileen Cottis, Sec.
Fee: £30
Membership Type: individual
Fee: £33
Membership Type: individual (overseas)
Description: University and college departments of drama, libraries, theatre professionals, theatre scholars, and other individuals. Aims to encourage research into the history and technique of the British theatre. Seeks to establish the International Federation for Theatre Research and the British Theatre Museum. Holds William Poel Festival. Sponsors periodic lecture in memory of Edward Gordon Craig (1872-1966), English actor, stage designer, and producer.
Publication: Book
Publication title: Research Book
Meetings/Conventions: annual meeting

04002
Society for Underwater Technology
SUT
80 Coleman St., London, EC2R 5BJ, UK
Tel: 020 73822601
Fax: 020 73822684
Email: info@sut.org
Website: http://www.sut.org.uk
Members: 1600
Staff: 6
Contact: R. L. Allwood, Chief Exec.
Fee: £70
Membership Type: full
Fee: £48.5
Membership Type: associate
Description: A multi-disciplinary learned society of individuals and organizations with a common interest in underwater technology, ocean science and offshore engineering, with members in more than 40 countries including engineers, scientists, other professionals, and students from industry, universities and government organizations.
Formerly: Absorbed, Engineering Committee on Oceanic Resources
Publication: Proceedings
Publication title: Offshore Site Investigation and Geotechnics
Meetings/Conventions: Life-Cycle of Flexible Risers and Flowlines Awareness – semiannual lecture

04003
Society of Academic and Research Surgery
SARS
Royal College of Surgeons of England, 35-43 Lincoln's Inn Fields, London, WC2A 3PE, UK
Tel: 020 78696640
Fax: 020 78696644
Email: sars@rcseng.ac.uk
Website: http://www.surgicalresearch.org.uk
Members: 450
Contact: N. Williams, Pres.
Fee: £60
Membership Type: ordinary, senior, corresponding
Description: Surgeons. Provides for the interchange of information about research related to surgery and surgical disease.
Publication: Journal
Publication title: British Journal of Surgery
Meetings/Conventions: annual conference – Exhibits.

04004
Society of Antiquaries of London
SAL
Burlington House, Piccadilly, London, W1J 0BE, UK
Tel: 0207 4797080
Fax: 0207 2876967
Email: admin@sal.org.uk
Website: http://www.sal.org.uk
Members: 2000
Staff: 12
Contact: John Lewis, Gen. Sec.
Description: Archaeologists, art historians, architectural historians and historians united for the encouragement, advancement and furtherance of the study and knowledge of the antiquaries of the U.K. and other countries. Operates a museum. Serves as a forum for discussion among members.
Publication: Journal
Publication title: Antiquaries Journal

04005
Society of Antiquaries of Newcastle-upon-Tyne
Great North Museum, Barras Bridge, Newcastle upon Tyne, NE2 4PT, UK
Tel: 0191 2312700
Email: admin@newcastle-antiquaries.org.uk
Website: http://www.newcastle-antiquaries.org.uk
Members: 800
Staff: 5
Contact: David Breeze, Pres.
Fee: £27
Membership Type: standard
Fee: £18
Membership Type: concessionary
Description: Promotes the study, investigation, description, and preservation of antiquities and historical records in the historic counties of Northumberland and Durham and the city and county of Newcastle upon Tyne.
Publication: Journal
Publication title: Archaeologia Aeliana

04006
Society of Antiquaries of Scotland
SAS
National Museums Scotland, Chambers St., Edinburgh, EH1 1JF, UK
Tel: 0131 2474133
Fax: 0131 2474163
Email: info@socantscot.org
Website: http://www.socantscot.org
Members: 3500
Staff: 8
Contact: Simon Gilmour, Dir.
Description: Individuals interested in the study of antiquities and the history of Scotland. Encourages greater interest and scholarship in Scottish history and archaeology; provides financial assistance for research, excavation, and publication. Organizes lectures and conferences.
Library Subject: archaeology, history
Library Type: reference
Publication: Proceedings
Publication title: Proceedings of the Society of Antiquaries of Scotland
Meetings/Conventions: Admission Election – annual meeting

04007
Society of Archer-Antiquaries
SAA
c/o Mr. H.D.H. Soar, Honorable Sec.
Yew Corner, 29 Batley Ct., Oldland, South Gloucestershire, BS30 8YZ, UK
Tel: 0117 9323276
Email: bogaman@btinternet.com
Website: http://www.societyofarcher-antiquaries.org
Members: 400
Staff: 1
Contact: Ken Arton, Pres.
Fee: £20
Membership Type: ordinary
Description: Individuals, archery clubs, universities, libraries, museums, and firms in 14 countries that are interested in the history and development of the bow. Studies matters relating to the history of archery and the development of the bow and arrow in all parts of the world from prehistoric times to the present day. Maintains museum of archery equipment.
Publication: Journal
Publication title: A Guide to the Crossbow

04008
Society of Architectural Historians of Great Britain
SAHGB
6 Fitzroy Sq., London, W1T 5DX, UK
Email: membership@sahgb.org.uk
Website: http://www.sahgb.org.uk
Members: 1300
Contact: David McKinstry, Membership Sec.
Fee: £35
Membership Type: ordinary
Fee: £90
Membership Type: institutional
Description: Exists to encourage an interest in the history of architecture. Provides opportunities for the exchange and discussion of ideas related to this subject.
Publication: Journal
Publication title: Architectural History

04009
Society of Archivists - United Kingdom
Prioryfield House, 20 Canon St., Somerset, Taunton, TA1 1SW, UK
Tel: 01823 327030
Fax: 01823 271719
Email: societyofarchivists@archives.org.uk
Website: http://www.archives.org.uk
Members: 1800
Staff: 5
Contact: Lorraine Logan, Membership Admin.
Fee: £12
Membership Type: student
Fee: £23
Membership Type: individual (unwaged, with annual income of 5,000)
Description: Archivists, records managers, and conservators in central and local government, universities, charities and the business sector. Aims to promote the care, preservation of archives, and the administration of archive repositories; to advance the training of members; and to encourage relevant research and publication.
Publication: Newsletter
Publication title: Society of Archivists Newsletter

04010
Society of Army Historical Research
SAHR
The Cavalry and Guards Club, 127 Piccadilly, London, W1J 7PX, UK
Tel: 07901951007
Fax: 02076299546
Email: guysayle@hotmail.com
Website: http://www.sahr.co.uk
Members: 1000
Staff: 6
Contact: Guy Sayle, Membership Sec.
Fee: £37.5
Membership Type: full
Fee: £80
Membership Type: in U.S. and Canada (airmail)
Description: Fosters an interest in and research into the history and traditions of the British army and of the land forces of the Empire, the Dominions, and colonies and the Commonwealth. Conducts lecture series.

04011

Society of Assistants Teaching in Preparatory Schools SATIPS

Cherry Trees, Stebbing, Great Dunmow, CM6 3ST, UK
Tel: 01371 856823
Fax: 01371 856823
Email: stebel@tesco.net
Website: http://www.satips.com
Staff: 1
Contact: E.R. Andrew Davis, Gen. Sec.
Fee: £21
Membership Type: individual
Fee: £115
Membership Type: school
Description: Preparatory schools and individual preparatory school teachers. Provides support for staff in prep schools; advances independent education, encourages the interchange of ideas, circulates relevant information. Holds conferences, sporting activities, festivals, and competitions.
Formerly: Formerly, Society of Assistants Teaching in Preparatory Schools

04012

Society of Authors - England SOA

84 Drayton Gardens, London, SW10 9SB, UK
Tel: 020 73736642
Fax: 020 73735768
Email: info@societyofauthors.org
Website: http://www.societyofauthors.org
Members: 8500
Staff: 13
Contact: Emma Boniwell, Membership Sec.
Description: Trade union for professional writers. Benefits include individual contract advice and advice on all of the business aspects of writing. Works for improved terms and conditions between authors and publishers. Also lobbies government authorities for legislation, which will enhance conditions for writers.
Publication: Journal
Publication title: Author. Advertisements.
Meetings/Conventions: bimonthly meeting

04013

Society of Biology

9 Red Lion Ct., London, EC4A 3EF, UK
Tel: 020 79365900
Email: info@societyofbiology.org
Website: http://www.societyofbiology.org
Members: 80000
Contact: Mark Downs, CEO
Fee: £162
Membership Type: fellow
Fee: £116
Membership Type: regular
Description: Promotes liaison, dialogue and interaction among bioscientists. Provides opinions and information to assist formulation of public policy concerning bioscience teaching, research and applications. Encourages open debate about practical and ethical issues in biosciences.
Formerly: Formerly, Biosciences Federation and Institute of Biology

04014

Society of Bookbinders SoB

c/o Hilary Henning, Membership Sec.
102 Hetherington Rd., Shepperton, TW17 0SW, UK
Email: info@societyofbookbinders.com
Website: http://www.societyofbookbinders.com
Members: 650
Contact: David Lanning, Pres.
Fee: £36
Membership Type: full
Fee: £75
Membership Type: corporate
Description: Represents the interests of bookbinders, book collectors and conservators. Provides a forum for the exchange of information thus promoting the highest standards of bookbinding both nationally and internationally. Conducts lectures, demonstrations, and regional programs throughout the country.
Library Type: open to the public
Publication: Journal
Publication title: Bookbinder. Advertisements.

04015

Society of Border Leicester Sheep Breeders

Rock Midstead, Northumberland, Alnwick, NE66 2TH, UK
Tel: 07891 245870
Fax: 01665 579326
Email: info@borderleicesters.co.uk
Website: http://www.borderleicesters.co.uk
Members: 235
Staff: 1
Contact: Ian J.R. Sutherland, Sec.
Description: Aims to encourage the breeding of Border Leicester Sheep and the maintenance of the purity of the breed by the publication of a book.

04016

Society of British Aerospace Companies SBAC

Salamanca Sq., 9 Albert Embankment, London, SE1 7SP, UK
Tel: 020 70914500
Fax: 020 70914545
Email: gill.pattison@sbac.co.uk
Website: http://www.sbac.co.uk
Members: 1500
Staff: 55
Contact: Allan Edward Cook, Chief Exec.
Description: Membership covers a cross-section of the aerospace industry in the areas of airframes, aero-engines, guided weapons and satellites. Seeks to improve the competitive performance of all United Kingdom aerospace companies by promoting communication between companies, the industry, and the government. Organizes the biennial Farnborough International exhibitions and flying displays.
Library Type: by appointment only
Meetings/Conventions: Farnborough International – biennial trade show – Exhibits.

04017

Society of British Neurological Surgeons SBNS

35-43 Lincoln's Inn Fields, London, WC2A 3PE, UK
Tel: 020 78696892
Fax: 020 78696890
Email: admin@sbns.org.uk
Website: http://www.sbns.org
Contact: Suzanne Murray, Sr. Admin.
Fee: £290
Membership Type: full
Fee: £145
Membership Type: associate
Description: Promotes the safe and effective neurosurgical treatment for patients throughout Great Britain and Ireland.

04018

Society of British Water and Wastewater Industries SBWWI

38 Holly Walk, Warwickshire, Leamington Spa, CV32 4LY, UK
Tel: 01926 831530
Fax: 01926 831931
Email: hq@bwwi.co.uk
Website: http://www.sbwwi.co.uk
Members: 76
Staff: 3
Contact: Carol Hickman, Exec. Dir.
Fee: £370-4850
Membership Type: regular (based on annual turnover)
Description: Trade Association. Covers the interests of contractors and manufacturers of pipeline equipment, metering systems, instrumentation and controls. Members meet regularly to discuss developments in the water industry and the effects of legislation and standards. Acts as a forum for discussions with water companies and other bodies associated with the industry. Represented on CEN, ISO and national standards committees.
Formerly: Formerly, Society of British Water Industries
Publication: Newsletter
Publication title: SBWWI News

04019

Society of Business Economists SBE

Dean House, Vernham Dean, Andover, SP11 0JZ, UK
Tel: 01264 737552
Fax: 020 79002585
Email: admin@sbe.co.uk
Website: http://www.sbe.co.uk
Members: 650
Contact: Katie Abberton, Sec.
Fee: £80
Membership Type: full
Fee: £35
Membership Type: student
Description: Represents economists in 14 countries working in commerce, finance, and industry. Seeks to help all those who use economics in a business environment. Aims to advance the use of economic analysis as a tool to support business decision-making. Aims to enhance the standing of the professional economist working outside the academia. Provides a forum for members to discuss and debate economic issues. Helps members keep in touch with practical and theoretical developments within the discipline.
Publication: Journal
Publication title: Business Economist. Advertisements.

04020

Society of Cable Telecommunication Engineers SCTE

Communications House, 41a Market St., Hertfordshire, Watford, WD18 0PN, UK
Tel: 01923 815500
Fax: 01923 803203
Email: office@scte.org.uk
Website: http://www.scte.org.uk
Members: 1200
Staff: 3
Contact: Roger Blakeway, Pres.
Fee: £35
Membership Type: technician/associate
Fee: £45
Membership Type: regular
Description: Individuals engaged in some branch of engineering directly or indirectly concerned with the design, development, manufacture and employment of materials and components used by the cable telecommunications industry.
Formerly: Formerly, Society of Cable Television Engineers
Publication: Magazine
Publication title: Cable Telecommunications Engineering
Meetings/Conventions: quarterly lecture

04021

Society of Cartographers SOC

University of Glasgow, School of Geographical and Earth Sciences, Glasgow, G12 8QQ, UK
Tel: 0141 3304780
Fax: 0141 3304894
Email: mike.shand@ges.gla.ac.uk
Website: http://www.soc.org.uk
Contact: Mike Shand, Honorary Sec.
Fee: £15
Membership Type: student
Fee: £25
Membership Type: full, overseas
Description: Supports practising cartographers. Encourages high standards of cartographic illustration. Provides members with information and opportunities to meet and exchange views and techniques with fellow practising cartographers.
Publication: Journal
Publication title: The SoC Bulletin. Advertisements.

04022

Society of Chemical Industry SCI

14-15 Belgrave Sq., London, SW1X 8PS, UK
Tel: 020 75981500
Fax: 020 75981545
Email: secretariat@soci.org
Website: http://www.soci.org
Contact: Joanne Lyall, Exec. Dir.
Fee: £75
Membership Type: full
Fee: £15
Membership Type: student
Description: Interdisciplinary network connecting industry, research, and consumer affairs at all levels throughout the world. Provides opportunities for forward-looking people in the process and materials technologies, energy, water, agriculture, food, pharmaceuticals, construction, and environmental protection areas to exchange ideas and gain new perspectives on markets, technologies, strategies, and people.
Publication: Magazine
Publication title: Chemistry and Industry. Advertisements.

04023

Society of Chiropodists and Podiatrists SCP

1 Fellmongers Path, Tower Bridge Rd., London, SE1 3LY, UK
Tel: 0207 2348620
Fax: 0845 4503721
Email: jb@scpod.org
Website: http://www.feetforlife.org
Members: 10000
Staff: 20
Contact: Joanna Brown, Chief Exec.
Description: State registered chiropodists. The principal activities are to fulfill both a pre-registration and post-registration education function, to act as a trade union for its members employed in the National Health Service, to monitor the professional and ethical conduct and standards of its members, to publish professional journals, and to fulfill a public relations role.
Publication: Journal
Publication title: The Journal of British Podiatric Medicine. Advertisements.

04024

Society of College, National and University Libraries SCONUL

102 Euston St., London, NW1 2HA, UK
Tel: 020 73870317
Fax: 020 73833197
Email: sitmui.ng@sconul.ac.uk
Website: http://www.sconul.ac.uk
Members: 200
Staff: 3
Contact: Toby Bainton, Sec.
Description: Works to improve the quality and extend the influence of the university and national libraries of the United Kingdom and Ireland. Promotes the science and practice of librarianship. Discusses, develops, and recommends policies for the efficient operation of higher education and national libraries. Fosters cooperation between libraries, and seeks to avoid duplication of efforts.
Formerly: Formerly, Standing Conference of National and University Libraries
Publication: Journal
Publication title: SCONUL Annual Library Statistics

04025

Society of Construction and Quantity Surveyors SCQS

24 Pennine Rise, Scissett, Huddersfield, HD8 9JE, UK
Tel: 01484 863686
Email: brian@scqs.org.uk
Website: http://www.scqs.org.uk
Members: 250
Staff: 1
Contact: Brian P. Kirkham, Chief Exec.
Fee: £45
Membership Type: individual
Fee: £30
Membership Type: associate
Description: Open to all quantity surveyors employed in senior quantity surveying posts of the public sector within the United Kingdom and extends to all those who, prior to promotion, held such a post and retain responsibility for quantity surveying within the public sector. Promotes discussion on professional, administrative, technical and other matters affecting the membership and affords advice to members in the execution of their duties; arranges annual conference, seminars and the interchange and publication of reports and information collated by members of the Society on Quantity Surveying and related subjects.
Formerly: Formerly, Society of Chief Quantity Surveyors
Publication: Magazine
Publication title: SCQS Newsletter
Meetings/Conventions: annual meeting

04026

Society of Construction Law SCL

67 Newbury St., Oxon, Wantage, OX12 8DJ, UK
Tel: 01235 770606
Fax: 01235 770580
Website: http://www.scl.org.uk
Members: 2055
Contact: Jackie Morris, Admin.
Fee: £65
Membership Type: admission
Fee: £100
Membership Type: full
Description: Barristers, solicitors, architects, surveyors, engineers, and other construction professionals. Is concerned with education, study, research and dissemination of knowledge of construction law and related subjects.

04027

Society of Consulting Marine Engineers and Ship Surveyors SCMS

202 Lambeth Rd., London, SE1 7JW, UK
Tel: 0207 2610869
Fax: 0207 2610871
Email: sec@scmshq.org
Website: http://www.scmshq.org/index.php
Members: 500
Staff: 1
Fee: £110
Membership Type: regular
Fee: £75
Membership Type: associate
Description: Consulting marine engineers and ship surveyors. Provides a central organization for those engaged in a consultative or similar capacity in technical maritime affairs.
Publication title: Marine Technical Consultancy

04028
Society of Cosmetic Scientists
SCS
Langham House East, Mill St., Ste. 6, Bedsfordshire, Luton, LU1 2NA, UK
Tel: 01582 726661
Fax: 01582 405217
Email: ifscc.scs@btconnect.com
Website: http://www.scs.org.uk
Members: 900
Staff: 2
Contact: Gem Bektas, Sec. Gen.
Fee: £58
Membership Type: regular
Fee: £53
Membership Type: associate, affiliate
Description: Represents scientists and technologists in the cosmetic industry. Works to advance the science of cosmetics and toiletries. Encourages education and research in cosmetics. Offers professional training programs.
Publication: Journal
Publication title: International Journal of Cosmetic Science. Advertisements.

04029
Society of County Treasurers
SCT
c/o Somerset County Council
Finance Dept., County Hall, Taunton, TA1 4DY, UK
Tel: 01823 358179
Email: technicalsupportteam@somerset.gov.uk
Website: http://www.sctnet.org.uk
Members: 36
Contact: Brian Roberts, Pres.
Description: Treasurers of all County Councils in England. Established for the discussion of financial, management and other matters affecting local government generally, and county councils in particular and for the representation of the views of the society on such matters.

04030
Society of Dairy Technology
SDT
PO Box 12, Appleby-in-Westmorland, CA16 6YJ, UK
Tel: 01768 354034
Email: execdirector@sdt.org
Website: http://www.sdt.org
Members: 500
Staff: 1
Contact: Maurice Walton, Exec. Dir.
Fee: £60
Membership Type: full
Fee: £30
Membership Type: retired
Description: Members from all sectors of the dairy and food industry producers, suppliers, consultants, technicians, students, academics, researchers. Provides a means for disseminating knowledge and application of dairy technology across the dairy and food industry. It is a focal point of reference for all matters concerning dairy science and technology. Meetings and conferences of international calibre are organized and technical education and training is encouraged and provided.
Publication: Journal
Publication title: International Journal of Dairy Technology. Advertisements.

04031
Society of Designer Craftsmen
SDC
24 Rivington St., London, EC2A 3DU, UK
Tel: 020 77393663
Fax: 020 77393663
Email: info@societyofdesignercraftsmen.org.uk
Website: http://www.societyofdesignercraftsmen.org.uk
Members: 7300
Staff: 2
Contact: Christopher Frayling, Pres.
Fee: £70
Membership Type: individual
Fee: £40
Membership Type: associate
Description: Qualified, full-time designer-craftsmen. Seeks to establish the professional status of craftsmen and designers and increase members' awareness of users of their products. Fosters and exhibits British craftsmanship; provides up-to-date information on leading craftsmen. Assists graduates trying to establish their own workshops. Maintains slide library depicting members' works.

04032
Society of Dyers and Colourists - England
SDC
Perkin House, 82 Grattan Rd., PO Box 244, Bradford, BD1 2JB, UK
Tel: 01274 725138
Fax: 01274 392888
Email: info@sdc.org.uk
Website: http://www.sdc.org.uk
Members: 2500
Staff: 30
Contact: Susie Hargreaves, CEO
Fee: £52.5
Membership Type: professional
Fee: £20
Membership Type: individual
Description: Colorists, technologists, and buyers involved in industry, fashion, retail and the supply chain. Promotes globally the advancement of the science of color concerning lectures, conferences, publications and technical standards work. Maintains Colour Museum. Offers educational and training activities.
Publication: Journal
Publication title: Coloration Technology

04033
Society of Editors
University Ctre., Granta Pl., Mill Ln., Cambridge, CB2 1RU, UK
Tel: 01223 304080
Email: info@societyofeditors.org
Website: http://www.societyofeditors.co.uk/index.php
Members: 400
Staff: 2
Contact: Bob Satchwell, Exec. Dir.
Fee: £230
Membership Type: full
Fee: £60
Membership Type: publication, academic
Description: Editors, deputy editors and senior editorial executives of national, regional and local newspapers, magazines and broadcasting organizations, journalism education, and media law. Seeks to defend and promote the independence of editors as an essential bulwark of media freedom. Fosters better education and training for journalists and monitors legislation for potential threats to media freedom.
Formerly: Formerly, Guild of Editors
Publication: Newsletter
Publication title: Briefing

04034
Society of Environmental Engineers
SEE
The Manor House, High St., Hertfordshire, Buntingford, SG9 9AB, UK
Tel: 01763 271209
Fax: 01763 273255
Email: office@environmental.org.uk
Website: http://www.environmental.org.uk
Members: 765
Contact: Patrick McHugh, Pres.
Fee: £108
Membership Type: corporate
Fee: £10
Membership Type: student
Description: Members drawn from many engineering disciplines. Provides a forum for the sharing of knowledge and expertise in environmental engineering and control over a wide field. Conducts technical meetings, training and education, symposia, exhibitions, workshops and conferences.
Publication: Journal
Publication title: Environmental Engineering

04035
Society of Equestrian Artists
SEA
174 Henwood Green Rd., Pembury, Kent, TN2 4LR, UK
Email: sec@equestrianartists.co.uk
Website: http://www.equestrianartists.co.uk
Members: 400
Contact: Alexander Hooton, Sec.
Fee: £25
Membership Type: friend
Fee: £30
Membership Type: overseas
Description: Exists to encourage the study of equine art and, by mutual assistance between members, to promote a standard of excellence in practice worthy of the subject's importance in British artistic tradition.

04036
Society of Feed Technologists
SFT
2 Highmoor Rd., Caversham, Reading, RG4 7BN, UK
Tel: 0118 9475737
Fax: 0118 9475737
Email: sfteurope@aol.com
Website: http://www.dustyoldbooks.com/sft
Contact: Mabel Foye, Sec.
Description: Serves as an animal nutrition industry, identifies advances in knowledge and technology and offers an opportunity to discuss the importance and implications of these changes.

04037

Society of Fine Art Auctioneers and Valuers SOFAA

2 Kingfisher Ct., Bridge Rd., Surrey, East Molesey, KT8 9HL, UK
Tel: 0208 9417861
Email: secretary@sofaa.org
Website: http://www.sofaa.info
Members: 41
Contact: Paul Viney, Chm.
Fee: £500
Membership Type: full
Fee: £140
Membership Type: associate
Description: Aims to provide clients the highest standards of service through proper guidance of its members. Instills good practice and ethics among member auctioneers and valuers.

04038

Society of Floristry SOF

Wilcot Chapel, Kinton, Shropshire, SY4 1AZ, UK
Tel: 0870 2410432
Email: info@societyoffloristry.org
Website: http://www.societyoffloristry.org
Members: 1000
Contact: Lucy Todman, Sec.
Fee: £45
Membership Type: regular, fellow
Fee: £20
Membership Type: student
Description: Professional florists and those in the floristry trade.
Publication: Magazine
Publication title: Focal Point. Advertisements.

04039

Society of Food Hygiene and Technology SOFHT

The Granary, Middleton House Farm, Tamworth Rd., Staffs, Middleton, B78 2BD, UK
Tel: 01827 872500
Fax: 01827 875800
Email: admin@sofht.co.uk
Website: http://www.sofht.co.uk
Staff: 2
Contact: Simon Houghton-Dodd, Chm.
Fee: £52.5
Membership Type: individual (standard)
Fee: £954
Membership Type: gold
Description: Promotes the production, distribution and sale of safe and wholesome food. Facilitates communication within the industry on all matters related to hygiene. Encourages training of personnel and provides an informal advisory service.
Publication: Magazine
Publication title: SOFHT Focus. Advertisements.
Meetings/Conventions: bimonthly symposium

04040

Society of Garden Designers SGD

Katepwa House, Ashfield Park Ave., Herefordshire, Ross-on-Wye, HR9 5AX, UK
Tel: 01989 566695
Fax: 01989 567676
Email: info@sgd.org.uk
Website: http://www.sgd.org.uk
Members: 1100
Staff: 1
Contact: Annabel Downs, Contact
Fee: £245
Membership Type: registered
Fee: £85
Membership Type: pre-registered
Description: Registered members/fellows have exhibited highest professional standards of garden design; correspondent members may be practising designers, students or interested in the subject. Emphasizes the excellence of work and the Code of Practice is designed to protect the interests of clients and members alike.
Library Subject: garden design
Library Type: open to the public
Publication: Journal
Publication title: Garden Design Journal. Advertisements.

04041

Society of Glass Technology SGT

Unit 9, Twelve O'clock Ct., 21 Attercliffe Rd., Sheffield, S4 7WW, UK
Tel: 0114 2634455
Fax: 0114 2634411
Email: info@sgt.org
Website: http://www.sgt.org
Members: 700
Staff: 5
Fee: £95-141
Membership Type: ordinary (aged over 30, with journal)
Fee: £23-29
Membership Type: concessionary (aged under 25, with journal)
Description: Associations and individuals interested in glass. Promotes the study of glass technology. Maintains five technical committees.
Library Subject: joint library of glass technology
Library Type: reference
Publication: Journal
Publication title: Glass Technology. Advertisements.
Meetings/Conventions: conference – Exhibits.

04042

Society of Headmasters and Headmistresses of Independent Schools SHMIS

12 The Point, Rockingham Rd., Leicestershire, Market Harborough, LE16 7QU, UK
Tel: 01858 433760
Fax: 01858 461413
Website: http://www.shmis.org.uk
Members: 106
Staff: 2
Contact: Peter Bodkin, Gen. Sec.
Description: Heads of smaller independent secondary schools. Aims to promote independent education; supports heads in their work and sharing of ideas and problems.

04043

Society of Heraldic Arts

12 Ridgeway, Ottery St. Mary, Devon, EX11 1DT, UK
Tel: 01404 811091
Email: sha.hon-sec@tiscali.co.uk
Website: http://www.heraldic-arts.com
Contact: Anthony Wood, Pres.
Fee: £25
Membership Type: craft
Fee: £15
Membership Type: associate
Description: Raises public understanding and appreciation of heraldic arts. Encourage excellence of heraldic arts. Provides a forum for the exchange of ideas and information relating to heraldic arts.

04044

Society of Homeopaths

11 Brookfield, Duncan Close, Moulton Park, Northampton, NN3 6WL, UK
Tel: 0845 4506611
Fax: 0845 4506622
Email: info@homeopathy-soh.org
Website: http://www.homeopathy-soh.org
Members: 2200
Staff: 17
Contact: Paula Ross, CEO
Fee: £44
Membership Type: student at a recognized school or college
Fee: £50
Membership Type: student at a non-recognized school or college
Description: Professional homeopaths on the Society's register. Aims to develop and maintain high standards for the practise of homeopathy and to promote public awareness of homeopathy. Supports the establishment of education and training in homeopathy.
Publication: Journal
Publication title: The Homeopath. Advertisements.

04045

Society of Hospital Linen Service and Laundry Managers

Bolton Hospital NHS Trust, Bolton, BL4 0JR, UK
Tel: 01204 390613
Fax: 01204 390693
Email: info@linenmanager.co.uk
Website: http://www.linenmanager.co.uk
Members: 80
Contact: Paul Gibson, Natl. Chm.
Fee: £40
Membership Type: regular
Description: NHS staff employed in linen services management or indirectly involved in linen services.
Library Type: not open to the public
Meetings/Conventions: annual seminar – Exhibits.

04046

Society of Independent Brewers SIB

PO Box 101, Thirsk, Y07 4WA, UK
Email: secretariat@siba.co.uk
Website: http://siba.co.uk
Members: 240
Contact: Julian Grocock, Contact
Description: Independent brewers and breweries. Seeks to obtain a sliding-scale tax exemption for breweries in the

United Kingdom. Represents members' collective commercial interests; conducts lobbying and promotional activities; facilitates communication and cooperation among members.

04047

Society of Independent Roundabout Proprietors
SIRP

66 Carolgate, Nottinghamshire, Retford, DN22 6ET, UK
Tel: 01777 702872
Email: sec@sirp.org.uk
Website: http://www.sirp.org.uk
Members: 120
Contact: Jack Schofield, Sec.
Fee: £30
Membership Type: regular
Description: Independent showmen who own vintage fairground equipment. Represents members' interests to the government.

04048

Society of Indexers
SI

Woodbourn Business Centre, 10 Jessell St., Sheffield, S9 3HY, UK
Tel: 0114 2449561
Fax: 0114 2449563
Email: info@indexers.org.uk
Website: http://www.indexers.org.uk
Contact: Wendy Burrow, Admin.
Fee: £95.5
Membership Type: individual (in UK and Europe)
Fee: £48
Membership Type: senior (in UK and Europe)
Description: Persons in 21 countries interested in all types of indexing, particularly of books and periodicals. Institutional membership is open to publishers, universities and colleges, firms, and other organizations concerned with or interested in indexing. Promotes high standards of indexing and works to develop indexing techniques. Maintains list of persons willing and qualified to undertake indexing work for authors, editors, and publishers; acts as advisory body on the qualifications and remuneration of indexers. Conducts discussions on various aspects of indexing. Organizes training course on principles of indexing.
Publication: Directory
Publication title: Indexers Available
Meetings/Conventions: Society of Indexers Conference – annual meeting

04049

Society of Information Technology Management
Socitm

F19 Moulton Business Park, Redhouse Rd., Northampton, NN3 6AQ, UK
Tel: 01604 497774
Fax: 01604 497610
Email: enquiries@socitm.net
Website: http://www.socitm.gov.uk/socitm
Members: 2000
Staff: 10
Contact: Jos Creese, Pres.
Fee: £135
Membership Type: senior
Fee: £95
Membership Type: public, third sector
Description: IS/IT Managers in Local Government and the Public Sector. The professional organization for local government officers responsible for recommending corporate information technology policy. Provides a focal point for local government IT; produces standards of good practice.
Library Subject: IT management
Library Type: reference
Publication: Survey
Publication title: IT Trends
Meetings/Conventions: semiannual conference – Exhibits.

04050

Society of International Gas Tanker and Terminal Operators
SIGTTO

17 St. Helen's Pl., London, EC3A 6DG, UK
Tel: 020 76281124
Fax: 020 76283163
Email: secretariat@sigtto.org
Website: http://sigtto.re-invent.net/DNN
Contact: Allyn Risley, Pres.
Fee: £3600
Membership Type: full (minimum)
Description: Companies from 27 countries operating natural and petroleum gas tankers. Promotes the safe operation of gas tankers and terminals. Represents members' interests before the International Maritime Organization.
Meetings/Conventions: biennial meeting

04051

Society of Laundry Engineers and Allied Trades
SLEAT

Ste. 7, Southernhay, 207 Hook Rd., Chessington, KT9 1HJ, UK
Tel: 0208 3912266
Fax: 0208 3914466
Email: admin@sleat.co.uk
Website: http://sleat.co.uk
Members: 35
Contact: David M. Hart, Sec.
Description: Suppliers of machinery, equipment and consumable to the laundry and dry cleaning trade. Supports and sponsors trade exhibitions; monitors safety and specification standards and publications. Promotes the interests of supply trade in liaison activities with user organizations.

04052

Society of Leather Technologists and Chemists
SLTC

8 Copper Leaf Close, Moulton, Northampton, NN3 7HS, UK
Tel: 01604 892059
Fax: 01604 711183
Email: office@sltc.org
Website: http://www.sltc.org
Contact: Pat Potter, Membership Sec.
Description: Represents people working in the leather-producing industry including technologists, chemists, analysts and production control as well as technical staffs in chemical supply industry. Works on the chemistry and technology of leather production involving histology of skins and protein chemistry particularly collagen, tanning materials, vegetable and synthetic tannins, inorganic materials based on chromium, aluminum, zirconium, titanium, dyestuffs, pigments and polymers for surface coating. Promotes tannery waste treatment, recycling and energy conservation and physical and chemical testing of leather.
Publication: Journal
Publication title: Journal of the Society of Leather Technologists and Chemists

04053

Society of Legal Scholars in the United Kingdom and Ireland
SLS

University of Southampton, School of Law, Highfield, Southampton, SO17 1BJ, UK
Tel: 023 80594039
Fax: 023 80593024
Email: s.j.thomson@soton.ac.uk
Website: http://www.legalscholars.ac.uk
Members: 2800
Staff: 3
Contact: Sally Thomson, Admin. Sec.
Fee: £60
Membership Type: teacher or researcher with 4 years of experience, practitioner
Fee: £20
Membership Type: teacher or researcher with less than 4 years of experience/student
Description: Individuals involved in legal research and the teaching of law at degree level or above in universities and other institutions; legal firms; chambers; other bodies.
Formerly: Formerly, Society of Public Teachers of Law
Publication: Membership Directory
Publication title: Directory of Members
Meetings/Conventions: annual conference September 5 to 8, 2011. Cambridge United Kingdom

04054

Society of Local Authority Chief Executives and Senior Managers
SOLACE

Hope House, 45 Great Peter St., London, SW1P 3LT, UK
Tel: 0845 6524010
Fax: 0845 6524011
Email: hope.house@solace.org.uk
Website: http://www.solace.org.uk
Members: 950
Staff: 8
Contact: David Clark, Dir. Gen.
Description: Serving local authority chief executives and senior managers. Provides an authoritative voice on all of the subject matters of local government and in embracing all types of local authority in the UK, it is able to speak for the whole of local government.

04055

Society of Local Council Clerks
SLCC

No. 8 The Crescent, Somerset, Taunton, TA1 4EA, UK
Tel: 01823 253646
Fax: 01823 253681
Email: admin@slcc.co.uk
Website: http://www.slcc.co.uk
Members: 4200
Staff: 1
Contact: Nick Randle, CEO
Fee: £30-365
Membership Type: full (based on the annual salary)

Fee: £160
Membership Type: full (affiliate)
Description: Clerks to parish and town councils in England and Wales. Serves local authority staff at parish and town council level of local government.
Publication: Journal
Publication title: The Clerk. Advertisements.

04056
Society of London Art Dealers SLAD

Ormond House, 3 Duke of York St., London, SW1Y 6JP, UK
Tel: 020 79306137
Fax: 020 73210685
Email: office@slad.org.uk
Website: http://www.slad.org.uk
Members: 105
Staff: 2
Contact: Patrick Bourne, Chm.
Description: Represents the interests of art dealers who have been in business for at least 3 years in the Greater London area. Promotes and protects the good name of the fine art trade and enhances public confidence in responsible art dealing. Has members that have a proven reputation in their field and have signed an undertaking to observe standards of fair and honest dealing.

04057
Society of London Theatre SOLT

32 Rose St., London, WC2E 9ET, UK
Tel: 020 75576700
Fax: 020 75576799
Email: enquiries@solttma.co.uk
Website: http://www.solt.co.uk
Members: 95
Staff: 20
Contact: Richard Pulford, Chief Exec.
Description: Comprises of managers and proprietors of theatres and producers of shows in the West End of London; both the commercial and subsidized sectors are represented. Negotiates minimum rates of pay and conditions of employment with the theatrical unions: British Actors Equity (covering performers, stage management, directors and designers), BECTU (theatre staff including technicians) and the Musicians' Union (musicians). Provides arbitration and conciliation service for disputes between managers and artists through the Society's partnership with Equity in the London Theatre Council.
Publication: Pamphlet
Publication title: Official London Theatre Guide. Advertisements.

04058
Society of Maritime Industries SMI

28-29 Threadneedle St., London, EC2R 8AY, UK
Tel: 020 76282555
Fax: 020 76384376
Email: info@maritimeindustries.org
Website: http://www.maritimeindustries.org
Members: 200
Staff: 10
Contact: John C. Murray, Chief Exec.
Description: Member companies supply equipment for all types of ships, for the offshore oil and gas industry and for pollution control. Acts as a collective voice of the marine equipment industry, liaising with and lobbying government in the interests of equipment suppliers for the benefit of international trade.
Formerly: Formerly, British Marine Equipment Council
Publication: Directory

04059
Society of Maritime Industries I British Naval Equipment Association BNEA

28-29 Threadneedle St., London, EC2R 8AY, UK
Tel: 020 76282555
Fax: 020 76384376
Email: info@maritimeindustries.org
Website: http://www.maritimeindustries.org/about/bnea.jsp
Members: 180
Staff: 2
Contact: Christopher McHugh, Dir.
Description: Represents interests of builders of warships and suppliers of equipment and services for naval vessels.

04060
Society of Metaphysicians

Archers' Ct., Stonestile Ln., The Ridge, Hastings, TN35 4PG, UK
Tel: 01424 751577
Fax: 01424 751577
Email: info@metaphysicians.org.uk
Website: http://www.metaphysicians.org.uk
Members: 2296
Staff: 5
Fee: £50
Membership Type: in UK
Fee: £100
Membership Type: in U.S.
Description: Seeks to create a new metaphysical system designed to optimize knowledge. Encourages members to develop personal parapsychological ability. Sponsors formalized research groups on international bases for parapsychology, paraphysics, social business, spiritual science, and its applications. Promotes a functional view of spiritual science through the media as the key to social harmony. Conducts meetings, discussions, research with workshop services, book sales, manufacturing and occult equipment sales, and correspondence courses.
Publication: Journal
Publication title: Borderline Science Series (Paraphysics)

04061
Society of Motor Manufacturers and Traders SMMT

Forbes House, Halkin St., London, SW1X 7DS, UK
Tel: 020 72357000
Fax: 020 72357112
Email: memberweb@smmt.co.uk
Website: http://www.smmt.co.uk/home.cfm
Members: 800
Staff: 140
Contact: Paul Everitt, Chief Exec.
Fee: £250
Membership Type: general
Description: Manufacturers and importers of cars, garage equipment, public service and commercial vehicles, and related equipment. Promotes the interests of the motor industry. Runs industry forum to improve quality and supply chain links in the U.K. automotive industry. Compiles statistics.
Publication: Bulletin
Publication title: Overseas Bulletin
Meetings/Conventions: Auto One – biennial trade show

04062
Society of Museum Archaeologists

Oxford Archaeology, Janus House, Osney Mead, Oxford, OX2 0ES, UK
Tel: 01865 263848
Email: n.scott@oxfordarch.co.uk
Website: http://www.socmusarch.org.uk
Members: 300
Contact: Nicola Scott, Membership Sec.
Fee: £20
Membership Type: full
Fee: £12
Membership Type: student
Description: Museum-based archaeologists. Aims to promote museum involvement in all aspects of archaeology, and to emphasize the unique role of museums within the essential unity of the archaeological profession.
Publication: Journal
Publication title: The Museum Archaeologist

04063
Society of Occupational Medicine SOM

6 St. Andrews Pl., Regents Park, London, NW1 4LB, UK
Tel: 020 74862641
Fax: 020 74860028
Email: admin@som.org.uk
Website: http://www.som.org.uk
Members: 2000
Staff: 5
Contact: O.H. Carlton, Pres.
Fee: £135
Membership Type: full
Fee: £106
Membership Type: overseas
Description: Doctors working in occupational medicine. Many of the members have specialist qualifications in occupational medicine but others may be family practitioners connected with or holding part-time appointments in the specialty. Strives to protect the health of people at work and the prevention and management of occupational diseases and injuries. Seeks to interest and inform members through publications and scientific meetings, organised regionally and nationally. Stimulates research and education in occupational medicine and actively liaises with professional organisations relevant to occupational health.
Publication: Newsletter
Publication title: Newsletter Periodical

04064

Society of Operations Engineers
SOE

22 Greencoat Pl., London, SW1P 1PR, UK
Tel: 020 76301111
Fax: 020 76306677
Email: soe@soe.org.uk
Website: http://www.soe.org.uk
Members: 18000
Staff: 27
Contact: Chris Grime, Pres.
Fee: £75
Membership Type: associate
Fee: £90
Membership Type: corporate
Description: Promotes safe, efficient, and environmentally sustainable operations engineering to the benefits of society. Seeks to improve professional education, training and competence and ethics. Represents members' interests.
Formerly: Formerly, Institution of Plant Engineers
Publication: Magazine
Publication title: The Plant Engineer. Advertisements.

04065

Society of Pension Consultants
SPC

Saint Bartholomew House, 92 Fleet St., London, EC4Y 1DG, UK
Tel: 020 73531688
Fax: 020 73539296
Email: info@spc.uk.com
Website: http://www.spc.uk.com
Members: 136
Staff: 4
Contact: John Mortimer, Sec.
Description: Accountancy firms, actuaries, consultants, external pension administrators, independent trustees, investment houses, investment performance measurers, life offices, and solicitors. Draws upon the knowledge and experience of members so as to contribute to legislation and other general developments affecting pension and related benefit provision. Maintains contact with a wide range of government departments and other groups, both in the UK and Europe.
Publication: Newsletter
Publication title: SPC News. Advertisements.

04066

Society of Petroleum Engineers - London Office
SPE

Threeways House, 40/44 Clipstone St., London, W1W 5DW, UK
Tel: 020 72993300
Fax: 020 72993309
Email: spelon@spe.org
Website: http://www.spe.org/spe-app/spe/index.jsp
Members: 79000
Contact: Behrooz Fattahi, Pres.
Membership Type: student (based on country)
Fee: £60-90
Membership Type: professional (based on country and age)
Description: Petroleum engineers. Provides the means to collect, disseminate and exchange technical information concerning the development of oil and gas resources, subsurface fluid flow, and production of other materials through wellbores. Encourages members to maintain and improve their technical competence. Conducts educational programs.
Publication: Journal
Publication title: Journal of Petroleum Technology

04067

Society of Pharmaceutical Medicine
SPM

9 Red Lion Ct., London, EC4A 3EF, UK
Tel: 020 79365903
Fax: 020 79365901
Email: spm@societyofbiology.org
Website: http://www.socpharmed.org
Members: 120
Staff: 1
Contact: Cliff Collis, Exec. Sec.
Fee: £55
Membership Type: individual
Description: Open to all those involved within drug development - both in the pharmaceutical industry and also in academic/clinical medicine and the drug regulatory agencies. Aims to provide a focus for questions relating to the development of medicinal agents.
Publication: Journal
Publication title: International Journal of Pharmaceutical Medicine

04068

Society of Ploughmen

Loversall, South Yorkshire, Doncaster, DN11 9DH, UK
Tel: 01302 852469
Fax: 01302 859880
Email: info@ploughmen.co.uk
Website: http://www.ploughmen.co.uk
Members: 1052
Staff: 1
Contact: Ken Chappell, Exec. Dir./Sec.
Fee: £25
Membership Type: personal
Fee: £40
Membership Type: family
Description: Individual members and local ploughing societies throughout the UK. Organises the annual British National Ploughing Championships, which are held in a different part of Great Britain each year. The Championships include modern tractor ploughing; vintage tractor ploughing and exhibitions; horse ploughing; trade stands and demonstrations; and country crafts.

04069

Society of Practising Veterinary Surgeons
SPVS

The Governor's House, Cape Rd., Warwickshire, Warwick, CV34 5DL, UK
Tel: 01926 410454
Fax: 01926 411350
Email: president@spvs.org.uk
Website: http://www.spvs.org.uk/new_site/v2
Contact: Jacqui Molyneux, Pres.
Fee: £140.79
Membership Type: full, associate
Fee: £28.12
Membership Type: recent graduate (0-2 years), undergraduate veterinary student
Description: Represents the interests of veterinary surgeons.
Publication: Magazine
Publication title: Bulletin

04070

Society of Procurement Officers in Local Government
SOPO

113-117 London Rd., Leicestershire, Leicester, LE2 0RG, UK
Tel: 0141 4311839
Email: k.may@espo.org
Website: http://www.sopo.org
Members: 2900
Contact: Peter Howarth, CEO/Managing Dir.
Fee: £1750
Membership Type: corporate
Fee: £80
Membership Type: affiliate
Description: Promotes the strategic procurement function within local government in England, Wales, Scotland, and Northern Ireland. Represents members' interests and advises local government associations. Promotes professional development.
Formerly: Formerly, Society of Purchasing Officers in Local Government

04071

Society of Professional Accountants
SPA

95 High St., Great Missenden, HP16 0AL, UK
Tel: 01494 864414
Fax: 01494 864454
Email: mail@spa.org.uk
Website: http://www.spa.org.uk
Contact: Peter Mitchell, Chm.
Fee: £100
Membership Type: basic
Description: Represents professionally qualified accountants in small practices. Maintains high standards of professionalism, integrity and ethics among its members. Promotes the educational and technical development of professional accountants.

04072

Society of Professional Engineers
SPE

Lutyens House, Billing Brook Rd., Weston Favell, Northampton, NN3 8NW, UK
Tel: 01604 415729
Fax: 01604 784220
Email: enquiries@professionalengineers-uk.org
Website: http://www.professionalengineers-uk.org
Members: 700
Contact: D. Hardcastle, Pres.
Fee: £52
Membership Type: associate (in UK/Ireland)
Fee: £80
Membership Type: regular (in UK/Ireland)
Description: Well-qualified professional engineers from the entire major engineering disciplines. Establishes and maintains a register that embraces all suitably qualified professional engineers of whatever discipline; protects and enhances the status of the professional engineer and promotes the concept of this title throughout the world and establishes and promotes the highest professional standards.
Publication: Magazine
Publication title: The Professional Engineer. Advertisements.

04073

Society of Recorder Players
SRP

c/o Dick Pyper, Chm.
35 Meads Rd., Guildford, GU1 2NA, UK
Tel: 01483 505104
Email: chairman@srp.org.uk
Website: http://www.srp.org.uk
Members: 1500
Contact: Peter Maxwell Davies, Pres.
Fee: £14
Membership Type: student
Fee: £18.5
Membership Type: full
Description: Recorder players of all ages and abilities. Aims to promote the education of the public in the study, practice and appreciation of the recorder and its repertoire.
Publication: Magazine
Publication title: The Recorder Magazine. Advertisements.

04074

Society of Saint Vincent de Paul - Scotland

113 W Regent St., Glasgow, G2 2RU, UK
Tel: 0141 2268833
Fax: 0141 2265050
Email: admin@ssvpscotland.com
Website: http://www.youthsvdpscotland.org
Contact: Michael Balfour, Pres.
Description: Catholic lay persons engaged in a spirit of justice and charity and united by a personal commitment to serve those who suffer. Seeks, through personal contact, to relieve suffering and promote the dignity and integrity of the individual. Conducts research.

04075

Society of Sales and Marketing
SSM

40 Archdale Rd., East Dulwich, London, SE22 9HJ, UK
Tel: 0845 6436832
Fax: 0845 6436834
Email: profblankson@ssm.org.uk
Website: http://www.ssam.co.uk
Members: 2500
Staff: 2
Contact: Robert A. Herbert-Blankson, Chief Exec.
Fee: £50
Membership Type: fellow
Fee: £40
Membership Type: associate
Description: Professionals engaged in sales, sales management, marketing, retailing, and international trade. Works to enhance the professional standing of members, and to encourage the study of sales, international trade, and related subjects. Conducts professional examinations; compiles statistics; maintains speakers' bureau.
Library Subject: sales, international trade, marketing, retailing
Library Type: not open to the public
Formerly: Formerly, Society of Sales Management Administrators
Publication: Journal
Publication title: Marketing Today. Advertisements.
Meetings/Conventions: annual dinner

04076

Society of School Masters and School Mistresses
SOSS

Queen Mary House, Manor Park Rd., Chislehurst, Kent, BR7 5PY, UK
Tel: 020 84687997
Email: sgbi@fsmail.net
Website: http://www.sossandsgbi.org.uk
Contact: J.C. Wolters, Chm.
Description: Provides relief as needed to masters and mistresses of all recognized schools, independent or maintained, and their dependants, provided that such persons have been in teaching for at least 10 years.
Formerly: Formerly, Society of Schoolmasters

04077

Society of Scottish Artists
SSA

2 Wemyss Ave., Glasgow, G77 6AR, UK
Tel: 0141 6162566
Email: ssa@tangledwebs.co.uk
Website: http://www.s-s-a.org
Members: 370
Staff: 1
Contact: Noreen Sharkey Paisley, Sec.
Fee: £40
Membership Type: ordinary
Fee: £75
Membership Type: ordinary/professional (with entry on the SSA website)
Description: Professional artists (elected), lay membership - open to anyone with interest in the visual arts. Aims to encourage interest in contemporary art; to show the work of young artists alongside work of more established artists, in the Annual Exhibition and smaller exhibitions throughout Scotland and Europe.
Publication: Catalog
Publication title: Annual Exhibition. Advertisements.

04078

Society of Scribes and Illuminators
SSI

6 Queen Sq., London, WC1N 3AR, UK
Email: gillianhazeldine@austwick.org
Website: http://www.calligraphyonline.org
Members: 600
Contact: Gillian Hazeldine, Honorary Sec.
Fee: £36
Membership Type: fellow
Fee: £28
Membership Type: lay
Description: Aims to advance the crafts of writing and illuminating. Fellows of the society are technically accomplished, with the ability to adapt historical models to contemporary work.
Publication: Handbook
Publication title: Calligrapher's Handbook

04079

Society of Shoe Fitters
SSF

The Anchorage, 28 Admirals Walk, Norfolk, Hingham, NR9 4JL, UK
Tel: 01953 851171
Email: secretary@shoefitters-uk.org
Website: http://www.shoefitters-uk.org
Members: 200
Staff: 1
Contact: Laura West, Honorable Sec.
Description: Aims to recognize fitting qualification and training in shoe fitting. Assists the public in finding shoes to fit. Offers foot health advice.
Library Type: not open to the public

04080

Society of Sports Therapists
SST

16 Royal Terr., Glasgow, G3 7NY, UK
Tel: 0845 6002613
Fax: 0141 3325335
Email: admin@society-of-sports-therapists.org
Website: http://www.society-of-sports-therapists.org
Members: 1500
Contact: Graham N. Smith, Chm.
Description: Open to anyone over the age of 18 years who has successfully completed a course in sports therapy and satisfies the criteria for membership of the Society. Aims to provide a professional body for sports therapists which will educate, monitor and legislate on all matters pertaining to sports therapy.

04081

Society of Teachers of Speech and Drama
STSD

73 Berry Hill Rd., Nottinghamshire, Mansfield, NG18 4RU, UK
Email: stsd@stsd.org.uk
Website: http://www.stsd.org.uk
Members: 600
Staff: 8
Contact: Felicity Amor, Chair
Fee: £44
Membership Type: full affiliate
Fee: £70
Membership Type: corporate
Description: Members are involved in all branches of speech and drama work schools, colleges of further education and universities. Works in the professional and amateur theatre as producers, directors and coaches; some are involved with the disabled whilst; others teach communication and presentation skills in the business world. Aims to uphold a high standard of teaching and support those working in the field. Each region has a representative who is responsible for promoting the work of the society. Holds conferences in London in February and during August in another region.
Library Subject: all aspects of speech, drama, theatre
Library Type: not open to the public
Publication: Journal
Publication title: Word Matters. Advertisements.

04082

Society of Teachers of the Alexander Technique
STAT

Linton House, 1st Fl., 39-51 Highgate Rd., London, NW5 1RT, UK
Tel: 020 74825135
Fax: 020 74825435
Email: office@stat.org.uk
Website: http://www.stat.org.uk
Members: 2500
Staff: 4
Contact: Ilia Daoussi, Contact

Description: Works to maintain professional standards and gain wider recognition of the Alexander Technique (a means of posture re-education). Encourages research and communication among members.
Library Type: by appointment only
Publication: Newsletter
Publication title: E-Newsletter

04083

Society of Technical Analysts STA

Dean House, Vernham Dean, SP11 0JZ, UK
Tel: 020 71250038
Fax: 020 79002585
Email: info@sta-uk.org
Website: http://sta-uk.org
Contact: Deborah Owen, Chair
Fee: £60
Membership Type: associate
Fee: £80
Membership Type: full
Description: Works to promote use and understanding of technical analysis as an investment tool serving all members of the investment community.
Publication: Journal
Publication title: Market Technician

04084

Society of Television Lighting Directors STLD

c/o Robert Horne
April Cottage, Church Rd., Scaynes Hill, West Sussex, RH17 7NY, UK
Email: secretary@stld.org.uk
Website: http://www.stld.org.uk
Members: 642
Contact: Stuart Gain, Chm.
Fee: £45
Membership Type: full
Fee: £25
Membership Type: affiliate
Description: Engages in the direction and design, or whose occupation is directly associated with, the creative aspect of television lighting. Stimulates a free exchange of ideas in all aspects of the television profession, including the techniques and design of new equipment.
Publication: Magazine
Publication title: Television Lighting. Advertisements.

04085

Society of Trust and Estate Practitioners STEP

Artillery House, 11-19 Artillery Row, London, SW1P 1RT, UK
Tel: 020 73400500
Fax: 020 73400501
Email: step@step.org
Website: http://www.step.org
Members: 13500
Contact: David Harvey, Chief Exec.
Fee: £185
Membership Type: full, associate, affiliate
Fee: £75
Membership Type: student
Description: Aims to bring together all practitioners in the field of trusts and estates. Raises the public profile of trust and estate work as a profession in its own right. Advances knowledge and learning in trusts, estates and allied subjects. Encourages and promotes the study of trusts and estate practice. Provides education, training, representation and networking for its members.
Publication: Journal

04086

Society of Wildlife Artists SWLA

Federation of British Artists, 17 Carlton House Terr., London, SW1Y 5BD, UK
Tel: 0207 9306844
Website: http://www.swla.co.uk
Members: 72
Contact: Harriet Mead, Pres.
Fee: £195
Membership Type: basic
Fee: £65
Membership Type: associate
Description: Professional wild life artists. Organises the exhibition of original works of art by wildlife artists; sales and commissions of wildlife art; educates the public in wildlife art through exhibitions; most work for sale at annual exhibition.
Publication: Catalog
Publication title: Annual Exhibition Catalogue. Advertisements.

04087

Society of Women Artists SWA

c/o Pamela Henderson, Exec. Sec.
1 Knapp Cottages, Wyke, Dorset, Gillingham, SP8 4NQ, UK
Tel: 01747 825718
Fax: 01747 826835
Email: pamhendersons@dsl.pipex.com
Website: http://www.society-women-artists.org.uk
Members: 138
Contact: Barbara Penketh Simpson, Pres.
Description: Upholds the tradition of fine art on behalf of women artists of today. Gives serious women artists the opportunity to exhibit.
Publication: Catalog
Publication title: Catalogue of Exhibits at Annual Exhibition. Advertisements.
Meetings/Conventions: annual convention – Exhibits.

04088

Society of Women Writers and Journalists SWWJ

14 Laburnum Walk, Rustington, West Sussex, BN16 3QW, UK
Email: wendy@stickler.org.uk
Website: http://www.swwj.co.uk
Members: 450
Contact: Wendy Hughes, Membership Sec.
Fee: £40
Membership Type: full
Fee: £30
Membership Type: associate, overseas
Description: Professional writers/journalists/poets. Encourages literary achievement, upholding of professional standards and social contact with other writers. Conducts activities including lunchtime meetings, discussions and seminars, manuscript advice service, competitions and visits.
Publication: Journal
Publication title: The Woman Writer

04089

Society of Wood Engravers

The Old Governor's House, Norman Cross, Peterborough, PE7 3TB, UK
Tel: 01733 242833
Email: swesec@geriwaddington.com
Website: http://www.woodengravers.co.uk
Members: 86
Contact: Geri Waddington, Gen. Sec.
Fee: £35
Membership Type: overseas
Fee: £25
Membership Type: regular, UK and Europe
Description: Full members wood engravers, elected by committee, on merit after exhibiting with the SWE; subscribers, individuals interested in wood engraving including prospective members, galleries, collectors, etc. Encourages a growing interest in wood engraving by exhibiting in well-established, as well as little-known venues; setting up courses for new engravers, welcomes wood engravers overseas in annual travelling exhibitions.
Publication: Newsletter
Publication title: Multiples

04090

Society of Writers to Her Majesty's Signet

Parliament Sq., Signet Library, Edinburgh, EH1 1RF, UK
Tel: 0131 2203249
Email: rpirrie@wssociety.co.uk
Website: http://www.thewssociety.co.uk
Contact: Robert Pirrie, Chief Exec.
Fee: £375
Membership Type: full
Fee: £120
Membership Type: affiliate
Description: Helps members and non-members keep up-to-date with aspects of the law and legal practice through education programme.

04091

Society of Young Publishers SYP

c/o The Publishers Association Limited
29B Montague St., London, WC1B 5BW, UK
Website: http://www.thesyp.org.uk
Members: 400
Contact: Angie Solomon, Chair
Fee: £30
Membership Type: standard (in employment)
Fee: £24
Membership Type: student, unwaged
Description: People, principally under the age of 35, working or interested in publishing and allied fields. Provides a forum for all young people in publishing and allied sectors to learn more about the industry and make contacts. Holds monthly speaker meetings, run a monthly reading group, an annual training conference and numerous social events throughout the year.
Publication: Handbook
Publication title: The Handbook

04092
Socio-Legal Studies Association
SLSA
Queen's University Belfast, School of Law, Belfast, BT7 1NN, UK
Tel: 028 90973468
Email: s.wheeler@qub.ac.uk
Website: http://www.slsa.ac.uk
Contact: Sally Wheeler, Chair
Fee: £30
Membership Type: full
Fee: £10
Membership Type: student
Description: Aims to advance education and learning and in particular to advance research, teaching and the dissemination of knowledge in the field of socio-legal studies.

04093
Soil Association
SA
South Plz., Marlborough St., Bristol, BS1 3NX, UK
Tel: 0117 3145000
Fax: 0117 3145001
Email: ff@soilassociation.org
Website: http://www.soilassociation.org
Staff: 200
Contact: Patrick Holden, Dir.
Fee: £24
Membership Type: single (with credit/debit card)
Fee: £33
Membership Type: joint
Description: Consumers, farmers, foresters, and agricultural and forestry researchers; food and timber companies. Promotes organic farming and sustainable forestry and researches the links between environment and health. Provides information to the public and health authorities. Licenses organic processors, producers, retailers, and wholesalers, and sustainable forestry and timber manufacturers.
Publication: Report
Publication title: Food & Farming Report

04094
Solar Energy Society
UK-ISES
PO Box 489, Abingdon, OX14 4WY, UK
Tel: 07760 163559
Fax: 01235 848684
Email: info@uk-ises.org
Website: http://www.uk-ises.org
Members: 300
Staff: 2
Contact: Tony Book, Chm.
Fee: £40
Membership Type: national
Fee: £79
Membership Type: international
Description: Promotes the use of solar energy.
Publication: Newsletter
Publication title: Solar News

04095
Solar Trade Association
STA
The National Energy Centre, Davy Ave., Knowlhill, Milton Keynes, MK5 8NG, UK
Tel: 01908 442290
Fax: 01908 665577
Email: enquiries@solar-trade.org.uk
Website: http://www.solar-trade.org.uk
Members: 210
Staff: 3
Contact: David Matthews, Chief Exec.
Description: Companies dealing with solar energy appliances and systems. Raises standards within the solar industry and promotes a greater understanding by public and media of the advantages of solar energy use. Maintains a Code of Practice to control members' activities; runs an arbitration service and acts as a centre for information about solar energy.
Publication: Booklet
Publication title: The Sun's Abundant Energy

04096
Solid Fuel Association
SFA
7 Swanwick Ct., Derbyshire, Alfreton, DE55 7AS, UK
Tel: 0845 6014406
Email: sfa@solidfuel.co.uk
Website: http://www.solidfuel.co.uk
Members: 35
Staff: 5
Description: Companies involved in mining coal, manufacturing or importing fuels or distributing fuels. Works with the promotion of the use of solid fuels and solid fuel appliances for domestic heating throughout Great Britain. Provides support services for users and specifiers.
Publication: Magazine
Publication title: The Complete Guide to Solid Fuel Heating

04097
Solids Handling and Processing Association
SHAPA
20 Elizabeth Dr., Oadby, Leicester, LE2 4RD, UK
Tel: 0116 2713704
Email: info@shapa.co.uk
Website: http://www.shapa.co.uk
Contact: John Whitehead, Sec.
Description: Represents manufacturers of equipment and systems used in the handling and processing of particulate solids.
Meetings/Conventions: meeting

04098
Solvents Industry Association
SIA
8 Saint Georges Ave., Dovercourt, Harwich, CO12 3RR, UK
Tel: 01255 240220
Email: info@sia-uk.org.uk
Website: http://www.sia-uk.org.uk
Members: 14
Staff: 1
Contact: Peter Davis, Gen. Sec.
Description: Producers and distributors of solvents. Aims to provide information, advice and services within the industry on technical, environmental and legal matters and to assist governments, authorities and other bodies in the promotion of environmental, health and safety and quality measures. Cooperates with authorities and institutes. Supports or opposes legislation affecting the interests of the industry.

04099
Somerset Chamber of Commerce and Industry
SCCI
Equity House, Blackbrook Park Ave., Somerset, Taunton, TA1 2PX, UK
Tel: 01823 444924
Email: manager@somerset-chamber.co.uk
Website: http://www.somerset-chamber.co.uk
Members: 260
Staff: 3
Contact: Rupert Cox, Chief Exec.
Fee: £2000
Membership Type: patron
Fee: £90
Membership Type: charity
Description: Represents members across Somerset at local, regional and national level on matters concerning trade, commerce and industry and lobbying. Facilitates networking, forums and events to enable members to exchange ideas, information, views and business practice.
Publication: Newsletter
Publication title: Chamber News. Advertisements.

04100
Soroptimist International
SI
87 Glisson Rd., Cambridge, CB1 2HG, UK
Email: hq@soroptimistinternational.org
Website: http://www.soroptimistinternational.org
Members: 90000
Staff: 4
Contact: Hanne Jensbo, Pres.
Description: Professional women. Works to uphold high standards of ethics and practice in business and the professions. Promotes respect for the civil and human rights of all individuals; seeks to enhance the economic and social status of women. Facilitates development of friendship and camaraderie among members; encourages voluntarism and the spirit of community service. Conducts research and educational programs; sponsors charitable activities; makes available children's services.
Publication: Newsletter
Publication title: International Soroptimist

04101
Soroptimist International of Great Britain and Ireland
SIGBI
127 Wellington Rd. S, Cheshire, Stockport, SK1 3TS, UK
Tel: 0161 4807686
Fax: 0161 4776152
Email: hq@soroptimistgbi.prestel.co.uk
Website: http://www.soroptimist-gbi.co.uk
Members: 12600
Staff: 5
Contact: Gina Coad, Admin.
Description: Individuals in 30 countries involved in elevating the status of women. Promotes human rights, goodwill, peace, and international understanding. Regional group of Soroptimist International. Promotes charitable programs.
Formerly: Formerly, Soroptimist Federation of Great Britain and Ireland
Publication: Magazine
Publication title: The Soroptimist. Advertisements.

04102

SOS Sahel International - UK

106-108 Cowley Rd., Oxford, OX4 1JE, UK
Tel: 01865 403305
Fax: 01865 403306
Email: mail@sahel.org.uk
Website: http://www.sahel.org.uk
Members: 50
Staff: 200
Contact: Sue Cavanna, Programme Mgr.
Description: Works in rural areas of the Sahel in sub-Saharan Africa. Supports community initiatives that focus on conservation of natural resources and sustainable agriculture and development. Implements long-term projects in Sudan, Ethiopia, Kenya, Mali, and Nigeria.
Publication: Book
Publication title: At the Desert's Edge: Oral Histories from the Sahel

04103

Sound and Music

Somerset House, 3rd Fl., S Wing, Strand, London, WC2R 1LA, UK
Tel: 020 77591800
Email: info@soundandmusic.org
Website: http://www.soundandmusic.org
Staff: 5
Contact: Matthew Greenall, Exec. Dir.
Fee: £25
Membership Type: individual
Fee: £10
Membership Type: junior/concession
Description: Advocates new music in Britain including contemporary jazz, classical, popular, music written for film, dance, and other media. Provides concerts, workshops, education projects, and collaborations.
Formerly: Formerly, Society for the Promotion of New Music, Sonic Arts Network
Publication: Magazine
Publication title: New Notes. Advertisements.

04104

South Chesire Chamber

Lyme Bldg., Westmere Dr., Crewe Business Park, Crewe, CW1 6ZL, UK
Tel: 01270 504700
Fax: 01270 504701
Email: info@sccci.co.uk
Website: http://www.southcheshirechamber.org.uk
Members: 448
Staff: 10
Contact: Steven Williams, Chm.
Fee: £111-452
Membership Type: company (based on number of employees)
Description: Represents members across South Chesire at local, regional and national level on matters concerning trade, commerce and industry and lobbying. Facilitates networking, forums and events to enable members to exchange ideas, information, views and business practice.
Publication: Survey
Publication title: Quarterly Economic Survey

04105

South East Folk Arts Network SEFAN

89 Hollingbury Park Ave., Brighton, BN1 78JQ, UK
Tel: 01273 541453
Fax: 01273 554189
Email: admin@sefan.org.uk
Website: http://www.sefan.org.uk
Members: 150
Staff: 1
Contact: Anthony Allen, Chm.
Fee: £16
Membership Type: individual/club/group/small organization
Fee: £48
Membership Type: large organization/festival/funded body
Description: SEFAN is an umbrella organisation serving as an advocate for performing traditional arts in the South East of England. It works to encourage folk content in arts and community events, provide information exchange within the community and to act as a "1st port of call" for all folk-related enquiries in region. Charity status awarded in 2005.

04106

South Eastern Welsh Pony and Cob Association SEWPCA

Flat 2, Rainbow Parade, Broad Oak, Heathfield, TN21 8SX, UK
Tel: 01435 863479
Email: angela.kember@btinternet.com
Website: http://www.sewpca.co.uk
Members: 450
Contact: Fiona Harding, Membership Sec.
Fee: £17.5
Membership Type: full, associate
Fee: £25
Membership Type: couple/joint
Description: Records the breeding details of Welsh ponies and cobs. Seeks to improve the breed and promote its excellence.
Publication: Newsletter

04107

South Wales Chamber of Commerce WWCC

Ethos, Kings Rd., Swansea, SA1 8AS, UK
Tel: 01792 653297
Email: info@southwaleschamber.co.uk
Website: http://www.southwaleschamber.co.uk
Staff: 4
Contact: Gillian Whitfield, Chm.
Description: Represents members across West Wales at local, regional and national level on matters concerning trade, commerce and industry and lobbying. Facilitates networking, forums and events to enable members to exchange ideas, information, views and business practice.
Formerly: Formerly, West Wales Chamber of Commerce

04108

South West Region Campaign for Nuclear Disarmament

c/o The Peace Shop
31 New Bridge St., Exeter, EX4 3AH, UK
Tel: 01392 431447
Email: cndsouthwestregion@yahoo.co.uk
Website: http://www.cnduk.org/index.php/regional-groups/south-west-region-cnd.html
Description: Aims to eliminate British nuclear weapons and other weapons of mass destruction.

04109

South Western Association of WPCS SWAWPCS

Briar Thicket, Ryme Rd., Yetminster, Dorset, Sherborne, DT9 6JY, UK
Tel: 01935 872069
Email: browanponies@hotmail.co.uk
Website: http://www.swawpcs.com
Contact: Sue Hardy, Honorary Sec.
Fee: £10
Membership Type: full
Fee: £2
Membership Type: family
Description: Records the breeding details of Welsh ponies and cobs. Seeks to improve the breed and promote its excellence.

04110

Southampton and Fareham Chamber of Commerce and Industry

Bugle House, 53 Bugle St., Hampshire, Southampton, SO14 2LF, UK
Tel: 023 80223541
Fax: 023 80227426
Email: info@soton-chamber.co.uk
Website: http://www.soton-chamber.co.uk
Members: 2000
Staff: 29
Contact: Jimmy Chestnutt, Dir. Gen.
Fee: £217.38
Membership Type: charity
Fee: £1468.75
Membership Type: company (maximum)
Description: Represents members at local, regional and national level on matters concerning trade, commerce and industry and lobbying. Facilitates networking, forums and events to enable members to exchange ideas, information, views and business practice.
Publication: Magazine
Publication title: Chamber of Commerce News. Advertisements.

04111

Southern Counties Folk Federation SCoFF

3 Cranbury Rd., Woolston, Southampton, SO19 7HZ, UK
Tel: 023 80434209
Fax: 023 80434209
Email: treasurer@scoff.org.uk
Website: http://www.focsle.org.uk/SCoFF
Contact: Sam Satyanadhan, Treas.
Fee: £35
Membership Type: arts centre
Fee: £25
Membership Type: guest club
Description: Promotes folk and related acoustic music and dance in the southern counties of England and the Channel Islands.
Publication: Magazine
Publication title: Folk on Tap. Advertisements.

04112
Southern Counties Welsh Pony and Cob Association
SCWPCA
Borderhill Stables, Clewer Hill, Waltham Chase, Southampton, SO32 2LN, UK
Email: scwpca@hotmail.com
Website: http://www.scwpca.com
Contact: Carla Fall, Membership Sec.
Fee: £8
Membership Type: single
Fee: £12
Membership Type: family (2 adults/2 children)
Description: Promotes educational and recreational activities for members. Encourages and helps small breeders and owners within the area of Hampshire, Berkshire, Wiltshire and Eastern side of Dorset.

04113
Southern Region Campaign for Nuclear Disarmament
Flat 12, Eliot House, 483 Portswood Rd., Southampton, SO17 2TH, UK
Tel: 023 80328335
Email: anna.maria@dsl.pipex.com
Website: http://www.cnduk.org/index.php/regional-groups/southern-region-cnd.html
Description: Aims to eliminate British nuclear weapons and other weapons of mass destruction.

04114
Southwark Habitat for Humanity
SHFH
93 Gordon Rd., London, SE15 3RR, UK
Tel: 020 77320066
Fax: 020 77326060
Email: gareth.hepworth@shfh.org.uk
Website: http://www.habitatforhumanity.org.uk/inv_gb_sou.htm
Contact: Gareth Hepworth, Contact
Description: Works in partnership with volunteers from all faiths who are committed to its goal of eliminating poverty housing. Brings families and communities in need together with volunteers and resources to build decent shelter sold with no profit.

04115
Spa Business Association
SpaBA
Ste. 5-6, Philpot House, Station Rd., Rayleigh, SS6 7HH, UK
Tel: 08707 800787
Fax: 08707 804477
Email: info@spabusinessassociation.co.uk
Website: http://www.spabusinessassociation.co.uk
Contact: Kerry Edwards, Office Mgr.
Fee: £246-4935
Membership Type: corporate (based on turnover)
Fee: £184.48
Membership Type: media, professional association
Description: Represents members who are engaged in spa business across the UK and Ireland. Encourages the highest standards of service among its members through leadership by example in making deals and establishing communications. Promotes the benefits of using spas for health and well-being of the public.

04116
Spanish Chamber of Commerce in Great Britain
126 Wigmore St., London, W1U 3RZ, UK
Tel: 020 70099070
Fax: 020 70099088
Email: info@spanishchamber.co.uk
Website: http://www.spanishchamber.co.uk
Contact: Silvia Estivill, Sec. Gen.
Fee: £265
Membership Type: regular (in UK)
Fee: £265
Membership Type: regular (in Spain)
Description: Works to promote and develop commercial relations and investments between Spain and UK.

04117
Speakability
1 Royal St., London, SE1 7LL, UK
Tel: 020 72619572
Fax: 020 79289542
Email: speakability@speakability.org.uk
Website: http://www.speakability.org.uk
Members: 3500
Staff: 12
Contact: Melanie Derbyshire, Chief Exec.
Fee: £10
Membership Type: bronze
Fee: £25
Membership Type: silver
Description: Works with people with aphasia to overcome the barriers by supporting people living with aphasia through information service and national network of groups; influences individuals and organizations in order to improve services for people with aphasia; raises funds to support these aims.
Formerly: Formerly, Action for Dysphasic Adults
Publication: Newsletter
Publication title: Speaking Up

04118
Specialist Access Engineering and Maintenance Association
SAEMA
19 Joseph Flectcher Dr., Wingerworth, Chesterfield, S42 6TZ, UK
Tel: 024 6224175
Fax: 024 7230357
Email: enquiries@saema.org
Website: http://www.saema.org
Staff: 1
Description: Serves as the national organization for permanent and temporary access industry.
Formerly: Formerly, Suspended Access Equipment Manufacturers' Association

04119
Specialized Information Publishers Association - United Kingdom
SIPA
Cliveden House, 19-22 Victoria Villas, Richmond, Surrey, TW9 2JX, UK
Tel: 020 82887415
Fax: 020 82887415
Email: uksipa@btconnect.com
Website: http://www.sipauk.com
Members: 65
Contact: Karen Hindle, Dir.
Description: Represents specialised information publishers. Provides training in the form of business lunches, workshops and annual conference. Assists members through legal helpline giving advice on health and safety, tax, employment and personnel or commercial legal problems.

04120
Specialty Coffee Association of Europe
SCAE
Oak Lodge Farm, Leighams Rd., Bicknacre, Essex, Chelmsford, CM3 4HF, UK
Tel: 01245 426060
Fax: 01245 426080
Email: secretary@scae.com
Website: http://scae.com
Members: 759
Contact: Nils Erichsen, Pres.
Fee: £135-610
Membership Type: grower, green coffee exporter, producer, roaster, wholesaler, coffee bar, restaurant, kiosk, retailer
Fee: £245-610
Membership Type: importer, trader, broker, agent
Description: Promotes specialty coffee across Europe. Provides a forum for discussion among cafe and coffee shop owners, baristas, exporters, wholesalers and others who are involved in the commercial coffee industry.
Publication: Newsletter
Publication title: Cafe Europa
Meetings/Conventions: Trieste Espresso Expo – annual show

04121
Spinal Injuries Association
SIA
2 Trueman Pl., Oldbrook, Milton Keynes, MK6 2HH, UK
Tel: 0845 6786633
Fax: 0845 0706911
Email: sia@spinal.co.uk
Website: http://www.spinal.co.uk
Members: 5000
Contact: Paul Smith, Exec. Dir.
Fee: £20
Membership Type: full, associate
Fee: £25
Membership Type: European
Description: National charity for spinal cord injured individuals, and all those concerned with their well-being. Offers information, advice and ongoing support to spinal cord injured people on all aspects of living with their disability. Provides helpline for information and advice; and assists those undergoing treatment in spinal injuries centres.
Publication: Book
Publication title: Are We There Yet?
Meetings/Conventions: Hydro Active Women's Challenge – annual competition

04122
Spohr Society of Great Britain
c/o Chris Tutt, Sec.-Treas.
123 Mt. View Rd., Sheffield, S8 8PJ, UK
Tel: 0114 2585420
Email: chtutt@yahoo.co.uk
Website: http://www.spohr-society.org.uk
Members: 70
Contact: Keith Warsop, Chm.

Description: Promotes the performance and recording of the music of Louis Spohr (1784-1859). Assists with research into Spohr's life and works.
Publication: Journal
Publication title: Spohr Journal

04123

Sports Journalists' Association of Great Britain
SJA

c/o Start2Finish Event Management
Unit 92, Capital Business Ctre., 22 Carlton Rd., Surrey, South Croydon, CR2 0BS, UK
Tel: 020 89162234
Fax: 020 89162235
Email: barrynewcombe@gmail.com
Website: http://www.sportsjournalists.co.uk
Members: 550
Contact: Barry Newcombe, Chm.
Fee: £30
Membership Type: domestic
Fee: £20
Membership Type: overseas
Description: All professional sports journalists with newspapers, magazines, television and radio, plus freelancers, photographers and cartoonists.

04124

Sprayed Concrete Association
SCA

Kingsley House, Ganders Business Park, Kingsley, Bordon, Hampshire, GU35 9LU, UK
Tel: 01420 471622
Fax: 01420 471611
Email: admin@sca.org.uk
Website: http://www.sca.org.uk
Description: Represents contractors and manufacturers of sprayed concrete. Promotes high standards in the application of sprayed concrete. Supplies technical guidance to assist engineers, consultants, and specifiers working in the industry. Provides education and training in the use and techniques of sprayed concrete. Promotes discussions and technical exchange of information to advance the technology of sprayed concrete.
Publication: Book
Publication title: Introduction to Sprayed Concrete

04125

Sri Lanka Project
SLP

c/o British Refugee Council
3 Bondway, London, SW8 1SJ, UK
Tel: 020 78203100
Fax: 020 78203107
Email: slproject@refugeecouncil.org.uk
Website: http://brcslproject.gn.apc.org
Contact: Nick Hardwick, Chief Exec.
Description: Promotes and facilitates provision of humanitarian assistance to displaced and dispossessed people in Sri Lanka. Maintains liaison and seeks to coordinate efforts of a network of nongovernmental relief and development organizations with programs in Sri Lanka. Gathers and disseminates to Sri Lankan refugees in Europe and North America information about political events in their home areas.

04126

St. Helens Chamber of Commerce

Salisbury St., Off Chalon Way, St. Helens, WA10 1FY, UK
Tel: 01744 742000
Fax: 01744 742001
Email: info@sthelenschamber.com
Website: http://www.sthelenschamber.com
Members: 1100
Staff: 90
Contact: Kath Boullen, Chief Exec.
Fee: £88.13
Membership Type: self-employed, charity
Fee: £164-1227
Membership Type: firm/company (based on number of employees)
Description: Represents members across St. Helens at local, regional and national level on matters concerning trade, commerce and industry and lobbying. Facilitates networking, forums and events to enable members to exchange ideas, information, views and business practice.

04127

Staff and Educational Development Association
SEDA

Woburn House, 20-24 Tavistock Sq., London, WC1H 9HF, UK
Tel: 020 73806767
Fax: 020 73872655
Email: office@seda.ac.uk
Website: http://www.seda.ac.uk
Contact: Mike Laycock, Co-Chair
Fee: £595-9750
Membership Type: institutional (associate, full)
Fee: £61
Membership Type: associate (independent)
Description: Improves all aspects of learning, teaching and training in higher education through staff and educational development. Sustains links with other organizations committed to enhancing the quality of learning in higher education. Helps all its members, whether staff and educational developers, teachers or learning staff, to enhance the quality of their capabilities in supporting learning.
Publication: Magazine
Publication title: Educational Developments

04128

Stage Management Association
SMA

89 Borough High St., 1st Fl., London, SE1 1NL, UK
Tel: 020 74037999
Email: admin@stagemanagementassociation.co.uk
Website: http://www.stagemanagementassociation.co.uk
Members: 720
Contact: Barbara Eifler, Exec. Dir.
Fee: £85
Membership Type: professional
Fee: £25
Membership Type: student
Description: Supports and represents stage management in the UK.
Publication: Magazine
Publication title: Cueline. Advertisements.

04129

Stair Society

c/o Thomas H. Drysdale, Sec.-Treas.
6 The Glebe, Manse Rd., Dirleton, East Lothian, Edinburgh, EH39 5FB, UK
Tel: 016 20850264
Email: stairsecretary@btinternet.com
Website: http://www.stairsociety.org
Members: 500
Contact: John W. Cairns, Chm.
Fee: £25
Membership Type: individual
Fee: £35
Membership Type: institution
Description: Encourages the study and advance the knowledge of the history of Scots law.

04130

Stand Up For Africa
SUFA

PO Box 46815, London, SW11 5SF, UK
Tel: 020 72287733
Email: info@standupforafrica.org.uk
Website: http://www.standupforafrica.org.uk
Staff: 9
Contact: Elsie Nemlin, Exec. Dir.
Description: Works to help eradicate poverty and suffering in Africa. Involves and supports young Africans in activism and development on behalf of Africa. Works in partnership with community organizations in Africa to address the root causes of poverty among children.

04131

Standing Conference on Library Materials on Africa
SCOLMA

The Library, School of Oriental and African Studies, University of London, Thornhaugh St., Russell Sq., London, WC1H 0XG, UK
Tel: 020 78984157
Fax: 020 78984159
Email: scolma@hotmail.com
Website: http://www2.lse.ac.uk/library/scolma/welcome.htm
Members: 70
Contact: Barbara Spina, Chair
Fee: £37
Membership Type: individual (with journal - by surface mail)
Fee: £42
Membership Type: individual (with journal - by air mail)
Description: Promotes the acquisition of library materials on Africa through a cooperative acquisition scheme between member libraries. Conducts bibliographical projects. Sponsors seminars.
Publication: Journal
Publication title: African Research and Documentation. Advertisements.
Meetings/Conventions: annual conference

04132

Stationers' and Newspaper Makers' Company

Stationers' Hall, Ave. Maria Ln., London, EC4M 7DD, UK
Tel: 020 72460999
Fax: 020 74891975
Email: marketing@stationers.org
Website: http://www.stationers.org

Contact: Susana De Sousa, Contact
Description: Represents the visual and graphic communications in the City of London, UK. Provides an independent forum for its members and events for members to network and share information about the industry.

04133
Steam Plough Club
SPC
Pant-y-Cae, Clyro, Hereford, HR3 6JU, UK
Tel: 01497 820750
Email: thesecretary@steamploughclub.org.uk
Website: http://www.steamploughclub.org.uk
Members: 480
Contact: Dick Eastwood, Sec.
Fee: £15
Membership Type: ordinary
Description: Encourages and expands interest in steam cultivation. Ensures that proper place in history of British agricultural engineering. Provides for the exchange of ideas and material to allow for steam ploughing engines and implements to be kept in the best possible working order for future generations to use and enjoy. Provides education, practical training, experience and competition for members in order to produce the best possible land work using steam ploughing engines and implements. Arranges meetings and visits to allow members to keep in touch. Maintains records and produces films to show the past and present history of steam cultivation.

04134
Steel Construction Institute
SCI
Silwood Park, Berkshire, Ascot, SL5 7QN, UK
Tel: 01344 636525
Fax: 01344 636570
Email: reception@steel-sci.com
Website: http://www.steel-sci.org
Members: 850
Staff: 70
Contact: Christine Roszykiewicz, Proj. Mgr.
Fee: £87
Membership Type: affiliate (UK and Ireland)
Fee: £305
Membership Type: sole trader
Description: Engineers, fabricators, architects, developers. All disciplines involved in the steel construction industry. Promotes and develops the proper and effective use of steel in construction. A range of technical publications result from industry led research projects and educational courses and seminars complement these. Provides advisory service for members.
Library Subject: specialist steel
Library Type: not open to the public
Publication: Magazine
Publication title: New Steel Construction. Advertisements.

04135
Steel Window Association
SWA
42 Heath St., Tamworth, B79 7JH, UK
Tel: 0844 2491355
Fax: 01827 310827
Email: info@steel-window-association.co.uk
Website: http://www.steel-window-association.co.uk
Members: 20
Staff: 2
Contact: Alain Skelding, Sec.
Description: Represents the majority of UK steel window manufacturers and supports member companies with a wide range of product development, market research and promotional activities. Offers a technical advice service and free literature distribution is available to specifiers.
Publication title: Specifier's Guide to Steel Windows

04136
Stephenson Locomotive Society
SLS
1A Lostock Ave., Cheshire, SK12 1DR, UK
Email: slsmembership@dickin.myzen.co.uk
Website: http://www.stephensonloco.org.uk
Members: 680
Contact: M.D. Dickin, Contact
Fee: £25
Membership Type: full
Fee: £10
Membership Type: young (under 21 years old)
Description: Aims to study the operation and history of railways, particularly locomotives and rolling stock.
Library Subject: railways, locomotives
Library Type: reference
Publication: Journal
Publication title: Journal of the Stephenson Locomotive Society. Advertisements.

04137
Steps Charity Worldwide
Warrington Ln., Cheshire, Lymm, WA13 0SA, UK
Tel: 01925 750273
Fax: 01925 750270
Email: info@steps-charity.org.uk
Website: http://www.steps-charity.org.uk
Members: 2500
Staff: 7
Contact: Sue Banton, Founder/Dir.
Description: Provides information and support for families of children with lower limb abnormalities. Brings families in touch with one another, and develops a network of local contacts providing support, help and advise. Gathers and exchanges information with parents and health professionals.
Library Type: reference
Formerly: Formerly, STEPS: Association for People with Lower Limb Abnormalities

04138
Stereoscopic Society
SS
6 Sheppards Ct., Horsenden Ln. N, Greenford, UB6 7QJ, UK
Email: info@stereoscopy.net
Website: http://www.stereoscopicsociety.org.uk
Members: 700
Contact: Bob Aldridge, Pres.
Fee: £21
Membership Type: within UK
Fee: £23
Membership Type: mainland Europe (outside UK)
Description: Individuals who are interested in the production of stereoscopic photographs. (Stereoscopy is the study of three dimensional imagery.) Seeks to advance stereoscopic photography by circulating prints or transparencies through the mail. Organizes meetings to encourage exchange of ideas and technical advice. Maintains small collection of books and stereoscopic production items. Computer group.
Publication: Journal
Publication title: Journal of 3-D Imaging. Advertisements.

Stichting Eurodata
see Teligen

04139
Stillbirth and Neonatal Death Society
SANDS
28 Portland Pl., London, W1B 1LY, UK
Tel: 0207 4367940
Fax: 0207 4363715
Email: support@uk-sands.org
Website: http://www.uk-sands.org
Members: 900
Staff: 5
Contact: Neal Long, Chief Exec.
Fee: £16
Membership Type: individual
Fee: £8
Membership Type: individual (benefits/low income)
Description: Offers support to parents and their families who have been affected by the death of a baby that has died before, during, or shortly after birth; also offers training to healthcare professionals involved in their care.
Publication: Book
Publication title: A Dignified Ending

04140
Stilton Cheesemakers' Association
PO Box 384A, Surbiton, KT5 9YL, UK
Tel: 0161 9234994
Email: enquiries@stiltoncheese.com
Website: http://www.stiltoncheese.com
Members: 5
Description: Stilton cheese makers. Protects registered certification trade mark "Stilton" throughout the world; maintains the high quality of the product; and promotes the sale of Stilton cheeses, primarily in the UK and the USA.

04141
Stop the War Coalition
STWC
231 Vauxhall Bridge Rd., London, SW1V 1EH, UK
Tel: 020 78012768
Website: http://www.stopwar.org.uk
Contact: Tony Benn, Pres.
Fee: £24
Membership Type: standard
Fee: £12
Membership Type: concession
Description: Aims to stop the war against terrorism. Organizes demonstrations against war and occupation of Iraq. Commits to oppose racist backlash generated by the erosion of civil rights.

04142
Storage and Handling Equipment Distributors' Association
SHEDA
Heathcote House, 130 Hagley Rd., Birmingham, B16 9PN, UK
Tel: 0121 4544141
Email: info@sheda.org.uk
Website: http://www.sheda.org.uk
Contact: Craig Powell, Pres.
Description: Members include stockists, designers and installers.

04143

Strategic Planning Society
SPS

Mayfair House, 14-18 Heddon St., London, W1B 4DA, UK
Tel: 0845 0563663
Fax: 0845 0563663
Email: membership@sps.org.uk
Website: http://www.sps.org.uk
Members: 4000
Staff: 6
Contact: Anthony Burton, Vice Chm.
Fee: £119.03
Membership Type: individual
Fee: £1242
Membership Type: corporate
Description: Corporations, educational institutions, and small companies and firms; executives, planners, government officials, and interested individuals. Promotes strategic planning in private, public, and governmental organizations. Seeks to: create and maintain networks for decision makers and planners; develop improved techniques for strategic planning; provide resources of knowledge and experience to aid businesses with planning problems; address political, economic, and social issues facing planners. Has established special interest and regional groups. Maintains Speaker's Bureau.
Library Type: open to the public
Publication: Journal
Publication title: Long Range Planning
Meetings/Conventions: Planning Directors' Strategy Forum – periodic meeting

04144

Stroke Association

Stroke House, 240 City Rd., London, EC1V 2PR, UK
Tel: 020 75660300
Fax: 020 74902686
Email: info@stroke.org.uk
Website: http://www.stroke.org.uk
Contact: Jon Barrick, Chief Exec.
Description: Works in England and Wales to control stroke in people of all ages. Funds research into prevention, treatment and better methods of rehabilitation, and helps stroke patients and families directly through community services.

Studium Polski Podziemnej (SPP)
see Polish Underground Movement (1939-1945) Study Trust

04145

Sudan Studies Society of the United Kingdom
SSSUK

c/o Mr. Adrian Thomas, Hon. Treas.
30 Warner Rd., London, N8 7HD, UK
Email: sudanstudies@sssuk.org
Website: http://www.sssuk.org
Contact: H.R. Davies, Honorary Ed.
Fee: £12
Membership Type: individual in UK
Fee: £20
Membership Type: institution in UK
Description: Promotes Sudanese studies in the United Kingdom and worldwide at all levels and disciplines.
Publication: Newsletter
Publication title: Sudan Studies

04146

Suffolk Chamber of Commerce

Felaw Maltings, S Kiln, 42 Felaw St., Ipswich, IP2 8SQ, UK
Tel: 01473 680600
Fax: 01473 603888
Email: info@suffolkchamber.co.uk
Website: http://www.suffolkchamber.co.uk
Members: 1300
Staff: 16
Contact: John Dugmore, Chief Exec.
Fee: £1835
Membership Type: organisation (based on number of staff)
Fee: £80
Membership Type: charity
Description: Promotes business and commerce.

04147

Sugar Association of London
SAL

154, Bishopsgate, London, EC2M 4LN, UK
Tel: 020 73772113
Fax: 020 72472481
Email: durhamn@sugar-assoc.co.uk
Website: http://www.sugarassociation.co.uk
Members: 120
Staff: 12
Contact: N. Durham, Sec.
Fee: £600
Membership Type: full (plus 1,000 joining fee)
Fee: £500
Membership Type: affiliate (plus 1,000 joining fee)
Description: Firms, companies, or organisations, which have a continuing interest in trading raw sugar. Works for the supervision of weighing and sampling of raw sugar cargoes, the provision of contract rules for the international raw sugar trade, and the provision of arbitrators for the settlement of disputes by commercial arbitration. Protects the interests of members and the international raw sugar trade in general.

04148

Sugar Bureau

25 Floral St., London, WC2E 9DS, UK
Tel: 020 71898301
Fax: 020 70318101
Email: info@sugar-bureau.co.uk
Website: http://www.sugar-bureau.co.uk
Members: 4
Staff: 10
Contact: Alison Boyd, Dir.
Description: Companies supplying sugar in the UK. Develops and communicates scientific facts about sugar to health professionals, universities, consumers, and the media. Offers technical and consumer information. Represents members' commercial and public relations interests.
Publication title: Dental Digest

04149

Support Organisation for Trisomy 13/18 and Related Disorders - UK
SOFT UK

48 Froggatts Ride, Walmley, West Midlands, Sutton Coldfield, B76 2TQ, UK
Tel: 0121 3513122
Email: enquiries@soft.org.uk
Website: http://www.soft.org.uk
Contact: Christine Rose, Contact
Description: Provides support, assistance and information for families affected by Trisomy 18, 13 and related disorders. Increases public and professional awareness of these syndromes. Promotes good relationships with the medical profession and the media.
Publication: Booklet
Publication title: Facts for Families

04150

Surface Engineering Association
SEA

Federation House, 10 Vyse St., Birmingham, B18 6LT, UK
Tel: 0121 2371123
Fax: 0121 2371124
Email: info@sea.org.uk
Website: http://www.sea.org.uk
Members: 450
Staff: 4
Contact: David Elliott, CEO
Description: Companies which provide surface finishing services, supplies, equipment, and finishing departments of manufacturing companies. Also surface finishing consultants. Aims to raise the awareness in designers, regulators and customers of the importance of surface finishing industry. Companies also supply paint and powder finishes, as well as heat treatment services.
Library Subject: surface engineering
Library Type: not open to the public
Formerly: Formerly, Metal Finishing Association
Publication: Bulletin
Publication title: Pricewatch. Advertisements.

04151

Surfers Against Sewage
SAS

Unit 2, Wheal Kitty Workshops, St. Agnes, Cornwall, TR5 0RD, UK
Tel: 01872 553001
Email: info@sas.org.uk
Website: http://www.sas.org.uk
Fee: £21
Membership Type: single
Fee: £15
Membership Type: unwaged
Description: Advocates for an end to the discharge of raw and partially treated sewage and toxic waste into the sea and inland waters through education, lobbying and promoting public awareness about the importance of a pollution free environment.

04152

Surgical Dressing Manufacturers Association
SDMA

17 The Crescent, Holymoorside, Chesterfield, S42 7EE, UK
Tel: 01246 568175
Fax: 01246 568175
Email: sdma@nigelb.fsworld.co.uk
Website: http://www.dressings.org.uk
Members: 15
Contact: Nigel Brassington, Sec.
Description: Encourages the expanding use of safe and effective surgical dressings products in health care markets. Creates a framework within which the surgical dressings industry can grow and prosper in an ethical and responsible manner.

04153

Surrey Chambers of Commerce

Unit 4a, Monument Way E, Woking, GU21 5LY, UK
Tel: 01483 726655
Fax: 01483 740217
Email: louis.punter@surrey-chambers.co.uk
Website: http://www.surrey-chambers.co.uk
Members: 1451
Staff: 22
Contact: Louise Punter, Chief Exec.
Fee: £264-1169
Membership Type: company (based on number of employees)
Description: Represents members across Surrey at local, regional and national level on matters concerning trade, commerce and industry and lobbying. Facilitates networking, forums and events to enable members to exchange ideas, information, views and business practice.
Publication: Newsletter
Publication title: Newslink. Advertisements.

04154

Surtees Society

Elvet Riverside Block 2, Durham, DH1 3JT, UK
Tel: 0191 3342908
Fax: 0191 3342911
Email: surtees.society@durham.ac.uk
Website: http://www.surteessociety.org.uk
Members: 227
Fee: £25
Membership Type: individual
Description: Promotes the advancement of public education in the region that constitutes the ancient kingdom of Northumbria in northeast England through the transcription, editing, translating, and publication of original historical documents.

04155

Survival

6 Charterhouse Bldgs., London, EC1M 7ET, UK
Tel: 020 76878700
Fax: 020 76878701
Email: info@survivalinternational.org
Website: http://www.survival-international.org
Members: 20000
Staff: 30
Contact: Stephen Corry, Dir. Gen.
Description: Worldwide organisation that supports tribal peoples. Stands for the right of tribal people to decide for the future, and helps to protect the lands, lives, and human rights of these people. Works through campaigns and education that focus on urgent situations and tend to deal with on the least contacted and so most vulnerable peoples. Currently working on about 80 cases in 34 countries around the world. Produces books and teaching packs; provides lessons in schools; organizes public talks; and arranges exhibitions. Aims to inform the public about tribal peoples. Opposes racism by demonstrating that tribal people far from primitive. Distributes materials in more than 70 countries. Supports projects in health and land rights for indigenous groups in areas such as Argentina, Australia, Botswana, Brazil, Canada, India, Indonesia, Kenya, Paraguay, Russia, the Philippines, and Venezuela. Provides films, slide shows, radio projects, publications, and photographic exhibitions for display in colleges, libraries, schools, teachers' centers, and at conferences and meetings.
Formerly: Formerly, Primitive Peoples Fund
Publication: Bulletin
Publication title: Urgent Action Bulletin

04156

Sussex Chamber of Commerce and Enterprise

Greenacre Ct., Station Rd., Burgess Hill, RH15 9DS, UK
Tel: 0845 6788867
Fax: 01444 259255
Email: info@sussexenterprise.co.uk
Website: http://www.sussexenterprise.co.uk
Members: 2500
Staff: 140
Contact: Mark Froud, CEO
Fee: £85
Membership Type: start-up
Fee: £99
Membership Type: small business
Description: Promotes business and commerce.

04157

Sussex Peace Alliance

67 Summerheath Rd., Hailsham, BN27 3DR, UK
Tel: 01323 844269
Email: geowcpuk@gn.apc.org
Website: http://www.cnduk.org/index.php/regional-groups/sussex-peace-alliance.html
Description: Aims to eliminate British nuclear weapons and other weapons of mass destruction.

04158

Sustain: The Alliance for Better Food and Farming

94 White Lion St., London, N1 9PF, UK
Tel: 020 78371228
Fax: 020 78371141
Email: sustain@sustainweb.org
Website: http://www.sustainweb.org
Members: 100
Contact: Jeanette Longfield, Coor.
Fee: £65-630
Membership Type: regular (based on annual income)
Description: Advocates for food and agriculture policies and practices to enhance the health and welfare of people and animals, improve the working and living conditions, promote equality, and enrich society and culture.
Publication: Report
Publication title: Bread Street: The British Baking Bloomer

04159

Sustainable Development Network SDN

PO Box 1356, Bristol, BS99 3BY, UK
Tel: 0117 9871300
Website: http://www.kabissa.org/members/sdnetwork
Members: 20
Contact: Idem Udoekong, Contact
Description: Promotes sustainable development at grass-roots community level in third world countries addressing environmental education, waste management, sustainable agricultural development, sustainable use of natural resources, ethical and socially responsible entrepreneurship.

04160

Swedenborg Society

20/21 Bloomsbury Way, London, WC1A 2TH, UK
Tel: 020 74057986
Fax: 020 78315848
Website: http://www.swedenborg.org.uk
Members: 815
Staff: 5
Contact: Richard Lines, Sec.
Fee: £5
Membership Type: individual
Fee: £50
Membership Type: life (individual)
Description: Individuals interested in Emanuel Swedenborg's writings. Promotes the printing and publishing of the works of Swedenborg into various languages, including English, most European languages, and some Asian and African languages. Provides free grants of Swedenborg's works to public libraries.
Publication: Newsletter
Publication title: Things Heard and Seen

04161

Swedish-English Literary Translators' Association SELTA

c/o Peter Linton, Sec./Webmaster
3 Roseacre Close, London, W13 8DG, UK
Tel: 020 89971218
Email: peter@lintononline.co.uk
Website: http://www.selta.org.uk/home.php
Members: 50
Contact: Eivor Martinus, Chm.
Fee: £15
Membership Type: full
Fee: £13
Membership Type: associate
Description: Swedish-English translators. Promotes publication of Swedish literature in English. Represents the interests of translators. Gathers and disseminates information.
Publication: Journal
Publication title: Swedish Book Review. Advertisements.

04162

Swimming Pool and Allied Trades Association SPATA

4 Eastgate House, E St., Hamspshire, Andover, SP10 1EP, UK
Tel: 01264 356210
Email: admin@spata.co.uk
Website: http://www.spata.co.uk
Members: 250
Staff: 2
Fee: £445
Membership Type: allied trade
Fee: £269
Membership Type: associate, affiliate
Description: Swimming pool installers, retail suppliers, trade suppliers, manufacturers, and companies associated with the swimming pool industry. Sets the standards for the industry and ensures that these standards are maintained. Maintains contact with Government Departments and all public and professional organizations concerned in any way with swimming.
Publication title: The Spata Standards
Meetings/Conventions: Spatex – annual meeting – Exhibits.

Syndicat Europeen de l'Industrie des Futs Fibre
see European Association of Fibre Drum Manufacturers

04163
Systematics Association
SA
Dept. of Botany, The Natural History Museum, Cromwell Rd., London, SW7 5BD, UK
Email: j.brodie@nhm.ac.uk
Website: http://www.systass.org
Members: 600
Staff: 7
Contact: J. Brodie, Pres.
Fee: £20
Membership Type: regular
Fee: £10
Membership Type: student, retired, unwaged
Description: Aims to provide a forum for discussing systematic problems and integrated new information from genetics, ecology and other specific fields into concepts and activities.
Publication: Newsletter
Publication title: The Systematist

04164
Talking Newspaper Association of the United Kingdom
TNAUK
National Recording Ctre., East Sussex, Heathfield, TN21 8DB, UK
Tel: 01435 866102
Fax: 01435 865422
Email: info@tnauk.org.uk
Website: http://www.tnauk.org.uk
Members: 18000
Staff: 30
Contact: Trevor McDonald, Chief Exec.
Fee: £30
Membership Type: domestic
Fee: £45
Membership Type: abroad
Description: Records newspapers and magazine on audio tape, computer disk, or CD-ROM for visually impaired persons.
Publication: Magazine
Publication title: Talking Newspaper News. Advertisements.

04165
Talyllyn Railway Preservation Society
TRPS
Wharf Station, Gwynedd, Tywyn, LL36 9EY, UK
Tel: 01654 710472
Fax: 01654 711755
Email: enquiries@talyllyn.co.uk
Website: http://www.talyllyn.co.uk
Members: 3500
Contact: John Robinson, Sec.
Fee: £500
Membership Type: life
Fee: £25
Membership Type: full
Description: Preserves the Talyllyn (narrow-gauge steam-operated) railway by voluntary work, financial assistance and publicity.
Publication: Magazine
Publication title: Talyllyn News. Advertisements.

04166
Tartans of Scotland
Scottish Tartans World Register, The Glack, Dunkeld, PH8 0ER, UK
Tel: 01350 728849
Fax: 01350 728849
Email: info@tartans.scotland.net
Website: http://www.tartans.scotland.net
Contact: Keith G.A. Lumsden, Registrar/Dir.
Description: Persons in 16 countries interested in preserving the heritage of Scottish tartans and highland dress. Conducts research into the identification of tartans, particularly the relation of clan and tartan to surnames. Maintains 2 museums and collections of books, manuscripts, paintings, drawings, and photographs of tartans and historic highland dress. Maintains register of tartans. Offers authentication service. Awards fellowships. Organizes school visits.
Formerly: Formerly, Scottish Tartans Society

04167
Tattoo Club of Great Britain
TCGB
389 Cowley Rd., Oxford, OX4 2BS, UK
Tel: 01865 715253
Fax: 01865 775610
Email: tcgb@tattoo.co.uk
Website: http://www.tattoo.co.uk
Members: 100
Staff: 1
Contact: Lionel Titchener, Contact
Description: Professionally registered tattoo artists working in accordance with Miscellaneous Provisions Act 1982. Aims to promote registered professional tattoo artists and to encourage clients to go to professionals not amateurs. Discourages tattooing of hands, face and neck. Has tattoo studio incorporating the Tattoo History Museum.
Formerly: Formerly, British Tattoo Artists Federation
Publication: Newsletter
Publication title: Tattoo International

04168
Tavistock Institute
30 Tabernacle St., London, EC2A 4UE, UK
Tel: 020 74170407
Email: hello@tavinstitute.org
Website: http://www.tavinstitute.org
Members: 120
Staff: 30
Contact: Eliat Aram, Dir.
Description: Aims to encompass the study of human relations in conditions of well being, conflict and change in the community, the work group and the larger organizations, together with the promotion of the effectiveness of individuals and organizations.
Publication title: Annual Review

04169
TE Lawrence Society
PO Box 728, Oxford, OX2 9ZJ, UK
Email: information@telsociety.org.uk
Website: http://telsociety.org.uk/telsociety/index.htm
Members: 600
Fee: £13-18
Membership Type: in UK
Fee: £16-23
Membership Type: overseas
Description: Aims to provide scholars and the public with accurate information about the life and works of T.E. Lawrence. Encourages serious research. Publishes information and research in a high-quality journal.
Publication: Journal
Publication title: Journal of the T.E. Lawrence Society

04170
Tea Council
9, The Courtyard, Gowan Ave., Fulham, London, SW6 6RH, UK
Tel: 020 73717787
Fax: 020 73717958
Email: info@teacouncil.co.uk
Website: http://www.tea.co.uk
Members: 50
Staff: 4
Contact: William Gorman, Exec. Chm.
Description: Generic promotion of tea and tea drinking in UK, on behalf of tea producing countries and UK tea companies.
Publication title: Guild of Tea Shops Guide

04171
Teaching Aids at Low Cost
TALC
PO Box 49, St. Albans, AL1 5TX, UK
Tel: 01727 853869
Fax: 01727 846852
Email: info@talcuk.org
Website: http://www.talcuk.org
Staff: 9
Contact: Hilary Heine, Gen. Mgr.
Description: Distributes low-cost books and teaching aids worldwide in order to help improve standards of health care worldwide.

04172
Tearfund
TF
100 Church Rd., Teddington, TW11 8QE, UK
Tel: 0845 3558355
Email: enquiry@tearfund.org
Website: http://www.tearfund.org
Staff: 270
Contact: Clive Mather, Chm.
Description: Religious organizations providing relief and development services worldwide. Promotes appropriate and sustainable development; seeks to ensure respect for the human rights of indigenous peoples in developing areas. Provides support and assistance to church-based development and relief projects; publicizes human rights abuses; makes available services to refugees and other displaced persons.
Publication: Magazine
Publication title: Teartimes

04173
Technical Advisors Group
TAG

Transportation Dept., Westminster City Council, 10th Fl. N, East City Hall, 64 Victoria St., London, SW1E 6QP, UK
Tel: 020 76413807
Email: mlow@westminster.gov.uk
Website: http://www.tagonline.co.uk
Members: 375
Staff: 3
Contact: Martin Low, Pres.
Fee: £95
Membership Type: regular
Fee: £75
Membership Type: associate
Description: Chief technical officers working with governmental and nongovernmental organizations on technical aspects of community and urban development and service provision. Disseminates information on community development projects and services.
Formerly: Formerly, Association of London Burough Engineers and Surveyors

04174
Telecommunications Heritage Group
THG

Dalton House, 60 Windsor Ave., London, SW19 2RR, UK
Tel: 020 80991699
Email: membership@thg.org.uk
Website: http://www.thg.org.uk
Members: 450
Staff: 5
Fee: £4.25-17
Membership Type: in UK
Membership Type: in Europe
Description: Promotes the study, collection, and preservation of telecommunications equipment. Works to preserve both individual articles and entire networks intact.
Publication: Journal
Publication title: Telecommunications Heritage Group Journal. Advertisements.

04175
Television and Radio Industries Club
TRIC

Hill Farm, Margaretting Rd., Essex, Galleywood, CM2 8TS, UK
Tel: 01245 290480
Fax: 01245 265963
Email: info@tric.org.uk
Website: http://www.tric.org.uk
Contact: George Stone, Dir.
Description: Supports professionals with careers in television and radio entertainment, communications, manufacturing, and related industries. Provides networking opportunities for members.

04176
Telework Association
TCA

The Warren, Polperro, Looe, Cornwall, PL13 2R, UK
Email: shirley@telework.org.uk
Website: http://www.tca.org.uk
Members: 2300
Staff: 2
Contact: Shirley Borrett, Exec. Dir.
Fee: £34.5
Membership Type: individual
Fee: £150
Membership Type: corporate
Description: Individuals (teleworkers) working from home supported by technology, people running centres supporting home based teleworkers, regional development agencies, companies introducing teleworking schemes. Concerned with the improvement in employment, training and services for people living in rural areas and the development of local economies through the use of IT and telecommunications including share facilities in local centers.
Library Subject: teleworking, telecottages, and telecentres
Library Type: not open to the public
Publication: Magazine
Publication title: Teleworker Magazine. Advertisements.

04177
Teligen

GreatWest House, GreatWest Rd., Brentford, TW8 9DF, UK
Tel: 02081 850402
Fax: 02081 850419
Email: info@teligen.com
Website: http://www.teligen.com
Contact: Halvor Sannaes, Dir., Tariff Services
Description: Serves as a key information provider to both telcos and the international user marketplace.
Publication: Newsletter
Publication title: Tariff Outlook

04178
Tenant Farmers Association
TFA

5 Brewery Ct., Theale, Reading, RG7 5AJ, UK
Tel: 0118 9306130
Fax: 0118 9303424
Email: tfa@tfa.org.uk
Website: http://www.tfa.org.uk
Members: 4000
Staff: 5
Contact: George Dunn, Chief Exec.
Description: Tenant farmers in Great Britain and Wales requiring professional advice and guidance on landlord - tenancy matters. Aims to promote the landlord - tenant system and seeks to create a fair environment in which the tenant farmer can flourish commercially without unsustainable rents and stifling restrictions.
Publication: Pamphlet
Publication title: Briefing Notes

04179
Tenant Participation Advisory Service
TPAS

5th Fl., Trafford House, Chester Rd., Manchester, M32 0RS, UK
Tel: 0161 8683500
Fax: 0161 8776256
Email: info@tpas.org.uk
Website: http://www.tpas.org.uk
Contact: Michelle Reid, Chief Exec.
Description: Seeks social housing policies and legal protection of occupation rights for all tenants. Acts as medium for cooperation among members.

04180
Tenants and Residents Organisation of England
TAROE

Jackson House, 2nd Ave., Runcorn, WA7 2PD, UK
Tel: 01928 701001
Fax: 01928 790281
Email: runcornoffice@taroe.org
Website: http://www.taroe.org
Members: 337
Staff: 4
Contact: Cora Carter, Chair
Fee: £10
Membership Type: individual
Fee: £20
Membership Type: single (individual tenant and resident association)
Description: Aims to support employment that enables people with disabilities who have not been successfully employed to work and contribute to society.

04181
Tennyson Society
TS

c/o Central Library
Free School Ln., Lincoln, LN2 1EZ, UK
Tel: 01522 552862
Email: kathleen.jefferson@lincolnshire.gov.uk
Website: http://community.lincolnshire.gov.uk/thetennysonsociety
Contact: Kathleen Jefferson, Contact
Fee: £10
Membership Type: personal, school
Fee: £12
Membership Type: family
Description: Individuals, libraries, universities, schools, and colleges seeking to promote the study and understanding of the life and works of Alfred, Lord Tennyson (1809-92), poet laureate of England from 1850 to 1892. Sponsors lectures, dinners, pilgrimages, annual memorial service and wreath-laying ceremony.

04182
Tenovus Scotland
TS

234 St. Vincent St., Glasgow, G2 5RJ, UK
Tel: 01292 443387
Fax: 01292 311433
Email: gen.sec@talk21.com
Website: http://www.tenovus-scotland.org.uk
Contact: Iain McFadzean, Gen. Sec.
Description: Individuals and organizations. Promotes advancement of medical research projects undertaken by Scottish hospitals and university medical schools. Provides financial support and other assistance to medical research programs. Conducts fundraising activities.

04183
Textile Institute
TI

St. James's Buildings, 1st Fl., 79 Oxford St., Manchester, M1 6FQ, UK
Tel: 0161 2371188
Fax: 0161 2361991
Email: tiihq@textileinst.org.uk
Website: http://www.texi.org
Contact: Andreas Weber, Pres.
Fee: £100
Membership Type: individual (non-UK/USA)
Fee: £625
Membership Type: corporate
Description: Companies and individuals in 100 countries involved in management, science, technology, design, information transfer, and marketing of textiles including clothing and footwear. Promotes interests of the textile industry worldwide; serves professional interests of members; confers qualifications and recognizes achievements in research, application of ideas, education, business, and public affairs. Maintains Information Service to collect information relating to textile industrial and economic conditions in different countries and economic sectors.
Library Subject: textiles
Library Type: by appointment only
Publication: Journal
Publication title: Journal of the Textile Institute

04184
Textile Recycling Association
TRA

PO Box 965, Kent, Maidstone, ME17 3WD, UK
Tel: 0870 428276
Fax: 0870 428276
Email: info@textile-recycling.org.uk
Website: http://www.textile-recycling.org.uk
Members: 42
Fee: £900
Membership Type: full voting (A)
Fee: £800
Membership Type: full voting (B)
Description: Textile recyclers/reclaimers and wiping cloth manufacturers.
Formerly: Formerly, Reclamation Association
Publication: Booklet
Publication title: Recyclatex Booklet for Schools

04185
Textile Services Association
TSA

5 Portland Pl., London, W1B 1PW, UK
Tel: 020 88637755
Fax: 020 88612115
Email: tsa@tsa-uk.org
Website: http://www.tsa-uk.org
Members: 600
Staff: 5
Contact: Murray Simpson, Chief Exec.
Fee: £157.5
Membership Type: single unit drycleaner
Fee: £40000
Membership Type: large company (based on turnover)
Description: Members are companies involved in laundry, dry cleaning and textile rental. Gives advice to members on health and safety matters, industrial relations and environmental and trade protection matters through its various publications and member Bulletins.

04186
Textile Society for the Study of Art, Design and History

PO Box 1012, St. Albans, AL1 9NE, UK
Tel: 020 73597678
Email: info@textilesociety.org.uk
Website: http://www.textilesociety.org.uk
Members: 400
Contact: Brenda King, Chair
Fee: £18
Membership Type: individual
Fee: £23
Membership Type: household
Description: Aims to unite scholars, designers, teachers, practitioners, artists, collectors, and others interested in the study of textile art, design, and history. Conducts an educational program with visits to exhibitions and lectures.
Publication: Journal
Publication title: TEXT

04187
Thalidomide Society

6 Abbis Orchard, Ickleford, Hitchin, SG5 3TN, UK
Tel: 01462 438212
Fax: 01462 438212
Email: info@thalsoc.demon.co.uk
Website: http://www.thalidomidesociety.co.uk
Members: 330
Staff: 1
Contact: Vivien Kerr, Contact
Description: Provides support, advice and information to thalidomide and similarly disabled people living in the U.K.

04188
Thames Valley Chamber of Commerce

467 Malton Ave., Berkshire, Slough, SL1 4QU, UK
Tel: 01753 870500
Fax: 01753 870501
Email: customerservices@tvchamber.co.uk
Website: http://www.thamesvalleychamber.co.uk
Members: 3000
Staff: 42
Contact: Paul Briggs, Chief Exec.
Fee: £150-1500
Membership Type: company (based on the number of employees)
Fee: £5000
Membership Type: business alliance
Description: Promotes business and commerce.
Publication: Magazine
Publication title: Business Voice. Advertisements.

04189
Thanet and East Kent Chamber
TEKC

Kent Innovation Centre, Thanet Reach Business Park, Millennium Way, Kent, Broadstairs, CT10 2QQ, UK
Tel: 01843 609289
Fax: 01843 609291
Email: admin@tekc.co.uk
Website: http://www.tekc.co.uk
Members: 230
Staff: 1
Contact: David Foley, Chief Exec.
Fee: £170-1495
Membership Type: band (based on number of employees)
Description: Represents members across Thanet and East Kent area at local, regional and national level on matters concerning trade, commerce and industry and lobbying. Facilitates networking, forums and events to enable members to exchange ideas, information, views and business practice.
Formerly: Formerly, Thanet and East Kent Chamber of Commerce

04190
The Arthur Ransome Society
TARS

Abbot Hall Museum, Kendal, Cumbria, LA9 5AL, UK
Email: tarsinfo@arthur-ransome.org
Website: http://www.arthur-ransome.org/ar
Members: 2400
Contact: Peter Hyland, Sec.
Fee: £42
Membership Type: adult in U.S.
Fee: £20
Membership Type: adult outside U.S.
Description: Promotes wider readership of the works of English author Arthur Ransome (1884-1967). Educates the public about Ransome's life, writing, and ideas. Sponsors activities for children that encourage sailing, fishing, or exploring in areas described in Ransome's books. Conducts research; publishes results. Also conducts charitable programs. Supports museum.
Formerly: Formerly, The Arthur Ransome Society
Publication: Journal
Publication title: Mixed Moss. Advertisements.
Meetings/Conventions: Literary Weekend – biennial conference

04191
The Churches Conservation Trust
TCCT

1 W Smithfield, London, EC1A 9EE, UK
Tel: 020 72130660
Fax: 020 72130678
Email: central@tcct.org.uk
Website: http://www.visitchurches.org.uk
Members: 340
Staff: 39
Contact: Loyd Grossman, Chm.
Description: Seeks to preserve redundant churches of historical, archaeological, or architectural interest. (Trust churches remain consecrated within the Church of England but are no longer used for regular worship. Currently, the Trust maintains more than 300 churches.) Encourages the holding of occasional services, concerts, art and history exhibitions, flower festivals, and other suitable events.
Formerly: Formerly, Redundant Churches Fund
Publication: Annual Report
Publication title: Annual Report and Accounts

04192
The Environment Council
TEC

PoBox 66755, London, WC1A9EA, UK
Tel: 020 81448380
Fax: 020 71609304
Email: info@envcouncil.org.uk
Website: http://www.the-environment-council.org.uk
Staff: 9
Contact: Winsome MacLaurin, Chief Exec.
Description: An independent charity dedicated to building awareness, dialogue and effective solutions to enhance

and protect Britain's environment. Administers: Business Programmes to help businesses become more environmentally aware; Environmental Resolve, an environmental mediation and training service.
Formerly: Absorbed, Conservation Trust
Publication: Handbook
Publication title: Business and Environment Programme Handbook

04193
The Event Services Association
TESA
Association House, 18c Moor St., Chepstow, NP16 5DB, UK
Tel: 01291 636331
Fax: 01291 630402
Email: jim@jandmgroup.co.uk
Website: http://www.tesa.org.uk
Members: 189
Staff: 6
Contact: Jim Winship, Dir.
Fee: £435
Membership Type: supplier
Fee: £50
Membership Type: event organizer
Description: Membership comprises both suppliers to the event industry and event organizers. Aims to work with other associations within the event industry to try and raise standards and increase safety measures. In particular, drawing up Codes of Practice to cover the different sectors of the industry e.g. safety, catering, marquees, seating, and staging. Collaborates with other industry bodies and supports appropriate guidelines/codes.
Publication: Magazine
Publication title: Event Organiser. Advertisements.
Meetings/Conventions: annual conference – Exhibits.

04194
The Federation of Image Consultants
TFIC
PO Box 31, Hemel Hempstead, HP3 0QZ, UK
Tel: 0844 5001018
Email: info@tfic.org.uk
Website: http://www.tfic.org.uk
Members: 200
Contact: Sue Donnelly, Pres.
Fee: £80
Membership Type: affiliate
Description: Represents professionals working or specializing in the field of personal image development. Sets and maintains standards for the profession. Supports and promotes consultants. Acts as a media source for the press and an information source for the general public.
Library Subject: image consultancy
Library Type: by appointment only

04195
The Fitness League
TFL
6 Sta. Parade, Berkshire, Sunningdale, SL5 0EP, UK
Tel: 01344 874787
Fax: 01344 873887
Email: info@thefitnessleague.com
Website: http://www.thefitnessleague.com
Members: 14000
Staff: 4
Contact: Peter Hobden, Council Chm.
Description: Charity organization. Promotes education for women in physical training, health, and fitness. Offers training courses and exercise classes.
Formerly: Formerly, Women's League of Health and Beauty

04196
Tho Roiki Association
TRA
Westgate Ct., Spittal, Haverfordwest, SA62 5QP, UK
Email: enquiries@reikiassociation.org.uk
Website: http://www.reikiassociation.org.uk
Contact: Sonia Thornton, Contact
Fee: £52
Membership Type: individual
Fee: £36
Membership Type: individual (first additional)
Description: Encourages people to deepen their practice of the art of Reiki. Provides information about Reiki to members and the wider community. Fosters the Reiki community locally, nationally and internationally. Encourages professional standards of Reiki practice.
Publication: Magazine
Publication title: Touch

04197
The Spelling Society
TSS
4 Valletta Way, Warwick, Wellesbourne, CV35 9TB, UK
Tel: 01789 842112
Email: membership@spellingsociety.org
Website: http://www.spellingsociety.org
Members: 1100
Staff: 1
Contact: John Gledhill, Membership Sec.
Fee: £15
Membership Type: full
Description: Raises awareness of the problems caused by irregularity of English spelling. Promotes remedies to improve literacy, including spelling reform.
Formerly: Formerly, Simplified Spelling Society

04198
The Survey Association
TSA
Northgate Business Centre, 38 Northgate, Notts, Newark-on-Trent, NG24 1EZ, UK
Tel: 01636 642840
Fax: 01636 642841
Email: office@tsa-uk.org.uk
Website: http://www.tsa-uk.org.uk
Members: 79
Staff: 3
Contact: Rory Stanbridge, Sec. Gen.
Description: Private sector firms engaged in all aspects of surveying; land, photogrammetric, aerial and hydrographic. Offers its members a comprehensive and professional service providing general and company specific advice, support and information on training, marketing, and health and safety, environmental matters etc. Monitors changes in UK and European Commission laws affecting the industry and issues guidance on the interpretation and application of legislation.

04199
The Tile Association
TTA
Forum Ct., 83 Copers Cope Rd., Beckenham, BR3 1NR, UK
Tel: 020 86630946
Fax: 020 86630949
Email: info@tiles.org.uk
Website: http://www.tiles.org.uk
Members: 750
Contact: Ian Crowther, Chm.
Fee: £190-2250
Membership Type: company (based on turnover)
Fee: £425
Membership Type: overseas manufacturer
Description: Open to tile distributors, contractors and manufacturers of ceramic tile and related products, ceramic tile retailers and agents. Aims to achieve professional regulation in the ceramic tile industry; to provide training and information; to be the voice of the industry; to give technical advice and help; and to strengthen relationships with related bodies in the tile industry.
Formerly: Formerly, National Association of Tile Distributors

04200
The Vermiculite Association
TVA
Whitegate Acre, Metheringham Fen, Lincoln, LN4 3AL, UK
Tel: 01526 323990
Fax: 01526 323181
Email: tva@vermiculite.org
Website: http://www.vermiculite.org
Contact: Michael J. Allen, Sec. Gen.
Fee: £3200
Membership Type: mining
Fee: £1850
Membership Type: regular
Description: Provides a forum for the exchange of technical, trade, and "best practices" for both producers and consumers of vermiculite products. Aims to promote the knowledge and use of vermiculite around the world. Develops standardized test methods and quality control procedures for vermiculite-based products.
Meetings/Conventions: annual meeting

04201
The Welding Institute
TWI
Granta Park, Great Abington, Cambridge, CB21 6AL, UK
Tel: 01223 899000
Fax: 01223 892588
Email: twi@twi.co.uk
Website: http://www.twi.co.uk
Members: 7500
Staff: 500
Fee: £26
Membership Type: student (full time)
Description: Represents individuals and companies using welding and joining technology or supplying equipment and consumable for welding and joining processes. Activities cover all aspects of welding and joining technology and materials engineering.
Library Subject: welding, international welding standards, welding materials and equipment
Library Type: not open to the public
Publication: Magazine
Publication title: Bulletin

04202

Thermal Insulation Contractors Association
TICA

TICA House, Allington Way, Yarm Rd., Business Park, Darlington, DL1 4QB, UK
Tel: 01325 466704
Fax: 01325 487691
Website: http://www.tica-acad.co.uk
Members: 218
Staff: 15
Contact: Ralph Bradley, Chief Exec.
Fee: £915
Membership Type: full, information subscriber, affiliate
Description: Represents the interests of thermal insulation contractors involved in various aspects of industrial insulation including power stations, oil refineries, chemical plants, on and off shore marine, fire protection, acoustics and asbestos removal and H & V in schools, hospitals and offices. Acts as joint signatory with the GMB and TGWU to the Thermal Insulating Industry's National Agreement.
Publication: Magazine
Publication title: Academy. Advertisements.

04203

Thermal Insulation Manufacturers and Suppliers Association
TIMSA

Kingsley House, Ganders Business Park, Hampshire, Bordon, GU35 9LU, UK
Tel: 01420 471624
Fax: 01420 471611
Email: admin@timsa.org.uk
Website: http://www.timsa.org.uk
Members: 36
Staff: 4
Contact: John Fairley, Contact
Description: Represents all the major manufacturers and many of the suppliers and distributors in the UK thermal insulation industry.
Publication: Handbook
Publication title: Thermal Insulation Handbook

04204

Thermal Spraying and Surface Engineering Association
TSSEA

38 Lawford Ln., Bilton, Warwickshire, Rugby, CV22 7JP, UK
Tel: 0844 8046898
Fax: 0844 8046899
Email: info@tssea.org
Website: http://www.tssea.co.uk
Members: 100
Contact: Andrew Cole, Sec.
Description: Companies worldwide involved in the metal coatings industry.
Formerly: Formerly, Association of Metal Sprayers

04205

Thomas Hardy Society
THS

c/o Dorset Country Museum
High West St., Dorchester, DT1 1XA, UK
Tel: 01305 251501
Fax: 01305 251501
Email: info@hardysociety.org
Website: http://www.hardysociety.org
Members: 1200
Contact: Mike Nixon, Sec.
Fee: £18
Membership Type: individual
Fee: £22.5
Membership Type: joint, overseas (individual)
Description: Individuals in 32 countries interested in the writings, life, and times of English novelist and poet Thomas Hardy (1840-1928). Serves to honor the memory of Hardy and to encourage the study and appreciation of his life and works.
Formerly: Formerly, Thomas Hardy Festival Society
Publication: Journal
Publication title: Thomas Hardy Journal. Advertisements.

04206

Thomas Lovell Beddoes Society

9 Amber Ct., Belper, DE56 1HG, UK
Email: john@beddoes.demon.co.uk
Website: http://www.phantomwooer.org
Members: 100
Contact: John Lovell Beddoes, Chm.
Fee: £5
Membership Type: individual
Fee: £8
Membership Type: joint, individual (overseas)
Description: Aims to research Beddoes' life, times and work. Encourages relevant publications. Aims to further the reading and appreciation of his works by a wider public.

04207

Thomson Foundation
TF

37 Park Pl., Cardiff, CF10 3BB, UK
Tel: 029 20353060
Fax: 029 20353061
Email: enquiries@thomsonfoundation.org
Website: http://www.thomsonfoundation.co.uk
Contact: Janet Boston, CEO
Description: Promotes excellence in journalism and broadcasting. Conducts educational programs and training courses for journalists and broadcasting technicians, particularly those working in central and eastern Europe. Maintains global network of freelance consultants; gathers and disseminates information on journalism, broadcasting, and media technologies; makes available financial aid and other assistance to individuals wishing to participate in training programs.

04208

Thomson Reuters Foundation

30 S Colonnade, London, E14 5EP, UK
Tel: 020 75427015
Website: http://www.trust.org
Staff: 13
Contact: Monique Villa, CEO
Description: Promotes professional development of journalists worldwide. Conducts study and training programs for journalists from the developing world and from central and Eastern Europe; sponsors research and educational programs and schools and universities; provides financial and technical support for charitable and cultural organizations. Provides AlertNet - online rapid news and communications service for international disaster relief organizations.
Publication: Newsletter
Publication title: ReutersLink

04209

Thoroughbred Breeders' Association
TBA

Stanstead House, 8 The Ave., Newmarket, CB8 9AA, UK
Tel: 01638 661321
Fax: 01638 665621
Email: info@thetba.co.uk
Website: http://www.thoroughbredbreedersassociation.co.uk
Members: 2700
Staff: 8
Contact: Louise Kemble, Chief Exec.
Fee: £110
Membership Type: United Kingdom, Ireland, Europe (airmail)
Fee: £135
Membership Type: America
Description: Breeders of thoroughbred horses, and others involved or interested in the bloodstock industry. Encourages by means of the provision of educational or research facilities or otherwise the science of producing and improving the thoroughbred horses in Great Britain.
Publication: Magazine
Publication title: The Pacemaker and Thoroughbred Breeder. Advertisements.

04210

Thrive

Geoffrey Udall Ctre., Beech Hill, Reading, RG7 2AT, UK
Tel: 0118 9885688
Fax: 0118 9885677
Email: info@thrive.org.uk
Website: http://www.thrive.org.uk
Staff: 38
Contact: David Aitchison-Tait, Chm.
Fee: £30
Membership Type: standard (in Europe), student
Fee: £60
Membership Type: enhanced (in Europe)
Description: Supports the disadvantaged, disabled, and older people to participate fully in the social and economic life of the community through promotion of gardening and horticultural activities.
Publication: Book
Publication title: A Garden for You

04211

Tibet Society of the United Kingdom

Unit 9, 139 Fonthill Rd., London, N4 3HF, UK
Tel: 0207 2721414
Fax: 0207 2721410
Email: info@tibetsociety.com
Website: http://www.tibetsociety.com
Members: 1500
Staff: 1
Contact: Philippa Carrick, CEO
Fee: £20
Membership Type: individual
Fee: £32
Membership Type: overseas (individual), family
Description: Assists Tibetan refugees to achieve a sustainable life in exile. Offers educational and training programs. Provides assistance to social and economic development programs for people within Tibet.
Formerly: Formerly, Tibet Relief Fund of the United Kingdom
Publication: Journal
Publication title: Tibet Society Briefing

04212
Tiles and Architectural Ceramics Society
TACS
27 Spurn Ln., Oldham, OL3 5QP, UK
Email: info@tilesoc.org.uk
Website: http://www.tilesoc.org.uk
Fee: £20
Membership Type: individual
Fee: £28
Membership Type: family
Description: Serves as Britain's national society responsible for the study and protection of tiles and architectural ceramics, uniting people with common interests.
Publication: Catalog
Publication title: European Industries Tiles

04213
Tilling Society
5 Friars Bank, Guestling, Hastings, TN35 4EJ, UK
Fax: 01424 813237
Email: society@tilling.org.uk
Website: http://www.tilling.org.uk/society
Members: 500
Contact: Cynthia Reavell, Sec.
Fee: £8
Membership Type: renewing, in UK
Fee: £10
Membership Type: renewing, outside UK
Description: Literary enthusiasts in 15 countries. Promotes enjoyment of the works of satirical English novelist Edward Frederic Benson (1867-1940). Encourages exchange of news and information, discussion, and speculation.
Publication: Book
Publication title: E.F. Benson as Mayor of Rye, 1934-1937: Reports from the *Sussex Express*

04214
Timber Decking Association
TDA
5 Flemming Ct., Castleford, WF10 5HW, UK
Tel: 01977 558147
Email: info@tda.org.uk
Website: http://www.tda.org.uk
Contact: Steve Young, Dir.
Description: Committed to help homeowners and design professionals source high quality and performance timber decks.
Publication: Brochure
Publication title: An Introduction to Creating Quality Decks

04215
Timber Packaging and Pallet Confederation
TIMCON
840 Melton Rd., Thurmaston, Leicester, LE4 8BN, UK
Tel: 0116 2640579
Fax: 0116 2640141
Email: timcon@associationhq.org.uk
Website: http://www.timcon.org
Members: 145
Contact: John Dye, Pres.
Fee: £360-2500
Membership Type: full (based on annual turnover)
Description: Represents companies throughout the United Kingdom including pallet manufacturers, case makers, export packers, pallet repairers, and suppliers of both timber and manufacturing equipment. Offers a complete interpretation and advisory service regarding relevant legislation.

04216
Timber Research and Development Association
TRADA
Stocking Ln., Hughenden Valley, High Wycombe, HP14 4ND, UK
Tel: 01494 569600
Fax: 01494 565487
Email: information@trada.co.uk
Website: http://www.trada.co.uk
Members: 1100
Staff: 190
Contact: Jeremy Vibert, Hd. of Information Center
Fee: £458-14981
Membership Type: corporate
Fee: £145-1400
Membership Type: professional (maximum)
Description: Represents timber importers, manufacturers, construction companies, architects, structural engineers, surveyors, and interested others from 38 countries. Promotes appropriate and economical use of timber and wood panels in the construction and packaging industries. Works in research and development in order to ensure that timber is used in the most efficient manner possible. Disseminates information to manufacturers and specifiers on topics such as surface finishes for wood, adhesives, and wood-based sheet materials. Advises members on European and international standards. Offers building design, consultancy, and structural appraisal services. Conducts product evaluations and mechanical tests for stress and fire resistance. Organizes professional training courses on subjects including visual stress grading, timber trade sales, and quality assurance services.
Formerly: Formerly, Timber Development Association
Publication: Newsletter
Publication title: Trada Update

04217
Timber Trade Federation
TTF
The Building Centre, 26 Store St., London, WC1E 7BT, UK
Tel: 020 32050067
Fax: 020 72915379
Email: ttf@ttf.co.uk
Website: http://www.ttf.co.uk
Members: 500
Staff: 11
Contact: Jean Rennie, Contact
Description: Serves as a UK trade association for timber agents, importers and merchants. Strives to create the best conditions in the market place for its members to trade. Promotes timber as a building material and its potential for other uses.
Publication title: Statistical Information

04218
Timeshare Consumers Association
TCA
Nornay, Nottinghamshire, Blyth, S81 8HG, UK
Tel: 01909 591100
Fax: 01909 591338
Email: info@timeshare.org.uk
Website: http://www.timeshare.org.uk
Contact: Sandy Grey, Chm.
Description: Provides help and specialist advice to consumers and their legal advisors to avoid pitfalls and to resolve problems. Supports owners and owners' clubs in realizing their benefits. Establishes a central resource of consumer-oriented information about timeshare. Lobbies for improved protection of timeshare consumers.

04219
Tissue Viability Nurses Association
TVNA
3 Ullswater Crescent, Looseleigh, Plymouth, PL6 5HB, UK
Email: chair@tvna.org
Website: http://www.tvna.org
Contact: Pauline Beldon, Chair
Fee: £15
Membership Type: full
Fee: £10
Membership Type: associate
Description: Stimulates research activities, disseminates research findings and promotes best practices in tissue viability nursing. Gives advice and information on the role, educational needs and professional development of the tissue viability nurse specialist. Acts as a primary point of contact for government and other agencies to any relevant issues in the field of tissue viability nursing.

04220
Tobacco Manufacturers Association
TMA
5th Fl., Burwood House, 14-16 Caxton St., London, SW1H 0ZB, UK
Tel: 020 75440100
Fax: 020 75440117
Email: information@the-tma.org.uk
Website: http://www.the-tma.org.uk
Members: 5
Staff: 10
Contact: Chris Ogden, Chief Exec.
Description: Represents the interests of the UK tobacco manufacturers. Represents the industry as a whole and does not promote particular brands or products. It provides factual information on smoking.
Publication: Newsletter
Publication title: Briefing

04221
Together
12 Old St., London, EC1V 9BE, UK
Tel: 020 77807300
Fax: 020 77807301
Email: contact-us@together-uk.org
Website: http://www.together-uk.org
Contact: Liz Felton, CEO
Fee: £15
Membership Type: waged
Fee: £5
Membership Type: unwaged
Description: Provides high quality services in communities, hospitals and prisons. Supports people with severe and enduring mental health needs and their carers. Works in partnership with health authorities, local authorities, housing associations and other voluntary agencies.
Formerly: Formerly, Mental After Care Association
Publication: Booklet
Publication title: Guide for Careers of People with Mental-health Needs

04222
Tolkien Society
Manches & Co., 3 Worcester St., Oxford, OX1 2PZ, UK
Website: http://www.tolkiensociety.org
Members: 1222
Contact: Cathleen Blackburn, Contact
Fee: £2
Membership Type: under 16 years old - in UK
Fee: £3.5
Membership Type: under 16 years old - outside UK
Description: Individuals in 44 countries interested in J.R.R. Tolkien (1892-1973), English scholar and author of fiction noted for its cogent use of fantasy. Promotes appreciation and study of Tolkien's works, particularly *The Lord of the Rings.*

04223
Tools and Trades History Society
TATHS
Woodbine Cottage, Budleigh Hill, E Budleigh, Devon, EX9 7DT, UK
Email: info@taths.org.uk
Website: http://www.taths.org.uk
Members: 550
Contact: Nick White, Chm.
Fee: £25
Membership Type: individual
Fee: £29
Membership Type: family
Description: Craft and tool collectors, historians of pre-industrial technology, antiquarians, archaeologists, museums, museum officials, libraries, and craft teachers in Europe, Australia, and North America. Promotes awareness and understanding of hand tools and the skills and techniques exercised by those who used them.
Publication: Catalog
Publication title: James Isaac and John Fussell

04224
Tools for Self Reliance
TFSR
Netley Marsh, Southampton, SO40 7GY, UK
Tel: 02380 869697
Fax: 02380 868544
Email: info@tfsr.org
Website: http://www.tfsr.org
Members: 300
Staff: 9
Contact: Janice Kidd, CEO
Description: Enables artisans in developing countries to better participate in the development of themselves and their communities. Works with local partner organisations to provide tools and skills training, and by raising awareness in the UK of the causes of poverty. Supports partner organisations in Ghana, Mozambique, Sierra Leone, Tanzania, Uganda, and Zimbabwe.
Publication: Newsletter
Publication title: Forging Links

04225
Tornado and Storm Research Organisation
TORRO
PO Box 972, Warrington, WA4 9DP, UK
Tel: 07813 075509
Email: sam.hall@torro.org.uk
Website: http://www.torro.org.uk
Members: 400
Contact: Samantha Hall, Admin./Sec.
Fee: £42.5
Membership Type: full (UK)
Fee: £58
Membership Type: full (Europe)
Description: Meteorologists, meteorological researchers, and weather observers worldwide. Seeks to advance scientific understanding of tornados and storms, particularly as they affect the United Kingdom. Gathers and disseminates information on tornados and storms; conducts visits to tornado touch down sites; undertakes climatological research.
Publication: Journal
Publication title: Journal of Meteorology

04226
Tourettes Action
TA
Southbank House, Black Prince Rd., London, SE1 7SJ, UK
Tel: 0207 7932352
Email: admin@tourettes-action.org.uk
Website: http://www.tourettes-action.org.uk
Members: 639
Staff: 4
Contact: Suzanne Dobson, Chief Exec.
Fee: £20
Membership Type: regular
Description: Works to provide support, education, and public awareness to the neurological disorder Gilles de la Tourette Syndrome. Promotes medical research in Tourette Syndrome.
Formerly: Formerly, Tourette Syndrome Association

04227
Tourism Society
Trinity Ct., 34 West St., Surrey, Sutton, SM1 1SH, UK
Tel: 020 86614636
Fax: 020 86614637
Email: admin@tourismsociety.org
Website: http://www.tourismsociety.org
Members: 1000
Staff: 3
Contact: Gregory Yeoman, Exec. Dir.
Fee: £95
Membership Type: individual
Fee: £50
Membership Type: overseas
Description: Provides a forum for professionals working in, studying or interested in tourism worldwide.
Publication: Journal
Publication title: Tourism

04228
Town and Country Planning Association
TCPA
17 Carlton House Terr., London, SW1Y 5AS, UK
Tel: 020 79308903
Fax: 020 79303280
Email: tcpa@tcpa.org.uk
Website: http://www.tcpa.org.uk
Members: 1000
Staff: 10
Contact: Gideon Amos, CEO
Fee: £43-123
Membership Type: overseas
Fee: £27-48
Membership Type: individual
Description: Promotes the art and science of urban, rural, and environmental planning with a particular focus on community empowerment and public participation in policy making.
Publication: Newsletter
Publication title: Planning Bulletin

04229
Toy Retailers Association
TRA
207 Mercury House, Willoughton Dr., Foxby Lane Business Park, Gainsborough, DN21 1DY, UK
Tel: 08707 537437
Fax: 08707 060042
Email: enquiries@toyretailersassociation.co.uk
Website: http://www.toyretailersassociation.co.uk
Contact: Derek Markie, Sec.
Fee: £125
Membership Type: independent retailer
Fee: £750
Membership Type: independent multiply
Description: Multiples and independents retailing toys.
Publication: Newsletter

04230
Trades Union Congress - England
TUC
Cong. House, Great Russell St., London, WC1B 3LS, UK
Tel: 020 76364030
Fax: 020 76360632
Email: info@tuc.org.uk
Website: http://www.tuc.org.uk
Members: 6700000
Staff: 280
Contact: Brendan Barber, Gen. Sec.
Description: Represents trade unions in the United Kingdom. Maintains the Educational Trust, offering courses to union staff and members, and the National Education Centre, a residential college available for use by trade unions. Operates Aid to provide charitable relief to famine, disaster, and poverty victims in Africa, Asia, and Latin America. Provides strategic framework to support the union role in learning and skills, and gives training and support to the growing number of Learning Reps.
Publication: Book
Publication title: Hazards at Work

04231
Trades Union Congress - Women's Committee
Cong. House, Great Russell St., London, WC1B 3LS, UK
Tel: 020 76364030
Fax: 020 76360632
Email: info@tuc.org.uk
Website: http://www.tuc.org.uk
Members: 3000000
Staff: 140
Contact: Kay Carberry, Asst. Gen. Sec.
Description: Promotes the interests of women workers within the trade union movement.

04232
Trading Standards Institute
TSI
1 Sylvan Ct., Sylvan Way, Southfields Business Park, Essex, Basildon, SS15 6TH, UK
Tel: 0845 6089400
Fax: 0845 6089425
Email: institute@tsi.org.uk
Website: http://www.tradingstandards.gov.uk
Members: 2500
Staff: 33
Description: Trading standards officers and organisations/companies with an interest in consumer protection and other related issues. Represents the views of its professional officers in promoting fair trading for the consumer and legitimate trader to their mutual benefit.
Library Subject: trading standards and related subjects
Library Type: not open to the public
Formerly: Formerly, Institute of Trading Standards Administration
Publication: Journal
Publication title: Trading Standards Review. Advertisements.

04233
Traidcraft
Kingsway, Tyne and Wear, Gateshead, NE11 0NE, UK
Tel: 0191 4910591
Fax: 0191 4976562
Email: comms@traidcraft.co.uk
Website: http://www.traidcraft.co.uk
Contact: Paul Chandler, Chief Exec.
Description: Promotes fair trade between industrialized countries and businesses located in economically developing areas. Works with institutions in developing areas to enable locally based businesses to enter global markets on an equitable basis.
Publication: Magazine
Publication title: The Traidcraft Magazine

04234
Tramway and Light Railway Society
TLRS
6, The Woodlands, Brightlingsea, CO7 0RY, UK
Email: tlrs.membership@tramwayinfo.com
Website: http://www.tramways.freeserve.co.uk
Members: 1000
Contact: H.J. Leach, Membership Sec.
Fee: £17
Membership Type: full
Fee: £12
Membership Type: senior, student
Description: Aims to bring together those interested in tramways. Collects archives, photographs, drawings and anything else related to tramways. Publishes books following research in all aspects of tramways. Encourages tramway modeling and exhibiting. Holds meetings and arranges visits for members.
Publication: Magazine
Publication title: Tramfare

04235
Translators Association
c/o Society of Authors
84 Drayton Gardens, London, SW10 9SB, UK
Tel: 020 73736642
Fax: 020 73735768
Email: sbaxter@societyofauthors.org
Website: http://www.societyofauthors.org/subsidiary_groups/translators_association
Members: 469
Contact: Sarah Baxter, Sec.
Description: Aims to protect the rights and interests of translators. Provides professional assistance on matters such as contracts, copyright, libel and tax.

04236
Transparency International - UK
TI(UK)
Downstream Bldg., 1 London Bridge, London, SE1 9BG, UK
Tel: 020 77856356
Fax: 020 77856355
Email: info@transparency.org.uk
Website: http://www.transparency.org.uk
Members: 200
Staff: 3
Contact: John Drysdale, Chm.
Description: Corporations, organizations, and individuals interested in reducing corruption in international business transactions. Eliminates corruption, particularly its corrosive impact on development in poorer countries and corruption's role in worsening poverty, increasing political instability and undermining the rule of law and democracy. Aims to encourage business to adopt commercial practices that are ethical. Formulates standards of integrity to govern international business dealings; maintains network of businesses agreeing to adhere to these standards. Priority areas are: construction and engineering sector; corruption in the official arms trade; money laundering in the UK; transparency in the extractive industries and reform of the UK law of corruption. Conducts anticorruption programs. Undertakes research and educational activities.

04237
Transport and General Workers' Union
TGWU
Transport House, 128 Theobalds Rd., London, WC1X 8TN, UK
Tel: 0207 6112500
Fax: 0207 6112555
Email: tgwu@tgwu.org.uk
Website: http://www.tgwu.org.uk
Members: 900000
Staff: 1000
Contact: Tony Woodley, Gen. Sec.
Fee: £2.3
Membership Type: care
Fee: £2.45
Membership Type: care extra
Description: Transport workers of all kinds, service sector, manufacturing and food and agriculture workers in the U.K., Republic of Ireland, Gibraltar, and Channel Islands.
Publication: Journal
Publication title: T and G Record. Advertisements.
Meetings/Conventions: biennial conference

04238
Transport Association
PO Box 374, Leatherhead, KT22 2EY, UK
Tel: 07507 785845
Fax: 0871 9005599
Email: marion@transportassociation.org.uk
Website: http://www.transportassociation.org.uk
Members: 60
Description: Promotes the qualities and values of medium-sized transport and distribution companies to potential and existing customers.

04239
Transport Planning Society
TPS
1 Great George St., Westminster, London, SW1P 3AA, UK
Tel: 020 76652238
Fax: 020 77991325
Email: tps@ice.org.uk
Website: http://www.tps.org.uk
Members: 750
Contact: Victoria Hills, Chair
Fee: £2500
Membership Type: stakeholder (multi-site)
Fee: £1000
Membership Type: stakeholder (single site)
Description: Facilitates, develops, and promotes knowledge, understanding and best practice in transport planning. Helps inform members, other institutions, companies and policy makers about key transport issues.
Library Subject: transportation, transport planning
Library Type: reference
Publication: Newsletter
Publication title: All Change

04240
Transport Salaried Staffs Association - United Kingdom
TSSA
Walkden House, 10 Melton St., London, NW1 2EJ, UK
Tel: 020 73872101
Fax: 020 73830656
Email: enquiries@tssa.org.uk
Website: http://www.tssa.org.uk
Members: 38492
Contact: Gerry Doherty, Gen. Sec.
Fee: £3.3
Membership Type: full-time worker (in UK)
Fee: £1.85
Membership Type: part-time worker (in UK)
Description: Represents workers in the transport and travel trade industry. Works with employers to provide their employees with better and more productive working conditions.
Publication: Newsletter
Publication title: Active

04241
Travel Trust Association
TTA
Albion House, 3rd Fl., High St., Surrey, Woking, GU21 6BD, UK
Tel: 01483 545787
Fax: 01483 730746
Email: info@traveltrust.co.uk
Website: http://www.traveltrust.co.uk
Description: Travelers and businesses whose employees travel frequently. Seeks to provide low-cost travel insurance to participants. Operates trust account to provide fidelity insurance to individual travelers.

04242
Tree Council
71 Newcomen St., London, SE1 1YT, UK
Tel: 020 74079992
Fax: 020 74079908
Email: info@treecouncil.org.uk
Website: http://www.treecouncil.org.uk
Members: 186
Staff: 4
Contact: Pauline Buchanan Black, Dir. Gen.
Fee: £250
Membership Type: full, consultative
Description: National organization concerned with trees. Aims to improve the environment in town and country by promoting the planting and conservation of trees and woods throughout the UK; to disseminate knowledge about trees and their management and to act as a forum for organizations concerned with trees, to identify national problems and to provide initiatives for cooperation.
Publication: Magazine
Publication title: Tree Guardian

04243
Triangles
3 Whitehall Ct., Ste. 54, London, SW1A 2EF, UK
Tel: 020 78394512
Fax: 020 78395575
Email: triangles.london@lucistrust.org
Website: http://www.triangles.org/?5cff7bd0
Description: Persons of all faiths united to use the power of thought and prayer to establish harmonious human relations. Aims to spread goodwill and understanding, and to strengthen and support practical and constructive action benefiting humanity.
Publication title: Energy Follows Thought

04244
Triumph Over Phobia
TOP UK
PO Box 3760, Bath, BA2 3WY, UK
Tel: 0845 6009601
Email: info@topuk.org
Website: http://www.topuk.org
Members: 28
Contact: Peter R. FitzGerald, Chm.
Description: Runs a national network of self-help groups to help people with phobia or obsessive-compulsive disorder to overcome their problems using graded self-exposure.
Publication: Newsletter
Publication title: Breakthrough

04245
Tropical Biology Association
TBA
Dept. of Zoology, Downing St., Cambridge, CB2 3EJ, UK
Tel: 01223 336619
Fax: 01223 336676
Email: tba@tropical-biology.org
Website: http://www.tropical-biology.org
Members: 40
Staff: 6
Contact: Rosie Trevelyan, Dir.
Description: Aims to meet the challenge of biodiversity conservation by establishing an informed, well-motivated community of tropical biologists both in Europe and in tropical countries.
Publication: Newsletter
Publication title: TBA Newsletter

04246
Tropical Forest Resource Group
TFRG
Crib, Dinchope, Shropshire, Craven Arms, SY7 9JJ, UK
Tel: 01588 672868
Fax: 08700 116645
Email: alan.pottinger@tfrg.co.uk
Website: http://www.tfrg.co.uk
Members: 9
Staff: 3
Contact: Alan Pottinger, Coor.
Description: Organizations, universities, research institutes, private companies, and government agencies seeking to inform development project and policy developers in areas of forest management and conservation. Gathers and disseminates information on subjects including national and regional forest planning, land and soil evaluation, economic and social system assessments, and biomass energy resource management. Conducts educational and training programs. Initiates and coordinates responses to charitable public and private organizations worldwide.

04247
Tropical Growers' Association
TGA
1st Fl., 20 St. Dunstan's Hill, London, EC3R 8NQ, UK
Tel: 0207 2832707
Fax: 0207 6231310
Email: contact@fosfa.org
Members: 70
Staff: 1
Fee: £15
Membership Type: individual
Fee: £50
Membership Type: company
Description: Individuals and companies in 30 countries interested in cultivating tropical trees or plants including rubber, oil palm, cocoa, and coconut. Organizes seminars; compiles statistics.

04248
Tropical Health and Education Trust
THET
1 Wimpole St., 5th Fl., London, W1G 0AE, UK
Tel: 020 72903892
Fax: 020 72903890
Email: info@thet.org
Website: http://www.thet.org.uk
Staff: 15
Contact: Pia MacRae, Chief Exec.
Description: Works with medical training institutions and hospitals in Africa to strengthen health worker training. Serves as a liaison linking medical education institutions in Europe and the developing world; supports locally led health training initiatives within the existing infrastructure.
Publication: Annual Report
Publication title: THET Annual Review

04249
Trussed Rafter Association
TRA
PO Box 571, Chesterfield, S40 9DH, UK
Tel: 01246 230036
Fax: 01246 230036
Email: info@tra.org.uk
Website: http://www.tra.org.uk
Members: 86
Description: Forges links with the public and private sectors to promote the industry's interests and liaises with research and regulatory bodies on product specification, health and safety and environmental issues. Participates in regular manufacturing and timber industry forums, providing members with current news on industry developments and key policies.
Formerly: Formerly, International Truss Plate Association
Publication: Handbook
Publication title: Trussed Rafter Association Technical Handbook

04250
Tuberous Sclerosis Association
TSA
PO Box 12979, Barnt Green, Birmingham, B45 5AN, UK
Tel: 0121 4456970
Website: http://www.tuberous-sclerosis.org
Members: 1600
Staff: 7
Contact: Diane Sanson, Hd. of Administration
Fee: £15
Membership Type: full
Fee: £20
Membership Type: overseas
Description: Supports families and individuals affected by tuberous sclerosis. Raises awareness of the condition and to educate professionals, sufferers and the general public.
Library Subject: tuberous sclerosis
Library Type: reference

04251
Tun Abdul Razak Research Centre
TARRC
Brickendonbury, Hertford, SG13 8NL, UK
Tel: 01992 584966
Fax: 01992 554837
Email: general@tarrc.co.uk
Website: http://www.tarrc.co.uk
Staff: 92
Contact: Kamarudin Ab-Malek, CEO/Vice Chm.
Description: Conducts research on the technological development, processing, and uses of rubber. Provides and supports technical and consulting services to rubber manufacturers.
Library Subject: rubber and polymer science
Library Type: not open to the public
Formerly: Formerly, Malaysian Rubber Producers' Research Association
Publication: Report
Publication title: Engineering Design with Natural Rubber

04252
Turkish British Chamber of Commerce and Industry
TBCCI
2nd Fl., Bury House, 33 Bury St., London, SW1Y 6AU, UK
Tel: 020 73210999
Fax: 020 73210989
Email: info@tbcci.org
Website: http://www.tbcci.org
Contact: Harvey Marshall, Chm.
Fee: £675
Membership Type: sustaining (UK/Turkey)
Fee: £325
Membership Type: general (UK/Turkey)

Description: Works to promote and develop bi-lateral trade, investments and joint ventures between Turkey and the UK.

04253

Turner Society

BCM Box Turner, London, WC1N 3XX, UK
Email: turnersociety@live.co.uk
Website: http://www.turnersociety.org.uk
Members: 400
Contact: Eric Shanes, Chm.
Fee: £25
Membership Type: individual in U.K., individual outside U.K. (surface mail)
Fee: £12.5
Membership Type: additional individual at same address
Description: Art collectors, scholars, and individuals worldwide interested in the work of J.M.W. Turner; libraries and galleries. Works to further appreciation and study of Turner (1775-1851).
Publication: Journal
Publication title: Turner Society News. Advertisements.

04254

Turners Syndrome Support Society TSSS

13 Simpson Ct., 11 South Ave., Clydebank Business Park, Clydebank, G81 2NR, UK
Tel: 0141 9528006
Fax: 0141 9528025
Email: turner.syndrome@tss.org.uk
Website: http://www.tss.org.uk
Contact: Arlene Smyth, Exec. Off.
Fee: £20
Membership Type: ordinary
Fee: £25
Membership Type: overseas
Description: Offers support and information to girls and adult women with Turner Syndrome, as well as to the families and friends.
Publication: Newsletter
Publication title: ASPECTS

04255

Twentieth Century Society

70 Cowcross St., London, EC1M 6EJ, UK
Tel: 020 72503857
Fax: 020 72518985
Email: caseworker@c20society.org.uk
Website: http://www.c20society.org.uk
Members: 1800
Staff: 5
Contact: Catherine Croft, Dir.
Fee: £35
Membership Type: individual
Fee: £55
Membership Type: household
Description: Works toward the protection of British architecture and design after 1914.

04256

TWIN

1 Curtain Rd., London, EC2A 3LT, UK
Tel: 020 73751221
Fax: 020 73751337
Email: info@twin.org.uk
Website: http://www.twin.org.uk
Staff: 18
Contact: Merling Preza, Pres.
Description: Serves as Trade Development NGO. Works with organizations and cooperatives of small scale farmers and artisans in the Third World. Facilitates trade and technology exchange; provides technical, marketing, and quality control assistance. Operates information service for Third World trade organizations; conducts training seminars on finance, technology, and trade.
Formerly: Formerly, Third World Information Network
Publication: Bulletin
Publication title: TwinCare

04257

Twins and Multiple Births Association TAMBA

2 The Willows, Gardner Rd., Surrey, Guildford, GU1 4PG, UK
Tel: 0148 3304442
Fax: 0148 3302483
Email: enquiries@tamba.org.uk
Website: http://www.tamba.org.uk/Page.aspx?pid=195
Members: 5500
Staff: 11
Contact: Samantha Jeffrey, Chair
Fee: £36
Membership Type: regular
Fee: £78
Membership Type: silver
Description: Parents with multiple birth children. Seeks to provide information and mutual support networks for families including multiple birth children; promotes increased understanding of the unique health and social needs of multiple birth children and their families. Gathers and disseminates information on multiple birth children; makes available specialist support services to members; serves as liaison linking members to local twins clubs; encourages research on the unique health, social, and educational needs of multiple birth children. Provides discounts on children's clothing and other supplies to members. Represents the interests of families with multiple birth children before government agencies and the media.
Library Type: not open to the public
Publication: Magazine
Publication title: Twins, Triplets, and More. Advertisements.

04258

Tylers' and Bricklayers' Company

3 Farmer's Way, Bucks, Seer Green, HP9 2YY, UK
Tel: 01494 689055
Fax: 01494 689055
Email: clerk@tylersandbricklayers.co.uk
Website: http://www.tylersandbricklayers.co.uk
Contact: John R. Brooks, Contact
Description: Represents and promotes data resource management professionals.

04259

Tyne and Wear Campaign for Nuclear Disarmament

1 Rectory Ave., Gosforth, Newcastle upon Tyne, NE3 1XS, UK
Tel: 0191 2857260
Email: gvickers@broadgate47.freeserve.co.uk
Website: http://www.cnduk.org/index.php/regional-groups/tyne-and-wear-cnd.html
Description: Aims to eliminate British nuclear weapons and other weapons of mass destruction.

04260

U.K. Irrigation Association UKIA

Moorland House, 10 Hayway, Northants, Rushden, NN10 6AG, UK
Tel: 01427 717627
Email: m.kay@ukia.org
Website: http://www.ukia.org
Members: 250
Staff: 1
Contact: Melvyn Kay, Exec. Sec.
Fee: £40
Membership Type: individual
Fee: £250
Membership Type: group
Description: Anyone interested in UK irrigation, particularly farmers and growers including manufacturers and suppliers of equipment, advisers, consultants, contractors, members of water authorities, trainers and researchers. Aims to promote interest in, and a better understanding of, all aspects of irrigation in the UK, through courses, open days, conferences and specialist meetings.
Publication: Proceedings
Publication title: Conference Papers
Meetings/Conventions: One-Day Tour – semiannual tour

Ughdarras a Chlo Hearaich

see Harris Tweed Authority

04261

UK Apitherapy Society

37 Cecil Rd., Hertfordshire, Cheshunt, EN8 8TN, UK
Tel: 01992 622645
Fax: 01992 622645
Email: peter.pebadale@virgin.net
Website: http://freespace.virgin.net/peter.pebadale/pages/UK_Api_Society.htm
Contact: Sue Claydon, Sec.
Description: Promotes the safe use of bee venom, whereby test stings are given before therapy begins.

04262

UK Association of Online Publishers AOP

55/56 Lincolns Inn Fields, Holborn, London, WC2A 3LJ, UK
Tel: 020 74044166
Fax: 020 74044167
Email: info@ukaop.org.uk
Website: http://www.ukaop.org.uk
Contact: Tim Faircliff, Chm.
Fee: £13500
Membership Type: full
Fee: £2000
Membership Type: affiliate
Description: Raises the profile, revenues and credibility of online publishing. Develops standards across all aspects of the online publishing industry. Offers online advertising, sponsorships, services and new technologies to online publishers. Facilitates share of knowledge and cross-fertilization of ideas.
Publication: Newsletter

04263
UK Cleaning Products Industry Association
UKCPI
1st Fl., Century House, Old Mill Pl., Cheshire, Tattenhall, CH3 9RJ, UK
Tel: 01829 770055
Fax: 01829 770101
Email: ukcpi@ukcpi.org
Website: http://www.ukcpi.org
Members: 70
Staff: 3
Contact: Philip Malpass, Dir. Gen.
Description: Companies engaged in the soap and detergent industry in the UK. Concerned with health and safety, consumer safety and environmental issues (excluding competitive issues). Actively involved with government, EC commission, consumer and environmental organisations, retail trade, academic institutions and the media.
Formerly: Formerly, Soap and Detergent Industry Association
Publication: Newsletter
Publication title: SDIA News

04264
UK Coalition of People Living with HIV and AIDS
UKC
250 Kennington Ln., London, SE11 5RD, UK
Tel: 020 75642180
Email: faq4you@hotmail.com
Website: http://www.ukcoalition.org
Contact: Bernard Forbes, Chm.
Description: Seeks to improve the quality of life of people with AIDS and HIV. Promotes health care access for individuals infected with HIV and AIDS. Seeks to increase public awareness of HIV and AIDS. Provides services and facilities that address the needs of people suffering from HIV.

04265
UK Committee for UNICEF
UNICEF House, 30A Great Sutton St., London, EC1V 0DU, UK
Tel: 020 74902388
Fax: 020 72501733
Email: media@unicef.org.uk
Website: http://www.unicef.org.uk
Contact: Elle Macpherson, Ambassador
Description: Raises funds for UNICEF programmes around the world. Works to raise public awareness of issues facing children around the world. Combats child labor, child trafficking and commercial sexual exploitation.

04266
UK Council on Deafness
Westwood Pk., London Rd., Little Horkesley, Colchester, CO6 4BS, UK
Tel: 01206 274075
Fax: 01206 274077
Email: info@deafcouncil.org.uk
Website: http://www.deafcouncil.org.uk
Members: 102
Contact: Susan Daniels, Chair
Description: Supports members in their work with deaf people. Provides support and funding opportunities for members. Compose of 101 member organisations.

04267
UK Fashion Exports
UKFE
5 Portland Pl., London, W1B 1PW, UK
Tel: 020 76365577
Fax: 020 76367515
Email: contact@5portlandplace.org.uk
Website: http://www.5portlandplace.org.uk
Members: 800
Staff: 7
Contact: Paul Alger, Exec. Dir.
Description: UK manufacturers, designers and wholesale suppliers of British-made apparel of all kinds including fashion accessories; associate members supplying various services related to the trade. Promotes increased sales abroad of British apparel by means of promotional events (e.g. exhibitions, trade missions) information to UK manufacturers and overseas buyers or agents.
Library Subject: industry, export
Library Type: not open to the public

04268
UK Forest Products Association
UKFPA
Office 14, John Player Bldg., Stirling Enterprise Park, Springpark Rd., Stirling, FK7 7RP, UK
Tel: 01786 449029
Fax: 01786 473112
Email: dsulman@ukfpa.co.uk
Website: http://www.ukfpa.co.uk
Description: Represents the technical and commercial interests of the forest products industry in the United Kingdom.

04269
UK Inbound
3rd Fl., 388 The Strand, London, WC2R 0LT, UK
Tel: 020 73957500
Fax: 020 72406618
Email: info@ukinbound.org
Website: http://www.ukinbound.org
Members: 330
Staff: 5
Contact: Rita Beckwith, Chair
Fee: £699
Membership Type: band 1 (for members with a turnover of less than 3 million per annum)
Fee: £849
Membership Type: band 2 (for members with a turnover of between 3-10 million per annum)
Description: Tour operators, hotels, restaurants, tourist attractions, transportation companies, heritage sites, restaurant and catering companies. Works to promote business between and on behalf of members, to lobby central Government on behalf of the industry and to pass on to member's commercial advantages gained through bulk purchase of goods and services.
Formerly: Formerly, British Incoming Tour Operators Association
Publication: Handbook
Publication title: BITOA Operators Handbook. Advertisements.

04270
UK Industrial Vision Association
UKIVA
PO Box 25, Royston, SG8 6TL, UK
Tel: 01763 220981
Email: info@ukiva.org
Website: http://www.ukiva.org
Members: 46
Staff: 2
Contact: Don Braggins, Contact
Fee: £750
Membership Type: UK
Fee: £1200
Membership Type: international
Description: Manufacturers of vision technologies and other industrial concerns making use of vision technology. Seeks to advance vision technologies and the manufacturing processes used to produce them. Represents members before labor and trade organizations, government agencies, and the public; gathers and disseminates information on vision technologies and their manufacture.

04271
UK Metric Association
UKMA
c/o Derek Polland, Sec.
34 Wroxham Gardens, London, N11 2BA, UK
Tel: 023 92755268
Email: secretary@metric.org.uk
Website: http://www.metric.org.uk
Contact: Robin Paice, Chm.
Fee: £15
Membership Type: individual
Description: Promotes the full adoption of the international metric system. Campaigns for better consumer protection through accurate and consistent use of metric units of measurement. Educates the public on the benefits of metric system.
Publication: Newsletter
Publication title: UKMA news

04272
UK Paruresis Trust
UKPT
PO Box 182, Cumbria, Kendal, LA9 9AE, UK
Email: support@ukpt.org.uk
Website: http://www.ukpt.org.uk
Members: 23
Contact: Andrew Smith, Chm.
Description: Provides support and help to men and women who have Shy Bladder Syndrome or problems urinating in the presence or vicinity of other people. Serves as a forum for information exchange and rehabilitation for people who suffer from the disorder.
Formerly: Formerly, UK Paruresis Association

04273
UK Public Health Association
UKPHA
94 White Lion St., 2nd Fl., London, N1 9PF, UK
Tel: 020 77138910
Fax: 020 30511769
Email: admin@ukpha.org.uk
Website: http://www.ukpha.org.uk
Contact: Angela Mawle, Chief Exec.
Fee: £5
Membership Type: unwaged/retired/full-time student
Fee: £25-50
Membership Type: individual (based on income)
Description: Promotes the development of public health policy at all levels of government, across all sectors, and supports those working in public health both professionally and in a voluntary capacity.

04274
UK Pyrotechnics Society
UKPS
c/o Christina Dunford, Membership Sec.
41 Kelmscott Rd., London, SW11 6QX, UK
Email: membership@pyrosociety.org.uk
Website: http://www.pyrosociety.org.uk
Contact: Richard Harwood, Chm.
Fee: £20
Membership Type: full
Fee: £15
Membership Type: junior
Description: Preserves the heritage, science, history and art of pyrotechnics. Promotes the education, research and advancement of pyrotechnic science. Encourages safe, responsible storage and use of fireworks. Represents the general public in all matters concerning fireworks legislation.
Publication: Newsletter
Publication title: Spark

04275
UK Society for Modelling and Simulation
UKSim
School of Computing and Informatics, Nottingham Trent University, Clifton Ln., Nottingham, NG11 8NS, UK
Email: david.al-dabass@ntu.ac.uk
Website: http://www.uksim.org.uk
Contact: David Al-Dabass, Contact
Fee: £20
Membership Type: individual
Description: Represents researchers, software vendors, end users, consultants and other individuals working in the field of simulation. Promotes all aspects of simulation, including continuous, discrete event and hardware. Offers support to all aspects of simulation work. Disseminates knowledge on simulation through research, training and education.

04276
UK Steel Association
Broadway House, Tothill St., London, SW1H 9NQ, UK
Tel: 020 76541518
Fax: 020 72222782
Email: steel@eef.org.uk
Website: http://www.eef.org.uk/uksteel/default.htm
Members: 40
Staff: 20
Contact: Ian Rodgers, Dir.
Description: Trade association for the steel industry in the United Kingdom. Represents the industry to policy and opinion farmers; promotes the industry and the importance of steel to the public; provides information and services to members.
Formerly: Formerly, British Independent Steel Producers Association
Publication: Membership Directory
Publication title: Member Companies List

04277
UK Timber Frame Association
UKTFA
The e-Centre, Cooperage Way Business Village, Alloa, FK10 3LP, UK
Tel: 01259 272140
Fax: 01259 272141
Email: office@uktfa.com
Website: http://www.uktfa.com
Members: 40
Staff: 5
Contact: Steven Streets, Technical Mgr.
Description: Membership ranges from complete design and build package companies, through to manufacturers of ancillary products, and other trade associations.
Formerly: Formerly, Timber Frame Industry Association

04278
UK Web Design Association
UKWDA
c/o Redstation Internet Ltd.
2 Frater Gate, Business Park, Aerodrome Rd., Hampshire, Gosport, PO13 0GW, UK
Tel: 01329 828224
Fax: 01329 828225
Email: sales@redstation.com
Website: http://www.ukwda.org
Members: 11115
Description: Works to promote and encourage industry standards within the British Web design sector.

04279
Ulster Archaeological Society
UAS
c/o School of Geography Archaeology and Palaeoecology
Queens University Belfast, 42 Fitzwilliam St., Belfast, BT9 6AX, UK
Email: arcpal@qub.ac.uk
Website: http://uas.society.qub.ac.uk
Members: 260
Contact: Barrie Hartwell, Pres.
Fee: £15
Membership Type: individual, family (includes journal)
Fee: £5
Membership Type: retired (without journal)
Description: Aims to promote and provide a forum for the interest in local archaeology and history through lectures. Organizes fieldtrips.
Publication: Journal
Publication title: Ulster Journal of Archaeology

04280
Ulster Architectural Heritage Society
UAHS
66 Donegall Pass, Belfast, BT7 1BU, UK
Tel: 028 90550213
Fax: 028 90550214
Email: louise@uahs.org.uk
Website: http://www.uahs.co.uk
Members: 1040
Staff: 3
Contact: Louise O'Neil, Admin./Business Development Off.
Fee: £25
Membership Type: single
Fee: £37
Membership Type: joint
Description: Promotes members' interests.
Library Subject: architecture
Library Type: reference
Publication: Newsletter
Publication title: Heritage Review. Advertisements.

04281
Ulster Cancer Foundation
UCF
40-44 Eglantine Ave., Belfast, BT9 6DX, UK
Tel: 028 90663281
Fax: 028 90668715
Email: info@ulstercancer.org
Website: http://www.ulstercancer.org
Staff: 40
Contact: Roisin Foster, Chief Exec.
Description: Encourages and facilitates research on cancer and its prevention and early diagnosis. Seeks to help patients and patients' families cope with cancer. Works for new and better treatments for cancer and helps people to reduce the risk of developing diseases. Conducts educational programs including clinics and training sessions for health care professionals; makes available children's services; sponsors competitions. Compiles statistics.
Publication: Book
Publication title: Cancer Control in Practice

04282
Ulster Farmers' Union
UFU
475 Antrim Rd., Belfast, BT15 3DA, UK
Tel: 028 90370222
Fax: 028 90371231
Email: info@ufuhq.com
Website: http://www.ufuni.org/portal.aspx
Members: 12500
Staff: 71
Contact: Graham Furey, Pres.
Description: Full membership is limited to persons actively engaged in farming; representatives of companies actively engaged in farming and retired farmers. Aims to defend rights and promote interest of members; to seek to secure for members a fair return from investment in agriculture; to stimulate social, educational, cultural and recreational activities in rural areas.
Publication title: UFU Diary

04283
Ulster Folk and Transport Museum
UFTM
153 Bangor Rd., Cultra, County Down, Northern Ireland, Holywood, BT18 0EU, UK
Tel: 028 90428428
Fax: 028 90428728
Website: http://www.nmni.com/uftm
Staff: 160
Contact: Lord O'Neill, Chm.
Description: Aims to further and support the study of the social history and popular culture of Ulster and its relationship to the rest of Ireland and northwest Europe.
Formerly: Formerly, Ulster Folk Life Society
Publication: Journal
Publication title: Ulster Folklife

04284
Ulster Society of Organists and Choirmasters
USOC

c/o Carolyn Hamill, Honorary Sec.
8c Beechwood House, Woodland Dr., Newtownabbey, County Antrim, Belfast, BT37 9SF, UK
Email: usoc@phoenix-organs.co.uk
Website: http://dnausers.d-n-a.net/dnetzMNU/usoc
Members: 200
Contact: Philip Stopford, Pres.
Fee: £20
Membership Type: individual
Fee: £7
Membership Type: overseas
Description: Church musicians of all denominations. Promotes: high standards in the selection and performance of church music; professional advancement of members; wider public interest in organ and choral music. Facilitates communication among members; sponsors social and educational activities.
Publication: Newsletter

04285
Ulster Teachers' Union
UTU

94 Malone Rd., Belfast, BT9 5HP, UK
Tel: 028 90662216
Fax: 028 90683296
Email: office@utu.edu
Website: http://www.utu.edu
Members: 6000
Staff: 7
Contact: Avril Hall-Callaghan, Gen. Sec.
Description: Teachers and other educational personnel. Promotes effective primary and secondary education. Works to enhance the professional status of members. Represents members' interests before government agencies, school administrative bodies, and the public.
Publication: Journal
Publication title: UTU News. Advertisements.
Meetings/Conventions: monthly meeting

04286
Ulster-Scots Language Society
USLS

68-72 Great Victoria St., Belfast, BT2 7BB, UK
Tel: 028 90436716
Website: http://www.ulsterscotslanguage.com
Contact: Michael Montgomery, Pres.
Fee: £8
Membership Type: individual
Fee: £12
Membership Type: joint, organization
Description: Promotes knowledge and use of Ulster-Scots language and cultural traditions.

04287
UNA International Service
UNAIS

Hunter House, 57 Goodramgate, York, YO1 7FX, UK
Tel: 01904 647799
Fax: 01904 652353
Website: http://www.internationalservice.org.uk
Contact: Matthew Snell, CEO
Description: Individuals aged 21 or older with an interest in global development. Promotes sustainable and locally administered economic and social development worldwide. Encourages international and intercultural exchange. Provides volunteer assistance to development programs.

04288
UNICEF - United Kingdom

30a Great Sutton St., London, EC1V 0DU, UK
Tel: 020 74902388
Fax: 020 72501733
Email: cards@unicef.org.uk
Website: http://www.unicef.org.uk
Contact: Lord Ashdown, Pres.
Description: Works with local communities to provide emergency relief and run long-term development programs in areas such as health, education and child protection; works specifically for children.
Publication title: Annual Review

Union Europeenne pour l'Agrement technique dans la construction
see European Union of Agreement

Union Internationale de Cristallographie
see International Union of Crystallography

Union Internationale des Assureurs Aviation
see International Union of Aviation Insurers

Union Internationale Humaniste et Laique
see International Humanist and Ethical Union

Union Internationale pour la Science, la Technique et les Applications du Vide
see International Union for Vacuum Science, Technique and Applications

Union Internationale Vegetarienne
see International Vegetarian Union

04289
Union of Construction, Allied Trades and Technicians - United Kingdom
UCATT

177 Abbeville Rd., London, SW4 9RL, UK
Tel: 020 76222442
Fax: 020 77204081
Email: info@ucatt.org.uk
Website: http://www.ucatt.org.uk
Members: 125000
Contact: Allan Ritchie, Gen. Sec.
Fee: £2.66
Membership Type: craft (excluding Northern Ireland)
Fee: £2.41
Membership Type: regular (excluding Northern Ireland)
Description: Represents the construction sector in UK. Provides legal assistance, insurance, loans and other benefits to its members.

04290
Union of Shop, Distributive and Allied Workers
USDAW

188 Wilmslow Rd., Manchester, M14 6LJ, UK
Tel: 0161 2242804
Fax: 0161 2572566
Email: enquiries@usdaw.org.uk
Website: http://www.usdaw.org.uk
Members: 367000
Staff: 400
Contact: John Hannett, Gen. Sec.
Description: Shopworkers in the distributive and allied trades. Seeks to improve the terms and conditions and to protect the interests of members. Works to promote equal opportunities and equal treatment for all members and oppose discrimination on grounds of sex, race, ethnic origin, disability, sexual orientation or religion.
Publication: Magazine
Publication title: Agenda: Magazine for Activists
Meetings/Conventions: annual meeting – Exhibits.

04291
UNISON

1 Mabledon Pl., London, WC1H 9AJ, UK
Tel: 0845 3550845
Email: direct@unison.co.uk
Website: http://www.unison.org.uk
Members: 1400000
Staff: 1200
Contact: Dave Prentis, Gen. Sec.
Description: Organizes those employed within areas that provide services to the public whether in public, private or voluntary sectors of the economy. Improves their pay and conditions of service and protects their rights. Provides a range of member directed services.
Publication: Journal
Publication title: Unison Journal. Advertisements.

04292
United Kingdom Association for European Law
UKAEL

King's College London, School of Law, Strand, London, WC2R 2LS, UK
Tel: 020 78481768
Fax: 020 78482443
Email: ukael@kcl.ac.uk
Website: http://www.ukael.org
Members: 320
Staff: 1
Contact: Andrea Cordwell James, Admin.
Fee: £30
Membership Type: individual
Fee: £100
Membership Type: corporate
Description: Promotes European law in the United Kingdom, closely linked to the Federation Internationale pour le Droit Europeen.

04293

United Kingdom Association for Milk Banking
UKAMB

The Milk Bank, Queen Charlotte's and Chelsea Hospital, Du Cane Rd., London, W12 0HS, UK
Tel: 020 83833559
Email: info@ukamb.org
Website: http://www.ukamb.org
Contact: Carolyn Westcott, Vice Chair
Fee: £125
Membership Type: milk bank
Fee: £25
Membership Type: individual professional (voting)
Description: Seeks to promote milk banking. Provides a forum for the exchange of information about milk banking. Reviews guidelines and sets standards for the practice of milk banking.
Publication: Newsletter
Publication title: UKAMB News
Meetings/Conventions: International Human Milk Banking Conference – annual conference

04294

United Kingdom Association of Professional Engineers
UKAPE

Hayes Ct., W Common Rd., Bromley, BR2 7AU, UK
Tel: 020 84627755
Fax: 020 83158234
Email: info@ukape.org.uk
Website: http://www.ukape.org.uk
Members: 2000
Staff: 3
Contact: Sydney Croft, Pres.
Fee: £144
Membership Type: full
Fee: £10
Membership Type: honorary
Description: Professional engineers who are chartered. Trade union established to promote the interests and status of engineers and the engineering industry. Upholds a code of conduct and maintains professional standards within the industry.
Publication: Newsletter
Publication title: Engineer Today

04295

United Kingdom Automatic Control Council
UKACC

Michael Faraday House, 6 Hills Way, Stevenage, SG1 2AY, UK
Tel: 01438 765636
Fax: 01438 767305
Email: info@ukacc.org.uk
Website: http://ukacc.group.shef.ac.uk
Members: 4
Staff: 1
Contact: Janine Mitchell, Honorary Sec.
Description: National member organisation of the International Federation of Automatic Control (IFAC). Seeks to act as an effective link between the UK and the international control communities, and to provide a focus for IFAC-related activities. Member institutions include: Institution of Electrical Engineers; Institute of Measurement and Control; Institution of Mechanical Engineers; and the Royal Aeronautical Society.

04296

United Kingdom Bartenders Guild
UKBG

Rosebank, Blackness, Linlithgow, EH49 7NL, UK
Tel: 01506 834448
Fax: 01506 834373
Email: ukbgjim@aol.com
Website: http://www.ukbg.co.uk
Members: 1000
Staff: 1
Contact: Jim Slavin, Natl. Admin.
Fee: £35
Membership Type: individual
Fee: £50
Membership Type: trade associate
Description: Bartenders and hotel and trade representatives. Serves as nonsectarian, non-political, non-union association, which is run by bartenders, for bartenders whose primary function is the advancement of the bartending profession.
Publication: Newsletter
Publication title: Bartender International. Advertisements.

04297

United Kingdom Cast Stone Association
UKCSA

15 Stone Hill Ct., The Arbours, Northampton, NN3 3RA, UK
Tel: 01604 405666
Fax: 01604 405666
Email: info@ukcsa.co.uk
Website: http://www.ukcsa.co.uk
Members: 51
Staff: 8
Contact: Neil Sparrow Haddonstone, Sec.
Description: Trade association of UK companies manufacturing cast stone to the strict technical specification laid down by the association, and companies in trades associated with the cast stone industry, whose mission statement is to encourage excellence in the manufacture of cast stone by the members and to increase the awareness and usage of the product.

04298

United Kingdom Committee of International Water Association
UKCIWA

Team Valley Gateshead Tyne and Wear, 4 Carlton Ct., London, NE11 0AZ, UK
Tel: 020 70828048
Email: jeni.colbourne@defra.gsi.gov.uk
Website: http://www.iwahq.org/templates/ld_templates/layout_633184.aspx?ObjectId=635975
Members: 35
Contact: Jeni Colbourne, Chair
Fee: £450
Description: Representatives from government agencies and departments, universities and research organizations, manufacturers and suppliers of water treatment equipment, water service companies, and regulatory agencies. Promotes Water Association activities.
Formerly: Formerly, United Kingdom National Committee of the International Association on Water Pollution Research and Control

04299

United Kingdom Council for Psychotherapy
UKCP

2nd Fl., Edward House, 2 Wakley St., London, EC1V 7LT, UK
Tel: 020 70149955
Fax: 020 70149977
Email: info@ukcp.org.uk
Website: http://www.psychotherapy.org.uk
Members: 79
Staff: 10
Contact: Andrew Samuels, Chm.
Description: Psychotherapy organisations. Protects the public by promoting appropriate standards for training, research, education and the practice of psychotherapy. Disseminates information and publishes a register of psychotherapist. Liaises with the government and the European Commission as necessary.
Publication: Directory
Publication title: Directory of Member Organizations
Meetings/Conventions: annual conference

04300

United Kingdom eInformation Group
UKeiG

Piglet Cottage, Redmire, Leyburn, DL8 4EH, UK
Tel: 01969 625751
Fax: 01969 625751
Email: cabaker@ukeig.org.uk
Website: http://www.ukeig.org.uk
Contact: Christine Baker, Contact
Fee: £24.47
Membership Type: individual (non-CILIP member)
Fee: £9.79
Membership Type: student, unwaged
Description: Serves as a body for information professionals and users, and developers of electronic information resources. Promotes and advance the effective exploitation and management of electronic information.
Formerly: Formerly, UKOLUG - the UK Online User Group

04301

United Kingdom Environmental Law Association
UKELA

PO Box 487, Surrey, Dorking, RH4 9BH, UK
Tel: 01306 500090
Email: ukela@tiscali.co.uk
Website: http://www.ukela.org
Members: 1000
Staff: 1
Contact: Peter Kellett, Chm.
Fee: £350
Membership Type: corporate
Fee: £55
Membership Type: individual, NGO
Description: Barristers, advocates, writers to the signet, solicitors, legal executives and academic lawyers, industry and environmental consultants and those interested in the development and practice of UK and EU environmental law. Aims to promote the enhancement and conservation of the environment and to advance the education of the public in all matters relating to the development, teaching, application and practice of law relating to the environment; encourage collaboration between those interested and concerned with environmental law.
Formerly: Formerly, Environmental Law Association

04302

United Kingdom Environmental Mutagen Society

UKEMS

1 Atholl Pl., Edinburgh, EH3 8HP, UK
Website: http://www.ukems.org
Members: 300
Staff: 11
Contact: Peter Farmer, Pres.
Description: Section of the European Environmental Mutagen Society. Individuals working in or interested in environmental mutagenesis. Promotes research and education in environmental mutagenesis. Offers professional training; sponsors workshops and annual meeting; provides student bursaries to members.
Publication: Journal
Publication title: Mutagenesis. Advertisements.

04303

United Kingdom Forum for Organisational Health

UKFOH

c/o Mrs. Mary Manolias, Sec.
43 Pemberton Rd., Surrey, East Molesey, KT8 9LG, UK
Tel: 0208 9793344
Email: mary.manolias@talktalk.net
Website: http://www.ukfoh.org.uk
Members: 30
Contact: Mary Manolias, Sec.
Fee: £15
Membership Type: individual
Fee: £100
Membership Type: group, company
Description: Professionals who share a common interest in the healthy development of organisations and includes occupational health physicians and nurses, researchers, counselors, personnel managers, general managers and occupational psychologists. Concerned with the development and maintenance of the psychosocial health of organisations and of the individual within the workplace. Believes that people are the most critical resource in any organisation, supports humanisation of the workplace and recognition of ways in which individual creativity and growth contribute to organisational effectiveness.

04304

United Kingdom Home Care Association

UKHCA

Group House, 2nd Fl., 52 Sutton Court Rd., Surrey, Sutton, SM1 4SL, UK
Tel: 020 82885291
Fax: 020 82885290
Email: enquiries@ukhca.co.uk
Website: http://www.ukhca.co.uk
Members: 1500
Staff: 10
Contact: Mike Padgham, Chm.
Fee: £245-495
Membership Type: full (depends on the number of branches)
Fee: £195
Membership Type: associate
Description: Represents independent home care organizations providing home care and nursing care to people in their own homes. Identifies and promotes the highest standards of home care.
Library Subject: home care
Library Type: not open to the public
Publication: Handbook
Publication title: Home Care Workers Handbook

04305

United Kingdom Housekeepers Association

UKHA

Flat 7, 14-15 Molyneux St., London, W1H 5HQ, UK
Fax: 020 77247378
Email: lynn.yambao@virgin.net
Website: http://www.ukha.co.uk
Members: 800
Contact: Lynn Yambao, Natl. Sec.
Description: Head housekeepers, domestic services managers or equivalent and deputies. Lecturers in housekeeping and domestic services and those linked with the housekeeping aspect of further or higher education. Associate and student membership is also available. Aims to improve the professional status of housekeepers, to promote housekeeping as a career and to provide a forum for the exchange of information and ideas.

04306

United Kingdom Hydrogen Association

UKHA

Owners Business Ctr., Newburn Enterprise Ctr., High St., Newburn Terr., Tyne and Wear, Newcastle upon Tyne, NE15 8LN, UK
Tel: 0191 2675724
Fax: 0191 2290591
Email: info@ukha.org
Website: http://www.ukha.org
Fee: £250
Membership Type: individual, university/education
Fee: £2500
Membership Type: related organization, industry
Description: Advocates for a positive social, political and economic environment for the development of hydrogen energy in the UK. Gives guidance on research and development priorities. Influences government and company policies to support hydrogen energy research and development.

04307

United Kingdom Industrial Vision Association

UKIVA

PO Box 25, Royston, SG8 6TL, UK
Tel: 01763 220981
Email: info@ukiva.org
Website: http://www.ukiva.org
Members: 40
Staff: 2
Contact: Jennie Harris, Contact
Fee: £750
Membership Type: in UK
Fee: £1200
Membership Type: outside UK
Description: Suppliers of industrial vision systems. Seeks to promote the use of vision technology by manufacturers in the United Kingdom. Encourages information exchange among members. Works to enhance international marketing efforts.
Publication: Brochure
Publication title: Guide to Machine Vision

04308

United Kingdom Institute for Conservation of Historic and Artistic Works

UKIC

1st Fl., Downstream Bldg., 1 London Bridge, London, SE1 9BG, UK
Tel: 020 77853807
Fax: 020 77853806
Email: training@icon.org.uk
Website: http://www.icon.org.uk
Members: 1600
Staff: 4
Contact: Simon Cane, Chm.
Fee: £146
Membership Type: full (accredited)
Fee: £110
Membership Type: low income/unwaged (accredited)
Description: Professional conservators and restorers who are engaged in practical conservation or whose main occupation is concerned with conservation (e.g. lecturers, managers, conservation scientists). Seeks to promote the highest standards of conservation by encouraging education, study and research in any relevant branches of practice or science and supporting efforts to increase proficiency. Assists in the dissemination of technical and professional information relating to the field of conservation.
Publication: Journal
Publication title: The Conservator

04309

United Kingdom Literacy Association

UKLA

University of Leicester, University Rd., Leicester, LE1 7RH, UK
Tel: 0116 2231664
Fax: 0116 2231665
Email: admin@ukla.org
Website: http://www.ukla.org
Members: 1100
Staff: 2
Contact: Lyn Overall, Gen. Sec.
Fee: £45
Membership Type: individual, U.K.
Fee: £55
Membership Type: school, U.K.
Description: Open to all interested in teaching of reading and language. Members are mainly teachers and teacher-educators/researchers. Covers the promotion and use of reading, language and communication.
Formerly: Formerly, United Kingdom Reading Association
Publication: Journal
Publication title: Journal of Research in Reading

04310

United Kingdom Major Ports Group

UKMPG

4th Fl., Carthusian Ct., 12 Carthusian St., London, EC1M 6EZ, UK
Tel: 020 72601785
Fax: 020 72601788
Email: richardbird@ukmajorports.org.uk
Website: http://www.ukmajorports.org.uk
Contact: Richard Bird, Exec. Dir.
Description: Represents commercial ports in the UK. Protects the interests of its members to policy makers and opinion formers in the UK and Europe.

04311
United Kingdom Maritime Pilots' Association
UKMPA

Transport House, 128 Theobald's Rd., Holborn, London, WC1X 8TN, UK
Tel: 020 76112568
Fax: 020 76112757
Email: ukmpaoffice@yahoo.com
Website: http://www.ukmpa.org
Members: 520
Staff: 1
Contact: G. Stevenson, Natl. Sec.
Description: Marine pilots (maritime navigation). Active in all relevant matters to promote the profession and the welfare of its members.
Formerly: Formerly, United Kingdom Pilots Association
Publication: Magazine
Publication title: The Pilot. Advertisements.
Meetings/Conventions: annual conference – Exhibits.

04312
United Kingdom Multiple Sclerosis Specialist Nurse Association
UKMSSNA

PO Box 63, Herefordshire, Ledbury, HR8 9AA, UK
Tel: 01531 670481
Email: admin@ukmssna.org.uk
Website: http://www.ukmssna.org.uk
Contact: Mary Fielding, Admin.
Fee: £35
Membership Type: full, associate
Description: Facilitates the development of a specialized branch of nursing in multiple sclerosis (MS). Educates the health and social care community about multiple sclerosis. Supports nurses and other healthcare professionals who care for people with MS. Supports multiple sclerosis nursing research, general research and clinical trials.

04313
United Kingdom Offshore Operators' Association
UKOOA

6th Fl. E, Portland House, Bressenden Pl., London, SW1E 5BH, UK
Tel: 0207 8022400
Email: info@oilandgasuk.co.uk
Website: http://www.oilandgasuk.co.uk
Staff: 25
Contact: Malcolm Webb, Chief Exec.
Description: Represents organization for UK offshore oil and gas industry.
Publication: Report
Publication title: Condensate in Produced Water - Genesis Report

04314
United Kingdom Onshore Operators Group
UKOOG

c/o Midmar Energy Ltd.
6 Dean Park Crescent, 1st Fl., Bournemouth, BH1 1HL, UK
Tel: 01202 780333
Fax: 01202 780444
Email: ukoog@oilmanuk.com
Website: http://www.ukoog.org.uk
Members: 10
Staff: 5
Contact: Steve Allen, Contact
Fee: £500
Membership Type: regular
Description: Licensed under UK landward to explore and produce oil and natural gas including coalbed methane. Provides a forum in which representatives of the oil industry discuss matters relating to the exploration and drill of oil and natural gas, including natural gas in coal seams. Represents the interest of the UK onshore oil and gas industry in negotiations with the government and other national and international authorities and organizations.
Library Subject: U.K. onshore oil and gas
Library Type: not open to the public
Publication title: UKOOG Guide to Legislation

04315
United Kingdom Petroleum Industry Association
UKPIA

Quality House, Quality Ct., Chancery Ln., London, WC2A 1HP, UK
Tel: 0207 2697600
Email: info@ukpia.com
Website: http://www.ukpia.com/home.aspx?tabid=11729
Members: 8
Staff: 8
Contact: Chris Hunt, Dir. Gen.
Description: Major oil supply companies with refining interests in the UK or Europe. Represents the supply, refining and distribution (downstream) sectors of the oil industry, in communication with government, industrial and commercial associations, the media and the public.
Publication: Newsletter
Publication title: Ukpia News

04316
United Kingdom Science Park Association
UKSPA

Chesterford Research Park, Little Chesterford, Cambridge, CB10 1XL, UK
Tel: 01799 532050
Fax: 01799 532049
Email: info@ukspa.org.uk
Website: http://www.ukspa.org.uk/home
Members: 71
Staff: 3
Contact: Paul Wright, Chief Exec.
Fee: £970
Membership Type: full, associate, overseas, affiliate
Fee: £1150
Membership Type: business affiliate
Description: Supports and encourages the startup, incubation and development of innovation led, high growth, knowledge-based businesses. Provides opportunity for larger and international businesses to develop specific and close interactions with a particular centre of knowledge creation for mutual benefit.
Publication: Magazine
Publication title: Innovation into Success

04317
United Kingdom Society for Trenchless Technology
UKSTT

38 Holly Walk, Warwickshire, Leamington Spa, CV32 4LY, UK
Tel: 01926 330935
Fax: 01926 330935
Email: admin@ukstt.org.uk
Website: http://www.ukstt.org.uk
Members: 212
Staff: 2
Contact: Russell Fairhurst, Chm.
Fee: £545
Membership Type: corporate
Fee: £55
Membership Type: individual
Description: Promotes the environmental, technical and commercial benefits of trenchless technology to the community, through explanation, education, training and research.
Library Subject: trenchless technology, utilities
Library Type: by appointment only

04318
United Kingdom Spring Manufacturers Association
UKSMA

Henry St., Sheffield, S3 7EQ, UK
Tel: 0114 2760542
Fax: 0114 2527997
Email: uksma@uksma.org.uk
Website: http://www.uksma.org.uk
Members: 100
Staff: 2
Description: Represents manufacturers of springs in England.
Library Subject: Technical publications relating to all aspects of spring technology
Library Type: reference

04319
United Kingdom Transplant Coordinators Association
UKTCA

c/o Philippa Stainton
PO Box 47, Kingsbridge, TQ7 4WG, UK
Tel: 07071 223171
Email: info@uktca.co.uk
Website: http://www.uktca.co.uk
Contact: Jayne Fisher, Chair
Fee: £60
Membership Type: full
Description: Represents the interests of transplant coordinators in UK. Promotes organ and tissue donation. Advances the education of the public and health care professionals in all matters relating to organ and tissue donation. Ensures that the standards of practice for donor transplant and recipient transplant coordinators are maintained.

04320
United Kingdom Warehousing Association
UKWA

Walter House, 418-422 Strand, London, WC2R 0PT, UK
Tel: 020 78365522
Fax: 020 74389379
Email: dg@ukwa.org.uk
Website: http://www.ukwa.org.uk
Members: 700
Staff: 8
Contact: Derrick Potter, Chm.
Fee: £575.75
Membership Type: associate corporate
Fee: £98.7
Membership Type: associate individual
Description: Companies providing public warehousing facilities for their customers. Represents member companies who, between them, operate around 800 million square feet of public warehousing space throughout the U.K. It aims to promote high quality storage conditions and a high level of customer service within the sector, to represent the view of its members to Government departments, trade and official organizations.
Publication: Membership Directory
Publication title: UKWA Directory of Members' Services. Advertisements.

04321
United Kingdom Weighing Federation
UKWF

Federation House, 10 Vyse St., Birmingham, B18 6LT, UK
Tel: 0121 2371130
Fax: 0121 2371133
Email: admin@ukwf.org.uk
Website: http://www.ukwf.org.uk
Members: 300
Staff: 10
Contact: Jeremy Sage, Pres.
Description: Dedicated to the needs of manufacturers of hardware, housewares and brushware to the U.K. consumer market. Offers a wide range of membership and consulting services, including export assistance service, legal and market information.
Publication: Newsletter
Publication title: Weighlog
Meetings/Conventions: annual general assembly

04322
United Kingdom's Disabled People's Council
UKDPC

Litchurch Plz., Litchurch Ln., Derby, DE24 8AA, UK
Tel: 01332 295551
Fax: 01332 295580
Email: general@uksdpc.org
Website: http://www.ukdpc.net
Members: 140
Staff: 10
Contact: Andy Rickell, Chief Exec.
Fee: £25
Membership Type: regional group
Fee: £50
Membership Type: national group
Description: Organizations controlled by disabled people and individual membership is now available to all disabled people and their supporters. The national umbrella organisation representing groups controlled by disabled people. Current concern is to secure anti-discrimination legislation. Has begun a 3-year group development programme to actively support the growth of regional organisations controlled by disabled people.
Formerly: Formerly, British Council of Organisations of Disabled People

04323
United Kingdom-Ireland Controlled Release Society
UKICRS

Devlab, Merck Sharp & Dohme, Hertfordshire, Hoddesdon, EN11 9BU, UK
Email: leab_sek@merck.com
Website: http://www.ukicrs.org
Contact: Leab Sek, Sec.
Description: Dedicated to the advancement of the science and technology controlling the release and delivery of active agents. Focuses on research about controlled release encompassing agriculture, veterinary, food, and cosmetic sciences.

04324
United Nations Association of Great Britain and Northern Ireland
UNA-UK

3 Whitehall Ct., London, SW1A 2EL, UK
Tel: 020 77663444
Fax: 020 79305893
Email: mulligan@una.org.uk
Website: http://www.una-uk.org
Members: 7000
Staff: 18
Contact: Philip Mulligan, Exec. Dir.
Fee: £25
Membership Type: individual
Fee: £35
Membership Type: joint (same address)
Description: Interested individuals, nationwide network of branches. Seeks to strengthen the role of the United Nations in global affairs through international cooperation. Acts as a forum for discussion of nonviolent conflict resolution, human rights, environment and development. Conducts educational and charitable programs. Maintains a speakers' bureau.
Publication: Newsletter
Publication title: New World. Advertisements.

04325
United Road Transport Union
URTU

Almond House, Oak Green, Stanley Green Business Park, Cheadle Hulme, SK8 6QL, UK
Tel: 0161 4862100
Fax: 0161 4853109
Email: info@urtu.com
Website: http://www.urtu.com
Members: 16874
Staff: 30
Contact: Robert F. Monks, Gen. Sec.
Fee: £148.2
Membership Type: driver
Fee: £130
Membership Type: non-driver
Description: Works to serve the interests of workers in the road haulage industry.
Publication: Magazine
Publication title: Wheels. Advertisements.

04326
Unity

Hillcrest House, Garth St., Hanley, Stoke-on-Trent, ST1 2AB, UK
Tel: 01782 272755
Fax: 01782 284902
Email: contact@unitytheunion.org.uk
Website: http://www.unitytheunion.org.uk
Members: 9000
Contact: Geoff Bagnall, Gen. Sec.
Description: Represents the pottery workers in UK. Aims to improve the working conditions and pay of its members.

04327
Universities Association for Lifelong Learning
UALL

21 De Montfort St., Leicester, LE1 7GE, UK
Tel: 0116 2859702
Fax: 0116 2046988
Email: admin@uall.ac.uk
Website: http://www.uall.ac.uk
Members: 240
Staff: 2
Contact: Lucy Bate, Admin.
Fee: £775
Membership Type: full, institutional
Fee: £300
Membership Type: associate
Description: Open to all UK universities and higher education institutions with international membership for overseas universities and associate membership for professional bodies. Provides a forum for the interchange of information on university continuing education and lifelong learning. Promotes all aspect of university continuing education. Encourages and conducts research on this subject and facilitates the dissemination of results to the general public and interested organizations.
Formerly: Also Known As, Universities Association for Continuing Education

04328
Universities Council for the Education of Teachers
UCET

Industry of Education, 20 Bedford Way, London, WC1E 0AL, UK
Tel: 020 75808000
Email: info@ucet.ac.uk
Website: http://www.ucet.ac.uk
Members: 94
Staff: 5
Contact: James Noble Rogers, Exec. Dir.
Description: All universities and university-sector colleges in the UK involved in the education of teachers. Acts as a national forum for the discussion of all matters relating to education of teachers and the study of education in universities. Contributes to the formulation of policy in these fields and makes representations to and collaborates with other groups in the UK with similar interests.
Publication: Pamphlet
Publication title: University Courses in Education Open to Students from Overseas

04329

Universities Federation for Animal Welfare
UFAW

The Old School, Brewhouse Hill, Wheathampstead, AL4 8AN, UK
Tel: 01582 831818
Fax: 01582 831414
Email: ufaw@ufaw.org.uk
Website: http://www.ufaw.org.uk
Description: Promotes and supports developments in the science and technology that underpin advances in animal welfare. Promotes education in animal care.
Publication: Journal
Publication title: Animal Welfare

04330

Universities UK
UUK

Woburn House, 20 Tavistock Sq., London, WC1H 9HQ, UK
Tel: 020 74194111
Fax: 020 73888649
Email: info@universitiesuk.ac.uk
Website: http://www.universitiesuk.ac.uk/Pages/Default.aspx
Members: 133
Staff: 70
Contact: Steve Smith, Pres.
Description: Members are executive heads of universities in the UK. Promotes, encourages and develops the university sector of higher education in the United Kingdom. Policy development, research, campaigning, lobbying, sharing best practice, conference and events.
Library Subject: higher education policy and research, legislation, government reports
Library Type: not open to the public
Formerly: Formerly, Committee for Vice-Chancellors and Principals

04331

University and College Union
UCU

Egmont House, 25-31 Tavistock Pl., London, WC1H 9UT, UK
Tel: 020 77562500
Fax: 020 77562501
Email: hq@ucu.org.uk
Website: http://www.ucu.org.uk
Members: 45000
Staff: 60
Contact: Sally Hunt, Gen. Sec.
Description: Academic and related research staff in university and similar higher education and research organizations. Concerned with the advancement of university education and research, the regulation of relations between academic and related staff and their employers. Also promotes common action by those staff and safeguards the interests of members.
Formerly: Formerly, Association of University Teachers - London and University and College Lecturers' Union
Publication: Journal
Publication title: AUTLOOK. Advertisements.

University and College Union Scotland

see Association of University Teachers - Scotland

04332

University Association for Contemporary European Studies
UACES

School of Public Policy, University College London, 29-30 Tavistock Sq., London, WC1H 9QU, UK
Tel: 020 76794975
Fax: 020 76794973
Email: admin@uaces.org
Website: http://www.uaces.org
Members: 1000
Contact: Luke Foster, Interim Exec. Dir.
Fee: £40
Membership Type: individual
Fee: £20
Membership Type: student
Description: Provides a forum for debate and a clearing house for information about European affairs. Directly involved in promoting research and establishing teaching and research networks. Brings together academics involved in researching and teaching on Europe with practitioners active in European affairs. Encourages people from all disciplines to become involved.
Publication: Journal
Publication title: Journal of Common Market Studies

04333

Urania Trust

12 Warrington Spur, Berkshire, Old Windsor, SL4 2NF, UK
Email: uraniatrust@f2s.com
Website: http://www.uraniatrust.org
Members: 2000
Staff: 16
Contact: Jonathan Powell, Chm.
Fee: £8
Membership Type: ordinary
Fee: £14
Membership Type: postal
Description: Anyone interested in man's relationship with the cosmos. Serves as an educational charity sponsoring any activities that explore man's relationship with the cosmos, philosophy, astrology, astronomy etc.

04334

Urostomy Association
UA

4 Demontfort Way, Uttoxeter, ST14 8XY, UK
Tel: 01889 563191
Email: secretary.ua@classmail.co.uk
Website: http://www.urostomyassociation.org.uk
Members: 2400
Staff: 2
Contact: Hazel Pixley, Co. Sec.
Fee: £12
Membership Type: individual
Description: Works to assist people who will undergo or have undergone surgery that results in a urinary diversion; assists caregivers in the rehabilitation process; provides support and information.
Publication: Magazine
Publication title: UA Journal. Advertisements.
Meetings/Conventions: annual conference – Exhibits.

04335

Valley of the Kings Foundation
VOKF

Chiddingstone Castle, Kent, TN8 7AD, UK
Email: vokf@aol.com
Website: http://www.nicholasreeves.com
Contact: Nicholas Reeves, Dir.
Description: Committed to the preservation and conservation of the site and its royal and private tombs and related archaeology, as well as to record the social history of those who have explored and continue to work in the Valley; disseminates information concerning the results of ongoing work in this area.

04336

Vegan Society of England
VS

Donald Watson House, 21 Hylton St., Hockley, Birmingham, B18 6HJ, UK
Tel: 0121 5231730
Fax: 0121 5231749
Email: info@vegansociety.com
Website: http://www.vegansociety.com/home.php
Members: 4500
Staff: 11
Contact: Nigel Winter, CEO
Fee: £7
Membership Type: additional family member living at same household
Fee: £21
Membership Type: basic
Description: Educational charity providing information on all aspects of veganism, which is a way of living that seeks to exclude, as far as possible, all forms of exploitation of, and cruelty to animals for food, clothing, or any other purpose. Promotes animal-free living for the benefit of people, animals and the environment. Provides information to the media, health care professionals, schools, caterers and the public.
Publication: Book
Publication title: The Animal-Free Shopper. Advertisements.

04337

Vegetarian Society of the United Kingdom

Parkdale, Dunham Rd., Cheshire, Altrincham, WA14 4QG, UK
Tel: 0161 9252000
Fax: 0161 9269182
Email: info@vegsoc.org
Website: http://www.vegsoc.org
Members: 22000
Staff: 25
Contact: Annette Pinner, Chief Exec.
Fee: £21
Membership Type: individual
Fee: £16
Membership Type: student, unwaged, senior
Description: Aims to increase vegetarianism in order to save animals, benefit human health and protect the environment and world food resources. Runs a cookery school, information sheets, teachers materials and has leaflets available free of charge.
Publication: Magazine
Publication title: The Vegetarian

04338
Vehicle Builders and Repairers Association
VBRA

Belmont House, 102 Finkle Ln., Gildersome, Leeds, LS27 7TW, UK
Tel: 0113 2538333
Fax: 0113 2380496
Email: vbra@vbra.co.uk
Website: http://www.vbra.co.uk
Members: 1200
Staff: 19
Contact: Malcolm Tagg, Dir. Gen.
Description: Car body accident repair centres and commercial vehicle bodybuilders in the United Kingdom. Promotes members' interests.
Publication: Magazine
Publication title: Body. Advertisements.
Meetings/Conventions: Business Forum – annual meeting

04339
Venture Scotland
VS

Norton Park, 57 Albion Rd., Edinburgh, EH7 5QY, UK
Tel: 0131 4752395
Fax: 0131 4752396
Email: admin@venturescotland.org.uk
Website: http://www.venturescotland.org.uk
Members: 130
Staff: 3
Contact: Jane Bruce, Dir.
Description: Participants in "Bothy Ventures" conducted by the organization. Promotes personal, social, and spiritual growth through participation in recreational outdoor activities; seeks to develop cooperation among members. Conducts ventures during which participants engage in activities such as raft building, mountain walking, and conservation and environmental protection projects. Conducts woodcraft education and training programs; participates in charitable activities.
Publication: Newsletter
Publication title: The Buchaille

Verband der Europäischen Angelgeratehersteller

see European Fishing Tackle Trade Association

Verband der Fluglinien Europäischer Regionen

see European Regions Airline Association

04340
Veterinary Association for Arbitration and Jurisprudence
VAAJ

c/o Graham D. Cawley, Honorary Sec.-Treas.
The Beeches, Rickerby, Carlisle, CA3 9AA, UK
Tel: 01228 521450
Fax: 01228 521450
Email: gdcawley@aol.com
Website: http://www.veterinaryexpertwitnesses.co.uk
Members: 130
Contact: Simon Newbery, Chm.
Fee: £25
Membership Type: regular
Description: Veterinary surgeons, students, and lawyers. Aims to promote and assist dispute resolution by all means. Offers training in all aspects of dispute resolution.

04341
Veterinary History Society

Netherton Lodge, Quenington, Cirencester, GL7 5DD, UK
Tel: 01285 750346
Fax: 01285 750053
Email: vivashbvj123@btinternet.com
Website: http://www.veterinaryhistorysociety.org.uk
Contact: Bruce Jones, Chm.
Description: Veterinarians and other interested individuals. Fosters all aspects of veterinary history.
Publication: Journal
Publication title: Veterinary History

04342
Victim Support

Hallam House, 56-60 Hallam St., London, W1W 6JL, UK
Tel: 020 72680200
Fax: 020 72680210
Email: contact@victimsupport.org.uk
Website: http://www.victimsupport.org
Members: 300
Staff: 1014
Contact: Gillian Guy, Chief Exec.
Description: All affiliated member schemes must adhere to the nationally agreed Code of Practice. Trained volunteers offer information, practical help and emotional support to victims of crime ranging from burglary to the murder of a relative. Service offered by home visit, or by the Witness Service at Crown Court centers and in a growing number of magistrates' courts. Aims to raise awareness of the effects of crime and the rights of victims.
Formerly: Formerly, National Association of Victims Support Schemes

04343
Victoria League for Commonwealth Friendship

55 Leinster Sq., London, W2 4PW, UK
Tel: 020 72293961
Fax: 020 72292994
Email: victorialeague@btconnect.com
Website: http://www.victorialeague.co.uk
Members: 300
Staff: 5
Contact: Lynn D. Hopkins, Chair
Fee: £25
Membership Type: general
Fee: £10
Membership Type: student
Description: Individuals and organizations. Promotes good fellowship among the peoples of the British Commonwealth. Conducts educational, cultural, and exchange programs.
Publication: Newsletter
Publication title: The Victoria League Newsletter

04344
Victorian Military Society
VMS

PO Box 5837, Newbury, RG14 7FJ, UK
Website: http://www.victorianmilitarysociety.org.uk
Members: 1000
Fee: £20
Membership Type: individual (UK residents)
Fee: £23
Membership Type: individual (European countries)
Description: Military historians, and enthusiasts; military museums and organizations. Aims to foster interest in the military history of the Victorian period, emphasizing the armies of the British Empire between 1837 and 1914. Conducts historical research. Sponsors competitions and special publications.
Publication: Journal
Publication title: Soldiers of the Queen. Advertisements.

04345
Victorian Society

1 Priory Gardens, London, W4 1TT, UK
Tel: 020 89941019
Email: admin@victoriansociety.org.uk
Website: http://www.victoriansociety.org.uk
Members: 3500
Staff: 6
Contact: Ian Dungavell, Dir.
Fee: £35
Membership Type: individual, young Victorian (aged 25 or under)
Fee: £45
Membership Type: household
Description: Prevents the needless demolition of Victorian and Edwardian buildings of architectural interest; promotes public understanding and appreciation of the architecture and decorative arts of the period.
Publication: Magazine
Publication title: The Victorian. Advertisements.

04346
Viking Society for Northern Research

University College London, Gower St., London, WC1E 6BT, UK
Email: vsnr@ucl.ac.uk
Website: http://www.le.ac.uk/ee/viking
Contact: Chris Abram, Hon. Asst. Sec.
Fee: £20
Membership Type: ordinary
Fee: £7
Membership Type: student
Description: Individuals and libraries of institutions in 23 countries. Promotes interest in the literature and antiquities of the Scandinavian North. Gives lectures; conducts seminars. Sponsors book auctions.
Formerly: Formerly, Viking Club
Publication title: Dorothea Coke Memorial Lectures

04347
VisitScotland

Level 3, Ocean Point 1, 94 Ocean Dr., Edinburgh, EH6 6JH, UK
Tel: 0845 2255121
Email: info@visitscotland.com
Website: http://www.visitscotland.com
Members: 140
Contact: Marco Truffelli, Chief Exec.

Description: Promotes and develops tourism in Scotland. Conducts research program. Maintains speakers' bureau. Compiles statistics.
Library Subject: tourism
Library Type: reference
Formerly: Formerly, Scottish Tourist Board
Publication title: The Conference and Exhibition Market in Scotland

04348
Vitalise
12 City Forum, 250 City Rd., London, EC1V 8AF, UK
Tel: 0845 3451972
Fax: 0845 3451978
Email: info@vitalise.org.uk
Website: http://www.vitalise.org.uk/Home-Page.aspx
Staff: 280
Contact: Neil McConachie, Interim Chief Exec.
Description: Provides respite care for physically disabled persons in the UK. Organizes holidays for disabled individuals and provides essential breaks and opportunities for carers and volunteers.
Formerly: Formerly, Winged Fellowship Trust
Publication: Magazine
Publication title: Let's Vitalise

04349
Vitreous Enamel Services
VES
Sherdley Rd. Industrial Estate, 12 Wharton St., St. Helens, WA9 5AA, UK
Tel: 01744 737274
Fax: 01744 739404
Website: http://www.vitreous-enamel.com
Description: Companies in the vitreous enamel and allied industries. Promotes the use of vitreous enamel in all its many uses. Works closely with the IVE, the professional institute of the industry.

04350
Voice of the Listener and Viewer
VLV
PO Box 401, Kent, Gravesend, DA12 9FY, UK
Tel: 01474 338716
Fax: 01474 325440
Email: info@vlv.org.uk
Website: http://www.vlv.org.uk
Members: 2000
Contact: Sue Washbrook, Membership Sec.
Fee: £25
Membership Type: individual (in UK)
Fee: £35
Membership Type: individual (outside UK)
Description: Individuals united to support public service broadcasting in the United Kingdom. Seeks to ensure the maintenance of high standards, independence, and diversity of broadcasting. Offers educational trust program; conducts research programs. Maintains speakers' bureau. Provides a forum for communication and exchange among those interested in broadcasting.
Library Subject: broadcasting issues
Library Type: reference
Formerly: Formerly, Voice of the Listener

04351
Voice: The Union for Education Professionals
2 St. James' Ct., Friar Gate, Derby, DE1 1BT, UK
Tel: 01332 372337
Fax: 01332 290310
Email: enquiries@voicetheunion.org.uk
Website: http://www.voicetheunion.org.uk
Members: 35000
Staff: 40
Contact: Philip Parkin, Gen. Sec.
Fee: £138-145
Membership Type: full-time teacher/lecturer (based on rate number)
Fee: £131-138
Membership Type: joint (based on rate number)
Description: Teachers, lecturers and student teachers, nursery nurses and nannies and education support staff in all parts of the UK, from nursery to tertiary and in both maintained and independent sectors. Promotes professional standards amongst teachers, support staff, and childcarers, emphasizing the need to give priority to the well-being of children and students; furthers the advancement of education and childcare by initiating proposals for reform and by resisting any lowering of standards; provides services to members and negotiates salaries and conditions of service.
Formerly: Formerly, Professional Association of Teachers - UK
Publication: Journal
Publication title: Your Voice. Advertisements.

04352
Voluntary Service Overseas - England
VSO
27A Carlton Drive, London, SW15 2BS, UK
Tel: 020 87807500
Email: enquiry@vso.org.uk
Website: http://www.vso.org.uk
Members: 40000
Staff: 298
Contact: Marg Mayne, Chief Exec.
Description: VSO is the world's leading independent international development organisation that works through volunteers to fight poverty in developing countries. VSO's high-impact approach involves bringing people together to share skills, build capabilities, promote international understanding and action, and change lives to make the world a fairer place for all.
Publication title: Orbit

04353
Volunteer Development - Scotland
VDS
Jubilee House, Forthside Way, Stirling, FK8 1QZ, UK
Tel: 01786 479593
Fax: 01786 849767
Email: vds@vds.org.uk
Website: http://www.vds.org.uk
Members: 500
Contact: George Thomson, CEO
Fee: £25-80
Membership Type: voluntary organization (based on annual turnover)
Fee: £25
Membership Type: individual, branch
Description: Management personnel overseeing voluntary activities. Promotes the professional advancement of members. Represents members' professional and economic interests; establishes standards of practice for managers of volunteers; serves as a clearinghouse on voluntary programs and volunteer management. Conducts research and educational programs; compiles statistics.
Publication: Newsletter
Publication title: SAVM Newsletter

04354
Volunteer Service Overseas - United Kingdom
VSOUK
317 Putney Bridge Rd., Putney, London, SW15 2PN, UK
Tel: 020 87807500
Email: enquiry@vso.org.uk
Website: http://www.vso.org.uk
Members: 1700
Staff: 780
Contact: Marg Mayne, Chief Exec.
Description: International development agency that works through volunteers in 74 countries worldwide. Enables people aged 17-70 to share their skills and expertise with communities and organizations across the developing world. Aims to make a difference in tackling disadvantage by helping people realize their potential.

04355
Volunteers for Rural India
VRI
12 Eastleigh Ave., Middlesex, South Harrow, HA2 0UF, UK
Tel: 0208 8644740
Email: enquiries@vri-online.org.uk
Website: http://www.vri-online.org.uk
Members: 90
Contact: Jyoti Singh, Gen. Sec.
Fee: £15
Membership Type: regular
Fee: £60
Membership Type: life
Description: Provides programs for people over the age of 18 who wish to learn about India. Places selected individuals in a rural development project in North India for a three-week trial period as paying guests. Organises seminars and conferences in both India and England on issues of human development, poverty, discrimination and the disadvantages suffered by the poor. Raises funds to help rural development projects in India.
Formerly: Formerly, Indian Volunteers for Community Service
Publication: Journal
Publication title: International Journal of Rural Studies. Advertisements.
Meetings/Conventions: triennial conference

04356
Vulval Pain Society
VPS
PO Box 7804, Nottingham, NG3 5ZQ, UK
Tel: 07765 947599
Email: info@vulvalpainsociety.org
Website: http://www.vulvalpainsociety.org
Members: 500
Staff: 3
Contact: David Nunns, Co-Founder
Description: Provides information and support to women who suffer from vulval pain and discomfort.
Library Type: not open to the public
Publication: Handbook

04357

Wales Craft Council WCC

Henfaes Ln., Powys, Welshpool, SY21 7BE, UK
Tel: 01938 555313
Fax: 01938 556237
Email: info@walescraftcouncil.co.uk
Website: http://www.walescraftcouncil.co.uk
Members: 165
Staff: 3
Contact: Philomena Hearn, Chair
Fee: £50
Membership Type: general
Description: Craft and giftware show organisers. Promotes increased demand for Welsh craft items. Publicizes Welsh crafts; gathers and disseminates industry information.
Publication: Catalog
Publication title: Trade Fair Catalogue. Advertisements.
Meetings/Conventions: semiannual trade show

04358

Wales Young Farmers' Clubs

YFC Centre, Royal Welsh Showground, Powys, Builth Wells, LD2 3NJ, UK
Tel: 01982 553502
Fax: 01982 552979
Email: information@yfc-wales.org.uk
Website: http://www.yfc-wales.org.uk
Members: 6000
Staff: 7
Contact: Tim John, Chm.
Description: Serves as voluntary youth organization. Offers educational, training, and social programs for rural young people. Works to raise environmental awareness.
Publication: Magazine
Publication title: CYFFRO

04359

Wales Young Farmers' Clubs - Carmarthenshire Federation

Agriculture House, Cambrian Pl., Carmarthenshire, Carmarthen, SA31 1QG, UK
Tel: 01267 237693
Fax: 01267 237693
Email: sir.gar@yfc-wales.org.uk
Website: http://www.yfc-wales.org.uk/carmarthen.php
Contact: Eirios Thomas, Contact
Description: Promotes the personal development of young people living in rural areas. Promotes the understanding of cultural diversity of Wales. Works to raise the profile of the Welsh language.

04360

Wales Young Farmers' Clubs - Clwyd Federation

Llysfasi College, Denbishire, Ruthin, LL15 2LB, UK
Tel: 01978 790403
Fax: 01978 790403
Email: clwyd@yfc-wales.org.uk
Website: http://www.yfc-wales.org.uk/clwyd.php
Members: 500
Contact: Eleri V. Roberts, County Organiser
Description: Promotes the personal development of young people living in rural areas. Promotes the understanding of the cultural diversity of Wales. Works to raise the profile of the Welsh language.

04361

Wales Young Farmers' Clubs - Eryri Federation

Meirion Dwyfor College, Safle Glynllifon, Clynnog Rd., Gwynedd, Caernarfon, LL54 5DU, UK
Tel: 01286 831214
Email: eryri@yfc-wales.org.uk
Website: http://www.yfc-wales.org.uk/eryri.php
Description: Promotes the personal development of young people living in rural areas. Promotes the understanding of cultural diversity of Wales. Works to raise the profile of the Welsh language.

04362

Wales Young Farmers' Clubs - Glamorgan Federation

Pencoed College, Tregroes, Mid Glamorgan, Pencoed, CF35 5LG, UK
Tel: 01656 864488
Fax: 01656 862398
Email: glamorgan@yfc-wales.org.uk
Website: http://www.yfc-wales.org.uk/glamorgan.php
Description: Promotes the personal development of young people living in rural areas. Promotes the understanding of cultural diversity of Wales. Works to raise the profile of the Welsh language.

04363

Wales Young Farmers' Clubs - Gwent Federation

Coleg Gwent, Usk Campus, Monmouthshire, Usk, NP15 1XJ, UK
Tel: 01291 672602
Email: gwent@yfc-wales.org.uk
Website: http://www.yfc-wales.org.uk/gwent.php
Contact: Nick Turner, Pres.
Description: Promotes the personal development of young people living in rural areas. Promotes the understanding of cultural diversity of Wales. Works to raise the profile of the Welsh language.

04364

Wales Young Farmers' Clubs - Meirionnydd Federation

Cae Penarlag, Gwynedd, Dolgellau, LL40 2YB, UK
Tel: 01341 423846
Fax: 01341 423723
Email: meirionnydd@yfc-wales.org.uk
Website: http://www.yfc-wales.org.uk/meirionnydd.php
Description: Promotes the personal development of young people living in rural areas. Promotes the understanding of cultural diversity of Wales. Works to raise the profile of the Welsh language.

04365

Wales Young Farmers' Clubs - Montgomery Federation

Old College, Station Rd., Powys, Newtown, SY16 1BE, UK
Tel: 01686 614028
Fax: 01686 614079
Email: maldwyn@yfc-wales.org.uk
Website: http://www.yfc-wales.org.uk/montgomery.php
Members: 700
Contact: Nicola Walker, Chair
Membership Type: individual (based on age)
Fee: £10
Membership Type: associate
Description: Promotes the personal development of young people living in rural areas. Promotes the understanding of cultural diversity of Wales. Works to raise the profile of the Welsh language.

04366

Wales Young Farmers' Clubs - Pembrokeshire Federation

Agriculture House, Winch Ln., Pembrokeshire, Haverfordwest, SA61 1RW, UK
Tel: 01437 762639
Fax: 01437 768996
Email: sir.benfro@yfc-wales.org.uk
Website: http://www.yfc-wales.org.uk/pembrokeshire.php
Contact: William Lawrence, Chm.
Description: Promotes the personal development of young people living in rural areas. Promotes the understanding of cultural diversity of Wales. Works to raise the profile of the Welsh language.

04367

Wales Young Farmers' Clubs - Radnor Federation

Rhoslyn, 11 High St., Powys, Llandrindod Wells, LD1 6AG, UK
Tel: 01597 829008
Fax: 01597 824096
Email: radnor@yfc-wales.org.uk
Website: http://www.yfc-wales.org.uk/radnor.php
Contact: Jimmy Hughes, Chm.
Description: Promotes the personal development of young people living in rural areas. Promotes the understanding of cultural diversity of Wales. Works to raise the profile of the Welsh language.

04368

Wales Young Farmers' Clubs - Ynys Mon Federation

Anglesey Show Ground, Gwalchmai, Ynys Mon, Holyhead, LD65 4RW, UK
Tel: 01407 720256
Email: ynys.mon@yfc-wales.org.uk
Website: http://www.yfc-wales.org.uk/ynysmon.php
Description: Promotes the personal development of young people living in rural areas. Promotes the understanding of cultural diversity of Wales. Works to raise the profile of the Welsh language.

04369

Walmsley Society

c/o Fred W. Lane, Honorary Sec.
April Cottage, 1 Brand Rd., Hampden Park, Sussex, Eastbourne, BN22 9PX, UK
Email: walmsley@mabarraclough.f9.co.uk
Website: http://walmsleysociety.org
Members: 200
Contact: Sean Walmsley, Pres.
Fee: £13
Membership Type: standard
Fee: £15
Membership Type: family
Description: Promotes and encourages an appreciation of the literary and artistic heritage left by Leo and James Ulric Walmsley.

04370
Walpole Society
The British Museum, Department of Prints and Drawings, Great Russell St., London, WC1B 3DG, UK
Tel: 020 77278739
Email: ss.jervis@btopenworld.com
Website: http://www.walpolesociety.org.uk
Members: 590
Contact: Simon Jervis, Chm.
Fee: £45
Membership Type: personal
Fee: £60
Membership Type: institution, library
Description: Publishes archival and other material relating to the history of the arts in Great Britain. The organization has published 65 volumes.

04371
War on Want
WOW
Development House, 56-64 Leonard St., London, EC2A 4LT, UK
Tel: 020 75490555
Fax: 020 75490556
Email: mailroom@waronwant.org
Website: http://www.waronwant.org
Members: 8000
Staff: 14
Contact: Sue Branford, Treas.
Description: Campaigns against the root causes of global poverty. Provides funding for projects in developing countries.
Publication: Report
Publication title: Annual Review

04372
War Resisters' International
WRI
5 Caledonian Rd., London, N1 9DX, UK
Tel: 020 72784040
Fax: 020 72780444
Email: info@wri-irg.org
Website: http://www.wri-irg.org
Members: 150000
Staff: 2
Contact: Howard Clark, Chm.
Description: Pacifist organization of individuals and movements participating in war resistance and peace activities in 35 countries. Disseminates information on training for nonviolent action and the problems of violent and nonviolent revolutionary change. Acts as information and coordinating center for conscientious objectors.

04373
Warrington Chamber of Commerce and Industry
WCCI
International Business Ctre., Delta Crescent, Westbrook, Warrington, WA5 7WQ, UK
Tel: 01925 715150
Fax: 01925 715159
Email: info@warrington-chamber.co.uk
Website: http://www.warrington-chamber.co.uk
Contact: Colin Daniels, Chief Exec.
Fee: £162-869
Membership Type: company (based on number of employees)
Description: Represents members across Warrington at local, regional and national level on matters concerning trade, commerce and industry and lobbying. Facilitates networking, forums and events to enable members to exchange ideas, information, views and business practice.

04374
Waste Care
Richmond House, Garforth, Leeds, LS25 1NB, UK
Tel: 011 33854325
Website: http://www.wastecare.co.uk
Description: Offers waste management, disposal, recycling and recovery for United Kingdom.

04375
Waste Watch
56-64 Leonard St., London, EC2A 4LT, UK
Tel: 020 75490300
Fax: 020 75490301
Email: info@wastewatch.org.uk
Website: http://www.wastewatch.org.uk
Contact: Gloria Hooper, Pres.
Fee: £25
Membership Type: individual, waged
Fee: £15
Membership Type: student, unwaged
Description: Promotes sustainable resource use. Campaigns through policy development for all areas of society to reduce, reuse and recycle waste. Promotes and encourages change of attitude and behavior toward waste management through projects and services in communications, education, information and research.

04376
Water Jetting Association
WJA
Thames Innovation Centre, 2 Veridion Way, Erith, DA18 4AL, UK
Tel: 0208 3201090
Fax: 0208 3201094
Email: info@waterjetting.org.uk
Website: http://www.waterjetting.org.uk
Members: 140
Staff: 2
Contact: David Kennedy, Dir
Fee: £500
Membership Type: full
Description: Contractors and manufacturers of high-pressure water jetting equipment. Promotes the safe use of jet cutting technology and represents the interests of members.
Formerly: Formerly, Association of High Pressure Water Jetting Contractors
Publication: Manual
Publication title: Code of Practice for Safe Use of High Pressure Water Training Manual and Operator Pack for Jet Cutting Training

04377
Water UK
1 Queen Anne's Gate, London, SW1H 9BT, UK
Tel: 020 73441844
Fax: 020 73441853
Email: info@water.org.uk
Website: http://www.water.org.uk
Members: 24
Staff: 14
Contact: Pamela Taylor, Chief Exec.
Description: Water supply companies. Exists to represent, promote and protect the common interests of members and to provide a forum within which members can consider and discuss matters of mutual interest and concern.
Library Type: reference
Formerly: Formerly, Water Companies Association
Publication: Newsletter
Publication title: The View from Water UK

04378
WEA Scottish Association
Riddles Ct., 322 Lawnmarket, Edinburgh, EH1 2PG, UK
Tel: 0131 2263456
Fax: 0131 2200306
Email: hq@weascotland.org.uk
Website: http://www.weascotland.org.uk
Fee: £15
Membership Type: individual
Fee: £5
Membership Type: optional concession
Description: Enables people to realize full potential through learning. Supports the educational needs of working men and women. Provides access to education and learning for adults from all backgrounds, and in particular those who have previously missed out on education.

04379
Welding Manufacturers Association
WMA
Westminster Tower, 3 Albert Embankment, London, SE1 7SL, UK
Tel: 020 77933039
Fax: 020 77933003
Email: wma@beama.org.uk
Website: http://www.wma.uk.com
Description: Welding manufacturers. Fosters the interests of its sector of industry by clarifying its policy and providing channels of communication and negotiation with other bodies.

04380
Well Drillers Association
WDA
PO Box 4595, Nuneaton, CV11 9DX, UK
Tel: 0788 5979583
Email: david.s.duke@gmail.com
Website: http://www.welldrillers.org.uk
Members: 17
Contact: Dave Duke, Sec.
Description: Membership is by application and acceptance by a majority of the members meeting and is available to all bona fide drilling contractors.

04381
Well Services Contractors Association
WCSA
PO Box 12089, Aberdeen, AB16 9BB, UK
Tel: 01224 868118
Email: chris.strang@wsca.co.uk
Website: http://www.wsca.co.uk
Contact: Chris Strang, Dir.
Fee: £500
Membership Type: associate
Fee: £6500

Membership Type: full
Description: Represents the interests of well services sector. Encourages safe and responsible exploitation of oil and gas. Ensures the sustainability of oil and gas industry. Improves health, safety and environmental performance in the well service sector.

04382

Welsh Amateur Dance Sport Association
WADSA

20 Carlton Terr., Troed-y-rhiw, Merthyr Tydfil, CF48 4EP, UK
Tel: 01443 691978
Email: m.webley@homecall.co.uk
Website: http://www.idsf.net
Contact: Michael Webley, Sec.
Fee: £10
Membership Type: junior, juvenile
Fee: £22
Membership Type: adult
Description: Amateur dancing organizations, dance instructors, and individuals with an interest in competitive dancing as a means of exercise and recreation. Promotes participation in dance programs, particularly those involving ballroom dancing; selects dance teams to participate in international dancing competitions.

04383

Welsh Amateur Music Federation
WAMF

Wales Millenium Ctr., Bute Pl., Cardiff, CF10 5AL, UK
Tel: 029 20635640
Fax: 029 20635641
Email: enquiries@tycerdd.org
Website: http://www.tycerdd.org/wamf.html
Members: 25000
Staff: 3
Contact: Keith Griffin, Dir.
Fee: £45
Membership Type: affiliate
Description: Supports and offers advice to affiliated amateur music promoting societies throughout Wales; represents some 25,000 performers.
Library Type: lending
Publication: Newsletter
Publication title: Annual Review of Activities

04384

Welsh Black Cattle Society
WBCS

13 Bangor St., Gwynedd, Caernarfon, LL55 1AP, UK
Tel: 01286 672391
Fax: 01286 672022
Email: welshblack@btclick.com
Website: http://www.welshblackcattlesociety.com
Members: 800
Contact: Andrew James, CEO
Description: Works to promote the improvement and maintain the purity of the Welsh Black cattle breed.

04385

Welsh Books Council
WBC

Castell Brychan, Ceredigion, Aberystwyth, SY23 2JB, UK
Tel: 01970 624151
Fax: 01970 625385
Email: castellbrychan@wbc.org.uk
Website: http://www.wbc.org.uk
Staff: 51
Contact: Elwyn Jones, Dir.
Description: Promotes the publishing industry in Wales.

04386

Welsh Centre for International Affairs
WCIA

Temple of Peace, Cathays Park, Cardiff, CF10 3AP, UK
Tel: 029 20228549
Fax: 029 20640333
Email: centre@wcia.org.uk
Website: http://www.wcia.org.uk
Members: 225
Staff: 10
Contact: Martin Pollard, Dir.
Fee: £25
Membership Type: individual
Fee: £50
Membership Type: voluntary organisation, charity, library, association
Description: Represents Welsh institutions including local government agencies, universities, churches, and the media. Fosters a sense of loyalty and obligation to the global community among the people of Wales. Conducts international volunteer and service programs; conducts citizenship education courses for young people.
Publication title: The UN at Fifty: The Welsh Contribution 1995
Meetings/Conventions: Anniversary Lecture – annual convention

04387

Welsh Liberal Democrats
WLD

Ground Fl., Blake Ct., Schooner Way, Butetown, Cardiff, CF10 4DW, UK
Tel: 029 20313400
Website: http://www.welshlibdems.org.uk/e-home.php
Members: 4000
Staff: 2
Contact: Ian Walton, Party Mgr.
Description: Political party in Wales. Conducts campaigns; disseminates information.
Formerly: Formerly, Welsh Liberal Party

04388

Welsh Music Guild

c/o Mr. Christopher Painter, Sec.
17 Broad St., Barry, CF62 7AG, UK
Email: chris@christopherpainter.co.uk
Website: http://www.welshmusic.org.uk
Members: 200
Contact: Geraint Stanley Jones, Pres.
Fee: £15
Membership Type: individual
Fee: £25
Membership Type: corporate
Description: Individuals in 10 countries united to promote the composition and performance of works by Welsh composers. Acts as source of information about Welsh music.
Formerly: Formerly, Guild for the Promotion of Welsh Music
Publication: Catalog
Publication title: Catalogue of Contemporary Welsh Music. Advertisements.

04389

Welsh Pony and Cob Society
WPCS

6 Chalybeate St., Ceredigion, Aberystwyth, SY23 1HP, UK
Tel: 01970 617501
Fax: 01970 625401
Email: info@wpcs.uk.com
Website: http://www.wpcs.uk.com
Members: 7140
Staff: 13
Contact: D.W.W. Lloyd, Pres.
Fee: £30
Membership Type: general
Fee: £750
Membership Type: life (under 21 years old)
Description: Owners, breeders and admirers of Welsh ponies and cobs. Records the breeding details of Welsh ponies and cobs and seeks to improve the breed and promote its excellence.
Publication: Journal
Publication title: Stud Book

04390

Welsh Women's Aid - Cardiff National Office

38-48 Crwys Rd., Cardiff, CF24 4NN, UK
Tel: 029 20390874
Fax: 029 20390878
Email: info@welshwomensaid.org.uk
Website: http://www.welshwomensaid.org/index.html
Members: 34
Staff: 10
Contact: Kirstie Pavey, Contact
Description: Advocates for the welfare of abused women in Wales. Offers shelter to women and their children fleeing domestic violence. Encourages women to be self-reliant and confident in building their futures. Provides counseling services to women and children. Raises awareness of abused women and domestic violence among the public, media, police, courts, social services, etc. List of publications available upon request.
Meetings/Conventions: periodic meeting

04391

Wensleydale Longwool Sheep Breeders' Association

c/o Mrs. Barbara Metcalfe
Oxmoor House Farm, Houghton Bank, Heighington, DL2 2UG, UK
Tel: 01388 777852
Email: mark.m.leech@btinternet.com
Website: http://www.wensleydale-sheep.com
Members: 200
Contact: D.L. Clouder, Sec.

04392
West Kent Chamber of Commerce and Industry
WKCCI
Castle Lodge, Castle St., Kent, Tonbridge, TN9 1BH, UK
Tel: 01732 366653
Email: jackie@wkcci.com
Website: http://www.wkcci.com
Members: 600
Staff: 5
Contact: Jackie Matthias, Chief Exec.
Fee: £252-658
Membership Type: company (based on the number of employees)
Description: Represents members across West Kent at local, regional and national level on matters concerning trade, commerce and industry and lobbying. Facilitates networking, forums and events to enable members to exchange ideas, information, views and business practice.
Publication: Magazine
Publication title: The Business

04393
West Midlands Campaign for Nuclear Disarmament
WMCND
54 Allison St., Digbeth, Birmingham, B5 5TH, UK
Tel: 0121 6434617
Email: wmcndall@gn.apc.org
Website: http://wmcnd.org.uk
Description: Aims to eliminate British nuclear weapons and other weapons of mass destruction.

04394
Whale and Dolphin Conservation Society
WDCS
Brookfield House, 38 St. Paul St., Wiltshire, Chippenham, SN15 1LJ, UK
Tel: 01249 449500
Fax: 01249 449501
Email: info@wdcs.org
Website: http://www.wdcs.org.uk
Contact: Sue Fisher, Contact
Description: Dedicated to the conservation and welfare of whales, dolphins and porpoises (also known as cetaceans). Seeks to reduce and eliminate the continuing threats to cetaceans and their habitats, to raise awareness about these animals, stop unnecessary death of cetaceans from manmade threats and the deliberate killing of whales and dolphins for commercial and scientific reasons; aims to prevent the extinction of endangered species and promote the recovery of all cetacean populations; promotes a worldwide interest in cetaceans.
Publication: Handbook
Publication title: Captive Cetaceans: A Handbook for Campaigners

04395
Whitebred Shorthorn Association
High Green Hill, Kirkcambeck, Cumbria, Brampton, CA8 2BL, UK
Tel: 01697 748228
Email: secretary@whitebredshorthorn.com
Website: http://www.whitebredshorthorn.com
Members: 54
Staff: 1
Contact: Rosie Mitchinson, Sec.
Description: Promotes breeding and herd book registers of Whitebred Shorthorn Cattle.

04396
Wholesale Markets Brokers' Association
WMBA
St. Clements House, 27-28 Clements Ln., London, EC4N 7AE, UK
Tel: 020 32079740
Fax: 020 71605244
Email: amcdonald@wmba.org.uk
Website: http://www.wmba.org.uk
Members: 10
Staff: 2
Contact: Alex McDonald, CEO
Description: Anyone interested in knitting. Aims to preserve the best of the old while exploring the new in knitting. Promotes members' interests.

04397
Wildfowl and Wetlands Trust
WWT
Slimbridge, Gloucester, GL2 7BT, UK
Tel: 01453 891900
Fax: 01453 890827
Email: enquiries@wwt.org.uk
Website: http://www.wwt.org.uk
Members: 100000
Staff: 340
Contact: Martin Spray, CEO
Fee: £17
Membership Type: youth (age 4-16)
Fee: £750
Membership Type: senior life (joint)
Description: Individuals with an interest in wetlands and wildlife. Promotes the preservation of wetlands and protection of animals. Conducts breeding programs to increase threatened wetland waterfowl populations; provides winter refuge for threatened wetland waterfowl; manages and restores wetland habitats; maintains a network of conservation and environmental education centers. Makes available educational and social opportunities to members; sponsors children's services; conducts research.
Formerly: Formerly, The Wildfowl Trust
Publication: Newsletter
Publication title: GooseNews

04398
Wildlife Aid
Randalls Farm House, Randalls Rd., Surrey, Leatherhead, KT22 0AL, UK
Tel: 09061 800132
Fax: 01372 375183
Email: simon@wildlife-aid.org.uk
Website: http://www.wildlifeaid.org.uk
Contact: Simon Cowell, Dir.
Fee: £24
Membership Type: adult
Fee: £10
Membership Type: junior (under 16)
Description: Seeks to redress the balance between man and nature and to preserve Britain's heritage; offers adoption of animals while they are receiving care.

04399
Wildlife Trusts
WT
The Kiln, Waterside, Mather Rd., Nottinghamshire, Newark, NG24 1WT, UK
Tel: 01636 677711
Fax: 01636 670001
Email: enquiry@wildlifetrusts.org
Website: http://www.wildlifetrusts.org
Members: 765000
Staff: 60
Contact: Aubrey Manning, Pres.
Description: Wildlife trusts comprising 726,000 individuals in the U.K. Cares for 2,200 nature reserves and protects wildlife in the United Kingdom; experiments with conservation management techniques; disseminates information; advises government departments; provides national catalog of sites. Offers children's services and educational programs. Serves as umbrella organization and works in conjunction with the Urban Wildlife Partnership.
Formerly: Formerly, Society for the Promotion of Nature Reserves

04400
Wilkie Collins Society
4 Ernest Gardens, Chiswick, London, W4 3QU, UK
Email: paul@paullewis.co.uk
Website: http://www.wilkiecollins.com
Members: 125
Contact: Paul Lewis, Contact
Fee: £10
Membership Type: local
Fee: £18
Membership Type: overseas
Description: Promotes members' interests.
Publication: Journal
Publication title: Wilkie Collins Society Journal

04401
William Barnes Society
31 Casterbridge Rd., Dorchester, DT1 2AH, UK
Tel: 01305 260348
Website: http://www.williambarnes.org.uk
Members: 200
Contact: Alfred Barrett, Chm.
Fee: £8
Membership Type: single
Fee: £10
Membership Type: joint
Description: Exists to enable its members to share fellowship and pleasure in the life and work of William Barnes.

04402
William Cobbett Society
WCS
c/o Barbara Biddell, Chair/Sec.
3 Park Terr., Petworth, West Sussex, Tillington, GU28 9AE, UK
Tel: 01798 342008
Website: http://www.williamcobbett.org.uk
Members: 160
Contact: Richard Body, Pres.
Fee: £8
Membership Type: general
Description: Individuals or associations interested in the life and works of William Cobbett (1763-1835), English journalist and essayist. Maintains 200 volume collection of works on or by William Cobbett. Sponsors annual memorial lecture and rural re-ride by motor coach.

04403
William Herschel Society
Herschel House, 19 New King St., Bath, BA1 2BL, UK
Tel: 01225 446865
Website: http://www.williamherschel.org.uk
Members: 500
Contact: Patrick Moore, Pres.
Fee: £10
Membership Type: in Europe/in UK
Fee: £13
Membership Type: overseas
Description: Conducts research and publicizes the life and works of William Herschel and his family.
Publication: Journal
Publication title: Speculum

04404
William Morris Society
WMS
Kelmscott House Museum, 26 Upper Mall, Hammersmith, London, W6 9TA, UK
Tel: 020 87413735
Fax: 020 87485207
Email: uk@morrissociety.org
Website: http://www.morrissociety.org
Contact: Fran Durako, Pres.
Fee: £18
Membership Type: individual
Fee: £8
Membership Type: student/concession
Description: Persons from 24 countries interested in the life and works of William Morris (1834-96), English poet, writer, craftsman, designer, printer, and socialist. Objective is to deepen understanding and to stimulate a wider appreciation of Morris and his work. Arranges study courses; encourages the republication of Morris' works and the continued manufacture of his wallpaper and textile designs. Sponsors exhibitions, lectures, and visits to places relevant to Morris' life and works. Maintains collection of Morris' original designs.
Publication: Journal
Publication title: Journal of William Morris Society. Advertisements.

04405
Wine and Spirit Trade Association
WSTA
International Wine & Spirit Centre, 39-45 Bermondsey St., London, SE1 3XF, UK
Tel: 0207 0893877
Fax: 0207 0893870
Email: info@wsta.co.uk
Website: http://www.wsta.co.uk
Members: 320
Staff: 8
Contact: Louise Vaux, Membership/Marketing Exec.
Description: Represents producers, importers, shippers, wholesalers, bottlers, warehouse keepers, freight forwarders, brandowners, licensed retailers and consultants. Provides one strong voice for the trade and represent its collective interests with national and international governments and agencies on social, regulatory, fiscal and technical issues. Offers unrivalled support and a range of competitive, professional business services that add value to member businesses.
Library Type: not open to the public
Formerly: Formerly, Wine and Spirit Association of Great Britain and Northern Ireland
Publication: Book
Publication title: Checklists

04406
Wine Society
Gunnels Wood Rd., Stevenage, SG1 2BT, UK
Tel: 01438 741177
Email: memberservices@thewinesociety.com
Website: http://www.thewinesociety.com
Members: 90000
Contact: David Caunce, Sec.
Fee: £40
Membership Type: life
Description: Sources well made, authentic wines from around the world and sells them to members at the best possible prices.

04407
Wirral Chamber of Commerce and Industry
Lord Leverhulme Chambers, 16 Grange Rd. W, Birkenhead, Merseyside, Wirral, CH41 4DA, UK
Tel: 0151 6478899
Fax: 0151 6500440
Email: info@wirralchamber.org.uk
Website: http://www.wirralchamber.org.uk
Description: Represents members across Wirral at local, regional and national level on matters concerning trade, commerce and industry and lobbying. Facilitates networking, forums and events to enable members to exchange ideas, information, views and business practice.

04408
Wobbly Parrot Rescue
631 Oxford Rd., Berkshire, Reading, RG30 1HP, UK
Tel: 0118 9595046
Fax: 0118 9676366
Email: wobbly@patrol.i_way.co.uk
Website: http://gurney.co.uk/parrots
Contact: Julie Scrase-Walters, Contact
Description: Committed to the rescue and protection of parrots.

04409
Womankind Worldwide
WW
2nd Fl., Development House, 56-64 Leonard St., London, EC2A 4LT, UK
Tel: 020 75490360
Fax: 020 75490361
Email: info@womankind.org.uk
Website: http://www.womankind.org.uk
Staff: 18
Contact: Sue Turrell, Exec. Dir.
Description: Promotes, supports, and funds women's initiatives in developing countries. Seeks to create a more peaceful society through the equal participation of women in determining values, directions and governance of society at all levels.
Publication: Journal
Publication title: Annual Review

04410
Women and Manual Trades
WAMT
52-54 Featherstone St., London, EC1Y 8RT, UK
Tel: 020 7251 9192
Fax: 020 7251 9193
Email: info@wamt.org
Website: http://www.wamt.org
Members: 200
Staff: 4
Contact: Niki Luscombe, Chief Exec.
Fee: £30
Membership Type: full individual, associate individual
Fee: £7
Membership Type: full concessionary
Description: Tradeswomen and women training in the trades. Encourages women and girls to pursue careers in the skilled trades of the construction industry. Provides information and advice to women working in the trades. Offers advice on areas of work, self-employment, and developing skills. Conducts self-employment classes including courses on business plans, tax, insurance, bookkeeping, self assessment, pricing and estimating, and health and safety. Works with the government agencies, training providers, unions and employers.
Library Subject: resources for self-employed women
Library Type: by appointment only
Formerly: Formerly, London Women and Manual Trades
Publication: Book
Publication title: Crossing the Border
Meetings/Conventions: conference – Exhibits.

04411
Women in Banking and Finance
WIBF
PO Box 122, West Wickham, BR4 9WW, UK
Tel: 020 87776902
Fax: 020 87777064
Email: christine.lawrence@wibf.org.uk
Website: http://www.wibf.org.uk
Members: 700
Staff: 1
Contact: Christine Lawrence, Chair
Fee: £55
Membership Type: individual
Fee: £50
Membership Type: individual (paid by standing order)
Description: Works for the advancement of the role of women in the banking and finance industry in England. Encourages networking; disseminates information.
Formerly: Formerly, Women in Banking
Publication: Newsletter
Publication title: In Focus. Advertisements.

04412
Women in Film and Television - United Kingdom
WFTV
12-13 Greek St., London, W1D 4BB, UK
Tel: 020 72871400
Fax: 020 72871500
Email: info@wftv.org.uk
Website: http://www.wftv.org.uk/wftv
Members: 800
Staff: 2
Contact: Kate Kinninmont, Chief Exec.
Fee: £117.5
Membership Type: within London
Fee: £58.75
Membership Type: overseas
Description: Women with a minimum of one year's work in the film and television industry. Provides information and professional support to members. Offers educational programs. Protects the interests of women in the film and television industry; promotes equal opportunities for members within the industry. Organizes events at major markets and festivals.

Publication: Newsletter
Publication title: Events Diary

04413
Women in Nuclear Global
WIN

c/o World Nuclear Association
Carlton House, 22a St. James's Sq., London, SW1Y 4JH, UK
Tel: 0207 4511520
Fax: 0207 8391501
Email: win@win-global.org
Website: http://www.win-global.org
Members: 2000
Contact: Cheryl L. Bogess, Pres.
Description: Informs the public about the role of women in nuclear science and related fields by providing educational programs, information exchange and arranging study visits. Addresses the general public's concerns about nuclear energy and the application of radiation and nuclear technology by objectively promoting the benefits of the peaceful uses of nuclear energy.
Publication: Newsletter
Publication title: WiNFO
Meetings/Conventions: annual meeting

04414
Women in Publishing
WIP

4 Barnard Hill, London, N10 2HB, UK
Email: info@womeninpublishing.org.uk
Website: http://www.wipub.org.uk
Members: 700
Contact: Claire Pimm, Treas.
Fee: £27.5
Membership Type: employed/self-employed
Fee: £17.5
Membership Type: unwaged/student
Description: Provides a forum for networking and mutual support among women in all areas of publishing.
Publication: Newsletter
Publication title: WiPlash. Advertisements.

04415
Women into Science and Engineering
WISE

Weston House, 2nd Fl., 246 High Holborn, London, WC1V 7EX, UK
Tel: 020 32060408
Fax: 020 32080401
Email: info@wisecampaign.org.uk
Website: http://www.wisecampaign.org.uk
Staff: 4
Contact: Terry Marsh, Dir.
Description: Encourages girls at schools, students, parents, teachers, career advisors, employers, politicians and the media to increase the number of women entering science and engineering professions. Provides printed material, videos, websites, awards and conferences.
Library Subject: science and engineering professions
Library Type: reference
Publication: Booklet
Publication title: A Girl Like You. Advertisements.

04416
Women Living Under Muslim Laws
WLUML

PO Box 28445, London, N19 5JT, UK
Email: wluml@wluml.org
Website: http://www.wluml.org/english/index.shtml
Description: International network that provides information, solidarity, and support for all women whose lives are shaped, conditioned, or governed by laws and customs said to derive from Islam. Aims to increase the autonomy of women by supporting the local struggles of women from within Muslim countries and communities and linking them with feminist and progressive groups at large; facilitating interaction, exchanges, and contacts and providing information as well as a channel of communication.
Library Subject: empowerment, fundamentalisms, law reform, militarization, sexual/reproductive rights and health, sexuality, state control, violence against women
Library Type: reference
Publication: Journal
Publication title: Dossier: A Collection of Articles

04417
Women Members Network of the Royal Society of Chemistry

Royal Society of Chemistry, Thomas Graham House, Science Park, Milton Rd., Cambridge, CB4 0WF, UK
Tel: 01223 432197
Website: http://www.rsc.org/Membership/Networking/WomenMembersNetwork/index.asp
Contact: Sarah Harrison, Specialist
Description: Organizes social and professional events for women members of the Royal Society of Chemistry.
Library Subject: women in chemistry, science
Library Type: not open to the public

04418
Women Welcome Women World Wide
5W

88 Easton St., Bucks, High Wycombe, HP11 1LT, UK
Tel: 0149 4465441
Fax: 0149 4465441
Website: http://www.womenwelcomewomen.org.uk
Members: 3000
Staff: 4
Contact: Frances Alexander, Founder
Description: Women of all ages interested in international cultural exchange. Fosters international friendship among women from different countries. Encourages members' travel excursions and visits with other members.
Publication: Newsletter
Publication title: WWWWW Newsletter

04419
Women Working Worldwide
WWW

MMU Manton Bldg., Rosamond St. W, Manchester, M15 6LL, UK
Tel: 0161 2476171
Email: contact@women-ww.org
Website: http://www.women-ww.org
Members: 20
Staff: 4
Fee: £20
Membership Type: general
Description: Promotes the interest of women employed in the work force in the United Kingdom. Encourages the improvement of employment, wages, and working conditions for women workers. Supports women employees through information exchange, international networking, and public education. Focuses efforts on industries that employ large numbers of women, such as clothing, textiles, and electronics. Conducts research and educational programs on health and safety issues, and employment legislation.
Publication: Book
Publication title: Common Interests: Women Organising in Global Electronics

04420
Women's Engineering Society
WES

Michael Faraday House, Six Hills Way, Hertfordshire, Stevenage, SG1 2AY, UK
Tel: 01438 765506
Fax: 01438 765506
Email: info@wes.org.uk
Website: http://www.wes.org.uk
Members: 797
Staff: 1
Contact: Dawn Fitt, Sec.
Fee: £40
Membership Type: regular
Fee: £32
Membership Type: associate
Description: From all disciplines of engineering and are professionals, incorporated and technicians. Includes students and juniors still at school and has associates who are not themselves women engineers, but are interested in what they are doing. Promotes awareness of engineering as the prime creator of wealth in society, and the contribution women can make to it; promotes the education and training of women engineers; ensures that women engineers can influence the process of policy formation and decision making in government and other organizations.
Publication: Journal
Publication title: The Woman Engineer. Advertisements.

04421
Women's Environmental Network
WEN

PO Box 30626, London, E1 1TZ, UK
Tel: 020 74819004
Fax: 020 74819144
Email: info@wen.org.uk
Website: http://www.wen.org.uk
Members: 2000
Staff: 12
Contact: Bernadette Vallely, Chair
Fee: £12
Membership Type: individual in UK concessionary
Fee: £40
Membership Type: overseas/supporting
Description: Works to educate, inform, and empower women and men who care about the environment. Campaigns and provides information on waste prevention, real (cloth) nappies (diapers), health, sanitary protection, and local organic food.
Publication: Handbook
Publication title: Stop Talking Rubbish! A Guide to Greening a Social Space

04422
Women's Food and Farming Union
WFU
Cargill plc, Witham St. Hughs, Lincoln, LN6 9TN, UK
Tel: 0844 3350342
Fax: 0844 3350342
Email: secretary@wfu.org.uk
Website: http://www.wfu.org.uk
Members: 2000
Staff: 1
Contact: Barbara Hughes, Acting Sec.
Fee: £34.5
Membership Type: individual
Fee: £135.13
Membership Type: business
Description: Farmers' wives, women farmers, and others engaged in agriculture and food production industries. Promotes farm produce and food manufactured in the UK. Encourages farmers and growers to improve marketing techniques. Lobbies against unfair competition.
Publication title: Annual Review. Advertisements.

04423
Women's International League for Peace and Freedom - United Kingdom Section
UK WILPF
52-54 Featherstone St., London, EC1Y 8RT, UK
Tel: 0207 2501968
Fax: 0207 4365637
Email: office@ukwilpf.org.uk
Website: http://www.ukwilpf.org.uk
Contact: Pat Pleasance, Pres.
Fee: £16
Membership Type: individual
Description: Works on issues of gender, peace, human rights and disarmament at the local, national and international levels. Promotes political and social equality and economic equity. Supports the continuous development and implementation of international and humanitarian law.
Publication: Newsletter
Publication title: Peace and Freedom Update

04424
Women's National Commission
WNC
2/J5 House, Bressenden Pl., London, SW1E 5DU, UK
Tel: 0303 4444009
Fax: 0303 4443314
Email: wnc@communities.gsi.gov.uk
Website: http://www.thewnc.org.uk
Members: 200
Staff: 7
Contact: Barbara-Ann Collins, Dir.
Description: Individual women in the United Kingdom, and women's sections of major political parties; trade unions; religious groups; professional organizations; other groups representative of women. Seeks to ensure by all possible means that the informed opinions of women are given their due weight in the deliberations of Government. Addresses such issues as: caring for the elderly; violence against women; social security; women and public appointments; women returners. Conducts studies and submits results and views to the Minister for women and other government bodies.
Publication: Directory
Publication title: Directory of Women's Organisations in United Kingdom

04425
Women's Royal Voluntary Service
WRVS
c/o Garden House
Milton Hill, Steventon, Abingdon, OX13 6AD, UK
Tel: 01235 442900
Fax: 01235 861166
Website: http://www.wrvs.org.uk
Members: 120000
Contact: Lynne Berry, Chief Exec.
Description: Strives to help people in need maintain independence and dignity in their homes and communities, particularly later in life. Provides home meals delivery, emergency support and help in hospitals. Aims to build stronger local communities.

04426
Women's Support Project
Granite House, 31 Stockwell St., Glasgow, G1 4RZ, UK
Tel: 0141 5522221
Fax: 0141 5521876
Email: wsproject@btconnect.com
Website: http://www.womenssupportproject.co.uk
Staff: 4
Contact: Jan Macleod, Development Worker
Description: Offers emotional and material support to women and children who are survivors of abuse. Administers training courses for organizations. Organizes discussion and support groups for women. Offers self-defense classes for women. Conducts research.
Publication: Report
Publication title: Is There a Correlation Between Child Sexual Abuse & Domestic Violence: An Exploratory Study of Links Between Child Social Abuse and Domestic Violence

04427
Woodworking Machinery Suppliers Association
WMSA
Cliff Farm, Plaistow Green, Derbyshire, Matlock, DE4 5GX, UK
Fax: 01629 530999
Email: info@wmsa.org.uk
Website: http://www.wmsa.org.uk
Members: 90
Staff: 4
Fee: £700
Membership Type: full
Fee: £425
Membership Type: overseas, associate
Description: Serves as trade association representing established suppliers of woodworking machinery, tooling, and dust extraction equipment, engaged in the manufacture and import of products. Aims to provide a high standard of service and reliability. Sponsors biennial Woodmex Exhibition in Birmingham, England.
Publication: Directory
Publication title: Directory of British Manufactured Woodworking and Sawmill Machinery and Equipment

04428
Woolmens' Company
The Old Post Office, 56 Lower Way, Buckinghamshire, Great Brickhill, M17 9AG, UK
Tel: 020 15261541
Email: clerk@woolmen.com
Website: http://www.woolmen.com
Contact: Gillian E. Wilson, Clerk
Description: Promotes and regulates the wool trade.

04429
Work Foundation
21 Palmer St., London, SW1H 0AD, UK
Tel: 020 79763565
Website: http://www.theworkfoundation.com
Members: 12000
Staff: 85
Contact: Will Hutton, Exec. Vice Chm.
Description: Works to improve the quality and productivity of U.K. work life, offers clients innovative solutions through research, consultancy, leadership and coaching programs.
Formerly: Formerly, Industrial Society
Publication title: Briefing Plus

04430
Workers' Educational Association - East Midlands Region
WEA
39 Mapperley Rd., Nottingham, NG3 5AQ, UK
Tel: 0115 9628400
Fax: 0115 9628402
Email: eastmidlands@wea.org.uk
Website: http://www.wea.org.uk
Description: Helps people to realize their full potential through learning. Supports the educational needs of working men and women. Provides access to education and learning for adults from all backgrounds, and in particular those who have previously missed out on education.

04431
Workers' Educational Association - Eastern Region
WEA
Cintra House, 12 Hills Rd., Cambridge, CB2 1JP, UK
Tel: 01223 417320
Fax: 01223 417321
Email: eastern@wea.org.uk
Website: http://www.wea-eastern.org.uk
Staff: 26
Contact: Carolyn Daines, Dir.
Description: Enables people to realize their full potential through learning. Supports the educational needs of working men and women. Provides access to education and learning for adults from all backgrounds, and in particular those who have previously missed out on education.

04432
Workers' Educational Association - London Region
WEA
96-100 Clifton St., London, EC2A 4TP, UK
Tel: 020 74261950
Fax: 020 77299821
Email: london@wea.org.uk
Website: http://www.wea.org.uk
Members: 40000
Contact: Soraya Patrick, Regional Dir.
Description: Enables people to realize their full potential through learning. Supports the educational needs of working men and women. Provides access to education and learning for adults from all backgrounds, and in particular those who have previously missed out on education.

04433

Workers' Educational Association - North East Region

WEA

21 Portland Terr., Jesmond, NE2 1QQ, UK
Tel: 0191 2126100
Fax: 0191 2126101
Email: northeast@wea.org.uk
Website: http://www.wea.org.uk
Description: Enables people to realize their full potential through learning. Supports the educational needs of working men and women. Provides access to education and learning for adults from all backgrounds, and in particular those who have previously missed out on education.

04434

Workers' Educational Association - North West Region

WEA

Cotton Exchange, Old Hall St., Ste. 405, Liverpool, L3 9JR, UK
Tel: 0151 2435340
Fax: 0151 2435359
Email: northwest@wea.org.uk
Website: http://www.nw.wea.org.uk/tiki-index.php
Contact: Greg Coyne, Regional Dir.
Description: Enables people to realize their full potential through learning. Supports the educational needs of working men and women. Provides access to education and learning for adults from all backgrounds, and in particular those who have previously missed out on education.

04435

Workers' Educational Association - Northern Ireland

WEA

1 Fitzwilliam St., Belfast, BT9 6AW, UK
Tel: 0289 329718
Fax: 0289 230306
Email: info@wea-ni.com
Website: http://www.wea.org.uk
Description: Enables people to realize their full potential through learning. Supports the educational needs of working men and women. Provides access to education and learning for adults from all backgrounds, and in particular those who have previously missed out on education.

04436

Workers' Educational Association - South Wales

WEA

7 Coppers Yard, Curran Rd., Cardiff, CF10 5NB, UK
Tel: 029 20235277
Fax: 029 20233986
Email: weasw@swales.wea.org.uk
Website: http://www.swales.wea.org.uk
Fee: £5
Membership Type: ordinary
Fee: £3
Membership Type: unwaged
Description: Enables people to realize their full potential through learning. Supports the educational needs of working men and women. Provides access to education and learning for adults from all backgrounds, and in particular those who have previously missed out on education.

04437

Workers' Educational Association - South Western Region

WEA

Bradninch Ct., Castle St., Exeter, EX4 3PL, UK
Tel: 01392 457300
Fax: 01392 457344
Email: southwest@wea.org.uk
Website: http://www.wea.org.uk
Contact: Steve Martin, Regional Dir.
Description: Enables people to realize their full potential through learning. Supports the educational needs of working men and women. Provides access to education and learning for adults from all backgrounds, and in particular those who have previously missed out on education.

04438

Workers' Educational Association - Southern Region

WEA

Unit 57 Riverside 2, Sir Thomas Longley Rd., Kent, Rochester, ME2 4DP, UK
Tel: 01634 298600
Fax: 01634 298601
Email: southern@wea.org.uk
Website: http://www.wea.org.uk
Description: Enables people to realize their full potential through learning. Supports the educational needs of working men and women. Provides access to education and learning for adults from all backgrounds, and in particular those who have previously missed out on education.

04439

Workers' Educational Association - United Kingdom

WEA

Corporate Services, 3rd Fl., 70 Clifton St., London, EC2A 4HB, UK
Tel: 020 74263450
Fax: 020 74263451
Email: national@wea.org.uk
Website: http://www.wea.org.uk
Members: 19000
Staff: 436
Contact: Maria Flemmer, Contact
Description: People requiring adult educational opportunities. Promotes adult education. Stimulates interest in adult education, particularly the needs of the educationally, socially, and financially disadvantaged. Provides courses.
Publication title: Cutting Edges

04440

Workers' Educational Association - West Midlands Region

WEA

Lancaster House, 4th Fl., 67 Newhall St., Birmingham, B3 1NQ, UK
Tel: 0121 2378120
Fax: 0121 2378121
Email: westmidlands@wea.org.uk
Website: http://www.wea.org.uk
Description: Enables people to realize their full potential through learning. Supports the educational needs of working men and women. Provides access to education and learning for adults from all backgrounds, and in particular those who have previously missed out on education.

04441

Workers' Educational Association - Yorkshire and Humber

WEA

6 Woodhouse Sq., Leeds, LS3 1AD, UK
Tel: 0113 2453304
Fax: 0113 2450883
Email: yorkshumber@wea.org.uk
Website: http://www.wea.org.uk/yh
Description: Enables people to realize their full potential through learning. Supports the educational needs of working men and women. Provides access to education and learning for adults from all backgrounds, and in particular those who have previously missed out on education.

04442

Working Families

1-3 Berry St., London, EC1V 0AA, UK
Tel: 020 72537243
Fax: 020 72536263
Email: office@workingfamilies.org.uk
Website: http://www.workingfamilies.org.uk
Members: 1500
Staff: 7
Contact: Sarah Jackson, Chief Exec.
Fee: £18
Membership Type: individual
Description: Campaigns to improve quality of life for all working parents and their children. Lobbies employers and policy makers for improvement of childcare facilities. Provides working parents with childcare information.
Formerly: Formerly, Working Mothers Association
Publication: Newsletter
Publication title: Balanced Lives

04443

WorkingAbroad Projects

The Coombe, Spring Barn Farm, Kingston Rd., Lewes, BN7 3ND, UK
Tel: 01273 479047
Email: info@workingabroad.com
Website: http://www.workingabroad.com
Contact: Andreas Kornevall, Co-Founder/Dir.
Description: Provides small scale organizations with need-based support from volunteers in order to create projects that are independent, small, effective and that work directly hands on with social, cultural, and environmental issues, specifically in the areas of cultural development, earth restoration, permaculture, indigenous rights, traditional art, and music.

04444
World Arabian Horse Organization
WAHO

Newbarn Farmhouse, Forthampton, Gloucester, GL19 4QD, UK
Tel: 01684 274455
Fax: 01684 274422
Email: waho@btconnect.com
Website: http://www.waho.org
Members: 2000
Staff: 1
Contact: Katrina Murray, Exec. Sec.
Fee: £50
Membership Type: individual, associate (one time fee)
Fee: £400
Membership Type: life
Description: National registries (62) and individuals (2000) interested in Arabian horses. Promotes the welfare and survival of the Arabian horse. Encourages uniform terminology, definitions, and procedures. Acquires and disseminates information regarding the Arabian horse worldwide.
Publication: Proceedings
Publication title: Account of Biennial WAHO Conferences

04445
World Association for Christian Communication
WACC

71 Lambeth Walk, London, SE11 6DX, UK
Tel: 020 77352877
Email: info@waccglobal.org
Website: http://www.waccglobal.org
Members: 800
Staff: 20
Contact: Randy Naylor, Gen. Sec.
Fee: £120
Membership Type: corporate in North America
Fee: £40
Membership Type: individual in North America
Description: Seeks to promote human dignity, justice and peace through freedom of expression and the democratization of communication. Provides professional guidance on communication policies and interprets developments in and consequences of global communication methods. Works towards the empowerment of women and assists the training of Christian communicators.
Publication: Newsletter
Publication title: Media Action

04446
World Association of Girl Guides and Girl Scouts
WAGGGS

World Bureau, Olave Centre, 12c Lyndhurst Rd., London, NW3 5PQ, UK
Tel: 020 77941181
Fax: 020 74313764
Email: wagggs@wagggsworld.org
Website: http://www.wagggsworld.org/en/home
Members: 140
Staff: 80
Contact: Mary Mc Phail, Chief Exec.
Description: National organizations representing in excess of 10,000,000 girls and young women. Promotes unity of purpose and common understanding in the fundamental principles of the Girl Guide and Girl Scout movement throughout the world; encourages friendship and mutual understanding among girls and young women of all nations. Holds training sessions at world centers. Conducts charitable programs through community development projects. At the cutting edge of issues affecting girls and young women.
Publication: Book
Publication title: Challenging Movement

04447
World Association of Professional Investigators
WAPI

212 Piccadilly, London, W1J 9HG, UK
Tel: 087 09099970
Fax: 087 09010209
Email: enquiries@wapi.com
Website: http://www.wapi.com
Contact: Stuart Withers, Chm.
Fee: £25
Membership Type: student
Fee: £50
Membership Type: associate
Description: Works to promote and uphold the image and status of investigation as an international profession; provides educational facilities and resources.
Publication: Newsletter

04448
World Bureau of Metal Statistics
WBMS

27a High St., Hertfordshire, Ware, SG12 9BA, UK
Tel: 01920 461274
Fax: 01920 464258
Email: enquiries@world-bureau.co.uk
Website: http://www.world-bureau.com
Description: Collects and disseminates current, accurate statistics on metal production, consumption, stocks, and international trade.
Publication: Manual
Publication title: Metallstatistik

04449
World Cancer Research Fund
WCRF

22 Bedford Sq., London, WC1B 3HH, UK
Tel: 020 73434200
Fax: 020 73434201
Email: wcrf@wcrf.org
Website: http://www.wcrf-uk.org
Contact: Marilyn Gentry, Pres./CEO
Description: Promotes research into cancer prevention.
Publication: Newsletter
Publication title: Informed

04450
World Coal Institute
WCI

Heddon House, 5th Fl., 149-151 Regent St., London, W1B 4JD, UK
Tel: 020 78510052
Fax: 020 78510061
Email: info@worldcoal.org
Website: http://www.worldcoal.org
Contact: Milton Catelin, Chief Exec.
Description: Coal producers and coal consumers worldwide. Promotes the merits and importance of coal as the single largest source of fuel for the generation of electricity and the manufacture of the world's steel. Provides a voice for the coal industry in international policy debates on energy and the environment; works to improve public awareness; encourages the efficient use of coal to reduce the impact of coal on the environment.
Publication: Report
Publication title: Coal: Meeting Global Challenges

04451
World Confederation for Physical Therapy
WCPT

Victoria Charity Centre, 11 Belgrade Rd., London, SW1V 1RB, UK
Tel: 020 79316465
Fax: 020 79316494
Email: info@wcpt.org
Website: http://www.wcpt.org
Members: 92
Staff: 2
Contact: Marilyn Moffat, Pres.
Description: Represents physical therapists around the world with a confederation of 92 national associations and supported mainly by subscriptions from its member organisations. Works to improve global health by: representing physical therapy and physical therapists internationally, collaborating with international and national organisations, encouraging high standards of physical therapy research, education and practice, and supporting communications of WCPT.
Library Type: not open to the public
Publication: Newsletter
Publication title: WCPT News
Meetings/Conventions: International Congress – quadrennial congress – Exhibits.

04452
World Dance Council
WDC

4 Dorset Gardens, Mitcham, CR4 1LX, UK
Tel: 07590 061170
Email: gensec@wdcdance.com
Website: http://www.wddsc.com
Contact: Hannes Emrich, Gen. Sec.
Description: National dance organizations. Seeks to popularize dancing as a social pastime and sport. Works to standardize international rules for teaching and judging. Promotes Annual world championships in ballroom and Latin dancing and encourages organization of area competitions. Sponsors meetings and seminars.
Formerly: Formerly, International Council of Ballroom Dancing

04453
World Development Movement
WDM
66 Offley Rd., London, SW9 0LS, UK
Tel: 020 78204900
Email: office@wdmscotland.org.uk
Website: http://www.wdm.org.uk
Members: 12500
Staff: 25
Fee: £24
Membership Type: voting
Fee: £36
Membership Type: overseas
Description: Achieves justice for the world's poorest people through campaigns that tackle the fundamental causes of poverty. Tries to change policies of governments, businesses and banks in wealthy countries and the controlled international agencies. Aims to create the conditions that will enable the world's poorest people to achieve equitable and sustainable development. Current campaigns call for: fair trade with the Third World, including controls on multinational companies; an end to government support for the arms trade; cancellation of Third World debts; and for aid to reach the poorest.
Publication: Magazine
Publication title: WDM in Action. Advertisements.

04454
World Energy Council - England
WEC
5th Fl. - Regency House, 1-4 Warwick St., London, W1B 5LT, UK
Tel: 020 77345996
Fax: 020 77345926
Email: info@worldenergy.org
Website: http://www.worldenergy.org
Members: 94
Contact: Pierre Gadonneix, Chm.
Description: Energy ministries, fuel and power corporations, engineering industries, universities, research organizations, and manufacturers in 94 countries involved in the production, supply, and study of energy resources. Promotes the development and peaceful use of energy resources by considering: potential resources and all means of production, transportation, and utilization; energy consumption in its overall relationship to the growth of economic activity in the area; and the social and environmental aspects of energy supply and utilization. Specific topics include worldwide survey of energy resources, national energy data profiles, and energy terminology. Maintains 8 technical and topical study committees.
Library Type: not open to the public
Formerly: Formerly, World Power Conference
Publication: Handbook
Publication title: Renewable Energy Projects
Meetings/Conventions: World Energy – triennial congress – Exhibits.

04455
World Federation for Culture Collections
WFCC
CABI Europe UK, Bakeham Ln., Egham, Surrey, TW20 9TY, UK
Email: d.smith@cabi.org
Website: http://www.wfcc.info
Members: 553
Contact: David Smith, Pres.
Fee: £20
Membership Type: ordinary
Fee: £100
Membership Type: affiliate
Description: Multidisciplinary federation of the International Union of Microbiological Societies and a multidisciplinary commission of the International Union of Biological Sciences. Groups 553 culture collections in 68 countries around the world, including private, public, national and industrial collections that relate to bacteria, fungi, plant and animal cell lines and viruses, or parts thereof (genomes, plasmids, cDNA banks). In total the collections preserve more than one million microbial cultures. Addresses practical questions such as the impact of postal regulations, quarantine rules, patent laws, and public health concerns on culture distribution. Conducts training courses in culture isolation, description, and conservation; offers individual training; sponsors periodic workshops. Operates speakers' bureau.
Library Type: reference

04456
World Federation of Neurology
WFN
Hill House, Heron Sq., Surrey, Richmond, TW9 1EP, UK
Tel: 0208 4399556
Fax: 0208 4399499
Email: info@wfneurology.org
Website: http://www.wfneurology.org
Staff: 2
Contact: Vladimir Hachinski, Pres.
Description: Neurologists and neuroscientists dedicated to improving the care of neurological patients and to preventing diseases of the nervous system. Disseminates information in the field of neurology. Organizes research groups on disease topics; compiles statistics. Maintains speakers' bureau. Conducts educational and research programs.
Publication: Journal
Publication title: Journal of Neurological Sciences. Advertisements.

04457
World Federation of Societies of Anaesthesiologists
WFSA
21 Portland Pl., London, W1B 1PY, UK
Tel: 020 76318880
Fax: 020 76318882
Email: wfsahq@anaesthesiologists.org
Website: http://www.anaesthesiologists.org
Members: 120
Staff: 1
Contact: Angela Enright, Pres.
Description: Societies of anesthesiologists. Objectives are to: promote research in anesthesiology; disseminate scientific information; encourage the establishment of safety measures including equipment standardization; recommend suitable standards for training in anesthesiology.
Meetings/Conventions: World Congress of Anaesthesiologists – quadrennial congress – Exhibits.

04458
World Federation of Surgical Oncology Societies
WFSOS
c/o Sarah Carney
The Royal Society of Medicine, 1 Wimpole St., London, W1M 8AE, UK
Tel: 0171290 29683904
Fax: 0171290 29893904
Email: sarah.carney@roysocmed.ac.uk
Website: http://www.aco-asso.at/internat/wfsos.html
Contact: W. Temple, Pres.
Fee: £100
Membership Type: general
Description: Promotes surgical oncology internationally. Encourages and assists the formation of surgical oncology societies.
Publication: Journal
Publication title: Journal of Surgical Oncology

04459
World Foundrymen Organization
WFO
47 Birmingham Rd., West Bromwich, B70 6PY, UK
Tel: 0121 6016976
Fax: 01544 340332
Email: andrew@thewfo.com
Website: http://www.jgp.ch/wfo
Members: 35
Contact: Jurg Gerster, Gen. Sec.
Description: National foundry technical associations. Represents the interests of the foundry and related industries.
Formerly: Formerly, International Committee for Foundry Technical Associations

04460
World Foundrymen Organization - United Kingdom
WFO
Winton House, Lyonshall, Herefordshire, Kington, HR5 3JP, UK
Tel: 0121 6016976
Fax: 0154 4340332
Email: andrew@thewfo.com
Website: http://www.thewfo.com
Members: 33
Staff: 1
Contact: Andrew Turner, Gen. Sec.
Description: Promotes the technology of the cast metals. Provides focus to all aspects of cast metals engineering.

04461
World Goodwill - Commonwealth
c/o Lucis Trust
3 Whitehall Ct., Ste. 54, London, SW1A 2EF, UK
Tel: 0870 7701646
Fax: 020 78395575
Email: worldgoodwill.uk@lucistrust.org
Website: http://www.worldgoodwill.org
Contact: Dominic Dibble, Contact
Description: Works to establish right human relations through the practical application of the principle of goodwill. Focuses on fundamental problems of humanity in the light of spiritual principles; cooperates with United Nations and its agencies.
Publication: Booklet
Publication title: Commentaries on Current Trends in World Affairs

04462
World Horse Welfare
Anne Colvin House, Ada Cole Ave., Norfolk, Snetterton, NR16 2LR, UK
Tel: 01953 498682
Fax: 01953 498373
Email: info@worldhorsewelfare.org
Website: http://www.worldhorsewelfare.org
Members: 50000
Staff: 150
Contact: Roly Owers, Chief Exec.
Fee: £52
Membership Type: champion plus
Fee: £36
Membership Type: champion
Description: Works to prevent ill treatment of horses exported to Europe. Aims to develop world-providing training courses demonstrating the economic importance of maintaining the health of a working horse. Rescues and rehabilitates horses in the United Kingdom.
Formerly: Formerly, International League for the Protection of Horses

04463
World Jersey Cattle Bureau
WJCB
Royal Jersey Showground, La Rte. de la Trinite, Trinity, Jersey, JE3 5JP, UK
Tel: 01534 866555
Fax: 01534 865619
Email: james.godfrey@royaljersey.co.uk
Website: http://www.wjcb.wildapricot.org
Members: 650
Staff: 1
Contact: James Godfrey, Sec.
Fee: £50
Membership Type: individual life
Description: National associations of Jersey cattle breeders; organizations interested in Jersey cattle breeding; individual life members. (Jersey cattle were developed on the Island of Jersey in the English Channel and are bred primarily for their production of high quality milk.) Coordinates the efforts of members in promoting the Jersey breed. Disseminates information; sponsors an international youth travel programme through which young people gain farming experience in different countries.
Publication: Magazine
Publication title: Global Jersey. Advertisements.
Meetings/Conventions: annual meeting

04464
World Jewish Relief
WJR
Oscar Joseph House, 54 Crewys Rd., London, NW2 2AD, UK
Tel: 020 87361250
Fax: 020 87361259
Email: info@wjr.org.uk
Website: http://www.wjr.org.uk
Contact: Paul Anticoni, CEO
Description: Individuals and organizations united to help Jewish people worldwide. Provides financial, medical, and educational assistance to Jews in Eastern European and former Soviet Union countries. Contributes food, clothing and medical support to the needy. Participates in retrieval of records of refugees who fled Europe.
Formerly: Absorbed, Czechoslovakian Jewish Aid Trust

04465
World Nuclear Association
WNA
22a St. James's Sq., London, SW1Y 4JH, UK
Tel: 020 74511520
Fax: 020 78391501
Email: wna@world-nuclear.org
Website: http://www.world-nuclear.org
Contact: John Ritch, Dir. Gen.
Description: Producers, processors, traders, consumers, electrical utilities with nuclear programs and government agencies in 30 countries, and other organizations whose work is related to uranium and the nuclear fuel cycle. Promotes the development of uranium for peaceful purposes and as a component of world energy supplies. Provides a forum for the exchange of information; conducts research concerning global requirements, resources, productive capacity of uranium, and conditions governing international nuclear trade.
Library Subject: all aspects of the nuclear field
Library Type: open to the public
Publication: Report
Publication title: WNA Market Report

04466
World Organisation of Systems and Cybernetics
WOSC
95 Finch Rd., Earley, Reading, RG6 7JX, UK
Tel: 0118 9269328
Email: alexandrew@tiscali.co.uk
Website: http://cybsoc.org/wosc
Staff: 10
Contact: Alex Andrew, Dir. Gen.
Description: National societies interested in cybernetics, systems, robotics, computer science, artificial intelligence, and related areas. Aims to sponsor national and international activities in the fields of cybernetics and systems, and generate interest in related disciplines. Tries to weed out pseudo-cybernetic claims and base cybernetics on sound scientific foundations; topics of interest include cybernetic modeling, computer simulation, biocybernetics, economic and social systems, ecosystems, adaptive systems, and philosophy of cybernetics. Acts as clearinghouse on robotics and promotes development in aspects such as: sensory perception; control devices; design of effectors. Organizes conventions and exhibitions.
Formerly: Formerly, World Organisation of General Systems and Cybernetics
Publication: Proceedings
Publication title: Congress of Cybernetics and Systems
Meetings/Conventions: International Congress of Cybernetics and Systems – triennial conference – Exhibits.

04467
World ORT
ORT House, 126 Albert St., London, NW1 7NE, UK
Tel: 0207 4468500
Fax: 0207 4468650
Email: wo@ort.org
Website: http://www.ort.org/asp/default.asp
Members: 120300
Staff: 13000
Description: Volunteer committees, women's groups, and professional groups in 46 countries. Aims to develop industrial and agricultural computer skills among Jews and others in an effort to help individuals become economically self-sufficient. Promotes the highest standards of production and improvement of the economy in affiliated countries. Provides vocational and technical training in schools in 46 countries; collaborates with various governments in sponsoring programs of technical assistance in developing nations; offers apprenticeship opportunities and placement services. Organizes apprenticeship programs.
Publication: Newsletter
Publication title: Front Line News
Meetings/Conventions: periodic seminar

04468
World Petroleum Council
WPC
1 Duchess St., 4th Fl., Ste. 1, London, W1W 6AN, UK
Tel: 020 76374958
Fax: 020 76374965
Email: info@world-petroleum.org
Website: http://www.world-petroleum.org
Members: 61
Staff: 15
Contact: Randy Gossen, Pres.
Description: National committees. Advances petroleum science and technology and the study of economic, financial, and management issues in the petroleum industry.
Library Subject: petroleum
Library Type: open to the public
Formerly: Formerly, World Petroleum Congress - A Forum for Petroleum Science, Technology, Economics and Management
Publication: Directory
Publication title: WPC Directory

04469
World Pheasant Association
WPA
Biology Field Station, Newcastle University, Close House Estate, Head-on-the-Wall, Newcastle upon Tyne, NE15 0HT, UK
Tel: 01661 853397
Fax: 01661 853397
Email: office@pheasant.org.uk
Website: http://www.pheasant.org.uk
Members: 1850
Staff: 3
Contact: Barbara Ingman, Admin.
Fee: £12.5
Membership Type: junior (under 16 years old) UK
Fee: £15
Membership Type: junior (under 16 years old) overseas and Eire
Description: Individuals and institutions from 35 countries dedicated to the conservation of pheasants and other galliformes (game birds), including currasows, francolins, grouse, guineafowl, megapodes, partridges, quail, and wild turkeys. Seeks to increase public awareness, understanding, and appreciation of nature and, in particular, gallinaceous birds and their requirements for survival. Works to improve and ensure sound avicultural methods in countries of origin and elsewhere, especially where conservation of natural habitats is difficult and wild populations are threatened. Facilitates the establishment of reserve collections and buffer stocks of threatened or endangered species.
Publication: Newsletter
Publication title: WPA News. Advertisements.

04470

World Ship Trust - United Kingdom WST

Iconoclast, Nine Elms Pier, Tideway Walk, London, SW8 5PZ, UK
Tel: 020 76271550
Fax: 020 70001251
Email: lynnmallet@worldshiptrust.org
Website: http://www.worldshiptrust.org
Contact: Lord Greenway, Chm.
Fee: £20
Membership Type: individual
Fee: £250
Membership Type: life
Description: Individuals in 48 countries interested in the preservation of historic ships. Seeks to display historic ships. Locates historic ships in distress and initiates preservation projects. Compiles information on the latest techniques and methods of ship preservation. Maintains liaison with ship preservation organizations worldwide.
Publication: Book
Publication title: International Register of Historic Ships, Third Edition

04471

World Society for the Protection of Animals - England WSPA

89 Albert Embankment, London, SE1 7TP, UK
Tel: 0207 5875000
Fax: 0207 7930208
Email: wspa@wspa-international.org
Website: http://www.wspa.org.uk
Members: 100000
Staff: 50
Contact: Dominique Bellemare, Pres.
Description: Promotes the conservation and protection of animals worldwide. Studies international and national legislation relating to animal welfare and promotes efforts that support the protection of animals and the conservation of their environment. Works to prevent and eliminate cruelty to animals. Operates Emergency Rescue Service.
Formerly: Absorbed, International Council Against Bull-fighting
Publication: Journal
Publication title: Animals International

04472

World Sugar Research Organisation WSRO

70 Collingwood House, Dolphin Sq., London, SW1V 3LX, UK
Tel: 020 78216800
Fax: 020 78344137
Email: wsro@wsro.org
Website: http://www.wsro.org
Members: 76
Staff: 3
Contact: Richard Cottrell, Dir. Gen.
Description: Represents sugar producers, refiners, and users; individuals interested in the sugar industry. Distributes information on sugar, nutrition and health and technical information related to sugar. Conducts symposia.
Formerly: Supersedes, International Sugar Research Foundation
Publication: Newsletter
Publication title: Abstracts

04473

World Travel and Tourism Council WTTC

1-2 Queen Victoria Terr., Sovereign Ct., London, E1W 3HA, UK
Tel: 020 74818007
Fax: 020 74881008
Email: enquiries@wttc.travel
Website: http://www.wttc.org
Contact: Jean-Claude Baumgarten, Pres./CEO
Description: Serves as a forum for global business leaders composed of the presidents, chairs and CEOs of the travel and tourism companies worldwide. Promotes awareness of the full economic impact of the travel and tourism industry. Encourages nations to adopt the council's policy framework for sustainable tourism development.
Publication: Handbook
Publication title: Blueprint for New Tourism
Meetings/Conventions: annual conference

04474

World Vision United Kingdom

Opal Dr., Fox Milne, Milton Keynes, MK15 0ZR, UK
Tel: 01908 841000
Fax: 01908 841001
Email: info@worldvision.org.uk
Website: http://www.worldvision.org.uk
Contact: Kate Nicholas, Hd. of Communications/Assoc. Dir.
Description: Helps transform the lives of children and families in need worldwide, without regard to religious beliefs, gender, race, or ethnic background.
Publication: Newsletter
Publication title: World View

04475

World War Two Railway Study Group

25 Woodcote Rd., Warwickshire, Leamington Spa, CV32 6PZ, UK
Tel: 01926 429378
Email: t.cane@btinternet.com
Website: http://www.saxoncourtbooks.co.uk/ww2rsg
Members: 130
Contact: Mike Christensen, Membership Sec.
Fee: £13.5
Membership Type: ordinary
Fee: £10
Membership Type: pensioner
Description: Documents all aspects of railways during World War Two and promotes interest in the subject.
Library Subject: railways, military
Library Type: not open to the public
Publication: Bulletin
Meetings/Conventions: annual meeting

04476

World Wide Opportunities on Organic Farms - UK WWOOF

PO Box 2154, Buckingham, Winslow, MK18 3WS, UK
Email: info@wwoof.org.uk
Website: http://www.wwoof.org.uk
Members: 10000
Staff: 1
Fee: £20
Membership Type: general
Fee: £30
Membership Type: joint
Description: Organizations placing volunteers on organic farms requiring assistance worldwide. Promotes organic farming; encourages voluntary farm work as an educational and cultural experience. Places volunteer farm workers with organic farms willing to provide room and board in exchange for help.
Formerly: Formerly, Willing Workers on Organic Farms
Publication: Newsletter
Publication title: WWOOFNews. Advertisements.

04477

World Wildlife Fund - UK WWK - UK

Panda House, Weyside Park, Surrey, Godalming, GU7 1XR, UK
Tel: 01483 426444
Fax: 01483 426409
Email: supporterrelations@wwf.org.uk
Website: http://www.wwf.org.uk
Members: 200000
Staff: 300
Contact: Ed Smith, Chm.
Fee: £48
Membership Type: family (with children aged 7 to 11 years)
Fee: £3
Membership Type: individual
Description: Strives to conserve the natural environment and ecological processes essential to life on earth. Encourages the use of renewable resources and sustainable development practices. Finances and supervises conservation projects.
Formerly: Formerly, World Wildlife Fund
Publication: Newsletter
Publication title: WWF News

04478

World's Poultry Science Association WPSA

2 Edengrove Park E, Ballynahinch, BT24 8DP, UK
Email: wpsa@hotmail.co.uk
Website: http://www.wpsa-uk.com
Contact: Kelvin J. McCracken, Asst. Sec.-Treas.
Fee: £25
Membership Type: individual
Fee: £10
Membership Type: associate
Description: Represents the interests of people concerned with poultry science and its application in the poultry industry. Encourages and facilitates liaison among research scientists and educators.
Publication: Journal
Publication title: The World's Poultry Science Journal

04479

World's Poultry Science Association - UK

61 Parkgate Rd., Connor, Ballymena, BT42 3PF, UK
Tel: 028 25892096
Email: wpsa@hotmail.co.uk
Website: http://www.wpsa-uk.com
Members: 320
Contact: Carolyn Preston, Sec.-Treas.
Fee: £25
Membership Type: ordinary
Fee: £50
Membership Type: affiliate, patron
Description: Individuals and companies associated with the poultry industry in the UK and abroad. The branch is one of about 40 throughout the world. Promotes advancement of knowledge of poultry production; disseminates the knowledge throughout the world. Promotes congresses, conferences, symposia and seminars; cooperates with other international organizations in achieving these aims.
Publication: Newsletter
Publication title: WPSA UK Branch Newsletter

04480

Worshipful Company of Bakers

Bakers Hall, Harp Ln., London, EC3R 6DP, UK
Tel: 0207 6232223
Fax: 0207 6211924
Email: enquiries@bakers.co.uk
Website: http://www.bakers.co.uk
Members: 400
Contact: David R. Goddard, Master
Description: Provides scholarships and prizes for young people in the baking industry and endeavors to encourage them to become first-class tradesmen/women.

04481

Worshipful Company of Farriers

19 Queen St., Chipperfield, Kings Langley, WD4 9BT, UK
Tel: 01923 260747
Fax: 01923 261677
Email: theclerk@wcf.org.uk
Website: http://www.wcf.org.uk
Members: 375
Contact: R.G. Howe, Master
Description: Works to ensure the welfare of the HORSE, by constantly encouraging and improving the practice of Farriery to the best possible standards to meet the requirements of the Farriers (Registration) Act 1975 amended 1977.
Formerly: Formerly, Farriers' Company

04482

Worshipful Company of Framework Knitters

86 Park Dr., Upminster, RM14 3AS, UK
Tel: 01708 510439
Fax: 01708 510439
Email: clerk@frameworkknitters.co.uk
Website: http://www.frameworkknitters.co.uk
Members: 225
Staff: 3
Contact: Alan J. Clark, Contact
Description: Liverymen of the company who are freemen of the City of London and have interests in the knitting and textile industry. Supports the city and the knitting industry. Runs alms houses for the elderly and poor of the industry. Maintains education bursaries for students of the industry.
Publication: Newsletter
Publication title: The Framework Knitter. Advertisements.

04483

Worshipful Company of Glaziers' and Painters of Glass

The Glazier's Co., 9 Montague Close, London Bridge, London, SE1 9DD, UK
Tel: 020 74036652
Fax: 020 74036652
Email: info@worshipfulglaziers.com
Website: http://www.worshipfulglaziers.com
Members: 300
Staff: 2
Fee: £6000
Membership Type: corporate
Description: Represents glass painters and stained glass artists. Provides technical and financial support for the restoration and conservation of historic and other important stained glass. Maintains active social program that provides special emphasis on enjoying stained glass.
Library Subject: stained glass
Library Type: not open to the public

04484

Worshipful Company of Grocers

c/o Grocers' Hall
Princes St., London, EC2R 8AD, UK
Tel: 020 76063113
Fax: 020 76003082
Email: enquiries@grocershall.co.uk
Website: http://www.grocershall.co.uk
Members: 900
Staff: 23
Contact: Allan Petrie, Contact
Description: Acts as a sounding board of informed responsible opinion. Strives to continue the traditions of the ancient fraternities. Performs charitable endeavors related to education and the church.

04485

Worshipful Company of Information Technologists WCIT

39A Bartholomew Close, London, EC1A 7JN, UK
Tel: 020 76001992
Fax: 020 76001991
Email: info@wcit.org.uk
Website: http://www.wcit.org.uk/members/anon/new.html
Members: 580
Staff: 3
Contact: Michael Grant, Clerk
Description: Promotes IT profession, charitable activities, education, and training.

04486

Worshipful Company of Musicians

6th Fl., 2 London Wall Bldgs., London Wall, London, EC2M 5PP, UK
Tel: 020 74968980
Fax: 020 75883633
Email: clerk@wcom.org.uk
Website: http://www.wcom.org.uk
Members: 340
Staff: 2
Contact: Margaret Alford, Clerk
Description: Musicians or those interested in music. Shows concern with the performing arts, education and promotion and the trades and crafts; works to the pursuit and recognition of excellence.
Publication: Newsletter
Publication title: Preserve Harmony

04487

Worshipful Company of Pattenmakers

3 The High St., Kent, Sutton Valence, ME17 3AG, UK
Tel: 01622 842440
Email: clerk@pattenmakers.co.uk
Website: http://www.pattenmakers.co.uk
Members: 220
Contact: R.W. Murfin, Clerk
Fee: £195
Membership Type: freeman, liveryman
Description: Pattenmakers.
Publication: Magazine
Publication title: The Pattenmaker Magazine
Meetings/Conventions: quarterly meeting

04488

Worshipful Company of Pewterers

Pewterers' Hall, Oat Ln., London, EC2V 7DE, UK
Tel: 020 73978190
Fax: 020 76003896
Email: clerk@pewterers.org.uk
Website: http://www.pewterers.org.uk
Members: 260
Staff: 5
Contact: Nicholas Bonham, Master
Description: Promotes and supports the pewter industry through organizations such as the Association of British Pewter Craftsmen and the European Pewter Union. Serves as custodians of the past of pewter.
Library Subject: pewter
Library Type: reference
Publication: Magazine
Publication title: Pewter Review
Meetings/Conventions: Pewter Live – annual trade show – Exhibits.

04489

Worshipful Company of Scientific Instrument Makers WCSIM

Glaziers Hall, 9 Montague Close, London, SE1 9DD, UK
Tel: 020 74074832
Fax: 020 74071565
Email: theclerk@wcsim.co.uk
Website: http://www.wcsim.co.uk
Members: 235
Staff: 2
Contact: Neville Watson, Clerk
Fee: £265
Membership Type: individual
Description: Private individuals working in or closely connected with the manufacture and development of scientific instruments in the UK. Supports the craft of instrumentation in the UK. Provides financial help to those studying about scientific instruments in higher education.

04490

Worshipful Company of Scriveners of the City of London

HQS Wellington, Temple Stairs, Victoria Embankment, London, WC2R 2PN, UK
Tel: 0207 2400529
Email: clerk@scriveners.org.uk
Website: http://www.scriveners.org.uk
Members: 200
Contact: Paul Elliot, Clerk
Description: Public Notaries of the City of London and its environs, and others in legal and related professions, including calligraphy and heraldry. Regulates the notarial profession within its jurisdiction.

04491

Worshipful Company of Shipwrights

Ironmongers' Hall, Shaftesbury Pl., Barbican, London, EC2Y 8AA, UK
Tel: 0207 6062376
Fax: 0207 6008117
Email: clerk@shipwrights.co.uk
Website: http://www.shipwrights.co.uk
Members: 400
Staff: 2
Contact: Andy Milne Royal, Clerk
Description: Members of the maritime trades and professions. Serves as livery company of the City of London, whose liverymen are all professional men and women in the maritime world (shipping etc), devoted to charitable and educational work in that field.
Publication: Handbook
Publication title: Members' Handbook

04492

Worshipful Company of Tin Plate Workers

Highbanks, Ferry Rd., Surlingham, Norfolk, NR14 7AR, UK
Tel: 08456 439967
Email: clerk@tinplateworkers.co.uk
Website: http://www.tinplateworkers.co.uk
Members: 280
Staff: 1
Contact: Michael Henderson-Begg, Clerk
Description: Tin plate and wire workers. Works to increase contact within the industries. Pursues and develops educational and charitable activities.

04493

Worshipful Company of Vintners

Vintners' Hall, Upper Thames St., London, EC4V 3BG, UK
Tel: 020 72361863
Fax: 020 72368177
Email: info@vintnershall.co.uk
Website: http://www.vintnershall.co.uk
Contact: Steve Marcham, Gen. Mgr.
Description: Vintners. Continues the traditional roles in providing shelter and supporting education, the wine trade and other organisations associated with the company.

04494

Worshipful Company of Wheelwrights

c/o Brian D. Francois
7 Glengall Rd., Kent, Bexleyheath, DA7 4AL, UK
Tel: 020 83065119
Fax: 020 83067426
Email: enquiries@wheelwrights.org
Website: http://www.wheelwrights.org
Members: 214
Staff: 2
Contact: Richard Proctor, Master
Description: Provides easy access to a wide range of information.
Publication: Book
Publication title: The Worshipful Company of Wheelwrights of the City of London 1670-1970

04495

Worshipful Society of Apothecaries of London

Apothecaries' Hall, Black Friars Ln., London, EC4V 6EJ, UK
Tel: 020 72361189
Fax: 020 73293177
Email: clerk@apothecaries.org
Website: http://www.apothecaries.org
Members: 1747
Staff: 16
Contact: Andrew M. Wallington-Smith, Clerk
Fee: £30
Membership Type: individual
Fee: £15
Membership Type: student
Description: Members of the medical profession. Functions as City of London Livery Company and medical examining body.
Formerly: Formerly, Society of Apothecaries of London

04496

Writers and Scholars Educational Trust WSET

6-8 Amwell St., London, EC1R 1UQ, UK
Tel: 020 72782313
Email: henderson@indexoncensorship.org
Website: http://www.indexoncensorship.org
Members: 8500
Staff: 10
Contact: Ursula Owen, Ed.-in-Chief
Fee: £108
Membership Type: institutional (includes online access)
Description: Writers, scholars, journalists, teachers, artists, publishers, and human rights organizations that monitor and report on censorship worldwide. Collects timely information on writers, artists, and others who have been silenced through censorship, persecution, and other forms of repression or assassination. Conducts research and provides funding for the Index on Censorship published by Writers and Scholars International. Operates library and documentation center of books, press cuttings, and graphics; offers lectures, talks, and advice to arts centers; provides newspaper, television, and radio reporters with background information.

04497

Writers' Guild of Great Britain WGGB

40 Rosebery Ave., London, EC1R 4RX, UK
Tel: 020 78330777
Fax: 020 78334777
Email: erik@writersguild.org.uk
Website: http://www.writersguild.org.uk
Members: 2000
Staff: 6
Contact: Bernie Corbett, Gen. Sec.
Fee: £150
Membership Type: full
Fee: £100
Membership Type: candidate
Description: Trade union for professional freelance writers. Aims to negotiate minimum terms agreements in all of those areas upon which members base the contracts. Protects members by lobbying at the Houses of Parliament and lobbying government organizations.
Formerly: Absorbed, Theatre Writers Union
Publication: Newsletter
Publication title: The Writers' Newsletter. Advertisements.

04498

Yacht Brokers, Designers and Surveyors Association YBDSA

The Glass Works, Penns Rd., Petersfield, GU32 2EW, UK
Tel: 01730 710425
Fax: 01730 710423
Email: info@ybdsa.co.uk
Website: http://www.ybdsa.co.uk
Contact: Richard Ayers, Pres.
Description: Yacht and small craft brokers, designers, and surveyors in 10 countries. Objectives are to: conduct and maintain standards of professional competence; agree on common forms of contract; arbitrate disputes; provide for discussion and exchange of information. Conducts teaching programs and workshops.
Formerly: Formerly, Yacht Brokers, Designers and Surveyors Association

04499

Yacht Harbour Association TYHA

Marine House, Thorpe Lea Rd., Egham, TW20 8BF, UK
Tel: 01784 223817
Fax: 01784 475870
Email: tyha@britishmarine.co.uk
Website: http://yachtharbourassociation.com
Members: 280
Staff: 1
Contact: Julie Goldie, Chair
Description: Operators, professionals, equipment suppliers overseas and UK. Concerned with the development of coastal and inland boating facilities.
Publication title: Code of Practice for the Construction and Operation of Marinas and Yacht Harbours

04500

Yachting Journalists' Association YJA

36 Church Ln., Hants, Lymington, SO41 3RB, UK
Tel: 01590 673894
Email: secretary@yja.co.uk
Website: http://www.yja.co.uk
Members: 268

Staff: 1
Contact: Rachel Nuding, Membership Sec.
Fee: £40
Membership Type: regular
Fee: £20
Membership Type: senior
Description: Specialist writers, radio and television presenters, photographers and illustrators with knowledge of every aspect of yachting and boating. Works to further the interest of yachting, sail and power in all its forms and to promote the interests of members.

Ymgyrch Diogelu Cymru Wledig

see Campaign for the Protection of Rural Wales

04501

Yorkshire Campaign for Nuclear Disarmament

2 Ashgrove, West Yorks, Bradford, BD7 1BN, UK
Tel: 01274 730795
Fax: 01274 414413
Email: info@yorkshirecnd.org.uk
Website: http://www.cnduk.org/pages/ctc/regoff.html
Contact: Hannah Tweddell, Contact
Description: Aims to eliminate British nuclear weapons and other weapons of mass destruction.
Publication: Newsletter
Publication title: Action for Peace

04502

Young Men's Christian Association - England YMCA

640 Forest Rd., London, E17 3DZ, UK
Tel: 020 85205599
Fax: 020 85093190
Email: enquiries@ymca.org.uk
Website: http://www.ymca.org.uk
Contact: Angela Sarkis, Natl. Sec.
Description: Promotes the spiritual and physical development of the youth. Cooperates with the International YMCA network to attain organizational goals. Sponsors programs in areas covered including refugee assistance, housing and education. Provides facilities for the activities of the members.

04503

Young Men's Christian Association - Ireland YMCA

Waring St., Belfast, BT1 2EU, UK
Tel: 028 90327757
Fax: 012 32438809
Email: stephen@ymca-ireland.org
Website: http://www.ymca.int
Contact: Stephen Turner, Contact
Description: Promotes the spiritual and physical development of the youth. Cooperates with the International YMCA network to attain organizational goals. Sponsors programs in areas covered including refugee assistance, housing and education. Provides facilities for the activities of the members.

04504

Young Women's Christian Association - Great Britain YWCA - GB

Clarendon House, 52 Cornmarket St., Oxford, OX1 3EJ, UK
Tel: 01865 304200
Fax: 01865 204805
Email: info@ywca.org.uk
Website: http://www.ywca-gb.org.uk
Staff: 250
Contact: Helen Wollaston, Chair
Description: Aims to be a force for change for women who are facing discrimination and inequalities of all kinds. Helps to enable young women facing disadvantage to identify and realize their full potential. Influences public policy in order to achieve equality and social justice for young women. Provides opportunities for participation in a world-wide women's movement.
Publication: Magazine
Publication title: Annual Review

04505

Youth Hostels Association of England and Wales YHA

Trevelyan House, Dimple Rd., Derbyshire, Matlock, DE4 3YH, UK
Tel: 01629 592600
Fax: 01629 592702
Email: customerservices@yha.org.uk
Website: http://www.yha.org.uk
Members: 230000
Staff: 1200
Contact: Chris Darmon, Chm.
Fee: £15.95
Membership Type: individual
Fee: £9.95
Membership Type: regular (under 26 years of age)
Description: Provides inexpensive accommodations for travelers worldwide. Welcomes individuals and groups of people. Facilities at some youth hostels for educational groups. Maintains 227 Youth Hostels in England and Wales.
Formerly: Formerly, Youth Hostels Association - England
Publication: Annual Report
Publication title: Guide

04506

YouthLink Scotland

Rosebery House, 9 Haymarket Terr., Edinburgh, EH12 5EZ, UK
Tel: 0131 3132488
Fax: 0131 3136800
Email: info@youthlink.co.uk
Website: http://www.youthlink-scotland.org
Members: 75
Staff: 40
Contact: Jim Sweeney, Chief Exec.
Description: Group involved primarily with the support and development of young people in Scotland. Supports member organizations; advocates for member organizations, develops, along with member organizations alternative methods and approaches to youth work, and promotes voluntary youth work, identifying and speaking up on issues regarding young people.
Formerly: Formerly, Scottish Standing Conference of Voluntary Youth Organisations
Publication: Magazine
Publication title: Link Magazine

04507

Zoological Society of London ZSL

Regent's Park, Outer Circle, London, NW1 4RY, UK
Tel: 020 77223333
Email: membership@zsl.org
Website: http://www.zsl.org
Members: 40000
Staff: 350
Contact: Patrick Bateson, Pres.
Fee: £65
Membership Type: adult
Fee: £53.5
Membership Type: concession
Description: Fellows of the Learned Society; Friends of London Zoo; Friends of Whipsnade. Promotes the worldwide conservation of animal species and their habitats by stimulating public awareness and concern through the presentation of living collections, by relevant research including captive breeding and by direct action in the field.
Library Subject: zoology, conservation, animal husbandry, taxonomy
Library Type: open to the public
Publication: Journal
Publication title: Animal Conservation

Alphabetical Index

Subject Index

Academic Freedom

Accounting

Acoustics

Actors

Adhesives

Administration

Administrative Services

Adoption

Adult Education

Advertising

Aerospace

Afghanistan

African

Agents

Aging

Agribusiness

Agricultural Development

Agricultural Education

Agricultural Engineering

Arachnology

Arbitration and Mediation

Archaeology

Architectural Education

Architecture

Archives

Arms

Art History

Art Therapy

Artifacts

Artists

Arts

Arts and Sciences

Asian

Associations

Astronomy

Attorneys

Authors

Subject Index

Autism

Automatic Control

Automatic Identification

Automotive Industries

Automotive Manufacturer

Automotive Services

Aviation

Baking

Banking

Behavioral Medicine

Bereavement

Beverages

Biochemistry

Bioethics

Biology

Biomedical Engineering

Biophysics

Bird

Birth Defects

Blood

Bone

Books

Botany

British

Broadcasting

Building Codes

Building Industries

Subject Index

Communications

Community Development

Community Service

Composers

Computer Science

Computer Software

Computer Users

Computers

Concrete

Conflict

Conservation

Construction

Consulting

Consumers

Contact Lenses

Containers

Contractors

Cooperatives

Cordage
Gold and Silver Wyre Drawers' Company 02305

Correctional
International Corrections and Prisons Association 02709

Cosmetic Surgery
British Association of Aesthetic Plastic Surgeons 01067
British Association of Plastic, Reconstructive and Aesthetic Surgeons 01106

Cosmetics
Cosmetic, Toiletry, and Perfumery Association - England 01792

Cosmetology
Barbers Company 00922
British Association of Beauty Therapy and Cosmetology 01071
British Association of Cosmetic Doctors 01077
Hairdressing Council 02356
International Federation of Societies of Cosmetic Chemists 02738
National Hairdressers' Federation 03282
Society of Cosmetic Scientists 04028

Counseling
Association for Careers Education and Guidance 00602
Association of Graduate Careers Advisory Services 00764
Institute of Career Guidance 02492
International Association for Educational and Vocational Guidance 02642
Irish Association for Counselling and Psychotherapy 00178
ISCO Careerscope 02900

Crafts
British Stickmakers Guild 01457
Craft Potters Association of Great Britain 01816
Crafts Council 01817
Embroiderers' Guild 01939
Federation of Crafts and Commerce 02142
Guild of Taxidermists 02342
Irish Woodturners' Guild 00304
Lace Guild 02951
Quilters' Guild of the British Isles 03595
Rural Crafts Association 03773
Society of Designer Craftsmen 04031
Wales Craft Council 04357

Creativity
Renaissance Universal 03631

Credit
Credit Protection Association 01819
Irish Institute of Credit Management 00243

Credit Unions
Association of British Credit Unions Limited 00689

Crime
ICC Commercial Crime Services 02429
ICC International Maritime Bureau 02431
Victim Support 04342

Criminal Justice
Howard League for Penal Reform 02415
International Association of Women Police 02681
Nacro 03157
National Association of Official Prison Visitors 03212
National Association of Probation Officers 03220
Penal Reform International 03461
Probation Boards' Association 03546

Criminology
British Society of Criminology 01430

Critical Care
Intensive Care Society 02622

Cromwell, Oliver
Cromwell Association 01821

Cryogenics
British Cryogenics Council 01178
Society for Low Temperature Biology 03969

Crystallography
British Association of Crystal Growth 01078
British Crystallographic Association 01179
International Union of Crystallography 02871

Cultural Exchange
British Mexican Society 01317
EIL Intercultural Learning 00090
Franco-British Society 02225
Hunterian Society 02423

Curriculum
Qualifications and Curriculum Authority 03589

Cybernetics
Cybernetics Society 01828

Cytology
British Society for Clinical Cytology 01396
National Association of Cytologists 03193

Dairies
British Sheep Dairying Association 01386
Royal Association of British Dairy Farmers 03676
Stilton Cheesemakers' Association 04140

Dairy Products
Dairy Council - United Kingdom 01831
Dairy UK 01832
Ice Cream Alliance 02432
Irish Creamery Milk Suppliers' Association 00209
Irish Dairy Board 00210
National Dairy Council 00341

Dance
British Association of Teachers of Dancing 01120
British Ballet Organization 01130
British Dance Council 01182
English Amateur Dancesport Association 01959
Imperial Society of Teachers of Dancing 02438
International Dance Teachers' Association 02715
ISTD Dance Examinations Board 02904
Laban Guild 02947
London Swing Dance Society 03025
Royal Academy of Dance 03663
Royal Scottish Country Dance Society 03738
Scottish Dance Teacher's Alliance 03836
Scottish Official Board of Highland Dancing 03867
Welsh Amateur Dance Sport Association 04382
World Dance Council 04452

Data Processing
Mobile Data Association 03123

Defense
Defence Manufacturers Association of Great Britain 01845
Institute of Civil Protection and Emergency Management 02502
International Institute for Strategic Studies 02762

Demography
Economic and Social Research Council 01919

Dental Hygiene
Association for Dental Education in Europe 00022
Irish Society of Periodontology 00290

Dentistry
British Dental Association 01185
British Dental Practice Managers' Association 01186
British Dental Trade Association 01187
British Endodontic Society 01203
British Orthodontic Society 01338
British Society for Dental and Maxillofacial Radiology 01399
British Society for Restorative Dentistry 01416
British Society for the Study of Prosthetic Dentistry 01424
British Society of Dental Hygiene and Therapy 01431
British Society of Periodontology 01442
Clinical Dental Technicians Association 01658
Commonwealth Dental Association 01697
Confederation of Dental Employers 01742
Dental Health Foundation 00078
Dental Laboratories Association 01848
Dental Practitioners Association 01849
European Academy of Paediatric Dentistry 00098
European Orthodontic Society 02057
European Prosthodontic Association 02066
Faculty of Dental Surgery 02116
General Dental Council 02263
Irish Dental Association 00212
Orthodontic Society of Ireland 00356

Dermatology
British Association of Dermatologists 01081
British Photodermatology Group 01351
International Foundation for Dermatology 02747
Irish Association of Dermatologists 00183
Irish Raynaud's and Scleroderma Society 00273
National Eczema Society 03262
Psoriasis Association 03576

Design
Design Business Association 01855
Design History Society 01857
Faculty of Royal Designers for Industry 02120
Feng Shui Society 02170
Institute of Designers in Ireland 00150

Detergent
Irish Cosmetics, Detergent and Allied Products Association 00207
UK Cleaning Products Industry Association 04263

Developmental Education
Staff and Educational Development Association 04127

Diabetes
British Association of Retinal Screeners 01113
Diabetes Federation of Ireland 00079
Diabetes UK 01864

Dictionary
Scottish Language Dictionaries 03853

Disabled
Action on Disability and Development 00453
Association for Higher Education Access and Disability 00024
Association of Disabled Professionals 00747
Association of Wheelchair Children 00883
British Dyslexia Association 01194
British Institute of Learning Disabilities 01278
British Society for Disability and Oral Health 01400
Cheshire Ireland 00054
Council for the Registration of Schools Teaching Dyslexic Pupils 01805
Disability Alliance 01875
Disability Federation of Ireland 00080
Disabled Birders Association 01876
Disabled Drivers' Association of Ireland 00081
Disabled Living Foundation 01877
Disabled Motorists Federation 01878
Dog Assistance in Disability 01884
Dyslexia Action 01905
Enable - Ireland 00092
Handicap International - UK 02360
Harrow Association of Disabled People 02363

Disarmament

Disaster Aid

Disease

Dog

Domestic Development

Domestic Services

Domestic Violence

Donors

Down's Syndrome

Driver Education

Drug Abuse

Dyslexia

Eating Disorders

Echocardiography

Ecology

Economic Development

Economics

Education

Educational Advocacy

Educational Reform

Elder Abuse

Elections

Electrical

Subject Index

Electronics

Emergency Medicine

Employment

Enameling

Endocrinology

Energy

Engineering

Engines

English

Entertainment

Entertainment Law

Entomology

Environment

Environmental Health

Environmental Law

Epidemiology

Epilepsy

Ergonomics

Estate Management

European

Euthanasia

Exhibitors

Footwear

Forensic Medicine

Forensic Sciences

Forest Industries

Forest Products

Forestry

Foundries

Fragrances

Franchising

Free Enterprise

French

Fruits and Vegetables

Fuel

Fundraising

Furniture

Gambling

Gardening

Gases

Gastroenterology

Gay/Lesbian

Genetic Disorders

Genetics

Geography

Geology

Geoscience

Gerontology

Gifted

Glass

Government Employees

Graphic Arts

Graphic Design

Graphology

Gravity

Holistic Medicine

Home Care

Homeless

Homeopathy

Horse Racing

Horses

Horticulture

Hospice

Hospital

Hospitality Industries

Housewares

Housing

Human Development

Human Engineering

Human Relations

Human Resources

Human Rights

Humanism

Humanities

Hunger

Hunting

Hypertension

Hypnosis

Imaging Media

Immigration

Immune Deficiency

Immunology

Impotence

Incontinence

Indigenous Peoples

Industrial Design

Industrial Development

Industrial Equipment

Industrial Security

Industrial Workers

Infants

Infectious Diseases

Information Management

Information Processing

Insolvency

Inspectors

Instructional Media

Instrument Makers

Insurance

Intellectual Property

Intercultural

Intercultural Studies

Interdisciplinary Studies

Interior Design

International Cooperation

International Development

Marine Industries

Maritime

Maritime Law

Marketing

Marriage

Massage

Materials

Mathematics

Meat

Medical

Medical Aid

Medical Education

Medical Identification

Medical Research

Medical Technology

Medicine

Medieval

Meeting Planners

Mental Health

Mentally Disabled

Metabolic Disorders

Political Federations

Political Parties

Political Reform

Political Science

Pollution Control

Population

Postal Service

Poultry

Poverty

Press

Primates

Professionals

Professions

Property Management

Property Rights

Prostitution

Psychiatry

Psychoanalysis

Psychology

Psychotherapy

Public Administration

Public Finance

Public Health

Public Policy

Public Relations

Public Speaking

Public Transit

Publishing

Purchasing

Pyrotechnics

Quality Assurance

Quality Control

Radiation

Radiology

Railroads

Real Estate

Recordings

Recreation

Recreational Vehicles

Refugees

Rehabilitation

Relief

Religious Administration

Religious Freedom

Religious Studies

Renaissance

Renting and Leasing

Reproductive Medicine

Reproductive Rights

Rescue

Research

Respiratory Diseases

Retail

Retailing

Retirees

Rheumatic Diseases

Right to Life

Robotics

Subject Index

Taxation

Teachers

Technology

Telecommunications

Television

Testing

Textbooks

Textiles

Theatre

Therapy

Thoracic Medicine

Time

Tires

Tobacco

Tourism

Toxicology

Trade

Translation

Transplantation

Transportation

Travel

Trees and Shrubs

Tropical Medicine

Tropical Studies

Unions

United Kingdom

United Nations

Urban Affairs

Urology

Utilities

Vacuum Technology

Vascular System

Vegetarianism

Vending

Veterinary Education

Veterinary Medicine

Vexillology

Victims

Visually Impaired

Vivisection, Anti-

Vocational Education

Voluntarism

War Resistance

Waste

Water

Water Resources

Acronym Index

Acronym Index